The Rt. Hon. David Lloyd George, O.M., M.P.

WAR MEMOIRS

OF

DAVID LLOYD GEORGE

VOLUME I

LONDON
ODHAMS PRESS LIMITED
LONG ACRE, W.C.2

COPYRIGHT

S 138

Made and Printed in Great Britain

FOREWORD

TO

NEW EDITION

I HAVE received many communications expressing a hope that my War Memoirs should be published at a price which would bring them within easier reach of readers of average means.

The publication of a popular edition has afforded me an opportunity for checking the statements published in the first edition in the light of public criticisms, of facts brought to light by subsequent writings, and of the numerous letters written to me by men who took an active part in the events I narrate. After a careful perusal of this fresh material I have not found it necessary to revise or correct any of the assertions I made or opinions I expressed in the original narrative.

I have added a sample of the letters that poured in during the last four or five years from eye-witnesses. I have specially chosen for publication a few of those I received on the Passchendaele episode, as the account I gave of that battle has been regarded as the most direct and detailed arraignment of the military command to which I have committed myself in these pages. A fair representative selection of this correspondence is given as an appendix to my Passchendaele chapter.

I aim to tell the naked truth about War as I saw it from the conning-tower at Downing Street. I saw how the incredible heroism of the common man was being squandered to repair the incompetence of the trained inexperts (for they were actually trained not to be expert in mastering the actualities of modern warfare) in the production of equipment, in transport, in tackling the submarine menace, in the narrow, selfish and unimaginative strategy and in the ghastly butchery of a succession of vain and insane offensives.   The last great struggle revealed not only the horrid and squalid aspects of war but its muddles; its futilities; its chanciness; its precariousness; its wastefulness of the lives, the treasure and the virtues of mankind—all that demonstrates the supreme stupidity of committing to such a brutal and blunder-headed tribunal as War the determination of issues upon which the happiness and progress of humanity so largely depend.

When all the people that on earth do dwell are gladly scraping the butter off their own and their children's bread in order to keep the god of war fit and sleek, it is necessary to show them clearly what a fool he really is.

Bron-y-de, Churt.   D. LLOYD GEORGE.
January, 1938.

PREFACE

TO

VOLUME ONE*

Most of the leading actors in the Great War, both Statesmen and Warriors, have committed to writing the story of the part they played in it. With one or two exceptions they have written their narrative themselves, although the composition of books has been to them as new a venture as it is now to me. With the exception of M. Briand, who never put pen to paper, all the dominant personalities of the War have told their tale of what they did and why they did it; amongst rulers, the Kaiser, the Crown Prince, M. Poincaré, President Wilson (through Mr. Baker); amongst statesmen, M. Clemenceau, Mr. Asquith, Lord Grey, Mr. Churchill, Colonel House, Prince Max of Baden, Von Bülow; amongst the warriors, Foch, Joffre, Hindenburg, Ludendorff, Hofmann, Cadorna, French, Haig (with the aid of another pen), Henry Wilson, Robertson, Pershing, and a host of others. My library shelves groan under the burden of war autobiographies. No wonder I hesitated for years to follow the example set me by those who figured so prominently on the stage where I also occupied a not inconspicuous position. I had almost decided to bequeath the undertaking to those with whom I should leave my papers, when two incidents occurred which influenced me to take up my pencil and relate my own story in my own words.

The first was an illness which released me from the irksome and peculiarly thankless duty of leadership in a political party unhappily poisoned and paralysed by internal dissension amongst its better known members. The other was a visit paid me during my convalescence by an old comrade of the Great War. He entreated me to take advantage of my seclusion from active political warfare to give my account of the events of the War. He reminded me that amongst statesmen I was the only one who went right through it from the declaration of War to the signing of Peace. He urged that the real history of the War might not—and probably would not— be written for another generation, but that the books written to-day by the men—generals and politicians—who had a share either in the

* This Preface is the result of the merging by the author of the Prefaces to Volumes I and III of the original edition in six volumes.

fighting or in the direction would constitute the principal material upon which the historian would draw for his facts and impressions. All these books gave the point of view of the individual writer, biased naturally either by limitation of his opportunities or by a controverted theory of events, or, too frequently, by the exigencies of a personal apologia. It was pointed out to me that I was the only person in authority who was in Mr. Britling's position. I " saw it through " from the outbreak of the quarrel to the settlement of the terms. There are multitudes who were better acquainted with certain aspects of the War; there are, or were, a few who for a limited period were in a better position to view the struggle as a whole; but there is no one (and I often recall the fact with horror) who was as intimately acquainted as myself with the war direction during the whole of its rending and tearing course through the vitals of mankind.

To tell the story at all is like repeating what was seen in a nightmare, and I shrank for years from writing my record of the horrifying details. It is not pleasant to remember how men and women devoted energy, intelligence, and zeal for four-and-a-half years to the work of destruction and pain. But it must be told if such a calamity is to be averted in the future. It is better that the real facts should be given. I do not pretend to know them all, but some of them I know better than my contemporaries. These I am doing my best to relate accurately in the following pages. I make my own contribution, not as one who claims to be an experienced author, but as a witness giving evidence on what he remembers of these tremendous transactions.

I have written of men and events as I saw and thought of them. That may involve criticism where others might praise and commendation where others might attach blame. Where I have indulged in any stricture, I have taken the utmost pains to test the accuracy of my recollection by reference to contemporary documents. I have also consulted men who took an active part in episodes I record. But the pathways and boundaries of memory are so obliterated and confused by time, that the most reliable witness often strays, unless the road is marked out with the " writing that remains." Luckily, I have in my possession—thanks to careful secretaries—a vast number of memoranda, minutes and letters concerning the War and Peace, all written at the time.

The only value which these volumes may possess for the future historian of war will depend upon the memories being genuine and upon the extent to which they are fortified by documentary or other contemporary evidence. These documents I have chosen and quoted or used with a full sense of the responsibility resting on every public servant not to reveal or publish anything which may injure the interests of his country. In the exercise of this discretion I owe much to the scrutiny of one of the most efficient and distinguished public servants of his generation—Sir Maurice Hankey. I owe thanks also to a great many kind friends who have assisted me by supplementing and stimulating my memory with their own as to occurrences where I enjoyed their valued co-operation.

The tale is one which does not always give me any pleasure to tell; quite the reverse. There is much of it which I wrote with intense reluctance. For I found it necessary in the interests of a truthful record to relate facts which constitute a severe criticism on the action of men whose memory is honoured by their fellow country-men for many sterling qualities which they possessed in a remarkable degree. My disinclination for revealing to the public unpleasant truths which reflect on distinguished public servants is naturally enhanced by the fact that some of them are no longer present to defend themselves. For that reason I felt disposed to pass on to others the duty of writing the true history of the occurrences recorded in these volumes. But as all these Great War figures had in their lifetime, either themselves or through the agency of authorised sub-stitutes, already given their version of affairs, in which they did not spare those of whom they disapproved—including myself—I felt I was justified in publishing information at my disposal which corrected wrong impressions. Moreover, I took the view that if you accept the responsibility of writing history, you cannot do so honestly without allocating blame as well as praise, where either is due to the men who take a leading part in the events which make that history. And the right and duty of criticism or approval for their contribution does not cease with their death. Warriors are in that respect in the same category as politicians. Apart from that general considera-tion, there are at least two imperative reasons why the facts should be told now and not later. It has been sagely remarked by Macaulay that the knowledge of past events " is valuable only as it leads us to form just calculations with respect to the future." The atmosphere of the world—East and West—is charged with the international suspicions, rivalries, ambitions and fears that have always hitherto ended in war. Nations are arming for war. Every nation throughout the world—almost without exception—is increasing its armaments. Every effort to arrest this menacing expansion of the mechanism of wholesale slaughter has failed. Nations with already enormous armaments are increasing and improving them. Formidable nations that were disarmed, are re-arming. Governments are making prepara-tions for war in defiance of treaties they signed, and they are doing so with an urgent anxiety that can only be explained by a general apprehension that war is impending. There is no confidence in any quarter that peace can be long preserved. In these circumstances it is essential first of all that nations should know, before they declare war, to what they are committing themselves. All nations alike enter into a war with an equal confidence in ultimate victory for their banners. Defeat is always a surprise to the vanquished. Elements they had not realised, defects in their own equipment, resources or qualities, or superiority in those of their foes, which they never suspected, mistakes attributable to inferior leadership which threw away good chances—and finally that play of chance and fate, which no genius can forecast or control, all make the issue of a war as doubtful as that of a serious disease. A good physician may pull through a man with a weak constitution—a poor or second-rate doctor may ruin the chances of a patient with the soundest natural physique. A good cause counts in any struggle, but it is by no means decisive in a particular conflict between right and wrong.

I remember forming one of a delegation of British Ministers (which included Mr. Asquith, Lord Kitchener, Mr. Balfour, Sir Edward Grey) which attended an important conference at Paris in 1915. When we left for London, M. Combe ("le petit père Combe") came to the station on behalf of the French Government to see us off. He was a small and vivacious octogenarian whose optimism had not been in the least dimmed by years or by the maledictions of the devout, whom he had offended by his attacks on the Church. As soon as he entered the saloon carriage where we were seated, he started to deliver an oration on the subject of the War and its prospects—all full of hope and confidence. He ended with a peroration about "*Justice, Liberté, le Droit et la Victoire.*" Mr. Balfour regarded the whole performance with ill-concealed disdain and turning to me said: "He must have strangely misread history if he thinks that '*Justice, Liberté et Droit*' are synonymous with '*Victoire.*'"

There is a melancholy justification for this cynicism in the events of the past. Victory may not always go to the big battalions, neither does it invariably incline to the righteous, for it is a historical truism that a just cause often contends in vain against the superior might or efficiency of its opponents or the weakness or greater stupidity of its adherents. Those who entrust the destiny of their country to war therefore incur unforeseeable risks which may be fatal to them and the land they love. No other arbitrament is so costly in its procedure as well as so uncertain in its event. Let those who doubt this read carefully what happened in the Great War and see how reckless and unintelligent handling brought us almost to the rim of catastrophe, and how we were saved largely by the incredible folly of our foes. But you cannot always rely on your opponents making greater mistakes than your own.

The next lesson is one we must not overlook in a world of armed nations—that if mankind should unhappily fail to abolish war from the category of its visitations, then, if we are involved in another, we must take earnest heed that we do not fall into the errors that cost us so dearly last time. That is also my excuse for giving an account, so detailed as to be weighted with dreariness, of the great improvisations which were set up to organise the resources of the nations for war. A study of these is essential to anyone who wishes to learn how a country can be organised to the best advantage either in War or in Peace.

But, whether in exposition, approbation or condemnation, I must emphasise the importance of this precept—that these lessons cannot be learnt unless they are truthfully taught. If out of respect for honoured memories or cherished delusions, the truth be suppressed and defects hidden under a varnish of glorification, then we shall learn nothing, and if there be a next time we may not then escape disaster as we did in the last calamity—by a shuddering breadth.

I regret more than words can express the necessity for telling the bare facts of our bloodstained stagger to victory. But I had to tell them or leave unchallenged the supremacy of misleading and therefore dangerous illusions.

Unfortunately, censure attracts more attention than laudation. I have criticised a few—very few—statesmen and generals. That attracts controversy, and controversy involves a publicity which casts the larger and more important part of the narrative into the shade. If in these pages I have resorted to criticism, I have also recalled with pleasure the great services of many. Bonar Law, Balfour, Churchill, Cecil, Geddes, Maclay, Reading, Smuts, Borden, Hughes, Milner, Northcliffe, Fisher, Ernle, Lee of Fareham, are amongst a multitude of statesmen and administrators to whom praise is due and has been accorded without stint. I have dwelt on the successes of Generals like Plumer, Allenby, Maude, Monash and Cowans, whose triumphs lit up the dismal narrative of military ineptitude displayed by a few others. There were great figures whose shortcomings added to our difficulties. In their case I have also called attention to the exceptional qualities they possessed. And as to the myriads of officers and men whose incredible valour and endurance saved their country from the consequences of every blunder perpetrated, whether by politicians, generals or admirals, if I have failed in bestowing on them the full measure of praise they merit, it is from lack of adequate power to express the emotion to which I am moved by a renewed contemplation of their heroism.

Bron-y-de, Churt.   D. LLOYD GEORGE.
1933-34.

CONTENTS

CONTENTS

CONTENTS

CONTENTS

LIST OF PLATES

The Rt. Hon. David Lloyd George, M.P., in
the robes of Chancellor of the Exchequer, 1914.

Elliott & Fry.

The Earl of Oxford and Asquith.

Press Portrait Bureau.

Viscount Grey of Fallodon, K.G.

Press Portrait Bureau.

The Lord Cunliffe.

E.N.A.

Count Paul Wolff-Metternich.

M. Albert Thomas (French Minister of Munitions), Sir Douglas Haig and General Joffre in earnest conversation with Mr. Lloyd George during his visit to the Somme front.

Cartoon by the late E. T. Reed. Reproduced by courtesy of the " Bystander."

A SLIGHT DISCREPANCY SOMEWHERE

HASQUITH (*to his pal Jawge*) : " 'Ere ! Not s'much o' your 'Too Late !' Wot's the blinkin' good o' me a-'ollerin' aht what I'm a-'ollerin' aht if you go a-'ollerin aht wot you're a-'ollerin' aht ? "

The famous poster placarded throughout the
country to help in recruiting Kitchener's Army.

Imperial War Cab

Downing Street.

xxiii

G. C. Beresford.

The Earl of Balfour, O.M., K.G.

Press Portrait Bureau.

The Rt. Hon. Sir Eric Geddes, G.C.B.

Russell.

Viscount Haldane, O.M.

Elliott & Fry.

Field-Marshal Sir William Robertson.

From a painting by J. B. Anderson.   Henry Dixon & Sons, Ltd.

The Rt. Hon. Andrew Bonar Law.

President Wilson.

Press Portrait Bureau.

Lord Carson.

Hay Wrightson.

The Rt. Hon. George Nicoll Barnes.

The Rt. Hon. Viscount Devonport.

The Rt. Hon. Lord Maclay.

Russell.

Elliott & Fry.

The Rt. Hon. Lord Ernle.

The Rt. Hon. Lord Lee of Fareham.

E. O. Hoppé.

Lord Northcliffe.

Lieut.-Colonel Sir Maurice Hankey, G.C.B.

E.N.A.

Rasputin.

Vandyk.

To a great man from his friend

J. C. Smuts

General the Rt. Hon. J. C. Smuts.

Admiral of the Fleet, Earl Jellicoe, bidding good-bye to Lord Kitchener on board *Hampshire*. Within half an hour of the taking of this photograph *Hampshire* struck a mine and Lord Kitchener was drowned.

WAR MEMOIRS

CHAPTER 1

THE BREWING OF THE STORM

1. FIRST CONTACT WITH FOREIGN AFFAIRS

In the year 1904, on the day when the Anglo-French Entente was announced, I arrived at Dalmeny on a couple of days' visit to the late Lord Rosebery. His first greeting to me was: " Well, I suppose you are just as pleased as the rest of them with this French agreement?" I assured him that I was delighted that our snarling and scratching relations with France had come to an end at last. He replied: " You are all wrong. It means war with Germany in the end! "

About a year after this prophetical utterance I became for the first time a Minister of the Crown. Had anyone then told me that before I ceased to hold office in the British Cabinet I should not only have witnessed a war between Britain and Germany, but have taken an active, and in fact a leading part in its prosecution, I should have treated such a forecast as one of the many wild predictions of good or evil with which every public man is assailed by persons of unbalanced minds.

Before my appointment I took very little part in the discussion of foreign affairs and had no pretence to a greater knowledge of their intricacies than that which is possessed by the average Member of Parliament who has read history, and brings it up to date with such information as is supplied by the leading newspapers and reviews of all Parties. My interests were definitely centred on more domestic matters; on the special concerns of Wales, and on the education controversy, free trade, Home Rule, the land question and social reform. In foreign policy I had always been, as I am to-day, an ardent advocate of the rights of small nationalities, and I had been trained to believe in a peaceable settlement of the differences which arose between the nations of the world. Notwithstanding the sinister growth of armaments and a feverish anxiety to perfect them in all countries, there had been unbroken peace for over forty years between the Great Powers of Western Europe, and this bred a cheerful if illusive hope that the world would ultimately abandon war as a tribunal for adjudicating international disputes. This happy confidence in the gradual and final escape of the world

from the perils of war (except against savages) was fostered, as I shall
show later, by the extent to which nearly all of us, even Cabinet
Ministers, were kept sedulously in the dark about our foreign
conversations and commitments.

I was, of course, well aware of the secular antagonism between
France and Germany and how that antagonism had been kept alive
by the tearing from the side of France of two of her best-beloved
provinces. The Franco-Prussian War was a memory of my boyhood.
After the fall of the Empire, Radical sentiment tended to be pro-
French in sympathy with the democratic institutions of our nearest
neighbour, whereas Conservative opinion inclined to be more
pro-German.

Inside the Liberal Party the tradition of its more advanced
elements ever since the days of Charles James Fox had been one of
constant friendliness towards the French Republic; English Conservatism had never quite got over the prejudices and apprehensions
roused by the French Revolution and the Napoleonic episode, and
Liberal Imperialism was inclined to follow in the track of the Anti-
Revolution Whigs.

Mr. Gladstone was passionately pro-French in his general attitude.
The Bismarckism of blood and iron never appealed to him. He was
essentially a Liberal in foreign affairs. When he visited Caernarvon-
shire in 1892, I was invited by Sir Edward Watkin to meet him at
dinner at the Watkin châlet on the slopes of Snowdon. It was a
small party. Apart from the members of the family, the late Tom
Ellis and I were the only other guests. Mr. Gladstone did practically
all the talking at the dinner-table and afterwards, and the rest of
us, only too thrilled to meet and hear this great figure from a past
world, were naturally content to listen in silence.

He was 83 years of age, but showed none of the usual symptoms
of senility. He was vital. His deep vibrant tones were music to
the ear whatever he said. That evening he was at times even gay
and merry.

His conversation ranged over a curious variety of topics. He talked
for some time on the development of transport in the country and
the improvement in the habits of the people who were associated
with it; the sodden driver and the drunken ostler of the past against
the sober engine driver and railway porter of to-day. To illustrate
this theme he told us one or two quite amusing stories of his
experiences in the old coaching days. I can only recall one of his
tales. When posting from Wales to London he sat on the box seat,
and in order to relieve the dreary hours he sought conversation with
the driver, who was a fine specimen of what much beef and more
beer could produce. Not achieving great success by ordinary
conversation he pulled out a handsome watch of which he was proud,
opened it, showed the works to the driver and explained to him the

function of the various wheels and levers. The only observation he elicited was: " What puzzles me is how you wind that 'ere watch when you get home drunk."

He then gave us a dissertation on corrugated-iron roofing, and the difficulties which had been encountered in keeping buildings of this kind warm in winter and cool in summer. The last subject was suggested by the fact that the châlet was built of this material. He then diverged to other reminiscences. He recalled with regret the prohibitive price of sugar candy when he was a boy and told us with gusto of his delight when he discovered recently, in walking along the streets of some obscure town in Cheshire, how cheaply you could to-day purchase this joy of his departed youth.

He then launched out into a wonderful panegyric on the people of France. I think it arose out of a reference to the Channel tunnel which Sir Edward Watkin was then promoting. Mr. Gladstone made it quite clear that in his judgment the French were a much more enlightened, broadminded and civilised people than those over whose destinies he was at the moment privileged to preside. The Radicals of that day might not have accepted his perfervid eulogies on the superiority of French intelligence, but apart from that his outburst more or less represented the Radical attitude towards the French Republic and its citizens at the time when I came into active politics. On the other hand, Germany, with her militarism, her autocracy and her constitutional devices to enhance the voting power of property and to depress and restrict the power of the worker in the State, and her resolve generally to keep democracy in its proper place, evoked a good deal of sympathetic approval amongst the more Conservative elements in the country.

Lord Rosebery and his friends did not share in these Radical sentiments towards French democracy. Their attitude was one of distrust of France and ill-concealed goodwill towards Germany. During Lord Rosebery's occupation of the Foreign Office in 1892-94, he had once or twice engaged the country in grave disputes with France and brought us to the brink of serious conflict. In the House of Commons his Under-Secretary, Sir Edward Grey,* in alluding to the menace of some French movement towards the British sphere of influence in the Sudan, had characterised it as " an unfriendly act." The Radical supporters of the Government resented the threat implied in the phrase, and they continued to view with great suspicion Sir Edward Grey's attitude towards France.

When the Campbell-Bannerman Administration was formed, it was sharply divided into two sections: the Radical element, of which the Prime Minister was the chief, and the Liberal Imperialists, relics of that element which deserted Fox and backed Palmerston. Chief

* The late Viscount Grey of Fallodon.

among them were Mr. Asquith,* Sir Edward Grey and Mr. Haldane.†
There was a perceptible difference of attitude between the two
sections on questions of foreign policy. The old pro-Boers inherited
the pacifist doctrines of Mr. Gladstone. The Liberal League
members of the Cabinet affected a more Palmerstonian attitude in
foreign affairs. The former suspicion of France which characterised
them in pre-Entente days had by this time altogether vanished, even
from the stubborn mind of Sir Edward Grey, but for it was
substituted a worrying distrust of the designs of Germany.

This was by no means confined to the Foreign Secretary.
Germany's naval shipbuilding programme was largely responsible
for this change in the Tory and Liberal Imperialist attitude towards
Germany. The Kaiser frequently boasted that he created the
formidable Navy of Germany, and he was always contemplating and
reviewing it with the pride of a Creator. He saw and said it was
good. What good it brought Germany is not evident, but the
story of evil it wrought will always remain one of the most
poignant chapters in the history not only of Germany but
of mankind. It was partly responsible for the World War. It
undoubtedly helped to range the British Empire amongst the
enemies of Germany and later on it brought America into the war.
Apart from these facts, it contributed to the spirit of arrogant
superiority which dictated the course of German diplomacy, and
consequently to the sense of apprehension which drew other
powerful nations to military and naval understandings. Its creation
undoubtedly helped to stimulate the Kaiser's fatal swagger.

The blustering zeal which he threw into the building of his
redoubtable navy was regarded as a threat not only to Britain's
supremacy at sea but to her actual security. Foolish speeches
delivered by men of no inconsiderable authority and influence in
Germany, hinting a challenge to Britain's fleet, were quoted
in the British Press and caused uneasiness in minds not readily
given to panic. The Radical section of the Cabinet were
just as much alive as their Imperialist colleagues to the menace which
rival warship programmes involved to the good relations they were
anxious to maintain with Germany as well as with all other nations.

I first became directly concerned with this issue when in 1908, on
the death of Sir Henry Campbell-Bannerman and Mr. Asquith's
accession to the Premiership, I left the Board of Trade to succeed
Mr. Asquith as Chancellor of the Exchequer. In this post it became my
duty to find the money for naval programmes, and Anglo-German relations thus became a subject in which I was departmentally interested.

I might here say a word as to the two crises which occurred in the
Asquith Cabinet over shipbuilding programmes submitted by the

* Afterwards Earl of Oxford and Asquith, d. 1928.
† Afterwards Viscount Haldane of Cloan, d. 1928.

Board of Admiralty. The first was in 1908, when Mr. M'Kenna was First Lord of the Admiralty; the second in 1913-14, when Mr. Winston Churchill held that post.

As Chancellor of the Exchequer, I never resisted any addition to the strength of the Navy which would provide a reasonable margin of security against the increases in the German Navy effected by the shipbuilding programme of the German Admiralty. My opposition to the demands of the Board of Admiralty in 1908 and 1913 might be summed up in the fourfold proposition: —

1. The Admiralty demand an extravagant margin which is burdensome and provocative;

2. We ought to concentrate more on small craft for the protection of our trade routes and less on mammoth ships;

3. There is a growing reaction in the world against the burden of increasing armaments, and a general desire for a better understanding between the nations. We ought therefore to concentrate more on seeking an arrangement with Germany as to competitive building than on provocative programmes;

4. During the 1913-14 dispute in the Cabinet over the Admiralty estimates I pointed out that Germany was now devoting her attention to strengthening her Army rather than her Navy.

In my first protest against what I conceived to be panic demands from the Admiralty I received the zealous and energetic support of Mr. Winston Churchill. Unfortunately, by 1913 he had become First Lord of the Admiralty, and his inflammable fancy had been caught by the fascination of the monster ship. The fight against "bloated armaments"—to use the old Disraelian phrase—was weakened by so formidable a defection.

I do not propose to discuss at this point the merits of the controversy, but I would like to mention two or three facts in justification of the attitude adopted by the Radical section of the Cabinet. I have consulted the memoranda and counter-memoranda which were put in during the 1913 discussions. The Treasury, which was not without information from expert naval sources, claimed that even if we proceeded with the old accepted programme, rejecting the new proposals, we should still have in 1917 the following margin of superiority: —

Dreadnoughts .... over 84 per cent.
Pre-Dreadnoughts .... 127 ,, ,,
Armoured Cruisers .... 278 ,, ,,
Light Cruisers .... over 70 ,, ,,
Torpedo Craft .... 60 ,, ,,

This estimate was based, not merely upon numbers, but upon a qualitative comparison which included speed, weight of guns and age. These figures were not accepted by the Admiralty. The Treasury computation assumed too great a margin of superiority in Dreadnoughts, but the sifted figures showed a secure margin. There was a further argument advanced by the Treasury and their supporters, viz., that, throughout the whole of the ship-building competition between Germany and ourselves for the past ten years, we had always forced the pace by increasing the size of the ships, the weight of guns, and the speed of our vessels, beginning this fatal competition with the laying down of superiority of strength against any possible combination of foreign fleets. The laying down of the Dreadnought seemed to many of us a piece of wanton and profligate ostentation.

As to the second Treasury proposition, that we ought to concentrate more on small craft and less on big ships, the experience of the War was a complete vindication of the point of view taken by the Treasury in 1913. We suffered severely from the shortage of cruisers and torpedo-boat destroyers for the protection of our vessels, mercantile and naval, against submarine attack; and the Admiralty, under the direction of Sir John Fisher, had to work with feverish energy to make up this serious deficiency. The shortage in itself was created, not so much by the fact that we had not a sufficient number of torpedo-boat destroyers, but because the vulnerability of our great battleships and battle cruisers to torpedo attack was such that we had to detach the best part of our torpedo-boat strength to defend them.

With the third and fourth propositions I shall have to deal in the course of my narrative.

It was of course impossible not to have an uneasy feeling that the German battle fleet was built with the design of challenging British naval supremacy. Grand-Admiral von Tirpitz in his memoirs is quite explicit about this, and so at times was the Kaiser. I do not say that they deliberately set before themselves as their goal a war with Britain that would destroy our fleet. They would have been content if their fleet grew so powerful that it frightened Britain into renouncing her supremacy at sea without a fight. But von Tirpitz, the real creator of the German Navy, avows openly that they would be content with nothing less.

Opposed as I was to inflated armaments, I never hesitated in the view that Britain could not afford and would not allow such a situation to arise. We had no army large enough to defend our country against the enormous conscript armies of the Continent. Our fleet was still just as much the sole guarantor of our liberties and independence as in the days of Napoleon. We should therefore have to go on building ship for ship, and three ships to two, against any effort of the Germans. Our financial resources and shipbuilding equipment were adequate to counter their utmost achievement in naval rivalry. But, this being the position, it was no less obvious that such unrestricted competition would involve quite needless financial exhaustion and growing irritation for both countries, and would only leave them at the end, with empty pockets and burdened backs, in the same position of relative strength as that from which they had started.

As one who had been taught to believe that peace was the only sane and sound basis for human progress, I sought to allay the growing antagonism between the two nations. As Chancellor of the Exchequer, I could not be indifferent to the cost of the useless naval competition. It was an exhausting drain upon resources sadly needed for social amelioration and national development. So I sought some means of reaching an agreement with Germany which would enable us on both sides to slow down the rate and volume of our naval construction.

An opportunity for this seemed to present itself when at the suggestion of Sir Edward Grey in July, 1908, I came into contact with the German Ambassador, Count Metternich. Of our meeting I made some years later a note from memory, which I reproduce here: —

" Soon after I became Chancellor of the Exchequer in 1908, Count Metternich, the German Ambassador, invited me to lunch at the Embassy. I had never met the Ambassador and I had a suspicion that the invitation had some political purpose. After lunch he soon made it clear why I had been asked. He knew that I belonged to the more pacifist group in the Cabinet. He introduced the subject of the growing suspicions between our two countries. I thought it a good opportunity for explaining to him that the real ground for the growing antagonism in this country towards Germany was not jealousy of her rapidly developing commerce, but fear of her growing Navy. I pointed out how completely dependent we were on our overseas supplies for our daily bread, and that any country that wrested from us the supremacy of the seas would be in a position to starve our population into abject surrender in a few months. I also urged that if our sea defences were overwhelmed by a superior naval force, our Army could put up no effective resistance against the huge military machines of the Continent. I thought it well to tell him that on the subject of maintaining the invulnerability of our shores by means of an adequately superior Navy there was no difference of opinion in the Cabinet, and that although I was one of those who were opposed to these huge armaments, I should, if our community were in the least imperilled, be the first to propose even a loan of £100,000,000 if that were necessary to inaugurate a programme for building a Navy adequate to our safety. I said to him, ' If this rival shipbuilding goes on to such an extent as to render our people seriously apprehensive of invasion we shall be driven inevitably to adopt conscription and thus raise an army capable of defending our shores against any invader.' He replied quite curtly, 'Do you think we should wait?'

M. Delcassé had just been driven out of the Quai d'Orsay largely owing to German hostility. He had, however, been well received in London on his visit to this country immediately after his dismissal. I forget how his name cropped up in our conversation. I only remember one passage. When I said, 'You dismissed M. Delcassé from his position of Foreign Secretary in France,' he cut in tartly, 'But evidently not in England!' I proceeded, 'If Germany had demanded the dismissal of the most unpopular Minister in this country he would by that very demand be translated to the highest altitude of popular favour.'

The luncheon party was, I fear, not a success."

Since the above note was written, I have, through the courtesy of the German Foreign Office, been able to study the German Diplomatic Correspondence for the period in question. From this I am reminded that there were, in fact, two interviews with Metternich, separated by an interval of about a fortnight.

The first was on 14th July, 1908, when I was invited by Sir Edward Grey to lunch, to meet Count Metternich, and the second was the lunch already referred to at the German Embassy on the 28th. Both of these interviews were reported very fully to Berlin by Metternich, and came before the Kaiser, whose annotations to the reports are highly significant of the German attitude at that time. They are also worth study for the light they throw on the character of the Kaiser—the quick leaps from sense to superciliousness which later on precipitated the world catastrophe. I reproduce the full text of the report on Grey's luncheon party, and extracts from the later interview with myself:—

SECRET.

London, July 16th, 1908.

Marginal Comments by the Kaiser.

The day before yesterday Sir Edward Grey invited me to breakfast* at his house with Mr. Lloyd George. The present Chancellor of the Exchequer has in a short time educated himself from an ultra-radical Welsh lawyer into a leading and esteemed personality in his Party and in the Cabinet. As he thinks imperially he is also respected by the Unionists. If I remember rightly, he allowed himself some years ago as a

* Lunch.

representative of the Opposition to have now
and then a dig at Germany in Jingo fashion.
As responsible Minister I found him to be of a
conciliatory attitude of mind.

When I touched upon the question raised in
Parliament regarding espionage, he agreed with
me that unfortunately every bit of nonsense was
believed here, as soon as it had to do with
Germany.

When I remarked that it was a pity that
English policy seemed to wish to exchange
French friendship for German hostility, and that
the Entente policy had called forth the uneasiness in Europe, Sir Edward Grey stated more or
less as follows: During the last ten years
England had several times very nearly got into
warlike complications with France and Russia.
Without an amicable arrangement it would
probably have come to a war already. There
was only an Entente with France. None " yet "
with Russia. Against this, Germany had the
Triple Alliance. It was incomprehensible how
one could speak in this connection of a policy
to isolate Germany.

Mr. Lloyd George joined in by saying that
it probably was the diplomatic support of France
by England which had upset Germany (1). Sir
Edward Grey replied that as far as Morocco was
concerned, England was pledged to give that
support.

I remarked that France was in an absolutely
safe position as long as she recognised the *status
quo* in Europe (2). Alone she could not attack
this. However, supported by England the idea
of revenge might one day come to life again (3).
Avis au lecteur: The article in the " Temps,"
which recommended England to have a strong
army in order to become qualified for an
alliance.

When Mr. Lloyd George expressed the
opinion that he did not believe France had
intentions of war, although the French had not
been able to make up their minds to recognise
the pact, I replied that I also did not believe
in any such intentions of the French. Also,
that I had not the slightest objection to England

(1) *Yes.*

(2) *German Territory!*

(3) *Well said!*

settling its disputes with other nations. On the other hand, in political journalism the friends and defenders of English foreign policy took care to spread the conviction that here one was not dealing merely with a settling of disputes, but simultaneously with the producing of a bulwark against the German Power. This procedure did not comply with a friendly tendency, and could not be taken as such in Germany, but was bound to call forth uneasiness there, and specially in Europe (4). Sir Edward Grey then remarked that the unpleasant part of the situation was caused by the fact that we mutually blamed each other for having hostile intentions. The belief in an eventual English attack existed in Germany; here, however, one believed that the German Fleet was built to threaten England's position.

Both Ministers were of the opinion that the situation between England and Germany turned round the naval question. The expenditure for the English fleet would as a result of the German naval programme (5) and the speeding up (6) in naval construction increase to such an extent, and at the same time apprehensions of the German danger would increase so in intensity, that relations between the countries could not improve as long as they were getting up against each other in naval rivalry (7). Every Englishman would spend his last penny to preserve their superiority at sea (8), on which depends not only England's position in the world, but also its existence as an independent State. The ruinous expenditure to which the naval rivalry led (9) could not make the relations between the two nations prosper. Anybody who only knew England a little, knew that there was no intention here to threaten (10) Germany with the English fleet or attack Germany at all. Taking into consideration the proportions of the English Army, a landing would be clearly out of the question. Mr. Lloyd George remarked jokingly that Prince Bismarck had said, when on some occasion or other the question of an English landing was discussed, that in a case like that he would leave it to the police to arrest

(4) *Quite right.*

(5) *Wrong! A result of England's ambitions for world empire and tendency to see phantoms.*

(6) *Has not been speeded up!*

(7) *Does not exist! Ours is limited by law!*

(8) *See Nauticus, they have it 3 times over already !!!*

(9) *Such insolent talk has never been heard from England, not even in the days of acutest tension with Russia about Afghanistan! It has never ventured to require Russia to withdraw its troops from the border, or to stop the reinforcements of its garrisons.*

(10) *?! They have done so permanently already.*

the English corps on landing. The conditions to-day were still exactly the same when it was a question of England threatening Germany. To England, on the contrary. a powerful German Fleet (11) with a still more powerful Army in the background, was a real danger (12).

I replied that a German invasion existed only in the imagination of the English. No sensible person was thinking of it in Germany (13). Unfortunately fleet building had become more expensive through the invention of the " Dreadnought " (13), through which England had lost its immense advantage and other seafaring nations had been compelled to adopt the same large types of ships and consequently to high expenditure in connection herewith. But, *à qui la faute?* During the last few days there had been a discussion in the House of Commons about the introduction of a still larger type of ship, a floating fortress. As long as the English defence policy tended to create uneasiness in Germany, I considered a curtailment in the armaments at sea as being out of the question (13). Sir Edward Grey would first have to introduce a political *détente* between both countries and through his policy in Central Europe re-establish the belief that his Ententes would not be one day misused against us (14) before the ground would be cleared for a possible discussion about the curtailment of sea armaments (15), not before. Mr. Lloyd George, who took a lively part in the discussion about the naval construction, answered that a slowing down of the tempo in our fleet building (16) would contribute more quickly to reassure public opinion than any political action could. We should find them on this side most ready to meet us half-way in establishing a joint basis for curtailment of the fleet building on both sides (17). The introduction of the Dreadnought type had been a great mistake from the English side. The Government here would give every possible guarantee (18) that no new type should be introduced (19) if we could come to an understanding. He had very much

(11) *Will never be powerful compared with England ! and still less of a danger than the already superior English fleet is to us.*

(12) *That after my speech at the Guildhall is first-class cheek !*

(13) *Quite right.*

(14) *Very good.*

(15) *Wrong ! We will not discuss that ! We shall never be dictated to as to how our armament should be constituted.*

(16) *We have no fast tempo. Neither are we building SECRET " Dreadnoughts " for other nations—which are then bought by England—or camouflaged as an armoured cruiser, suddenly turn up as battleships.*

(17) *This unheard-of demand the English Minister should put first to Roosevelt, Clemenceau, Mirabello* or Japan ! The replies would be cheerful ! Why only to us ? Because they believe that my diplomacy is fed up, and is being impressed by their shouting for war.*

(18) *We don't need it.*

(19) *Is the same to us.*

* Italian Naval Minister.

regretted that the correspondence between His
Majesty the Kaiser and Lord Tweedmouth had
not been published at the time.   From that
correspondence the friendly feeling of His
Majesty the Kaiser for England would have
become clear to the public and he would also
have seen in His Majesty's letter a justification
for entering into confidential discussion with us
about naval expenditure (20).   If he had at the
time had the responsibility for the State Finances
he would indeed have insisted in the Cabinet
on the publication of the correspondence (21).
A conference at The Hague was not the proper
way (22) to reach curtailment in naval expenditure.   If, as he fervently hoped, it should ever
come to this, it must not be tried in an official
manner, such as with an exchange of notes (23).
Unofficial confidential discussions which must
not be made public at all (24), would, if an
understanding between England and ourselves
in this matter were at all possible, be more likely
to conduce to the desired end (25).

Sir Edward Grey agreed with his colleague
except on the point where the latter had recommended the timeliness of the publication of the
correspondence.

I told Mr. Lloyd George he was right: that
neither a conference at The Hague nor even
less an official proposal by way of a note (26)
from the English to the German Government,
would solve the question of decreasing the fleet
expenditure (27); that I even considered an
official movement (28) in this direction under
the circumstances very dubious (29) and grave
and dangerous, but for the rest I would not be
moved from the safe ground which I had taken
up with my demand: First a policy of reassurance, then we can talk about the fleet (30).

In reporting this discussion I have left out a
good deal and have, in order to be brief, only
mentioned the most important parts.   The
incidental things, however, contribute to the
right colouring of the whole picture.   I allow
myself, in order not to be misunderstood, to
add the following supplementary final remarks.

Your Highness knows that for a long time the

(20) *He would have re-
ceived a nice reply from
me. Would have no
result !*

(21) *Aha !*

(22) *Right.*

(23) *I should answer
them with bombs.*

(24) Out of the ques-
tion !   *So that the
German people don't
rise and smash the
windows of the Minister
in with bricks !*

(25) *No.*

(26) *That would be a
declaration of war !*

(27) *Right.*

(28) *We should look upon
that as a declaration of
war.*

(29) *Definitely war.*

(30) *No ! There will be
no talk about that at
all !*

English Government has entertained the wish to come to an agreement with us about naval expenditure (31). Before and during the second Conference at The Hague an abortive attempt was made in this direction. If I have been rightly informed, the fear has already arisen on our side that the English Government might, alone or with others, put an official proposal to us for limitation of our naval programme and that from this an immediate danger of war would result (32). It is my firm belief that the present Government is far (33) from setting before us, through any sort of ultimatum, the issue of either giving in or going to war. She has no sort of intention of putting a threatening question to us (34). She desires much more to prevent later possibilities of war through timely agreement. If I decline somebody's wish, I need not for that reason fight with him at once. This comes only then into consideration when I see that the other one puts on the air of forcing (36) his wish (35) upon me.

(31) *Out of the question! They will first have to achieve this with other great Powers!*

(32) *Yes.*

(33) *??*

(34) *In the conversation of the Ministers lies already a hidden threat! Let them compare themselves first with America. The latter is much stronger than we are!*

(36) *He does that.*

(35) *In our position it is better that such a wish should not be expressed!*

To both Ministers I have made the fulfilment of their wish dependent on one condition, the explanation of which lies in our hands. I would have needlessly constricted future possibilities, and made the position more acute, if I had given them to understand that we never and under no circumstances would be prepared to come to an arrangement with them about naval expenditure. The price which I mentioned for this will certainly not soon be paid to us by Sir Edward Grey.   (*Signed*) P. Metternich.

Final Remarks of the Kaiser:—

Bravo! Metternich! Has done his business very well, except in one point, which is the most important. The Ambassador has overlooked entirely that he was not permitted, even if entirely non-committally and only as a private opinion, to [? agree]* to the insolent demands of the English Ministers to make their peacefulness dependent on the diminution of our sea force. Through that he has put himself on a very dangerous slope. I am sorry for him because of that. It must be pointed out to him that I do *not* wish a good understanding with England at the expense of the extension of the German fleet. If England only intends graciously to hold out her hand to us with the indication

* Word missing in original.

that we should curtail our fleet, then this is an excessive impudence, which contains a great insult for the German people and its Kaiser, and which should be refused *a limine* by the Ambassador! By the same rights France and Russia could then demand a curtailment of our land force. As soon as one allows any foreign Power under any pretext whatsoever to have something to say about our own armaments, then one may retire, like Portugal and Spain! The German fleet is not built *against* anybody and not *against* England either? But according to *our* needs! This has been said quite clearly in the Navy Law and has remained unchanged for eleven years! This law is being carried out to the very last tittle: whether the British like it or not does not worry us. If they want a war, *they* may *start* it, we are not afraid of it!

(*Signed*) Wilhelm R.I.

Here are the most important passages in the report Count Metternich sent to Berlin of our second conversation—with the Kaiser's marginal notes:—

Kaiser's Marginal Notes.

" . . . On the same day I had a long discussion with the Chancellor of the Exchequer, Mr. Lloyd George. . . . I explained to him why the political course followed by England during the last six years was bound to lead to the present uncomfortable situation: formerly on the side of the Triple Alliance, now on the side of Germany's opponents; Morocco thrown as an apple of discord between Germany and France; France encouraged in the idea of *revanche* through hope of help from England; Entente politics as a bulwark against alleged German expansion and aggressivenesss; spy scares and fears of invasion; a twisting of German intentions in political journalism, a slandering of the motives of German politics, and nothing done

(1) *A very good summary!*

to stop it (1). Through the unchecked poisoning of public opinion, I said, we are being pushed unwillingly into the perilous position of seeing the spectre of war rising on the horizon—a spectre which Mr. Lloyd George and I are alike convinced that both our Governments as well as both our countries wish to expel (2).

(2) *That's not my idea at all! If England wants to have war, just let her start it, we'll give her what for!*

The Minister showed an understanding of all this, but, like every one of his countrymen, he sees in the naval question the central point of German-English relations, around which everything turns and of which all other happenings are a result. . . . England, he said, had the money and would strain every nerve to retain supremacy at sea (3). With a race in fleet building (4) the tension would unavoidably be increased, and therewith at the same time the danger of a collision would grow. At the end of the crushing armaments (5) the distance between the two fleets would still be great, and we should not be any nearer to our object (6). We should be playing into the hands of two tendencies here which he was fighting against, and which were not in our interest. With the growth of expenditure for the Navy in the race between Germany and England, new financial sources would have to be found and all thoughts would be turned to the Tariff Party, which promised new receipts at the expense of foreign countries and without further burdening the Englishman. . . . Further: the more the German fleet approached the English in strength (7) the stronger the thought would become that English safety no longer depended on its fleet alone, but that England must also develop an Army. In order to have a really strong Army there was only one means: Conscription. With the quick growth of the German Navy the possibility of an invasion increased—although he did not at all believe in such (8) an intention—and then England would be pushed into the introduction of Conscription (9). The military party and a great number of Conservatives were already anxiously wishing for this. With the approach of the German menace, the great mass of the people, which as yet would not have anything to do with conscription, would soon be won for it (10). . . . I replied that Germany had sufficient means at its disposal to produce a very respectable fleet, apart from its army. . . . Even if the burden were heavy, it would be necessary in view of the international situation. At least ten (11) years' hard work would be necessary to produce an armed country, and an army equal to the Continental pattern. If we saw that England was going over to Conscription, with its eyes on Germany, in order to reach an alliance with France, I did not believe that we should wait

(3) *Nobody wants to dispute that!*

(4) *Does not exist at all; only in the English brain!*

(5) *? Not for us!*

(6) *But that is not our object.*

(7) *Absolutely out of the question and has never been attempted.*

(8) *! !*

(9) *It would do them good.*

(10) Tant mieux.

(11) Sancta Simplicitas! 50!

B

(12) *We should be totally indifferent.*

(13) *This is unheard of! and is a result of Metternich going into the idea at all.*

(14) *This is talk which until now has been only used against fellows like China or Italy! It is unheard of!*

(15) *We have not got that far yet!*

(16) *! !*

(17) *Bluff!*

(18) *No! Three times no. After the above words NEVER!*

(19) *Bosh!*

patiently for this process to be carried to completion (12). . . . Mr. Lloyd George then returned to his pet idea, the slackening down in the speed of naval construction (13) and exhorted me to make use of the time during which the peace-loving Liberal Government was at the helm. . . . Considering how much greater importance the fleet has for England than it has for Germany, the English fleet must always be a good bit stronger than ours, in order to be able to furnish that feeling of security which England requires from it, and at the same time sufficiently powerful to keep any wanton idea of attack on her from arising on our side (14). The German fleet, however, should be strong enough to give adequate protection for our overseas interests, and at the same time to give the English fleet, despite the latter's necessary superiority, the feeling that it would be risky to pick a quarrel with us (15). The relative strength of 2 : 3, it seemed to him, would establish the right balance (16) at sea between us. He could not cite the authority of the English Government for this, but only uttered his own personal view; he knew, however, that we should find the greatest friendly response from the Liberal Cabinet (17) if we should be inclined to discuss the slackening down of the speed of naval construction (18). If even we only agreed to build one Dreadnought less every year, this would result in a complete change of the feeling in England towards us (19). . . ."

The above extracts give a fairly good picture of the course of my discussion with Metternich. How the whole report, and in particular my unspeakable impertinence in daring to suggest, on any grounds and for any consideration, that there should be an agreed limit to the German Navy, affected the Kaiser is best seen in his footnote to the report, which I transcribe in full:—

"This sort of conversation as it has been carried on between Lloyd George and Metternich is utterly unworthy and provoking for Germany! I must beg him in future to have nothing to do with that sort of expectoration. Here he has accepted very patiently as a listener the opinions and orders of English statesmen, and has only ventured protests which had no effect at all. He should give these gentlemen, *who do not wish to see ' our wanton ideas of an attack,' realised,* an answer like ' Go to H——,' etc. That would bring these fellows to their senses again. That Lloyd George even dared to come out with an order for defining the speed of OUR building is beyond the limit, but is a result of Metternich putting himself during the first discussions on the dangerous path of *' a possibility not being out of the question.'* The clever British are trying to hook him, and sooner or later they will pull the string and drag him out; despite this ' private talk,' ' non-committal character of expression of opinion,' etc.! He should *ab ovo* refuse everything with such remarks as, ' No country allows itself to be dictated to or admonished by another country about the size and kind of its armaments.' ' I refuse to discuss such a matter.' For the rest, let them read the Navy Law —known for eleven years—and Nauticus!

Metternich should give that sort of fanatic a kick in the ——; he is too soft!"

The luncheon party had a further sequel, of which I was not made aware at the time, and have only recently learned through a perusal of the German Diplomatic papers.

At the time of my interview with Metternich, I was planning to visit Germany in the following month of August, 1908, in order to study on the spot the German systems of industrial insurance, with a view to preparing my own scheme of health and unemployment insurance for this country. Metternich, reporting this to Berlin, had urged that the British Chancellor of the Exchequer, whom he described as " one of the most outstanding personalities in England, and one who most probably would be called upon one day to stand at the head of a Liberal Government," should be treated with the utmost consideration. The Kaiser accordingly arranged that I should be invited to pay him a visit. But in the meantime Metternich came over hurriedly to talk to the German Imperial Chancellor, von Buelow, who had reprimanded him for his incautious conversation with me. I understand that von Buelow was warned that I should certainly discuss the Navy with His Imperial Majesty, and that if Wilhelm used to my face the sort of remark he had noted on Metternich's report, a grave instance of *lèse-majesté* would be liable to ensue. A hasty warning was sent to Court and I never received the Kaiser's suggested invitation.

I was, however, successful in securing an interview with the Vice-Chancellor, von Bethmann-Hollweg, who was in Berlin at the time. He was then in charge of Health Insurance and had a very thorough acquaintance with its working. He was very helpful to me in my investigations on that subject. He was good enough to invite me and my party to be his guests at a big dinner which he gave at the Zoologischer Garten.

Von Bethmann-Hollweg was an attractive but not an arresting personality. He gave me the idea of an intelligent, industrious and eminently sensible bureaucrat, but he did not leave on my mind an impression of having met a man of power who might one day shake destiny. He gave us a good dinner, and at its close great tankards of lager beer were brought round, and von Bethmann-Hollweg grew talkative and combative.

He embarked upon a discussion of the European situation, and was very bitter about what he called " the encirclement of Germany with an iron ring by France, Russia and England." I did my best to assure him that, so far as England was concerned, there was not the slightest desire to enter into any hostile combinations against Germany, and that we were most anxious to live in peace and neighbourliness with his great country. I told him, however, that England was very uneasy about the growth of the German Navy, and felt that it was aimed straight at her heart; and I repeated all that I had said to Count Metternich about our being an island and completely dependent upon the sea for our very existence. He was not very enthusiastic about the German Navy, and I perceived that he was no advocate of a shipbuilding programme that would be regarded as a menace by Great Britain; but he did his best to convince me that the German people had no desire to attack England. The impression he left on my mind was that official Germany was genuinely apprehensive of the *rapprochement* between France and England, and England and Russia. They were quite convinced that King Edward was organising a Confederacy with a hostile purport against Germany. The King was regarded as an inveterate enemy of German might.

This led to one extraordinary outburst in the course of his conversation, when he reverted to the theme of the growing hostility of England, France and Russia against Germany, and the " iron ring " they were pressing round her. " An iron ring! " he repeated violently, shouting out the statement, and waving his arm to the whole assembled company. " England is embracing France. She is making friends with Russia. But it is not that you love each other; it is that you hate Germany! " And he repeated and literally shouted the word " hate " thrice. He became very excited, and his discretion was certainly not under control, for he went on to show a distinct antipathy even to Bavaria, when he contrasted the attachment of the eastern provinces of Prussia, and of Berlin, to the Kaiser, and their readiness to die at a word from him, with the more lukewarm attitude of Bavaria.

Incidentally, he let in a flood of light upon the view of the ordinary German as to the decadence of England. He was clearly of the opinion that we were no longer a hard-working people; he thought that we loved our ease too much, and that we were a nation of week-enders. He gave a description of his own day: how he rose at seven o'clock, and worked until eight; then went for a ride until nine, then had his breakfast; afterwards resumed his daily tasks; worked practically till dinner, and kept going right through the week. He said, " In England, you go to your office at eleven; you have a long luncheon hour; you leave at four; on Thursday you go to the country; you remain there until Tuesday morning, and you call it a week-end!"

It is fair to say that this was after dinner! But I am not at all sure that this revelation of the Continental pre-war idea of English degeneracy had not something to do with the contempt with which military Germany contemplated the possibility of our intervention later on. It was very generally assumed that English fibre had been softened and disintegrated by prosperity. The poor show we had made in the Boer War had confirmed this idea.

What made it more significant was that his personal attitude towards England and Englishmen was extremely friendly, and this was not a mere matter of words, for he had sent his son to Oxford. His view was that the German worker was a better man than the English worker; that the German scientists were easily superior in quality and numbers to the insignificant band of British scientists. On the other hand, he seemed to have a better opinion of the English than of the German upper and middle classes. He attributed the superiority of the German worker to the fact that in his early years he received a stern military training in obedience which taught him habits of discipline and continuity.

I left Berlin gravely disturbed by the expressions of distrust and suspicion I had encountered in so high and friendly a quarter. It seemed to me to be ominously significant of what must be the general opinion at the time in leading German circles.

At the other end of the scale, I was also deeply impressed by a scene I witnessed at Stuttgart during the same tour. On our arrival there we learnt that a " Zeppelin " was about to make an exhibition flight. We went along to the field where the giant airship was moored, to find that by a last-minute accident it had crashed and been wrecked. Of course we were deeply disappointed, but disappointment was a totally inadequate word for the agony of grief and dismay which swept over the massed Germans who witnessed the catastrophe. There was no loss of life to account for it. Hopes and ambitions far wider than those concerned with a scientific and mechanical success appeared to have shared the wreck of the dirigible. Then the crowd swung into the chanting of " Deutschland über Alles " with a fanatic fervour of patriotism. What spearpoint of Imperial advance did this airship portend? These incidents were cracks in the cold surface, through which the hot, seething lava of unrest could be seen stirring uneasily underneath.

After these few glimpses of our foreign problem, I was drawn back during the succeeding years into the anxious preoccupations of domestic affairs. I understood, nevertheless, that there was a growing menace to peace abroad, and social order at home, which we must strive to avert if possible by peaceable methods, though I realised that we could not altogether rule out of account the possibility of a failure of such methods.

2. PLAN FOR A PARTY TRUCE

My observation to Metternich, in the conversation already reported, about the possibility of our being driven to adopt Conscription, was by no means a casual sentence thrown out by me as a debating point in the course of an argument. Still less was it a piece of bald bluff, used in the hope of convincing or impressing the German Ambassador.

I had for some time past been growingly concerned with the precariousness of our position in the event of our naval defence being broken through. We had depended upon it for centuries to protect us against invasion from the Continent. Hitherto it had not failed us, and this immunity had given us a sense of complete security. This feeling was expressed by Sir John Fisher in his famous remark that " We could sleep soundly in our beds because of the invincibility of our Navy." But the rapid march of scientific discovery, constantly revealing the existence of hitherto unsuspected forces, which were capable of the most formidable utilisation for service and disservice to mankind, made me feel that it was quite within the realm of possibility that one day there might be an invention which would neutralise our superiority, and reduce us to equality with, if not inferiority to, our neighbours. Inventions which portended such a menace had already appeared. Whether the peril would come from the air or from under the waters, I knew not; but no one could feel assured that such possibilities were altogether out of the reckoning. In such an event our position would be one of complete helplessness in the face of an invader with a powerful army.

We had two fundamental weaknesses in such a contingency. The first was that our army was too insignificant to stand up against the gigantic forces of the Continent. The second was that we were so overwhelmingly dependent upon overseas supplies for our food, that if these were cut off we should, within a few months, be brought to the very verge of starvation. It was this consideration amongst others that always led me to urge that we ought to devote more thought to the development of the resources of British soil.

I did not agree with Lord Roberts' case that a large force could at that time be landed from the Continent to capture London. In the absence of some invention which had not yet been found, or at least had not yet been developed, our Navy was powerful enough to prevent any emergency of that kind arising. My apprehension was entirely as to what the unknown future had in store for us if science neutralised the efficiency of our warships.

There were ominous clouds gathering over the Continent of Europe and perceptibly thickening and darkening. The submarine and the Zeppelin indicated a possible challenge to the invincibility of our defence. I felt we should be safer if we had in this country a system of training for our young manhood which would fit it for the defence of the Realm in the possible event of an invasion of our shores. I was opposed to conscript armies of the Continental type, and thought them designed rather for aggression than for defence. For the latter purpose it seemed to me that something resembling the Swiss militia system would suffice and might be adopted here.

It was with these thoughts in my mind that I ventured in 1910 to submit to the leaders of both political parties in this country a series of proposals for national co-operation over a period of years, to deal with special matters of urgent importance.

In the year 1910 we were beset by an accumulation of grave issues —rapidly becoming graver. The gravest have not yet been solved. It was becoming evident to discerning eyes that the Party and Parliamentary system was unequal to coping with them. There was a jam at the legislative dock gates and there was no prospect of the growing traffic being able to get through. The shadow of unemployment was rising ominously above the horizon. Our international rivals were forging ahead at a great rate and jeopardising our hold on the markets of the world. There was an arrest in that expansion of our foreign trade which had contributed to the phenomenal prosperity of the previous half-century, and of which we had made such a muddled and selfish use. Our working population, crushed into dingy and mean streets, with no assurance that they would not be deprived of their daily bread by ill-health or trade fluctuations, were becoming sullen with discontent. Whilst we were growing more dependent on overseas supplies for our food, our soil was gradually going out of cultivation. The life of the countryside was wilting away and we were becoming dangerously over-industrialised. Excessive indulgence in alcoholic drinks was undermining the health and efficiency of a considerable section of the population. The Irish controversy was poisoning our relations with the United States of America. A great Constitutional struggle over the House of Lords threatened revolution at home, another threatened civil war at our doors in Ireland. Great nations were arming feverishly for an apprehended struggle into which we might be drawn by some visible or invisible ties, interests, or sympathies. Were we prepared for all the terrifying contingencies?

Moved by this prospect I submitted to Mr. Asquith a Memorandum urging that a truce should be declared between the Parties for the purpose of securing the co-operation of the leading party statesmen in a settlement of our national problems—Second Chamber, Home Rule, the development of our agricultural resources, National Training for Defence, the remedying of social evils, and a fair and judicial enquiry into the working of our fiscal system.

Mr. Asquith regarded the proposal with considerable favour, and it was decided to submit it to four or five members of the Cabinet for their observations. So far as I can recollect, the only Cabinet Ministers who were called into consultation were Lord Crewe, Sir Edward Grey, Lord Haldane, and Mr. Winston Churchill. I cannot recall any criticism in detail from any of them. They all approved of the idea in principle, and it was agreed that the proposal should be submitted to Mr. Balfour, who was still the Leader of the Conservative Party. The only outsiders to whom I showed the document were Mr. F. E. Smith (subsequently Lord Birkenhead) and Mr. Garvin. They were very pleased with the whole conception.

Mr. Balfour was by no means hostile; in fact, he went a long way towards indicating that personally he regarded the proposal with a considerable measure of approval. He was not, however, certain of the reception which would be accorded to it by his party. Unfortunately, at that time he was not very firmly seated in the saddle. The Die-Hard cry against his leadership was getting audibly shriller each day. However, he consulted some of his leading colleagues, and he received from them replies which were by no means discouraging. I understood that Lord Lansdowne, Lord Cawdor, Lord Curzon, Mr. Walter Long, and Mr. Austen Chamberlain favoured the plan. When he came to summon a more formal and general meeting of his colleagues, he again found that the ablest members of the Conservative Party were by no means antipathetic to the idea. So far as I can recollect, the only opposition came from the late Lord Londonderry. But when Mr. Balfour proceeded later on to sound the opinion of less capable and therefore more narrowly partisan members of his party, he encountered difficulties which proved insurmountable. He called upon me one evening at 11, Downing Street to discuss the matter, and I found him then much more hesitant and reluctant. I gathered from him that the chief objection entertained by his colleagues was to my presence in such a combination. I was so completely associated in their minds with extreme radical proposals, I was so much in the front of the offence at that time, and I had said so many wounding things in the scrimmage, that they were more than doubtful whether they could secure the adhesion of their supporters to any Coalition of which I was a member.

I instantly assured him that, as far as I was concerned, I would not make my inclusion in the Ministry a condition of my support. On the contrary, I was quite prepared to keep out of it and give it my whole-hearted and zealous backing as an independent member of

the House of Commons, so long as it tackled its job with courage and
conviction. He then told me that there was one other man he felt
he would have to consult. He said: "You will be surprised when
I give you his name." When I heard it, I think I was rather
surprised that this individual should still hold such an important
and influential position in the councils of the Party, for he had
retired from active political life for a good many years: it was Mr.
Akers-Douglas, who had formerly been Chief Whip of the Conservative Party, and was then Lord Chilston. I remember one of
the last things Mr. Balfour said to me on that occasion. Putting his
hand on his forehead, looking down and more or less soliloquising,
he said: "I cannot become another Robert Peel in my party!"
After a short interval he added: "Although I cannot see where the
Disraeli is to come from, unless it be my cousin Hugh, and I cannot
quite see him fulfilling that rôle!" Mr. Akers-Douglas, however,
turned down the project for co-operation in settling these momentous
national issues, and there was an end to it. It very nearly came off.
It was not rejected by the real leaders of the Party, but by men who,
for some obscure reason best known to political organisations, have
great influence inside the councils of a party without possessing any of
the capabilities that excite general admiration and confidence outside.

I am not concerned, in these War reminiscences, to examine the
possibilities of this project, had it been adopted and carried out,
except in so far as it might have altered or modified the international
situation. Had it materialised then, there would by 1914 have been
a body of trained young men aggregating between a million and one-
and-a-half million, fit for incorporation in our armies, shortly after
the declaration of war. What is still more important, there would
have been rifles and other equipment for them, which it took us over
eighteen months to manufacture in the Great War, and the requisite
machinery for manufacturing still more for ourselves and our Allies.
There would also have been a staff of trained and competent officers
fit to lead such an army into the field. Had such a force been in
existence when the crisis arose in 1914, and had Germany been
conscious of the fact that the British contribution would not be
limited to her "contemptible little army" of six divisions, but that
there was a large body of trained and equipped men behind that
small Expeditionary Force which could soon be made fit to take an
effective part in the fighting line, Germany would have hesitated
before plunging the world into the disaster of the Great War. The
young men who were sent to the trenches during the last two years
of the War had received much less training than an application of
the Swiss Militia System would have given to those who would have
been called to the Colours in 1911, 1912, 1913, and 1914.

Even if the existence of such a formidable force had not influenced
the course of events in the direction of peace, the contribution made

by it in the earlier stages of the War might well have been decisive and have shortened the term of this devastating struggle.

I have heard it said that, at the battle of Ypres, the troops on both sides were so tired out by the end that the irruption of one fresh division on either side would have achieved victory for the army lucky enough to secure so timely a reinforcement. A number of Territorial battalions, not one of which had received anything like the Swiss training, were thrown into the battle line before the end of the fight, and, according to the testimony of Sir John French, rendered invaluable aid to our exhausted troops. If, instead of 19 battalions of Territorials with able but amateur officers, there had been three or four hundred battalions of more fully trained men, led by thoroughly equipped officers, the battle of Ypres would not have been a stalemate, but a victory which might have liberated Flanders and ended the War.

The same observation applies to the Dardanelles, where the fatal delays in landing troops which enabled the Turks to bring reinforcements were due to the fact that we could not spare the one extra division necessary to make up an Expeditionary Force—not even a spare division—until it was too late to achieve any results. Even from the point of view of filling up the serious gaps in the ranks of our Regular Army, due to the disastrous retreat from Mons, the heavy fighting on the Marne and at Ypres, the possession of a trained Militia would have been invaluable. Young men with an aggregate training of about a year, mixed up with the Regulars, would have been more useful than the Reservists, a large number of whom had been softened and debilitated by years of civilian occupation. All these considerations constantly leapt to my mind during the progress of the campaign, and always brought with them a regret for the "Great Refusal" of 1910.

There is much to be said in favour of the Party system. The open conflict of Parties is better for a country than the squalid intrigues of personal ambitions or of rival interests conducted in the dark. But there are times when it stands seriously in the way of the highest national interests. On these occasions it hinders, delays and thwarts real progress, and in the event the nation suffers heavily. I shall always regard the rejection of the proposals for co-operation in 1910 as a supreme instance of this kind of damage. On the other hand, the ground for co-operation must be one of genuine national well-being. A suspension of party hostilities merely in order to ensure a distribution of patronage and power amongst the leading contestants, degrades and enervates politics.

3. THE AGADIR CRISIS, 1911

As to the part I took in the Agadir incident, it is hardly necessary for me to write at any length. The story has been so fully and fairly told by both Mr. Winston Churchill and Sir Edward Grey that there is little which I need add.

My intervention was due largely to the fear that if things were allowed to drift, we might find ourselves drawn into a great European War on a question in which we were inextricably involved. For the French position in Morocco was part of the Lansdowne Treaty, and Sir Edward Grey in his book, "Twenty-Five Years," makes it clear that he regarded a dispute on anything which constituted a challenge to that settlement as something which we were bound to put in a different category from any dispute which might arise between France and Germany outside the four corners of that arrangement. I still think there is very great force in his contention in that respect.

The situation can be outlined in a few words. France, who had been accorded a zone of influence in Morocco by the Treaty of Algeciras, found it necessary to send an expedition to Fez. Germany, conceiving with some reason that France had annexationist designs, thought she would be entitled to corresponding compensations elsewhere, and promptly took steps to indicate her claim, and opened the negotiations by sending a gunboat to the Moroccan harbour of Agadir. This was a blundering and blustering kind of diplomacy, and when Britain, naturally concerned at its meaning and possible outcome, sent a communication to Berlin on the subject, our letter was left unanswered for weeks, while we learnt from France that the German Government was pressing quite impossible demands upon her as the price of withdrawal from Agadir.

It is hard to say whether there was real danger of war. There is an ominous passage in a dispatch from von Bethmann-Hollweg to the Kaiser, dated 15th July, 1911, when the German silence *vis-à-vis* Britain had already continued for eleven days. The Imperial Chancellor reported that Herr von Kiderlen, the German Foreign Secretary, had gathered from his discussion with the French Ambassador the impression that "in order to reach a favourable result, we shall certainly have to take a very strong line!" To this the Kaiser makes a marginal note:—

"Then I must return home at once. For I can't let my Government take that sort of action without being right on the spot so as to keep a careful watch on the consequences and have them well in hand! Anything else would be unpardonable, and too parliamentary! *Le Roi s'amuse!* And meantime we are steering straight for mobilisation! That must not happen WITHOUT ME!

Besides, our Allies must first be informed about this! For it may draw them in, in sympathy!"

There can be no doubt as to the meaning of those words. The Kaiser clearly contemplated the mobilisation of his armies as a not unlikely result of the diplomatic situation. In 1914 mobilisation made for war—it meant war.

When the rude indifference of the German Government to our communication had lasted for seventeen days—from the 4th to the 21st July—I felt that matters were growing tensely critical and that we were drifting clumsily towards war. It was not merely that by failing even to send a formal acknowledgment of the Foreign Secretary's letter the Germans were treating us with intolerable insolence, but that their silence might well mean that they were blindly ignorant of the sense in which we treated our obligations under the Treaty, and might not realise until too late that we felt bound to stand by France. These reasons prompted me to make the Mansion House speech which has already been so fully dealt with by Sir Edward Grey and Mr. Churchill.

On the 21st July I was due to speak to the Bankers at their annual banquet to the Chancellor of the Exchequer and I decided to take advantage of the occasion to make a statement which would warn Germany of the peril into which her Ministers were rushing her so heedlessly.

I felt that I had no right to intervene in a matter which was in the sphere of the Foreign Office, and to make a declaration which might involve our relations with Germany, without obtaining the consent of both the Prime Minister and Grey. Before delivering it, therefore, I submitted its terms to the Prime Minister. He fully approved, and sent immediately to the Foreign Office to ask Sir Edward Grey to come to the Cabinet Room in order to obtain his views and procure his sanction. My recollection is that when he arrived, he cordially assented to every word of my draft, and I delivered the speech later on to the Bankers at the Mansion House.*

The genesis of that speech is, as I have said, quite correctly recorded by both Grey and Churchill, but I have here given my own confirmation of their narrative, because my public intervention at

* The passage of my speech in question was as follows:

"But I am also bound to say this—that I believe it is essential in the highest interests, not merely of this country, but of the world, that Britain should at all hazards maintain her place and her prestige amongst the Great Powers of the world. Her potent influence has many a time been in the past, and may yet be in the future, invaluable to the cause of human liberty. It has more than once in the past redeemed continental nations, who are sometimes too apt to forget that service, from over-whelming disaster, and even from national extinction. I would make great sacrifices to preserve peace. I conceive that nothing would justify a disturbance of international goodwill except questions of the gravest national moment. But if a situation were to be forced upon us in which peace could only be preserved by the surrender of the great and beneficent position Britain has won by centuries of heroism and achievement, by allowing Britain to be treated, where her interests were vitally affected, as if she were of no account in the Cabinet of Nations, then I say emphatically that peace at that price would be a humiliation intolerable for a great country like ours to endure. National honour is no party question. The security of our great international trade is no party question. The peace of the world is much more likely to be secured if all nations realise fairly what the conditions of peace must be. . . ."

that time in the sphere of foreign affairs was so unusual that a rumour gained currency, and even finds place in German and Austrian official diplomatic correspondence, that I was merely acting as a mouthpiece to read out a statement prepared by the Cabinet, and was at most but vaguely aware of its implications. Even E. T. Raymond avers that what I read was a passage carefully prepared for me by Sir Edward Grey. But I have not the least desire to shuffle off my true responsibility in this connection. The initiative in this matter was my own, as was the wording of the statement. Certainly I secured authoritative approval before I made it, but it was not actually submitted to the whole Cabinet in advance.

The effect of the speech was unquestionably to clear the air, and avert any danger of Europe drifting unawares into war. The German Government, naturally, was furious, for its gunboat diplomacy had received a severe and well-merited rebuff. Metternich was instructed to make representations about my speech to the British Foreign Office. He did so in a very stern manner, but found little to cheer him in his reception. He reported to von Kiderlen-Waechter that " with reference to the speech of the Chancellor of the Exchequer, Grey was thoroughly uncompromising, defended it as moderate, and stated that it had been entirely right for this speech to be made." The truth was, of course, that the Wilhelmstrasse had over-reached itself, and taken a course which it was difficult either to explain or to explain away. The Austrian diplomatic correspondence shows that the Kaiser and his Minister thought the Government then in office in France was a weak one and lacked backbone. The German Foreign Office doubtless conceived that a sudden and dramatic rattling of the sabre would terrify this feeble Ministry and that by this means Germany would win substantial concessions in Morocco. But they were not prepared to go to war with both France and England, to make good this gamble.

Von Kiderlen-Waechter described my speech to the Austrian Ambassador at Berlin as " an unfair and colossal bluff." However, it was bluff he was not prepared to call. It was in truth by no means bluff, and if an equally clear statement of our attitude had been made in a July only three years later, it is conceivable that once again the peril of a recklessly incurred war might have been averted.

4. NO CABINET CONSIDERATION OF FOREIGN POLICY

During the eight years that preceded the war, the Cabinet devoted a ridiculously small percentage of its time to a consideration of foreign affairs. This was partly, but not altogether, due to the political conditions under which we worked. The 1906-14 Governments and Parliaments were engaged in a series of controversies on home affairs, each of which raised more passion than any dispute between the rival political parties within living memory.

Education, Temperance, Land Taxation—culminating in the most serious constitutional crisis since the days of the Reform Bill—the Parliament Act, Home Rule, and the Disestablishment of the Church in Wales: these subjects challenged an infinite variety of human interests, sentiment, and emotion, and the partisan warfare that raged round these topics was so fierce that by 1913 this country was brought to the verge of civil war.

Of course, certain aspects of foreign policy were familiar to those Ministers who attended the Committee of Imperial Defence, but apart from that the Cabinet as a whole were never called into genuine consultation upon the fundamental aspects of the foreign situation. There was a reticence and a secrecy which practically ruled out three-fourths of the Cabinet from the chance of making any genuine contribution to the momentous questions then fermenting on the continent of Europe, which ultimately ended in an explosion that almost shattered the civilisation of the world. During the whole of those eight years, when I was a member of the Cabinet, I can recall no such review of the European situation being given to us as that which Sir Edward Grey delivered to the Colonial Conference in 1907, or to the Prime Ministers of the Dominions at the Committee of Imperial Defence in 1911. Even there the information that was withheld was more important than that which was imparted. For instance, nothing was said about our military commitments. There was in the Cabinet an air of " hush hush " about every allusion to our relations with France, Russia and Germany. Direct questions were always answered with civility, but were not encouraged. We were made to feel that, in these matters, we were reaching our hands towards the mysteries, and that we were too young in the priesthood to presume to enter into the sanctuary reserved for the elect. So we confined our inquisitiveness and our counsel to the more mundane affairs in which we had taken part in Opposition during the whole of our political careers. Discussions, if they could be called dis-cussions, on foreign affairs, were confined to the elder statesmen who had seen service in some previous ministerial existence. Apart from the Prime Minister and the Foreign Secretary there were only two or three men such as Lord Loreburn, the Lord Chancellor, Lord Morley, Lord Crewe, and, for a short time, Lord Ripon, who were expected to make any contribution on the infrequent occasions when the Continental situation was brought to our awed attention. As a matter of fact, we were hardly qualified to express any opinion on so important a matter, for we were not privileged to know any more of the essential facts than those which the ordinary newspaper reader could gather from the perusal of his morning journal. I recollect the late Lord Northcliffe, at a dinner at Lord Birkenhead's house, where he was invited to meet a number of Cabinet Ministers in the Liberal Administration, telling us all quite bluntly that the Editor of a great London journal was better informed about what was happening in the capitals of the world than any Cabinet Minister. He maintained that all the information we got was carefully filtered. He might have gone further and said that much of the information essential for forming a sound opinion was deliberately withheld. When a Cabinet Minister first takes office, nothing gives him a greater sense of his personal importance than the stout little leather bag with a specially constructed key which is sent after him every night to any address which he may give. It is supposed to contain communications of the most deadly import and secrecy as to what is happening in Courts and Chancelleries throughout the world. As a matter of fact it is just a series of harmless dispatches from our representatives in every foreign country, great and small. There is not a dispatch which contains anything that the Foreign Office clerks who copied it, and the Foreign Office printers who set the type, and the numerous Private Secretaries who have access to these printed copies, could not read without the danger of any indiscreet revelation by any of them disturbing our relations with the most insignificant Kingdom or Republic in the world. All the things that mattered were conveyed in private and confidential letters from our Diplomatic Representatives abroad to the Foreign Secretary personally, in his private and unpublished replies, and in the interviews which he held with the Ambassadors at the Foreign Office in Downing Street. What mattered just as much, perhaps even more, were the secret arrangements arrived at between the military and naval staffs of Britain, France, and Russia as to the part their respective forces were expected to play in the event of war with Germany. None of these vital communications were placed at the disposal of the Cabinet. They were passed on to the Prime Minister, and perhaps to one or two other Ministers. The rest of us were kept in the dark and were therefore not in a position to assess the realities of the foreign situation. When Lord Ripon* was made leader of the House of Lords, having been in Cabinets since the days of Palmerston he knew from previous experience of the existence of secret interchanges of this character, and he asked Sir Edward Grey for an opportunity of perusing them, as he was leading the House of Lords and could hardly do so with judgment unless he were really informed.

There is no more conspicuous example of this kind of suppression of vital information than the way in which the military arrangements we entered into with France were kept from the Cabinet for six years. They came to my knowledge, first of all, in 1911, during the Agadir crisis, but the Cabinet as a whole were not acquainted with them before the following year. There is abundant evidence that both the French and the Russians regarded these military arrangements

---

* When I first entered the Cabinet, Lord Ripon was the oldest member and I was the youngest.

as practically tantamount to a commitment on our part to come to the aid of France in the event of her being attacked by Germany. When the British Government was hesitating at the end of July, 1914, as to whether it would support France in the event of a German attack, French statesmen almost reverted to the " Perfidious Albion " mood, and even the meek M. Paul Cambon said that the only question was whether the word " honour " was to be expunged from the British dictionary. On the whole, the view summarised in that pungent comment is the one I heard expressed by most supporters and opponents of our intervention in the Great War; and yet the Cabinet were never informed of these vital arrangements until we were so deeply involved in the details of military and naval plans that it was too late to repudiate the inference. To attempt then to set right the impression produced in the minds of our Allies would have created a new situation, involving a return, in an aggravated form, of the unpleasant relations with France which the Lansdowne Agreement of 1904 had, for the time being, brought to an end. In 1906 both Sir Henry Campbell-Bannerman and Mr. Asquith expressed grave doubts as to the wisdom of proceeding with these discussions. They ultimately assented to that course being pursued under pressure from Sir Edward Grey and Lord Haldane. When in 1912 (six years after they had been entered into) Sir Edward Grey communicated these negotiations and arrangements to the Cabinet the majority of its Members were aghast. Hostility scarcely represents the strength of the sentiment which the revelation aroused: it was more akin to consternation. Sir Edward Grey allayed the apprehensions of his colleagues to some extent by emphatic assurances that these military arrangements left us quite free, in the event of war, to decide whether we should or should not participate in the conflict. The Prime Minister also exercised his great authority with the Cabinet in the same direction. In spite of these assurances a number of Cabinet Ministers were not reconciled to the action taken by the Foreign Office, the War Office and the Admiralty, and these commitments undoubtedly added a good deal to the suspicions which made the task of Sir Edward Grey in securing unanimity in 1914 very much more difficult.

Personally, I was prepared to accept the Foreign Secretary's assurances that we were not committed. I was strengthened in my conviction that there was no definite commitment to give military support to France in her quarrels with Germany by the meetings of the Committee of Imperial Defence during the Agadir crisis. There Sir Henry Wilson, with the aid of a pointer and a big map, explained to us the whole of the arrangements which had been entered into with the French Foreign Office; they were contingent upon a German attack upon Belgium, and the march of German divisions through that country to attack France. In that contingency our

Expeditionary Force was to be taken to the Belgian frontier along the French railways, for the purpose of giving every support to the army which was resisting the invader in that quarter. I never doubted that, if the Germans interfered with the integrity and independence of Belgium, we were in honour bound to discharge our treaty obligations to that country.

CHAPTER II

THE CRASH

1. UNEXPECTED PLUNGE INTO WAR

How was it that the world was so unexpectedly plunged into this
terrible conflict? Who was responsible? Not even the astutest and
most far-seeing statesman foresaw in the early summer of 1914 that
the autumn would find the nations of the world interlocked in the
most terrible conflict that had ever been witnessed in the history of
mankind; and if you came to the ordinary men and women who were
engaged in their daily avocations in all countries there was not one of
them who suspected the imminence of such a catastrophe. Of those
who, in the first weeks of July, were employed in garnering their hay
or corn harvests, either in this country or on the Continent of Europe,
it is safe to say that not one ever contemplated the possibility that
another month would find them called to the Colours and organised
in battle array for a struggle that would end in the violent death of
millions of them, and in the mutilation of many more millions. The
nations slithered over the brink into the boiling cauldron of war
without any trace of apprehension or dismay.

When I first heard the news of the assassination of the Grand Duke
Ferdinand, I felt that it was a grave matter, and that it might provoke
serious consequences which only the firmest and most skilful handling
could prevent from developing into an emergency that would involve
nations. But my fears were soon assuaged by the complete calm with
which the Rulers and diplomats of the world seemed to regard the
event. The Kaiser departed for his usual yachting holiday in the
Norwegian fiords. His Chief Minister left for his usual shooting
party on his estate in Silesia. The acting Head of the German
Foreign Office went off on a honeymoon trip. A still more reassuring
fact—the military head of the German Army, von Moltke, left for
his cure in a foreign spa. The President of the French Republic and
his Prime Minister were on a ceremonial visit to Russia and only
arrived back in Paris on July 29th. Our Foreign Office preserved its
ordinary tranquillity of demeanour and thought it unnecessary to
sound an alarm even in the Cabinet Chamber. I remember that
some time in July, an influential Hungarian lady, whose name I have
forgotten, called upon me at 11, Downing Street, and told me that we
were taking the assassination of the Grand Duke much too quietly;

that it had provoked such a storm throughout the Austrian Empire as she had never witnessed, and that unless something were done immediately to satisfy and appease resentment, it would certainly result in war with Serbia, with the incalculable consequences which such an operation might precipitate in Europe. However, such official reports as came to hand did not seem to justify the alarmist view she took of the situation.

I cannot recall any discussion on the subject in the Cabinet until the Friday evening before the final declaration of war by Germany. We were much more concerned with the threat of imminent civil war in the North of Ireland. The situation there absorbed our thoughts, and constituted the subject-matter for the major part of our deliberations. Mr. Churchill recalls the fact that on that Friday, the 24th of July, we met in the Prime Minister's room in the House of Commons to discuss once more the Irish crisis, which was daily becoming more menacing. When the discussion was over the Cabinet rose, but the Foreign Secretary asked us to remain behind for a few more minutes as he had something to impart to us about the situation in Europe. When we resumed our seats he told us, for the first time, that he thought the position was very grave, but he was hopeful that the conversations which were proceeding between Austria and Russia might lead to a pacific settlement. So we separated upon that assurance. On Saturday Sir Edward Grey left for his fishing lodge in Hampshire, and all other Ministers followed his example and left town. On Sunday came the news of the landing of arms by Nationalists at Howth, near Dublin, and of a conflict with the military which arose out of that incident. The excitement over this event overshadowed, for the time being, the Continental situation. At that very hour Isvolzky, the Russian Ambassador in Paris, who was then at St. Petersburg, and M. Paleologue, the French Ambassador in Russia, both said: " It is war this time"; and later on the same Sunday afternoon, Monsieur Sazonow, the Russian Foreign Minister, made a similar statement to Monsieur Paleologue, and added: " It is too terrible to contemplate." Mr. Harold Nicolson, in his Life of his father, the late Lord Carnock, who was then Permanent Head of the Foreign Office, states that Sir Arthur Nicolson, as he then was, became so alarmed about the situation on this Sunday, that he took immediate steps to bring Sir Edward Grey back to London. War was declared by Austria on Serbia two days later and by Germany and Russia five days later.

Even then I met no responsible Minister who was not convinced that, in one way or another, the calamity of a great European war would somehow be averted.

2. NOBODY WANTED WAR

In looking back upon the incidents of those few eventful days one

feels like recalling a nightmare, and after reading most of the literature explaining why the nations went to war, and who was responsible, the impression left on my mind is one of utter chaos, confusion,
feebleness and futility, especially of a stubborn refusal to look at the
rapidly approaching cataclysm.   The nations backed their machines
over the precipice.   Amongst the rulers and statesmen who alone
could give the final word which caused great armies to spring from
the ground and march to and across frontiers, one can see now clearly
that not one of them wanted war; certainly not on this scale.   The
possible exception is the foolish Berchtold, the Austrian Premier,
upon whom must be fixed the chief personal responsibility for most
of what happened.*   As to the rest, they all shrank from the prospect.
Least of all could it be said that the aged Franz Joseph wanted
war.

The last thing the vainglorious Kaiser wanted was a European
war.   The feeble and simple-minded but sincere Czar of the Russias
certainly did not desire war.   During his reign the occasional outbursts of truculence against strikers, Jews, and revolutionaries, for
which he was held responsible, were not any expression of natural
ferocity on his part.   They always occurred as a result of official
incitement, usually as a means of countering some domestic crisis.
But on this occasion his principal official adviser, Sazonow, displayed
a real horror at the prospect of a great war, and in the Czar's more
intimate circles, even Rasputin warned the Court of the danger to
the Dynasty which would be involved in plunging Russia into a
great conflict with his powerful neighbours.

Austrian and German rulers and statesmen had a hankering desire
for a small war against a tiny neighbour who, standing alone, would
easily and speedily be overwhelmed.   It would soon be over, the
prestige of Austria would be restored by this exhibition of her
irresistible might, and Germany would once more prove herself the
undoubted master of Europe and the unchallengeable arbiter of its
destinies. But the last thing any of these Rulers and Statesmen wanted
was a prairie fire that would scorch up a whole continent.   Those who
directed affairs amongst the Central Powers only felt that they must
burn out that " wasps' nest," as they called Serbia, and they never
seemed to take cognizance of the fact that the grass on the plains of
Europe at that time was all tinder.   There was no arresting voice

---

* That Berchtold was prepared if necessary to launch a European war in furtherance
of his projects is evidenced by a dispatch from him on 25th July, 1914, to the Austrian
Ambassador at St. Petersburg, where he gives him the following instructions:—
   " . . . When your Excellency reaches this point in your conversation with Herr
Sazonow, it will be a suitable opportunity for stating in connection with your account
of our motives and intentions, that we—as your Excellency would be already in a
position to make clear—are seeking for no territorial gain, and have no intention
of impairing the sovereignty of the Kingdom (of Serbia) but that on the other hand
we shall go to the utmost limit in carrying through our demands, *and shall not even
recoil from the possibility of European complications.*"   (My italics.)

anywhere to call a halt: no dominant personality to enforce attention or offer acceptable guidance amidst the chaos.   The world was exceptionally unfortunate in the quality of its counsellors in this terrible emergency.   Had there been a Bismarck in Germany, a Palmerston or a Disraeli in Britain, a Roosevelt in America, or a Clemenceau in authority in Paris, the catastrophe might, and I believe would, have been averted; but there was no one of that quality visible on the bridge in any great State.   Von Bethmann-Hollweg, Poincaré, Viviani, Berchtold, Sazonow and Grey were all able, experienced, conscientious and respectable mariners, but distinctly lacking in the force, vision, imagination and resource which alone could have saved the situation.   They were all handy men in a well-behaved sea, but helpless in a typhoon.

In Germany, which counted most in this crisis, navigation was complicated by the august presence on the bridge, of a weak, fussy and egotistical personage, who, at critical moments, overawed and overrode all his subordinates.   He never contemplated a great war as a possibility when in the early days of July he issued his first directions as to the course of German diplomacy, and then sailed away to the Norwegian fiords, where he depended for his information as to the course of a crisis whose issue was in his hands, upon some local newspaper.*   When he came back and realised that he might be involved in a great European struggle, he visibly shrank from the prospect, but he had not the strength to countermand his orders.   He was afraid of being taunted with cowardice in the face of danger. So he allowed himself to be dragged into a conflict, for leadership in which he was utterly unfitted by training, talent or temperament.

The picture which the events of the last fateful days present to me is that which you see in an estuary, when a river, which has been gliding steadily along towards the sea for a long distance without any consciousness of the final destiny which awaits it in the direction in which it flows, suddenly finds itself confronted with the immensity of the ocean and the terror of its waves.   The confusion and tumult of waters which ensue mean that its reluctance has come too late.   If I were on a jury trying any of the men who were in control of affairs at that date, I should bring against most of them a verdict of manslaughter rather than of murder.   A brief summary of what

* " . . . My fleet was cruising as usual in the Norwegian fiords, while I was on my summer vacation trip. During my stay at Balholm I received but meagre news from the Foreign Office and was obliged to rely principally on the Norwegian newspapers, from which I received the impression that the situation was growing worse. I telegraphed repeatedly to the Chancellor and the Foreign Office that I considered it advisable to return home, but was asked each time not to interrupt my journey. . . .
" . . . When, after that, however, I learned from the Norwegian newspapers—*not from Berlin*—of the Austrian ultimatum to Serbia, and, immediately after, of the Serbian Note to Austria, I started upon my return journey without further ado. . . ."
(" My Memoirs," 1878-1918, ex-Kaiser Wilhelm II, pp. 241-2.)

happened will give an idea of the aimlessness and muddle that prevailed.

Grey wanted Russia and Austria to talk it out amongst themselves. He then suggested the mediation of Germany with Austria, of France with Russia, and of Russia with Serbia. On the other hand, Germany preferred to leave Austria to talk it out alone with Serbia without any intermediary or intervener. Sazonow leaned towards conversations between Russia and Austria; Germany, later on, but much too late, inclined in the same direction. Grey then cut athwart this idea with his proposal for a conference of Ambassadors in London, but he wished to leave both Austria and Serbia out of this gathering —a fatal omission which undoubtedly led Germany to reject the proposal. In von Bethmann-Hollweg's opinion a Conference so constituted looked too much like a tribunal to try Austria's case, when the country which was arraigned would not even be present to state her defence, and, in any event, all the judges being biased and the majority definitely hostile, would have but one friend on the Bench. Germany still preferred a continuation of the Austro-Russian talks. And, besides, it was quite clear that the Germans did not care for the idea of a meeting in London. England, France, and Russia would be represented there by skilled and experienced diplomatists, rootedly opposed to the Austrian objectives in the Balkans; on the other hand, the German Ambassador had not the full confidence of the German Foreign Office, for many reasons. Amongst others, he was suspected of hesitancy and lukewarmness in his attitude towards the Austrian pretensions. Even Russia was not enthusiastic about the notion of a Conference, preferring to continue direct negotiations with Austria. Sazonow only accepted the proposal of a Conference in the event of these direct negotiations breaking down. The Four-Power Conference was, therefore, turned down. The suggestion had only served to waste invaluable time. It was not wisely framed, and it was not put forward with conviction; it was not pressed home and it was finally dropped; in fact, it was dropped at the first objection. It was a timid and half-hearted approach, and at the first difficulty it encountered it was abandoned by its distracted author. Then came the muddle about mobilisation and semi-mobilisation of the Austrian, Russian, and Serbian Armies. The Willy-Nicky letters followed with the Czar's suggestion of a reference to the Hague, and the Kaiser's counter-suggestion of a cancellation by the Czar of his Decree for mobilising the Russian Army. The letters were written to the tramp of battalions and the rumble of cannon pressing on towards frontiers, and the inevitable clash that was to come. A multitude of moidered Counsellors, by their conflicting advice, now hustled Wisdom into the arms of the bravoes who had for years waited eagerly for this hour, and were standing impatiently outside the Council Chambers ready to strangle their victim.

3. ATTITUDE—MILITARY, POLITICAL AND CIVILIAN—TO WAR

Whilst diplomacy desired peace and worked for it by confused and bewildered methods, there were powerful elements in every community that thirsted for war. The Military Chiefs, high and low, in at least three of the countries principally concerned were not averse from putting their theories, plans, and hopes to the test. All of them believed in the machine they had helped to perfect, and they were confident that if tried it would prove triumphant. In this country this desire did not count in the estimation of a hair! Our overwhelming confidence in the power of our Navy may perhaps have influenced opinion in certain quarters, but that influence was not decisive. In Germany, on the other hand, military sentiment counted a good deal. I am inclined to believe, after a careful perusal of the evidence, that it was a decisive factor. The Kaiser had, owing to certain incidents and indiscretions, lost much of his popularity. His popularity with his Army was definitely on the wane. They realised that he had not the heart of a soldier, and that he was not the man who would lead them into battle—if he could avoid a fight. The Crown Prince was their favourite. The Kaiser was becoming sensitive to this rather contemptuous opinion formed of his courage by the Army he idolised. He knew that any symptom of shrinking or shuddering at the prospect of a great fight would finally forfeit the last remnant of respect for him in the breasts of the soldiers he adored. This he could not face. So the last fatal days before the War present the pitiable spectacle of a man torn between fear, common sense and vanity, the two former pulling him back from the chasm—the latter pushing him relentlessly over the brink. His letter of the 28th of July to von Jagow is a perfect specimen of the distracted state of mind which was produced by this inward struggle. In it he said : —

"That the requests of the Danube Monarchy had been broadly met; the Serbs' few reservations could probably be cleared up by negotiation; the reply amounted to a ' capitulation in the humblest style,' and with it there disappeared *all reason for war*." (The italics were the Kaiser's.)*

This part of the letter is often quoted. What is not so often quoted is the following sentence in the same note in which he stated that he considered that a guarantee was needed for the execution of the demands upon Serbia, and also that as "a visible *satisfaction d'honneur* for Austria the Austrian Army should temporarily occupy Belgrade as a pledge." The letter is a proof of the fatal hesitancy in the Kaiser's will, prompted by conflicting appeals. His subordination of judgment to the will of the Army is further illustrated by his attitude towards the invasion of Belgium. When

* Lutz : " Lord Grey and the World War " (pp. 257-8).

he realised that a march across Belgium without the consent of its
Government would bring Britain into the War, he sent for Von
Moltke and asked him whether it would not be possible to change
the war plan and concentrate on Russia. Von Moltke replied that
it was too late, as all the preparations had been made on the assumption that the German Army would immediately march through
Belgium and capture Paris in a given time. The Kaiser is stated
to have replied: "Your uncle would have given me a different
answer." Nevertheless he surrendered.

The "little war" to occupy Belgrade was the bait of the General
Staff to land the Great War. Once its hook was in the gills of the
Kaiser he was dragged along. The "little war" involved the
mobilisation and declaration of war by Austria. That brought on
the partial mobilisation of Russia. That drove Germany into the
declaration of war against Russia. Then we were already in the
World War.

In Austria and Russia the High Command were finally responsible
for the War. They insisted on mobilisation whilst not unhopeful
negotiations were still going on. Austrian mobilisation led to
Russia mobilising her army so as to prevent any surprise movement
across the frontier. Austria mobilised to strike at Serbia. Russia
mobilised for a counterblow. When the Kaiser, frightened by the
thunder clouds, intervened personally with the Czar to avert war,
he begged "Nicky" to cancel his Decree which had already gone
forth, for the mobilisation of the Russian army. The Czar was
willing to accede to this not unreasonable request, but the army
leaders assured him that the "technical" difficulties of cancellation
and even of partial demobilisation were insuperable. It was thus
that the military chiefs in the leading countries of the Continent
thrust the nations into war, whilst their impotent statesmen were still
fumbling for Peace. Each army believed in its own invincibility and
was anxious to demonstrate it.

The belief in the superiority of the German Army was by no
means confined to the Germans. I remember two or three years
before the War, Lord Kitchener, who was then Sirdar of Egypt,
calling upon me at the Treasury in connection with a loan for the
development of the Sudan. As it was shortly after the Agadir crisis,
we got on to the subject of the Franco-German position. He had a
poor opinion of the French Army, and thought the Germans would
"walk through them like partridges." Shortly afterwards, there
was a banquet at Buckingham Palace to entertain some foreign
potentate, and I sat next to a foreign Prince, who was not a German.
He also entertained the same opinion of the invincibility of the
German Army, and used exactly the same metaphor as Lord
Kitchener about the way it would scatter all other armies like
partridges.

The French Army, on the other hand, were equally confident of their powers. They believed they had the best gun in the field— the famous *soixante-quinze*—and they were not far wrong. It is not the first time that rapture over the possession of a new military invention has made a nation less averse from war. The French had also great confidence in the training given to their officers and in the fine quality of their troops. They knew their organisation was excellent and they had the inevitable "plan." There never was a time since 1870 when the French Army had less fear of its great rival. The Russians had improved their Army in equipment and organisation since their defeat in Manchuria. They felt infinitely superior to the Austrian Army, and deemed themselves quite a match for what was left of the German Army, after the better half of it had marched to the West. Generals in this frame of mind hungered for war and had no difficulty in manœuvring statesmen who did not know their own minds into positions where war became inevitable. Thus great armaments made war.

But the Army was not the only element that desired war. The populace caught the war fever. In every capital they clamoured for war. The theory which is propagated to-day by pacifist orators of the more cantankerous and less convincing type that the Great War was engineered by elder and middle-aged statesmen who sent younger men to face its horrors, is an invention. The elder statesmen did their feckless best to prevent war, whilst the youth of the rival countries were howling impatiently at their doors for immediate war. I saw it myself during the first four days of August, 1914. I shall never forget the warlike crowds that thronged Whitehall and poured into Downing Street, whilst the Cabinet was deliberating on the alternative of peace or war. On Sunday there was a great crowd. Monday was Bank Holiday, and multitudes of young people concentrated in Westminster demonstrating for war against Germany. We could hear the hum of this surging mass from the Cabinet Chamber. On Monday afternoon I walked with Mr. Asquith to the House of Commons to hear Grey's famous speech. The crowd was so dense that no car could drive through it, and had it not been for police assistance we could not have walked a yard on our way. It was distinctly a pro-war demonstration. I remember observing at the time: "These people are very anxious to send our poor soldiers to face death; how many of them will ever go into battle themselves?" It was an unworthy doubt of the courage and patriotism of the demonstrators. A few days later recruiting stands were set up in the Horse Guards Parade, and that great open space beheld a crowd of young men surging around these stands and pushing their way through to give their names for enlistment in the Kitchener Armies. For days I heard, from the windows of Downing Street and the Treasury, the movement of a myriad feet towards the stands and the shouting of names of eager volunteers by the recruiting sergeants. The War had leapt into popularity between Saturday and Monday. On Saturday the Governor of the Bank of England called on me, as Chancellor of the Exchequer, to inform me on behalf of the City that the financial and trading interests in the City of London were totally opposed to our intervening in the War. By Monday there was a complete change. The threatened invasion of Belgium had set the nation on fire from sea to sea. By then Sir Edward Grey had ample evidence that his stipulation to Monsieur Cambon that we could only come to the aid of France if public opinion demanded it, was completely fulfilled. But Belgium was responsible for the change. Before then the Cabinet was hopelessly divided—fully one third, if not one half, being opposed to our entry into the War. After the German ultimatum to Belgium the Cabinet was almost unanimous. Had Germany without any provocation attacked France, I have no doubt that public sentiment in this country would have demanded that the Government should go to the aid of the victim of such wanton aggression. But it was thoroughly understood that on this occasion France was drawn into the quarrel by her Treaty obligations with Russia, and that if France had stood out of the dispute, Germany would only have been too pleased to leave her alone. The Franco-Russian Alliance was offensive and defensive. France was therefore bound to support Russia, whether she was interested in the *casus belli* or not. But Britain was not in that position. We had given no undertaking to come to the aid of Russia in any dispute, whether in the East or in the West. Russian autocracy was almost as unpopular with the people of these islands as Bolshevism is to-day. It was identified with Siberian prisons for political offenders, and with wholesale pogroms of harmless Jews, and with the massacre of workers whose only crime was the presentation of a petition for the redress of their undoubted wrongs. So long therefore as the war was likely to take the form of a contest between the autocracies of Germany and Austria on the one hand, and of Russia and her Allies on the other, British opinion was definitely opposed to intervention. It is a misfortune that Sir Edward Grey did not play sooner and more boldly this card of our treaty pledges to Belgium. It might have averted war altogether.

The London demonstrations had their counterparts in St. Petersburg, Berlin, Vienna and Paris. Blood was up and blood must flow. The populace and the military were at last of one mind. This combination took decision out of the hands of quivering and hesitant statesmanship, which desired peace but had not the resolution and boldness to do the simple things that could alone ensure it. Mr. Emil Ludwig's description of huge assemblies in the London squares demanding peace, whilst a small mob of French residents in London gathered together to clamour for war, is nonsense—and mischievous nonsense, because such a false picture deludes and misleads the statesmanship of the future as to the real perils against which it has to guard.

There is no better evidence of the change which came over public opinion than the following extracts from the *Daily News*. The great Liberal journal came tardily to the conclusion that war was justifiable. It represented the reluctance with which Liberals throughout the country contemplated the prospect of Britain entering into the War. Its testimony as to the state of public opinion during these eventful days is therefore not biased by any bellicosity. Here is a paragraph which appeared in that paper on the 3rd of August, which gives a very faithful account of the temper of the nation up to and including Sunday:—

" There is no war party in this country. On the contrary, the horrors of war have already seized on the popular imagination, and in the highways and public vehicles in London yesterday, the populace were heard to express their indignation at the swift and tragic movements on the Continent."

Here is an account of the crowds on the following day, after it came to be known that Germany was threatening Belgium:—

" The crowd continued to grow and grow. It extended from Trafalgar Square where it formed a dense mass, right along to the House of Commons, where its greatest number gathered about Downing Street, opposite the War Office. Groups of young men passed along in taxi-cabs singing the ' Marseillaise.' During the earlier part of the day there had been little disposition to demonstrate by the wearing of colours, but the tendency spread, and hundreds were buying Union Jacks. At seven o'clock in the evening, when Mr. Asquith left the subsequent Council Meeting to go to the House of Lords, the crowds cheered him with extraordinary fervour. It was a scene of enthusiasm unprecedented in recent times."

Here follows an extract from the account of the temper of the crowd of the 4th of August, after it had been known that we had delivered out ultimatum to Germany:—

" In anticipation of the receipt of Germany's reply, huge crowds gathered in Whitehall and outside Buckingham Palace, and extraordinary scenes of enthusiasm were witnessed. . . . Ministers entering 10, Downing Street were loudly cheered.

Not for years—since Mafeking night—have such crowds been seen in London, and Whitehall, the Mall, and Trafalgar Square, were all packed with excited throngs."

Then follows an account of the frenzy with which the Declaration of War was received: —

The enthusiasm culminated outside Buckingham Palace when it became known that war had been declared. The word was passed round by the police that silence was necessary, inasmuch as the King was holding a Council for the signing of the necessary proclamations. . . . The news that war had been declared was received with tremendous cheering which grew into a deafening roar when King George, Queen Mary and the Prince of Wales appeared on the balcony. . . .

Westminster, Charing Cross, and the main thoroughfares round Westminster were thronged all last night with excited throngs, who displayed marked tendencies towards mafficking. Both in numbers and in noisiness it far exceeded the crowds of Monday. Union Jacks were everywhere to be seen, and the air was filled with the sound of patriotic songs; Trafalgar Square was almost impassable.

A hostile crowd assembled outside the German Embassy, and smashed the windows. A special message was sent to Cannon Row, and a force of mounted and unmounted police was quickly on the scene, but had considerable difficulty in restoring order."

In face of these reports, given by a witness whose leaning was definitely against war, what becomes of the suggestion that we entered into the War against the vocal opposition of the people of this country? All wars are popular on the day of their declaration. To quote Walpole's famous observation upon a war into which he had been reluctantly forced: " They are ringing the bells now: soon they will be wringing their hands." But never was there a war so universally acclaimed as that into which Britain entered on the 4th of August, 1914.

4.   4TH AUGUST, 1914

The 4th of August, 1914, is one of the world's fateful dates. The decision taken on that day in the name and on behalf of the British Empire altered the destiny of Europe. It is not too much to say that it gave a different turn or direction to the advance of the human race. The trumpets of war had already sounded in the East and in the West, and colossal armies were hurrying to the slaughter. Millions of men were either on the march or strapping on their armour for the conflict, and roads and railway tracks trembled with the weight of guns and munitions and all the sinister devices and mechanisms of human destruction!

Was there any hope that the great catastrophe could be averted? There were continuous meetings of the Cabinet on Friday, Saturday and Sunday. I experienced much difficulty in attending throughout because of the Conference at the Treasury to deal with the grave financial situation into which we had been plunged by War. But I heard and took part in most of the discussion. It revealed serious differences of opinion on the subject of British intervention in a Russo-German war even although France was forced by her Russian alliance to join in. Grey never definitely put before the Cabinet the proposition that Britain should, in that event, declare war. He never expressed a clear and unequivocal opinion either way and no decision was therefore taken on that point. But it was quite clear from the course of the debate inside the Cabinet and the informal conversations which took place outside during our short adjournments that we were hopelessly divided on the subject of Britain entering the War on the issue as it had developed at that date. Had the question of defending the neutrality and integrity of Belgium been raised there would not have been a dissentient voice on that issue. Lord Morley and John Burns might conceivably have stood out. Of that I am not convinced had a decision on that point alone been reached in time as a means of circumscribing the area of war and possibly of persuading Germany of the futility of waging it at all under conditions which would have been unfavourable to her preconcerted military schemes. But such a proposal was never submitted to our judgment.

The one faint glimmer still visible in the lowering sky was in the direction of Belgium.

The dark clouds were rapidly closing up, but there was still one visible corner of blue. The Germans had signed a treaty not merely to respect, but to protect the neutrality of Belgium. Would they honour their bond? Great Britain was a party to that compact. If anyone broke its terms, Britain was bound to throw in her might against the invader. Would the faith of Prussia, strengthened by the fear of Britain, prevail? If the treaty stood, the situation might yet be saved.

The policy I urged upon my colleagues was not one merely of passive non-intervention in the struggle between Germany and Austria on the one hand and Russia and France on the other. We were not in the position of France. She was bound by Treaty to support Russia in her quarrels with Germany. We were under no such obligation. I proposed, therefore, that we should take immediate steps to increase and strengthen our Army in numbers and equipment, so that when we judged the time had come for intervention, none of the belligerents could afford to disregard our appeal. Had Germany respected the integrity of Belgium, that policy would have been the wisest course to pursue. There would have been plenty of time for passions to exhaust their force and for the sanguine expectations of military enthusiasm to evaporate. The problem of France would have been a different one; the march of events would have been slower. France, instead of having to defend a frontier of over 500 miles, without fortresses or artificial barriers, could have concentrated all her strength on defending a frontier of 250 miles protected by formidable fortresses. An army (including reserves) of 3,000,000 men, holding entrenched positions on this narrow frontier, would have been invincible, and Germany might well have been content merely to defend her frontiers in the West, and throw her armies into Poland. There, difficulties of transport, bad roads, inadequate railways, immense distances, would have postponed decision for weeks if not for months. It took Germany over 12 months' hard fighting to conquer Poland. Even then the Russian Army was still in being and ready to resume the conflict in 1916. British intervention in the cause of peace might then have induced saner counsels. Britain was the one Power in Europe that had never yet been beaten in a European war. With her immunity from attack, with her immense fleet manned by the most skilful seamen in the world, with her enormous resources, she could be reckoned upon to wear down any Power. Had Britain been able to throw into the scale a well-equipped army of a million men to support her fleet, Germany would have hesitated before she rejected terms of peace and thus brought the British Empire into the conflict on the side of her enemies. These were the arguments I advanced in favour of non-intervention in the struggle if the neutrality of Belgium were respected.

The invasion of Belgium put an end to all these possibilities. Then our Treaty obligations were involved. On Sunday, the 2nd of August, the omens were not propitious. There were clear indications that the German forces were massing on the Belgian frontier. Germany had appealed to Belgium for permission to march through her territories to attack France. Belgian Ministers hesitated, but the answer given by Belgium's heroic King constitutes one of the most thrilling pages of history. The British Government, on hearing the news, issued an ultimatum to Germany warning her that unless by twelve o'clock on August 4th assurances were received from Germany that the neutrality of Belgium would be treated as inviolate, Britain would have no alternative but to take steps to enforce that treaty. Would Germany realise what war with Britain meant, arrest the progress of her armies, change her strategy, and perhaps consent to a parley? How much depended upon the answer to these questions! We could suspect then what it meant: we know now. There were many of us who could hardly believe that those responsible for guiding the destiny of Germany would be so fatuous as deliberately to provoke the hostility of the British Empire with its inexhaustible reserves and with its grim tenacity of purpose once it engaged in a struggle.

Amongst those who criticise the intervention of Britain there are two sections. There are those who pretend to believe that this was a war intrigued and organised and dictated by financiers for their own purpose. In Germany and amongst the friends of Germany in other lands there are those who ascribe our action to the irritation produced by a growing jealousy of Germany's strength and prosperity, and British politicians are pictured as eagerly on the pounce for an opportunity to destroy this redoubtable rival. As to both, the tale of these days is a complete answer. I was Chancellor of the Exchequer and, as such, I saw Money before the war; I saw it immediately after the outbreak of war; I lived with it for days, and did my best to steady its nerve, for I knew how much depended on restoring its confidence; and I say that money was a frightened and trembling thing: money shivered at the prospect. It is a foolish and ignorant libel to call this a financiers' war. As to the second form of attack on British action, big businesses everywhere wanted to keep out of it, and as to the rest this narrative will be a reply. Here were no eager men praying for the hour to arrive when they could strike down a great commercial rival.

It was a day full of rumours and reports, throbbing with anxiety. Hour after hour passed, and no sign came from Germany. There were only disturbing rumours of further German movements towards the Belgian line. The evening came. Still no answer. Shortly after nine o'clock I was summoned to the Cabinet Room for an important consultation. There I found Mr. Asquith, Sir Edward Grey, and Mr. Haldane all looking very grave. Mr. M'Kenna arrived soon afterwards. A message from the German Foreign Office to the German Embassy in London had been intercepted. It was not in cipher. It informed the German Ambassador that the British Ambassador in Berlin had asked for his passports at 7 p.m. and declared war. A copy of this message was passed on to me, and I have it still in my possession. A facsimile of this fateful document as it was submitted to us at this solemn conference is reproduced overleaf:

"Time: 9.5 p.m.
Date: Aug. 4th, 1914.

The following message has been intercepted by W.O. Censor: —
To German Ambassador from Berlin.
English Ambassador has just demanded his passport shortly after seven o'clock declaring war.

(Signed) Jagow."

No news had been received from Sir Edward Goschen.*
We were therefore at a loss to know what it meant. It looked

---

* We learnt subsequently that his telegram to us announcing his action had been held up by the German authorities. It never reached us, and not until Sir Edward Goschen arrived back in Britain some nine days later did we hear of its dispatch and obtain a copy of its text.

opposite:

TELEPHONE MESSAGES RECEIVED BY CHIEF CENSOR

FROM CHIEF CENSOR. WAR OFFICE.

Time: 9.5 p.m.

Date: August 4th 1914.

The following message has been intercepted by W.O.Censor:-

To:.German.Ambassador.........................

From.....Berlin...............................

        English Ambassador has just demanded his passport
shortly after seven o'clock declaring war

/Signed/   Jagow

Ass^t Chief Censor

Cochrane

The British Cabinet's first intimation of the outbreak of War conveyed in an intercepted telegram from the German Government to the German Ambassador in London, Prince Lichnowski.

like an attempt on the part of the Germans to anticipate the hour of the declaration of war in order to effect some *coup* either against British ships or British coasts. Should this intercept be treated as the commencement of hostilities, or should we wait until we either heard officially from Germany that our conditions had been rejected, or until the hour of the ultimatum had expired? We sat at the green table in the famous room where so many historic decisions had been taken in the past. It was not then a very well-lighted room, and my recollection is that the lights had not all been turned on, and in the dimness you might imagine the shades of the great British statesmen of the past taking part in a conference which meant so much to the Empire, to the building up of which they had devoted their lives—Chatham, Pitt, Fox, Castlereagh, Canning, Peel, Palmerston, Disraeli, Gladstone. In that simple, unadorned, almost dingy room they also had pondered over the problems which had perplexed their day. But never had they been confronted with so tremendous a decision as that with which British Ministers were faced in these early days of August, 1914.

And now came the terrible decision: should we unleash the savage dogs of war at once, or wait until the time limit of the ultimatum had expired, and give peace the benefit of even such a doubt as existed for at least another two hours? We had no difficulty in deciding that the Admiralty was to prepare the fleet against any sudden attack from the German flotillas and to warn our coasts against any possible designs from the same quarter. But should we declare war now, or at midnight? The ultimatum expired at midnight in Berlin. That was midnight according to Central Europe time: it meant eleven o'clock according to Greenwich time. We resolved to wait until eleven. Would any message arrive from Berlin before eleven informing us of the intention of Germany to respect Belgian neutrality? If it came there was still a faint hope that something might be arranged before the marching armies crashed into each other.

As the hour approached a deep and tense solemnity fell on the room. No one spoke. It was like awaiting the signal for the pulling of a lever which would hurl millions to their doom—with just a chance that a reprieve might arrive in time. Our eyes wandered anxiously from the clock to the door, and from the door to the clock, and little was said.

" Boom! " The deep notes of Big Ben rang out into the night the first strokes in Britain's most fateful hour since she arose out of the deep. A shuddering silence fell upon the room. Every face was suddenly contracted in a painful intensity. " Doom! " " Doom! " " Doom! " to the last stroke. The big clock echoed in our ears like the hammer of destiny. What destiny? Who could tell? We had challenged the most powerful military empire the world has yet brought forth. France was too weak alone to challenge its might and Russia was ill-organised, ill-equipped, corrupt. We knew what brunt Britain would have to bear. Could she stand it? There was no doubt or hesitation in any breast. But let it be admitted without shame that a thrill of horror quickened every pulse. Did we know that before peace would be restored to Europe we should have to wade through four years of the most concentrated slaughter, mutilation, suffering, devastation, and savagery which mankind has ever witnessed? That twelve millions of the gallant youth of the nations would be slain, that another twenty millions would be mutilated? That Europe would be crushed under the weight of a colossal war debt? That only one empire would stand the shock? That the three other glittering empires of the world would have been flung to the dust, and shattered beyond repair? That revolution, famine, and anarchy would sweep over half Europe, and that their menace would scorch the rest of this hapless continent?

Has the full tale yet been told? Who can tell? But had we foreseen it all on the 4th of August we could have done no other.

Twenty minutes after the hour Mr. Winston Churchill came in and informed us that the wires had already been sent to the British ships of war in every sea announcing the fact that war had been declared and that they were to act accordingly. Soon afterwards we dispersed. There was nothing more to say that night. To-morrow would bring us novel tasks and new bearings. As I left I felt like a man standing on a planet that had been suddenly wrenched from its orbit by a demoniac hand and that was spinning wildly into the unknown.

On the morrow Ministers woke up to a new and unaccustomed outlook. Hitherto we had been dealing with Britain and the world at peace. Now we were confronted with the problems of Europe, including Britain, plunged into the vortex of war.

Measures which conferred unheard-of powers on the Executive were passed through both Houses of Parliament after a few hours' discussion. Most of them had been carefully thought out during the tranquil years of peace by the numerous sub-committees of the Committee of Imperial Defence. Of what was accomplished by that remarkable body in the years before the War, and of its foresight, nothing has yet been written. Its founder—Earl Balfour—when he set up the Committee of Imperial Defence as an essential part of the organisation of defence, rendered a service to his country which deserves immortality. Under Mr. Asquith it carried on its task and traditions with undiminished vigour and persistence. It therefore came to pass that when war was thrust upon us, plans which played a vital part in our achievement of victory lay at hand in the pigeon-holes of the Committee of Imperial Defence, prepared down to the last detail and ready to be put into execution. Credit must be given to Lord Balfour for the creation and direction of this body and to Mr. Asquith for making the fullest use of its powers and for further developing its area and scope, but above all it is due to three indefatigable secretaries, Sir George Clarke, later Lord Sydenham, Admiral Sir Charles Ottley, and the ablest and most resourceful of them all, Lieutenant-Colonel Sir Maurice Hankey. The War Book, perfected under Mr. Asquith's chairmanship, and the work of Lord Haldane at the War Office—his organisation of the Territorials, creation of a General Staff as a thinking brain for the Army, and the foundation of the Officer's Training Corps—constitute a powerful answer to those who taunt the Liberal Government with being quite unprepared for the contingency of war.

To these instances may be added the preparedness of the Navy, more especially in the matter of capital ships, under the guidance of Lord Tweedmouth, Mr. M'Kenna, and Mr. Winston Churchill.

But the C.I.D. had by no means completed its exhaustive survey of the possibilities and demands of war, when the storm broke upon us. That probably accounts for the fact that two contingencies which turned out to be of vital consequence had not yet been explored. The first was the financial chaos which would inevitably ensue, especially in a country which transacted most of the intricate business of financing international trade.

The second was the enormous expenditure of munitions which would be involved in war under modern conditions. No one had contemplated the construction of earthen fortifications on so gigantic a scale as that which developed in the Great War upon which Europe had now entered. The Torres Vedras lines were a matter of a few miles. So were Todleben's earthen ramparts at Sebastopol. The colossal earthworks of 1914-18 extended over hundreds of miles. The myriads of heavy guns, trench mortars, and machine guns, the millions of projectiles which became an essential part of the equipment of armies engaged in such vast operations, were beyond the contemplation of any student of the exigencies of war. With these two unforeseen emergencies it was my destiny to be called upon to deal.

5.   CABINET IGNORANCE OF FRENCH'S STRATEGICAL ADVICE

To weave the events of the War into a consecutive narrative is no part of my undertaking. That task has already been discharged by other and more expert pens than mine. I simply set myself to contribute to the story of the War more or less detached incidents with which I was especially concerned. The Cabinet were told very little about military or naval movements. In so far as there was any civilian consultation it was confined to the Prime Minister, Mr. Winston Churchill, and occasionally Lord Haldane and Sir Edward Grey.

The Cabinet was ignorant of the fact that in the Councils of War held immediately after the declaration, Sir John French was opposed to the Expeditionary Force being taken to the Belgian frontier. The first War Council held after the entry of this country into the War was on 5th August. Ministers were represented by the Prime Minister, Lord Haldane, Sir Edward Grey and Mr. Winston Churchill; the Navy by Prince Louis of Battenberg, and the Army by Lord Kitchener, Lord Roberts, Sir John French, Sir Ian Hamilton, Sir Charles Douglas, Sir H. C. Sclater, Sir John Cowans, Sir Stanley von Donop, Sir Douglas Haig, Sir J. M. Grierson, Sir A. J. Murray and Sir Henry Wilson. At this Council Sir John French said: —

" that the prearranged plan to meet this situation had been that the Expeditionary Force should mobilise simultaneously with the French and concentrate behind the French Army at Maubeuge by the fifteenth day of mobilisation. The intention then had been for it to move eastward towards the Meuse and act on the left of the French Army against the right German flank. It had, however, always been felt that, if we were late in commencing our mobilisation, as had actually happened, we should have to change our plan. Maubeuge, in his opinion, was no longer a safe place at which to concentrate. He suggested that Amiens would now be the safer place at which to concentrate. The general tenor of his opinion was that the Expeditionary Force should be sent to France; a safe place for concentration should be selected, and events should be awaited. He added that, as an alternative, and owing to the existing conditions, he was inclined to consider a landing at Antwerp with a view to co-operation with the Belgians and Dutch. The three forces would form a considerable army, and would necessarily contain a large German force, and they might be able to advance southward. The feasibility of this plan, however, was largely a naval question. As an alternative to a landing at Antwerp, he proposed a landing in France and a movement to Antwerp by the coast route."

He does not seem to have received any support from any quarter for his suggestions and he appears not to have pressed them any further. The general effect of the consultations which took place on that and the following day was that we should conform our strategy with that of the French Army.

Had either of the two courses been adopted, it is clear now that the whole course of events would have been different, and particularly would this have been the case if five British Divisions had occupied Antwerp. There would have been then on the German flank five excellent Divisions of picked troops. This would have provided the necessary stiffening for the Belgian militia. The Germans would not have considered it safe to penetrate as deeply into France as they subsequently did without clearing their flank from this redoubtable menace. They would thus have lost valuable time, and time was the essence of their plan.

This advice given by the Commander-in-Chief of the Expeditionary Forces was withheld from the Cabinet and was therefore never discussed by Ministers. During the three or four weeks that followed the declaration of War the attention of the Cabinet was concentrated upon questions of recruiting, the escape of the *Goeben*, the conjecture as to what Turkey was likely to do, messages from Greece, and occasional obscure reports from the Front, which were delivered to us at the beginning of each sitting by Lord Kitchener in his loud staccato voice, and with that remote look in his eyes, directed at no one in particular, which was a sure indication of his unease amid surroundings with which he was not familiar. He was sitting in council with men, belonging to the profession with which he had wrestled all his life, and for which, in his heart, he had the usual mixture of military contempt and apprehension. His main idea at the Council table was to tell the politicians as little as possible of what was going on and get back to his desk at the War Office as quickly as he could decently escape. Now and again he flashed out an illuminating sentence of information. Just before the first German blow was delivered, I recollect that Lord Kitchener departed from his usual secretiveness so far as to reveal to us what General Joffre's intentions were. The French Commander-in-Chief, according to him, did not believe that the Germans would march through the Central and Western Provinces of Belgium, because it was an industrial area where the roads were not good and not in the least suited to the movement of large bodies of men with transport and artillery. His idea was that the German Army would swing towards the South-Eastern corner of Belgium, and attempt to pierce the Allied defences in the direction of Namur. Lord Kitchener said that Joffre's idea of the French strategy was that of a boxer who covered himself from his antagonist's blows with his left arm whilst he came round with the right and hit an unexpected blow at his antagonist's weakest point. Lord Kitchener informed us that he thought General Joffre's conception of the German plan of operation was all wrong. He was firmly convinced the Germans would march along all the eleven roads that made for the frontier, and would endeavour to outflank the Allied forces at a point much higher up than that indicated by General Joffre. However, he said, Joffre held stubbornly to his view. We were soon to know the result of this fatal miscalculation.

One morning I was engaged in the Treasury disposing of a few urgent financial problems before the meeting of the Cabinet when Mr. Winston Churchill walked into my room with an unusually gloomy mien. He had clearly some grave news to communicate, and as I was surrounded by officials he beckoned me to come outside.

We went into another room, and he then told me what he had just heard from Kitchener: that the Germans had advanced with enormous forces along the upper Belgian roads; had driven our troops from Mons, and that the whole British force was now in full retreat pursued by a German force of overwhelmingly superior strength. Mr. Churchill records that he was " relieved and overjoyed at my response," but I certainly felt, more than ever, that we were up against it, and that nothing but a mobilisation of the whole of our strength could save Europe and the world from an incalculable disaster.

For several days we had no reports as to what was happening. We heard nothing of the great struggle in Lorraine where the French invading army was hurled back across the frontier after a pitched battle in which the Germans won a decisive victory more by a superiority in artillery than in numbers. We heard nothing of the defeat of the French on the Meuse and the advance of the German Army from that direction towards Paris. We were in a complete fog as to the movements and plans of our own little army. All we knew was that they quitted their positions on the Belgian frontier and were pressed—if not pursued—southwards by overwhelming German forces. We were assured, however, day-by-day, that the retreating army had at last taken up a position in which they were prepared to make a stand with every hope of successfully repelling their assailants. And then on the following morning we were informed that they had abandoned this position and resumed their retreat, but were prepared to fight on a more defensible line, which, we observed, was many leagues nearer Paris.

We heard nothing of the hurried crossing of the Somme, the Aisne, the Marne, the Oise, and we were not told for days of the retirement behind the Seine, miles to the south of Paris. The Cabinet was bewildered by the scrappy and incoherent reports given to it each morning by Lord Kitchener. He was pressed to give us a more satisfactory account of what was really happening. But he protested that he had imparted to his colleagues all the information which had been vouchsafed to him from our Headquarters in France. The first intimation we received of the seriousness and the magnitude of the defeat inflicted upon the Allied Armies was a report in *The Times*—published in defiance of the Censor—giving a graphic account of the march of the German troops through Amiens singing the " Wacht am Rheim " along its deserted streets.

The Cabinet ultimately decided to send Lord Kitchener to France to find out. Conflicting accounts of what passed on this occasion between our great Generals have already appeared, and I feel it is no part of my task to reconcile them. It was my first experience of the fallibility of the Military Leaders—the stubborn miscalculation, muddle and lack of co-ordination, which resulted in mowing down the flower of the finest armies ever put in the field by France and England.

I need hardly say that we were surprised and disappointed by a collapse that had not in the least been anticipated by us or our military advisers. But there was no panic. Reinforcements were hastened to France. Soon afterwards the victory of the Marne—one of the great historical battles of the world—checked the German advance. For the moment utter disaster was averted, and we had time to make fresh plans for the future.

From the fighting of the first two months of the War there emerged two facts of supreme importance in their relation to the strategy of the War. Had these facts been fully appreciated by the Allied Generals at the time and had they conformed their plans to this understanding the War would have taken a different course. The first fact was the enormous superiority of the Germans in artillery— not so much in numbers as in weight and the definite advantage enuring to them in this respect. For the first time the heavy gun was treated as a mobile weapon and its superiority in range and destructive effect to the ordinary field gun broke up the French offensive and crumpled up the French plan of campaign.

The second was the difficulty—even with superior gun power— of dislodging a brave and tenacious enemy from prepared positions where the defender operated under cover. The French failed completely in open warfare in Belgium and Lorraine. The longer range and more shattering power of the German artillery broke up their attack, demoralised their troops and forced them to a speedy retreat to save their armies from utter destruction. On the other hand the defeated troops successfully repelled all attacks by the victorious foe on the Grand Couronne of Nancy, although made with the same overwhelming gun superiority. The French dug themselves in on these hills and the Germans were beaten off with great loss in spite of their more powerful artillery.

Marshal Foch in his Memoirs, writing of the lessons taught (but not learnt) by the fighting of August and September, 1914, says: —

" Generally speaking, it seemed proved that the new means of action furnished by automatic weapons and long-range guns enabled the defence to hold up any attempt at breaking through long enough for a counter-attack to be launched with saving effect. The ' pockets,' which resulted from partial attacks which were successful and seemingly even decisive, could not be maintained, in spite of very costly losses, long enough to ensure a definite rupture of the adversary's line. They could be too quickly rendered uninhabitable and useless for the assailant.

When a defensive front has been forced by superior numbers to fall back, it has not thereby been broken. Counter-attacks on the assailant's flank have often consumed the latter's reserves and threatened his communications, to the extent of eventually stopping his partial advance and causing him to retire.

Many new subjects for reflection are offered when we examine the limitations and the weaknesses of an offensive which, while tactically successful at first, is continued in violation of the principles which modern weapons have now imposed; . . ."

When did the Allied Generals come to these wise conclusions? Not before the bloody assaults of Artois and Champagne in 1915— not even by the still more sanguinary battles of the Somme in 1916.

CHAPTER III

SIR EDWARD GREY*

I CANNOT give a fair presentation of the events that led to the War, prolonged its duration, and aggravated and extended its desolation, without a candid picture of the personalities who controlled and directed these events. Their characteristics were responsible for much that happened—for better or for worse. It is a mistaken view of history to assume that its episodes were entirely due to fundamental causes which could not be averted, and that they were not precipitated or postponed by the intervention of personality. The appearance of one dominating individual in a critical position at a decisive moment has often altered the course of events for years and even generations. A gifted and resolute person has often postponed for centuries a catastrophe which appeared imminent and which but for him would have befallen. On the other hand a weak or hesitant person has invited or expedited calamity which but for him might never have happened or which at least could have been long deferred. I cannot therefore tell my tale of the Great War without giving some idea of the men whose qualities either hastened or failed to avert it, or had the effect of prolonging its devastating course once it had started.

I have found it an exceedingly difficult and occasionally disagreeable task to give an accurate account of the prominent figures in the War when so many of them were colleagues with whom I always enjoyed the most pleasant personal relations: some of them men with whom I worked in perfect amity for over a decade; some to whom I owed many personal courtesies and kindnesses; some who accorded help in the kind of attacks which now and again threaten to overwhelm any man who in politics chooses the more controversial role.

These considerations more especially apply to my examination of the attributes of Mr. Asquith, Sir Edward Grey, Mr. Bonar Law, Mr. Churchill and the other distinguished political leaders with whom I was privileged to work for so many years in cordiality and good fellowship.

As Lord Grey (or as he then was, Sir Edward Grey) was among those who played a decisive part in the movements and occurrences

* The late Viscount Grey of Fallodon.

that led to the War, it is necessary to an understanding of my narrative that I should give a frank estimate of his qualities. His tenure of the crucial office of Foreign Secretary constituted an essential part of what happened, and his personality was distinctly one of the elements that contributed to the great catastrophe. I cannot, therefore, leave out my impressions of his character in my tale of events. It would not be worth while doing so—it would not be fair to my readers—unless I gave a frank analysis of the man who strove honestly to avert war but failed, and said something of the characteristics and shortcomings that were largely responsible for that failure. I appreciate the imperative duty of not allowing any irrelevant considerations to influence judgment. For that reason in my character sketches of political personages I have sternly repressed every tendency to partisan bias.

The public know less of Sir Edward Grey than of any conspicuous statesman of his time. His reputation is therefore on a purely conjectural foundation. Sir Edward Grey's position in public life was always entirely different from that which Mr. Asquith established for himself. The latter had neither rank nor wealth to help him along. He won his way to Premiership entirely by superb talent and parliamentary achievement. No Prime Minister in history—with the notable exceptions of Gladstone and Disraeli—possessed a better mental equipment for a political career. Sir Edward Grey had high intelligence but of a more commonplace texture. It was reflected in his speeches, which were clear, correct and orderly, but were characterised by no distinction of phrase or thought. His handling of foreign affairs was of the same conventional type. His influence was derived from other sources. He had qualities, largely of appearance, manner and restraint, which gave the impression of the " strong, silent man " whom the generation brought up on Carlyle earnestly sought, and, when they thought they had discovered him, fervently adored. In the War and post-War days of Clemenceau, Foch, Lenin, Mussolini, Roosevelt and Hitler—all talkers—that legend has become a little mildewed. The strongest men of history have never been silent. One of the strongest—Napoleon—could on occasion even be garrulous. Just before 1914 the vogue of the taciturn was still prevalent and no man profited as much by it as Grey. His striking physiognomy with the thin lips, the firmly closed mouth, and the chiselled features gave the impression of cold hammered steel. Add to this exterior the reticence of speech and the calm level utterance on the rare occasions when he spoke, and you were led to expect imperturbable strength in an emergency. He did not command the flaming phrase that illumines but sometimes also scorches and leaves behind an irritating burn. On the other hand he possessed to perfection that correctitude of phrase and demeanour which passes for—and sometimes is—diplomacy, and that serene flow of unexceptionable diction which is apt to be reckoned as statesmanship until a crisis comes to put these urbanities to the test.

Apart from these attributes, Grey's unique position was due to the care with which he kept almost entirely out of the clash of Party conflicts, and never measured his prowess against the formidable gladiators who held the arena in his time. It is not that he was less contentious than Mr. Asquith: for Mr. Asquith was the least contentious of politicians. He shrank from the combat until duty forced him into it. But he never failed then to play a redoubtable part in the front of the fight whatever the hazard. He was therefore subjected to every kind of assault fair and foul to which all active politicians are liable from exasperated adversaries. On the other hand, although Sir Edward Grey's uneasy attitude towards all his various leaders in turn proved him to be temperamentally fractious, he was fortunate throughout his political career in avoiding any trial of dialectical strength or skill with the deadly swordsmen who held the arena during his political life. Even when he was busily negotiating faction inside his Party he preferred to remain behind the lines, leaving the actual fighting to Lord Rosebery, Mr. Asquith, and Mr. Haldane. He thus succeeded in attaining high position in Party Governments without incurring any of the risks of active engagement in Party struggles. The only office he ever held was by tradition deemed to be immune from the slings and arrows of partisan warfare. In opposition he substantially confined his sparring activities to impartial comments on foreign affairs. His administration in office and his allotted function out of office alike were therefore not subjected to the fierce onslaughts that test the quality of political leaders. His face was never disfigured by any blows received in action, for he consistently shunned the political battlefield. He was specially fitted to discharge the duties of an office administered under such tranquil conditions with a dignity and grace which appealed to all Parties alike. Hence the unique position of immunity from severe criticism which he had always enjoyed.

In the policy which led up to our participation in the War, Sir Edward Grey, amongst British statesmen, played the leading part. His navigation of foreign waters was not seriously challenged. Whether he could have steered Europe clear of the rocks must always be a matter of conjecture and inference from the facts. Men who are at all interested in that aspect of the problem will for some time draw differing conclusions. I am inclined to believe that the verdict of posterity will be adverse to his handling of the situation.

Of one thing there can be no doubt; he failed calamitously in his endeavours to avert the Great War. As to Sir Edward Grey's hesitations during the fateful days when the thunderclouds were deepening and rapidly darkening the sky, I have endeavoured to give an accurate summary of the facts. They tell their own tale of a pilot

c*

whose hand trembled in the palsy of apprehension, unable to grip
the levers and manipulate them with a firm and clear purpose. He
was pursuing his avowed policy of waiting for public opinion to
decide his direction for him. He reminded me of a Chairman of
Committees whom I knew in the tumultuous days of the 1892-95
Parliament. It was peculiarly a Parliament that demanded firmness
as well as fairness in the occupant of the Chair. Mr. Mellor was an
able, cultured and upright man of gentlemanly exterior and
demeanour, who would have been acclaimed by all parties as an ideal
Chairman in quiet times. But the Home Rule Parliament of
1892-95 was the most tempestuous I have seen, and there Mr. Mellor's
suavity and judicial courtesy were a pitiable sight. I can hear him
now, rising in his place and looking at neither side lest it be suggested that he was accusing one or other of being responsible, and
calling out in an appealing but not compelling voice: " Order,
Order!" Sir Edward Grey's impartial but weak and uncompelling
appeals to the raging nations of Europe to keep the peace always
recall this parliamentary incident to my memory. In the din he was
barely heard—he certainly was not heeded. Had he warned
Germany in time of the point at which Britain would declare war—
and wage it with her whole strength—the issue would have been
different. I know it is said that he was hampered by the divisions in
the Cabinet. On one question, however, there was no difference of
opinion—the invasion of Belgium. He could at any stage of the
negotiations have secured substantial unanimity amongst his colleagues on that point. At the very worst there would have been only
two resignations, and those would have followed our entry into war,
whatever the issue upon which it was fought. The assent of all the
Opposition leaders was assured, and thus in the name of a united
people he could have intimated to the German Government that if
they put into operation their plan of marching through Belgium they
would encounter the active hostility of the British Empire. And he
could have uttered this warning in sufficient time to leave the
German military authorities without any excuse for not changing
their dust-laden plans. When the ultimatum was actually delivered,
war had already broken out between Germany and her neighbours,
and the German staff were able with some show of reason to inform
the Kaiser that it was then too late to alter their arrangements without jeopardising the German chance of victory. As a matter of fact,
the Kaiser was even then anxious, in order to avoid a conflict with us,
to divert his forces from the Belgian frontier, and turn their faces
towards the East. Von Moltke gave him the answer which I have
already indicated.

It was a temperamental failure. Grey's mind was not made for
prompt action. It is reported of the late Sir Hugh Bell, the great
northern industrial magnate, who was a colleague of Sir Edward

Grey for years on the N.E. Railway, that he once said of him: " Grey is a good colleague because he never takes any risks: and he is a thoroughly bad colleague for the same reason." That saying explains why he did not take his stand on Belgium in time to give those who dreaded war in Germany a chance of reconsidering their plans in time. He would not take the risk involved in making such a bold declaration. He was still hoping that war could be averted by quieter and more conventional methods. He altogether lacked that quality of audacity which makes a great Minister.

His Arbitration Treaty with America was a notable event. The rest of his big efforts came to naught. His Balkan Settlement in 1913 fell to pieces as soon as it left our shores. His London Convention was luckily rejected, for had it been in operation during the War, it would have deprived us of our most effective weapon against Germany. He failed to keep Turkey, and afterwards Bulgaria, out of the War. His stiff and formal beckonings to them to cross over to our side could only provoke ridicule. There were many obvious expedients—including the sending of a special envoy to Turkey and Bulgaria who would be empowered to promise financial support— that he might have employed to keep both or either out of the War. He resorted to none of them. These last two failures, which a more strenuous or resourceful Foreign Minister would have converted into success prolonged the War by years, and very nearly caused the defeat of the Allies. His advice to Greece in 1914 not to join forces with the Allies was a calamity which cost us the Gallipoli Peninsula, and conduced to the overthrow of Serbia. He hesitated and fumbled in his negotiations to bring Italy into the War. As Luigi Villari says in his interesting and illuminating book, " The War on the Italian Front ": " The negotiations had been shilly-shallying for months." Had it not been that Grey had taken a few weeks' holiday and left Mr. Asquith—who was quite capable of coming to bold decisions— in charge of the Foreign Office in his absence, Italy might have sulked at the cold, critical treatment accorded her advances. In a few days Mr. Asquith brushed aside trivialities and brought the negotiations to a stage that led to a speedy decision. Had he not done so, what would have happened to the Allies? The Austrian Armies could have concentrated their whole strength on Russia, and that great country would have succumbed in 1915 to the joint attack of Germany and Austria. Throughout, Grey mistook correctitude for rectitude.

Sir Edward Grey belonged to the class which, through heredity and tradition, expects to find a place on the magisterial bench to sit in judgment upon and above their fellow-men, before they ever have any opportunity to make themselves acquainted with the tasks and trials of mankind—and some of them preserve those magisterial airs through life. They are remote from the hard work of the community.

They take it for granted. The men drawn from that class who attained pre-eminence, like Palmerston, Randolph Churchill, Salisbury and Balfour, threw themselves into the arduous conflicts of politics and fought their way to the top, giving and taking on the way the blows that hammer character. Sir Edward Grey stepped into generalship without ever doing any soldiering—not a good training for facing real danger. It was all right when things went smoothly, and all you had to do was to put forward a soldierly appearance on parade. It is a different thing when you are suddenly confronted with the greatest and most deadly diplomatic struggle ever seen between great nations. The conflicts of politics are as good a discipline and hardening for the troubles of an official career as war is for the military leader. The veteran who never fought a battle may escape the perils of shot and shell through which his comrades have passed, but he also misses the experience which would be useful to him when at last he finds himself thrown into action.

He was the most insular of our statesmen, and knew less of foreigners through contact with them than any Minister in the Government. He rarely, if ever, crossed the seas. Northumberland was good enough for him, and if he could not get there and needed a change, there was his fishing lodge in Hampshire. This was a weakness—and it was a definite weakness in a Foreign Secretary, and especially in a Foreign Secretary with no imagination—which accounted for some of his most conspicuous failures. He had no real understanding of foreigners—I am not at all sure that for this purpose he would not include Scotland, Ireland and Wales as foreign parts. Moreover, when a conference in some foreign capital might have saved the situation, his dislike of leaving England stood in the way. When he suggested a Conference of Ambassadors of the Four Powers a few days before the War, he proposed that it should be held in London. I shall point out later on how this egotistic insularity prevented the summoning of a conference which might, and I think would, at that stage have brought Bulgaria on to the Allied side. The ideal Foreign Secretary would be a cross between a recluse and a tramp, e.g., between Sir Edward Grey and Mr. Ramsay MacDonald.

A Cabinet which was compelled by political and economic exigencies to concentrate its energies on domestic problems left the whole field of foreign affairs to Sir Edward Grey. Anyone reading with care and impartiality the record of the way in which he missed his opportunities must come to the conclusion that he lacked the knowledge of foreign countries and the vision, imagination, breadth of mind and that high courage, bordering on audacity, which his immense task demanded.

CHAPTER IV

THE FINANCIAL CRISIS

1. HOW WE SAVED THE CITY

THE political situation naturally did not develop without immediate and violent reaction on the inherently unstable financial equilibrium of the whole world, which is maintained by perhaps the most sensitive organisation devised by man; and the financial crisis which marked the outbreak of the War began some days before hostilities actually commenced.   This was inevitable, because finance, or indeed the conduct of business operations of every nature, is based on successful anticipation and the ability to foresee and to discount or prepare for coming conditions.   It was in July, 1914, before the Austrian ultimatum was presented, that uneasiness showed itself on the bourses of the world, when Vienna, Berlin, and Paris commenced to sell securities to an unusual extent.   These transactions were for the most part effected in New York, where the stream of orders to sell quickly grew into a torrent.   On the 27th, after diplomatic relations between Austria-Hungary and Serbia had been broken off, the volume of selling became such that the foreign exchange market in New York gave way under the unprecedented pressure to remit to Europe the proceeds of sales.   From New York this breakdown spread to other foreign exchanges generally and was, in fact, the immediate cause of the world financial crisis.   It affected this country to a special degree, since London was the financial centre of the world, and more sensitive than any other capital to disturbances in the complex credit system through which international economic relations function. The business of London as a financial centre depends for its smooth working upon the punctual payments by foreign debtors of the money owing to British creditors.   This is particularly the case where liability of the debtors arises out of bills of exchange " accepted " on their behalf by the creditors, so much so that mercantile tradition, embodied everywhere in law, insists on the prompt payment of a bill of exchange on maturity.   This special obligation, indeed, is considered paramount; and default is looked upon as a deadly sin.   And every accepting house which accepts a bill and assumes the obligation implied by it on behalf of a foreign trader does so on the understanding that the latter will provide the necessary funds in good time.

London was not the only but easily the first of all the " accepting " cities of the world. The crackle of a bill on London with the signature of one of the great accepting houses was as good as the ring of gold in any port throughout the civilised world. A long experience maturing into a sure instinct taught these commercial financiers what to endorse and what to reject. When I asked the Governor of the Bank, Sir Walter Cunliffe, how he knew which bills were safe to approve, he replied, " I smell them." When the delicate financial cobweb was likely to be torn into shreds by the rude hand of war, London was inevitably thrown into a panic. The sudden paralysis of the foreign exchanges and of the London money market made it impossible for the very numerous foreign traders whose bills had been accepted in London to acquire money in London—wherewith to meet their obligations of this nature—in exchange for the money which they possessed in their own countries. In the aggregate the liabilities of this type amounted to hundreds of millions of sterling. If there were a general default it followed that the accepting houses would fail to pay bills upon which the whole business of the discount market depended, and which were among the most important assets of the London banks. In the last week of July, therefore, there was every prospect of such a crash in London as had never been known. The position of the banks, upon whose continued operation depends the supply of the means of payment in all business transactions, was also menaced from another direction. So soon as it became possible for the proceeds of the sale of securities to New York to be remitted to Europe, the pressure of sales was diverted to the London Stock Exchange, and there naturally followed a great depreciation in prices of stock all round. Though it was possible for the banks to withstand the depreciation of the investments they themselves owned, it was another matter when the solvency of the very large number of borrowers on the security of stocks was endangered. Thus, during the week, everything contributing, prices continued to move in a vicious circle of depreciation. So far there had been no real panic, the difficult situation which had arisen being due almost entirely to the inability of other nations to meet their liabilities. Though in this particular I do not think the actual course of events had been generally anticipated, something of the kind had been foreseen by the Sub-Committee of the Committee of Imperial Defence which considered the question of Trading with the Enemy in 1911 and 1912, and was referred to in its report.* The declaration of war by Austria precipitated matters. The outlook on that day was so serious that Mr. Montagu, the Financial Secretary to the Treasury, collected together a number of financial and business men to meet me at luncheon to discuss the situation.

* Report of Proceedings of the Standing Sub-Committee of the C.I.D. on Trading with the Enemy, Sept. 1912, pp. 8 and 9.

On Friday, 31st, the London Stock Exchange was closed, all the other stock exchanges except that of New York and the official market in Paris having closed the previous day.

Up to this point the Government, though keeping in close touch with developments in the City and watching events, had refrained from any action. But on Friday the Bank of England, which had this time felt the pressure for several days, found its reserve position seriously weakened and raised the bank rate (which had already been raised from 3 per cent. to 4 per cent.) to 8 per cent. Next day the Governor of the Bank applied to me as Chancellor of the Exchequer for permission to exceed the fiduciary issue of the notes prescribed by the Bank Charter Act 1844. This request was granted in a letter signed by the Prime Minister and myself, modelled on the precedents of 1847, 1857, and 1866, when a similar course was forced on the Government. As permission had, on those occasions, been made conditional upon no discounts or advances being granted at less than 10 per cent., the bank rate was raised to that figure. On this day, though no panic was shown by the public, there were unusual demands for gold on the Bank of England on the part of people seeking to cash the notes supplied to them by their own banks.

It was fully realised, of course, that increasing the issue of notes was a first step to ease the immediate situation in one direction only, and that it did nothing really to relieve the accepting houses or the Stock Exchange. But the two days, Sunday, 2nd, and Monday, 3rd August, which happened to be a Bank Holiday, gave a breathing space, and nearly the whole of Sunday was taken up in conferences at the Treasury, at which the situation was reviewed and a policy formulated. During these discussions, in addition to the help of Sir John Bradbury, the able permanent head of the Treasury, and of other permanent officials, I had the advantage of the advice of Lord Reading and Sir George Paish.

The outcome of our deliberations was a decision that the next step to be taken should be one calculated to relieve the accepting houses; and a proclamation was issued that evening granting a moratorium of one month to the acceptors of bills. This emergency measure obviously afforded no help to the banks or the discount houses. In fact, it ratified and consolidated a position which was detrimental, especially to the latter, in so much as it definitely froze up their chief liquid assets.

Partly in consequence of this, many of the leading representatives of these two financial interests and of trade generally met together to consider the situation from their point of view. After sitting till 2 a.m. on Monday, this conference formulated certain resolutions which were forwarded to the Government. To one of their recommendations effect was given on the 3rd, when it was announced that the 4th, 5th, and 6th August would be additional Bank Holidays.

This was done in order to obtain a further respite and to gain time to devise measures appropriate to the situation; but there was some doubt as to its advisability, owing to the fear that the cash circulated during the holidays might be accumulated by the trading community, and not be passed to the banks where it would be put into circulation again. On the same day an Act was passed through all its stages in both Houses regularising the proclamation in regard to a moratorium and giving the Government power to declare a general moratorium. ⁄ These three holidays were some of the busiest and most anxious days I ever spent. I had summoned a conference composed of Ministers and other officials and some of the leading bankers and traders, which sat morning and afternoon under my chairmanship. Ultimate decisions had to be taken by me subject to consent and if necessary revision by the Cabinet in so unprecedented a situation, where a mistake might injure the credit and confidence so essential to full strength and use of " the sinews of war." I resolved to consult every person whose ability, knowledge and experience would assist me in coming to the right conclusion. Mr. (later Sir) Austen Chamberlain, the Chancellor of the Exchequer in the preceding Unionist Government, was, amongst others, invited by me to the Allied War Conferences and assisted in the deliberations. This was an unusual, if not an unprecedented step to take; but the situation warranted any measures that might help, however novel. I well remember Mr. Chamberlain's surprise when I asked him in the House of Commons if he could give us the benefit of his experience and knowledge, and the prompt manner in which he placed himself entirely at our disposal. During the morning of the 5th, indeed, when I was obliged to leave the conference to attend the Cabinet, Mr. Chamberlain took my place as chairman; and so was brought about the unique situation of a member of the Opposition presiding at a Government Conference, a foretaste of the Coalition. I gladly acknowledge the value of the service he rendered in helping to unravel the complexities of the financial crisis and to succour those who had been caught in the tangle. He had that admixture of experience, authority, common sense and courage which is so essential in an emergency. A point which impressed me specially at the beginning of our discussions was the difficulty of reconciling the interests of the different sections of the banking community. Nevertheless, during the whole of our deliberations I was most ably backed up and advised in my position as chairman by all my colleagues, of whom five notable members have since died, i.e., Lord Cunliffe, Governor of the Bank of England, Sir Austen Chamberlain, Sir Edward Holden, Chairman of the London City and Midland Bank, Mr. Huth Jackson, and Lord St. Aldwyn. It was the first time I had been brought into direct contact with the latter since 1891, when as Sir Michael Hicks-Beach he piloted the Tithe Bill through the House of Commons. The late Sir Samuel Evans and I fought it for several nights. Sir Michael was a consummate Parliamentarian. He had a reputation for explosive irascibility in his private dealings, but in the House of Commons he was a model of suavity and address. He was chosen by the distracted and specially vocal financiers as their chief spokesman at these Treasury Conferences, where he handled his duties with all his old tact and mastery.

Our labours were not completed till the 6th August, the last day of the holidays, but we had advanced far enough by the 5th for me, on that day, to give the House of Commons an interim account of our activities and recommendations, and after announcing that steps had already been taken to suspend the Bank Act, to state definitely that it had been decided not to suspend specie payments. The latter decision, which marked the main difference between our treatment of the situation and that adopted by other countries, was one which in fact did greatly help us to recover financial normality, because it tended towards a restoration of confidence which was so vitally necessary at the moment. In accordance with this view, I made an appeal to the public to refrain on patriotic grounds from attempting to hoard gold, and accentuated the great part that finance was going to play in the struggle upon which we were entering. In order to deal with the need for currency, I explained that the Government was about to issue Government notes of the value of £1 and 10s., and that though the preparation and printing of these notes in the short time available entailed an immense effort, the Treasury officials and others concerned had made such progress that three million pounds would be ready at the end of the holidays, after which notes would be available at the rate of five million pounds a day. Postal orders were temporarily to be legal tender. Another announcement I was able to make, which was a sign of the strength of the Bank of England and would tend to reassure the business community, was that after the holidays the bank rate would be reduced from 10 per cent. to 6 per cent. I explained the reasons for the limited moratorium which had already been announced and that a more general moratorium extending for a month would be proclaimed, during which period bankers would pass cheques through the clearing houses as usual, and would supply cash to their customers for the payment of wages and the normal requirements of daily life. Mr. Chamberlain also spoke with a view to allaying alarm. As a matter of fact, the 10 per cent. bank rate was in actual operation on one day only, Saturday, the 1st August, before the holidays intervened.

In the House next day I introduced the Currency and Bank Notes Bill legalising the issue of the new currency notes and the suspension of the Bank Act, and it passed through all its stages in both Houses during the day. As the conference had by then completed its deliberations, I was also able to give further details of the extended moratorium, which was announced that day in what was known as the First General Proclamation. Not the least of the numerous anxieties weighing on the Government at this time of general upheaval and stress was this problem of establishing the financial stability of the nation itself, and as the responsible Minister I awaited with great anxiety the moment when business should again start, to learn the outcome of our experiments. It was with great relief, therefore, that on Friday, 7th, I was able, after the banks had reopened, to communicate to the Commons the favourable nature of the reports on the banking situation which had come in from all parts of the country, to the effect that there was no panic and that cash was being freely paid in.

Nevertheless, though much had been done, we had by no means reached the end of our difficulties. As I have said, the moratorium had originally been instituted to save the accepting houses from bankruptcy, but it was no more than a temporary expedient and it did not settle what was going to happen after the month had elapsed —still a real and very urgent question. So long as the accepting houses were threatened with bankruptcy the position of the banks and discount houses which held bills drawn upon them was precarious; and credit remained paralysed. The first remedial measure taken was in the form of an arrangement announced on the 12th August, by which the Bank of England undertook to discount pre-moratorium bills and to relieve the holders of the bills of all liability in respect of them. The bills so discounted amounted during the next few weeks to over a hundred million pounds, and the Bank, of course, could only take them subject to a guarantee against loss, being in reality merely the agent of the Government in the matter. This was a bold and important step, for by it the Government, in order to re-establish the foreign trade situation through the speedy rehabilitation of the discount market, temporarily assumed immense liabilities; and its action was generally approved. But sweeping though the measure was and valuable as was the relief it afforded, it did not accomplish all that was required, since the accepting houses still remained liable for the bills at maturity, and being still uncertain of their own solvency hesitated to enter upon fresh business, the very course which was essential to the re-establishment of the situation. In other words, the normal machinery for financing international trade, which was so vital a factor in our economic existence, was not working. To help the accepting houses, therefore, the Government took a further step. By an arrangement which was made public on the 5th September, the Bank of England, still with the indispensable guarantee, undertook to advance funds to acceptors to pay off the bills at maturity, and to postpone until a year after the end of the War any claim against them for repayment. By this means time was given to the accepting houses to recover the sums due from their clients, and they were enabled to proceed and carry on business free from embarrassment.

Thus at last was the problem of the pre-moratorium bills solved, and the position of the accepting houses consolidated. But we were not yet out of the wood. There were several other sources of danger to be dealt with before the moratorium could be removed. The Courts (Emergency Powers) Acts, passed on the 31st August, relieved the hardships of debtors who could not pay owing to war conditions. Schemes, into details of which I need not here enter, were also devised to meet the difficulties arising out of advances to the Stock Exchange and of debts due from foreign countries to British traders. The next important point was both a grave and difficult one to settle and occasioned long and anxious discussion, for there was room for great difference of opinion. The moratorium had undoubtedly saved the situation during the height of the crisis, but, once it should have served its purpose and helped to restore the normal flow of international business, its continuation could only be detrimental in many ways. The trend of events during August and September, however, had furnished considerable experience upon which to form a judgment, and at the end of the latter month it was decided that the moratorium should come to an end on the 4th November. The adoption of this course, which proved to be the correct one, was very largely due to the advice of Lord Reading and Sir George Paish, by both of whom it was urgently pressed. There was another matter which was of no slight moment to us as Ministers. In the various schemes which had been improvised against time and carried out during the crisis, the guarantee of the Government, it must be remembered, had been given on our sole responsibility. It was imperative, therefore, that Parliamentary authority should at the earliest opportunity be given to our actions. This was done by the Government (War Obligations) Act, which received the Royal Assent on 27 November, and was in essence an act of indemnity for the Ministers.

Thus were matters tided over. During the worst part of it, whether it be regarded as a week or ten days, which covered the period whilst Europe changed from a state of unstable peace definitely to war, the City of London could not guess how near to ruin it was. But it suspected the worst, and many of its leaders were too overwhelmed by the great dangers to which they saw themselves exposed to be able to think with their accustomed composure and to preserve unshaken their wonted touch. Financiers in a fright do not make an heroic picture. One must make allowances, however, for men who were millionaires with an assured credit which seemed as firm as the globe it girdled, and who suddenly found their fortunes scattered by a bomb hurled at random from a reckless hand. The strongest and sturdiest figure amongst them was Sir Edward Holden, with the brogue and stout heart of Lancashire in all his utterances. He stood out amongst all these money barons. Not unnaturally the Ministers and officials, who could afford to take a more detached and impersonal view of the affairs of the country, were better able to perceive what was required from the larger point of view and to act immediately. One great difference between our policy and that of other nations was that we definitely endeavoured as soon as possible to re-establish our economic system on a normal basis, a task which was frankly abandoned by most of the other governments. And this we succeeded to a very great extent in effecting immediately. In fact so successful was our recovery that the pendulum perhaps swung too much in the opposite direction and led on the part of some to the attitude expressed by the catchword " business as usual." This, though valuable at the moment of doubt to help re-establish confidence, later on led to an entire misconception in many quarters of the effort demanded by what proved to be a struggle for our very existence.

Throughout these conferences I found Lord Reading's aid invaluable. His knowledge of finance, his mastery of figures, his dexterity and his calm and sure judgment helped at many turns.

The nation passed through the great financial crisis in a marvellous way. There was no sign of panic on the part of the public in a situation that for us as a nation was unprecedented. In this emergency the main duties of the Government were to keep things going and to restore normality as quickly as possible by prompt and wise and, if necessary, drastic action, and meanwhile to maintain the community as a whole in that state of composure which is barren soil for the breeding of panic. In doing the former the Government and the Treasury were greatly assisted by the steadfast attitude of the Governor of the Bank of England, whose wise, far-sighted and broad point of view on the national aspect of affairs, and whose massive strength were a source of comfort and good counsel. His sense of humour, which he concealed under a dour and almost surly countenance, was an encouragement in those trying days. He was fond of little practical jokes to lighten the dismal anxieties of our common burden. He affected a deep resentment at our issuing the £1 notes as Treasury and not Bank of England Notes. He scoffed at the inferiority of our issue in the quality of its paper and its artistry as compared with the crisp £5 note of the Great Bank over which he presided. (The first issue of Treasury Notes was a temporary one and very rough.) I can see his impressive figure with its rolling gait, coming one morning through the door of the Treasury Board Room. He had a scornful look on his face. He came up to my desk with a mumbled greeting, solemnly opened the portfolio he always carried, and pulled out a bedraggled £1 Treasury Note, dirty and barely legible. He said: "Look at that. It came into the bank yesterday in that condition. I told you the paper was no good —far better to have left it to us." He had scrubbed the note in order to reduce it to this condition of effacement for the pleasure of ragging me. I told him so and he laughed. His manner was not propitiatory to strangers, but when you got to know him he was a genial, kindly man, and I liked him. I relied on his shrewdness, his common sense and instinct.

He was a man of very few words. I cannot recall a single sentence he uttered at any of these numerous conferences. What he said was half whispered in my ear. He accompanied me later on to Paris to meet M. Bark, the Russian Finance Minister, and M. Ribot, the French Finance Minister, at a conference to discuss the subject of financing Russian contracts in America. When a question arose as to a transhipment of gold the Governor of the Bank of France expressed himself with great fluency. I then said: "The Governor of the Bank of England will state the British view on the subject." He rose slowly, and after a few preliminary puffs he said: "We do not mean to part with our gold," and then subsided into his seat.

During his visit we drove to Boulogne to catch the boat. On our way I was anxious to make a detour through Bethune, which I was eager to see. It was occasionally bombarded, but the risk was trifling. However, the Governor would not consent to my proposal. I was surprised, for he was a man of undoubted courage. He said: "A predecessor of mine was killed visiting the trenches at Namur. But he was there on business with the King, and the city said, 'Poor fellow!' But if I were hit in the stomach at Bethune they would all say, 'D——d fool—what business had he to go there?'" That was conclusive, and I never saw Bethune.

To revert to our financial arrangements in the first few weeks of the war: The risks of every course were undoubtedly great. But decisions had of necessity to be prompt. Panic had to be anticipated at every turn. It was no time for sitting indefinitely in Council in order to evolve the perfect course of action which would reduce to a minimum the eventual cost to the National Exchequer. The possible consequences of delay or of the adoption of inadequate measures, which did not at once restore public confidence, were so appalling that immediate action was imperatively demanded. In the result the Government loss was negligible. We guaranteed about £500,000,000 of securities in respect of debts incurred across the seas—some of these on enemy security. In due course it was all gathered in except a few millions. In this aspect the problem before us was akin to that presented at the same time by the State Insurance of Shipping, though in the latter case it was only necessary to put into operation a scheme, worked out under the auspices of the Committee of Imperial

Defence, and all ready to be applied. I had gratifying proof, indeed, that the share I had taken in the policy of the Government met with the approval and gained the confidence of a section of the business and financial world which had not previously regarded my efforts as Chancellor of the Exchequer with any favour.

Amongst those whose advice I sought was Lord Rothschild. My previous contact with him was not of a propitiatory character. He had led the opposition in the City to my scheme for Old Age Pensions and to my Budget proposals in 1909, and I had assailed him in phrases which were not of the kind to which the head of the great house of Rothschild had hitherto been subjected. My attack was strongly resented by all his friends. However, this was no time to allow political quarrels to intrude into counsel. The nation was in peril. I invited him to the Treasury for a talk. He came promptly. We shook hands. I said, "Lord Rothschild, we have had some political unpleasantness." He interrupted me: "Mr. Lloyd George, this is no time to recall those things. What can I do to help?" I told him. He undertook to do it at once. It was done.

When he died, shortly afterwards, I attended his funeral. On a grey, damp morning the streets to the cemetery were lined with poor Jews who were there to pay their humble tribute of reverence to the great Prince in Israel, who never forgot the poor and the wretched amongst his people.

In the long run not only did the measures undertaken achieve their object, but the liabilities incurred by the Government at that time did not result in appreciable loss. Having, after an interval of eighteen years, carefully considered all the circumstances, I am of opinion that it was the bold policy of the Government, relying on the strength of the national character, which enabled the City of London to recover quickly from the stunning blow at the outbreak of war, and to continue to pulsate and fulfil one of its functions as the economic heart of the whole Empire of which it was the centre.

2. SUPPLEMENTARY BUDGET AND THE FIRST WAR LOAN

On 17th November, 1914, I introduced my first War Budget. Virtually it was my only War Budget, for although on 4th May, 1915, I made the customary Budget statement, shortly before vacating the Exchequer to undertake the office of Minister of Munitions, I did not on that date introduce any new features or modifications of taxation. My reasons were twofold: In the first place, the additional taxes I had already imposed in November, 1914, were only beginning to fructify, and I pointed out that while additions to taxations would be necessary, we should have to wait till the autumn to decide what they should be; and in the second place, the only extra charges I had in mind in May for immediate application, were on alcoholic liquors; and the storm of opposition which these encountered made it impossible to introduce them at that time without raising most violent and undesirable political controversy. This is a story which I deal with more fully in a subsequent section when discussing the drink problem in the War.

The real 1915 Budget was that introduced in September by my successor, Mr. M'Kenna, and it was memorable for the imposition of the M'Kenna Duties, which in subsequent years were to play so important a part in political controversy, and were the prelude to a revolutionary change in our fiscal system.

By November, 1914, it was obvious that the additional expenditure caused by the War would far outrun anything provided for by the peace-time Budget I had introduced in the spring. Already on 8th August the House of Commons had voted the Government a credit of £100,000,000 for War purposes, and it was now necessary to ask it for a further credit of more than twice that amount. If the War were to continue far into 1915, much greater sums still would be required.

The issue before the country, and particularly before myself as Chancellor of the Exchequer, was whether these huge sums should be raised entirely by loans, and added in full to the National Debt, or whether we should aim at paying our way as far as possible by current taxation, and thus reduce the debt burden to be handed on to the next generation.

I took the view that the immense spending of the Government was bound to cause a very considerable inflation of our currency. War-time demands would stimulate our industries to unprecedented activity; and in addition, the closing down of the international commerce of Central Europe and the crippling of the industrial capacities of France and Belgium, would, for the time being, mean that a heavy extra demand for goods by other countries would fall on us. The result would be a much bigger circulation of money here, and it would be far easier to pay for the War while this state of things lasted, than later on, when trade depression supervened and deflation removed our spare cash.

Accordingly, when Parliament reassembled in November, 1914, for an unexpected Autumn Session, and I laid before the House of Commons a proposal for a second vote of credit for £225,000,000, I introduced at the same time a supplementary Budget, with the object of raising a portion of this sum by additional taxation.

The additions were as follows: I doubled the income tax—raising it from 1s. 4d. to 2s. 8d. in the £ I also doubled the super-tax. Already I had in the spring introduced the graduation of this tax, making it range up from 5d. in the £ on income exceeding £3,000, to a maximum of 1s. 4d. on income in excess of £11,000. These charges I now doubled. The beer duty I raised from 7s. 9d. per barrel to 25s., and the tea duty from 5d. to 8d. per lb. On the other hand, as a compensation to publicans for the sharp restrictions on facilities for drinking which were being introduced, I cut down their licence duty—a concession involving about half a million.

The beer and tea duties went on, of course, at once. But the higher income and super-taxes only took effect for the final quarter of the current financial year. Had there been no additional taxation, the revenue realised in 1914-15 would have been below the estimate, through reduced yield of certain taxes and duties. As a result even of the short currency of these added levies, the 1914-15 revenue exceeded my estimate of May, 1914, by about $19\frac{1}{2}$ millions. In a full year these extra taxes would produce upwards of £60,000,000 of additional revenue.

When I decided to frame a supplementary budget, I asked Mr. Austen Chamberlain, who had been Chancellor under the last Conservative administration, to co-operate with me in working out its details, in order that the party truce might be fully preserved in the matter. He accepted my invitation, and we entered on consultations; but before long he resigned his connection with the Government. This was not the outcome of any personal disagreement. Indeed, when making a statement on this matter in the House on 24th November, he declared: —

> " During the confidential conversations I have had with the Chancellor of the Exchequer and his colleagues since he invited me to discuss the details of his Budget with him, I could make no complaint whatever of the spirit with which the Right Honourable gentleman approached the questions with which we dealt, and I desire to state that he has looked on the questions which came before him as revenue questions pure and simple, and that he has not allowed his mind to be diverted by any ulterior object."

But Mr. Austen Chamberlain was in a difficult position when it came to the additional duties I proposed to levy on beer. The links between the Conservative Party and the " Trade " were very strong. As a representative of that party he could not possibly associate it in advance with proposals to more-than-treble the tax on beer. " Even as a compromise," he declared, he could not assume personal responsibility for such a measure.

The House of Commons, however, did not shrink from the beer taxes, and the Budget with its drastic additions to our fiscal imposts was passed speedily into law. Such complaisance may not strike us to-day as very wonderful, faced as we are by annual budgets which in a time of peace are four times as large. But the Britain of 1914 had no experience of such burdens, and would have been aghast at my suggestions had it not been for the moment too elevated by the enthusiasms of its war task.

In the course of my Budget speech of November, 1914, I made a statement which is not without interest to-day. Urging the importance of raising as much as possible of our war expenditure by immediate taxation, in place of leaving it all for repayment in future years, I predicted that immediately after the War there would be a short spell of booming industry, while here and abroad the deficits of goods which had been held up by the War were being made good. " But," I continued, " when that period is over we shall be face to face with one of the most serious industrial situations with which we have ever been confronted. We shall have exhausted an enormous amount of the capital of the world which would otherwise have been available for industries. Our purchasers, both here and abroad, will be crippled. Their purchasing power will have been depressed. Let us make no mistake. Great Britain will be confronted with some of the gravest problems with which it has ever been faced."

Unhappily, the last fifteen years have conspired to verify this prophecy all too thoroughly.

In bringing forward this supplementary Budget, I also announced the issue of the first War Loan. The vote of credit granted in August for the War had been for £100 million, and I was now asking for a fresh credit of £225 million. It was clear that further votes would before long be required. For the present, however, I contented myself with the proposal of a War Loan of a face value of £350,000,000. It was to be 3½ per cent. security, issued at 95, and thus yielding the Government £332½ million of actual cash. Of this total, £45 million were required for loans to our Allies and Dominions. The remainder would be used, along with the yield of the additional taxes imposed, for financing our own immediate war expenditure.

The loan was made redeemable at par in 1925-28. In view of its issue price of 95, its interest yield was approximately 3⅔ per cent. The whole loan was very quickly over-subscribed.

This was the only War Loan for which I was immediately responsible. The second War Loan was that issued on 21st June, 1915, by Mr. M'Kenna. It was for an unspecified amount (with an upper limit of £910 million), and consisted of stock issued at par, bearing interest at 4½ per cent. It brought in about £570 million of new money by the time the list was closed on 10th July, as well as Consols and other Government securities for conversion, to an amount equalling about £276,500,000 of the new War Loan stock.

Looking back, I cannot help regretting that Mr. M'Kenna should have thought it necessary to raise the interest rate of a Government loan to 4½ per cent. Maybe this corresponded to the price that was being offered in the money market for other gilt-edged securities. But in view of the increase in our nominal capital reserves due to war inflation and to the restriction of an overseas market for investment money which was also one of the effects of the War, there can be little doubt that the Government could have continued to obtain as much money as it required by voluntary investment, without raising its interest rate beyond the level of $3\frac{2}{3}$ per cent. at which my first loan had been negotiated. Investors would have had to take this, for lack of an alternative. And if they had been unwilling to do so, there would have been a clear and popular ground for the conscription of capital for war purposes—a step which would have been an appropriate corollary to the conscription of man-power which we were soon to introduce.

As it was, the adoption of the principle that the British Government had to pay the commercial rate for money needed to defend the country had a costly sequel. This principle governed the plans for the Third War Loan, for which arrangements were begun toward the end of 1916, and carried through in January, 1917, by Mr. Bonar Law, who had just replaced Mr. M'Kenna at the Exchequer. That loan was issued at 95, bearing interest at 5 per cent., and over £2,000 million was raised at this penal figure. The same rate governed subsequent borrowings, which by the end of the War had added a further £4,000,000,000 to our National Debt. It cost the country a dozen years of remorseless deflation and concomitant depression to bring interest rates down again to a level that would enable this vast sum to be reconverted to $3\frac{1}{2}$ per cent. Throughout the interval, not only was the country taxing itself to pay a sum ranging at one time as high as £100,000,000 a year more than it would otherwise have done, but the high yield of a gilt-edged Government security kept up rates all round, and made money dearer for all enterprises, industrial, commercial and national. It would be hard to estimate the sum total of the price paid by the nation in every department of affairs for the decision of Mr. M'Kenna in 1915 to increase the rate of interest paid by the Government on its war-time borrowings. His action had, no doubt, the fullest authorisation from the leading circles of banking and finance. But the country has since then had ample evidence that these circles are by no means to be reckoned as infallible advisers.

CHAPTER V

THE FIGHT FOR MUNITIONS

1. INTRODUCTORY

THE outbreak of war found this country totally unprepared for land hostilities on a Continental scale. Our traditional defence force has always been our Navy, and this weapon has been kept efficient and ready at all times. But our Army, mainly used for policing our widely scattered Empire, was a small, highly trained force of professional soldiers, excellent for their normal tasks, but lacking both the numbers and the equipment for large-scale fighting against European armies.

Unhappily, too, the War Office was hampered by a traditional reactionism. Its policy seemed ever to be that of preparing, not for the next war, but for the last one or the last but one. The Boer War found us still in the mentality of the Crimea, and the Great War caught our military thinkers planning for the next war under the conditions of the Alma in so far as these were modified by the irrelevant experiences of the African veldt. Unfortunately, they only remembered the lessons that were better forgotten because they were inapplicable, and forgot all the experiences by which they ought to have profited because they were a foretaste of the methods of future warfare. Todleben's famous earthworks had no meaning for them, nor had the trenches of Magersfontein and the Tugela, where our massed troops were slaughtered by riflemen they never saw. But the thin red line of Inkerman and the glorious charge which sabred the gunners at Balaclava, and the Boer horsemanship which rushed Methuen's camp at Klip's Drift dominated the military mind. Military imagination makes up in retentiveness what it misses in agility.

The man-power needed for our new armies was fortunately not dependent for its production on the unsympathetic organisation of the War Office. Lord Kitchener's outstanding name and fame constituted a great appeal, which was organised with expert efficiency and understanding by the agents of the two great political parties. From farm and village and city street young men thronged into the recruiting offices at the sound of Lord Kitchener's call to arms. The first half-million managed within the first month to press its way through the recruiting stations, and it speedily grew to a million, then to two, then three. The immortal story has been told and retold, and it is not my business to tell it again. In the magnitude and grandeur of the response it has no parallel in history. Considering the fact that there were neither rifles, machine-guns, cannon nor mortars available for training, the dug-out officers and non-commissioned officers achieved wonders in the turning of their material into armies.

The equipment of these armies, however, is another story; and in so far as that equipment included the provision of munitions, that duty was eventually placed upon me. The story is therefore mine to tell.

The whole business was at the outset jealously retained by the War Office in its own hands, even to the tailoring contracts. The result was shortage, delays, misfits and muddles.

Happily for the world, the weapons of modern slaughter do not grow naturally. They have to be designed and manufactured; and although Britain was the leading manufacturing country in the world, its industries were almost entirely concerned with the arts of peace. It was deficient in machinery for the production of rifles, machine-guns and artillery especially of the heavier calibres. Armament firms were few, and the methods of the national arsenals were obsolescent and primitive to a degree. The Army Chiefs were mostly horsemen—Lord French and Sir Douglas Haig were both cavalrymen, and won their reputations as cavalry generals. Lord Kitchener was a sapper. His only experiences of war, however, would have left him with the impression that mobility counted more than weight and quantity of shell.

High-explosive shell, which the German forces were using against us with such shattering effect, was regarded up to the outbreak of war by our own Ordnance Department as being merely in the experimental stage, and the problem of a satisfactory filling and fuse for it had not be solved. It had not been seriously and systematically investigated. The War Office was obsessed with the importance of shrapnel. It was the only artillery lesson of the Boer War which they remembered, and in September, 1914, our War Office Generals were still preparing to slug African kopjes with Boers hiding behind bushes or boulders. It was the most useful shell in Africa. Why not in Europe? They had been criticised in 1900 because the supply was inadequate, they were not going to be caught and castigated this time. Their mental arsenals had no room for anything but shrapnel.

As to heavy artillery, the regular establishment of the Army at the outbreak of war did not provide for anything beyond the 60-pounder. The 4.7 was considered almost too cumbrous a weapon for the field. There were a few specimens of six-inch howitzers in existence, of obsolescent pattern, and some six-inch guns, which could be gleaned here and there, partly from coastal forts. There was only one 9.2-inch howitzer just completed. There was very little ammunition for any of these heavy guns. Our old siege train guns were muzzle-loaders! It had been the official view of the General Staff that the tendency of field operations to approximate towards siege warfare, displayed in the Russo-Japanese fighting in Manchuria—the most recent example of modern war—should not be accepted as a general tendency, and they had made no plans or preparations for dealing with such a situation. The Japanese armies walked round the field defences of the Russians without attempting to destroy them or storm then, just as French did with his cavalry at Magersfontein. Why not in France? A trench hundreds of miles long from Switzerland to the sea, which you could not outflank, either on the right or the left, was beyond their limited vision.

Some of our old-fashioned six-inch howitzers arrived in France in time to be used in the battle of the Aisne, but even by the end of January, 1915, the British had only 24 of these weapons in the field, or one battery per corps—one-sixteenth the number that were being used against us by the Germans. And the Germans had shells for their howitzers; we had a very scanty ration for ours. The official allowance of machine-guns to our troops was two per battalion, and even this meagre dole was not available for our new armies during the first months of their service, although they were sent to fight against German forces equipped with 16 machine-guns per battalion. As to shells, the production of shell cases was absurdly inadequate, but such as it was it greatly exceeded the provision for filling the empty cases with explosives or for manufacturing fuses to detonate them. When I paid a visit to Woolwich Arsenal some months after the outbreak of the War, I found stacks of empty shells which were being slowly and tediously filled, one at a time, with ladles by hand from cauldrons of seething fluid. The production of the fuses for detonating the shells was governed by the same lack of imagination, and consequently there was a similar deficiency in output.

It was not so much a question of unpreparedness at the outbreak of war. No one before the War contemplated our raising armies aggregating hundreds of thousands of men for any war in which we were ever likely to be engaged. Our military arrangements with France never went beyond the dispatch of an Expeditionary Force of six divisions to support the French armies on their left flank. When the Cabinet decided to appeal for volunteers they only asked for a recruitment of 100,000. What followed that appeal exceeded the most sanguine anticipation. When the German armies overran Belgium and broke the French front, marching up to gates of Paris, the youth of Britain rolled up in such numbers that the whole idea of our contribution to the War was changed by this uprising of indignant valour. The Cabinet, excited by the spectacle to a fit of audacity, raised the limit of enlistment to 500,000. The flood did not take long to overflow even that limit.

No blame can, therefore, be attached to the War Office or its responsible heads for failing to have in store, at the outbreak of the War, a reserve of equipment and munitions for the hitherto un-dreamed-of forces we were compelled to raise and put into the field. But they cannot be held guiltless of mental obtuseness in their neglect to keep abreast of modern development in pattern of munitions and machinery for munition production, and still more of a most pitiable breakdown of initiative in facing the new task which confronted them, of bringing munition production up to the standard demanded by the actual conditions of warfare as they soon manifested themselves in the campaign of 1914.

Modern warfare, we discovered, was to a far greater extent than ever before a conflict of chemists and manufacturers. Man-power, it is true, was indispensable, and generalship will always, whatever the conditions, have a vital part to play. But troops, however brave and well led, were powerless under modern conditions unless equipped with adequate and up-to-date artillery (with masses of explosive shell), machine-guns, aircraft and other supplies. Against enemy machine-gun posts and wire entanglements the most gallant and best-led men could only throw away their precious lives in successive waves of heroic martyrdom. Their costly sacrifice could avail nothing for the winning of victory.

This question of munitions supply thus emerged as the crucial issue of the War. Before long it became clear that unless we could solve it, and solve it promptly, we were doomed to certain futility in this War.

2.   FINANCE OF PRODUCTION

At the outbreak of the War my only connection with the problem of munitions supply was the responsibility, as Chancellor of the Exchequer, for finding money to pay the bills.

My instruction as to what the actualities of war were likely to be was confined to a visit which the Secretary of State for War (Mr. Haldane) invited me to pay with him to Army manœuvres in the vicinity of Hungerford in the summer of 1908. I was thrilled with the anticipation of viewing a battle, even although it was only a stage fight. I felt that, under such auspices, one would see something of what the terrible reality would be like. There were real soldiers, real rifles, bayonets, swords, cavalry, cannon, commanded by real generals who had fought more than once in real wars. Mr. Haldane and I were perched, with the staff of one of the opposing armies, on a hill which was defended by infantry supported by field guns. When some years later I saw the Messines Ridge and Kemmel

I realised with what prevision the General Staff had chosen the terrain for the military manœuvres of 1908. It was explained to us that the hill was to be attacked by a force not visible at the moment but which was expected soon to deploy from a valley about a mile off. It was an exciting moment when we saw the skirmishers of the enemy emerge from the defile, whence they were followed by masses of infantry spreading and swarming over the plain. The volleys fired by attackers and defenders and the roar of the cannon on both sides were deafening. This must be something like real war! The issue did not tremble long in the balance, for a regiment of cavalry hitherto hidden in the woods dashed out of cover, and, half-concealed by a heavy shower of rain which then fell providentially, galloped along to the foot of the hill, gallantly scrambled up the slopes in the face of shot and shell, reached the parapet, swept over our poor guns and captured the position. I felt then that I knew something of what our Generals expected the next war would be like. When Mr. Haldane asked me afterwards to find out of the Exchequer an additional sum for the provision of light guns I felt they were quite necessary to avert the possibility of such a catastrophe happening in a Continental war when the mounted hordes of the Continental armies attacked our Expeditionary Forces on the hills of Flanders. Machine-guns were too trivial a toy to be included in the schedule of fresh demands on the Exchequer. This interesting military experience came to my mind when eight years later I saw masses of cavalry ride up to the lines to storm the trenched and wired plateau of the Somme above Guinchy. I remembered the Hungerford manœuvres and I understood better than ever that a military obsession, however fantastic it may be, is stronger than death—than many deaths.

Let me state at the outset that neither at the outbreak of war nor at any subsequent period in its course was the provision of munitions hampered by failure to furnish the money for their purchase or production. On the contrary, I repeatedly made it clear that as far as the Treasury was concerned no obstacle would come from that quarter in providing every supply that could possibly aid us to victory. If the choice were between spending gold or British lives, I was ready to take the responsibility of calling on the nation to yield its last coin, provided it were wisely and effectively spent. Nor did the country itself ever hesitate to support this attitude.

On the 5th August, 1914, the day after the declaration of war, the House of Commons was invited by me to vote an initial sum of £100 million towards the cost. I let the War Office know that it could have whatever funds it needed to expedite supplies, and in September I took the further step of definitely setting aside a sum of £20 million and earmarking it as a fund to be drawn on to finance extensions of factories and works for the production of munitions. I must add that

D

the Master-General of Ordnance decided in his wisdom not to inform the trade at first of this provision, as is proved by the following extract from a minute by him, dated 2nd October, 1914: —

> " The Secretary of State told me on 30th September that the Cabinet had decided that day that the various firms supplying munitions of war were to be called upon to increase their plant so as to allow of large orders over and above those already placed to be executed in order that we should be able to obtain additional supplies of guns, rifles, ammunition, etc., in the same time if possible as those already ordered and promised, and that in addition our Allies should also be able to procure the same.
>
> He informed me that the Chancellor of the Exchequer had agreed to place twenty millions sterling at the disposal of the trade for the purpose of increasing their plant. . . .
>
> *It has been considered by me inadvisable at this stage to inform the trade that grants of money will be made,* as hitherto I have received no hint or notice of difficulties of that sort. . . ."

That last sentence illuminates the War Office horror at the thought of adopting to meet this unprecedented emergency any method not sanctioned by " pigeon-holed " tradition wrapped in red tape.

I soon realised that the ordinary methods of Treasury approval for expenditure were inapplicable to the exigencies of war and that to make orders for essential supplies dependent on discussions of every detail between the War Department and Treasury officials would delay and hamper action.

Pointing out that in the present emergency it was not possible to insist on the normal routine and Treasury control in regard to departmental commitments for contracts which now often had to include abnormal financial conditions, I suggested that throughout the War such contracts should be concluded without reference to the Treasury. The departmental heads in the War Office were thus given freedom to take full and immediate responsibility for whatever contracts they held necessary. I assented to this procedure all the more readily because there was installed at the War Office as its financial adviser an able Treasury official—Sir Charles Harris. Not in the whole public service could be found a more faithful and vigilant watchdog for the public money.

3. RED TAPE AT THE WAR OFFICE

But although a financial *carte blanche* had thus been offered to the responsible authorities for all measures necessary to supply munitions, and although the needs of our troops at the front were urgent and terrible, the shortage of munitions continued and increased. The War Office neglected to utilise to the full its powers to remedy the lamentable shortage from which our armies were suffering so severely.

Admittedly the authorities were faced with an unprecedented situation. To cope with it, measures equally unprecedented were necessary. The gravamen of the charge against them is that they completely failed to show the resource and flexibility of mind requisite to grapple with that situation and to improvise those exceptional measures. The only defence they have been able to produce is the plea that the demands on them were out of all proportion to previous experience; that they strove to meet them through their traditional channels of supply; and that those channels became choked in the effort. But that was obvious from the outset. Their task should have been to increase those sources of supply in original ways available to us as one of the three greatest and most resourceful and adaptable manufacturing countries in the world. Any powers they sought for the purpose would instantly have been accorded to them by Parliament. They not only failed to do this; they put all kinds of obstacles, both at the outset and later on, in the way of everyone who tried to help them, or relieve them of some part of their burden.

Up to the beginning of the War the normal routine was for the Minister of War as the instrument of Government to decide what operations he would sanction. The Commander-in-Chief would notify him of his requirements for carrying out those operations. On the basis of this information the Master-General of Ordnance would decide what stores must be obtained, and would in turn inform the Director of Army Contracts, who would approach the recognised armament firms, and refer their quotations for consideration to the Financial Secretary of the War Office. After due discussion, a contract would eventually be placed.

As soon as the War started, however, the Financial Department, on the suggestion of the Treasury, informed the Director of Army Contracts that he need not refer quotations to them before closing contracts, so long as he let them know of all liabilities incurred. This should have considerably expedited procedure. I am inclined to believe that in practice this relaxation had the effect of increasing the delays. It turned out to be a psychological blunder. The explanation casts an interesting light on the limitations of Departmentalism. As long as the officer ordering the supplies had the check of scrutiny and sanction by the officer of another department, he put forward his requisitions boldly. His responsibility in the event of any accusation of extravagance was by this means shared if not altogether transferred. But now the whole undivided burden of decision was cast upon him. Responsibility to the strong is a stimulus—to the weak it is a palsy. There were many unpleasant memories lingering in the military mind of select committees and commissions appointed in past wars to investigate extravagant orders inefficiently executed. The Master-General of Ordnance hints that he felt most uneasy without the support of his customary financial strait-waistcoat, and complains that it " threw increased responsibility for the expenditure on the shoulders of the Master-General of Ordnance, who, feeling that he had not every item checked as usual before commitment, had to look still closer into each proposal involving expenditure, whether for contracts placed with the Trade for finished war material or for buildings, machinery and staff required for his own department." The Ordnance Department therefore felt constrained by the sense of an unaccustomed responsibility to find good and sufficient excuses for going slowly, and halting and hesitating in front of the munitions problem.

The War Office had always dealt direct with the Government arsenals and a certain small circle of contractors only, and could not bring itself to launch out into dealings with a wider circle. The taking in hand of an array of new and untried firms and the organisa-tion of them for munitions production would beyond question have been a serious and unprecedented responsibility. The Ordnance Department recoiled from that risk.

When, therefore, prominent industrialists all over the country clamoured to be of assistance, and made offers to supply military stores and munitions, the War Office did all it could to keep them at bay. Complaints reached me that they were treated as if they were greedy suppliants for profitable war contracts. The general policy of the War Office was to give these would-be helpers a list of the traditional contracting munition firms, and invite them to approach these firms with offers to sub-contract for supplies. It must be borne in mind that these firms were already working at full pressure, choked with orders from the War Office for not only their maximum output, but for whatever extended output they could hold out any hope of developing. It was obvious that their overworked staffs would neither have the time to organise a large system of subsidiary firms, nor the inclination to spare some of their best skilled men to train workers in other concerns in the processes of munition manu-facture; and furthermore, they would naturally be none too eager to teach other firms which might develop into awkward rivals and competitors with themselves in days to come. In peace time there had been between Admiralty, War Office and foreign orders only barely sufficient orders for armaments to go round, and few guessed how long it would be before peace returned.

It was subsequently discovered that not only had some of the arma-ment firms accepted contracts from the British War Office which were far beyond their capacity to execute, but that some of them had undertaken orders on a gigantic scale from the Russian Government. When they accepted these Russian contracts they must have known that they had not the faintest chance of executing them in time if they were to deal fairly with their British orders. Their failure to execute these orders was largely responsible for the disasters which befell the Russian armies in the campaign of 1914-15. War is the harvest of the armament firms. But in all countries they were inclined to over-estimate the capacity of their own fields and barns.

The policy of the War Office relieved it of the dreaded responsibility for the control of work from these outside firms, but at the cost of interposing between the crying needs of our front line on the one hand, and the vast manufacturing capacity of Great Britain on the other, the narrow bottle-neck of a handful of overworked firms, far too busy with their own tasks to undertake the gigantic duty which the War Office sought to thrust upon them, of organising the whole potential productive capacity of the country for munitions manufacture.

The military organisers appear to have been handicapped by that ingrained distrust, misunderstanding and contempt of all business men (not on the War Office register) which was traditionally prevalent in the Services; and doubtless the business men on their side were—to say the least—puzzled by their contact with the military mind and army manners. The Master-General of Ordnance has explained that the method adopted with some of these would-be helpers was to send them down to one of the arsenals to see the work being carried out and form an opinion as to their firm's capabilities of undertaking it; and he adds that while many went, comparatively few returned to say that they could do it. In the light of the subsequent achievements of such men under the direction of the Ministry of Munitions, one has an idea of the sort of encouragement these men must have received at official hands. And it shows that there was a genuine, though mistaken, under-estimate of the capacity, skill and adaptable engineering ability of the nation at large. Doubtless there were many incompetents and exploiters among those eager applicants for orders. But a filter of red tape was ill adapted to sift them out and still retain the really efficient business men, who are often the first to recoil, perplexed and disgruntled, at such treatment. The good men and the rubbish alike failed to squeeze through the fine and resistant mesh. Meantime the War Office, aware that it was not in sight of obtaining the gigantic supplies required by the front line, spent much time begging the soldiers not to use up shells so quickly.

4. FIRST SIGNS OF SHELL SHORTAGE

After the first rapid fluctuations of the War in the retreat from Mons and the advance from the Marne to the Aisne, the battle-front began to settle down, in September and October, 1914, into that long line of deep entrenchments which were to characterise the Western Front up to the end of the War.

The utilisation of the 5.9 howitzer by the Germans as a field gun was a surprise to the French and British alike. Its effect on the nerve of the troops was shattering, and it contributed largely to the break-up of Allied resistance in the early stages of the War.

Already the Allied forces had experienced the immense weight of the German artillery, and the crashing moral effect of the high-explosive shells which they freely employed. The ability of the Germans to use, even when it was a war of movement, heavy guns of a calibre far greater than we had begun to think of as practicable in the field of battle, and the devastation wrought by their " coal-boxes " and " Jack Johnsons," as their giant shells were irreverently nicknamed, had been a revelation to our military chiefs, British and French alike. Such defences as were hastily improvised proved quite inadequate to protect the retreating armies against the attacks of this deadly gun. No trenches had been prepared, and such shallow trenches as were here and there hurriedly scratched in the soil during the retreat offered no shelter from the explosives rained upon them by Germany's heavy artillery. On the other hand, when it came to the German turn to retreat, their engineers dug deep into the earth, and the bombardment by light guns was quite ineffective against such defences. As the War thus passed to the stage of trench warfare, we found that the shrapnel of our field guns was powerless not only to level parapets, to destroy trenches and to obliterate machine-gun emplacements, but even to tear down barbed-wire entanglements, and that the only way to save British lives was to churn up enemy defences with a crashing barrage of high-explosive shells that would smash the machine-guns, level trenches and break lanes through the wire before an attack was attempted.

At that time the War Office was supplying only shrapnel for the field guns, and of the shell even for field howitzers and 60-pounders, 70 per cent. was shrapnel. The few six-inch howitzers and the lonely 9.2-inch howitzer which was sent out in October, fired high explosive, but had only a limited amount of ammunition.*

By the first week in September, 1914, General Headquarters in France were writing to the Master-General of Ordnance, asking for supplies of H.E. (high explosives). The request was emphatically reiterated on the 15th, and by the 21st a definite request for 15 per cent. of H.E. shells for the field guns was made—a proportion raised presently to 25 per cent. and by the 6th of November to 50 per cent. A week later this request was modified to 25 per cent. but raised on 31st December again to 50 per cent. The War Office refused to supply this proportion, on the plea that " the nature of the operations may again alter as they have done in the past." Thus persistent was

---

* H.E. was first used by 18-pounders on 31/10/14.

the refusal of the War Office to recognise the fact, demonstrated ten years earlier by the Russo-Japanese conflict in Manchuria, that modern warfare tended to become a war of entrenchments and siege operations. I may add that on the 22nd October, 1914, the French General Deville had informed the War Office that the French were giving up shrapnel altogether and concentrating on H.E.

But even more serious than the failure of a supply of H.E. was the general shortage of shells of any kind whatever. By 17th September, Sir John French was wiring for increased supplies of shells for his howitzers, pointing out that the reserves in stock on the lines of communication had fallen dangerously low, and that " in view of the large expenditure of this ammunition now taking place and to be expected, this is a serious matter. No effort should be spared to send out further supplies at once."

The War Office replied that they were sending out what they could—it would increase Sir John French's stock to about ten days' supply at his then rate of expenditure—and warned him that " this will run our stock very low, and we cannot supply at this rate until manufacturers reach their maximum output." The shortage of ammunition for the larger guns became the theme of almost daily telegrams of Sir John French. By 28th September he was writing to draw attention also to a pending shortage of field-gun ammunition. He said: " For 18-pounders the proposal is to dispatch 15,000 rounds a week, or less than 7 rounds per gun a day. This is by far too small an amount. During the last fortnight there has been an average daily expenditure of 14 rounds per gun, notwithstanding the fact that these guns, as a whole, have been, comparatively speaking, but lightly engaged during the action on the Aisne. I need hardly say that a shortage of ammunition for Field Artillery might be attended with the gravest results. It may be thought that the nature of the recent operations have been abnormal, but in my opinion future operations in this campaign will to a great extent be of a similar kind, and in order to maintain the Army in an efficient fighting condition I am compelled to represent that the proposed rate of ammunition supply cannot possibly suffice to meet demands." In its reply, dated 7th October, to this letter, the War Office excused itself in the following terms: " With reference to your letter of 28th September, I am commanded by the Army Council to point out that they have provided in the first instance, and have also sent out, replenishments in almost every case fully up to *the quantities of gun ammunition which were laid down before the War*." (My italics.) This letter went on to promise increased amounts, and Sir John French answering it on the 10th October, retorted that even this larger rate of supply would provide the army with only 9 rounds per gun per day for the 60-pounders, 11 rounds per day for the 4.5-inch howitzers, and if all the divisions were counted, only 6 rounds per day for the 18-pounder field artillery. Thereafter a series of urgent telegrams came from France for more shells. The tremendous attempt made by the Germans to throw the British Army into the Channel and to capture the ports had just started. The first battle of Ypres, the last fought in the open field on this front, had developed, and in the middle of that terrible struggle the Field-Marshal wired Lord Kitchener: " If the reserve on the lines of communication is not at once made up to at least the authorised scale and maintained on that scale, it is possible that the troops may soon be required to fight without the support of artillery. The great battle which has now lasted for several days still proceeds, and the gravest result will be entailed by a shortage of artillery ammunition." In reply he was told by the Secretary of State for War: " As soon as I can work out the rate you are expending ammunition I will answer the last paragraph. . . . You will of course see that economy is practised. . . ." Three days later, the Master-General of Ordnance wrote to G.H.Q. declaring: " I cannot say what our future supplies will be, as it entirely depends on the promises of the firms to whom we have given large orders being kept up to date." He added that he could not increase supplies of 4.7-inch shell without depleting the equipment of the fresh divisions now being made up. French replied that he had been compelled to reduce supplies for the howitzers to 10 rounds per gun a day, and would shortly have to bring down the 18-pounder field guns to the same ration. He begged for the ammunition which the Master-General of Ordnance was holding up as equipment of batteries not yet sent overseas—" I submit that it is of greater importance to keep the batteries which are already here adequately supplied with ammunition, than it is to retain ammunition in England for the batteries which are to come out later "—and in an urgent postscript added: —

" I *must press* this point: *The offensive is of the last importance during the next two weeks or so!* I wish to emphasise third paragraph of my letter.—J.F." (His own italics.)

Two days later, on the 31st October, French wired repeating his plea, to which the War Office acceded. Kitchener also suggested to him that Joffre ought to send more French guns with a plentiful supply of ammunition. But, as a consequence, when two days later Sir John French asked for another infantry division, he was offered a choice of Stuart Wortley's Territorial Division " without artillery, for which we have not got ammunition," or the incompletely trained VIIIth Division,* with its artillery depleted by the supplies sent out already.

Throughout November and December the shortage of ammunition

---

* " The Official History of the War: Military Operations, France and Belgium," Vol. II, page 450, notes that the 8th Division " was ' untrained ' according to home standards. . . . The Division assembled at Hursley Park, near Winchester, between the 19th September and 2nd November; it began embarking on the 4th November. There was, therefore, no opportunity for training in brigade and division."

was growing. On the 12th November G.H.Q. wired for more shells for the 4.7-inch guns, and the War Office stated in reply what they had sent in the last week, and added: "We cannot continue to supply at this rate." On the 12th December, Sir John French wired Lord Kitchener: "I am very anxious about our supply of ammunition." Kitchener replied that the output was insufficient for the guns already in the field, and that he doubted the wisdom of sending more batteries to France, as "it is obviously uneconomical to keep batteries in France that cannot be used because of the want of ammunition." On the 31st December French wrote to the War Office: "The present supply of artillery ammunition has been found to be so inadequate as to make offensive operations, even on a small scale, quite out of the question. Recent experience has shown that the ammunition available suffices for scarcely one hour's bombardment of a small portion of the enemy's line, and that even this operation leaves no ammunition to repel a counter-attack or to give the assaulting columns sufficient support. Owing to the nature of the operations in which we are, and shall continue to be, engaged, *the supply of artillery ammunition is the governing factor. . . . It is on the supply of ammunition for artillery that the future operations of the British Army will depend.*" (My italics.)

The members of the Cabinet saw none of these letters from Sir John French at the time, and knew nothing of their existence.

5. THE FIRST CABINET COMMITTEE

It was not perhaps obvious at first to everyone how vital this question of munitions was, or how urgent and grave it was to become. The eyes of the nation during those early months were set more upon the spectacular massing of our man-power, and the enrolment of the first million of the new Army. Indeed, this public attitude caused an accentuation of the difficulty, for vast numbers of highly skilled workers, whose technical ability was of the first importance for increasing the output of munitions, were swept by the torrent of public enthusiasm or driven by the undiscriminating taunts of their neighbours into the ranks of these recruits. But it was clear to some of us that the arming and equipment of our forces would be no less essential than their numbers, and far harder to attain. And when the first warning echoes of the shortage in France began to be heard, the rumours of the congestion in our munition firms at home came to our ears, we felt that special action must be taken to deal with the matter.

In September I urged the appointment of a special Committee of the Cabinet to look into the question of guns, shells and rifles. At first, Lord Kitchener resisted so strongly that the Cabinet turned down the proposal. He was held in such awe at this date that his colleagues did not dare challenge his authority. Eventually, however, early in October, I prevailed upon the Cabinet to appoint a Committee to examine the question of our munition supplies, and to advise as to means of increasing production and expediting deliveries. The Committee consisted of the following seven persons: —

The Secretary of State for War (Lord Kitchener).

The Lord Chancellor (Lord Haldane).

The Chancellor of the Exchequer (Mr. Lloyd George).

The First Lord of the Admiralty (Mr. Churchill).

The Home Secretary (Mr. M'Kenna).

The President of the Board of Trade (Mr. Runciman).

The President of the Board of Agriculture (Lord Lucas).*

This Committee met altogether six times between the 12th October, 1914, and the 1st January, 1915, and took the initiative in some of the more important questions of policy and procedure which arose. As the work done by this short-lived Committee formed the basis of later developments for the supply of munitions, I give some brief account of it. At the first meeting on the 12th October, it reviewed the question of the provision of guns for the new armies and recommended that orders should be given for the manufacture of artillery on a much larger scale than had hitherto been contemplated by the War Office. Instructions were given for the ordering of 3,000 18-pounder field guns, to be delivered by May, 1915, instead of the 892 already ordered for delivery in June. I pressed hard that the capacity of the existing armament firms should be extended, that the great engineering capacity of this country outside the armament works should be immediately mobilised for the production of munitions and that the works of large engineering firms should be taken over and converted to that purpose. The Master-General of Ordnance objected on the grounds that the manufacture of guns, rifles and shells was a very delicate operation and needed long experience and trained skill of a high order; that the few firms who possessed the necessary experience and training subcontracted in respect of all work which outside firms were capable of doing; and that by this means all the engineering capacity which could safely be trusted was fully engaged. To go beyond that process and leave the whole production of any munitions of war to inexperienced establishments would be too risky. He dwelt on the dangers arising from faulty shells. The whole of our guns might burst. Such was his case for the existing procedure. There can be no doubt that any great expansion under the pressure of necessity was bound to lead to some defective work, but the sequel proved that the risk was far greater from badly designed fuses—for which the Ordnance Department was responsible—than from the carelessness of British manufacturers. The rifle shortage was also considered. There was no prospect of supplying our recruits with rifles for many months to

* Subsequently killed in action.

come unless special efforts were made to quicken supply. A message was sent to the representative of the War Office in the U.S.A., instructing him to ascertain the maximum output which could be secured from firms capable of manufacturing field guns or rifles to a total of 1,500 18-pounder guns and half a million rifles. I may say that the reply to this inquiry showed that there appeared to be little hope of securing additional output from that source before September, 1915.

On the next day, 13th October, representatives of the Ordnance Factories, and of Messrs. Armstrong, Vickers, the Coventry Ordnance Works, and Beardmore, met our Committee. In regard to finance, I promised the representatives of the armament firms who were called in that the Government could find the capital required to extend the works of the armament firms or those of their sub-contractors, and would compensate them for any resulting loss. Thus encouraged, the contractors engaged to increase their output by every possible means, and as a result of this meeting the commitments of the works represented were raised from 878 guns to 1,608—deliveries in all cases to be completed not later than August, 1915.

It was after this second meeting that I decided to pay a visit to France to inspect methods employed there to expand and quicken production.

At successive meetings on the 20th and 21st October we took up the question of propellent and explosives, which was left to the Secretary of State for War to investigate further, and that of the supply of rifles—it being decided to increase largely the number already ordered for delivery in July, 1915. As a result, big orders were placed in the United States, and grants of money made to firms in this country for the increase of their plant. Then, in regard to the organisation of trade resources, it was decided that a Committee of the armament firms should be formed to distribute the orders to individual firms.

This summary gives some of the main points dealt with during the first four meetings of the Committee in October; but it was not long before I discovered that grants of money, though essential, were not all that was necessary to meet the situation.

The difficulty at this time of increasing the orders for munitions, or of accelerating delivery of existing orders under the War Office procedure, was becoming every week more apparent, for the existing armament workshops were already working to their full capacity, and the War Office seemed unable to organise any effective increase in their capacity or their number. This country was richer than any other in a wide variety of manufacturing plant, a vast amount of which we subsequently found ways and means of adapting to the production of munitions. Labour difficulties were systematically pleaded by the munition firms as an excuse for failure to carry out

D*

their contracts; yet there was still in the country an ampler supply of labour than we enjoyed at any subsequent period of the struggle. The numbers of skilled workmen were dwindling day by day owing to indiscriminate recruiting. The head officials at the War Office, who were responsible for the whole field of munition design and production, made no effort to retain pivotal men in our engineering works, and they clung most tenaciously to their methods of assigning contracts. They refused stubbornly to adopt the only effectual measures for utilising and organising the manufacturing and labour resources of this country in order to secure an adequate output.

In order to obtain a further insight into the possibilities of increasing our munition supply, I decided after the second meeting of the Cabinet Committee to visit France to see what was being done there in the way of expanding production.

On this visit I was accompanied by Lord Reading, then Lord Chief Justice, and by Sir John Simon, then Attorney-General.

Our party—Lord Reading, Sir John Simon and myself—left Newhaven at midnight on October 16th and crossed on a destroyer to Dieppe. It was my first experience of the physical proximity of war. As soon as we left Newhaven the lights were put out, as a German submarine had been seen off Cherbourg that morning. We had to steam out of the ordinary route and hang about a good deal, so that the crossing took twice as long as the ordinary packet boat would have taken.

At Dieppe we were met on behalf of the French Government and were taken to visit some of the battlefields north of Paris. One of the cars which met us was driven by the dramatist Henri Bernstein, who had recently taken a prominent part in denouncing M. Caillaux during his wife's trial. We were taken to Senlis and Beauvais among other places. The lower part of Senlis was a complete ruin after its bombardment by the Germans. That was our first view of the ruin caused by war. At Creil the bridge over the river had been blown up by the French to cover their retreat from the Germans, and we passed over a pontoon bridge. Motoring through a country which seemed in some districts to have been almost abandoned by its inhabitants, for we were on the track of the German march, we reached Paris in the evening. Paris itself looked like a deserted city. All the gaiety, bustle and vivacity had gone. The Government was still at Bordeaux, whither it had fled during the panic of August. The Elysée, the Chamber of Deputies, the Luxembourg and all the Government offices were locked up and left in charge of a few heroic caretakers. The President, the Ministers, the Deputies—almost all except Clemenceau and Briand—had gone. It will be recalled that M. Clemenceau, when asked whether he thought the Government ought to leave Paris as the Germans were almost at the gates, replied: " Yes, Paris is too far from the front! " The young men of Paris were away at the front: older men were outside on guard armed with obsolete rifles with long bayonets. A considerable number of the remaining population, especially in the richer quarters, had sought safety further south when the Germans were approaching with great strides towards the *banlieue*. The hotels were closed, and shops which did not dispense the necessaries of life had neither purchasers nor window-gazers. The sparse population of the streets looked grave and preoccupied. Before the war the dress of the ordinary Parisian women always seemed to me to be sombre, just as the apparel of the average British women gave one the impression of being drab; but on this occasion garments, both male and female, were blacker than ever, for the French army during the terrible battles of September had suffered casualties more appalling than had ever been inflicted on any armies within so short a space of time. It was, indeed, a grim city.

On Sunday morning, at ten o'clock, we achieved the object of our journey, which was to ascertain how far the French Government had organised private industry for the purpose of producing munitions of war, and how far, in view of French experience, similar organisation could be undertaken in the United Kingdom. General St. Clair Deville, the inventor of the famous 75-millimetre gun, had been authorised by the French Government to give us all the information he procured, and he and Captain Cambefort placed their knowledge and experience at our disposal. General Deville struck us as a splendid type of the quiet, thoughtful, and efficient Frenchman. Cambefort spoke English excellently (he was a big merchant and manufacturer at Lyons in times of peace), and knew England well. They explained to us what arrangements the French were making to increase their supplies of guns, shells, etc., and what provision they were making for future development. They explained how the Government, as soon as war broke out, called engineers and manufacturers together in order to make the best available use of all factories and workshops capable of assisting in Government work. The great difficulty was shortage of skilled workmen, because at the mobilisation no thought had been given to this necessity, and all of military service age, not then actually engaged in munition work, had gone to the front. The Government was now doing its utmost to get them back, though this was very difficult, as they were scattered over different regiments and in different parts of the battle front. Still, a number of these skilled men had now been recovered. Munitions were being manufactured by private firms, and private production would rapidly increase.

The return of essential and pivotal skilled men who had been drafted either into the Territorials or Kitchener Armies was not seriously taken in hand in Britain until after the formation of the Ministry of Munitions in May, 1915. By that time many of these workers had already fallen in futile battles, owing largely to lack of guns and ammunition they could have helped to provide. Production suffered seriously from this mistake.

General Deville said that England had such an immense number of splendidly equipped engineering works, with every variety of machines, plant and tools, that our situation was, for the purposes of increasing supplies, better than that of France. He offered to be at the disposition of our Government for advising us on the method of munition production they had evolved. We reported this offer to the War Office, but I never heard that it came to anything. If he repeated to the Ordnance Authorities at home the advice he gave to me it certainly did not fructify.

While in Paris I received a visit from Lord Robert Cecil, who had been on a search for his sister's son, reported missing. He learned as a result of his inquiries that the boy had been badly wounded, and taken with others in the same condition to a French country house. Here their wounds were being attended to when the Germans took possession of the mansion. The men's wounds were only partially dressed, the hæmorrhage in many cases being only temporarily stopped. The doctor who was attending them warned the German officer that to move these men meant their death, but in spite of this the officer insisted on their being bundled into carts and taken away as prisoners. As a result of this they all died. Had they been left behind and recovered, they might have returned to the front and helped to kill German soldiers. Such are the ruthless alternatives of war.

Lord Robert was also arranging for a burial service for the dead British soldiers, who were to be exhumed where that was possible, and buried again with religious rites—a rather gloomy and gruesome task. He was anxious that the British Government should arrange a mission for this purpose. I promised to see to it.

We were privileged to have an interview with General Gallieni, who was Military Governor of Paris. He was certainly a very remarkable person. He was evidently a very ill man; he looked sallow, shrunken, and haunted. Death seemed to be chasing the particles of life out of his veins. Afterwards we learnt that he was suffering from a serious internal disease. He died from this disease in 1916. Still, he was fearless, resolute and confident. He had just made a notable contribution to the victory of the Marne. We discussed with him very fully the whole military position.

Early on Monday morning we left Paris and motored to Amiens, the General Headquarters of the Northern Army of France. On the way we passed through Montdidier. German aeroplanes had just bombed the town and the fragments of their bombs were hardly cold when we arrived. Here I heard, for the first time in my life, the crack of shells fired with murderous intent against human beings, and my first experience of it gave me a shudder. At Amiens we came to the Headquarters of General Castelnau, one of the ablest military leaders in the War. He had already won a great reputation in the fierce battles of the Grand Couronne in front of Nancy, where under his leadership the French repulsed the German efforts to break through on that critical front. His personality created a deep impression on our minds. He was a short man with a high forehead and intelligent dark eyes—quiet and grave in demeanour. I drove with him up to the French lines beyond Doullens. On the road the General explained how the War was progressing and how differently things had turned out from what military staffs on both sides had anticipated and planned. It was clear that neither German nor French generals had foreseen that the War would develop into a siege operation on a colossal scale.

"I imagined," he said, "that we should have had great pitched battles, with a fortnight or so in between for rest and preparation. But here am I—I have marched with my men from Lorraine to Normandy, and they have been fighting incessantly for 79 days and nights—and are still fighting."

He had a habit of giving answers to my questions which were curiously irrelevant, but always striking. On the way up to the front we met an ambulance, and I asked him whether that was carrying the wounded to the hospital behind the lines. His answer was: "The man who is responsible for this war has the soul of a devil!" He discussed the losses, which had been enormous on both sides. The Prussian Guards, he said, had been wiped out, and the French had lost too many brave men. He deplored their loss, and said: "I look at the lists of these dead heroes, and learn how they died, and I weep, and say: 'There is not one of these men who is not a greater man than I'."

Two of his own sons had been on these lists of the killed. He was in the habit of reading out to his staff every morning the names of fallen officers. One morning the list contained the name of his own son. When the name was reached his only sign of emotion was a gulp, a catch in the throat, before the name "Charles Castelnau" passed his lips, and he then proceeded calmly to the end of the list. In commenting on the military position he grew grave when talking of the clutch in which the two armies were locked, and the apparent impossibility of breaking it. I asked how many men were under his command, and he said there were nine army corps. "Well," I remarked, "that is a greater army than Napoleon ever commanded in any single battle."

His answer was a kind of soliloquy. "Ah, Napoleon, Napoleon! If he were here now, he'd have thought of the 'something else'." Asked what he thought of the chances of the War, and whether the French would succeed in driving the enemy out of France, Castelnau's answer was: "*Il le faut!*"

The answers which both General Castelnau and subsequently Generals Foch and Balfourier gave to my questions on the military situation left on me the impression that even the ablest of the French military leaders were, for the time being, completely baffled by the military dilemma presented to them by the unexpected change in the tactics of the German Army. A war of movement had been anticipated and provided for in the equipment and organisation of the Army. A great siege operation where the *soixante-quinze* and the Chasseurs played a subordinate part had clearly not been thought of. They had attempted here and there to penetrate this earthen fortress and had everywhere failed with heavy losses. They were now looking for the "something else." Unfortunately for the Allies they looked for possibilities straight in front of them only and failed to look around and far beyond.

General Castelnau seemed very popular with his men, visiting them in the trenches and cheering them, calling them "*mes infants*" and enquiring whether they had enough to eat. "*Trop!*" said one soldier, who was marching to take his place in the trenches with a yard of the delicious French bread under his arm.

I was told that the men were entirely different in spirit from what they were at the beginning of the War. Then they were terrified of the big shells of the enemy and recoiled in horror from the hideous explosives. It needed a very firm hand to put a stop to the effect of this terror. We heard that General Maud'huy, who had by that time joined our party, and who had the record of being one of the most daring of French Generals, had dealt with his men in a very drastic way. A section of them had broken under the fire of the German artillery. The next day, therefore, the General marched them out again until they were under shell fire, when he ordered them to halt and face about. He then began to put them through their ordinary drills, on the understanding that any man who attempted to run away would be shot immediately. When he thought that they were used to shell fire, he marched them back again. I asked Maud'huy if this story I had heard about him were true. He smiled, and said "Ah, but I gave them their reward afterwards!" "And what was that?" I asked. "*Monsieur*," was the answer, "when we were attacking I permitted them the next time to advance two hundred metres in front of the rest." "Was there any further trouble with their *morale*?" "*Jamais!*" was the reply. The complaint about *morale* arose mainly concerning soldiers drawn from certain French departments remote from the German frontiers and with no memories of any Teutonic invasion in the past; peasants drawn from these areas were inclined to treat the fight as something which more particularly affected the northerners. The spirit of the men from these districts had now been completely established. They all knew that it was a struggle to the death for France to which their devotion was beyond challenge or fear. I observed the countenance of men who had passed through the fiery furnace. Though they were resigned and calm, yet the horror of it all was stamped on some of their faces—a horror that habitude and resignation had not yet been able to smooth out.

We proceeded to General Balfourier's headquarters, and there for the first time saw something of the bombardment of villages by the German artillery. It was continuous but leisurely. There was no serious fighting going on, and I have no doubt that the report on both sides would be: "All quiet on this front!"

I did my best during this visit to inform myself by question directed to General Castelnau and General Balfourier, and everyone I met, as to the real character of the problem with which the Allies were confronted owing to the digging in of the German Army.

This was the first occasion on which I met General Foch. He was a totally different type from General Castelnau. The part he had taken in the recent victory on the Marne added to my eagerness to meet him. He corresponded more with the British idea of what a typical Frenchman is like—vivacious, demonstrative, emphatic and gesticulatory. He talked just as much with his hands and arms as he did with his tongue. But whether he expressed himself with hand or voice he always talked well and to the point. His high broad forehead and his penetrating eye proved him a man of exceptional gifts. I asked him if he had any message for the British Cabinet and he said, "Tell them there will be no more retreats." I asked him whether I could also tell them there would be any more advances. He hesitated and was evidently perplexed by the question. After a perceptible halt he replied: "That depends on the men and material you will be able to throw into the battle line." He said that the Belgians had been obliged to retreat before the German advance, but his advice to them had been, "If you want to keep your country, dig yourselves into it, and hang on to it!"

At the Headquarters of Balfourier's Division we saw a German prisoner who had just been brought in—a Prussian Guard. He was wounded in the arm, and evidently in pain. The Lord Chief Justice spoke to him, and ascertained that he came from Berlin. The prisoner behaved with great dignity, being neither surly nor communicative, but evidently feeling his position keenly. He had every appearance of an educated man. "Well," said the French General, "you need not worry. You will be taken to the hospital, and looked after just as well as our own men." "Your men are well treated by us, too," replied the German. The General shrugged his shoulders. "At any rate," he said, "for you it is now only a question of time. When the war is over you will be free to return to your home." "Ah!" said the prisoner, with weary longing, "home is the only thing that matters in life!"

I inquired of a young French officer who was helping to guide us round the front whether the stories of German cruelty to women were true. "No," he answered. "They leave them alone as a rule." And he added with a cynical shrug, "They do not appreciate women."

At this stage of the War there was not much outward visible sign of its devastation. The hundreds of long-range guns which later on smashed towns and villages and churned up fields had not yet begun their ruinous activities. The country as a whole showed no signs of pillage or destruction. The peasants were in the fields, often working stolidly within range of the German shells. I heard of one old woman who was working in a potato field when a shell burst dangerously near. She stopped for a moment, looked at it and then went on with her work. Everywhere there was a sense of everyone having calmly settled down to an established condition of things which threatened to last for some time. The inhabitants of villages which were being bombarded were leaving the villages during the day and returning at night to sleep. It was early in the morning when we met an old man and woman who had left their home in a bombarded village just for the day. The old woman was carrying under her arm a duck, probably destined for their midday meal. They were engaged in deep conversation, but to all appearances were taking the situation very philosophically.

When we reached the British Headquarters at St. Omer, Sir John French had left for the Menin road where "some fighting" was reported to be going on. It was the beginning of the terrible battle of Ypres.

CHAPTER VI

THE FIGHT FOR MUNITIONS—*continued*

I. A POLICY OF SHORT VIEWS

In spite of the recommendation of the Cabinet Committee that it was advisable to mobilise the engineering resources of this country more fully for the production of munitions, the War Office adhered to its dependence on the established armament firms. Had the War been " over by Christmas," then the official policy might have carried us through. Although Lord Kitchener, on 4th December, 1914, in one of the very few interviews he granted to the Press, spoke of the possibility that the War would last three years, the authorities at the War Office responsible for the supply of munitions were slow to envisage the character and the probable duration of the struggle. This came to light in the course of negotiations for the purchase of rifles from America.

The War Office decided that no more rifles than those already on order should be arranged for unless delivery was promised by 1st May, 1915. In this connection I transcribe a letter I wrote to the Master-General of Ordnance on 23rd November, 1914, relative to the War Office action: —

" Dear General von Donop,—Lord Reading has shown me your letters to him on the subject of further American orders for rifles. I understand that you are of opinion that unless delivery by the 1st of May is promised the Army will not stand in need of additional rifles beyond those which have already been promised to you after that date. I must say this rather surprises me in the face of the figures supplied to the Committee of which I was a member. Unless you have arranged for an enormous addition to the supplies which you then foresaw, we shall certainly be very seriously short even in the month of September. We were then working on the assumption that the Kitchener Armies were limited to the figures which Parliament had then sanctioned. Since then Parliament has ordered the enlistment of another million men. Do the promises received by you from various sources for the delivery of rifles provide for the equipment of this additional million?

I should have thought that as long as you had a responsible firm in America who were prepared to undertake the delivery to you of additional rifles—even although they were only received in substantial numbers late next year—it would have been worth while accepting their services.

Kindly let me know, as I promised to inform Mr. Grenfell definitely what the decision of the War Office is on the point.— Yours sincerely,

D. Ll. GEORGE.

P.S.   Further supplies of rifles will be required for the Central Association of Volunteer Corps, which has been quite recently sanctioned by the War Office, in which there are already some 200,000 men and which, according to War Office anticipation, will amount eventually to a million."

I have no record of any reply to this letter, but the Master-General of Ordnance probably spoke to me on the matter when he saw me.

This failure to realise the scale of warfare to which we were committed, and the corresponding scale of armament and munition output that would be required, was characteristic of the War Office during those early months.   When it was discovered in December that the deliveries of gun ammunition promised by the main con-tractors were not coming forward, it was not inferred that the scheme of production was at fault.   The contractors' estimates had been too sanguine; the sub-contractors had broken down over unforeseen difficulties.   These failures were, indeed, taken by the War Office to be proof of the fundamental soundness of their contention that the technical difficulties of armament work were likely to defeat the inexpert manufacturer, and could only be tackled by the established firms.

Accordingly the War Office enlisted the aid of the Board of Trade for a scheme to transfer skilled workers from other engineering firms in the country to the established munition works.   Though in regard to its intended object this scheme was a fiasco, it had the effect, not foreseen by its originators, of helping to break down the War Office policy of dealing exclusively with the traditional sources of supply. For when these independent firms were approached as to transfer of their men, many of them protested that they were already doing a certain amount of Government work as sub-contractors, or were supplying materials to firms engaged in sub-contracts; and even those which as yet were doing nothing of this kind raised the strongest objection to handing over their best skilled men to private armament firms, and offered instead to undertake munition production themselves.

The canvass of employers was carried out during the first fortnight of January, 1915, and Sir H. Llewellyn Smith, of the Board of Trade, reviewing its meagre results in a note dated 23rd January, said:—

" I have therefore been led to the conclusion that, if a large amount of labour in addition to what can be obtained from among the unemployed British and Belgian workpeople is required for armament purposes, it is necessary in the first place to ascertain precisely how much additional work can be devolved on other engineering firms by the armament firms, or given to them direct, and to distribute this work judiciously so as to take advantage to the fullest extent of the plant and labour available. . . ."

One useful outcome of the action of the Board of Trade was that the Master-General of Ordnance was persuaded to sanction a proposal that firms should be informed through the Labour Exchanges that they might make requests for contracts for Army supplies, subject to having been inspected and found to be capable of undertaking the task in question. In the course of the first eighteen months of the War about 11,000 firms were thus inspected through the Labour Exchanges. This led to a scheme by the Board of Trade for a survey of engineering firms, a project which, however, broke down when the Engineering Employers' Federation, which was to have taken an active part in carrying through the survey, took objection to the absence of any specific information as to the types of contract which the War Office might be prepared to offer. The Home Office also arranged to carry out a census of machinery, which was conducted in March by the factory inspectors, and its results communicated to the War Office. No substantial progress, however, was made with the utilisation of the full engineering resources of the nation.

2. THE SHELL SHORTAGE GROWS

A memorandum issued by Lord Kitchener to the G.H.Q. of the Expeditionary Force on 9th January, 1915, states the ammunition position at that date with a frankness which must have had a discouraging effect upon the Commander-in-Chief and his army in France:—

" It is impossible at the present time to maintain a sufficient supply of gun ammunition on the scale which you consider necessary for offensive operations. Every effort is being made in all parts of the world to obtain an unlimited supply of ammunition, but, as you are well aware, the result is still far from being sufficient to maintain the large number of guns which you now have under your command adequately supplied with ammunition for offensive operations. You have pointed out that offensive operations under the new conditions created by this war require a vast expenditure of artillery ammunition, which may for even ten or twenty days necessitate the supply of 50 or 100 rounds per gun per day being available, and unless a reserve can be accumulated to meet an expenditure of this sort it is unwise in embarking on extensive offensive operations against the enemy's trenches. It is, of course, almost impossible to calculate with any accuracy how long offensive operations once undertaken may last before the object is attained, but it is evident that the breaking-off of such operations before accomplishment owing to the want of artillery ammunition, and not on account of a successful termination or a convenient pause in the operations being reached might lead to a serious reverse being sustained by our forces."

Neither this memorandum nor the purport of it was communicated to the Cabinet.* It was not merely a question at that time of supplying a sufficiency of shells for an offensive, but enough to reply to the German bombardment of our trenches. There were no offensive operations undertaken until the following March and then only on a limited scale. The evidence pouring in from the front proved that the shell supply was pitifully unequal to making even a show of defence by artillery. Throughout January and February the burden of telegrams from G.H.Q. to the Master-General of Ordnance is continually: "Stock of shell very low;" "Amount received much below proportion;" "Request that further supplies may be expedited as much as possible." On 21st January, General von Donop wrote to the Chief of the General Staff in France: "It seems quite hopeless for me to give you any dates for delivery of guns or ammunition."

Such information as I was able to obtain, despite the reticence of the military authorities, about the situation increased my already acute uneasiness. I therefore circulated a memorandum to the Cabinet, four days later, on 22nd February, 1915, submitting some Considerations on the Conduct of the War, from which I quote the following:—

" The first and the greatest difficulty is equipment. The number of men we could put in the field is seriously limited by the output of guns and rifles. In this respect we have a great advantage. We are at a disadvantage as compared with the Germans in one material respect, but we are at a great advantage in other respects. As to the disadvantage, the Germans and Austrians between them had, even at the commencement of the War, much larger supplies of war material and more extensive factories for the turning out of supplies than the Allied countries possessed, and they have undoubtedly since made much better use of their manufacturing resources for the purpose of increasing that output. Germany is the best organised country in the world, and her organisation has told.

Those are the disadvantages. What about the advantages? The

---

* The first week of the battle of the Somme we had 3½ times as many guns in France as on 1st January, 1915, and the expenditure of shells during that week by the artillery taking part in the battle was 237 per gun per day.

manufacturing resources at the disposal of the Allies are enormously greater than those which Germany and Austria can command. In this computation Russia barely counts, but the manufacturing resources of France and Great Britain between them are at least equal to those of Germany and Austria, and the seas being free to them they can more easily obtain material. But apart from that they have practically the whole of America, which is the greatest manufacturing country in the world, and Japan to draw upon.

I believe that France has strained her resources to the utmost, and she can hardly do much more. She has now abolished the sale of absinthe, and that will have an appreciable effect upon the productivity of her workmen. She is, therefore, doing all she can to contribute. I do not believe Great Britain has ever yet done anything like what she could do in the matter of increasing her war equipment. Great things have been accomplished in the last few months, but I sincerely believe that we could double our effective energies if we organised our factories thoroughly. All the engineering works of the country ought to be turned on to the production of war material. The population ought to be prepared to suffer all sorts of deprivations and even hardships whilst this process is going on. As to America, I feel confident from what I have heard that we have tapped only a small percentage of this great available reserve of supply.

Special attention should be given to the laying down of machinery which is essential to the turning out of rifles and cannon. I hear it takes months to complete these machines, but even if they are only ready in September we shall need them all.* My first suggestion, therefore, would be that full powers should be taken, if we do not already possess them, as I think we do, to mobilise the whole of our manufacturing strength for the purpose of turning out, at the earliest possible moment, war material. I have always thought that our complete command over the railways equips us with the necessary powers without resorting to legislation. But legislation which would enable us to commandeer all the works in the United Kingdom, and, if necessary, to deal with labour difficulties and shortcomings, would undoubtedly strengthen our hands. We might even take full powers to close public-houses altogether in areas where armaments were being manufactured. As to our railway powers, I made the suggestion some time ago to the War Office that they should be used. I am not sure of the extent to which that has been done."

* Without the necessary machines and gauges manufacture could not start. These additional machines were not ordered by the War Office and by the armament firms in any appreciable quantities for another six months. It was done then after the big gun programme which had followed the Boulogne Gun Conference. It was one of the first steps taken by the Ministry of Munitions.

At this time the Ordnance Department had manœuvred the political meddlers with munitions out of action. The Cabinet Committee on Munitions had ceased to exist. Its last meeting was held on 1st January, 1915. The Board of Trade was supposed by the rest of the Cabinet to be functioning entirely in the direction of organising our engineering skill. As a matter of fact it was then conforming to the War Office policy and trying vainly to carry out its scheme for transferring skilled workers from factories and workshops not engaged in war work to the traditional armament firms. The War Office seemed to be carefully shutting its eyes to the magnitude of the task confronting it, and our army in the field was watching with dismay the approach of the summer campaign, conscious that its supplies were quite inadequate, and that the outlook for any increase was of the blackest.

At a Conference held at 10, Downing Street on Friday, 5th March, 1915, at which the Prime Minister, Lord Kitchener, myself, General von Donop, Mr. M'Kenna, Lord Crewe, Sir George Gibb and Sir George Askwith were present—a conference of which some account appears in a letter to Mr. Balfour, which I reproduce a little farther on—I urged again that there should be a fuller utilisation of existing engineering firms, and in particular I drew attention to the need for expediting the supply of rifles, which was still so inadequate that many of our troops in training had no rifles to drill with. Both Lord Kitchener and General von Donop seemed quite satisfied with the prospects about rifles, of which they hoped we should have about two million by the beginning of 1916. When I pointed out that the House of Commons had already voted 3,000,000 men, Kitchener was taken aback, and declared that they had not yet begun to calculate the military equipment—guns, ammunition, etc.—for such a force.

The conference decided that an investigation should be set on foot to find out what machinery was lying idle which could produce war material, and that Lord Kitchener should be asked to calculate what munitions would be required for an army of 3,000,000.

3. CORRESPONDENCE WITH MR. BALFOUR

With the disappearance in January of the Cabinet Committee on Munitions there had ceased to be any effective instrument either for prodding along the War Office officials in regard to this vital issue, or for carrying out the tasks they were leaving undone.

Some time before the conference on March 5th, I had established contact with Mr. Balfour, who was a member of the War Council and of the Committee of Imperial Defence. Mr. Asquith had retained him on these bodies in order to secure his experience and advice in the national interest. From time to time I had poured into his ears my misgivings as to the whole position, and I had especially impressed upon him the delays in providing our troops with adequate support owing to the refusal of the War Office to make full use of our manufacturing resources. I had an implicit belief in his patriotism and a great admiration for his high intellectual gifts. Moreover, he had some war experience. He knew his Generals well. He had not forgotten the incompetent complacencies of the Boer War. He had suffered from them at that time. Their blunders had helped to discredit his administration. On returning from the Conference I received the following letter from him: —

> "4, Carlton Gardens,
> Pall Mall, S.W.1.
> March 5th, 1915.

My dear Chancellor of the Exchequer,

I know you won't take it amiss my dictating this letter, for my own handwriting is rather a trial to my correspondents. I most earnestly trust that you are not letting slide the matter about which we talked the day before yesterday. Putting labour troubles altogether on one side, the position seems to me to be most unsatisfactory, and unless you will take in hand the organisation of the engineering resources of the country in the interests of military equipment, I do not see how any improvement is to be expected. I am afraid it really *is* the fact that the Contracts Department of the War Office deliberately rejected the opportunity of getting the rifle-making plant which was offered to them some time ago. They supposed, poor things, that they had already had enough! !

I find it very difficult to understand how we have enough even for our own needs, putting aside the needs of our Allies. Apart from what we can purchase abroad, I gather that our output at the present moment is quite insufficient for our own needs. We make about 45,000 *new* rifles a month, and we enlist 60,000 a month; and large numbers of our existing levies are unarmed.

Lord K. seems, however, more preoccupied about the shell question than about the rifle question.

Everybody seems to admit that there would be no difficulty in making the *metallic* framework of the shell to any extent we may desire. It is the *fuses* which present all the difficulty. Now will anybody tell me that with proper organisation it is materially impossible greatly to increase the output of fuses? It may be so, but I do not feel at all inclined to accept it on the authority of the Ordnance people at the War Office. They are admirable people, and are doing splendid work, but their training cannot have been of the kind which would enable them successfully to exploit the manufacturing resources of the country.

In this connection I cannot help feeling surprised at the attitude which the Russian Foreign Office are now taking up. They are not only indifferent to the augmentation of the Allied Forces by the adhesion of fresh States to the Entente; they appear positively

to dislike it. This would be perfectly intelligible if they themselves possessed an overwhelming strength in well-equipped armies.
But if they are as ill-provided as in our moments of pessimism we
suppose, their confidence is truly amazing.

Personally, I should rather like to see the Greeks sent off to
occupy Smyrna and the adjacent country. This might bring in
the Italians, and it would be an additional reason for not employing the Greeks in Gallipoli. I do not quite understand why the
Admiralty ever expressed a strong desire for their assistance; and
their plan of landing a large force on the Peninsula and fighting
the Turks inch by inch seems to me altogether absurd. With the
only road over which supplies can reach the Turks partly destroyed
and effectively enfiladed by ships of war, we can well afford (it
seems to me) to leave the garrison at Gallipoli to stew in its own
juice—provided always the ships of war are able unassisted
successively to reduce the forts, which the Admiralty assures us is
the case.*

I did not mean, however, to trouble you with all this; my object
in writing was merely to beg you to do what is possible to bring
in outside manufacturers to the assistance of the War Office.

Yours sincerely,

ARTHUR JAMES BALFOUR."

Before I received the letter I had written Mr. Balfour as follows:—

"March 6th, 1915.

Dear Mr. Balfour,

Yesterday we had an informal meeting to discuss the labour
difficulties on the Clyde and on the Tyne. The Prime Minister
and Lord Kitchener were there; M'Kenna, Sir George Gibb and
Sir George Askwith were also present, but the Admiralty were not
represented. After disposing of the issue raised by the Clyde
strike we proceeded to discuss the important question of munitions
of war.

Von Donop assured us as far as rifles were concerned that the
position was satisfactory. He is confident that he will be able to
supply the men now in course of training with rifles of sorts by
the end of September. This equipment will include resighted
rifles; it also includes 130,000 to 140,000 rifles which von Donop
said were not worth resighting but were good enough to kill
Germans with in this country.

If recruiting goes on at the rate at which it is proceeding now
we shall be able to equip the whole of our new forces with rifles
by about the beginning of February next year. All this is accepting von Donop's optimistic estimate of the output. Now they are

---

* I did not accept Mr. Balfour's views as to the possibility of forcing the Straits
for navigation without occupying Gallipoli. Had we deputed this task to the Greek
Army early on in the war, all our subsequent difficulties would have been averted.

being turned out at the rate of 30,000 or 40,000 a month, and von Donop is entitled to say that they are well ahead of contract time. Gradually he hopes to expedite the rate of output until in September it becomes 100,000 a month, and in December 155,000 a month. HE CANNOT QUICKEN THE PACE NOW BECAUSE IT TAKES NINE MONTHS TO CONSTRUCT THE NECESSARY PLANT AND MACHINERY FOR THE PURPOSE OF TURNING OUT A RIFLE. Had this been done in August of last year we should have had our rifles ready for the new armies by June instead of September—the difference being a vital one, for the present figures mean that we cannot send all our new forces into the field until the summer is past. They are much better than I hoped, but there is no provision made in them for supplying a single rifle to our Allies, and that is the most serious feature in the outlook. The Russians, as you know, are deplorably short of rifles; they are better off for shells.*

Once more we decided yesterday to take the step in industrial organisation which we resolved upon in October and which until recently we were all under the impression had actually been taken. The War Office admit that they were deplorably short of shells, of rifle ammunition and of fuses; they also admit that they can do nothing this year in this country to supply the deficiencies of our Allies. That is almost a disastrous admission as far as the prospects of the War for the next twelve months are concerned. Nothing can remedy this state of things except the placing at the head of this new Executive of an energetic, fearless man who will not be cajoled and bamboozled by von Donop nor bullied by anyone else.

I sincerely wish you had been present. These views have to be pressed on the War Office, and as the mere fact that it should be necessary to do so at the end of eight months' war is in itself a reflection upon War Office organisation, it is quite an unpleasant function to undertake, and I am sorry to say I had very little support. It is essential that your influence and position should be behind this pressure. There will be an adjourned meeting for Kitchener to produce further figures. I hope it will be held early in the week and that it will be possible for you to attend. THE FATE OF THE WAR DEPENDS UPON STRONG ACTION BEING TAKEN IMMEDIATELY TO ORGANISE OUR ENGINEERING RESERVES FOR THE PURPOSE OF INCREASING THE OUTPUT NOT MERELY FOR OURSELVES BUT FOR OUR ALLIES. During yesterday's discussion it was assumed that we could do nothing in this country to aid Russia, and that it was quite as much as we could do between now and the end of the year to equip our new forces.

Yours sincerely,

D. LL. G."

* The War Office had withheld from the Cabinet all information as to the serious shell shortage on the Eastern Front.

4. D.O.R.A. AND MUNITIONS

Four days after the conference above described I laid before the House of Commons, on 9th March, 1915, a Bill to amend and extend the provisions of the Defence of the Realm Act.

This was the third edition of D.O.R.A., and was designed to give very greatly increased powers to the Authorities to secure munition production.

The first " Defence of the Realm Act " had been carried on 8th August, 1914, and gave general powers to His Majesty's Government to make regulations for the conduct of affairs under war conditions; the second, passed on 28th August, 1914, extended these powers and included powers of control over armament factories and their workers.

This third D.O.R.A. extended the power of control so as to enable the Government to take over and use any factory or workshop whatever, to control its processes and output, to remove its plant elsewhere if necessary, to commandeer empty premises for the housing of workmen engaged on war work, and to annul any contracts which stood in the way of firms carrying out the production of war material.

The possession of the powers conferred on the Government by this new measure undoubtedly strengthened its hands in subsequent negotiations with firms and workers. Had those powers been resolutely and intelligently applied, without loss of time, they might have gone far to solve some if the most serious difficulties with which we were at the time confronted. An attempt was indeed made by the Board of Trade to apply the power of taking over armament works as a means of checking the excessive profits these were making —profits which had led to grave discontent among the workers, who felt with some reason that the appeals made to them to put forth their utmost efforts were in fact appeals to increase the wealth of war profiteers. But the negotiations over this proposal broke down, and later on this matter was dealt with by me by means of provisions with regard to Excess Profits incorporated in the Munitions Act.

In the course of the discussions on the Bill, Mr. Bonar Law made some very helpful observations which are relevant to the story. He began by saying: —

" . . . I wish to say at once that the powers which are now demanded are probably the most drastic that have ever been put to any House of Commons. They enable the Government to go to any factory and tell them what they are to make and what they are not to make, or to go to any factory and tell them that their machinery is not being employed to the best advantage, and that we are going to take it away and use it for another purpose."

The Chancellor of the Exchequer: " For war material."

Mr. Bonar Law proceeded to say that the mere fact that the

Government were asking for such drastic powers and rushing the Bill through gave him ground for anxiety, and he continued: —

". . . I have said, speaking in this House last Monday, that I had some doubt whether in one respect the Government were doing everything they could to end this war. I expressed that doubt. I had no knowledge, and I have none now; but I did express the doubt whether we had shortness of ammunition or of other munitions of war, and I said I believed that if that was so after seven months of war, in a country like this, which is the greatest manufacturing country in the world, and where there is immense power of adapting one form of manufacture to another— that if there is that shortage, I do not think the industrial resources of the country have been used to the greatest advantage. I cannot understand why, if this Bill is necessary to-day, the necessity of it could not have been foreseen in August or September, and why it should not have been introduced then."

This quotation shows that the uneasiness as to the failure of the War Office to make the best use of our manufacturing capacity was spreading. It was in the course of this discussion that I said that "the Government were on the look-out for a good, strong business man with some ' push and go ' in him who would be able to put the thing through." The phrase caught on and the public anxiously awaited the advent of the "man of push and go." There were several experiments made by Lord Kitchener in the way of satisfying the demand.

The Bill was passed without any division or challenge. The Ordnance Department could not complain that they were not equipped with the fullest powers to make the best use of the manufacturing capacity of this country. There were no symptoms, however, of any eagerness on their part to exploit these new powers by setting works outside the Armament ring to the manufacture of war material. I therefore urged the Prime Minister to summon another Council meeting to discuss the position once more. At this meeting it was decided to appoint a special Committee to deal with the questions I raised. On 22nd March the Committee met and drew up the outlines of a plan, as the result of which the Prime Minister wrote me the following letter: —

" 10, Downing Street,
Whitehall, S.W.

22nd March, 1915.

My dear Chancellor of the Exchequer,
In reference to the discussions of this afternoon, and the conclusions to which we came, I wish to submit to you one or two supplementary observations.

(1) I think, on reflection, that the scheme as a whole is on right lines.

(2) It is essential to its working that Kitchener should be brought in.

(3) As regards the composition of the proposed Committee, I am disposed to think that (on the political side) in addition to yourself and A.J.B. you should have a working financier, such as Montagu.

(4) That given your two (more or less capable) business men, say Grant and Arthur Pease (as to both of whom I hope you will make further enquiries), you ought to have—in what Balfour calls a session—*two* representatives of the Admiralty and War Office. The Admiralty men might be Black and perhaps Hopwood. The War Office, von Donop and Sir Charles Harris (the latter a man of really high quality). You might tell me what you think of these suggestions at or after the Cabinet.

Yours always,
(Signed) H. H. A."

But on the 25th March, Lord Kitchener wrote to him, requiring that the Committee should be subject to a variety of strict limitations; it must not interfere in any way with any of the regular armament firms, nor must it place any contracts with any firms who were already doing any contracting or sub-contracting for the War Office; nor make any use of labour from any firms which might in future be registered at the War Office as possible sources of supply of war material. It was, in short, to be a quite powerless body, which would act as an adviser to the War Office—all pertinent and serviceable advice being rejected in advance, as a condition precedent to the acceptance of the Committee.

Mr. Balfour, to whom this letter was shown, wrote me:—

". . . I cannot help suspecting that K. has only an imperfect grasp of the problem with which he has been faced for seven months.

I do not believe you will get ' forrader ' by correspondence. The only thing is to talk it over with K. directly, although I know how difficult it is to make this operation a success. . . ."

But no discussion was successful in inducing the Secretary of State for War to agree that this Committee should have really effective executive powers. Its constitution was in the main that of an advisory body. The conversations which led to this lame conclusion occupied three weeks. In the course of these discussions a very trenchant memorandum was put in by the late Mr. Edwin Montagu, a man of exceptional insight and grasp of realities. This memorandum is worth reading as a contemporaneous statement of the difficulties experienced in dealing with the War Office:—

" The Prime Minister.

The Chancellor of the Exchequer, Mr. Balfour and I are going to see von Donop and Booth this afternoon, but I want to put once again, in a nutshell, the position as I see it.

You can have alternatively in contemplation two Committees or kinds of Committee. On the one hand you may leave Lord Kitchener directly responsible for the supply of munitions of war, working through the agency of the various men he collects for the purpose. You can have all the contracts, all the opportunities for resource, initiative energy and large view concentrated through von Donop and an overworked Secretary of State who admits again and again that he is incompetent by reason of his lack of knowledge of English conditions. If you do this, Lord Kitchener will welcome a Committee to tell him when he is wrong. Neither he nor his subordinates will be under any necessity to accept the advice of the Committee, the Committee will have no responsibility and will, I do not hesitate to say, suffer the same fate as your Cabinet Committee of last September. You can appoint such a Committee but I am quite certain it will not lead to the production of any new munitions of war and you will not find the Chancellor of the Exchequer or Mr. Balfour or anybody who does not wish to waste his time serving on such a Committee.

It is not for me to suggest any explanation of the War Office's . . . continued, bigoted, prejudiced reluctance to buy rifles or to increase the munitions of war, but that the solution of the suggestion above is most unsatisfactory can be supported by the evidence that : —

(1) Lord Kitchener, as he says, knows nothing about the problem.

(2) Lord Kitchener is overworked.

(3) Lord Kitchener admits that it would have been better to take the advice (and he did not take it) of the Committee in September.

(4) Lord Kitchener views with complete complacency figures which *mean nothing* unless labour is obtained, looks with complete satisfaction at machinery provided at Government expense which is idle because there is no labour, and works quite happily to a maximum of 350,000 shells a month, a maximum not yet by any means in sight. If you assume that an Army Corps wants 100 guns and each gun wants 17 shells per day, that shows a requirement of 1,700 shells per day per Army Corps, or 51,000 shells per Army Corps per month, which means that 350,000 will supply shell for seven Army Corps and we are talking of an Army of one million men.

On the other hand you can have a Committee which will be responsible and take the blame for any shortage of munitions of war from this time forward, which will try to infuse new life into von Donop, Lord Kitchener having failed, which will be responsible directly, under whatever scheme of devolution it may work, for all Army contracts for munitions of war in the future. There need be no necessity for strict terms of reference, for Lord Kitchener can rest secure that the members of the Committee have no motive but to increase the supply of munitions of war. All that it requires is an assurance that the War Office will not continue to bonnet it, to hoodwink it and to neglect its advice and to conduct its own business independently of the Committee. The Committee wants not only existence but power. It wants the surrender by Kitchener of this part of his activities and he will be represented on it by Baker, von Donop and Booth. This Committee Kitchener will not have. That he will not have it is evidenced by his continued objections and his repeated attempts to forestall its appointment. In a private letter to you I am sure you will forgive me in describing as impertinent to you his treatment of the suggestions you made for the working of the Committee, for he accepted them when you sent them across after they had been approved by the Chancellor of the Exchequer and then inserted words in putting them into his own document which made them quite useless for the purpose you and the Chancellor of the Exchequer had in mind. You stipulated that the Committee should concur in all new contracts; he made you stipulate that the Committee should concur in all new contracts which the Committee placed. This is making a meaningless farce out of a practical suggestion.

Therefore it really seems to me that there is a difference of principle which cannot be bridged except by you. The responsibility is now yours. George's view or Kitchener's must prevail. If you take the first alternative above, very well then, the project fails and Kitchener stews the British Army in his own juice. If you take the second alternative, Kitchener is relieved of responsibility, which falls on George and Balfour (and as an accidental result George negotiates in his own way with the men working on munitions of war). I submit most respectfully that the situation is serious, that delay does not improve it, that if you think the situation is as satisfactory as it can be, if Kitchener has his way, then I say no more. If you think that the situation demands that George's suggestion should be carried out, then you must impose your will on Kitchener, for I am certain that there can be no accommodation of this vital difference of principle except by the surrender of one or the other to your wishes."

In the event the Prime Minister seems to have decided on a compromise which turned out to be quite unworkable. The first meeting of the Committee was held on 12th April, 1915, three weeks after the War Council had decided to appoint it as a matter of extreme urgency. There were in all five further meetings between that date and 13th May. With the reconstruction of the Government and the formation of the Ministry of Munitions at the end of May, its functions were taken over by that new Department.

Five days before its first meeting Lord Kitchener had constituted at the War Office an "Armaments Output Committee" with the help of Mr. George M. Booth, of the Booth firm of engineers. It was he who became known as the "man of push and go," with the ostensible function of securing labour for the established armament firms, which had been subsidised considerably to extend their works, and were finding difficulty in staffing the extensions.

This Armaments Output Committee became informally, though not technically, subordinate to the Munitions of War Committee, and from the outset Mr. Booth consulted with me as to the steps he was proposing to take to organise labour in different areas for munition production.

With the work of the Munitions of War Committee it is hardly necessary to deal here in much detail. It was given, by the Prime Minister, terms of reference that nominally empowered it to take all steps necessary for the purpose of ensuring the promptest and most efficient application of all the available productive resources of the country to the manufacture and supply of munitions of war for the Navy and Army. Actually it was doomed to futility, first by the extreme reluctance of the War Office to supply it with information which was essential to the proper discharge of its duties, and ultimately by the blank refusal of the War Office to relinquish to it the task of organising munition production. The first difficulty is referred to by Mr. Balfour in a note he sent to the Committee.

"The War Office have a natural objection to stating the number of men they propose to put in the field on any particular date, and probably the Committee would be reluctant to press them upon such points of policy. This reticence, however, makes it extremely difficult to draw up trustworthy statistical estimates of the amount of munitions of war that will be required at different dates."

But it was historically of importance because its setting-up marked the clear recognition by the Government that the War Office and Admiralty could not be expected to carry out in addition to their other duties a task so vast as the supply of munitions in war-time had become; and thus it proved a stepping-stone to the creation of a Ministry of Munitions.

The original members of the Committee were myself, as its chairman, supported by Mr. Balfour, Mr. Edwin Montagu,

E

Mr. George Booth, and Mr. Arthur Henderson, together with General von Donop and Mr. Harold Baker from the War Office, and Sir Frederick Black and Admiral Tudor from the Admiralty. Sir H. Llewellyn Smith from the Board of Trade was co-opted at the first meeting, and Sir Percy Girouard on 26th April.

Among the tasks which this Committee undertook was the carrying out by means of a deputation to France of a further and more detailed survey of the way in which the French were organising their munition production, and the adoption of a scheme prepared for its consideration by Sir Percy Girouard, for the regional organisation of munition firms.

It is significant that at the last meeting held by the Munitions of War Committee, on 13th May, the first business considered was a memorandum prepared by Mr. Balfour in which he pointed out that there were not enough field-guns to supply the divisions then being sent out, and that even for the guns they had, there would be only half the necessary ammunition in June and less than half in July.

5. THE GREAT SHELL SCANDAL

But although the munition shortage with which we were faced in the spring of 1915 covered all or most branches of war material, the most pressing need in the field was for shells for our artillery.

On 31st December, 1914, Sir John French had informed the War Office, on the basis of his experience during the first five months of war, what his requirements in the way of shells would be in order to maintain the regular defence of the front and the exceptional expenditure necessitated by special attacks. For the principal artillery of his forces—the 18-pounders, the 4.5-inch howitzers and the 4.7-inch field-guns—he laid down his requirements as:—

50 rounds per gun per day for the 18-pdrs.
40   „   „   „   4.5-in.
25   „   „   „   4.7-in.

The number of rounds per gun per day actually supplied to him for these weapons, month by month, were:—

	Month	18-pdr.	4.5-in.	4.7-in.
1914	Nov.	9.9	6.8	10.8
	Dec.	6.0	4.6	7.6
1915	Jan.	4.9	4.2	7.6
	Feb.	5.3	6.5	5.3
	Mar.	8.6	6.5	5.3
	Apr.	10.6	8.2	4.2
	May	11.0	6.1	4.3

These figures require no comment from me. They speak for themselves. The consequences of this deficiency were tragic for the troops who had to hold the line during these months. Throughout those months our men were being battered by the Germans without any effective means of retaliation. Retaliation meant protection. The Germans would have hesitated to open fire on our trenches had they known we could return shell for shell. But they knew too well that they could rain explosives on our poor fellows with practical impunity. And when we attacked, our advance was not supported by adequate artillery preparation or counter-battery work, and our men were held up by unbroken wire and there slaughtered by machine-guns. This calamity was due to the utter inadequacy of the preliminary bombardment. It was not the fault of our artillery; their guns were not heavy enough and their shell supply for heavy and light guns was not only painfully inadequate but inappropriate to the task, for it was mostly shrapnel.

On 21st December, 1914, I stated in the House of Commons: "What we stint in material, we squander in life; that is the one great lesson of munitions." The truth of that statement was brought home to us in the following months, when our men were left without any means of replying effectively to the German fire.

I have already shown how Sir John French constantly called for more munitions at the end of 1914. He continued to send urgent messages for greater support. When the battle of Neuve-Chapelle had been in progress three days, Sir John French had to wire Lord Kitchener on the 13th March, 1915: —

"Cessation of the forward movement is necessitated to-day by the fatigue of the troops, and above all by the want of ammunition. If we are to obtain results of value, we must have all possible support in men and ammunition from home."

On the 16th March he wired: —

"The supply has fallen short, especially in 18-pounder and 4.5-inch, of what I was led to expect and I am, therefore, compelled to abandon further offensive operations until sufficient reserves are accumulated."

And in a reinforcing telegram of the same date he added: —

"The delay is really most deplorable. Now is the time to strike. Can nothing be done to expedite action operations now?"

Sir John French followed up these telegrams by a letter to the War Secretary, dated 18th March, in which he declared that the results of the Army Council's efforts to supply him with ammunition had been "consistently disappointing."

"If the supply of ammunition cannot be maintained on a considerably increased scale it follows that the offensive efforts of

E

the Army must be spasmodic and separated by considerable intervals of time. They cannot therefore lead to decisive results. . . .

Up to the present time the mud and the shortage of artillery munition have been the most potent factors in restricting us to the defensive. But the weather and the state of the ground have no longer to be reckoned with as limiting the scope of our operations. . . .

. . . I desire to state with all the weight of my authority as Commander-in-Chief of the British Army in France, that the object of His Majesty's Government cannot be attained unless the supply of artillery ammunition can be increased sufficiently to enable the Army to engage in sustained offensive operations, and I further desire to impress on them the very serious nature of the effort that it is necessary to make to achieve this end."

The War Office reply to this letter complained that the artillery had used, in the first 16 days of March, 200 to 220 rounds per gun —about 13 rounds per gun per day! This included the shells fired at the battle of Neuve-Chapelle. For this operation shells had been saved up for weeks. The War Office asked that "*in view of the effects achieved, which appear to have been to reduce the defence to a dazed and demoralised condition* [my italics] the utmost economy will be made in the expenditure of ammunition," and begged that less ammunition of the heavier natures should be expended.

There was an explanation for Lord Kitchener's abnormal frugality in the matter of shells, apart from the natural bent of his mind. The one campaign that had brought him renown and rank—in fact made him "Lord K. of K."—was waged on the basis of a tender for the total cost of the operation, which he submitted to that most austere of all Chancellors, Sir Michael Hicks Beach. The latter refused to give his sanction to operations against the Mahdi without having a most careful estimate of the cost, and the expenses were consequently cut down to the lowest figure. Lord Kitchener undertook to keep within this estimate and succeeded in doing so. The formidable Chancellor had won for himself a reputation by fighting every proposal, from whatever quarter it came, which would involve any additional expenditure. He looked at every project entirely from that angle. Sometimes this provoked a combination of all the spending Departments against the Treasury. There is a story told of those days which illustrates the internal conflicts in the Cabinet which were aroused by this attitude of mind. A Conservative Minister was asked after a Cabinet meeting whether anything important had been decided that day. He replied: " Nothing, except that we gave Hicks Beach the usual 19 to 1." Lord Kitchener, knowing the Chancellor's reputation, very astutely played upon it by contracting with him to run the expedition on the cheap.

It is a curious illustration of the way in which Lord Kitchener's mind worked about these matters, that just after this battle of Neuve-Chapelle, Kitchener stalked into the Cabinet with his most military stride, and with that ominous cast in his eye exaggerated and emphasised—a sure sign of surging anger—and as soon as he sat down he exclaimed in husky tones charged with suppressed emotion: "Oh, it is terrible—terrible!"

"Were the casualties very heavy?" we inquired, anxiously. "I'm not thinking for the moment about the casualties," replied Kitchener, "but for all the shells that were wasted!" He had just been given the actual figures of the artillery ammunition fired in the course of the battle.

Sir John French's retort to the War Office complaint (quoted above) about his rate of ammunition expenditure, was that he had said nothing about the German defence being "dazed and demoralised" and that such impression as had been made on them was due to the high-explosive shells from our heavier artillery. He added: "There is no evidence in my possession to show that the preliminary bombardment of Neuve-Chapelle was unnecessarily severe. In fact, at two places it was inadequate, and very heavy losses resulted. . . . Our losses and the amount of ground gained are the best indication as to whether the expenditure of artillery ammunition was on an unnecessarily extravagant scale."

(The total ground gained by us was equal to about one square mile in area; and our casualties were 12,892—i.e., 583 officers and 12,309 other ranks.)

Speaking in the House of Lords on 15th March, 1915, on the Second Reading of the Defence of the Realm (Amendment) Bill, to which I have already referred, Lord Kitchener so far departed from his habitual reticence as to state:—

"The work of supplying and equipping new Armies depends largely on our ability to obtain the war material required. . . . Notwithstanding these efforts to meet our requirements, we have unfortunately found that the output is not only not equal to our necessities but does not fulfil our expectations, for a very large number of our orders have not been completed by the dates on which they were promised.

The progress in equipping our new Armies and also in supplying the necessary war material for our forces in the field has been seriously hampered by the failure to obtain sufficient labour and by delays in the production of the necessary plant. . . ."

This open admission by Lord Kitchener of the serious nature of the munitions situation created some uneasiness in the public

mind, and considerably helped the negotiations in which I was
engaged during the next few days with representatives of the Trade
Unions, to arrange for the prevention of strikes and lock-outs in
establishments engaged on war work, and for the dilution of labour
by the introduction of unskilled workers—negotiations which resulted
in the " Treasury Agreement " on this matter, of which I give an
account later on.

For the next few weeks there was a comparative lull in the reports
about munition shortage. No very big operations were undertaken
on the British Front in France, and possibly the fact that we were at
the time engaged in negotiations with Italy, with a view to her intervention in the War on our side, made the military authorities chary of
allowing any fresh details of our munition difficulties to leak out.

The illusion that things were going well in this respect was
heightened by a letter which Lord Kitchener wrote to Mr. Asquith
on 14th April, in the following terms:—

" War Office,
April 14, 1915.

My dear Prime Minister,
    I have had a talk with French. He told me I could let
you know that with the present supply of ammunition he will
have as much as his troops will be able to use on the next forward
movement."

On the strength of this assurance, the Prime Minister delivered
on 20th April his famous Newcastle speech, in which he declared
that there was no truth in the statement that our Army or that of
our Allies were being crippled or hampered by our failure to supply
the necessary ammunition; and that it was neither true nor fair
to suggest that there had been anything in the nature of a general
slackness in the armaments industry on the part of either employers
or employed.

On the following day I had to take part in a debate on munitions
in the House of Commons, and in the course of my speech I gave
full credit to the War Office for their actual achievements, and
stressed the magnitude of the task with which they had been confronted. The telegrams from the front complaining of the shell
shortage were not communicated to the Cabinet. I have no knowledge as to whether the Prime Minister saw them. Lord Kitchener
had given me his assurances as to the present adequacy of the Army's
equipment, and on the strength of such information as was given
me by the War Office I put up the best defence I could for the
shortage. I was anxious to conciliate the War Office and carry it
along with us in the efforts we were making to increase the munitions
supply. I knew this could not be done without persuading those
who were in supreme control to depart from traditional ideas and
practices, and I was at that time doing my best to convince them. I

therefore dwelt in my speech in the House rather on their achievements than on their shortcomings. I pointed to the fact that whereas we had only promised the French six divisions we had already put six times as many in the field. " That was the problem which confronted the War Office, and which they had to face. I do not say that they could not have done more, but I want the House of Commons to know what has actually been done by the War Office."

I passed on to make a brief reference to some of the difficulties we were experiencing: drink, short time, trade union restrictions; and to the efforts which were being made by the Munitions of War Committee and the Armaments Output Committee to cope with these matters.

I ended on a note of optimism, based on my confidence that there was nothing in the problem confronting us which our nation was incapable of meeting and overcoming. But I was in fact far from optimistic about the progress we were making at the time, though to have given public expression to my views would at that moment probably have done more harm than good, in view of the diplomatic situation in reference to Italy.

The Opposition drew attention to the discrepancy between what Mr. Asquith had said at Newcastle on the previous day and Lord Kitchener's statement five weeks previously in the House of Lords, about the output of ammunition being equal neither to our expectations nor to our necessities. They put in a plea for more information as to the situation and for better co-ordination of effort in the production of ammunition, with which latter recommendation I expressed myself in my speech as in full agreement.

It must, I think, be accepted that Lord Kitchener had somehow misunderstood what French said to him about the adequacy of the shell supply in France. Certainly the statement, expanded emphatically as it was by Mr. Asquith at Newcastle, received a prompt and dramatic refutation only two days later, when the Germans opened a fresh offensive at Ypres, with the new and added horror of the first gas attack; for our army found itself deplorably deficient in artillery ammunition with which to extricate the doomed infantry from the death-cloud that was annihilating them.

The introduction of gas gave fresh emphasis to the lesson that the technical side of this war was supremely important. It was a method of fighting which we were not ready to employ; we were, therefore, not prepared to meet such an attack. A feeling of anger and horror ran through the whole nation. The main criticism we had to face was the fact that no preparations whatever had been made to protect our men against this deadly weapon, although we had received through French sources more than one warning—on 30th March and 15th April—that the Germans were reported to be preparing this new method of attack, and on 17th April, five days before they

Published on April 21st, 1915.   *Reproduced by courtesy of " Punch."*

" DELIVERING THE GOODS."

themselves used it, the Germans published the false charge that the British had been using shells and bombs with asphyxiating gas. That was obviously designed as a defence in advance for the use they were proposing to make of this cruel weapon of war. I may add that the French, though warned before ourselves, were equally unprepared.

Rough-and-ready methods of protecting troops against the chlorine fumes were improvised by the officers at the front, and at home Lord Kitchener took a deep personal interest in the providing of appliances for anti-gas defence, which were promptly put in hand by the War Office; but the episode added to the growing public anxiety as to our unpreparedness to cope with a foe that had at his disposal the resources of science directed by a skilled and highly organised industrialism, and who was resolved to make the most ruthless use of all his advantages.

The serious breach which had been made by this weapon in our front induced the Army Commanders to attempt a counter-attack at Festubert on 9th May, in an effort to relieve the pressure on the troops at Ypres. In his book " 1914 " Sir John French wrote of this battle: —

> " After all our demands, less than 8 per cent. of our shells were high explosive, and we had only sufficient supply for about 40 minutes of artillery preparation for this attack. On the tower of a ruined church I spent several hours in close observation of the operations. Nothing since the battle of the Aisne had ever impressed me so deeply with the terrible shortage of artillery and ammunition as did the events of that day. As I watched the Aubers Bridge, I clearly saw the great inequality of the artillery duels, and, as attack after attack failed, I could see that the absence of sufficient artillery support was doubling and trebling our losses in men."

Our losses at this battle were very heavy—gains there were none. Three days after this battle started I received an unexpected visit from two gentlemen—one being Sir John French's secretary, Brinsley Fitzgerald, and the other one of his A.D.C.'s, Captain F. Guest. They had been sent over by the Commander-in-Chief to lay before Mr. Balfour, Mr. Bonar Law, and myself certain facts and documents referring to the shortage of ammunition. They had with them copies of correspondence and a memorandum by Sir John French, emphasising the need for high-explosive shell and containing a demand for a monthly supply of gun ammunition to be furnished within the next three months. The Commander-in-Chief was tired of remonstrances to the War Office which produced nothing but counter-remonstrances, so he decided to appeal over their heads to leading politicians and Press men. This was the first communication on the shell question that I had received from the Commander-in-Chief.

Sir John has since stated that the reason why he selected me to be a recipient of his complaint was because I had always shown a special interest in the subject. As part of his campaign to expose what he considered a dangerous situation, he also furnished information and gave his views to the Military Correspondent of *The Times,* and on 14th May there appeared a report from him in that paper, under the headlines: "NEED FOR SHELLS: BRITISH ATTACKS CHECKED: LIMITED SUPPLY THE CAUSE."

As this report is practically an epitome of the information communicated to me by Sir John French's emissaries, I quote the following passages:—

> "The results of our attacks on Sunday last in the districts of Fromelles and Richeburg were disappointing. We found the enemy much more strongly posted than we expected. We had not sufficient high explosive to level his parapets to the ground after the French practice, and when our infantry gallantly stormed the trenches, as they did in both attacks, they found a garrison undismayed, many entanglements still intact, and Maxims on all sides ready to pour in streams of bullets. We could not maintain ourselves in the trenches won, and our reserves were not thrown in because the conditions for success in an assault were not present.
>
> The attacks were well planned and valiantly conducted. The infantry did splendidly, but the conditions were too hard. *The want of an unlimited supply of high explosive was a fatal bar to our success.* . . .
>
> The value of the German troops in the attack has greatly deteriorated, and we can deal easily with them in the open. But until we are thoroughly equipped for this trench warfare, we attack under grave disadvantages. . . .
>
> To break this hard crust we need more high explosives, more heavy howitzers, and more men. This special form of warfare has no precedent in history.
>
> It is certain that we can smash the German crust if we have the means. So the means we must have, and as quickly as possible."

This article created very considerable public anxiety and consternation. It was the first time the public had ever been so plainly told from the army front how serious was the munition shortage; and I may add that the visit of Sir John French's representatives similarly gave me my first clear and authoritative information as to the full gravity of the position. As I have said, the Cabinet had not been shown the Commander-in-Chief's frequent telegrams on the subject, and we had been compelled to form our opinions on the basis of general statements, rumours, and a common-sense interpretation of the facts known to us. Although I had taken an active interest in increasing the output of munitions and had assisted the War Office by every means at my disposal to achieve this aim, all vital telegrams from the front on the subject of the shell shortage had been withheld from me, even when I was Chairman of the Committee appointed by the Prime Minister to consider the munition question.

Now, however, it was clear that after eight months we were still fatally short of munitions for the kind of war in which we were entangled. An even graver trouble was that as far as I could see, there was no prospect of our getting an adequate supply with the present methods of organisation. The unavailing sacrifice of the lives of our men would continue, the War would be prolonged, and ultimate victory would be jeopardised, unless someone took the matter in hand.

So strongly did I feel on the subject that I addressed the following letter to Mr. Asquith:—

"May 19th, 1915.

My dear Prime Minister,

Certain facts have been brought to my notice on the question of munitions which I have felt bound to call your attention to. I write to you inasmuch as my appointment as Chairman of the Munitions Committee came direct from you.

In order properly to discharge our functions as a Committee it was essential that all information as to the character of the explosive most urgently needed and the present supply available should be afforded to us. I am now informed, on what appears to be reliable information:—

(1) That in order to attack highly developed trenches protected by barbed-wire entanglements, shrapnel is useless, and high-explosive shells indispensable;

(2) That those who are responsible for conducting operations at the front have for months impressed this fact upon the War Office, and asked in the first instance that 25 per cent. of the shells sent to France should be high explosive, and that afterwards this percentage was increased to 50 per cent.;

(3) That notwithstanding these urgent representations, the percentage of high-explosive shell provided for the 18-pounders has never exceeded 8 per cent.; that when the great combined attack to break through the German lines was made by the French and British armies last Sunday week, the French prepared the attack with an overwhelming bombardment of high explosive which utterly demolished the German trenches and barbed-wire entanglements, thus enabling the French to penetrate the German lines for four miles without any excessive loss of life. In spite of the fact that the French spent their high-explosive shells lavishly, they have still in reserve hundreds of thousands of shells of the same kind for the purpose of

continuing their operations. On the other hand, our armies had less than 45,000 high-explosive shells in all. Of these about 18,000 were 18-pounders. They therefore had to rely on shrapnel, so that when our troops advanced to the attack the German fortifications were barely pockmarked. The Germans rose in their trenches and mocked at our advancing troops, and then calmly mowed them down in thousands. The Germans themselves have barely lost 200 men.

I am also told that the attack on Saturday last had to be made by night—a risky operation—because of the deficiencies in high-explosive shell, and that after the battle there were not more than 2,000 high-explosive shells left for all our guns.

(4) That a full report on ammunition was sent to the War Office weeks ago from Headquarters in France, and that later on another report on guns was sent. Neither of these reports has ever been shown to the Munitions Committee, and I gather they have not been seen by you.

If these facts are approximately correct, I hesitate to think what action the public would insist on if they were known. But it is quite clear that the proceedings of a Munitions Committee from which vital information of this character is withheld must be a farce. I cannot, therefore, continue to preside over it under such conditions. *It is now eight months since I ventured to call the attention of the Cabinet to the importance of mobilising all our engineering resources for the production of munitions and equipments of war.* In October of last year I brought a full report from France showing how the French Ministry for War had coped with the difficulty. The Cabinet at that date decided that the same course should be pursued here, and a Cabinet Committee was set up for that purpose. We met at the War Office, and it was there agreed, with the Secretary of State in the chair, that steps of that kind should be taken in this country. *I regret to say after some inquiry that action on those lines has not been taken even to this hour except at Leeds.*

A Cabinet Committee cannot have executive power; it can only advise and recommend. It is for the department to act. They have not done so, and all the horrible loss of life which has occurred in consequence of the lack of high-explosive shell is the result.

Private firms cannot turn out shrapnel because of the complicated character of the shell; but the testimony is unanimous that the high explosive is a simple shell and that any engineering concern could easily produce it. That has been the experience of France.

Ever sincerely,

D. LLOYD GEORGE."

This letter played its part—an important one—in the course of events which led to the reconstruction of the Government by the formation of the first Coalition—a matter with which I deal in more detail elsewhere in this narrative.

Lord Northcliffe (who at that time owned *The Times* as well as the *Daily Mail*) was personally responsible for the publication by *The Times* of the dispatch from its Military Correspondent, Colonel Repington. Lord Northcliffe had for some time been receiving an unending stream of letters and statements from men at the front about the shell shortage, but all efforts to give publicity to these complaints had been diligently blacked out of his proofs by the Censor. He was not content with the news that the Ministry was to be reconstructed. He attributed the blame for the shell shortage to Lord Kitchener, and he resolved to drive him out of office if he possibly could. On hearing that he would be retained in the reconstructed Ministry, he came out on 21st May with an article in the *Daily Mail* with a headline that ran: "THE SHELLS SCANDAL: LORD KITCHENER'S TRAGIC BLUNDER."

The *Daily Mail* and *The Times* were solemnly burned on the Stock Exchange that afternoon. But the campaign for more shells went on. On 25th May *The Times* published a letter from Bishop Furse, at that time Bishop of Pretoria, now Bishop of St. Albans, who had just returned from a visit to the Front. The following extracts from his letter give some picture of the situation which the Bishop had found:—

" . . . When battalion after battalion of infantry—and, as was recently the case in the Ypres salient, regiment after regiment of cavalry, too—have to sit in trenches day after day, night after night, being pounded by high explosives from enemy guns, with no guns behind them capable of keeping down the enemy's fire, then the conclusion they draw is obvious—namely, that the nation has failed to provide sufficient guns or ammunition to meet those of the enemy.

When, night after night and day after day, the men in the trenches know that for every one hand grenade or rifle grenade or trench mortar bomb which they throw at the enemy they will get back in answer anything from five to ten, then the conclusion they draw is also obvious—namely, that the nation does not somehow realise the situation, or, if it does, has not made it its business to supply what is necessary. . . . They know that it is little short of murder for a nation to ask men, however full of the right spirit, to face an enemy amply equipped with big guns and the right kind of ammunition, unless they are at least equipped with equally effective munitions of war.

There can only be one impression left on the minds of men

in such a case, and that is that somehow or other the nation does not know the truth, does not understand, and is not backing them, for, knowing the old country as they do, they have no doubt that if Germany can produce these things, we can, if we will. . . ."

An officer home from the front stated in the *Northwich Chronicle* of 22nd May, 1915:—

" . . . People at home do not appear to realise how critical the position is out here. . . . The Germans have still unlimited supplies of munitions. . . . You can rub it in about our need for men and munitions of war. I am sorry to say that in the ten days' battle about Ypres our men suffered heavily owing to lack of ammunition. The Germans poured shells into our lines. . . . For our men it was a terrible time, while the Germans shelled us heavily and we, owing to shortage of ammunition, could not reply effectively. It is up to everybody at home to realise what such a situation means, and for people to understand that successful war cannot be waged without enormous supplies being available on the spot."

The two foregoing extracts represent the point of view of an onlooker and of a man in the trenches. I will quote, as the view of the man behind the guns an extract from a striking letter written to me at the time by Captain H. FitzHerbert Wright, M.P. for Leominster, who was serving as an artillery officer on the Western Front. The address on his letter was " Belgium, 29/5/15." He said:—

" . . . . I rejoined the 4th North Midland Brigade (Howitzer) on the outbreak of the War and have been serving out here for nearly 13 weeks as a Captain and Officer Commanding the Ammunition Column. . . . As O.C. Amm. Col., all the shells fired by my brigade pass through my hands. We have been attached to two divisions—the 4th and the 46th, both in the 2nd Army. When we first got into the firing line in the first week of March we were allowed 20 rounds per gun per day: 80 *rounds per day per battery*. We have been in action throughout. Our allowance is now two rounds per gun per day, *or eight rounds per battery per day*. It isn't that our fellows have made bad practice, or that there are not any targets suitable for our 50-pound lyddite shells. General Smith-Dorrien has publicly and privately given us the highest praise for the accuracy and effectiveness of our fire, and our fellows are made much of by all the infantry over whom they have fired; and, as to targets, we daily see the German trenches, and works growing and growing, simply asking to be pounded. I have to-day returned from having a week with our 1st Battery, spent mainly in an observation station, and I speak of what I have seen. The battery commanders in our Brigade, the Q.F. brigades, the R.H.A. and the Heavy are now not allowed to fire except by order of the General even one round.

The R.H.A. adjutant told me he had to send 1,500 rounds down to the 1st Army for the recent fighting down South, and he had now an empty park and column; one of the officers of the Heavies told me his park and column are at this moment empty (4.7-inch shells) and he may not fire even in the event of an attack without express orders. My batteries in 12 weeks have averaged a little over 60 rounds per battery a week. Naturally, I don't know the reason, but I suspect, and we all suspect, that there are no shells for us. Anyhow, here we are inviting attack, seeing the enemy firing daily 20 or 30 rounds into our lines to our one into theirs. We don't know or care who is to blame; we only know that we are being starved to death for want of shells, and our infantry fated daily to a more and more terrible task if an attack either by the Germans or ourselves takes place in our zone. I know nothing of other zones except by hearsay. We want to be fed; soldiers do not live by bread alone. . . .

Nor is that all; we are outclassed in guns, number and quality; we are outranged; I am not now speaking of our Brigade, but generally. So far as our Brigade is concerned, our guns were pretty old in South Africa, and are, therefore, getting into years now. The 5-inch Howitzer never should have come out here. I raised this matter last September through Talbot and tried to get the 4.5-inch Howitzer, the Regular gun, but got the answer direct from W.O. that it was impossible as there were none, and the output of guns hadn't yet overtaken the wastage. However, we are doing our best and, having had good positions well concealed, at short ranges have, as I already quoted, done well. If we got into the open or had to shoot at anything over 3,500 yards we should be off the map in five minutes. We fire one round a minute, and the shell takes 20 seconds to go the distance. A q.f. at from 10 to 15 rounds a minute would find us easy victims.

Nor is that all: outclassed in guns; little or no ammunition; that sums up the Artillery part of the show, except to say that much of the shells we have are shrapnel—that does not apply to my Brigade, which has only lyddite—which is less useful than rain, against the German trenches.

Now for the infantry—and more magnificent infantry will never be seen. In our division there are two machine-guns per battalion. The Germans have 16; our Regulars have six or eight; in our Division we have two trench mortars on a front of not less than three miles; the Germans have them at frequent intervals all along; our hand grenades are in many cases " hand "-made and truly " hand " grenades; a few are thrown and the Germans

promptly answer with 50-pound bombs. We call that showing
our superiority. I suppose of courage—certainly not of equipment.
Our lights are ridiculous beside the German lights . . . we do
not use gas. Personally, I hope we shan't have to, though if it
is true that our air reconnaissance reports that what were supposed
to be light railways coming up their lines are in reality 18 inch
pipes conjectured to be used for gas on a large scale, it is probable
we shall never have the chance, even if we want to.

Now are these facts anything for England, the richest country
in the world or nearly, anything to be proud of? Are they not
a matter rather for sackcloth and ashes?

If we get ammunition we can hold on, though the poor infantry
will go on getting cut to pieces. If we get plenty of ammunition
we can go ahead. I suppose you know that the Artists, now a
training corps for officers, rejoices in the name of the Suicides
Club—magnificent, cheery fellows? Where is the responsibility
for that name being more than justified by the casualty lists?

Never mind where is the responsibility; get the mess cleared
up. You have the pluck and go of ten. More power to you!

I hope I haven't by any fault of diction or over-emphasis led
you to think I am exaggerating. I am but dotting the 'i's' and
crossing the 't's' of the Bishop's letter. He and I are old friends
since the Eton days. . . ."

I have in my possession a bundle of letters, blue-pencilled by
the censor or stamped by him "NOT TO BE PUBLISHED" which were
sent to me by Northcliffe about this time to show me the sorts of
reports he was receiving from France, but was not allowed to print.
The circumstances in which these came to me from him are described
as follows by Tom Clarke in his interesting book, " My Northcliffe
Diary " : —

"May 25, 1915: Several stories from officers at the front supporting Northcliffe's allegation re shell shortage having been
refused publication by the censors at the Press Bureau, the Chief
has given instructions that we must not submit them to the Censor.
When it was pointed out that we might be trapped on a technical
point, he said, ' I have been threatened so much in the past few
weeks that I do not mind now. Send all these censored proofs to
Lloyd George and Curzon. They know the truth, and it will let
them see how the Press Bureau is keeping it back.' "

Here are a few specimens culled from this collection of appeals
and complaints : —

" We had some artillery officers to mess the other evening, and
they were very worried. They had had orders from General
Headquarters to fire only a certain number of shells a day and

their requests for supplies were always avoided by some excuse. . . ."

" . . . We have just to sit tight in the trenches while the German high explosives batter them to bits, and the main part of our casualties in the 16-hour bombardment which I described in the last letter were from this cause. . . . Out of our company of from 150 to 200 men only 13 came out of the trenches after the last attack."

" . . . It makes your heart break to see those men going forward and then held up—one after another, fighting and struggling, until, wearied out, they collapse like a wet cloth. And why? Because there is not an adequate supply of high explosives to blow the wire to bits, and let our men go at the enemy."

" . . . I have often heard the wish expressed that a representative of the manufacturing population at home might be present in one of our front trenches to witness the eagerness and anxiety of officers and men as they watch the enemy's trench being bombarded preparatory to an assault. There is not one who does not realise that on the intensity and volume of that fire his life and all his chances of success depend. On these occasions shrapnel gives no confidence to those who have had a little experience; they know that it has as much effect as one would expect from a handful of gravel on a German machine-gun emplacement, and they know that over some 200 yards it is only machine-guns that can stop them. When the first line has been destroyed by them (i.e., by German machine-guns) many of us have seen the second immediately throw themselves over our parapet to certain and conscious destruction.

Actually to witness this heroic perseverance and self-sacrifice of a fighting body which in quality and war experience cannot soon —if ever—be replaced, and to know that it is all due to the tardy organisation of the war machinery at home raises thoughts that cannot be expressed ' in print.' "

Although statements of this nature were banned by the Censor from the columns of the Press, the facts they set out were becoming common knowledge in every newspaper office, and in countless homes throughout the land. That knowledge doubtless played an important part in making the country ripe for the change of Government which was announced on 19th May, when Mr. Asquith, having invited his fellow-ministers of the Liberal Government to resign their offices, reconstructed his Ministry as a Coalition Government, including the leaders of the Conservative Party.

CHAPTER VII

THE POLITICS OF THE WAR

No nation engaged in a struggle with a redoubtable foe can afford
to dissipate its energies and distract its executive by party controversy.
The last days of July, 1914, found the traditional British parties
confronting each other in the fiercest political conflict waged since
the suppression of the last Jacobite rebellion. We were faced with
the prospect of an internecine struggle which would have rent the
nation into warring factions such as these islands have not witnessed
since the great Civil Wars.   The threatened uprising of Ulster
against the dominion of an Irish Parliament was not a bluff. The
Orange North would have fought before it submitted. The Curragh
incident, the gun-running in Ulster, followed by the arming of the
South (which was the beginning of the bloodshed of the six years
that followed) all pointed towards the possibilities of bloody strife
once more on a political battlefield. Political and religious issues
had not so long ago been referred in these islands to the arbitrament
of the sword. It is never safe to say that such things will not
happen again. "The thing that hath been, it is that which shall
be, and that which is done, is that which shall be done, and there
is no new thing under the sun." This saying, uttered over 2,000
years ago, is being verified in every generation, and it is never quite
wise to assume that it has exhausted its application to any branch
of human thought or activity. The thinker and the striker have
always worked in a close partnership—more or less willing, and less
rather than more understanding. Unionists who attended Ulster
meetings in England tell me that they never saw such depths of
fierce indignation as that aroused by the threat of force to subject
the Protestants of the North to the rule of the Catholic South. On
the other hand, I myself never witnessed such an outburst of ferocious
anger as that which was aroused in the House of Commons when
the late Mr. John Ward and Mr. J. H. Thomas denounced the
attempt of certain Army officials to override the constitution by
threatening to disobey orders and refusing to carry out laws of which
they disapproved. The North had armed, the South was arming.
What would have happened?

There was no surety that if bloodshed ensued its flow could have
been confined to Ireland. There are towns on this side of the

Channel where it would have been difficult to keep the peace amongst the votaries of warring creeds if their fellow-religionists in Ireland on either side were being slain. Wisdom might have intervened. But it might not. Mankind was only too ready for the shedding of blood, as we were to discover in a few days.

Then there came real war, like a mighty rushing wind, the struggle not of sects and factions, but of nations and continents, and the incipient fires of civil war were swept into the great conflagration. All the same the spreading flame of national dissension in Britain encouraged the warmongers of Germany and Austria to plunge. England was supposed to be temporarily out of the reckoning. Without her tenacious aid, France and Russia would soon collapse. The Ulster trouble was an undoubted factor in precipitating the Great War. How little the German rulers knew the temper of the British people! At the sound of the trumpet they all fell into line and wheeled against the common danger. There was not a perceptible break or gap in their ranks. This coming together of all creeds and sections to face a national peril was immediately reflected in the House of Commons. Its mood quickly changed. A few days before the outbreak of war the Prime Minister had been howled down by Unionist members excited beyond the bounds of Parliamentary decorum. A little later and the same members were cheering to the rafters the moving eloquence with which he called the nation to wage war with all its strength against the invaders of Belgium. In the course of a single day angry political passions were silenced and were followed by the just wrath which is too deep to be easily lashed into the frothing fury that so often churns the shallow waters of party recrimination. During the autumn and winter of 1914 and the early spring of 1915 this temper continued in the political world. Party politics and party bitterness disappeared. In fact, the Liberal Government received more unanimous and cordial support from Unionists confronting them than from the Liberal and Labour benches behind.

The reasons for this attitude are interesting and significant, and account to a large extent, if closely examined, for the political developments of the next six years. Previous wars in which this country had been engaged by no means closed down the hostilities of parties. They rather stoked political and personal antagonisms into fiercer enmity. Some of these wars actually became the dividing line of parties. The change which took place in 1914 cannot be explained by the supposition that we are more patriotic than our ancestors. The Conservative Party had in recent years become increasingly Germanophobe. Rivalry between the two Empires for supremacy on the seas and in the marts of the world accounted largely for the remarkable swing round in the Conservative attitude towards Germany. The Conservatives were far from desiring war anywhere. But when war with Germany came, there could be no doubt as to its popularity with Conservatives, Press and rank and file. It was something many of their most ardent spirits had hoped for. Others feared it was inevitable that we should be forced sooner or later to try conclusions with a Power that seemed to be preparing to destroy us. So when it came with a Liberal Government in power it was an auspicious combination of events of which they had not dreamed. There was a note of exhilaration in their support of the War. On the other hand, the Liberals felt the obligation of honour involved in the Belgian Treaty, and they promptly if unhappily followed a course prescribed by the greatest of their leaders in 1870 when he protected Belgium from invasion during the Franco-Prussian War. So the Conservatives entered the War with enthusiasm and the Liberals with reluctant conviction. Conservatives in particular were well pleased by Mr. Asquith's choice of Lord Kitchener as War Director inside his Cabinet. Lord Kitchener had no Party associations; but if he had any leanings they were towards Conservatism. Even those leanings were inherited prejudices rather than convictions. The latter he had neither the time nor the inclination to acquire during his busy life on duties for his country in environments far removed from our Party conflicts. At any rate his appointment to the War Office was a guarantee of the Government's intention to prosecute the War vigorously, and that Party considerations should not enter into its conduct. His selection for what was practically a War Dictatorship gave satisfaction and confidence to the nation generally and to the Conservative Party in particular. It undoubtedly had the effect of restraining criticism, for doubts cast on the War direction implied censure of Lord Kitchener. For the first few months of the War his influence was paramount. His very picture on the walls counted more than all the appeals of all the political leaders of all parties.

The Liberal Government commanded a working majority in the House of Commons. It is true it was dependent for that majority on a Coalition of groups—the Liberal, Nationalist, and Labour groups. The country has been governed by Coalitions for the greater part of the last half-century. In the 1914 Parliament the Conservatives, in fact, constituted the largest party in the House, but they could not attract the support of any other section. It followed that the Liberal Government could not be dismissed except by dissolution, and that was unthinkable in the agony of the Great War. It would have been an unspeakable crime to divide the nation when even united it could barely be saved from defeat, so formidable was the foe we had challenged. The Conservatives were led by men of high character and capacity whose patriotism was above suspicion—Mr. Bonar Law, Mr. Balfour, Lord Lansdowne, Sir Edward Carson, and Lord Curzon. Such men were much too high minded to desire electoral victory bought at such a cost to their country. Liberals will admit that their actions throughout the War were dictated by the highest motives of patriotism and that during that period they were willing to sink all Party dealing and rivalries and maintain their opponents in full possession of power so long as that power was wielded in the achievement of victory for their country's banner.

The men of the Army and Navy who at the bidding of their country were undergoing hardships and facing death on the seas from Scapa Flow to Coromandel, and in strange lands from Nieuport to Nineveh, were of many different political faiths, and there were multitudes whose faith had not yet been cast in any party mould. Men of political parties and unions left their badges at home and joined the new fraternity of sacrifice, and others whose opinions were unformed and who were still unattached entered the same comrade-ship. They expected—and they had a right to expect—that their jeopardy should not be increased by the irrelevant bickerings at home of those men who could afford to indulge in untimely animosities with complete immunity to themselves. Diversion and dissipation of thought and energy in attack or defence in time-honoured Party quarrels which had no bearing on the issues of the War (and which could not be dealt with during the War) would have weakened a front which had no superfluous strength to spare and intensified dangers already almost too appalling for human nature to bear. That is why France with her face all wrinkled with Party lines, displayed the *union sacrée* to the eyes of the world, and Britain, also riven with Party schisms, presented the spectacle of a united front.

There was an undoubted advantage from the point of view of national unity in having a Liberal rather than a Tory Government in power when war was declared. There was a further advantage in having a Government at the head of affairs which had the support of Labour. This secured the adhesion of the great Labour organisa-tions whose action and sympathetic aid was essential to its vigorous prosecution. Had Labour been hostile the War could not have been carried on effectively. Had Labour been lukewarm victory would have been secured with increased and increasing difficulty. The most prominent and influential leaders of trade unionism worked for victory throughout the War. Without their help it could not have been achieved. But beyond and above all these considerations, as a factor in the attainment of national unity, was the circumstance that the War had been declared by a party which by tradition and training regarded war with the deepest aversion, and has more especially since the days of Gladstone, Cobden and Bright, regarded itself as specially charged with the promotion of the cause of peace.

The spring of 1915 witnessed a growing change in the attitude of Parliament. Questions multiplied, debates became more prolonged,

the atmosphere became more critical, the note more challenging.
Mr. M'Kenna's administration of the Home Office provoked much
dissatisfaction, and not merely on the Unionist benches. His policy
towards residents of enemy extraction in this country was thought
to be too protective, too indifferent to the dangers which might
arise from espionage. The country was all camp and arsenal, and
valuable information for the enemy was visible everywhere without
speering or spying. Mr. M'Kenna's rigid and fretful answers, though
always technically complete, were provocative. Whilst administering
the letter of his trust, he showed too clearly that he had no sympathy
with its spirit. And the nation was uneasy. Its sons were falling, and
information was undoubtedly getting through from the shores of
Britain which helped the enemy in the slaughter. Subsequent events
proved that intelligence of great value to the enemy percolated to
Germany through the agency of persons living unmolested in
England under Mr. M'Kenna's indulgent regime. War is a ruthless
business and those who wage it cannot afford to be too discriminating.
The nation was right in thinking that this was not the time to risk
the national security on glib pedantries. The anxiety of the people
found expression in both Houses of Parliament, and the challenge,
at first friendly, quickly became more insistent and ended on a note
of undisguised anger.

Then came the rumours that our gallant troops were being
inadequately provided with ammunition. Men were falling fast
under the continuous bombardment of an enemy well equipped with
the most formidable guns lavishly provided with an overwhelming
supply of high explosives. Casualties were multiplying at an alarming rate. Though the figures were withheld from the public by a
prudent War Office there was, as I have already shown, a growing
feeling that our losses were great. With that in the mind of the
nation, information leaked through as to the helplessness of our
troops under the hammering of the Teutonic Thor. The facts were
too poignant not to provoke a cry from those who knew them. The
article in *The Times* would have forced Parliament to take sharp
cognisance of the lamentable deficiency had not Mr. Asquith
anticipated its intervention by a dramatic move.

CHAPTER VIII

THE POLITICAL CRISIS IN MAY, 1915

POLITICAL crises never come out of the blue. Clouds gather in the sky, sometimes from one quarter, sometimes from many. Suddenly one of those clouds is black with menace, approaches with surprising speed, hangs right overhead, and breaks into angry flashes.

The political crisis of May, 1915, was no exception to this meteorological rule. It was due to a combination of factors which had been at work for some time. The final addition of one extra cause for discontent at the existing conditions provoked the storm which swept away the Liberal Government, which had weathered many tempests. It is not correct to ascribe the change in government solely, or mainly, to the shortage of shell for our armies. The general dissatisfaction with the conduct of the War, of which there were many symptoms, and of which the culmination was reached in the second half of May, was not only due to the realisation of the munitions situation. Other contributing factors were the failure of the offensive in France, as to which expectations had been unduly raised; and disappointment over the result of the Dardanelles, with a growing feeling that the expedition was either misconceived or muddled. The disagreement between the First Lord of the Admiralty and the First Sea Lord deepened this feeling.

Underlying the various specific grounds for anxiety in different directions was a sense of revolt against the attitude of the Government and what was regarded as its leisurely and take-for-granted attitude in dealing with vitally serious matters, matters of life and death to the whole of the Allies and the British Empire, and to hundreds of thousands of gallant young men who had offered their lives to their country. The War was not being treated either with sufficient seriousness or adequate energy. So far back as the beginning of this year I had urged that more constant attention should be paid to the higher conduct of the War. *And for five and a half weeks, from the 6th April to the 14th May, the War Council had not been convened,* and the machinery set up by the Government for exercising a general supervision over the conduct of the War had not been afforded an opportunity to exercise the functions for which it had been created and for which it was responsible.

There was a genuine conviction on the part of many who had no desire to provoke a Ministerial crisis that if an improvement were not soon effected we should lose the War. This opinion was held very strongly by many members of the Opposition, who had so far loyally supported the Government, but were becoming increasingly restive. In fact, it was obvious that unless prompt action were taken to convince the country that a fresh urge was being put into the direction of affairs there would be a most dangerous division in the nation, and that this division might develop on party lines. Nothing could have been more fatal to that national unity which was essential to victory in so deadly a struggle.

On 14th May the War Council sat again for the first time after a long period of coma. Its meeting was purely formal, and only one or two members were summoned. On that day there appeared in the Press the violent outburst on the shell situation to which I have already referred in a previous section, and next day occurred the incident which actually brought matters to a head. This was the resignation from the Admiralty of Lord Fisher over our Dardanelles policy. In view of the controversy which arose later on as to the interference of the political with the naval chiefs in the matter of strategy, it is interesting to note that this particular crisis arose partly from the complete subservience of Ministers to our chief military adviser in the conduct of the War on land, and partly from the overriding of our principal naval adviser by a combination of generals and statesmen in the conduct of the War at sea. It had long been known that Lord Fisher was opposed to the attempt to force the Dardanelles by the Navy alone, but his resignation, which deprived the country of the services of its most distinguished naval expert, was the match which, applied to the discontent generated everywhere, blew up the complacency of statesmen. With it went the Government under which the War began.

I heard of Lord Fisher's contemplated resignation quite accidentally. On the morning of Saturday, 15th May, as I was passing through the entrance lobby of No. 10, Downing Street, I met Lord Fisher, and was struck by a dour change in his attitude. A combative grimness had taken the place of his usually genial greeting; the lower lip of his set mouth was thrust forward, and the droop at the corner was more marked than usual. His curiously Oriental features were more than ever those of a graven image in an Eastern temple, with a sinister frown.

"I have resigned!" was his greeting, and on my inquiring the reason he replied, "I can stand it no longer." He then informed me that he was on his way to see the Prime Minister, having made up his mind to take no further part in the Dardanelles "foolishness," and was off to Scotland that night.

I tried to persuade him to postpone his departure until the

Monday, which would give him an opportunity of placing his case before a War Council, but he declined to wait another hour. I told him that so far as the Council was concerned he had never expressed any dissent from the policy or the plans for the expedition; that though I was a member of the War Council and had been opposed to that venture from the start I had not heard one word of protest from him; and that it was only right that we should be given an opportunity of hearing his objections, weighing his advice, and taking the appropriate action. His answer was that Mr. Churchill was his Chief, and that by the traditions of the service he was not entitled to differ from him in public. On being reminded by me that the Council was a Council of War, and that he was bound as a member of that Council to speak his mind freely to all his colleagues around the table, he stated that he had at the outset made an emphatic protest against the whole expedition to the Prime Minister privately, and had left to him the responsibility of communicating or withholding that knowledge. Here he was referring to a conversation he and Mr. Churchill had with Mr. Asquith before the War Council meeting on the 28th January. This protest had never been passed on to the Council.

Failing to shake him in his purpose, I sent a message to Mr. Asquith. He was at Mr. Geoffrey Howard's wedding. (He had a queer liking for weddings and funerals and rarely missed one which he might be expected to attend.) I conveyed to him that I thought it was important he should see Lord Fisher at once. But the Prime Minister's powers of persuasion and authority were equally unavailing with the First Sea Lord, who subsequently visited Mr. M'Kenna, his former Chief at the Admiralty. Mr. M'Kenna was also an opponent of the Dardanelles expedition. At this period Mr. Winston Churchill was Mr. M'Kenna's pet aversion, for Mr. Churchill had supplanted him at the Admiralty. He was, therefore, not in a mood to extricate his supplanter from his troubles. Whatever happened at this interview, the impulsive old sailor left for Scotland that night, his departure producing an inevitable crisis, for political circles in London were seething with disquieting rumours, and there was a general feeling that things were being muddled badly and that the War was therefore not going well for us. The next I heard of the matter was when I saw Mr. M'Kenna that afternoon. Lord Fisher had reported to him the conversation he had with me. Mr. M'Kenna said that the " old boy " was quite obdurate and was not open to persuasion.

The following Monday morning Mr. Bonar Law, who had for years been a personal friend of mine and on terms of greater cordiality with me than is usual between political adversaries who are taking a strenuous part in party conflicts, came to see me at the Treasury.

Informing me that he had received a communication which seemed to him authentic indicating that Lord Fisher had resigned, he asked me point-blank if that were the case. He alluded to an unsigned letter received by him which had obviously been written by the First Sea Lord. Lord Fisher's characters and style were so dashing and on so bold a scale that no one could fail to know at a glance who had written a letter of his. The signature was superfluous.

On being told by me that his information was correct Mr. Bonar Law emphasised the grave nature of the political question raised, especially as he was convinced that the Government were misinformed about the shell situation. His party had supported the Government consistently throughout the months of the War, without seeking party advantage, but there was a growing discontent amongst Conservatives at this attitude of unqualified support, especially over the treatment of alien enemies, the deficiency of shells, and the failure of the Dardanelles expedition. Matters indeed, had come to such a pitch that it would be impossible for him to restrain his followers, and yet it was essential to avoid any division in the nation in face of the enemy. He was specially emphatic as to the impossibility of allowing Mr. Churchill to remain at the Admiralty if Lord Fisher persisted in his resignation. On this point he made it clear that the Opposition meant at all hazards to force a Parliamentary challenge. After some discussion we agreed that the only certain way to preserve a united front was to arrange for more complete co-operation between parties in the direction of the War. I asked him if he would wait a few minutes while I went to No. 10 to see the Prime Minister. I went alone to see Mr. Asquith and put the circumstances quite plainly before him. The Prime Minister at once recognised that in order to avert a serious Parliamentary conflict, which would certainly lower the prestige of the Government, if it did not actually bring about its defeat, it was necessary to reconstruct the Cabinet and admit into it some of the leaders of the Unionist Party.

This decision took an incredibly short time. I left Mr. Asquith and returned to Mr. Bonar Law and invited him to accompany me to the Cabinet Room to talk things over with the Prime Minister. In less than a quarter of an hour we realised that the Liberal Government was at an end and that for it would be substituted a Coalition Government. It was decided that Mr. Bonar Law should write a letter to the Prime Minister explaining the position in order to enable the latter to sound his leading colleagues.

Later in the day I received the following letter from Mr. Bonar Law. The enclosure fairly represented the attitude he adopted in the morning conversations, first with me and then with the Prime Minister.

"Lansdowne House,
Berkeley Square, W.
17th May, 1915.

Dear Lloyd George,

I enclose copy of the letter.

You will see we have altered it to the extent that we do not definitely offer Coalition but the substance is the same.

Yours sincerely,
A. BONAR LAW."

"Lansdowne House,
17th May, 1915.

Dear Mr. Asquith,

Lord Lansdowne and I have learnt with dismay that Lord Fisher has resigned, and we have come to the conclusion that we cannot allow the House to adjourn until this fact has been made known and discussed.

We think that the time has come when we ought to have a clear statement from you as to the policy which the Government intend to pursue. In our opinion things cannot go on as they are, and some change in the constitution of the Government seems to us inevitable if it is to retain a sufficient measure of public confidence to conduct the War to a successful conclusion.

The situation in Italy makes it particularly undesirable to have anything in the nature of a controversial discussion in the House of Commons at present, and if you are prepared to take the necessary steps to secure the object which I have indicated, and if Lord Fisher's resignation is in the meantime postponed, we shall be ready to keep silence now. Otherwise I must to-day ask you whether Lord Fisher has resigned, and press for a day to discuss the situation arising out of his resignation.

Yours, etc.,
A. BONAR LAW."

The story of the formation of the new Ministry has been told from different angles by many writers great and petty. The actual appointments were a subject of something which in business might be termed haggling between the parties. The worst controversy came over Lord Haldane and Mr. M'Kenna. The Conservatives had taken a fierce dislike to both on quite unreasonable grounds, and were bent on leaving them out. They were both personal friends of the Prime Minister—his friendship with Lord Haldane being of very long standing. What was the offence of these special objects of Conservative animosity? Lord Haldane was the originator and organiser of the Expeditionary Force, which had served the Allies so promptly and so effectively. It was a fine piece of organisation. He was the creator of the General Staff, which might have saved us many a tragic error had it not been practically dismantled by Lord Kitchener. The Officers' Training Corps, which equipped the new armies with a splendid team of young lieutenants, was also his idea. But in one of those philosophic dissertations which gave him and his friends equal pleasure he had referred to Germany as his "spiritual home." That was an *ex post facto* crime for which he must be banished from the sight of all patriotic men. There was also a rooted conviction in the Unionist mind that Lord Haldane, after his visit to Berlin, had failed to warn the Cabinet as to the German preparations for war which he must have observed. All these criticisms were in my judgment fundamentally unjust, and inflicted a deep wrong on a man whose patriotic energy had rendered greater service to the nation in the reorganisation of the Army than any War Secretary since the days of Cardwell. However, temper was bitter and unconscionable on this subject, and Mr. Asquith and Sir Edward Grey sacrificed friendship to expediency.

Mr. M'Kenna's crime, as I have already explained, was that in his administration at the Home Office he had been too tender to aliens. And in days when a rush-light at a farm building on the coast became a signal to the enemy the Home Office indulgence to alien enemies dwelling within our gates was considered to be treason. So he also must go. Mr. Asquith saved him and sacrificed Haldane. Lord Haldane was not qualified to fight a personal battle for himself. Mr. M'Kenna was. So Lord Haldane was driven in disgrace into the wilderness and Mr. M'Kenna was promoted to the second place in the Government.

Meanwhile, on the same day the subject of munitions was debated in the House of Commons, where, as a member put it, the one word impressed on the hearts of most members would be "Shells." Arguments were put forward for the formation of a Coalition Cabinet, and the Government were pressed to have a debate on the whole subject of munitions. This was refused by Mr. Asquith. The next day, in the House of Lords, Lord Kitchener admitted the delay in producing the material which it had been foreseen would be required, and attributed it to the unprecedented and almost unlimited calls on the manufacturing resources of the country. On the 19th, the Prime Minister announced to the House that steps were in contemplation which would involve the "reconstruction of the Government on a broader personal and political basis." In other words, he had been persuaded by the general discontent with the conduct of the War shown on all sides to form the first Coalition Government. On the same day I again wrote to Mr. Asquith who had been responsible for my appointment as Chairman of the Cabinet Munitions Committee, a letter on the subject of munitions, which has already been recorded in an earlier section of this narrative. I was anxious that the munitions situation should be recognised as an essential part of the problems which the new Coalition would have to face at the outset of its existence. I did not think it was in the national interest that it should be submerged in controversies about the Dardanelles or the treatment of aliens.

As the whole political situation was in the melting pot, I decided to postpone for a few days a tour I had contemplated making round some of the centres of munition production in order to address the workers. On the 21st some of the Ministers and the leaders of the Opposition met in conclave at Downing Street in what was really the first joint meeting of the new combination. The main subject of our deliberations for that meeting and for almost all the rest of the week was the composition of the new Government. It was only settled at a late hour on the 25th. The task was a difficult one, for it entailed much consideration of the balancing of parties, as well as of personal claims inside the parties.

Mr. Asquith honoured me with his particular confidence during these discussions. The appointments took up valuable time, but at last they were concluded. The most notable change was the taking of Mr. Winston Churchill out of the Admiralty and placing him in charge of the Duchy of Lancaster, a post generally reserved either for beginners in the Cabinet or for distinguished politicians who had reached the first stages of unmistakable decrepitude. It was a cruel and unjust degradation. The Dardanelles failure was due not so much to Mr. Churchill's precipitancy as to Lord Kitchener's and Mr. Asquith's procrastination. Mr. Churchill's part in that unfortunate enterprise had been worked out by him with the most meticulous care to the last particular, and nothing had been overlooked or neglected as far as the naval operations were concerned. The fatal delays and mishandlings had all been in the other branch of the Service. It is true that the conception of a one-sided Naval operation without simultaneous military action was due to Mr. Churchill's impetuosity, but both the Prime Minister and Lord Kitchener were equally convinced that it was the right course to pursue. When I learned the office finally offered to Mr. Churchill, it came to me as an unpleasant surprise. I reckoned it would have been impossible to keep him at the Admiralty, in view of the dispute which had precipitated the crisis. The Unionists would not, and could not in the circumstances, have assented to his retention in that office. But it was quite unnecessary in order to propitiate them to fling him from the masthead, whence he had been directing the fire, down to the lower deck to polish the brass. In the first sorting out and allotment of offices in which I had taken part, it had been arranged that he should be placed in the Colonial Office, where his energies would have been helpfully employed in organising our resources in the Empire beyond the seas; and I cannot to this hour explain the change of plans which suddenly occurred. The brutality

10. Downing Street.
Whitehall. S.W.

Tu. 25 May 1915

My dear Lloyd George,

I cannot let this
troubled & tumultuous chapter
is on its long close without
trying to let you know
what an incalculable help
& support I have found in
you all through. I shall
never forget your
devotion, your unselfishness,
your power of resource. What

is (after all) the best of all
things from self-forgetfulness.

These are the rare things that
make the drudgery and squalor
of politics, with its constant
revelations of the large part
played by petty & personal
motives, endurable, and
give to its drabness a lightening
streak of nobility

I thank you with all my
heart

Always your affecte

H. H. Asquith

May, 1915, by Mr. Asquith to Mr. Lloyd George.

of the fall stunned Mr. Churchill, and for a year or two of the War his fine brain was of no avail in helping in its prosecution.

Apart from the appointment of individuals, one of the most important decisions reached, and one which concerned me most particularly was that taken to form a separate department under a Minister of Cabinet rank, to undertake the difficult and complicated work of mobilising the national resources for the production of munitions, and so to relieve the executive military authorities from a duty which had grown far too heavy to be carried out by them. Since I had consistently taken a great interest in the subject, had shown by every means in my power the importance I attached to it, and had been the head of the Cabinet Committee dealing with it, the Prime Minister invited me to take charge of the new Ministry of Munitions.

On 26th May, 1915, the names of the first Coalition Cabinet were published, and the following announcement appeared in the Press:

"The Prime Minister has decided that a new department shall be created, to be called the Ministry of Munitions, charged with organising the supply of munitions of war. Mr. Lloyd George has undertaken the formation and temporary direction of this department, and during his tenure of office as Minister of Munitions will vacate the office of Chancellor of the Exchequer."

The change in the Government had taken place; the Coalition was formed, and the War Council reorganised under the title of the Dardanelles Committee, which more accurately described its scope. Owing to the general upheaval occasioned by the political change, the newly formed Committee did not actually meet until the 7th June, or three weeks after the last session of the body it superseded. In fact, at this stage, when both in the east and west there were urgent questions awaiting decision, those especially charged with the control of our war policy met only once during a period of nearly nine weeks. So fully occupied was I in organising the new Ministry of Munitions, that for a time I was personally unable to pay as much attention as I had done to the general conduct of the War, and did not, during June, attend any of the sittings of the new Committee.

CHAPTER IX

THE MINISTRY OF MUNITIONS:
ESTABLISHMENT AND LABOUR PROBLEMS

1. MY APPOINTMENT

It was on Whit-Monday, 1915, that I finally left the Treasury to take up my duty as Minister of Munitions. It was a serious decision for me to make. As Chancellor of the Exchequer I had been holding the highest and most responsible office under the Prime Minister—the post which ranked next to his in Parliamentary importance, and in that position had been initiating and carrying through schemes of social amelioration which were very congenial to my disposition and upbringing. I was exchanging all that for the terrible task of manufacturing engines for human mutilation and slaughter.

Whatever I had done directly or indirectly to hasten or assist in the creation of this department, which I regarded as most urgently necessary, the last thing I desired was to have to assume control of it. I had no wish to give up the Chancellorship of the Exchequer for something of an unknown nature. I cannot say that I undertook the functions of my new office with any feelings of exhilarate confidence. I was taking in hand the organisation of a business that was quite new to me. The only insight given me into its workings had revealed a state of utter confusion and chaos. I was leaving a well-established and well-organised department, staffed by some of the picked men of the Civil Service, and directed in all its ramifications by well-defined rules and traditions which worked with perfect smoothness. I was taking in hand a department with no staff, no regulations, no traditions. All new departments are viewed with a certain measure of suspicion by the older establishments. But the department which mattered most to the success of the new Ministry regarded it not only with distrust but with profound dislike, veiled behind a mask of contempt. Its very existence was a statutory expression of a national verdict of failure delivered by the High Court of Parliament against the War Office. It was cut out of the living body of the War Office, and that hurt. There is no historical testimony as to Adam's sensations after the rib had been torn out of his side. But he must have felt sore and resentful. In his case, however, the knowledge

that by the operation he had secured a helpmate more than reconciled him to the excision. The War Office was surly, suspicious, and
hostile, and no help the new Ministry tendered or gave softened the
animosity of the War Lords towards it. Although Lord Kitchener
personally treated me with every courtesy, his entourage were
unsympathetic to the new venture, and later on he was stimulated by
the hostility of his own and other departments to acquiesce in the
erection of barriers in my way. This antagonism was one of the
difficulties I foresaw and certainly endured.

Politically it was for me a wilderness of risks with no oasis in sight.
There were numerous possibilities of serious conflict with organised
labour over trade union regulations, hours of labour, wages, restrictions on modility, and, most serious of all, over what I called dilution,
i.e. the mixing of the skilled labour with unskilled. Here you
touched one of the most sensitive nerves of trade unionism. The
question of drink had to be tackled, foreboding quarrels with a
powerful trade in England and Wales, Scotland and Ireland. No
wonder my old uncle and foster-father, Richard Lloyd, whose advice
I was wont to listen to above all others, wrote to me and counselled
me not to leave the Treasury. Yet in spite of all this, I felt as I
reviewed all the circumstances of the national situation, and realised
beyond a shadow of doubt the supreme and vital importance of a
proper supply of munitions for our success in the war, and
remembered the insistence with which I had urged this upon the
Government, that I was in honour bound to accept if the Prime
Minister thought I was the man best fitted for this post. I made my
decision; and I never had cause to regret it. As I look back to-day
upon the problems which were then presented to me, the extraordinary difficulties that surrounded the work which I took in hand, my
own inexperience in that kind of work, the chaos and tangle with
which I was confronted, I feel that in many ways the creation of the
Ministry of Munitions was the most formidable task I ever
undertook.

I was heartened to face the overwhelming responsibility of this
step by a letter which I received at the time from Mr. Asquith. It
ran as follows: —

" 10, Downing Street, S.W.
25th May, 1915.

My dear Lloyd George,
    I cannot let this troubled and tumultuous chapter in our history
pass without letting you know what incalculable help and support
I have found in you all through. I shall never forget your devotion,
your unselfishness, your powers of resource, and what is (after all)
the best of things, your self-forgetfulness.

These are the rare things which make the squalor and drudgery
of politics, with its constant revelations of the large part played by

petty and personal motives, endurable, and give to this drabness the lightning streak of nobility.

I thank you with all my heart,

Always yours affectionately,

H. H. ASQUITH."

This letter from the man who had been my colleague for ten years, and to whom I had been principal Parliamentary lieutenant for seven years, gave me great delight. The black squad of envy had not yet succeeded in poisoning the wells of confidence between captain and second officer.

I received further encouragement from many quarters from friends near and far who wished me well and realised the terrific responsibility of my new venture. Amongst the letters which came to me was one which I specially prized for its understanding and sincerity from a great American statesman whose vision and superb courage I had always admired—Theodore Roosevelt.

" Oyster Bay,

Long Island, N.Y.

1st June, 1915.

My dear Lloyd George,

In a sense it is not my affair, but as one of your admirers and sympathisers I wish to congratulate you upon the action that has been taken in getting a Coalition Cabinet, and especially upon your part therein. More than all I wish to congratulate you upon what you have done in connection with this War. When the War is over, you will again take up the work of dealing with the Labour question, with Irish Home Rule, with many other matters. But the prime business at present for you to do is to save your country; and I admire the single-hearted manner with which you have devoted yourself to this great duty. I am sorry Redmond could not see his way to take office also, but, of course, there may have been reasons of which I know nothing that made it inadvisable for him to do so.

Give my regards to Edward Grey,

Faithfully yours,

THEODORE ROOSEVELT."

The contiguity of these three famous names—Roosevelt, Asquith and Grey—reminds me how, shortly before the War, I met the former at a luncheon party given by Sir Edward Grey to Mr. Roosevelt when Mr. Asquith and I were the only other guests. Mr. Roosevelt was not the type of man who would attract Mr. Asquith. His vehemence repelled the unexcitable Englishman. Asquith was a man of refractory prejudices which he never concealed. This gave a certain arrogance to his manner when dealing with men he did not care for. It was obvious during the table talk that Mr. Asquith had an instinctive dislike, which was not far removed from contempt, for the dynamic American. The Prime Minister made no allowance for the real greatness of the man. He was irritated by his mannerisms. Roosevelt flung out commonplaces with the same forceful and portentous emphasis as he uttered truths which showed penetration and breadth of judgment. The more stale the platitude the greater the emphasis. This kind of conversation always annoyed the British Premier and gave a note of supercilious derision to his mien and voice. Roosevelt felt it and gradually his torrential flow of sense and sentiment dried up. The meal was hardly a success.

The Royal Warrant formally appointing me Minister of Munitions was not actually issued until 9th June, the day on which the Ministry of Munitions Act became law. But without waiting for this I had begun immediately to set about the organisation of the new department.

The quarters allotted to the Ministry were at No. 6, Whitehall Gardens—a pleasant, old-fashioned house, just off Whitehall, not at all designed for office purposes. It had been vacated a short time before by that well-known art dealer, Mr. Lockett Agnew. It was more suitable for the residence of a man of artistic proclivities than for the head office of a manufacturer.

I went there with my two secretaries, and found that before I could even start to build up a new Ministry it was necessary to provide at least the bare requirements of an office. My first encounter with red tape was characteristic of the action of this departmental bindweed.

The sole articles of furniture in the office of the new department were two tables and a chair. My secretaries gave urgent orders for an adequate supply of furniture, but before this had been delivered, a squad from the Office of Works appeared on the scene to take away the little we had, on the ground that it did not belong to the new department and therefore must be removed. They were ultimately prevailed upon to be merciful, and until the new equipment arrived, I was allowed one table to write upon and one chair to sit at the said table.

This is Colonel House's description of his visit to me at this time:

"This was, I believe, George's first day as Minister of Munitions in his new Whitehall quarters. There was no furniture in the room except a table and one chair. He insisted upon me taking the chair, which I declined to do, declaring that a seat on the table was more suitable for me than for a Cabinet official.

He spoke again and again of 'military red tape,' which he declared he would cut out as speedily as possible. He was full of energy and enthusiasm, and I feel certain something will soon happen in his department. He reminds me more of the virile, aggressive type of American politician than any member of the Cabinet. . . . He has something dynamic within him which his colleagues have not and which is badly needed in this great hour. . . ."

Red tape, then, was worsted in its first round—the only casualties being a temporary general inconvenience. I retained my table and chair against all rules and orders until a reasonable consignment of suitable furniture was allocated to me. I was soon to find that this was not a serious attack but a reconnaissance to investigate and to rattle. Later on red tape resorted to all the devices in its well-stocked armoury to delay, impede and thwart. A more formidable and unexpected antagonist next appeared in the person of human vanity. My room was an old Adam drawing-room, where every panel glittered with long pier-glasses. They no doubt would be an essential accessory to a hairdresser's or haberdasher's trade, but I found them fatal to the transaction of business in armaments. When callers came in I noticed that their eyes wandered from my direction, and that their minds soon followed the rambling gaze. I realised the cause of this distraction. The glistening mirrors reflected the face and figure of my interviewers from every angle. This was too much for the most hard-faced business man. I do not pretend to be above the ordinary human weakness in this respect, but a day's contemplation of a countenance full of anxiety and dubiety more than satisfied my own appetite. I ordered the glasses to be covered over. Difficulty number two was thus blotted out.

I sat in my bare room to survey my problem. What was it? On the one hand I had to envisage all the wide range of activity covered by the supply of munitions—the innumerable requirements of the Army in the field, and the multiplicity of different materials, processes, and co-ordinations necessary to produce those goods; and on the other I had to inform myself as to the available resources of material, machinery and labour, here and abroad, for supplying those requirements. I had to ascertain the existing state and organisation of production of munitions under War Office direction. The whole field had to be plotted out and suitable men selected to take charge of each section of it.

First came the creation of a staff. The Ministry of Munitions was from first to last a business-man organisation. Its most distinctive feature was the appointment I made of successful business men to the chief executive posts. On 14th June, 1915, I announced in the House of Commons my intention of utilising, as far as possible, the " business brains of the community . . . some of them at my elbow in London, to advise, to counsel, to guide, to inform, to instruct, and to direct," others " in the localities, to organise for us, to undertake the business in each particular locality on our behalf." The first position in every department was entrusted by me to one of these distinguished captains of industry, to whom I gave authority and personal support that enabled them to break through much of the routine and aloofness which characterised the normal administration of Government contracts. I had no office staff except my two able Private Secretaries, Mr. J. T. Davies (now Sir John T. Davies) and Miss F. L. Stevenson, both of whom accompanied me from the Treasury. Miss Stevenson was the first woman secretary appointed by a Minister. The precedent, I see, has since been followed by most Ministers and heads of departments. Later on Mr. (now Sir) William Sutherland volunteered to assist when the correspondence and the interviews overwhelmed my small staff. He was an experienced Civil Servant, and a man of outstanding abilities. During the troublous times which were in store for me his shrewdness and vision served to help me to avoid many a hidden political trap. The Labour Department of the Board of Trade offered to assist in supervising and directing my arrangements with Labour. For this I was profoundly grateful. The Ordnance Department had little to spare me in the way of staff. For this also I was equally grateful. The War Office placed Sir Percy Girouard at my disposal. Of him I shall have something to say later on. But the men who were to organise and drive the production of guns, rifles, machine-guns, shell, and trench mortars were still to be found. What kind should I look for? I received hundreds of letters from " push-and-goes " and their admiring friends. I had a large number of genuine offers from Company Directors, who offered to place at my service the temporary assistance of managers in whose capacity they had acquired confidence. I had first of all to decide in my own mind the type of man I needed for the highest posts. Sir Eric Geddes told me that when he came to visit me at my new department it seemed to him that I was pulling names out of a hat and distributing them to the different jobs that waited to be done; but I am afraid the task of putting suitable men to departments could not be carried out quite so simply as that.

I knew that upon my success or failure in attracting the right sort of man and placing him in the right sort of place depended the efficiency of the new department and its chances of achieving its purpose. It was not sufficient to peruse testimonials or letters of recommendation—not even honest ones—testifying to the efficiency shown by men in the perfectly organised branches where they had served, and which they were prepared temporarily to quit in order to serve the State. Here each man would be called upon to build up a business of which he knew nothing, and do it better than experts who had been trained and spent their professional lives in that line of activity. The most difficult task was to choose wisely between two types of successful business men. The failures were easily spotted and eliminated. The knowledgeable men who knew all about the subject, but did not possess the essential gift of translating their knowledge into effective action, constituted the most dangerous trap, but it was discernible by judicious inquiry as to antecedents, and could then be evaded. But those who have made a success in their business careers can be divided into two classes. There is the careful and cautious man who has a complete mastery of all the details of his trade and attends to them steadily and assiduously. By this means he gradually builds up a business, or if he has acquired control of an already established concern keeps it going and slowly extends it. He does not command those gifts of intuition, rapid decision, and force which enable an improviser to create and hustle along a gigantic new enterprise, and certainly not with material of which he has no previous experience. He is useful in a secondary position, but as an initiator he would be a disappointment if not a disaster. The great improvisers who constitute the second class are rare men anywhere, but in an emergency their value to a country is beyond price, and these were the men I needed for first place. In any great crisis, time is a determining factor, and these men save the days, weeks and months which make the difference between victory and defeat. In selecting the leading hustlers I had to bear all these considerations in mind.

I cannot claim that my first choices were always the best. They were, I think, the best available at the time. I found that some were admirable workers provided they were under the control and direction of others, but not equal to the responsibility of a supreme position. It was then that I realised thoroughly for the first time that men ought to be marked like army lorries with their carrying capacity: " Not to carry more than three tons." The three-tonners are perfect so long as you do not overload them with burdens for which they are not constructed by Providence. I have seen that happen in Law and Politics. The barrister who acquired a great practice as a junior and failed completely when he took silk; the politician who showed great promise as an Under-Secretary and achieved nothing when promoted to the headship of a department. As I went along I discovered that one or two first-rate men were better suited for duties inside the department other than those for which I had originally chosen them.

During the War the neglect of this maxim was a fruitful source of our disasters; the excellent Brigadier who was promoted to a corps and the successful Corps Commander who was given an army, neither of them being equal to the higher responsibility cast upon them. In the Navy also there are many such illustrations of dashing captains who were lifted above their capabilities. However, with all able misfits, I shifted them about and found substitutes. But in the quality of the men themselves I was never disappointed, for when they found the post that suited them best they proved themselves to be first rate. Men who did not seem to fit into the functions originally designated for them became quite indispensable in equally responsible positions where they were finally placed. And some of them were promoted from tasks where they were rendering conspicuous service to other more important positions where their compelling powers were more urgently needed.

No more remarkable collection of men was ever gathered together under the same roof. Between them they had touched the industrial life of the country and of the Empire at every point. To use a current phrase " All the means of production, distribution, and exchange " were aggregately at their command.

One of the first to tender his services was Sir Eric Geddes. He came from the North-Eastern Railway, and he had the make of one of their powerful locomotives. That is the impression he gave me when one morning he rolled into my room. He struck me immediately as a man of exceptional force and capacity. I knew that he was a find, and I was grateful to Lord Knaresborough, the chairman of the company, for offering to release him during the period of the War. He turned out to be one of the most remarkable men which the State called to its aid in this anxious hour for Britain and her Empire. He will appear again and again in my story of the War.

There was also Sir Ernest Moir, who had constructed some of our finest docks and harbours, a man of exceptional ability and tact. Sir Frederick T. Hopkinson, a man of similar experience, came to our aid. There was Sir Hubert Llewellyn Smith. When I first met him at the Board of Trade in 1906 I considered him to be the most resourceful and suggestive mind in the whole of our Civil Service at that time—and withal a man whose long service at the Board of Trade had brought him intelligently into direct contact with every branch of commerce and industry throughout the world. There was Sir John Hunter, who had directed the construction of our largest and most famous bridge. There were Sir Hardman Lever and Sir John Mann, two of the ablest accountants in this country. There were expert financiers like Sir Alexander Roger, who turned out to be an energetic and efficient organiser. The iron and steel industry lent us of the very best. The armament firms placed at our disposal not only Sir Percy Girouard, but Sir Glyn West, who had a much longer practical experience of the actual processes of gun making. We also had Sir Charles Ellis, whose suave and attractive personality served us so well in the handling of this collection of men of clashing temperaments. There was James Stevenson (afterwards Lord Stevenson), whose experience in organising throughout the country business dealings in a famous brand of Scotch whisky was voluntarily transferred to the business of organising in the provinces the activities of an even more potent spirit—that of patriotism. With Sir Hubert Llewellyn Smith there was Mr. Beveridge (now Sir William Beveridge), a man who was credited with an unrivalled knowledge of labour problems. In the organisation of the welfare branch of our new factories we had the valuable direction of Mr. Seebohm Rowntree, who is not only a highly successful man of business, but a student of social conditions of world-wide fame. Coal gave us the dynamic personality of Sir L. W. Llewellyn. The railways lent us not only Sir Eric Geddes, but Sir Henry Fowler and Sir Ralph Wedgwood. There was Sir Arthur Duckham, one of the ablest engineers in the land—a man of unusual capacity and attainments. The publishing world gave us Sir Edward Iliffe, who carried out with remarkable success the vital task of organising machine tool production. Shipping was represented by Sir George Booth, a member of the well-known firm of Booth Brothers. Though known, as I have said, as the man of " push-and-go," he was neither, but he had other invaluable qualities. He was rather a conciliator than a compeller. I found his tact and geniality invaluable in a Ministry of energetic talents. And through the portals of the Board of Trade there wafted into this Ministry of solid and material industrialism a breeze from the foothills of Parnassus in the person of Mr. Umberto Wolff. The statistician of the Ministry of Munitions is now one of the most eminent economists in the world —Sir Walter Layton. The Parliamentary Under-Secretary, Dr. Addison, was a man with a high order of intellectual capacity, full of ideas, resourcefulness and courage. My military secretary, whom I designed as liaison officer with the War Office, was Sir Ivor Philipps, an experienced soldier and a good business man. The Explosives Department gave me that eminent judge, Lord Fletcher Moulton. He was one of the subtlest brains in England. As usually happens his subtlety caused distrust and misunderstanding amongst blunter minds. He was not only one of the greatest lawyers of his day, he was also a man of distinguished scientific attainments. When he placed his great gifts at the disposal of the War Office for the solution of the new problems created by the unprecedented demand for explosives, he rendered service of incalculable value to the country. Of such were the personal components of this strange Ministry. If not a Ministry of all the talents it was undoubtedly a Ministry of all the industries—war and peace, production, transport, law, medicine, science, the Civil Service, politics, and poetry—and all at their best. It was a wonderful array of talent. It was a formidable battery of dynamic energy. But I saw that unless firmly controlled and carefully watched there would be constant explosions which would make the whole machine unworkable. At first I placed Sir Percy Girouard in charge as chief engineer of the concern. He was an out-and-out Kitchener man. He had worked with and for him in Egypt. When the War broke out and Lord Kitchener took charge, Sir Percy was taken out of Armstrong's and put in charge of part of the munition organisation at the War Office. He was delivered over to me with the munitions problem.

Sir Percy Girouard had a great reputation, honourably won by distinguished engineering achievements in our Colonial Empire. He was a man of great natural gifts and accomplishments, and he was credited with possessing a resourcefulness which approximated to the genius of purposeful action. In addition to that he was a man of considerable charm, with a pleasant sense of humour fortified by much interesting and entertaining reminiscence. I discovered that he had a gift of persuasive speech which was invaluable at the meetings we held in London and in the provinces to stimulate co-operation. Although he was primarily a railway man and his success had been achieved in that sphere, his association with Armstrong's had furnished him with experience in the manufacture of every kind of munition of war. But I soon discovered that he suffered from the same drawback as his old chief, Lord Kitchener. They had both spent their exceptional physical reserves in hard work under climatic conditions which are not congenial to men born and bred in a temperate clime. His stock of vitality had been burnt out in great tasks driven through under tropical suns—the vivid spirit was still there and the habits and movements of an old energy were also visible, but these took the form of an unsettling restlessness rather than that of a steady activity. He dashed about from the War Office to the Ministry and back from the Ministry to the War Office, where he spent most of his time, to and from one department after another attending to no detail of any kind in any of them. When he came to see me he was always in such a hurry that he never sat down. He rushed into my room like a man who was chased by a problem and could not stay too long lest it caught him up.

He had one curious mannerism. I observed that when I pressed him with inconvenient questions of detail as to the progress made, he seemed to hide behind his eyeglass, and I could get no farther. From him I learnt less than nothing of what the various departments of the Ministry were doing, for such information as he acquired he gleaned from the War Office, and it was, therefore, misleading. All this feverish bustle gave the impression of a propelling eagerness to urge everybody along, but I soon discovered that it was the symptom of a spent nervous system. Reluctantly I felt he had no longer the steady nerve and the calm industry which are essential in the chief organiser of a new department where there were so many men quite new to the tasks entrusted to their charge, and I felt that a man of a totally different calibre would be more useful. So we parted company.

His place was not filled. I soon realised that all the hustling that was necessary would have to be done by myself, with the aid of the energetic departmental chiefs whom I had chosen.

Describing these appointments in a speech in the House of Commons on 29th July, 1915, when I was reporting progress on the arrangements of the new Ministry, I said: —

"We have had practically to create a new staff. That is a very difficult undertaking if you have to do it immediately, because, obviously, everything depends upon the staff and the men you select. And under ordinary conditions you would take a very long time to choose your instruments. You cannot do that when you are engaged in emergency work. Fortunately we have had placed at our disposal the services of very considerable men in the business world—men of wide experience, men, some of them, who are in charge of very considerable undertakings. They have placed their services voluntarily at the disposal of the Minister of Munitions, and are rendering excellent services each in his own department. I think I can say that there are at least 90 men of first-class business experience who have placed their services voluntarily at the disposal of the Ministry of Munitions, the vast majority of them without any remuneration at all. [Cheers.] Some of them were managers of very great concerns, and the firms with which they were connected are in most, if not in all, cases paying them salaries which the State could not afford to pay. These men are exceedingly helpful; in fact, without their help it would have been quite impossible to have improvised a great department on the scale on which this department necessarily had to be organised and arranged."

After going as thoroughly into the actual munition position as the time and information at my disposal would permit, there were visible a few outstanding and dominant facts: —

(1) The War Office had not made any thorough survey of its needs on the assumption that the British Army was to develop into a gigantic force of at least 70 divisions, that its task would necessitate breaking through formidable double and often multiple lines of entrenchments, defended by masses of artillery, heavy as well as light, and thousands of machine-guns, and that this operation would be a prolonged one. It had not, for instance, come to any final decision as to the number and calibre of the guns which would be required for this purpose. The quantity and type of the guns ordered were both obviously inadequate to the undertaking in front of it. Nor had it calculated the number of machine-guns required for so great a force.

(2) Until the number and especially the size of the guns had been decided no one could be expected to compute the numbers and sizes of the shells required.

(3) There had been no computation made of the number of machine-guns required for an army fighting under modern conditions.

(4) There had been no survey of the capacity of this country or America to produce the number of guns, shells, machine-guns, and rifles needed. It was found later on, when the programme was settled, that we did not possess in Britain and could not purchase in the States the necessary machine tools to execute the agreed programme. We had to make a start with manufacture of those tools before we began on the extra guns, etc.

(5) The War Office had instituted no inquiry into our capacity for filling shells with explosives. Investigation by the new Ministry revealed the facts (a) that our capacity in this respect was not more than one-tenth of the need; and (b) that even if we had the necessary filling appliances, we possessed only a small proportion of the explosive hitherto used. We therefore had to encourage experiments to be made in order to find other equally effective explosives, and to provide a different set of appliances to suit the result of these experiments.

It horrifies me to imagine what would have happened if this state of things had been allowed to go on for a few more months without any perception of its existence, and therefore without any attempt at amendment. What if all Ministers had retained complete confidence in the military direction of the War? The sensitiveness of the War Office to any suggestion that established methods were not the best and the repression of civilian inquisitiveness as to these methods or their results might have postponed discovery of this fatal neglect until it was too late to set them right. Even with all the strenuous endeavour put by some of the ablest business and scientific heads in the country into survey, investigation, consultation and construction, with a view to ascertain needs, defects and remedies, and then to drive through to production, we were only just able to fulfil the requirements of the Army for the summer campaign of 1916. It is such an incredible story of lack of forethought and intelligent inquiry that it is necessary to give more detailed and documented information on these vital points. That I propose to do later on in the course of my narrative. The tale has its lessons for every form of bureaucratic enterprise. It also contains its warning to those who heedlessly lead nations towards war. They should understand something of the risk they incur and the precarious character of the gamble into which they are plunging.

The work which fell upon me was by no means wholly of a kind which could be done sitting at a desk. One very urgent problem was to secure the hearty co-operation of employers in converting their factories and workshops to the production of arms. Another was equally vital: the securing of the good will of the workers and their agreement to the further speeding-up of production and the dilution of labour which it would involve. Labour, I knew, would be one of my chief difficulties. So during the first week of June I made a tour of the districts which were the centres of the engineering industry, in order to harness local enthusiasm to munition production in the service of the new Ministry.

At Manchester, Liverpool, Birmingham, Cardiff and Bristol, I met representatives of the chief engineering firms and of the trade unions affected, and urged them to organise local committees to assist in producing munitions of war and to arrange the allocation of contracts between them in such a way as to ensure the maximum output from the engineering works of the district. I stressed the importance of local responsibility and of systematic decentralisation as a means of saving time and red tape, and I appealed to both business men and trade unionists to work together with one will.

I will quote a passage from a speech I delivered at Manchester in order to show the nature of the appeal I made to employers and workers alike: —

"I have only held this office for a few days, it is true. I had some insight before then into the position of things, but what I have seen has convinced me from overwhelming testimony that the nation has not yet concentrated one half of its industrial strength on the problem of carrying this great conflict through successfully. It is a war of munitions. We are fighting against the best-organised community in the world; the best-organised whether for war or peace, and we have been employing too much the haphazard, leisurely, go-as-you-please methods, which, believe me, would not have enabled us to maintain our place as a nation, even in peace, very much longer. The nation now needs all the machinery that is capable of being used for turning out munitions or equipment, all the skill that is available for that purpose, all the industry, all the labour, and all the strength, power, and resource of everyone to the utmost, everything that would help us to overcome our difficulty and supply our shortages. We want to mobilise in such a way as to produce in the shortest space of time the greatest quantity of the best and most efficient war material. That means victory; it means a great saving of national strength and resources, for it shortens the War; it means an enormous saving of life. . . ."

I pointed out why the Government had taken powers under the Defence of the Realm Act to control the workshops of the country, and to insist that Government work—the work of the country—must take precedence over all civil work. I then discussed the relations of the Government with labour. Two things were essential to the efficiency of the new organisation for munitions of war—to increase the mobility of labour and to secure greater subordination in labour to the direction and control of the State. The State must be able to say where and under what conditions it required a man's services. "When the house is on fire, questions of procedure and precedence, of etiquette and time and division of labour must disappear." I added: —

"... I can only say this, that to introduce compulsion as an important element in organising the nation's resources of skilled industry and trade does not necessarily mean conscription in the ordinary sense of the term. Conscription means raising by compulsory methods armies to fight Britain's battles abroad. Even that is a question not of principle but of necessity. If the necessity arose I am certain no man of any party would protest. But pray do not talk about it as if it were anti-democratic. We won and saved our liberties in this land on more than one occasion by compulsory service. France saved the liberty she had won in the great Revolution from the fangs of tyrannical military empires purely by compulsory service. The great Republic of the West won its independence, saved its national existence, by compulsory service. And two of the greatest countries of Europe to-day, France and Italy, are defending their national existence and liberties by means of compulsory service. It has been the greatest weapon in the hands of democracy many a time for the winning and preservation of freedom. . . ."

I appealed to the workmen to give up, for the period of the War, the unwritten rules by which output was limited, and I gave an undertaking that piece rates should not be reduced. In the same way I urged suspension of trade union rules forbidding dilution in order that unskilled men and women might be brought in to make up for the shortage of skilled men. I pointed out that the refusal of unenlisted labour to submit to discipline contrasted strangely with the position of the voluntary army at the front: —

"The enlisted workman cannot choose his locality of action. He cannot say, 'I am quite prepared to fight at Neuve-Chapelle, but I won't fight at Festubert, and I am not going near the place they call "Wipers."' He cannot say, 'I have been in the trenches eight hours and a half, and my trades union won't allow me to work more than eight hours.'"

With special reference to what I expected from Lancashire, I added in my Manchester speech: —

"Lancashire's private works, when they are fully engaged, and after you have mobilised them, can turn out a quarter of a million of high-explosive shells a month. A gentleman near me tells me that you can turn out a lot more. Well, the more the merrier; but we want you to start from that and then work up in the direction of a million."

I quote a Press report of this meeting, because it gives a fair idea of the spirit which commanded all classes to whom I appealed: —

" Manchester, Thursday (June 3).

Lord Derby and the Lancashire men gave a hearty reception to Mr. Lloyd George's speech. . . . Separate munition committees were appointed for three divisions of Lancashire, embracing the whole county. . . . A satisfactory preliminary discussion took place as to the best means of mapping out the work. Mr. Lloyd George had said that he aimed at an output of a quarter of a million shells per month from Lancashire alone, and the reply was a promise of a million a month within a short time.

All this is excellent, but the bitter tragedy is that the organisation was not accomplished six months ago. Manchester masters tell me that, in the past, they have asked the War Office again and again for a statement of what was wanted, only to be put off with a polite acknowledgement or a reference to the Labour Bureau."

On the following day I spoke in similar terms at Liverpool. I repeated my reassurance to the workers about the temporary nature of the relaxations of ordinary rules and practices which they were being asked to accept.

A resolution was carried, pledging those present to do all they could to increase the output of munitions. This resolution was seconded in a significant speech delivered by one of the workmen's representatives. It is worth quoting: —

" Mr. Clarke, a representative of the Amalgamated Society of Engineers, seconded the resolution. He said: ' We have learned now that things are not going so well at the front as we thought they were. Certain newspapers have hidden the truth from us, and have presented too rosy a picture. It was only yesterday when they heard Mr. Lloyd George's speech* that the workmen realised the terrible urgency of the matter. Now that we know, I am sure that there will be no difficulty.' "

Press comment on this speech stated: —

" The general feeling in representative trade union circles in London with regard to Mr. Lloyd George's speech is one of unanimous agreement. One prominent trade unionist said: ' We are delighted with the definiteness of the speech, and only wish it had been given eight months ago. We have been annoyed at the

* My speech at Manchester.

campaign in favour of conscription, because we knew there were hundreds of thousands of men for whom no equipment could be immediately obtained. . . ."

While I was thus engaged in stimulating the organisation of the country for munition production, the Ministry of Munitions Bill was carried through Parliament. This measure set up the new Ministry and gave it its powers. They were laid down as follows in Clause 2 (1) of the Act. I quote that section as it is a good example of the comprehensiveness and elasticity required in legislation for coping with an emergency.

" The Minister of Munitions shall have such administrative powers and duties in relation to the supply of munitions for the present War as may be conferred on him by his Majesty in Council, and his Majesty may also, if he considers it expedient that, in connection with the supply of munitions, any powers or duties of a Government Department or authority, whether conferred by statute or otherwise, should be transferred to, or exercised or performed concurrently by, the Minister of Munitions, by Order in Council make the necessary provision for the purpose, and any Order made in pursuance of this section may include any supplemental provisions which appear necessary for the purpose of giving full effect to the Order."

In other words, the job of the new Ministry—the responsibilities hitherto held by the War Office or Admiralty which it was to take over and the new tasks it was to undertake, were not defined by Act of Parliament, but left to be fixed by Orders in Council, which, without the waste of valuable time involved in Parliamentary procedure, could adopt the power to the need as it arose.

At the outset it was broadly laid down that the new department should be guided by the " general requirements and specific requisitions " of the Army Council. This might have been taken to mean—and indeed, the Army Council did its best to impose such an interpretation—that the Ministry was no more than a Supply Department unable to exercise any initiative and only empowered to act on programmes and orders transmitted to it from the military authorities. Fortunately, however, the Order in Council defining my functions was more explicit. It set out that my duty was:—

" to ensure such supply of munitions for the Present War as may be required by the Army Council or the Admiralty, *or may otherwise be found necessary.*"

This final saving clause which I have italicised, gave me authority, of which I made full and industrious use, to acquaint myself directly with the needs present and future of the Army and make plans to meet them. Had I been limited by the shortsighted vision of the Army Council we should have continued to be in arrears with supplies to the end of the War.

On this matter I am tempted to quote an extract from the official history of the Ministry of Munitions. This book was written years after I had left the Ministry. I had no responsibility for its preparation, and as a matter of fact was not consulted as to any part of its contents. Referring to the interpretation I placed upon my functions at the Ministry, it says: —

"This wide view of his position and responsibilities is reflected throughout his career as Minister of Munitions, and his vision of the character and probable length of the conflict that lay ahead not only had a profound effect on the munitions programmes actually adopted in his period, but enabled the Ministry to meet much larger programmes later on. He laid the foundations of the Ministry's productive capacity on a scale so vast that it was almost sufficient—as far as guns, gun ammunition, rifles, machine-guns, and trench warfare supplies were concerned—to carry the country to the end of the War. The great developments undertaken under his successors were principally directed to meet new demands for aircraft, for chemical warfare, and for increased quantities of steel for shipbuilding, motor transport, tanks and railways."

A good deal of play has been made in some quarters with the fact that the new factories organised by the Ministry of Munitions, and the fresh orders for shells which it issued, only began to bear fruit on a large scale by the spring of 1916, and that until that time the bulk of the supplies reaching our armies in the field were in respect of orders given by the War Office before the new Ministry was created.

I have not the slightest desire to claim any unmerited approbation for the Ministry of Munitions, or to rob the War Office of the smallest of its true titles of praise. But in loyalty to the many splendid colleagues who co-operated with me for munitions production, and to the magnificent work they performed, I am bound to point out that this suggestion is ill-founded.

It is true that, partly under pressure from the Cabinet Committee on Munitions, and the Munitions of War Committee, appointed in the spring of 1915, to the activities of both of which I have already referred, the War Office had by the beginning of June, 1915, placed extensive orders at home and abroad for shells. But it was one thing to order, and quite another to ensure delivery. By the 29th May, 1915, out of 5,797,274 shell bodies ordered by the War Office for delivery by or before that date, only 1,968,252 had actually been delivered—this after ten months of war. A more important consideration is the fact that of the shells actually manufactured a comparatively large number were not fitted with fuses and filled with explosive. They were just a collection of harmless steel mugs. The steps taken by the Ministry to reorganise the munitions industry throughout the country and to speed up production during these first seven months of its existence were successful in bringing up the total of deliveries on War Office orders from the two millions at which it stood on 1st June to 14 millions by the end of December, 1915, and for the first time adequate measures were taken to complete these with fuse and explosive.

The failure of the War Office orders to materialise was largely due to its stubborn and stupid adherence to the policy of dealing only with the recognised armament firms, and leaving these firms themselves to organise—or leave unorganised—the rest of the engineering industry in the country. The Ordnance Department could have exercised complete control over the manufacturing resources of the country; powers for that purpose had indeed been thrust upon them by the Defence of the Realm Act which I brought in on 9th March, 1915, but no great use had been made of them. The Ordnance Department was still convinced that it was too risky to entrust the manufacture of munitions to inexperienced firms, and that the only safe course was to give the order to the well-established armament manufacturers, leaving it to them to peddle out the simplest components. As far as American orders were concerned, a departure from this principle was enforced by the Cabinet Committee, although control was impossible and supervision difficult over production in the States. At home, where both supervision and control were practicable, War Office stubbornness was invincible. One of the attributes of small minds is that they resent a change in their accustomed methods merely because it implies a censure on their past record.

So far as the yield of War Office orders was concerned, the difference between the deliveries from August, 1914, to June, 1915, and those from June, 1915, to April, 1916, was due largely to the fact that during the latter period the Ministry of Munitions had taken on the direct organisation of the outside firms and of the labour for munition production, and after August, 1915, had also taken charge of the Government ordnance factories, including the Royal Laboratory at Woolwich, which at that time was still responsible for nearly the whole of the shell filling and completion, and was doing the job by tedious and antiquated pre-War methods. M. Albert Thomas, the French Munition Minister, who visited Woolwich at this date, called it " *une vieille boîte.*"

As I have already indicated, the lack of foresight on the part of the War Office was further shown by its failure to set up a programme authority to study the necessities, possibilities and probabilities of the future—as distinct from the mere tabulation of quantities due on contracts placed. It is necessary that I should develop the full effect of this oversight.

When certain munitions or components had to be manufactured, the Ordnance Department never undertook a careful survey of the reserves of manufacturing capacity available in this country for that purpose and how that capacity could be best utilised for the provision of an adequate supply. Had they done so they would have discovered that in order to exploit these reserves to their full capacity it was necessary to secure certain machine tools, gauges and gadgets, the manufacture of which would occupy several months. The fact that this had not been seen to at the very beginning of the War had not merely wasted the period of ten months which had already elapsed, but the delays involved a further wait of several anxious and fateful months before the process of manufacturing guns, rifles, machine guns and even shells on an adequate scale could be even commenced. A third and in some respects a more disastrous failure was their complete neglect to investigate the explosives problem. They had taken no steps to enlarge their capacity for filling shells even to the limit of the orders which they themselves had already given for shell bodies. In fact, they had not even considered the question of whether there was a sufficient supply available of the explosive material with which these shells were charged to meet even the requirements of their own limited programmes. As I shall point out later on, the War Office had been already warned by Lord Moulton that the available supplies would not be forthcoming in sufficient quantities and that the nature of the explosive would therefore have to be changed. Had this deplorable blunder not been remedied in time, the British Army could not have been equipped in 1916 with a third of the material needful for the operations.

The Ordnance Department administered a prescribed system, and it was passive, if not hostile, where new expedients were concerned. This passivity was shown in the matter of Lord Moulton's request for executive powers in regard to the high explosives in December, 1914; in the proposed extension of his sphere to propellants in the spring of 1915; in the delay in the adoption of newer forms of high explosives, and in the reluctance to approve the Stokes gun. Perhaps the most striking illustration of the limited horizon of the War Office authorities can be found in their refusal (backed, it may be observed, by the Secretary of State) to admit the necessity for the guns which in August, 1915, I ordered in excess of War Office demand. This is an incident with which I deal more fully elsewhere.

Most of the special steps that were taken after the formation of the Ministry of Munitions to stimulate production could equally well have been taken in 1914. It was to those special steps that the greatly accelerated yield on account of outstanding War Office orders in the latter part of 1915, as well as the immense augmentation of output in 1916 on direct orders of the Ministry, was mainly due.

In the month of July the Ministry of Munitions took over from the War Office responsibility for the administration of outstanding contracts. Its work therefore had a dual character. It had, on the one hand, to speed up these existing contracts, consulting closely and co-operating actively with the existing armament firms in order to relieve their difficulties in regard to materials and labour, while on the other hand it was at the same time opening up fresh sources of supply, both by organising outside firms for munition production, and by establishing new Government factories, and securing equipment, labour and materials for their use.

It requires some effort to envisage the wide range of our task. Few people would at the outset imagine how much is covered by the phrase: " Munitions of war," or dream of the colossal ramifications of the industries concerned in their production.

The making of a gun or shell-case, for instance, involves the metal trades, blast-furnaces, steel works, iron and steel foundries, forges, stamps, drops and dies, rolling-mills, drawn rod and wire works—and behind them, the colliery and the iron-ore quarry.

It requires factories, and these in turn require machinery, covered electrical plant, factory equipment and machine tools; engines, pumps, turbines, road and rail transport; boiler-making and constructional engineering work.

The explosives for filling and propelling the shell from the gun involve the output of chemical works, dye works, gas works, and a great deal of very careful laboratory experiment, investigation and testing.

Small arms and ammunition, and all the miscellaneous stores used in trench warfare, involve numerous components all requiring ferrous and non-ferrous metals in manufactured forms, woodwork, textile products, optical glass, vulcanite.

Shells loomed so large in the public eye at the time when the Ministry was formed, that there is a danger of the fact being overlooked that the department became responsible for the production and supply, not only of ammunition and guns, of rifles and machine-guns, but also of mechanical transport, trench warfare stores, optical munitions and glassware, metals and materials, tanks, bombs, poison gas, railway material, machine tools, timber, electrical power, agricultural machinery, mineral oils and building materials.

In place of the War Office method of contracting with a few experienced firms for supplies of finished articles—a method which had worked satisfactorily in peace-time, but had proved quite inadequate to this war—the Ministry of Munitions had to concern itself directly with the production of every raw material and intermediate stage of manufacture of each component in its munitions supplies;

and this in regard to a range and variety of armaments hitherto undreamed of.

2. CENTRAL AND AREA ORGANISATION

When the Ministry of Munitions Act was laid before Parliament at the beginning of June, 1915, the existing bodies for the providing of munitions were three in number, viz.: —

(a) The Munitions Supply Organisation under the War Office, presided over by the Master-General of Ordnance, run almost exclusively by Army Officers, with the addition of one important civilian intruder in the person of Lord Moulton, who had been given a position as chairman of the Committee of High Explosives supply;

(b) The Armaments Output Committee, which Lord Kitchener had set up with Sir Percy Girouard and Mr. G. M. Booth at its head, originally to take up the problem of labour supply, though it had actually made an extremely useful but limited start on the question of area organisation;

(c) The Munitions of War Committee—now virtually defunct, as its Chairman had become Minister of Munitions (designate).

In the course of the month of June most of the supply functions for which General von Donop's department had been responsible were transferred to the Ministry, which also amalgamated with itself the work of the Armaments Output Committee; so that by 1st July, in place of the three bodies I have mentioned, there was now the one Ministry in charge of output and supply. Woolwich Arsenal remained under the Ordnance Department until August, 1915, and responsibility for design and invention until the end of the year.

Four departments were at first set up; Sir Percy Girouard undertook munitions supply; Lord Moulton explosives supply; Brigadier-General L. C. Jackson the Engineers' Munitions Department, and Mr. Beveridge took charge of the Secretariat and the organisation of labour.

Supporting them was an array of the experienced business men I have mentioned. I will not detail the whole of this original organisation, but illustrate its structure along one branch. Sir Percy Girouard, the Director-General of Munitions Supply, had immediately under him nine men, each in charge of a particular job or group of jobs. One of these, Mr. Eric Geddes, held the position of a Deputy Director-General of Munitions Supply. He was set to supervise a group of sub-departments, each in charge of an experienced man; Mr. Moir was responsible to Geddes for machine-guns; Mr. Hopkinson for small arms ammunition; Mr. Brown for rifles; Major Symon for guns and equipment, ammunition wagons and optical munitions; and Mr. D. Bain for horse-drawn transport vehicles. As the War progressed, several of these sub-departments grew in importance, and required the undivided attention of a Deputy Director-General. Before I left the Ministry, munitions supply was one of three supply departments (the others being explosives supply and trench warfare supply), and was divided into ten main sub-departments, half of which were again sub-divided into four or five sections; and these various departments, sub-departments and sections were being run by experienced business men on business lines.

It was in such fashion that we modelled our headquarters. In the same spirit we approached the organisation of the country into areas for munition production.

I have already mentioned how the Armaments Output Committee, acting under the direction of the Munitions of War Committee and with my active support, had in April and May made a beginning with this task of area organisation.

In a number of areas district committees were set up to co-ordinate munition production, and they undertook the establishment of national shell factories in their centres. The first of such schemes was the one adopted at Leeds, which received Government sanction on 13th May, on the recommendation of the Munitions of War Committee. A description of this Leeds experiment was published in leaflet form, entitled *National Munitions Factories: Working Model,* with a view to stimulating similar movements in other districts.

The tour which I undertook during the first week of June had as one of its objects the encouragement of this system. At all meetings I urged that no time should be lost in setting up committees, and recommended that as far as possible districts should co-ordinate their efforts so as to form one organisation rather than several.

Very widespread zeal and activity was aroused by this appeal, and the effect was greatly to accelerate local organisation in the districts I had visited. This spirit of energetic devotion to the task of making good the munition shortage became general during June. Deputations from local committees called daily at the new Ministry. Many of these I saw and did my best to stimulate, direct, and assist. A copious correspondence poured in from business men offering their services and asking for information in regard to requirements, specifications, contracts, labour. Business men were encouraged to offer their services and they responded to the more sympathetic treatment accorded to them. It was imperative that anything in the nature of delay and confusion at this stage should be avoided, and I quickly saw that the branch in the Ministry dealing with local matters would have to be strengthened.

Early in June Mr. Stevenson, who had joined Mr. Booth's " District Department " almost immediately after the formation of the new Ministry and had taken up work in connection with the organisation of local committees, was asked by me to submit a scheme of area organisation.

I give the outline of the plan adopted for area organisation as it may be of value to those who will be called upon to organise the national energy for other tasks.

The scheme adopted was generally described by me in a speech in the House of Commons on 23rd June as follows: —

" No staff, however able, could adequately cope from the centre with the gigantic and novel character of the operations which must be put through during the next few weeks if the country is to be saved. We have, therefore, decided to organise the country in districts. I am relying very considerably upon the decentralisation which I have outlined. There is no time to organise a Central Department which would be sufficiently strong and which would be sufficiently well equipped to make the most of the resources of each district. . . . There is only one way of organising the resources of the country efficiently within the time at our disposal. That is that each district should undertake to do the work for itself, and that we should place at their disposal everything that a Government can in the way of expert advice and in the way of material, because we have ourselves offered to supply the material wherever it is required. Anything in the way of expert advice, specifications, samples, inspection and material— that we can supply; but we must rely upon the great business men of each locality to do the organisation in those districts for themselves; and they are doing it."

Here is Stevenson's description of his methods: —

" The first thing I did was to call for a map. I might as well have called for the moon. But, nothing daunted, I went out and bought one, for the price of which the Government still owe me. I divided the map into ten areas, the limits of which (with a few exceptions) followed county boundaries, and proceeded on the ordinary commercial lines of decentralisation. This scheme was approved by Mr. Lloyd George, and an Area Office was established in each (viz. Newcastle, Manchester, Leeds, Birmingham, Cardiff, Bristol, London, Edinburgh, Glasgow, Dublin, and Belfast) with the object of relieving the pressure at headquarters, securing local information and disposing of sectional difficulties. Curiously enough, one county was left out—Hereford—with the remark: ' We will leave that to the Board of Agriculture! ' But in that neglected county the greatest shell filling factory in the Kingdom was later built. . . ."

Within the main Areas nearly fifty Boards of Management were appointed. The procedure was somewhat as follows: The Boards of Management would undertake orders for specified quantities, say of shell, to be delivered within specified dates at a specified price. These orders were distributed amongst various engineering firms in the district or entrusted to National Factories managed by the Board, and the Boards were responsible to the Government for the shells manufactured.

The Area Offices exercised a general supervision over the local Boards of Management within their areas, and were each provided with an Organising Secretary, a Superintending Engineer, and a Labour Officer. The Secretary combined with secretarial duties the work of Establishment Officer and of sub-accountant for the district; was responsible for dealing with applications for petrol by firms engaged on munition work and a variety of other tasks. The Engineer was charged to develop the resources of the Area as fully as possible along the lines laid down from time to time by the Minister of Munitions, to ascertain details of and report on available machinery, to inspect National Shell Factories, advise on the capabilities of firms, and report on the progress of contracts. The Labour Officer had, of course, to supervise the supply and distribution of labour; and the great expansion of the work in connection with dilution, and the investigation of general conditions of labour led later on, in November, 1916, to the splitting-up of this work between two independent officers, dealing respectively with dilution and investigation.

'. It would be a mistake to suppose that all this harnessing of local energy and creation of district organisation went through easily and smoothly. Particularly in the early stages it required constant attention and very careful handling to ensure that the machinery worked.

Frictions and hitches had constantly to be overcome, and an agreed method of working settled. I had constantly to settle local and general questions—some important, many trivial—which delayed action. On 26th August, 1915, I issued a memorandum entitled: " Decisions for the Guidance of Boards of Management," which summarised the conclusions I had come to with them on the basis of our conferences, and this served thenceforward as their charter.

Summarising briefly some of the results obtained by these Boards of Management in the recruiting of hitherto inexperienced firms for munition production, I may say that in the course of the War they secured an output of 65 million empty shell, and over 606 million components; nearly 10 million trench warfare articles and over four million items in connection with aeronautical supplies. Nor was this great work done regardless of cost to the State, for it is estimated that the National Factories managed by these Boards saved the country £1¾ million based on the standard prices hitherto charged by contractors for the various articles produced.

There are many things which were done in the War that experience has taught should be done differently another time—

though Heaven forbid there should be another time! But the ultimate opinion of everybody acquainted with the Area Organisation and the Boards of Management, as war-time organisations, is that exactly the same policy should be again adopted, were it ever to become necessary once more to harness the outside resources of the country to armaments supply.

Such was the machine we constructed. My next concern was to devise methods which would ensure that every department got ahead with its job at full speed, and that breakdown or failure in any quarter should be promptly remedied instead of being allowed to drift on unnoticed till disaster occurred.

The Ministry had set things moving in the country as a result of my tour of some of the industrial districts and of the communications with industrial leaders, employers and workmen throughout the country. I had gathered a very able staff of first-class men at headquarters to do the work. It remained now to drive the machine at full speed as soon as it was put together.

So I proceeded to institute a system under which, as each department of the Ministry was organised—guns, explosives, shells, machine-guns, bombs, factory construction, labour supply, and so on—its head should make a weekly report of the progress of the branch to Mr. W. T. Layton (now Sir Walter Layton), who had been appointed Director of Statistics, and that he should collect these reports and furnish me with a weekly summary. As soon as each branch definitely got into working order and was in a position to start production it was asked to submit a statement showing its anticipated output week by week. The weekly reports of results actually achieved were constantly checked against the figures of anticipation, and we were thus able to see just how far each single section was keeping abreast of its task.

The weekly budget prepared by Mr. Layton, showing the promises and performances of each department, would be handed over to me at the week-end, and I would take it down with me to my cottage at Walton Heath; for whenever I could, I would escape from London on Saturday. There I would take this weekly budget, and go carefully through it, scribbling notes to be subsequently dictated and sent to the departmental heads on points which struck me in regard to the progress of the work. A few specimens taken at random will serve to illustrate these minutings: —

DR. ADDISON.

Weekly Report.   Trench Warfare.

The discrepancy between promise and deliveries is discouraging. What steps have been taken to speed it up?

Bomb deliveries are also disappointing.   D. LL. G.
30/9/15.

SIR FREDERICK BLACK.

Notes on Weekly Report for Week Ending Sept. 18th.

The contrast between shells promised and shells delivered is most discouraging, and the discrepancy is bad enough for contractors; but when you come to the national shell factories it is grotesque. Is there no means of improving the situation? Whose duty is it to call for explanations from individual contractors and from Boards of Management, and whose duty is it to keep them both up to the mark?

I am afraid that the department dealing with this phase of our work is considerably overtaxed. The men in charge are exceptionally able men, but they have too much to do.

Filling Factories.

Having regard to the urgent importance of increasing our filling capacity, this report is not as encouraging as I would wish it to be. The interviews at the conferences we have had the last two or three days will improve matters, but I hope special attention will be directed to this all-important branch. Both in the matter of national projectile factories and filling factories I urge that the great builders should be called into conference and invited to assist us by placing at our disposal men who can speed up erection of these buildings. Please see that this is done. D. LL. G.

30/9/15.

GENERAL DU CANE.

I understand that the lag in the delivery of six-inch Howitzer shell is partly attributable to the delay in delivery of certain cartridges for N.T.C. charges. Could this be hurried up?

D. LL. G.

14/3/16.

GENERAL DU CANE.

As there has been a good deal of trouble about ineffective fuses and gaines, I am very anxious there should be no further failures. You spoke very highly of the latest designs, but I should like to feel that the test has been of such a character that nothing is left to chance. So much depends upon these latest designs; if they fail, the ammunition at a very critical time would not achieve the necessary results. I should be very glad if you would, therefore, take the necessary steps for proving on a considerable scale the efficiency of the new designs. D. LL. G.

10/5/16.

In addition to firing this bombardment of notes and queries at the departmental heads of the Ministry, I was, of course, in constant personal touch with them through the week, providing them as far as possible with stimulation, correction and counsel. I was at the office from 9 a.m. until 8 p.m. and often later, and available for consultation with the officials of the Ministry when any difficulty arose.

Very early in the working of the Ministry I began the system of calling a weekly meeting of the heads of departments, at which I could discuss verbally with them the features in their weekly reports, and any matters arising in my minutes to them which required further consultation.

It was a great advantage and saving of time to have them all together for these meetings. For when one of them was asked why his output was failing to keep up to the level estimated for it he might give the explanation that he had not been supplied with some raw material, semi-manufactured product, or other component which was essential for the output of his particular section. In such a case, as the officer responsible for the supply of that missing component would also be present, the matter could be thrashed out without delay and a great deal of time and paper saved which would otherwise have been used in following a conventional routine of noting one man's complaint, sending it to another for comments, and thereafter having a docket flying about like a shuttlecock from department to department, while excuses instead of output were being multiplied.

My aim throughout was to tone up this staff to a pitch of high endeavour by every appeal that moves men to do their best—by praise; by emulation; by fear of exposure to criticism; and, above all, by the urge of a genuine spirit of patriotism. I think all those who were familiar with the working of the Ministry will agree that this aim was very successfully realised.

These meetings also stimulated healthy competition. No departmental head cared to have attention drawn to deficiencies in adapting performance to promise at meetings attended by his colleagues. There was no time to consider susceptibilities. The nation was in grave jeopardy and time counted. We had already lost months, we could not now afford to lose even a day.

The work of the whole Ministry was very closely interlocked. Failure to keep abreast of shell-filling might be the result of a failure to supply fuses or high explosives. This might proceed from a labour shortage in a particular district. In the weekly conference the trouble could be tracked down immediately to its root, and the responsible officer charged to rectify it. Meantime some arrangement might be improvised to get temporarily round the difficulty.

One immense advantage of these meetings was that in course of time they built up a very strong team-spirit among the men I had gathered round me. They were a diverse crowd—each an experienced leader accustomed to run his own business and to give orders rather than to receive them. It was essential for the success of the Ministry that they should learn to curb their independence, and to co-operate with each other. They began the process at these weekly meetings, even if at first it was occasionally in the role of mutual accusers. By degrees they grew to be really friendly, and with one or two possible exceptions they ended by becoming a close-knit band of fellow-workers, with a healthy *esprit de corps*.

My efforts to stimulate progress could not, of course, be confined to the staff of the Ministry. I had to be in continuous touch with industry all over the country. Frequently I would send for the manufacturers in some particular line—guns, rifles, machine tools— to consult with them about their output and stir them up to greater activity. I travelled round the country, visiting works and speaking to the workers, smoothing over labour difficulties, composing quarrels, urging increased output. The honour of the nation at home was pledged to our men at the front, that they should be furnished as fully and as speedily as was humanly possible with the weapons and defences that they needed in their struggle; and I held myself responsible that no effort should be spared and no reasonable expedient neglected to secure the fulfilment of that pledge.

I have been a pretty hard worker all my life, from boyhood right up to the present day. But I have never worked harder than during the period when I was carrying through the organisation of our munition supplies—not even during my Premiership, strenuous and arduous as those years were.

I generally worked an hour or two before breakfast, perusing essential papers and annotating them. It was my custom to invite to breakfast people who wished to see me, or whom I wished to see on munition business; sometimes important and influential American visitors wanted to discuss matters of moment with me, not necessarily connected with the Ministry of Munitions, and breakfast was a convenient opportunity for meeting them.

But my day would have started much earlier than this. As I have already mentioned, I would from the moment of waking have been at work upon papers and reports which I had taken overnight to my bedside.

By nine o'clock I was at work in my office at the Ministry of Munitions. The pressure of the task made it inevitable that many ancient traditions should be broken. After dealing with any import- ant letter or documents which had come to hand, there would be some matter which I had already decided to tackle that morning— maybe guns or shell-filling or rifles—and there would be depart- mental heads to see and their problems to settle; arrangements to make about division of raw material, perhaps, between rival claimants for its use, and so on. Often, too, there would be Cabinet Meetings to attend in the morning, although for the first few weeks of my tenure of the Ministry, imperative business prevented my attending. I was told that at one meeting Mr. Balfour asked: "What has become of the Minister of Munitions? I have not seen him for some time."

Lunch would probably be used, like breakfast, as an opportunity to meet someone with whom I had urgent munition business to discuss. In the afternoon the House of Commons claimed me, though as soon as I had replied to the numerous questions affecting my department which were habitually on the Paper, I would escape, if the nature of the succeeding business made it possible, to get on with my job.

Constant difficulties arose with the War Office, which necessitated consultations with Lord Kitchener, and frequently with the Prime Minister. These were often lengthy matters. The War Office was at that period a perpetual source of obstruction.

Labour difficulties involved me in frequent visits to industrial centres, and consultation with deputations of workers or shop stewards. Especially in the earlier days, before the control of profits had become general, there was a bad spirit stirring among the men, and syndicalist agitators caused a good deal of trouble. In this respect the Glasgow district gave us the most trouble, although there was considerable agitation of an obstructive character in the Newcastle, Sheffield, and other areas.

I need not refer to the various public meetings I had to address from time to time round the country, in order to rouse the nation to the vital issues confronting us, and keep up enthusiasm for munition output. My recollection of those days is one of an unceasing drive. Although I was urging on the Ministry and all my staff there as hard as I could, I think I can claim that I asked from none of them an effort greater than I was myself making.

3. THE PROBLEM OF LABOUR

Looking back to-day upon the problem which from the outset of the War confronted the nation in regard to the arming and equipping of our troops, it seems a little curious that at the beginning of the hostilities there was in some quarters expectation and fear of acute unemployment. Within the first week, the Cabinet Committee on the Prevention and Relief of Distress, of which the President of the Local Government Board, Mr. (now Sir) Herbert Samuel, was chairman, invited the Mayors and Provosts throughout the country to form local committees to provide against unemployment. Local authorities were urged to expedite public works and to frame schemes which might be put in hand if serious distress should arise. Acting on this impulse, employers and workers in the engineering industry held a meeting on 19th August, 1914, " to discuss ways and means whereby the unemployment contingent upon the national distress may be minimised." The Director of Army contracts issued in the same month from the War Office a circular entitled: " Memorandum as to minimising of unemployment during the War," in which he recommended the abandonment of overtime work as a means of spreading the available employment among as many hands as possible.

By mid-September, however, the Board of Trade discovered that the feared unemployment was not materialising; by November there was an unsatisfied demand for 6,000 armament workers, and the shortage of labour grew as the need for munitions increased until the deficiency of workers became one of our greatest problems.

The Cabinet Committee on munitions, the appointment of which in October, 1914, I have already described, was not called together from 23rd October until 23rd December; and at this latter meeting the supply of labour was found to have become a matter of acute difficulty.

There were three main causes operating to accentuate the labour difficulty. The first was the fact that enlistment had been particularly heavy in the big industrial districts, especially those associated with engineering. Between 4th August and 4th November, 1914, the enlistment per 10,000 of the population had been only 80 in the East of England and 88 in the South-West, while it was 150 in Yorkshire, Durham and Northumberland, 196 in Warwickshire and Midland Counties and 237 in Southern Scotland, in all of which areas the population was mainly industrial. The same high percentage of recruitment obtained also in South Wales and other industrial centres. By October, 1914, 12.2 per cent. of the male workers in the engineering trades had enlisted—a proportion which rose by July, 1915, to 19.5 per cent. In far too many cases it was the most energetic and competent skilled workers who rushed to the colours and the less efficient who were left behind.

The second cause was the fact that as labour grew less plentiful and the demands on it increased, workers found themselves in a stronger bargaining position than they had ever experienced. Employers were unwilling to quarrel with and dismiss a worker whom they would find hard to replace, and there was a growing competition to secure the services of the skilled artisan. If dismissed from one post he could get another job immediately, often at higher pay. This led to a tendency among some workers to bad timekeeping, slackness at their work and in certain cases to excessive drinking. The number against whom such charges would be brought was no doubt a relatively small percentage of the whole body of workers. None the less, the failure of a few men in a factory to keep their own process up to time had often the effect of holding back all the other workers engaged on the job. As a result, we were getting nothing like the full possible output even from the staff of workers which the nation still retained in its factories.

A third cause of the shortage of labour for munition production was the fact that the War Office policy was, as I have said, to deal only with a limited number of firms. In consequence, most of the engineering shops in the country were doing little or no work for munition production, but were carrying on with private contracts, on the principle of " business as usual." This meant that a considerable proportion of the engineering labour in the country was not being mobilised for munition production.

For solving the labour problem, therefore, it was obvious that the steps needed were: —

(a) To check the enlistment of skilled men; if possible to recover from the Army those who had already joined up; and ultimately to dilute the available supply by bringing in as much additional unskilled labour as could be safely utilised in the processes of manufacture.

(b) To induce workers to keep better time and abstain from slacking at their work and continually changing their employer.

(c) To ensure a more rigid control of drinking facilities in munition areas.

(d) To train and employ women for the class of work for which they were suitable.

(e) To bring the needed munition work and the available labour in the kingdom together, either by transferring all workers to the established armament firms, or by spreading our production among all the shops in the kingdom.

Prior to the setting up of the Ministry of Munitions, the handling of the labour problem was primarily the duty of the Board of Trade, working in consultation with the War Office. The Board of Trade gave a great deal of time and effort to this task and worked out various schemes for dealing with it. A number of causes, however, combined to hinder these schemes from having the desired effect.

At the Committee of Imperial Defence on the 27th of January, 1915, Lord Kitchener expressed fears that any attempt to conserve to British manufacturers their pivotal men might directly or indirectly prejudice recruiting more than seemed likely at first sight. He objected to any system which entailed the rejection of any willing recruit. In consequence of Lord Kitchener's attitude, the only conclusion reached by the Committee was a recommendation that when a valuable man in industry was recruited the firm should fill his place with some man or woman ineligible for the Army.

In the course of January, 1915, arrangements were made whereby valuable skilled men serving with the colours could be released and sent back to the munition firms from which they had gone out. But no considerable numbers were actually released under this system until the late summer. A War Office scheme for " badging " was brought into existence in March, 1915, but during the first seven or eight months of the War, when enthusiasm for enlistment had been at its height, the most vital industries suffered losses which no subsequent efforts could altogether repair. When once a man had joined the colours no power could make him return to civil work against his will, and the influence of all his military superiors, from the General Officer to the youngest corporal, was exerted to keep him in the Army if he looked like becoming a useful soldier.

Broadly, therefore, it may be said that the activity of the recruiting officer in denuding the country of its best skilled workers was subject to no effective check during the first year of the War. Every outside influence was against the retention of the artisan at home—especially the patriotism of the worker, who often could not be persuaded that his work was necessary to the equipment of the Army. Moreover, during the period of voluntary recruitment the man who remained at his home post was liable to be taunted as a coward and insulted in the streets with white feathers.

Arising out of the discussion in the Cabinet Committee on munitions on 23rd December, 1914, various efforts were made to bring about the expansion and dilution of the available labour. Belgian workmen were taken on as fully as possible, and a certain number of women were brought into armament work. The first systematic attempt to enrol women for replacement of male labour was made by the Board of Trade on 16th March, 1915. In two-and-a-half months, to 4th June, 1915, some 78,946 women were enrolled on the Special War Register for women for work connected with munitions, but only 1,816 of these were actually given jobs.

The subsequent history of women's work in the production of munitions is one of the brightest chapters in the story. I give elsewhere some account of their efficiency and of their fine devotion and courage in connection with shell-filling. It was one of the many curious revolutions effected by the War that the lead in organising women and girls for national service was taken by the very people who, prior to the War had been, in the cause of women's suffrage, the thorniest opponents of the Government. Mrs. Pankhurst and her daughter Christobel, Miss Annie Kenney, Mrs. Drummond and other prominent suffragettes were prime movers in this new crusade.

On 18th July, 1915, they headed a great Women's War Pageant, in which thousands of women demonstrators marched for miles along London streets through rain and mud, escorting a deputation that waited on me, as Minister of Munitions, to express their welcome of the National Register and to offer their services to help the country. While voicing the demand of the women to be permitted to take part in war work, Mrs. Pankhurst also put in a plea for wage conditions which would safeguard their standard of living and prevent them from being sweated or exploited by manufacturers. In reply I gave a guarantee that they should have a fair minimum wage for time work and should receive for piece work the same rates as were paid to men. These conditions, sedulously enforced by the Ministry throughout the duration of the War, had a permanent effect upon the status of women workers in this country. For although the emergency work upon which they were engaged was only temporary, and the regulations in which the agreement was embodied applied only to women engaging on what previously had been regarded as men's work, yet a standard was set up which could not easily be set aside afterwards; and it may confidently be claimed that the low and variable wages which were paid to women in the metal trades before the War are gone never to return.

In the War Office establishments, and the metal and chemical industries, which by mid-1916 were engaged in munition production to the extent of at least 75 per cent. of their total output, the women and girls employed rose from 82,589 in July, 1914, to 340,844 by July, 1916. By November, 1918, the grand total of women employed on work directly or indirectly to Government order was 1,587,300. These figures give some indication of the immense growth of the effort made by women on behalf of their country during the War.

The difficulties which had to be overcome to secure the admission of women workers on this scale into branches of industry which had previously been a male preserve were, of course, immense. But I will not further digress here to deal with them, as they were a part of the general problem of dilution of labour which I discuss in the following pages.

During the opening months of 1915 the Board of Trade made a series of efforts to draw supplies of labour to the established armament firms from other engineering concerns. This was in accordance with the War Office policy of giving its contracts only to the recognised munition firms, and was based on the assumption that outside firms were doing only civilian work. The results achieved were very meagre, partly because it transpired that many of these firms were devoting a part at least of their energy to sub-contracts for munition production, partly because they resented most intensely the proposal to filch away from them their best workmen and demanded as an alternative that they should themselves be given War Office contracts to execute. A further difficulty was that the workmen themselves were unwilling to leave their homes and take up work in some distant part of the country for a strange concern. It soon became clear that the transference of labour from commercial to Government work could only be achieved by compulsory measures.

In one respect, indeed, many outside firms intimated that they would welcome compulsion. They were tied up by contracts they had entered into for civilian commercial work, and although they

G

were anxious to assist the Government they could not break these contracts without incurring penalties. If, however, the Government would either give them statutory release from their obligations, or would take over their works under the system of Government control laid down in the Defence of the Realm Act, this difficulty would be surmounted.

On legal advice being taken, it was found that the existing powers were not adequate for this matter, and the outcome was the new Defence of the Realm Act which I laid before the House of Commons on 9th March. That measure authorised the Government " to require any work in any factory or workshop to be done in accordance with the directions of the Admiralty or Army Council given with the object of making the factory or workshop, or the plant or labour therein, as useful as possible for the production of war material." And it further provided that " where the fulfilment by any person of any contract is interfered with by the necessity on the part of himself or any other person of complying with any require-ment, regulation or restriction of the Admiralty or the Army Council that necessity is a good defence to any action or proceeding taken against that person in respect of the non-fulfilment of the contract in so far as it is due to that interference."

Owing, however, to the persistence of the War Office in clinging affectionately to its traditional policy of dealing only with the established munition firms, comparatively little use was made of these powers prior to the establishment of the Ministry of Munitions.

Quite the most difficult problem in regard to labour was that of securing their wholehearted co-operation in the urgent task of munition production—by sticking in the same workshop, keeping good time, working steadily and avoiding strikes; and in particular by consenting to those relaxations of their trade union rules which would make possible an extensive dilution of skilled by unskilled workers, and a considerable use of overtime in cases of emergency.

When the first drafts for the new D.O.R.A. were under consideration, as submitted on 26th February, it was at first proposed to insert clauses which would have made illegal under penalty any strike or lock-out in any firm engaged on the construction of war material, and which would have provided compulsory arbitration in the case of all disputes. I decided, however, to see what could be done to achieve the same end by a voluntary agreement with the trade unions.

Accordingly, on 17th March, 1915, a representative meeting of trade unionists was summoned " to consult with the Chancellor of the Exchequer and the President of the Board of Trade on certain matters of importance to labour arising out of the recent decision of the Government, embodied in the Defence of the Realm

(Amendment) Act, to take further steps to organise the resources of the country to meet naval and military requirements."

ᐟ The Conference was held in the gloomy board room of the Treasury, with the gilt throne of Queen Anne at one end of the room. There was a tradition that once upon a time it had been occupied by kings and queens who came to discuss their finances with the Lords of the Treasury. The last sovereign who sat upon it was the first Hanoverian George. Since he understood no English and the Lords of the Treasury understood no German our sovereigns ceased to go through the formality of attending these meetings at the Treasury to arrange their finance, and the once glistening and plushed throne has now a sad look of tarnished and torn neglect. The room was so crowded with the representatives of workers in many trades that some of them had to lean against this rickety throne of the last of the Stuarts. I had invited Mr. Balfour to be present. He had addressed many an assembly largely composed of workmen, but this was his first experience of sitting down to confer with them on a basis of equality. So far he had only talked to them; now he was talked to by them. The expression on his face was one of quizzical and embarrassed wonder.

He was surprised to find the workmen's representatives talked so well. They put their points clearly and succinctly, wasting neither time nor words. On the other hand, there was just a note of aggressiveness in manner and tone to which he was not quite accustomed from such quarters. For the moment it almost quelled him, and he was silent throughout. He did not quite recover his ease even after they left. He liked new experiences, but not of this sort. This was a portent which had for the first time appeared in the quarter of the sky where he had shone for a generation, and it came uncomfortably near. His ideas of Government were inherited from the days when Queen Anne sat on that throne. They were only changed to the extent that the fact of her being the last occupant constituted a triumph for the subject and thus modified the Constitution in a popular direction. But this scene was fundamentally different. He saw those stalwart artisans leaning against and sitting on the steps of the throne of the dead queen, and on equal terms negotiating conditions with the Government of the day upon a question vitally affecting the conduct of a great war. Queen Anne was indeed dead. I had watched his mood for years from an opposing bench. In looking at him now I felt that his detached and enquiring mind was bewildered by this sudden revelation of a new power and that he must take time to assimilate the experience.

The Conference met on 17th-19th March, 1915.

Opening the proceedings, I said that those present were being invited to consider the need for a larger output of munitions, and the steps which the Government proposed to take to organise industry to that end. Every belligerent country had found the expenditure of war material exceeded all anticipation. I referred to the very drastic powers which the Government had now assumed to control or take over any works in the country which were either turning out munitions of war or were capable of being adapted for that purpose, and told them that this was the matter on which I wanted to consult with them.

The " taking-over " of these works would not mean that their present owners and managers would be turned out adrift, and some admiral or general put in charge. The works would be run as formerly, except that they would be entirely turned over to munition production, and, of course, under such control there would have to be a limitation of private profits.

But if the Board of Trade were going in this manner to interfere with the rights and interests of the capital, the owner and managements of these concerns, it was only just that they should similarly ask the workers to consent to such limitations as might be found vitally necessary in the national interest of their ordinary privileges. In particular, I wanted to ensure that certain trade union regulations which might be more than justified in peace-time should be modified in such a way as to avoid hampering the nation's munition supplies in the existing emergency, and particularly that if any disputes arose, either about such relaxation of normal trade union rules, or about hours or rates of pay, the matter should be settled by peaceful arbitration, and pending a settlement the workers should carry on with their job. The Government did not say that workmen ought never to complain, or to ask for an increase in wages. " Our point is that during the time the questions at issue are being adjudicated upon, the work shall go on. . . . We want to get some kind of understanding with you about that before we undertake the control of these works."

I then laid before the representatives of the trade unions a series of propositions which had the object of providing that there should be no stoppage of work for Government purposes by strike or lock-out, pending a settlement of any disputes that might arise between employers and workpeople, and that all such disputes should be referred to arbitration; and that for the duration of the War, all trade union restrictions tending to limit output or the employment of semi-skilled or female labour should be suspended.

The workers' representatives were then left together to prepare their own draft of the undertaking they were prepared to give on these points. This draft was discussed and amended, and finally on 19th March a memorandum was presented by Mr. Arthur Henderson which had been accepted with only two dissensions. It was accordingly signed on behalf of the Government by myself and by

Mr. Runciman, and on behalf of the workmen's representatives by Mr. Henderson and Mr. Mosses. I undertook to provide enough copies for every union to send one to each of its members.

This document was known as the "Treasury Agreement." It occupied an important place throughout the War in the negotiations with labour, because it set out clearly, in terms which the trade union leaders recognised to be fair and just, the conditions under which munition labour was thereafter progressively organised. It stipulated for the admission of unskilled and semi-skilled workers to dilute the existing body of skilled labour, provided that they were paid the same wages as had customarily been paid for the work; it furnished a scheme of arbitration to take the place of strikes; and it laid down that the private profits of the manufacturers were to be subject to limitation.

In the following week an agreement on similar lines was specially negotiated by me with the Amalgamated Society of Engineers, whose representatives, though present at the previous conference, had attended without power to sign.

These two agreements, though important because of the solutions they reached, failed to become immediately operative. There was one difficulty remaining. The workers, quite naturally, declined to confirm the suggested proposals limiting their own freedom until the Government implemented its undertaking to restrict private profit. Mr. Runciman was at the time busily engaged in negotiation with the heads of the armament firms in an effort to arrive at an agreed basis of limitation of profits, but in the end these negotiations came to nothing. The matter was ultimately dealt with by the Munitions of War Act in June, 1915, which provided that the establishments engaged in munitions work could be brought under the control of the Ministry, that their profits should be limited, and that in such controlled establishments trade union rules restricting output should be suspended.

This question of controlling private profits was in fact vital to the whole issue of labour supply. It was useless to ask the workers on the plea of a grave emergency to put their whole effort into manufacture and to stop striking or agitating for higher wages or to accept modifications of rules and restrictions designed for their protection, which they had won from employers through years of struggle, when they saw those same employers busily amassing colossal fortunes out of the emergency. In a "Memorandum on Labour for Armaments," by Sir H. Llewellyn Smith, dated 9th June, 1915, this situation is expressed as follows: —

"The difficulty, as it has been expressed, both by workmen's representatives at the two Treasury Conferences and by employers themselves (as in the shipbuilding employers' deputation received to-day) is that the workmen, though engaged on armament work, still feel themselves to be working essentially for private employers, with whom they have only a ' cash nexus,' and that in the present circumstances a ' cash nexus ' is quite inadequate to secure control. . . .

So long as contractors' profits are not brought under control, the workmen feel that any sacrifice they may make of their rules and restrictions will directly increase the profits of private persons, and their unwillingness to make the sacrifice is made almost insuperable by this suspicion."

It is true that during this period there had been a steady tendency for wages to rise, and that in addition, on account of the regular full work available in this country, combined with overtime, the workers were earning considerably more than they had previously done. But on the other hand, prices of food and other necessities had also been rising at a pace which in some cases almost outstripped any advance in wages. Strikes were in consequence occurring with ever-increasing frequency. Mr. I. H. Mitchell, of the Industrial Commissioners Department, when reviewing the tendencies of the last six months in June, 1915, wrote : —

" I am quite satisfied that the labour difficulty has been largely caused by the men being of opinion that, while they were being called upon to be patriotic and refrain from using the strong economic position they occupied, employers, merchants and traders were being allowed perfect freedom to exploit to the fullest the Nation's needs. This view was frankly submitted to me by the leaders of the Clyde engineers' strike in February last. As soon as Labour realised that nothing was being done to curtail and prevent this exploitation by employers, it let loose the pent-up desire to make the most they could in the general scramble. This has grown until now many unions are openly exploiting the needs of the Nation. If the work is Government work, it is the signal for a demand for more money. Trade union leaders who, from August last year until February this year, loyally held their members back from making demands, are now with them in the rush to make the most of the opportunity."

I may sum up as follows the labour situation as it presented itself when the Ministry of Munitions was formed in June, 1915 : —

Recruiting had taken away from industry a considerable number of its most essential workers and was still being pushed forward without any limitation other than that resulting from the belated badging of key men in the more important armament firms. Arrangements had been made by Lord Kitchener to permit the release from the colours of skilled workers badly needed by firms engaged on war work, but of a quarter of a million men employed in the metal trades who had joined the forces, only about 5,000 had actually been brought back.

The principle of dilution of skilled labour, though adopted in the Treasury agreement, had not yet been confirmed by the trade unions and put into force.

Profits of the firms engaged in war work were still unlimited, and were attaining unprecedented dimensions. Industrial unrest, stimulated by this spectacle, was growing rapidly. Whereas the number of disputes involving stoppage of work known to the Board of Trade at the beginning of 1915 was 10, 47 fresh disputes arose in February, 74 in March, 44 in April, and 63 in May. As regards labour this was the general situation with which the Ministry of Munitions was at the outset of its existence called upon to deal.

My first step for coping with this situation was to lay before Parliament, on 23rd June, 1915, the Munitions of War Bill. This was a measure designed to implement by Statute the various proposals which had already been discussed with the employers and workers in the munition industry. It dealt with the settlement of labour differences, the prohibition of lock-outs and strikes, the controlling of establishments engaged in production of munitions and the limitation of their profits, the control of munition workers and the issue to them of badges; and it also provided for voluntary enrolment of a body of munition workers to be at the disposal of the Ministry and work where the need for their services was the greatest. Introducing this Bill, I reminded the House of the tremendous task which production of munitions for modern war had turned out to be, and outlined the steps I was taking to organise the available national resources for this end. I mentioned some of the difficulties, such as the question of supply of raw material. I hinted that the Government might find it necessary to take complete control of the metal market. It might have to deal firmly with people who attempted to hold up necessary supplies in order to exploit higher prices. It might have to take steps to prevent a coal shortage. Existing machinery was often idle because there were no skilled men to use it. Many such men had enlisted in the Army, and must be found and brought back from the firing line to the workshop. The holding up of work through the slackness of a minority had to be remedied, and the restriction of output because of yard regulations, written and unwritten, must be avoided. The question of compulsory service in the production of munitions of war, I said, had been the subject of a very frank discussion between the leaders of the trade unions and myself, and I was bound to point out that if there were an inadequate supply of labour for the purpose of turning out the munitions of war which were necessary for the safety of the country, compulsion would be inevitable. The trade union leaders put forward as an alternative the proposal that the

Government should give them an opportunity of securing the men required. They said: " Give us seven days, and if in seven days we cannot get the men, we will admit that our case is considerably weakened." To this I had agreed. But even if the required workers were forthcoming voluntarily, I explained that it would still be necessary to take powers in the Bill to enforce contracts with them and to secure discipline in the workshops. Here again an agreed solution had been reached for the setting up of a Munitions Court.

I then came to the very important provisions in the Bill with regard to limitations of profits from munition work : —

" The trade unions insisted, and I think properly insisted, on their share of the bargain. They said, workmen are quite willing to work for the State, to put their whole strength and to suspend their trade union regulations, as long as they know that the work is of advantage to the country. But the objection in their minds always is that they are suspending trade union regulations important to them in order to increase the profits of individual employers. That they will not assent to, and they say, as a condition of all the other provisions to which they have given their assent, there must be a clause in the Bill which will limit the profits of those establishments which are working for the State, and that the provisions which I have enumerated only apply to establishments where the profits are limited. That is why we propose to set up controlled establishments, so that where the State assumes control of a workshop all the conditions which I have referred to shall apply to that workshop. That means the workshops where the munitions of war are being supplied at the present moment. It means practically that the State assumes control of the profits of these establishments, that whatever suspension of regulations takes place it will be entirely for the benefit of the State and not of the individual employer, and upon those conditions the trade union leaders are prepared to accept those suggestions which I have already made."

The Munitions of War Bill quickly passed through its Parliamentary stages and received the Royal Assent on 2nd July. No time was lost in bringing to the solution of the labour problem the aid which its powers afforded.

I made a systematic effort to get back skilled men serving with the Colours to resume their work in the munition firms. On 9th June I sent a circular letter to engineering and shipbuilding firms to get lists of the skilled men in their employ who had enlisted, and telegrams were sent by the Adjutant-General to certain Commanding Officers to ascertain what skilled men were in their units. But Lord Kitchener stipulated that, for the time being, only those men should be released who were not yet overseas or in units ready to be sent out.

The recovery of skilled mechanics from the ranks, however, under this strict limitation was not very successful. From July to the end of October, 1915, the total number thus brought back, either under the "bulk scheme" for release of those known to be skilled mechanics, or the individual release of men specially asked for by their own firms, barely exceeded 5,000. The flower of the skilled mechanics who had joined the Army was either already abroad or in the "barred" units at home. Speaking on 20th December, 1915, in the House of Commons, I said:—

"We are trying to get men from the Colours. . . . It is like getting through barbed-wire entanglements without heavy guns. There are entrenchments behind entrenchments. You have not merely the Army, the Corps, the Division, the Brigade, the Battalion, and the Company, but the Platoon, and even the Squad—everybody fighting to prevent men from coming away. I am not surprised. I am not blaming them. Skilled men at any trade are skilled men at every trade. Your intelligent skilled man is a good man in the trenches, and nobody wants to lose him. Therefore, every corporal fights against parting with a good, intelligent, skilled workman. As my honourable friend points out, the men themselves feel that they are running away from danger in order to go back to comfort and high wages and emoluments, and they don't like it. It is a very creditable story. . . ."

By August I had discovered that the bulk of the men we wanted were in the "barred" units, and I wrote to Lord Kitchener making a very urgent plea for the release of at least the most valuable of these. Throughout August and September, 1915, a correspondence was in progress between the Ministry and the War Office, and eventually arrangements were made in September for a census of skilled munition workers in all units not yet sent out of the country, and of those offering themselves some forty thousand were passed by investigators as suitable. By the end of October steps were being taken to allocate these men to munitions works.

Great as were the difficulties of carrying out the schemes for return of skilled workers from the Colours, the difficulties in the way of introducing dilution of labour were far greater, though the ultimate results of this policy were more fruitful.

The fundamental opposition to dilution came from the craft unions. Through long years they had built up as a protection against the dangers of cut wages, unemployment, and blackleg labour an elaborate system of rules and customs which were designed to control the rate of output and narrow the doorway into the industry. The rules were highly artificial in many cases; men appertaining to certain crafts alone were permitted to touch certain work, even though it might be of a kind which any handy man could do with little or no special training; and a man doing one job might not carry out the simplest task ancillary to it which ought by these rules to be allocated to another class of craftsman, but must stand by and wait till the other type of craftsman was called in, and executed that limited operation. Experience of a restricted market for their labour had made the unions develop every means of restricting its supply, and they were afraid, not without reason, that if the door were thrown open they would after the War suffer from a congested labour market, and that if sharp demarcations between the crafts were once broken down they would be difficult to re-establish. It was not a fear of falling wages during the War which troubled them. I had guaranteed that this would not occur. It was rather a dread of losing the tradition of mystery and technical difficulty which they had built up to protect their craft, and the apprehension of an overcrowded supply of workmen in their particular trade, leading to unemployment, lower wage rates, and a reduced standard of craftsmanship and of living in years to come. The patriotic appeal of our national necessity made difficult headway against these quite natural and—as the event proved in some cases—justifiable fears. Clemenceau once said that there was no difficulty in inducing Frenchmen to give their lives for their country, but they would not give their money. This is not to be wondered at when we remember that in actual fact the fires of patriotism are too often quenched when they come up against the cool waters of " business." Trade unionists flocked to the standard of their country when volunteers were called for to face death, but I was told that men at the front, daily confronted with death and needing shells to protect and defend themselves, wrote home to their fellow trade unionists entreating them not to surrender any of the privileges of their craft, although strict adhesion to these privileges was impeding the supply of the munitions they so sadly needed. The war-time profiteers were not infrequently brothers or fathers of those who suffered and died at the front, and with altered circumstances might have shown equal self-sacrifice. But unhappily for sentiment, when you come to business matters you discover that business is business, and admits of no divided loyalties. Our statesmen more recently have rediscovered this truism at Ottawa.

It was perhaps unfortunate that the first branch of the engineering industry where it was found necessary to raise the issue of dilution was the machine tool trade, since this was regarded as the very special preserve of the skilled worker, and was one the output of which, unlike that of shells or machine-guns, would continue its importance after the War. When we attempted to increase munitions manufacture in this country we found that our first need was machine tools, which did not as yet exist in quantities sufficient even to permit the carrying out of the orders already placed by the

War Office, far less the greatly augmented production at which the Ministry aimed. At a conference I summoned of machine tool makers on 15th July, an agreement with the trade unions was reached for a programme of night shifts and labour dilution. But when the officers of the Ministry tried to carry through this arrangement they came up against bitter opposition from shop stewards and local trade union committees. At Woolwich Arsenal the local committee resolved: "That we refuse to entertain the proposal to allow the introduction of semi-skilled men on work now done by fully qualified mechanics, as it is not proved there is the shortage claimed." And at the works of Messrs. J. Lang and Sons, Johnstone, the workers' committee declared: "That no woman shall be put to work a lathe, and if this is done the men will know how to protect their rights." This was in August, 1915, and I had to weigh carefully the alternatives of taking drastic action or trying conciliation. Had stern action proved successful without rousing wide antagonism, it would greatly have expedited the process of dilution. If it had failed against a massed opposition on the part of the skilled workers —for it would obviously have been impossible to punish them all— the campaign for dilution might have been permanently lost. As yet the Ministry was in its early stages, and a realisation of the immense and urgent need for greater munition output had not fully captured the minds and imaginations of the whole body of workers. I decided to try persuasion first.

On 9th September, 1915, I visited the Trades Union Congress at Bristol, and addressed it on the subject. I told them how German trade unions had organised and expanded their services for munition production. The War, I declared, had become a conflict between the mechanics of Germany and Austria and the mechanics of Great Britain and France. But as yet this country was not doing its best in the struggle. Only 15 per cent. of the machinery which could be used for turning out rifles, cannon and shells (in all of which there was a shortage) was working night shifts. The problem, I pointed out, was largely one of labour. If every skilled man were working his utmost there would still not be nearly enough. The issue of dilution was not one of turning off a skilled man to make room for an unskilled, but one of concentrating the skilled men on the work which only they could do. At present highly skilled workmen with years of training were doing work which could as easily be done by those who had only a few weeks' or a few days' training, and we could not equip our armies unless organised labour was prepared to assist by suspending during the War all restriction which made it difficult to use skilled labour in the best way by employing unskilled under skilled direction wherever possible.

I then proceeded to explain the bargain which had been made with the trade union leaders at the Treasury Conference. "Has the State kept the bargain? [A voice: 'No.'] I am going to tell you. Profits, restrictions of profits. Does anybody say we have not kept the bargain? [A voice: 'Nobody knows!'] Nobody knows? We have declared 715 establishments producing munitions of war to be 'controlled establishments'; we have put them under control of the State . . . and do not forget this, we have not asked any trade union to suspend any regulations except in an establishment where we control the profits. What have we done about controlling the profits? We have controlled them by an Act of Parliament. . . . We are restricting them on the basis of what they earned before the War. . . . They are only going to get the standard which is based upon the profit made before the War, with any allowance which is made by us in respect of increased capital which they have put in. What do we do with the balance? We put it into the Treasury to carry on the War. [Cheers.] It is the first time it has ever been done in the history of any country. You have practically taken over the whole of the engineering works of this country and controlled them by the State. I have seen resolutions passed from time to time at Trade Union Congresses [laughter] about nationalising the industries of this country. We have done it. [Cheers and laughter.] . . ."

I told the Congress about the undertaking, embodied in an Act of Parliament, that conditions would be restored at the end of the War, and, further, I gave them a guarantee that piece rates should nowhere be cut down in munition works as a result of any increase in output; and that unskilled men and women should be paid the same rate as had been given to skilled men for the jobs transferred to them. Having dealt with the way in which the Government was keeping its side of the bargain, I indulged in some plain speaking on the failure of the trade unionists to do their share. I referred to the refusal of men to admit semi-skilled workers, the squabbles between coppersmiths and plumbers as to the dividing line between their jobs, and the penalising of men who worked faster than the average "A complaint came to me from Woolwich that there was a deliberate attempt to keep down the output. The Labour Advisory Committee investigated it, and a trade unionist defended the men in this particular case. The significance of his testimony was this —and I am quoting now from the report of the investigators: 'The trade unionist witness regretted having to acknowledge that the workmen in several departments restricted output in order to maintain the prices obtained before the War, and this was continued up to the present time.' Well, that is not carrying out the bargain. [A voice: 'It is not playing the game.'] I agree."

It is fair that I should record the fact that a crowded assembly of trade union delegates listened to this plain speaking not only without resentment but with a swelling appreciation. A week later there was held a conference of trade union executives to discuss dilution, and a series of resolutions favourable to the plan was adopted. Following on this expression of approval, I set up a Central Munitions Labour Supply Committee, containing representatives of the Ministry, of the Employers and the Employed, presided over by Mr. Arthur Henderson, which proceeded to co-operate with the Ministry in organising labour dilution and dealing with the multitudinous problems of wage rates and local conditions of employment, transfer of labour, etc., which arose in this connection.

By the end of 1915 labour troubles were interfering seriously in some areas with the output of munitions. I suspected that in some cases the failure of a firm to deliver up to schedule was due to a certain degree of slackness and inefficiency on the part of the management, but in a great many cases it was traceable to the activities of men inside the works who deliberately fostered discontent. The trouble did not come from the trade unions or their officials. They honourably adhered to their agreement with the State. But an agitation known as the " shop steward " movement arose in the greatest of the munition works. These " stewards " were chosen by the workers in a given factory or workshop to present grievances to the management. They felt they must justify their existence by searching out wrongs which had escaped the notice of the local trade union secretary. It gradually became a formidable element of disturbance in the largest munition areas. Glasgow was one of the worst districts, and the agitation amongst the workers seriously interfered with the output, especially with the delivery of big guns. I decided to visit the works to see for myself what the position was, and put before the men and their leaders the exact facts with regard to the military position, and the peril in which their fellow-workmen at the front were placed by the absence of adequate artillery of the heavier kinds to enable them to contend with their foes on equal terms.

Accompanied by Mr. Arthur Henderson I arrived at Glasgow on Christmas Eve, and we both went to Beardmore's works, where the delivery of heavy artillery was being seriously retarded by labour difficulties. At my request, the shop stewards were brought together and I then told them why I had come and made my appeal for their assistance in stimulating greater activity in production. A man who seemed to be their leader stepped to the front and started haranguing me on the servitude of labour in private establishments. He was a strong man, with a fine open face, the natural pleasantness of which was overlaid by a theatrical frown which he had succeeded in implanting upon a kindly countenance. He struck an attitude, and in a loud, challenging voice he said, " I am as much a slave of Sir William Beardmore as if I had the letter ' B ' branded on my brow," his hand passing across the wrinkled forehead. This was my first acquaintance with Mr. David Kirkwood. I discovered that he was fundamentally a reasonable man to deal with. He promised that if Mr. Henderson put our case before a free assembly of workers, he would do his best to secure a fair hearing.

There was another spokesman who seemed to me to be a natural savage. He came right up to me with threatening mien and locked fists, talking in an ill-tempered and angry voice. I must say the rest of his comrades were not too pleased with his attitude. Later on I met Mr. Gallagher, a Communist, whose manners were quite perfect, and whose tones were soft, but he left no doubt in my mind that his was the most sinister influence.

The following morning (that is Christmas morning) we addressed a great gathering of workmen at the St. Andrew's Hall. Mr. Henderson took the chair; four-fifths of the workmen were anxious to hear all that was being said, but a minority were determined to disturb the proceedings and deprive us of a hearing. They were specially annoyed with Mr. Henderson, and he had by far the worst time. On the whole I was heard quite well, with a few surmountable interruptions. Mr. Kirkwood played the game and got up in the middle of the most turbulent elements, and put in a plea for a fair hearing. The visit, for a time at least, had a quieting effect and a quickening influence upon production. Some weeks later we had further trouble, and then strong action had to be taken in the way of deportation of some of the leaders, and the prosecution of others.

We were as yet, however, far from having reached full victory; there were still some entrenched obstructions and restrictions to break through. Even the greatest convulsion fails to tear out of the soil a well-grounded suspicion.

In this case its roots were so deep that they resisted the shattering bombardment of a year of horror. Throughout the autumn of 1915 discussion and disagreements continued as to the application of the principle of dilution, and in December I brought forward the Munitions of War (Amendment) Bill in order to give statutory force to the various points on which agreement had been reached. Even at this stage the Amalgamated Society of Engineers was still holding out, and when the Bill had reached its Committee stage, they sent a deputation to wait on Mr. Asquith and myself, armed with a resolution declaring that a series of amendments which they proposed—

"... are essential as an element of justice in the administration of the Munitions of War Act, 1915, and should be incorporated in the Amended Act if we are to maintain our influence with our members in securing the high standard of production required. Further, that a Committee representative of the conference be instructed to wait upon the Prime Minister and the Minister of Munitions and intimate the decision of this conference *as the basis of our continued co-operation.*"

The veiled threat in the last line of this resolution naturally stirred Mr. Asquith to anger. When challenged the deputation protested that they had not meant it in that way, and that all they wanted was to secure that the various provisions of the protection of wage levels and conditions of employment which had been set out in two circulars issued by the Ministry (Circulars L.2 and L.3) as conditions under which dilution was to be carried out should be given the force of statute. To my challenge whether they could cite a single instance in which an unskilled man, introduced into a controlled establishment, had been refused these rates, Mr. Brownlie, the engineers' secretary, had to admit they could not, and Mr. Asquith and I pointed out to them that some of their people had persistently tried to block dilution, and were at present making objections with little real substance as an excuse for their attitude. I would be willing to meet them in regard to incorporating the provisions of the two circulars in the Bill, if they on their side would guarantee that henceforward they would really co-operate in the dilution scheme, and not merely fall back upon some new demand as a pretext for doing nothing.

The deputation accepted this offer, and signed a document pledging the Conference and membership of the Society to accept the scheme of dilution and co-operating actively therein if the Government incorporated in the Bill the rates of pay and conditions of labour in controlled establishments set out in the Ministry's two circulars.

The Bill was re-committed and amended in accordance with this agreement, and thereafter dilution made rapid headway.

4. THE ROYAL ENCOURAGEMENT OF MUNITION WORKERS

The story of the steps taken to organise labour for the munition factories, and to induce them to put forward their best efforts and submit to control and the suspension of cherished trade union regulations and practices, would not be complete without a tribute to the vitally important help rendered by the late King George V. to the nation by heartening and encouraging the munition workers and those who were creating the district organisations.

It would be hard to over-estimate the value of the national service rendered by the Sovereign's visits to munitions areas and the personal relations he established with the workers there. I have shown in my narrative how dangerous a gulf had threatened to open between the outlook of the men in the trenches and that of the men at home in the workshops. While those who joined the Army felt they were serving King and Country, and put on with khaki a spirit of loyal comradeship and unquestioning service, those who remained in the familiar civilian environment of the workshop found it hard to escape from the old traditional atmosphere of jealous care for their rights as against their employers, the fear of exploitation, the readiness to " down tools " at any threat of encroachment upon their hard-won privileges. It was no easy task to persuade them that they too were in the service of the State for the defence of the nation; and to this end nothing could have been happier than the spontaneous resolve of the King to go about among them, to shake them by the hand, talk with them, and make a direct appeal to their patriotism and citizenship.

In the spring of 1915, when labour troubles were beginning to make themselves felt, King George began this practice of visiting the places where munitions were being produced. On 17th March he went to Woolwich Arsenal, and inspected the royal gun and carriage factories there, and the royal laboratory where explosives were made and tested. At the end of April he similarly visited the other royal factories, the small arms factory at Enfield and the gunpowder factory at Waltham Abbey. He followed up this visit by sending a special royal message to the workers at these factories, expressing his keen interest in their work, and his conviction that all engaged in the workshops would do their utmost, individually and collectively, to support their comrades at the front. On 12th May the King paid a two days' visit to Portsmouth, and went through the dockyards there, and again sent them a message on his return expressing " appreciation of the part which, by their devotion to duty, they are taking in maintaining the strength and efficiency of the Fleet."

Hardly had he got back to Buckingham Palace before he was off again on a week's tour of the shipyards and armament factories of the north. He spent May 17th and 18th on the Clyde, touring round from early morning to visit shipbuilding yards. At one of the largest, that of the Fairfield Shipbuilding and Engineering Co., the workmen presented him with a resolution expressing their loyalty and determination to press forward as efficiently and rapidly as possible with the Government work on which they were engaged. Replying, he said this resolution " will be universally welcomed, and will strengthen the confidence of the Nation in ultimate victory. It will indeed be a happy outcome if my visit to the Clyde has in any way conduced to this expression of patriotic resolve on the part of the men of one of the most important shipyards in this renowned industrial centre."

From the Clyde the King went to the Tyne, where he also spent two days, and spoke personally with a number of foremen and workers in the armament works and shipyards. He met the members of the North-East Coast Armaments Committee, and encouraged them in their task. He thanked the workmen in a speech for what had been done, but urged that more was still required. He voiced the hope " that all restrictive rules and regulations would be removed, and that all would work to one common end and purpose." This was a courageous gesture on the King's part to help forward the solution of the very difficult problem of suspending the trade union restrictions, which at that time were seriously hampering output. He followed it up a fortnight later by sending a message to the Armaments Committee urging "workers to do all they can." King George concluded this tour by visiting Barrow-in-Furness on 21st May. Whilst there he received a message from the Wallsend workers declaring their resolve to get ahead with the Government work, and replied expressing his appreciation. On 10th June he sent a message to the Barrow workers, appreciating "their assurances of loyalty and of resolution to do their utmost to assist in bringing to a victorious conclusion the great war which has now been raging for ten months."

The formation of the Ministry of Munitions called forth the King's keen any sympathetic interest. I have the most grateful recollections of the good will he showed to me in my anxious task, and of his readiness to give that personal help and encouragement which was so valuable a means of maintaining and improving the spirit of the munition workers. On 22nd July he started off and toured the munition areas of the Midlands. At Coventry he went round the works, and spoke personally to the foremen in all the shops. The members of the Coventry Armaments Output Committee were presented to him. Then he went on to Birmingham, where he spent the next day. So much interested did he show himself to be in the process of munition manufacture that it was difficult for the members of his suite to draw him away and enable him to keep to his time-table. Here again he insisted on having the members of the Munitions Committee and of the District Board of Management presented to him, and spoke warmly to them of the "zeal and cheer-fulness" he had noted amongst the workers. This he followed up ten days later with a special message of encouragement.

Towards the end of September the King made another munitions tour, this time in Yorkshire, where he spent three days at Leeds and Sheffield. He moved among the munition workers, chatting freely with them. He picked out one worker at Sheffield, whom he recognised as having served with him when he was a midshipman in H.M.S. *Bacchante*. He watched another making shells, and remarked to him: "I am glad you realise the importance of the work in hand. Without an adequate supply of shells we cannot expect to win."

Words like these, uttered "man to man" by the Head of State to the artisan, naturally ran like wildfire through the works. It was this directness of personal contact, free from pomp or any trace of arrogance and aloofness, which made the King's visits to the muni-tion areas such a valuable aid in the task of rousing the workers' enthusiasm and breaking through their reluctance to accept new methods and regulations.   It was a real service to the men fighting our battles at the front who were in such peril of being overwhelmed by the superior equipment of the enemy.

The stimulation of the munition workers was of course only one among the myriad tasks imposed upon the Sovereign by the War— tasks to which he applied himself with indefatigable zeal, after a fashion which established him more firmly than ever in the affection of his people.   His was the only throne in all the combatant countries which did not rock throughout all those critical years.   Most of them, indeed, were overthrown.   As one who was privileged to hold high and responsible office under the Crown all through the War I had special opportunities of witnessing how thoroughly the King discharged his duty to the country.   Nowhere was the part he played more fruitful and valuable than in the encouragement of our munition workers.

5. THE DRINK TROUBLE

One of the most serious obstacles encountered in the way of increasing the output of munitions was the heavy drinking in certain areas.   France had dealt drastically with the problem by prohibiting absinthe: Russia by forbidding vodka.   The question of drinking facilities has always been a dangerous topic for Governments to tackle, and the War Government, being naturally anxious to avoid controversial subjects, shrank from tackling it for many precious months.   We consequently lost substantially in production.   It is difficult for us to-day to realise how seriously excessive drinking contributed to diminish the output.   Britain to-day is a much more sober country than it has ever been in my memory.   There is still a good deal of heavy drinking, drunkenness still occurs, and the national health suffers from it, but the sight of a drunken man or woman reeling down the street has grown a rare spectacle, and the consumption of alcohol has fallen off very heavily.   The discipline and restriction compelled by the exigencies of the War is largely responsible for this salutary change.   This must ever be counted as one of the good things occasionally garnered from things evil.   The memory of pre-war conditions is growing fainter, and it is becoming quite hard to remind oneself of the very different state of affairs which too often prevailed then.   Cases of drunkenness appearing before the courts were three times as numerous in pre-war years as they are now.   The quantity of spirits (alcoholic content) drunk in 1913 was two and a half times what it is to-day.

That may give the rising generation, growing up to the new and better tradition of to-day, some idea how commonplace and widespread insobriety must have been in some areas of this country up to the Great War.   During the first five months of the War it became a serious element in the struggle to avert defeat. On the home front alcoholic indulgence shared with professional rigidity the dishonour of being our most dangerous foe. It is one of the themes of my book to tell how both of them were beaten off, though not without heavy casualties. The first effect of the War was rather to increase the habit of excessive drinking, and, indeed, to raise it into a real menace to the nation. It is easy to understand that this would be so. The sudden onset of unaccustomed danger drove many who were out of the danger zone to the vicarious philosophy of " Let us eat and drink —especially drink—for to-morrow our comrades may die! "

The disorganisation of social habit through the War, the reckless excitement that thrilled the air, the feeling that the tables of the law had once more been smashed amid the thunders of a grimmer Sinai, led some of both sexes to excesses in all directions, and as war work increased the earnings of multitudes, those who drank, drank deeply, for they could afford the indulgence as they never did before. The evil was not confined to men—it spread to women. My attention was specially directed to this problem through the reports that excessive drinking among the workers in the firms engaged on armament production was gravely hindering the output of munitions. The reports of eye-witnesses were very grave and alarming, especially when taken in conjunction with the fact—of which I was already aware—that deliveries of munitions of war were in arrears, and that there were persistent rumours of serious shortage in France.

Liquor consumption had certainly gone up rapidly. Drunkenness was greatly on the increase, particularly in the industrial areas which we relied on for munitions. A considerable percentage of the workers failed to turn up on a Monday morning, and when they appeared on Tuesday they were much the worse for their week-end debauch. Some of them took to extending their leisure at both ends of the week. One bank holiday a great number of men failed to turn up for a whole week. No wonder output was unsatisfactory. I passed on such reports as I received to the War Office and Admiralty. They replied that they were only too painfully aware of the facts and that their official reports showed an even worse state of affairs than anything revealed in mine. I decided that the time demanded that this peril to our armies ought to be instantly and firmly tackled, and on 28th February, 1915, I began to stir up public opinion on the subject of this increasing and menacing evil, with a view to making strong action possible. Speaking at Bangor on that day I said: —

" I hear of workmen in armament works who refuse to work a full week's work for the nation's need. What is the reason? They are a minority. The vast majority belong to a class we can depend upon. The others are a minority. But, you must remember, a small minority of workmen can throw a whole works out

of gear. What is the reason? Sometimes it is one thing, sometimes
it is another, but let us be perfectly candid. It is mostly the lure
of the drink. They refuse to work full time, and when they return
their strength and efficiency are impaired by the way in which they
have spent their leisure. Drink is doing more damage in the War
than all the German submarines put together. . . . We have got
great powers to deal with drink, and we mean to use them. We
shall use them in a spirit of moderation, we shall use them
discreetly, we shall use them wisely, but we shall use them quite
fearlessly, and I have no doubt that, as the country's needs demand
it, the country will support our action, and will allow no
indulgence of that kind to interfere with its prospects in this
terrible war which has been thrust upon us."

A month later, on 29th March, 1915, I received a deputation from
the Shipbuilding Employers' Federation, who were unanimous in
urging that the sale of excisable liquors should be totally prohibited
during the period of the War. In particular, they asked for the
closing of public-houses and clubs in the areas where war munitions
were being produced. They pointed out that in spite of Sunday
labour and all overtime the total period worked on the average in
almost all shipyards was below the normal number of hours per
week, and though work was in progress night and day for seven days
a week, less productiveness was being secured from the men than
before the War. The deputation was of the opinion that this was
principally due to drink. The figures of weekly takings in public
houses near the yards were convincing evidence of the increased sale
of liquor. Allowing for the enhanced price of intoxicants and for
the greater number of men now employed in shipbuilding, the
takings had in one case under observation risen 20 per cent., in
another 40 per cent.

The damage done by the drink habit was sufficiently illustrated
by the case of a battleship coming in for immediate repairs and
having those repairs delayed a whole day by the absence of the
riveters through drink and conviviality. This case, they said, was
one of hundreds. Nor was this the only reason in favour of prohibition as against curtailment. As long as public-houses were open there
would be found men to break the rules of the yard and come late to
work in order to secure drink beforehand. And the indisposition to
work after the consumption of excessive alcohol was too obvious to
need elaboration. They urged total prohibition during the War.
It was certainly not a teetotal deputation. Neither in figure nor
physiognomy did they give any indication of having spent their
leisure hours in the service of the Band of Hope. When prohibition
came in in America this incident explained to me why the majority
of employers were stout prohibitionists. It also explained the

rumours that they drew a definite line between national prohibition and personal abstinence.

The evidence was not to be lightly disregarded. Replying to the deputation, I said:—

> "Success in the War is now purely a question of munitions. I say that, not on my own authority, but on the authority of our great General, Sir John French. He has made it quite clear what his conviction is on the subject. I think I can venture to say that that is also the conviction of the Secretary of State for War, and it is the conviction of all those who know anything about the military problem—that in order to enable us to win, all we require is an increase, and an enormous increase, in the shells, rifles, and all the other munitions and equipment which are necessary to carry through a great war. You have proved to us to-day quite clearly that the excessive drinking in the works connected with these operations is interfering seriously with that output. I can only promise you this at the present moment, that the words you have addressed to my colleagues and myself will be taken into the most careful consideration. . . . I had the privilege of an audience with his Majesty this morning, and I am permitted by him to say that he is very deeply concerned on this question—very deeply concerned—and the concern which is felt by him is, I am certain, shared by all his subjects in this country."

His Majesty had indeed shown the most anxious interest in the problem of drink, and had talked over with me the various possible methods of combating it. Reports had been coming in to him from many quarters as to the damaging effect of drink on production. He was himself prepared to go to any length of personal self-sacrifice for this end, and on 30th March, the day after I had received this deputation, he sent me, through his secretary, Lord Stamfordham, a remarkable letter, which, after saying that "nothing but the most vigorous measures will successfully cope with the grave situation now existing in our armament factories," proceeded:—

> "We have before us the statements, not merely of the employers, but of the Admiralty and War Office officials responsible for the supply of munitions of war, for the transport of troops, their food, and ammunition. From this evidence it is without doubt largely due to drink that we are unable to secure the output of war material indispensable to meet the requirements of our Army in the field, and that there has been such serious delay in the conveyance of the necessary reinforcements and supplies to aid our gallant troops at the front.
> The continuance of such a state of things must inevitably result in the prolongation of the horrors and burdens of this terrible war.

I am to add that if it be deemed advisable, the King will be prepared to set the example by giving up all alcoholic liquor himself, and issuing orders against its consumption in the Royal Household, so that no difference shall be made, so far as his Majesty is concerned, between the treatment of rich and poor in this question."

This royal gesture became known as " The King's Pledge," which the nation at large was urged to adopt in conformity with the King's example. There was sound wisdom in the scheme, for the workers habitually complained, and with all-too-good reason, that while their employers and the members of the so-called upper classes were eternally lecturing and rebuking them for drinking, they were themselves freely and often excessively enjoying the alcohol which they sought to deny to their employees. "The King's Pledge," and the fact that a number of distinguished persons and prominent men in every branch of industry followed his Majesty in subscribing to it, very greatly strengthened the hands of the Government in the measures which it subsequently took to limit and control the supplies of intoxicants. Lord Kitchener was amongst those who gave practical support to the King's initiative and adhered to it to the end. It was always a subject of general debate at Ministerial and Military tables whether total abstinence had increased or diminished the vision and efficiency of the Secretary of State for War, or whether it had left it *in statu quo*, and there were three distinct views on this point, each emphatically held and controverted.

Unfortunately, despite its considerably moral value, the King's example was not adopted widely enough to make any deep impression on the problem itself. The House of Commons flatly declined to pass any such self-denying ordinance for its own observance, and this attitude on the part of the nation's legislators helped to prevent " The King's Pledge " from becoming the starting-point which King George and his advisers had hoped it might prove for a big voluntary movement of national sobriety. It remained, therefore, to reinforce this initial impulse by statutory powers.

I was at this time giving very serious consideration to the idea of dealing with the drink traffic by buying out on behalf of the State all the private interests, and thus enabling the Government to obtain a perfectly free hand to carry through whatever measures were felt to be in the national interest, unhindered by the immensely powerful influence which the trade has always been able to exert on politics in this country. To this end I caused an investigation to be made by Sir William Plender as to the probable total value of the interests it would be necessary to acquire. On 30th March, he furnished me with a preliminary memorandum which showed that the market value of the shares in Breweries was approximately £68,786,000, while the value of the property owned by Breweries in Great Britain, including all tied houses, together with the value of all free public-houses and other on-licences would be £225,000,000 to £250,000,000.

It will be observed that this rough estimate did not include the value of distilleries.

I then secured the appointment of a " Liquor Trade Finance Committee " to advise the Government on the financial arrangements that would have to be made if it should be decided by the State to purchase the properties of the Breweries in England and Wales, to control the branches of the Retail Liquor Trade not so purchased, and to prohibit temporarily the retail trade in spirits, while permitting the continuance of the sale of beer below a certain alcoholic strength. The Committee reported on 15th April, 1915, submitting a series of recommendations as to the extent and manner of effecting the State acquisition of liquor interests, should such a step be decided on. This Committee estimated the total cost of transfer to the State of the properties of Breweries and the interests of the licensees of free houses in England and Wales at £250 million, excluding allowances in respect of certain off-licences for compensation to the holders of grocers' licences, compensation to officials and employees, and any other expenditure involved in the carrying through of such acquisition.

To politicians bred in pre-war traditions of national expenditure, the sum involved in this purchase seemed prodigious. It was held by some that in view of the heavy burdens we were already bearing to finance our war effort, it would be folly to choose this moment to incur this further heavy outlay. The sum required was barely one-fortieth of the ultimate cost of the War. In return the nation would have secured an asset which, on the basis of present profits would have given a return of 8 per cent.

The real statesmanship of the temperance cause was on my side. But a powerful section of temperance advocates were up in arms against the abhorrent suggestion that the State should sully its soul by becoming the manufacturer and distributor of alcoholic poison. They had no objection to share by taxation in the profits made by selling this poison to their fellow citizens. But the conscience of a devotee is an eccentric thing and argument never converts but only exasperates a true believer. The resistance of this section grew. On the practical side I was faced with the difficulty that the interests which would have to be dealt with by way of purchase or compensation were so numerous and varied in character that the negotiations threatened to take many months. I secured the adhesion of some of the leading brewers to my scheme. I did not despair of securing the adhesion of the rest. The Conservative leaders were consulted as to their attitude and they intimated that they would offer no opposition to the deal if the Government came to the conclusion that it was essential as a war measure. But a number of influential local optionists brought such pressure to bear on the Prime Minister that he feared serious trouble inside the Party, and in view of the urgency of the problem of reducing excessive drinking in the interests of munition output I decided for the time being to proceed with a more limited reform.

During the course of the negotiations I received from Mr. Edwin Montagu the following contribution to the discussions in a letter which he wrote me. As it puts the case against restriction forcibly and wittily, I think it worth reproducing: —

"(1) I believe and believe firmly that almost without exception, except in the cases of apoplexy, a shot in the stomach, or a congested liver, a man with a moderate amount of alcohol is a better citizen, a better man, a more vigorous individual, than he would be without it. Medical evidence shows that alcohol is a poison; like so many other poisons in moderation, it is beneficial, and total abstinence seems to me to be morally as great a weakness as insobriety.

(2) I cannot find myself in agreement with you that there is any evidence that drink has hampered us in this War on any substantial scale which calls for heroic remedies. Evil exists— there is broken time, there is disinclination to work; it is true that, even with Sunday labour and overtime, the average hours worked are less per week in many important trades than before the War. I believe this to be largely to due to overtime itself. If a man is called upon to work substantially longer one day than he is accustomed to work, the next day he is disinclined to work, and if he is a free agent may refuse to work. Our party anyhow, believes that trade unions are good institutions. They fixed the working day and its length probably empirically because experience showed them that, let us say, eight hours was the maximum which a member of their union could work regularly to produce the full economical output of which he was capable. They insisted that overtime should be treated as overtime because they found that it was economically bad, and it seems to me that the War has proved that insistence upon overtime leads to irregular work and a smaller output, and it should be avoided as much as possible.

(3) It is true that receipts from the sale of drink are large, but this is due mainly to your own taxation, which has increased the price of beer, and to the increase in the price of raw material and of labour, which has increased the price of whisky.

(4) It is true that employers and officials alike attribute everything that is wrong not to drunkenness, but to drink; but you must remember that although the Tory habit of mind is to be found on

both sides of the House of Commons you are now for the first time coming into contact with the Tory mind, naked and unashamed, in bulk, and I cannot help feeling alarmed that you regard it as honest, as unprejudiced as the habit of mind to which you are accustomed. I regard it as being a worse habit of mind. It is a habit of mind which treats the working man as a machine with no vested interest in his habits and with no right to humane consideration. Just as if an engine can do 500 revolutions a minute it can do 30,000 in an hour and 300,000 in 10 hours, so they think a man who can drill 6 holes in an hour ought to drill 60 in 10 hours and 600 in 100 hours. Anything wrong with their system they are accustomed to put down to the unpatriotism, to the want of a sense of duty, the gross habits of these animals whom they regard as their inferiors. When you say to me that it is not only the evidence of the employers but also the evidence of the War Office and the Admiralty I am more emphatic in regarding the source of information as tainted. Likely it was these gentlemen, who would like to work on paper according to theory, dismissing from their minds all human factors, found the British working man an intolerable nuisance. They would like to regulate him in all his actions, to measure his food like sailors on a ship or prisoners in a gaol, to dictate to him what time he went to bed and what time he arose, where he should live and even what he should think, to drill and perhaps to flog him to approximate him to the ideal nigger working for an average mine-owner in a Rand mine.

(5) It is said that holidays would not be so attractive to the labourers if the public-houses were closed. But you are not going to close the public-houses; you are, I think, driven by a belief that you cannot with fairness deny a stimulant to a man in the Black Squad who works under horrible climatic conditions in the open air and you are going to allow him to have light beer. He will go to the public-house to get his light beer just as he goes now to get his strong beer. His holidays will be just as attractive, and if your object is to make it unattractive you will have to close picture palaces and deprive him of all opportunity for amusement.

(6) Every one of the deputation which waited on you the other day drinks moderately—they told you so—but they would be insulted if you told them that they were unfitted for work because of this habit, and I really believe that you run grave danger by insulting or being understood to insult the people of this country of all classes by interfering with their liberty. The agricultural labourer, the honest, self-controlled artisan, the small tradesman, inspired by patriotic motives and doing his duty, may feel that those who are running the War do not trust them, and you may impair the fighting enthusiasm of your country. I hear rumours from all sources, from the Opposition, from the Labour Party, from

total abstainers and excessive drinkers, from political 'wire-pullers' that you will be met with opposition. But you will, of course, succeed in overcoming all this and I would only urge in conclusion two important things:—

(1) You must consult Labour so that you may find your difficulties lessened by their acquiescence. You may have to persuade employers to give them something else whilst you are doing this.

(2) You ought, I think, to consult some financial expert on the finance. You will, of course, not be misled by the desire of the brewers and the distillers to get out of the trade which is continually having to fight hostility on the part of the community.

But I think the Governor of the Bank would be able to give us information as to the best way of carrying out your project. If you issue £200,000,000 of 4 per cent. stock you must, I fear, create a disastrous effect upon our credit. The Irish Land Stock is an example of the effects of a particular stock in a particular interest. I do not see how you can expect your brewer friends to hold your stock; they will run to the market and unload it, and when it approximates to a price of 50, it will bring down with it the price of all other Government stock, not to the same level, but down, and I would urge that at once you ought to get the Stock Exchange Committee to fix a minimum price for it in order to make it unsaleable, at any rate, for the present.

You will notice that I make two suggestions at the end, after letting myself go in the earlier part of what I have written. I am now going to assume that I am wrong in all my objections, and that you are going full steam ahead."

This pungent letter will give an idea of the division inside the Government on the drink issue. With regard to Mr. Montagu's suggestion that diminished production was due to fatigue arising from long hours, the figures I give later on as to the average hours actually worked in the yards and factories at that time supply a complete answer.

Having decided for the time being to abandon the attempt to purchase the whole of the liquor trade, I prepared a measure to secure its more effective control—a measure which further enabled the experiment to be made of State purchase and management of the liquor traffic on a small scale in particular areas. With this programme in view I laid before the House of Commons on 29th April a further instalment of D.O.R.A.—the Defence of the Realm (Amendment) (No. 3) Bill—designed to deal with the evil of drink in those munition-making areas where it was proving especially disastrous to the nation, and at the same time I outlined other plans for a nation-wide limitation of the peril.

In commending this Bill to the House I drew attention to the very alarming evidence which had come to hand of the effects of excessive drinking. A selection of this was published a couple of days later as a Government White Paper. This gave statistics of time lost in the shipyards and engineering shops of the Clyde and Tyne, and reports by officers of the Admiralty and the Home Office.

The reports were almost unanimous in making the same assertions as to lost time and energy due to alcohol. Statistics compiled from 15 firms in the Clyde district, for example, showed that of the iron-workers, 27.6 per cent. were working more than 53 hours per week, 39.4 per cent. between 40 and 53 hours, while 33 per cent. were working less than 40 hours per week. It was a minority that slacked, but a minority large and important enough to be disastrous to our national output.

The measure I proposed was to the effect that any area of importance for the production and transport of war materials might be placed under special control as regards the sale and supply of alcohol. The areas were to be defined by Orders in Council, and regulations applied to them which might empower the Government to close down the private liquor industry in the area, and become itself the sole supplier of intoxicants; to acquire, either temporarily or permanently, all licensed premises and businesses; to open, without licence, places of refreshment in which liquor could be sold; and generally to control the licensing and sale of intoxicants within the area. The Bill was duly carried, and a Central Control Board was set up to deal with Liquor Traffic. This Board issued on 12th June a set of regulations by which it took power, in any area placed under its control, to close any licensed premises or clubs, to regulate their hours of opening, to prohibit the sale or supply of any specified class of intoxicant, to impose conditions and restrictions upon licensed premises or take them under its supervision and to regulate the amount of liquor that could be brought into an area or transported within it. It further took power to prohibit in an area all sale of liquor except by the Board of Control, to prohibit treating, etc.

In July a series of Orders in Council was issued, defining the chief munition areas in the country and placing them under the Board of Liquor Control. During the following months the Board began to make effective use of its powers, issuing the " No Treating " Order in October, 1915, and drastically restricting the hours of sale of intoxicants. For the London area the hours of opening were in November narrowed down to what had previously been the " Sunday " hours.

It will be noted that I avoided total prohibition, despite the earnestness with which this policy was urged on me, in all good faith, by many who had not previously been associated with the "blue ribbon" movement. I realised clearly enough, what has since then been demonstrated in the United States, that it is futile to legislate far in advance of popular opinion or the public conscience. Restriction and limitation the nation would accept, and a considerable degree of reform could be achieved under State control, where the element of private profit and exploitation was eliminated. I confined my objective to this practical programme.

Even this reasonable scheme encountered very bitter opposition, and in my further proposals for a general discouragement of drinking I was at first compelled to swallow an almost complete defeat. In my speech on the 29th April I had said that I intended in my Budget to impose a graded surtax on the heavier beers, to quadruple the tax on wines, to double the taxes on spirits, and to raise the maximum permissible dilution of spirits from 25 per cent. to 36 per cent. under proof. These proposals roused considerable opposition both in and out of the House of Commons. The Irish Party was particularly angry in view of the big brewing and distilling interests in that country. One by one I was compelled to abandon, for the time being, these proposed taxes, and could only retain one insignificant but quite useful little restriction in the shape of a prohibition on the sale of spirits less than three years old, the object being to prohibit the newer and more fiery spirit. Even round this a fierce controversy arose between the rival distilling interests—the "Pot versus Patent" fight —for manufacturers of pot-still whisky made a practice of keeping their product several years to mature, whereas the output of the patent still was marketed straight away.

But although I lost this opening round I succeeded in subsequent years in carrying through the policy of high taxation of alcoholic beverages, dilution of spirits and encouragement of lighter beers. In this campaign I was able to utilise the aid of the Food Controller, under whose care the supplies of grain required for brewing and distilling had been placed. Not only was the total amount brewed and distilled restricted, but the release of such grain as was allowed was made conditional upon a proportion of the beer being of a light character, and the spirits being considerably diluted. The nation sang music-hall ditties bewailing "Lloyd George's Be-e-e-er," but the statistics of insobriety showed a rapid decline. The compulsory dilution of spirits and the elimination of the heavier beers had an especially beneficial effect, for they reduced the quantity of alcohol content of the beverages imbibed by a high percentage. The weekly average of convictions for drunkenness in England and Wales, which in 1913 were 3,482, had by the first part of 1917 fallen to 929.

The following are the figures for the total consumption of absolute alcohol in Great Britain during the War years:—

1914...................89 million gallons
1915...................81 „   „
1916...................73 „   „
1917...................45 „   „
1918...................37 „   „

These figures represent the amount of alcohol estimated to have been consumed in all forms of alcoholic beverages—spirits, wines and beers—and the rapid decline in the last two years is only partly due to the fact that millions of men had left our shores. It is mainly attributable to the effectiveness of the drink restriction policy which was instituted and enforced.

While by means of progressive measures of taxation, dilution and limitation of the intoxicating beverages in the country, we were able to reduce very considerably the effective supplies of them obtained by the people, and especially the quantity of proof spirit and alcohol consumed, we were pressing forward in the industrial areas devoted to munition production the limitation of hours and drinking facilities. But I was by no means satisfied to adopt a purely negative policy. The Liquor Control Board had been given powers to take over the whole business of liquor supply within an area, and in four of the areas it experimentally adopted these powers, the first area so treated being that of Gretna Green—from which was developed the Carlisle experiment in State management of the liquor trade, an experiment which is still with us, and on which I will forbear comment beyond the unchallengeable statement that in the opinion of many highly competent observers it has more than justified the faith of those who authorised the venture, and has demonstrated that State management is capable of giving an orderly and adequate provision of alcoholic refreshment under conditions which promote sobriety and social amenity. The positive policy of the Control Board was shown in another very important direction—that of finding a satisfactory substitute in the scheduled areas for the drinking-dens whose opportunity of catering for the leisure of the workers was being curtailed. This led it to the appointment of a Canteens Committee. In its first report, dated 12th October, 1915, the Control Board stated:—

". . . The Board incline to the view that excessive drinking may often be traced to the want of adequate facilities for food, refreshment, and recreation, particularly in conjunction with long hours and overtime. The improvement of public-houses and the provision of canteens may therefore do much to render less necessary the imposition of purely restrictive measures. . . ."

The Board pointed out that drink was often resorted to when food was inadequate or improper; and that it was important

"to supply for large numbers of persons at specified times a suitable dietary . . . at a reasonable cost.

In endeavouring to meet this requirement, the Board have proceeded on two collateral lines of action: —

(a) The increase of facilities for obtaining suitable meals at public-houses, and

(b) The establishment wherever necessary of industrial canteens inside or within easy access of the works, supplying both substantial meals and light refreshment at reasonable prices."

A number of voluntary organisations rendered great help in the promotion of these canteens, such as the Y.M.C.A. and Y.W.C.A., Lady Lawrence's Munition Makers' Canteen Committee, the Salvation Army, and the Church Army. As to the actual provision of canteen premises and equipment, however, there was a question whether the Board or the employers should finance this; and it seemed much more desirable that the employers should undertake this responsibility, as it ensured their interest and gave a better prospect of permanence to the canteens. Accordingly, I secured Treasury sanction for an arrangement whereby the cost of building and equipping canteens might be charged by controlled establishments against their current profits under Part III of the Munitions of War Act, 1915, on condition that such buildings were maintained thereafter permanently as canteens, save by permission of the Ministry or of the Government Department which should inherit its duties.

This concession operated from November, 1915, until November, 1918, during which period 867 schemes of canteens at controlled establishments were approved, the total cost of them which was recommended for writing off gross profits being £1,909,135. About a million workpeople were employed in the establishments to which these canteens were attached.

The habit of regular and wholesome meals which these canteens encouraged, combined with the limitation and dilution of alcoholic beverages, helped to establish the post-war tradition of moderation in drinking and an improved standard of healthy living with which we are now familiar.

The progress which was made amply warranted me in stating to a temperance deputation which waited on me in 1917 to urge total prohibition, that by confining our objectives to practical and attainable limits we had been able in the last year or two to achieve a far bigger advance toward national sobriety than had hitherto been effected in a far longer period by all persuasive and legislative efforts in combination.

6.   WELFARE CONDITIONS IN THE WORKSHOPS

One of the most welcome features of my post as Minister of Munitions was the opportunity it placed within my reach of doing something to better the social and industrial conditions in the manufacturing establishments which came under my direct or indirect control. Legislation reflected the growing desire in industry among both workers and employers for better standards in the workshops. In matters of this kind the law cannot move very far in advance of public opinion, save at the risk of becoming a dead letter. Various measures were sanctioned to a greater or less extent by the demands of workers, the successful experiment of enlightened employers, the zeal of practical reformers, and the growth of a progressive public opinion.

They represented, of course, only the minimum demand enforceable by law upon industry. Their incidence was limited and partial, and they did not go very far to ensure the highest attainable measure of amenity, health or comfort for the worker. Some employers were doing good pioneer work in the voluntary creation of improved conditions for their staffs, but they were in those days the exception rather than the rule.

The establishment of the Ministry of Munitions and the new industrial development which it organised gave an impulse to important changes in the general situation.

In the first place, the State as represented by the Ministry became a large-scale direct employer of industrial labour, and on an even larger scale an indirect employer of labour in the establishments engaged in munition work which were brought under its control. It was thus in a position to exercise persuasion, pressure, and, if necessary, compulsion, upon employers throughout the country to adopt higher standards for ensuring the welfare of their workers during the hours of employment.

In the second place, the withdrawal of a large part of the male population from industry into our fighting forces brought about the introduction of female labour on a scale never previously contemplated, and into industrial occupations which had formerly been staffed exclusively by men. There had, of course, before the War been a considerable body of female labour employed in certain types of factory—particularly in textiles—but it now invaded unusual fields of the heavy industries, the shell-filling factories, and even shipbuilding. In most of these establishments rough and unseemly conditions prevailed and had hitherto been put up with by the men workers, but it was recognised as impossible to ask women to submit to them.

A singularly favourable opportunity thus presented itself for introducing into industry a great forward movement for improving the general conditions of the welfare of the workers—an opportunity of which as Minister of Munitions I proceeded forthwith to take full advantage.

One of the first tasks of the Ministry of Munitions was the creation of national filling and explosive factories; and from August, 1915, a woman staff inspector of the Ministry was at work visiting these as fast as they were opened up and keeping in touch with the Boards of Management regarding the very important and varied questions of the welfare of women in this often dangerous work. Her duties included advice and help in the selection of woman supervisors, in the training of the special types of labour required, and in the provision of doctors and nurses for its care. In September, 1915, I appointed a Health of Munition Workers Committee to advise on questions concerning " industrial fatigue, hours of labour, and other matters affecting the personal health and physical efficiency " of the munition worker. It was a strong Committee representing the concentrated experience of the Home Office, of employers, labour, and medical experts. The Chairman was Sir George Newman and the members included Sir Thomas Barlow, Dr. Leonard E. Hill, three leading officers of the Home Office factory department, Sir W. M. Fletcher, Secretary of the Medical Research Committee, Mr. Clynes, Professor Boycott, Mr. Samuel Osborne, and Mrs. H. J. Tennant. It rendered invaluable service throughout the War by recommendations which supplied us with a practical programme for welfare work, and became a forerunner of the Industrial Fatigue Research Committee which has since the War carried out such important investigations into the conditions of industrial efficiency. Throughout the autumn of 1915 the supply departments of the Ministry of Munitions, working in consultation with this Committee, were organising measures to promote the welfare of munition workers in the national factories. In December, 1915, I took the further step of appointing Mr. B. Seebohm Rowntree Director of the Welfare Section of the Ministry, which I invited him to organise. Mr. Rowntree is well known, not only as a great employer of labour, but as one of the foremost and most successful pioneers in the development of improved conditions in his works. I should like to pay tribute here to the skill, energy, sympathy, and address with which he organised this new department. The work he did helped to transform the conditions for munition labour during the War, and has left a permanent mark upon conditions in our industries.

It was a difficult problem which confronted the new Welfare Section. In a large number of the existing factories conditions were very rough and primitive, and there was no tradition of care for the health or comfort of the employee beyond the minimum that was already compulsory under the Factory Acts. The pressure of work had, of course, been greatly intensified by the necessities of the War. Hours were long, and premises often crowded. New factories and extensions of existing factories were being rapidly run up, and these temporary erections were often occupied and buzzing with activity before any thought had been given to the provision of accessories in the shape of lavatories, cloak-rooms, mess-rooms, or canteens. And, in addition, they were being increasingly staffed by women and girls, for whose supervision no appropriate arrangements had been made.

The Health of Munition Workers Committee, in a memorandum issued in January, 1916, urged the need for attention to this side of the problem of production:—

" If the present long hours, the lack of healthful and sympathetic oversight, the inability to obtain good wholesome food, and the great difficulties of travelling are allowed to continue, it will be impracticable to secure or maintain for an extended period the high maximum output of which women are undoubtedly capable."

Under the Munitions of War (Amendment) Act of January, 1916, I had taken powers to control not only the wages but the conditions of employment of women workers on munitions, and also of semi-skilled and unskilled men and boys taking the work of skilled men in controlled firms. The Welfare Section of the Ministry, however, while holding these powers in reserve, adopted the deliberate policy of educating rather than compelling the firms engaged on munition work to put in hand arrangements for the welfare of their employees. Mr. Rowntree held that this was the only way of ensuring that the improved conditions so created would continue permanently after the War.

In the first instance the Welfare Section naturally devoted its principal effort to securing proper conditions for the women workers. At the outset they were often worse off than the existing male staffs, for no special accommodation or provision had in most cases been furnished for them, and they had no person of their own sex in authority to whom to appeal. In April, 1916, I ruled that women supervisors should be appointed in all national factories where women or young persons were employed, and that they should be approved by the Welfare Section. Their introduction into these national factories served as a precedent for their introduction into controlled establishments. In the same month a start was made by the Section with the development of welfare supervision for boys.

The welfare arrangements which were initiated included the provision of staffs and proper accommodation. The staffs comprised supervisors and assistant supervisors of welfare, and in the larger works, matrons, nurses, lady doctors, cloak-room attendants, etc. The provision of welfare accommodation included such matters

H

as washing facilities, sanitary conveniences, cloak-rooms, canteens, seats in work-rooms, supplies of overalls and caps, and recreation facilities. It was necessary to persuade some employers that one broken basin and a jug of cold water was insufficient washing provision for a staff of 300 workers; that workers engaged in hot, heavy and exhausting work should be able to have convenient access to clean drinking water and not to be reduced to running the risk of typhoid by drinking water intended only for manufacturing purposes; that the efficiency of workers would be increased if they were not required to work all day in clothes drenched in the morning on the way to the factory, and if they could take their meals in comfort in a mess-room, or—better still—get cheap and wholesome food in the canteen, instead of gobbling scrappy meals beside their machines.

The policy of persuasion was, however, justified by its results. The demand for welfare supervisors grew to such an extent that special training courses were arranged by the department—a function later on taken over by the London School of Economics and by most of the provincial universities. Over 1,000 supervisors of varying grades were working in munition factories at the date of the Armistice. Allowing for the fact that their appointment had been made compulsory in T.N.T. factories and practically compulsory in national factories, probably some 700 had been appointed voluntarily by heads of firms or boards of management.

The welfare policy of the department ensured the standard of physical comfort for nearly 350,000 workers in the national factories and Government establishments, much above the minimum required under the Factory and Workshop Acts, and it stimulated a similar provision of canteens, rest rooms, ambulance rooms, and other material comforts, to a greater or less degree in a large proportion of the other controlled establishments, in which at least 400,000 women munition workers were employed. This increased comfort was extended in some measure at least among a million and a quarter men and nearly a quarter of a million boys similarly employed by controlled firms and in national factories.

The department built, or promoted the building of, 11,738 flats and houses for munition workers. It provided hostels for more than 23,500 workers and secured further accommodation in a large number of other cases, together with lodgings and billets in private houses for munition workers. It provided directly for canteens and mess-rooms in the great majority of the 150 national and Government factories, while the Central Liquor Control Board approved on behalf of the Department the canteens of some 740 controlled establishments.

Its work in promoting intelligent care for the health and comfort of employees, the convenience of their hours, the hygienic conditions of their work, is perhaps less susceptible to statistical statement, but was at least as important in the permanent impression it made on our national industrial conditions.

As early as 1917-18 the " Factory Inspectors' Annual Report " bore witness to the effect of the welfare movement stimulated by the Ministry of Munitions in permeating the standards of non-munition trades, such as : —

> " Cotton and woollen and worsted textiles, in laundries, in potteries, in biscuit factories . . . where conditions, with honourable individual exceptions, have long been stationary, but here too . . . the new movement has begun to take effect. . . . In these and many other developments moving towards social welfare in non-munition factories in 1917, there is really less sudden a growth than it is apt to be considered. Enlightened workers have been asking for these things, and enlightened manufacturers have been demonstrating for many years that these improving conditions are both rightly demanded and practicable. Now common sense awakened sees that the pace must be greatly quickened. . . . It is not only in controlled and national factories that material advance has been made. The whole spirit of management has quickly changed in many factories and industries where no new welfare order runs, and where State control of profits has not entered."

Legislative provision for the extension of the welfare movement was in full operation when the work of the department ceased. The principles established by the Ministry through persuasion were being gradually followed up by the Home Office with definite legislation. As early as August, 1916, the Police, Factories, etc., Miscellaneous Provision Acts gave definite powers of enforcing welfare provision. The Trade Boards Act of 1918 authorised trade boards " to make representations " to Government departments with regard to working conditions in their trade, while in the organised industries an increasing number of Joint Industrial Councils were beginning to consider questions of hours, conditions, and training. The prospect of legislative provision for a 48-hour week for all factory workers had appeared on the horizon.

In the light of these and other subsequent developments, there seems to have been a certain note of prophecy in a speech made by me as Minister of Munitions in February, 1916, when I remarked : —

> " It is a strange irony, but no small compensation, that the making of weapons of destruction should afford the occasion to humanise industry. Yet such is the case. Old prejudices have vanished, new ideas are abroad; employers and workers, the public and the State, are favourable to new methods. This opportunity

must not be allowed to slip.   It may well be that, when the tumult
of war is a distant echo, and the making of munitions a nightmare
of the past, the effort now being made to soften asperities, to
secure the welfare of the workers, and to build a bridge of
sympathy and understanding between employer and employed,
will have left behind results of permanent and enduring value to
the workers, to the nation and to mankind at large."

CHAPTER X

THE STRATEGY OF THE WAR

EASTERN v. WESTERN FRONTS

IN the foregoing pages I have told something of the way in which the Ministry of Munitions was inaugurated, and of the human side of the problems with which it was faced. Before proceeding further to describe its practical achievements in the sphere of munition production, I must turn back to give some account of the battlefields for which these supplies were required, and the strategy they were designed to support.

For if it had involved tedious and incessant effort to break down the barriers of routine and military inertia which hampered the equipment of our forces, the parallel task of ensuring that our resources of man-power and munitions should be used in the most effective manner was still harder, and in fact was never carried out satisfactorily until the closing period of the War. I will now give a brief sketch of this problem, and of the efforts made to secure what I conceived at the time to be a wise solution.

There was during the early months of the War practically no effective War Council in the country keeping the position in constant review by directing and co-ordinating our efforts. There was a sense of leisureliness, if not of casualness, in our exertions.

After the great battles of the Marne and Ypres the War seemed to be settling down to normality. It was becoming accepted as if it were an ordinary part of the daily existence of nations. The people everywhere were adapting themselves to war conditions. The population of Whitehall, high and low, were no exception. That may account for the fact that there was a "no great hurry" atmosphere about our movements. The Germans had failed to capture Paris. It is true their armies were clamped firmly in Belgium and some of the richest departments of France, but they were kept within the limits of these autumnal conquests and could get no farther. The safety of the Channel ports had been assured by the battle of Ypres. There was some fighting in Poland and the Russian steam-roller had been pushed back by the Germans, but it had made up for that by rolling forward in Galicia. The Central Powers had been checked. We could now take our time to enrol and equip. That was the official temper—I am not sure that it did not represent the national attitude towards the end of 1914.

The fact that we were lavishing life and treasure away every day the War was prolonged; that Russia had revealed a dangerous weakness in the matter of equipment of her great armies, and that another campaign might therefore lead to her collapse and leave all the fighting to France and ourselves; that the position of Serbia was precarious and that the Central Powers might any day sweep her out of the way and open the road to the East; that unless we stirred ourselves up immediately we might not be able to put a well-equipped army in the field until the third year of the War: all these possibilities never seemed to come into the reckoning to disturb the general equanimity.

As far as the people at large were concerned, this composure was attributable to their unshaken confidence in our military chiefs and naval captains. What I had already seen of the official military attitude towards the equipment of our armies and their failure to grasp the new conditions of war as they had developed in France, convinced me that there was no justification for this remarkable complacency.

This induced me to write the following letter to the Prime Minister:—

" 11, Downing Street, W.

31st December, 1914.

My dear Prime Minister,

I am uneasy about the prospects of the War unless the Government take some decisive measures to grip the situation. I can see no signs anywhere that our military leaders and guides are considering any plans for extricating us from our present unsatisfactory position. Had I not been a witness of their deplorable lack of prevision I should not have thought it possible that men so responsibly placed could have so little forethought. You remember the guns and ammunition incident. When I raised the question in the Cabinet, the War Office had only ordered 600 guns in all. These were to be delivered before next September. The immense manufacturing resources of the country had not been organised for cannon, rifles, or ammunition, and America was not even explored. As a result of the activities and suggestions of the Cabinet Committee, 4,000 guns are now promised before that date. Ammunition has also been provided for those guns. Rifles not yet satisfactory. . . .

No real effort has been made until this week to ascertain the Russian position. Now K. has invited a Russian officer to come over to confer with a view to helping Russia with ammunition. Two months ago I pressed it on the War Office. Had it been done then we could have helped Russia, whilst Archangel was still open, and saved her from the peril of exhausted caissons.

Could we not have a series of meetings of the War Committee of the C.I.D. at an early date?   Occasional meetings at intervals of a week or a fortnight will end in nothing.

Forgive me for intruding on your well-earned rest, but I feel that a continuation of the present deadlock is full of danger.

Sincerely yours,

D. LLOYD GEORGE."

This letter led to the calling of a War Committee at an early date to review the position. In order to form an opinion on the discussions and decisions of this Committee it is necessary to recall the military position at that date.

When the campaign of 1914 on all fronts came to an end owing to weather conditions, the Supreme Command, political, military and naval in the belligerent countries, had time to review the position and to decide upon their future course of action. Every army found its first plans baffled and broken by the fighting that had taken place. Not one of the elaborate schemes so carefully prepared and perfected for years by experts and lying in their bureaux ready to put into resistless operation on " the day "—for they all had their eagerly expected " day "—survived the actual clash of battle. Something went wrong with them all.

There was the long-prepared and pigeon-holed German plan for crushing France in a few weeks by an outflanking march of overwhelming forces through Belgium, followed by an immediate turning to the east with the victorious troops to roll up the armies of Russia. It had been worked out to the last detail. Nothing had been overlooked except the extent and effect of Britain's military intervention, and also perhaps the equally important fact that the execution of the plan would be in the hands of different men from those who originated it. That scheme had now failed utterly and its fragments were scattered along the banks of the Marne and the Yser. The pigeon-hole at Berlin was empty. The thwarting of the invincible plan had not been anticipated. A new plan must therefore be worked out.

The French plan of attacking with the first and second armies south of Metz, and with the fourth and fifth north of it never had a chance of success. It was based on an assumption that never materialised. The British idea of holding the Germans on the Belgian Front whilst the French dealt with them lower down was based on the same complete miscalculation of the German strategy as that which misled the French generals. This was merely conforming to the French strategy. Had Sir John French's idea of the occupation of Antwerp been adopted there would have been a different situation to deal with.

The Austrian dream of an easy march from Belgrade to Nish had a rude awakening, for the Serbian peasants inflicted two disastrous defeats on their jaunty invaders. The Russians had some successes against Austria. Against Germany, if they ever had a plan, it never came off. The invasion of East Prussia was little more than a chivalrous improvisation to save France from the blunders of her generals. It came to a bad end at Tannenberg.

The great struggles of 1914, therefore, had shattered every military dream and wrecked every military hope on both sides. The military leaders were bereft of any clear idea how ultimate victory could be attained. Every army had its failures. Every army had its successes. At the end of the 1914 campaign they all rejoiced in the victories and forgot the defeats. That was the general state of mind in and behind the lines. But no one had any clear notion what to attempt next. New plans must therefore be thought of for the 1915 campaign.

I was bold enough to form an opinion as to the general situation and rash enough to express it. As I have been severely criticised in certain professional quarters for my impertinent activities in this direction, I feel bound to state the considerations that led me to challenge the policy or lack of policy which in the event was responsible for prolonging the War, added enormously to its sacrifices in human life, increased its burdens and brought the cause of the Allies to the very brink of irretrievable disaster.

Why should a civilian who had made no study of the science of war have concerned himself at all with strategical questions? Why not leave that phase of the war problem to men who had devoted their lives to such a study? My answer to those who charge me with meddling in a business of which I knew nothing except what I had learnt by a reading of past wars, and conversations with soldiers whom I had met here and in France, is that as events developed it became increasingly evident to the rawest amateur mind that the military were fumbling badly with their job. The Allied strategy in France had been a sanguinary mistake which nearly brought us to irretrievable defeat. When it failed the High Commands had no rational alternative to propose. The Allied generals were completely baffled by the decision of the Germans to dig in. They could think of nothing better than the sacrifice of millions of men in a hopeless effort to break through. Even then they had not worked out what mechanical aid was necessary to carry out such an operation, nor had they given any real systematic thought to the methods of providing their armies with the requisite machinery for putting into effect their hazy and crazy plans.

How crazy were their ideas at this stage can be ascertained by reading the painful story of a succession of foolish offensives which for years were to mow down the flower of British and French youth by the million in vain efforts to rush machine guns, skilfully concealed and effectively protected.

The primary responsibility for success or failure rested with Governments, and they could not shuffle off any part of that responsibility by pleading that they had placed their trust in experts who were obviously unequal to their task.

By the end of the year over a million young men had volunteered and had been duly enrolled either in the Kitchener armies or in the Territorials, and thousands were still streaming in. Amongst them were the pick of the youth of the country in physique, brain and character. In every sphere of life all that was best amongst the young men of the land joined the Army. It cannot be said as yet that they had donned the King's uniform, for in the best-equipped of all countries for the manufacture of men's apparel, the War Office had not yet succeeded in procuring the necessary supply of uniforms for all their recruits. But it was already evident that the human material which was everywhere being trained into soldiers was of a higher quality than anything to which drill sergeants had hitherto been accustomed. The Universities were drained of all the physically fit—so were all the professions. Artisans, miners, labourers—all contributed of their choicest.

In some quarters the prejudice against leaving home to join the Army still lingered. Recruiting agencies had still in some areas a difficulty in overcoming the tradition about the youth who for some unsatisfactory reason " ran away to become a soldier." And it took some time and much appeal to break it down. I had taken my part in these recruiting appeals especially amongst Nonconformists, who had always been inclined to hold aloof from the Army, and also amongst my Welsh fellow-countrymen of all creeds. For these reasons, apart altogether from my responsibility as a Member of the Cabinet that declared war, I felt a special obligation to see that the men who volunteered to face death for their country's honour, should be equipped with the best their country could provide them with in order to fight its battles, and that the most effective use should be made of their valour in the battlefield. The events of the last few months had shaken any confidence I ever had in the wisdom of military leadership and I was full of apprehension lest the flower of Britain's youth should be mown down through professional rigidity, narrowness and lack of vision.

I had no pretence to any knowledge of strategy, but there were certain obvious facts which were apparent even to the uninitiated in the mysteries of war.

The first was that if the resources of the belligerents on both sides were assessed—in men, material and money—the Allied Powers possessed an overwhelming advantage over their foes provided their resources were effectively utilised and wisely directed.

This Allied superiority was, however, completely neutralised by the fact that two out of the three Great Powers (Britain and Russia) that constituted the Alliance against Germany and Austria were inferior in equipment to their foes. As far as heavy artillery went France was also inferior. Equipment was therefore the most urgent problem for the Allies. Unless they exerted themselves to the utmost to make up their deficiencies in this respect, victory was unattainable. Two out of the three (Britain and France) had great manufacturing capacity, and America with its infinite resources was also at their call for that purpose. The third, Russia, was very deficient in manufacturing capacity and had no credit for purchase abroad, but had an inexhaustible reserve of the best human material. As to equipment, therefore, the problem was first to utilise all our available resources at home and across the seas to increase the numbers and power of our machinery of war and to do so without loss of time, and secondly to pool the output fairly and distribute it where it could be most effectively used for the Allied cause.

The second and outstanding fact was that Germans had largely neutralised the Allied superiority in man-power on the Western Front not only by better equipment but by constructing the most extensive and formidable line of entrenchments ever known in the history of war.

There was no way of outflanking the German lines in France and Flanders, and any attempt to force them by frontal attacks would involve losses so colossal that no sane man would contemplate such a sacrifice of human life as a possibility, if there were any other means available of breaking through on a more vulnerable front. At any rate the Allies had not the necessary gun-power to make any effort to break through on the west a feasible operation, and it would take years to equip them with an artillery numerous and heavy enough for such an attempt.

The third was that, whilst the Central Powers had an entire front of 600 miles on the west which presented no great physical difficulties for them in the way of entrenchment in length or in the character of the soil, on the Eastern and South-Eastern Fronts they had a line of thousands of miles to defend, much of it swamp which was too soft in summer and too hard in winter for any entrenching tools to handle. Moreover, their man-power would not suffice to garrison effectively so extensive a fortress.

The fourth was that on that front, Germans and Austrians were confronted with a foe who could turn out millions of brave men traditionally fearless and skilful in war, who only needed efficient equipment to make their numbers and their valour irresistible.

On the South-Eastern and Southern sections of that Front the

Central Powers had to defend their positions with an army drawn from a population, three-fifths of which belonged to races hostile to the governing races in the two Empires and entirely sympathetic to the Allied population on their frontiers. The Slavs, Roumanians, and Italians who constituted the majority of the people ruled by Franz Joseph had been straining for freedom from the dominion of a privileged racial caste, and their prospect of gaining it would be accelerated by the defeat of the German regime, whilst it might be indefinitely postponed by a Teutonic victory.

Out of a total population of over 50 millions in Austria-Hungary, only 12 millions were Germans and 10 millions Magyars. Almost 30 millions belonged to populations which were kith and kin to the nations with which Austria was either at war, or was about to wage war. Even the Magyars were not too eager to follow the rash lead of Vienna. It was known that Count Tisza, the ablest and calmest of all the Hungarian statesmen, was rootedly opposed to the mad plunge into war with the Serbian Slavs. What made Austria specially vulnerable was that the provinces contiguous to her actual or contingent foes were populated by the races who by blood were nearly related to the enemies of the Empire. This proved to be a source of weakness to the Austrian armies during the whole course of the War, and a danger against which they found it impossible to guard. Whenever the Russians gained an appreciable advantage in their attacks, Slavonic regiments surrendered with ease and even with ill-concealed satisfaction, to the onslaught of ill-equipped Russian armies. One Czech regiment marched through into pre-destined captivity in Russia with the band playing.

It was also quite obvious to anyone who surveyed the possibilities of the Balkans with some knowledge of the disposition and quality of its peoples, that if the Allied Powers had taken strong and timely action they could have organised out of the warlike races that inhabit this turbulent peninsula from the Danube down to the Chersonese and thence southward to the Peloponnesus, a formidable confederation with an army of trained men already tempered in the fires of war. The Serbians had at that time an available force of 300,000 men. The Roumanians could put at least half a million men in the field. The number of fighting men available in Roumania was placed by the War Office at 900,000. The Greeks had 400,000 trained men. The Bulgarians owed a deep debt of gratitude to Russia for the part she had played in their liberation, and their memories of Gladstone's fiery crusade on their behalf against Turkish oppression turned their hearts towards Britain. If attached to the Allied side they could have placed another 400,000 men at the disposal of the Alliance. All the contingents were of the doughtiest fighting material with recent war experience. The organisation of such a confederacy would have involved loans which in the aggregate would not have amounted to one week's cost of the War to the British and French taxpayer. There would also have been some difficulty in the way of a preliminary arrangement of the spoils. But this was by no means an insuperable obstacle to agreement. There was plenty of honest loot awaiting the plunderers without transgressing any principle of racial liberty or self-determination. The Slavonic provinces of Southern Austria would have satisfied Serbia. Roumania would have been only too pleased at the prospect of annexing Transylvania with its three millions of men of their own blood. The Bulgarians could have been brought in by the prospect of the re-annexation of Adrianople and a port on the Aegean; and the Greeks had an eye on the littoral of Asia Minor, where their own people had built up prosperous towns and brought the valleys into fruitful cultivation. It would have been necessary to take in hand immediately the equipment of the various armies that composed the confederation. That would have been a gradual process. At first an addition of light artillery and ammunition, with a few machine guns, would have sufficed in these mountain fastnesses. The presence of 100,000 British troops, or a composite army of British and French, equal to half the forces subsequently sent to the Dardanelles or one-third of the numbers sacrificed in the spring and summer of 1915 in vain attacks on infrangible German redoubts in France and Flanders, would have given that moral strength to the Balkan Armies imparted by the physical presence of the banners and soldiers of the great Western Powers. Such a contingent would have had an incalculable effect in welding, inspiring, sustaining and restraining all the other elements in this formidable combination.

The Central Powers were much better equipped in the matter of heavy artillery than were the Allies. A break through in France demanded superiority in guns of the heaviest calibre and an overwhelming supply of ammunition. The Allies could not hope to achieve supremacy in this respect for two years. The question of inferior equipment in the heavier calibres did not present so formidable a difficulty in a great operation on the Eastern and South-Eastern Fronts as it did in the west. The Eastern Front not being so well fortified, the Allies could then, with lighter guns and less ammunition, make more effective use of their superiority in numbers. The Russians repeatedly demonstrated this fact in their attacks on the Austrians. They only failed to exploit their victories because of the shortage of gun ammunition for their field artillery and of the lack of rifles. These deficiencies could have been supplied by their western allies, had they consented to forego their unpractical and costly offensives.

Apart from the heterogeneity of the Austrian Armies their organisation, training, munitionment and direction were not comparable to that of their great military neighbour.   For these reasons Austria was often a source of weakness, and constantly a source of anxiety, to the German Supreme Headquarters, and more than once they had to detach troops which they could ill dispense from their own special tasks and their own frontiers, in order either to save Austria from collapse or to clear some impending menace from her frontiers.   This weakness, which was so painfully apparent to the German Staff, was completely overlooked by both the French and British military direction.   The French and British commands were therefore implored by statesmen and soldiers of position and experience in both countries not to commit their armies to repeated and wasteful attacks delivered against an impregnable front defended by an invincible armament, whilst completely neglecting a vulner-able front which could have been penetrated with a third of the troops wasted so prodigally in the ghastly carnage of the western battlefield.

Before coming to these conclusions I had made a careful study of the main facts of the military position with such information as was available to me.   I never missed an opportunity of seeking the opinions of such military experts as were accessible to a civilian minister on every aspect of the situation.

It is a mistake to assume that a competent opinion can only be formed by general officers who have taken no part in the actual fighting, and who have never had any personal acquaintance with the physical conditions under which modern warfare is conducted.   Men who have passed months of vigilance, anxiety and horror in the fighting line have also their contribution to make to the facts upon which strategy must be based.   It is a curious reflection on the methods of promotion in the British Army during the Great War that scarcely one of these men ever reached the topmost ranks—except amongst the Dominion troops.   I saw many of these fighting officers right through the War and learned much from them.

As to equipment, I have already given an idea of the efforts I made up to the end of 1914 to quicken manufacture at home and in America.   I had also drawn attention to the pressing need for helping Russia.   As to the general strategy of the War, at the end of December, 1914, I wrote the following memorandum, which I circulated to the War Council.

2, Whitehall Gardens, S.W.
   January 1, 1915.

SUGGESTIONS AS TO THE MILITARY POSITION

Now that the new armies are in course of training and will, with the Territorials, be ready by the end of March to the extent of at least half a million men, I suggest that it is time the Government should take counsel with the military experts as to the use which shall be made of this magnificent force. It is a force of a totally different character from any which has hitherto left these shores. It has been drawn almost exclusively from the better class of artisan, the upper and the lower middle classes. In intelligence, education and character it is vastly superior to any army ever raised in this country, and as it has been drawn not from the ranks of those who have generally cut themselves off from home ties and about whose fate there is therefore not the same anxiety at home, the people of this country will take an intimate personal interest in its fate of a kind which they have never displayed before in our military expeditions. So that if this superb army is thrown away upon futile enterprises such as those we have witnessed during the last few weeks, the country will be uncontrollably indignant at the lack of prevision and intelligence shown in our plans. I may add that operations such as those we have witnessed during the past few months will inevitably destroy the *morale* of the best troops. Good soldiers will face any dangers and endure any hardships which promise ultimate progress, but this intermittent flinging themselves against impregnable positions breaks the stoutest hearts in the end.

There are therefore three or four considerations I wish to urge on the military situation.

1. STALEMATE ON THE WESTERN FRONT

I cannot pretend to have any military knowledge, but the little I saw and gathered in France as to the military position, coupled with such reading on the subjects as I have been able to indulge in, convinced me that any attempt to force the carefully prepared German lines in the west would end in failure and in appalling loss of life, and I then expressed this view to my colleagues. General Foch told me that there would be no more retreats on the French side, and I could well appreciate his confidence after I had driven past trench behind trench from Paris all the way to the Aisne. The French generals are confident that even if the whole of the German Army now occupied in Poland were thrown on the Western Front, the French and British troops would still be able to hold their own. The same observation, of course, must apply to the German military position. We were told the other day that the Germans had, during the last few months, prepared a series of trenches of the same kind on their side right up to the Rhine. After three or four months of the most tenacious fighting, involving very heavy losses, the French have not at any one point on the line gained a couple of miles. Would the throwing of an additional half-million men on this front make any real difference? To force the line you would require at least three to one; our reinforcements would not guarantee two to one, or anything approaching such a predominance. Is it not therefore better that we should recognise the impossibility of this particular task, and try and think out some way by which the distinct numerical advantage which the Allies will have attained a few months hence can be rendered effective?

2. EXTENSION, AND CONSEQUENT ATTENUATION, OF ENEMY'S FRONT

Another consideration which ought to weigh with us is the importance of attenuating the enemy's line by forcing him largely to extend it. The Germans now defend a front of 600 miles. No wastage in sight will so reduce their forces to such numbers as would make any part of this line untenable. The French returns of wounded prove that 79 per cent. of the wounded return to the line: 54 per cent. of the French wounded have already returned; 25 per cent. are convalescent and will soon be back. It is a fundamental mistake always committed by the press to exaggerate the enemy's losses; the slight and curable character of most wounds is always overlooked. But if the length of the German line is doubled, even at the present rate of attrition, it might become at an early date so thin as to be easily penetrable.

3. FORCING THE ENEMY TO FIGHT ON UNFAVOURABLE GROUND

The enemy is now fighting in country which is admirably adapted to his present entrenching tactics. He would be at a disadvantage if he were forced to fight in the open.

4. NECESSITY OF WINNING A DEFINITE VICTORY SOMEWHERE

There is another consideration which is political as well as military, but which nevertheless cannot be overlooked in an exhausting war like this, where we have to secure continuous exertion and sacrifice on the part of our people, and where we have also to think of hesitating neutrals with large armies who are still in doubt as to their action. There is a real danger that the people of Great Britain and of France will sooner or later get tired of long casualty lists explained by monotonous and rather banal telegrams from headquarters about " heavy cannonades," " making a little progress " at certain points, " recovering trenches," the loss of which has never been reported, etc., with the net result that we have not advanced a yard after weeks of heavy fighting. Britishers have ceased to be taken in by reports which exaggerate slight successes and suppress reverses; neutral states have never been deceived by these reports. The public will soon realise that the Germans are now in effective occupation of a larger proportion of Allied territory than they were in possession of at the date of the Battle of the Aisne. This is true of Belgium, of France, and of Poland. These occupied territories contain some of the richest coalfields and industrial centres in Europe, and the most sanguinary attacks have not succeeded in moving the Germans (on an average) a single yard out of these territories. A clear definite victory which has visibly materialised in guns and prisoners captured, in unmistakable retreats of the enemy's armies, and in large sections of enemy territory occupied, will alone satisfy the public that tangible results are being achieved by the great sacrifices they are making, and decide neutrals that it is at last safe for them to throw in their lot with us.

5. AN ALTERNATIVE SUGGESTION

Inasmuch as these objects cannot be accomplished by attacks on the Western Front, some alternative ought to be sought. I venture to make one or two suggestions. I have heard of a proposal that there should be an attack in the direction of Denmark upon the north coast of Germany. This proposal is associated with the name of Lord Fisher. For the moment I cannot venture to express any opinion upon it, as I should like to know more about the military and naval possibilities of such an enterprise. It strikes me as being very hazardous, and by no means certain to fulfil the purpose which its originators have in view. Schleswig-Holstein, with its narrow neck, could be easily defended by a comparatively small German force, strongly entrenched against a hostile army seeking to advance into Prussian territory, and there is no room for flanking operations. But at the present moment I would rather not criticise this plan. My purpose is rather to put forward another alternative, and I think more promising scheme for consideration by the Prime Minister and his advisers. It would involve *two independent operations* which would have the common purpose of bringing Germany down by the process of knocking the props under her, and the further purpose of so compelling her to attenuate her line of defence as to make it more easily penetrable. I will explain these two propositions in a little more detail.

6. THE FIRST OPERATION

I suggest that our new forces should be employed in an attack upon Austria, in conjunction with the Serbians, the Roumanians and the Greeks. The assistance of the two latter countries would be assured if they knew that a great English force would be there to support them. Roumania could put 300,000 men in the field, whilst retaining a sufficient force to keep the Bulgarians in check. As this move might decide the Bulgarians to remain honestly neutral, the Roumanians could spare another 200,000. The Greeks and Montenegrins have an army of 200,000 available. How many men could we spare? By the beginning of April we shall have in this country 700,000 men who will have undergone a six months' training. Of these 400,000 would be Territorials, 200,000 of whom will have been in camp continuously for eight months. We shall have in France a force of 300,000 men, provided we do not waste it on barbed wire. The French can easily defend their lines against the troops which Germany can spare from defending Silesia after the Austrian armies have been withdrawn to defend their southern frontier. We should require 200,000 experienced troops to stiffen the new armies. We should thus have a force of 1,000,000 available. Four hundred thousand men might be left here as reserve to throw into France in case of need if the French were hard pressed before the southern diversion against Austria had developed. Some of them might be sent to Boulogne so as to be at hand in case of emergency. Subsequently this force could be used to reinforce the new Expeditionary Force from time to time. This would leave 600,000 available for the Austrian expedition. Gradually this force could be increased as the new armies were equipped.

This would mean an army of between 1,400,000 and 1,600,000 men to attack Austria on her most vulnerable frontier. Here the population is almost entirely friendly, consisting as it does of Slavonic races who hate both the Germans and the Magyars. We could send our troops up either through Salonika or, I believe, by landing them on the Dalmatian coast. We could seize islands there which might make an admirable base for supplies not far removed from the railway through Bosnia into Austria. This operation would force the Austrians to detach a considerable army from the defence of Cracow, and thus leave Silesia undefended. The Austrians could not withdraw the whole of their army to face this new attack, because in that case the Russians could pour through the Carpathians and capture either Vienna or Budapest. The front which would be developed would be much too lengthy for the Austrian forces to entrench and hold. The Germans would be compelled either to send large forces to support their Austrian allies or to abandon them. In the first case Germans would have to hold an enormous length of extended front, in the aggregate 1,200 miles, and the Allies would, for the first time, enjoy the full advantage of the superior numbers which by that time they can put into the field.* On the other hand, if the Germans decline to quit their own frontiers, and leave the Austrians to their fate, that empire would be rapidly disposed of as a military entity, and about 2,500,000 men (including Russians), engaged in the task of attacking it would be free to assail the Germans.

7. TWO INCIDENTAL ADVANTAGES OF THIS COURSE

1. Something which could be called a victory would be thus within our reach, and the public would be satisfied to support with all their resources the conduct of the War for a much longer period without grumbling or stint.

---

* The Germans would also render themselves liable to a dangerous attack in the rear from the immense forces which by that date Russia will have placed in the field.

2. Italy would not only be encouraged by this formidable demonstration, she would be forced to come in in her own interest, because the operations would be conducted largely along the coast which she is looking forward to annexing to her kingdom, as the population is predominantly Italian. She must view with very great jealousy any occupation of this territory by Serbian troops, and Italian public opinion would not countenance any proposal on the part of the Italian Ministry to come to the aid of Austria if we made it clear that the whole of this littoral would become Italian territory if Italy helped to conquer it.

8. THE SECOND OPERATION

This involves an attack upon Turkey. There are four conditions which an attack on Turkey ought, in my judgment, to fulfil: —

1. That it should not involve the absorption of such a large force as to weaken our offensive in the main field of operations;

2. That we should operate at a distance which would not be far from the sea, so as not to waste too many of our troops in maintaining long lines of communication and so as also to have the support of the Fleet in any eventualities;

3. That it should have the effect of forcing Turkey to fight at a long distance from her base of supplies and in country which would be disadvantageous to her;

4. That it should give us the chance of winning a dramatic victory, which would encourage our people at home, whilst it would be a corresponding discouragement to our enemies.

Perhaps I ought to add a fifth: it would be a great advantage from this point of view if it were in territory which appeals to the imagination of the people as a whole.

What operations would meet these conditions? It is supposed that the Turks are gathering together a great army for the invasion of Egypt. The sections show that they have collected something like 80,000 troops in Syria, and that they are slowly moving them along towards the Egyptian frontier. I would let them entangle themselves in this venture, and whilst they were engaged in attacking our forces on the Suez Canal, I would suggest that a force of 100,000 should be landed in Syria to cut them off. They could not maintain themselves in that country very long once their railway communications were cut. They would therefore be forced either to fight or to surrender. The distance from Constantinople to Syria would not permit them to bring up reinforcements in time to produce any impression upon the situation. A force of 80,000 Turks would be wiped out and the whole of Syria would fall into our hands. The pressure upon Russia in the Caucasus would be relieved; the Turkish Army in Europe could not effectively attack our lines of communication as they would be bound to take steps to redeem the situation in Syria, and, if possible, recover the country.

Unless we are prepared for some project of this character I frankly despair of our achieving any success in this War. I can see nothing but an eternal stalemate on any other lines. The process of economic exhaustion alone will not bring us a triumphant peace as long as Germany is in possession of these rich allied territories. No country has ever given in under such pressure, apart from defeat in the field. Burke was always indulging in prophecies of victory as a result of France's exhaustion. The war with France went on for twenty years after he indulged in his futile predictions. Germany and Austria between them have 3,000,000 young men quite as well trained as the men of the Kitchener Armies, ready to take the place of the men now in the trenches when these fall. At that rate the process of exhaustion will take at least ten years. In soil, in minerals, in scientific equipment, Germany is a country of enormous resources. In the number of men who have a scientific training it is infinitely the richest country in the world. That must not be left out of account when we talk about the process of exhaustion. No doubt they will suffer a good deal from lack of copper. We must not depend too much on this. German industries dependent on copper will suffer, but one way or another copper will be found for ammunition. Copper in small quantities will get in through neutral countries; neutrals cannot resist the prices offered by Germany for their copper supplies. Moreover, they have some copper mines in Germany. Some of them were working at a profit at the date of the War. There must be many more lower grade copper mines which would not have paid under ordinary conditions, just like the copper mines of North Wales, but which would become immediately profitable when the price of copper is doubled or trebled. Moreover, they have inexhaustible supplies of coal and iron, and as long as they have the Hungarian plains they can frugally feed themselves. There is an enthusiasm and a spirit, according to every testimony, which cannot be worn down by a two or three years' siege of German armies entrenched in enemy territory. The German spirit will not be broken by the bombardment of Dixmude or Roulers.

We cannot allow things to drift. We ought to look well ahead and discuss every possible project for bringing the War to a successful conclusion. Supply and ammunition difficulties, severe economic pressure, financial embarrassments, even privation and distress—nations will face them cheerfully as long as their armies in the field are in unbeaten possession of their enemies' land. But once defeat which is unmistakable comes their way, moderate economic troubles make a deep impression on their judgment. Such defeats are not to be compassed along our present lines of attack, and we ought to seek others.

If a decision were come to in favour of some such plan of campaign as I have outlined, it will take weeks to make the necessary preparations for it. I cannot recollect that in our discussions at the C.I.D. such an operation was ever contemplated. The ground therefore has not been surveyed. It would take some time to collect the necessary intelligence as to the country, so as to decide where to land the Army and what shall be the line of attack. Transport would have to be carefully and secretly gathered. Large forces might have to be accumulated in the Mediterranean, ostensibly for Egypt. It might be desirable to send an advance force through Salonika, to assist Serbia. Military arrangements would have to be made with Roumania, Serbia, Greece and, perhaps, Italy. All this must take time. Expeditions decided upon and organised with insufficient care and preparation generally end disastrously. And as similar considerations will probably apply to any alternative campaign, I urge the importance of our taking counsel and pressing to a decision without delay.

D. Ll. G.

When I wrote this memorandum I had five months' experience of what war under modern conditions meant. After four and a half years of the closest acquaintance with its problems I stand by the main thesis of this document.

Both the rival armies had attempted to break through the defences of their opponents in the west and had failed after the most sanguinary battles. The Germans recognised the impracticability of attempting to force the western barrier and decided to go for the east. By strengthening their entrenchments in the west they reckoned on being able to hold the Allied forces with two men to the combined French and British three. When in 1916 they changed their strategy and attacked the strongly fortified French positions at Verdun, their effort failed and they wasted irrecoverable time and opportunity. On the Allied side there was considerable division of opinion on the issue of the " way round " by the eastern flank.

The controversy that arose on this subject has been represented as a struggle between the amateur and the professional soldier—between the ignorant politician and the trained warrior. This is a wanton and rather silly misrepresentation of the origin of that conflict of ideas which divided those who were responsible for war direction in the Allied countries from 1915 up to the end. There were highly placed politicians on both sides of the controversy. But there were also military men of outstanding ability who took different sides. I had a conversation with Lord Kitchener on my memorandum. His attitude towards it was certainly not that of the professional who resents the intrusion of amateurs. Quite the contrary. He expressed a considerable measure of agreement with my general theme. He was emphatic about the impossibility of penetrating the German lines on the Western Front, and driving the German Armies out of France and Flanders, without incurring sacrifices which he rightly considered prohibitive if another way could be found of defeating the Central Powers involving the payment of a smaller toll in human life.

The day after I circulated my memorandum, Lord Kitchener, in one of his periodic flashes of insight, wrote this remarkable letter to Sir John French to the headquarters in France: —*

> " January 2nd, 1915.
>
> There does not appear to be much sign of the contemplated push through on the part of the French Army. Probably they find themselves up against the same problem all along the line as you do in your part, viz. trenches that render attack only a waste of men for a few yards gained of quite worthless ground. The feeling is gaining ground that, although it is essential to defend the lines we hold, troops over and above what are necessary for that service could be better employed elsewhere.
>
> I suppose we must now recognise that the French Army cannot make a sufficient break through the German lines of defence to cause a complete change of the situation and bring about the retreat of the German forces from Northern Belgium. If that is so, then the German lines in France may be looked upon as a fortress that cannot be carried by assault, and also cannot be completely invested—with the result that the lines can only be held by an investing force, while operations proceed elsewhere.
>
> The question of *where* anything effective can be accomplished opens a large field, and requires a good deal of study. What are the views of your staff? Russia is hard pressed in the Caucasus, and can only just hold her own in Poland. Fresh forces are necessary to change the deadlock; Italy and Roumania seem the most likely providers; therefore some action that would help to bring these out seems attractive, though full of difficulties."

At that moment Kitchener was definitely opposed to the Western Front superstition and had turned his mind to the " way round."

In coming to this conclusion I do not suggest that Lord Kitchener had been influenced by the arguments submitted to him in my memorandum the day before he wrote this letter, but in giving expression to views he had no doubt already formed as to the unwisdom of wasting his new armies on impossible frontal attacks in France and as to the desirability of forcing the issue on some other front, he was sustained by the fact that he discovered he had political support inside the Cabinet for his ideas. At the same time Mr. Winston Churchill's mind was moving in the same direction. Lord

* Sir George Arthur's " Life of Lord Kitchener," Vol. II, p. 35.

Kitchener, Mr. Churchill and I arrived at similar conclusions independently of each other.

A few days later Sir John French, when brought over from France to attend a Committee that was examining the strategical position, expressed his opinion that "complete success against the Germans in the western theatre of war, though possible, was not probable. If we found it impossible to break through, he agreed that it would be desirable to seek new spheres of activity in Austria, for example."

It is a rather significant coincidence that a proposal almost identical with mine was submitted on 1st January, 1915, by General Gallieni to M. Briand and to the French Premier, M. Viviani. Gallieni was a man of tried genius, and was recognised as being one of the most resourceful of the Allied Generals. M. Poincaré in his "Memoirs" refers sympathetically to the Gallieni plan and he goes on to say that General Franchet d'Esperey, one of the soundest and most successful of the French Generals, had already suggested it to him when he saw him at his Army Headquarters at the French Front. General Gallieni's views on the subject are recorded by his secretaries in their highly interesting book "Gallieni Parle. . ."

" The participation of France in the War in the East, the intervention of one of our armies in the Balkan theatre, is perhaps the question which interested him most deeply from the time he became Minister! He saw in it consequences such as no one then anticipated.

From 1914 on a French Expedition to the Balkans could and should be for us the happy solution; in fact the only one which would permit a prompt ending of the War in victory. ONE CANNOT BREAK THROUGH ON THE WESTERN FRONT, he complained. The German offensive on the Yser, made under excellent conditions and which nevertheless failed, proves that to us. Therefore we must find another way. Towards the East! Take Constantinople. How? We need a harbour, quays, in order to disembark troops, and a railway, in order to transport them. Therefore Salonika. Therefore through Salonika march on Constantinople. From there go up the Danube with the Balkans people who will have joined us. AND THAT WOULD HAVE SOLVED THE IMPORTANT QUESTION OF CORN: The Roumanians, even the Russians whose ports we would have opened up, would not be obliged to sell at a miserable price to Germany and so supply her.

Such was my plan. I had been to see Briand. He, Briand, went to consult Joffre, who said: ' That is a personal ambition of Gallieni who wants to get a command. I won't give a man. Why search elsewhere and far off for what I shall get here in March [1915]. I feel sure I shall break through and drive the Germans back home.'

We had spoken about this plan with the English who agreed. The matter had been studied very closely here and with the Allies. It was in view of Joffre's opposition that the English decided—an idea from their Navy—to take Constantinople from the sea; to force the Dardanelles. And the French followed them."

I have been informed on unimpeachable authority that General Castelnau was also of the same opinion.

A contemporary historian, who had obviously drawn his inspiration from the War Office, rather contemptuously refers to the Salonika idea as " Mr. Lloyd George's fancy." The fact that some of the ablest statesmen and soldiers in France had conceived the same " fancy " reconciles me to this flippant and ill-informed comment.

I have quoted sufficient military authority of unchallenged distinction to make it clear that my idea of an attack on the Central Powers through the Balkans was not the wild phantasy of an inexpert civilian mind, wandering recklessly into regions which he was not qualified to explore.

When these great soldiers expressed a doubt as to the feasibility of battering a way through the barriers erected by the Germans in the west, they did not mean it could never be done at any time and at any cost. They meant that it could not be achieved without an expenditure of time, treasure and life which no normal person would be prepared to contemplate. The " Westerners " never visualised a massacre of millions of the best young men of France and Britain. At first they deluded themselves with the assurance of speedy victory. Later on, the Western Front became the shrine of Moloch, demanding and justifying such sacrifice as even its most infatuated priest would not have dreamt of offering had he known in 1915 what this worship meant.

The policy of western holocausts was only tolerated by British, French and Italian public opinion owing to an elaborate system of concealing repulses and suppressing casualties.

We did not " break through " until the autumn of 1918, although we made several attempts in 1915, 1916 and 1917, all ending in terrible slaughter. In every case the losses we actually sustained were appreciably greater than those we inflicted, although officially they were less. Until the Germans had been weakened by poor and scanty food, and were confronted with the overwhelming Allied reinforcements pouring in from America, our offensives on the Western Front invariably failed to accomplish the object we sought to attain. Even then we had not succeeded in driving them out of France and Belgium at the date of the Armistice, and they only gave up their resistance when the Turks and Bulgarians had been broken in the south-east and Austria had consequently decided to relinquish the fight. The French and ourselves lost over 5,000,000 men in killed and wounded in attack after attack upon the scientific frontiers erected by the Germans in the west. Sir Willian Robertson, in one of the several memoranda he submitted to the Cabinet for its enlightenment on the true principles of sound strategy, once stated that "Every fool knows that you cannot be too strong at the decisive point." This is an observation none the less sensible because it is a platitude. But every wise man also knows that the decisive point is the one at which you have the best chance of beating your enemy with the least risk and at the lowest cost, and that only "every fool" would deliberately choose to fight him at the point which presents the greatest difficulty in overcoming him, and offers him the best opportunity for beating off your attacks and inflicting the heaviest losses on your troops. "Every fool" would also know that the attack at the decisive point must be made at the decisive moment. In 1915 the moment had certainly not arrived which made the Western Front the decisive point. The poor fools to whose judgment Sir William Robertson referred in his memorandum know now what the strategy of attacking the foe at his strongest point has cost the world. But unfortunately they could not foresee it then—except for a few "meddlers," military and amateur.

There was, at least, some excuse for French reluctance to detach their troops from their own country. As M. Clemenceau almost daily reminded the French public: "The Germans are at Noyon" —that is, they were within 40 miles of the cherished capital, which at one moment they had within their clutch, had they but closed their fingers before withdrawing their hands. Some of the fairest provinces of France were in German occupation: and only a leader who commanded the unchallenged confidence of his countrymen could possess the influence necessary under those conditions to induce them to acquiesce in the withdrawal of French men and French guns from the defence of the *patrie,* and ship them hundreds of miles away to the east to fight alongside and on behalf of races, and to liberate provinces, in which they had no particular interest.

But the British military direction had no such excuse. Wellington was not sent to Spain because Castlereagh preferred Spaniards to Prussians, but because some one in authority had the sense to perceive that the Spanish Peninsula was the flank where British troops could direct the most dangerous blow against the might of their great foe. Sherman in the famous march through Georgia acted upon the same principle.

It was these considerations that prompted Lord Kitchener, Mr. Winston Churchill and myself simultaneously, but without previous consultation, to come to the conclusion that the greatest help that Britain with her command of the sea could afford to the Allies, was to organise, equip and strengthen an attack upon the weakest point of the great fortress in which the Central Powers were entrenched.

CHAPTER XI

THE WAR COUNCIL AND THE BALKANS

DURING the first two months of the War there was no established War Council. There were sporadic and irregular consultations from time to time between the Secretary of State for War and the First Lord, between each of them individually and the Prime Minister and, now and again, between the two War Lords and the Prime Minister sitting together. The Foreign Secretary was occasionally brought in. I was not summoned to these conferences except when there were matters to be decided that directly affected finance. At the end of November the Prime Minister decided to establish a War Council and early in January he assembled it to examine the various proposals put forward by Mr. Winston Churchill, Sir Maurice Hankey, and myself. Mr. Churchill urged with all the inexorable force and pertinacity, together with the mastery of detail which he always commands when he is really interested in a subject, the merits of his Dardanelles scheme. I gave my reasons for preferring a landing at Salonika. The plan of forcing the Dardanelles by naval action had been examined more than once in the past by naval authorities when the possibility of bringing pressure to bear upon the Turkish rulers at Constantinople had been contemplated. Each time it had been condemned as being too risky an operation without the occupation not merely of Gallipoli but of the Asiatic shores as well. Every time the project was explored the dangers were foreseen which were actually experienced when it was tried later on by the Allies. The difficulty was obvious—that of forcing by marine action a passage through narrow straits commanded on both sides by defensible heights. It was always apprehended that even if the Narrows could be forced in spite of mines and fortifications, they might be closed against the return of the Fleet as long as either of the two shores remained in the hands of the enemy. When the Greeks offered to join the Allies earlier on in the War they were prepared to send an adequate contingent to occupy the Gallipoli Peninsula. Had they done so the whole story of the Dardanelles would have been different. The story of the whole War would also have differed fundamentally from that which was told by the event. But for some inscrutable reason Sir Edward Grey rejected Greek overtures of help. His tiresome hesitancies helped us into the War, but they hindered us when we were well in it. A more virile and understanding treatment of the Balkan situation would have brought Greece and also Bulgaria into the War. Italy could also have been brought in sooner.

If Lord Kitchener had had at his disposal an adequate force to subdue the Gallipoli garrison, and also to occupy the Asiatic side of the Straits and to hold their own there against the attacks of the Turkish Army on the mainland, then there was a great deal to be said for the Dardanelles plan. But he stoutly insisted that he could not spare more than a Brigade at that time. That, I was convinced at the time, was an underestimate of the reserves of men at his disposal, and I know it now. It was due primarily to apprehension that the Russian Army might collapse, enabling Germany to concentrate great forces on the Western Front. In addition, Lord Kitchener was from time to time afflicted by incomprehensible fear of denuding this country of regular troops and thus leaving it open to all the peril of an impossible invasion from an enemy that dare not sail his ships in any part of the German ocean, except for a few hours' dash half-way across and back at full speed.

There was another factor which played a great part in Lord Kitchener's estimate of our available military strength at this stage of the War. He had the old regular general's contempt for the quality of our Territorial Army. He had always in his mind the volunteers of his younger days—imperfectly organised, deficient in equipment, with inadequate fire practice and hardly drilled at all. The Volunteer Force was the bedraggled starveling of the War Office, eking out its meagre finances by local concerts, entertainments and subscriptions. I recall its financial straits. The lawyer to whom I was articled was the local captain in his little town. Such training for war as I ever acquired was given me by a sergeant-major in that company of Volunteers to which I belonged. He drilled the men, played the cornet in the band, and sold tickets for the concerts. When Kitchener returned to England to take over the direction of the War and found a great force of 270,000 men called the Territorial Army, he thought of it in the terms of the Volunteers who were the joke of the Regulars—a few hundred thousand young men officered by middle-aged professional men who were allowed to put on uniform and play at soldiers. He did not realise the revolution which had been effected in this force by Haldane's genius. On the first occasion when I had any lengthy and intimate conversation with Kitchener on the War one evening after the declaration, he spent nearly the whole of the time in deriding the Territorial Army. He was full of jest and merriment at its expense. This miscalculation had quite an important effect upon the course of the War during the first few months. There are competent soldiers who maintain that Lord Kitchener could easily have thrown at least ten more divisions of excellent troops into the battle line during the decisive days of the Battle of Ypres had he placed greater trust in the Territorials that were available. And there is no doubt that if he had known their full value he could by the spring of 1915 have sent several divisions to Salonika. They were excellent material and by that time they had received six months of constant training in camps. The Balkan Expeditionary Force need not have been made up exclusively of Territorials. Some of the Territorial divisions might have been sent to France to relieve Regular divisions who were garrisoning sloppy trenches, and these highly trained soldiers could have been spared for the Balkans as a stiffening for the Expeditionary Force. The weather was not propitious for fighting in Flanders. There was also a substantial force of Australians and New Zealanders mustered in Egypt. These might have been sent to Salonika. We all know now what first-class fighters they were.

But unless one takes the Territorials and Dominion troops into account, even if there had been a division or two of Regulars available and these had been doubled by the accession of an equivalent French contingent, Lord Kitchener was clearly not in a position at that time to send a sufficient number of troops for the double operation of driving the Turks out of Gallipoli and of holding Chanak against the main Turkish Army. On the other hand, the occupation of Salonika was not a big military operation. The Greeks would have offered no real protest against the landing and there was no enemy within striking reach to prevent it. The first two or three months of the year would have been occupied in improving the railway communications—a very necessary operation. Parts of the line could have been doubled. Locomotives, carriages and wagons for the conveyance of troops and material could have been landed, sidings could have been erected and roads could have been improved.* By the time the winter snows had melted in the Balkans and the river floods from the Danube to the Vardar had subsided, Lord Kitchener could have accumulated a considerable force on the spot, and with the aid of the French troops which by that time could have been spared, the Salonika Army would have been so formidable that the Bulgarians would have hesitated to intervene on the side of our foes. The Official War History is emphatically of that opinion.† Long before Germany disentangled herself from

* The Official Military History of the Military Operations in Macedonia discussing the suitability of Salonika for a landing says: " The carrying-power of the railways was low, but, according to the estimate of the British General Staff, it could have been greatly increased under British, or French control—it was indeed considered that the six trains a day in each direction on the Belgrade line could have been at least doubled if an understanding had been reached with Greece at an early stage. The road communication with and in New Serbia was very much worse than that of the railways, but that again could have been bettered. . . ."

† Page 48. Military Operations: Macedonia.

her great drive in Russia, the combined Allied forces in that area drawn from Serbia, Britain and France with a probable accession of over half a million men from Greece and Roumania would have been so powerful that it would have been a hopeless enterprise for Austria, even with German assistance, to launch an attack in so difficult a terrain. The bastion of the Balkans would have been behind us as an impregnable fortress, and not in front of us, impenetrable and unscaleable when defended by resolute troops as we found it to be from 1916 to 1918.

Even the equipment at our disposal at that date would have been sufficient to enable us to defend such a position against any enemy.

Shrapnel, of which we had a fair supply, would have been effective against troops advancing in the open across slopes visible from the high ground which the Allied forces would have occupied. We could then at our leisure have perfected the equipment and organisation of our Balkan allies, and when all was ready launched an attack on Austria in combination with Russia and Italy. Italy came in on the Allied side in May and would have come in sooner had there been resolute action on an effective scale in the Balkans.

We had several discussions at the War Committee on the various and rival proposals that were put forward. These lasted several days. Sir John French was brought over from France to take part in one of the discussions. His opinions, which I have already quoted, were favourable to an attack on the south-eastern flank.

I presented the case for a Salonika landing to the War Council, but I was at a disadvantage in converting my colleagues. Mr. Winston Churchill had been in constant touch with Lord Kitchener, and when the former has a scheme agitating his powerful mind, as everyone who is acquainted with his method knows quite well, he is indefatigable in pressing it upon the acceptance of everyone who matters in the decision. On the other hand, I saw Lord Kitchener only on very rare occasions. At that date the War Lords were very exclusive and kept very much to themselves. They were both naturally very busy and had no time to spare for civilian amateurs.

The First Lord of the Admiralty had another advantage in urging his proposal, and that was decisive. He was prepared to act without waiting for an immediate dispatch of troops. His proposal was a purely naval operation in its initial stages. Troops would only be called for after the Narrows had been forced, and therefore after all the forts had been demolished. Even then their role was to be a modest one. Lord Kitchener knew that the completion of such a task by the Navy would take some time. Meanwhile, there would be no call for troops or ammunition from the Army. On the other hand, the Salonika plan did involve the immediate landing of a certain number of troops, with guns, ammunition, stores, sea and land transport. This idea of a purely naval operation was a welcome relief to an embarrassed Secretary of State who was always being pressed to send more troops and munitions to every theatre. His worries in this quarter would be shouldered for two or three months by the Admirals. So Lord Kitchener swung round to the Dardanelles plan, and that settled it. Every Minister at that Council, including the Prime Minister, Sir Edward Grey, Mr. Balfour and Lord Crewe, followed Lord Kitchener's lead as to the Dardanelles attack. I stood alone in expressing a different and doubting view. Lord Fisher was dumb. I was not aware at the time that he and other Admirals were opposed to the venture as a purely naval operation unsupported by troops.

The Dardanelles scheme was, therefore, resolved upon and preparations were immediately made to carry it through. Mr. Churchill threw into the execution of his scheme all his impulse and ardent energy. I pressed at a later meeting of the Committee that some action should be taken to make the Salonika expedition more practicable in the event of the attack on the Dardanelles failing. Accordingly, after the Dardanelles decision had been taken I secured the unanimous consent of the Committee to a proposal that Lord Kitchener should take steps immediately to improve the transport arrangements from Salonika to Nish by doubling the line where feasible, and by increasing the number of locomotives, sidings, carriage wagons, and other transport facilities on the Salonika railway. Lord Kitchener undertook to take the matter in hand. But nothing was done to carry out the order of the War Committee, and no further notice was taken of it. When we were compelled to send an expeditionary force at the end of the year to prevent the victorious Central Powers and Bulgaria from marching through to the Mediterranean, not a single additional rail had been placed, not an additional siding had been constructed, not an additional wagon had been landed. Not a road had been widened or mended. Not even a survey had been made of the transport facilities available on rail or road and the means by which they could be improved. The result was that when Serbia was attacked in the autumn by the Central Powers the General Staff gave it as one of their reasons against sending an expeditionary force at that date to the aid of the hard-pressed Serbians, that there were no means of transporting such a force up the line. Even at the end of 1916, when General Joffre had been thoroughly converted to the importance of Salonika, and the Allies had been in occupation of that part for twelve months, the number of troops that could be dispatched and effectively used in that area was limited by the fact that up to that date no steps had been taken to improve the transport accommodation. A force adequate to the need could not be sent there for that reason.

As soon as the Cabinet Committee had come to a final decision that the attack on the Dardanelles was to proceed, I ceased to challenge the wisdom of the enterprise, feeling that it was better to press forward energetically with one or other of these outflanking operations than to abandon all idea of taking action in that direction. I continued to urge the dispatch of troops to Gallipoli in time and sufficient numbers, and especially with an adequate equipment of guns and ammunition. Whilst discussions and preparations were proceeding, reports came in from the Balkans that emphasised the peril of delay. A very striking letter from Mr. George Trevelyan, the eminent historian, written to Mr. (Now Sir Francis) Acland, was passed on to me amongst other members of the Cabinet, including the Foreign Secretary. He was at the time travelling in the Balkans with Mr. Seton Watson, the great authority on Balkan politics, and his letter is a very calm and informative view of the position and the attitude of the various Balkan States at that time.

"Sofia,
January 15th, 1915.

Dear Francis Acland,

We* came here from Nish yesterday and are going on to Bucharest to-morrow. We had a long conversation with Sir Henry Bax Ironside, who is as much impressed as Mr. Des Graz by the danger Serbia will be in if a big Austrian army with German corps to stiffen it comes to the attack. As everything we have seen and heard in Serbia leads us to suppose that Serbia cannot resist such an attack successfully if unaided, we have to-day telegraphed to Grey urging that every diplomatic and military effort should be made to save Serbia and prevent the annihilation of our influence in the Near East which will certainly result from a disaster to Serbia.

I wrote to you in much the same sense from Nish—you may even get this letter and that one together—urging that British troops should be sent from Egypt or anywhere else, if the Germans come against Serbia or a fresh and overwhelming number of Austrians. The moral effect would be very great on a mercurial people like the Serbians, just as the moral effect of the arrival of the ammunition was very great in December. On the Austrians also the moral effect would be great—they were much disconcerted in December by a false report that the Russians had joined the Serbians at the time of the Serbian *retour* offensive—because ten Russian N.C.O.'s were seen. Even the presence of our Blue-jackets at Belgrade has done the Austrians intellectual damage.

We did not wire from Nish, not because Mr. Des Graz† was opposed to this view, but I talked the matter over with him and he was most deeply impressed with the danger of Serbia and the

---

* Mr. Seton Watson and himself.
† The British representative in Serbia.

need for military help if the expected invasion in force took place, especially with German aid. I deferred wiring till I came here, because I wanted to know whether there was any danger of Bulgaria marching against Greece, if Greece came up the Vardar valley to help Serbia. Bax Ironside is confident there is no longer such a danger, that Bulgaria has now decided on neutrality at least unless and until Serbia is crushed and the whole Entente game lost in these parts. If this is so we could use the Vardar valley to convey British troops to aid Serbia and Greece herself ought to march. Watson points out that British troops might also or alternatively be sent via Antivari or Dalmatia—but there we trench on military questions where I am out of my depth. The *principle* is that we must save Serbia or lose the whole Near East with results on the whole War imaginable by you.

We have not yet been to Bucharest and may not be much wiser when we have been. But though all have hopes, none we have yet seen, Serbian or English, has any confidence that Roumania will march till after the battle is lost and won. Other measures must, therefore, be taken to save Serbia if she is attacked in force, besides efforts to bring Roumania in.

You may wonder why we have wired and written so little about the Macedonian question. I have told you what the general Serbian attitude is about it—I did so in my last letter. But as we don't know what Prince Trubetskoi has been and is doing about it, we don't know enough to proffer advice or to judge whether any special treatment of the Macedonian question now can help to save Serbia *now*—for the crisis of the invasion, if it comes, may be on her any week. In general, however, we can say from numerous conversations with Serbians from the Crown Prince downwards that the more Yugo-Slavia and Adriatic expansion are dwelt upon, the more Serbians will be willing to concede to Macedonia. And that Serbia will only concede at the friendly dictation of the Great Powers her Allies.

It should be borne in mind that the Serbians are a mercurial people, though they have such stout stuff in them. They may begin retiring, even in disorder and despair, and then if something is done, or something turns up to put fresh heart in them, they may do wonders.

Diplomatically everything seems uncertain and fluctuating from hour to hour with regard to the action or inaction of Roumania and Bulgaria—perhaps of Greece. It is no very wild guess to suppose that the ultimate choice of Roumania and Bulgaria respectively or jointly, will depend on the result of the coming attempt to conquer Serbia if such attempt is made. Of course, the Roumanians ought to help to save her during that invasion, and they *may*, and every effort should be made to make Roumania do so. But other plans should be prepared to save Serbia, on the assumption that Roumania will not march till she sees who is the victor, for that is the only safe assumption. We do not wish to give the impression that Serbia is at the last gasp. Her spirit is splendid and her Army, if halved by losses, is in good estate. But if, as at present expected, Germany and Austria can mobilise against her numbers that are beyond her power to resist, the result of the whole War may be affected by an abnormal effort to help her.

GEORGE TREVELYAN."

We were to discover too soon how accurate were Mr. Trevelyan's and Mr. Seton Watson's prognostications about Bulgaria and Serbia. We had other communications which confirmed the impression given by Mr. Trevelyan's letter. The Balkans were a frightful mix-up, and it was clear that they might be consolidated on the side that took the boldest action in that quarter ere it was too late.

At the end of January a report was received from our Minister at Sofia referring to a message from the Russian Foreign Minister, which expressed great apprehension as to the possible attitude of Bulgaria. The Minister thought these fears well founded, that there was a growing feeling at Sofia that Russia was not succeeding in her military operations, and that when the weather improved sufficiently to enable the Germans to advance, Warsaw would fall into their hands. That was the opinion of the Bulgarian generals, and the Minister warned us that unless Bulgaria was persuaded we were on the winning side no territorial bribe would bring her into the Alliance. They were not as much concerned about territorial extensions as with the drift of the War, which they were watching with anxious eyes before deciding which side to join. I called Lord Kitchener's attention to this telegram, and the following correspondence ensued: —

" January 29th, 1915.

Dear Lord Kitchener,
    You will I am sure have seen Telegram Number 14 in last night's sections from Sofia. It is so obviously the German interest to crush Serbia in order to detach Bulgaria from the Triple Entente and to free a way to Constantinople that it is risky to doubt the accuracy of the telegram. The French delayed assistance to Antwerp until it was too late. This time the responsibility is ours and we shall not be held blameless if a catastrophe occurs.

Ever sincerely,

D. LLOYD GEORGE."

"War Office,
Whitehall.
29th January, 1915.

My dear Lloyd George,
I think we all see the danger. The difficulty is that our forces are tied up in France and that the situation requires a fighting force in Serbia. To go there with a small force such as a Brigade would be useless unless followed by others, as we should be laughed at as soon as it was discovered that we were only an Army *pour rire*. We might force Greece in as a belligerent, but very few Greek troops would reach Serbia while Bulgaria maintained the attitude she has adopted.

I cannot help thinking Bulgaria wishes to see Serbia perish and with that object stops all assistance being given her by Roumania and Greece. See enclosed which please return.

Yours very truly,
KITCHENER."

As to Lord Kitchener's plea that he could only spare a Brigade for the occupation of Salonika, he had at home at that time a fine division of regular troops not yet sent to any front. This would have provided the necessary nucleus and stiffening for the 14 Territorial divisions available at that date at home. Two or three divisions of these gallant Territorial troops he soon after sent to Flanders and found fit enough to take their place in the first-line trenches to defend the British position against Germany's best soldiers. There were also 39,000 Australians and New Zealanders in Egypt. They were all equal, to say the least, to anything the Bulgarians or Austrians could have brought against them. On the Western Front the French and ourselves already considerably outnumbered the Germans, and, although we lacked the heavy artillery necessary for attack, we had shown ourselves, even when we were much weaker, strong enough to resist a German attack. Had we sent a few of these available divisions the French could and would also have sent an equal number of troops. Their pride would not have permitted them to go unrepresented in equal strength in so important a theatre. On that point they always displayed a certain useful touchiness, if not jealousy. If the French and ourselves had, in consequence of this expedition to the East, been compelled to economise our men on the Western Front, the foolish offensives which cost the Allies over 100,00 men during the first four months of 1915 would have been avoided. There were plenty of men for rash and ill-considered ventures on the Western Front, but only a Brigade could be spared for an enterprise which, as events proved before the end of the year, was essential to save the Allied cause from a great disaster.

As the enclosure of Lord Kitchener's letter was concerned with the attitude of Roumania, which was also represented as waiting and watching, but not yet willing to take the risk of joining the Allies, I replied to Lord Kitchener: —

> "Treasury Chambers,
> Whitehall, S.W.
> January 29th, 1915.
>
> Dear Lord Kitchener,
> I return the Sofia despatch. Thanks.
> I am fairly confident you will not get these Balkan States to decide until they see Khaki!
>
> Ever sincerely,
> D. Lloyd George."

At a meeting of the War Council on January 28th Lord Kitchener had one more of those flashes which now and again cast their rays deep into the gloom of the stormy problems which were raging around us. He said "that he was impressed by the advantages which Germany derived from her central position. This enabled the enemy to co-ordinate their efforts. The Allies, on the other hand, were all acting independently. In his opinion there should be some central authority where all the Allies were represented and full information was available. Attacks should be arranged to take place simultaneously. This would cause appeals for assistance to be made to the German Great General Staff from all parts of the War simultaneously. These attacks might be continued for ten days or so, after which there would be a period of rest. During these offensive operations he would suspend all communication between the Allied countries and Germany."

I was entirely in favour of Lord Kitchener's suggestion, and I said that I was going to Paris shortly to meet the Finance Ministers of the Allies. Possibly an opportunity might occur to make the suggestion informally and to get one or other of the Allies to put forward a more formal proposal. Mr. Balfour agreed. The conclusion arrived at was that I was to avail myself of any favourable opportunity which might present itself in Paris to start the idea of a central body to provide the Allies with facilities for consultation, with a view to greater co-ordination of effort.

Somewhere about the end of January and the beginning of February the French Secretary for War, M. Millerand, had visited London to discuss the position. He was a sturdy and aggressive exponent of the views of the French Commander-in-Chief. He held a brief for General Joffre and fought his case with all the tenacity and forensic skill of a tenacious advocate. General Joffre did not want to part with a single battalion from his French command. He was convinced that he could break through the German lines that year. Later on this confidence received a horrible interpretation in a succession of sanguinary and futile offensives which culminated in that climax of stubborn folly—the Champagne attack, which was repelled with a loss of 200,000 men. However, all the decisions of the War Cabinet were unfolded to him, including the preparations that were to be made for a landing at Salonika when troops were available. When I visited Paris I found that M. Millerand had never repeated these conversations to his colleagues.

I visited France in company with the Governor of the Bank of England (the late Lord Cunliffe) and we met M. Ribot, the French Finance Minister, and M. Bark, the Russian Foreign Minister, to discuss the terms on which advances should be made to Russia with a view to enabling that country to make necessary purchases in America. As suggested, I took occasion to discuss the whole military position with the leading members of the French Cabinet.

Nothing came of the discussions at the time, the French military authorities being obsessed by the notion that their Great Headquarters had, and ought to have, the supreme control of the land war. The naval direction they were prepared to leave to us. But their view was that as far as the Continent was concerned we had neither the forces nor the experience that entitled us to equality of authority in the strategy of the War. Joffre was at that time the unchallenged dictator as far as the War direction was concerned.

I also visited Sir John French's Headquarters and there met Sir William Robertson for the first time. He had hitherto taken no part in the fighting, either directly or indirectly. For the first part of the War he was Quartermaster-General, and as such was reported to have organised supplies in the confusion of the hurried retreat from Mons, to the general satisfaction of the Army. He was then promoted from stores to strategy, and was now chief of Sir John French's staff. So far he had not been responsible for planning any of the battles. Later on he was the Commander-in-Chief's principal adviser in deciding the strategy and planning the tactics of Neuve-Chapelle and Loos. He was an impressive personality, with that slowness of speech and positiveness of statement which gives confidence to the uninitiated in the mysteries of a profession. He also possessed a blunt humour which pleased the Army, especially when it was expressed in ranker language and when exercised at the expense of someone other than the person who repeated the scornful witticisms.

On my return there was a further discussion on the Serbian intentions. I greatly regretted our delays in taking action in the Balkans. I pointed out that the War Council had approved this Serbian project in principle some weeks ago. When I was in Paris I had discussed it with members of the French Government, with the result that they had brought it to the attention of their Cabinet

Meeting, and the French Government had now expressed approval in principle.

I thought it certain that if we made it clear that we intended to send a division the French would do the same. They were very anxious to co-operate in any military enterprise in the Near East.

I subsequently embodied in a letter to Sir Edward Grey the result of my conversations in Paris and at the British Headquarters:—

"February 7th, 1915.

My dear Grey,

During my visit to Paris I had several opportunities of discussing with Ministers the question of the Balkans. When I first mentioned it to the Minister of Finance I found that Millerand had never repeated to his colleagues that the suggestion of an expeditionary force to Salonika had been made to him when he was in England. I found subsequently, in conversations with the Prime Minister, Delcassé, and with Briand, that they had also been kept in the dark as to the conversations which took place in England between Millerand and British Ministers. They were astonished, and not a little annoyed, that the matter had not been reported to them. I found that their attitude was much more friendly to the idea than was that of Millerand. Briand, who is much the ablest man in the Ministry, was strongly for it—in fact, he told me that he had been for some time urging some diversion of this kind upon General Joffre. I met Briand at Sir Francis Bertie's and the three of us had a prolonged talk on the position. Briand told us that the Cabinet had considered the suggestion on Thursday: that Millerand stood absolutely alone in his opposition to it, Delcassé hesitating a little, not knowing what the attitude of Russia would be towards it: the rest of the Cabinet being perfectly unanimously in favour of the principle of an expeditionary force of two divisions being sent to Salonika at the earliest practicable moment, preparations to be made at once, and the troops to be sent as soon as Generals Joffre and French could be persuaded to spare them. The French wished for an expeditionary force in which the French Army should be represented. They therefore suggested that one British and one French division should be sent. The President of the Republic was present at the Council; he also approved of this course.

It is now a question of persuading Joffre. Briand was of opinion, and so was the President, that if a joint note were addressed to Roumania and Greece, asking them whether they would be prepared to declare war immediately if an expeditionary force of two divisions were sent to Salonika, and if they replied in the affirmative, then no doubt General Joffre would gladly spare the necessary force. Briand said it was too preposterous to imagine that if 40,000 men from the west brought in 800,000 from the east, thus withdrawing German pressure on the west, any General could possibly object to such a plan.

Briand told Bertie and myself that he would propose at yesterday's meeting of the French Cabinet that a joint note should be sent in those terms to Roumania and to Greece. Bark, the Russian Finance Minister, who was present, strongly supported the proposal and thought Russia would gladly send a small force to occupy Serbian Macedonia, so as to make an attack by Bulgaria impossible. Isvolsky, whom Bark consulted on the subject, was also emphatically of the same opinion.

The French are very anxious to be represented in the expeditionary force. Briand thinks it desirable from the point of view of a final settlement that France and England should establish a right to a voice in the settlement of the Balkans by having a force there. He does not want Russia to feel that she alone is the arbiter of the fate of the Balkan peoples.

I found the President, Briand and the Prime Minister very sceptical as to what Russia would or could do in the immediate future. They were very doubtful as to whether Russia was in a position, owing to her lack of rifles and ammunition, to bring in anything like an overwhelming force on the eastern frontier for some months; in fact, they were very inclined to take our War Office view as to the effective number of the Russian troops in the coming spring and summer.

I have no idea what Delcassé's view is after yesterday's Cabinet Council, but I hope you will bear in mind in discussing the question with him that with the exception of Millerand he was the only man amongst the French Ministers who expressed any doubt at all as to the feasibility of this plan. Briand is in favour of an operation on a much larger scale, *and he told me that he had had the idea examined by experts in the War Office, and that they reported favourably on the proposal, provided troops could be spared by General Joffre and Lord Kitchener.*

Bertie was present and heard the whole of the conversation, and he may have reported to you its purport separately. When he and I first saw the President he examined all the objections, but I could see that even then he was quite friendly to the idea and at the Council on the following day, as I have already pointed out, he spoke in favour of its adoption.

Yesterday I saw Sir John French and General Robertson, the new Chief of Staff. Every soldier I have met since the beginning of the War has placed Robertson in the forefront as the most conspicuous success amongst our generals, and he made a deep impression on the Governor of the Bank, Montagu, and myself yesterday. He is a shrewd, clear-headed, strong man. No general except Kitchener made quite the same impression on my mind as Robertson did yesterday. French introduced the idea of an expedition, and at first he was hostile, not in principle, but on the ground that he could not spare the troops. *However, he called Robertson in, and when I explained to him exactly what the proposal was, he had no hesitation in saying that it was ' good strategy.' He maintained that view throughout the discussion.* This influenced French's attitude very considerably. I told him we were very anxious to carry his judgment along with ours in any scheme which affected the military operations for which he was responsible. Ultimately he agreed that if the Roumanians and the Greeks promised to march on our undertaking to send an expeditionary force to Salonika, he would spare at least a Division for the purpose. He is willing, and, I think, anxious, to come over to discuss the project with the War Council. He suggested that he should be invited, and I hope that the Prime Minister and Kitchener can see their way to asking him to attend an early meeting of the War Council.

Robertson would have gone further than French: he would send not merely one but two Divisions at once if Greece came in, and even on the offchance of forcing a decision in the Balkans. He thinks it will compel Bulgaria to at least neutrality. If Briand is as successful in the mission which he promised to undertake to General Joffre, then there is no reason why the expeditionary force should not start within a week or ten days at the outside.

I am sure you will agree that there is every reason why the joint note should be sent without delay. It is quite clear from the telegrams which have appeared in the sections during the last few days that anything in the nature of an arrangement between the Balkan States is impossible. I think the attitude of the Serbian Prime Minister as revealed in our telegrams from Nish is unalterable. I doubt whether it would be possible for him to give up a substantial part of his territory in advance until he actually gets something in return. It would produce such a feeling of discouragement in his army as to paralyse their efforts. They have done so brilliantly that it would be a misfortune if this were to happen.

There are several ominous telegrams which indicate clearly that Bulgaria is hardening into opposition to the Triple Entente. There is the telegram about the success of their borrowing mission to Berlin. The Germans are not such fools as to advance money without receiving some assurance as to Bulgaria's action in certain contingencies. There are the telegrams from Dedeagatch about the laying of mines. Those mines can only be used against the Entente Powers. There are the rumours about bands being organised to attack the railways: and there are one or two others, all pointing in the same direction. Then the Roumanian news is for the moment discouraging—the trouble they have taken to explain away the loan raised in England, amongst other items of news. I am afraid that they have a better appreciation of the Russian position than we have, and that they are losing confidence in the Russian strength. *Unless, therefore, we mean to allow the great possibilities of the Balkans to slip out of our hands, we ought not to dilly-dally any longer. If we fail to take timely action here, our condemnation will be a terrible one.* As I read the sections I feel that even days count now. My experience yesterday shows that the generals, if properly taken in hand, can be persuaded. No general likes to have his troops taken away to another sphere of action. His mind is naturally concentrated on the trenches in front of him, unless he is a very big man indeed, and a man, moreover, who has the responsibility, not merely for the success of the operations under his immediate control: and neither Joffre nor French are quite in this position.

I should like to see you to-morrow to give you a fuller account of my interviews, but I thought it well to send you a summarised report before you see Delcassé.

Yours sincerely,
D. Lloyd George.''

In the conversations which I had subsequently with the Prime Minister and the Foreign Secretary, I strongly urged that a conference should immediately be summoned either at Salonika or one of the Greek islands which the Foreign Ministers of France, Russia, Serbia, Greece and Roumania should be invited to attend, in order to deliberate on the whole of the position in the Balkans, and endeavour to establish the basis of an understanding for effective co-operation between all these States against the Central Powers. I was strongly of opinion that the Bulgarian Government should also be asked to send a representative to this conference. Sir Edward Grey objected to such a gathering on the ground that it would be quite impossible for him to leave the Foreign Office at so critical a moment for the length of time it would take to attend a meeting at such a distance. I pointed out that proceeding by way of Brindisi it would take him less than a week to get there, and that he need not be absent for a longer period than a fortnight or three weeks in all. There would be no difficulty in getting M. Sazonoff there as far as travelling was concerned, for Petrograd to Salonika would be a matter of three or four days' journey at the outside. The Foreign Secretary was, however, so unwilling to entertain this proposal that it fell through.

Had this suggestion been adopted a Balkan Confederation on the

Allied side could have been negotiated. It would have been necessary to give our plenipotentiary full powers not only to arrange geographical terms, but also to dispense liberal financial aid. The Balkan kingdoms—never rich—had been impoverished by a succession of wars with Turkey and amongst themselves. Loans from Britain and France would have encouraged them to take the risks of war. It was not a question of bribery but of sheer necessity, if they were to equip themselves adequately to encounter the hazards of alliance. The Germans realised that. They therefore did not trust their interests to the ordinary diplomatic representation, but sent to Sofia a special emissary of high standing and great ability. He knew the importance of giving financial help to Bulgaria and accordingly promised a handsome advance. It was not the decisive factor in her choice, but it was one of the inducements. Grey might not have been the best man to manipulate and persuade the fractious elements that had to be brought together. In fact, he was not. But he might have found a suitable colleague or a substitute. The Czar Ferdinand was not at that date as pro-German as was generally assumed. On the contrary he was definitely anti-Kaiser. He was a man who possessed an inordinate pride of pedigree. He was a Bourbon. And Wilhelm in one of his fits of boyish recklessness had offended his vanity when they were visiting at the same Schloss. He had been tempted to greet the self-important Bulgarian Emperor rather rudely as he was leaning over a parapet in deep contemplation of the view. The Bourbon blood never forgave the insult. Ferdinand would have been personally better pleased to co-operate with the Czar of Russia and the Kings of England and Italy. But as the issue of the War was very much in doubt he waited for some clear indication of the way things were going on the battlefield. By September the chances of Bulgarian expansion seemed more likely to be realised by throwing in his lot with the Central Powers than by joining the Allies, so he declared finally, but after considerable hesitation, for the former. A meeting with him in the spring would have produced different results. We were then about to attack the Dardanelles. By September our attacks had been beaten off. It is true that in the early spring Russia was not doing too well, but her position was by no means irretrievable. By the autumn her armies had been driven helter-skelter out of Poland and beyond. Ferdinand then came to the conclusion that the Bulgarian opportunity was with the victorious Germans. We missed our chance of organising a confederation that would have decided the War by 1916, and all through lack of enterprise and gumption.

If special diplomatic methods were not to be tried in the Balkans I begged the War Council to send more troops to that theatre so as to secure a favourable military decision there.

On 19th February the War Council met and the discussion is very illuminating because of the light it throws upon the views taken at the time of the prospects of the War.

"LORD KITCHENER said that the War Committee ought to consider very seriously before advising the removal of the XXIXth Division to the East. The situation in Russia had greatly deteriorated during the last week or two. The Russians had lost very heavily in men and, what was more serious, they had lost very heavily in rifles, of which they were short. If the Germans could inflict a sufficiently decisive defeat on the Russians they would be in a position to bring back great masses of troops very rapidly to France, and there would be a great demand for reinforcements in the western theatre of war.

MR. LLOYD GEORGE agreed that the position was very serious. Russia might receive a knock-out blow. Had we to admit that we were impotent in view of such a contingency? *In his opinion the Germans would not send their forces west, but would endeavour to smash Serbia and settle the Balkan question. The view appeared now to prevail that Germany would aim at the conquest of the north-east corner of Serbia with a view to establishing through communication and direct access to Bulgaria and thence to Constantinople.* (My italics.)

THE PRIME MINISTER agreed, but considered that the most effective way would be to strike a big blow at the Dardanelles.

LORD KITCHENER agreed with the Prime Minister. If the fact of not sending the XXIXth Division would in any way jeopardise the success of the attack on the Dardanelles he would dispatch it. *He doubted whether the Germans would attack Serbia as suggested by Mr. Lloyd George.*

MR. LLOYD GEORGE suggested that we ought to send more than three divisions. It was worth while to take some risks in order to achieve a decisive operation which might win the War. From the discussion he gathered that the maximum force available for operations in the East was as follows: —

The Australian and New Zealanders (including mounted troops)	39,000
The XXIXth Division	19,000
Naval Division ....,...	10,000
Marines	4,000
French Division	15,000
Russians	10,000
Total	97,000

LORD KITCHENER said he had every intention of supporting the Dardanelles operation, but considered two divisions on the spot to be sufficient at first. There was no object in sending out troops from here which he might require.

Sir Edward Grey asked if we were safe in the West.

Mr. Lloyd George said he had spoken on this subject with a great many officers who had been at the Front. There was a general agreement that our army could not carry out a successful attack without a very heavy loss of life, and the same was true of the French Army. No doubt it was also true of the Germans; for the Germans to attack, therefore, would be the best thing that could happen. It was just as costly for them to try and break us as for us to try and break them. . . ."

On 24th February there was a further discussion which constitutes a very useful addendum to the report of the last meeting.

". . . Mr. Lloyd George agreed that a force ought to be sent to the Levant, which could, if necessary, be used after the Navy had cleared the Dardanelles to occupy the Gallipoli Peninsula or Constantinople. He wished to know, however, whether in the event of a naval attack failing (and it was something of an experiment) it was proposed that the Army should be used to undertake an operation in which the Navy had failed.

Mr. Churchill said that this was not the intention. He could however, conceive a case where the Navy had almost succeeded, but where a military force would just make the difference between failure and success.

Mr. Lloyd George hoped that the Army would not be required or expected to pull the chestnuts out of the fire for the Navy. If we failed at the Dardanelles we ought to be ready immediately to try something else. In his opinion we were committed by this operation to some action in the Near East, but not necessarily to a siege of the Dardanelles."

CHAPTER XII

ALLIED PROCRASTINATION

SUCH meagre and cautious reports as were vouchsafed to Cabinet Ministers as to the progress of the War did not enlighten us as to what was really happening on or behind the battlefields. There was an impression left on our minds that the military authorities thought it better we should not be told too much. Secrecy was essential to success. The Prime Minister and Mr. Churchill knew a good deal more about the situation than we did. But they were not fully apprised of the facts. Casualties were scrupulously withheld. In fact, there was no considered statement submitted to the War Council on the military position, showing the relative strength of the Allies and of the Central Powers in men or machinery. I often doubt whether anyone inside the War Office had taken the trouble to make a careful survey. We therefore knew nothing of the numbers on the various fronts, either our own or those of our Allies or our foes; what reserves were available; what was the equipment in guns, machine-guns, rifles or ammunition on both sides; or when our new armies would be ready. Lord Kitchener told us he had no troops to send to the Dardanelles. We had to accept it on his authority for he never condescended to details. We had to decide every issue without being informed as to the most relevant facts. Those of us who were members of the so-called Council of War were not much better off in that respect than other Ministers who had to be satisfied with a perfunctory statement from Lord Kitchener at the beginning of a Cabinet sitting. We had to forage here and there on our own initiative for information essential to our utility as war councillors. Sometimes we scrounged an important fact, more often we picked a snub.

I was a diligent seeker after truth. In spite of travestied and medicated reports I was convinced we were not doing well. I was equally convinced we were not doing our best. We had decided to launch a serious adventure in the Dardanelles. We had also resolved to prepare the ground for an alternative in Salonika if the Dardanelles failed. I saw clearly that we were tackling neither of these plans with the whole of our available military strength. We just dawdled and put off. In the Dardanelles both Lord Kitchener and the Prime Minister were hopeful that the Navy would do the trick, in which case very few troops would be needed.   If the Navy failed altogether then no soldiers would be required for that enterprise. Elsewhere there was nothing in particular happening in France. Germany had abandoned any idea of attempting a further advance in the west. We were building up an army to turn her out altogether. We were raising great new armies but not taking adequate steps to equip them. We were very dependent for ultimate success on Russia. But we knew nothing about her plans, and very little about the resources in men or munitions with which these plans had to be carried out. All we knew about Russia was that she was being beaten, that she was short of rifles and getting shorter because she was losing more in retreat than she gained in manufacture. But we were not at pains to ascertain the truth. There was no co-ordination of effort. There was no connected plan of action. There was no sense of the importance of time. We were still much too leisurely and casual for a matter of life and death. It was not an absence of fussing but a lack of clear vision and resolute drive. I began to realise that it was not composure but confusion. In spite of official reticence, disquiet- ing scraps of news and rumours percolated through. They made me uneasy as to the course of events, still uneasier as to the way events were directed on the Allied side.

On the 22nd February I circulated to my colleagues the following memorandum : —

" I am anxious to put before my colleagues a few considerations on the general situation. It must be acknowledged to be one of the utmost gravity, and one which, if it is not taken in hand at once firmly and boldly, may end in irretrievable disaster for the cause of the Allies and for the future of the British Empire. This may very well appear to some of my colleagues to be the language of morbid pessimism, but I hope, before they come to that con- clusion, they will do me the honour of perusing the reasons set forth here which have led me to this conclusion.

The Press and the Country have up to the present treated the progress of the War as one of almost unbroken success. Their method is a simple one. Every trivial military incident which turns to our advantage is magnified and elaborated in headlines which occupy half a column and descriptions which take a page. On the other hand, grave misfortunes such as those which have befallen the armies of our Russian Allies in the course of the last few days are relegated to a few lines of type, whilst they are explained away in a column of leaded matter. I am afraid that many who have a more intimate acquaintance with the facts are pursuing the same mental process. They concentrate their gaze upon those incidents and aspects of the military situation which suit their hopes, whilst they deliberately shut their eyes to the developments which might conduce to the awakening of their fears. The only pathway to ultimate success is paved by reality. Unless we look facts, however unpleasant, in the face, we shall never grapple with them.

What are the salient facts of the situation? Not a yard of German territory is now in the occupation of the Allies. Practically the whole of Belgium is in German occupation. Some of the richest departments of France and Russia are now firmly held by the enemy. The Germans are now in possession of larger tracts of allied territory than they have ever held before. A still more serious fact: whilst they maintain possession of the country occupied by them in the west with comparative ease, they have at last established a complete military predominance in the east. It is true that they drove the Russians out of East Prussia some months ago, and the Russians came back afterwards; but as Lord Kitchener pointed out, there is a serious difference between what happened then and what is occurring now. Then the Russians were in a position to bring up considerable reserves to overpower the enemy, and the German reserves were not ready to take the field. Now the position is entirely reversed. Large German reserves have taken the field. The remarkable report circulated by Lord Kitchener from the pen of a Dutch officer points out that after sending huge reinforcements to East Prussia and North Poland to overwhelm the Russians, they have still numbers behind them they could throw in, but which have not been sent to the frontiers because there is no room for them.

That is the German position now. What about the Russian position?"

I then proceeded to examine in detail the seriousness of the Russian position in reference to rifles and the present situation and the future prospects of the Allies and the Central Powers in respect of man-power. I dwelt on the fact that it was useless to reckon the enormous reserves of men available in Russia without taking into account the possibility of arming them. And I drew the inference that unless and until we took steps to equip the Russians, the Central Powers had more fighting men than the Allies at their disposal. I then proceeded: —

"Having regard to the superior equipment of the German-Austrian forces and to the fact that when we come to attack them they will be found to have entrenched their positions in allied soil, it is idle to hope for victory unless we secure a great numerical superiority over these forces. Where can we hope to find it? Russia cannot now, according to the War Office report, put and maintain 2,000,000 of fully armed and equipped men on all her assailed frontiers. Even if she could, that leaves us with a deficiency of 2,000,000. It will be observed that in the figures which I have given I have credited Great Britain with 2,000,000. When can she put 2,000,000 into the field? When can she put 1,000,000 into the fighting line? Is it quite certain that by the time 1,000,000 are ready Germany will not have added at least another 1,000,000 to her reserves?

I am sorry to draw so menacing a picture, but I should, indeed, be happy if I thought the appearance of the landscape did not justify the gloomy colours with which I have attempted to paint it. The Dutch report circulated by Lord Kitchener gives still more alarming figures. If these be even approximately accurate we could not hope to bring the War to a successful termination for years to come. But even with my more moderate figures, the problem is the most serious with which British statesmen have ever been faced.

The first thing to do is to find out exactly where we stand. Who can present a reliable estimate of the military resources of the Allies? We ought to have a conference between the military authorities of the three countries, at which a candid exposure of the position of each country is made and some military convention agreed to as to our future action. General Paget is a good soldier, but his qualities are not altogether fitted for a detailed investigation into questions of equipment. We know approximately, at any rate, how France is situated. We have not the slightest notion of what the position of Russia is. I strongly urged as far back as October that we should take drastic measures to ascertain accurately the Russian position as to equipment and munitions. We are entitled not merely to ask but to demand frankness from our Russian Allies. Russia is not in this war to help France and Belgium and ourselves. France came in to assist Russia when she was menaced; Belgium came in on account of France; we came in to protect Belgium; so that indirectly we are in because Russia was attacked. Germany was not merely at peace with us but was extremely anxious to maintain the peace not merely with us, but with France as well. She engaged in this war to try conclusions with Russia before Russia was prepared to attack her. We are helping Russia with men, with material, with money. France and ourselves have already advanced £50,000,000 or £60,000,000 of money to Russia and we have promised another £100,000,000. We are, therefore, justified in demanding candour from Russia. Germany knows all about the Russian forces, their numbers, disposition and equipment. All we want is that our great ally should supply us with information which her enemies already possess.

What next? Every effort must be made to increase the number of men whom we can put into the field and to shorten the period in which they could be put into the fighting lines. How is that to be done? If France could put 3,000,000 of men under arms and Germany 5,000,000, then the whole of the Allied countries ought to be able, on the basis of population, sooner or later to count on 20,000,000. That may be an impossibility, but it is an indication of the enormous reserves of men fit to bear arms that the Allies have to draw upon. The problem resolves itself into one of: —

1. The training and equipping of these men in the shortest space of time.

2. The maintaining of the *status quo* without any appreciable aggravation until the Allied countries are prepared to throw overwhelming forces into the battlefield.

How are these two objects to be attained?"

Here followed a passage on the urgent need for developing our potential resources for munition production which I have already quoted on page 100 in telling the story of the fight for munitions. After dealing with the issue of materials, I proceeded as follows: —

" Now with regard to the raising of men. France has probably brought every available man she can spare into line. That is far from being the case with either the British Empire or with Russia. Great Britain, on the French basis, ought to have 3,500,000 now under arms, instead of 2,000,000. The Dominions and the Colonies ought to have, on the same basis, 1,200,000 men instead of 100,000. I believe we could with a special effort raise our 3,500,000, or, if that be found inconsistent with the turning out of the necessary equipment, we could certainly raise 3,000,000. I still think it is unnecessary to obtain compulsory powers. The young men of this country will enlist in our armies if it is brought home to them that their services are needed. I ventured to suggest some time ago that the best method of doing so would be by determining the quota each county and town ought to contribute in proportion to its population, and leaving it to local pressure and local patriotism to do the rest. If we officially announce that a particular county is expected to contribute, say, 10,000 men; that up to the present 6,000 have been enrolled in that county, and that 4,000 more ought to enlist in order to make up the quota, local pride will fill up the ranks for us.

Some means ought also to be taken to induce our self-governing colonies to take upon themselves a larger share of responsibility in the matter of levies. They are under the impression now that they are doing all that is expected of them. The peril ought to be brought home to them. The optimistic telegrams which we publish have deluded them into the belief that all is going well, and that all they need do is to send a few thousand to the Mother Country as a token of their sympathy and esteem for her. When they realise that she is in real peril, I do not doubt their response.

Russia, on the French basis,* ought to have 12,000,000 men under arms. That is probably more than she could equip for some years, but having regard to her primary responsibility as far as the Allies are concerned for the struggle, the numbers of her men ought to bear some relation to her enormous resources in vigorous manhood.

All this must necessarily take time. We have hitherto proceeded as if the War could not possibly last beyond next autumn. We should now take exactly the other line—assume that it will last not merely through the year, but conceivably through next year as well. Capital, therefore, ought to be spent on laying down machinery which will enormously expedite the output of rifles, cannon and all other machinery and munitions of war towards the latter end of the year and the beginning of the next. If it turns out that my estimate errs on the side of pessimism the worst that happens will be that we shall have spent a considerable amount of money, we shall have caused a considerable amount of inconvenience to the population. But all that is nothing compared with the disaster of having to face another year of war with inadequate preparation. This the public will never forgive after the warning we have received, nor ought they to be expected to forgive.

But what is to be done in the meantime? It looks as if during the best part of the present year the Allies must content themselves to be in a position of military inferiority to Germany. During this period the best we can hope for is that we shall be able to hold our own. Can we even accomplish this without summoning some fresh forces to our aid? Having regard to the overwhelming forces at the disposal of Germany there is at least an element of doubt. There are only two directions in which we can turn for any prospect of assistance—the Balkan States and Italy. The Balkans we might conceivably have brought in some months ago, but the Allies have been unfortunate in this quarter. We have only succeeded in bringing in the Turks against us without engaging any other Balkan Power on our behalf. Is it too late to do anything now? Lord Kitchener pointed out the other day at the Council that the Germans had taken risks by attacking the Russians with their full forces before they were quite ready, in order to be prepared to meet the attack of our reinforcements in April. With the one exception of our initial action against Turkey, where our promptitude was unmistakable, our risks have all been in the contrary direction; we have generally taken them too late. The

* Of the proportion of recruits to population.

momentous step we have taken in attempting to force the Dardanelles must have a decisive effect one way or the other on the Balkans. Are we prepared for either or for any event?

If this great movement succeeds—then, if we are prepared to take immediate advantage of it—its influence may be decisive as far as the Balkan States are concerned. This means that if we have a large force ready, not merely to occupy Gallipoli, but to take any other military action which may be necessary in order to establish our supremacy in that quarter, Roumania, Greece, and, I think, very probably, Bulgaria will declare for us. If, on the other hand, we have no force on the spot adequate to cope with the Turkish Army, it may be that most of the effect of such a brilliant *coup* might be lost. To bring Bulgaria, Roumania and Greece in with Serbia means throwing an aggregate army of 1,500,000 on to the Austrian flank. This will not only relieve the pressure on Russia, but indirectly on France. It will tend to equalise things, and thus give time to re-equip the Russian Army.

Now let us take the other contingency—the failure of the Dardanelles effort. Unless it is at once countered, such a failure will be disastrous in the Balkans, and might very well be disastrous throughout the East. The Bulgarian general pointed out that not merely Bulgaria but Roumania and Italy have a good deal to gain in the way of territory by throwing in their lot with Germany. There is only one guarantee against a catastrophe being precipitated in that quarter as a result of a repulse in the Dardanelles. There must be a strong British force there available to support our friends. Is it quite out of the question that we should anticipate our April preparations by three or four weeks and thus follow the German example of taking risks so as to arrive in time?

The sending of a large expeditionary force undoubtedly involves large preparations—ships, transports to carry troops and their equipment to Salonika or Lemnos, also preparations for transporting them up country; and the Committee of Imperial Defence decided some weeks ago that these preparations should be immediately undertaken, so that if an expedition was at any time determined upon, no delay need ensue owing to lack of sea or land transport. I understand that the Admiralty have done all that was entrusted to them in this respect; I know nothing of the steps taken by the War Office respecting the railways and the roads.

My final suggestion is that a special diplomatic mission, based on our readiness to dispatch and maintain a large expeditionary force in the Balkans, should immediately be sent to Greece and Roumania to negotiate a military convention. Germany has not depended upon her ordinary diplomatic representatives where the situation presented any greater possibilities friendly or hostile to her welfare. She has sent von der Goltz to Constantinople, Sofia, and Bucharest; von Buelow to Italy; Dernberg to America. She has not yet depended upon her X——s in critical situations. No doubt they are very good men in their way, but the mere fact that they have remained so long in inferior diplomatic berths proves that, in the opinion of the Foreign Office, their qualities are not of the first order.

D. LL. G.

P.S.—Since writing the above I have read a remarkable report from General Paget, which confirms in essentials the view I have repeatedly expressed as to the Balkan situation. I was privileged to see this document through the courtesy of the Prime Minister. I respectfully suggest that every member of the War Council should have an opportunity of perusing reports which bear so intimately on decisions they are asked to come to. To consult them without trusting them with the only information which makes their judgment worth having is worse than futile.

D. LL. G.

February 22, 1915."

On receipt of this memorandum Lord Fisher sent me a letter which is worth reproducing as a characteristic comment from a very remarkable man.

" Admiralty.

Dear Mr. Lloyd George,

I am in complete accord with your phenomenal paper! Yesterday I had to write these following words to a most influential personage:—

' Rashness in War is Prudence, and Prudence in War is Criminal.

The Dardanelles futile without soldiers!'

23/2/15.   Yours, FISHER."

Lord Kitchener had sent General Paget to the Balkans to report on the position there. That report confirmed all the information I had previously gathered as to the prospects and probabilities in that quarter. According to him, the Serbian Army, after a series of brilliant victories against overwhelming Austrian forces, had succeeded in clearing their country of all enemy troops, and were now in a strong position behind their Danubian frontier. They had neither the numbers nor the transport and equipment which would enable them to take the offensive, but the very able generals which they were fortunate enough to possess were satisfied that if Roumania could be persuaded to join the Entente and advance against the Austrians with a force of 300,000 men, the Serbian Army would conform and take up the offensive. The Report urged that one or two Divisions of British, French or Russians troops should co-operate with the Serbian Army and that the presence of British troops would most certainly tend to induce Bulgaria to maintain neutrality, if indeed she would not seize the opportunity of attacking the Turks. Such action on our part, or even the definite proposal of such action, would in his opinion cause Roumania to enter into the War, at such a time when her aid would be most invaluable. During the passage of the Russian Army across the Carpathians, the Roumanian Army of even 200,000 men operating against the southern flank of the already somewhat demoralised Austrian Army, would assist the Russians to an almost invaluable extent. Roumania was hesitating, but her action would be most prompt if British troops were to co-operate in a campaign on the Danube. There were no fortifications of modern standard between Belgrade and Vienna. That was the substance of the Paget report. It was a soldier's opinion confirming that which had already been formed by other soldiers as well as civilians.

Eighteen months later Roumania came in with an army of four or five hundred thousand men, but by that time Russia was beaten and broken. Her armies had been driven hundreds of miles nearer Petrograd. They could no longer hold their own when attacked, even in their own country. The Balkans were in the hands of the Central Powers; communication between the west and Roumania was completely cut off; we could afford no aid in either men or material, and fighting alone she fell without rendering any service to the Allies by her sacrifice. The poor aid Russia was able to give to the last remnant of her beaten army could not avail, and the very effort to afford that aid finally exhausted the Russian strength.

Two or three days after my memorandum was circulated, Lord Kitchener circulated a reply to it. The document recalled the curious mixture of sagacity and opacity which constituted the make-up of this extraordinary man:—

" REMARKS BY THE SECRETARY OF STATE FOR WAR ON THE CHANCELLOR OF THE EXCHEQUER'S MEMORANDUM ON THE CONDUCT OF THE WAR.

I would like to make the following observations on the Chancellor of the Exchequer's very interesting paper on the state of the War.

I will not now refer to the figures quoted by the Chancellor, as the seriousness of our position can be realised and considered quite apart from the question of the numbers of the combatants on either side. The Chancellor rightly points out that the Russian Colossus, as some people described our Russian ally, has not produced that effect on the progress of the War which those who took an optimistic view anticipated. Nevertheless, in my opinion

Russia has done remarkably well, and, according to my view of the situation, she will be found to have saved us six months out of the three years which, as my colleagues will remember, I estimated, in the House of Lords, might be the duration of the War. We must remember that at the outset our chief requirement was time, and though the Germans have strained every effort they have not succeeded in giving a knock-out blow at any time during the seven months of hostilities. It is true that they occupy a large expanse of territory outside their country, but the War is not on that account more likely to end in their favour.

If we are victorious the end of the War must come through one of the two following causes: (1) by a decisive victory, or a succession of decisive victories, of the Allies, which may take place just as well outside German territory as within it; or (2) by attrition, for when Germany is no longer able to support her armies in sufficient strength in the field she must sue for peace. I think it would be interesting to obtain, and I am arranging with Lord Moulton to furnish, a mathematical calculation of approximate dates when attrition might force our enemies to sue for peace. *As far as I can judge now, I think that about the beginning of 1917 this state of affairs may be reached.* [My italics.]

I leave out of calculation the possibility of the starving of Germany and Austria, where 105 millions of civilian population have to be fed.

With regard to the Chancellor of the Exchequer's practical suggestions, I am glad to think that there are more factories available for the output of war material in this country, but the real crux of the situation is, in my opinion, the organisation of the skilled labour required to work the machinery, and, if the Chancellor of the Exchequer could help us in this and in the many labour difficulties with which we are confronted, I have little doubt that in time an increased number of men, up to a total of 3,000,000, may be recruited and trained fit to take the field.

In the efforts we are now making to raise, arm and equip 2,000,000 men we are faced with grave difficulties, not the least of which is that, constantly, our manufacturers find themselves unable, owing to shortage of skilled labour, to keep their promises of delivery of arms, ammunition, etc. This shortage could be very much lessened by the employment of unskilled together with skilled labour on the same machines, but trade union rules do not admit of this. One of the first essentials, therefore, is to secure the requisite modifications of those rules.

A committee is sitting, on which Sir George Gibb represents the War Office, for the purpose of organising labour. I understand that they have been more or less successful in some of their efforts to induce trade unions to agree to modify the restrictive regulations which they now impose on labour; but if the Chancellor of the Exchequer could use his great powers to persuade the trade unions to deal with this matter at once, he would be doing a great deal to help us in preparing an army of the dimensions he regards as necessary.   I quite agree with him that the closing of public houses in areas occupied by our labouring classes would have a very good effect, but such a measure would no doubt have to be carried out with care, as the men might resent any interference with their present habits.   I would suggest, in this connection, that by keeping the public-houses closed up to 11 a.m. it would be possible to get the men into the works before they had had an opportunity of obtaining intoxicants.

We are making a great effort to increase our armies in the theatre of the War up to 2,000,000 men, including those required to maintain the force in the field.   We are just beginning to see the results that have been achieved, and the difficulties that we have to face in the creation of these new armies.   Until we can actually put into the field a considerable number of our new forces I doubt whether it would be advisable to attempt further increases, except as regards the placing of orders for the necessary armament.   Our present output will, of course, be continuous, and will not cease when any specific quantities of articles are delivered: every effort is continually being made to increase production, but the great difficulty I foresee is that to which I have referred, viz. the labour question.

When our new armies are prepared to take the field, it will be undoubtedly a matter of vital importance that they should be employed in the most effective manner, so as to secure decisive results, and that they should not be scattered on subsidiary enterprises.

Much depends upon the success of the Navy in forcing the Dardanelles, but we have not sufficient men available at present to attack the Turkish troops on the Gallipoli Peninsula.   As the situation develops in the Near East, we shall be better able to judge how our troops could be best employed when ready.   K.
February 25, 1915."

This document is the first in which our Generals committed themselves to the idea of a " War of Attrition."   Their avowed aim was to " break through " and drive the Germans back across the Rhine, a routed and broken mob, chased by cavalry.

It is no part of my task to describe military operations and I shall therefore not attempt even to summarise the story of the Dardanelles Campaign with its incomprehensible blunders and its tragic failure. The poignant tale has been told by a master hand in Mr. Winston

Churchill's volumes of the "World Crisis." A small force of a few thousands landed in time would easily have overwhelmed the wretched garrison to whom the defence of Gallipoli had been entrusted by the careless Turks. When we sent an army numbering tens of thousands to attack in April, Turkish reinforcements had arrived which were strong enough to prevent us from capturing one of our objectives. We were always too late. We ran race after race with the sluggish Turk and each time he invariably won, and arrived first at the winning post. He delayed and procrastinated according to his wont, but we beat him at the dawdling game. He gave us many chances and we never took one.

Whilst that tragedy was visibly developing scene by scene and act after act, I was a helpless spectator who possessed neither the official position nor the personal influence with the War Directors which would enable me effectively to intervene.

During the whole of the summer months the Serbians remained on the defensive, whilst our strength was being muddled away on the Western Front in attack after attack upon German positions defended by much more powerful artillery than any the Allies could command. Hundreds of thousands of British and French troops were killed and wounded, and ammunition was lavished upon fruitless and costly attacks against impregnable fortresses. The Germans soon became convinced that they need feel no anxiety as to these onslaughts. As soon as they saw how feckless our efforts were in the Dardanelles they ceased to worry about that operation and postponed dealing with it until the autumn. They were right. Scores of thousands of the Allied troops fell in belated and therefore fruitless assaults on Achi Baba and the heights above Suvla and in clinging on to the rocky slopes of Anzac. In the east, as well as in the west, the German game of attrition was a great success. So they left the south-eastern flank to the Turk and in the west they left their entrenchments to be defended by numbers which were considerably inferior to those which were arrayed against them, and they turned their attention to the east with a resolve not merely to relieve the pressure upon their sorely tried allies in the Carpathians but to defeat the Russian Army along the whole front, and if possible, to destroy it.

CHAPTER XIII

THE RUSSIAN COLLAPSE

POIGNANT APPEALS FROM THE RUSSIAN SOLDIERS

THE failure of the Allied military chiefs to realise that the event of this war would ultimately be determined by equipment on land, sea and air ought to have been brought home to the most blinkered mind by the Russian defeats in 1915, and by the grave consequences that ensued.

On the Western Front we hailed a recovery of ground on a front of two or three kilometres to a depth of one kilometre as a victory. We had several triumphs of that kind during the year 1915. They were attained at a heavy cost of human life on our own side, and comparatively small losses to the Germans. In the aggregate we succeeded in tearing out of German claws a few square miles of French and Flemish soil. The balance of advantage was every time with the enemy. We captured nothing of any strategic value. We expended over 10,000,000 shells and added hundreds of thousands to the ghastly casualty lists of the War. During the same period on the Eastern Front the Germans drove the Russian armies on a front of 500 miles to a distance ranging from 90 to 300 miles from their original entrenchments. Every shell told. The price they paid in German lives for their vast conquests was not half what we sacrificed in the attainment of trivial results. They captured more great cities and provinces than we did hamlets and shell-harrowed fields.

The great retreat of 1915, in which, with unexampled carnage the Russian armies were driven pell-mell out of Poland and the Baltic provinces up to Riga, was entirely due to Russian inferiority in artillery, rifles and ammunition of all kinds. Amongst my papers there are reports written at that date by British officers who were observers of the actual fighting, and I have had the advantage of perusing some of the dispatches sent from the Russian generals at the front to their Government. They afford poignant and convincing evidence of the fact that the Russian rout was due to lack of material. Even before the end of the campaign of 1914, the Russian Army's resistance threatened to break down altogether through lack of equipment. There were some distressing appeals sent in November and December, 1914, from General Yanushkevitch, the Chief of the Staff of the Grand Duke Nicholas, Commander-in-Chief of the Russian Armies, from the fighting front to General Sukhomlinoff, the Secretary of State for War.

Here are a few specimens couched in language which might well be called hysterical had it not been fully justified by the tragic facts:—

"22/XI-1914.

Yanushkevitch to Sukhomlinoff.

. . . . I should be infinitely obliged to you, on behalf of the Army, if you would consider it possible to hurry up Rudsky [a well-known metallurgical works in the Baltic provinces] for the promptest output of shells. This is a nightmare to me. With the reduction in the number of guns and quantity of cartridges, 50 to 60 per cent. more casualties have started."

He went so far as to suggest that even the appearance of shells without any means of explosion might encourage the troops.

"Would it not be possible in addition to everything else to increase the quantity of shells (fuses are not necessary, but there will be shots). At any rate the spirits of the troops will be kept up. (A drowning man always catches at a straw.) The matter of the provision of rifles has been successfully arranged: up to 50 per cent. has been secured. . . ."

General Sukhomlinoff, in reply sent a telegram which he intended to be reassuring, but which must have had a very depressing effect upon its recipient. He was doing his best to speed up production, and ends up by saying:—

". . . I myself visit the works and urge them, but come upon strikes, shortage of coal, non-delivery of lathes from abroad—and we have none."

Workmen, miners, railwaymen and foreigners were all to blame. The Czarist Ministers were alone blameless. How completely the equipment of the poor Russian soldiers had been neglected is revealed in a fuller message from Yanushkevitch to Sukhomlinoff dated 6th December, 1914:—

"I know that by my wailing I caused you trouble and worry, but what is to be done? You know that my hair stands on end at the thought that, owing to the shortage of cartridges and rifles, we shall have to submit to Wilhelm. . . . *The fewer the cartridges the greater the loss.* If it were possible to throw in 150,000 to 250,000 men at once, it would be possible in 1 to 1½ weeks to hurl back the enemy and secure an advantageous position immediately. . . . That is why I consider it my duty to make a humble appeal to you. Many of the men are without boots and have frost-bitten feet; they are without short fur coats or sweaters, and are beginning to catch severe colds. As a result, where officers have been killed off, mass surrenders and captures have started, in some cases on the initiative of ensigns. They say, ' Why should we perish of hunger and cold, without boots, the artillery is silent, and we are killed like partridges. The Germans are better off. Let us go.' The Cossacks, who in an attack had recovered 500 that had been captured, were abused by the latter: ' Who asked you, fools; we do not want to hunger and freeze again.' These occurrences are truly sad—but they are threatening. That is why I am now raising my voice. The English offer to help in executing the orders in their country, in America and Japan. Be merciful and give us instructions for everything possible to be ordered (horse-shoes, cartridges, rifles). Nothing will be in excess. The Army will absorb everything like an insatiable monster. Forgive me, for God's sake. Believe me that I am not exaggerating. I am speaking from my conscience. . . ."

Here was a war that had been foreseen for years past by the Government of the Czar. For this contingency preparations had been made; at least the French peasants had supplied cash in plenty for such preparations. How had it been spent?

The Grand Duke Nicholas, who commanded this Army, was a fine soldier, and an honourable man. He took for granted that his colleagues and comrades at the War Office were of the same pure metal. His disappointments come out in the telegrams of the Chief of his Staff. Here is another to the egregious Sukhomlinoff:—

" 10/12/14.

In order not to worry you, I have, by order of the G.D. [Grand Duke], sent an S O S by wire to General Vernander, describing to him the picture in regard to the cartridges. Both Commanders-in-Chief [at the fronts] have sent such telegrams that my hair stands on end. Cartridges are disappearing. In Germany articles have already appeared that ' we are at our last gasp, as we are almost not replying to their firing; that on the evidence of our soldiers [prisoners] our numbers are shrinking without being replaced, and the artillery has been forbidden to shoot.' The deduction to be made from this is that victory is at hand. And the reinforcements promised for the 1st December have not as yet come to hand."

General Yanushkevitch to General Sukhomlinoff.

" February, 1915.

. . . 2-3 times a day cartridges are asked for from the fronts, and there are none. My heart is heavy. . . ."

General Sukhomlinoff to General Yanushkevitch.

"24th February, 1915.

. . . The eighth month of a fierce campaign is making itself felt by an exhaustion of stocks with all armies, and with use of projectiles.

Positively all possible measures are being taken, and the Grand Duke Serge Mikhailovitch, who is now at the head of this business, can convince himself that the constant orders abroad have not promoted the development of our private industry, and with Government factories one does not get very far, especially when, moreover, the means therefore had to be acquired by sheer force —at the bayonet point and at a risk of losing one's position in the service. . . ."

At that time such information as I was able to secure about the Russian situation, despite the reticence of the military authorities, increased my already acute uneasiness. In February I laid my views before Mr. Asquith in writing as follows:—

"Treasury Chambers,
Whitehall, S.W.
February 18th, 1915.

My dear Prime Minister,

The situation revealed by Lord Kitchener's statement at this morning's Cabinet is a grave one, and I strongly urge that the War Council should take it into consideration at once. After seven months' war we do not even now know approximately the position of the Russians. Sir John French told me that he had been assured by the Russian officers who visited him that Russia would have 3,000,000 of men fully equipped in the field next month, and that they could then sweep back the German and Austrian armies opposed to them. The War Office compute the Russian forces now at 1,200,000. If Sir John French's information be correct the Russian reinforcements available in March would come to 1,800,000. Now we learn that the Russians have no rifles to equip their new men with and that they can only turn out rifles at the rate of 40,000 per month. At that rate they can only bring 500,000 more men into the field by this time next year. The Germans are capturing more than 40,000 Russians with their rifles each month. What is the truth about their equipment? We surely ought to know. Our fate depends upon it.

I ventured in October last to express my doubts as to the Russian equipment, and I suggested then that we should take definite steps to ascertain how they were situated. I thought then it might be possible to arrange a meeting between the three

War Ministers—or responsible representatives. X is a futile person with no authority and but little intelligence. Y, for this kind of work, is no better.

We ought to have a searching and candid survey of the whole military situation with a view to devising the best means of meeting it—otherwise we shall drift into irretrievable disaster.

There has been deplorable lack of co-ordination between East and West, and as long as it lasts the Germans will continue winning. *Mere optimistic bluff is not going to float us through this hurricane.*

Ever sincerely,

D. LLOYD GEORGE."

Nothing was done, however, to improve the position. The same kind of messages as I have already quoted continued to come from Russian generals at the front, and much the same sort of reply came from the self-complacent ministers at Petrograd.

General Yanushkevitch to General Sukhomlinoff.

" March, 1915.

. . . Our strategy is now dead, as we cannot undertake anything, since we are helpless materially. If we could only repel attacks; it is painful that instead of being able to throw in every month 1,440 companies we must be satisfied with 350. . . ."

Yanushkevitch to Sukhomlinoff.

" March, 1915.

. . . You know that during the Russo-Japanese war they fought for about two weeks and vegetated for 2-3 months but now there are divisions that have already been fighting for 85 days. That is no longer fighting, but a titanic struggle to the death. . . . I feel quite heavy at heart. At night I imagine I hear someone's voice: ' You have been sold, you have missed, you have overslept.' "

As usual in Russia when failure was due to an incompetent and corrupt system the blame was attributed to other causes. The Jews always come in handy on occasions when corrupt or incompetent Gentiles make a mess of national affairs.

Yanushkevitch to Sukhomlinoff.

" 27th April, 1915.

. . . In some places they are already blowing up bridges, stores. This is all done for money; probably the Jews are doing it. *There is no one else to do it.*

The question of cartridges and rifles is, I may say, a bloody one."

Yanushkevitch to Sukhomlinoff.

" 21st May.

. . . Ivanoff, reckoning 40 shots per day per rifle, and 5,000 rifles to the division, requires five million rifle cartridges per day and 40 parks of light cartridges per month. If one compares this with the colossal expenditure of the French during the last operations in Champagne (100,000 per 24 hours for 10 days, over 50,000 along the whole front daily) one's tongue clings to one's throat. . . .

From all armies the cry goes up: Give cartridges!"

Yanushkevitch to Sukhomlinoff.

" 27th May.

. . . Yesterday the Germans dropped on to a section of one of the regiments 3,000 heavy shells. They demolished everything. And we fired barely 100. . . ."

Some hint of the difficulties which beset the Russian arrangements for munition production may be gleaned from the following extracts taken from a report sent us at the time from a British officer who was then in Russia:—

" May 26th, 1915.

It is rumoured that Manikovski is to be nominated as Chief of the Artillery Department . . . and that the Grand Duke Serge is to be asked to take sick leave . . . He [Manikovski] said that the Grand Duke Serge was a man of great ability, but he had never smelt powder, and he loved the Artillery Department and all its ways ' like a man will still love a woman, though he knows all the time that she is a bad lot.' . . . He has worked hard and has all details at his finger-tips, though he is very ill and should be in bed. His fault is that he obstinately underestimates the number of shells required per gun per month, and sees no necessity for an adequate reserve. *He has trusted too much to the promises of Vickers and Creusot, whose failure has upset all calculations. . . .*"

Yanushkevitch wrote on the same date that the Commander-in-Chief " was appointing Lord Kitchener his agent, with ' carte blanche' to procure shells, rifles and ammunition." He added that " it was against the law of Russia to give such powers to a foreign General, but ' since it is a question now whether Russia should be victorious or defeated, we will spit on those laws. . . .'"

A despatch on 30th May, 1915, stated:—

"The powder expert in the French Mission thinks it would be impossible to form new factories, as there is already a want of trained personnel. . . . The Russian Government should be urged to give larger orders for machinery, provided Lord Kitchener really sees his way to providing fuses."

The Russians had a pathetic belief in Lord Kitchener and talked with confidence of shells provided on the guarantee of Lord Kitchener.

Here is a telegram from Yanushkevitch to the Russian War Office:—

"June, 1915.

Orders have been given to Kitchener, as the political situation and the phantom of strikes, etc., do not entitle one to ignore this not very profitable offer from abroad, *but one secured by the guarantee of Kitchener* [to give prompt assistance] . . . The III and VIII Armies have melted away. Three corps from three divisions with 5,000 bayonets each. Staffs of officers are vanishing, and the supplementary units, on receipt of rifles on the fighting days vie with each other in surrendering!"

Yanushkevitch to Sukhomlinoff.

"June, 1915.

. . . A bilious telegram was sent to Ivanoff. The reply was 'in 12 corps there are seven divisions, representing 12,000 bayonets! There are no rifles and 150,000 are without rifles. . . . From hour to hour it is worse. We await the heavenly manna from you. The chief thing is—cannot rifles be purchased? . . .'"

A further despatch of 8th June throws a sinister light on the working of the professional mind when confronted with the consequences of its inefficiency, lack of vision and energy:—

". . . The French Technical Mission regards Smislovski as the real enemy of all progress. They say he has opposed their work in every way in his power because, if they show themselves able to produce shell in Russia, it will be direct proof of inefficiency in the Artillery Department, which people will say might have increased the output months ago. . . ."

The story reads painfully like an echo in a higher key of the lethargy, the lack of vision, the conflict between patriotism and professional vanity which hampered munition supply everywhere.

In July and August we also had reports from British officers at the Russian Front as to what was happening there. They wrote within sound of the German guns: —

" The First Army was hopelessly weak in heavy artillery. For instance, north of Tysekanov the 1st Turkestan Corps had to fight 42 enemy guns of big calibre with only two. As a result, the 11th Siberian Division was practically destroyed. The German preponderance in heavy artillery seems to have created something of a panic."

It was not that the Russians had not entrenched. They were driven out of territory which for 30 years had been prepared for defence by highly skilled engineers. Great fortresses, which had been devised with ingenuity and constructed with an immense amount of labour, were destroyed in a few hours by the terrible cannon brought up by the German Army. The Russians, with their inferior equipment and serious shell deficiency, were quite unable to reply. Retreat was the only expedient open to them to save their armies from complete destruction. They were short of the machine-guns which would have enabled them to fight rearguard actions to delay the enemy and inflict upon his advancing troops losses which, in course of time, would have exhausted his strength and forced him to pause. In this unequal contest between machinery and men the great losses were almost entirely amongst Russian men, and these are described as "appalling." They had no guns which would stand up for one hour against the massed cannon of their ruthless foe, and when they had a few they were either silenced by the crashing missiles that rained on and around them, or their scant supply of ammunition was soon exhausted.

From another part of the front where the Russians had made considerable progress against the Austrians it was reported that the victorious Russians had been forced to retreat because of the lack of ammunition. Such ammunition as Headquarters could spare was urgently needed to meet the German onslaught. The vanquished Austrians then avenged their retreat in perfect security against the disarmed victors. The report further stated (18th June, 1915): —

" As we are forced to save shells the enemy can inflict loss unpunished."

Another account states: —

" All the late advances have been pure murder, as we attacked against a large quantity of field and heavy artillery without adequate preparation. I think the casualties in the ordinary sense of the word must have been 1½ million."

Here is another extract from another quarter of the 900-mile battlefield, where the Germans were still pursuing their long-range massacre of defenceless Russians: —

"This Army [the Third Russian Army] is now a harmless mob. We are very short of ammunition and guns. All realise the futility of sending men against the enemy; they with their artillery and we with ours."

At this time—ten months after the outbreak of war—Britain was just beginning to set about the task of systematically organising her enormous manufacturing resources to produce suitable weapons and sufficient supplies of ammunition for herself.

Until the Germans arrived with their superior equipment and technique, the Russians had been doing very well against the Austrians. But when Mackensen came with his great guns and his efficiently trained German soldiers, the Russians were quite unable with their inferior equipment to withstand the onslaught. As one British officer said during the retreat in May: "To-day is the eighteenth day of uninterrupted battle and retreat. I fancy they have had very little to eat. This army has been thoroughly spoilt up to now [30th May] by having only Austrians against them. They did not know what real fighting meant . . . The Russians even now are possibly in numerical superiority, but the *morale* of the Third Army has been temporarily shattered." And by June he reported that "the Third Army is reduced to a quarter of its strength, and its *morale* has been crushed owing to losses from artillery fire to which the Russians are unable to reply in consequence of lack of shell and rifle ammunition." The Russian General Staff, in their official apology for the retirement, point out how over-whelming was the German concentration of guns, and proceed "as a natural result all the Russians in the beaten zone who were not killed or wounded were stunned and contused." In this remarkable document there is a paragraph which is reminiscent of something I heard from the lips of an eminent British General as to the stupidity of spoiling troops by teaching them to expect that their enemies should be crushed by a preliminary bombardment before they were called upon to attack them. "It is evident that the enemy infantry which has been pampered and spoilt by such artillery support, and has been accustomed to attack only when the enemy is poisoned and overwhelmed by it, will soon be forced to fight in far more difficult conditions."

A comment written at the time (30th May) upon that observation by Colonel Knox, the shrewdest and best informed of the British officers at the Russian Front, was: "It is a pity that the poor Russian infantry cannot get a little pampering and spoiling of the same kind."

It was not merely an inferiority in guns that contributed to this disaster. There was a shortage of rifles and of rifle ammunition. Of the units which were sent to the front to replace the enormous casualties, only 25 per cent. came with a rifle. And there were no rifles at the front to supply the deficiency. Once more to quote from one of the British observers (18th June): —

"The Russian guns are everywhere outnumbered by the German, and we have, of course, far less shell. The Russian infantry has not only to fight without proper artillery support; many of the units are much below strength, for there are insufficient rifles to arm the drafts, and, to crown them all, there seems to be serious danger of shortage in rifle ammunition."

When the Russians held their own they could pick up and pass on to the unarmed living the rifles of the fallen, and the unexhausted bandoleers of the stricken multitude also provided a reserve of cartridges; but when the retreat began these sources of supply failed, and the shortage became more and more serious.

That was early in June, and the fighting went on until the end of September. By July the Russians had ceased to fight with any hope of victory; strategy was confined to the problem of an extrication which fell short of annihilation. The Russian strategy was reduced to an effort to frustrate the German effort to Sedanise them on a grand scale. Their highest idea of tactics was a skilful retreat.

"August 29, 1915.

The men were tired out from retiring every night and digging trenches in the morning, only to be shelled in the afternoon by an artillery to which they could hardly reply. The casualties were appalling. They were put at one million and a half in this summer drive."

As one Russian officer said: "The munitions shortage is bleeding the Russian Army to death."

At first the Russian generals were sustained by the thought that the Germans had exhausted all their reserves of ammunition in their first overwhelming attack, that they would not be able to continue to bombard on such a formidable scale, and that once they left depots which they had taken weeks to stock and store, the advantages which their superior artillery had given them would disappear.

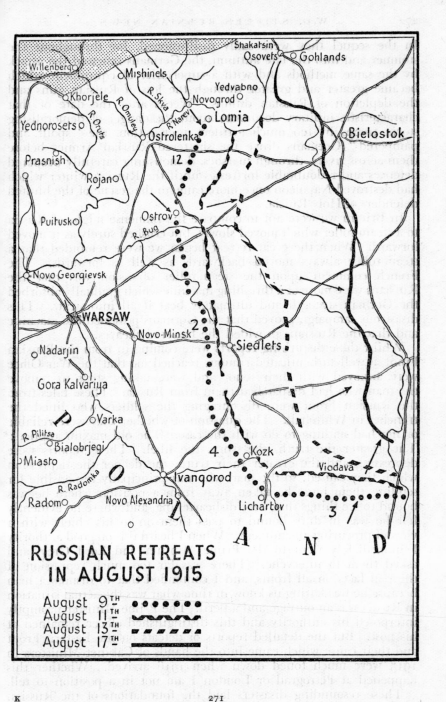

Shakatsin
Osovets • • Gohlands
W.llenberg
Mishinels
Khorjele
R. Skva
R. Omuley
R. Oruts
Yednorosets ○
Yedvabno
Novogrod
R. Narev
○ Lomja
Ostrolenka
BIELOSTOK
Prasnish
○
Rojano
12
Puitusko
Ostrov ○
R. Bug
○ Novo Georgievsk
1
●WARSAW
Novo-Minsk
2
Nadarjin ○
Siedlets
Gora Kalvariya
P
○ Varka
R. Pilitsa
Bialobrjegi
4
○ Kozk
○Miasto
Ivanqorod
Viodava
R. Radomka
Radom○
Novo Alexandria
○ Lichartov
3
O
L
A
N
D

RUSSIAN RETREATS
IN AUGUST 1915

August	9TH	• • • • • •
August	11TH	
August	13TH	
August	17TH	

In the sequel they were sadly disillusioned, for throughout the summer and into the late autumn, the Germans renewed the attack by the same methods and with a superiority of equipment which became greater and greater through the loss of Russian guns and the depletion of Russian dumps. Weeks after the date of that characteristic military document about the danger of demoralising storm troops by too much artillery preparation, the " spoilt and pampered " Germans drove the shattered Russian Armies before them across rivers, through marshes, demolishing carefully prepared defences and redoubtable fortresses until the Russian winter which had destroyed Napoleon once more came to the rescue of the hunted defenders of Holy Russia.

In Britain we were apt to compare the immense might of Russia to a steam-roller which moved slowly, but crushed surely as it moved forward. When the great retreat began we were reminded that a steam-roller always moved backwards as well as forwards. The French comment upon the steam-roller obsession was that the Russians were more of a threshing machine which gradually absorbed the German strength and ultimately beat it all into straw. This disastrous campaign proved that the Germans possessed the machine and that the Russians provided the battered sheaves.

Whilst these disturbing reports were coming in from the Russian Front, a well-authenticated rumour reached me that the War Office were annoyed with their tenor and were taking steps to remove the man who had despatched them from Russia. These tales from the Russian Front were discouraging the soldiers who lined the trenches in Whitehall. The question of whether they were reliable or not had nothing to do with the case. The old maxim applied: The greater the truth, the worse the libel. These reports were depressing and the greater their truth, the deeper the depression which they caused; so the man who was principally responsible for sending them must be taken away from a position where he was bound to see things that were disheartening, and where he evidently felt he was in duty bound to pass them on to his chiefs with a view of procuring amendment. When I heard this on good authority I immediately went to the Prime Minister and Lord Grey, and asked them to intervene. There was far too much repression of the real facts on all fronts, and I contended that to dismiss a man because he was letting us know in time what was the actual situation in Russia was an outrage and a peril. The Prime Minister promptly interposed his authority and this distinguished officer remained at his post. But the detailed reports of defeats on the Eastern Front and their cause which came into the hands of Cabinet Ministers in 1915 were much toned down when 1916 arrived. Whether this happened at Petrograd or London I am not in a position to tell.

These resounding disasters laid the foundations of the Russian

Revolution. The true state of affairs might be kept from British Cabinet Ministers, and, with the help of the censor, from the British public, but they could not be concealed for any length of time from the people they most concerned—the people of Russia. When mutilated soldiers returned to their homes and carried the news to the Russian villages of defeat after defeat and of the fact that these defeats were attributable to lack of preparation on the part of their rulers, and told their neighbours of the ghastly casualties which had been inflicted upon their fellow-countrymen in consequence of this neglect, the effect was, first of all, one of consternation, and gradually of smouldering resentment. In one small village, out of 26 young men who had gone to the front, 24 had been destroyed in the murderous campaign. The Russian peasant moved slowly but the town workers expressed their indignation in alarming riots which were only quelled by the rifles of the police. From the Moscow rioters came the cry: " Beasts! Beasts! You have no ammunition to fight the Germans, but you have plenty to shoot down Russians."

Inside the Army the deficiencies in equipment naturally created a sense of growing dissatisfaction and distrust. At first it was directed against the Allies: later on it turned against the Czar and his advisers, and then both Czardom and the Alliance fell together into the same pit of righteous wrath. Here is a report from the Russian Front which came into my hands just as I entered upon my duties as Minister of Munitions: —

" August 29, 1915.

Officers cannot understand why England, with her highly developed industries, is unable to help Russia with munitions. They come to me and ask why we do not send out shell and rifles. When I tried to explain that we have not sufficient for our own requirements, they simply do not believe, and go on to argue that it is in our own interest to help, for they will do the fighting if we will only give them the wherewithal to do it."

CHAPTER XIV

WHY WERE THE RUSSIAN ARMIES ILL EQUIPPED?

THE bitter rebuke of those bewildered Russian officers whose men had been slaughtered for lack of proper munitions is true in substance and in fact, and history will return a true bill against the military directors of France and Britain for their selfish obtuseness in abandoning their Russian comrades in arms to hopeless carnage, when they might so easily have saved them and in so doing have rendered the most effective help to their own countries. They never could be taught to appreciate the fact that a great victory over the Germans in Poland would be a greater service to France and Belgium than a slight advance into the German lines in Champagne, or even than the capture of a molehill in Flanders.

They could unquestionably have saved Russia had they taken the right action and taken it in time. For instance, had the manufacturing resources of our country been mobilised for the production of munitions of war as soon as we decided to fight in August, 1914, and had the military chiefs foreseen in time (as they ought to have realised as soon as the Germans dug themselves into the soil of France after the Marne) that the War would resolve itself into an attack and defence of formidable earthworks, impenetrable except by overwhelming artillery, then the same systematic methods for increasing the output of rifles, machine-guns and guns of heavier calibre with abundant ammunition as were inaugurated by the Ministry of Munitions in 1915, might just as easily have been taken in August or September, 1914—in fact, more easily, for all the pivotal skilled men would have been kept at home. The result of prompt action on an adequate scale would have been that by the end of the year we could have increased our output of the lighter type of shell by hundreds of thousands, and by the summer of 1915 we should have had at our disposal a fine equipment of guns of every calibre—light, medium and heavy, with a full complement of shells. We could have added hundreds of thousands to our stocks of rifles, and what is quite as important, we should have had thousands of machine-guns, which owing to the delays, were not available until late in 1916. In 1915, this great equipment would have exceeded the needs of our armies for defence in the field at that time. The new recruits were not ready to take part in the fighting until September, 1915, and those who were then placed in the battle line were barely one-tenth of the total recruitment up to that date. That fact would have enabled us, without impinging on our own requirements, to double the Russian equipment of medium and heavy guns, and to more than treble their meagre supply of shells. Had we postponed efforts to break through in the west until we were quite ready, the Russian Armies could have been supplied with an equipment which would have enabled them to break up the Austrians, whilst repelling the Germans. We could have furnished them with sufficient rifles for their fighting men, and with hundreds of machine-guns to assist them in defending their fortified posts. Had the French contributed even a moderate quota out of their more considerable supplies of guns and ammunition, the Russian Armies instead of being a mere target for Krupp's great guns, would have become a redoubtable weapon for attack and defence. That would have compelled the Germans to weaken their forces on the Western Front in men and mechanism and thus make their defensive line in France and Flanders more vulnerable.

The way the Allied War direction failed to utilise the gigantic resources of Russia in men is the best proof of the lack of vision and of ordinary business intelligence which nearly lost the War and succeeded in prolonging it for years with increasing havoc, ruin and ghastliness.

Russia had such reserves of vigorous and sturdy youth that four and a half years of devastating war, followed by many more years of ravaging disease and the wholesale massacre of revolution and counter-revolution, seem to have made no appreciable impression upon their inexhaustible numbers. By the end of 1916 over 13,000,000 had been called up, and it was estimated then that there were still left several millions of fit men of military age never yet summoned to the colours. As to the 13,000,000 that joined the army, the first contingent of these millions were highly trained and well officered. Most of the number who were waiting their turn at the gates of the slaughter house had received quite as thorough a training for military service as that which either Britain, France, or America could afford to give to their recruits the last year or two of the War. As one Russian general was reported to have said when the Duma complained of the horrible casualties: " Don't worry yourself. Thank God, of men at all events we have enough." In courage and endurance they had no superior on either side on any battlefield. But their equipment in guns, rifles, machine-guns, ammunition, and transport was the poorest in the field (except later on, when our Salonika Army was deliberately kept on quarter rations of shot and shell), and for that reason they were beaten in action by troops inferior in numbers and sometimes in quality, and slaughtered by the million without the means of defence or retaliation. Their country was a half-primitive peasant land, unskilled in industrial arts and therefore unable to provide her gallant young

defenders with adequate weapons. In spite of the infinite natural
resources of the country, it had none of the developed or accumulated
wealth which commanded the credit that would have enabled it to
purchase essential equipment or supplies in the only available neutral
market in the world that could furnish it with its needs—the United
States of America. When that credit was partially forthcoming it was
frittered away by corrupt incompetence. On the other hand France
with a population less than a third that of Russia soon came to the
end of her man-power, and for filling up the gaps made by war in her
armies had to depend upon successive combings from her workshops
and farms, upon the patch-ups turned out from the hospitals, and
upon the young boys who became of military age during the years of
the War. She supplemented these by coloured men from French
Colonies in Africa and Asia. Any and every material for soldiering
she could lay her hands on was thrown into the fiery furnace. Her
divisions at the commencement of the War each numbered 20,000
men. By 1918 many of them had been reduced to less than half this
strength, and even at that were kept up with difficulty. But France
has some of the finest arsenals in the world for the production of
weapons, especially for land warfare, and her engineers in other
departments were highly skilled craftsmen. Her resources for turning
out every machine and device for waging a mechanical war were
capable of an expansion which seemed to be limited only by the
demand. France was also a country rich in wealth accumulated by
generations of toil and frugality. Her credit thus stood high in the
world.

As for Great Britain, when the War broke out she had millions of
young men of military age, but not four per cent. of them had
received any military training. As soon as war was proclaimed
hundred thousand after hundred thousand flocked to the colours.
But only gradually were they absorbed, drilled and fashioned into an
army. It was the end of the second year of the War before a million
of them could be placed in the battle line. By that time France had
lost over 2,000,000 and the Russian casualties were 5,000,000. We
did not possess the officers, the training sergeants, and all that constitutes a *cadre* capable without loss of valuable time of making out of
the best raw material soldiers fit to encounter the finest army in the
world. But we were the greatest manufacturing country in Europe.
There are no finer craftsmen in the world than those employed in our
metal trades of all kinds. Their resourcefulness and adaptability
were amply demonstrated as soon as they were put to the test. We
were also the richest nation in Europe. Britain was the greatest
creditor nation in the world. She had lent £4,000,000,000 to the
nations of the earth and in the main the security was good. So British
credit in America was good enough to guarantee any order for equipment which that country had any reasonable hope of executing.

Britain and France jointly arranged a substantial credit for Russia in America, but when I entered the Ministry of Munitions I found that the more powerful financial countries had managed to hustle and trample down Russia's best chances of utilising her foreign credits. M. Albert Thomas and I did our best to secure a fair distribution and co-ordination of the Allied orders in America. It was then almost too late.

Had Britain explored her unsuspected resources and then organised them for war as soon as she risked her own greatness and the lives of her own children in the demoniac venture she could, in the late summer of 1915, have equipped 2,000,000 Russians with almost as powerful an armoury of machines and missiles as that with which she sent 1,500,000 Britons into action in the summer and autumn of 1916. With some help from France, which her armies could, as I shall point out later on, easily spare and spare to their own advantage, and with the further aid of the American factories which our credit could purchase, Russia would easily, in the campaign of 1915, have held Germany in check and overthrown the inferior armies of Austria. Instead of which what happened? I have endeavoured to summarise the pitiful story of the disaster that befell a great country and the mutilation and death that came to millions of her brave sons through the incompetency of her rulers and the blind and selfish folly of her friends.

The Russian failure to make the best of the resources at their command, natural and acquired, was not due to any lack of mental quality in the race. They are an exceptionally gifted nation. But they have the leisurely and casual habits of a peasant people. With them time does not count and organisation has no meaning. They wait for the seasons, and for months of the year there is nothing they can do to help fruition but keep warm until the sun comes round to call them to their labours. When their first spell of toil is over they have another period of loitering about, doing little until the fructifying rays have completed their task. The industrialism of the west, which demands incessant, well-directed, wasteless toil, has never entered the lives or fashioned the habits of 90 per cent. of the Russian people. One or two illustrations of the way this ingrained and hereditary tendency of mind affected all their work came to my notice during the War. A Russian officer whom I met at a Conference during the War told me that the real Russian was essentially an unpractical dreamer, and he challenged me to name one who had ever displayed any aptitude for business in trade, finance or politics. I named several. He annotated each name by saying: " He is not a Russian, he is a German," or again, " He is an Armenian." " He is a Georgian." " He is a Scandinavian." " He is a Jew." Then I said: " What about yourself?" He replied: "I am a Greek." That is much too wholesale an indictment of a race that numbers well over a hundred millions and has accomplished great things. But my experience of doing business with them taught me that there was an unwelcome ingredient of truth in this cynicism.

Here is a fair illustration of their strange combination of genius and ineptitude. Their chemists were men of exceptional knowledge, ingenuity and imagination. Early in 1915 the Russian munitionment encountered the same class of difficulty as arrested our activities at one point. There was an inadequate supply of the kind of explosive which had hitherto been used for the purpose of filling their cartridges and shells, and it was essential that another source of supply should be discovered without loss of time. In their case as in ours the matter was referred to chemists for investigation. After weeks spent by these scientists apparently without any practical issue, inquiry was made at the laboratory to ascertain what progress had been made with the solution of the difficulty. It was discovered that the chemists had forgotten all about the urgent task which they had been specifically invited to solve. They had in the course of their experiments got on the track of a new chemical discovery which was infinitely more important to them than the explosive ingredients of a shell, and they were pursuing this trail with an eagerness and an enthusiasm which made them quite oblivious of the fact that their country was engaged in a life and death struggle with a foreign foe, and that they had been called upon to use their scientific skill to save it from an impending catastrophe. Here is another illustration of the same kind of practical defect in the Russian temperament. When the Germans let loose their first gas attack in Russia there were at first the same crude improvisations to protect the troops as we were forced to attempt. These proving ineffective, British and French aid was invoked. We were asked to send immediately a supply of the masks which had been invented for the protection of the Allied troops in the west from these chemical horrors. We instantly sent to Petrograd hundreds of thousands of our latest pattern. Before they were forwarded to the front they were submitted to a preliminary examination by a Russian chemist, who had no hesitation in coming to the conclusion that they were by no means perfect. The consignment was, therefore, detained at Petrograd, whilst Russian professors were devoting their time to devising something better. The perfect mask was never invented. The English masks were ultimately transmitted to their destination, but meanwhile thousands of gallant Russian soldiers had been choked by the agonising fumes.

Had we not known something of the inefficiency of Russia under its autocracy we might have pointed to the great arsenals of Perm and Petrograd and many another finely equipped workshop planted here and there in their vast country. For our neglect we could have put in the plea that we honestly thought Russia was quite able to furnish the needs of her own armies without much outside aid. M. Albert

Thomas told me on his return from a visit to Russia in 1916 that he was filled with envy when he went through the Putiloff works near Petrograd. They were equipped with the most modern machinery. In that respect they surpassed the finest of the French arsenals. But the management was incompetent, indolent and muddled. The incompetence of Russian management, however, was not a new discovery, and it needed no special journey to reveal it to western eyes. At any rate, it was known by 1915, and Britain and France in co-operation ought to have averted its calamitous results to the Allied cause by supplying the equipment which Russian management had failed to provide. When the Teutonic hurricane burst on the doomed armies of the Muscovites in May, 1915, their fine arsenals had succeeded in turning out the first four heavy guns manufactured there since the War began. But not a gun above the calibre of three inches reached Russia from abroad in 1914, and in 1915 Russia had to face the calamities of that year without any adequate help in heavy artillery and ammunition, for lack of which her valiant army was perishing.

CHAPTER XV

WHAT WOULD HAVE HAPPENED HAD THE ALLIES POOLED THEIR RESOURCES

WHILST the Russian armies were being shattered and pounded by the overwhelming artillery of Germany, and were unable to put up any defence owing to the lack of rifles and ammunition, the French were hoarding their shells as if they were golden francs, and were pointing with pride to the enormous accumulation of reserve dumps behind the lines. I recollect a munition conference in Paris where French generals flourished their statistics of accumulated millions with all the pride of possession and of achievement. What about Britain? When Britain began to manufacture in earnest, and turned out her hundreds of guns, great and small, and her hundreds of thousands of shells of all calibres, the British generals treated the production as if we were preparing to enter for some great race or contest where it was essential that the British equipment should be equal to and if achievable better than that which had been provided for any competitor in the field. The military leaders in both these countries never seemed to have grasped what ought to have been their dominant thought—that they were engaged with Russia in a common enterprise where it was vital to the attainment of a common end that they should pool their resources, and each of them be put in the best position to contribute his share to the speedy accomplishment of that aim. The team spirit was conspicuously absent during the first years of the War. Each player was thinking too much of his own scoring and too little of victory for his side. The recognition by the French generals of the towering fact that Russia had an overwhelming superiority in men never had any effective practical outcome, except a constantly expressed demand that Russia should send a large contingent of these men to France to aid the French Army in its defence of French territory, and to save French manhood from an undue share of the sacrifice which such defence involved. Quantities of guns, rifles and ammunition were sent from Britain and France to Russia before her final collapse, but they were dispatched reluctantly; they were quite inadequate to the need, and when they reached the hard-pressed armies of Russia, they came too late to avert the final collapse.

The answer of the French and British generals to every suggestion for the remunitionment of Russia was that they had nothing to spare in 1914, 1915 or 1916, and that when they gave anything away to Russia it was out of their own dire need. That was a complete answer if fatuous and wasteful efforts to crash through the formidable German entrenchments were the best strategy for either of those years. Allied Generalship on the Western Front never gave any weight to the fact that up to the third quarter of 1916, the Germans had a definite superiority in heavy guns in the west as well as the east. I am not sure that they even realised it. They could see their own guns; they could not visualise those of the enemy. And yet their own Intelligence Officers supplied them with abundant evidence of the Allied inferiority in artillery. In 1916 I was shown a French memorandum which gave the comparative strength of the German and French artillery in the greatest battle of the War—the battle of Verdun—three months after it had commenced, when both sides had brought up every gun they could spare in the west.

The following is a translation of this memorandum, in which I have, for the convenience of the reader, rendered the French measurements of calibres into their equivalents in inches:—

SUB-SECRETARIAT OF STATE   9th July, 1916
for Artillery and Munitions

CABINET

Technical Service

COMPARATIVE TABLE OF FRENCH AND GERMAN ARTILLERY IN LINE ON THE VERDUN FRONT

Subdivisions.			On the German side on 26th May, 1916.		On the French side. Average between 21st February and 20th May, 1916.	
			%	Description of calibres.	%	Description of calibres.
Very heavy	..	..	2	16½ in., 15 in., 12 in.	1	A.L.G.P. (very powerful heavy guns*)
Heavy	..	..	35	8.3 in., 5.9 in.	13	6.1 in., 8.7 in., 10.6 in.
Medium	..	..	43	4.1 in.	19	3¾ in., 4.1 in., 4.7 in.
Light	..	..	20	3 in.	67	2.95 in., 3.1 in., 3½ in.
TOTAL OF PIECES IN THE LINE			2,000		1,600	

* 5½ in., 7½ in., 7.9 in., 9½ in., 11 in., 12 in., 14.6 in.

This table shows that the Germans not only possessed a total numerical superiority of guns on the Verdun Front, but that they had approximately 740 heavy and very heavy guns against the French 224—or more than three times their equipment of these powerful weapons. They had more guns and heavier guns than the French in the west, although they were engaged in massing all the artillery they could spare for their campaign in the east against Russia.

The western generals will point to these figures as a proof that they could not send a single gun or shell away from their front to help at any other. What it does demonstrate is the folly of attempting with inferior artillery to attack a highly trained army skilfully entrenched and armed with superior weapons. Anyone who has seen the German entrenchments will realise how formidable an enterprise it was to capture them. The fortresses of Beaumont Hamel, Posières and Thiepval will serve as specimens. They were excavated deep down under the surface. These dug-out fortresses were strengthened by iron girders and concrete so that no shell could hope to penetrate their well-equipped depths. To shell them was like bombarding the Catacombs. On the other hand, the German task in attacking the French lines was equally hopeless. The Allies had considerable numerical superiority on the Western Front. They also could entrench, and they had a sufficient equipment of guns, machine-guns, rifles and grenades to repel every advance by German troops. That was the lesson of Verdun.

On the Russian Front there was not the same need for heavy artillery as on the west. Neither Austrians nor Germans could dig such a tremendous line of triplex entrenchments along so vast a front. It was more of a war of movement. There the *soixante-quinze* would have come by its own, provided there were plenty of ammunition. The millions blazed away in stubborn and stupid offensives in the west would have served. Had there been enough heavy artillery to effect a break in the Austrian lines the lighter and more mobile guns would have done the rest. And a few hundred machine-guns with adequate ammunition would have completely held up the German advance.

To anyone who had the advantage of perusing the despatches from our able military representative on the Eastern Front, or any reliable history of the 1915 campaign, it must be evident that the overwhelming defeats sustained by the Russian Armies were not due to any inferiority in numbers (the Russians outnumbered the Germans along the whole line) or to any lack of courage, endurance or discipline on the part of Russian soldiers whose undaunted valour under dismaying conditions must always remain a marvel. Neither were these disasters attributable to lack of skill on the part of the Russian generals in the field. By common consent their conduct of the retreat was at least competent. The enveloping tactics of the German marshals were thwarted at every turn and the Russian Armies escaped without any wholesale loss of equipment. This was due to a combination of skilful generalship on the part of the leaders and fine fighting qualities in the men they led. It is easy to lead into action a well-equipped army hopeful of victory. It is not so easy to lead broken and discouraged troops out of a succession of fields where they have been stricken and stricken again by a foe whom they know to be much better equipped than they are. Let us give the Grand Duke Nicholas and his generals the credit of having achieved this feat. But why was so gallant an army, so competently led, driven like

a herd of cattle across the plains and marshes of Poland? The answer
is to be found in the extracts I have given from the reports of
impartial British officers, who witnessed this agony of brave men who
had been deprived by official stupidity of the means of defending
themselves and the country for which they were prepared to die. They
were not vanquished by better troops—they never had a chance of
measuring their quality as fighting-men with the soldiers who were
arrayed against them. They saw millions of German shells hurtling
through the air in their direction and bursting into destructive fury
amongst them, they heard the deadly rattle of the machine-guns
carried forward by the advancing Germans, but they rarely came up
against the foe that pelted them at a safe distance with bullet and
shell. Their defences were shattered by the monster guns of Germany.
The survivors of this bombardment were left among the debris without a shelter to protect them from such a rain of fire and brimstone as
has not fallen on mankind since the days of Gomorrah. Had they
advanced machine-guns would have mowed them down. Orderly
retreat was their only chance of saving themselves and their country.
Even in retreat hundreds of thousands were destroyed in the open
by the terrible blizzard of shrapnel and high explosive.

Had the Russian artillery been doubled, especially in the medium
and heavy calibres; had there been an abundant supply of shell for
light as well as heavy; had the Russian posts been defended by an
adequate quota of machine-guns, the German troops would have
encountered the same resistance on the Eastern Front as they
experienced whenever they attacked in the west, and they could not
have afforded the cumulative losses inflicted upon them in a series of
attacks. On the Austrian Front, where the quality of the enemy
troops was distinctly inferior for a variety of reasons which I have
already given—reasons which do not in the least reflect on Austrian
valour—the impetuous onslaught of the Russians following a sufficient
preliminary attack would not only have successfully broken the
Austrian lines, but that success could have been exploited and pushed
perhaps to the gates of Vienna. The Austrian Armies were a different
proposition from the German. The German Armies were homogeneous and bore an equal intensity of hatred against Slav and Gaul.
In a struggle between Teuton and Slav three-fifths of the Austrian
troops had a deeper detestation of their Teutonic comrades than of
their Slavonic foes. The Russians partly for that reason won comparatively easy victories against the Austrians, and they were only
unable to take advantage of the victories owing to lack of ammunition.
A well-equipped Russian army could have crossed the Carpathians,
penetrated through the Hungarian and Austrian plains up to their
Slavonic kinsmen in Croatia or Czecho-Slovakia and then imperilled
the capital of the Empire. Roumania would, under those conditions,
have felt safe in throwing her 500,000 on the Austrian flank, and

Bulgaria would have known it was better to fight on the Allied side or to keep out of it altogether.

It may be said that the Germans would then have come to the rescue of their chief ally. Of course they would. They would have been bound to do so for their own preservation. But they could not have afforded Austria effective assistance without dangerously weakening their own Western Front. They could not have withdrawn any part of their troops from the Polish Front, as that would have placed in jeopardy the roads that led to the heart of Prussia. The battles of Loos, Artois and Champagne, if they had been fought at all, would have been fought under conditions twice as favourable to the French and British Armies as those which turned them into a futile massacre of myriads of brave young men. These gallant fellows were sacrificed on the altar of misguided and antiquated theories which had already been discredited by repeated exposure. The sacrifice was in vain. It did not liberate France and it failed to save Russia. The excuse they put forward, after their failure, for fighting these profligate battles, was that hard-pressed Russia demanded these attacks in order to prevent the Germans from increasing their forces on the Eastern Front. The Germans never arrested their victorious march for a single hour, because hundreds of miles to the west the French and British generals were piling up shell dumps behind the front and making other elaborate preparations to send their infantry to be shot down by German machine-guns in fruitless efforts to break through impregnable German defences. Each time French and British generals were sure of victory. Previous experience ought to have taught them to know better. The best help we could have given Russia would have been to send her artillery a portion of the ammunition we wasted in battles that achieved nothing but the building up still higher of the ghastly pyramid of casualties amongst our own troops.

To sum up: Had we sent to Russia half the shells subsequently wasted in these ill-conceived battles and one-fifth of the guns that fired them, not only would the Russian defeat have been averted, but the Germans would have sustained a repulse by the side of which the capture of a few blood-stained kilometres in France would have seemed a mockery. What more? Austria would have been crumpled up. Only prompt transference to the Austrian Front of several divisions of German infantry and several batteries of German guns from France could have saved the Dual Monarchy from utter collapse. Had Russia been victorious, then Bulgaria would have entered the War on the Allied side. A Balkan Federation—including Serbia, Roumania and Greece, and perhaps Bulgaria—on the south, and an Italian army on the west, with a victorious Russia on the east marching against a routed and divided Austria, might have ended the War in 1915. That may be a sanguine estimate of possibilities. The certainty is that if the Russian equipment had been strengthened Austria would, by the end of the 1915 campaign, have been tottering towards her fall. Germany would have been hard put to it to keep her troublesome ally from collapsing. By the spring of 1916 Britain, Russia, Italy and the Balkan Confederation, all now fully equipped (certainly if we had started manufacturing in time), could have directed a convergent attack on Austria which would have completed her disintegration. An isolated and weakened Germany would then have had to face the full strength of France and Britain and would gladly have made the peace of a foe outmanœuvred and overwhelmed.

Instead of this we left Russia to her fate and we thereby precipitated the Balkan tragedy, which had such an influence on the prolongation of the War.

Surveying the position twelve months after we had entered into the War, I felt that things were going badly for the Allies in the east and in the west. All our attacks in France had turned out to be costly failures, and I had a conviction, shared to a certain extent by Lord Kitchener, that the one in which we were then engaged would turn out to be a sanguinary defeat for the Allied cause. The armies of our greatest Ally were in a position where they hailed a mere escape from complete destruction as a triumph of strategy. The bumper harvest of a conquered Poland was pouring into the depleted granaries of Germany (whose harvest had failed), thus neutralising our blockade. In the East we were making no progress in Mesopotamia, and we were not only held up in Egypt but we lived in daily dread of an invasion of the Delta by the Turkish forces across the Canal. In Gallipoli we had suffered defeat after defeat and there were rumours, which proved to be only too true, that Serbia was soon to be trampled down under the ruthless heel of the advancing legions of the Teuton. My ten weeks at the Ministry of Munitions had driven home to my consciousness the painful truth that most of this could have been avoided, had we organised our resources in time and distributed them wisely. This prompted me to write the following statement in September, 1915, as a preface to a collection of my War appeals published by Messrs. Hodder and Stoughton. I was anxious to rouse public opinion from a complacency created by official reports concocted out of spurious victories. I felt it was the only way to enforce a change. Reading it now, 17 years after it was written, when one is able to peruse the story of 1914-15 and to ruminate upon it in the quiet of one's study, I cannot find any essential inaccuracy or exaggeration in the survey which I then gave of the Allied position.

" After twelve months of war my conviction is stronger than ever that this country could not have kept out of it without imperilling its security and impairing its honour. We could not have looked on cynically with folded arms whilst the country we had given our word to protect was being ravaged and trodden by one of our co-trustees. If British women and children were being brutally destroyed on the high seas by German submarines this nation would have insisted on calling the infanticide Empire to a stern reckoning. Everything that has happened since the declaration of war has demonstrated clearly that a military system so regardless of good faith, of honourable obligations, and of the elementary impulses of humanity, constituted a menace to civilisation of the most sinister character; and despite the cost of suppressing it, the well-being of humanity demands that such a system should be challenged and destroyed. The fact that events have also shown that the might of this military clique has exceeded the gloomiest prognostications provides an additional argument for its destruction. The greater the might the darker the menace.

Nor have the untoward incidents of the War weakened my faith in ultimate victory—always provided that the allied nations put forth the whole of their strength ere it is too late. Anything less must lead to defeat. The Allied countries have an overwhelming preponderance in the raw material that goes to the making and equipment of armies, whether in men, money, or accessible metals and machinery. But this material has to be mobilised and utilised. It would be idle to pretend that the first twelve months of the War have seen this task accomplished satisfactorily. Had the Allies realised in time the full strength of their redoubtable and resourceful foes—nay, what is more, had they realised their own strength and resources, and taken prompt action to organise them, to-day we should have witnessed the triumphant spectacle of their guns pouring out a stream of shot and shell which would have deluged the German trenches with fire and scorched the German legions back across their own frontiers.

What is the actual position? It is thoroughly well known to the Germans, and anyone in any land, belligerent or neutral, who reads intelligently the military news must by now have a comprehension of it. With the resources of Great Britain, France, Russia —yea, of the whole industrial world—at the disposal of the Allies, it is obvious that the Central Powers have still an overwhelming superiority in all the material and equipment of war. The result of this deplorable fact is exactly what might have been foreseen. The iron heel of Germany has sunk deeper than ever into French and Belgian soil. Poland is entirely German. Lithuania is rapidly following. Russian fortresses, deemed impregnable, are falling like sand castles before the resistless tide of Teutonic invasion. When will that tide recede? When will it be stemmed? As soon as the Allies are supplied with abundance of war material.

That is why I am recalling these unpleasant facts, because I wish to stir my countrymen to put forth their strength to amend the situation. To dwell on such events is the most disagreeable task which can fall to the lot of a public man. For all that, the public man who either shirks these facts himself, or does not do his best to force others to face them until they are redressed, is guilty of high treason to the State which he has sworn to serve.

There has been a great awakening in all the Allied countries, and prodigious efforts are being put forth to equip the armies in the field. I know what we are doing, our exertions are undoubtedly immense. But can we do more, either in men or material? Nothing but our best and utmost can pull us through. Are we now straining every nerve to make up for lost time? Are we getting all the men we shall want to put into the fighting line next year to enable us even to hold our own? Does every man who can help, whether by fighting or by providing material, understand clearly that ruin awaits remissness? How many people in this country fully apprehend the full significance of the Russian retreat? For over twelve months Russia has, in spite of deficiencies in equipment, absorbed the energies of half the German and four-fifths of the Austrian forces. Is it realised that Russia has for the time being made her contribution—and what an heroic contribution it is!— to the struggle for European freedom, and that we cannot for many months to come expect the same active help from the Russian Armies that we have hitherto received? Who is to take the Russian place in the fight while those armies are re-equipping? Who is to bear the weight which has hitherto fallen on Russian shoulders? France cannot be expected to sustain much heavier burdens than those which she now bears with a quiet courage that has astonished and moved the world. Italy is putting her strength into the fight. What could she do more? There is only Britain left. Is Britain prepared to fill up the great gap that will be created when Russia has retired to re-arm? Is she fully prepared to cope with all the possibilities of the next few months—in the west, without forgetting the east? Upon the answer which Government, employers, workmen, financiers, young men who can bear arms, women who can work in factories—in fact, the whole people of this great land— give to this question, will depend the liberties of Europe for many a generation.

A shrewd and sagacious observer told me the other day that in his judgment the course pursued by this country during the next three months would decide the fate of the War. If we are not allowed to equip our factories and workshops with adequate labour to supply our armies, because we must not transgress regulations applicable to normal conditions; if practices are maintained which restrict the output of essential war material; if the nation hesitates, when the need is clear, to take the necessary steps to call forth its manhood to defend honour and existence; if vital decisions are postponed until too late; if we neglect to make ready for all probable eventualities; if, in fact, we give ground for the accusation that we are slouching into disaster as if we were walking along the ordinary paths of peace without an enemy in sight; then I can see no hope; but if we sacrifice all we own, and all we like for our native land; if our preparations are characterised by grip, resolution, and a prompt readiness in every sphere, then victory is assured."

CHAPTER XVI

THE FUTILE ALLIED OFFENSIVES ON THE WESTERN FRONT

WHILST the Germans were engaged in these tremendous operations to rout and wreck the great armies of Russia, the military authorities in France, Britain and Italy could think of no more effective means of coming to their aid than to hurl great masses of their troops against impregnable positions in France, Flanders, and the Austrian Alps. No decision on the part of their enemies could have suited the Central Powers better than this course, pursued with an obstinate and senseless determination which sacrificed the flower of the Allied armies in vain efforts to break through defences bristling with cannon and machine-guns, and with two or three equally powerful positions to fall back upon in the event of the first being carried. The Allies at the same time pursued in listless and ineffective fashion, with inadequate troops, inefficiently equipped, and always timed to arrive too late, their efforts to capture Gallipoli. Had they spared in time one-fifth of the soldiers sacrificed in these futile attempts in France to reinforce the Dardanelles Expedition, Gallipoli could have been captured with comparative ease. We encountered defeat after defeat in that quarter, each defeat being a telling blow which resounded throughout the Balkans where Bulgaria and Roumania were watching the turn of events. As the collapse of Russia became more and more complete, as our failure to force the Dardanelles was becoming more and more evident, the fight of our friends in Bulgaria became fainter and feebler, the pro-German party in military circles at Sofia became more buoyant and insistent, the wily Bulgarian Monarch thought he saw more clearly on which side his bread was buttered, and the brave Serbian Army behind the Danube became more and more despondent. They saw now the approaching doom of their isolated country.

The infatuation of a break-through which haunted the western generals like a disease of the mind still prompted them to organise another and, as they thought, overwhelming attack on the German entrenchments. This was timed to take place in September, 1915. After the decision had been taken, a lingering doubt seems to have entered Lord Kitchener's mind as to the wisdom of such a proceeding. According to the " Official History of the War," published under the auspices of the War Office, the British Military Authorities, after the Boulogne Munitions Conference in June, seem to have undertaken for the first time a careful survey of the equipment of the armies on the Western Front—French, British and German—more especially in heavy guns and ammunition. They discovered what they ought to have ascertained and provided against in September, 1914—that the German proportion of heavy artillery was twice that of the Allies and that the German shell production per day was also double that of France and Britain together and that:—

"Taking these several important factors into consideration, the British Military Authorities arrived at the conclusion that an offensive on the Western Front, if it was to have a reasonable chance of success, would have to be delivered on a continuous front of twenty-five miles, by a force of not less than thirty-six divisions, supported by 1,150 heavy guns and howitzers and the normal complement of field artillery. They maintained that this quantity of guns and the necessary ammunition could not be provided before the spring of 1916, and that until then it was preferable, whatever the general situation, to remain on the active defensive in the western theatre of war."

This sensible conclusion was not conveyed by the generals to their respective Governments in time to influence a decision. I have no recollection that Lord Kitchener ever communicated to the Cabinet or the War Council the resolution now revealed by the Official History.

It was not good for civilians to be told that events had proved them to be right and the military wrong. But Lord Kitchener did at last inform the Cabinet that he was opposed to the autumn offensive which General Joffre contemplated launching in September, and in which the latter was anxious that the British Army should participate by an attack on the German right. Sir John French was fully alive to the drawbacks and dangers of the proposed operation, and I believe that at first Sir Douglas Haig shared his opinion. These risks of the proposed operation were pointed out with great force by members of the Cabinet, including the Prime Minister. Nevertheless, the Cabinet as a whole (there were at least two exceptions) adopted Lord Kitchener's view that we had no option in the matter but to fall in with the plan to which the French Commander-in-Chief so stubbornly and stupidly adhered. In consequence of this weak decision the great autumn offensive was undertaken. The Allied armies were badly beaten with terrible casualties. Our new armies entered into action for the first time and fought with conspicuous valour, and tens of thousands of them fell in the futile carnage of the Loos offensive.

On the eve of this offensive Lord Kitchener was authorised to visit France in order to persuade General Joffre to postpone the attack, but his mission was a failure. He reported that " General Joffre was quite determined both on political and military grounds (the main element in the former being the situation in Russia) to take the offensive without delay and on a considerable scale. Sir John French agreed with the French Commander-in-Chief as to the urgency of the step from the military point of view." Lord Kitchener, though far from sanguine that any substantial military advantage would be achieved, was strongly of opinion that we could not without serious and perhaps fatal injury to the Alliance refuse the co-operation which Joffre expected.

Even after the failure of this last ill-judged offensive of the 1915 campaign had become quite evident to any sane observer, General Joffre persisted for weeks in attack after attack. When he became convinced that further efforts were fruitless except to add to the already appalling casualty list, he intimated to his Government that he had no intention of persevering with his plan that year. Accordingly he said he would be prepared to assist in carrying out the project which had been urged upon him by the ablest members of the French Government for sending a force to Salonika to help Serbia. Before General Joffre was convinced by lacerating facts that his offensive had failed, the losses in the Champagne attack were three times those in the Dardanelles. Millions of shells were also wasted—10,000,000 in all, including French and British. Half of the men who fell in these criminal attacks would either have stormed Gallipoli or, had they been sent to Salonika, would have enabled Serbia to throw the invading army into the Danube. One third of the shells would have averted the Russian retreat.

CHAPTER XVII

THE SERBIAN TRAGEDY

WHILST the billy-goat tactics of western generals in butting away the strength of their armies against unbreakable walls was proceeding in a succession of sickening thuds, what was happening to the Allies on the Eastern and South-Eastern Fronts? I have told the story of how the might of Russia was broken through lack of equipment. What about Serbia? Ominous warnings came from Sofia, Bucharest, Athens and Nish in the summer of 1915 that Austria was gathering a great force in the valleys that pointed towards the Danube. Later on we heard that German troops were arriving in great numbers. It was known that Bulgaria had practically decided to throw in her lot with the Central Powers and join them in the attack on her neighbour.

The sinister effect of the Russian disaster was soon felt in the changed attitude of Bulgaria. About the third week in August, 1915, when what was supposed to be the impregnable fortress of Kovno fell before the German guns and the Russian armies were still being driven daily league after league towards Petrograd, a message reached the British Foreign Office from its representative at Sofia warning us that " the capture of Kovno had made a deep impression on the governing and military circles at the Bulgarian capital and had given rise to anticipation of a crushing disaster to Russian arms." He further warned us " that the elements most favourable to us had, during the last few days, become so impressed with Germany's military strength that they would hesitate to take the course which would expose Bulgaria to a German attack." A few weeks later the crafty Ferdinand, who had been crouching behind a complacent Ministry until he found which belligerent alliance was the highest bidder and the likeliest winner, thought the time had come to throw in his lot openly with Germany and Austria. If the blow fell upon Serbia it was not for lack of timely information as to what fate was being prepared for her by the Central Powers. Late in September there percolated through the news that the Austrians were massing troops in the valleys that ran toward the Danube and that several German divisions had already arrived to reinforce them. There could be no doubt as to the intention and imminence of their movements.

The probability of a German-Austrian attack on Serbia was alluded to in the Press, and was even discussed in the House of Commons about the end of September, 1915. When the matter was raised in Parliament, Sir Edward Grey made a statement to the House in the following terms: —

" If, on the other hand, the Bulgarian mobilisation were to result in Bulgaria assuming an aggressive attitude on the side of our enemies, *we are prepared to give to our friends in the Balkans all the support in our power, in the manner that would be most welcome to them, in concert with our Allies, without reserve and without qualification. We are, of course, in consultation with our Allies on the situation, and I believe the view that I express is theirs also.*"

As Sir Edward Carson subsequently said, after the blow had fallen: —

" That was one of the most important declarations that could be made in this House. I believed it, when I was a party to it, to be the policy of His Majesty's Government, but I believed more. I believed that our military advisers never would have allowed us to make that declaration unless we had actual preparations and plans which were ready when the moment came to enable us to strike and assist our gallant little Ally in the field of battle."

The Grey declaration satisfied an anxious House of Commons. It was hailed with delight throughout Serbia as a promise that her powerful friends in the west would come to her rescue if any evil befell her, and, of course, come in time to save her. The Germans had a better understanding of the value of Allied pledges than either Parliament or the Serbian people. They never faltered or halted in their march. The German military leaders had come to the conclusion that there was nothing to apprehend from an attack which was being carefully engineered on the Western Front. In fact, they welcomed it. They knew their General Joffre, and they felt that whilst his mind was concentrated on his plans in Champagne he had none left for any other theatre of war. The Allied generals were preparing a smoke screen, not to conceal their own designs—those were visible from any aeroplane—but to hide from their own vision those of the Central Powers lest the spectacle should induce the Allied statesmen to divert their forces from the pursuit of the impracticable. The western offensive began on 25th September. In two days it was obvious to any intelligent observer that the French had failed in their main purpose of breaking through the German lines and that the British attack had equally failed at Loos. The

Germans knew it, and continued to pour division after division into the Danubian basin. General Joffre, however, persisted in hurling troops against German entrenchments only to discover after he had captured them what he knew before, that there was an equally formidable position a few hundred yards behind. Still he persevered week after week, making no perceptible indent in this succession of entrenchments. There was nothing new in this. Every soldier in France could have told him in advance what he had rediscovered with the loss of scores of thousands of precious lives. Sir William Robertson, in a memorandum he issued about that time, said: " We know perfectly well there is no insuperable difficulty in breaking through the first-line defence. It has been done several times in this theatre during the summer. It is the second and third lines which give the trouble." These lines were never reached, or at least were not retained. Whilst this was going on, the western generals, heedless of the pitiful appeals of the Serbian people watching the fall of the avalanche towards their home, continued to waste valuable time on a hopeless task in France. Once engaged on it, the French and British generals found it difficult to extricate their armies without further hard struggling. They threw all their reserves into the cruel German trap with its teeth of steel that pierced and crushed flesh and blood with a relentless grip.

On 7th October, the Germans and Austrians crossed the Danube at five different points. A telegram announcing that fact reached here the same day. As I shall point out later on, Lord Kitchener did not see that telegram until the following day, and when a War Council met to discuss the military position on the 8th he was not aware that the armies of the Central Powers had already invaded Serbia. When at last he heard of it and communicated the news to the Cabinet, it was decided that he should go over to France to confer with General Joffre on the new situation which had arisen in the east. They discussed the sending of French and British troops to help the hard-pressed Serbs. On 9th October, General Joffre submitted to Lord Kitchener a memorandum, which is summarised as follows:—

" The reasons for the intervention of the Allies in the Balkans are:—

The necessity to check German projects in the new theatre of operations which they have now commenced, and the moral obligation not to leave our Ally Serbia alone to bear the brunt of our common enemies.

The initiative of the operations in the Balkans belongs to our adversaries and they are capable of keeping a numerical superiority whatever we do. There can, therefore, be no question of our engaging in a general action which would offer no chances of success.

Our rôle should be to prevent the crushing of the Serbs, to ensure their communication with the sea, and eventually to secure a zone of retreat. Also we should thus bar the way to the Germans from access to Salonika.

He considers therefore: —

1. That the mission of the troops should be to hold Salonika strongly as a base for the French, English and Serbian Armies.

2. To cover and hold the railway line between Salonika and Uskub in order to ensure our communication with the Serbian Army and the supplies of that army.

3. To cover the right of the Serbian Army, preventing any attempt of the enemy on Central Serbia.

To attain these objects a force of 150,000 men, which is more than the Bulgarians can put in the field on this side, appears sufficient.

In case events such as, for example, a new distribution of Greek and Roumanian forces, lead the Allies to take a different attitude, and to increase later the amount of their effort, General Joffre states that France, having a limited number of men at her disposal, cannot take part in such an effort, the responsibility for which would fall entirely on the British Government.

General Joffre strongly advocates that the Italian Government should be urged at first to send forces to Salonika and eventually to open the road to Serbia via Durazzo."

This document contains proposals so like those I had repeatedly pressed on the Cabinet that I feel entitled to call attention to the similarity. The only difference is one of date—a fatal divergence.

If the document had been penned three—even two—months earlier and acted upon immediately, the Balkans would not have fallen into German hands and Lord Kitchener's prediction of victory in 1917 would have been realised. It was now too late to avert disaster, and this was obvious to anyone who could see beyond the trenches in front of him. General Joffre was not gifted with such vision.

This report was discussed at a full meeting of what was still known as the Dardanelles Committee on 11th October. The military advice given to that Committee was that no troops should be sent to the Mediterranean, either to the Dardanelles or to Salonika, until the offensive in France had been brought to a conclusion. Both Sir Douglas Haig and General Joffre had stated that their object was " to gain further ground in order to consolidate what we had already won." In their judgment " our position was such that in certain sections we had either to go forward or to go back." Sir William Robertson thought that "to do this would entail a considerable amount of fighting generally in the neighbourhood of Loos." When asked whether, if the result of this contemplated action were favourable, it would lead to any modification of the strategic position, he admitted " it would not, unless General Joffre was also able to supply pressure and make progress in Champagne." We were given to understand that General Joffre had practically come to the conclusion already that the general offensive must be postponed for three months. The great offensive was an admitted failure. All the same, the French Commander-in-Chief declared he could not send any troops away from France until he knew definitely whether the Germans contemplated a counter offensive. Of that he could not be certain for another fortnight. That meant, according to Sir William Robertson, that no troops could be moved, either British or French, from the battle area for another two or three weeks. Whilst this discussion was taking place the Germans and Austrians were advancing in Serbian territory (they had already marched onward for four days) and the Bulgarians on that very day were hurling 300,000 men across the lines of communication between Serbia and Salonika. What strategy! What generals! What statesmen to tolerate either!

The military experts were pressed for information as to the date when they could be in a position to spare troops from France. There was a good deal of desultory and confusing talk on this point as to what ought to be the destination of these troops, assuming they could be spared. Some suggested that they should be dispatched to the Dardanelles to reinforce the army in Gallipoli, to enable it to make another attack on the Turkish positions in that Peninsula. The French were opposed to this plan unless at the same time an army was landed to occupy the Asiatic shore. They were strongly of opinion that the mere capture of Gallipoli, and the forcing of the Narrows would only entice the Allied fleets into a trap, which would be closed as soon as they entered the Marmora. The Allied fleets would there have no means of replenishing their fuel supplies, and would soon be reduced to impotence. They ought to have thought of that before agreeing to the Gallipoli Expedition. Others, notably Mr. Bonar Law and Sir Edward Carson, were for landing the troops at Salonika and pushing along immediately to the help of Serbia. The Chief of the Staff objected that the Salonika railway was not equipped with the necessary means of transport to enable the Allies to carry any considerable body of troops even as far as Uskub. That revealed the fact that although the War Committee had decided in January last to take immediate steps to double the line where feasible, to construct sidings, and to increase the rolling stock, nothing had been done to carry out that order. I supported the view urged so strongly by Mr. Bonar Law and Sir Edward Carson. I supplemented this with a suggestion that we should immediately communicate with the Greeks and the Roumanians, pledging the Allies to send 250,000 troops without delay to Salonika, if they on their part were prepared to join in a combined effort to rescue Serbia. I pointed out that the Roumanians could put 400,000 men in the field, and the Greeks at least 200,000, which with our 250,000 would make an aggregate of 850,000; that with such a force Bulgaria could be neutralised, or if she intervened could be crushed; and that at any rate it would enable the Serbians to hold their own against the attack which was being made upon them. Lord Curzon and others thought it was too late to send any support, and that we had better utilise our troops as reinforcements for the Gallipoli expeditionary force with a view to making a fresh attack on the Turks. Others suggested a landing at Alexandretta, and others that we should dispatch our forces to Egypt without prejudice to their ultimate destination or action, and for this purpose neither Alexandretta nor Salonika, nor the Adriatic side of the Straits would be ruled out. Meanwhile some distinguished general officer should be sent out to the Mediterranean to survey the situation, report upon it, and advise as to the best course to be adopted.

A " too-late " council is necessarily desperate and distracted. The conclusions of this distracted council were an embodiment of its despair. They were as follows: —

" 1. Immediate instructions to be given for the dispatch, *so soon as the present operations are over*, of an adequate substantial force from France to Egypt without prejudice to its ultimate destination, transport for which is to be prepared by the Admiralty.

2. A specially selected general to proceed without delay to the Near East and to consider and report as to which particular sphere, and with what particular objective, we should direct our attention.

3. The General Staff, War Office, to state in what way their views given in their Appreciation of the 9th October would be modified if both Greece and Roumania were to act with the Allies."

These conclusions meant the practical abandonment of Serbia to her doom. The combined armies of Germany, Austria and Bulgaria had no difficulty in sweeping the depleted, outnumbered and ill-equipped army of Serbia out of the way, capturing the Balkans and clearing the road to Constantinople.

In the meantime it was decided to send General Monro to the Mediterranean. On 31st October he recommended the evacuation of the Gallipoli Peninsula. At the first meeting of the new War Committee on 3rd November (to which I shall refer later on) it was decided to send Lord Kitchener to view the situation for himself. Their decision was not dictated solely by military considerations. Lord Kitchener's influence in the Cabinet was not what it had been in the first year of the War. It had waned very rapidly in recent months. In 1914 he was practically military dictator and his decisions upon any questions affecting the War were final. The Members of the Cabinet were frankly intimidated by his presence because of his repute and his enormous influence amongst all classes of the people outside. A word from him was decisive and no one dared to challenge it at a Cabinet meeting. I think I may say I was the first to do so on munitions and on subsidiary questions like the Welsh Division and the appointment of Nonconformist chaplains. But my colleagues regarded my intervention on these questions with a certain amount of uneasiness approaching dismay. Gradually one mistake after another committed by the military, for which he was held responsible as the Supreme War Lord, lowered his prestige and weakened his influence; and there was a very general feeling that his usefulness had been exhausted. This feeling subsequently found practical expression in the appointment of Sir William Robertson, as Chief of the Imperial General Staff, with exceptional powers all carved out of Lord Kitchener's authority. On this occasion there was a mute hope that once Lord Kitchener went to the Mediterranean, and especially if he returned to Egypt, the sphere of his greatest triumphs, he might find it worth while to remain there to direct the great forces accumulated in the western Mediterranean, in Egypt, Gallipoli, and either Salonika or Alexandretta. When the appointment was made, a member of the Cabinet pushed a note to me on which was written: " *Malbrouck s'en va t'en guerre*. But will he return?"

I was much disturbed about the abandonment of Serbia and the gross neglect to take the most obvious precautions to avert it. On 12th October I circulated the following memorandum on the position to my colleagues:—

" The helplessness of four great Powers to save from destruction one little country after another that relied on their protection is one of the most pitiable spectacles of this War.

The appreciation of the existing situation in the Balkans circulated by the General Staff is a distressing document! It might all be compressed into two words: Too late! It might easily have been foreseen that a march through Serbia into Bulgaria would be one of the most obvious and profitable of moves for the German General Staff to contemplate, by connecting up their railway system with Turkey:—

1. They could aim a most direct and effective blow—in fact,

the only direct and effective blow they could possibly aim—at the British Empire.

2. They could have at their disposal a reserve of two or three millions of men of the best fighting quality added to their own reserves, and thus more than redress in their favour the balance in the war of attrition which is now proceeding.

3. They could have a fair chance of destroying a great British force which is holding on by tooth and claw to a rim of the Gallipoli Peninsula.

4. They could strike a ringing blow at our prestige in the East.

5. They could render perfectly nugatory our sea-power in so far as South-Eastern Europe and a large part of Asia are concerned.

6. By the process of equipping the Turks and ultimately perhaps the Persians and Afghans, they could force us in 1916 to divert large masses of troops from the main theatre of operations in France to defend our own possessions in Egypt and in the Far East.

7. They could, by the same means, divert a large number of Russians to defend their frontiers in the Caucasus and their interests in Persia.

8. All this they could achieve by overcoming the resistance of an ill-equipped army of 300,000 Serbians, a considerable portion of these having their attention engaged by the prospect of a hostile Bulgarian army attacking them from behind. Not a very formidable proposition for the military power that has rolled up the great armies of Russia, whilst, at the same time, holding in check the combined forces of France and Britain! It was therefore obvious even to the civilian mind that it was too tempting a project for the Germans not to seize upon.

There were two reasons why it was clear that they could not postpone putting this project into execution: —

1. The Turkish ammunition was gradually being exhausted, and Turkey could not have sustained a series of attacks such as those we had been making on the Gallipoli Peninsula much longer without having her store of ammunition replenished.

2. The winter was coming on, when Serbian roads and passes would be very difficult to negotiate.

3. This year the Germans have an undoubted superiority over the Allies in: —

(a) Material of war;
(b) Equipped and trained men.

Next year the position will be equalised in both respects. It

would not be like the Germans if they did not take full advantage
of their temporary superiority.

It is, of course, easy to be wise after the event, but these are
considerations which have been repeatedly urged during the past
few months at the War Council and Cabinet meetings. I have
often braved my colleagues by the frequency with which I have
called attention to them. I circulated two papers calling attention
to the possibilities in the Near East as far back as December and
February last. It perplexes the mere civilian to find any explanation for the neglect of the military authorities to provide against
so disastrous a blow to our Empire, when it was so clear to any
careful observer that it was impending. It is incredible that the
fifth day after the blow had actually fallen finds us without a plan
—unless the sending of some general—not yet fixed upon—to the
eastern Mediterranean to scout for a scheme of operations can be
called a plan. The Cabinet may depend upon it that when it
becomes clear to the British public that we have been taken by
surprise and that we have not made the slightest preparation to
counter the German thrust, confidence will vanish in our capacity
to conduct the War, and rightly so.

It may be asked: What would you do now? The question is
not who is to blame, but how are we to set it right? I am not at
all sure that they are not more or less the same questions. This
is a matter which I propose to return to later on, because I think
it is essential. We have been let down so often that it is criminal
folly on our part to depend any longer for the safety of the Empire
on our present military organisation. But dealing merely with the
Balkan tangle, I think even now we ought to make one great effort
to save Serbia. There are two reasons for doing so. The first
is that the abandonment of Serbia to her fate would be fatal to
the prestige of Great Britain among the Allies and throughout the
world. The hostility of Bulgaria and the neutrality of Greece
and Roumania are attributable to the conviction which has permeated all neutral countries that Germany is irresistible and that
we are impotent to protect nations which have incurred her wrath.
Our complete failure to protect Belgium started this idea. Our
inability to give effective support to Russia has confirmed it: and
the abandonment of Serbia to her doom will root it deeper than
ever in the mind of the world. The effect in the East will be
incalculable.

The second reason is that Serbia now provides the only barrier
between us and the military reconstruction of a great hostile Moslem
Power, which would be a menace to Egypt, Tripoli, Tunis, Algiers
and Morocco, and also to our hold on India. Surely the averting of
such a catastrophe is worth one great final effort? Is such an effort
beyond our compass?

The General Staff reckon that the German and Austrian armies engaged in the operations aggregate 200,000 men; that the Bulgarians number 300,000. We have, therefore, a total force of 500,000 to cope with in the Balkans. It is also, I understand, the reckoning of the General Staff that unless the Germans withdraw troops either from Russia or from France they cannot materially increase the strength of their armies in the Balkans. Serbia has an army of 300,000 men, very brave, very ably led. Their defeat of the Austrians last year demonstrated these two facts. They are fighting in a country they thoroughly understand, and they are fighting with all the ferocity with which a small mountain race always defend their native land. In numbers, therefore, the combined Bulgarian and Teutonic forces only overtop the Serbians alone by 200,000 men. Is it quite out of the question to make up this deficiency when so much depends on it for the Allies? Could not Roumania and Greece be persuaded or pressed to come in even now? Mere appeals to their sense of honour and their treaty obligations will not affect them in the least. They are naturally thinking about the security of their own countries, and they are paralysed by the German power and our impotence. It must be shown to them that we are quite capable of giving them all the necessary military support to protect them and enable them to carry through their undertaking. Why should we not promise them support, provided they come to the aid of Serbia immediately? They have men and equipment quite adequate to the conducting of a three months' campaign. Roumania, Serbia and Greece between them could put nearly a million men into the field, as against the Germano-Bulgarian combination of half a million. We could hold the Turkish forces in Gallipoli so as to prevent Turkey from sending any considerable reinforcements to the aid of the Bulgarians. Turkey has plenty of men available, but until the Germans arrive in Constantinople she has not the necessary munitions to equip fresh armies. If we said to the Greeks and the Roumanians that if they took the field immediately we could place at their disposal straight away 30,000 men who have already landed at Salonika, and that in a month's time we would guarantee that those 30,000 would be 100,000; that in two months' time the 100,000 would become 150,000; and that by the end of the year we could undertake to have at least 250,000 men operating the Balkans; that in addition to that we could help them with ammunition—a promise which France and ourselves could afford to give if we dropped the offensive in the west—their whole attitude would be changed. In addition to this we could undertake, with the aid of Italy, to furnish the Russians with 500,000 rifles, thus enabling Russia to place another three-quarters of a million men in the line. If this were done, Roumania would feel herself secure from any Austro-German attack as the Austro-German armies would have as much as they could possibly do to hold their own against the increased pressure of the Russian armies. Russia might, under those circumstances, even promise definitely to detach 100,000 men to assist the Roumanians against any attack which might be made upon them.

The situation is desperate, and nothing but prompt, courageous, and even daring action can retrieve it. What risks do we run by making this promise?

1. We should have definitely to postpone the offensive in the west. When it has failed now, after the most prolonged and careful preparation, why should it be assumed that it will succeed three months hence? The French and ourselves will not be appreciably better off in the matter of big guns—not until the late spring of next year. We have already lost—French and British—between 500,000 and 600,000 men in the two great attempts made since May last to pierce the German line. To ignore the costly lesson thus given us and to make another effort of the same kind without adequate equipment of heavy guns and ammunition would be wantonly to throw away the lives of the very fine body of men who have volunteered for the new armies.

2. We might fail to redeem our promise to the Roumanians and Greeks. The French have promised 64,000 men when the offensive is over. I am not sure whether those 64,000 include the 15,000 French troops already landed at Salonika. But let us assume that they do. I understand that there are considerable drafts on their way to the Dardanelles. These might be safely diverted to Salonika so long as the Turks on the Gallipoli Peninsula are cut off from the fresh supplies of ammunition they are hoping to get from the Germans. That would bring our forces at Salonika up to about 100,000 men.* We should have to find the remaining 150,000. I understand that on the Western Front the French claim that with our army they have a superiority of very nearly 1,000,000 over the Germans. If even 400,000 men were taken away from the west our superiority would still be overwhelming. The Germans have already demonstrated clearly that a superiority of three to two does not enable the offensive to break through a well-entrenched line. Why, then, should it be supposed that when the Germans are in inferior numbers they could break through our lines? Are the French soldiers and ours so inferior in quality to the German *Landsturm*?

If the Germans brought half a million from the east they would still be in a slight minority in the west. With the increased

---

* French 64,000
British withdrawn from Gallipoli plus drafts, about.............................35,000
99,000

pressure the Russians could bring to bear by means of reinforcements, we had enabled them to equip and put into the field, the Germans, so far from being in a position to withdraw troops from the east, might have to draw heavily on their reserves in order to hold their own on that frontier.

3. The risk that we could not furnish the 500,000 rifles for Russia. Why not? Our American rifles will be coming in shortly, and we could, for the sake of a great effort to save a desperate situation, spare 150,000 rifles to equip 200,000 Russians who are ready in every other respect for the field. The temporary risks we might have to face by parting with the rifles are not comparable with those we run if nothing effective is done to save the situation in the Balkans. The Italians must be financed to part with their 300,000 Vitalis, and the French would surely spare 50,000 rifles to help the Allied cause out of the worst plight it has yet been in.

I earnestly press that the offer should be definitely made to Russia and Greece without loss of time. If Greece shows any reluctance to come in, the appeal to her might take the form of a demand that she should redeem her treaty obligations to Serbia. We are in this War to enforce international treaties, and a demand of that kind could not be interpreted as the bullying of a small nationality when we are actually engaged in a war with the greatest military power in the world on the same ground. Greece is always at the mercy of a great Sea Power. Germany cannot protect her against us, and I have information from reliable Greek sources that this line would have much greater effect upon the King of Greece than an appeal to his honour to redeem his bond to Serbia.

The notion that we are satisfying the needs of this critical situation by making another attack on the Gallipoli Peninsula is, to my mind, an insane one. We have failed repeatedly when the Turks were short of ammunition. Are we now to succeed when they are reinforced with German heavy guns and abundance of ammunition? It is by no means improbable that the Turks, thus re-equipped, might drive us into the sea before reinforcements ever reached our army on that Peninsula. This probability is indicated in clear terms in Colonel Hankey's report. If we neglect his warning our responsibility will be great. But even assuming we can hold our own, an attack on positions which have been proved to be impregnable against gallant assaults would end in the loss of another 50,000 or 60,000 men with nothing achieved. It is quite clear to anyone who reads the document prepared by the General Staff that this was no part of their original plan. It has simply been spatch-cocked into their document by strong Dardanellian influences. It has been done so badly that the simplest of us can see it. The recommendations of the General

L

Staff were that it would confine ourselves to the offensive in France
We are now not merely to send out a general to trawl the eastern
Mediterranean for a new policy, but before he reports we are
to send 150,000 men away from France—from the only objective
which the General Staff are prepared to stake their reputation upon
recommending!

D. LL. G.

October 12th, 1915."

To this Sir Edward Grey replied:—

" FOREIGN OFFICE,
October 13th, 1915.

My dear Lloyd George,
    Your memorandum has come to me since the telegrams to
Bucharest and Athens were sent last night, and for the moment
I suppose they settle one point in your memorandum.
    I am no judge of the military consideration involved, but as
Kitchener agrees and you desire it and the Prime Minister
authorises it I sent the telegrams at once. From the political point
of view I am as strongly in favour of the line now taken as you
can be, and I am glad to be able to say anything diplomatically
which is backed by action or the prospects of action.
    What I do feel to be useless is constant diplomatic effort based
neither on military nor naval success, without the prospect of such
success, and without any offer of action. These last telegrams are
not open to that criticism.
    For the rest I wish to avoid drift in our strategy, and if I differ
from the conclusions of your paper at all it is that I think our
strategic decisions should be based on naval and military opinion
founded upon good staff work. I urged strongly and I understood
you also to urge the same thing, and I hope the staff work now
being done under Murray will be encouraged and continued. I
do not like to discard its conclusions. But I agree that the opinion
expressed by the Staff about the Gallipoli Peninsula is more provisional and tentative than final.
    It is, however, vital to come to a decision quickly either to
attempt to force the Dardanelles or to evacuate—so it seems to
me, and I would accept either decision rather than none.
    I was not sure whether your memorandum was addressed
specially to me or not; it deals mainly with military strategy on
which I am qualified to be guided rather than to guide.

Yours sincerely,
E. GREY."

    The irony of his sentence about " military and naval opinion based
on good staff work " is withering. But the greatest irony of all

fter what had happened, was that he meant every word of it. The
vay he had been betrayed by the Military to give in the House of
Commons pledges to Serbia they had no hope of redeeming did not
eem to diminish his childish faith in their advice.

Considerable delays ensued in sending troops to the
Mediterranean. On 19th October M. Millerand, the French
Secretary of State for War, came over to discuss the position. He was
accompanied by General Joffre. I find amongst my papers the
following note made by a secretary of what took place at the
discussions: —

" Ll.G. saw Millerand to-day, who says that Ll.G. was right after
all and that an expedition in the Balkans should have been undertaken last spring. He is now concerned that the Dardanelles
operations are a failure, and though he fears it is too late to render
very effective assistance in the Balkans, yet he is in favour of
France and Britain sending troops there. He and Ll.G. together
drew up a plan upon which France and England are to act for a
campaign in the Balkans."

Our plan suggested that: —

" The prevention of the German effort to get through to Constantinople should be regarded as the primary objective of the
joint expeditionary force. If, by the time the new force can arrive
at the eastern Mediterranean, Serbia is still blocking the way, the
French and British forces should proceed to Salonika to help the
Serbians to keep the railway free to Uskub.

If by the date of the arrival of the troops the Germans have
forced their way through to Constantinople, the two Governments
to decide their course then on the advice of their Generals. . . .
The two Governments have agreed to go on sending to the help
of Serbia sufficient contingents to constitute a force of 150,000
men.

Should the present situation become greatly altered owing to
unforeseen circumstances arising, both Governments would then
take steps in common as to the new directions to give to their
troops."

Greece was pressed to send troops to assist in saving Russia, but the
appeal to her came too late, because by that time the armies of the
Central Powers and of Bulgaria had overwhelmed Serbian resistance,
and the Greeks put in the plea that they were afraid of standing up
against the victors when there were no Allied troops within sight to
assist them. They had the fate of Serbia before their eyes. Serbia
had been abandoned by the Allies in defiance of the solemn pledges

of timely support. The Greeks were naturally apprehensive of a
repetition of the same desertion in their own case. The sweeping
victories of the Central Powers on the Eastern Front naturally
impressed all the South-Eastern States more than the capture by the
Allies of a few kilometres in France. Russia had collapsed; Serbia
had been overrun; the Dardanelles expedition had been a complete
failure, and even in the west the Allies had not succeeded in breaking through, and the Germans, victorious on every front, were
advancing southwards with seven-league boots. They were already
in the defiles of the Balkans, soon they would be on their Southern
slopes. At that time there was nothing between them and the Greek
frontier. Greece with her small army would be easily devoured by
this terrible monster.

Sir Edward Carson, disgusted with what he conceived to be the
deception practised upon Serbia, had resigned. Mr. Bonar Law and
I shared his opinion about the whole transaction, but on the whole
decided that we could not withdraw from the Ministry at this critical
juncture. I am not sure that we were right.

There was a general feeling that there was a disastrous lack of
grip in the direction of the War, and that the Cabinet ought to take
upon itself a more direct responsibility in controlling its conduct.
Suggestions were put forward for the setting-up of a War Committee
which would exercise a more constant supervision over the direction
of the War. I was amongst those who made representations to the
Prime Minister upon this point. On the 29th October I received
from him the following memorandum: —

" CONDUCT OF THE WAR

The proposal, as I understand it, is that there should be a small
Committee of the Cabinet, not less than three or more than five
in number, to deal executively with the conduct of the War.

It is understood that the Committee will from time to time call
to their aid, for the purposes both of discussion and decision, other
members of the Cabinet, either because their departments are
concerned in the particular matter which is being dealt with or
for other special reasons.

The Cabinet to remain as it is in numbers and composition.

The plenum of the Cabinet to be constantly informed of the
decisions and actions of the Committee, and in all questions which
involve a change or new departure in policy to be consulted before
decisive action is taken.

Parliament to be informed that this method of procedure has
been adopted, and to be told the names of the members of the
Committee.

October 28, 1915.   H. H. A."

On 31st October I replied: —

"11, Downing Street,
Whitehall, S.W.
October 31, 1915.

My dear Prime Minister,

I am sorry to trouble you when you must be worried with the anxieties of the situation, but I feel I must put to you my view of the position before you come to a final decision. The appointment of a small Committee with fairly full powers will undoubtedly be a great improvement on the sort of Duma which has been sitting on war problems up to the present. But unless there is a complete change in the War Office the new Council will be just as impotent as the Cabinet and old Council have proved themselves to be. Our war Administration have committed every blunder that the enemy could wish them to be guilty of. It was quite clear, even to the civilian mind, soon after the War began that this War would ultimately be decided by superiority in quality and quantity of material, and by the wearing down of the enemy in numbers. The Allies had the advantage in both respects, and the War Office have by an incredible lack of foresight and energy thrown away both these advantages.

As to material, whilst the Germans were spending the whole of the late autumn and winter of 1914 in increasing their guns, rifles and ammunition for the summer campaign, our War Office did nothing substantial till the end of 1914 and in the spring of 1915. Then they did it under pressure from outside, and even then they were satisfied with giving orders whilst taking no steps to see that they were or even could be executed. The result has been that the campaign of 1915 has been lost to us. We could not help Russia in ammunition because we have not even now an adequate equipment, more especially in rifles and heavy guns and trench appliances, for ourselves. The full story of the neglect of the War Office in this respect has not yet been told. It is worse than I expected it would be when I first took up the work of the Ministry of Munitions—how they ordered shell without taking measures to see that there were fuses and primers, cartridge cases, gaines and the necessary arrangements for filling, so that huge stocks of empty shells were piled up at Woolwich with no means of completing them which was in the least commensurate with the demand.

As to attrition, by prompt action in the Balkans we could have added a million and a half to our reserves of men, most of it excellent fighting material. Roumania, Greece, and, I think, Bulgaria, could have been brought in, not by words, but by prompt and strong action. On the other hand, we could have cut off the enemy from the magnificent reservoir of men in the Turkish Empire who are only awaiting equipment to become one of the most formidable fighting machines in the world. *In July the Intelligence Department of the War Office warned Kitchener that the Germans were likely to break through to Constantinople. We were constantly warned that Bulgaria was becoming more and more hostile.* One or two Cabinet Ministers, including myself urged that steps should be taken to prepare for this probable German move. Nothing was done; even when information came in that the Germans and Austrians were accumulating forces in the valleys of Hungary and in the Bukovina, no plan of action was thought out. *Kitchener never knew that they had crossed the Danube 20 hours after the news reached the War Office that they had effected a crossing at five points.* A fortnight after the crossing his only plan was to send a general to the Mediterranean to report on the situation. Days after the road to Constantinople had been cleared through Bulgaria and weeks after the actual commencement of the struggle upon which the fate of our rule in Egypt may depend, we are forced by the French to take some action. You will recollect that the Committee of Imperial Defence as far back as February last decided that all the necessary preparations should be made for rendering a landing at Salonika effective whenever the Cabinet decided to take that course. Kitchener never took the slightest notice of that decision, and not even a mule had been bought for transport when the German blow fell on Serbia.

The public may have delusions now about Kitchener, but the moment these facts are told in the House of Commons I have very little doubt what will be thought and said by all sections.

If I thought the appointment of a small Committee would put an end to all these amazing series of blunders, I should be satisfied. But I have gone on for months always thinking that every mistake must surely be the last, and finding myself constantly surprised by the capacity of our great War Lords for blundering. I wrote you in December last calling your attention to the stupidity of the War Office, and telling you that, in my judgement, unless we showed greater grip as a Government in the management of the War, it must end in inevitable disaster. I have protested at each stage, sometimes in writing, sometimes by intervention in the Cabinet and at the War Council. I did so long before the Northcliffe Press began its campaign. At best the chances are against the next few weeks bringing much cheer—they might bring ruin to Serbia and for us retreat in the Balkans and disaster in Gallipoli. The nation would endure this and a good deal more if they knew everything was being done that human effort and foresight could compass to ensure final victory; but their confidence has been rudely shaken by what they can see of our unpreparedness in the

Balkans. The friendly Press are showing marked symptoms of mutiny. The steadfast loyalty of our own party to your leadership has so far saved the Government, but you will forgive me for saying that I doubt whether that would save us if a catastrophe befell Serbia or our forces in the Dardanelles and all the facts on the conduct of the War were dragged out as they would be. Every mistake and omission would then be brought out with accumulative force. The row in the Commons will come last. Press and public will be moved before the party politician, but in the end he will follow public opinion, and we must have a good answer when the time comes. There is only one answer that can satisfy the public, and that is that you have already made an end of the futile regime that tumbled along from one fatuity to another. I am quite willing to face the inevitable tumult when it comes if this answer can be given, but I have very reluctantly come to the conclusion that I can no longer be responsible for the present war direction, and at the Cabinet to-morrow I propose with your permission to raise the real issue.

Ever sincerely,
D. LLOYD GEORGE."

The allusion in my letter to the fact that Lord Kitchener never knew the Germans had crossed the Danube for 20 hours after the news had reached the War Office is explained in the following note made after the Committee meeting by one of my secretaries: —

"At a Cabinet last week, before the German advance into Serbia had begun, but when news of it was being expected at every moment, Ll. G. asked K. in the Cabinet whether there was any news of the Germans having crossed the Danube. K. said that up to the time when he came to the Cabinet he had received no news. Ll. G. suggested that the news might have come in since and said he would get the P. M.'s secretary to telephone to the War Office and ask if any news had been received, as he considered it most important to know when the Germans had begun to cross the Danube. The following is the reply which Ll. G. received and which he read out to the Cabinet. A telegram had been received in the War Office the day before. K. did not express the least surprise that he had not seen the telegram. Here is a copy of it: —

'Late *yesterday* afternoon enemy xd. Danube with one batt. at   . Aust. troops xd. the Slava in 5 difft. places between Sabac and Belgrade. They are so far not in large force. Fight is continuing.'

10, Downing Street,
Whitehall. S.W.

K does not read the
telegrams — & we dont
see them — it is intolerable

E. C

Facsimile of a note passed by Lord Carson (then Sir Edward Carson)
to Mr. Lloyd George, during a Cabinet Meeting, in September, 1915.

Immediately this telegram was read to the Cabinet, Sir Edward Carson passed Ll. G. the following note:—

' K. does not read the telegrams—and we don't see them—it is intolerable.

E. C. "

On 4th November I received the following letter from Mr. Asquith:—

10, Downing Street,
Whitehall, S.W.
3rd Nov. 1915.

" *Secret.*

My dear Lloyd George,

What I wanted you to know before to-morrow's Cabinet was that, in view of the conflicting opinions now to hand of Monro and the other generals in regard to the future of the Dardanelles, I arranged to-day that K. should proceed without delay (to-morrow, Thursday night) to Alexandria, and after visiting Gallipoli and Salonika, and conferring with all our military and diplomatic experts in that quarter of the world, advise us as to our strategy in the eastern theatre.

In the meantime I propose to take over the War Office, and I am confident that in the course of the next month I can put things there on a better footing, and in particular come to a complete understanding with you on all the important problems which are connected with the design, fabrication and supply of munitions.

We avoid by this method of procedure the immediate supersession of K. as War Minister, while attaining the same result. And I suppose even B. L. [Bonar Law] would hardly object to such a plan.

Yours very sincerely,
H. H. A.

P.S.—This is for yourself alone; I have not said anything to any of our colleagues. But I regard it as of the first moment that in this matter you and I should act together."

The Germans invaded Serbia on October 7th. The Cabinet decided on 11th October that a general should be sent to the Mediterranean to examine the position there and decide what action should be taken. As already mentioned, General Monro was chosen. Appointed on 15th October, he started on his voyage of discovery for methods of helping Serbia on 22nd October and arrived at Mudros on 28th October. On 31st October he recommended that our troops should be withdrawn from the Gallipoli Peninsula and transported to Egypt for re-equipment. In the meantime, a certain number of British and French troops had landed at Salonika, the first contingent reaching that port on 3rd October. Two divisions only were disembarked by 7th October, the day on which the offensive against

ʟ*

Serbia was launched by the forces of the Central Powers. Had we dropped the fatal offensive in France as soon as it became clear that it could not succeed in its main purpose, and sent immediately to the Mediterranean a number equal to those who fell in futile attacks after that date, the bastion of the Balkans would have been held by us with the help of what was left of the Serbian Army; and neither Germans, Austrians, nor Bulgarians possessed the necessary strength to force those defiles against such a garrison.

The growing feeling of anxiety, developing into criticism of the military direction, is reflected in a letter which I received at this time from the late Lord Charles Beresford. At that time, he was still a figure of some distinction and he had attracted to himself a good deal of popular esteem. He always possessed a certain flair which revealed itself even in his most histrionic performances and in his most exuberant and extravagant utterances.

" 1, Great Cumberland Place,
London, W.
16th October, 1915.

Dear Mr. Lloyd George,
    Please excuse dictation.

I hope I shall be able to see you in the House some day next week, as I do not think it would be wise or politic to meet you except at a private house or in the House of Commons; there are many people who jump to conclusions, and such people would at once think that there was an intrigue afoot.

We are, in my opinion, drifting to certain destruction. We have no policy, no objective, and nothing has been thought out ahead. It is imperative that we leave the Gallipoli Peninsula. Suvla Bay and Anzac must be evacuated shortly owing to their being under water. It is too late now to land an army in Asia Minor; the country will soon be a marsh. We shall have to lose a rearguard in the evacuation, but that would be better than losing 140,000 men there now, plus another 140,000 or 200,000 necessary for reinforcements, owing to casualties and the ravages of disease which has now set in. We cannot get through the Dardanelles, and we are wasting life and destroying prestige by remaining in the Gallipoli Peninsula. I believe the Fleet could secure the retreat, even to a portion of the rearguard.

In every way fronts are changed, new military situations created, and new objectives undertaken. We have now taken a new objective and formed a new front at Salonika—an excellent reason for withdrawing from an impossible position in Gallipoli.

We want about 200,000 men of the Allies landed at Salonika. It would be fatal to send them in driblets. If the Serbians are crushed the Germans will get to Constantinople. They will open up the whole of Asia for supplies. Roumania and Greece will out of fear probably throw in their lot with Germany.   There is a spark in Islam now which would under these circumstances be fanned into a violent flame, more particularly if we remain in the Gallipoli Peninsula.   Looking ahead, we should probably have to denude our Allies in France of a large portion of our army in order to fight for the defence of our Empire in the East and Egypt. Surely some dispatch should be sent or method taken to show the Greeks that they must come out on one side or the other.

There will be a tremendous reaction in the country when the people know the truth, and I am afraid that the whole of the Cabinet will go down.   Democracy are not reasonable when they are excited.   If the people bring about the downfall of the Cabinet what have we got to put in its place?   We should have a reign of chaos during the greatest crisis the Empire has ever faced.

One of the great dangers consists in having Lord Kitchener in the Cabinet.   The people believe in him, but they do not know he is wasting his time talking on political subjects.   I have been to him several times and pointed out that he ought to leave the Cabinet on the plea that he cannot devote his time to it.   His business is to take an envelope, write on it what men he wants, and what munitions he wants, and present that to the Cabinet. The question of how they are to be got has nothing whatever to do with him.   It is a political question of tremendous difficulty which must be argued out by the Cabinet.   Lord Kitchener's difficulty would be well illustrated if there was a debate in the Cabinet on conscription or voluntary service.   Which side would he take?

In war, quick decisions and prompt actions are wanted.   Neither are possible without a definite policy, and a clear objective for the military and naval forces, upon which depends the success or failure of the policy.   The Government have no policy, and the military have no objective.   It does not require that a man should be in the Cabinet to see the danger that exists to our Empire through this lamentable state of affairs.   We are wasting days and weeks, when every hour, indeed, every minute, is of vital importance to us in the near future.

In my opinion, our policy should be: —

1. Evacuate the Dardanelles;
2. Send 200,000 (an allied force) men to Salonika with plenty of guns;
3. Get across the railway between Belgrade and Constantinople by some means between Nish and Sofia.

I know the country and the difficulties attending such a proposition, but risks and difficulties must be met in war provided a substantial result is possible of attainment.   Risks such as we are undertaking in Gallipoli have no excuse whatever. It was a risk courting defeat, and is certain to affect our prestige in the Balkans, with the Allies, and worse than all, with our great Eastern Empire.

Yours very sincerely,

CHARLES BERESFORD.

The Rt. Hon. D. Lloyd George, M.P."

This letter reflects the rising and spreading sense of dubiety amongst men who were watching the course of events with some accumulated knowledge and experience. As yet the general public were still trustful if a little mystified. Their faith in Kitchener and their invincible belief in British luck had not yet been shaken.

One culminating illustration at this period of our military leaders' capacity for blundering remains to be recorded. Upon the return of Lord Kitchener, at the end of November, 1915, from his expedition to the Balkans, the antipathy of the British General Staff to any operations in that theatre crystallised into a definite recommendation that the Salonika expedition should be recalled. Rumour had it that Kitchener had somehow been talked over by the plausible and adroit King Constantine of Greece into favouring this step. The General Staff advised that we should withdraw from both the Dardanelles and Salonika and concentrate our forces on the defence of Egypt.

The French Government had vision enough to be furious at this suggestion. It urged very wisely that such an action would be naturally regarded throughout the East as a token of weakness and irresolution, and would mean the utter loss of the Balkans. Not only would it spell the final abandonment of the last shattered remnants of the army of our ally, Serbia: it would also drive both Roumania and Greece into the arms of Germany, adding something like another million men to their forces in that war theatre, imperilling the southern flank of the Russians, and turning the whole Balkan coast, including the harbours of Greece, into enemy bases for submarine activity in the Mediterranean. On Friday, 3rd December, 1915, the French sent an angry telegram, challenging the shilly-shallying attitude of the British Government—the proposal to leave Salonika and the lack of firmness we were showing in our handling of Greece. They complained bitterly that we had gone back on our decision at the Paris Council which had taken place a week previously, and that Lord Kitchener had evidently made arrangements with the King of Greece which were quite outside the intentions of the French. They requested that representatives of the British Government should meet them the following day at Calais to discuss the position.

As yet the British Cabinet had not reached a definite decision upon the issue. It had been postponed from one meeting to another.

Upon receipt of the French Government's telegram, the Prime Minister went to Calais, taking Lord Kitchener and Mr. Balfour with him. He did not invite me to join the party, doubtless because my strong opposition to any abandonment of the Balkans was well known, and I did not even hear of the telegram from France till the Saturday morning when our representatives had already departed for Calais.

On their return we were informed that they had succeeded in talking the French round to their point of view and that the evacuation of Salonika had been agreed upon. But the telegrams on Monday from Paris were far from supporting this interpretation of the proceedings, and showed that the French were still very dissatisfied, and that no satisfactory arrangement had really been arrived at on the Saturday.

While everything was in this state of chaos, a telegram came to say that M. Albert Thomas was on his way over to have a talk with me on the subject of the Calais Conference, and to explain to me the real opinion of the French. Meanwhile at the War Council that morning (6th December, 1915) the matter was discussed. Mr. Bonar Law was the only one present who agreed with my view of the matter, all the rest being for immediate evacuation. Lord Kitchener read a telegram from Greece which said that the Germans demanded the evacuation of the Balkans by the Allied troops, and were willing to allow the Greeks to cover the re-embarkation. I am recorded as having said " It is a good thing that the Germans and the British have found something to agree upon at last. Surely this must be the beginning of peace! "

Shortly afterwards M. Albert Thomas arrived, and explained to me the reason for his visit. I learned that when the French deputation to the Calais conference returned to Paris and admitted that they had agreed to the evacuation of the Balkans, the rest of the French Cabinet expressed the greatest dissatisfaction with this conclusion. The deputation insisted that they had been told that this was the view taken unanimously by the British Government, and that in those circumstances they had felt bound to acquiesce: whereupon M. Thomas interposed that he knew it was not the view of the whole British Cabinet, as I had told him when he was last in London that I was entirely opposed to evacuating the Balkans and was very much in favour of engaging in a Balkan campaign this year or next. The French Cabinet ultimately refused to accept the decision arrived at on the previous day at Calais. Thereupon, M. Thomas offered to come over to London and see me in an effort to obtain a reconsideration of their decision by the British Government.

Naturally I promised him all the help and backing I could furnish. He attended more than one prolonged meeting of our leaders at which he set forth very passionately the desire of the French to remain at Salonika. Perhaps the best help I afforded him was an arrangement I made for him to lunch at 10, Downing Street with the Prime Minister. I am not sure that the favourable personal impression he made on his host and hostess was not more helpful to his cause than all his eloquence in Council. However that may be, the final outcome of these discussions was that Lord Kitchener was sent over to Paris to consult with the French Cabinet, with full powers to make any arrangements on behalf of our Government. He did not much like the idea of going. "The French are not very keen on me at present for some reason," he said. However, he went, and the upshot was an agreement for the Allies to remain at Salonika and fortify it in preparation for an effective campaign in 1916. So narrowly was averted an act of incredible folly. But the effective campaign was not waged in 1916. The French and British military chiefs took care that the Salonika expedition should not be equipped with the guns and ammunition which would justify offensive operations. And in order further to deprive General Sarrail of all temptation to attack they deprived him of all the means of transport essential to an advance.

Speaking on 20th December, 1915, in the House of Commons, having in mind the fatal tardiness which had brought so much disaster to the Allied cause in the Dardanelles, the Balkans, Russia and Mesopotamia, I used the following words:—

"... Too late in moving here, too late in arriving there, too late in coming to this decision, too late in starting with enterprises, too late in preparing! In this war the footsteps of the Allied forces have been dogged by the mocking spectre of 'too late,' and unless we quicken our movements damnation will fall on the sacred cause for which so much gallant blood has flowed. . . ."

That summed up my considered opinion at the time on the muddled campaign of 1915. That is my judgment to-day after a careful perusal of all the documents and histories written on the subject from every point of view.

CHAPTER XVIII

THE BALKANS AND THE SOMME

THE whole strategic possibilities of the War for the Allies was changed by the Serbian collapse. The opportunities offered for a formidable movement against the eastern flank of the Central Powers had been, if not entirely lost, at least made more difficult and doubtful. The constant allurement to amateur and other strategists of such a chance to divert troops from the Western charnel-house was shut down. The general staffs of France and Britain had not won *the* War, but they had won *their* war. The Dardanelles had been evacuated; the Balkans had been transferred from Allied to enemy hands; the road to the Danube, to Constantinople and the Black Sea had been finally blocked; Serbia had been wiped out; Russia was tottering to her fall; Roumania was isolated. What consummate strategy! The Germans had not been beaten, but the politicians had been thwarted. The Brass Hats were triumphant. They sang their chortling *Te Deums* from Chantilly to Whitehall. The East with its opportunities, which were also temptations, was no more. Hail to the blood-red sun of the West!

It is true that forces which numerically appeared to be very powerful were sent to Salonika; and there was every appearance of a formidable army of British, French, Serbians and Greeks, numbering in the aggregate hundreds of thousands, being assembled in that theatre. It was for all offensive purposes reduced to stagnation and impotence by an equipment so inadequate as to render this conglomerate army quite incapable of making any effective attack upon the enemy. The General Staffs were determined that all temptation to action must be removed from generals performing in that theatre. There were two possible uses to which the Salonika Expeditionary Force could be put. One was that it should be sufficiently strong to hold up the Bulgarians and a certain number of Austrian and German and Turkish troops, and to prevent them from being thrown on to other points where their accession might have been harmful and perhaps decisive. This plan would also have had the effect of preventing the surly and suspicious King of Greece, who was only too sympathetic to the Germans, from throwing in his lot with them under the pretext that he could not resist the invasion of such a powerful force. As it was, he handed over Kavalla and a Greek Division to the enemy as an offering to propitiate an idol he feared as well as adored. He might have given them the whole of the Greek Army had we not been there. If that was to be the sole purpose of the occupation of Salonika, the force was much too large, and a smaller army well entrenched at Salonika, supported with an adequate quota of guns, would have answered equally well. It could easily have been reinforced by sea had there been an attack; there was no object in accumulating large forces there and providing them with powerful offensive armaments.

The second alternative was that we should have an army at Salonika which could either have attacked the Turks on the right flank, cut their communications with Germany, and possibly captured their capital; or, on the other hand, stormed the defiles of the Balkans, broken through and defeated the Bulgarian Army, re-established relations with Roumania, and through Roumania with Russia; in fact, recreated the chance which had been lost through the fatal strategy of the early autumn of 1915. The fine achievement of the Serbian Army under General Misitsch later on, when it fought its way through to Monastir, proves that this was not outside the region of attainment by an army which was even moderately equipped with artillery and ammunition.

The military chiefs pursued neither of these policies. As I shall point out later on, the Salonika Army was left practically without any guns or ammunition which would have enabled it to bombard its way through the crudest defences in such a difficult terrain. It was camped on the malarial plains of the Struma and the Vardar for two years without being given the means of fighting its way to healthier ground. The British Staff were in favour of the first course and would have reduced the force to dimensions sufficient for the discharge of this rôle. The French Staff hesitated between the two. The argument between them went on for months. The French Commander-in-Chief, once an obdurate Westerner, now feigned conversion to some of the tenets of the Eastern faith. Here undoubtedly the reasons were political and personal. The influence of General Joffre in France had considerably diminished, owing to his failure to put the defences of Verdun in order for a whole month after he had been warned that an attack was impending. The autocratic authority which he once exerted, and which up to that date was quite sufficient to intimidate Governments and to compel them against their judgment to conform to his stubborn will, had faded almost to vanishing point, since the German guns at Verdun had laid bare his limitations. The leading statesmen of France, including the President and the President of the Council, believed in attacking the enemy on the south-eastern flank. In this they were supported by—in fact they were acting on the suggestion of—the most gifted soldier in the French Army, General Gallieni.

General Joffre, therefore, in order to placate the men who for the first time had become his masters, deferred to their wishes about reinforcing the Salonika Front. It was his offering on the altar of the offended gods. The Moloch of the Western Front had been temporarily satiated. Some sacrifice might now be spared for the idols of the Élysée. General Joffre's influence had been strong enough to resist their plan when it would have been useful and perhaps decisive; but his authority was too weak to offer any effective opposition when the plan had ceased to have anything like the same value. This is one of the comic interludes which are woven into every tragedy.

Joffre came over to London on 9th June, 1916, to persuade the British Cabinet to join the French in strengthening the forces at Salonika. At that time the great offensive on the Somme had been agreed to by both Staffs and both Governments. I was one of the members of the Cabinet who accepted Lord Kitchener's view as to the futility of launching this attack. Lord Kitchener reluctantly withdrew his objections and the rest of us were overruled. The preparations were now far advanced. It was part of General Joffre's case that the offensive was essential in order to relieve the pressure on the French at Verdun. For the same reason we had been asked to take over a considerable sector of the Western Front hitherto occupied by French troops. The French needed every battalion they could spare for the defence of Verdun. It is one of the incomprehensible episodes of the War that the French Commander-in-Chief, the ruthless advocate of the " all for the west " policy, should at such a juncture come over to Britain to beg us to join the French in sending a considerable contingent of French and British soldiers to Salonika in order to launch a stage attack which must fail for lack of guns and ammunition.

At the Conference which was held in Downing Street, General Joffre presented his case with great force and eloquence. As to whether he was a good soldier or not, let others judge. Although I may not be competent to express an opinion I still hold one, and hold it strongly. As to his gifts as an orator, I feel that as an old Parliamentarian I am quite equal to forming a judgment, and quite entitled to state it. He was one of the most forceful and dramatic speakers I heard at any conference which I ever attended. But although on this occasion he spoke with all the outward visible manifestations of earnestness and sincerity, in voice, gesture, language, and facial expression, it was difficult to believe that he was convinced even by his own eloquence. He was urging an attack with forces devoid of the armament necessary to achieve their purpose, and he made no suggestion that the equipment should be strengthened up to the point of effectiveness. It was one of the most cynical performances I have ever listened to. Having regard to the inevitable loss of brave lives which would have been entailed in such a futile enterprise, it would have been wicked had it not been that he was relying upon our turning his proposal down. I realised that he did not mean business and that an offensive at Salonika unsupported by the necessary guns and ammunition must fail; I also knew that such a failure must discourage any future attempt under more favourable conditions.

Here is an official summary, taken down at the time, of the part I took in the discussion: —

" Mr. Lloyd George said that he had always been in favour of an advance from Salonika, but that unless there was a fair chance of success he considered it fatal; and because the facts before him were not convincing that it would be successful, he, as a supporter of the principle of an advance, was doubtful. We had had a bad experience at the Dardanelles, where we lost about 200,000 men as well as prestige. Unless there was a reasonable chance of success he was entirely opposed to it. The facts given by our General Staff had not been seriously controverted by General Joffre to-day. To attack a good army, in strong positions, with only twenty-four French and six British heavy howitzers was very dangerous. General Joffre said that we should be keeping the enemy busy and quoted the Russians. But the Russians were occupying the attentions of the Austrians, the Bulgarians were not helping anyone. If there was a fair chance of breaking right through and threatening the enemy's flank, the Roumanians might come in on our side. But General Joffre does not say there is this chance; he did not contemplate breaking through the Bulgarian lines—he was only thinking of comparatively trifling victories. To attempt the operation with inadequate strength was to discredit it. Sir Douglas Haig has in front of him very serious operations undertaken merely to relieve the pressure on France. This consideration had appeared conclusive to the War Committee, otherwise they were opposed to the offensive at the present time, considered purely as a military operation. The Ministry of Munitions were sending heavy guns to France, but nothing like what Sir Douglas Haig wanted, and therefore Sir Douglas Haig would prefer to undertake his operations later, when he was sure of a full supply of these guns. The test was whether General Joffre in these circumstances would like to see, say, fifty howitzers diverted from France to Salonika. Mr. Lloyd George said that he was as firm a believer in an eventual offensive from Salonika as M. Briand himself, and urged that we should not begin any advance from Salonika until we were quite ready, as an unsuccessful offensive would prejudice any further offensive on this flank. No Government after the failure would try it a second time. This indeed was the main reason for his opposition. The Allies were not yet equipped to defeat the Bulgarians—to say nothing of the possibility of Turkish opposition in addition."

So, much to the secret satisfaction of General Joffre, we turned our backs on Salonika and our faces once more to the Somme. It ranks with Verdun as one of the two bloodiest battles ever fought on this earth up to that date. The casualties on both sides were well over a million. It was not responsible for the failure of the German effort to capture Verdun. It was only an element in slackening up a German offensive which had already slowed down and was by now a practical and almost an acknowledged failure. The French Commander-in-Chief said in May that the Germans had already been beaten at Verdun. Had the battle continued to rage around the remaining forts which held up the German Army we could have helped to reinforce the hard-pressed French Army either by sending troops to the battle area or by taking over another sector of the French Front. The Somme campaign certainly did not save Russia. That great country was being rapidly driven by the German guns towards the maelstrom of anarchy. You could even then hear the roar of the waters. That is, we might have heard it had it not been for the thunders of the Somme. This deafened our ears and obscured our vision so that we could not perceive the approaching catastrophe in Russia and therefore did not take measures to avert it. One-third of the Somme guns and ammunition transferred in time to the banks of another river, the Dnieper, would have won a great victory for Russia and deferred the Revolution until after the War.

It is claimed that the battle of the Somme destroyed the old German Army by killing off its best officers and men. It killed off far more of our best and of the French best. The battle of the Somme was fought by the volunteer armies raised in 1914 and 1915. These contained the choicest and best of our young manhood. The officers were drawn mainly from our public schools and universities. Over 400,000 of our men fell in this bullheaded fight and the slaughter amongst our young officers was appalling. The "Official History of the War," writing of the first attack, says: —

> "For this disastrous loss of the finest manhood of the United Kingdom and Ireland there was only a small gain of ground to show. . . ."

Summing up the effect on the British Army of the whole battle it says: —

> "Munitions and the technique of their use improved, but never again was the spirit or the quality of the officers and men so high, nor the general state of the training, leading and, above all, discipline of the new British Armies in France so good. The losses sustained were not only heavy but irreplaceable."

Had it not been for the inexplicable stupidity of the Germans in provoking a quarrel with America and bringing that mighty people into the War against them just as they had succeeded in eliminating another powerful foe—Russia—the Somme would not have saved us from an inextricable stalemate. I was not surprised to read in the British " Official History of the War " that M. Poincaré is reported to have said that the greatest of all French soldiers, General Foch, was opposed to the Somme offensive. When the results came to be summed up they reminded me of an observation made by Mr. Balfour when the project of this great offensive first came from the French Staff. He said: " The French are short of men; yet they want to do something which would reduce their numbers still more." At that time he was in favour of telling the French that we thought they were going to make a mistake.

Whilst the French generals and our own were reporting victory after victory against the German Army on the Western Front; whilst our Intelligence Departments at the front were assuring their Chiefs, and through them, their Governments at home, that five-sixths of the German divisions had been hammered to pulp and that the remaining divisions would soon be reduced to the same state, the German General Staff were detaching several divisions from the battle area in France and sending them to the Carpathians to join the Austrians and Bulgarians in an attack on Roumania. No one on the Allied side seemed to have anticipated this move—at least, no one made any plans to counter it, if and when it came. The whole mind of the western strategists was concentrated on one or other of the hamlets along the Somme. They exaggerated the effect of every slight advance, and worked themselves into a belief that the Germans were so pulverised by these attacks that they had not the men, the guns, nor the spirit to fight anywhere much longer. They were only waiting, with hand cupped to ear, for the crack which would signify the final break of the German barrier, and they were massing cavalry immediately behind the French and British battle line in order to complete the rout of the tattered remains of the German Army. This is no exaggeration of their illusions. I saw them at this moment of exaltation.

When the battle of the Somme was being fought, I traversed the front from Verdun to Ypres. With M. Albert Thomas I visited General Haig at his Headquarters, and with him I drove to General Cavan's Headquarters to meet General Joffre. The latter and M. Thomas were anxious to secure a number of six-inch howitzers for the French Front. We had followed the advice given by the young French artillery officer at the Boulogne Conference (described in the next chapter) and manufactured these howitzers on a great scale, with a view to concentrating a plunging fire to demolish the enemy trenches. The French had gone in more for the long-range gun, and they were short of howitzers.

When we reached General Cavan's quarters there was a heavy bombardment going on from our eight-inch howitzers assembled in the valley below, known to the soldiers as the Happy Valley. The roar of the guns beneath and the shrill " keen " of the shells overhead were deafening. We could hardly carry on a conversation. We found the noises were worse inside Lord Cavan's quarters than outside. After we had arranged the matter of the howitzers we got on to a general talk about the offensive. Both Generals—Joffre and Haig— were elated with the successes already achieved. On my way to this rendezvous I had driven through squadrons of cavalry clattering proudly to the front. When I asked what they were for, Sir Douglas Haig explained that they were brought up as near the front line as possible, so as to be ready to charge through the gap which was to be made by the Guards in the coming attack. The cavalry were to exploit the anticipated success and finish the German rout.

The Guards could be seen marching in a long column through the valley on their way to the front line preparatory to the attack. Raymond Asquith was amongst them. Before I reached Ypres I heard that the attack had failed and that the brilliant son of the British Prime Minister was amongst the fallen. When I ventured to express to Generals Joffre and Haig my doubts as to whether cavalry could ever operate successfully on a front bristling for miles behind the enemy line with barbed wire and machine-guns, both Generals fell ecstatically on me, and Joffre in particular explained that he expected the French cavalry to ride through the broken German lines on his front the following morning. You could hear the distant racket of the massed guns of France which were at that moment tearing a breach for the French horsemen. Just then a Press photographer, of whose presence we were all unaware, snapped us.

The conversation gave me an idea of the exaltation produced in brave men by a battle. They were quite incapable of looking beyond and around or even through the struggle just in front of them. That would have been all right had the Allied Governments been advised on the whole field of the War by independent advisers, who were superior or equal in capacity and will power to these resolute soldiers, whose vision was clouded by the smoke of the battle in which they were engaged. But neither the French nor ourselves had military counsellors at the side of Ministers comparable in ability and force to Joffre, Foch and Haig. General Gallieni had been a sick man for years and therefore did not possess sufficient vitality to enforce the advice which his genius counselled. Of Sir William Robertson I shall have something to say later on. A mistaken loyalty to Sir Douglas Haig fettered his common sense. The result was that the break through was postponed from victory to victory. We suffered enormous losses. Some of them were irreplaceable—in the case of officers and in the picked men who had joined the Kitchener armies in the first moments of enthusiasm. The Germans flaunted our wild onslaught on the Somme and advertised its failure by their

Roumanian campaign. They marched to the Danube to celebrate and exploit their victorious repulse of the Allied Armies on the Western stream. Mackensen crossed the great river from the Bulgarian side and marched on Bucharest. Falkenhayn's army had already fallen like an avalanche from the Carpathian heights and overwhelmed the ill-equipped Roumanian Armies on the plains. Roumania, with its oil and wheat, fell into German hands, and thus months and years were added to the War.

Before the attack on Roumania came, I was disturbed by news from the Balkans, which indicated a movement on the part of Bulgaria against her Trans-Danubian neighbour. We had also received a disquieting memorandum from Colonel Thomson (afterwards Lord Thomson), our military attaché at Bucharest, as to the equipment of the Roumanian Army. In guns and ammunition it was quite unequal to the armament which the forces of the Central Powers could easily spare for the attack. I spoke to one of the military staff at the War Office on the subject, but he tried to comfort me by assuring me that apart from the fact that the Germans had no troops or guns to spare from the Somme, where he said their losses in men and material were gigantic, it was getting too late for German action in Roumania, as snow would already have fallen on the Carpathians, and the passes were impervious to artillery. Moreover, he did not think much of Colonel Thomson or his report. I was not completely reassured, and a day or two later I sent in to the Chief of the Imperial General Staff the following note: —

"D.M.O.

I have just seen the telegram announcing the declaration of war by Bulgaria against Roumania. This is an additional ground for the anxiety which I expressed to you on Saturday as to the possibilities in the immediate future in the Balkans. I then expressed some apprehension that Hindenburg, who has strong Eastern proclivities and has always been opposed to the concentration of Germanic forces in the west, would direct his attention to the crushing of Roumania, and that we ought to be thinking out every practicable plan for giving effective support to Roumania in the event of her being heavily attacked. We cannot afford another Serbian tragedy. We were warned early in 1915 that the Germans meant, in confederation with the Bulgars, to wipe Serbia out. In spite of that fact, when the attack came we had not even purchased a single mule to aid the Serbians through Salonika. The result was that when our troops landed there, owing to lack of equipment and appropriate transport, they could not go inland and Serbia was crushed.

I hope that we shall not allow the same catastrophe to befall Roumania through lack of timely forethought.

There are four disquieting facts in the situation: —

1. Hindenburg's well-known Eastern inclinations.

2. The declaration of war by Bulgaria against Roumania. I cannot believe Ferdinand would have taken this risk where it was quite unnecessary unless he had received substantial guarantees of German assistance in the attack on Roumania.

3. The slackening of the German attack on Verdun. Hindenburg will certainly give up this foolish attack at the earliest possible opportunity. The abandonment of this operation will release hundreds of heavy guns and hundreds of thousands of good troops. If in addition to this he were prepared gradually to give ground on the Somme, making us pay for it as he retires, he could transfer several more divisions from the West to the East. He could give up four or five times as much ground as we have won during the past two months without surrendering any vital positions.*

4. I can hardly think that the equipment of the Roumanian Army would enable it long to resist an attack from an Austro-Germanic-Bulgarian force, armed with hundreds of heavy guns and supplied with enormous quantities of heavy shell. The Roumanians are very scantily supplied with heavy guns and I doubt whether their supplies of ammunition are sufficient to enable them to get through a continuous fight lasting over several weeks.

I therefore once more urge that the General Staff should carefully consider what action we could take in conjunction with France and Italy immediately to relieve the pressure on Roumania if a formidable attack developed against her. There may be nothing in my fears, but no harm could be done by being prepared for all contingencies.

D. LLOYD GEORGE.

4/9/16."

The Russians made a gallant effort to help the outnumbered and out-gunned Roumanian Army. But by Christmas the greater part of Roumania was in the hands of the enemy. The Roumanian King was forced to an abject peace, and a country which had been a menace and a peril to the Central Powers became to them a fruitful source of much-needed supplies of oil and corn. Roumania and Serbia were both *hors de combat*; Greece had been neutralised, with the pro-German elements in its Government right on top. Three

---

* I am entitled to point out that five months later the Germans actually adopted this plan and by doing so completely upset the strategy of the Nivelle offensive.

countries which between them could have thrown more than a million excellent soldiers into action on the side of the Allies had been eliminated from the calculations. The effort to save Roumania had finally exhausted the great strength of Russia. The Allied generals, in contemplating the results of their strategy, found refuge in grotesque computations of German losses on the Somme. They were placed at a million on the British Front alone. We were left to imagine what havoc the French had wrought with their guns. Our great offensive had failed in the avowed objective of a break through and we took refuge in statistics. Sir Douglas Haig had not achieved his strategic aim, but a distinguished academician more than made up for the failure by a great statistical triumph he achieved in one of the back rooms of the War Office. The learned professor was acting under the direction and on information supplied by the "Intelligence" Department of the War Office. Surely its officials never displayed greater intelligence than when they played up to the urgent need of the army chiefs for some symbol of victory. As a matter of fact we lost on our front 50 per cent. more men than the Germans did. The French casualties were not as heavy as ours but they also were heavier than the German losses.

Thus ended the third campaign of the Great War.

CHAPTER XIX

MINISTRY OF MUNITIONS: PRACTICAL ACHIEVEMENTS

DURING a considerable part of the time occupied by the events described in the foregoing pages, my own departmental work was the development of our munition production. I have already told how, upon my appointment at the beginning of June, 1915, as Minister of Munitions, I proceeded to organise this new Department of State. I must now give some account of the work we were able to carry out during the thirteen months that I was responsible for its direction, until my translation to the War Office in July, 1916.

I shall not, of course, attempt to write a detailed history of the immense range of activities covered by the Ministry; but shall confine my notice to a few only of the developments of outstanding importance which took place during that period. They will serve as samples to illustrate the infinite variety of problems we were faced with, and the measure of success with which we achieved their solution.

1. GUN CONFERENCE AT BOULOGNE

When I undertook the official task of manufacturing munitions for the British Army, the War Office view of my duty was that my sole business was to comply with the demands which came from their Ordnance Department. Once I fulfilled these requisitions my statutory responsibility was, according to their interpretation, at an end. In a letter dated 5th June, 1915, from the War Office, detailing the relations between that Department and the Ministry of Munitions, it was laid down that " the duties of the new Department with regard to the supply of each kind of munitions will begin when the requirements of the War Office have been made known to it, as regards the kind, quantity, and quality of such munitions, and they will end when the delivery of such munitions has been made to the War Office."

I took a different and a much wider view of my responsibility. The rigid and hardened mentality of the War Office refused to bend or give to any facts that were not stale with age, and chronicled in accepted military histories. They rejected all experience which they had not been taught during the training they received in the days of their remote youth. I had been driven by their stubborn attitude to the conclusion that if we waited until our Whitehall generals woke up to the realities it might be too late then to save the situation. For months the Commander-in-Chief in the field had called their attention to the difference between this war and any other war which had ever been waged before by the British or any other army, because of the unexpected substitution of siege warfare for the anticipated war of movement. This altered the munitions problem so far as cannon were concerned in at least three respects: (1) It called for much bigger calibre guns and mortars than any hitherto sent to the field; (2) It necessitated a quite unprecedented expenditure of shell; and (3) shrapnel which was invaluable against masses of men moving in the open field or in searching out inadequate cover, became useless when the opposing troops were sheltering in a deep trench; and therefore the need of the Army was for high explosive of the heaviest calibre to tear up wire and to crash into trenches and parapets. I had learned from the correspondence placed at my disposal by Sir John French that he had repeatedly urged this point of view upon Lord Kitchener. I therefore came to the conclusion that I had to take the risk of a personal initiative, not merely in methods adopted for executing orders which came from the War Office but in determining for myself what the needs of the Army were and in organising my programme accordingly.

Not having the training of a soldier, and having no personal knowledge of these matters beyond what I had acquired during the past few months by contact with French generals and British officers —and these talks were not adequate to enable me to formulate a detailed and reliable programme for guns, machine-guns, and rifles —I decided to take immediate steps to consult with men of authority, and especially with men who had personal experience of the practical exigencies of the situation in the battlefield. It was useless to rely upon the Ordnance Department of the War Office. I was convinced that with them shrapnel was not a necessity of war but had become a point of honour. They felt that they could not desert it without a reflection upon their own prevision and patriotism. I decided, therefore, to go behind them to men who had first-hand knowledge of the actualities and requirements of the present War. This decision was reflected in the following note which I find amongst my papers:

" That a conference be arranged at the earliest moment between the French Military Authorities and M.M. (Minister of Munitions) on the one hand and the British Military Authorities and M.M. on the other with a view to arriving at a common basis for computing the number and calibres of guns and the quantity and natures of ammunition necessary to ensure the success of the next great offensive operation on the Western Front."

This turned out to be a momentous decision, for in the sequel it undoubtedly revolutionised the whole of our ideas as to the scale and character of the requirements of our Army. The conference was fixed for 19th June, 1915, at Boulogne. Before this conference I was confronted with a gun programme which even those who then framed it afterwards admitted was quite unequal to the needs of the military situation. I decided to test its sufficiency by drawing upon the best experience available from the battle front. I made arrangements with M. Albert Thomas, who was organising munitions in France, for the attendance of representatives of the French artillery. I asked him to bring along not merely the official adviser of his Ministry on these matters, but also, if possible, someone from the front who had actual experience of the effect of both the French and German artillery, with a view to ascertaining what kind of guns it would be most useful to manufacture, and in what proportions. Boulogne was crowded up to the attics and the only accommodation available for the conference was a frowsy room at a second-rate hotel (later in the War the whole hotel was completely demolished down to the cellars by a bomb). I had communicated with Sir John French and asked him to send his very best artillery expert to the conference. When I arrived at Boulogne I was met by General Du Cane, who had been sent as the Commander-in-Chief's representative. As I discovered at the time, and even more completely later on, he was a man of great intelligence, and what was even more important to me under these conditions, he was more accessible to the influence of fresh facts and new ideas than most men high up in his profession with whom I had business dealings. The French were not present at the first conference, but I had a full discussion with General Du Cane and handed to him the following note for consideration:—

" Given an army of 1,000,000 men, what equipment would you require in guns of all natures—number of shells before you commenced a serious and sustained attack with a view to breaking through the German lines?"

This gives an idea of my views before the conference began.

Later on in the course of the proceedings this further question was posed:—

" What weekly output of ammunitions should we aim at developing month by month in order to supply an army in France of 18 army corps of 54 divisions, so as to allow it to develop its full power of offence?"

The following day we had two meetings, and there were present, in addition to the British delegates, M. Albert Thomas, General Gossot, of the French War Office, and a young French officer of the French Headquarters Staff of the name of Colonel Walch.

Before we came to the discussion of the guns there were some very important questions of co-ordination between the various Govern-ments to be cleared up. The situation that had arisen abroad was illustrated in the lack of touch between the Allies on vital matters. Each of the Allied countries was running its own war on and behind the various fronts. I found that on munitions supply it was imperative that there should be much more intimate contact between the respective Governments. At the beginning of the year the Allies were still competing in the American market and putting up prices against each other. The Russians and ourselves were competing for T.N.T. whilst all the Allies were doing the same for other explosives and other materials. In one case the British Government withdrew from purchasing when it was discovered that it was being played off against the Russians. The price of picric acid was forced up by the demands of the French, and the whole metal and machinery market was deranged owing to the activity of certain people acting for Russia. Even amongst the Allies themselves there was no efficient system of controlling purchases and no co-ordination. France, for example, could not obtain export licences for coke from this country; and whilst demanding shell steel from us suddenly stopped the export of ferro-silicon.

We then proceeded to consider the question of artillery. For hours we discussed the whole problem of the kind of guns which the experience of the War had proved to be most useful, especially since the War had resolved itself into a question of attacking and defend-ing earthen fortresses. I soon discovered that the ideas of the French general were just as antiquated as our own. He had the same superstitious belief in the efficacy of the wonderful light French gun, the *soixante-quinze,* for all purposes as our own generals had in the all-round potency of shrapnel. I had to contend not with a profession but with a priesthood, devoted to its own chosen idol. General Gossot had not much, if any, experience at the front in this war and his ideas were purely historic. On the other hand, Colonel Walch had keen a kind of artillery liaison officer, and in that capacity he had seen the French and German artillery in action from Switzerland up to the British lines, and he had observed with scientific care and accuracy the results produced by the different kinds of guns and shells. He was a young man not only of great intelligence but of reckless courage, for he threw over his commanding officer with some approach to contempt for his ignorance. That demands more fear-lessness for an army officer than crossing no-man's-land in the face of a machine-gun. I found afterwards that he was an Alsatian Huguenot, and he was certainly imbued with a full measure of the spirit of Protestant revolt against authority. The conference soon resolved itself into a dialogue between Colonel Walch and myself, neither Thomas, the French General nor General Du Cane taking much part. It was hardly a dialogue; it was rather a cross-examination

on my part with a view to extracting from Colonel Walch all the
information which he undoubtedly possessed, and obtaining from
him his definite opinion as to the kind of gun it would be most useful
for us to manufacture for the service of our army, having regard to
the kind of warfare to which we were now committed.

The hotel was situated opposite the English Episcopal Church. A
few yards lower down was the Scottish Presbyterian Church. After
this talk had been going on for hours, I heard through the open
windows a distant sound of hymns being sung in these churches and
soon after saw the congregations pouring out from the two churches,
carrying prayer and hymn books in their hands. It suddenly occurred
to me that this was Sunday morning and that I had been discussing
earnestly with these officers the problem which was repeatedly
referred to by Colonel Walch as a question " which was the best
gun for destroying material " and " which was the best gun for killing
men." And this on a day consecrated to the worship of the Prince
of Peace. The thought made me shudder. I pulled myself together
only by reflecting that this was a war that had been forced upon us
by the arrogance of brute force crushing down the weak, and that
I had been driven by the relentless hand of Fate to choose between
giving my individual assent to the shedding of blood and
assenting to a surrender of international right and liberty in
Europe.

By this time both General Du Cane and I had a very clear idea
as to the lines upon which our gun programme ought to proceed.
I had the best evidence afterwards that, although he had taken no
part in the proceedings, he had listened with great intentness and
had not missed a word of the clear and emphatic statements of the
young French artillerist.

By that time we had both come to the definite conclusion that our
ideas as to the manufacture of artillery would have to be considerably
enlarged, and that we should have to develop our gun construction
on a very much larger scale than anything that had been hitherto
contemplated, both as regards quantity and calibre. On leaving the
hotel for the boat, General Du Cane expressed his satisfaction with
what he regarded as the most fruitful Council of War he had ever
attended, and then he said to me: " What I am about to say to you
now will make you think much less of me." I asked him what it
was and he replied: " After this conference I have completely
changed my mind as to the requirements of the Army." I told him
that his admission made me think far more highly of him and that
it was creditable both to his intelligence and integrity. He promised
that after consultation with the Commander-in-Chief he would prepare a revised estimate of the needs of the Army.

At that date the War had been going on for ten months. Guns and
shells had been a subject of vexatious and fretful correspondence

between the soldiers at the front and the War Office, and yet this was the first conference that had taken place on that subject between the artillerists with actual battle experience on the French and British Fronts.

As a result of this conference, Sir John French sent to the War Office on 25th June, 1915, a revised estimate of his requirements of heavy guns. The War Office forwarded this letter to the Ministry of Munitions on 30th June, for observations, accompanied by a table showing the additional heavy guns which equipment on this scale would involve for a force of 70 divisions. After an exchange of correspondence, the Ministry submitted a programme of its expected monthly gun deliveries up to the following spring, and towards the end of July drew up a revised programme showing a faster rate of delivery of heavy guns.

I was not, however, satisfied with these programmes. In view of the information I had gathered at Boulogne, I was convinced that for the success of our operations, an overwhelming mass of guns of the heaviest calibres was essential—an opinion confirmed by the success of our advance at Hooge, after a thorough preliminary bombardment with heavy guns, in early August. After careful enquiry as to possible sources of supply in this country and abroad, I decided to put in hand a very greatly increased programme, which would provide guns on a scale ranging for some types up to 25 per cent. above the War Office allowance, and this not for 70 but for 100 divisions.

I felt that to break through the formidable entrenchments of the Germans would involve a battering by artillery far heavier than the War Office yet realised, and that there should also be a margin available to provide for contingencies. If the guns were not all required for the various fronts of the British Army, the surplus would be available to supply the urgent needs of the Russians, who were at that moment suffering severely from the superior artillery of Germany and Austria.

Sir H. Llewellyn Smith, on behalf of the Ministry of Munitions, sent to the War Office a statement showing my new programme, and explained in his covering letter:—

" I am therefore directed to state that orders have already been placed which will not only cover the additional numbers suggested in your letter of 8th September, but will also provide a very considerable margin for possible future needs. The Minister has been influenced in providing such a margin by the important consideration that the ordering of these large quantities will make it worth while to have new machinery on a larger scale installed, both at home and abroad, which will hasten the dates at which considerable deliveries can take place in 1916. A larger number of heavy guns will by this plan be delivered during the critical first months of 1916 than would otherwise have been possible. . . ."

It might have been imagined that the War Office would be delighted to learn that its desires were thus being more than fulfilled. On the contrary, it was furious at the presumption shown by the Ministry in daring to increase or anticipate the programme laid down for it. The preliminary warning of a storm came in the shape of a letter from the War Office, dated 1st October, 1915, which stated that on learning that " the purchase of a large number of heavy howitzers over and above any demand made by the War Office was contemplated by your Ministry," Lord Kitchener had consulted with Sir John French to find out how many he wanted, and obtained his confirmation that the schedule submitted by him in June represented his requirements. The Army Council, therefore, had no wish for my extra guns, and suggested that the orders for them should be transferred to Russia's account.

I directed an impenitent answer to be sent to the War Office. The letter pointed out that the large orders were necessary to secure early delivery of even the War Office figure of requirements, while early delivery of the extra guns might well prove to have a decisive effect on the campaign. The letter continued: —

" Should the Secretary of State differ from the above views, the Minister of Munitions is prepared at any time to discuss the matter with him, or if he should prefer, he might bring it before the attention of the Cabinet. The Minister is not, in any case, prepared to cancel the orders he has placed for the provision of heavy howitzers, unless the Government as a whole will take the responsibility of deciding that the proposed provision is excessive."

If in fact there proved to be a surplus, I said that it would still be possible to pass this on to the Allies. But I made no offer to adopt the suggestion that some of the guns should be manufactured to Russian patterns, as such an alteration of the orders I had placed would have upset the existing arrangements and caused considerable delay in gun production. This called forth the wrath of Lord Kitchener, who expressed his disapproval of the action of the Ministry of Munitions in a memorandum, entitled: " Supply of Heavy Guns to the Army," which he circulated to the Cabinet. In this memorandum he called on the Cabinet to judge between him and me. He recounted the history of the dispute, and pointed out that the additional programme which I had put in hand entailed a provision of the following heavy guns over and above the requirements of the War Office: —

60-pdr.	120 guns, equivalent to 15 divisions
6-in. howitzer	220 " " " 27 "
8-in. " ⎫	
9.2-in. " ⎬	259 " " " 49 "
12-in. " ⎫	
15-in. " ⎬	40 " " " 45 "

639

After describing the latest exchange of correspondence with the Ministry on the matter he declared: —

"The point I wish to emphasise is that, if these extra guns are ordered for the War Office, the War Office will not be able to provide the personnel for the batteries required to place them in the field, for, even if the men were forthcoming, it would be quite impossible to find the artillery officers necessary for this service."

He urged, therefore, that these guns should be allotted to Russia, and should be manufactured to Russian calibres and patterns.

Thereupon the matter was thrashed out in the Cabinet. But I gave way neither on the issue of reducing my orders nor on that of making the guns to the Russian pattern, for if surplus guns should be available for the Russians it would be possible to furnish them with ammunition as well. I had for some time been urging that arrangements should be made to equip the Russians; but to change these orders to Russian calibres and patterns would have involved delays and complications in production. The Cabinet appointed a Committee under the chairmanship of Lord Crewe to deal with the matter. It sat once, at the Ministry of Munitions, and examined General von Donop, who repeated his objections to the enlarged programme. I did not state my case in reply. Here is an extract from Sir William Sutherland's notes, taken at the meeting: —

". . . I was somewhat mystified as to what was the official finding of the meeting; the various speeches being severely critical as described, and Mr. Lloyd George, beyond outlining the position generally, not making the spirited and continuous fight so often showed by him in similar circumstances.

'I suppose, sir,' said J. T. Davies when the meeting was over, ' that means the end of your programme.'

'No,' said Mr. Lloyd George, ' it means the end of the Committee,' and straightaway started his orders for the prodigious work."

In fact the Committee adjourned without coming to any decision, and never met again. The subject was dropped—but not the programme. I pushed that through. Before I ceased to be Minister of Munitions, it turned out that even more guns were needed by our Army than the large number I had ordered. When they were furnished by the machinery and facilities the Ministry of Munitions had ordered for the enlargement of production, no difficulty was experienced in finding the necessary complement of officers and men for the batteries. I may here anticipate the course of events so far as to point out that when the Ministry of Munitions finally produced this " unhouselled and unannealed " surplusage of guns, the War Office resolutely refused to part with them to help Russia, on the ground that they were all needed by our own troops in France, and a good many more. It was with difficulty that I persuaded the Staff to dispense with a few of the lighter guns for Russia.

But at first there was a good deal of gibing and sniping about what was called my mad production of heavy guns, and I had evidence that the War Office meant to neutralise my extravagance by refusing to train artillerists to man this wasteful surplus. I decided to take the matter up with the Prime Minister, and if necessary with the War Committee, and in order to check the facts upon which I intended to base my case, I wrote on 15th November, 1915, to General Sir Ivor Philipps, who had been Military Secretary to the Ministry at the time the order was given, to ask him for his recollection of my instructions. He was at that time preparing to leave for France with the Division he commanded. His reply was as follows:—

" Headquarters,
38th (Welsh) Division,
Avington Park Camp,
Winchester.

My dear Minister,

When the Big Gun Programme was under discussion you repeatedly urged on your staff that your main object in increasing the order for guns was to ensure the maximum possible delivery at the earliest possible date. This you specially impressed on us, both verbally and in writing. The necessity for impressing early deliveries by giving larger orders to contractors was passed on by me to the departments concerned, and we did our utmost to see that your very clear orders on the subject were carried out.

In many conversations with me you stated that your main objects in placing the Big Gun orders were:—

1. To ensure earliest possible deliveries by giving large orders to firms to encourage them to increase their power of output.

2. To provide guns for 100 divisions, should necessity arise hereafter to put that number in the Field.

3. To provide a surplus of very heavy guns to meet the latest views of advanced French artillery experts, that the teachings of the War tended to show that in future more and more heavy guns would be required to secure victory.

4. That if these guns were in excess of our own requirements, they would be invaluable as a reserve to assist our Allies.

It must be remembered that you laboured under great difficulties. You got no assistance from the War Office.

After your Conference at Boulogne with M. Thomas and the French artillery experts, as a result of the information you then collected the War Office at once put forward an increased and entirely revised programme.

No suggestion of this increased programme had been mentioned by the War Office while the ordering of guns was in their hands. When, however, the responsibility was on your shoulders, the demands of the War Office were at once increased.

I do not think you need fear that you have ordered too many guns or shells. What you have to consider in the War Council is, whether you are preparing to man the guns or even half of them when delivered. I fear that the War Council is neglecting this point. You will remember that I prepared a note on the subject when at the Ministry. You have done your share of the work of providing guns and shells; the country will one day appreciate your great work in this respect.

Yours sincerely,

IVOR PHILIPPS."

I have quoted this letter in full because it gives in compact form, and from the pen of a distinguished Army officer, a summary alike of my attitude to this issue and of the War Office reluctance to admit the need for the guns I was providing. In contrast to their attitude then, I may add that a year later, Sir William Robertson, writing in November, 1916, said: —

"We must have a much greater amount of heavy artillery than we now possess, and be able to turn out an almost unlimited amount of ammunition."

At the same time Sir Douglas Haig wrote: —

"An ample supply of munitions is also an essential. The enormous quantities required have been furnished this year with unfailing regularity. But the great reserves required in readiness for next year can only be accumulated by reducing expenditure to an absolute minimum during the winter, and then only provided the output can be maintained at the full rates estimated."

The "Official History of the War" makes it clear that even the

" extravagant " programme, for which I took responsibility, was insufficient for the purpose of bombarding the elaborate entrenchments constructed on the Somme plateau by the Germans. The official historian points out that we had a shortage of guns, more especially in the heavier calibres. These were the very calibres where I had exceeded the amended requisition of the War Office and thus drawn on myself Lord Kitchener's censure.

By November, 1916, a whole series of increased demands for big guns had been made by the War Office, and the Ministry of Munitions had been compelled to expand considerably the programme which I had been pressed so hard to curtail. Fortunately I had acquired machinery which was equal to the manufacture of this expanded requisition.

2. NATIONAL FACTORIES

To increase the supply of shells was our most immediate aim, for it was the shell shortage which had chiefly impressed the popular imagination and brought about the crisis which gave birth to the Ministry. But along with shells I had undertaken the responsibility for all the rest of the wide range of military supplies—guns, rifles, machine-guns, bombs, trench-warfare equipment, military transport, and optical instruments. Soon after the formation of the Ministry, tanks were handed over by the Admiralty. Control of the output of the finished article led inevitably to control of the preliminary stages of manufacture, back to the raw materials involved.

The consequence was that the scope of control exercised by the Ministry widened steadily and ineluctably until before the end of the War it covered practically the whole industrial life of the nation. The form of control became increasingly stringent with the progressive shortage of materials, until by the end of the War no one could start a new business or enlarge an old one except for war purposes. Everyone was liable to have buildings, plant or machinery requisitioned for more urgent work. None of the industrial metals and few raw materials could be used by anyone without Government licence. The nation concentrated all its great strength and skill on victory.

The materials which the Ministry of Munitions brought under its control included nearly a hundred main categories, and extended not only to more obvious articles such as iron, steel, copper, chemicals, and machine tools, but to bricks, flax-seed, glass-ware, waste paper and yarn. Ultimately the Ministry assumed responsibility for all visible supplies of such materials, controlled all private importation and the distribution of materials to non-munition as well as to munition trades, thereby virtually bringing all the industries using materials which entered into production of munitions under the control of the department.

It was not an arbitrary bureaucracy; for the Ministry acted through-out in very close co-operation with the particular trade or industry controlled. Frequently, important members of the trade had official posts and executive authority in the Ministry; while in these and other cases an Advisory Committee representing the trade was con-stituted as a consultative body to advise the department or section of the Ministry concerned. Where a trade had already a representative association, we discussed matters with it; and if no such body already existed, we sought to promote its formation. By contributing to, or bearing the whole cost of, needed extensions and adaptations of factories on the one hand, and by arrangements for limitation of profits and the operation of the Excess Profits Duty on the other, our national industry was welded into a great public undertaking for the winning of the War.

Even after utilising every workshop and factory capable of turning out munitions, we found that the output would be inadequate unless we supplemented our resources by the setting up of emergency buildings. This was more particularly the case when we came to the larger calibre shells and facilities for shell-filling. I therefore took steps to press forward as soon as the Ministry of Munitions was set up the policy which I had already been promoting as Chairman of the Munitions of War Committee, or organising special national factories for the definite purpose of supplementing our existing resources for munition production; particularly for making shells and explosives, for shell-filling and completing ammunition.

The first few months of the Ministry's existence saw the establish-ment of an imposing group of these national factories. By the end of December, 1915, when the Ministry had been in existence only seven months, there were, in addition to the Royal Factories at Woolwich, Waltham Abbey, Enfield Lock and Farnborough—which had been transferred from the War Office in the course of the autumn —and certain factories for explosives, no less than 73 new national factories. Of these, 36 were national shell factories for turning out the lighter natures of shell; 13 were national projectile factories, mainly concerned with heavier shell; 13 were national filling factories. There were eight new factories for making explosives, a new factory for filling trench mortar bombs, and two gauge factories which I took over to ensure an adequate supply of gauges for the new concerns which were springing up everywhere to produce munitions. Progress had been hampered in every direction by the inadequate supply of gauges.

As time went on, this array of national factories was steadily increased, both in number and in the variety of the products for the manufacture of which they were erected or adapted. By the end of the War they numbered in all 218; and covered not only every kind of munition, from cannon and aeroplanes to small-arms ammunition, but saw-mills, factories for boxes, tools, optical instruments and ball-bearings, and establishments for sorting and storing salvage.

The total of 218 included the four Royal Factories which were in existence before the War, the wood alcohol factory at Coleford set up by the Woods and Forests Department in 1913, and three or four explosives factories initiated by the War Office or by Lord Moulton's Committee on High Explosives between November, 1914, and May, 1915. Two of the national shell factories had already been begun under the Munitions of War Committee before the Ministry of Munitions was set up. Over nine-tenths of the remaining two hundred odd factories were constructed under the auspices of the Ministry, or with the aid of Government advances, leaving less than a score of establishments which were already engaged on production of necessary supplies such as gauges, ball-bearings, cotton waste or acetone, before they were taken over and nationalised.

The total covers only concerns engaged in manufacture or repair. It excludes the large classes of inspection and storage depots, mines, quarries, and other similar undertakings which were controlled by the Ministry. It excludes also the State-owned plant within the works of contractors, even where operated by servants of the department. And, of course, it does not touch the vast array of private firms which, frequently with the aid of substantial Government subsidies, were busily engaged upon munition manufacture. The great nucleus of national factories stood at the heart of the munitions industry as a colossal supplement to the Royal Ordnance Factories and a guarantee, within the hand of the Government, that the supplies for our armies could be expanded to meet the rapidly increasing demands from the front.

The first group of these factories which I was responsible for setting up was the group of national shell factories. The pioneer of these was the factory at Leeds, started by the Local Munitions Committee in May, 1915. The Leeds engineering firms had been urged to arrange a scheme of co-operation for production of munitions, and like practical men, they went to Woolwich in April to study the processes involved. Thereupon they came to the conclusion that the best way for them to work was to take or erect premises where, with their joint assistance, tools, workmen, supervision and inspection could all be assembled and the work carried out on a non-profit basis by a committee of management.

By 7th May, a draft scheme had secured general approval, and the next day the formal sanction of the Government was given and the work was put in hand forthwith. On 31st May, a national shell factory was approved for Keighley, and when at the beginning of June, I made my tour, as Minister of Munitions-elect, of the industrial districts, I was able to point to the Leeds effort as an example which could be widely applied. The idea was eagerly taken up, and as a result seventeen of these factories had been approved by me before the end of June, and ten more were added before the end of September.

These national shell factories were co-operative undertakings run by Boards of Management approved by the Ministry and provided by the local Munitions Committees. They represented in the main engineering talent which had not hitherto been engaged in any shell production, and at first they were chiefly concerned with the manufacture of the lighter types of shell. As time went on they were able to extend their range to include some of the heavier natures, and before the end of the War three factories at Leeds which had begun as shell factories were transferred to the ordnance factory class.

The national shell factories harnessed the ability of the engineering industry outside the existing armament firms. I was also concerned to make fuller use of the experience inside these firms, particularly for the production of heavy shell. In July, 1915, the actual output of this shell was far below the promises which had been made, and the demands of the army in the field for large high-explosive shell were rapidly growing. I was arranging a big increase in the programme of heavy artillery, and I had to ensure an adequate supply of ammunition for these additional guns, as well as for those already in the field.

Accordingly, on 13th July, 1915, I held a conference with the representatives of nine leading armament firms to see what steps must be taken to ensure the completion not only of existing programmes, but of the new and much bigger programmes which would be required.

The method hitherto adopted by the War Office of relying upon the existing works, extended with the aid of the grants from the Exchequer which I had authorised in the previous autumn, had proved definitely inadequate. But the armament firms strongly disliked the idea of my proceeding to found new and independent national factories for the production of heavy shell. So we reached a compromise. The armament firms would themselves build and manage new factories, additional to their existing works, the Government providing all the capital, both for the building and the running. The new factories would be Government property and the armament firms would provide managers to run them as Government agents, and under the control of the Ministry. The firms setting up and managing these works for the Ministry would get a percentage commission on the output. I must add that Messrs. Cammell Laird refused to take any commission for erection or management of the factory they set up in Nottingham. These factories were known as national projectile factories, as distinct from the national shell factories which I have already described. Seven national projectile factories were started in the following month,

August, 1915, and four in September; and by the end of 1915 the number had risen to thirteen. Before the War ended there were fifteen, and, in addition, five of the national shell factories were transferred to the department of the Ministry managing the projectile factories, on account of the nature of the work they were carrying out.

Some indication of the speed with which these national factories got into their stride, and of the service they were able to render, can be gathered from the following figures. Output from the national shell factories started, in the case of the first-established among them, in the summer of 1915, and from the earlier national projectile factories in the autumn of that year. In these closing months of 1915 their combined output was 200,400 empty shell, nearly all of the lighter natures. In 1916, their total output was 6,712,300, more than half of which was medium and heavy shell.

In just over three years, from mid-1915 to the close of hostilities in 1918, the combined total output of empty shell from the national shell and national projectile factories was 40,143,300.

Further, the cost of shell produced by these factories was decidedly lower than that of supplies from outside firms—so much so that in the case of the national projectile factories it amply compensated for the loss of value incurred through the difference between the original cost of their erection and equipment and the sums ultimately realised by them on disposal, while the lower costs achieved by the national shell factories not only made a large direct saving in expenditure on supplies, but enabled the charges of outside firms to be checked and reduced.

Like the national shell factories, the national projectile factories were used as time went on for a variety of other purposes in addition to shell production. In 1917, seven of them were busy on gun repair, one on making gun parts, and another on making guns. Yet another, Cathcart, turned over to aeroplane work from May, 1917. Grenade mortars, aero-engines, and shells for the Italians were among the supplies turned out by these factories; and before the end of the War five of them had become classified as ordnance factories, and were mainly occupied in making and repairing cannon.

3. FILLING THE SHELLS

The two groups of factory I have described, the shell and the projectile factories, ensured a provision of empty shell, but it was also necessary to provide explosives to fill and propel them, and works to carry out the filling and completion of rounds of ammunition. The story of the arrangements made for shell filling by the War Office is a sardonic comment on the attack directed against civilians for their presumptuous interference with the professional soldier in the discharge of his duties.

The need to secure outside sources of supply for high explosives had been realised early in the War by the War Office, for the excellent reason that the manufacture of high explosives had never been undertaken by the ordnance factories. There was practically no trade capacity for the manufacture of military tri-nitro-toluene, commonly known as T.N.T., a coal extract which eventually became an important ingredient in the bursting charge of high-explosive shell, and the stocks of the commercial explosive which were available needed treatment to bring them up to service standards.

The Defence of the Realm (Consolidation) Act, 1914, became law on 27th November, 1914. Under it the Government had power to take over factories engaged in the production of warlike stores, and the very next day the War Office descended on the Rainham Chemical Works, on the Thames opposite Woolwich, and commandeered them for the purification of crude T.N.T. At this time, however, the available supply was only about 10 or 12 tons a week, provided by a single firm.

The Board of Trade, when approached by the War Office, recommended that a distinguished civilian, Lord Moulton, should be entrusted with the organisation of an adequate supply of explosives. He was the ablest scientific lawyer of his generation. He was appointed Chairman of a Committee of High Explosives. He insisted that a new State factory must be set up for T.N.T. production, and made an arrangement with a firm of acid manufacturers, Messrs. Chance and Hunt, in December, 1914, whereby they set to work in January, 1915, to erect at Oldbury a factory for the Explosives Supply Branch of the War Office. This was the first national factory for manufacturing T.N.T.

Lord Moulton further entered into an arrangement with the Admiralty to set up a big factory at Queen's Ferry for production of gun-cotton. But the site could not be secured until May, 1915, and at the end of that month the Admiralty backed out of the arrangement. The new factory thus fell to the Ministry of Munitions, and was developed for the production of not only gun-cotton, but T.N.T. On becoming Minister of Munitions I found that there had been no survey of the prospective demand for explosives in view of orders already given, and that the provision then made for the production of explosives was quite inadequate to supply prospective requirements. In July, 1915, four more national explosives factories were established by the Ministry, including the huge factory at Gretna for the production of cordite. The construction of this factory had been recommended in May by the Munitions of War Committee, of which I was chairman, and was authorised by me as Minister of Munitions in the following month. It was also based on plans and proposals prepared, at the request of the Committee, by Lord Moulton.

The assistance rendered to the nation by Lord Moulton in this matter of explosives has never been sufficiently recognised.

By the end of the War there were no fewer than 32 H.M. explosives factories among the national factories controlled by the Ministry. We had been compelled to build these factories ourselves, because for some explosives, such as T.N.T., there was before the War an entire lack of industrial capacity, while for others like cordite there appeared to be no prospect of a large-scale demand after the War which would induce existing manufacturers to extend their works. In consequence of these arrangements in the case of explosives, the bulk of our home-produced war supplies came from these new national factories.

At the outbreak of the War, State production was limited to the Royal Gunpowder Factory at Waltham Abbey, which made about 75 short tons (i.e., 150,000 lb.) of cordite and gunpowder a week. By 1917, the national explosives factories were producing over ten times this quantity of cordite weekly, and of explosives of all kinds more than 2,000 tons a week. In the course of the War, the grand total of their output of explosives was over 317½ thousand tons: being 236,251 tons of high explosive (mainly T.N.T.) and 81,341 tons of propellants (mainly cordite). The need for these factories is illustrated by figures given by Lord Moulton in a paper dated 13th April, 1915, which he prepared for the Munitions of War Committee. He showed that the total estimated amounts of high explosives required by the Navy and Army in the months of February and March, 1915, were 4,505,600 lb. The actual supplies obtained and used were 1,038,802 lb., or considerably less than a quarter of the requirements.

Like the national shell and projectile factories, these explosives factories proved of great value, apart from the essential importance of their output, in furnishing data for simplification of process and reduction of cost in the production of supplies by other firms. The system of cost and efficiency returns which was established in them gave rise to a general competition in economy, not only between different national factories, but between these and the trade manufacturers. They provided a very economical source of supply as compared with either American sources or British contractors, and enabled very considerable reductions to be made in 1917 in the contract price for explosives.

But our troubles over explosives were not confined to the difficulties and delays of construction and equipment of our factories in war-time, when there was so much competition for labour and material. The most formidable obstruction I had to overcome came from the tardiness with which the War Office adapted itself to new conditions and fresh demands. It led to an emergency so critical that it very nearly wrecked the whole of our shell programme. This choice specimen of military rigidity in high quarters is best told in the words of Lord Moulton himself. Soon after I was nominated Minister of Munitions I received from him a letter, which apart from the fact that it is a startling exposure of military bureaucracy, is an interesting account of the kind and quantity of explosives fired in the War: —

> " Ministry of Munitions of War,
>   Explosives Department,
>   Institution of Mechanical Engineers,
>   Storey's Gate,
>   Westminster, S.W.
>   16th June, 1915.

Dear Mr. Lloyd George,

There is a matter of the greatest importance as to which I must request your advice and help in your position as Minister of Munitions.

From the time that I was first consulted on the question of the provision of high explosives I recognised that the lavish expenditure of these explosives which is characteristic of the present War made it absolutely impossible to proceed on the lines which up to that time had regulated our naval and military services. The adoption of T.N.T. as our principal high explosive was but two or three months old when the War began, and I doubt whether there was at that time a production of 20 *tons per week* of this explosive in the whole of Great Britain, while the production of lyddite must almost have ceased by reason of the belief that it would be substantially superseded by T.N.T. Would-be suppliers were told by War Office officials that it would not be used. Of neither of these explosives was there any Government manufacture or even any industrial manufacture except such as I have mentioned. *When I add that in little more than two days the Germans fired off over 800 tons of such explosives* * you will see how absolutely impossible it was to rely on the sources of supply which then existed. . . .

The only hope of obtaining an adequate supply of explosive lies in the proper production and utilisation of T.N.T.

This produce has the property of animating explosives, of which it forms only a small part, the remainder being principally nitrate of ammonia, a substance which can be obtained in practically unlimited quantities. Schneiderite, which is at the moment the favourite explosive of the French, is of this type. Only one-tenth of it is T.N.T. . . .

So soon as I had realised the position I put it before the naval and military authorities, and pointed out that it was absolutely

* My italics. D. Ll. G.

necessary to widen the list of high explosives and not to be content with using T.N.T. or lyddite alone. I fear it produced little impression at the time. But two or three months after I had done so, the Research Department at Woolwich demonstrated that by mixing T.N.T. with nitrate of ammonia they produced an explosive which was much more powerful than T.N.T. and equally safe. They showed that this could be done to an extent of one to four without lessening its explosive force and that it could be done to an extent of nearly half and half without even interfering with the existing convenient method of filling shells by melting the T.N.T. and pouring it into the shells. Some two months ago the use of this mixture was approved and directions were given that it should be applied to the whole of the land service for six-inch shells downwards and experiments were directed to be made with regard to the larger shells. . . .

To my great regret I find that those who have charge of the loading of shells have for the last two months completely disregarded the direction and now say that they do not propose to use the mixture for another month. I know of no reason except that they say that they have not got their warming cupboards for the nitrate of ammonia and it will take them some time to get them fitted up. I have no hesitation in saying that such a matter is quite trivial in comparison with the importance of so vital an improvement in our explosive supply at a critical period like this, and that to overcome such a difficulty should not have required more than a few days. . . .

I am certain that the possibility of an adequate supply of high explosives for the needs of the Services depends on the cordial acceptance of the means of economising the T.N.T. such as I have indicated, by artillerists and more especially by those in charge of the loading of shells. *It is hopeless for me to struggle to meet the extraordinary demands created by the War if there is on their part a disregard of or a reluctance to accept the necessary modifications of our artillery methods, which good sense and an appreciation of the magnitude of the problem before us dictate.**

You will excuse my speaking thus frankly, but I am satisfied that I have not said a word that I cannot support, and it is only by your coming to my help as Minister of Munitions that I can hope to obtain immediate and implicit acceptance of these all-important conditions of the supply to the Services.

Yours sincerely
MOULTON."

I realised that unless I could persuade the War Office to accept some considerable modification in the character of the explosive used

---

* My italics. D. Ll. G.

for filling, it was no use pressing forward the manufacture of shells, for we should not possess a sufficient quantity of the necessary ingredients to complete them. But here I was up against the inveterate rivalry between soldier and sailor. The Admiralty would not forgo their full quota of T.N.T. Why should the War Office be satisfied with a shell which was less perfect than that which the Admiralty insisted upon. This was not a question of factory supplies, but of departmental prestige. However, after a protracted struggle involving a loss of valuable time in the output of complete shell, a certain relaxation was achieved of the maximum requirements of the War Office. This enabled me to get along for a few weeks. But there was not enough T.N.T. to supply all the requirements of the shell programme, even in the reduced proportions which the War Office was prepared to allow. The delay was holding up the orders for machinery for the new filling factories, even the building of these factories. The character of the machine depended on whether the filling should be liquid or dry, and that again depended on the proportions of T.N.T. and ammonium nitrate, and the lay-out of the building depended on the kind of machinery which would be installed. The fight went on, and the consequent delays became more serious until the whole responsibility for design was wrenched from the War Office. We were turning out stacks of empty shell, but owing to these delays in deciding the mixture for the filling, the supply of complete shell was lagging seriously behind.

Two men in particular helped me to overcome this barrier erected by professional suspicion and procrastination. One was Sir Eric Geddes, of whom I have already spoken, the other was Colonel Arthur Lee (now Lord Lee of Fareham). When Sir Ivor Philipps was appointed to the command of the Welsh Division in October, 1915, I invited Colonel Arthur Lee to become his successor. By training he was an artillery officer and thus possessed first-hand knowledge of some of our difficulties. I had known him for years as a Member of the House of Commons He was an able critic of the policies in which I was concerned as a Minister. I recognised his efficiency and intelligence as an opponent. He had taken a leading part in the agitation for eight dreadnoughts in 1908, and I am not sure he was not the inventor of the very telling phrase " We want eight and will not wait." I had on more than one occasion crossed swords with him in debate. He was a skilful swordsman, who gave few openings because he had the gift of both mastering his case thoroughly and presenting it forcibly. Early in the year 1915, on his temporary leave from France, he had brought me some startling information as to the failure of our artillery to make any impression on the barbed-wire entanglements of the enemy. He was a man of untiring industry, great resource, and practical capacity. Although an officer in the Army and proud of his profession, he was one of the few whose judgment was not paralysed by an opinion expressed by a senior in rank. I found that in every crisis he had a cool head, a clear eye, and a stout heart. During the many ensuing years of almost crushing responsibility through which I was destined to pass I found his understanding, his loyalty, and his courage of immeasurable support. As soon as he joined me at the Ministry of Munitions he spent his first few days in scouting around to see what was—and what was not—going on. With unerring judgment he fastened on the shell-filling snag. He it was who also perceived that Eric Geddes was the best man in the Ministry to undertake the task of reorganising that essential part of our business.

Among the interesting developments to which the chemical side of warfare gave rise I must mention the story of acetone. Here again we nearly came to grief for lack of timely forethought. This chemical, which was an essential element in the process of manufacturing cordite, for cartridges great and small, was commonly produced by destructive distillation of wood.

Before the War there was a small factory in the Forest of Dean set up by the Office of Woods and Forests to utilise waste cordwood. In May, 1915, this Office set up two fresh factories at Bideford and Dundee, which were transferred together with the Coleford factory, to the Ministry in October. Messrs. Kynoch's also set up a factory in the New Forest, which was nationalised in 1917. But this country is not one of the great timber-growing lands, and it takes a great deal of wood to produce a ton of acetone, so in practice we were dependent for the great bulk of our supply on imports from America.

But by the spring of 1915 the position in the American acetone market had become extremely delicate. British cordite firms were competing with each other and with the agents for the Allies. Prices were being forced up. American contractors were selling their output twice over and defaulting on their contracts. They even went to the length of insisting upon an advance in price upon their existing contracts with the British Government, and in the case of their default it proved impossible to recover damages from them.

Prompt steps were taken over here to eliminate the competition between British cordite makers for American acetone. But when this had been done and arrangements had been made for the purchase of all overseas supplies immediately available, I was confronted by a much more serious crisis. In the survey we made of all the various prospective requirements, it soon became clear that the supplies of wood alcohol for the manufacture of acetone would prove quite insufficient to meet the increasing demands, particularly in 1916. The matter was urgent, for without the acetone there would be no cordite for our cartridges, for either rifles or big guns.

As Chairman of the Munitions of War Committee I took this matter greatly to heart. While I was casting about for some solution of the difficulty, I ran against the late C. P. Scott, Editor of the *Manchester Guardian*. He was a friend in whose wisdom I had implicit faith. I told him of my problem and that I was on the look-out for a resourceful chemist who would help me to solve it. He said: "There is a very remarkable professor of chemistry in the University of Manchester willing to place his services at the disposal of the State. I must tell you, however, that he was born somewhere near the Vistula, and I am not sure on which side. His name is Weizmann." Scott could guarantee that whatever the country of origin, Weizmann was thoroughly devoted to the cause of the Allies, that the one thing he really cared about was Zionism, and that he was convinced that in the victory of the Allies alone was there any hope for his people. I knew Mr. Scott to be one of the shrewdest judges of men I had ever met. The world renown of his great paper had been built up on the soundness of his judgment—of men as well as of affairs. But I also trusted his patriotism implicitly. Pacifist as he was he believed in the essential justice of our intervention in this War. I took his word about Professor Weizmann and invited him to London to see me. I took to him at once. He is now a man of international fame. He was then quite unknown to the general public, but as soon as I met him I realised that he was a very remarkable personality. His brow gave assurance of a fine intellect and his open countenance gave confidence in his complete sincerity. I told him that we were in a chemical dilemma and asked him to assist us. I explained the shortage in wood alcohol and what it meant in munitionment. Could he help? Dr. Weizmann said he did not know, but he would try. He could produce acetone by a fermentation process on a laboratory scale, but it would require some time before he could guarantee successful production on a manufacturing scale.

"How long can you give me?" he asked. I said: "I cannot give you very long. It is pressing." Weizmann replied: "I will go at it night and day."

In a few weeks' time he came to me and said: "The problem is solved." After a prolonged study of the micro-flora existing on maize and other cereals, also of those occurring in the soil, he had succeeded in isolating an organism capable of transforming the starch of cereals, particularly that of maize, into a mixture of acetone butyl alcohol. The generations of these organisms die very quickly, and in quite a short time, working night and day as he had promised, he had secured a culture which would enable us to get our acetone from maize.

Now maize contains about two-thirds its weight of starch, and our sources of supply were very wide; so that this discovery enabled us to produce very considerable quantities of the vital chemical. To-day this discovery is the centre of an important industry.

In King's Lynn there was an oil-cake factory which had been converted in 1912 to make acetone from the starch content of potatoes. It had come into the field with promises of supply, but the quality of its output was not satisfactory, and financially the company was unsteady. So in March, 1916, it was nationalised, and by June it was making acetone from maize by the Weizmann process with highly successful and valuable results. The shipping shortage in 1917 which forced us to restrict all unnecessary imports, introduced yet another experiment. In the autumn of that year, horse-chestnuts were plentiful, and a national collection of them was organised for the purpose of using their starch content as a substitute for maize. The King's Lynn factory carried out the manufacture, and though at first the poor quality of the material hampered output, these difficulties were overcome, and the Weizmann process was turning out acetone from horse-chestnuts by the time the factory closed in 1918.

When our difficulties were solved through Dr. Weizmann's genius, I said to him: "You have rendered great service to the State, and I should like to ask the Prime Minister to recommend you to His Majesty for some honour." He said: "There is nothing I want for myself." "But is there nothing we can do as a recognition of your valuable assistance to the country?" I asked. He replied: "Yes, I would like you to do something for my people." He then explained his aspirations as to the repatriation of the Jews to the sacred land they had made famous. That was the fount and origin of the famous declaration about the National Home for Jews in Palestine.

As soon as I became Prime Minister I talked the whole matter over with Mr. Balfour, who was then Foreign Secretary. As a scientist he was immensely interested when I told him of Dr. Weizmann's achievement. We were anxious at that time to enlist Jewish support in neutral countries, notably in America. Dr. Weizmann was brought into direct contact with the Foreign Secretary. This was the beginning of an association, the outcome of which, after long examination, was the famous Balfour Declaration which became the charter of the Zionist movement. So that Dr. Weizmann with his discovery not only helped us to win the War, but made a permanent mark upon the map of the world.

Dr. Weizmann is still the same busy, devoted, self-forgetful enthusiast. When I saw him recently he had just returned from a collecting trip abroad for the Zionist cause, in which he raised £70,000. He has collected something like fifteen or sixteen million pounds sterling for the rebuilding of Zion. It is the only reward he seeks, and his name will rank with that of Nehemiah in the fascinating and inspiring story of the children of Israel.

I have paused to tell of Professor Weizmann and his work, because it illustrates the multiplicity of different personalities and interests which were blended into the munition effort of this country. It is, too, a page of world history, the opening sentences of which were written in the Ministry of Munitions.

The story of our successful efforts to produce explosives brings me to the tale of our national filling factories. They really represented the most worrying aspect of the shell problem, for even more serious than the failure of the War Office arrangements for making shells, was their neglect to realise practically that ere shells were fired they must first of all be filled and fused.

At the outbreak of the War, practically the whole of the gun ammunition used by both Army and Navy was filled or assembled at Woolwich. There were five firms in the country which could fill shells. One of them had filled lyddite in the South African War. The other four had done some shell filling for foreign countries. But throughout the opening months of the war Woolwich was and remained substantially the only place where shell was filled.

In May and June, 1915, the national shell factories had started. In July I arranged, at the conference of armament firms of which I have already told, for the erection of national projectile factories. But the provision for shell filling in the country was at that time quite inadequate to deal with the growing supplies of empty shell coming from these factories, from the trade, and from American and Canadian orders. Woolwich was getting choked with stacks of empty shell, while our Army was without ammunition. It was therefore essential to my task that Woolwich should be under the control of the Ministry. Without it I could only manufacture shell carcases. At first the War Office refused to surrender the famous Ordnance Factory to the Ministry. They were supported in this refusal by the Admiralty. It soon became evident that I could not provide complete shells unless the means of filling these were transferred to my control. We were short of shells for the great battle which was being fought in France in September. We had a large stock of empties, but we were short of the completed article. The only practical result of Loos was to transfer Woolwich to the Ministry of Munitions. It was the first War Office institution of whose working I had any experience.

Soon after I entered its mysterious portals I came up against a ghostly potentate known as "The Extract." What was "The Extract"? I received account of it in a carefully prepared report that was presented to me as soon as I took over Woolwich.

In order to understand the procedure which governs the productive power of Woolwich and similarly of Enfield and Waltham Abbey with slight modifications, one must realise that the mainspring of the whole fabric, from a procedure point of view, is this document— "The Extract." "The Extract" is a term with an historical origin, which I need not enter into here, save to say that it was an extract from the proceedings of a Board of Ordnance which met at the Tower, and that this "Extract" was passed from official to official of equal rank who were not in a position to give orders to each other. An "Extract," however, is merely an order to do certain work. This phantom of "The Extract" was backed up by a frightening array of capital letters: M.G.O., D.D.O.S., S.O.S., D.E.O.S., I.R.E.S., C.S.O.F., etc., with a host of other alphabetical combinations glowering in the background. They were entrenched in well-worn professional traditions behind entanglements of red tape, and all ready from Alpha and Omega to die in their ditch rather than surrender the fortress held by them and their official forefathers to the barbarians who threatened their empire from the dark forest of politics.

When I took over Woolwich I soon found why, in the words of Monsieur Albert Thomas, it was "*une vieille boîte.*" It was due to the working of "The Extract" by the Capital Letters. They jostled each other, they were in each other's way, hindering but never hustling, and only acting together when there was any resistance to be offered to the political Hun. They were an alphabetical nightmare. My first duty was not exactly to lay these ghosts, but to put them in their proper places; to see that each of them pushed his own trolley without running into anybody else's. I saw why we had been delayed in divers ways. The men or Ministry that ordered "The Extract" controlled the output, and until Woolwich was transferred to the Ministry of Munitions and at least a few capital letters were on my side, I could not really get along with shell filling and components.

The first step taken by me in the reorganisation of Woolwich was the promotion of Sir Frederick Donaldson, the head of the Arsenal, to an important post I created for him outside Woolwich. He was a man of high intelligence and great knowledge of the technique of his job. To this he added undoubted charm. But years of routine in tranquil days when time did not count, when shells were manufactured to fire at safe targets, when all that mattered was that you should keep the Admiralty and the War Office Sections at Woolwich from interfering with each other, and, above all, ensure that the last penny provided by the estimates should be judiciously expended within the financial year, disqualified him for an emergency where hours were precious to the safety of the State, and improvisations had to supersede routine and regulation. I appointed in his place Mr. Vincent Raven, of the London and North-Eastern Railway, and his quickening influence was soon felt throughout the

Arsenal and resulted in an increased production of completed shell.

Woolwich, with the best management, could not provide anything like the facilities for shell filling demanded by the number of shells already ordered or about to be manufactured. I decided, therefore, to extend the range of national factories by setting up a number of national filling factories. Two were arranged for in July—one at Aintree and one at Coventry. Four more were begun in August, six more in September. Before the end of the War there were eighteen national filling factories engaged in filling shell. Some of them were directly controlled by the Ministry; some by agents, like the national projectile factories; some by Local Boards of Management, like the shell factories, the members serving without fee or reward.

The chief technical difficulties in connection with the carrying through of successful filling operations were not those of skilled labour. The actual filling was a simple process, and the great bulk of the labour in the filling factories was that of unskilled women workers. Such labour difficulties as arose were associated rather with the danger of the work, such as the scare of T.N.T. poisoning which towards the end of 1916 temporarily depleted the staffs; the difficulty of getting workers to observe the regulations for minimising risk of explosions; the repellent character of some of the precautions which had to be adopted, such as the wearing of respirators when handling fulminate of mercury compounds, or the smearing of the face with special grease if engaged with work on tetryl.

The courage of the girls and women engaged in these factories has never been sufficiently recognised. They had to work under conditions of very real danger to life and limb, and what some of them probably dreaded still more, of grotesque disfigurement—for one of the perils which was associated with the shell-filling factories was toxic jaundice resulting from T.N.T. poisoning. This ailment turned their faces a bright and repulsive yellow. The poor girls for this reason were nicknamed by their associates outside as " canaries." They were quite proud of this designation, for they had earned it in the path of duty.

Plutarch relates that at the battle of Pharsalus, Julius Cæsar told his legionaries to thrust their spears at the faces of Pompey's cavalry —patrician exquisites of Rome; and that these young gallants, who would have been brave enough in facing bodily wounds and death, were so terrified of facial disfigurement that they turned in horror and galloped away, holding their hands before their eyes. For girls and women, whose natural instinct it was to prize their looks and complexion, the blotching ugliness of T.N.T. poisoning was a peril which tested their courage perhaps even more than the risk of explosion. In 1916 there were 181 cases of this toxic jaundice, of which 52 ended fatally, and in 1917 there were 189 cases with 44 deaths. But in the course of that year the methods of preventing it were being rigidly perfected, and by 1918 the figures were brought down to 34 cases, of which 10 ended fatally. Despite the number so stricken, and the scare which found expression in the Press, there was no labour shortage at the filling factories.

Another fine story of courage comes from the factory at Hayes, where girls and women were employed to fill gaines. A gaine, it should be explained, is a tube filled with explosive, attached under the nose-cap of a high-explosive shell, and sticking down into the T.N.T. filling. Its purpose is to ensure that the detonation of the fuse in the nose-cap shall effectively detonate the contents of the shell.

In 1915 the frequency of prematures and blinds led to the discovery that a large stock of gaines sent from America had a left-hand instead of a right-hand screw, and tended to come unscrewed in the shell as it rotated in flight. To prevent this, the screwed-in gaines had to be stabbed in two places with cold chisel and hammer to break the thread so that they could not unscrew.

Women workers in the factory at Hayes undertook a large part of this work—risky work, for if a trace of the fulminate were ignited by the blow, the gaine would explode and disembowel them. One morning news came that there had been a terrible explosion at Hayes, in which several women had been killed. My representative went down to visit the scene. Work was being done in a number of little huts, separated off from each other. One of them was badly shattered. At its entrance Lord Lee ran against a busy little woman, about five feet high, white-faced but resolute. " Is this where the explosion took place?" he asked. "Yes," she answered. She was in charge of the hut, and when he entered it he saw bloodstains on the floor, and the survivors carrying on at full speed, with hammer and cold chisel, stabbing gaines.

Lord Lee spoke with the little forewoman. She had at one time been a lady's maid. Now she was doing her bit for the country in the munition factory, and when the explosion had occurred that morning she had calmed and steadied her girls and headed them back to their grim and dangerous task. All she would say was: " I am not going to run away, especially when I think of those poor boys in France who are facing more dangers than we are here."

Before long a safety device was produced to guard workers against the dangers of explosion when stabbing gaines; and later on the introduction of an improved pattern made such stabbing unnecessary. But till that time the girls and women carried on their risky work in the pluckiest fashion, and if one of them was blown to horrible destruction the others would keep up their spirits by singing at their work—singing songs with words of their own composition, which had little perhaps of literary grace, but plenty of crude vigour and unfaltering courage.

That was the kind of spirit shown by our women munition workers. Granted efficient direction, there was nothing it could not accomplish.

The experiences I have narrated in regard to our dealings with Woolwich Arsenal, and the facts set out in Lord Moulton's letter, give some slight hint of the official obstacles which continually interfered with our progress. It has to be borne in mind that we were not carrying on a smooth-running concern, but building from the ground up a vast new range of industries for the production of articles—many of them never before manufactured in this country. We had to find out how to make the best use of whatever materials were available, and this meant that it was impossible to rest content with standard specifications for ingredients, and standard processes of manufacture, however ideal these might be for the leisurely and limited munition production of peace-time.

At the beginning of the War, for example, lyddite was our only high explosive for shell filling. That was all very well when a few tons would satisfy our needs for months, but not when we wanted to fire off hundreds of tons a day; for besides being expensive, lyddite was a substance for the manufacture of which imported materials were needed. Hence the adoption of T.N.T. But again, T.N.T was costly and limited in amount, and as the demand for high-explosive shells grew it became obvious that the supply of pure T.N.T would be nothing like adequate. Hence the development of the amatol mixtures of T.N.T. and ammonium nitrate. But the approved method of filling a shell with T.N.T. was to melt the explosive and pour it in through the opening at the nose where the fuse would eventually be screwed on. When ammonium nitrate was mixed with the hot melted T.N.T.—like sand mixed into treacle—the mixture poured more and more stiffly, and with more than 40 per cent. of the nitrate it would not pour at all. So some way had to be found of mixing the two ingredients dry, and filling shells with the powder, if the maximum economy in the use of T.N.T. was to be observed.

For solving this problem fertile and original minds were needed. Britain is rich in such, and one of my most interesting tasks at the Ministry of Munitions was to get hold of men of real inventive and administrative ability and harness their capacities to the service of our immense task. Often they were men with a holy terror of red tape and official formalities, who would not readily submit to dictation, but if given their head would do work of the very greatest value. They had to be chosen with discrimination so as to separate the men of practical, if somewhat intractable, genius from the mere inventing cranks.

To help us with the problem of shell filling, I had the good fortune to secure the services of Lord Chetwynd, who was recommended to me by Mr. Ellis as the best man to help us in our difficulty. He had, as far as I remember, no practical experience in dealing with explosives, but he had a tremendous store of resource and ingenuity. I was, however, warned that he was very sensitive to any attempt to control him by a bridle of red tape.

We told him he was wanted to build and run a factory that would fill a thousand tons a week of high explosive into shells. He stipulated for and got a very free hand, without control by the departmental managers of the Ministry, and a contract valid till after the cessation of hostilities.

Thus equipped, he went straight ahead in glorious independence. He found a site at Chilwell, near Nottingham, and designed and built his own factory there. While it was being erected he went over to France in October, 1915, as one of a deputation I sent to study the French methods of shell-filling, and satisfied himself that the French practice of filling powdered explosives, by pressing it in through the nose of the shell, could be adapted for amatol. This was important, for to make our supplies of T.N.T. go as far as possible it was desirable to use it with 80 per cent. of ammonium nitrate, which involved filling dry, as such mixture could not be poured. At Woolwich they had designed a process for filling with this 80:20 amatol by compressing the powder into cakes and insetting these in the shell. But that meant either having a detachable bottom for the shell or a detachable tapered end, and both these devices proved in practice not only an additional complication and delay, but unsatisfactory and a cause of premature explosion.

Lord Chetwynd went back to Chilwell and determined to fill 80:20 powder by pressing through the nose. He hastily designed and ran up a small experimental plant to show it could be done, and when there was a talk of abandoning the 80:20 amatol on account of the unsatisfactory results achieved by the Woolwich shells, he challenged a test of those filled by him by pressing through the nose—a test from which they emerged triumphantly. His initiative in this matter was of incalculable benefit to the country, and made possible an immense increase in both the speed and the volume of shell-filling. The Chilwell factory was an amazing place, where powerful explosives were milled and mixed like so much flour. Lord Chetwynd designed his own plant and processes, aiming always at speed, simplicity, and the fullest use of machinery on mass-production lines. He passed his raw material through machines originally used for coal crushing, stone pulverising, sugar-drying, paint-making, sugar-sifting. The T.N.T. he ground between the porcelain rollers of a flour mill. A bread-making plant did the mixing. He bought up a derelict works that had been producing lace-making machinery and used them to manufacture the appliances he designed for filling shells. People objected that it must be highly dangerous to treat high explosives so unceremoniously. Lord Chetwynd's retort was to move to a house at the end of his press-houses. " If anyone is to be blown up, I'll be the first!" he remarked: and his action greatly encouraged his workers. A Zeppelin hunted up and down the Trent all through a January night in 1916 trying to locate and bomb the factory, but without success. A rumour spread next day in true war-time fashion that Lord Chetwynd had caught three German spies trying to signal the Zeppelin with lights, and had shot them out of hand. He was prompt to turn it to account, so he set a policeman as sentry all day over an empty room, and at night made a labourer dig three graves on the hillside. Into these he put stones and filled them in, with a black post at the head of each. That turned the rumour into unquestioned history, and discouraged would-be spies and the unwanted curious from prying round the place.

I have given these notes about Chilwell because they will convey some idea of the difficulties with which we were faced in our task of producing filled shell; and some idea, too, of the men who came to our aid. Besides, Chilwell was the largest of our national filling factories, and was our principal source of supply for the heavier natures of filled shell. Of the high-explosive shell filled during the War in the national factories, of sizes from 60-pounder to 15-inch, over 50 per cent. were filled at Chilwell, which turned out $19\frac{1}{4}$ million of these heavy shells, in addition to a considerable number of lighter shells, aerial bombs, etc.

Chilwell started shell-filling in January, 1916. Some of the national filling factories had begun filling of components—gaines, fuses, etc.—even before this. I had placed Geddes in charge of the whole filling section at the end of 1915, and such were his energy and resource that by the middle of 1916 the new filling factories had got into their stride and were furnishing the Army with complete ammunition on a scale which made possible the terrific bombardments of the Somme offensive.

4. MACHINE-GUNS

During 1914 and the first half of 1915, responsibility for the design and supply of machine-guns rested with the Master-General of Ordnance at the War Office. How completely the military direction failed to appreciate the important part this arm would play in the War is shown by the fact that between August, 1914, and June, 1915, four contracts only were placed by them with Messrs. Vickers for a total of 1,792 machine-guns. This would work out at two machine-guns per battalion, with none left for training at home as provision for machine-gun companies and no margin for losses or breakages.* The first order was dated 11th August, 1914, and was for 192 guns. The second, on 10th September, was for 100. The third, dated 19th September, was for 1,000, and the fourth, a few days later, for another 500. A provision in the third contract laid it down that the rate of delivery should be 50 guns per week. Only 10 to 12 had been the rate specified under the first order. The whole 1,792 guns were to be delivered by June, 1915. In fact, however, only 1,022 had been received by that date.

At the outbreak of the War the allotment of machine-guns to each battalion was only two. This was the equipment of our first Expeditionary Force. An explanation of the failure of the military authorities to realise the importance of this weapon is to be sought in the fact that as one distinguished officer wrote: "The machine-gun was regarded by British authorities as a weapon of opportunity rather than an essential munition of war."

It took our generals many months of terrible loss to realise the worth of the machine-gun. They were converted by representations from officers who had witnessed its deadly effect in action. The farther they were from the fighting line the less impressed were military commanders with the power and peril of the machine-gun. Brigadier-General Baker-Carr, the founder of the Machine-Gun Training Corps, has given in his recent book† a piquant account of the difficulties he experienced in establishing his training school and in convincing the higher command of the importance of the machine-gun. As it bears upon the attitude of the War Office in reference to the manufacture of this devastating weapon, I may be permitted to quote one or two passages.

This is the attitude before the War:—

"At that time, the sole mention of machine-guns was confined to a dozen lines in the 'Infantry Training Manual.' Nobody in authority concerned himself with this weapon of enormous potential importance, and battalion commanders before the War frankly and cordially disliked it.

'What shall I do with the machine-guns to-day, sir?' would be a question frequently asked by the officer in charge on a field day.

'Take the damned things to a flank and hide 'em!' was the usual reply."

In 1915 he was urging an increase in the number of machine-guns:—

"The fighting line, at any rate, had awakened to the realisation of the automatic weapon and many commanders were showing

---

* In 1918 our equipment of machine-guns was 36 Lewis guns per infantry battalion and 64 Vickers guns per machine-gun battalion. Deficiencies were replaced immediately from reserves at home.

† "From Chauffeur to Brigadier."

themselves eager to learn anything they could, which would help to strengthen their front without increasing the number of men.

Already I was urging the advisability of doubling the number of machine-guns per battalion, i.e. raising it from two to four. I had put forward the suggestion very tentatively to G.H.Q. and had been promptly told to mind my own business. The commanders of larger units, such as armies and army corps, did not at that time appreciate the vast saving of man-power that could be effected by the substitution of machinery for brawn, and it was only when we got within the danger zone that the proposals drew forth a cordial response."

He states that after having met with very little encouragement he set up his machine-gun school behind the lines.

"Not one single member of the Staff of G.H.Q. ever took the trouble to pay a visit to the School during the six months that it was quartered in the Artillery Barracks, a quarter of a mile distant from the General Staff Office."

He talks about the enormous fire power of the German machine-gun and the faith of the German Army in its potency both in attack and defence, and he adds: —

"Although this fact was flagrantly and terribly patent to the soldier in the front line, who was called upon to face the enemy machine-guns, the High Command was unable to realise the crucial importance of it, even after the Battle of the Somme, and it was only in the following year, during the ghastly and bloody fiasco known as the Third Battle of Ypres, that the full truth was forced upon them."

At last, after great pressure from the fighting line, sanction was given to increase the number of machine-guns per battalion from two to four. This was in the summer of 1915. He then says: —

"Within twenty-four hours of hearing the news I put forward a proposal to double this amended establishment. G.H.Q. was horrified.

'Look here, Baker,' I was told indignantly. 'We've given you two extra guns per battalion. You ought to be satisfied.'

Vainly I pointed out that the additional guns were not a personal present to me, but a badly needed increase in the arrangement of the fighting troops. But it was useless to argue."

It is an incredible story for anyone who had no actual experience of the fanatical hostility displayed by the Higher Commands to any new ideas.

Despite the meagre output for our own Army, plant was laid

down in this country in October, 1914, to provide 50 guns a week for the French Government, subject to the proviso that the output for the British Forces should not thereby be delayed. When the Ministry of Munitions was established, it was discovered that negotiations were actually taking place for the payment of £50 premium upon each gun delivered in excess of an average of 50 per week up to the end of December, 1915.

The Vickers gun had been adopted to replace the Maxim, which was obsolescent at the outbreak of the War. Maxims already in service were retained; but the total output of these guns from the Royal Small Arms Factory, Enfield, during the first two or three years of the War amounted to only 666 guns, and production of them ceased entirely in March, 1917, in accordance with the policy, already settled before the War, of abandoning this weapon for land service.

The growing importance of machine-guns became more and more manifest as reports came in from battle after battle describing the appalling casualties inflicted upon our men by this deadly little mechanism. The Germans were the only nation which had realised before the War the potentialities of the machine-gun, and they were arming their troops with 16 per battalion.

But this estimate of the value of the machine-gun was not shared in the War Office. The echo of its devastating racket had not yet penetrated that tranquil sanctuary of the God of War.

The manufacture of machine-guns raised the very important issue of priority as between rifles and machine-guns, of both of which there was a serious and immediate shortage; for the manufacture of both these weapons called for the same raw materials, the same machinery, and the same class of workmen. Geddes, whom I had placed in charge of the output of both machine-guns and rifles, found it impossible to get from the War Office any satisfactory estimate either of the numbers of each that would be required, or of the relative priority to be given to their production. Eventually he went, with Sir Percy Girouard, his immediate superior, to lay the matter before the Secretary for War himself, so as to obtain a ruling for the guidance of manufacture during the next nine months. The report of that interview is perhaps best told in Geddes' own words:—

"I told Kitchener that rifles and machine-guns were the same as shillings and pounds: that nine rifles were equal to a Lewis automatic gun and 13 rifles to a Vickers machine-gun in the productive effort required for their manufacture. I wanted to know the proportions of each wanted for nine months ahead so that I could make my plans. His reply was, 'Do you think I am God Almighty that I can tell you what is wanted nine months ahead?' I replied, 'No, sir! And I do not think that I am either. But we have to work it out between us and try to get it right.' Then he gave me the old War Office answer. ' I want as much of both as you can produce.'

My patience was wearing thin, and I think I spoke fairly definitely. I told him of the weeks I had spent trying to get these very elementary facts out of his subordinates. Eventually he said that the proportion was to be two machine-guns per battalion as a minimum, four as a maximum, and anything above four was a luxury. That was the opinion of the Secretary of State, who was looked upon generally as our greatest soldier, on 26th July, 1915.

I sat down in the War Office and wrote this down. So elated was I at my success in having at last got something upon which I could work that I spelt ' luxury ' wrong. I asked Kitchener to sign it. He always had a reluctance to sign documents and said that he gave orders and expected them to be obeyed. I replied that doubtless that was the military way, but I had been brought up to accept a signature as an authority for money I spent, and unless he would sign it, the document was no good to me. He walked out of the room. Girouard caught him in the doorway and said, ' Geddes is like that: he won't act unless you sign a paper.' So Kitchener came back and initialled the document."

Elated at his success in getting this documentary statement from the War Secretary, Geddes brought it to me. As Minister of Munitions I was officially expected only to fulfil the requirements of the War Office, and was not authorised to go beyond them. But I had made inquiries of my own amongst the fighting soldiers who had been in action and they were all in agreement as to the need for more and more machine-guns, so that, when I read this miserable estimate, I was so indignant that I would have torn it up if Geddes had not rescued it from me. He always treasured it.

According to Geddes I said to him: " Take Kitchener's maximum (four per battalion); square it; multiply that result by two; and when you are in sight of that, double it again for good luck."

This calculation gave 32 machine-guns per battalion with another 32 for a margin. That of course meant not that each battalion should take 64 machine-guns into action, but that manufacture should be on that scale to provide for all contingencies. As a matter of fact, in November, 1915, the War Office raised their establishment requirements to 16 machine-guns per battalion, and this was progressively raised by suggestive stages until before the end of the War the total number of these guns issued to the fighting forces and kept in reserve for contingencies exceeded a figure equivalent to an average of 64 per battalion. These included the guns issued to the Machine-Gun Corps and the Air Force, and we had also an ample margin for losses, which were very heavy. The numbers we

Memo of meeting with Lord
Kitchener on machine
guns.

———

Essential 2 per Battalion

If possible run to 4 per Battalion
and above it may be counted
as a luxury

26/6/15

Facsimile of a memorandum, drafted by Sir Eric Geddes and initialled by Lord Kitchener, dealing with the supply of machine-guns to the Armies.

had in France at the date of the Armistice were the equivalent of over 80 per battalion. In addition there was ample supply in England to replace inevitable losses and breakages.

As a matter of history, what with the demands from our own forces and the assistance we gave to our Allies, I do not think we ever had too many machine-guns up to the end of the War. On the contrary, the proved utility of this weapon was so great that on 23rd February, 1918, I find the programme we authorised for that year was an output of 138,349 further machine-guns, and another 192,000 in 1919; this, in comparison with a total stock of 1,330 of this arm, old or new, in the hands of our troops in 1st June, 1915.

Nor do I think that the Army ever had cause to regret that the supply proposed by Lord Kitchener in July, 1915, was increased sixteenfold. Photographs taken of dead Highlanders lying in swathes in front of a single German machine-gun on the battlefield of Loos, which I saw some weeks later, taken by Colonel Arthur Lee and brought to me, finally disposed of any qualms I may have had at having taken upon myself the responsibility for overriding military opinion.

The realisation of this expanded programme naturally involved very careful planning on the part of the Ministry. A long view was needed for machine-gun contracts, and as Geddes pointed out at the time, to create a new output of this class of weapon one must formulate a definite concrete plan 9 to 12 months in advance.

The Ministry began by placing a contract with Messrs. Vickers on 19th July, 1915, for 12,000 Vickers machine-guns. Financial assistance was given to enable the firm to extend their plant at Erith and Crayford. The productive capacity of these factories ultimately reached 5,000 machine-guns a month.

We also turned our attention to the Lewis gun. This weapon had been rejected for land service by the military authorities in 1912, on the ground that it was undesirable to multiply types of arms. At the outbreak of the War, they were still emphatic in their preference for the Vickers rather than the Lewis gun. The latter was a much lighter weapon than the Vickers gun, and could therefore be moved about by the soldiers with greater ease. It was indispensable for an advance and for aeroplanes.

But during August, 1914, 45 Lewis guns had been ordered for the Air Service, and in the first week of September contracts were placed for 200 more for general service to be delivered at the rate of 25 per week. The orders were subsequently increased by the War Office, but no effective steps were taken to increase facilities for manufacture and to expedite delivery, so that despite increased requisitions during the nine weeks ended 12th June, deliveries to the War Office averaged only 36 per week.

When the Ministry assumed control I had the position investigated, and found that any effective increase in output was dependent upon the placing of larger orders, which would justify the Birmingham Small Arms Company and the manufacturers in making a considerable extension of their plant. It also depended on arrangements being made to increase the output of the necessary machine tools and gauges for manufacture. Hitherto the War Office and the Admiralty between them had given contracts for under 2,000 Lewis guns—just enough to keep the firm from accepting foreign orders. So an order was placed with them for 10,000 machine-guns to be delivered before the end of May, 1916, and while this contract was running I negotiated a further agreement with them whereby the output was to be extended to 750 guns weekly, with a running contract for this number for the duration of the War. In May, 1917, arrangements were made for this to be increased to 1,800 a week.

In February, 1915, plant and skilled workmen had been brought over to Coventry from France for the manufacture of Hotchkiss guns, and a factory started, from which the Admiralty ordered 1,000 of these machine-guns. The anticipated output of the factory was 25 to 50 guns a week.

On 13th August, 1915, I decided to sanction a scheme for doubling the output of this factory, although the British military authorities did not then accept this type of gun for service use. Accordingly, in September, 1915, the Ministry placed an order for 3,000 machine-guns, and by the beginning of June, 1916, the factory had delivered 1,013. Its output rose to 690 guns a month by the end of October, 1916. The ultimate importance of this weapon, especially for the armament of the tanks, is of course familiar history.

It would be a mistake to suppose that these immense expansions of the supply of machine-guns were carried through with a reckless disregard for expense. Output was of course the chief concern, since the lives of our soldiers were in the balance. But cost was carefully studied. For example, the orders placed by the War Office with Messrs. Vickers in August and September, 1914, ranged from £167 to £162 per gun. The price fixed by the Ministry of Munitions in July, 1915, was £125 per gun. In 1916, it was reduced to £100. In 1918 it was still further brought down to £74.

Our progress in the task of supplying our forces with machine-guns may be summarised as follows:—

At the outbreak of the War, if we ignore the obsolescent Maxim, of which a few were still being turned out at the Royal Small Arms Factory at Enfield (which produced just over 80 of them during the first 18 months of the War), the only supply of machine-guns was the 10 to 12 a week which were the maximum that Vickers could then turn out.

By the end of May, 1915, the total machine-guns delivered to the War Office since August, 1914, were 1,039—775 Vickers and 264

Lewis; and the total number in service, including Maxims, was 1,330. Guns so far ordered numbered 2,305.

How the output of machine-guns rose thereafter is shown by the following little table: —

Year.						Total output.
1914	...	...	...	...	...	287
1915	...	...	...	...	...	6,102
1916	...	...	...	...	...	33,507
1917	...	...	...	...	...	79,746
1918	...	...	...	...	...	120,864
					Total	240,506

Out of this total of 240,506 machine-guns which were manufactured in this country during the War we supplied 26,900 to our Allies, or twenty times as many as our whole stock at the time the Ministry of Munitions was formed.

5.   MACHINE-GUN CORPS

It was my duty as Minister of Munitions to furnish the machine-guns required by the Army—and, as I have related, I went at one time considerably in advance of their official requirements in the direction of an intelligent anticipation of the numbers of guns they would presently find it necessary to apply for.

Officially, it was perhaps hardly a part of my duty to ensure that the best use was being made of the large supply of machine-guns, but obviously this was a matter in which I could not fail to be keenly interested. In October, some three months after the question of the number of guns to be provided had been settled by me and when their production was getting into its stride, the project of forming a special Machine-Gun Corps received the Royal Assent.* This was a plan which I strongly supported. I had been informed of the very effective methods employed by the enemy to get the best results from this weapon—methods involving the use of special machine-gun companies, not permanently attached or allotted to any battalion or division.

But I was greatly alarmed to hear, shortly afterwards, that although this Machine-Gun Corps had been authorised, little was being done to make it a reality, and hardly any men were being brought into training for it, out of the millions of men that had been recruited. Orders had, in fact, been issued that no man should be recruited for it or transferred to it from other units. By this date my capacity for amazement at professional repugnance to new ideas or formations had reached saturation point. The estimated deliveries of machine-guns would by March, 1916, reach a cumulative total of more than

* Royal Warrant.   Army Order No. 416 of 22nd October, 1915.

10,000, and by midsummer of over 20,000. No doubt there were many other demands for men being made upon the War Office, but the machine-gun was obviously such a formidable factor in defence and attack that only some curious form of unbelief and opposition could be responsible for this, to my mind, otherwise inexplicable and unintelligent failure to train men especially to make the best use of it. I determined, therefore, at the risk of once again interfering in something which was not departmentally my concern, to ascertain the exact position.

In the War Committee of 13th November, 1915, I took up this matter. I laid before the Committee a memorandum setting out the estimated deliveries of machine-guns, and urging adequate preparation for the effective use of this weapon. The memorandum continued:—

"I believe that one machine-gun, with its detachment of ten men, is at a very low estimate equivalent in destructive power to fifty riflemen, especially on the defensive. If that is a correct basis of comparison we could make up for our shortage in men and obtain equivalent fighting value by training 200 machine-gunners instead of 1,000 riflemen. In other words, with 50,000 machine-gunners we could do the work of 250,000 infantry. We could also save in rifles, in which, so far as I can see, the Allies are never going to obtain the numerical superiority over the Germans necessary for a decisive victory.

It seems also, that if our machine-guns are employed on a large scale, on a comprehensive plan, they will, in conjunction with barbed wire and fortification, give us the strategic power *so far enjoyed by the Germans alone* of taking large numbers of troops away from one front, where no offensive is in contemplation, and transferring them to a quarter where active operations are intended.

This is what the Germans have done on the Western Front, to release men for the thrust against Russia, and what they are doing on their Eastern Front, to set free men for attacking Serbia, and for action on the Western Front. This power to replace men, which amounts to strategic elasticity, applies especially, I think, to our present intentions on the Western Front."

General Sir Archibald Murray, who was then acting as Chief of the Imperial General Staff, under Lord Kitchener (at the time away in the Mediterranean), was present at the War Committee, and supported my view. He said that the General Staff had actually started a machine-gun school at Grantham, intended to train a corps of men in machine-gun handling and tactics; but the Adjutant-General would not supply them with any men. They wished to train 10,000 men at a time, taking in a fresh supply every two months, but so far had only had 3,000 men. He confirmed my estimate that one machine-gun was equal to fifty rifles, and contradicted Mr. M'Kenna's suggestion that mobility was lost with machine-guns.

As a result of my pressure, the War Council decided to ask the Army Council to provide for 10,000 men to be put continuously under instruction. Actually some considerable delay occurred before this instruction was carried out, but eventually a number of men were drafted from various units to the Corps Training Centre, and even they were not especially picked men like the German machine-gunners, whom Sir Douglas Haig has described as a *corps d'élite*. None the less, they added immensely to the efficiency of our army. Four years later, in November, 1918, the strength of this new branch of the Army which had been initiated under such difficulties amounted to 6,427 officers and 123,835 other ranks.

When one recalls the devastating use made by the Germans of their picked machine-gunners both in attack and defence, and how they saved their own infantry by that process, one is astounded at the tardiness with which our military leaders came to any realisation of the power of the most lethal weapon of the War.

6. DESIGN AND INVENTION

In this War the engineer and the chemist dominated the battle-field. When war broke out the Central Powers were much better prepared than the Allies on the mechanical and chemical side in this respect. The great howitzers of the Germans played a decisive part in the opening conflicts of the War. Even in 1916 the French artillery was inferior in this type of weapon. We had practically nothing that counted in trench warfare until late in 1915. The Teutonic heavy guns (German and Austrian) smashed the concrete fortifications of Liège, compelling in a few hours the surrender of defences which we reckoned would hold out for days if not weeks. The Germans who captured Antwerp were in numbers but a third of the garrison, and in quality they were the second best of the German troops. Big guns did the work for them. The German 5.9 shell with its terrifying explosion stopped the French advance, and hurled their armies back towards Paris. Whilst the German engineers in their workshops gave their comrades superior weapons for attack, their field engineers constructed for them the best defences. Deep and skilfully constructed entrenchments protected by wire and defended with machine-guns, *Minenwerfer,* and grenades defied the repeated efforts of the Allies to push the German invaders back out of France and Belgium. Their use of poison gas broke the French and British fronts at Ypres in 1915, and helped to scatter the Russians in Poland.

On their Eastern Front the Germans could defeat and hurl back Russian armies thrice as strong numerically, but destitute of the guns, shells, mortars and gases which the Central Powers possessed. Human valour is no shield against high explosives or machine-gun bullets. As deadlock gripped the battle front it became increasingly clear that if Allied strategy declined to seek a back-door, the only hope of gaining a decisive victory was to produce some new contrivance or improvement in our weapons which might turn the balance. And even a back-door, if barred, needs smashing in.

It soon became evident to clear eyes and gradually to the most obtuse vision that the War would be fought and ultimately decided in the workshop and the laboratory.

Unhappily, at the outbreak of the War and all through its opening months we were definitely behindhand in the field of munition design. Our artillery had not been tested in a great war. Our little stage manœuvres taught us nothing as to what real war would be like. Our heavy artillery was a joke to our foes. We had no trench mortars or grenades. We had vested our confidence so much in shrapnel that we had not worked out a safe high-explosive shell. When we started manufacturing high-explosive shells we had not thought out the problem of how we were to produce a sufficient quantity of explosive for so stupendous a demand, nor had we invented a competent fuse to explode such shells as we were able to fill. Our only modern big gun was the solitary experimental 9.2 inch, which was sent out to the front in September, 1914, and which was nicknamed "Mother" by the troops. Our machine-guns were few in number, and many of them obsolescent in design. The War Office had refused to consider the Lewis gun for land service. We had no trench mortars and no reliable hand grenades. The enemy had both.

Research and design for munitions of war were under the control of the Master-General of Ordnance. During the opening months of the War, he held that, as it would soon be over, it would be foolish to divert to the lengthy and tedious process of working out and approving designs for new weapons the energy which could be better used for producing existing standard types. Thus, when early on in the War a request came from the Front that specimens of captured German *Minenwerfer* should be examined with a view to providing the Army with trench-mortars, the proposal was postponed on the ground that other demands on the capacity of the Ordnance Factory and armament firms were more immediate.

But as the War progressed the military authorities were compelled to face ever multiplying problems of new designs and types of munition which were required by the army in the field. They had also to arrange for the immense growth of output of all supplies, new or old, and this threw a great deal of extra work on the drawing-office at Woolwich. It was inevitable that it should become thoroughly congested and hopelessly in arrears. The Admiralty,

N

which also relied on Woolwich for the same class of work, became so impatient that in May, 1915, it established its own drawing-office at headquarters, and gradually developed it to include simple designing.

Britain is very rich in scientific and inventive ability, and in November, 1914, the General War Committee of the Royal Society was appointed to " organise assistance to the Government in conducting or suggesting scientific investigation in relation to the War, the Committee to have power to add to their number and to appoint Sub-Committees not necessarily restricted to Fellows of the Society." By this step the Government mobilised the most distinguished body of scientists in the world to assist the nation. The Admiralty made considerable use of this body, and referred to it such inventions and suggestions sent in as seemed to hold out some promise of being useful. But the procedure of the War Department remained practically unaltered. Apart from some slight co-operation with the Chemical Sub-Committee which had been set up by the Royal Society, little use was made by the War Committee of the Society for military purposes.

When the Ministry of Munitions was first set up, the Army Council retained responsibility for the kind and quality of the stores we were to supply. The fixing of designs and specifications and the tests to be applied, the research and experimental work in connection with munitions, were still under the War Office, and though the Ministry of Munitions was responsible for providing guns, ammunition, rifles, and other munitions, it was entirely dependent upon the War Office authorities for decision and investigation in respect of the patterns, ingredients, and specifications of these stores.

I soon discovered that the separation of design and manufacture was a serious mistake and led to blunders and delays. It was not improved by the reactionary attitude of the War Office. Our soldiers in the battle line were more progressive. Sir John French set up, early in June, 1915, an Experimental Committee at G.H.Q. to deal with inventions and the application of modern science to the needs of war. At home there was a popular demand for a similar organisation to serve the needs of both the Army and the Navy, and on 22nd June, 1915, Mr. Balfour, who was then First Lord of the Admiralty, definitely formulated a scheme for this purpose. The War Office held aloof, and in July the Admiralty set up an Admiralty Board of Inventions and Research to serve the needs of the Senior Service alone. A similar organisation was shortly afterwards established by me for the Ministry of Munitions.

A very short experience convinced me that the unnatural divorce of design and production was quite unworkable. In particular, I felt it important that the Ministry of Munitions should be able to examine new suggestions and inventions of possible value—a view confirmed by the history of the Stokes gun—and I proceeded to press for the transfer to the Ministry of the authority at least to deal with such new ideas and designs.

The history of the Stokes gun affords an illustration of the impracticability of the dual system. The Army were clamouring for a mortar that would enable them to reply to the bombing appliances with which the Germans harried our trenches. As early as January, 1915, Mr. Wilfred Stokes, an East of England manufacturer of agricultural machinery, had submitted to the War Office a design for a trench mortar of extreme simplicity—a plain steel tube, into which a bomb could be dropped with a cartridge fitted to its base, which would explode on hitting a striker at the base of the tube, and propel the bomb into the enemy trench. You could fire the gun as rapidly as you could drop bombs into it.

The War Office did not approve the type of fuse fitted to the bomb, and turned down the invention. It was brought forward again in March, and again rejected.

Hearing favourable reports of this gun, I arranged to see it for myself, and on 30th June I witnessed it in action in a demonstration at Wormwood Scrubs. I was accompanied by Major-General Ivor Philipps, the Military Secretary to the new Ministry. Both of us were very impressed with its performance. It struck me as having great possibilities.

Officially I was limited at this time in the Ministry to the manufacture of those stores which the War Office approved. It was impossible to pretend that it had passed the design for the Stokes gun—on the contrary, it had twice rejected it.

Happily I had received just before this a donation of £20,000 from one of the Indian Maharajahs, to be expended by me on whatever war purpose seemed to me most useful for the Empire. On the strength of this fund, and in spite of my knowledge that the War Office was opposed to using the Stokes gun, I gave instructions for 1,000 of them to be made forthwith, together with 100,000 bombs—these last not to be completed till a satisfactory fuse had been prepared for them. Meantime I set about reopening the issue with the War Office.

By the second week of August they had been brought to the point of carrying out a further test of the mortar at Shoeburyness. By this time a fuse had been fitted to the bombs, similar to that used on the Mills hand grenade. The Ordnance Board now reported that the gun was better than a 3.7-in. trench mortar which the War Office had been manufacturing, and it was formally approved on 28th August. This was just as well, for already on 22nd August General Headquarters in France had telegraphed the War Office for as many Stokes mortars as could possibly be supplied by 1st

September, and had sent over an officer to consult with the Trench Warfare Department about the smoke bombs it was desired to use in them for a smoke screen in the coming Battle of Loos. Thirty were hastily improvised and sent out.

During the remainder of the War, the Stokes gun became and remained the trench mortar in highest favour and most constant demand. Out of 19,000 trench mortars and trench howitzers issued during the War to our troops, 11,500 were Stokes guns. Throughout 1917 and 1918 the 3-in. Stokes gun was the only form of light trench mortar manufactured, as by this time it had clearly proved its superiority to all rival patterns. And this was the weapon which the Ordnance Department of the War Office had done its best to fling aside as worthless.

Naturally after this experience I was more than ever anxious to bring the supervision of new inventions and improvements in design under the control of a progressively-minded body, which would not suffer from an ingrained habit of rejecting every fresh idea on principle. The fact that we were at that time being held up by the delay in settling the ingredients of shell filling and the design of fresh fuses and gaines made me still more desirous of having complete control in those vital matters. The Admiralty, as I have said, was showing itself far more alert in this respect than the War Office, and in face of the failure of the Ordnance Department to do anything in the matter, was even studying new ideas for land warfare. On the plea that they would be of value to the Royal Naval Air Service, Mr. Churchill had as early as January, 1915, begun investigations into the possibilities of armoured cars, and had set up in February the Admiralty Landships Committee, which carried out work of immense value for the evolution of the tank.

I was, naturally, being deluged at the Ministry of Munitions with letters and calls from people who had some new invention or improvement to propose. The great majority of these ideas were, of course, useless, and many of them came from cranks and lunatics. But it was clear, as in the case of Mr. Stokes, that some of them might prove of value, and it was also evident from the result of the Admiralty researches into land warfare and the rejection of Lord Moulton's recommendations about explosives, that the War Office was failing to carry out the work urgently required in this field. Early in June I arranged with Mr. Balfour to take over all the work of the Admiralty in reference to expedients and inventions for land warfare. This meant, amongst other things, that the manufacture of tanks was handed over to the Ministry.

In reply to a request I made to him, Lord Kitchener sent a message through Sir Reginald Brade that he was agreeable to my taking over the inventions work relating to munitions, for the supply of which my Department was responsible.

Accordingly, on 13th July a meeting was held at which a new Department of the Ministry was set up for dealing with inventions having relation to Munitions of War.

To carry out the duties of this Department I appointed Mr. Ernest Moir. This development was described by me as follows, in the course of a speech which I made in the House of Commons on 28th July on the work of the Ministry:

" I should like to say one word as to what we are doing with regard to inventions. It is essential for the conduct of the War that the fullest use should be made of the best brains of inventors and scientific men. Perhaps hitherto there has been a want of co-ordination among the various methods of dealing with the projects of inventors. So far as naval inventions are concerned, the First Lord of the Admiralty has set up an Inventions Board under the distinguished presidency of Lord Fisher.

I have just concluded arrangements to constitute an Inventions Branch of the Ministry of Munitions, and I hope it will do for inventions for land warfare what Lord Fisher's Committee will do for sea warfare.

The War Office is handing over the whole question of inventions to us, and careful arrangements have been made to secure that the new branch shall keep in close touch with Lord Fisher's Board to avoid duplication and overlapping, and also with the War Office experts and Army authorities who must have the ultimate voice in deciding whether any particular invention is of service in actual warfare.

I have appointed Mr. E. W. Moir, a distinguished engineer who has already given valuable assistance to my department on a voluntary basis, to take charge of the new branch, and he will not only have an expert staff, but also a panel of scientific consultants on technical and scientific points. It ought to be clearly understood that only a very small minority of inventors' projects are of practical value [laughter]. Many projects fail from technical defects, and many others, though technically perfect, are unsuited to the practical conditions of warfare.

The new branch will have justified its existence if one project in a hundred, or even in one thousand, turns out to be of practical utility in the present emergency.

We have got a good many which we are experimenting upon very hopefully."

Despite the optimism of that speech, it turned out that the setting up of this Inventions Department was only the beginning of our troubles. Although their political heads had given consent to the transfer, the officials of the War Office were most reluctant to part with any vestige of their authority, and a duel began between them and my own officials.

By the beginning of September very little progress had been made. I accordingly saw Lord Kitchener and secured his consent to an arrangement whereby Colonel Hickman, of the War Office, and Mr. Moir should keep in touch with each other so that new ideas and suggestions received by the War Office should be passed along to the Ministry.

But despite this friendly effort to come to a satisfactory arrangement, and the accommodating spirit displayed by the Secretary for War, the trouble with the War Office went on unabated. At the end of September the Ordnance Board set up rival bodies analogous to the Advisory Panel of the Ministry of Munitions. On 16th October I received a letter from Moir which I will transcribe, as it gives a vivid picture of the campaign of obstruction which was at that time being waged by the War Office against the Ministry on this and other issues.

"MINISTRY OF MUNITIONS.
Princes Street,
Westminster, S.W.
16th October, 1915.

The Rt. Hon. David Lloyd George, M.P.,
    6, Whitehall Gardens, S.W.

Dear Mr. Lloyd George,

Having been asked by General von Donop to call on him on Thursday the General informed me that he saw some difficulty in transferring to the Inventions Branch of the Ministry of Munitions the powers granted to the Secretary of State for War by Clause 30, Sub-Section 12, of the Patents Act, 1907. This Sub-Section provides that the submission of an invention to the War Office or the Admiralty shall not act as publication, and on the 2nd October application was made through Sir Herbert Llewellyn Smith for a transfer of that provision to the Ministry of Munitions.

General von Donop's point was that in sending on from the War Office to the Munitions Inventions Department such inventions as the War Office thought were of no use (for these are admittedly the only suggestions that they are sending us at the present time) they might be running some risk of complaint by the inventor should such ideas leak out through their submission to our Panel of Experts. In such cases the War Office might be blamed. My answer to this was that up to the present as they had only sent to this Department things that, according to their lights, were of no use, I naturally had not insulted our Panel by putting these before them, and had dealt with them myself.

Incidentally, I went on to say that I hoped there would soon be some arrangement made by which this Department would not only see the worthless but also the possible ideas that were useful from the War Office point of view.

I also enlarged on the fact that this Department could get no military assistance, and that the assistance which we already had in the shape of Colonel Goold-Adams and Colonel Heffernan was going to be withdrawn from our Panel for, so far as I could ascertain, no sufficient reason. These two experts on artillery, I told General von Donop, were of immense value to us, and far from wanting to reduce the military members of the Panel we wanted to increase them. The reason for suggesting their removal, General von Donop said, was because the balance of the Ordnance Board was overworked and consequently Colonel Goold-Adams and Colonel Heffernan must return to Woolwich. I asked him if he could get someone to take these two gentlemen's places temporarily on the Ordnance Board. *He said that if they did not return he would have them removed from the Board and would not allow them to return even after the War.*

During the course of conversation I pointed out that although this Department had been informed that we could not be given any military assistance the War Office had been able to get together an Inventions Board numbering 14, and including seven Generals, three Colonels, and three Majors. I also told him that my view of the matter was that our Inventions Department had probably relieved the War Office of a good deal of work.

The whole matter seems to me to be a further indication, if any were necessary, of the spirit of objection to civil assistance by the military authorities, and I think that a good deal of the resistance comes from the gentleman with whom I had the interview.

I have not seen Colonel Goold-Adams, but Colonel Heffernan, with some trepidation, admitted to me recently, that he enjoyed his work with us very much, and that he did not want to give it up. He would be quite willing to carry it on on Saturdays or Sundays if he could not do so in any other way. Unfortunately an engagement of this sort would be a very difficult one to carry out except so far as concerns the attending of experiments or visiting work which is going on.

Both Colonel Goold-Adams and Colonel Heffernan are highly intelligent men, and I consider that they should not be removed from your department either in connection with inventions or anything else. The other six members who are left behind on the Ordnance Board should, I imagine, under stress of war conditions, either be reinforced or could probably find it possible to do the work among themselves.

Of course, we can get on without anybody, but there is, I think,

an obvious effort to defeat the objects that you have set yourself
out to attain, at least in some of their departments, on the part of
the military Authorities.

Yours faithfully,

E. MOIR."

The two officers mentioned in this letter were members of the
Inventions section of the Ordnance Board, who had been seconded
for work with the Ministry's Inventions Board as a means of keeping
liaison with the military authorities.   This was part of the arrangement I had come to with Lord Kitchener at the time when it was
agreed that inventions should be transferred to the Ministry of
Munitions for research and investigation.

A fortnight later Mr. Moir wrote me with the news that Colonel
Goold-Adams had been recalled by the War Office.   He enclosed the
Colonel's letter, which was in the following terms:—

"Ordnance Board Office,

Royal Arsenal,

Woolwich.

29th October, 1915.

Dear Mr. Moir,

. . . I regret to say that I have been officially informed to-day
that I am to sever my connection with the Ministry of Munitions,
and no reason is given.

I am more than sorry to have to do so, but it cannot be helped.
When you have had an opportunity I hope you will express my
regret to Mr. Lloyd George.

Sincerely yours,

H. GOOLD-ADAMS.

P.S.—I need hardly say that if my services or advice are wanted
officially at any future date I shall only be too glad to be of
assistance.

H. G. A."

The whole position was unsatisfactory.   Had the Design Department of the War Office been not only efficient and energetic, with an
appreciation of the value of time in war, and had it also worked
harmoniously and with good will with the new Manufacturing
Department, then no serious mishaps or delays would have ensued.
But that was not the case.   The process of manufacture in every
direction was being held up by mistakes here and procrastination
there.

It must be remembered that up to this stage, the Ministry of
Munitions had merely been accorded power to make researches and

investigations with regard to new inventions and improvements. It had no control over the design of either new or old patterns of munitions. That was still in the hands of the War Office, which retained its Inventions Board with overriding authority over the Ministry's researches.

Moreover, in connection with the expansion of manufacture there constantly arose questions of the possibility of modifying or adapting specifications to suit the exigencies of production; and in these questions the Ministry, which was responsible for production, was powerless until a lengthy process of consultation with the War Office and experimentation by these officials produced ultimate sanction. Such questions arose daily, for the practical experience of war was making matchwood of old theories and traditional patterns of munitions. The standard fuses proved unreliable and caused prematures and " duds," the guns and gun-carriages were seen to be capable of improvement, and the new forms of warfare which developed were calling constantly for new types of weapons, or modifications of existing types. The difficulties with regard to the composition of shell explosive and the ingredients of cordite were causing grave anxiety and delay, and the fuses were thoroughly unsatisfactory. The Ministry, responsible for meeting all these changing demands, was unable to move because of the division of authority with the Ordnance Board. While the Board had been responsible for design and production, it had been able to co-ordinate the two, if it so willed, without delay. Obviously, it was desirable, since the Ministry had taken over production, that it should also have the responsibility for design. This divided authority, with the consequent delays on the part of the War Office in coming to vital decisions on fuses and explosives, seriously impeded the work of production of completed shells. Shell cases multiplied at a great rate, but the same pace could not be kept in the matter of the completion until the design of the fuses and the ingredients of the explosives were finally settled.

As I have pointed out, the position with regard to explosives was critical and threatened us with a disastrous shortage of shells for the front. The delays of the War Office in coming to a decision were seriously impeding production. A letter written by General Du Cane on 22nd October, 1915, to Colonel Arthur Lee, who had just taken over Sir Ivor Philipps's position as Military Secretary to the Ministry of Munitions, revealed other directions in which the handling of design by the War Office was proving a source of danger as well as of delay. General Du Cane presided over the Experiments Committee at G.H.Q. in France. The gaines which detonated the shells were so ill-designed that they caused premature explosions which burst our guns at an alarming rate. The total number of our guns at that date was not high.

N*

Here is an extract from General Du Cane's letter:—

". . . I feel pretty confident that you will never get your show running smoothly until you get full responsibility for pattern and experiments. I am pretty sure that you will find that the system by which the War Office and Ordnance Board retain the responsibility for these matters is your great stumbling-block. The M.G.O.'s people seem to me to be mentally exhausted and the Ordnance Board and Experimental Department at Shoebury to be hopelessly congested.

K.'s great argument for keeping control was that he must be responsible for the safety of the troops, because being voluntary soldiers they would all run away or desert if we burst guns like the French. He has failed hopelessly as regards safety, and the result of his control now is to prevent the causes of the trouble being definitely ascertained.

At present our H.E. for 13 and 18 pounders is so unreliable that we cannot use it in large quantities. We have lost 36 guns since the 21st September for an average of one accident to something between 4,000 and 5,000 rounds. That is worse than the French ever were.

During the recent operations the French accidents were one to 120,000 rounds. We have a long way to go yet. I suggested to L.G. that he shall ask the French for 200,000 of their fuses so that we could use them while we are getting our own right. . . .

The loss of 36 guns in a month by prematures represents the highest percentage of bursts ever suffered by any artillery on either side in this war."

Accordingly in mid-November I wrote the following letter to the Prime Minister:—

"6, Whitehall Gardens,
Whitehall, S.W.

My dear P.M.,

I hope it will now be possible to come to a decision as to the future of the Ordnance Board.

Important munitions are being held up or retarded, and I am receiving serious complaints from the Department as to the position of matters. The present situation is an impossible one. M. Thomas has complete control of design as well as manufacture, but I am helpless.

Yours sincerely,
D. LLOYD GEORGE."

Mr. Asquith was at that time temporarily acting as Secretary for War, in the absence of Lord Kitchener, who had gone to the Mediterranean, and he supported my attitude. Strong protests were raised

by the officials at the War Office.   General von Donop foresaw a
general relaxation of strictness of design which would endanger the
safety of the Army.   Sir Charles Harris, the Assistant Financial
Secretary, protested against the breach with precedent and the overthrowing of the remarkable instrument of efficiency existing in the
Ordnance Board.   Manufacturing questions were, according to him,
a part only, and that not the most important part, of the Board's work.
" To make a civilian department responsible for the design of
munitions as well as for their supply would be to head straight back to
the inefficiency that had been experienced in the Egyptian campaign
of 1880.   The Ordnance Board ought to be strengthened, not
abolished."

But in November, 1915, people were more impressed with the
hindrances to action before their eyes than with what a Treasury clerk
witnessed in 1880, and despite these protests the Prime Minister
decided to transfer design of munitions to the Ministry, and to
abandon the Ordnance Board control.   This decision was embodied
in the following memorandum noted by Sir Reginald Brade : —

> " The transfer to the Ministry of Munitions of the responsibility
> for designs, patterns, and specifications for testing of arms and
> ammunition, and for the examination of inventions bearing on such
> munitions, leaves to the War Office the following functions only
> in regard to munitions of war, viz. : —
>
>   1.   The duty of fixing the requirements of the Army both as
> regards the general nature and amount of the munitions
> required, together with the duty of allocating all such material.
>   2.   The duty of receipt, custody and actual distribution of
> all such supplies.
>
> These functions fall to the General Staff and the Quartermaster-
> General's department respectively.   This is the system in force
> with the Army in the field, and, in altered conditions, should be
> followed in the War Office during the War.
> As regards the staffs hitherto employed in this work, such officers
> and others as are necessary for the performance of the limited
> functions remaining to the War Office should be retained; the
> balance being placed at the disposal of the Ministry of Munitions.
> The exact details must be worked out in conference between repre-
> sentatives of the two offices.
> The above was dictated to me by the Prime Minister with
> instructions to notify it as his decision arrived at after consideration
> of the relative positions of the War Office and the Ministry of
> Munitions in which each stands now that the transfer of duties
> . . . has been approved."

Following this decision, on 29th November, 1915, the new duties in regard to design were formally undertaken by the Ministry, and the control of experimental and research bodies, such as the Research Department, Woolwich, was also transferred from the War Office. The Department of Munitions Design, formed within the Ministry, was placed under the control of General Du Cane. The Ordnance Board was dissolved on 4th December, 1915, and reconstituted as the Ordnance Committee and advisory body to both the Ministry of Munitions and the Admiralty.

I quote an extract from a letter I wrote at this date, 30th November, 1915: —

"Lord Kitchener comes home to-day. They have not been able to keep him away. However, in his absence the Prime Minister has handed over the Ordnance Board to me. I have been fighting for this for months, but the War Office have dodged me, and by keeping the Ordnance Board have been able to limit very considerably the energies of all this department. Moreover, when anything *was* accomplished it was only after hard fighting and much unpleasantness."

One last fight remained. Whatever else the War Office failed to do, they at least lived up to the old tradition of the British Army of never knowing when they were beaten. Not only inventions, but design and inspection had now, in set terms, been transferred to the Ministry of Munitions. "Very well," said the War Office in effect, "go ahead, and design and inspect your munitions. But before we issue them to the Army, *we* reserve the right to submit them to our own tests and inspection, and to send out only those designs of which we also approve."

Accordingly the War Office refused to transfer their testing and experimental staff at the school of musketry at Hythe, maintained the department of the Director of Artillery at the War Office as an over-riding authority superior to the Ministry of Munitions, and generally set themselves to nullify wherever possible the change which had been decided on.

General Du Cane, fresh from the battle zone, found himself pitch-forked into this internecine conflict. On 14th December he submitted the following memorandum upon the position: —

"RELATIONS WITH THE WAR OFFICE.

When the Prime Minister and Mr. Lloyd George first discussed with me the formation of a Military Department in the Ministry, to be responsible for the design of munitions, I pointed out to them that this proposal would depend for success on two conditions being fulfilled, viz.: —

1. The necessary officers being placed at the disposal of the Ministry.

2. The removal of possible causes of friction that might result from the maintenance of a rival technical department in the War Office.

The first of these conditions has been fulfilled, but the second has not.

Before I was appointed to my present position I had an interview with the Prime Minister at the War Office, at which he said that he fully recognised the difficulties that must result from my having personal relations with the M.G.O. and the officers of the D. of A.'s directorate in the circumstances that must result from the contemplated measure of reorganisation, and instructions were issued by him that the General Staff would deal with the ' requirements and allocation,' and the Q.M.G. with ' distribution.'

These instructions have not been carried out, and the D. of A.'s directorate still exists at the War Office and deals with these subjects. It is true that arrangements have been made for references from the Ministry on the subject of ' requirements,' to be sent to the Director of Staff Duties, but this officer refers them again to the D. of A. and merely passes on his replies.

The difficult situation that it was hoped to avert, therefore, actually exists. There is still a rival technical department at the War Office, tenacious of its position. The officers of this department feel deep resentment at being deprived of their most important functions, and while they are the officers who should be in the closest possible touch with my department, working harmoniously with my officers, the relations are so strained that they result in their avoiding one another as much as possible. The bad effects of this situation are already beginning to be felt, and if it is allowed to continue it will inevitably result in acute friction and loss of efficiency.

I submit that it is essential that effect should be given at once to the Prime Minister's decision, that a proper channel of communication should be established with the War Office, and that cordial and harmonious relations should be established without any further delay. If this cannot be brought about, I must confess my inability to look forward to the task before me with confidence.

J. P. Du Cane, D.G.M.D., M.G.

14/12/15."

This was plain speaking, and not by a civilian, but by a highly placed staff officer of acknowledged ability and of long military experience. But the War Office still fought on, and on 5th January, 1916, a letter was received at the Ministry, in the following terms: —

"War Office, London,
January 5th, 1916.

Sir,

With reference to your letter No. D.G.M.D./General/8, dated the 13th December, 1915, I am commanded by the Army Council to inform you that they observe that it is proposed in the letter under reply that the final approval to new designs, or amendments to existing designs, should be given by the Director-General Munitions Design. The Army Council, however, consider it most desirable that the approval should not be given until they have expressed their concurrence as to its suitability for adoption as meeting the requirements of the Service. I am to add that the Army Council are strongly of opinion, confirmed by experience, that in most cases before final approval is given to inventions or designs, practical trials on conditions formulated by the Army Council, carried out by troops under the orders and observation of responsible military commanders selected by the Council, are essential. Any special conditions which the Ministry of Munitions desired would be added to those formulated by the Army Council.

In accordance with the views expressed above, the Council desire to retain at their own disposal an experimental staff at Hythe, but they will be glad to arrange for the Director-General Munitions Design to obtain from this staff and that of the Machine-Gun School any assistance that he may desire, and, so far as is possible, they will endeavour to meet the wishes of the Ministry of Munitions as regards the transfer, or loan to that Department, of individual officers now serving at Hythe.

I am, etc.,

R. H. BRADE."

I do not need to point out that this letter was, in effect, a flat refusal on the part of the Army Council to acquiesce in and carry out loyally the decisions already made as to the transfer of design and inspection to the Ministry. I had no option but to bring the matter before the Cabinet War Committee—somewhat, I think, to the Prime Minister's bewilderment, for he had assumed that this was all settled and done with. It was thrashed out in two meetings, on 26th January and 3rd February, 1916, and a formula ultimately agreed which laid it down that:—

"(a) The responsibility for designs, patterns, and specifications and for testing arms and ammunition rests with the Ministry of Munitions.

(b) The Army Council is responsible for the general nature and amount of the weapons and equipment required, but there shall be no court of appeal set up in the War Office from the decisions of the Ministry of Munitions under (*a*).

(*c*) When it is necessary that new weapons, stores, or articles of equipment should undergo practical trials by troops, either at home or in the field, the co-operation of the Army Council should be sought by the Ministry.

(*d*) The Army Council should be represented on Advisory Committees or bodies under the Ministry of Munitions to the extent that the Army Council think desirable."

By this time the War Office had shot their last bolt, and the decisions embodied in the above clauses formed the basis upon which the work of munition design was carried forward thereafter by the Ministry with ever-increasing smoothness and efficiency. But after what an expenditure of time, mental concentration and energy! Meanwhile we had to put up with unsatisfactory gaines and fuses which often caused more trouble to our troops than to the enemy. In February, 1916, a decision was arrived at which ought to have been reached in June, 1915. It naturally took the new department some time to perfect their designs. Manufacturers proceeded with the mechanisms already settled and sanctioned, and when the great battle was fought later on in the year we suffered in the quality of our shells from the delay.

7. TANKS

British in conception, design and manufacture, the Tank was the one outstanding and dramatic innovation brought forth by the War in the sphere of mechanical aids to warfare. It was the ultimate British reply to the machine-guns and heavily fortified trench systems of the German Army, and there is no doubt whatever that it played a very important part in helping the Allies to victory. It might have played a still greater part if it had been developed more promptly through a livelier display of sympathy and encouragement on the part of the War Office, and if its use in the field had been more intelligently exploited. Even in spite of blunders in these respects, the Tank saved an immense number of British lives, and gave invaluable stimulus to the morale of our troops, while spreading terror and alarm among those of the enemy.

I am not concerned here to enter upon the controversial question of the origin of the Tank. The idea of a mechanically propelled, travelling fortress was one which had occurred to a number of inventive minds, even before the War. My own connection with its development only started after I had entered on my duties as Minister of Munitions. In that office, and subsequently as Secretary of State for War and as Prime Minister, I had a good deal to do with the later stages in the evolution and manufacture of this new weapon. The first tentative experiments, mainly carried out by the Air Department of the Admiralty, and backed by the foresight and enthusiasm of Mr. Winston Churchill had already been undertaken when I came on the scene.

My first encounter with the early attempts to produce a self-propelled machine, capable of crossing trenches and forcing its way through entanglements, was when on 30th June, 1915, I was invited with Mr. Winston Churchill to witness an exhibition by R.N.A.S. officers at Wormwood Scrubs of experiments with a wire-cutter affixed to a caterpillar tractor. This was not a tank, nor indeed anything like it; but it was one of the early experimental models, tested and later abandoned in the search for a device which would accomplish what the Tank ultimately achieved.

I was surprised to find that these experiments were being conducted by naval men, mostly temporary officers and ratings of the armoured car division of the Royal Naval Air Force. On enquiry I found that the Admiralty had till then been, and still were responsible for the experimental work of developing this machine for land warfare, and were carrying out their work with funds voted for the Navy and with naval personnel! This was sufficiently astonishing. But my astonishment was succeeded by admiration of Mr. Churchill's enterprise when I discovered that he alone of those in authority before whom the idea of a mobile armoured shelter was placed, had had the vision to appreciate its potential value, and the pluck to back, practically and financially, the experiments for its development.

Later I discovered that the project for a machine-gun destroyer, propelled on the caterpillar principle, had in fact been put forward in October, 1914, by a soldier, Colonel Swinton, who realised how deadly the German machine-guns were proving to our infantry, and laid his idea before the Secretary to the Committee of Imperial Defence, Colonel Hankey, who quickly appreciated its value and importance. Colonel Swinton had followed this up at the beginning of January, 1915, by pressing the matter personally on the War Office. Colonel Hankey had put forward the suggestion, along with other new ideas, in a memorandum dated 28th December, 1914, to the Committee of Imperial Defence. Mr. Churchill wrote to the Prime Minister on 5th January, 1915, supporting the proposal, and fortunately he also proceeded to initiate independent measures for investigation and experiment financed from the Navy vote. "Fortunately," because though the War Office set up a Committee to investigate Colonel Swinton's suggestion, it dropped the project after a few experiments and decided to take no further action. As Mr. Churchill, when Secretary of State for War, said four-and-a-half years later in his evidence before the Royal Commission on Awards to Inventors, with reference to the part played by the War Office:

" Certain investigations and experiments were made, but the matter came to a dead end. . . . I formed the opinion that no real progress was being made and that the military authorities were quite unconvinced either of the practicability of making such engines or of their value when made."

After seeing the experiments at Wormwood Scrubs, I arranged with Mr. Balfour, the new First Lord of the Admiralty that the Ministry of Munitions should undertake responsibility for the manufacture of tanks, while the Admiralty Committee continued experiments. Major Albert Stern, as Chairman of the Ministry's Tank Committee, threw great energy into their production.

The first-fruits of this arrangement appeared when, at the beginning of February, 1916, I went with other Ministers, including Lord Kitchener and various naval and military officers and some representatives from G.H.Q., France, to witness the official trial of the first machine—later known as the " Mother " Tank—at Hatfield Park. The experiment was a complete success, the tank achieving even more than it was asked to accomplish. And I can recall the feeling of delighted amazement with which I saw for the first time the ungainly monster, bearing the inscription " H.M.S. Centipede " on its breast, plough through thick entanglements, wallow through deep mud, and heave its huge bulk over parapets and across trenches. At last, I thought, we have the answer to the German machine-guns and wire. Mr. Balfour's delight was as great as my own, and it was only with difficulty that some of us persuaded him to disembark from H.M. Landship, whilst she crossed the last test, a trench several feet wide.

Sir William Robertson was also very favourably impressed, but Lord Kitchener scoffed as the huge, clumsy creature lumbered and tumbled about, though always moving forward, and expressed the opinion that it would be very quickly knocked out by artillery. He certainly gave me the impression at the time that he thought little of the invention; but a different light is shed upon his attitude by a letter I have quite recently received from General Sir Robert Whigham, who in 1916 was a member of the Army Council, and accompanied Lord Kitchener to the Hatfield trial. He writes:—

". . . Lord Kitchener was so much impressed that he remarked to Sir William Robertson that it was far too valuable a weapon for so much publicity. He then left the trial ground before the trials were concluded, with the deliberate intention of creating the impression that he did not think there was anything to be gained from them. Sir William Robertson followed him straight away, taking me with him, to my great disappointment as I was just going to have a ride in the tank! During the drive back to London, Sir William explained to me the reason of Lord Kitchener's and his own early departure, and impressed on me the necessity for maintaining absolute secrecy about the tank, explaining that Lord Kitchener was rather disturbed at so many people being present at the trials as he feared they would get talked about and the Germans would get to hear of them. It is a matter of history that after these trials fifty tanks were ordered and that Lord Kitchener went to his death before they were ready for the field. I do know, however, that he had great expectations of them, for he used to send for me pretty frequently while he was S. of S. and I was D.C.I.G.S., and he referred to them more than once in the course of conversation. His one fear was that the Germans would get to hear of them before they were ready."

Out of fairness to Lord Kitchener's memory I insert this letter here. If this is the correct interpretation of Lord Kitchener's view, I can only express regret that he did not see fit to inform me of it at the time, in view of the fact that I was responsible as Minister of Munitions for the manufacture of these weapons.

The mention of this tank test recalls to my mind an incident which amused us all at the time, on the occasion of another similar test which took place on Lord Iveagh's estate. The elephantine monstrosity crashed through shrubberies, smashing young trees and bushes into the earth, and leaving behind it a wide trail of destruction. I went to inspect this mashed and mutilated track, and there in the middle of it I found a partridge's nest full of eggs—and incredible to relate, not a single egg had been broken!

The work of production and supply naturally fell to the Ministry of Munitions, and on 12th February, 1916, only a few days after the trials at Hatfield, the War Office formally placed an order for 100 tanks. Soon after manufacture had started, the number of tanks asked for was increased to 150, and work was pressed on at full speed, since the necessity was urgent; but production presented special difficulties, because the type was entirely new and parts had still to be improvised. Shortly after the commencement of the Somme battle, the military authorities decided to make use of a number of the machines as soon as they could be produced, to help on our renewed offensive before the winter months, and in August, 1916, upwards of 50 were shipped over to France. On 15th September, just seven months after the signature of the "charter" authorising their construction, some 49 of these were thrown into the battle.

Not the least remarkable thing about the introduction of these new weapons is the fact that although thousands of persons of all grades necessarily knew all about them, the secret of the tanks was so well kept that their first appearance came as a real surprise to the enemy. The very name "Tank" reflects the fact that during construction they were camouflaged even in name by being described as tanks and water carriers. Hence the tests at Hatfield were described on the programme as a " Tank Trial."

But the decision of the army chiefs to launch the first handful of these machines on a comparatively local operation in September, 1916, instead of waiting until a much larger number were available to carry out a great drive, has always appeared to me to have been a foolish blunder. It was contrary to the views of those who had first realised the need for such a weapon, had conceived it, fought for its adoption, designed it, produced it, and carried out the training of those who were to man it in the field. We made the same error as the Germans committed in April, 1915, when by their initial use of poison gas on a small sector alone, they gave away the secret of a new and deadly form of attack, which, had it been used for the first time on a grand scale, might have produced results of a decisive character.

Mr. Montagu, who succeeded me as Minister of Munitions, supported the " tankers " in their earnest endeavours to keep the tanks from being thrown into action until several hundred had been manufactured and manned by trained crews. I saw the Prime Minister, and begged him to intervene authoritatively. He did not disagree, but referred me to Sir William Robertson. I urged the C.I.G.S. to exert his influence with the Commander-in-Chief. He answered in his most laconic style, " Haig wants them." So the great secret was sold for the battered ruin of a little hamlet on the Somme, which was not worth capturing.

In spite, however, of this decision of the Commander-in-Chief in the field, and of the remarkable moral effect produced by the tanks when they went into action, an atmosphere of doubt and prejudice lingered for some time at the War Office. On 26th September, 1916, the Army Council asked for an additional 1,000 tanks; but after the orders for these machines, and for the vast number of component parts required had been placed, and the complicated machinery for the production of this mass of materials had been set in action, I discovered that the demand had without my knowledge been cancelled by the Army Council. I at once countermanded this cancellation, and took steps to ensure that production should continue.

I retained my belief in the tanks, and my interest in their development and use, throughout the War. Even when I ceased to be directly concerned in their production or employment, the subject not infrequently came under my notice as Chairman of the War Cabinet to which questions were referred, owing to the disagreement of some of those responsible for the origin of the tanks with the methods and tactics employed in their use. Questions of delay in production and supply, sometimes due to lack of continuity in the policy of G.H.Q., sometimes due to difficulties of manufacture, also came up. Indeed, there were moments when I regretted that in the case of the tanks I

Comparison of Shell Filling.

Nature.	Week Ending Sept 25th 1915.	Week Ending Jany 8th 1916	Week Ending July 15th 1916
H.E.			
18 Pr.	—	18,492	264,207
13 Pr.	—	2,000	1,144
4.5"	20,989	36,985	180,411
4.7"	626	7,284	8,538
4.7" Chemical	—	—	3,512
5"	—	3,770	3,071
60 Pr.	3,153	7,912	30,288
6"	5,451	5,025	39,181
8"	1,585	4,019	30,469
9.2" Howr.	1,227	529	23,322
9.2" Gun.	—	638	544
12"	80	283	2,491
15"	—	—	218
Forward	33,111	86,937	593,396

	Total Rounds	Total Round 4.7" & Above
Week ending Sept 25th 1915	119,901	15,426
Week ending Jany 8th 1916	281,613	37,477
Week ending July 15th 1916	1,179,021	168,881
%age increase July 1916 over Sept 1915	883	995

Facsimile of table supplied by Sir Eric Geddes to
in Shell Production during the first year of the

Weeks Ending Sept. 25th 1915, Jan.y 8th 1916 and July 15th 1916.

Nature.	Week Ending Sept 25th 1915	Week Ending Jan.y 8th 1916	Week Ending July 15th 1916.
Brought Forward.	33,111	86,937	593,396
Shrapnel.			
18 Pr. Home.	50,964	125,084	338,554
18 Pr. Abroad.	—	43,300	153,362
15 Pr.	6,924	—	—
13 Pr.	14,740	1420	20,252
4.5"	10,858	11,803	—
4.5" Incendiary	—	—	.790
10 Pr.	—	4,297	—
2.75"	—	499	1,971
4.7"	—	—	5,900
5"	442	127	131
60 Pr.	2,862	7,890	20,861
6"	—	—	355
Anti Aircraft Special	—	256	43,449
Total { Home	119,901	238,313	1,025,659
{ Abroad		43,300	153,362

ns of H.E.	Tons of Propellant	
123	110	*Lt H.S.W. mc... Compliments of Mr Lloyd George 15 July 1916*
239	217	
1,651	1,111	
1,242	910	

r. Lloyd George, showing the remarkable increase
inistry of Munitions, September, 1915, to July, 1916.

had not taken the same course as I had adopted in regard to heavy artillery and machine-guns, and organised at the outset for a larger supply than the War Office demanded.

I do not consider that the tanks were correctly used until the Battle of Cambrai in November, 1917. This action, though indecisive, if not sterile of result—through no fault of the new arm—will, I think, go down to history as one of the epoch-making events of the War, marking the beginning of a new era in mechanical warfare. Nevertheless, even after the remarkable success of the machines, there was a slowness to realise and a reluctance to admit their potentialities, alike as savers of life and as begetters of victory. But by the summer of 1918 their value was definitely established. Joint arrangements were made by the British, French and Americans for their production on a great scale, and the plans for the continuation of operations during 1919 contemplated their employment, as well as that of cross-country tractors, in immense numbers. In fact, had the advance of the Allies in 1919 taken place, it would have been a devastating march of hordes of mechanical caterpillars.

8.   SUMMARY OF ACHIEVEMENTS OF THE MINISTRY

I will not weary my readers by further details of the complex problems which the Ministry of Munitions had to tackle. Some indication of their variety may be gleaned from the fact that the preparation of a single product such as a complete round of 18-pounder high-explosive shell involved the manufacture and assembly of 78 accurately gauged components—15 for the cartridge, 11 for the shell, and 52 for the fuse, gaine, etc. And the main types of shell ran to some twenty-six different sizes and kinds.

By September, 1915, three months after I had taken over the Ministry of Munitions, we were producing 120,000 filled shells of all kinds weekly, as against the 70,000 a week when I took over the job of munitions. In January, 1916, the figure had risen to 238,000 per week; and in mid-July, just after I had left the Ministry of Munitions to go to the War Office, the total weekly output of filled shell rose to 1,025,659.* These figures exclude our purchases from abroad. In commemoration of the passing of the million mark, Sir Eric Geddes supplied me with a table, signed by himself showing this remarkable progress, which I reproduce.

To show the progress which was achieved by the methods we instituted in the Ministry of Munitions, I also give the following table which sets out the total supplies of filled shell which were forthcoming from all sources during the ten months from 1st August, 1914, to 30th June, 1915, and in the twelve months July, 1915, to June, 1916: —

---

* These figures do not represent the full scale and weight of the increase. The most valuable results were in the increased production of heavy shell.

Total output of filled shell or complete rounds:—

				Aug. 1914, to June, 1915.	July, 1915, to June, 1916.
Light	...	...	...	1,877,300	14,748,800
Medium	...	...	...	389,000	3,895,800
Heavy	...	...	...	26,500	566,500
Very Heavy	...	...	...	14,000	288,300
Total	...	...	...	2,306,800	19,499,400

On 6th July, 1916, the day on which I left the Ministry of Munitions to become Secretary of State for War, I was furnished with a report signed by Sir Walter Layton, which stated that:—

" A year's output at the rate prevalent in 1914-15 can now be obtained in the following periods:—

Shell.	18-pdr. Ammunition	...	...	Three weeks
	Field Howitzer ditto	...	...	Two weeks
	Medium Gun and			
	Howitzer ditto	...	...	Eleven days
	Heavy Howitzer ditto	...	...	Four days

The present weekly output in the first three classes is practically equivalent to the whole stock in existence before the War. There was no stock of heavy howitzer ammunition before the War.

A statement could be made on similar lines for other munitions."

I have already shown how, when I took over the Ministry of Munitions in June, 1915, the allowance of shells per battery was eight rounds per day (two rounds per gun). Contrast this with the following extract from the diary of an Artillery Officer (taken from the Royal Artillery Commemoration Book):—

" August 18th, 1916.

The men are very tired, and the layers are nearly exhausted, although we have changed them as often as possible.

My guns have already fired nearly 1,000 rounds each and are almost too hot to touch. . . . At three in the morning I got a telephone message to say that the remainder of the programme was cancelled, and that I was to drop back to my normal 400 rounds a day."

The same officer, under date 1st August, 1916, writes:—

" There are 15 batteries altogether. . . . on a piece of ground four hundred yards long by two hundred wide."

Similar progress can be recorded with respect to artillery. At the outbreak of the War the total number of guns available was 1,902, of

which 1,573 were light, and 329 were ranked as heavies at that date
(i.e., 4.7-inch guns and upwards). In the following ten months to
30th June, 1915, there were manufactured 1,105 fresh guns, 1,011
light and 94 heavy. Between 1st July, 1915, and 30th June, 1916, the
number of guns manufactured was 5,006—4,112 light and 894 heavy.
The number of guns of 6-inch calibre and upwards was multiplied
nearly fivefold.

I have given elsewhere the figures for the notable growth in our
machine-gun supply in this period. Of grenades our output during
the year July, 1915—June, 1916, was 27,000,000 as compared with
68,000 produced from August, 1914, to June, 1915. We similarly
produced 4,279 trench mortars as compared with the War Office 312.

The effect of this artillery can perhaps best be understood by the
evidence of some German records which I will quote. The history
of the 27th (Württemberg) Division, one of the best divisions which
fought at the Somme, states:—

"... A culminating point was reached which was never again
approached. What we experienced surpassed all previous conception. The enemy's fire never ceased for an hour. It fell night
and day on the front line and tore fearful gaps in the ranks of the
defenders. It fell on the approaches to the front line, and made all
movement towards the front hell. It fell on the rearward trenches
and the battery positions and smashed men and material in a
manner never seen before or since. It repeatedly reached even the
resting battalions behind the front, and occasioned there terrible
losses. *Our artillery was powerless against it.* ... In the Somme
fighting of 1916 there was a spirit of heroism which was never again
found in the division, however conspicuous its fighting power
remained until the end of the War."

The history continues that the men of 1918 had not the " temper,
the steadfastness and the spirit of sacrifice of their predecessors. . . ."

Captain von Hentig, of the General Staff of the Guards Reserve
Division, writes:—

" The Somme was the muddy grave of the German field army,
and of the faith in the infallibility of the German leadership, dug
by British Industry and its shells. . . ."

Captain Hierl, an acute critic of the War, says of the Somme:—

" The immense material superiority of the enemy did not fail to
have its psychological effect on the German combatants. The
enemy commanders may put this down to the credit side of their
account as the profit of their attrition procedure. . . . The great
enemy superiority in war apparatus and men was thus made to
pull its weight, whilst the superiority of the German leadership
and training did not get its proper return. . . ."

This evidence from the other side of the battle front demonstrates beyond challenge the importance of the success achieved by the Ministry of Munitions in equipping our forces for battle.

The figures I have given for the increase of output in 1915-16 represent only the first-fruits of the hard work put into the organisation of the Ministry of Munitions. But its greatest claim to recognition is due to the fact that it was organised with a view to expansion if the necessity arose. The business was planned from the commencement not to furnish adequate supplies for one final battle in 1916, but on the assumption that the War might last for years, that there might be a succession of prolonged fights on a great scale and that the demand for munitions of every kind would probably increase and not diminish. That is why up to the end of the War manufacture kept pace with the growing need for more guns, more trench mortars, more machine-guns, more rifles, more ammunition, more explosives, more tanks, and more lorries.

When we organised our factories and ordered our machinery it was on the basis of a demand far beyond that which was contemplated by the Military Staffs in 1915. I was then accused of megalomania because I took this view of the undertaking which was entrusted to me. But in 1916, 1917, and 1918, the generals were very pleased that the swollen-headed plans of 1915 had all materialised and that the stocks in hand were ready to answer to every call made upon them by the soldiers at the front.

It was a much criticised Ministry. When we had hardly begun to pull things together, and to restore order out of chaos, all the confusion was attributed to the new Ministry. "The house that is building is never like the house that is built" and we were blamed for all the untidiness, for the mortar and material scattered about, for the girder skeleton, the unfilled framework, and the unfinished state of the structure.

When I first went to the Ministry of Munitions there was no organisation—when I left it there was no better organised Department in Whitehall, and I should like any of its critics to name one of the old-established Departments which was superior to it in all-round efficiency. The organisation of a big business from the foundation is not an easy task when all the circumstances are favourable. It is none the easier when the ground is cumbered with ill-designed, badly-constructed and ramshackle buildings thrown about at random. It is specially difficult if the old directors from whom this part of the business has been wrenched, and who are thoroughly unfriendly to the new management, still retain an over-riding jurisdiction in vital details.

That we should have succeeded in spite of these difficulties was a triumph for the capable men who threw the whole of their energies into the performance of their arduous duties. Without their ceaseless toil, and their great resourcefulness, achievement would have been quite unattainable in the time and under the conditions.

My view of the functions of the head of such a concern was that its success would depend upon his having a clear idea in his own mind as to the objectives which he should strive to attain, and a definite plan as to the best way of reaching them. After that success would depend upon his gift of choosing the right persons to direct every branch of the business, upon his power of drawing the best service out of them by encouragement, stimulation and support; upon the exercise of such a close and constant supervision over every detail (without getting lost in a jungle of details) as would enable him to discover where things were going wrong, and upon his taking the right steps to remedy deficiencies when he found them, and taking them in time.

I claim for my competent staff and for myself, that when at a critical moment in our history this crucial task devolved upon us, we did not fail our country.

CHAPTER XX

ALLIED RELATIONS WITH AMERICA

DURING the first part of the War, I was not departmentally concerned with our diplomatic relations with the Neutral Powers. I had, however, a very definite interest in the attitude adopted by the United States of America towards the Allies, inasmuch as that great country represented the one important outside source of supply for munitions of war—a matter with which, as I have already related, I very early concerned myself. As a member of the first Cabinet Committee on Munitions Supply, I was already in October, 1914, promoting arrangements for large orders of munitions from the States, and as Chairman of the Munitions of War Committee, and later as Minister of Munitions, I was responsible for a steadily growing stream of supplies from across the Atlantic, which swelled by degrees to considerable dimensions, up to the point when we perfected arrangements for manufacture at home.

During this period, therefore, I had a very special incentive to watch the course of our relations with America. The maintenance of a good understanding with her was not only a necessary condition if our munition supplies were to continue uninterrupted, but a factor of vital importance in ensuring a just and satisfactory settlement of the struggle, whenever the hour of peace should strike.

When a war is in progress, neutral countries are often placed in an embarrassing position. Themselves at peace with all the world, they naturally seek to maintain their normal commercial relations with both the belligerent parties. In addition, they endeavour if possible to improve the shining hour by doing an increased and more profitable business, by supplying the additional demands created by the war at the inflated prices made possible by war's restriction of supplies. But while they thus earn greater profits, they are subject to greater hazards and less consideration. Nations fighting for their lives cannot always pause to observe punctilios. Their every action is an act of war, and their attitude to neutrals is governed, not by the conventions of peace, but by the exigencies of a deadly strife.

The country which is determined at all costs to remain neutral must therefore be prepared to pocket its pride and put up with repeated irritations and infringements of its interests by the belligerents on both sides; compensating itself for these annoyances by the enhanced profits of its war-time trade. Should the difficulties of neutrality prove too great, it is left with the choice either of treating the violation of its rights by one of the belligerent parties as a *casus belli*, or of taking sides, not on the strength of war-time incidents, but rather on its view of the rights and wrongs of the principal conflict. Such, briefly stated, was the problem which confronted the United States of America during the course of the World War. Prior to Armageddon, the firm tradition of the States was to hold utterly aloof from all concern with the tangled relations of the Old World—a tradition enshrined in its doctrine of America for Americans, and let Europe keep its greedy hand off our Continent. In turn, America would leave the rest of the world to Europe alone. Up to the date of the Great War Americans maintained with ostentatious stiffness this traditional attitude. They sought to return to it with a snap when they let go their end of the Treaty of Versailles. Gradually in Europe, Asia and Polynesia alike American statesmen have been driven out of this position by inexorable facts.

It is true that Colonel House, President Wilson's *alter ego,* was keenly interested in international affairs, and visited Europe in the summer of 1914 in the rôle of disinterested and benevolent adviser, to urge a better understanding between everybody and everybody else. It is to his credit and that of Mr. Theodore Roosevelt that they both understood that the theoretical aloofness of America no longer had any basis in realities, and that she would be intimately affected by any European upheaval, whether she professed to ignore it or not. The affable Colonel's visit to Europe was, through no fault of his own, fruitless. Wisdom expressed in gentle tones could not be heard above the roar of the nearing cataract. He found hearty sympathy for his ideas in England, a trumpeting militarism in Germany and political chaos in France. The mass of the American public was as remote in its thoughts and interests from these things as though they were happenings on another planet.

During the opening stages of the war, opinion in the United States was quite as overwhelmingly in favour of maintaining firm neutrality towards the European struggle as opinion was in Britain three days before the declaration of war. With regard to the merits of the respective belligerents, the predominant opinion in America was supposed by this country and France to be pro-Ally, though there was a strong pro-German section among the large German-American population of the Middle West, and a chronic hostility to England amongst the Irish. The intellectuals were believed to be pro-Ally. A careful sounding of opinion among American Universities and Colleges carried out by Sir Gilbert Parker, the distinguished Canadian novelist, in October, 1914, showed an overwhelming sympathy for the Allies. But despite this general tendency, it would be true to say that on the whole, opinion in the States was neither pro-Ally nor pro-German, but simply and solely pro-American. In war, sympathy is a long way off support. President Wilson was universally acclaimed when in mid-August he made a speech calling on the citizens of the United States to observe strict neutrality in act and speech, and at that date even Mr. Theodore Roosevelt rejoiced that his country was geographically able to keep out of the fight. An analysis of the American Press made by Sir Gilbert Parker, at the end of September, 1914, showed that while far more of the leading papers were friendly to the Allies than to Germany, the majority were definitely neutral, and viewed the merits on both sides with a detached impartiality.

Belgium was thousands of miles away from Illinois. German destroyers and submarines at Ostend were not within a few steam hours of New York. German guns at Calais could not block the principal highway to America's powerful ports. German Zeppelins could not bomb Washington and kill women and children in their homes. These things were very remote. We cannot impute this indifference to callousness. An earthquake in Japan with a loss of tens of thousands of lives does not occupy as many columns of a British newspaper as does a railway accident near Carlisle with the loss of a score of lives.

Apart from this, the moral issues were not so free from ambiguity to the American conscience. Many people in this country were unreasonably astonished at this attitude on the part of America. Filled with anger at Germany's wanton aggression in Belgium, and with fear of the threatening monster of Prussian militarism, they could not understand how the great Democracy of the New World should hesitate for an instant about the merits of the issue upon which we had drawn our sword, or should fail to ally itself with us in defence of liberty and justice.

But to the onlookers in America, the issue was not so simple. On 22nd August, 1914, Colonel House wrote to President Wilson:—

" The saddest feature of the situation to me is that there is no good outcome to look forward to. If the Allies win, it means largely the domination of Russia on the Continent of Europe; and if Germany wins, it means the unspeakable tyranny of militarism for generations to come."

Britain and France never quite realised the handicap to their propaganda in neutral countries which was involved in their alliance with the Czarist regime. America shuddered at the idea of any close association with the Government of Russia—brutal, tyrannical and corrupt, in fact, rotten to the core—and that went far to neutralise the horror felt at the Belgian tragedy. America also had a large and politically important Irish-American population, trained to hatred of England as to a religion. Let us be fair. Britain had for centuries given cruel cause for this rooted animosity, and we had not yet repaired the wrong we had burnt into the sensitive and retentive Irish soul. Add to this the fact that Americans were by long tradition accustomed to think of Britain as the despotic monarchy from whose greedy clutch the States had wrested themselves free in the heroic struggles of the War of Independence. There were other considerations which compelled neutrality. The German population in America were a highly respected, diligent, and peaceable element of the community, with characteristics that furnished little evidence in support of the legend of Prussian ferocity. Moreover, they commanded millions of useful votes, which might determine the issue of crucial elections. In these circumstances it will be clear that the general sympathy of America with the Allied cause was bound to be considerably qualified and non-committal. Americans might strongly desire to see the Allies victorious, but not strongly enough to be prepared to endure with patience losses or inconvenience to themselves, or risks to their respective political parties, as the price of Allied victory.

In short, America was not bound by treaty commitments to enter the War on either side. While the predominant opinion (whenever an opinion was formed) was that, on balance, the Allies were in the right, that verdict was too qualified to impose an obligation of honour to march with them to and through the gates of Hell. Failing such obligation, the issue of neutrality or participation in the War became one purely of relative expediency for America. It was her interest to maintain her trade, her prestige, the security of her citizens, and to keep her young men out of the shambles. She would only be forced to fight if fighting was better calculated than neutrality to defend these interests.

It so fell out that while American intellectual sympathies were in the main with the Allies, American commercial interests were open to more frequent and obvious interference by them. Germany's chief power was on land, Britain's on the sea. Germany's invasion of Belgium, her devastation of France, might rouse disinterested wrath in America. But it did not touch American pockets. On the other hand, Britain's firm measures to prevent contraband of war from reaching Germany, and her wide and constantly widening interpretation of contraband, caused serious inconvenience to American shipping and direct interference with American business. Time and time again, the friction created by this interference generated between the two countries a perilous heat which seemed to be within an ace of producing a rupture of diplomatic relations. Once or twice the language of protest bordered on the minatory. These protests undoubtedly introduced a certain element of timidity into our blockade, and Germany profited by the relaxation. Later on, Lord Robert Cecil tightened up our clutch.

To be weighed against these annoyances was the fact that Britain was far and away the wealthiest of the belligerents and was able to place in the United States—and pay cash for—orders for colossal war supplies for herself and her Allies. If we were interfering with America's potential trade with our enemies, at least we were providing her with a magnificent market in Britain, France, and Russia, which stimulated her industries to an unprecedented level of activity and profitableness. This fact had its influence in holding back the hand of the American Government whenever, excited to intense irritation by some new incident of the Blockade, it contemplated retaliatory measures.

Throughout 1914 and 1915, until the prospect of the Presidential election of 1916 began to loom high above the horizon and import a new complication of the issues, the story of the relations between America and the belligerents is that of a country driven backwards and forwards between the two sides by an alternation of incidents, any one of which might easily have tipped the scales for war, had it not been counterpoised by new troubles on the other side; and had it not also been for the stubborn determination of President Wilson to keep his country out of the fight if he possibly could.

The opening weeks of the War found American opinion, as I have said, strongly on the Allied side. We never quite knew where President Wilson's real sympathies lay. We felt that, in the tremendous struggle which was constantly before his eyes, he would have been more than human had his heart not been engaged on one side or the other, whatever his hand might do or his tongue might speak. But his deportment was so studiously unpleasant to both sides that they each suspected him of being antipathetic to their own side. We only knew for a fact that the President was severe in his judgment of Allied actions, and we did not realise that this was due to the fear lest his private sympathies should pervert the strict impartiality of attitude which he was imposing on himself.

Very shortly, the use which Britain made of her sea-power to prevent supplies reaching the Central Powers, even through neutral countries, provoked an outcry in America, particularly from the powerful Copper Trust. Copper was a vital necessity for munitions, and we did our best to stop any supplies of it from reaching Germany. Had Germany been confined to the use of her own ports, this would have been quite a simple matter. But she was bordered by neutral States—Holland, Scandinavia, and at first Italy—and consignments, ostensibly destined for these countries, were really being sent for her benefit. And the United States were very large producers of copper.

On 5th October 1914, Sir Cecil Spring-Rice, our Ambassador in Washington, wrote:—

" The copper interests here are very powerful. . . . We shall have to find some means of crippling Krupp without ruining the mining states here, who possess the ear of the Secretary of State and have a commanding influence in the Senate."

On 3rd November he wrote : —

" We have command of the seas and this is a reason why we are likely to fall foul of all the neutrals. The American conscience is on our side, but the American pocket is being touched. Copper and oil are dear to the American heart and the export is a matter of great importance. We are stopping the export and the consequence is a howl which is increasing in volume. We should probably do the same. But the howl may become very furious soon. . . ."

Early in November, 1914, in accordance with a plan prepared by Mr. Leverton Harris, an agent was sent to New York from this country to attempt to solve this problem by buying up as much as possible of the American stock of copper on condition that the producers should undertake to sell only to purchasers approved by us. But this business proposition was not successful, for pro-German influences were exerted to defeat it. We then proceeded, at Gibraltar and elsewhere, to hold up all copper consignments to neutral countries until we were satisfied as to the bona fides of the consignees. The Governments of the neutral countries in Europe came to the aid of their manufacturers by prohibiting the export of copper, which simplified our release of cargoes to meet their bona fide requirements. We then told the American copper producers that if they continued to sell copper to Germany, we should buy none from them ourselves, but should hold up all their European consignments. Two of the largest American refining companies promptly entered into an agreement with us, and before long most of the others were glad to come into line. One of the last to come in was the great Guggenheim group. Its hand was forced by an announcement made, in reply to a question in Parliament, that the firms whose consignments were safeguarded by agreements with us were welcome to announce the fact, so that orders might be placed with them. Thereupon Guggenheim cabled their representative in London to sign an agreement with the Admiralty.

By the beginning of March, 1915, we had secured control of 95 per cent. of the exportable copper of the United States, and the powerful influence of the Copper Trust was no longer a menace to good relations between us and the States.

Fortunately for the Allies, American annoyance at any action on our part which hampered their trade would ere long be counterbalanced by anger at some more exasperating deed by the Germans.

If in the autumn of 1914 we were holding up neutral vessels and requiring certificates of ultimate destination before we would release their cargoes, the Germans were sowing mines all round the narrow seas, which sank neutral shipping without warning, and were brutally bombarding the unprotected watering places of Scarborough and Whitby. In January, 1915, the Germans took the further step of bombing with Zeppelins the towns of King's Lynn and Yarmouth, and at the end of that month their submarines began a form of attack which was in the end to bring the United States into the War, by sinking unarmed merchant vessels in the open sea.

While these acts increased the moral condemnation of Germany by American opinion, it remained the case that our actions regarding contraband were a more frequent irritation. From a well-informed source we learnt in January, 1915, that the United States was growing less interested in the War as a main item of news: " The air-raid has been commented on in the strongest terms in every paper I have seen, but these things no longer excite surprise. I think I told you that I had seen signs of the public being bored with the War. The proof came last week when the earthquake was reported and the War went to the second or third page." And from another source we were told: " There is a lack of proportion in the information we have concerning the British Navy. We scarcely ever hear of it except when some British ship is blown up by a German torpedo, or when a British ship holds up an American cargo. You can readily see the dangerous psychological effect of this. . . . 'War news' no longer sells. But 'interference with American trade' does sell. It sells, and it has a certain unfortunate effect upon what I call the ' headline mind.' "

As to the general sentiment in the Middle West, we were told: " The German Army wins admiration for its efficiency and courageous performance, but sympathy with its purposes or ideals was lost the day it stepped into Belgium. The War is deplored as unnecessary and preventable, and no one desires anything more than a speedy and conclusive peace. But it must be conclusive. Peace without definite victory would satisfy no one. ' This thing has got started,' they say, ' so let's have it finished once for all.' Meanwhile everyone out here is very busy with his own affairs."

Towards the end of January, 1915, an adroit attempt was made to embroil us with America. The *Dacia*, a German merchantman, laid up in America since July, 1914, was bought by a German-American, registered as an American vessel and sent with a cargo of cotton for Bremen, via Rotterdam. We made it known that we refused to recognise the transfer of flag, and Germans waited hopefully for us to seize the American ship and thus produce a storm in the States. The *Dacia* was duly seized, but by the French Navy, and the plot miscarried. The French cause was popular in the

o

States, and hitherto they had played a minor part in the capture of contraband. President Wilson could of course protest to France, and did so without avail. But his protest did not mark a culmination —perhaps critical—of a series of protests, as it would have done had Britain been the culprit.

Germany thereupon proceeded to announce a submarine blockade of Britain, and declared she would sink every merchant vessel in the seas surrounding these islands after 18th February, 1915, and would not guarantee safety to passengers or crews, even of neutral shipping, since British vessels might be hoisting neutral flags in these dangerous waters, and her submarines would therefore ignore the nationality of flags. This called forth a very strong note from President Wilson, to which Germany only replied that if he would stop all export of munitions to the Allies, and take steps to ensure supplies of raw materials and food to Germany, they would reconsider their attitude.

Britain replied to the submarine campaign by an Order in Council virtually blockading Germany. We did not actually use the technical term "Blockade," as what we announced was not merely or mainly a close investment of German ports, but a cutting off of supplies for Germany by detaining all vessels carrying goods of presumed enemy destination, ownership, or origin. This was of course a novel though obvious variation of the principle of blockade, made necessary by modern progress in transport, which turned every neutral harbour on the Continent into a potential German port. Naturally the flutter of notes backwards and forwards across the Atlantic grew denser and intenser.

During these months, Colonel House was visiting the belligerent countries of Europe as the President's emissary to take soundings as to the possible terms of peace. His presence and the understanding he achieved of the practical realities of the situation, doubtless helped to ease friction between us and America. But his peace efforts were doomed to frustration. At that stage of the War, he found in Britain a readiness to consider a peace based on restoration and indemnity for Belgium, but Germany refused to promise restoration, and would not hear of indemnity.

On 7th May, 1915, while Colonel House was in London, news came of the sinking of the *Lusitania*. That put a sharp end to all possibility of promoting peace talk between England and Germany. The question of the moment became rather whether the United States themselves could any longer maintain their neutrality. The Colonel himself held that they could not and should not hold back any longer. He wrote on 9th May to President Wilson:—

". . . Our intervention will save, rather than increase, the loss of life.

America has come to the parting of the ways, when she must

decide whether she stands for civilised or uncivilised warfare. We can no longer remain neutral spectators. Our action in this crisis will determine the part we will play when peace is made, and how far we may influence a settlement for the lasting good of humanity. We are being weighed in the balance, and our position amongst the nations is being assessed by mankind."*

President Wilson sent a strong note to Germany; but it was a protest, not an ultimatum. The Austrian Ambassador at Washington sounded Bryan, the Secretary of State, and got the assurance that America did not mean to fight. He promptly advised Berlin, which was encouraged to be unaccommodating to Wilson. The click of the President's typewriter had no deadlier rattle behind it. House, meantime, was trying to arrange that Germany would abandon her submarine warfare if England ceased to stop food supplies for Germany. Sir Edward Grey was prepared to consider this.† But he never consulted the Cabinet as to this proposal. Had he done so they would have turned it down emphatically. Whether he consulted the Prime Minister before expressing his readiness to enter into an arrangement on this basis I am not prepared to say. Germany, however, stiffened by the reassurance that America would in no circumstances fight, refused the proposal, and said that she had plenty of food. What she wanted was raw materials. Naturally there could be no thought of letting these in for her munition manufacturers, and the proposal fell through. Had Germany accepted Colonel House's suggestion, the whole course of the War might have been changed. There certainly would have been no starving population in Germany in 1918. That means there would have been no revolution in November, 1918, and the War would have been prolonged for another year. But apart from that, Germany might not have declared that indiscriminate sinking of all ships which brought America into the War. Once more German military arrogance had blundered and by doing so had saved us from one of our worst blunders.

In connection with our blockade policy I should like to pay tribute here to the services rendered by Lord Robert Cecil in pressing forward the firm maintenance and full development of our activities in this field. When he became Under-Secretary of State for Foreign Affairs on 31st May, 1915, the Reprisals Order was already in force. Nevertheless, there was hesitation in high places about maintaining its provisions, as exemplified by Sir Edward Grey's readiness to consider abandoning an essential part of it on Colonel House's suggestion. Such hesitation was not shared by Lord Robert Cecil. In Council and in public he urged its strict observance. His advice

* " Intimate Papers " of Colonel House. Volume I, page 434.
† ibid., page 443.

was consistently in favour of bold measures. His activities in the
Foreign Office were directed to the same end. Ultimately, in
February, 1916, it was decided to appoint a Minister of Blockade,
with Cabinet rank, to co-ordinate the work of all the various Committees and Departments dealing with this matter in its various
aspects. Lord Robert Cecil was the obvious choice for this post,
and he agreed to undertake it—without salary—in addition to his
work as Under-Secretary to the Foreign Office. He was appointed
on 23rd February, 1916, and it was largely due to him that the great
national and international organisation of the blockade weapon was
tightened so that it became one of the decisive factors in our ultimate
victory.

Notes continued to pass between the United States and Germany
throughout 1915 about the *Lusitania*. That a thousand non-
combatant passengers—men, women, and children—including over
a hundred American citizens, should have been thus massacred in
cold blood was a severe strain on the President's pacifism. He stood
it, although Germany repeatedly refused his request that she should
at least disavow the action of her submarine commander. Gerard,
the American Ambassador in Berlin, wrote to Colonel House on 1st
June that: " It is the German hope to keep the *Lusitania* matter
' jollied along ' until the American people get excited about baseball
or a new scandal and forget." President Wilson put the best face
he could upon the matter by making a speech in which he suggested
that the American people were " too proud to fight." He shrank
from taking the action urged upon him by his principal adviser.
Mr. Theodore Roosevelt launched a characteristic attack on the
President's inaction: —

> " Unless we act with immediate decision and vigour we shall
> have failed in the duty demanded by humanity at large, and
> demanded even more clearly by the self-respect of the American
> Republic. . . .
> For many months our Government has preserved between right
> and wrong a neutrality which would have excited the emulous
> admiration of Pontius Pilate, the arch-typical neutral of all
> time . . ."*

The situation was complicated by the fact that while notes were
passing about the *Lusitania*, another liner, the *Arabic*, was also
torpedoed and sunk. Colonel House now wanted the President to
proceed to war without further notes, and for a time the situation
was exceedingly strained. But the German Government promised
to instruct their submarine commanders not to sink further liners
without warning, and after very strong pressure even went so far

* " Fear God and Take Your Own Part," page 353.

as to proffer a tentative disavowal of the action of the submarine commander who sank the *Arabic*. This belated action just—only just—enabled the "will to peace" of the President to survive the Presidential election.

The situation was not eased by information coming to light just at this time, through an indiscretion of the Austrian Ambassador, that the Austrian Embassy, aided by Von Papen, the German military attaché, was planning to cripple American munition plants, so as to interfere with supplies for the Allies. Von Papen and Boy-Ed, the German attachés, and Dumba, the Austrian Ambassador, were sent home, but President Wilson still kept his temper. The Presidential election was drawing nigh, and Wilson was determined to stand for re-election as the man who kept America out of the War.

Probably there was no very powerful desire among the American people at this stage to join in the fight. On 17th September, 1916, Spring-Rice wrote: "The majority want to make money and not to make war." In November he reported that anti-German feeling was growing stronger, together with the view that a victory of the Central Powers would be an immense calamity to the States. But in practice this sympathy showed itself rather in a greater eagerness to do business with the Allies than to make war on Germany. At the beginning of October we raised a loan on the American market to finance purchases of supplies. The loan was for 500,000,000 dollars, secured on the joint credit of France and Britain, in the form of 5 per cent. five-year bonds. In two days it was over-subscribed by about 200,000,000 dollars. As a proof of good will to the Allied cause, this was very gratifying. But Sir Cecil Spring-Rice, writing on 7th October, 1916, of the success of the loan, declared again: "It cannot be too often repeated that the American people are determined to hold aloof if they possibly can, and that the Government cannot take any action of which the great mass of the people do not approve."

Such, in brief outline, was the course and temper of American neutrality prior to the winter of 1916, when the re-elected President made his public bid for peace, to which I shall have later on to refer.

But even in the course of these first two years of War, President Wilson was continually on the alert for an opportunity to intervene and shorten or end the conflict. One effort in particular which he made, in the winter and early spring of 1915-16, was of special interest. As I was called into the discussion that followed, it is an essential part of my War Memoirs.

CHAPTER XXI

PRESIDENT WILSON'S PEACE MOVES

SEVERAL tentative movements were made in neutral countries for mediation during the first few weeks of the War, but they came to nothing. Whether President Wilson could have succeeded in arresting the mad plunge of Europe into war, had he intervened authoritatively and in time, will always remain a matter of conjecture. He made no effort. The suddenness with which the negotiations flared up and exploded the powder magazine probably took him by surprise. In that respect he was not alone.

When the War broke out, President Wilson made a well-intentioned but quite ineffectual gesture. He wrote on August 5th, 1914, to each of the belligerent monarchs a letter in the following terms: —

" Sir,

As official head of one of the Powers signatory to the Hague Convention, I feel it to be my privilege and my duty under Article 3 of the Convention to say to your Majesty in a spirit of most earnest friendship, that I should welcome an opportunity to act in the interest of European peace, either now or at any time that might be thought more suitable as an occasion to serve your Majesty and all concerned in a way that would afford me lasting cause for gratitude and happiness.

WOODROW WILSON."

While that letter was crossing the Atlantic, the Austrians were pressing down on their coveted prey, Serbia; French troops were singing as they swept over the frontier into the lost provinces of Alsace and Lorraine; the German General Staff was at last putting into effect its darling plan, minutely elaborated for years past, of an advance through Belgium that would encircle and destroy the army of France, and bring decisive victory in six weeks. To attempt to hold back the momentum of these vast forces with an offer of mediation was at that stage as futile as to think of arresting the descending blade of the guillotine with an appeal for mercy. Where Sir Edward Grey's proposal for a conference, made before war was declared, was scarcely heard (it certainly was not heeded) in the confusion, the polite and formal plea of a comparatively un-weaponed America for pause and reflection, coming as it did when armies were on foreign soil, could serve only to place on record her goodwill to all parties alike.

The replies were not hurried, and when they came they were universally discouraging. Having started, however reluctantly, the combatant nations all meant to fight it out to the bitter end. Germany was on the whole winning, so her rulers were in no mood for peace. France was pulling herself together after an inglorious beginning. Britain had barely started, but her stubborn spirit had caught a fire which could not easily be put out. Austria, in the act of inflicting what she thought would be an easy castigation on Serbia, had the whip wrenched out of her hand by the gallant army of the Serbs, and her flesh stung with the shame of a scourging inflicted upon her by the people she had despised. She was in a mood to revenge the humiliation by overwhelming force. The Russian tradition had always been to make a clumsy start. The defeat of Tannenberg did not, therefore, dismay this loose-limbed but stout-hearted giant. No one wanted peace. Every nation engaged in the struggle resented the idea of stopping the fight once it had begun. There were far fewer pacifists amongst them on 1st January, 1915, than on 1st August, 1914. There was a deep instinct in the minds of men that this conflict had been coming for a long time, and once it had begun it was better to get it over and done with. The voice of the mediator was, therefore, not heard in any land, and his rôle was everywhere an unpopular one. President Wilson's time for intervention had already passed, and it could not be resumed until the nations were beginning to feel the strain.

The message sent in November, 1914, by Mr. Thomas Nelson Page, the American Ambassador in Rome, to Mr. J. W. Bryan is remarkable, not only for its picture of the belligerent frame of mind but also for the prophetic vision of post-War troubles:—

"American Embassy, Rome,
November 19, 1914.

[received December 7.]
. . . I am conscious here of a strong undercurrent of conviction that when one side or the other in the present war prevails, America will become the next object of attack, either on the part of Germany or of Japan, as the case may be. It seems to be considered that the War will not end until one or the other party is absolutely discouraged and that no tenders of friendly offices will avail before that crisis. Also there is frequent expression of the thought that even should the War be ended in its present status, it would only be a truce until the belligerents, more especially

Germany, had recuperated sufficiently to attack again with better success, and that permanency of peace will depend on a condition in which absolute disarmament can be insisted upon. . . .

THOMAS NELSON PAGE."

At the close of 1915 there was some peace talk whispered about. The losses on all sides had been beyond anything the students of war had ever contemplated. The advantage was still with the Central Powers, but it was becoming increasingly clear to them that they could not cash their gains without incurring further sacrifices even more appalling than those which they had already sustained. The great new army of the British Empire, well drilled and fully equipped, would come into action in its full strength for the first time in the impending campaign of 1916. Neutral spectators had, therefore, some hope that the hour was propitious for taking definite steps towards mediation.

President Wilson was anxious for peace. Apart from the fact that his humane instincts were horrified by the slaughter and barbarity of the War on land and sea, his embarrassments as a neutral were increasing and intensifying each successive month. As I have already related, the British were searching his ships and the Germans were threatening to sink them. The British blockade was interfering daily with American commerce. That roused angry resentment in the American breast. On the other hand, the German counter-measures were an outrage on humanity. The reverberations of the War in the American Electorate were complicating American politics, and the Presidential election was not so far off. There was a powerful German vote which resented the tolerance extended by the Administration to the manufacture of munitions of war for the Allies. There was a still more powerful Irish vote which hated Britain. Apart from these groups, American sentiment was on the whole on the side of the Allies. The wanton trampling down of Belgium by the German legions was largely responsible for the creation of that opinion. War against the Allies was impossible. No Government could have carried the American public into such a war. Intervention on the other side would also mean a divided nation. The poor President was, therefore, harassed and perplexed by a terrible dilemma. What would suit him best would be the part of peacemaker. It fitted in with his temperament as well as with his political difficulties. He therefore sent Colonel House from the ark as a dove of peace to spy out the waters of the deluge in Europe and to report to his chief whether there was a sign of subsidence and any peak visible on which the harbinger of peace could plant her feet.

In this capacity Colonel House visited France, Germany, and Britain with a view to taking soundings about the possibility of bringing the War to an end, and as to the response which would be accorded to any proposal made by President Wilson in that direction. He flew from capital to capital. In Germany he found no prospect of any readiness to consider a peace which would conform to the President's ideals, let alone to the aims of the Allies. The furthest he got with von Bethmann-Hollweg was that Germany might consent to relinquish her conquests of Belgium and French territory in return for a sufficient indemnity. In his highly interesting " Intimate Papers " he gives a graphic account of the American Ambassador's interview with the German Emperor : —

"The Kaiser talked of peace and how it should be made and by whom, declaring that ' I and my cousins, George and Nicholas, will make peace when the time comes.' Gerard says to hear him talk one would think that the German, English, and Russian peoples were so many pawns upon a chess-board. He made it clear that mere democracies like France and the United States could never take part in such a conference. His whole attitude was that war was a royal sport, to be indulged in by hereditary monarchs and concluded at their will. . . ."*

Colonel House reached Paris with an intensified conviction that the German Government would not agree to peace terms which even the most moderate of Allied statesmen could accept. Thereafter he developed the line that any American intervention must take the form of a threat to Germany, followed if necessary by open hostilities, with a view to shortening the War; and, moreover, that such intervention was necessary not only to shorten the duration of the conflict, but to ensure that the peace ultimately made should be one of justice embodying the ideals of the President, rather than one of victorious allies carving up their defeated foe.

To this end, Colonel House urged both in Paris and in London that at a suitable moment the Allies should accept an offer from the President to call a conference of all the belligerents to discuss terms on which the War might be ended; it being understood that if terms acceptable to Wilson were agreed to by the Allies but rejected by Germany, the United States should come in on the side of the Allies to compel Germany's agreement.

It is difficult to come to any clear conclusion as to the reception accorded to the House mission in Paris. He himself clearly formed a favourable impression of the attitude of M. Briand, who was then Prime Minister of France, towards his pacific efforts. But M. Briand was one of those pleasant men who take a long time to understand, and after a prolonged acquaintance you were never quite sure that you knew him sufficiently well even then. He was an enigma even to his closest friends, and no one ever knew what his innermost

* " Intimate Papers," Vol. II, page 139.

O*

thoughts were on any subject. However, by disposition he was a conciliator. He had a greater personal delight in reconciliation than in strife. But although inscrutable where his own individual opinions were concerned, there could be no doubt as to his sensitiveness to parliamentary opinion. And any suspicion of leanings towards pacifism was a crime in Paris. M. Clemenceau was a typical representative of the general attitude of the governing classes in the French metropolis. As for the French peasantry, they had resigned themselves to the leadership of Paris, and they were prepared to go through right to the end if those who were in supreme charge of the interests of their country felt it was necessary for the honour and safety of France to fight on. M. Briand could hardly have dragged France into a Peace Conference at that date unless he had had the most complete assurance that the terms offered would be favourable to France and would contain a guarantee for her future safety. Any rumour of a disposition on his part to countenance such a parley would have ensured his immediate downfall. British Ministers therefore, felt that Colonel House's sanguine disposition had misled him into taking too hopeful a view of the co-operation of France in an endeavour to initiate *pourparlers* with an enemy whose arms, taking the terrain of the War as a whole, were triumphant in the East and the West.

In Britain, the British Cabinet was divided between two points of view. It was not so much that there were some Members of the Cabinet in favour of peace and others opposed, as that the majority were still convinced of the certainty of ultimate victory, while a formidable minority entertained doubts of the possibility of success if the War were prolonged beyond this year. The leading members of this defeatist junta were the Chancellor of the Exchequer and the President of the Board of Trade. Their pessimism had deepened Sir Edward Grey's natural gloom. Mr. Runciman was anxious as to the effect of the submarine campaign upon our sea transport. In his opinion our shipping capacity had already been strained to the utmost by the demands made upon it for the feeding of our population and of our armies, and the carriage of essential raw material for ourselves and our Allies. A few more thousands of our tonnage sunk by the German swordfish that swarmed around the approaches to our harbours, and we could not carry on. Mr. M'Kenna had also serious misgivings as to the financial position. He doubted whether it would be possible much longer for us to raise the funds necessary to enable us to finance essential purchases for ourselves and the Allies in countries across the sea, at the rate we were then expending our reserves on the War. He circulated to the Cabinet in September 1915, two dismal papers from Sir John Bradbury and Mr. J. M. Keynes respectively. Sir John Bradbury was an exceptionally able man, with exceptionally orthodox ideas about finance and the gold standard. He ends an elaborate and discouraging review of the financial possibilities as follows : —

" It seems clear . . . that unless there is either an early and very large reduction of civil and military consumption, an increase of production by the withdrawal of a part of our forces in the field and their return to civil employment or a drastic curtailment of credits to Allies, further borrowing here will only be possible at the price of such an inflation of credit in relation to available commodities as will finally upset the balance of exchange and seriously impair our power to purchase either munitions or food-stuffs in America."

Mr. Keynes was more alarming and much more jargonish in his formidable paper. With the help of what he hints is an over-sanguine estimate of our borrowing possibilities in America we would get through to the end of the financial year, i.e., the 31st of March, 1916, provided our liabilities were not increased by fresh orders (he does not specifically mention our orders at the Ministry of Munitions for machine tools and rifles), but after that, the Deluge —unless peace intervenes. As to our existing commitments : —

". . . We ought to be able to do this without producing a catastrophe in the current financial year [i.e. up to 31st March, 1916], *provided peace puts us in a position to cancel the infla-tionism immediately afterwards. Otherwise the expenditure of the succeeding months will rapidly render our difficulties insupportable. This leads us to the meaning of ' inflationism ' and the consequences of depending upon it."*

Then comes a professional exposition on the character and inevitability of " the catastrophe," and he concludes : —

" The alternatives presented to us are, therefore, alternatives of degree. If by flinging out our resources lavishly we could be sure of finishing the War early next spring, I estimate that they might be about equal to our needs. If, on the other hand, it would be over-sanguine to anticipate this, it must be considered whether it is more desirable to average our expenditure, or alternatively, to be lavish until about next January, to appreciate the prospects in front of us somewhat suddenly at about that date, and then, having regard to the near future, to curtail rigorously, and tell our Allies that for the future they must look to themselves.

It is certain that our present scale of expenditure is only possible as a violent temporary spurt to be followed by a strong reaction; that the limitations of our resources are in sight; and that, in the case of any expenditure, we must consider not only as heretofore, whether it would be useful, but also whether we can afford it."

Mr. Winston Churchill in one of his amusing outbursts, once said that this country was governed by the 31st March. Put the British Empire at one end of the scale and the 31st March at the other, and the latter would win every time. That was Mr. M'Kenna's view.

Chancellor and President of the Board of Trade more than hinted at the possibility of starvation for our sea-fed island. Mr. M'Kenna's nerve was shaken by these vaticinations of his chief adviser, Mr. J M. Keynes. The latter was much too mercurial and impulsive a counsellor for a great emergency. He dashed at conclusions with acrobatic ease. It made things no better that he rushed into opposite conclusions with the same agility. He is an entertaining economist whose bright but shallow dissertations on finance and political economy, when not taken seriously, always provide a source of innocent merriment to his readers. But the Chancellor of the Exchequer, not being specially gifted with a sense of humour, sought not amusement but guidance in this rather whimsical edition of Walter Bagehot, and thus he was led astray at a critical moment Mr. Keynes was for the first time lifted by the Chancellor of the Exchequer into the rocking-chair of a pundit, and it was thought that his very signature appended to a financial document would carry weight. It seems rather absurd when now not even his friends—least of all his friends—have any longer the slightest faith in his judgment on finance.

Luckily Mr. Bonar Law and I knew well what value to attach to any counsel which came from the source of the Chancellor's inspiration and, therefore, we both treated the fantastic prediction of British bankruptcy " in the spring " with the measure of respect which was due to the volatile soothsayer who was responsible for this presage of misfortune. I was still less impressed by these prophecies of evil because I knew it was part of the campaign which the Treasury were waging against my great gun programme. They had succeeded in scaring Lord Kitchener. I knew more about the resources of credit of this country. Mr. Bonar Law urged that American (North and South) securities held in this country should be mobilised and sold or pledged to pay for purchases overseas. This practical suggestion was subsequently adopted and all went well.

When the hour of indicated doom struck and we still bought greater quantities than ever of food, raw material and munitions from abroad and were paying for them and our credit was still high the date of impending collapse was postponed until the autumn The fall of the year and the fall of the British Empire would arrive on the scene arm in arm. In his forecasts Mr. Keynes made the same mistake which had brought the late Mr. Baxter's prophecies into disrepute. He had been too definite in the dates for the end of the world. Some of these had already passed. When the fateful days arrived without any indication of the heavens above us being rolled together as a scroll, a fresh date further on was chosen. You may do that kind of thing once and perhaps twice, but repeated failures discredit the prophet. The Cabinet as a whole were not, therefore, at this time unduly depressed by Mr. M'Kenna's pictures of approaching famine, because they had ceased to believe in the impish Baxter who at the Chancellor's invitation had wandered into the Treasury.

After Colonel House had put his views before Sir Edward Grey and the Prime Minister, the latter decided that it would be desirable that other Ministers should be brought into consultation. It was therefore arranged that on 14th February, 1916, Mr. Asquith, Sir Edward Grey, Mr. Balfour and myself should be invited to meet Colonel House at dinner at Lord Reading's house. He there placed before us his ideas as to the summoning by President Wilson of a conference of all the belligerents to discuss peace terms. Colonel House has given some account of this important talk in his " Intimate Papers," but that account is by no means complete, and unless the whole purport of the conversations is given the public cannot judge the reasons for the failure of this peace move. He states in his book that at the Reading dinner the terms of an acceptable peace were outlined by me, who, " somewhat to his surprise and apparently also of Sir Edward Grey " was ready to agree to intervention by the President. As the sequel was determined by these terms, I propose to set out exactly what my proposal was. I was opposed to the summoning of a conference without some preliminary understanding with the President as to the minimum terms which the Allies were to insist upon with his sanction and support. A conference without such an agreement would have been productive of the most serious consequences to the *morale* of the Allied Countries, in the event of its failure. Having regard to the unpropitious military situation such a fiasco was quite within the realms of probability. In my opinion, therefore, it was undesirable to take such a risk unless we were practically assured beforehand that if Germany proved intractable on these terms the U.S.A. would throw in her lot with us.

These terms were acceptable to the Prime Minister, Sir Edward Grey, Mr. Balfour, Lord Reading, and also to Colonel House. The latter, who knew President Wilson's mind better than any living man, was convinced that the terms would also meet the President's view of the justice of the case. It is interesting to recall these terms in order to show the conditions of peace which would have satisfied the British leaders of that date. They included the restoration of the independence of Belgium and Serbia, and the surrender of Alsace and Lorraine to France, provided that the loss of territory thus incurred by Germany would be compensated by concessions to her in other places outside Europe. There were to be adjustments of the frontiers between Italy and Austria so as to liberate Italian communities still under the Austrian yoke. Russia was to be given an outlet to the sea. There were also to be guarantees against any future recurrence of such a catastrophe as this World War.

Colonel House promised to cable to President Wilson a full report of the proceedings and to obtain his assent to the conclusions arrived at before the British Government notified their acceptance of President Wilson's proposal. Sir Edward Grey insisted that before any final decision was taken the Allies should be consulted.

Why was this conference never summoned? Who was responsible? Had it come off either Germany would have accepted the terms as soon as she realised that President Wilson was committed to their enforcement, or, in the event of their rejection, America would have come into the War in the spring of 1916, instead of 12 months later. The world would have been saved a whole year of ruin, havoc and devastation. What a difference it would have made! Was the fiasco due to Sir Edward Grey's reluctance to press the idea upon our French Allies, or was it attributable to the insertion by President Wilson of one fatal word in the gentleman's agreement suggested by Colonel House? The document as cabled by Colonel House definitely committed the President to war (subject of course to the assent of Congress) in the event of rejection by Germany of a conference into which he was prepared to enter with a pledge to the Allies of support for minimum terms. The President in his reply inserted the word "Probably" in front of the undertaking. Sir Edward Grey's view was that this completely changed the character of the proposal, and therefore, he did not think it worth while to communicate the purport of the negotiations to the Allies. As far as I can recollect he made no effort with President Wilson through Colonel House or any other intermediary to restore the position as it was left by the Reading dinner conversations. The real explanation probably is that President Wilson was afraid of public opinion in the U.S.A. and Sir Edward Grey was frightened of our Allies. The world was once more sacrificed to the timidity of statesmanship. This great and at one time promising plan thus fell through. The bloody campaigns of 1916 were fought without any decision. Hundreds of thousands of brave young men fell on the scarred heights of Verdun, on the muddy plateau above the Somme, in the foothills of the Istrian and Tyrolese Alps, in the forests and swamps of Russia, on the slopes of the Carpathians, and in the torrid regions of Mesopotamia and Central Africa. Every military staff in all the armies at every stage of the sanguinary road was convinced that victory was awaiting their strategy just round the next corner. Politicians must not be allowed to snatch triumph out of their grasp just as it was all but within reach. Peace discussions were therefore postponed until the deafening sound of the great guns abated.

Looking back on this period in the light of the information which

:ame later to hand, it is clear that if Colonel House's plan had been
acted upon, the most that could have been hoped from such a conference as President Wilson could then have assembled would have
been the earlier entry of the United States into the struggle, and the
shortening of the War which that event would have brought about.
Nothing is more certain than that Germany in 1916 would have
insisted on terms which would have been entirely incompatible with
those that the President's Vicar-General in the outside world, Colonel
House, had agreed upon with us. A secret dispatch from Washington in the spring of 1917 advised us that when Bernstorff handed to
the State Department of the U.S.A. the note informing them of
Germany's intention to embark upon unrestricted submarine
warfare, he made simultaneously a confidential communication to
Colonel House, putting in writing Germany's peace terms. These
were: —

1. The practical occupation of Belgium;
2. The straightening out of their French frontier in order to
include the French iron fields;
3. Indemnity from France;
4. Full compensation for all commercial losses.

It will be seen that these terms were not only entirely at variance
with those which had been suggested by America, but were obviously
utterly inacceptable to the Allies. They were in fact terms which
assumed Germany to be victorious, and no peace could possibly have
been based on them.

Whether the declaration of these terms by Germany at a conference
would have brought President Wilson into the War on the Allied
side in 1916 is perhaps slightly less certain. The President was at
that time resolutely pacifist, and it is possible that Colonel House
credited him with a greater readiness to participate in the struggle
than he would actually have shown when it came to the test. While
he could not have accepted the German terms, he might at that stage
have contented himself with trying to balance them against the
proposals of the Allies, and urge the *via media* of an inacceptable
and inconclusive peace. Count Bernstorff noted in the course of a
report on 6th September, 1916, that: "Wilson regards it as in the
interest of America that neither of the combatants should gain a
decisive victory." President Wilson fought his election in the late
autumn on his policy of keeping America out of the War. On this
he won.

In this connection I am tempted to quote an interesting letter
which Theodore Roosevelt wrote after the American Presidential
Election in November, 1916, to Lord Lee of Fareham. At that time
Roosevelt was an energetic supporter of the Allied cause, and Lee
had suggested that he should visit England and lecture on the issues

of the War. Writing to decline the invitation, he hints—what was
in fact the case—that his uncompromising support of the Allied
cause had lost him the sympathy of both the political parties in the
States to such an extent that no one, least of all Wilson, would dare
to associate himself with a policy publicly advocated by him. His
letter was in the following terms:—

> " Sagamore Hill,
> November 10th, 1916.

Dear Arthur,

I have carefully considered your letter (no letter from Grey has
come). My dear fellow, I hate not to do anything you ask. But
my judgment is most strongly and unqualifiedly that it would be
a grave error for me to do so in this case. I have consulted
Whitridge and Bacon, both of whom are at this moment more
interested in the success of the Allies than in any internal
American questions, and they agree with me—Whitridge feeling
at least as strongly as I do in the matter. Wilson has probably
been elected, and if Hughes were elected it would only slightly
alter the case so far as this particular proposal is concerned. For
a number of months to come the American public would positively
resent any conduct on my part which would be construed as
indicating my presuming to give advice about, or an expression of,
American opinion. Wilson would certainly endeavour to do
exactly the opposite to what he thought I had indicated; even
Hughes, if elected, would resent any seeming desire of the British
and French to consult me; and my coming over would give every
greedy sensation-monger in the Yellow Press, and even in the Pale
Saffron Press, the cue to advertise the fact, with statements and
inferences grotesquely false but very mischievous. Moreover, those
whom I spoke to on your side of the War could not but feel that
my words carry weight, and to this extent I cannot be guilty of
deception towards them, for my words carry no weight, and it
would be unwise to pay any heed to what I said as representing the
American people. At the moment I am as completely out of
sympathy with the American people as I would have been out of
sympathy with the English people in 1910 or the French people in
1904. The Wilson " policies " are those of the Democrats, who
have just polled a bare plurality of the popular vote. Mr. Wilson
would like to antagonise every proposition I make. The Repub-
licans by an overwhelming majority nominated Hughes precisely
because he did *not* represent my views; they thought it wise to
dodge the issues I thought it vital to raise. No other man of
national importance (for Root really exerted not the slightest
weight in the campaign and only spoke once to a half-empty hall)
took the stand I took—which I took in every speech. I was the

only man who raised my voice about Wilson's iniquity in suffering the German submarines to do as they did on our coast.

If I went abroad I could give you no advice of even the slightest worth. I would diminish my already almost imperceptible influence here at home. I would expose myself to bitter malefications—no matter how much one condemns one's own country, one cannot stand condemnation of it by promiscuous outsiders (*you* may say *anything* and I will say ditto to it). I would like to visit the front at the head of an American division of 12 regiments like my Rough Riders—but not otherwise.

Always yours,

THEODORE ROOSEVELT.

P.S.—The amiable Bryce steadily exerts what influence he has here on behalf of the Pacifist crowd, who are really the tepid enemies of the Allies."

This rather bitter and disillusioned letter shows the doubts and uncertainties with which the strongest American leader of his time viewed the prospect of his country taking a really bold and decided course in its dealings with the combatant nations of Europe. Later on, history was to afford another proof that the bold course is the best one.

CHAPTER XXII

THE IRISH REBELLION

THE long-drawn-out and wearisome tragedy of the relations between
Great Britain and Ireland played an important part in the World
War. There can be little doubt that the expectation on the Continent
that Britain had for the moment sunk so deep in the quagmires of the
Irish bog as to be unable to extricate her feet in time to march
eastward, was one of the considerations which encouraged Germany
to guarantee Austria unconditional support in her Serbian adventure.
The continued unrest in Ireland, and the political differences
between statesmen here as to the proper method of dealing with
them, imported an undercurrent of divided counsel and party feeling into our deliberations about our principal task. And ultimately,
the rebellion of Easter, 1916, quickly though it was suppressed, interposed a deplorable distraction and left an aftermath of bitterness and
danger which hampered us throughout the remainder of the War
and for years afterwards.

Nor can it be forgotten that the Irish situation formed an abiding
ground of antagonism to Great Britain amongst the large and
politically powerful Irish-American section in the United States.
Had there been no Irish grievance, it is by no means improbable
that America would have come much earlier into the War, and
by so much shortened its duration.

I do not propose to enter on a discussion of the Irish question.
But in considering the events of 1916, and the part I was called
on to play in bringing about some alleviation of the trouble, it is
important to bear in mind the background against which those
events were set.

In the early summer of 1914, in view of the fact that the Liberal
Government had succeeded after a three years' fight in carrying
through a measure of Home Rule, the Protestant North had reached
a state of incipient rebellion, and was arming and drilling for
resistance to the decision of the Imperial Parliament. The Catholic
South had begun to copy these tactics, and raise National Volunteers
to match the Ulster Volunteers of the North. There was a gun-
running at Larne to supply Ulster with guns from Germany; and
then one at Howth to supply Southern Ireland. The paradox of the
situation was that Ulster's rebellion was acclaimed by a powerful

section of British opinion as loyalty, while Southern Ireland's preparations to defend the decision of the Imperial Parliament were
denounced as sedition.

At the outbreak of the Great War, the Home Rule Act was suspended in order to allay the threatened rebellion of Ulster, backed
by the Unionist party in Great Britain, and to procure a measure of
unity, in face of the common danger. For the moment this action
achieved its purpose, but it may be doubted whether in the long
run it proved profitable. For Southern Ireland, seeing its hopes
dashed at the moment when they were about to be realised, at first
sulked in resentment and soon became a mass of seething disaffection;
and, after an interlude of strife and suffering of a deplorable
character, it had to be pacified by concessions far more extensive
than would have satisfied it in 1914.

The irritation of Southern Ireland was exacerbated by a number
of needless follies. When the World War broke out, its spokesman,
Mr. Redmond, pledged its full support to Britain in the conflict, and
heartily encouraged the efforts to recruit its young men for the army.
But with extraordinary tactlessness, old officers were let loose on
Munster, Connaught and Leinster to lure men to the colours to the
strains of " God Save the King." Both the tune and the tone were
anathema in those parts, and roused every instinct of sedition. I
relate further on, in my sketch of Lord Kitchener, how he approved
the embroidery of the Red Hand of Ulster on the banner of the
northern division, but banned the South Irish Harp on the southern.
The slap in the face which this curious procedure administered to
Southern Ireland stamped out every spark of kindling enthusiasm
there, and caused a serious set-back to recruiting.

Throughout 1915 and early 1916, seditious movements grew in
strength. The Irish Volunteers, a body openly formed to enforce
the Sinn Fein policy of complete independence for Ireland, drilled
publicly and rapidly recruited their numbers. Funds came to them
from America, with leaflets designed to increase disaffection. In
Dublin especially the note of rebellion was everywhere to be heard.
Full information of these developments was supplied to the Irish
Secretary, Mr. Augustine Birrell, but he, wisely or unwisely, refused
to sanction any drastic action to suppress the movement. He was
content to hope and pray that matters would not come to a head till
the War was over—after which the coming into force of the postponed
Home Rule Act would solve the difficulty.

Admittedly the problem was an awkward one for statesmanship.
How could action be taken against the Irish Volunteers unless corresponding action were also taken against the Ulster Volunteers, who
were also armed to resist the Government and to oppose an Act now
on the Statute Book? How could we defend the rights of Belgium
and in the same breath coerce Ireland for arming to secure for herself

a measure of independence which the majority of the House of Commons had admitted to be just? How could we resort to coercion in Ireland—unless events made it inevitable—and maintain with America the friendly relations which were essential to our success in the War? There seemed plenty of excellent reasons for doing nothing. There always are. So nothing was done.

In April, 1916, the inevitable happened. Encouraged by Germany and the Irish-Americans, the Sinn Fein leaders in Dublin decided to bring matters to a head by an open rebellion. A ship was to come over from Germany to Ireland, bringing the Irish revolutionary leader, Sir Roger Casement, and an outbreak was timed to take effect on Easter Day, 23rd April, two days following his arrival.

Sir Roger Casement failed to turn up in Ireland on the 21st, and on the following day the news appeared that he and the ship which bore him had been captured by the British. Notices were sent out by the Irish Volunteer headquarters to postpone the Sunday arrangements. But on Easter Monday, 24th April, a rising occurred in Dublin and some parts of the country.

The provincial disturbances were small and easily suppressed. The Dublin outbreak was far more serious, and for a time the Irish capital was held by the forces of revolt. Troops were hastily summoned, martial law proclaimed, and in a couple of days the rising had been quelled, not without bloodshed. Several of the rebellious leaders were tried by court martial and shot.

Obviously matters could not be allowed to rest there, and after going into the matter carefully, Mr. Asquith went over to Dublin to examine the situation on the spot. Martial law was still in force, and the three principal officers of the Crown—the Lord Lieutenant, Lord Wimborne, the Chief Secretary for Ireland, Mr. Birrell, and his Under-Secretary, Sir Matthew Nathan—had all resigned their posts.

On his return, Mr. Asquith approached me with the suggestion that I should take up the task of trying to negotiate a settlement with the Irish revolutionary leaders. My sympathy with their cause was known. On the other hand, I had been recently very much detached from the Irish developments, as I had been fully immersed in my task of equipping our armies with munitions, specially in view of the coming campaign on the Somme.

The request came at an awkward moment. For some time I had been urging on our leaders a measure of closer co-ordination with our Russian Ally, and had at last got them to agree to a practical step in this direction. Lord Kitchener was to proceed to Russia via Archangel to consult with the military authorities there about closer co-operation in the field, and it had been arranged that I should go with him to find out for myself the truth about the appalling shortage of equipment of which we had heard, and see in what way the Ministry of Munitions could best help to remedy it. These were

10 Downing Street.
Whitehall. S.W.

Secret   22 Aug 16

My dear Lloyd George,

I hope you may
see your way to take
up Ireland: at any
rate for a short time.
It is a unique opportu-
nity, and there is
no one else who could
do so much to
bring about a permanent
solution

Yrs very sincerely.

H.H. Asquith

Facsimile of the letter written by Mr. Asquith which induced Mr. Lloyd
George to abandon his proposed visit to Russia with Lord Kitchener.

matters in which I was for the moment far more closely interested than I was in the pitiable and rather squalid tragedy which had overtaken our lack of policy in Ireland.

But my plans were upset by Mr. Asquith's proposal. It was conveyed to me in a letter which I reproduce in facsimile, the terms of which were as follows:—

" 10, Downing Street,
Whitehall, S.W.

SECRET.   22nd May, 1916.

My dear Lloyd George,

I hope you may see your way to take up Ireland; at any rate for a short time. It is a *unique* opportunity and there is no one else who could do so much to bring about a permanent solution.

Yours very sincerely,
H. H. ASQUITH."

For me at least this letter has a peculiar interest, for it saved my life! Much against my own inclination, I decided that I could not refuse Mr. Asquith's request, so I had to tell Lord Kitchener that I could not accompany him on his voyage, and I asked him to do his best to find out for me the munition position there and the way in which he thought the British Munitions Ministry could render any help in the equipment of the Russian Armies. Even while Mr. Asquith was penning his letter, an obscure German vessel was steaming across the North Sea towards the cold northern waters around the Orkneys, bearing a mine which it was presently to loose at a venture off the Scottish coast in the hope of sinking some vessel from the Grand Fleet cruising around these wind-swept Scottish islands. A fortnight later that mine struck the *Hampshire* with the renowned and almost legendary figure of our British Minister of War aboard. But for this letter, I should have been with him and shared his fate. This escape, at least, I owe to Ireland.

On 25th May, Mr. Asquith announced in the House of Commons that I had undertaken to devote my time and energies to seeking a solution of the Irish situation, and he explained that my decision was the outcome of the unanimous request of all my colleagues in the Government. I had already begun to consult with the political leaders of both the Irish Nationalist and the Ulster Unionist parties. The negotiations were conducted at the Ministry of Munitions. The Nationalists were represented by Mr. John Redmond, Mr. John Dillon, Mr. T. P. O'Connor and Mr. Devlin. Ulster was represented by Sir Edward Carson and Mr. James Craig.

Redmond was not only a great orator but possessed elements of statesmanship of a high order. The fact that he was given no chance to apply his qualities in the rebuilding of his native land is one of the myriad tragedies of Irish history. Devlin had all the charm, wit and eloquence of Irishmen at their best. To these graces and powers he added fundamental shrewdness and sagacity. Of Carson—one of the most remarkable products of Irish soil—I speak later on. Craig (afterwards Lord Craigavon, the Irish Premier) possessed all the gifts of an American political boss of the nineteenth century. T. P. O'Connor had a much wider experience of the world than his colleagues and that made him more tolerant and accommodating as a negotiator. Redmond, O'Connor, Devlin, Carson and Craig displayed a genuine anxiety to reach a settlement. Dillon was difficult. He had the temperament and mental equipment of the fanatic. He always found it hard to accommodate his ideas to the tyranny of facts. In private he was genial, pleasant and gentle of speech. In public he was a scold. In negotiation he was inclined to be truculent and unyielding. His stubbornness over comparatively trivial details helped to wreck the Buckingham Palace negotiations just before the War. When he ultimately gave assent to the terms reached in these negotiations he did so with a mental reservation, and his rigid and niggling interpretation of the arrangement arrived at proved to be fatal later on, for it made it impossible for Redmond and Devlin to meet Unionist misgiving by even the slightest appearance of concession.

After a discussion I laid before them a series of proposals. These proposals were:—

1. To bring the Home Rule Act into immediate operation;

2. To introduce at once an Amending Bill, as a strictly War Emergency Act to cover only the period of the War and a short specified interval after it;

3. During that period the Irish members to remain at Westminster in their full numbers;

4. During this war emergency six Ulster counties to be left as at present under the Imperial Government;

5. Immediately after the War an Imperial Conference of representatives from all the Dominions of the Empire to be held to consider the future government of the Empire, including the question of the Government of Ireland;

6. Immediately after this Conference, and during the interval provided for by the War Emergency Act, the permanent settlement of all the great outstanding problems, such as the permanent position of the exempted counties, the question of finance, and other problems, which cannot be dealt with during the War, would be proceeded with.

The above is an abbreviated summary of my proposals, which in their full form extended to fourteen clauses. Sir Edward Carson and Mr. Redmond promptly went over to Ireland to consult with their respective followers about the scheme. Despite the fact that it contained proposals most unpalatable to each of the disputing factions in Ireland, both sides agreed to accept it, and to do their best to work it loyally.

I wish the story could end there. But it cannot. The plan which held out such promise for a settlement of the ancient grievance of Ireland, and which was accepted by both parties in Ireland itself, was thereafter deliberately smashed by extremists on both sides. My first warning of this opposition came in the shape of a memorandum sent to me on 11th June, 1916, by a prominent Unionist member of the Cabinet—the day before my scheme was accepted without opposition by the Ulster Unionist Council, and a week before it was also unanimously approved by a gathering of Nationalists at Belfast. The memorandum was as follows:—

" Information reaches me from both England and Ireland, North and South, that there is no disposition to come to a settlement, that the line taken by the leading Unionists, as the result of their interviews in London, is that the Unionist Party in Ireland are being driven by the Prime Minister and Minister of Munitions into accepting a situation which they know to be morally wrong and wrong politically, that the Nationalist Party are sullen and hostile and have no intention of abandoning their policy and programme whatever may be the decision of their leaders.

At the same time I hear the gravest accounts of the condition of Ireland. If one half of what I have heard is true it seems to me to be quite clear that this is not the moment to embark upon any political experiment. The situation is very different from what I believed it to be when we first discussed this question, far graver and more serious, and unless I am wholly misinformed I don't think it would be possible for me to give my assent to any agreement including the adoption of Home Rule, the more so as I have excellent authority for the opinion I hold very strongly that, whatever may be said or written, the U.S.A. will not interfere with the supply of munitions or other supplies."

This unexpected communication by one of my own Cabinet colleagues, who had been a party to the decision authorising me to carry out the negotiations, and who had talked over with me my scheme before I finally submitted it to the leaders of Irish opinion, was characteristic of the type of bitter partisan hostility which the prospect of a settlement of the Irish trouble called forth from extremists who would rather see no settlement at all than one which did not fully conform with their ideas. On 23rd June—the very day on which final approval of the proposals was recorded by a representative Conference of the Ulster Nationalists—a manifesto denouncing it was issued by five Unionist Peers—Lords Balfour of

Burleigh, Cromer, Halsbury, Midleton and Salisbury. Two days later Lord Selborne, the President of the Board of Agriculture, resigned from the Cabinet as a protest against the scheme.

Lord Lansdowne, the veteran Tory leader, fired the next shot. On 28th June I received the following note from Mr. Asquith:—

> " 10, Downing Street,
> Whitehall, S.W.
> 28th June, 1916.
>
> My dear Lloyd George,
> Please look at enclosed which has just come from Lansdowne.
> Yours,
> H. H. A."

The enclosure was the following letter:—

> " Lansdowne House,
> Berkeley Square, W.
> 28th June, 1916.
>
> My dear Asquith,
> You will, I am sure, have noted that my consent to the postponement of further discussion as to the Irish settlement was given with considerable reluctance and not without misgivings. I agreed, not because I was convinced that further inquiry was likely to produce satisfactory results, but because it seemed to me that, having regard to the extreme gravity of the situation, no suggestion which gave us breathing time ought to be put aside.
> The discussion towards the close was hurried, and I am not sure that we were *ad diem* as to the scope of the enquiry. I may, therefore, perhaps be allowed to make my own views clear.
> What we want to know is, not merely whether under a Nationalist Government, Sir John Maxwell, with his 40,000 men, will be able to put down another Sinn Fein rebellion, or whether our military and naval resources would be sufficient to prevent a German-Irish landing. The question seems rather to be whether, with a Nationalist executive, it would be possible to deal effectively and promptly with domestic disorder, e.g., with sporadic but organised disturbances, occurring simultaneously all over the country. Could we deal with them as effectively and as promptly as we could if they were to occur now?
> Another point which it seems to me requires to be cleared up is this. Do Messrs. Redmond and Devlin understand that, if a Nationalist Government is set up, we shall still make use of the Defence of the Realm Acts, and that their suggestion that under the new dispensation the ordinary law will suffice cannot be entertained?
> And do they understand that Mr. Devlin's promise of an

immediate amnesty for the persons who are now imprisoned owing to the part which they took in the recent rebellion is not one which can be entertained?

I understand that you advised the S.W. Unionists yesterday to formulate their demands as to the safeguards which they considered indispensable.

Would it be possible to press them to put in a statement of their requirements, and, if we find that they are reasonable, could the Nationalist leaders be required to accept them as one of the conditions of settlement?

Believe me, yours sincerely,

LANSDOWNE."

On 10th July Mr. Asquith made a statement in the House of Commons in which he set out the main features of the agreement which had been reached. The following night Lord Lansdowne spoke in the House of Lords about the proposals, in terms which Mr. Redmond characterised as " a gross insult to Ireland . . . a declaration of war on the Irish people, and the announcement of a policy of coercion."

On 17th July a meeting was held at the Carlton Club of Conservative members of both houses of the Imperial Parliament, at which an " Imperial Unionist Association " was formed to " watch negotiations as to the Irish question between the Government and the Nationalist Party." This Association proceeded to adopt a resolution calling for stern measures of repression in Ireland, and opposing any idea of immediate Home Rule. In conformity with the wishes of their followers, the Unionist members of the Coalition Cabinet insisted on serious modifications in the terms which had been agreed between me and the Irish leaders, when a Bill was being drafted to carry them into law.

This situation was exposed by Mr. Redmond on 24th July, when he raised the question on a motion for adjournment of the House of Commons. Sir Edward Carson, placated by the proposed exclusion of the six counties from the scheme, urged strongly that a settlement should be made with the South. But the other Conservative members of the Cabinet were obdurate, and mangled the terms which I had originally put forward until Mr. Redmond was no longer willing to accept them.

The matter was concluded by Mr. Asquith's announcement in the House of Commons on 31st July that Mr. H. E. Duke, the member of Parliament for Exeter, was to be appointed Chief Secretary for Ireland. With this step we reverted to the old and unsatisfactory system of control, of which the Royal Commission on the Rebellion of Ireland had already stated in its report, issued on 26th June and published on 3rd July, 1916, that: —

" If the Irish system of government be regarded as a whole, it is anomalous in quiet times, and almost unworkable in times of crisis."

The revival of that "anomalous" and "almost unworkable" system led to the persistent growth of further disaffection, culminating in the chaos of the immediate post-war years, and the ultimate settlement of the problem on lines which involved far bigger concessions to Southern Ireland than would have been made in the scheme I had proposed. The last word has not yet been spoken in this unhappy feud that Britain has inherited from a foreign foe, who, having conquered England first, then proceeded to annex Ireland.

CHAPTER XXIII

THE COMING OF CONSCRIPTION

APART from the proposals I had placed before the Liberal and Conservative leaders in 1910 for a National Militia, no statesman had ever contemplated that the military contribution of this country to a European war should exceed the limits of our normal regular army. Our ideas were embodied in the Expeditionary Force created by Mr. Haldane. After the declaration of war an appeal was made for 100,000 men. Their main use was intended to be as units for filling gaps in the ranks. It was only when the numbers who volunteered reached a figure which was beyond the highest hopes of enthusiasts that the Cabinet and Parliament widened their view of the part we were destined to play on the battlefields of Armageddon.

We had always visualised Britain playing her traditional rôle in Continental wars. Our Navy would keep the seas for the Allies. Our wealth would help them to finance their foreign purchases. Our Army would play a subordinate part in the struggle.

But why was not Conscription adopted from the moment the Cabinet decided to raise an army on the Continental scale? Obviously it would have provided the most effective method for organising the man-power of this country.

To the British people the idea was unfamiliar, and we move slowly in these islands. Bred on a soil for centuries inviolate, we were accustomed to send abroad only small, professional armies, the ranks of which, in so far as they were British, could be filled by the recruiting sergeant on a voluntary basis, with the allurement of uniform and the King's shilling. Our national defence had been the fleet, which requires far fewer men than does an army, and for whose needs in the darkest moments of the Napoleonic struggle, the Press-gang—long since passed into the limbo of forgotten evils—had troubled only the sea-port towns and their vicinity.

Not only were we unused to the idea of universal and compulsory national service for war; we also had a strong traditional objection to the creation of large armed forces, as potential instruments of tyranny and an infringement of personal liberty; and, moreover, among wide sections of the nation there was a tendency to look down on the common soldier's vocation.

Besides, in the early days, few conceived that the War would be a long-drawn-out affair. It was surmised that no nation could sustain war on the modern scale for more than a short time. Pacifist and militarist writers agreed about that. " Over by Christmas " was the popular slogan, which was used to excuse the corresponding cry, " Business as usual."

For these reasons it was thought by all those who had the supreme responsibility of interpreting public opinion that it would have been impossible at the outset of the War to carry through a scheme for the mobilisation of the whole country, such as was adopted in France. And to add to these negative arguments against such a procedure, there was the positive fact that recruits during the first months were pouring in, on a voluntary basis, far more rapidly than the military authorities could handle them. In the first three months of the War, 900,000 new recruits were enlisted, at an average of 300,000 a month, in addition to the reservists recalled to the Colours and the Territorials already enlisted. The army authorities had neither barracks in which to house these men, uniforms in which to clothe them, nor weapons with which to drill and train them. Far from needing to adopt special measures to secure men for the forces, we were driven to raise and stiffen the physical standard for recruits, in order to check this unmanageable spate.

As time passed, however, a series of developments occurred to modify the situation.

The military authorities, for their part, improvised by the time the first rush of recruits was over, a technique for handling supplies of men on this unprecedented scale. The stream itself dwindled by the end of the year to an average of 30,000 a week.

Already before the close of 1914, it was becoming clear that the unregulated process of voluntary recruiting had swept into the Army large numbers of men who were vitally necessary in the workshops, for the production of munitions of war and in other civilian avocations essential even in war. Many of them, from their skill, intelligence, and experience, were pivotal men and irreplaceable. Efforts were made to get some of them back, but the salvage operations were not very successful. The obvious lesson was that if the War were not to be bungled and lost, our resources of man-power must be more intelligently applied.

The War had not ended by Christmas. On the contrary, it was settling down into a long-drawn-out struggle, which would demand from us not only a far bigger military force on the Continent and elsewhere than had at first been expected, but would require a continuous stream of fresh men to replace casualties and keep the armies up to strength.

As the magnitude of the struggle, and its life-and-death importance for us, was borne in upon the nation, the popular antipathy to military service died away, and was replaced by a healthy

impatience at the spectacle of sturdy young men " skrimshanking "
at home while fathers of families were in the trenches.

These developments weakened the case for persistence in the
voluntary system, and helped to prepare men's minds for its
abandonment when eventually it proved incapable of furnishing the
Army with an adequate supply of fresh recruits.

Not the least of the difficulties which had to be overcome before
conscription was eventually adopted, was the hostility engendered by
its advocates. These were associated before the War in the popular
mind with extreme Jingoism, and in consequence opposition to any
suggestion of national military service had become an article of faith
with some Liberals and Socialists. An agitation for conscription was
begun early in the struggle from the same quarters, which kept alive
the feud and gave it the semblance of a party issue. It would have
been far easier for the Government to introduce national service at
an early date, if the matter had not taken on such a violently controversial colour, so that its adoption looked like a Chauvinist
triumph.

My own attitude to this question has never been based on considerations of political orthodoxy. Long before the War I had
formed the opinion that there was much to be said in favour of some
system of national training, and of universal liability to military
service for national defence. I have told how I advanced this suggestion when talking with the German Ambassador years before the
War, and how the matter was also discussed as a practical proposition
with the leaders of the Conservative Party by the Liberal Government
in 1910.

Looking backward, there is no doubt at all that we should have
been able to organise the nation for war far more effectively in 1914,
and bring the conflict to a successful issue far more quickly and
economically, if at the very outset we had mobilised the whole nation
—its man-power, money, materials and brains—on a war footing and
bent all our resources to the task of victory on rational and systematic
lines. Towards the end, something approaching this condition was
in fact reached, but there had intervened a long and deplorably
extravagant prelude of waste and hesitation. But a majority of the
Cabinet opposed conscription not only as inexpedient, but because
at that time they were strongly antagonistic to it on principle, and
there was no pressure from the Conservative opposition to apply
conscription.

A decision having been reached, with something like national
unity, to rely as long as possible upon the voluntary principle, every
effort was made to stimulate its successful working. At first, recruiting meetings, posters, literature, and other forms of popular appeal
were employed. The recruiting crusade was well organised. The
services of expert propagandists, political agents, advertising agents,

and public speakers, lay and clerical, were requisitioned, and their combined work in agitation and enlistment was a triumphant success. By degrees, other more systematic approaches to the manhood of the nation were improvised, and only after these repeated promptings and combings proved unavailing to maintain our supply of recruits did we turn of necessity to compulsory service.

The first of these systematic steps was the "Householders' Return," organised early in November, 1914, by the Parliamentary Recruiting Committee. This was a return of men eligible and willing to serve, and was secured by means of forms sent to every householder in the Kingdom, with a covering letter signed by Messrs. Asquith, Bonar Law, and Arthur Henderson, the leaders of the three political parties, appealing to every eligible man to hold himself ready to enlist in the forces of the Crown.

This scheme, reinforced by the appeals of poster and public meeting, helped to maintain the steady flow of recruits well into 1915. At the beginning of the year, on 8th January, 1915, when conscription was being debated in the House of Lords, the official attitude of the Government at that time was stated by Lord Crewe in the following phrase: "We do not regard the possibility of compulsion as being within the landscape, as we now see it." More than three months later, on 20th April, I myself stated in reply to a question in the House of Commons that: "The Government are not of opinion that there is any ground for thinking that the War would be more successfully prosecuted by means of conscription." Both of these statements as to the Government's attitude were determined by the fact that as yet the voluntary system was continuing to yield as adequate a flow of recruits as could be absorbed by our training and equipping facilities at that date.

That the attitude of some of us on this issue was purely realist, and not doctrinaire, is illustrated by a weighty pronouncement which Lord Haldane made in the course of the debate on 8th January, 1915, to which I have already referred. After declaring that hitherto the voluntary system was proving adequate, and showed no signs of breaking down, he added:—

"... By the Common Law of this country it is the duty of every subject of the Realm to assist the Sovereign in repelling the invasion of its shores and in defence of the Realm. That is a duty which rests on no Statute, but is inherent in the Constitution of the country. It has been laid down ... that any subject at a time of emergency may be asked to give himself and his property for the defence of the nation. Therefore compulsory service is not foreign to the Constitution of this country. Given a great national emergency I think it is your duty to resort to it. I can conceive a state of things in which we might resort to it. ... At a time of national necessity every other consideration must yield to national interest, and we should bar nothing in the way of principle if it should become necessary."

This statement was of importance, not only for its value as a summary of the Common Law position with regard to compulsory national service, but as showing that Lord Haldane himself and others like-minded in the Cabinet were approaching the issue purely on the basis of practical expediency, and held no theoretic objection or prejudice against its adoption. I may also refer here to the statement made by me at Manchester on 3rd June, which I have already quoted in my account of the Ministry of Munitions, where I emphasised that there was nothing anti-democratic in conscription; on the contrary, every great democracy had resorted to it in times of national danger as a fit and proper democratic weapon for self-defence; and if necessity arose we ought without hesitation to apply the same weapon ourselves in this present conflict.

As a matter of fact, I had become painfully aware, long before I actually became principally responsible for creating a Ministry of Munitions, that the haphazard results of the voluntary system in a national emergency of this magnitude were leading to deplorable waste and mismanagement of our available man-power. I was eager to press forward some scheme for a more systematic co-ordination of these resources, and one of the first acts of the new Cabinet formed by Mr. Asquith at the end of May, 1915, when he established the first Coalition Government, was to instruct Mr. Walter Long to draft a Bill for the setting up of a National Register. The aim of this Register was twofold. By providing a complete record of the number and distribution of men at different age levels throughout the country it would enable us to calculate our available resources of men for military service, and also inform us what supplies of men were available for production of munitions.

Some time was lost in discussion of the points raised, but ultimately on 5th July the National Registration Bill was laid before Parliament and carried by a large majority. Opposition to it, based mainly on the presumption that it was a preliminary to conscription, came from a small group of Liberal and Labour Members, and, of course, from Messrs. MacDonald and Snowden, who throughout the War persistently opposed every effort to secure recruits for the national defence. Indeed, three months earlier, the Independent Labour Party, of which Mr. Ramsay MacDonald was the leading light, had carried in their Norwich Conference a resolution censuring the official Labour Party for its work on behalf of recruiting.

The returns obtained by the National Register showed that there were about five million men of military age in Great Britain who were not already serving with the Forces. Of these, there were, of course, a considerable number physically unfit for military service, and, further, a number in " barred" occupations who were held non-recruitable because indispensable to the maintenance of national industry and in particular of munitions. It was estimated that Great Britain contained a residue of 1,700,000 to 1,800,000 fit men available as recruits not yet serving with the Forces. This figure was proved later on to be an under-estimate of our reserves of man-power.

While this register was being compiled, a Cabinet Committee on our national resources in men and money had carried out in August, 1915, an investigation into the situation, and in a Report dated 2nd September, 1915, it pointed out that voluntary recruiting was not enabling us to make a military effort comparable to the resources of the country. Lord Kitchener was aiming at an army of 70 divisions in all theatres by the latter part of 1916. The Committee held that " a 100-division army would bear a truer relation both to our dangers and to the exertions of our Allies." After making all allowance for our naval, financial, and industrial contributions, " it cannot be claimed that an army of 70 divisions represents our true proportionate contribution of men to the Allied line of battle."

Taking the 70-division scheme, however, as the standard to be reached, the Committee showed that present methods would be insufficient. In addition to the Regular reserves and Territorial forces mobilised at the beginning of the War, the fresh recruits accepted and passed into the Army in 13 months totalled 1,888,000. " The recruiting records for the last six months, show an average yield of 20,000 a week, resulting in an effective yield to our military forces of probably 19,000 men." Lord Kitchener was asking for at least 30,000 a week, a figure which a month later he raised to 35,000. " Even the yield of 20,000 a week can only be maintained by repeated canvassing of individuals and by every form of social, and in some cases of economic, pressure upon all classes of men (except munition workers) from 17 to 45, whether married or single, whether usefully employed or not, and whether or not they can be spared from their trade or district."

The Committee reported the evidence it had received in statements to it by the President of the Board of Trade, the Chancellor of the Exchequer, Lord Kitchener, and myself. From its record of my own evidence I cull the following extracts: —

Asked by the Committee what form of compulsion the Minister of Munitions considered necessary, " Mr. Lloyd George said he would take the same powers exactly as were taken in France. He would make everybody between certain ages liable to serve in the Army at home or abroad, and only during the duration of the War. With this general and basic authority ' you could work the rest all right.' "

And in my concluding remarks I am reported as saying: —

"You will not get through without some measure of military compulsion or compulsion for military service. The longer you delay the nearer you will be to disaster. I am certain you cannot get through without it. I do not believe, for instance, that you can keep your armies at the front without it, unless you are going deliberately to cut their numbers down to a figure which will be inadequate, and which is known to be inadequate in advance. The number of men you should put at the front does not depend on us in the least. It is going to depend on the Germans and what the Germans are going to do during the next three months in Russia. If they succeed in putting the Russians out of action during 1916 as a great offensive force, for us simply to keep 70 divisions at the front is suicide.* Not only that, it is murder, because to send a number of men who are obviously inadequate is just murdering our own countrymen without attaining any purpose at all. . . ."

The President of the Board of Trade, Mr. Runciman, argued to the Committee that on the basis of the statistics he had at his disposal there would, after leaving a sufficient number of men in industry, be less than half the number available for the Army which Lord Kitchener considered indispensable to maintain his 70 divisions, and not more than half of these could be secured by voluntary recruiting. The Committee felt that this argument "would appear to lead directly, if unconsciously, to compulsory military service" (of which Mr. Runciman was a leading opponent). But they did not agree with his sweeping exclusion by whole classes of large numbers of potential recruits from his calculations.

The statement of the Chancellor of the Exchequer, Mr. M'Kenna, was to the effect that Britain could not afford to carry on her financial aid to her Allies and at the same time maintain an army of 70 divisions in the field. One or other of the two tasks we might compass, but not both. The Committee found his arguments ingenious but unconvincing, and reminded the Cabinet that "whereas a few months ago the possibility of raising a substantial loan in the United States was scouted altogether, and whereas a few weeks ago we were assured that £20,000,000 was the utmost limit, the Chancellor of the Exchequer now hopes to borrow £100,000,000 sterling from this quarter during the present year, and to repeat the operation in a subsequent year."

Lord Kitchener told the Committee that "it would be his duty to ask Parliament before the end of the year for a Bill giving him compulsory powers." He added, however, that he regretted the

* In 1918 we had 89 divisions including Dominion, etc., troops.

raising of the question of compulsory service at the present time, because he had intended to choose his own time for rushing it on the country as a non-party measure of military emergency, whereas it was now being revived as a party issue. Before deciding on his scheme for compulsion he wanted to see the results of the National Registration.

The Committee concluded in their report dated 2nd September, 1915, that " the men are available for the 70-divisions army, but the number cannot be obtained on a voluntary basis." They posed as questions for the Cabinet: —

"First: Whether the 70-divisions scheme is to be cut down to the limits which can be supplied by voluntary enlistment, or whether it is to be carried out by compulsory measures.

Secondly: Assuming that the 70-divisions scheme is to be carried out and that compulsion is to be used, whether a decision should be taken now or some time later in the year."

At this time the Cabinet was broadly divided into three sections on the question of conscription. There was the group of those who had come to regard a measure of compulsory national service as vitally necessary for the successful prosecution of the War, and in consequence were anxious to bring it in with the smallest possible delay. At the other extreme stood those who through principle or prejudice were as strongly opposed to it, and prepared to fight it to the last ditch. Between them were some, who were not opposed in principle, and admitted that we might have to resort to compulsion, but were loath to admit the need for so radical a change of system until it was proved to be unavoidable, and only then if they were sure it would command general approval by the mass of the people. They anticipated that any attempt to carry and enforce compulsory universal service would excite such opposition as to make the proposal unworkable.

On 8th October, 1915, Lord Kitchener laid before the Cabinet a memorandum on " Recruiting for the Army," which began with the ominous statement: —

"The voluntary system, as at present administered, fails to produce the number of recruits required to maintain the armies in the field."

He proposed that a scheme of conscription by ballot should be introduced, based on the returns of the National Register. Each district should be expected to furnish a quota of recruits in accordance with the numbers of men available within the area, as shown by the Register. If voluntary recruiting failed to produce the full quota, the balance would be obtained by a ballot of the eligible men not yet enlisted.

This scheme was, however, severely criticised as clumsy and unworkable, and it was not further proceeded with. It was recognised that if the voluntary system could not be continued the alternative must be a national measure of compulsory service.

The opponents of this argued in the Cabinet and outside that conscription was impracticable because the volunteers already enlisted would be unwilling to serve alongside pressed men, and while a separation of conscript and volunteer armies was unworkable, their mingling would be disastrous. Lord Curzon took the trouble to have extensive enquiries made from officers and men of all ranks in France on this question, and the quite unanimous verdict returned was that these fears were without foundation. The army in the field felt strongly that those at home who would not come out otherwise should be fetched, and while it was suggested that the conscripts might at first have to put up with a certain measure of chaff and ragging, this would soon pass, and the difference in their conditions of enlistment be forgotten.

Actually, of course, this was what took place when conscription was put into force. Here again it turned out that those who raised imaginary objections to a firm policy were flinching at shadows. Our bane throughout those early periods of the War was the incurable tendency of a number of people in high places to argue that measures vitally necessary for the success of our effort could not, for some reason or other, be taken. Thus we were told that the outside firms could not learn to make munitions; that the finances of the country could not stand the strain of our total effort; that the men needed for our Army could not be spared from industry; that gunners could not be trained to operate our programme of big guns; that the country would not stand conscription; that volunteers would not fight beside pressed men; and so on. Every one of these arguments was falsified by the event. Unhappily, each one of these objections served for a greater or less time to hold up and paralyse the efforts we should have been making to win the War. The advice of these prophets of the impossible cost us months and years of prolonged warfare, and hundreds and thousands of British lives.

In deference to the objections of the anti-conscriptionists, and to the hesitations of the middle group of the Cabinet, one final effort was made, in the form of the Derby Scheme, to galvanise the voluntary system into renewed vigour. It was generally recognised, both in the Cabinet and in the country, that if this failed, conscription would be inevitable.

The Derby Scheme owes its name to the fact that Lord Derby, although for many years a strong supporter of the introduction of Universal Military Service, consented to become Director of Recruiting and to carry through a last canvass of the country's man-power, in order to give the voluntary system the utmost opportunity of

furnishing the men needed for the Army. He was appointed on
5th October, 1915, and the post carried, at his request, no pay and
no military rank.

The authorship of the plan which he set himself to administer
has not hitherto been made public.

The main feature of the Derby Scheme was a personal canvass of
every man in the Kingdom between the ages of 18 and 41, working
on the basis of the National Register. Each man was asked to attest
—to pledge himself to join up when called for—subject to the
undertaking that all attested men would be divided into two classes,
the single and the married, and each of these into 23 groups according
to age; that the military authorities would call the men up by class
and group as wanted for the Army, beginning with the younger
single men, and would call up none of the married men till all the
single men had been summoned to the colours.

The married men were encouraged to put down their names in
the light of an assurance that not only would they be left at home
till the single men had all been called in, but that if the single men
did not attest in adequate numbers the married men would not be
bound by their attestation pledge. This was stated by Mr. Asquith
in a speech he delivered in the House of Commons on 2nd November,
1915:—

"I am told by Lord Derby that there is some doubt among the
married men who are now being asked to enlist as to whether they
may not be called upon to serve, having enlisted, while younger
and unmarried men are holding back and not doing their duty.
Let them disabuse themselves of that notion at once. So far as I
am concerned, I would certainly say that the obligation of the
married men to enlist is an obligation which ought not to be
enforced, and ought not to be held binding on them unless and
until we can obtain, I hope by voluntary effort, but if it were
needed, and as a last resort by other means, as I have stated, the
unmarried men."

This position was rendered still more definite and explicit by
correspondence between Lord Derby and Mr. Asquith, which confirmed the pledge that no attested married men should be called
up unless and until the unmarried men had been recruited
voluntarily or conscripted by Act of Parliament.

Every possible effort was made to ensure the full success of the
Derby Scheme. His Majesty the King wrote a special appeal: "To
My People," supporting the scheme, which was issued on 23rd
October. The instructions to the local Recruiting Committees as
to carrying out the canvass were jointly considered, approved and
signed by Lord Derby, by the Chairman of the Parliamentary

Recruiting Committee, and by Mr. Arthur Henderson, Chairman of the Labour Recruiting Committee. The closing day for the canvass, originally fixed as November 30th, was extended to December 15th.

The result was rather what might have been anticipated. Married men attested in considerable numbers, secure in the assurance that they would not be expected to fulfil their promise unless and until all the single men had been called up. The single men attested much less generally. Out of 2,179,231 single men of military age not enlisted before 23rd October, 1915, the number presenting themselves under the Derby Scheme, and enlisted, attested or medically rejected, was 1,150,000, leaving 1,029,231, or nearly half the total, outside the scheme. Of those who put down their names, so many were either the medically unfit or " starred " men—men employed in jobs from which it was held that in the national interest they could not be spared for the Army—that Lord Derby estimated the net number of single men he would actually get for the Army through his scheme would be only 343,386 out of the total of 2,179,231 in the country.

In face of these figures, it was obviously impossible to pretend that Mr. Asquith's pledge to the married men had been fulfilled. Over a million single men had refused to attest, and the policy of recruiting them compulsorily was the inevitable sequel. As regards popular support for such a policy, all the attested married men were naturally insistent on it. They protested that it would be a breach of the promise made to them to summon them to the colours while so many unmarried men were left at home.

Accordingly, on 5th January, 1916, after much heated discussion in the Cabinet, the first definite measure of conscription was introduced, when Mr. Asquith laid before Parliament a Military Service Bill to compel the attestation of all unmarried men, and widowers without children or dependents, between the ages of 18 and 41. Defending the Bill against the objections of anti-conscriptionists inside and outside the Government, he urged that it was necessary in redemption of the pledge he had given to Lord Derby—a pledge which he certainly considered to be within the limits and upon the general line of policy which had been agreed upon by the Cabinet. He was himself of the opinion that no case had been made out for general compulsion, and he thought the Bill would be sincerely supported by those who either on principle or—as in his case—on the ground of expediency were opposed to compulsion.

This line of argument failed to convince some of his opponents. Sir John Simon resigned from the Government rather than support conscription in any form, and rallied about three dozen other Liberal members into an opposition to attack the measure.

Sir John Simon, speaking on 5th January, 1916, in the debate on the Military Service Bill, declared that his opposition to any measure of conscription was one of fundamental principle, and he added that there were other members of the Government who had not resigned whose views on the matter were indistinguishable from his own. The reference was, of course, recognised as applying to Mr. M'Kenna and Mr. Runciman, who had both opposed the measure strongly in the Cabinet. They did not, however, carry their principles to the point of resigning. When it came to the direct issue they based their objection, not on the fundamental principle with which Sir John Simon credited them, but on the argument that we could not spare from our national industries as many men as would be taken into the Army through conscription, nor afford to keep them under arms when we had got them. During the days immediately prior to the introduction of the measure it was thought that they also might resign if they could not get the Bill so modified as to limit and reduce the numbers liable to be called up under it.

Mr. Redmond and his Irish Nationalists opposed the Bill on its first introduction, but when they knew definitely that Ireland would be excluded from its scope they withdrew their opposition. The reason for the exclusion of Ireland was that the Bill was intended to implement the pledge given in connection with the Derby Scheme, and this scheme had not been worked in Ireland.

Mr. Arthur Henderson and the Labour Party were placed in a rather difficult position by a resolution of the Trades Unions at their Bristol Conference on 5th January condemning the Government's proposals. Mr. Asquith was, however, able to give Mr. Henderson official assurance that nothing in the nature of industrial conscription was contained in or implied by the Bill, and in consequence Mr. Henderson spoke and voted in support of the Second Reading. A minority of the Labour Party, led by Messrs. Ramsay MacDonald, Snowden, and Thomas, opposed the measure.

Carried through all its stages by overwhelming majorities, the Bill became law on 27th January, 1916. At midnight on 1st March all single men who had not already joined up were automatically reckoned as enlisted in His Majesty's forces for the period of the War. The single men attested under the Derby scheme had already been all called up, and a first call was now made on the attested married men, of whom the groups aged 19 to 27 were summoned to the colours.

So ended the first round. But the issue could not rest there. Forces were at work which, with a march as inevitable as destiny, pressed the nation forward into a complete system of compulsory service.

With the advance of the spring of 1916 there came a call from the military authorities for more recruits. This meant summoning the older groups of attested married men. But at the rumour of this a violent agitation broke out. These fathers of families declared that before they were called for, a much closer comb-out ought to be made of the single men, very many of whom were still at home, exempted from military service because they were in starred occupations. Further, it was insisted that the younger unattested married men ought to be called up before their elders were sent to the trenches. And the older men, with serious responsibilities for children, for houses, for businesses, ought to have some arrangement made to relieve them of their financial difficulties—leases, mortgages, and so on—before they were taken for the Army.

Fierce and long were the debates in the Cabinet on this issue. The calling up of the older classes of married men was postponed while the new phase of the problem was being studied. Mr. Asquith promised that on 18th April he would make a statement about recruiting, but on that day he had to announce a postponement because of Cabinet disagreements; and he followed this on the 19th by announcing a further postponement, as disagreement in the Cabinet was so serious as to threaten the break-up of the Government. He adjourned the House of Commons till 25th April, on which date a secret session of the House was held to thrash out the problem.

The existing shortage of men for the Army was proving itself serious, and the methods so far available for securing new recruits were proving insufficient. A month previously, on 21st March, 1916, the Chief of the Imperial General Staff, Sir William Robertson, had submitted a memorandum in which he stated that:—

". . . As regards personnel we are not now in an appreciably better position for making that 'maximum effort' . . . than we were when I raised the question nearly three months ago. At the present time the infantry serving abroad is 78,000 below its establishment; the 13 Territorial Divisions at home are also deficient of 50,000 men. . . . Of the 193,891 men called up under the Military Service Act no fewer than 57,416 have failed to appear. . . ."

A note by the Army Council on 15th April, 1916, showed that the estimated deficit would on 30th June be 179,000 men, and that while as yet there were only 52 divisions abroad instead of the intended 62, there was a deficit of 66,000 men in their establishment.

At the Secret Session of Parliament on 25th April the situation was passed under review, and the Prime Minister put forward the Government proposals to deal with it. These were officially announced afterwards to include the extension of service of time-expired men, transfer of recruits from territorial to regular units, prompt enlistment of men whose exemption certificates had expired, and recruitment of all youths as they reached the age of 18. Further efforts were also proposed to enlist unattested married men, and if in a month's time 50,000 of these were not forthcoming and 15,000 a week thereafter, then compulsion would be resorted to.

A second secret session was held on 26th April, and on the following day Mr. Walter Long introduced a Bill embodying the Government's proposals; but it was so adversely criticised that Mr. Asquith withdrew it. There was by now a quite general impatience with any further paltering or half-measures, which Mr. Asquith, with his usual good sense, clearly recognised. On 2nd May he announced that the Government would bring in a measure to impose general and immediate compulsory military service. This was introduced on the following day, and on 25th May it received the Royal Assent. The opposition to it was of quite a trivial nature. Sir John Simon's band of non-co-operators had sunk to 27, and Mr. Ramsay MacDonald's Labour group to 10.

I was in charge of the measure on its second reading in the House of Commons, and speaking on that occasion I challenged the appeal to principle made by its opponents, in the following passage: —

" I have waited for this great overriding principle and I have not heard it yet. Is this Bill inconsistent with the principles of either Liberalism or democracy? Is it inconsistent with the principles of democracy that the State should demand the services and help of every man to defend its life when it is at stake? There is not and never has been a country yet faced with a great military peril that has ever saved itself without resort to compulsion. Never. It is true of autocracies, it is even more true of democracies. Where is the principle? I have a personal interest in finding out, because I have been told that I am a traitor to Liberal principles because I supported conscription; therefore I am personally interested in seeking it out. I cannot find it. Every great democracy which has been challenged, which has had its liberties menaced, has defended itself by resort to compulsion, from Greece downwards. Washington won independence for America by compulsory measures; America defended its independence in 1812 by compulsory measures. Lincoln was not merely a great democrat, but his career was in itself the greatest triumph that democracy has ever achieved in the sphere of government. He proclaimed the principle of ' Government of the People, by the People, for the People,' and he kept it alive by conscription. In the French Revolution the French people defended their newly obtained liberties against every effort of the autocracies of Europe by compulsion and by conscriptionary levies. France is defending her country to-day by conscription. In Italy the Italian democracy are seeking to redeem their enthralled brethren by compulsion. In Serbia the Serbian peasants defended their mountains by compulsory measures, and they are going to win them back by the same means. When honourable members say that conscription is contrary to the principles of liberty and true democracy, they are talking in defiance of the whole teaching of history and of common sense."

I also remarked that in the face of the national emergency which made this measure imperative, I would submit to be driven out of my party, and out of public life altogether, rather than refuse it my support.

I had in fact been pressing the need for compulsory military service on the Government for a considerable time, and the importance of the part I had played in finally carrying it through was attested by two letters which I received at the time from Sir William Robertson. The first of these was of some length, and in it Robertson was good enough to comment in warm terms on my "great courage and patriotism," and wound up with the assertion that "but for you it would not have been done." The second was shorter, and I transcribe it in full: —

" War Office.

2/5/1916.

Dear Mr. Lloyd George,

The Bill introduced to-day should more than compensate you for the rubbishy Press attacks of the last week or two. The great thing is to get the Bill, and for it the Empire's thanks are due to you—alone.

Yours very truly,

WM. ROBERTSON."

These expressions of appreciation are perhaps the more important, because Sir William Robertson was not always in as cordial sympathy with my ideas. But if my zeal for this cause won me some approval in quarters not uniformly favourable to me, it added a fresh edge to the bitterness of those who held that my determination to fight the War through without hesitation or reserve, was a most improper and, indeed, unholy attitude. The distrust and hostility of this section of Liberal opinion was thenceforward confirmed and ineradicable. Speaking at Conway on 6th May, 1916, in advocacy of the Military Service Bill, I found myself compelled to reply to a series of attacks which had been directed against me by a prominent Liberal journalist who was at that time in close touch with some of my colleagues, for " abandoning Liberalism," " throwing such fervour into the prosecution of the War," and " having differences of opinion with my chief." To the first charge, the fact that a vast majority of Liberals in the House of Commons had supported the Conscription Bill sufficiently gave the lie. To the second charge I pleaded guilty on the ground that while I hated war I held, once we had decided to wage war, that we must wage it effectively. " That is why I have had no sympathy with those who seem to think that because war is hateful, you ought to fight it with a sort of savour of regret in your actions. Doubting hand never yet struck firm blow."

Of my relations with Mr. Asquith I declared: —

" I have worked with him for ten years; I have served under him for eight. If we had not worked harmoniously—and we have —let me tell you here at once it would have been my fault and not his. I have never worked with anyone who could be more considerate, and I disdain the things they have said. But we have had our differences. Good Heavens! What use would I have been if I had not differed? I should have been no use at all. He has shown me great kindness during the years I have worked with him. I should have ill requited them if I had not told my opinions freely, frankly, independently, whether they agree with his or not.

Freedom of speech is essential in everything, but there is one place where it is vital and that is in the Council Chamber. The councillor who professes to agree with everything that falls from his leader has betrayed him."

Looking backward after the event, no one can now doubt that the adoption of conscription was vitally necessary for carrying the War through to victory. Without it we should have been overwhelmed when Russia, Roumania and Serbia had all cracked and the French Army was threatening mutiny.

The effect on our Allies was heartening. Lord Esher in a memorandum dated 4th May, 1916, reported an interview he had just had with M. Briand, and stated: —

" M. Briand spoke with enthusiasm and deep content of yesterday's proceedings in the English Parliament. He is certain that it will have far-reaching results in Germany, and will accentuate the uneasiness, growing fast among the Central Powers, as to the ultimate issue of the War. . . . The adoption of compulsory service in England will, he thinks, have a lowering effect on German mentality and *morale*.

The effect in France will be even greater.

In spite of all that England has done, which is well known to the French Government, there are many people in France in whose minds doubts still linger as to the determination of England to go through with the War to the bitter end. To these people the adoption by the English Parliament of a procedure so foreign to the traditions and habits of the English people will be a ' *coup de massue.*' The whole French nation, he says, will now recognise that England means to make every necessary sacrifice, and any doubts that existed will be at once dispelled."

While recognising the necessity for the introduction of compulsory service, I have always emphasised and paid tribute to the magnificence of the voluntary effort which the manhood of the country put forward in 1914 and 1915. In my speech at Conway on 6th May, to which I have already referred, I said:—

" The achievement of the nation in raising by voluntary methods those huge armies is something of which we may very well be proud. It is almost unparalleled in the history of war, and nothing which has happened since in the way of compulsory measures can ever detract from the pride we possess in the fact that we are the first nation in the history of the world that has raised over three millions of men for any great military enterprise purely by voluntary means. Young men from every quarter of this country flocked to the standard of international right as to a great crusade. It was a glorious achievement, and well may Britain be proud of it!"

According to a memorandum of the Committee of Imperial Defence, dated 17th April, 1916, the number of men who had by that date actually gone into service with the forces, naval and military, including those already serving at the outbreak of war, was 3,769,659, to which there should be added those in attested groups of married men not yet called up, and single men attested but retained in starred occupations, to a total of 697,000, making a grand total of 4,667,000 men as our full volunteer force, exclusive of contingents from the Dominions and India, which would bring the sum to well over 5,000,000.

On the day when the Military Service Bill received the Royal Assent, the King issued a " message to his people," in the following terms:—

" Buckingham Palace,
25th May, 1916.

To enable our country to organise more effectively its military resources in the present great struggle for the cause of civilisation, I have, acting on the advice of my Ministers, deemed it necessary to enrol every able-bodied man between the ages of eighteen and forty-one.

I desire to take this opportunity of expressing to my people my recognition and appreciation of the splendid patriotism and self-sacrifice which they have displayed in raising by voluntary enlistment since the commencement of the War, no less than 5,041,000 men, an effort far surpassing that of any other nation in similar circumstances recorded in history, and one which will be a lasting source of pride to future generations.   I am confident that the magnificent spirit which has hitherto sustained my people through the trials of this terrible war will inspire them to endure the additional sacrifice now imposed upon them, and that it will, with God's help, lead us and our Allies to a victory which shall achieve the liberation of Europe.

GEORGE R.I."

CHAPTER XXIV

DISINTEGRATION OF THE LIBERAL PARTY

The fissures which showed themselves in the ranks of Liberalism during the debate on conscription were not of sudden growth. They had been steadily forming and widening during the previous twelve months. At the first challenge in 1914 a gust of patriotic fervour had swept the party forward in united resolve, and there were very few who felt compelled by their principles to join with Lord Morley, Mr. Trevelyan, and Mr. Burns in withdrawing from the Government and deciding to hold aloof from the conflict. The leaders of the National Liberal Federation issued on 8th August a circular announcing the indefinite suspension of party propaganda and calling on Liberals to sink political differences and give themselves to the service of the country; and the *Liberal Magazine* declared, " In the great war in which we are engaged, at whatever cost we must win."

But as the War went on the men brought up on the peace-loving precepts of Cobden and Bright and Gladstone disliked it more and more. They had no doubt or hesitation as to the justice or inevitability of our part in it. But they gradually became depressed at the sight of the dread machinery which thrust itself upon them everywhere in the highways and byways, and at the evidence of the accumulating horror which spread desolation throughout the land. The larger and more sagacious half of the party treated the War as a disagreeable necessity forced upon us in the defence of liberty, and to be brought to an end all the sooner by a vigorous organisation of all our available resources into a great national effort. But the real political sectary in his heart argued thus: " War is a hideous thing. You must show your aversion by waging it half-heartedly. Wield the sword with your left hand, and let your right nurse its strength until the blessed day arrives when it will be needed once more for swinging the sword of the Lord and of Gideon in the eternal fight for the principles to which we are attached." The men who threw the whole of their strength and spirit into waging war effectively were disliked and distrusted more and more by the sectarians. Every cannon and shell turned out by these men weighed them down deeper into perdition. Hence the heavier the guns they turned out the deeper their damnation. The men who won their admiration and trust were those leaders who proved the sincerity of their shudder by waging war nervelessly. The more ineffective they became the greater was the trust which was placed in the integrity of their leadership by these high-minded followers. Even under the accommodating Premiership of Mr. Asquith there were ominous growls and occasional outbursts of impatience from the straitest of his supporters. They resented conscription, which had consequently to be carried in two steps. There is no greater mistake than to try to leap an abyss in two jumps.

The Opposition Lobbies, it is true, were not overcrowded with malcontents. Real Parliamentary opinion can rarely be gathered from a perusal of divisions lists. There were sinister grumblings in the corridors and tea-rooms. The activities of the Ministry of Munitions in turning out guns, rifles, shot, and shell on an unprecedented scale provoked irritation and even resentment amongst certain Liberals in Press, Parliament and Club. The personal attitude of old political friends towards me changed and chilled after I became Minister of Munitions. It found petulant expression in speeches and articles, and I felt myself shunned and even spurned by men who once had greeted me with cordiality and enthusiasm. I was treated as one tainted with the leprosy of war. I had a sense of political isolation more complete than I had ever experienced during the whole of my lifetime. My old friends were turning their backs on me. The Conservatives had not yet forgotten the part I had played in the bitter controversies of the last few years, and the Liberals were resentful and sulky.

This attitude hurt me deeply, but it did not slow down by one pulsation my resolve to work energetically and to the limit of my power at the terrible task to which I had been called. I had assented to the declaration of war with tenacious reluctance, but once I was persuaded of its inevitable justice I threw myself with all my energy into the task of helping my country to vindicate the right. I was encouraged during these difficult times by a message which I received, early in 1916, from Theodore Roosevelt through a friend of his, Colonel Arthur Lee (now Lord Lee of Fareham), who acted as my military liaison officer at the Ministry of Munitions. Roosevelt's letter ran as follows: —

" Dear Arthur,
    Your letter was most interesting and I am more pleased than I can say that you are so hard at work and in so congenial and useful a way. Give my heartiest regards to Lloyd George. Do tell him I admire him immensely. I have always fundamentally agreed with his social program, but I wish it supplemented by Lord Roberts's external program. Nevertheless, my agreement with him in program is small compared with the fact that I so greatly admire the character he is now showing in this great crisis. It is often true

that the only way to render great services is by willingness on the part of the statesman to lose his future, or, at any rate, his present position in political life, just exactly as the soldier may have to pay with his physical life in order to render service in battle. In a very small and unimportant way I have done this myself during the last eighteen months. I have paid no heed, and shall not pay the slightest heed, to the effect upon my own fortunes, of anything that I say. What I am trying to do is to make this country go right, and I don't give a damn as what my countrymen think of me in the present or the future, provided only I can make them wake up to the sense of their duty. In an infinitely greater emergency, Lloyd George seems to me to be following the same line of conduct in trying to serve Great Britain at present.

Don't make any mistake about me. I don't believe there is any chance of my being nominated, because, as I wrote Lodge the other day, it would be utter folly to nominate me, unless the country was in heroic mood. If they put ' Safety First ' ahead of honour and duty, then they don't want me, and they need not expect that I will pussy-foot in any shape or way on the great issues that I regard as vital, and to which I regard all others as subordinate.

I hope you have by this time seen a copy of my book. Read the first chapter and the conclusion. Perhaps Lloyd George might be interested in looking at two or three sentences that you may care to show him. . . ."

As long as the party was united there was no organised secession. Sir John Simon's feeble efforts to lead a " cave " on conscription were a ridiculous failure. He is a very able man, but he commands neither the boldness, the breadth, nor the inspiration that are essential to great leadership. But apart from these issues there was inside the Cabinet a definite group which sought to drive a wedge between the Prime Minister and myself. As long as I was at the Exchequer I saw Mr. Asquith almost every morning before the Cabinet and discussed with him matters of urgency. Interviews were easily arranged when I worked at the Treasury Buildings, which had a door opening into 10, Downing Street.

On my way to the Treasury from 11, Downing Street I passed through the Prime Minister's residence. We invariably got on well and pleasantly together when we met. But when I went to the Ministry of Munitions I had to be there by nine o'clock and I found it difficult to leave until late in the evening. I thus saw much less of Mr. Asquith. In fact I saw very little of him alone for months. That was the opportunity of the mischief-makers and they took full advantage of it. When I left the Exchequer and Mr. M'Kenna took my place it was understood that his appointment was to be provisional. I was to return to my post at the Treasury as soon as I had set munitions going. This arrangement was a mistake and did much harm. The very possibility of its ever materialising made of Mr. M'Kenna a bitter enemy and poisoned his personal relations towards me. Ever afterwards they remained septic. This condition made business transactions in which I was engaged as Minister—all involving finance—very difficult. I ought to have assured him from the outset that I had no intention of ever claiming the redemption of the Prime Minister's pledge. Mr. M'Kenna possessed many of the gifts that make a good administrator in times that do not call specially for imagination, breadth of vision, or human insight. He knew the details of his job as Chancellor, he was a competent arithmetician, a ready reckoner (Mr. Balfour once said he was " an adroit accountant "), he was, in fact, a master of finance in blinkers. His chief defect, as I have already pointed out, was that he was apt to divide his more conspicuous colleagues into those he liked and those he viewed with distrust, suspicion, and jealousy. This peculiarity made him a source of weakness and distraction in a team. His was the most active personal element in the disintegration of the Asquith Coalition. A lady with a gift of satirical analysis of character once said to me that he was like one of those shilling paint-boxes given to children. The blocks were hard and angular, the colours were all very definite and crude. He possessed none of those delicate tints which you find on an artist's palette.

From June, 1915, to June, 1916, I was so immersed in the hurrying on of munitions for our hard-pressed Army that I had very little time to watch the political situation or to keep in touch with politicians in or out of the House of Commons, and I did not quite realise how far hostile intrigues had gone. When, later on at the end of 1916, the definite split came in the party and most of the Liberal members of the Cabinet declined further responsibility for the conduct of the War except under conditions of personal leadership which were inacceptable to the nation, all restraint disappeared and no likely opportunity was missed for criticising and occasionally embarrassing the Government of the day. The attacks were generally left to guerillas, but the sympathy and encouragement of leaders to these snipings were not wanting and were barely concealed. On two or three conspicuous occasions which appeared to be propitious, leaders and all joined in the assault, horse, foot and artillery. The official organisation set to work energetically in the country to spread suspicions and undermine confidence in the War Cabinet which was prosecuting the War with such excessive zeal. Multitudes of true Liberals did their best to save Liberalism from the eternal reproach of presenting this factiousness as the only contribution which their party was able to make to the security of the nation at a time of unparalleled danger in its history. For this they were persecuted, and for this they have never been forgiven by those whose futility in a grave emergency has doomed Liberalism to a generation of querulous impotence.

What would have happened had the party kept together to the end? It is impossible to surmise. There was one man who, if he had survived the War, might have kept the Liberal leaders from separating—the late Mr. Percy Illingworth. Without his powerful help as Chief Whip, Mr. Asquith was unequal to the task of reconciling personal differences and imposing unity. Percy Illingworth was the best type of Englishman—straight, competent, fearless, with a complete subordination of self to duty. He was devoted to Mr. Asquith as his leader—he was proud of him as a Yorkshireman. He was attached to me as a friend. He was loyal to us both, and we both knew and trusted him implicitly. He had a thorough cognisance of the intrigues of little men who plotted incessantly to separate us, and as long as he was there he kept a vigilant eye upon their activities and intimidated them with his Yorkshire bluntness of speech. In January, 1915, he died of typhoid acquired by eating a bad oyster. Had he been alive in 1916 there would have been no split between Mr. Asquith and myself. Of that I am convinced. What trifling incidents often precipitate important events! A rotten mollusc poisoned the whole Liberal Party for years and left it enfeebled. Later on the bite of a monkey in Greece altered the whole course of events in the Levant and had its reactions much further afield.

War has always been fatal to Liberalism. " Peace, Retrenchment, and Reform " have no meaning in war. Moreover, a nation, to make war effectively, must be prepared to surrender individual right and freedom for the time being. If the war is prolonged, that submission becomes a habit. Victory is the triumph of force and not of reason. After every great war there is a period during which belligerent nations incline to divide into two extreme camps—roughly known as revolutionary and reactionary. In that temper Liberalism is at a disadvantage. That is why it is to-day at a discount throughout Europe. Even in America its doctrines assume the form of a dictatorship. The temporary collapse of the Liberal Party in this country was inevitable from the moment it became responsible for the initiation and conduct of a great war. The instinct of the ordinary Liberal in that respect was sound. The War therefore made him uneasy.

1914 was a catastrophe for Liberalism. That was unfortunate, but the issues at stake were too big for treatment in terms of party interests. The challenge to international right and freedom was so tremendous that Liberalism—above all Liberalism—could not shirk it. When millions of men placed their lives at the disposal of their country without giving a thought to the political complexion of the Government or Minister to whose call they were responding or whose decrees they were obeying, it would be but a sorry boast for politicians who face no such danger to claim that they also had forgotten party interests in their country's peril. But there are certain obvious principles which should govern politics in such circumstances. Any combination of parties in a national emergency, if it is to be effective, involves a readiness in all the parties concerned to give and take. The moment it becomes a blind or subterfuge for the attainment of its aims by one party in the combination, then it is a selfish fraud practised on the nation. The two War Coalitions were honestly worked for patriotic ends. I saw Mr. Asquith at the head of two War Governments, one Liberal, the other Coalition, and from a close acquaintance with him during both administrations, I am able to say, and do say unhesitatingly and without qualification that, once war was declared, in neither of his Governments did he give any thought to party advantage. Indeed, so completely did he forget even party principles during his second administration that, in his desire to propitiate old opponents and so ensure unity, he assented to a Protectionist Budget, and even went so far as to pledge the country, by an agreement entered into with its Allies at the famous Paris Conference, to a drastic and far-reaching policy of protection after the War.

Whether general danger to a community comes from flood, fire or war, the instinct that leads to common action rather than to divided counsels is the same. It is evinced primarily by a readiness to co-operate with anyone who is willing and fit to climb the ladder, play the hose, handle the axe, or in any useful way face and fight the fire.

This elementary parable represents my views on the correct position of the party system during a war great enough to demand the undivided attention and whole energy of a nation.

For my own part, throughout the whole War, I never made inquiries as to a helper's political past. And when I knew the party to which he belonged, that fact exercised no influence whatever on my judgment of his qualification. I only wanted to ascertain his fitness for his job.

The two men of whom I saw most during the last two years of the War, when I had supreme direction, were Mr. Bonar Law and Lord Milner, both of whom belonged to the political side opposed to my own. And yet at our numerous conferences and consultations I was never even remotely conscious of their party associations. Why should I have been? When specialists are called into consultation on a case of serious illness, foolish indeed would be the relative and even criminal would be the doctor who thought more of the political views of these experts than of their qualifications to assist in pulling the patient through the crisis. Unhappily for the Liberal Party it included, at that supreme time of trial, many doctors and kinsmen who took another and narrower view of their responsibilities, and who protested stoutly that consultants tainted with political heresy should be excluded from the sick-room. And these bigots have never forgiven those who adopted a different attitude.

CHAPTER XXV

LORD KITCHENER:
A CHARACTER STUDY

To me Lord Kitchener is one of the unsolved mysteries of the War. Was he a great man, or was he a great disappointment? There were many competent observers who knew him well, but took different views of his character—there were many who held conflicting estimates alternatively and simultaneously. But no one who ever saw him regarded him as an ordinary man, for his very appearance had a distinction all its own. What he did well he did with a sway that was peculiar to himself. When he saw his vision was penetrating. Even his failings were not ordinary. He held childish opinions on some matters, but they were not commonplace. When he did silly things, as the wisest men occasionally do, they were extraordinarily silly. His intuitions, his improvisations, his visions—yes, even his stupidities—were all far removed from the average.

A lady with a pernicious gift for stinging epigram described him as " Not a great man, but a great poster." He was, indeed, the greatest " poster " since Boulanger, but he was far more. He was certainly not a Boulanger, for he was conspicuously free from the vice of the *poseur*. After having been in close touch with him and having seen him at work every week and almost every day, for nearly two years, I could not even then quite make up my mind about his qualities. Of this I feel certain, he had flashes of greatness. He was like one of those revolving lighthouses which radiate momentary gleams of revealing light far out into the surrounding gloom and then suddenly relapse into complete darkness. There were no intermediate stages. Now and again he would express an opinion or give utterance to an illuminating phrase that penetrated the fog of war, and then sometimes he would indulge in a garrulousness which displayed the greatest ignorance of the elementary conditions with which he had to deal. He had an ineffable contempt for the Territorials and a puerile fear of the Senussi. I heard him talk of the Territorials as if they were a worthless rabble of make-believes. On the other hand, I heard him talk with woe of the possibility of a million Senussi horsemen sweeping into the Egyptian Delta.

Whether he had always been so, or whether the tropical sun had scorched and parched some of his intelligence, leaving merely oases of verdure and fertility, I cannot judge, for I only met him once previously, some three years before the War. He was then full of admiration for the German Army and pitying contempt for the French Army. " They will walk through them like partridges," was one of his phrases. I discovered that his opinion was not based on military but on political reasons. There is no greater fatuity than a political judgment dressed in a military uniform. What convinced him of the superiority of the German to the French soldier was that the latter had been demoralised by democratic views and concomitant ideas of liberty which were utterly incompatible with true discipline, whereas the former was trained to obey his superiors. He was right and he was wrong. The German system proved superior for the short course, but French democracy was the better in the long run. The autocratic system of the German Empire crashed hopelessly when it had to bear the burden of a great defeat.

Kitchener's rigid point of view and its reactionary arrogance showed itself in other directions. Some of his mental veins had hardened and any pressure on them produced apoplectic results. He vehemently opposed the recognition of Nonconformist denominations not already included in the Army List, and his refusal to appoint chaplains of what he evidently thought were superfluous and eccentric sects provoked the most angry scenes I have ever witnessed at a Cabinet. The Army only recognised three or four denominations. The others, not being on the Army List, had no existence for him. He did not realise that with an army that was being multiplied tenfold and drawing recruits from classes, or types, untapped by the ordinary recruiting sergeant, the variety of religious beliefs held must necessarily be greater. To his mind the religious services provided for the regulars of the old army ought to be good enough for these amateur soldiers. The vital importance of encouraging national co-operation by deferring to all legitimate susceptibilities did not occur to him. This showed the light occulted. When he gave way, however, he did it thoroughly. I well remember how, when he had been overruled by the Cabinet on the question of chaplains he took a piece of paper, started writing, and turning to me said: " Come now, tell me the names of these sects for which you want padres. Is this list right? Primitive Baptists, Calvinistic Wesleyans, Congregational Methodists. . . ?" It was not intended to cast ridicule; he simply had never heard the correct names of these great religious bodies. I gave him the right titles. He wrote them all down carefully. As soon as he returned to the War Office he took steps to invite representatives of all these denominations to attend a Chaplains Committee there. It functioned right through the War without any friction.

A smaller man, according to the wont of small men, would have pretended to signify agreement, and then have placed every obstacle in the path of execution. Lord Kitchener may or may not have been a great man, but he certainly was not a small one, and here his action was one of greatness, for having been overruled he loyally accepted defeat.

His attitude towards the various nationalities that constitute the people of the United Kingdom was more obdurate, and his obstinacy had far-reaching and fatal results. Scotchmen had by tradition established a military title to their nationality, and it was a title Lord Kitchener respected and honoured. But although Welshmen and Irishmen had also their separate national regiments, he declined to encourage their national sentiments when it came to the point of raising separate Welsh and Irish divisions. The case of the Welsh division was one with which I was naturally particularly concerned. In order to encourage recruiting in the Principality, a number of influential Welshmen, with the Earl of Plymouth at their head, decided to form and raise a purely Welsh division. Colonel Owen Thomas took a very active part in this effort. But when the proposal came before Lord Kitchener he promptly vetoed it. The question was thereupon raised by me in the Cabinet, and there was a fierce fight. In the end the cause of the Welsh division was carried. Lord Kitchener came to me afterwards and said: " What was the name of the officer who pressed this scheme forward?" I told him it was Colonel Owen Thomas. " Can you bring him along to me?" asked Kitchener, and I promised to do so. The Colonel was summoned post haste to London, and I took him round to Kitchener, at the War Office. Kitchener bent on him a terrific frown, and Thomas, though a stout-hearted fellow, visibly quailed on seeing that imposing personage with his stern face and his terrifying eyes. Lord Kitchener rumbled forth: " I understand you are a Colonel." Thomas timidly signified assent. " Would you like to become a Brigadier-General?" Thomas could not find his tongue, and I answered promptly for him, " Of course he would!" " Then I will make you a Brigadier-General for this Welsh division. Carry on!" said Kitchener.

In the case of the Welsh division he thus made a handsome surrender. But unhappily for the country, he maintained his dislike for the Irish division. This formation represented poor John Redmond's last effort to bring Ireland effectively into the War. He addressed recruiting meetings throughout Ireland, and his eloquence won thousands of young Irish Nationalists and Catholics to fight under the standard of freedom and justice raised by the British Empire. His brother, William Redmond, one of the best loved members of the House of Commons, took a commission in this new unit, and he subsequently fell fighting under the British flag in France. But Lord Kitchener did his best to damp the ardour of the Redmonds. He refused commissions to educated young Irishmen of the class and type who were being made officers in England, Scotland,

and Wales, for no conceivable reason except that he distrusted and disliked their nationalism. The culminating incident will take an invidiously prominent place in the tragic history of Irish relations with Great Britain. Nationalist ladies, fired with enthusiasm for the new Irish division, for Mr. Redmond and for the cause to which they were devoting themselves, embroidered a silken flag with the Irish harp emblazoned upon it. At the same moment the patriotic ladies of Ulster were embroidering the Red Hand of Ulster on the flag which they designed to present to a division which was being raised in Ulster. In due course the two flags were presented to the respective divisions. One was taken and the other was left. When Lord Kitchener heard of the green flag and its Irish harp he ordered that it should be taken away. But the Ulster flag was allowed to fly gloriously over the heads of the Orange soldiers of the Protestant North. Ireland was deeply hurt. Her pride was cut to the quick, her sense of fair play was outraged, her sympathy with the Holy War against the military dictatorship of Europe was killed, and John Redmond's heart was broken. He ought to have appealed to Parliament, but he probably knew it was too late to avert the evil. From that moment the effort of Irish Nationalism to reconcile England and Ireland by uniting the two peoples in a common effort for the oppressed of another land failed, and Lord Kitchener's sinister order constituted the first word in a new chapter of Irish history.

Like all great men he had a sense of humour. Amongst my papers I came across a pleasant reminder of this fact. A Welsh mariner interned at Ruhleben had sent home a letter in which he had sought successfully to convey without censorship to his relations at home some notion of the severity of the conditions in that camp. The letter was sent on to Kitchener. Here is the letter: —

" Englisches Lager,
Barake 11,
Ruhleben,
Bei Spandau,
BERLIN.

Dear Wife and Children,

I have your letter of the 1st, and am pleased to know you are all well. I am afraid we are here for a long time and we dread the winter. I wish I were at home with you.

I am still keeping well and I cannot say any more. My love to you all, and my respects to Cig, Tan, Menin, and Siwgr, whom I have not seen this long time, but hope to see when I get home.

&c., &c."

A footnote by Lord Kitchener's correspondent explains that: —

" The words as above (Cig, Tan, Menin, Siwgr) are Welsh, and the interpretation of them respectively is: —

Meat
Fire
Butter
Sugar."

A copy was sent on by Lord Kitchener to Sir Edward Grey and myself with this endorsement: —

" Sir Edward Grey.
Mr. Lloyd George.
    The value of the Welsh language in dealing with the cultured Teuton.   K."

When I met him subsequently at the Cabinet he chortled over the incident.

His was a hypnotic personality and the impulse of his magnetism moved multitudes of men to willing action. Was he a great organiser? I cannot tell, even though I saw his greatest tasks. He undoubtedly possessed some of the rarest qualities of the great organiser—the gifts of improvisation, of driver, of leadership. But he had developed two patent defects, a reluctance to delegate and, more serious still, an inability to choose the right men.

Lord Kitchener was one of the first to realise the magnitude of the War. When most men talked of peace before Christmas he predicted a three years' struggle and set out—as far as men were concerned—to prepare for it. He made a call first for half a million and then for a million more. He knew that with the means at his disposal not one half of them would be available for the field for a full year. As a matter of fact the first battle of the first divisions of the " K " army was fought in September, 1915. His views as to the duration of the campaign changed somewhat from time to time, and in the spring of 1915, he predicted that the German reserves would be exhausted by September. But nothing can rob him of the credit for the vision that foresaw in August, 1914, a three years' campaign, and for the energy and wisdom with which he set out at once to prepare for it.

I doubt whether any other man could at that moment have attracted the hundreds of thousands who rallied to the flag at his appeal. And those who were responsible for placing the striking portrait of Lord Kitchener's strong face on the appeals to fight for " King and Country " had a genius for publicity. It was eminently the face of a commander. The resolution of its firm lines, the mixture of calm penetration and determination in the steady eyes, the intelligence of the broad square brow, all gave an impression of irresistible strength that inspired everyone who saw it. And in those stormy days who was there who did not gaze on those granite features with a confidence of the kind that led the nation to heights of sacrifice? Kitchener was cast in nature's mould for a hero.

Another proof of Lord Kitchener's military vision was given in August, 1914, when the intention of the Germans to advance through Belgium was still unknown. General Joffre and his advisers were confident that the real blow would come from the Ardennes and that no serious German forces would advance in the Mons direction. Their view was that the roads in that quarter were not suited for the progress and maintenance of a great army. Lord Kitchener took a different view; and I have a distinct recollection of his expressing his opinion to the Cabinet. The event proved he was right. The French Commander's mistake was very nearly fatal to the Allied cause.

Kitchener had not the mind for directing a great war conducted along lines to which he was completely unaccustomed either by training or experience. He never took to the manufacture of heavy guns for field warfare and he was sceptical of the prodigal expenditure of shells in trench warfare. He did not realise the part which the machine-gun was destined to play in the War.

As the operations developed on lines which were farther and farther removed from his conception of warfare he became less and less effective and his judgment was less and less trusted by his colleagues. It is not too much to say that during the last few months of his stay at the War Office he was a *roi fainéant*. Sir William Robertson was appointed to the position of Chief of the Imperial General Staff, with powers that reduced Lord Kitchener's position to that of a signatory Minister. He held the Seals of Office, but so far as war direction was concerned he had to use them under Sir William Robertson's orders. It was no doubt a humiliating position for a great soldier, because he was in every respect a greater man and a greater soldier than the keeper of his seals. Nevertheless, his hold on the public never diminished, and to the end there was always a small crowd waiting outside the War Office watching to catch a glimpse of him. And when the sad news broke upon London that he had gone down with the *Hampshire* in the cruel waters of the North Atlantic, a pall of dismay descended on the spirit of the people. Men and women spoke of the event in hushed tones of terror. The news of a defeat would not have produced such a sense of irreparable disaster. The tidings of the German advance of March, 1918, did not send such a shudder of despair through Britain as did the news of the tragic end of this remarkable man. I am not capable of analysing Lord Kitchener's attributes or gifts. But he was one of the great personalities of the War who exercised an indubitable effect on its course and thus on the destiny of the whole world. Great Britain and her Allies owe to the memory of Lord Kitchener the undying gratitude and the enduring fame which are the due of great service rendered greatly in a great cause.

CHAPTER XXVI

AT THE MINISTRY FOR WAR

On the 6th day of June, 1916, I walked across from the Ministry of Munitions to attend a War Council at 10, Downing Street. Before I entered the Cabinet Chamber the Prime Minister's Secretary, Mr. Bonham Carter, beckoned me into his room and jerked out something about the *Hampshire*. Usually quiet and composed, he was obviously labouring under some suppressed emotion which rendered his speech scarcely articulate. At last he was able to convey to me the startling news that the cruiser in which Lord Kitchener had sailed for Russia had struck a mine off the Orkneys and that Lord Kitchener and his staff had all been drowned. When I entered the Cabinet Room I found the Prime Minister, Sir Edward Grey, Mr. Balfour and Sir Maurice Hankey sitting at the table all looking stunned by the tragedy. One realised how deep was the impression made by the personality of this extraordinary man on all who came in contact with him. Sir Maurice Hankey and I quite forgot for the moment that had it not been for the Irish negotiations we also would have shared the same fate.

The passing of Lord Kitchener left an empty place at the War Office. I realised that this post might be offered to me. But I was far from eager to go to the War Office under present conditions. Although the post of Secretary of State for War was a much more exalted one than that of the Minister of Munitions, and during the present hostilities came second in importance only to that of Prime Minister, it had during recent months declined very much in real influence. Lord Kitchener had lost much of his grip, and, as I have related above, the effective direction of War Office matters had been delegated by a special Order in Council to his Chief of Staff. I had no liking for the prospect of finding myself a mere ornamental figurehead in Whitehall. It is a part I would play grudgingly and gracelessly. Had the Secretaryship of State been a live office where the Minister exercised supreme control subject to Prime Minister and Cabinet, I should have welcomed the promotion. It would have afforded the opportunity to pull things together and alter the direction of affairs. I was becoming increasingly dismayed and dissatisfied at the course along which affairs were drifting, and seriously considered whether I could not render more effective help to our country by resigning office altogether, in order that, as an independent critic, not bound by the traditions of Cabinet unity, I might urge in Parliament and in the country a more vigorous and intelligent prosecution of the War.

Among my papers I find the draft of a memorandum which I prepared on 17th June, 1916, for the purpose of laying before Mr. Asquith my views in reply to his offer of the Secretaryship for War. This is what I had set down: —

" I wrote you the other day asking you to let me have an opportunity of placing before you certain serious considerations before you made up your mind finally about the War Office. Let me at once relieve your mind of one possible anxiety. During the eight years I have had the privilege of serving under you I have no doubt given you from time to time a good deal of worry, but it has never been due to any personal claims I have ever pressed upon you. You were good enough to admit that, when the present Coalition Administration was formed. I do not now propose to ask you for any personal consideration or advancement, as you will realise later on. I have made other plans. But that emboldens me to place before you one or two considerations of a very urgent character. . . .

1.   If the Allies are to be pulled together and to be induced to co-operate, you must have a Secretary of State for War who, apart from possessing personality, will possess real power and influence. No statesman with any self-respect would consent to occupy office under the humiliating conditions to which poor Kitchener had been reduced during the last few months of his life. Many a time I have seen him wince under the indignity of his position. Unless the Secretary of State has the ultimate say in patronage he will be treated with supreme contempt in his own department, and by the whole of the Army. Such a man would have no weight in the councils of the Allies, at a time when it is most urgent that his voice should be cast on the side of unity and co-operation.

2.   There are many important spheres of activity in the British Army which would be better placed under civilian than under military direction. It is no use referring to what is done in Continental armies. Those armies numbered millions, and the best brains of the nation were attracted by the great prizes which were to be won by service in them. Ours was a small thing. The rewards were necessarily limited in number and scope. Where good brains are to be found in the British Army they ought to be put into tasks which civilians cannot discharge. They are wasted on mere business and contractual jobs. On the other hand, if the brains devoted to that class of work are not

good, the Army suffers very severely and there is extravagance without efficiency. I never can get a soldier to realise this; he has a rooted prejudice against giving what has always been regarded as a military job to a civilian.

3. Soldiers are not very eager to promote brilliant subordinates, who may, if very successful, dim their lustre. They are not consciously influenced by such rivalries, but unconsciously they undoubtedly are. They prefer a safe, second-rate man in a position affording great opportunities, to running the risk of creating formidable rivals by choosing men of exceptional powers. This undoubtedly accounts for one or two appointments in the British Army, and still more for two or three non-appointments. A civilian on the other side would have no sense of rivalries in military promotion and he would insist upon the best man being appointed.

4. No wise civilian would ever dream of embarking upon strategy. A man who did that would be fit for no post in any ministry. He would be a danger. There you must be advised by the expert. But the expert must also have his schemes checked by the common sense of the civilian. That is what happens in the War Committee. Great strategical enterprises ought to be submitted not merely to the Secretary of State, but to the War Committee. The soldiers in this war have not been a conspicuous success. Up to the present there has not been a plan conceived and carried out by them which has not ended in bloody failure.

These are some of the thoughts I wanted to put before you determined your action. As I have already stated, I have no personal interest in the matter. I propose now to take a course which I had determined upon long ago. I have been profoundly dissatisfied for a long time with the progress and conduct of the War. I have expressed my dissatisfaction in writing and orally to you, the War Committee and the Cabinet. Had it not been for the fact that I had undertaken a task the carrying out of which was vital to the success of our Army, I should long ago have joined Carson, with whom I have been in the main in complete sympathy in his criticisms of the conduct of the War. But when there was trouble with labour, when the organisation which I had with the help of others created had not yet borne fruit, I felt as if I were running away from the post of difficulty. But now the Munitions Department has been an undoubted success. Ammunition is pouring in. When I came in we were manufacturing in this country 70,000 shells a week; that is about one-sixth of what we spend now in a single week of ordinary trench warfare activity. The whole ammunition reserve was under 75,000; we produce more than twice that per day now. The guns are coming in by the hundred. The policy for which I was mainly responsible in respect of heavy guns—a policy, by the way, which I heard described by one of my colleagues as "sheer lunacy," and which has been consistently opposed by him and by others for months—has now been demonstrated by the facts of the War to be the only one that can possibly achieve success. Our Army in France is now sending in a requisition for hundreds more of heavy guns than had ever been ordered by the War Office. Had it not been that I had in defiance of all authority high and low made arrangements for the manufacture of these guns, the requisition would be in vain.

I am only pointing out these things in order to show that the Munitions Department ought almost to be able to run itself now. I therefore feel that my position in the Ministry is an anomalous one, as I am completely out of sympathy with the spirit and the method of the War direction. I feel we cannot win on these lines. We are undoubtedly losing the War, and nothing can save us but the nation itself. The people do not realise how grave the situation is. I feel they ought to be told. They ought to have a chance of saving themselves, otherwise they have a right to turn round on those who hold these views and say when disaster comes: 'Why did you not tell us in time?' I know you have always taken a more optimistic view of the prospects, but I think you will agree that up to the present my gloomy forebodings have been realised. I hope to God I am wrong; but if I am not, I should feel I had been guilty of a gross neglect of duty if in order to retain a pleasant office I had chosen to muzzle myself and not warn them in time of the danger impending their country. This is no newly formed resolution on my part, as the Lord Chief Justice can tell you, for I intimated to him many weeks ago my intention on the subject. There are things which must be said not merely to our own countrymen, but to the Allies, which cannot be said by one who is still a member of the Cabinet, and yet it is essential to the winning of the War that these warnings should be uttered. I have found it very difficult to refrain from expressing my opinion in conversations, and I am conscious that to do so whilst I am still a member of the Government lays me open to the charge of disloyalty, so that I find myself in the unhappy position of having to choose between disloyalty to my colleagues and the betrayal of my country.

It is with deep regret that from an overwhelming sense of public duty I feel that I must sever my association with you and with some of my other colleagues who have shown me great kindness and goodwill, but I am profoundly convinced that I can render better service to my country in a very dark hour by standing outside and telling them what I know. I believe the Government is rapidly losing the confidence of the nation. It cannot retain it by artificially prolonging the life of Parliament. The nation ought to have an opportunity of choosing its own policy and its own representatives to expound it, and I specially feel that the men in the trenches ought to have an opportunity of choosing the Parliament and the policy on which their lives depend. Here again I am conscious of being out of touch with several of my colleagues and I cannot help seeing that there is an attempt being made to put off a decision on this important question until it is too late to act.

As to Ireland, as far as I am concerned it must be either through or off in the course of the next few days; but I feel that outside the Government I can be more helpful even in the settlement of that question."

That memorandum gives a pretty definite indication of the views I had formed by that time about the situation; and it shows some of the reasons why I was reluctant to take on the position of Secretary of State for War. However, after further talks with Mr. Asquith, with Lord Reading, who was strongly opposed to resignation, with Mr. Bonar Law, and also with Lord Beaverbrook, who was present at all my conversations with Mr. Bonar Law on the subject of the conduct of the War from this time onward until the reconstruction of the Government, I was persuaded to give up the idea of resignation. I also consulted a very old and always a very good friend of mine, the late Sir Edward Russell (afterwards Lord Russell) of the *Liverpool Post*. I sent my memorandum on to him, but he advised against resignation. Mr. Bonar Law urged that if I resigned and joined Carson in criticism it would make his position in the Government quite intolerable. He also would have to retire. Thus we should break up the national unity. I therefore decided not to send in my memorandum, and to postpone for the time my intention of leaving the Government. I accepted the War Office with considerable misgivings, partly on the ground of general War policy and partly because I disliked working in fetters.

On 6th July, 1916, therefore, Mr. Asquith, who had been once again in temporary charge of the War Office pending the appointment of Lord Kitchener's successor, handed it over to me.

I was at the War Office for only five months—too short a time to effect much change in its internal organisation and policy, particularly since the Chief of Staff, Sir William Robertson, regarded any effort to exercise authority on my part as an impingement upon his special powers, so he thrust out all his prickles whenever he suspected I might be about to attempt any rash civilian interference with the sanctities of military matters. The two chief tasks which I was able to carry out during my brief tenure—tasks of which I give some account in following sections—were the tidying up of the appalling muddle in Mesopotamia, and the reconstruction of the Transport system on the Western Front. I also stirred up recruiting in the Empire outside these islands.

In these problems, which I inherited with my new office, I claim to have achieved a good measure of success. In the case of another inherited problem I was less happy. This was the matter of a military mission to Russia. I had from time to time since the War began pressed the Government to establish closer relations between the Western Allies and Russia. I was anxious not only to secure a more effective co-ordination between East and West, but also to find out what could be done towards re-equipping and thus reorganising the Russian Armies.

Lord Kitchener was on his way to Russia when he lost his life. It was a mission of extreme urgency, for the critical state of affairs in that allied country could hardly be exaggerated, and if she were to be saved from collapse it was vital that we in the West should come to a good understanding with her on matters of strategy, finance, and equipment supply.

Lord Kitchener had pre-eminently possessed the right qualifications for this mission. Now that he was gone, it became a question of finding someone suitable to replace him.

The obvious and in fact inevitable person for this mission was Sir William Robertson. As Chief of the Imperial General Staff he possessed the necessary status, prestige and qualifications. The only conceivable alternative would have been General Haig, the Commander-in-Chief, who clearly could not be spared from France in the middle of a great offensive. True, Robertson was not an authority on finance, but this could be got over by sending Lord Reading with him to deal with questions of that nature which needed to be settled.

Robertson made difficulties. The Somme offensive was in full blast, and he was very busy with the arrangements it involved. Time slipped by, and when we reached the latter part of September I felt it was imperative to bring matters to a head; for Archangel was ice-bound in winter, and winter would soon be here.

Accordingly I wrote the following letter to Mr. Asquith:—

CONFIDENTIAL.   " War Office,
                                        26th September, 1916.
My dear Prime Minister,

Before you come to a final decision on the suggestion that I made to you this morning, as I attach very great importance to something being done on those lines, I should like to put before you once more the considerations which convinced me that action on this matter is essential. I have thought so for some time.

1.   The tone of some of the communications from Petrograd indicates a good deal of irritation against us in Russian official, and specially in Russian military circles.

2.   The Germanophile influences have been considerably strengthened in the Russian Government by recent changes. Our friends have disappeared one by one and there is no man now of any influence in the Russian Bureaucracy who can be said to be favourable towards this country.

3.   The Russians, like all peasant peoples, are very suspicious of a trading and financial community.   They always imagine that we are trying to get the better of them in a bargain. The mere fact that their suspicion is a ridiculous one to a business man does not in the least affect the peasant mind. They have undoubtedly got it into their heads that we are anxious to make money out of them.   This suspicion must be removed.

4.   It is not a question of terms but of atmosphere.   The Russian is a simple and, I think, a good fellow, and once we win his trust there will be no difficulty in doing business with him.   We must therefore take some striking action which would clear away these suspicious vapours that obscure the real issues. I therefore urge the importance of sending immediately to Russia emissaries of high standing with full powers to clear up the situation.   It is a misfortune that Bark and Bylaeff left before an agreement was arrived at.   But that is past.

5.   Whoever is sent must not merely possess authority, but must be known by the Russians to be a person or persons of high standing and influence in this country.   I would strongly urge that Sir William Robertson and Lord Reading be asked to go.   As to Sir William Robertson, his standing here is known to the military authorities in Russia, and for the moment they are the only people who count in Russia.   The bureaucrats are poor creatures.   He could discuss with General Alexeieff the military dispositions for next year.   It is important these two men should meet.   Up to the present the Russians have never conferred with the Western Powers as to military plans.   Men like General Gilinski, who represented the Russian Armies in Paris, are worse than of no account; and I am afraid that if there is a second Chantilly conference Alexeieff either cannot or will not send anyone who will have full power to decide the outlines of the next campaign.   The eastern generals probably concentrate their minds too exclusively on the east, and I am not sure that the western generals are not inclined to commit a similar error by limiting their views too much to the countries where their forces are operating.   It would be a good thing for both General Robertson and for General Alexeieff that they

should interchange views, and the decision arrived at by these two great soldiers after such an interchange might very well be decisive.

As for Lord Reading, he has the high standing and the necessary diplomatic gifts and the knowledge of finance which would enable him successfully to achieve an understanding with Russia.

I am afraid of the present misunderstanding developing into strained relations. It would probably not produce a rupture during the progress of the War, but it would certainly have a very sinister influence upon the peace negotiations.

Ever sincerely,
D. LLOYD GEORGE.

P.S.—There has already been a delay of some months in ordering essential military material for Russia, and I am apprehensive that Russian generals will attribute failures—due to their own shortcomings—to our delay in furnishing them with financial assistance."

My proposal in regard to Sir William Robertson was shattered against the rock of personal suspicions. He was already predisposed to imagine that I would welcome his absence from the War Office, and there were those in the Cabinet who were resolutely hostile to anything I did or suggested, who deliberately encouraged Robertson to refuse the proposed mission. Indeed, one of them subsequently admitted that he had advised Robertson not to go. As a consequence, I received on the next day this letter from the C.I.G.S.:—

" War Office.
27/9/16.
6.15 p.m.

Dear Mr. Lloyd George,

The Prime Minister has just sent for me to discuss the Russian visit. I have thought it well over since you spoke to me this morning and have concluded that it is impossible for me to make the visit without losing entire control over the War, and this at an important time. I quite realise the force of what you say, but if I went I should be away for at least a month and that is much too long if I am to keep my hand on the many problems we are dealing with.

I am honestly very sorry not to be able to fall in with your proposal, and as I told the P.M., if I am asked to go—I shall go, but my opinion is that I ought *not* to go, if I am of any use as C.I.G.S.

Callwell got on well when he went. He would be better than no one!

Believe me, I am sorry, but I must tell you what I feel about the necessity for my remaining at my post.

Yours very truly,

W. R. ROBERTSON."

With this refusal the proposed mission to Russia collapsed, and our chance of coming to a real understanding with our great Ally in the east was lost until it was too late to save Russia from her final collapse.

Such news as came through to us during the autumn of 1916 from Russia showed what a fatal blunder the abandonment of the mission was proving. All the omens were pointing to a breakdown of the Russian military effort and to a separate peace with Germany. At the end of July, Sazonow, faithfully pro-Ally, had been intrigued out of the Russian Foreign Ministry and been replaced by Sturmer, who was suspected, not without reason, of pro-German leanings. The King of Sweden (who was pro-German in sympathy) had remarked to the British Ambassador at Stockholm, on hearing this news, that there would be peace between Russia and Germany in two months! Though this prophecy was unfulfilled, it was based on a true insight into the trend of affairs in Russia.

Sir George Buchanan, the British Ambassador in Petrograd, mentioned in a private letter to Lord Charles Beresford on 17th October the prevalence of rumours of a separate peace, which Sturmer had officially denied, and reported the growth of a pro-German sentiment in influential circles. In a further letter of 28th October he stressed the progress which pro-German and anti-British propaganda was making, and added: "The losses which Russia has suffered in this war are so colossal that the whole country is in mourning; and so many lives have been uselessly sacrificed during the recent unsuccessful attacks against Kovel and other places that the impression seems to be gaining ground with many people that it is useless going on, more especially as Russia, unlike Great Britain, has nothing to gain by prolonging the war . . . with the people becoming every day more discontented and with a man like Sturmer at the head of the Government, I cannot help feeling anxious."

On 30th November, Lord Rhondda sent me a series of memoranda written by a British officer stationed at Archangel, recording his impression gleaned on a visit to Petrograd and Moscow. He, too, was impressed with the strength of German propaganda and war weariness among the mass of the nation. "From the highest to the lowest all are of opinion that the spirit of the Russian populace in the big cities of late has fallen very greatly," he wrote. "The chief cause, of course, of this change in national *morale* is the extreme difficulty of getting the first necessities of life, even at any price, and the now universal necessity of standing in long queues in the big

owns to get a small supply of such articles as milk, black and white
read, butter and/or cheese, sugar, tea and coffee, meat, fish, etc.
. . These queues form an excellent field of operations for agents
f German propaganda, where it is subtly hinted and often even
penly asserted by people standing waiting their turn that all
his misery is merely being suffered for the aggrandisement of
England. . . ."

Then came the following prophetic sentences: —

". . . The next three months are the critical period. . . . Either
he Government will yield or there will be a *coup d'état,* or, if
either of these things happen, Russia will have to stop fighting and
make peace, with disastrous results."

This informant urged that measures of counter-propaganda should
be initiated with the utmost dispatch. " It is only with the most
assiduous and patient nursing that the Russian Government and
people can be led through another one or two years of war and
hardship, and no effort or comparatively trifling expense should be
spared in achieving this. . . ."

But the warning was too late. The ice had already closed round
Archangel. Before it melted again in the spring, Russia had crashed
into revolution, and all hope of reinforcing her as an Allied Power
was at an end.

EFFECTS OF GERMAN PROPAGANDA

CHAPTER XXVII

SIR WILLIAM ROBERTSON

SIR WILLIAM ROBERTSON was one of the enigmas of the War. He was not a great soldier, but that he possessed an outstanding personality is beyond question. The fact that there was such a wide diversity of opinion and such an acute controversy as to his gifts and character is sufficient proof that he was no common man. No one in so exclusive a profession as the Army, where social prestige and accomplishment count for so much, could have risen from the humblest upbringing and the lowliest rank to the topmost heights which he occupied unless he possessed talents well above his fellows. He was industrious, steady, intelligent; all the administrative tasks entrusted to him, whether as ranker, N.C.O., or commissioned officer, he discharged competently and with distinction. He was an excellent organiser. He had, during his military career, few opportunities, if any, of leading men in the field. His experience had been of an administrative kind, and here he was a conspicuous success. In that respect amongst all the generals, he was second only to Sir John Cowans. He had other qualities which made for speedy promotion in the Army. He was cautious and discreet. His massive reticence made a deep impression on all whose duty it was to seek his opinion.

A laconic sentence, or often a mere grunt which might signify anything, was all that he vouchsafed in answer to the most anxious searcher after truth on our military position. He was non-committal but he was sternly orthodox. Such mistakes therefore as he committed were all of the negative kind, and as these were always in accordance with Army regulations and traditions they counted in his favour and helped his promotion. He understood the Army better than any of his rivals.*

Such men always get on in any vocation. These qualities of

---

* Extract from *Times* obituary leading article: " . . . he was not a genius, except in CARLYLE'S definition. There was no meteoric brilliance about him; his imagination was commonplace. . . . That is the true lesson of ROBERTSON'S career. Genius dazzles by its splendour; but it is possible to see this man exactly as he was, to watch each of the struggles which he made, and to understand completely the reason why he triumphed. There is excuse in genius for failure to emulate it; ROBERTSON'S career offers no excuse. What he did any man or boy of ordinary attainments can do also, provided that he is willing to make the necessary sacrifices of immediate leisure and comfort."

circumspection in judgment and speech lead even shrewd and experienced observers of all sorts and conditions of men to infer that there is a vast mental hinterland unexplored and unrevealed. Mr. Asquith declared Robertson to be " the greatest strategist of the day." That he most certainly was not. But his oracular mono-syllables and grunts misled much abler men than himself. Of his abilities I have already spoken. Some of his limitations I have indicated. His mind was sound but commonplace. He was cautious to the point of timidity. There lay his strength—that also accounted for his drawbacks. A general who takes no risks or leaves them to others never won a difficult campaign.

When I first met him he had reached a very considerable position in the military hierarchy. He was Chief of the Staff to the Commander-in-Chief of the Expeditionary Force in France. I was certainly impressed at my first acquaintance with him. I saw a good deal of him later on in the War and I came gradually to understand his powers and his limitations.

He had a profound and disturbing suspicion of all foreigners; if I may use a fruit grower's vocabulary, Robertson had the canker of xenophobia in his very sap and that vitiated the quality of his product. In a war conducted by an alliance of several nations it was essential to victory that there should be a sound and broad inter-pretation of the policy of the single front. In the order of his distrust came Frenchmen, first and deepest of all, then Italians, Serbians, Greeks, Celts, and last of all—if at all—Germans. The Austrians had no existence for him except in his arithmetical tables. They were not near the Western Front and did not otherwise obtrude their hostile presence into his strategical conceptions. The French always irritated him and brought out all his stubbornness. That is why they called him " General Non-non "; that represented his first impulse towards all their requests and proposals. Briand once said to me: " Rob-berrt-son says ' Non ' before he has heard what your proposal is about."

Of the Germans he had a very high opinion and no dislike. In 1916, when the German Army was making its stubborn defence of the slush on the Somme plateau, he said to me: " If we and the Boche were together, we would have beaten the whole lot of them long ago." When the fighting was at its worst he did not hesitate to express his opinion in a discussion on Peace Terms, that a strong Germany in Central Europe was vital to the preservation of Peace. His memorandum on that subject rose in parts to the heights of statesmanship. After a week's reflection on his own temerity he withdrew the memorandum and cancelled it. He would have been much more effective as a politician than as a soldier. Since he has already passed away I can express this opinion without inflicting the hurt it would inevitably have caused him.

I shall have a good deal to say later on as to his fitness for the position of Chief of the Imperial General Staff. I do not believe he ever visualised the full significance and responsibility of that great position. His function ought to have been that of Chief Military Adviser to the Cabinet on the War as a whole. Sir Douglas Haig, Sir Archibald Murray, Sir John Maxwell, General Milne and General Maude were all sectional generals, and their minds were bound to be concentrated in the main, if not entirely, upon the problem of defeating the army immediately in front of them, but the C.I.G.S. ought to have realised that it was his duty to supervise and to co-ordinate efforts on all the battlefields. He came into full authority when the British contribution to the War in men, material money and ships had grown to vast dimensions and was still growing We were therefore entitled not indeed to impose our ideas upon the Allies or to dictate to them, but to impress and insist much more than we did. Our chief failure in the first three campaigns of the War was in co-ordination of forces and resources, in a full realisation of what the united front meant strategically. Robertson rendered no help in overcoming this calamitous defect. From the moment he became C.I.G.S. he hindered and thwarted at every turn every effort to concentrate and distribute the aggregate power of the Allies in such a way as to achieve the surest and speediest results. I felt profoundly that in this respect he completely failed the statesmen whom he derided, but ought to have guided.

Sir Douglas Haig was a stronger man. I doubt whether he was abler than Robertson, but he had better fighting qualities. He was a man of more indomitable will and courage. He was also Robertson's senior; that counts in every profession but most of all in the Army and Navy. Other qualifications being fairly equal seniority has always the say. That is why, whenever I saw these two men together, I felt that Haig dominated, over-awed and almost bullied his junior. Robertson was not endowed with that intrepidity in thought and action that makes great generals.

There was a rigidity about Robertson's physical movements which gave an indication of his lack of mental suppleness and adaptability He did not argue, he shrank from being involved in argument and he hated contention; one reason being that he was very sensitive about any challenge to his personal or official dignity in word or deed. When the Woolwich workers were making some trouble on a question of time or wages, Dr. Addison invited Sir William Robertson to address them on the urgency of their work. He thought that a few words from so distinguished a soldier might appease them When, however, the two reached the hall they found it filled with a raging and noisy crowd who hurled questions at the visitors without respect to stars or stripes. The Chief of the Imperial Staff was offended at that kind of reception. He felt his dignity would be impaired by arguing with a tumult, so he declined to speak and left the meeting to Dr. Addison.

He rarely intervened in Council and I never heard him take much part in discussion with Allied generals. At these conferences between the soldiers and sailors of the Allies, Robertson usually sat at the table in gruff silence. His protests were frequent, but generally inarticulate. He thoroughly disapproved of Foch, Nivelle, Joffre, and Lyautey, but he never condescended to dispute with them. He seemed bored, if not overpowered by the voluble confidence of the French generals. When I attended the Rome Conference in 1917, M. Briand and General Lyautey, who was then Secretary of State for War in France, travelled by the same train. Late at night Lyautey sent for Sir William Robertson and myself to his saloon. He had a map of Palestine in front of him, and from this he proceeded to deliver a very lengthy lecture on the strategy of a campaign for the conquest of Jerusalem. Robertson never uttered a word of approval or dissent; he let out an occasional grunt, and when Lyautey had concluded his address, he turned to me and said: " Has he finished?" I told him I thought he had. We got up, and' on our way back to the British carriage he said to me: " That fellow won't last long." Nor did he, for his demission ensued in a very few weeks.

Robertson's appearance gave no idea of the essential geniality and kindliness of the man. In repose his facial expression was sullen, if not rather morose; in conversation he melted and often became entertaining, so long as you did not venture on a topic on which he disagreed with you. In that case he found refuge in glumness.

He could be full of fun. I recollect returning from a visit to Paris with him and Lord Kitchener. In the train there was a good deal of pleasant chaff interchanged between us. Lord Kitchener was giving an account of his house down in Kent to which he was very attached. He complained, however, that there was no water in the particular valley in which he had built his residence, but it added to his grievance that there was plenty of water in the valleys on either side. Robertson said: " Then why don't you make a tunnel from one of these valleys to draw water into your own?" This idea amused the sapper.

Personally I was attracted by Robertson and would have liked to have been able to work with him to the very end. That is a story I must tell in later chapters.

CHAPTER XXVIII

TRANSPORT

SIR DOUGLAS HAIG once told Sir Eric Geddes that the problem of warfare consisted of "three M's": Men, Munitions, Movement. I tell elsewhere in this story the way men were supplied to our military authorities by civilian organisers, and the use or misuse that was made of them; I have shown how those same authorities proved unable to organise the production of their munitions, and had to remit this task to politicians and men of business. Now I have to show how the professional soldiers who fought so valiantly in the stricken area also found themselves unable to cope with the vast problem of Movement which this unprecedented war set before them, and how here again disaster was narrowly averted by the aid of the civilian expert. I am not arraigning the professional soldier, but only the supercilious folly miles behind the shell area which stigmatised all civilian aid in the construction or direction of the war machine as unwarranted interference by ignorant amateurs.

It is of course hardly surprising, when one recalls the gigantic scope of the transport problem—the millions of men with their equipment, baggage, horses, etc., which had to be moved to and from France and from one front to another; their colossal daily supplies of food, fodder, ammunition, tools, trench warfare supplies; medical and surgical stores and evacuation of wounded—that elderly officers who had reached seniority after years of service under the rather rigid conventions of a small army, and with no practical experience of traffic on a large and continuous scale, would not necessarily be competent to work out the best method of dealing with this vast tangle of unanticipated transport. It required an exceptional experience which they had never obtained, and exceptional organising ability which the process of their selection could not guarantee.

Quite early in the work of the Ministry of Munitions I encountered this failure of the military to organise unprecedented transport, and that no further away than within the walls of Woolwich Arsenal When I took over Woolwich in August, 1915, and I put Mr. Vincent Raven in charge of it, he found himself responsible for a bewildering range of factories and departments, occupying an area of about $3\frac{1}{2}$ miles long by $2\frac{1}{2}$ miles wide, with about 150 miles of internal railway track for bringing in and distributing its supplies of raw material and evacuating its output. There was not enough rolling stock. The system was so confused that it was impossible to get the raw material into the Arsenal, to get the finished goods out, or to move stuff efficiently from place to place within the Arsenal itself. Traffic was hopelessly congested. He had to get a special expert in from one of the railway companies to take charge, and organise the system of transport. He speedily got things on to an efficient footing.

But the real crux of the transport problem was the connecting links between the French ports and the front line. On this side, the movement of goods and men in Britain, and their dispatch to the French coast, were organised by our own highly efficient railway chiefs and shipping services. Once landed in France, they came on the French railway system, and were badgered and disorganised by inexpert officers who were trying to wring from it services on a scale hitherto unconceived. As might have been expected, the result was confusion, congestion and delay.

While I was Minister of Munitions I sent Geddes over to France on one occasion, with the permission of the War Office, to look into some matter of the recovery and transport of salvage. The account he gave me on his return of the transport situation was so disquieting that I suggested to Lord Kitchener that he should be sent to make an investigation and report, with a view to its better organisation. But Lord Kitchener held the opinion that these were purely military matters, into the sanctity of which no profane civilian must be allowed to intrude. He was by this time suffering from that growing inertia and ossification of the mind which so gravely impaired his usefulness during his last months of office.

Shortly before I left the Ministry of Munitions it was reported to me from France that there was a shortage of ammunition. On enquiry I found that this was in no way due to failure on our part to produce it. In fact our munition factories were becoming choked up with completed output because the base depots in France were too congested to receive it.

On the day on which the death of Lord Kitchener was reported, Sir Eric Geddes, whose special work had been so much hampered by the failure in transport facilities, came to see me on the subject of transport. It appeared that in reply to a request from the War Office for an estimate as to output of artillery ammunition from 1st July onwards, the figure of 1,000,000 rounds per week had been given. Of the possibility of this production the War Office was frankly sceptical, and stated that even if it were produced it could not be conveyed either across the Channel or to the front owing to the congested state of the ports and roads, and that in any event the guns could not fire it. In view of the fact that the last advance estimate of the Ministry had been exactly fulfilled, and in view of all our efforts to produce

ϱ*

what the Army wanted, this attitude was, to say the least of it, somewhat exasperating.

As soon as I became Secretary of State for War in July, 1916, I sent
through Lord Derby, who was then my Under-Secretary, a request to
Sir Douglas Haig that he should invite Sir Eric Geddes to go over and
look into the matter of transport.   But my suggestion was not
favourably received.   The day after I learnt this I was going over
myself to France to visit the whole of the front from Verdun to
Flanders.   When I reached Paris I saw Lord Esher, who was located
there in his usual post of general adviser to everybody and liaison officer
between everybody and anybody—a most useful kind of person if he
possesses tact, discernment, and experience.   Lord Esher had these
qualities in a superlative degree.   He was a friendly and helpful
personage with a great knowledge of military things and people.   I
told him all my misgivings about transport and Haig's polite snub
to Derby.   I said that I had sent Derby because I thought he was a
special favourite of the Commander-in-Chief!   He did not confirm
that impression and said: "Go there yourself and talk quite frankly
about the whole position.   Talk to Haig himself about it and refuse
to be referred to his staff.   Your only difficulty will be that although
Haig is not a good judge of men he stands by them with stubborn
loyalty to all, whatever their quality.   But if you can show him that
essential supplies are being kept from his army during the progress
of a great battle, he will listen and look into the matter."   I took his
advice, drove straight to G.H.Q. and stayed the night at Sir Douglas
Haig's château.   He received me with great cordiality, and gave me
the usual sanguine estimate of the progress and prospects of the
Somme offensive.   Casualties were omitted from the narrative.   When
I approached him on the subject of transport I decided that it would
be better not to discuss merits or details, but to ask him to see Sir Eric
Geddes and afford him an opportunity for seeing the transport
arrangements and reporting to him on their condition.   To this
suggestion he assented with alacrity, as it enabled him to get out of
what might turn into a disagreeable discussion with the new Secretary
of State for War.   I was equally pleased because I felt assured that he
would now treat the proposal for a change not as an arraignment of his
organisation of the war front but as a method of helping him at a
critical moment.   With his agreement I wired Sir Eric Geddes an
invitation to pay a visit to G.H.Q. and inspect transport arrangements.

Sir Eric went over and spent two days there.   He was treated, needless to say, with perfect courtesy.   At the end of the time the
Commander-in-Chief asked him if he had seen everything, and
Geddes answered that he had seen enough to think about, but did not
know what to think yet.   He stayed a few days longer, but then had
to tell Haig that he had been shown nothing which the ordinary

distinguished tourist would not have been shown; and that what he wanted was a month, in which time he would analyse the problem and produce a report and programme.

Very fortunately, Sir Eric Geddes and Sir Douglas Haig had by this time taken warmly to each other. Sir Douglas later on stated that he " recognised in him the very qualities which the army in the field required." The upshot was that the Commander-in-Chief invited the railway expert to come and spend a month making a thorough investigation and evolving a programme for the transport system. Sir Eric went as a civilian, with a small expert civilian staff to assist him. There never was a more efficient group. He also took with him Sir George Beharrell and General Mance, D.D.M. at the War Office, whom I lent him for the purpose, and Sir Philip Nash, who with Beharrell had been working under Geddes in the Ministry of Munitions. In France he further added to his staff General Freeland, who was on the staff of the Director of Railways at G.H.Q. With these assistants he prepared a programme of transport improvement, including a light railway system for serving the forward areas behind the front line.

On Sir Eric's return I appointed him Director of Military Railways at the War Office. This brought me to my first conflict with the military members of the Army Council. The appointment had to be sanctioned by the Council. One of the generals sitting around the table, speaking obviously on behalf of the rest, protested against a civilian appointment which overrode or circumscribed the authority of experienced and respected generals already discharging these functions to everybody's satisfaction. I challenged this statement and submitted facts which proved serious confusion and congestion, from the ports to Amiens, at Amiens, and from Amiens to the front. Sir William Robertson sat glum during the discussions. Ultimately the appointment was sanctioned. The military members met and decided to send me a formal written protest. Immediately I received it I summoned another meeting of the Army Council and asked the protestors to state their case. The same spokesman repeated his arguments—the rest were silent and once more the appointment was confirmed. The following morning Sir John Cowans came to see me. He looked a little shy and embarrassed. He told me the military members of the Council had met and drawn up a document which they had asked him to present to me. He put on his great horn spectacles and drew a foolscap paper from his pocket. I stopped him and asked him whether it had anything to do with the Geddes appointment, and when he answered in the affirmative I told him that this matter was finally settled and I declined to re-open it. He smiled and said " I thought you would say so. This paper is therefore of no use." He then tore it up and laughed. Thus ended my first encounter with the military members. I got on much better with them afterwards.

No sooner had Geddes taken up his post than Sir Douglas Haig wired that he wanted Geddes to join his staff in France as Director-General of Transportation. This created a difficult situation, for I did not want to lose him, in view of the important transport reforms I wished him to inaugurate at the War Office, and Geddes himself was by no means eager to go to France, knowing as he did what bitter jealousy of the interloper would be felt by some of the staff officers who had hitherto had charge of transport there. However, General Butler, who had come over from the Commander-in-Chief as a special emissary to secure the services of Geddes in France, was so insistent and persuasive that we eventually made a compromise. It was agreed that Sir Eric should hold the two positions simultaneously; while remaining Director of Military Railways, he should also become Director-General of Transportation in France, and thus be in a position to place his railway experience and remarkable gifts of organisation alike at the service of the War Office and the Expeditionary Force. He had two experienced railway managers as deputies, Sir Guy Granet at the War Office and Sir Philip Nash at G.H.Q. in France.

There was the inevitable and anticipated disgruntlement in some quarters among the staff at G.H.Q. over this appointment. Certain indignant generals tendered their resignations. They started a rumour—only too readily believed in some quarters—that I was up to the politicians' trick of forcing unwanted civilians on the Army, and interfering with the military authorities.

To dispose finally of the suggestion that I exercised my authority to force Sir Douglas Haig to dismiss a competent military staff in order to substitute civilians who knew nothing of war conditions, I would like to quote a letter written to Sir Eric by the Commander-in-Chief:—

> "General Headquarters of British
> Army in France,
> Friday, September 22, 1916.
>
> My dear Geddes,
>   Butler has told me of his interview with you, and I am very pleased to think that you are prepared to join me here and help in beating the Germans for the good of the Empire.
>   I should be grateful if you would come over and see me in order that there may be no misunderstanding as to the conditions on which you are prepared to help.
>   After full consideration of the organisation which you proposed to me on your last visit, I am most willing and anxious that you should take over complete charge of TRANSPORTATION services of the Army in France. That is to say that you would have under your control:—

(a) Broad gauge railways.
(b) Narrow gauge railways.
(c) Inland water transport.
(d) Roads.

and that whilst working under instructions from my Q.M.G. you will have direct access to me, and will be in the closest touch with me and my General Staff in order to know our plans so as to look ahead *in time* and provide for our future needs. . . .

Looking forward to seeing you,
Believe me,
Yours very truly,
D. HAIG."

The appointment also called forth the following exchange of letters between the Commander-in-Chief and myself: —

" War Office,
27th September, 1916.

My dear General,
Geddes has told me that you have asked him to become your Chief Executive Officer for Transportation in France. I had as you know already appointed him to a similar position in this country. I have told him that I would approve his undertaking complete responsibility for the work upon both sides of the Channel if you wish him to do so. The main thing, to my mind, is that he should be given a very free hand and the personal support of yourself and myself. If you decide to appoint him on your Staff I hope you will find it possible to make these conditions so far as France is concerned. I am doing so in England. He will have direct access to me and then I shall be able to take a close personal interest in supporting the full development of your transportation policy.

Yours sincerely,
D. LLOYD GEORGE.

General Sir Douglas Haig, G.C.B., etc."

The General's reply was as follows: —

" General Headquarters,
British Armies in France,
1st October, 1916.

My dear Mr. Lloyd George,
I thank you for your letter of the 27th September. I am writing officially to the War Office on the subject of Geddes' appointment, but reserving various details for further discussion here with my Quartermaster-General and Inspector-General of Communications.

It is my intention to give Geddes as free a hand as possible and to give him my personal support, but it is essential that changes shall be made gradually and without upsetting the existing organisation, which has done excellent work under very difficult conditions and has never failed me up to date.

Yours very truly,

D. HAIG."

Within a month Sir Eric had established his headquarters for the B.E.F. Transport at a little place three miles from Montreuil, called Monthouis, and before long destined to become famous under the soubriquet of "Geddesburg." From this centre Geddes organised the improved transport system which functioned so splendidly during the latter part of the War.

For a man of Sir Eric's railway experience the problem was not a very difficult one. It called chiefly for expert knowledge in the handling of traffic and the capacity to think on an adequate scale and then act promptly. The military transport authorities had been trying all along to "make do" with a totally insufficient transport system. The French railways in the area had been placed at their disposal, and over these and over French country roads, neither of which had been designed to bear a tithe of such weight and volume of traffic, they were trying to move their troops and stores. Naturally the machine broke down. There was an efficient service from depot or factory in Britain up to the French port. But the assembling yards behind the ports were the point of greatest weakness, having become a real bottle-neck which strangled the traffic flow. When the goods finally got past and on to the railheads, which were placed perhaps as much as fifteen miles behind the front line, they had to be conveyed forward this distance over broken-down roads which were simultaneously being used for movement of troops.

Putting experienced railway men in charge of the assembling yards helped to relieve the congestion there. But the first big innovation which Sir Eric undertook was the construction of light narrow-gauge railways in the forward areas to move supplies from the broad-gauge railheads up to the line. Till this time there were no light railways at all. He framed a programme for an eventual 1,000 miles of light railway with rolling-stock to correspond. The first stage in the execution of that programme involved an order for 1,000 miles of light steel rails, and one stormy autumn night I was awakened in the small hours at the Hotel Crillon, where I was staying during a visit to France, by a dispatch rider bringing Sir Eric's report setting out the proposal for this requisition. I read and initialled it, and it was rushed back to "Geddesburg" in time for Beharrell to fly with it to Boulogne and catch the 9 o'clock boat in the morning. He arrived in London and dismayed Sir Ernest Moir with the size of the requisition. But Sir Ernest duly produced the goods, and by June, 1917, the whole 1,000 miles of light railway were complete. The dimensions of the task may be judged when I say that the 1,000 miles of narrow-gauge track involved 60,000 tons of steel for rails and sleepers, apart from the requirements of rolling stock. I may add here that in the autumn of 1917 a further 900 miles of light railway were ordered, and that up to the end of the War the total length supplied reached well over 4,000 miles.

The congestion behind the ports in France could only be removed by increasing the capacity of the standard-gauge lines to clear the imported goods away. Sir Eric made arrangements with Sir Ernest Moir about the provision of supplies for this purpose.

At the end of November he put forward his programme for additional standard-gauge lines. Hitherto the Army had relied mainly on the existing French lines, and though in the two years 1915-16 Britain had supplied the French Government with over 150 locomotives and 2,300 tons of railway material for maintenance of its railways, very little had been done to supplement the existing system with any British military railway additions. Sir Eric's new programme was for 1,200 miles of standard-gauge line, 300 new large main-line locomotives, and about 9,000 wagons. Sir Douglas Haig backed this up by paying a personal visit to this country at the beginning of December, and on 12th December wrote asking for means to carry out large schemes of doubling lines and building new lines, connecting lines, depots and extensions.

When I say that 1,200 miles of standard-gauge track involved 160,000 tons of steel, or 6,000 tons a week for six months, it will be seen that Sir Eric was not afraid to "think big." The support accorded to him by the Commander-in-Chief shows also that he had taught G.H.Q. to share his outlook. By June, 1917, nearly all this huge order had been completed, and a requisition for a further 1,000 miles had been received.

With the expansion of the railways, the congestion at the ports was reduced. It was possible to clear the quays and speed up the discharge of cargoes when the bottle-neck beyond had been broadened.

The roads were another vital link in the transport system. They are, of course, the first requisite for organised military operations, a fact of which the Romans were well aware when they constructed their great military highways. Throughout the War the roads of France were subject to terrific strain, and in the forward area, before the light railways were constructed, they were the only means of movement for both troops and stores. Of course, they got knocked to pieces, and for some time no proper effort was made to keep them in repair.

Sir Eric Geddes made arrangements for the systematic repair and construction of roadways. The stone for them was mainly quarried in France. The work was done to a large extent by prisoners of war.

Before leaving the subject of roads, I should like to pay a tribute to the fine work which Sir Henry Maybury did in organising this branch of our transport facilities. On the formation of the Transportation Department at "Geddesburg," Sir Henry Maybury was brought over to take charge of the road construction work, the maintenance of the existing roads, and building of new ones, particularly where the front moved forward. The mobility of our road transport in the latter part of the War was due in a high degree to his efforts.*

Closely connected with the transport developments was the recruitment of the Chinese Auxiliary Corps by Sir Eric Geddes, who sent an officer to China to recruit 15,000 Chinese labourers for work in France, out of whom some 6,000 were required for work on the railways and 1,000 for inland water transport, the others being employed at various tasks on the road, railheads, dumps, etc.† They were immensely powerful fellows, and it was no uncommon spectacle to see one of the Chinese pick up a balk of timber or a bundle of corrugated iron

---

* To illustrate the dimensions of motor transport used by the Army, I quote the following figures showing the total numbers of mechanical transport vehicles acquired by the War Office from the outbreak of War to 1st September, 1916, and the numbers supplied by the Ministry of Munitions between the latter date and the end of December, 1918: —

(a) Lorries: heavy and light:

Acquired by War Office from every source before 1/9/16	21,705	
Supplied by M. of M. from 1/9/16 to Dec., 1918	37,785	
Total		59,490

(b) Cars, vans and ambulances:

Acquired by War Office, etc.	9,630	
Supplied by M. of M., etc.	24,170	
Total		33,800

(c) Steam wagons:

Acquired by War Office, etc.	440	
Supplied by M. of M., etc.	714	
Total		1,154

(d) Tractors:

Acquired by War Office, etc.	936	
Supplied by M. of M., etc.	2,505	
Total		3,441

(e) Motor cycles:

Acquired by War Office, etc.	18,750	
Supplied by M. of M., etc.	22,300	
Total		41,050

* These figures are, of course, exclusive of the motor vehicles supplied to our Allies.

† I am told that when I was asked to sanction the recruitment of "Chinese labour" for the British Army in France, I replied, "For Heaven's sake don't give it that name. What about Chinese Auxiliary Corps?" The former appellation would have recalled an unpleasant political controversy still fresh in party memory on both sides.

sheets weighing three or four hundredweight, and walk off with it as calmly as if it weighed only as many stone!

At times, of course, these Chinese coolies came under aerial bombing or long-distance shelling. That did not greatly perturb them; they were far less nervous under fire than the British West Indian Auxiliaries, who were similarly engaged on Labour Corps duties. But it tended to disorganise their work in another way, because if they suffered any fatal casualties, they would all break off work to attend the funeral, and neither threats nor cajolery had the least effect on them, nor would bombing or shelling by the enemy scatter their cortège, until the obsequies had been duly completed.

The whole story of British achievement in the sphere of transport during the War has never yet been told. It would be well worth telling in detail, and would reflect very high credit on those who were responsible for its development, most of all on Sir Eric Geddes. The following extracts from Sir Douglas Haig's final dispatch, while they exhibit some remarkable reticences about certain points in the story, pay a merited tribute to the "civilian experts" whose advice I persuaded him to consider in 1916 : —

"The successful co-ordination and economic use of all the various kinds of transportation requires most systematic management, based on deep thought and previous experience. So great was the work entailed in the handling of the vast quantities, of which some few examples are given above, so complex did the machinery of transport become and so important was it that the highest state of efficiency should be maintained, that in the autumn of 1916 *I was forced to adopt an entirely new system for running our lines of communication.* * The appointment of Inspector-General of Communications was abolished, and the services previously directed by that officer were brought under the immediate control of the Adjutant-General, the Quartermaster-General, and the Director-General of Transportation. The last-mentioned was a new office created with a separate staff composed for the greater part of civilian experts to deal specifically with transportation questions. . . .

The Director-General of Transportation's branch was formed under the brilliant direction of Major-General Sir Eric Geddes during the autumn of 1916, as above stated. To the large number of skilled and experienced civilians included by him on his staff, drawn from the railway companies of Great Britain and the Dominions, the Army is deeply indebted for the general excellence of our transportation services."

* My italics. D. Ll. G.

CHAPTER XXIX

THE MESOPOTAMIA MUDDLE

THERE are three reasons why I incorporate a chapter on the Mesopotamia scandal in my reminiscences of the War. One is that I opposed the initiation of the campaign. I quote the following minute from the War Council held on February 24th, 1915: —

> "Mr. Lloyd George suggested that the Mesopotamia Expedition was merely a side issue. The Turks knew how far-reaching the effects of a disaster there would be and would spare no efforts to bring it about. The Mesopotamia force ought, in his opinion, to be withdrawn and concentrated on the Dardanelles."

The second is that when I became Secretary for War on 6th July, 1916, the first urgent task which I found awaiting my attention was the problem of dealing with the mess and muddle of the British Expedition to Mesopotamia. My last reason for telling it as part of my War story is that it is a perfect example of what military administration is capable of if entirely freed from civilian "interference." It was an ideal professional soldiers' campaign lacking even a minimum of supervision from the meddlesome politician. Tradition places the Garden of Eden in the land between the Euphrates and the Tigris. In this blissful enclosure there reappeared in 1916 the Paradise of the Brass Hat. He reigned alone in unfettered and unrestricted sway over this garden for nearly two years. There was no serpent or consort to mislead or meddle with him. Where there were any politicians roaming about they were as meek as any beast in the ancient Garden. He ran his Eden alone. Let us see what kind of a Paradise he produced.

It is a gruesome story of tragedy and suffering resulting from incompetence and slovenly carelessness on the part of the responsible military authorities. Attempts had been made to smother up the story through a campaign of secrecy and deliberate misrepresentation, but despite these efforts enough had leaked out early in 1916 to make it clear that strong action on the part of the Home Government was demanded.

The history of the expedition up to that date can be briefly outlined as follows. Towards the close of September, 1914, it became evident that Turkey was likely to join the enemy powers. This made it at once important to take steps for safeguarding the oil supplies in the

Persian Gulf, which were owned by the Anglo-Persian Oil Company, a concern in which the Government had become large shareholders as a means of ensuring supplies of oil fuel for the Navy.

Troops were at the time being dispatched from India to France, and the Imperial Government—through Lord Crewe, who was then Secretary of State for India—arranged with the Government of India for one brigade to be diverted to the Persian Gulf, to occupy the island of Abadan at the mouth of the Euphrates, and protect the oil tanks and pipe-lines. This force was duly sent, and landed on 23rd October, 1914.

Within a fortnight after this, on 5th November, 1914, war was declared on Turkey. Thereupon two fresh brigades were dispatched to Mesopotamia, and on 22nd November the town of Basra was captured and occupied. Basra was the seaport of Mesopotamia, and was on the west bank of the Shatt-el-Arab (the wide joint stream of the Tigris and Euphrates) about 70 miles up river from the open sea.

This expedition, though sent by arrangement with the British Government at home, and subject to the general agreement whereby all expenses of the Indian Expeditionary Forces beyond their ordinary cost of maintenance should be borne by Imperial Funds, was in respect of its administration under the sole control and responsibility of the Indian Army authorities.

Under threat of Turkish attacks, the Indian Government reluctantly sent another brigade in February, and when the danger to the force grew more acute they were peremptorily ordered in March to send a fourth. Meantime the expedition had extended its area in December by capturing the town of Kurna, where the Tigris and Euphrates join, 50 miles above Basra. It had thus occupied the whole length of the Shatt-el-Arab.

The Indian Government decided on 1st April, without obtaining the consent of the India Office at home, to organise the expedition as an army corps. They sent two more brigades to complete a second division, and appointed General Nixon to be Commander-in-Chief of the force. He was instructed to make plans for occupying the whole of the Basra Vilayet, and eventually advancing on Baghdad.

The oil-field lay to the east of the Shatt-el-Arab, up a tributary, the River Karun, and the pipeline ran down its left bank to the island of Abadan. On 19th April the Home Government asked the force to move against the Turks in this region. General Nixon asked on the same day for more forces, which were refused by India. The Home Government concurred, and added a warning against extensive operations, saying, " Any proposal involving possible demands for reinforcements of undue extension is to be deprecated. . . . Our present position is strategically a sound one and we cannot at present afford to take risks by extending it unduly. In Mesopotamia a safe game must be played."

General Nixon then sent part of his force, under General Gorringe, up the Karun river, and the other part under General Townshend, to capture Amara, 90 miles up the Tigris, getting a last-minute sanction from the British Government.   Both operations were successful, and on 3rd June Amara was taken.   Then, in boiling heat, an advance was made up the Euphrates to Nasariyeh, 68 miles beyond Kurna. The Indian Government now became eager for more progress, and got the consent of Sir Austen Chamberlain, who was then Indian Secretary, for Townshend to advance on Kut, 150 miles up the Tigris beyond Amara.   Kut-el-Amara was entered after severe fighting on 29th September, 1915.

In November, 1914, the idea of an eventual advance on Baghdad had been turned down both by the India Office and by the Viceroy of India, who gave strong reasons against it.   But subsequent successes had led the Indian Government to favour the project, and they sought permission from the Home Government for General Nixon to carry out his plan for this advance.   On 6th October, 1915, it was definitely vetoed by Sir Austen Chamberlain, but later he relented to the point of saying that if the General Staff approved and thought the operation feasible, with the aid of two fresh divisions which might presently be placed at the disposal of the Mesopotamian force, the India Office would be prepared to consider it.   The Indian General Staff, also after some hesitation, agreed that with two fresh divisions Baghdad could be taken and held.   In the end General Nixon told General Townshend to go ahead and capture Baghdad with the tired men he had at his disposal, on the strength of the hope that presently another two divisions would arrive in Mesopotamia.

Townshend advanced as far as Ctesiphon, a few miles from Baghdad, where he found the enemy strongly entrenched, and numerically equal or superior to his own exhausted troops.   After a fierce fight the British forces retired, and had to retreat down the river, compelled by lack of supplies and medical accommodation for casualties, and fighting a series of rearguard actions till they reached Kut, which they prepared to hold until relieved and reinforced by the further troops which were expected.   More than 30 per cent. of the force had been killed or wounded.

General Townshend reached Kut on 3rd December, where he was told by the military authorities to defend himself till relieved.   By 7th December the town was fully invested by the Turks.   After suffering severely in attempts to take it by storm they settled down to beleaguer it.

The remainder of the British forces hastily improvised efforts to relieve the town.   They were reinforced by the two promised divisions from France.   These were Indian divisions, already severely punished in the French fighting, and they arrived piecemeal during December at Basra, where 12,000 troops were immobilised through lack of transport to take them to the front. The attempts of the Tigris force to relieve General Townshend were heavily defeated. They made some progress in their attacks on the beleaguering lines, but owing to lack of reinforcements they abandoned the attempt to break through. Ultimately, on 29th April, 1916, after having gallantly defended the town for 147 days, Townshend's brave men were starved into surrender.

Long before this tragic climax, it had become clear that the expedition was being hopelessly mismanaged in some way or other, and early in February, 1916, the War Office took charge of the expedition. The forces there were, however, parts of the Indian Army, and immediately under the Indian General Staff in Simla. It was not until July, 1916, when I went to the War Office, that the administration of matters connected with the expedition was transferred to the control of the Home Government.

This transfer was my first step towards clearing up the muddle. My second was to promote the appointment of a Commission to make an investigation into the muddle and its causes. This Commission was set up in August, 1916, and issued its report on 17th May, 1917. The report was signed by seven of the eight Commissioners, while Commander J. Wedgwood put in a separate report, substantially agreeing with the other, but emphasising more forcibly certain aspects of the blunders and errors which had been committed, particularly by the Viceroy and Commander-in-Chief in India.

The facts revealed by this Commission's report cast a baleful light upon the mismanagement, stupidity, criminal neglect and amazing incompetence of the military authorities who were responsible for the organisation of the expedition, and on the horrible and unnecessary suffering of the gallant men who were sent to failure and defeat through the blunders of those in charge.

The General Staff in India knew perfectly well the nature of the country to which the force was being sent, and the kind of equipment which would obviously need to be supplied to it. Mesopotamia is a flat, alluvial tract, largely covered by floods in the wet season, while in the summer the rivers dwindled to very shallow streams. There are no proper roads, and water transport was the principal means of moving either men or supplies. It is a country of torrid heat in summer, though the nights throughout a considerable part of the year are cold, and during the winter and spring the country is subject to cold winds and icy storms. It was a primitive and backward country, some distance by sea from the nearest civilised base.

Obviously, therefore, the first essential for sending any expedition to Mesopotamia was to ensure that it was very well found; that it had an ample supply of suitable river boats for its transports; that clothing and food should be suited to the conditions of the country; that medical equipment, especially for the wounded and the sick, should be above the average, to meet the dangers of a sterile and disease-ridden land; that provision was made for establishing a well-equipped base at the port of Basra; and that arrangements for reinforcements should be carefully planned and promptly executed.

Every single one of these obvious duties was not merely done badly, but left undone to the point of incredibility. In the opening months of the War the Indian Government showed an extraordinary tardiness in rendering any help at all to the Empire in its struggle. Only under strong pressure would it send a single soldier to the front, and despite its enormous population it declared itself incapable of recruiting substantial additional forces. It would not spend an extra pice on the War; indeed, in the Budget debate of March, 1915, at Simla, a member boasted that although it was a War Budget, military expenditure had not been increased, and was, in fact, below the original estimate. The Indian troops which came to France came under the control of the British authorities; but those which were sent to Mesopotamia were entirely in the hands of the reluctant and parsimonious authorities at Simla, and were stinted and starved of every kind of equipment and support. " Every general who appeared before us agreed," said the Commissioners, " that the Mesopotamia Expedition was badly equipped."

It was short of artillery, particularly of heavy guns. The Indian Military Authorities do not appear to have thought of asking for any. It was not till December, 1915, when the ill-starred attack on Baghdad had been already attempted and failed, and General Townshend was beleaguered in Kut, that the first request was received for heavy guns for Mesopotamia, and not till 26th May, 1916, that India sent a definite statement of its requirements for these weapons.

Even as late as the spring of 1916 the expedition was deficient in many things which India could have supplied, such as wire-cutters, rockets, Véry lights, water-carts, tents, mosquito nets, sun-helmets, bombs, medical supplies, and even blankets and clothing. The Commander-in-Chief in India excused himself before the Commission by saying that some of these articles had not been heard of before the War, at least in India. But they had not been supplied to this expedition when the War had been in progress 18 months. Even the Turks were using Véry lights in Mesopotamia before our troops had any.

Despite the severities of the weather at certain seasons, the military authorities proposed at first to leave the provision of warm clothing for the troops entirely to private benevolence, sending them out with nothing but "shorts" and tropical clothing. The Viceroy himself protested against this.

There were no aeroplanes at all for the first six months, though the need for them in that wide, roadless land was obvious. For this failure the authorities at home must share the blame.

But it is when we come to the question of river transport that the blundering and incompetence of the military authorities is seen in its full functioning. So long as the expedition was confined in its objectives to the original landing on the island of Abadan, or the port of Basra, it was mainly dependent on ocean-going transport. But from the moment when, in December, 1914, it advanced, with the approval of the authorities at Simla, up river to Kurna, special river transport became a vital necessity, and with each further advance, which lengthened the line up the river, the need for transport vessels increased.

As early as 23rd November, 1914, after the capture of Basra, General Barrett was advised by Commander Hamilton, R.I.M., who knew the Tigris intimately, to apply at once for 12 special steamers, as they would have to be built to an unusual pattern, and would take 12 months to construct. But the General and his staff did not think the matter urgent, and did nothing about it till in January they were asked by India what further transport they needed. He then asked for seven steamers and two lighters. In February he asked for four tugs. These were obtained in India in March, and sent out; but when in May General Nixon took over, he found that they were useless for the hot weather, when the river ran low. He asked for vessels drawing not more than 3 feet or 3 feet 6 inches.

After delays in India, this request was ultimately incorporated in a requisition telegraphed to the India Office on 4th August, 1915. Nothing was done till confirmation in writing turned up in September. Then the officials at the India Office made inquiry of the firm recommended to them for this work, but rather than pay them a commission amounting to one-third of one per cent. for supervising the execution of the order they turned to their expert naval architect, who without special knowledge of the conditions of the Tigris, proceeded to secure them the building of vessels differing in a number of respects from the type ordered—vessels which were sent out in sections between April and December, 1916. It may be briefly stated that on account of the alterations of the pattern these boats were useless for the purpose of up-river transport; that the fact that they had to be assembled at Basra meant considerable further delay after they reached Mesopotamia; and that owing to lack of facilities for shipbuilding at Basra, and the large size of some of the sections, they were very difficult to handle—particularly as no drawings, descriptions or instructions came with them. Some sections sank in 30 feet of water, and the rest had to be towed to Bombay to be erected there. The Commission remarks: —

" More inept proceedings than those connected with the purchase and shipment of river craft in England in 1915 and early in 1916 would be hard to find."

When in October, 1915, General Nixon learnt that the paddle-steamers wanted would take a year to build he asked for stop-gap boats from India. The Indian authorities replied as they had done previously in June, that no suitable tugs were available. A month later they admitted that there were 13 available. The Commission gives a picture of the circumlocution and red tape which created the long delays before any request from Mesopotamia got even a negative reply. "Correspondence was usually conducted between the G.O.C. in Mesopotamia and the Chief of the Staff in Simla or Delhi. From the latter officer, anything about river craft would be transmitted to the Quartermaster-General, who would thereafter communicate what he thought necessary to Captain Lumsden, R.N., the Director of the Royal Indian Marine at Bombay." How that officer spent his time is thus described by the Commission:—

"The Director of the Royal Indian Marine was not granted—at any rate did not exercise—any initiative in maritime or nautical matters. . . . The time of the Director and Senior Officers of the Indian Marine is much taken up with mere office or desk work. The amount of writing which they have to get through—or at all events do get through—can only be described as enormous. . . . The Director of the Royal Indian Marine gave to the Commission a list of the duties, the discharge of which he considered rendered it impossible for him to visit Mesopotamia and see for himself the actual state of things there. Most of the duties specified required neither maritime experience nor nautical knowledge, and could have been performed by any alert business man, even though he may never have been on blue water in his life."

The report, in fact, makes several references to the fact that the Indian officials never went to look at things for themselves, and when they were told of conditions, refused to pay attention to the reports. Worse, they blankly misreported the facts. "So much out of touch was Simla with the actual situation in Mesopotamia that we find the Indian General Staff, in 'appreciations' in June and September, 1915, definitely stating that the expedition was well supplied with river craft, and using this among their arguments for the advance to Baghdad."

The lack of river transport up to the spring of 1916 was a direct cause of the failure of military operations carried out by the troops with the utmost bravery. On account of the shortage it took nearly two months to concentrate troops and supplies for the advance from Amara to Kut, and the advance to Baghdad was fatally delayed through the same cause. It seems almost certain that, but for the shortage of river transport, the Turkish Army would have been destroyed between Amara and Ctesiphon; and the evidence shows conclusively, according to the Commission, that shortage of river transport was the chief cause of the failure to relieve Kut.

Since the vital importance of such transport was clearly understood both in India and at home, it is natural to ask what on earth possessed the military authorities to allow the advance up the Tigris in face of the shortage. The report of the Commission brings out that General Nixon, the commander on the spot, when he found the Indian authorities unable or unwilling to provide the needed transport, was optimistically ready to try his luck with what he had; and the Indian authorities themselves, having failed to provide what they must have known was necessary, made no effort to impress the gravity of the shortage on the India Office at home. This Office was allowed to get the impression that all was well, an impression perpetuated by a typically official incident. General Nixon's appeal for more vessels, sent to the India Office by the Indian Government, was not laid before the Secretary of State. The Military Branch of the India Office sent it on to the Stores Branch as an indent; and though it was forwarded to the War Office, no letter was sent drawing attention to the shortage of transport it revealed. Thus military officials both in India and in London suppressed or ignored facts which, had they been known by either the War Council or the Cabinet, would have prevented the granting of consent to the ill-fated advance on Baghdad.

Allied to the failure to furnish river transport was the neglect to develop wharfage and storage facilities at Basra.

The boats available had their usefulness heavily reduced through this failure. General Gorringe stated that " no improvement in the unloading wharves for ships was made until December, 1915 . . . although the accommodation was bad and congested for stores of every kind being unloaded." To the physical drawbacks was added the incompetence of the military officials. The Commission reports that delays to steamers were at first occasioned, not so much by inability to get cargoes out into lighters, as by inability or unwillingness of the military departments ashore to receive it rapidly.

" It is clear that management of the traffic of a port and discharge of cargo was not work to which officers of the Royal Indian Marine had previously been accustomed. . . . Men with these qualifications were known to be employed in one or other of the great Indian and Burmese river ports. Their advice was not asked for; and their assistance was not utilised until more than a year after the landing of the expedition in Mesopotamia when conditions in Basra had become serious."

In January, 1916, the Indian Government at last sent an expert civilian, Sir George Buchanan, formerly in charge of the Port of Rangoon, to become Director-General of Basra and reorganise its traffic and facilities. Characteristically, they omitted to define his status and duties; and General Nixon proceeded to limit and circumscribe these in such a way that Sir George Buchanan found it impossible to carry on, and soon returned to India. In his report to Simla he said: —

"I found it difficult to realise that we had been in occupation of Basra for a year, as the arrangements for the landing and storing of goods of every description were of the most primitive order, and in the absence of roads, the whole area was a huge quagmire. To a newcomer appearances were such that troops and stores might have been landed, for the first time, the previous week. . . . The military expedition to Basra is, I believe, unique, inasmuch as in no previous case has such an enormous force been landed and maintained without an adequately prepared base."

But if the neglect of transport by the military authorities was directly responsible for the failure and defeat of the expedition, their neglect of medical equipment turned disaster into horror.

Tales of the atrocities resulting from inadequate provision for the wounded and sick were so widespread that even Sir Beauchamp Duff, the Commander-in-Chief of the Army in India, felt himself compelled in March, 1916, to set up a Commission to inquire into the matter. Their report was, however, such a sickening exposure of official negligence and incompetence that the Indian Government would not publish it. The Mesopotamia Commission appointed by the Home Government had this report before them, and published it as an appendix to their own report. It was known as the "Vincent-Bingley" Report, as Sir William Vincent and General Bingley were the chief members responsible for it.

The evidence of both reports is that the expedition was systematically starved by the Indian military authorities in regard to every vital medical provision, and that protests were stifled and outside offers of help refused.

The standard of the Indian Army in this respect was low to begin with. A witness from the Indian Medical Service told the Commission: "I doubt whether you gentlemen would consider that the Sepoys' Hospitals in peace-time India are hospitals at all." Sir Alfred Keogh, Director-General of Army Medical Services at the War Office, said: —

"I have no hesitation whatever in saying that the medical arrangements connected with the Army in India have been for years and years most disgraceful. . . . Anything more disgraceful than the carelessness and want of attention with regard to the sick soldier in India it is impossible to imagine."

But if things in India were bad, they were far worse in Mesopotamia. The expedition was sent out with a medical establishment, even according to its organisation orders, lower than that laid down for a frontier campaign; and " the actual amount of medical personnel in Mesopotamia was during long periods far below even this meagre scale."

There was at times a serious shortage of essential drugs. Necessary appliances for the hospitals were scanty or altogether lacking. Often there was no ice. For months there were no electric fans. There were not enough bandages, blankets, bed-pans, and splints. Even when the wounded got to the military hospital at Bombay it was to find there an appalling state of neglect—no X-ray apparatus, a lack of splints and surgical appliances, a shortage of doctors, surgeons, nurses, and attendants.

The doctors and ambulance staffs with the expedition performed miracles of heroic work, but there were very few of them. At the first battle of Kut some of the fighting units were without stretcher bearers, and wounded men were left on the field of battle all night, some of them being stripped, mutilated, and killed by the Arabs.

No wheeled transport for seriously wounded cases was sent out. Instead, a number of riding mules were supplied! The Commissioners say: " We have no evidence that these riding mules were ever used by the wounded, though their presence on one occasion in a very restive state is recorded by a witness. They are obviously useless for serious cases."

In default of wheeled ambulances, the medical officers were forced to move the more seriously wounded in springless army transport carts, drawn by mules, ponies, or bullocks. The A.D.M.S., 3rd Division, said that this cart, " which is without springs, has no cover to give protection against rain or the direct rays of the sun; and the bottom of which consists of bars of iron which, even when liberally covered with mattresses or other padding, renders the placing of a wounded man, especially cases of fracture, in such a conveyance, a practice which can only be designated as barbarous and cruel."

In some cases, we learn, dead bodies were used as cushions on these carts, in default of any other means of padding them.

But it is when we come to the transport of wounded and sick men down the river to Basra that the story reaches its culminating horror. There were no river steamers at all fitted as medical transports, nor any personnel to attend to casualties on the journey. Use had to be made of the scanty river transport employed in bringing men, stores and animals up stream, and as congestion grew it became impossible to clean or disinfect these boats in any way before sending the wounded, thickly packed, in them, down to Basra, and detailing from the scanty and overworked field ambulance staffs a few men to accompany them—too few to give proper attention or even to feed them.

" Wounds which required dressing and re-dressing were not attended to, and the condition of many of the patients who travelled by these steamers was, when they reached Basra, deplorable. There the wounds of many were found to be in a septic condition, and in urgent need of re-dressing. In some cases bed sores had developed, more than one patient arrived soaked in fæces and urine, and in a few cases wounds were found to contain maggots."

The Commission quote a description, by Major Carter, I.M.S., which I cannot repeat without apologising for its repulsive horror, of how the wounded, after Ctesiphon, arrived in Basra. Yet it is necessary for us to face frankly the record of what actually happened to a number of valiant men who fought for Britain and her Empire in the Great War. Our soldiers had not merely to read of, but to suffer this. Here is the account : —

" I was standing on the bridge [of the hospital ship *Varela* from Bombay] in the evening when the *Medjidieh* arrived. She had two steel barges without any protection against the rain, as far as I can remember. As this ship with two barges came up to us I saw that she was absolutely packed, and the barges too, with men. The barges were slipped, and the *Medjidieh* was brought alongside the *Varela*. When she was about 300 or 400 yards off it looked as if she was festooned with ropes. The stench when she was close was quite definite, and I found that what I mistook for ropes were dried stalactites of human fæces. The patients were so huddled and crowded together in the ship that they could not perform the offices of nature clear of the edge of the ship, and the whole of the ship's side was covered with stalactites of human fæces. This is what I then saw. A certain number of men were standing and kneeling on the immediate perimeter of the ship. Then we found a mass of men huddled up anyhow—some with blankets and some without. They were lying in a pool of dysentery about 30 feet square. They were covered with dysentery and dejecta generally from head to foot. With regard to the first man I examined . . . . [I omit a still more terrible passage of the description] . . . . The man had a fractured thigh, and his thigh was perforated in five or six places. He had apparently been writhing about on the deck of the ship. Many cases were almost as bad. There were a certain number of cases of terribly bad bed sores. In my report I describe mercilessly to the Government of India how I found men with their limbs splinted with wood strips from ' Johnny Walker ' whisky boxes, ' Bhoosa ' wire, and that sort of thing."

" Were they British or Indian?"

" British and Indian mixed."

This state of affairs was thus described by the G.O.C. of the expedition : —

" Wounded satisfactorily disposed of. Many likely to recover in country comfortably placed in hospitals at Amara and Basra. Those for invaliding are being placed direct on two hospital ships that were ready at Basra on arrival of river boats. General condition of wounded very satisfactory. Medical arrangements under circumstances of considerable difficulty worked splendidly."

What about Major Carter's report to the Indian military authorities? The Commission gives the following account of its reception: — " He [Major Carter] was treated with great rudeness. Surgeon-General Hathaway, in writing to the D.M.S. in India on this subject, says: ' The Army Commander, realising the injustice, ordered the D.A. and Q.M.G. and myself to deal with him [Major Carter] with reference to his objectionable remarks.' And General Cowper, then D.A. and Q.M.G., told us: ' I threatened to put him under arrest, and I said that I would get his hospital ship taken away from him for a meddlesome, interfering faddist.' " General Cowper was passing on treatment he had himself received, for the Commander-in-Chief in India, Sir Beauchamp Duff, had threatened to dismiss him for sending to India too insistent demands as to the need for River Transport.

Not only would the authorities do nothing themselves; they would let no one do anything to help them. On 11th August, 1915, the Secretary for India wired the Viceroy with an offer from the Lord-Lieutenant of Hampshire to raise funds for the sick and wounded soldiers in Mesopotamia, and send out doctors, nurses, medicines, and hospital comforts. After consulting the Commander-in-Chief, the Viceroy answered that money was ample and sufficient for supplying comforts for sick and wounded in Mesopotamia and in India; that everything necessary was being done, and that his Government had arranged for doctors and nurses. Electric fans were offered by the Madras Fund in December, 1914, for installation in the hospitals at Basra, but by the middle of 1915 none had been actually installed. The British Red Cross Society cabled General Nixon to accept two petrol-driven motor-launches. The offer was repeated on 28th December, and the reply was: —

" Nothing required at present. If anything needed in future will not hesitate to ask you."

This was just after the total breakdown of medical services following the battle of Ctesiphon.

I need not particularise further the failures of the military authorities to deal with other medical and sanitary issues; the insufficient and inappropriate food they supplied, which led by 1915 to an outbreak of scurvy among the troops, and a much more serious outbreak the following spring; the neglect of water supply, so that the troops were reduced to drinking from the nearest river, and an outbreak of cholera resulted. The report of the Commission makes it clear that on every hand there was utter failure to make the most elementary provision for the obvious needs of the expedition. In their "Findings," they remark:—

"Looking at the facts, which from the first must have been apparent to any administrator, military or civilian, who gave a few minutes' consideration to the map and to the conditions in Mesopotamia, the want of foresight and provision for the most fundamental needs of the expedition reflects discredit upon the organising aptitude of all the authorities concerned."

I need not refer to the way in which the military authorities in India starved the expedition of drafts and reinforcements—although they were in charge of a country of 315,000,000 people, of whom 50,000,000 belonged to fighting races. But one amazing incident deserves mention. When in October, 1915, the advance on Baghdad was in prospect, and the need for reinforcements to support the force there was urgent, the Imperial Authorities asked the Indian Government to provide a division temporarily, as the two divisions from France might not get there in time. "With the intention of evading this liability," says the Report, "the Indian Government resorted to procedure which, to say the least of it, was disingenuous." There were, in fact, certain artillery batteries, cavalry regiments, and infantry brigades which could be spared in India, but the Home Government was not informed of this, and the reason given in a minute from the Military Secretary of Sir Beauchamp Duff to the Viceroy's Military Secretary ran as follows:—

". . . It is proposed by the Chief that the force he has named should be assembled . . . for eventualities, but that the Home Government should not be informed of this. . . . The Home Government are very anxious that Baghdad should be taken, and they will send us the required force if we hold out, but they will give us nothing if the least sign of willingness to find reinforcements is shown by us."

So the Viceroy cabled on 17th October:—

". . . In no case could I undertake to supply from India, even temporarily, a further force of the strength of a division."

The Indian Government, as Commander Wedgwood remarks, "held out" while Serbia was being overrun, and while our last man was being put in at Loos.

It is hardly necessary to add that the Commission passed severe censures upon the Commander-in-Chief in India, Sir Beauchamp Duff, and the Viceroy, Lord Hardinge; on the Surgeon-General, the Director of Medical Services, the Indian Marine, and the Commanding Officer in Mesopotamia, General Nixon. It further condemned the whole military system of administration as "cumbrous and inept" and recommended its drastic reform.

When I was appointed Secretary of State for War in July, 1916, my first task was to take in hand the Mesopotamian situation. The most urgent call was for improved transport and medical arrangements. It was my good fortune to secure the assistance of the Q.M.G., Sir John Cowans, a man whom I have always considered to be the most capable soldier thrown up by the War in our Army. I shall never forget the quiet efficiency with which he detailed the steps that he thought should be taken. He had no hesitation in utilising experienced civilian assistance and some of the ablest of his transport officers in the Barge department were promoted civilians. All that could be done from this end was put in hand and pressed through without delay and there were no further scandals in the administration of the Mesopotamian Army.

The Commission also stated that "it was not until London took over the sole charge that there was any marked improvement in the management of the campaign. The improvement and success since effected are a striking illustration of the all-importance of unity of control in time of war." A number of references are made through the report to the better state of things which had supervened since July, 1916.

I feel that I cannot conclude this rather gruesome chapter without quoting a first-rate example of official circumlocution. It might serve a useful purpose to insert it here as a warning.

The Report of the Mesopotamian Commission gives a graphic description of the cumbrous procedure and circumlocution which at that time hedged round any proposal to make provision for the needs of the Army. It was supplied by Mr. Brunyate, Financial Secretary to the Indian Government, and for some years Financial Adviser to the Commander-in-Chief and Military Member of Council. When asked to give a concrete case of how a paper relating to a proposal for army equipment would pass through the two departments, he replied:—

"The Quartermaster-General, it may be supposed, wishes to have more mules. Probably before putting forward the proposal at all he sees the Commander-in-Chief personally as Commander-in-Chief and ascertains from him that he is willing to have that proposal ventilated. He then writes a note stating his facts, probably supported by a note from the Director of the Army Remount Department, makes a definite recommendation, estimates the cost, and marks his note to the Army Department of the Government of India. The office clerks of the Army Department note on the case, the Assistant Secretary notes, the Deputy Secretary may note, and it reaches the Army Secretary—we will call him General Holloway, though he is not actually Army Secretary now.   He criticises the proposal if he thinks fit . . . the office of the Financial Adviser then note upon it . . . the clerks in the Finance Adviser's office note, the Assistant or Deputy Financial Adviser notes, now Mr. Fell. Mr. Fell may be prepared at once to accept the proposal on behalf of the Finance Department, and may intimate that he does not intend to refer it to the Finance Member. The file then goes back to the Army Secretary, and in that case he at once arranges for the necessary orders to be issued to give effect to the Quartermaster-General's proposal, unless he thinks the case of sufficient importance to refer it to the Army Member.

Such reference will, of course, practically always be required if the proposal is one requiring the sanction of the Secretary of State. In that case the Army Secretary would take the Army Member's orders at this stage, and a dispatch to the Secretary of State would then be drafted in the Army Department. . . . Or again, Mr. Fell, when the case first reached him, might have criticised the proposal, and indicated a desire to see it modified or rejected. In that case the file would still go back to the Army Secretary, and he would doubtless at that stage take the orders of the Army Member unless before doing so he wished to have the opinion of the Quartermaster-General on the criticisms and suggestions which had been made in the military finance branch. Mr. Fell, when criticising the proposal, would probably have indicated whether he intended to refer the case eventually to the Finance Member. Thus when the Army Secretary brought these criticisms before the Army Member, the latter would know that if he decided to override the Financial Adviser's criticisms, he might have to face opposition from the Finance Member. The Army Member would then pass his orders. If he adhered to the scheme as put forward by the Quartermaster-General and the Army Department he would record a note to that effect. The file would then go back to the Financial Adviser, and the latter would not note again, but would submit the case to the Finance Member. If the Finance Member decided not to press the objections raised by Mr. Fell, the proposal would become a fully accepted proposal, and orders would be issued for putting it into effect. If, however, the Finance Member definitely objected to the scheme, the case would then go back to Mr. Fell for return to the Army Secretary for re-submission to the Army Member. The Army Member might then defer to the Finance Member's objection, in which case the whole proposal would be dropped with the Army Member's concurrence, though a reluctant concurrence. If, however, the Army Member, in spite of the Finance Member's objections, considered that the proposal was a necessary one, he would intimate to the Army Secretary that the case should be referred to His Excellency the Viceroy, under our Rules of Business, which prescribe that when two Members of Council differ the case must be referred for the orders of the Viceroy. The Army Secretary would then lay the case before the Viceroy. The latter might very possibly indicate a personal opinion that, in the circumstances, as a particular case, he thought it perhaps desirable that the views of the Army Member should be deferred to, and any expression of the Viceroy's wish in an ordinary case is very frequently—I might almost say generally—deferred to. Or the Viceroy might, pursuing the ordinary procedure under our Statutory Rules of Business, simply instruct the Army Secretary that the case was to be brought up in Council the following week. It would then be discussed in Council, the Army Secretary being present, but not taking any part in the discussion, and would be settled by the views of the majority of the Council."

Asked how long a disputed case might take, he replied:—

" At the best a disputed proposal would, I think, ordinarily take a good many weeks. I cannot put it more exactly than that, but a great deal depends on whether the responsible secretary takes a grip of the case and prevents it being constantly remitted backwards and forwards between the Financial Adviser on the one side and the Administrative Authority, the Quartermaster-General, or whoever he may be, on the other, inviting each in turn to reply to the other's rejoinders and criticisms. Where a case was not taken hold of and put to an end, I have known it very lamentably protracted from this cause. . . ."

This fantastic picture is not a page from some Dickensian work of fiction. It is a sober account by a highly responsible official of the actual procedure adopted up to 1916 by the military authorities at Simla—procedure to which any request for vitally necessary supplies for the Mesopotamian Expeditionary Force would be subjected. It helps to explain the tragedy which befell that gallant company.

As Sir John Cowans was the General Officer who undertook the reorganisation of the transport system in Mesopotamia, and as his work was a triumphant success, it would not be out of place here to give my impressions of this genial and competent soldier. The first time that I recollect seeing Sir John Cowans—" Jack " Cowans as he was known to all his numerous friends—was at the first meeting of the Munitions Committee which was set up at the end of 1914. We met at the War Office, in the Secretary of State's room, and when the discussion on the supply of munitions had come to an end, and our interviews with General von Donop and others were over, Lord Kitchener suggested that we might like to see the man who was responsible for the other war supplies—the Quartermaster-General. General Cowans was sent for, and my first impression was that of a large, rather ungainly, awkward and weather-beaten man with a

R

stolid face and shrewd eyes. He did not in the least resemble my idea of a Staff General. He had rather the visage and demeanour of a successful corn merchant in an agricultural town. He sat down without a glimmer of expression on his face, and when asked for particulars as to food supplies for the Army, he slowly and clumsily pulled out a shabby spectacle case and extracted a pair of horn-rimmed glasses. When these were adjusted he pulled out of his pocket a worn note-book that bore a distinct resemblance to a laundry book, and casually gave us extracts from the notes therein for the answers. Then the clothing—another book. We listened and gradually realised that we were being given a lucid summary of the organisation of supplies which was so completely satisfactory that when Lord Kitchener inquired of us whether we wanted to put any questions, we all felt there was nothing left to ask. This perfunctory soldier surprised me with his quiet, unostentatious efficiency. It was borne in upon the Committee that here was a man who understood organisation—that he was an organiser to his finger tips. When I came to know him better I realised that under his rough exterior and stolid look there was a simple and kindly nature and inexhaustible fund of good humour and joviality. Once you knew him it took little to awaken the twinkle in his eye and to provoke his hearty, noisy, infectious laugh.

With an appearance of being extraordinarily casual, Cowans was an excellent business man. His own department was perfectly ordered, and he himself was thoroughly acquainted with all the workings of it. He discharged his duties throughout the four and a half years of the War in such a way as to give complete satisfaction to everybody concerned, soldiers and civilians. Whatever doubts and grumbles there were about the deficiencies and shortcomings of other war leaders, there never was a murmur from any quarter as to the efficiency with which Sir John Cowans did his work. That is more than can be said about any other prominent figure in the War, military or civil.

I have already described the appalling state of affairs in Mesopotamia when Cowans took the job in hand. Quickly, with almost incredible speed, the state of affairs changed completely. Without fuss and apparently without effort he straightened things out and no more was heard of scandals in Mesopotamia.

When as Secretary for War I came to grips with the Army Council because I insisted upon putting civilians into jobs which soldiers had hitherto been responsible for, it was Cowans who was sent as representative of the irate generals to put their protest before me. He was certainly the best person for the job as far as I was concerned, for his efficiency and good humour made him an acceptable mediator. You could not quarrel or get angry with Jack Cowans. He smiled wrath away.

CHAPTER XXX

THE KNOCK-OUT BLOW

THE latter half of 1916 saw a succession of sporadic and untraceable attempts in certain quarters to bring about an inconclusive peace. Kites were flown and hints broadcast in Holland, in Spain, at the Vatican, in Sweden, and the U.S.A. There was good reason to think that some at least of these movements were being stimulated by German agents, as this was a propitious moment for securing favourable terms for the Central Powers. In the early months of the War, Germany with her elaborately prepared and highly efficient military equipment and organisation had pressed her attack upon the Allied Powers, who were far less skilfully directed, less adequately equipped, and, in the case of the British forces, only just beginning to improvise their military resources. The tide of German conquest had now reached its height, but there was a good deal in the military and naval situation to engender misgiving and even despair of a clear, unmistakable victory being secured on either side.

The uneasy stirring of this peace talk brought to the fore the question of the aims with which we were pursuing the War, and the terms on which we hoped to end it. In August, 1916, the matter was raised in the War Committee, and Sir William Robertson, amongst others, was asked by the Prime Minister to prepare a memorandum setting forth the views of the General Staff on the peace terms desirable from the military point of view. Sir William Robertson's memorandum, dated 31st August, 1916, is in many respects a very remarkable document to have been written in the circumstances of the time. It reads:—

" 1. Although the end of the War is yet by no means in sight, negotiations for peace, in some form or other, may arise any day, and unless we are prepared for them we may find ourselves at a great disadvantage, not only as compared with our enemy but also as compared with our Allies. It is not unlikely that M. Briand already possesses very decided views on the subject, carefully worked out for him under his general direction by the clever people who serve him, and who do not appear on the surface of political life. At a hastily summoned council we should have no chance against him, armed with a definite policy to which he may beforehand, and unknown to us, have committed the Russians and perhaps other Powers of the Entente. If this should happen, the Germans might take advantage of it to drive in a wedge between us and the other Entente Powers, with the result that we might find ourselves without support in those claims which we may be compelled to make, more especially in regard to the disposal of the captured German colonies. We need therefore to decide without loss of time, as to what our policy is to be; then place it before the Entente Powers and ascertain in return what are their aims, and so endeavour to arrive at a clear understanding before we meet our enemies in conference.

2. For centuries past—though unfortunately by no means continuously—our policy has been to help to maintain the balance between the Continental Powers which have always been divided by their interests and sympathies into opposing groups. At one time the centre of gravity has been in Madrid, at another in Vienna, at another in Paris, and at another in St. Petersburg. We have thwarted, or helped to thwart, each and every Power in turn which has aspired to Continental predominance; and concurrently as a consequence we have enlarged our own sphere of imperial ascendancy. As part of this traditional policy we have aimed at maintaining British maritime supremacy, and at keeping a weak Power in possession of the Low Countries. In more recent years a new preponderance has been allowed to grow up, of which the centre of gravity has been in Berlin, and the result of it is the present War.

3. It is submitted that the basis of peace negotiations must be the three principles for which we have so often fought in the past and for which we have been compelled to fight now, namely:—

(a) The maintenance of the balance of power in Europe;
(b) The maintenance of British maritime supremacy; and
(c) The maintenance of a weak Power in the Low Countries.

4. If and when these general principles, and such others as are deemed necessary, are accepted by His Majesty's Government it will be possible to formulate the conditions upon which, and upon which only, we would be prepared to negotiate. No useful purpose would be served by discussing these conditions until the general principles have been settled, but some of the many questions demanding examination may be mentioned by way of showing how important it is to commence investigation with as little delay as possible. It may be added that this paper is written mainly from a military standpoint, and in this connection it cannot be too often remembered that the conditions upon which peace is concluded will govern, or at any rate ought to govern, the size and nature of the army subsequently required by us.

5. If the balance of power in Europe is to be maintained it follows that the existence of a strong Central European Power is essential, and that such a State must be Teutonic, as a Slav nation, the only other alternative, would always lean towards Russia, which would accordingly obtain a preponderant position and so destroy the very principle which we desire to uphold. On the other hand, as Germany is the chief European competitor with us on the sea, it would be advantageous to make such terms of peace as would check the development of her navy and of her mercantile marine. In other words, it would be to the interests of the British Empire to leave Germany reasonably strong on land, but to weaken her at sea. The full extent to which His Majesty's Government have already been committed is not known to the General Staff, but apparently it is the intention to break up Austria-Hungary. By the Roumanian Political Convention a large part of Eastern Hungary will be transferred to Roumania; Italy will no doubt insist on retaining Trieste with Istria and some of the neighbouring districts; and Serbia is to be given part at least of Herzegovina, Bosnia and Slavonia. The chief problems to be determined are the disposal of Austria proper, of the Magyar district of Hungary, of the Northern Slav provinces of Bohemia, Moravia and Galicia and finally, whether there shall be access to the Adriatic from the north otherwise than through Italian or Serbian territory. It is clear that all these provinces cannot become independent States. Galicia may be absorbed in a new Polish Kingdom, but Bohemia and Moravia on the one side and Hungary on the other will be difficult of disposal. Acting on the principle of maintaining a strong Germany, it might be advantageous if Austria proper were incorporated in that Empire, more especially as thereby ten million South Germans would be brought in as a counterpoise to Prussia. The other alternative, which has the advantage of settling the question of the disposal of the various provinces, is to maintain a diminished Austria-Hungary, and in that case an Adriatic port, Fiume for choice, should be allotted to it. This new Austria-Hungary would very probably form a very close union with Germany, but such a union might be not altogether to our disadvantage on land as limiting the power of Russia and the Slav States, and on sea as preventing the Mediterranean from becoming a French and Italian lake.

6. As regards the western boundaries of Germany we will presumably be obliged to agree to the wishes of the French with regard to Alsace and Lorraine. Belgium must be restored to her pre-war condition, and it may be desirable that the Grand Duchy of Luxembourg should be added to her territories. It would be advantageous if Belgium could be given free access from the sea to Antwerp by transferring to her that part of Seeland which lies

south of the Scheldt. In this case Holland might be given con pensation in East Friesland and in the East Frisian Islands.

7. On the north it is to be wished that the whole of Schleswi and possibly a part of Holstein should be restored to Denmarl From a naval point of view it would be of the highest importanc to take away from Germany the Kiel Canal—which might b internationalised—the Harbour of Kiel, the North Frisian Island and the eastern shores of the Heligoland Bight. These question as all others of a naval nature, are of course matters for th Admiralty to advise upon.

8. On the east the boundaries of Germany will depend on thos that may be given to Poland. A difficulty in the way of creatin this new State is to provide it with a sea port. The Poles then selves are desirous of having Dantzig, and state, in support of th claim, that 60 per cent. of the population of West Prussia Polish. It would, however, scarcely seem feasible in any circun stances to cut off East Prussia from Germany, and it is hard t believe that Germany will ever be so crushed as to consent to th transfer of Posen to Poland, unless the latter were to form a Stat of the German Empire under a German Prince, a contingenc which presumably could only occur in the event of a Germa victory. As regards Poland, we shall probably be obliged t conform to Russian wishes.

9. Bulgaria may either secede from the Central Powers and l allowed to retain her existing territories, plus the uncontested zor of Macedonia, or she may fight on to the end. In the latter cas if and when Russia is established in Constantinople, it is possib that she may try to annex Bulgaria, and eventually to link it u with Bessarabia by wresting the Dobrudja from Roumania.

10. The principal suggestions here made for examination ar that Germany should be reduced on the west and north by th cession to other Powers of parts of Alsace and Lorraine, Ea Friesland, Schleswig, and part of Holstein; that there should l some rectification of frontier due to the creation of Poland; an that in the south she should be strengthened either by the i corporation of Austria proper, or by a close union with a muc diminished Austria-Hungary; and that her naval power should l shaken by taking away from her the Kiel Canal and vario districts on the North Sea and Baltic which are of great maritin importance.

11. It is apparently the intention to break up the Turkis Empire by handing over Constantinople and the Straits to Russi and by dividing up Mesopotamia, Syria, and parts of Asia Mino This intention does not affect the question of the future boundari of Germany in Europe, but it is of importance as preventin German development in the Near East.

12. In Asia outside the Turkish Empire, our main concern is with Persia, and there seems no reason why any agreement that it may be necessary to make with Russia concerning that country should be discussed at the Peace Conference.

13. Our future relations with our Allies demand as close consideration as our relations with our enemies. What is our policy to be towards the French in Salonika, towards the Italians and French in Albania, towards the Italians in Asia Minor, towards the Russians in the Balkans, and towards the Slav world generally in connection with the creation of Poland? It is well to remember that the present grouping of the Powers is not a permanency, and indeed it may continue but a very short time after the War is over.

14. With regard to her colonies, Germany will have lost the whole of them when the campaign in German East Africa has been completed. They are:—

    Kiauchau
    Togoland
    The Cameroons
    German South-West Africa
    German East Africa
    German New Guinea
    The Bismarck Archipelago
    The Caroline, Marshall, Marianne, Solomon and Samoan Islands, in the Pacific.

Germany is certain to make strenuous efforts to recover all or most of these Colonies in order that she may keep her " place in the sun" and preserve at least the semblance of a position as a world power. She is therefore likely to put forward tempting bargains to those Powers who are not interested in order that pressure may be brought to bear upon those Powers who are interested to relinquish their claims. We alone are interested in all these Colonies, and France only in the Cameroons, Belgium in East Africa, and Japan in Kiauchau and the Northern Pacific Islands. It is easy to see therefore that if the cession of a portion of, say, Poland to Russia, or of Alsace-Lorraine to France, or even the complete evacuation of Belgium is made conditional by Germany upon our giving up Togoland, South-West and East Africa, and the Southern Pacific Islands, we may be placed in a difficult position.

15. Kiauchau, the Marianne, Caroline and Marshall Islands have been occupied by, and are being administered by, the Japanese, and Japan is unlikely to release her hold on them without a substantial *quid pro quo*, which it will not be easy to find.

16. The Samoan Islands were occupied by, and are now

administered by, the Government of New Zealand, which is likely
to attach a high sentimental value to this, the first conquest of a
young people. The same applies to German New Guinea, the
Bismarck Archipelago and the Solomon Islands, which were occupied by and are now in the hands of the Australian Government,
who have the further inducement to keep what they have got,
that these islands form a valuable buffer between the mainland and
possible Japanese encroachment.

17. In Africa the difficulties are even greater. The Union of
South Africa, with the experience of this war behind it, is unlikely
to tolerate the neighbourhood of a great foreign power. They
have conquered German South-West Africa with their own
resources, and taken a leading part in the campaign in East Africa.
We are, therefore, likely to enter the Peace Conference with Togoland as the only possession which we can use freely for the purpose
of bargaining.

18. The many problems which the future disposal of the
German Colonies involve require very full consideration, and no
time should be lost in obtaining the views of the Dominions, and
in deciding on the attitude to be adopted in regard to the other
Entente Powers.

19. Another question requiring discussion and settlement, as
far as possible, is that of enemy proposal for an armistice pending
negotiations for peace. The existence of the Entente blockade
makes it extremely difficult to suggest any equitable terms on
which an armistice could be arranged. From the point of view
of the Entente the maintenance of the blockade during the
armistice is absolutely essential, as otherwise the Central Powers
would be able to provision themselves during the armistice and
would consequently be in a much better position to recommence
hostilities if the negotiations for peace were to collapse. The
enemy would no doubt strongly oppose a maintenance of the
blockade because it would progressively weaken him every day
that it continued, with the result that at the end of the armistice
he would be in a worse position than at the commencement. But
we may hope that during the same period his position would, if
there were no armistice, become worse, and we cannot allow him
to reap an advantage from an armistice which he would not obtain
if there were no armistice. In fact we need not concern ourselves
with him. The last thing Germany would do, in similar circumstances, would be to give the least consideration to the difficulties
of her enemy. Moreover, our desire will be to conclude the
negotiations as quickly as possible, whereas the removal of the
blockade will almost certainly tend to lengthen them indefinitely

20. There seem, therefore, to be three courses which require
consideration: —

(*a*) Refuse an armistice altogether and continue fighting during peace negotiations or until the enemy surrenders unconditionally.

(*b*) Limit the armistice to land and air operations; maritime operations, whether submarine or otherwise, being continued.

(*c*) Agree to some kind of rationing policy during the armistice, calculated to leave the Central Powers in the same economic position at the close as at the beginning of the armistice.

21.   All three courses have their objections.   As regards (*a*) it would not be easy to conduct peace negotiations while active operations were in progress, as the constant fluctuations in the fighting might have a corresponding influence on the negotiations. It must also be remembered that the negotiations would necessarily take a long time as so many different Powers are concerned, to say nothing of the conflicting interests and large areas involved.

22.   On the other hand it will be difficult to draft satisfactory terms for an armistice even if it is confined to land and air operations alone, for unless the terms are most precise and can anticipate all possible contingencies, constant complaints will be made as to infringements of its conditions and innumerable disputes may in this way arise.   Further, if it were decided to grant an armistice as in (*b*), and submarine attacks on passenger and merchant vessels were continued, the Conference proceedings might become embittered and a settlement rendered the more difficult.   Course (*c*) is not recommended.   The more hungry the enemy is kept the better, and after all he probably has enough to live upon.   Also, it would be difficult to arrange a scale of rations that would be acceptable to all parties.

23.   It is quite evident that the question is beset by numerous difficulties and therefore its examination is the more urgent.   On the whole it seems hardly possible to refuse an armistice, but it is necessary that we should have some definite guarantees of good faith, and therefore it is suggested that the granting of an armistice should at least be made conditional on: —

(*a*) The immediate withdrawal of all enemy troops inside their pre-war frontiers;

(*b*) Immediate release of all prisoners of war held by the enemy;

(*c*) Tentative surrender of a certain portion of the enemy fleet.

W. R. ROBERTSON, General,
Chief of the Imperial General Staff.

War Office,
31st August, 1916."

Apart from the interest of this document as setting out the ideas of the military authorities upon the territorial measures that should

R*

be taken to limit the perils of a recurrence of the German menace, it is of value in that it reflects the expectation current at the time that peace negotiations might not be far distant on the horizon.

There were, however, marked differences in the attitude adopted by various influential people to this prospect. Many who had entered the War reluctantly felt that once it had been forced upon us, it would be a real disaster if peace were made before it had been demonstrated clearly that no military machine, however perfect, could prevail in the end against the roused conscience of civilisation. But this view was by no means fully appreciated and shared in all quarters. In face of our dubious military position and unsatisfactory outlook, there were those who felt attracted towards the possibility of a prompt if inconclusive peace.

The third campaign of the War was now drawing to a close and the Allies seemed further than ever from achieving a favourable determination of the issue. At the end of the first campaign Belgium had been almost entirely occupied by the enemy; a large and important section of Northern France had also been overrun by the Germans, and even after the retreat from the Marne ten of the richest provinces of France remained in enemy occupation. At the end of the second year's campaign Serbia had fallen entirely into the hands of the Central Powers, Bulgaria with its brave army had joined the enemy and thousands of square miles of Russian territory had been conquered and were adding to the resources of the enemy in food, timber and labour.

By the end of the third summer Roumania had been crushed and most of its territory, including its capital, was in enemy occupation. Invaluable reserves of oil and corn were added to the enemy stores of essential supply. The Balkans were thus almost entirely in the hands of the Central Powers, for whose munitions the road to Constantinople had been cleared. Turkey had been resuscitated and was making a formidable contribution to the military strength of its allies. She was holding up at one point or another hundreds of thousands of British and French troops. We had been driven by Turkish forces out of the Dardanelles, and a British army had surrendered to the Turks in Mesopotamia. In the west, attempts made with colossal losses to release the fierce grip of the German Army on the soil of France had not succeeded in producing any tangible result. The Germans had been hammered by the most formidable artillery ever mobilised on a battlefield and they had suffered severely, and had to abandon some territory, but their casualties were not comparable with those inflicted on the French and notably on the British Army, and the territorial gain was insignificant, whether computed in superficies or strategy. The German attack on Verdun had failed, but the French had even there lost considerably more men than the Germans.

The French nation was bleeding at every pore, and no one could visit France without feeling that although the courage of this gallant people was undaunted and its spirit unbroken, its ardour was being quenched in the blood of its sons. Official reports from Italy were far from encouraging. The Italian people were by no means as united in their decision to enter the War as the other belligerents. Their inadequately equipped troops had since May, 1915, performed prodigies of valour and triumphs of engineering skill in scaling fortresses drilled and blasted out of the great mountains that lowered over the Italian plains; but progress had been slow, and losses had been heavy. Recently, there had been a serious setback. The Cabinet were informed early in November by Sir Rennell Rodd, our Ambassador in Rome, upon the accuracy of whose reports on the Italian position we all placed implicit confidence, that—

" there were already in Italy certain symptoms of war weariness and discontent at the protraction of the struggle. Great Britain is represented as the only country anxious to prolong the struggle *à outrance* for her own ends. It would be wrong to pretend that there exists here the same grim determination to carry through as prevails in France and in the British Empire."

The Russian armies were broken and quite unable to offer any effective resistance to the German attack, and although their position in respect of ammunition and rifles was supposed to have improved during the year it was quite clear that their equipment would not enable them to stand up much longer to the formidable artillery at the disposal of Hindenburg's armies. Ten thousand tons of ammunition stacked at Archangel had, either through carelessness or treachery, been blown up. The whole administration was slack, incompetent, and drenched with corruption. No wonder that the Russian people were seething with discontent. The peasantry were permeated with sullen disaffection. The workers in the towns were becoming more difficult and insubordinate. Strikes multiplied and street demonstrations were becoming a menacing feature. The soldiers had ceased to believe in the possibility of victory, and whether they were called upon to advance or to resist they obeyed mechanically, but their response lacked spirit or confidence. Discipline alone held them in the trenches. Food everywhere throughout Russia was becoming scarce. Revolution was only a question of time. It was taken for granted on all hands. Although we were assured by our representative in Russia that it would not occur until the War was over, the Allies could not rely upon a population saturated with a spirit of disgust with its Government to go on risking precious lives at the behest and for the sake of an autocracy which no longer commanded respect, and which in fact had become universally despised among all classes high and low. There were hopes that Russian resistance might last long enough to hold up a considerable proportion of the Central Powers' Armies until the Allies on the Western and Italian Fronts had at last achieved the long-expected " break through." But that hope was becoming increasingly precarious and in the event it proved to be illusory. A complete collapse of the Russian resistance meant two or three million German and Austrian troops, with their formidable train of artillery, released for the Western and Italian Fronts, to attack an exhausted France and discouraged Italy.

There was another impending peril which threatened the very life of Britain—the sinking of our merchant ships by enemy submarines. The German Admiralty had set itself the task of increasing its submarine fleet fourfold in numbers. The increase in size and power of these elusive vessels of destruction was more menacing than the augmentation in their numbers. It meant that the area of attack was widened. The newer types could travel into the ocean and hunt far and wide for their prey. The difficulties of organising effective protection were thereby considerably enhanced. The output of the German yards was multiplying at an alarming rate, and the figures of our losses leapt up steeply week by week. The defence was by no means equal to the assault. It had to fight an invisible foe—an enemy who left no spoor behind, but who destroyed and then disappeared, pursuing his course in the trackless depths, unseen, unseeable, and untraceable, leaving nothing behind to indicate direction or distance.

The following table shows the rate at which British merchant vessels were being sunk by submarines during 1916:—

Date.	No.	Tonnage.
January, 1916	5	62,288
February ,,	7	75,860
March ,,	19	99,089
April ,,	37	141,193
May ,,	12	64,251
June ,,	11	36,976
July ,,	21	82,432
August ,,	22	43,354
September ,,	34	104,572
October ,,	41	176,248
November ,,	42	168,809
December ,,	36	182,292

This is how the position appeared at that time to Lord Robert Cecil, who was then an influential member of the Cabinet:—

" One thing is clear. Our situation is grave. It is certain that unless the utmost national effort is made it may become desperate, particularly in the matter of shipping. The position in Allied countries is even more serious. France is within measurable distance of exhaustion. The political outlook in Italy is menacing. Her finance is tottering. In Russia there is great discouragement. She has long been on the verge of revolution. Even her man-power seems coming near its limits."

This was a situation that must necessarily invite doubt in the stoutest hearts and recruit patriotic and humanitarian sentiment to the side of immediate peace. But for reasons which I give later on I felt that any attempt to make peace at a time when the Germans were at the climax of strength and achievement, whilst we were only just beginning to mobilise our full power, would necessarily be unsatisfactory and inconclusive.

The attitude of France towards any peace overtures at this stage was one of uncompromising hostility, despite the gloom of the out-look. It was set out very clearly at a sitting of the French Chamber in a speech of exceptional power by the Prime Minister, M. Briand. A Socialist by the name of M. Brizon had delivered a speech on 19th September, 1916, in the course of which he dwelt upon the losses of France and ended by asking if France had not suffered enough, and whether she could not now negotiate peace. M. Briand in reply delivered one of the most eloquent speeches of his life. I quote an extract from that speech. When he sat down he received from the Chamber what is said to be " such an ovation as has never been accorded to a Prime Minister," and the House by 421 votes to 26 ordered the speech to be placarded throughout France. It may therefore be assumed that it represented the determined and even fierce resistance of the country which had suffered most from the War to any premature efforts to make peace.

"Look at your country, M. Brizon. It has been violently attacked. It stands for something in the world as a propagator of those ideas which have done work for the world's progress. When your country, which has for two years had the honour to be champion of right, has stayed the invader, and defends the whole world, when its blood flows, you say, ' Negotiate peace.' What a challenge, what an outrage to the memory of our dead! [Loud cheers, and a shout, ' debout les morts! '] What, M. Brizon! Ten of your country's provinces are invaded. Our old men and women and children have been carried off. They bear their misery bravely, awaiting deliverance at your hands. Is it then that you come to us saying, ' Negotiate, go and ask for peace '? You little know France if you imagine that she can accept economy of milliards, or even of blood in such humiliating circumstances. What peace would you get for France? It would be a peace of war. If you wish that peace should shine upon the world, M. Brizon, if you wish the idea of liberty and justice to prevail, ask for victory, and not for the peace obtainable to-day, for that peace would be humiliating and dishonouring. There is not a Frenchman who can possibly desire it."

On the other hand Germany had her troubles. A blockade had been tightly drawn around the Central Powers, while on the other hand the Allies had developed very extensive arrangements for securing their own essential supplies. Austria and Turkey were broken reeds. Germany could not lean her hopes too heavily upon them. In Britain the work of the Ministry of Munitions was now bearing copious fruit, and the adoption of national service was securing hundreds of thousands of men for our armies.

It was natural, therefore, that Germany should be ready to welcome and foster suggestions from any quarter urging an early peace settlement, while her strength remained intact and her position on the War map lent colour to the suggestion that she was substantially a victorious Power. Rumours indeed reached us that her emissaries in the United States were angling for intervention by President Wilson with a view to an early and favourable peace.

The President himself would not have been without his own reasons for being attracted by the suggestion of proposing such an intervention. The Presidential election was at hand—it was due at the beginning of November—and there was the very large and influential German-American vote to consider. He was, moreover, standing on his reputation as the man who had kept America out of the War, and anything he could do to reduce the very real danger —a danger which not long after took concrete form—that America would after all be drawn into the conflict, would obviously help his election campaign. The moment was, however, in my view utterly inappropriate for the discussion of any peace terms which would be remotely satisfactory to the Allies. I will not pretend that my opinion was shared by all members of the British Cabinet. There were those among them who had grave doubts about the military position and the outlook for our shipping, our food supplies, and financial reserves. Lord Grey, Lord Lansdowne, Mr. M'Kenna, and Mr. Runciman in particular were obviously uneasy about the prospect. They had misgivings as to the possibility of continuing the War beyond Christmas, 1916. It has become clear from statements which have since been published that a similar impression was widely held abroad.

I felt it vitally important to throw out a sharp challenge to the defeatest spirit which was working from foreign quarters to bring about an inconclusive peace, and which appeared to find an echo even in some responsible quarters in our own country.

I was no friend to war. It was only with the utmost reluctance that I had at the last minute agreed to the ultimatum of Britain. My pacifist attitude was very well known, and had it not been for

Germany's violation of Belgian neutrality, I should up to the last have refused to remain in a Cabinet which implicated the country in war with all its carnage and organised barbarism. But once having entered on the War, I was no less resolute to pursue it until at least the object of our sacrifice had been achieved. It was not merely a question of abiding by the Shakespearian counsel: —

> " Beware
> Of entrance to a quarrel: but being in
> Bear't that the opposed may beware of thee."

A conference under existing conditions might have involved a peace which would have been a virtual and practical abandonment of the cause which compelled us to take up arms.

Accordingly, copying an example which had been set shortly before by Lord Grey himself, I granted, on 28th September, 1916, an interview to an American correspondent—in this case Mr. Roy W. Howard, the President of the United Press of America—in which I outlined my views as to the attitude this country and her Allies should adopt towards any talk of an immediate peace.

I began by pointing out that Britain had only now got into her stride in her war effort, and was justifiably suspicious of any suggestion that President Wilson should choose this moment to " butt in " with a proposal to stop the War before we could achieve victory. " There had been no such intervention when we were being hammered through the first two years, as yet untrained and ill-equipped. Our men had taken their punishment without squealing. They had held grimly on while the winning Germans talked of annexing Belgium and Poland as their spoils of victory, and of making it a fight to a finish with England."

" The whole world—including neutrals of the highest purposes and humanitarians with the best of motives—must know that there can be no outside interference at this stage. Britain asked no intervention when she was unprepared to fight. She will tolerate none now that she is prepared, until the Prussian military despotism is broken beyond repair."

It was idle for people now to deplore the horror of continued conflict, when their pity had not moved them to stop it while British troops were being gassed, and exposed to an overpowering attack that used ten shells to their one.

" But in the British determination to carry the fight to a decisive finish there is something more than the natural demand for vengeance. The inhumanity and pitilessness of the fighting that must come before a lasting peace is possible is not comparable with the cruelty that would be involved in stopping the War while there remains the possibility of civilisation again being menaced from the same quarter. Peace now or at any time before the final and complete elimination of this menace is unthinkable. No man and no nation with the slightest understanding of the temper of the citizen army of Britons, which took its terrible hammering without a whine, or a grumble, will attempt to call a halt now."

"But how long do you figure this can and must go on?" I was asked.

"There is neither clock nor calendar in the British Army to-day," was my reply. "Time is the least vital factor. Only the result counts—not the time consumed in achieving it. It took England 20 years to defeat Napoleon, and the first 15 of those years were black with British defeat. It will not take 20 years to win this war, but whatever time is required, it will be done.

"And I say this, recognising that we have only begun to win. There is no disposition on our side to fix the hour of ultimate victory after the first success. We have no delusion that the War is nearing an end. We have not the slightest doubt as to *how* it is to end."

"But what of France?" I was asked. "Is there the same determination there to stick to the end; the same idea of fighting until peace terms can be dictated by Germany's enemies?"

"The world at large has not yet begun to appreciate the magnificence, the nobility, the wonder of France," I replied. "I had the answer to your inquiry given me a few days ago by a noble Frenchwoman. This woman had given four sons—she had one more left to give to France. In the course of my talk with her I asked if she did not think the struggle had gone far enough. Her reply, without a moment's hesitation, was: 'The fight will never have gone far enough until it shall have made a repetition of this horror impossible.' That mother was voicing the spirit of France. Yes, France will stick to the end."

I pointed to the defence of Verdun as evidence of French staying power. While the British were buoyed up by a sporting spirit, the French were burning with an unquenchable patriotism. The motto of the Allies was "Never again!" I was myself fresh from a visit to the battlefields, and the ghastliness I had witnessed was something which must never be re-enacted. The War must make that certain.

This was the substance of my interview, which was given very wide currency, and was discussed in every country. The "Policy of a Knock-Out Blow," as it was called, caused great exasperation, not only to the Central Powers (as witnessed by the constant reference to it in their Press and in the speeches of their politicians), but even to several of my colleagues in the British Cabinet, who, if not exactly pacifists, were leaning towards an early peace of accommodation. Several of my colleagues regarded the interview as provocative, and many held that it did not accurately represent the attitude of the Government towards the idea of an immediate peace.

It was not long before I discovered that this interview had caused a great deal of perturbation and animadversion amongst the members of the Cabinet. I received the following letter from Lord Grey: —

"29th September, 1916.

My dear Lloyd George,

The more I think of it the more I am apprehensive of the possible effect of the warning to Wilson in your interview, and I want to explain why this is so.

1. Briand's speech, and I think steps taken in Washington, has made any further warning to Wilson unnecessary for the present.

2. We shall now be held responsible in America for warning Wilson off the course. He will now point to your words as the reason why he can do nothing, and this will tend to bring him and Bethmann-Hollweg together.

3. Wilson will be more disposed to put upon us the pressure that Congress has urged him to put, which may be very inconvenient.

4. The extreme submarine warfare will be precipitated by Germany, who will tell Wilson that as he can do nothing because of us, Germany must use every means against us. Wilson and his supporters will be less inclined than before to resent submarine warfare against us.

5. It has always been my view that until the Allies were sure of victory the door should be kept open for Wilson's mediation. It is now closed for ever as far as we are concerned.

I am still anxious about the effect of submarine warfare.

I hope you won't think me captious in questioning one point in our interview of which the rest not only draws my assent but my admiration. I may be quite wrong in my view, but a public warning to the President of the United States is an important step, and I wish I had had an opportunity of putting these considerations before you and discussing them with you.

No answer needed now as nothing more can be done till we see the effect.

Yours sincerely,

GREY OF F."

To this I replied: —

"October 2, 1916.

My dear Grey,

Thanks for your letter. I wonder whether you are still of the same opinion after reading M.I.I.'s secret information? Have you seen it?

Spring-Rice's telegram 2943 seems to be also very significant.

If the hands of Wilson had been forced—and there is every indication that the Germans and Irish co-operation could do so—
then we should be in a very tight place. Any cessation of hostilities
now would be a disaster; and although we could always refuse or
put up impossible terms, it is much better that we should not be
placed in that predicament. *You* could not have warned off the
United States without doing it formally. I could commit a serviceable indiscretion; you could not. It would ruin you; I am
inoculated!

. . . In so far as callous impenitence will allow me, I am
genuinely sorry for adding one dram to your cup of anxieties.

Ever sincerely,

D. LLOYD GEORGE."

Lord Grey committed himself to a series of forecasts in this letter
all of which were falsified by the event. He predicted that it would
encourage Wilson to " do nothing and would tend to bring him and
Bethmann-Hollweg together." A few months later, when I was Prime
Minister, Wilson broke off diplomatic relations with Germany, and
a few weeks after doing so entered into the War on the side of the
Allies. Grey predicted that another result of my letter might be an
increase in the pressure which the President would bring to bear
upon us. That also turned out to be an unrealised apprehension.
He foresaw that my interview would precipitate an extreme submarine warfare by Germany, and that President Wilson as a result
of it would be less inclined to resent submarine warfare against
us. Germany had decided at the beginning of 1916 to increase fourfold the number and potency of her submarines. At the end of
August she had already launched a large number of these new, more
powerful craft. And so far from Wilson and his supporters being
less inclined than before to resent submarine warfare, it was the
intensification and extension of the submarine campaign that
provoked America to declare war against Germany early in 1917.

As to Grey's prediction that the door against Wilson's mediation
would, as a result of my interview, be " closed for ever as far as we
are concerned," two or three months later President Wilson issued
his famous Peace Note.

It is, however, significant of Lord Grey's frame of mind at this time
that he seemed to have a doubt as to the victory of the Allies—and
that he was relying as a means of escape from the consequences of
defeat upon the mediation of the President of the United States.

How little Lord Grey's estimate of the probable effect of my interview corresponded with reality is made clear by the reports which
came to hand from our Ambassador in the United States, Sir C.
Spring-Rice. In a telegram to the Foreign Secretary, dated
4th October, 1916, Spring-Rice said: —

" I am informed from a very reliable source that the President has no intention of making peace proposals. The Secretary of State for War's statement has had a great effect.

I have also reason to believe that action will not be taken on the Retaliatory Clauses. . . ."

He followed this up with a letter dated 6th October, 1916, in which he wrote : —

" Mr. Lloyd George's statement, which had an immense and instantaneous effect in this country, put a stop to the peace rumours which for some time have been prevalent here. It seems generally acknowledged now that the President has no intention of offering his mediation at any rate in the near future."

The letter also said that the American Government was maintaining uncompromising opposition to Germany in regard to any extension of the submarine campaign, and explained that the peace rumours emanating from German sources were being used by them to assist their deals on the stock market.

" The publication of a peace rumour is at once followed by a general decline on the Stock Exchange, and the authoritative quarter which launches such a rumour is in excellent position to profit by its power."

In a later telegram, dated 20th October, 1916, Sir C. Spring-Rice reported : " Lloyd George's interview had the most excellent effect here." There is in fact no evidence that my " Knock-Out Blow " interview did anything to injure our cause in the States. On the contrary, it steadied opinion there and helped to increase the sympathy felt with us in our desperate fight.

CHAPTER XXXI

THE LANSDOWNE PEACE MOVE

SHOULD we make or encourage peace overtures whilst the issue of the
War was still in doubt and the enemy had good reason to claim that
he had won on points? The British Cabinet was brought by the
intervention of one of its most respected members to a searching and
considered examination of the question.

The type of partisan pacifist who maintains that an honourable
and satisfactory peace could have been negotiated long before
November, 1918, is generally anxious to cast the whole of the blame
for prolonging the War on the Coalition that came into existence
at the end of 1916. In order to sustain their criticism they assume
that 1917 afforded the first real opportunity for making peace. The
discussions which took place in the Asquith Cabinet on the desirability of encouraging peace overtures and the decision arrived at by
the Cabinet are either unknown to these critics or are wilfully
ignored by them.

The first serious peace movement in Europe started immediately
after the termination of the sanguinary battle of 1916. The horrible
and futile carnage of the Somme following on the ghastly losses of
Verdun had sent a thrill of horror through all the belligerent lands
and there was a distinct movement for an interchange of views as to
the possibility of a settlement.

In the middle of November Lord Lansdowne startled the Cabinet
by a memorandum which he circulated amongst members with the
consent of the Prime Minister. It was written the day before Mr.
Asquith and I left England for the Paris Conference, and was in the
hands of members of the Cabinet on our return. This bold document frankly suggested doubts as to the possibility of victory. It was
at least courageous, and proved that he at any rate was quite alive to
the perils of the Allied situation. It was clear that Lord Lansdowne
thought a condition of stalemate had been reached and that there
was no prospect of any improvement.

The text of this memorandum was as follows: —

" The members of the War Committee were asked by the Prime
Minister some weeks ago to express their views as to the terms
upon which peace might be concluded. I do not know whether

there has been a general response to this invitation, but the only reply which I have seen is one written last month by the First Lord of the Admiralty, in which he deals at some length with the problems which might have to be discussed at any Peace Conference. Mr. Balfour observes truly that these questions cannot be profitably examined except upon an agreed hypothesis as to the military position of the combatants at the end of the War, and he proceeds to assume, though merely for the sake of argument, that the Central Powers, either through defeat or exhaustion, have to accept the terms imposed upon them by the Allies.

I venture to suggest that the attention of the War Committee might with advantage be directed to a somewhat different problem, and that they should be invited to give us their opinion as to our present prospects of being able to 'dictate' the kind of terms which we should all like to impose upon our enemies if we were in a position to do so.

We are agreed as to the goal, but we do not know how far we have really travelled towards it, or how much nearer to it we are likely to find ourselves even if the War be prolonged for, say, another year. What will that year have cost us? How much better will our position be at the end of it? Shall we even then be strong enough to 'dictate' terms?

It seems to me almost impossible to overrate the importance of these considerations, because it is clear that our diplomacy must be governed by an accurate appreciation of them.

We have obtained within the last few days from the different Departments of the Government a good deal of information as to the situation, naval, military and economic. It is far from reassuring.

From the President of the Board of Trade we received on the 26th October a most interesting and carefully compiled memorandum tending to show the daily growing shortage of tonnage and its consequences. Mr. Runciman comes to the conclusion that our shipbuilding is not keeping pace with our losses, and that, although the number of our vessels is down, the demands on our tonnage are not diminished. We must look forward to depending more and more on neutral ships, but we can be under no illusions as to the precarious nature of that resource. I do not think I exaggerate when I describe this most important document as profoundly disquieting. But in a later memorandum, dated 9th November, the President paints the picture in still gloomier colours, and anticipates, on the advice of his experts, 'a complete breakdown in shipping . . . much sooner than June, 1917.'

The President of the Board of Agriculture has recently presented to the Cabinet his report on Food Prospects in 1917. That report goes to show that there is a world's deficit in breadstuffs, that the price of bread is likely to go higher, that there had been a general failure of the potato crop, that the supply of fish is expected to be 64 per cent. below the normal, that there is considerable difficulty in regard to the supply of feeding-stuffs, that the difficulties of cultivation steadily increase, that land is likely to go derelict, the yield to decline, and the number of live-stock to diminish greatly.

Lord Crawford's later note, dated 9th November, on Home Food Supplies, shows that these anticipations were not unduly pessi-mistic. The position has, he tells us, become much worse, and, owing to the inroads made upon the agricultural population by the demands of the Army, it is in some parts of the country ' no longer a question of maintaining a moderate standard of cultiva-tion, but whether cultivation will cease.'

Turning to our naval and military resources, we have a report from the First Lord of the Admiralty, dated 14th October, from which we learn that, in spite of the tremendous efforts which we have made, the size of our Home Fleets is still insufficient, that we have nearly reached the limit of immediate production in the matter of capital ships, that we have not got nearly enough destroyers to meet our needs for escort and anti-submarine work, that we shall certainly not have enough for our Allies, and that the position in regard to light cruisers is not much better. From the same report we may infer that the submarine difficulty is becoming acute, and that, in spite of all our efforts, it seems impossible to provide an effectual rejoinder to it. The increasing size of the enemy submarines, the strength of their construction (which will apparently oblige us to re-arm our merchantmen with a heavier gun), and their activity in all parts of the world, point to the same conclusion.

The papers which we have from time to time received from the General Staff and from the War Committee prove that in the matter of man-power we are nearing the end of our tether. The last report of the Man-Power Distribution Board seems, in particu-lar, to sound a grave note of warning. The unexhausted supply of men is, they tell us, now very restricted, and the number avail-able can only be added to by a still further depletion of industry. In the meanwhile Ireland still declines to add to the available supply the 150,000 men who would be obtainable from that country, and I am not aware that any serious attempt is to be made to secure them.

All these seem to me to be very serious factors in the calculation which it is our duty to make. It will be replied, and no doubt truly, that the Central Powers are feeling the pressure of the War not less acutely than we feel it, and I hope we shall also be told that our staying powers are greater than theirs; but, even if this be so, it is none the less our duty to consider, after a careful review of the facts, what our plight and the plight of the civilised world will be after another year, or, as we are sometimes told, two or three more years of a struggle as exhausting as that in which we are engaged. No one for a moment believes that we are going to lose the War; but what is our chance of winning it in such a manner, and within such limits of time, as will enable us to beat our enemy to the ground and impose upon him the kind of terms which we so freely discuss?

I do not suppose for an instant that there is any weakening in the spirit of the people of this country, and I should hope, although I do not feel absolute confidence on the subject, that the same might be said of our Allies, but neither in their interests nor in ours can it be desirable that the War should be prolonged, unless it can be shown that we can bring it to an effectual conclusion within a reasonable space of time.

What does the prolongation of the War mean?

Our own casualties already amount to over 1,100,000. We have had 15,000 officers killed, not including those who are missing. There is no reason to suppose that, as the force at the front in the different theatres of war increases, the casualties will increase at a slower rate. We are slowly but surely killing off the best of the male population of these islands. The figures representing the casualties of our Allies are not before me. The total must be appalling.

The financial burden which we have already accumulated is almost incalculable. We are adding to it at the rate of over £5,000,000 per day. Generations will have to come and go before the country recovers from the loss which it has sustained in human beings, and from the financial ruin and the destruction of the means of production which are taking place.

All this it is no doubt our duty to bear, but only if it can be shown that the sacrifice will have its reward. If it is to be made in vain, if the additional year, or two years, or three years, finds us still unable to dictate terms, the War with its nameless horrors will have been needlessly prolonged, and the responsibility of those who needlessly prolong such a War is not less than that of those who needlessly provoke it.

A thorough stocktaking, first by each Ally of his own resources, present and prospective, and next by the Allies, or at all events by the leading Allies, in confidential consultation, seems indispensable. Not until such a stocktaking has taken place will each Ally be able to decide which of his desiderata are indispensable, and whether he might not be prepared to accept less than 20s. in the £ in consideration of prompt payment. Not until it has taken place will the Allies as a body be able to determine the broad outline of their policy or the attitude which they ought to assume towards those who talk to them of peace.

I think Sir William Robertson must have had some such stock-taking in his mind when he wrote the remarkable paper which was circulated to the Cabinet on the 31st August. In that paper he expressed his belief that negotiations for peace in some form or other might arise any day, and he urged that ' we need therefore to decide without loss of time what our policy is to be, then place it before the Entente Powers, and ascertain in return what are their aims, and so endeavour to arrive at a clear understanding before we meet our enemies in conference.' The idea may, for all I know, have been acted on already.

Many of us, however, must of late have asked ourselves how this war is ever to be brought to an end. If we are told that the deliberate conclusion of the Government is that it must be fought until Germany has been beaten to the ground and sues for peace on any terms which we are pleased to accord to her, my only observation would be that we ought to know something of the data upon which this conclusion has been reached. To many of us it seems as if the prospect of a ' knock-out ' was, to say the least of it, remote. Our forces and those of France have shown a splendid gallantry on the Western Front, and have made substantial advances; but is it believed that these, any more than those made in 1915 with equally high hopes and accompanied by not less cruel losses, will really enable us to ' break through '? Can we afford to go on paying the same sort of price for the same sort of gains?

Judging from the comments supplied by the General Staff, I should doubt whether the Italian offensive, however successful, is likely to have a decisive effect.

At Salonika we are entangled in an extraordinarily difficult enterprise, forced upon us, against our better judgment, by our Allies, and valuable only because it occupies enemy troops who would otherwise be fighting the Russians and the Roumanians. On the Russian and Roumanian frontiers we shall be fortunate if we avoid a disaster, which at one moment seemed imminent. General Brussiloff's language is inspiring, but is it really justified by the facts? The history of the Russian operations has been very chequered, and we shall never, I am afraid, be free from the danger of miscarriages owing to defective strategy, to failure of supplies, to corruption in high places, or to incidents such as the disastrous explosion which has just lost us 10,000 tons of munitions at Archangel.

Again, are we quite sure that, regarded as political rather than military assets, our Allies are entirely to be depended upon? There have been occasions upon which political complications have threatened to affect the military situation in France. I quote the following sentences from a letter written a few days ago by a very shrewd Frenchman: ' Rappelez-vous bien que la Démocratie française n'est pas menée par son gouvernement; c'est elle qui le mène; un courant d'opinion publique en faveur de la cessation de la guerre pourrait être irrésistible. . . . Au feu, le soldat français se battra toujours comme un héros; derrière, sa famille pourra bien dire: en voilà assez!' Italy is always troublesome and exacting. Sir Rennell Rodd, in a dispatch dated the 4th November, asks us to take note of the fact that there are already in Italy 'certain symptoms of war weariness and discouragement at the protraction of the struggle. . . . Great Britain is represented as the only country anxious to prolong the struggle à outrance for her own ends. . . . It would be wrong to pretend that there exists here the same grim determination to carry through as prevails in France and the British Empire.' The domestic situation in Russia is far from reassuring. There have been alarming disorders both at Moscow and in Petrograd. Russia has had five Ministers of the Interior in twelve months, and the fifth is described as being by no means secure in his seat.

Our difficulties with the neutrals are, again, not likely to diminish. It is highly creditable to the Foreign Office that during the last two years we have escaped a breakdown of our blockade policy, which, in spite of continual obstruction and bad faith, has produced excellent results; but we have been within an ace of grave complications with Sweden and the United States. As time goes on the neutrals are likely to become more and more restive and intolerant of the belligerents, whose right to go on disturbing the peace of the civilised world they will refuse to admit.

I may be asked whether I have any practical suggestion to offer, and I admit the difficulty of replying. But is it not true that, unless the apprehensions which I have sketched can be shown, after such an investigation as I have suggested, to be groundless, we ought at any rate not to discourage any movement, no matter where originating, in favour of an interchange of views as to the possibility of a settlement? There are many indications that the germs of such a movement are already in existence. One cannot dismiss as unworthy of attention the well-substantiated reports which have come to us from time to time upon this subject from Belgian, Scandinavian, Japanese and Russian sources, or such circumstantial stories as those told in Sir Esmé Howard's dispatch of the 24th August as to the meeting held at Prince Lichnowsky's house, and in Lord Eustace Percy's memorandum as to the intimations made by the Rector of the Berlin University. The debates in the Reichstag show that the pacifist groups are active and outspoken. From all sides come accounts of the impatience of the civil population and their passionate yearning for peace.

It seems to me quite inconceivable that during the winter we shall not be sounded by someone as to our readiness to discuss

terms of peace or proposals for an armistice. Are we prepared
with our reply? Lord Crawford has dealt with the question of
an armistice. I am not sure that I agree with some of his suggestions, but I am sure that he is right in holding that
an unconditional refusal would be inadmissible.

As to peace terms, I hope we shall adhere steadfastly to the main
principle laid down by the Prime Minister in the speech which he
summed up by a declaration that we could agree to no peace which
did not afford adequate reparation for the past and adequate
security for the future, but the outline was broadly sketched and
might be filled up in many different ways. The same may be said
of the not less admirable statement which he has just made at the
Guildhall, and of the temperate speeches which the Secretary of
State for Foreign Affairs has from time to time delivered.

But it is unfortunate that, in spite of these utterances, it should
be possible to represent us and our Allies as committed to a policy
partly vindictive and partly selfish, and so irreconcilably committed to that policy that we should regard as unfriendly any attempt,
however sincere, to extricate us from the *impasse*. The interview
given by the Secretary of State for War in September last to an
American correspondent has produced an impression which it
will not be easy to efface. There may have been circumstances
of which I am unaware, connected perhaps with the Presidential
election, which made it necessary to announce that at the
particular moment any intervention, however well meant, would
be distasteful to us or inopportune. He said, indeed, that ' the
world must know that there can be no outside interference *at this
stage* '—a very momentous limitation. For surely it cannot be
our intention, no matter how long the War lasts, no matter what
the strain on our resources, to maintain this attitude, or to declare,
as M. Briand declared about the same time, that for us, too, ' the
word peace is a sacrilege.' Let our naval, military and economic
advisers tell us frankly whether they are satisfied that the knock-out
blow can and will be delivered. The Secretary of State's formula
holds the field, and will do so until something else is put in its
place. Whether it is to hold the field, and, if not, what that something else should be, ought surely to depend upon their answer,
and that again upon the result of the careful stocktaking, domestic
and international, which, I hope, is already taking place.—L.
November 13, 1916."

" The above note had been written before the discussion, which
took place at to-day's Cabinet, from which we learned that the War
Committee had already decided to take important steps in the
direction which I have ventured to indicate.—L.
November 13, 1916."

Coming from a statesman of Lord Lansdowne's position and ante-cedents, this document made a deep impression. No one could accuse him of being a mere " pacifist." He was the author of the Entente Cordiale in 1904. He was an unflinching advocate of the policy of standing by all the implications of that fateful Treaty.

Before the Cabinet came to any conclusions on the Lansdowne memorandum, the Prime Minister invited the opinions of the military and naval authorities on the suggestion of a possible stalemate. The Chief of Staff, Sir William Robertson, truculently repudiated such a possibility. Ultimate victory was assured the Allies, provided the advice of the War Office was obediently followed in every particular and its demands patriotically fulfilled in every detail. There must be more men and material hurled at the enemy, and the hurling must be done exclusively on the Western Front. It was made quite clear that there would be still heavier casualties than those already suffered. From that Sir William Robertson did not shrink, but this further slaughter of British lives must occur in France and Flanders and not elsewhere.

Sir Douglas Haig put in a memorandum on similar lines. In this note, which Sir William Robertson appended to his answer to the Lansdowne memorandum, the Commander-in-Chief stresses the difficulties of maintaining any offensive in France during the winter, but points out that the conditions of which he complains represent only the normal situation at that time of the year. On the other side of the picture, the Germans had been badly defeated on the Somme, and their casualties had been undoubtedly heavy—far heavier than those of the Allies. Their *morale* had been lowered seriously. Indeed, he reached the conclusion that—

" an appreciable proportion of the German soldiers are now practically beaten men, ready to surrender if they could find opportunity, thoroughly tired of the War, and hopeless of eventual success."

The Allied troops, on the other hand, were all confident of victory.

" It is true that the amount of ground gained is not great. That is nothing. Our proved ability to get the enemy to move at all from his defensive positions was the valuable result of the fighting."

Sir Douglas Haig further said that he regarded the prospects of success on the Western Front in 1917 as most favourable. For this, however, he wanted many more troops, and an ample supply of munitions—of which " the enormous quantities required have been furnished this year with unfailing regularity." More aircraft, more road and railway material, etc., were also wanted. Given these supplies, he and his army were confident of being able to achieve ultimate victory. From the memoranda put in by the Chief of the Imperial Staff and the Commander-in-Chief there could be no doubt as to military opinion about our prospects.

Lord Grey's contribution was characteristic. His position as Foreign Secretary was pivotal when it came to a question of making peace or continuing war. We all anxiously awaited his guidance. He was the most departmental of Ministers, and had always been buried in his office, with hardly a thought for anything else. He scarcely ever expressed any opinion on any Cabinet questions outside his own department. His aloofness was monumental. He had a habit—entirely his own—of drafting his dispatches at the Cabinet table whilst discussions were proceeding on home affairs. This lofty detachment he carried into the War Cabinets. In the discussion bearing on the most effective methods of prosecuting the War he had little to say or suggest. Having been forced to declare the War from which he had failed to save his country, it was for others to direct it and find the means for its successful prosecution. But here was a question pre-eminently affecting his department. Should any peace approaches be encouraged or entertained? The initiative had been taken by one of his immediate predecessors at the Foreign Office— Lord Lansdowne.

In spite of the confidence manifested by the military authorities, Lord Grey expressed his misgivings as to the effect of the submarine campaign, and said he thought it had not been mastered and for the present seemed to be getting more and more beyond our control. He went so far as to say, however, that as long as the military and naval authorities considered that the position of the Allies was likely to improve, even though it might not result in the ultimate and complete defeat of Germany, it would be premature to make peace. Should it at any future time become evident that the Allies could not improve further their position, they should proceed forthwith to make the best peace terms they could.

Ever non-committal and hesitating, he neither associated himself with Lord Lansdowne nor did he dissent from his views. He neither approved nor disapproved. Whatever the decision or the event his intervention would conform to either. Was he in favour of the Lansdowne thesis? If it were turned down and its author and his supporters were taunted with faintheartedness, no one could fairly quote one sentence of unequivocal commendation from Lord Grey. On the other hand, if either then or later Lord Lansdowne's brave memorandum were justified, then no one could say that Lord Grey had offered any hostile criticism to its purport.

Sir William Robertson in his memorandum had arraigned the Foreign Secretary's diplomacy both before and during the War and had ascribed to its feebleness most of our misfortunes. The attack occupied one short paragraph in Sir W. Robertson's contribution. Lord Grey devoted pages to an explanation and defence of his failures —his failures to avoid war; to keep Turkey out of the War; to secure the timely help of Greece; and to lure Bulgaria on to our side. He had done everything of which diplomacy was capable without adequate military support. The failure was military and not diplomatic. All very interesting, but having no bearing on the momentous issue raised by Lord Lansdowne—whether it was better to make peace now or to fight on in the hope that we might be in a better position later on to dictate terms.

It is rather surprising that no constructive suggestions for peace were ever put forward by him either now or at any time. If he gave any thought to the terms of peace which he had in his mind as the end and aim of the War he never favoured his colleagues with his ideas. The only concrete proposals as to peace terms submitted to the Asquith Cabinet came from another pen. It was shortly before the Lansdowne discussions that the Government for the first time had submitted to its judgment any categorical, concrete and comprehensive scheme of a peace settlement. This was the document, to which reference has already been made, which came from the pen of Mr. Balfour, then First Lord of the Admiralty. It is a truly remarkable document and will bear careful perusal. The sentences in which he refuses to commit himself to any expression of opinion as to the possibility of future wars are ominous, coming from such an experienced statesman and so clear and penetrating an intellect. Apart from that it is the first time any statesman of the first rank committed himself to a written forecast of the conditions of peace.

"THE PEACE SETTLEMENT IN EUROPE
Memorandum by Mr. Balfour

The Prime Minister asked the Members of the War Committee to express their views on the peace settlement; and the present paper is an attempt—a very tentative and halting attempt—to comply with this request.

Even the most tentative suggestions must, however, proceed upon some hypothesis with regard to the military position of the combatants at the end of the War. What this will be no human being can foresee with any assurance. But inasmuch as it is convenient to proceed upon a hypothesis which is clear and determinate, I shall assume in what follows, though merely for the sake of argument, that the Central Powers, either through defeat or exhaustion, have to accept the terms imposed upon them by the Allies.

Let me add this further preliminary observation. The number

of questions which will have to be discussed at any Peace Conference is obviously very large.   In what follows I desire to do no
more than to offer some stray reflections upon the most important
group of these questions—that which is concerned with the
redistribution of population in the European area.   By this
limitation will be excluded not merely such subjects as the restriction of armaments, the freedom of the seas and the revision of
international law, but also Heligoland, the Kiel Canal, strategic
modifications of frontiers,* and the extra-European problems
connected with Asia Minor and Germany's Colonial Empire.

On some of these subjects I may perhaps trouble the Committee
at a later date.

The principal object of the War is the attainment of a durable
peace, and I submit that the best way of securing this is by the
double method of diminishing the area from which the Central
Powers can draw the men and money required for a policy of
aggression, while at the same time rendering a policy of aggression
less attractive by rearranging the map of Europe in closer
agreement with what we rather vaguely call 'the principle of
nationality.'

The second of these methods, if successfully applied, would
secure many objects which are universally desired by the Allies.
It would give Belgium her independence, restore Alsace and
Lorraine to France, provide some kind of home rule for Poland,
extend the frontiers of Italy, and establish a Greater Serbia and
a Greater Roumania in South-East Europe; I should greatly like
to see it applied in Bohemia also.   To Bohemia, Germanic
civilisation is profoundly distasteful.   The Czechs have been waging war against it for some generations, and waging it under grave
difficulties with much success.   Whether an independent Bohemia
would be strong enough to hold her own, from a military as well
as from a commercial point of view, against Teutonic domination
—surrounded as she is at present entirely by German influences—
I do not know; but I am sure the question deserves very careful
consideration.   If the change is possible it should be made.†

Now, a map of Europe so modified would not only carry out the
second of the two methods of preserving peace which I have
described above, but would also help to carry out the first.   The
resources of men and money on which the Central Powers could
draw for purposes of aggressive warfare would be greatly
diminished.   Alsace-Lorraine, Austrian Poland, with, possibly,
parts of German Poland, Transylvania, Italian Austria, Bosnia

---

* Of course such strategic modifications might involve transfers of populations,
which could not properly be described as negligible.   But their object would not be
to acquire territory, but to increase security by making frontiers more defensible.

† I presume that arrangements will be made by which the frontier of Bohemia
would, to some small extent at least, become coterminous with the New Poland.

and Herzegovina would cease to be recruiting grounds for supplying German or Austrian Armies; and the men of military age thus withdrawn from the Central Armies would be added to the nations with which the Central Powers are now at war; thus, as it were, counting two on a division.

The populations thus transferred would, I suppose, be more than 20 millions. I take no account in this argument of the non-Italian population which Italy will no doubt obtain if the Allies are successful; nor do I discuss the uncontested zone coveted by Bulgaria. If the principle of nationality be rigidly applied, I suppose that, without doubt, Bulgaria ought to have it. Whether she deserves it, and whether, in view of Serbian sentiment we can give it to her, is quite another question.

I conceive that this general scheme is, broadly speaking, what public opinion in this country would desire to see carried out. The point on which there might be most difference of opinion would perhaps be the fate of Poland—since the fate of Constantinople and the Banat is already settled so far as the Allies can settle it. Almost the only thing on which Russia and Germany seem to be agreed is that the status of Poland should be altered by the War, and that, while receiving some measure of autonomy, it should remain dependent upon one of its two great neighbours. But as to what the limits of the new Poland should be, and on which of its two great neighbours it is to be dependent, there is, it need hardly be said, a fundamental divergence of opinion between Petrograd and Berlin.

Looking at the Polish question from a purely British point of view, I should like to see the new State include not merely Russian Poland, but as much of Austria and German Poland as possible. This, of course, is in strict accord with the two principles laid down earlier in the paper. But I should *not* like to see the old Kingdom of Poland restored. I should fear that the new Poland would suffer from the diseases through which the old Poland perished; that it would be a theatre of perpetual intrigues between Germany and Russia; and that its existence, so far from promoting the cause of European peace, would be a perpetual occasion of European strife.

Moreover, even if such a Poland were capable of playing the part of an efficient buffer State (which I doubt), I am not sure that a buffer State between Germany and Russia would be any advantage to Western Europe. If Germany were relieved of all fear of pressure from Russia, and were at liberty to turn her whole strength towards developing her western ambitions, France and Britain might be the sufferers; and I am not by any means confident that cutting off Russia from her western neighbours might not divert her interests towards the Far East to an extent which

British statesmen could not view without some misgivings. The more Russia is made a European rather than an Asiatic Power, the better for everybody.

I therefore conclude that the solution of the Polish question which would best suit our interests would be the constitution of a Poland endowed with a large measure of autonomy, while remaining an integral part of the Russian Empire—the new State or province to include not only all Russian Poland, but also Austria's and (part at least of) Prussia's share in the plunder of the ancient kingdom.

Personally I should like to see the Danish portions of Schleswig-Holstein, filched by Prussia and Austria from Denmark in 1863, again restored to their former owner. But Denmark would hardly accept the gift unless it was accompanied by some form of territorial guarantee which she would think effective; and even then the memory of Belgium might act as a deterrent. But the question should be seriously considered. I ought, parenthetically, to add that unfortunately the region through which the Kiel Canal passes is German both in language and sentiment.

So far I have indicated the kind of changes which I should like to see attempted when peace comes to be discussed. But there are some projects advocated by those who believe in the complete victory of the Allies which I regard with great suspicion. Among these perhaps the most important are the projects for breaking up or reconstituting the German Empire. If I had my way, I should rule out any attempt to touch the internal affairs either of Germany or of Austria. It may be that, under the stress of defeat, ancient jealousies—forgotten in the hour of victory—will revive. South may be divided from North, Roman Catholic from Protestant, Württemberg, Bavaria and Saxony from Prussia, or from each other. A revolution may upset the Hohenzollerns, and a new Germany may arise on the ruins of militarism.

Any or all of these things are possible, but I would certainly deprecate any attempt on the part of the victorious enemy to bring them about. One of the few recorded attempts to crush militarism in a defeated State was Napoleon's attempt to destroy the Prussian Army after Jena. No attempt was ever less successful. As everybody knows, Napoleon's policy compelled Prussia to contrive the military system which has created modern Germany. It may be—I hope it will be—in the power of the Allies to strip Germany of much of her non-German territory; but, whatever be the limits of the new Germany, I hope no attempt will be made to control or modify her internal policy. The motto of the Allies should be ' Germany for the Germans—but only Germany.'

This formula, however, even if it be accepted, does not solve the problem of Central Europe. It says nothing, for example, of the future relations between Germany and Austria. I should myself desire to see the Dual Monarchy maintained, shorn indeed of a large portion of its Slav, Italian, and Roumanian territories, but still essentially consisting of Austria and Hungary. If this were to occur, we should have in the future, as we have had in the past, a German Empire and an Austrian Empire side by side and probably kept in close alliance—political if not also economic—for purposes of mutual protection. Other possibilities, however, have to be considered. The result of the War may be the complete break-up of the Dual Monarchy; and if the Dual Monarchy breaks up, it is reasonable to suppose that the German portion of it would coalesce with the German Empire, leaving Hungary either isolated or dependent. Apparently such a change would create a great German-speaking State more formidable than Germany before the War; and this may be, in fact, what would happen. On the other hand, it must be remembered that such a change would profoundly modify the position of Prussia. The Roman Catholics and South German elements would become overwhelmingly strong; and if the driving force behind German aggression be due, as most observers think, to Prussian organisation and Prussian traditions, the change might in its ultimate effect be a defeat for German militarism.

But I do not disguise from myself either that the dangers of such a Teutonic reorganisation are considerable, or that the likelihood of its occurring may be increased if the result of the War is to convince the German-speaking peoples that their only hope of national greatness lies in their consenting to forget all causes of difference and welding themselves into a single powerful State. Those who think the future must necessarily resemble the past may perhaps be disposed to remind us that for the five centuries preceding the Bismarckian era the political tendencies prevailing in Germany have been, on the whole, centrifugal and separatist. They will argue that this inveterate tradition, interrupted though it has been for forty-five years by a united and triumphant Germany, nevertheless represents the real tendencies of the race; and that to this tradition it will revert after a war for which Prussian policy and a Prussian dynasty have been responsible.

Personally, I am inclined to doubt this conclusion, plausible as it seems; nor do I believe that anything which we and our Allies can accomplish will prevent the Germanic Powers, either united by alliance or fused into a single State, from remaining wealthy, populous, and potentially formidable.

For this reason I do not share the fears of those who think that the triumph of the Slav countries is likely to menace German predominance in Central Europe. When we remember that the Slav populations are divided by language, religion and government;

that they fought each other four years ago; that they are
fighting each other at this very moment; that the only one among
them which can count as a Great Power is Russia; and that Russia,
according to most observers, is likely to be torn by revolutionary
struggles as soon as the pressure of war is removed; when (I say) we
remember these things, we shall probably be disposed to think
that the Germanic States will be very well able to take care of
themselves, whatever be the terms of peace to which they may have
to submit.

This is a fact (if it indeed be a fact) which is sometimes ignored.
Many of those who speculate about the future of Europe seem to
fear that Germany will be so weakened by the War that the
balance of Power will be utterly upset, and Britain will be left face
to face with some other Great Power striving in its turn for
universal dominance. I doubt this. In any case it seems to me
quite clear that, measured by population, Germany—and still
more, Germany in alliance with Austria—will be more than a
match for France alone, however much we give to France, and
however much we take from the Central States. If, therefore,
Europe after the War is to be an armed camp, the peace of the
world will depend, as heretofore, on defensive alliances formed by
those who desire to retain their possessions against those who desire
to increase them. In that event the Entente is likely to be maintained. Germany may suffer a spiritual conversion; Russia may
break up; France and Britain may be rendered powerless by
labour troubles; universal bankruptcy may destroy universal
armaments; international courts may secure international peace;
the horrors of 1914, 1915, 1916, and 1917 may render the very
thought of war disgusting to all mankind. On these subjects it
is vain to speculate. All I would for the moment insist on is that
the greatest territorial losses which the Allies can or ought to inflict
on the Central Powers will leave them powerful both for defence
and offence. Whatever trouble Russia may give us in Mesopotamia, Persia and Afghanistan, I do not think she will attempt the
domination of Europe, still less succeed in securing it.

There are two subsidiary points on which I may say a word
before concluding—rights of way and indemnities. If the shores
of the Adriatic are in Italian hands, if Salonika is in Greek hands,
how are we going to provide the Central Powers with commercial
access to the Mediterranean and the South? That they should not
be denied such access seems to be fairly clear. It is one thing to
cut off Germany from her megalo-maniacal designs upon Asia
Minor, Mesopotamia, Persia, and India; it is quite another to put
the commerce of Austria-Hungary with the Eastern Mediterranean
and the Suez Canal at the mercy of the States which lie between it
and the sea. There could, it seems to me, be no more powerful

incentive to new wars. Some method of guaranteeing to States which have no convenient seaboard the free flow of commerce through selected channels is therefore urgently required. I have had no time to give to the subject, but I have sometimes idly wondered whether the treaties which apply to navigable rivers flowing through different States might not—with the necessary modifications—be applied also to ports and railways.

My last topic is war indemnities. I have, for the sake of argument, assumed that the success of the Allies is going to be complete. On this assumption—ought indemnities to be demanded?

Germany has never made any secret of her intention of beggaring her enemies and reducing them, if she got the power, to complete commercial subservience. My own inclination would be strongly against imitating Germany's behaviour in 1871 and imposing a commercial treaty on my opponents for my own advantage. Such treaties are needlessly humiliating, even when they are not onerous. When they are, they are sure, sooner or later, to be broken.

But there are two things I should like to do, and which in the interests of international morality I think ought to be done. I think the Central Powers should be made to pay for the damage they have done in Belgium, Northern France, and Serbia; and I think they ought to surrender shipping equivalent in amount to that which they have sent to the bottom in the course of their submarine warfare. These are charges which it should be within their power to meet; and if within their power to meet, then certainly within our right to demand. Whether more can or ought to be exacted is a point on which I feel incompetent to give an opinion; but it may be worth remembering that to take territories from the German or Austrian Empires free of debt, is in effect to increase the burdens on the States from which they are taken, and to relieve the burden on the States to which they are added.

A. J. B.

Oct. 4, 1916."

Mr. Henderson, one of the ablest and most influential of Labour leaders, at this time publicly as well as in private, threw in the whole weight of his great influence with organised labour against "a premature peace." His words are worth quoting: —

"The War has gone on too long for some of the people of this country. It is possible that in the military situation of the case we may become war-weary, and I want to warn everyone of the danger of a premature peace. I am as strong for peace as any man or woman can be, but I must be satisfied that the peace we expect places us, above any doubt, beyond the recurrence of such a catastrophe. . . . We are in the War, and to talk about peace with all the most unscrupulous military forces against us would be a step to having the whole thing fought over again. That would not be ending the War by a permanent peace. A peace under such conditions, with Belgium and France, Serbia and Roumania, in the condition they are! No! We want not a dishonourable peace, but a lasting, permanent peace, peace based upon national right and national honour, and I say these two words in spite of the fact that one of my own colleagues has described them as platitudes."

This speech fairly expressed the view I also took at the time as to the mistake of encouraging peace overtures until the military situation had considerably improved.

Another member of the Government whose attachment to the cause of peace is above suspicion, Lord Robert Cecil, came to the conclusion that in view of the military estimates of our prospects: —

" A peace now could only be disastrous. At the best we could not hope for more than the *status quo* with a great increase in the German power in Eastern Europe. Moreover, this peace would be known by the Germans to have been forced upon us by their submarines, and our insular position would be recognised as increasing instead of diminishing our vulnerability. No one can contemplate our future ten years after a peace on such conditions without profound misgiving. I feel, therefore, that we are bound to continue the War."

He then proceeds, in the memorandum from which I am quoting, to make certain practical suggestions as to the organisation of the nation. Lord Robert Cecil's memorandum has a further interest because it contains a review of the military position at that date by a very able observer: —

" Whether we agree with Lord Lansdowne's conclusions or not, one thing is clear. Our situation is grave. It is certain that unless the utmost national effort is made it may become desperate, particularly in the matter of shipping. The position in Allied countries is even more serious. France is within measurable distance of exhaustion. The political outlook in Italy is menacing. Her finance is tottering. In Russia there is great discouragement. She has long been on the verge of revolution. Even her man-power seems coming near its limits.

On the other hand, our enemies, though badly injured, are not disabled. The economic position of Germany may or may not be alarming. It is certainly not yet desperate. No certain information as to her supplies is available. There is no trustworthy ground for thinking that she is starving, although she may be—very possibly she is—in want of other necessaries, such as wool, cotton, lubricating oils, rubber, which will hamper and diminish her military strength, and there is great political discontent. In Austria the position is probably worse."

The Prime Minister, having, according to his wont, carefully gathered or received opinions amongst his colleagues without attempting to influence them, decided ultimately that the time had not yet arrived for peace feelers. No member of the Cabinet expressed his dissent from this conclusion.

I have given a fairly exhaustive account of the Lansdowne episode because I am anxious to demonstrate that the Governments that conducted the War never lost sight of the importance of seizing any favourable opportunity that might offer itself to make an honourable peace. The Lansdowne discussions have also their special value because they are the first occasion on which any of the belligerent Governments courageously faced the possibility that peace might have to be considered without victory. The Asquith Government examined the whole position with great care and came to the unanimous conclusion that to enter into peace negotiations with Germany before inflicting a complete defeat upon her armies, would be disastrous. The principle of President Wilson's subsequent dictum in favour of peace without victory was thus carefully studied and emphatically repudiated in advance by the Asquith Government. What is more to the point, when one considers the kind of criticism levelled at the Government of 1917, is the conclusion come to by the Asquith Administration that without acknowledgment of defeat on the part of the Central Powers overtures of peace should not be encouraged, as they would settle none of the issues raised by this colossal struggle, and might and probably would be dangerous to the *morale* and solidarity of the Allies.

Mr. Asquith himself gave no countenance to a timorous or defeatist attitude. A fortnight after my " knock-out blow " interview had been published, he delivered, on 11th October, 1916, a speech in the House of Commons, in the course of which he said:—

" The strain which the War imposes on ourselves and our Allies, the hardships which we freely admit it involves on some of those who are not directly concerned in the struggle, the upheaval of trade, the devastation of territory, the loss of irreplaceable lives— this long and sombre procession of cruelty and suffering, lighted up as it is by deathless examples of heroism and chivalry, cannot be allowed to end in some patched-up, precarious, dishonouring compromise, masquerading under the name of Peace. No one desires to prolong for a single unnecessary day the tragic spectacle of bloodshed and destruction, but we owe it to those who have given their lives for us, the flower of our youth, the hope and promise of our future, that their supreme sacrifice shall not have been in vain.   The ends of the Allies are well known; they have been frequently and precisely stated.   They are not selfish ends, they are not vindictive ends, but they require that there shall be adequate reparation for the past and adequate security for the future.   On their achievement we in this country honestly believe depend the best hopes of humanity."

Here we had a fine and firm resolve expressed in the splendid eloquence of which Mr. Asquith was a master.   The fact that his eldest son Mr. Raymond Asquith, a young man of great brilliance and promise, had fallen in action a few weeks before the delivery of this speech, gave tragic force to this passage.

Hardly less emphatic was a statement made less than a fortnight later by Lord Grey.   It is indeed somewhat curious to note that while Prince Max of Baden in his " Memoirs " describes Germany watching through the late autumn of 1916 what it regarded as the approach of a " trial of strength between Lloyd George and Lord Grey," for and against the policy of the " knock-out blow," Lord Grey himself, speaking on 23rd October to a gathering at the Hotel Cecil, was declaring : —

" There must be no end to this war, no peace except a peace which is going to ensure that the nations of Europe live in the future free from that shadow and in the open light of freedom. For that we are contending.   It is our determination, which the progress of the War but deepens, in common with our Allies, to continue the War till we have made it certain that the Allies in common shall have achieved the success which must, and ought, to be theirs, till they have secured the future peace of the whole continent of Europe, till they have made it clear that all the sacrifices we have made shall not have been made in vain."

These valiant words lend little colour to the rumour which for some reason or other was then evidently widespread, not only in this country but even more throughout Central Europe, that Lord Grey was one of those who were angling for an inconclusive peace.

Can anyone doubt now, on a calm review of the position, that Mr. Asquith and his colleagues were right in the conclusion to which they came?   Could we have made a peace at that time which would not have recognised Germany as a victor?   Could we have made it at any time before the final breakdown of Germany's prowess?   Would Germany have agreed to restore the complete independence of Belgium?   Even if she consented to evacuate Belgium, would she have agreed to impose no military and commercial conditions which would have meant the practical incorporation of Belgium in the sphere of German domination and military and trading expansion? All the evidence is in the negative. The few far-seeing German statesmen who foresaw the perils which encircled the Fatherland and were anxious that peace should be made whilst the German military power was intact, never ceased to urge the German Chancellor to make an unequivocal statement about the full restoration of Belgium. Their efforts and urgent appeals were in vain right up to the final collapse. Prince Max of Baden, who later on became Chancellor, pointed out to the German leaders that even so pronounced a pacifist as Mr. Ramsay MacDonald, speaking in the House of Commons in the spring of 1916, had insisted that a declaration by Germany of her intention to restore a complete Belgian sovereignty and every " portion of it " was a condition precedent of any peace settlement. That declaration never came.

Would Austria have given up her conquests in Serbia? Would there have been no terms imposed as to the fortification of the Serbian capital, which would have left Serbia helplessly at the mercy of Austria, and thus reduced her to a state of vassalage to the Austrian Empire? Would no part of Serbian territory have been carved out to requite Czar Ferdinand's loyal rapacity? Then what about the Baltic provinces of Russia and Russian Poland? Would Germany have given up all her marvellous conquests in Russia and added nothing to her territories in that quarter? A suggestion that Alsace-Lorraine be restored to France as a condition of peace would have been greeted throughout the Fatherland with a Teutonic guffaw. France at the end of 1916 was certainly not in a position to ask for more than the restoration of the German conquests of 1914. Even then were the German industrialists prepared to give up the Briey mines? All the contemporary evidence points the other way. Apart from that there was not one chance in a million that peace negotiations could produce a settlement in the east or west satisfactory to the most moderate Allied statesman.

Would real disarmament have been any part of a 1916 peace? Would Germany have consented to dismantle the redoubtable military machine that had placed her in such a commanding position in the world? And if Germany did not disarm, no other country could have afforded to do so. To quote again the words then used by a statesman whose name is a guarantee for pacific intentions— Lord Robert Cecil—" A peace now could only be disastrous. At best we could not hope for more than the *status quo* with a great increase in the German Power in Central Europe." The only result would have been a bigger Germany, better armed, confident that her armies were unbeatable in the field even by overwhelming numbers, and with a military staff which had learned how war under modern conditions could be best and most effectively conducted.

It is often said now by men who are seeking busily to find fault with those who shouldered the terrible responsibilities of decision in the War, that no harm would have been done had the Allies taken the initiative in approaching the Central Powers with a view to the Convocation of a Peace Conference in 1916, even if such a conference failed. It is urged that if Germany and Austria made unreasonable conditions the Allied populations would have firmly supported their representatives in rejecting these terms and would then have continued the fight with renewed zeal and conviction. Would they? If Germany had offered to withdraw all her forces from Northern France and from Belgium, merely imposing certain conditions in the case of Belgium as to the uses of the ports of Belgium and as to the dismantlement of her frontier fortresses, could the Allied Governments have roused once more the spirit of 1914 to the pitch of facing for more than two years the horrible losses of the preceding two and a half years, merely in order to restore Alsace-Lorraine to France or to hand back Courland and other conquered territories to the incompetent hands of Russian autocracy? The inhabitants of these lands are no more Russian than they are German. Once the carnage of war had stopped, would Britain have consented to renew it and send her sons to fight other bloody battles like the Somme in order to restore the useless fortifications of Belgrade, or to rescue some obscure vilayet in Macedonia from the clutches of the Bulgarian king? At any rate, the risk that nations would have accepted any humiliations inflicted upon foreigners, rather than send millions more of their own kinsmen to the wholesale slaughter of modern warfare, were too great for those who looked forward to the permanent triumph of international right, justice and peace as a result of the sacrifices of this generation. We should have met at the Congress a Germany which had victoriously held up Europe for two and a half years, shattered completely the power of three of her enemies, Russia, Roumania and Serbia, and was still in occupation of the territory of two more, and had successfully defied every effort to dislodge her hold on her conquests. The best that could be hoped for would be a completely liberated France and Belgium, with a Germany swollen through its eastern conquests by scores of thousands of square miles and tens of millions of population. With a war so ended we should have been confronted with a triumphant Prussian militarism which had demonstrated its invincibility in the field against overwhelming odds in numbers, material and wealth. Mr. Asquith and his Cabinet were emphatically right in refusing to assent to the Lansdowne proposition. Had they done so, even if they had secured the adhesion of France, it could not have ended in a great and workable peace. France would not have agreed readily to make any overtures, because no peace possible at that time would have satisfied her essential conditions—the restoration of her lost provinces and reparation for her damaged towns and villages. Italy would have been fooled, for she had banked on Allied success for the redemption of the Italian valleys in the Austrian Empire, and notwithstanding her heavy losses she would have had nothing out of any peace settlement which was attainable in 1916. It would have been said that Britain was anxious for peace and was prepared to sell her Allies to attain it. Such an impression would have had a shattering effect on Allied *morale*—east and west. The failure to make peace or a refusal by France to follow a peace initiative from Britain would have distracted and divided opinion in America, at the moment when opinion in that great country was being driven rapidly in our direction by the reckless and indiscriminate methods of the submarine campaign.

s*

CHAPTER XXXII

THE MILITARY POSITION AT THE END OF THE 1916 CAMPAIGN

IF we were resolved to continue the War, it was vital that we should fight in a way that would give us a reasonable chance of achieving victory. But when I surveyed the outlook both on land and sea in the closing months of 1916, I saw the gravest grounds for disquietude. There was as yet little sign that the efforts and sacrifices we had made were leading us towards a victorious conclusion; and the information which came either to the War Office or to the Admiralty was by no means reassuring.

In October, 1916, at one of the stilted and formal morning interviews which the Chief of the Imperial Staff in the course of his duty accorded to me as his civilian chief, after he had exhausted a few secondary and trivial matters upon which he had gone through the form of consulting me, I probed him as to the position on the Somme, the terrible casualties, and the insignificant gains. He returned the familiar answers to the effect that the German losses were greater than ours, that the Germans were gradually being worn down, and their *morale* shaken by constant defeat and retreat. All the same it struck me that his answer was not given with the usual rigid confidence. I then asked him whether he would mind telling me whether he had formed any views as to how this sanguinary conflict was to be brought to a successful end. For the time being the question took him aback, and he looked like a general in full dress who thought to himself " This is one of those fool questions that ignorant civilians always fire at you, and they must not be encouraged." He just mumbled something about " Attrition." I asked him whether he would mind giving me a memorandum on the subject. In due course it was written, and here is a summary of it: —

The Western Front is still held to be the main theatre of operations for the British forces.

As to the secondary theatres: In Mesopotamia the British force is improving its position, and will be in a condition to meet any effort the Turks can make against us by the time they are ready to attack. In Egypt there is similar reason to expect that the Western Front against the Senussi will be safe by the end of the year, and arrangements complete for an advance on the east into the Sinai desert. At

Salonika the Allied forces have held the Bulgarian-German Armies. General Milne has asked for a reinforcement of 15 divisions and heavy artillery to achieve a victory on the Macedonian front, but the C.I.G.S. considers such a transfer from the main theatre of the Western Front undesirable. He thinks the only decisive campaign in the Balkans this winter must be on the Roumanian front. He regrets that the Allies have agreed to send reinforcements of 39,000 rifles to Macedonia.

In German East Africa we hold the coast line, and have driven the German forces into the unhealthy interior.

On the Western Front we are now superior to the Germans in numbers, in aircraft, in artillery, and probably to some extent also in the supply of ammunition. The effect of the Somme offensive has been to unsettle the enemy and weaken their *morale*. They are not actually demoralised, and we cannot expect them to collapse, but their prospects are worse than ours when we were being subjected to similar assault in 1914, as they have not behind them the undeveloped resources we had then. So our relative superiority is growing greater every day. But the C.I.G.S. holds that we must keep up the western pressure, as if the Central Powers can transfer more of their troops to the east the result will be disastrous. He gives figures to show the extent to which such transfers have taken place in the last five months. Since 1st June, the German forces have increased by $27\frac{1}{2}$ divisions, most of which have been added to the Eastern Front, where the number of battalions has risen (between 1st June and 23rd October) by 221, while on the west it has been reduced by 74.

He then goes on to show how we have increased our mechanical strength on the Western Front. The following figures show the growth of British artillery in France.

	1st Jan. 1916.	End Oct. 1916.
Field guns	1,938	3,060
Howitzers & heavy guns ...	785	1,879
Daily income of ammunition ...	30,000 rds.	210,000 rds.

Howitzers and heavy guns would number over 2,000 by the end of the year, and the increase in machine-guns, trench mortars, etc., has been on a corresponding scale. But in man-power the Army in France is 80,000 below establishment, and should be reinforced. There should be a further comb-out, and the Home Defence Force should be reduced after the Navy had been induced to make more effective arrangements to prevent invasion. The greatest possible force should be available in France by the spring of 1917.

The Entente Powers are suffering from bad communications and defective co-operation, apart from France and England. The value of the Entente troops of Roumania, Belgium, Serbia, Portugal and

Russia is low—in the case of Russia through lack of equipment. The enemy troops are more mobile and have a moral superiority. The duration of the War depends on the staying power of Germany's allies. Austria and Turkey are growing exhausted, and Bulgaria is weakened by its previous wars. Germany is, however, fighting with undiminished vigour, and can continue the War for as yet an indefinite period. But her supplies of food would become very short in another six months.

The C.I.G.S.'s conclusion was that the end of the War could not yet be predicted. We must be prepared to put our whole effort, tighten the blockade, rally every available man, and face still greater strain and sacrifice, to secure the peace we desired.

Sir William Robertson ended his memorandum with a table setting out the estimated numbers of troops and of still available reserves at the disposal respectively of the Allies and of the Central Powers. It is worth studying, for it contains ominous figures upon which I comment later on. The following is a summary of this table: —

	Entente Armies, including troops in home territory, and excluding coloured troops.	Reserves still available.
British	3,517,000	?
French	2,978,000	775,000
Russian	4,767,000	6,500,000
Italian	1,676,000	1,250,000
Roumanian	590,000	380,000
Belgian	128,000	10,000
Serbian	117,000	22,000
Portuguese	65,000	
	13,838,000	8,937,000
Enemy Forces.		
German	5,470,000	2,000,000
Austro-Hungarian ...	2,750,000	800,000
Turkish	500,000	300,000
Bulgarian	400,000	112,000
	9,120,000	3,212,000

The C.I.G.S.'s picture did not present a cheerful outlook. We could now hold our own against the Turks in Mesopotamia and Egypt—but nothing more just yet. At Salonika we could stand up to the Bulgarians if they attacked, but we were in no position to attack them. On the Western Front we were doing better. We were shaking the German *morale*. His solitary proof of it was disturbing. Several German divisions had fled from the western battlefield to the east. Why? Not because they were beaten but because they felt they could hold their own in the west with 74 fewer battalions. What a commentary on the smashing triumphs of the Somme!

The statistical table showed that so far as existing effectives and reserves at any rate were concerned, we had an overwhelming majority of men compared with the enemy powers. But our superiority in numbers depended entirely on Russia and Roumania remaining effectively in the War. That was becoming increasingly problematical. Once they were eliminated the numerical superiority passed over to the enemy countries. Equality of numbers then would only be attainable by a further heavy drain on our man-power. It was an ominous fact that of the 13,838,000 Allied troops, 5,357,000 were Russian and Roumanian; and of the reserves 6,880,000 were Russian and Roumanian. Roumania, with her 970,000, was about to disappear from the Allied schedule. Russia, with her 11,000,000, was to follow soon after. As to the general military position I have summarised it in a preceding chapter. It was not encouraging.

The conviction was borne in upon me that a much more serious effort must be made to co-ordinate the Allied efforts in east and west; Sir William Robertson admitted the Allied weakness in that respect. In thinking this matter over I made up my mind to have a confidential talk with the Prime Minister about the situation, and I accordingly invited him to come round one evening to dinner at my house. The invitation was accepted and the dinner duly took place. Besides Mr. Asquith there were present Lord Crewe, Lord Grey, Mr. Balfour, Lord Curzon and, I think, Lord Lansdowne. I laid before them my views as to the seriousness of the situation and as to the steps which should be taken. Mr. Asquith heard me sympathetically and recommended me to bring the matter forward for discussion at the next meeting of the War Committee.

This meeting took place on 3rd November, 1916, and, in anticipation of it, I secured from Sir William Robertson a further statement, which I reproduce here, setting out his views as to the probable end of the War: —

" 1. You tell me the War Committee wish to have my opinion with respect to the probable duration of the War, and I must at once confess that I feel it very difficult to express any opinion which can usefully be relied upon. Hindenburg is alleged to have stated recently that no man can foresee the end of the War, and I certainly cannot. This inability to forecast events is not peculiar to this war, but is more or less common to all wars. It is, in fact, greatly accentuated in the present war, both by the colossal scale of the War and the conditions under which it is waged. Never before, for instance, have such large questions of international finance and commerce been involved.

2. Further, we are not fighting for some comparatively minor object which we might hope to attain after giving the enemy a sound beating, but we are to continue the War ' until the military domination of Prussia is wholly and finally destroyed.'

3. The question you ask me is by no means merely, or even mainly, a military one. For example, I am ignorant of: —

(a) Probable solidarity of the Allies and of enemy countries.

(b) Social and economic conditions in the enemy countries.

(c) Comparative staying power in money and commerce of the two opposing sides.

(d) Possible submarine developments.

(e) The power of our Navy to keep open sea communications and preserve adequate mercantile marine for the supply of ourselves, our Allies, and the Allied Armies overseas.

(f) Advantages and disadvantages which may accrue from Allied diplomacy.

4. The staying power in men counts for very much, but I do not know what men we ourselves are capable of putting into the field, or when they can be put there. Nor do I think, for reasons explained in my paper of the 26th ultimo,* that in the case of the other belligerents any really useful purpose would be served by attempting to find the answer to your question by the manipulation of figures. In the first place the figures we use are to a great extent guess-work. Secondly, although the Entente have on paper more men than the enemy, they cannot be nearly so easily liquidated in practice. Russia is corrupt, badly armed and administered, and will not improve her communications; Italy refused to move men from her own country; Roumania is in retreat. Finally, Germany's interior position and complete control over the policy and operations of the Central Powers give her an advantage worth many hundreds of thousands of men.

5. On the Western Front we and the French have been steadily gaining a moral and material ascendency over the enemy, and as regards ourselves it is still within our power to put more men and more guns and munitions into the field. If we do this, and if we do not fritter away our efforts in non-vital theatres, and if Russia can be supplied with a reasonable amount of heavy artillery and other necessary war material, we may hope that in the future the pressure upon the enemy on both fronts will not be less severe than it has been in the past. How long we can continue to apply this pressure, and when we may expect to derive decisive results from it are questions which mainly depend upon the factors

* Summarised on pages 537-38.

mentioned in para. 3. It also depends upon the strategy of the Entente, over which my control is very limited. I am, therefore, quite unable to form any opinion as to when the end of the War may be, but I think we shall be well advised not to expect the end at any rate before the summer of 1918. How long it may go on afterwards I cannot even guess. One thing is quite certain, as I have many times said during the present year, and that is that we cannot hope for a conclusion in our favour unless and until we make full and appropriate use of all our resources. We have not yet taken the steps to do this and we ought to take them at once. I referred to some of them in the final paragraph of my paper of the 26th ultimo, and I may add here that we must : —

Have a full day's work from every man and woman.

Make all possible use of foreign labour.

Check present waste and extravagance in the national life.

Become as self-supporting as possible.

Clearly explain to the nation the grave nature of the task in front of us.

Secure a control over the War in all its aspects equivalent to the contribution we are making towards it. (I emphasised this in January last, but little, if any, improvement has been effected.)

W.R.R.
C.I.G.S.

November 3, 1916."

Basing myself upon this document, I made a statement at the War Committee, of which I give the following extracts from the summary contained in its minutes : —

" Mr. Lloyd George . . . read to the War Committee a minute by the Chief of the Imperial General Staff, dated the 3rd November, 1916, regarding the probable duration of the War.

Mr. Lloyd George said that this was one of the most serious documents on the War that he had read. We were not getting on with the War. We were now at the end of the third campaign of the War, yet the enemy had recovered the initiative. He had in his occupation more territory than ever before, and he had still some four millions of reserves. At no point had the Allies achieved a definite clean success. . . .

How then, Mr. Lloyd George asked, is the War to be brought to an end?"

I then summarised the facts of the Allied military position in terms which were subsequently embodied in the memorandum which appears later.

The minute then goes on: —

"So far as the public was concerned, the responsibility for the conduct of the War attaches to the politicians, and more especially to the Cabinet Ministers who compose the War Committee. The public will forgive anything except inaction and drift. He urged that the politicians responsible for the conduct of the War in the principal Allied countries, ought to meet together to take stock of the situation. In the first place, the representatives of France, Italy, and Great Britain should confer together. . . .

He suggested that the first object of the Conference should be to insist that West should confer with East. . . .

Mr. Lloyd George concluded by urging: —

1. A small conference composed of two ministers each from France, Italy, and this country.

2. A military conference to take place subsequently in the East, which should be attended by the principal generals from the West, preferably Generals Robertson, Joffre, Castelnau and Cadorna."

In the discussion which followed, so the minutes state, a general agreement was expressed with the tenor of my remarks, though they were criticised by some members as unduly pessimistic in regard to the general situation of the Allies.

It was generally agreed that the offensive on the Somme, if continued next year, was not likely to lead to decisive results, and that the losses might make too heavy a drain on our resources, having regard to the results to be anticipated. We decided, therefore, to examine whether a decision might not be reached in another theatre. As a preliminary step my proposals were approved in principle, and it was left to Lord Grey and myself to draft a telegram to Paris and one to Rome with regard to the proposed conference in Paris.

The War Committee agreed that before the meeting of the military conference at Chantilly, arranged for 15th November, it was essential that there should be consultation between the heads of the principal Allied Governments, in order to take stock of the situation and of the broad principles of policy and strategy that should decide the next phase of the campaign and the operations next year. They considered that the question should be first discussed by the statesmen, who had the real and ultimate responsibility for the whole conduct of affairs, and that the presence of expert advisers at this stage of the conference would be undesirable. They regarded a large conference as useless and suggested that it should be limited to two statesmen each from this country, France, and Italy, the British representatives being the Prime Minister and myself. The difficulty about Russian representation appeared insuperable, as no one could take the place of the Emperor and his chief political and military advisers, who could not leave Russia at present.

The War Committee further agreed that, if the Paris Conference arrived at important conclusions these should be discussed with Russia, and that this could probably best be done by sending representatives of the Allies to Russia, where they could be received by the Emperor, and confer with the chief persons who, under the Emperor, directed policy and strategy. Without a visit to Russia, no final agreement affecting both West and East could be adopted, and in no other way than a visit to Russia could full consultation and effective discussion be assured.

It was arranged that Lord Grey and I should concert a telegram to Paris and Rome on these lines.

The military conference at Chantilly, to which reference is made in the above quotations from the War Committee minutes, was one that had already been arranged to take place in November between representatives of the military staffs of the Allied Armies. While there would be obvious advantages in arranging our conference of statesmen at a time when we could have these military authorities available for consultation, it seemed no less important to claim priority for the political conference, since, as was pointed out at our Committee, we were the authority ultimately responsible for decisions.

At the next meeting of the War Committee, on 7th November, it transpired that there appeared to be some difference of opinion among our Allies as to the proposal for a further conference in Russia. Italy was dubious about the possibility of sending representatives to such a conference. Further, it seemed that the military chiefs were proposing to hold their meeting at Chantilly a week before the Paris conference could be held, and this I considered to be undesirable; for as I pointed out to the Committee, there would be a tendency among the generals to commit themselves at this conference as to their strategical views, before the responsible heads of the Governments had been able to reach a decision as to what they felt it necessary to take in hand in the way of preliminary consultation with our Eastern Allies, and there might be difficulty subsequently in inducing the generals to modify or reconsider their opinions.

A telegram was accordingly dispatched on that day to Rome and Paris in the following terms: —

"We are of opinion that the only way to secure effective consultation on the future conduct of the War ensuring the best co-operation in east and west and the co-ordination which is essential to success, is for a conference to be held in Russia and preferably at the Russian General Headquarters if the Emperor would allow it.

We regard conference at Paris as preliminary to conferring on the spot in Russia and the main object at Paris should be to arrange this. To postpone consultation at Paris as suggested by Italy would involve very considerable delay. The Prime Minister and Secretary of State for War will, therefore, go to Paris on Monday in order to have informal conversation with M. Briand on Tuesday, the day which he has chosen. After this we hope it will be agreed to ask the Russian Government to fix a conference in Russia at the earliest possible date at which Great Britain, France and Italy should be represented. We consider that the conference to be of any use must be small in numbers and be in Russia. The other Allies can be called into conference subsequently at Paris if need be.

Meanwhile we urge that military conference at Chantilly should be postponed for a week. We think it would serve no useful purpose till the considerations which we wish to put before M. Briand have been examined and without these considerations before it the conference at Chantilly might be committed to conclusions that it would be necessary to revise."

The views here expressed were ultimately agreed to by our Allies, and the Paris conference was arranged to take place on Wednesday and Thursday, 15th and 16th November, 1916; but General Joffre refused to postpone the military conference at Chantilly, and it was held on the same date as the Inter-Allied conference. In the event it dominated and to a large extent stultified the political conference. The soldiers successfully torpedoed our efforts to secure a joint examination by soldiers and statesmen from the east and west, of the strategy of the Allies for the campaign of 1917. The disastrous military offensives of that year were hatched at Chantilly by the generals, and their selfish action in precipitating momentous decisions without consultation was largely responsible for failure to avert the Russian crash.

In preparation for this Paris conference I drafted a statement setting out my view of the military situation, and of the need for a further conference in Russia to co-ordinate the Allied efforts in east and west. This statement was revised and very extensively abridged by Mr. Asquith, and the condensed version of it, rendered into French, was taken by us to Paris. I give below a copy of this document, re-inserting, in italics, the principal passages in my original draft which were blue pencilled by Mr. Asquith from the memorandum as laid by him before M. Briand. The omissions were due not so much to disagreement about the accuracy of the statement as to the Prime Minister's reluctance to append his signature to a document which the French might regard as critical of the higher commands in both countries. In effect he took all the sting out of the document.

" The time has come for the Allies, in their innermost counsels, to look the facts of the situation in the face. The war environment is always peopled with illusions, many of them deliberately fostered in order to keep up the spirit of the combatants, many others created by the electric atmosphere engendered by all great wars.

We are at the turning-point of the campaign. *Upon the decisions we take now will depend the ultimate issue. In 1914-15-16 we could afford to blunder without throwing away the chance of final victory. If we take the wrong turning in 1917, I do not believe that our fortunes can be retrieved.* The situation is undoubtedly grave.

We are approaching the end of the third campaign. After months of hard fighting we have made no appreciable impression on the strongholds of our enemies. On land they hold all their conquests, with hardly any diminution in the area of the conquered territories. At sea they are more formidable and destructive than they have ever been since the commencement of the War. On land they have recovered initiative which some months ago they lost. Our new ally, Roumania, whose irruption into the field on our side was *confidently predicted by one of the highest military authorities* to mark the end of Austria, is now fighting for very life on her own soil, and *is barely holding her own with the help of Russia. Nearly 50 per cent. of the army with which she entered the field has already been put out of action. She has been deprived of hundreds of square miles of her territory and* the German forces are within 20 miles of the richest oil wells in Europe.

At sea, the British, Allied and neutral shipping, on which depends not merely the active co-operation of England in the alliance, but the very life of the English people, its food, its munitions, and those of its Allies, is being destroyed at an alarmingly increasing rate.

On land, what is the prospect? We were confidently assured in February, 1915, by a high military authority* that in a few months' time the Germanic federation would have exhausted its reserves. This is the end of 1916. The Germans since June have added twenty-seven new formations to their gigantic armies; this week they have added another. Their army has increased since June by 300,000 and our military advisers, after careful investigation of the facts, now inform us that the reserves of man-power available for Germany and her allies exceed 3,000,000 men, without reckoning the additional 1,000,000 of young men who march every year into military age.

As to the blockade, Germany will be saved from famine, and

* Lord Kitchener.

will even be able to make headway against every difficulty, so far as its most essential war needs are concerned, if it succeeded in securing the Roumanian cornfields. On the Somme, the Allies have achieved a succession of brilliant victories, but what has been the result of these operations? What were the results which the Somme offensive was designed to provide?

1. To draw closer the bonds of the Franco-British Alliance. That has been achieved beyond all doubt.

2. To raise the siege of Verdun. We have succeeded there.

3. To break through the German lines and roll the enemy back to the Meuse. Here we were not successful.

3a. *The capture of some important strategic position then held by the enemy and the occupation of which by the Allies would have placed him at a serious disadvantage in the next push —something comparable to what the capture of Verdun would have been for the Germans. That object has failed.*

4. To divert great forces from the Eastern Front so as to enable the Russian offensive on that front to succeed. The movement of enemy troops has been the other way. *Since the Somme offensive began, nineteen divisions have left the West for the East, and as a result, the* Russian offensive, which started so brilliantly in the spring, and from which so much was hoped, has been stopped, and has given place to complete immobility.

Another object has been recently added to the occupation of such a number of German divisions as to make it impossible for the Germans to concentrate such forces on Roumania as would crush that country. That event is still doubtful. All we know is that Germany has as many troops and guns there as the difficult terrain will permit.

The most brilliant success scored by the Allies this year has been the recapture of the Verdun forts by a single *coup de main,* without great losses to the assailants. This is a feat of arms, the planning and execution of which displayed the highest qualities of generalship. In barely fifteen days the French Army completely wiped out the results of the grim and costly German attacks, which have gone on for eight months. In consequence, the western line is a little more favourable to the Allies than it was at the end of 1915. *If anyone this time last year had ventured to predict the actual position to-day he would have been denounced as a morbid and malignant pessimist.*

We must now take such measures as will prevent the situation next year from being only a repetition, if not an aggravation, of the present situation. Time is no longer in our favour.

The outstanding features of the conduct of the War which gave me the greatest concern as to the future are twofold:—

    1. That in the main decisions taken during the last three campaigns every military estimate of what could be accomplished with the resources at our disposal has not only been mistaken, but conspicuously falsified by events.

    2. That the same mistakes are repeated time after time without any reference to the disastrous experience gained by the failure of the preceding ones.

Let us take the campaign of 1915 as an example. This campaign was ruined by two obsessions.

The first was that the Germans intended a great attack on the Western Front.

As a matter of fact their great attack was on the East and South-East.

The second was that by frontal attack, backed up by such artillery preparation as the Allies were then capable of, their forces would break through the German lines. This mistake was committed at Neuve Chapelle, repeated at Artois, Festubert, Loos, and Champagne. When the attack failed to accomplish its full purpose, it was always thought to be due to the absence of something which could easily be supplied if a second attack of the same kind were made. Then when the second failed, it was said that it came very near success, and that a few more guns or more divisions of infantry would have ensured complete triumph.

The failure to conceive what was possible and what was not under present conditions of warfare was responsible for the failure of the experiments, which were repeated each time with greater forces, and consequently ended each time in enormously greater losses. Still the same old obsession has taken a firmer grip than ever of the military brain.

There is no fundamental difference in the character of any of these attacks. There is no essentially novel form of strategy or attack introduced.

The nearest approach to a new resource or device has been the employment of the tanks, and that came from entirely non-military sources.

Another example of the failure to estimate the real obstacles in the path of victory was the Dardanelles. The military attack on Gallipoli was entirely conceived and planned by soldiers, and the greatest soldier amongst them told me shortly before the attack that Gallipoli would be carried with the forces then at the General's command with losses not exceeding 5,000. How lamentably the military diagnosis failed is now a matter of history, but in each succeeding attack there was the same under-estimate of obstacles, the same conviction that we could butt through by throwing great masses of men and guns on the enemy lines as though we were fighting in the eighteenth century and not in the twentieth.

I hold in the history of 1915 the case of Serbia to be the most unpardonable and, I fear, the most irreparable of all the Allied failures. We realise now how important it was for us to block the German road to the east. We could have cut off their supplies We should have given the German people the sense of being hemmed in, and what would have been more destructive to their morale than the consciousness of that fact? We could have won Bulgaria and organised a great Balkanic Federation with a reserve of 2,000,000 fighting men, which we could have gradually equipped and made formidable armies out of for attacking the Germanic Powers on their southern flank. We could have encircled the Powers in a ring of flame. Turkey, with very little ammunition and hardly any power to manufacture it, would soon have collapsed from sheer exhaustion. This could have been accomplished by the timely occupation of the Vardar Valley with half the forces which are now in Salonika, and a third of the men who fell in fruitless and fatuous attacks on German barbed-wire entanglements in the Western campaigns of 1915. Instead of this what has happened? The German road to the east is open from Belgrade to Baghdad; she is supplied with corn, cotton, coffee tea, copper, and, what is still more important, with first-class fighting men. These facts have given her people new hope Bulgaria is equipped, Turkey is reorganised; Greece is overawed with a third of her people hostile to the Allies; Serbia is destroyed, Roumania is fighting for her life. An attempt was made to occupy the Vardar Valley in November, 1915. We realised at last how vital it was to seize the bridge to the east. But it was then too late. The Balkans, which might have been an asset, are now a heavy burden.

In 1916 we have repeated in the case of Roumania the fatal error of 1915 in the case of Serbia. The volcanic energy which Russia has displayed in retrieving the blunder made may yet redeem the situation. Nevertheless, it was a blunder of the most inexplicable character. What are the facts? We all knew exactly what the Roumanian equipment consisted of. We knew that the Roumanian Army had no heavy guns, and that her supply of ammunition even for field-guns was quite unequal to the stress of a sustained attack or defence. As long as the Austrian Armies were engaged elsewhere Roumania might be all right; but our military advisers must have known that if the Germans chose to withdraw their forces from the attack on Verdun and send a few of their *reserve divisions to Roumania, Roumanian guns and ammunition were quite unequal to facing such a concentration. This, however, does not seem to have been foreseen by any of the advisers of the Allies; at least, no one seems to have made any provision against this contingency. Either no Government contemplated it as possible, or each Government thought it was the business of the other to make plans for meeting that eventuality. It was only after the German attack had developed that the Allies improvised hurried expeditions to rescue Roumania from her doom. It is no exaggeration to say that Roumania may be the turning-point of the campaign. If the Germans fail there it will be the greatest disaster inflicted upon them. Afterwards it will only be a question of time. But should Germany succeed I hesitate to think what the effect will be on the fortunes of the campaign. Eight hundred thousand men who constitute excellent fighting material if well equipped will have been thrown away.* The Germans' stores, much depleted, will be stocked with great quantities of oil and corn, which will place the Central Powers above any anxiety in these two important respects—and yet no one seems to have thought it his particular duty to prepare a plan which would bring such triumph to the Allies if it succeeded, and which would certainly avert a possible disaster of the first magnitude to their cause. And this is the third year of a campaign which has seen many muddles of the same sort committed through this fatal lack of co-operation and forethought.*

The Salonika expedition is another illustration of the two fatal defects which have pursued the Entente—tardiness and lack of co-operation. The Salonika expedition launched in time would have saved Serbia and given us the Balkans. At best all that can be said for it now is that it is holding 250,000 Bulgarians and Turks with a force which is nominally at any rate double that number. Why so many Bulgarians should think it necessary to confront it I am at a loss to know. General Milne's figures show that the aggregate number of Allied rifles available do not very much exceed 100,000. The equipment in guns and in transport of these troops is ludicrously inadequate even for the modest rôle which it is supposed to play. Neither General Foch nor Sir Douglas Haig would ever dream of attacking the tiniest Somme village defended by a single German regiment with the guns and ammunition General Sarrail and General Milne have at their disposal for the storming of over 200 miles of the strongest positions in Europe held by over 200,000 of the finest infantry. The ammunition of the two combined forces would hardly last out a couple of days in a Somme bombardment. No wonder when the Roumanians came

---

* Sir William Robertson's memorandum placed the Roumanian effectives and reserves at 970,000 men.

to discover the depleted condition of our ammunition they concluded that we had not altogether kept the spirit of the bargain into which we had entered with them.   The whole state of the Salonika Army gives the impression that the generals in command had as a matter of policy been deprived of every temptation to make too effective a use of the armies under their control.   It is true that we have recently sent large reinforcements of men and a few batteries of heavy guns, and a further stock of ammunition. If they had been dispatched two months ago—and it is just as difficult to spare them now as it was then—General Sarrail might have really threatened the Bulgarian flank on the Monastir side and compelled them to withdraw perhaps a couple of divisions from the Roumanian Front in order to save Macedonia.   Sarrail failed for lack of transport, lack of troops, lack of guns, and what the Roumanian and Russian public know now about this, the French and British public will know soon.

The history of our dealings with Greece is a dreary picture of paralysing indecision.   The Greek people are with us, and have indicated their sympathies repeatedly by their votes, but the King is now, and always has been, the Kaiser's friend and the Entente's foe.   He has never missed an opportunity of serving the former and selling the latter.   He gave valuable information to the enemy as to our troops, our positions, our intentions, and our movements.   Under our very eyes, with our troops looking on, he handed over an important strategic position like Fort Ruppel to the enemy—a fort which it would take us thousands of valuable lives to storm.   He gave the Germans a whole division of infantry and most valuable mountain guns.   He has fooled us all round the ring and made us the laughing stock of the East whilst we were writing lawyer's letters to his military advisers.

It is only by a relentless scrutiny of our shortcomings in the past to find out wherein we have failed that we can hope to avoid failure in the future.   Our first duty is to calmly face the facts of the situation, however painful, and to acknowledge, at any rate to ourselves, and in our own councils wherein we are responsible for the unsatisfactory conditions with which we are now confronted. To attempt to ignore them or to gloss them over amongst ourselves is a sure guarantee of disaster.   I quite realise the importance of keeping up the public faith in victory, and that it is not always necessary to call the attention of the people to the dangers and defects of our position; but in the War Councils of the Allies the facts must be exposed as they really are, and, unless this is done, someone must take the public into his confidence and give the people a chance of saving themselves before it is too late.

But so far as the British Government can judge, the operations in the west, if continued on the present footing, hold out no hope of our inflicting on the German armies in 1917 a defeat sufficiently crushing to put an end to the War, unless we are able to reinforce them by much greater efforts in the other theatres of war.

The position in the southern theatre does not offer any much greater hope of a decisive success. It is true that the Italian Army, by means of a campaign admirably conceived and well carried out, has made appreciable progress and gained considerable victories. All the same, trench warfare generally predominates on this front, and one can see no dawning of a day of big results.

On the Eastern Front the Russian attack, starting under such happy auspices, has been brought to a full stop, and it is clear that on the principal Russian Fronts there will be great difficulties to overcome before serious progress can be made.

As we have already said, the entry of Roumania on to the scene did not produce the decisive results which had been hoped for, and if the situation in this theatre is a little less grave than it has been, it continues, none the less, to be an object of serious pre-occupation for the Allies. As we foresaw, the difficulty of communications by land and sea has prevented a decisive success on the Salonika front. The greater part of the Bulgarian Army, it is true, has been held there, and on the flanks there are slight advances to record. All the same, these operations do not allow us to count on a decisive success in that region, unless the operations are combined with others on other fronts in such a way as to divert a considerable part of the forces opposed to us. Even in that case, the lack of roads and railways will hold up our advance, which would, in any case, be difficult in face of the resistance awaiting us.

The effect of our inability to obtain a decisive result on the Salonika front is that the Central Powers still keep open the route which leads them to their objectives in the East.

What is the prospect in front of us? What is our policy? *Has anyone mapped out a road to victory? If he has, I have not yet been privileged to see that document. Words will not win. We must have a definite plan. I have only heard of one.* People talk of hammering, and of a war of attrition. The success of hammering depends entirely upon whether you are making a greater impression on the barrier or the hammer. The success of a war of attrition depends upon the time it takes, and who can last out the longest. In examining the chances of success of a war of attrition, certain essential factors must always be present to the mind.

The first is the reserve man-power of the Central Powers and their allies. Our General Staff places these reserves at three or four millions. They reckon in addition that each year a million young men become available for service.

We shall be wise not to conclude that even these appalling figures exhaust the man-power of the enemy. Polish conscription may well give him between 500,000 and 1,000,000 men. Prisoners, Polish and Lettish labour, are constantly releasing young men from essential trades. The German military leaders are also clearly giving a good deal of attention and thought to the substitution of machine power for man-power. They believe that owing to the perfection of their machinery they can reduce the numbers of their infantry men by several thousand in each division, and they have one considerable advantage over the Entente, that being in possession of enemy ground, they can gradually give way, selling land dearly as they retreat without any serious damage to their military position. This last point is illustrated by the difference between the fighting on the Somme and the fighting at Verdun. The French Army could not retreat five miles at Verdun without giving up something of considerable strategical value and of infinitely greater moral importance. They were consequently bound to defend every kilometre at the most appalling cost. On the other hand, the Germans could give up 5, 10, even 20 kilometres on the Somme without surrendering any point of much strategic or moral importance.* The only thing that matters to them is that in reconquering French or Russian territory their enemies should pay more for its capture than it cost them in its defence.

Another factor, if we wish to measure the chances of a war of attrition, is the effect of the submarine campaign against our merchant shipping. The importance of this cannot be exaggerated. Undoubtedly during the last few weeks the destruction of Allied and neutral tonnage has taken on alarming proportions, and unless effective steps can be taken to check it, the consequences may be of the most serious character to the armies of the Allies. Our success depends so much upon our maintaining the unchallenged supremacy of the sea that if we fail to protect our transports and our supplies, it will be impossible for Great Britain to maintain her present forces either in the east or the west. It will become equally impossible for France and Italy, Russia or ourselves to keep up the present supply of munitions. We feel confident of being able to defeat this latest and most pernicious development of the German submarine attack, but it would be idle to pretend that it does not fill us with serious anxiety, when we contemplate the prospect of a campaign lasting over a period of years.

The difficulties which we have experienced in making payment for our purchases from abroad must be as present to the minds of French statesmen as to ourselves. Our dependence upon America

---

* This they did in the spring of 1917, thereby disarranging the whole of the Nivelle plans.

is growing for food, raw material and munitions. We are rapidly exhausting the securities negotiable in America. If victory shone on our banners our difficulties would disappear. *Success means credit: financiers never hesitate to lend to a prosperous concern: but business which is lumbering along amidst great difficulties and which is making no headway in spite of enormous expenditure will find the banks gradually closing their books against it.* The fall of Roumania would have a serious effect on our American credit. On the other hand, if Roumania succeeded in resisting the tide of invasion then the victories of Verdun and our advance on the Somme would have their maximum effect, and the Americans would open their purses and send us their merchandise. The problem of finance is the problem of victory . . . *not debatable victory, but unchallengeable victory; not victory won here countered by disaster there.*

Another consideration to be taken into account is the morale of the four nations behind the armies. As the War drags its weary and bloodstained path, the sacrifices and the sufferings must necessarily increase; the casualties will become heavier, and the gloom cast by the appalling losses over the homes of the country will become darker and deeper. Then food will become scarcer and costlier, the burdens of taxation will be heavier. Efforts will be made perhaps by powerful neutrals to patch up peace on what would appear to be specious terms, and there is a real danger that large masses of people, worn out by the constant strain, may listen to well-intentioned but mistaken pacificators; and, last of all, there is the danger, which one hardly likes to contemplate but which is ever present in our minds, of one of the four great Allies being offered terms which seem better than an indefinite prolongation of the horrors of war. No alliance has ever borne the strain of a protracted war without breaking. These are considerations which it would be well for us to bear in mind when we are urged to depend upon attrition as the sole means of bringing this terrible war to an end.

What, then, is our suggestion? It is that the responsible military and political leaders of the four great Allied nations should for the first time since the commencement of the War meet together to discuss the situation and to formulate their policy or strategy. The responsible leaders of the Central Powers and their Allies are constantly meeting to discuss plans, to devise new plans, to revise old ones. The real military leaders of Russia never had five minutes' conversation with the military leaders of the West. Such communications as I have read between them indicate a good deal of divergence in essential points of strategy. Take, for instance, General Alexeieff's despatches on the Balkans. These are questions not merely of strategy, but of equipment, which have never yet

*been discussed by the Higher Commands at the various confer-
ences. I do not regard discussion about Russia with General
Jillinski, or even General Palitzine, as an interchange of views
between East and West. History will mock at us for our neglect
to insist upon a meeting of the responsible military and political
leaders of the various fronts for three whole campaigns. The whole
policy of the Allies ought to be co-ordinated; there ought to be a
complete understanding between the East and West. Surely
Generals Joffre and Robertson have something to say about their
experiences in the West which it would be worth General
Alexeieff's while to hear. On the other hand, General Alexeieff
must have had a good deal of experience and must have learned
many lessons which it would be valuable for his Western colleagues
to hear something of. There is no other business which would
have been conducted for three years without some sort of interchange of opinions between the men that matter in the direction
of affairs. If a conference is decided upon, it would be a farce
to send anyone there except the men who matter; the men who
represent France, Russia, Italy, and Britain must not merely be
men of the highest capacity, they must also be men whose decisions
could practically be accepted, not because they have been tied
down by their instructions and therefore cannot assent to anything
which their colleagues or superiors had not already given previous
assent to, but accepted because of the high positions which the
representatives hold.*

What, then, is our proposition? We have shown above all the
importance of the rôle played in the present war by Roumania and
the Balkan countries. We have shown that the conquest of
Roumania would furnish the enemy with very considerable
resources of man-power, and would be an incalculable aid to the
re-establishment of their economic equilibrium. On the other
hand, we have shown that the elimination of Bulgaria would
complete the encirclement of the Central Empires, would isolate
Turkey, which would then be compelled to die of exhaustion, and
would bring the Entente Powers markedly nearer to final
victory.

Although these advantages are so evident that they justify the
greatest efforts for the achievement, we do not hide from ourselves the considerable difficulties to be anticipated. Our military
advisers have more than once explained to our Government and to
the French Government how difficult and uncertain every operation must be that is based on Salonika.

Our proposition is that the statesmen and generals of the great
Western Powers should confer with the statesmen and generals of
the Eastern Front, taking for their programme the examination
of the situation in its entirety, and more particularly the military

situation in the east. The object of the conference must be to determine what it is possible to do on the Eastern Front, and what is the nature and importance of the help which the west ought to give to the east for those operations which are judged to be necessary. Moreover, the statesmen and generals of the west ought to explain clearly to the statesmen and generals of the east the limits which are imposed on our possible effort in the Salonika region. In Russia, since the dismissal of M. Sasonoff, there are only two men who can speak with authority; the Emperor and General Alexeieff. At the present moment it is impossible for either of these to come to the west. That is why—and we insist on this point—it is of capital importance that generals and statesmen competent to represent the Western Powers with the fullest authority should go to Russia as promptly as possible in order to discuss these questions, the interest of which is vital for the conduct of the War."

A meeting of the Cabinet was held on Monday, 13th November, and on the following morning the Prime Minister and I proceeded to Paris accompanied by Sir Maurice Hankey. He had arranged to have a private conversation with M. Briand on the morning of 15th November before the Allied Conference opened that afternoon, with a view to placing before him confidentially the opinions of the British War Cabinet. This private meeting was fixed for the Quai d'Orsay at 10.30 a.m. on 15th November. When Mr. Asquith, Sir Maurice Hankey and I arrived we found there was no M. Briand. We were informed that the *President de Conseil* had been unexpectedly detained at a meeting of one of the Committees of the *Chambre des Députés* to which he had been suddenly summoned, but that he expected to arrive soon. We waited for another half an hour and then came another message that he had found it impossible to get away, but that we might expect him in another quarter of an hour. Then Sir Maurice Hankey learnt from an amused official that the Chairman of this Committee was M. Clemenceau, and that he was subjecting the French Premier to a fierce cross-examination on certain unsatisfactory aspects and episodes in the conduct of the War and that M. Briand was having a very *difficile* time. We then realised that M. Briand was detained by circumstances over which he had not the least control, and that one of the circumstances was the redoubtable " Tiger " over whom no one had any control.

Another three-quarters of an hour passed and M. Briand hurried into the room looking flustered, unhappy and altogether rather badly mauled. We learnt that he had escaped the ruthless claws of the great political cat this time, but with difficulty, and only by the exercise of every fibre and sinew of his renowned dexterity and suppleness. He was not, however, in a state of mind which would enable him to give cool and concentrated attention to our memorandum. We felt that the conditions were not propitious for a calm examination of the military position. The problems raised needed all the concentration and composure which every member of that small gathering could command. However, after an interchange of the usual civilities and conventional inquiries Mr. Asquith explained the purpose of the informal meeting he had sought. He pulled out of his pocket the memorandum and read it, or rather rushed through it, without emphasis or pause. M. Briand, whilst preserving the pose of a courteous and attentive listener, was evidently too ruffled and distracted to take in ideas at such a speed. He asked Mr. Asquith to leave a copy and promised to study it all with great care before the afternoon meeting. That was all, and then we shook hands and Mr. Asquith and I drove off to the Hotel Crillon, feeling like men whose proposals, to which weeks of thought and debate had been given, had been received with civil torpidity. Here was the country that had so far sustained the most serious damage in the War and had the enemy in occupation and control of its finest provinces, and yet there seemed no evidence of any racking pre-occupation on the part of its leaders with the problems of liberation. That was the burden of M. Clemenceau's satire, and I felt that there was some justification for his bitterness. No man has a greater admiration for M. Briand's gifts, but as a War Minister he was much too easy-going. My mind inevitably travelled on to contemplate the obvious similarity between French and British leadership. Both Mr. Asquith and M. Briand were men of rare intellectual gifts, but unfortunately they both lacked driving power. Once again we were captained by men who were distinguished figures on the bridge in normal weather; skilful navigators in ordinary storms, but not qualified for command in the most raging typhoon that ever swept the seas. France as well as Britain were both led by men devoid of vigour and initiative. Yet the fortunes of the Alliance depended upon their leadership.

The first session of the Inter-Allied Conference from which so much was hoped took place that afternoon. The importance of these meetings is shown by the list of those attending, which included, for the British Government, Mr. Asquith and myself, accompanied by Lord Bertie and Sir Maurice Hankey; for the French Government, M. Briand, President of the Council and Minister for Foreign Affairs, Admiral Lacaze, Minister of Marine, with M. de Margerie, Director of Political and Commercial Affairs at Quai d'Orsay; for Russia, M. Isvolsky, Ambassador in Paris; for Italy, Signor Carcano, Minister of the Treasury, Senator Tittoni, Minister of State, and the Marquis Salvago Raggi, Ambassador in Paris.

The President of the Council (M. Briand), after welcoming those present, made a characteristic speech, eloquent but inconclusive, the minute of which I quote verbatim.

" M. Briand recalled that at the moment when the former Conference of March, 1916, met, the whole of Europe was still suffering from the anguish caused by the attack on Verdun. The advance made in the last days of February by the German Armies had given rise to the keenest apprehension; but the Allies on that occasion reviewed the situation in all its aspects, and co-ordinated their efforts, and as a result of that co-ordination they had been able to carry out an offensive which had already given satisfactory results, and of which one of the first consequences had been to relieve Verdun.

At the same time the Russian Armies had taken the offensive on their side, and one of the effects of these operations had been to relieve the congestion on the Italian Front, and to allow our Allies to score a brilliant revenge against the Austrians.

The results obtained, however satisfactory they might be, were not, strictly speaking, decisive, but they had at least the consequence of removing the initiative in the field from the Germans and transferring it to the Allied troops. But that was not enough to bring victory.

The War was about to enter upon a serious—one might say a decisive—phase, and the Allies would have to close their ranks in order to bring the War to a speedy end by achieving a final victory over their enemies, since the patience of the nations could not be indefinitely submitted to such an ordeal.

Before discussing this problem, a question of principle arose: What ought to be the attitude of the Governments towards the General Staffs; whatever might be their confidence in the General Staff—a confidence indeed fully justified—ought the Governments to abandon absolutely to them the conduct of operations?

The French Government did not think so. It held, on the contrary, that it was the Governments which, since they bore the whole responsibility for the conduct of the War, should take the initiative in regard to operations, it being always understood that the execution of the plan adopted should be left to the military authorities, who had the means to carry it out.

If there was agreement on this point, the moment would seem to have come for the Government to envisage the direction which it would be desirable to give to the War. On that very day the delegates of the General Staffs were studying at Chantilly the elements of the problem, and their labours would be of great service in enabling the Governments to take a decision in full cognisance of the circumstances.

What struck the Premier first of all when studying the situation on the basis of the documents furnished by the military authorities and carefully checked by General Headquarters, was the fact that the Allies had altogether at their disposal effectives superior by at least 50 per cent. to those which the combined strength of the Germans, Austrians, Bulgarians and Turks could put against them. That was a consideration well calculated to give courage and to justify an absolute confidence in final victory.

These hopes showed a still firmer foundation, added M. Briand, if the present fighting value of the armies were compared. While our troops had not only lost nothing of their attacking qualities, but on the contrary had never ceased to improve, as the success of our last Anglo-French offensive on the Somme had demonstrated, the soldiers of the German Army were far from possessing to-day even among their officers, the same qualities as at the time of their formidable attack on Verdun.*

Furthermore, the Allied situation from the point of view of munitions was growing stronger and stronger every day.

Such considerations should not, however, be allowed to lull our courage to sleep, or make us lose sight of the great goal we had to reach. They should, on the contrary, stimulate our ardour, encourage us to intensify our efforts, and make us understand the great advantages which we have reaped from putting into the common store our strength and our resources.

And now, what course of action ought we to adopt on all fronts? It was on this point that it would seem worth while to deliberate, in order to discover the swiftest solution of the War. The French Government considered, and its opinion would doubtless be shared by the military authorities, that it was absolutely necessary to manifest an incessant activity on all fronts. This activity could not bring about a decisive result all at once, but it was indispensable in order to retain the initiative in the Allies' hands. The offensives of the armies of General Brussiloff and General Lechnisky had frankly not been decisive, but they had enabled the Russians to take 400,000 prisoners and disorganise the Austrian Army.† On its front, the Italian Army had dealt the Austrian Army terrible blows, which had greatly weakened it; while on our front our valiant troops and those of our friends and Allies the English, had undertaken an offensive which had already had happy consequences which were familiar to his hearers.

All these operations, without being decisive had had the effect of preventing our enemies from continuing the tactics of which we had been the victims at the outbreak of war, and from dealing us blows, first on one front, and then on the other. Since our activity had shown itself everywhere, the Austro-German Armies had been everywhere condemned to act on the defensive. Let that

---

* A few weeks later the 50 per cent. superiority had already disappeared, and the mutiny in the French Army did not quite bear out M. Briand's claim as to the superior " attacking qualities " of the Allied troops.

† The greater numbers of Russian and Roumanian prisoners captured by the Central Powers are not mentioned.

lesson profit us and encourage us to keep on! But what operations could be undertaken in winter? The French Government considered, and it had made its views on this subject known to its Allies, that it was in the Balkans that the most effective efforts could be put forth. What, in fact, was Germany doing?

Pressed on all sides, it was not hesitating to violate the rights of nations in an attempt to procure new reserves of men in Poland. It was said that it could find in this way 300,000 or 400,000 men. Suppose these figures correct, would it not take several months more to train these new recruits and make soldiers of them? Were we going to wait without doing anything until Germany and Austria were able to use these troops against us? Would it not be much more worth while to make straight away an effort to stop, or at all events to render useless this violation of the rights of nations?

But what could be done? Let us ask ourselves. *It seemed to him indispensable to try by energetic action in the Dobrudja and against Sofia to put Bulgaria out of action, and thereby Turkey.*

That effort was not impossible, and he thought that Russia would be disposed to make it, if we could second her action by an offensive on the Salonika Front. There could not be for the army of the east any question of undertaking an operation of large scope. The narrowness of its base rendered this task almost impossible. But it could, for instance, continue its pressure on the German-Bulgarian Armies, and try to recapture Monastir.

The Salonika Army, although inadequately supplied with men, had at all events carried out the promise made to Roumania to immobilise the Bulgarian Armies on its front. Since the entrance of Roumania into the picture, not a single Bulgarian soldier had been able to leave the Salonika Front to take part in operations against our new Ally. That in itself was an appreciable result, *but it was necessary for those operations to continue so as to free Roumania, and at the same time the activity of the Allied Armies must be intensified on all the other fronts.*

If Bulgaria and Turkey were put out of action before the end of the winter, public opinion in Germany and Austria would certainly be demoralised, and next spring we should be able to deal our enemies decisive blows.

That was how the French Government saw the course of the War. If the Allied Governments were in agreement with it in deciding that it was the Governments which should take in hand the general conduct of the War, and if they shared its way of looking at things, he had the firm conviction that we should be able next year to obtain decisive results.

We had come to a grave hour—maybe to a critical hour, if there was wobbling in the decisions of the Allies and a dispersal of their efforts.

T

' I have shown you the goal that we wish to reach,' said the
President of the Council in conclusion. ' It is worth our while
to give it serious study, for if we adopt a definite solution, we shall
have rendered a signal service to the cause which we support.' '

It was then the turn of the British Prime Minister to urge upon
the conference the definite proposal set forth in our memorandum.
The minute of the Conference continues: —

" Mr. Asquith thanked M. Briand, in the name of the British
Government, for the eloquent words he had just uttered. But,
added the Prime Minister, to attain the goal which has been
indicated with such precision, it will be needful for statesmen and
generals from the Great Powers of the west to proceed to Russia
to confer with the Russian statesmen and generals, to determine
what it is possible to do on the Eastern Front, and what is the
nature and the importance of the help which the Western Powers
can render to Russia and Roumania, to bring to a favourable issue
those operations which are considered necessary. This conference
would have for its object the examining of the situation in its
entirety, and more particularly the military situation in the east.
It is necessary that this meeting should take place as soon as
possible, and that the statesmen charged to represent the Western
Powers should have full authority to discuss the grave problems on
which the conduct of the War depends.

The British Prime Minister was of the opinion, that it was not
the military authorities but rather the Governments which ought
to undertake responsibility for the political and strategical conduct
of the War, and he proposed that the representatives of the Powers
met here to-day should forthwith, and *without prejudice in any
respect to the conclusion of the conference which would be held in
Russia,* enter on an engagement to submit themselves to the
decisions of this Assembly.

The Chief Italian Delegate thought, like M. Briand, that as the
Governments had the responsibility of power, it was to them that
the right belonged of deciding the conduct of the War, but he was
of opinion that no decision ought to be definitely fixed before
there had been consultation with the competent military authorities. With this reservation, M. Carcano entirely associated himself
with the point of view of the French Government. The Minister
of the Treasury pointed out at the same time that he was in this
expressing only a personal opinion, and that he did not think
himself authorised to enter on an engagment in the name of the
Royal Government. He would wish to refer the matter to the
President of the Council, who had been unable through sickness
to be present at the conference, but with whom the final decision
rested.

M. Briand pointed out that at present they were concerned only with an exchange of views between the delegates of the Allied Powers, and that the solutions arrived at by them did not bind their Governments, and were only taken *ad referendum*. It could not indeed be otherwise, since it was a question of summoning a conference in Russia, the principal theatre of war during the winter, to discuss these problems there and take the necessary decisions.

M. Tittoni declared that the Italian Government had been in agreement with the French Government since the coming into power of M. Briand in considering that the Balkan theatre was that in which the War would reach its decision. But when it was a case of discussing in what manner the Allies ought to concert their efforts to attain a definite result, it was evident that they would have to discuss in the first place among themselves the conditions of the joint military and financial co-operation.

The President of the Council did not disagree with this, but he pointed out that it was necessary for the Governments to take into their hands the direction of the War. The front on which operations were taking place was so extended that it was difficult to embrace with a single glance, *and there was no army chief who would not be tempted—it was human nature—to consider the front on which he was in command as the most important, just as each soldier did—hence the necessity for the Governments to be the arbiters of operations.* Our enemies had shown that they would not hesitate, even at the risk of a sacrifice of *amour propre*, to keep in view only the end to be reached. Did they not, the moment that Roumania entered on the scene, give up the pursuit of their attack on Verdun, despite even a dynastic interest therein, to transfer their principle effort to the Balkans?

That example should not be lost on us. *It was not a question of obtaining a success at one point or at another, but of envisaging the final result, and of co-ordinating our effort to obtain as soon as possible the ultimate victory.*

The Russian Ambassador, although without instructions and without special powers, undertook to state that the proposal to hold a conference of the Allies in Russia would be met with the liveliest sympathy on the part of His Majesty and his Government. M. Isvolsky added that he personally considered that it was the Governments, and not the Staffs, which ought to have the direction of the War, but that question did not arise in Russia, since the Emperor was at once the supreme head of the armies and of the Government.

As to the question of the principal theatre of operations during the winter it was clear from all communications received from Russia that the Imperial Government and everyone in Russia were well aware of the capital importance of the operations in the Balkans.

M. Briand noted with satisfaction that all the delegates were agreed in principle in recognising that the Eastern Front would be during the winter the principal theatre of operations. Since that was the case, and while leaving to the conference which would be held in Russia the task of deciding what should be done by the Russian and Roumanian Governments, we could examine straight away to what extent these efforts could be seconded by the army in the east.

Mr. Lloyd George noted with satisfaction that all the delegates had approved in principle the proposition of the British Government for summoning a conference in Russia to decide on the general conduct of the War, and that they were in agreement as to the necessity of adopting a common line of action.

'But that is not enough,' added Mr. Lloyd George. '*We must not rest content with taking these decisions. We have still to see that they are carried out.* After having decided on the Salonika expedition, the English and French Governments entrusted its execution to persons who were not perhaps sufficiently convinced of the importance of this front, and have not given sufficient attention to it to know whether the effectives were adequate, whether the transport was well organised, and in particular whether the artillery corresponded to the needs of the operations. Certain military authorities had said, it is true, that heavy artillery could not be utilised in this theatre on account of the bad state of the roads and of the topographical conditions; but the Germans have shown us the contrary in the Carpathians. *When Governments have taken a decision, they ought to see that it is carried out.*

'The goal towards which our efforts ought to be directed has been indicated with much eloquence by the President of the Council. It is a matter of encircling Germany more and more every day, of cutting its communications with the East, of hindering the formation of new armies.

'To get there, we shall have to unite all our resources. One cannot in fact avoid the thought that the magnificent offensive of the Russian Armies, despite the valour of the troops and the skill of the generals, has not perhaps yielded all that was hoped for, solely because of the inadequacy of heavy artillery on the Eastern Front. These armies ought then to be given the cannon and the munitions of which they stand in need, and that without waiting until the French, English and Italian Armies have been furnished with all the material that is necessary to them. We have got to help Russia and Roumania, not by taking from the surplus of our production, but by drawing if it must be upon what is necessary for ourselves, for it would be a shortsighted policy not to put these armies straight away into a position to fulfil the task which falls upon them.'

Mr. Lloyd George proposed, in consequence, that the Assembly should adopt the following resolutions:—

1. The three Governments of France, Italy and Great Britain undertake to participate in a political and military conference which shall be held in Russia as soon as possible.

Each Government will send to this conference, as its representatives, statesmen and officers of high rank, possessing full authority to speak in the name of their respective Governments.

2. The aim of the conference will be to examine the political and military situation in all its aspects, and in particular to fix the nature and the importance of the military effort which the Allies ought to carry out in the east during 1917. The object of the conference shall be at the same time to estimate the importance of the help which ought to be provided by France, Italy and Great Britain, to Russia and Roumania, in order to enable these Powers to carry out the operations which shall have been decided on.

3. The Governments represented at the present conference shall enter into an engagement to furnish in the fullest possible measure to their Allies the full military equipment asked for by the conference, which will be held in Russia, even if this should result in a certain slowing down in the equipment of their own armies, and Russia shall on its side enter into an engagement to conform to the decisions adopted by this conference.

This last phrase does not in any way imply that the conference will impose certain conditions on Russia, it simply means that Russia will take the necessary steps to enable her to make use as promptly as possible, and with all the desired intensity of the resources put at her disposal by the Allies. It turned out that 300 pieces of heavy artillery sent to Russia at the beginning of the year could not be used until a quite recent date through lack of artillery-men to serve them.

M. Tittoni, after stating that the Italian delegates could only take part in these deliberations *ad referendum,* asked permission to tell the meeting the reflections which Mr. Lloyd George's proposition suggested to him. One could not doubt, said he, the good will of the Italian Government; its solidarity with the Allies was whole and entire; but he did not want to rest content with theoretical formulas, and was trying to do practical work. Now, it was no use hiding the fact that the realisation of the programme advanced by the President of the Council and by Mr. Lloyd

George would come crashing against difficulties independent of the good will of men. He had to speak freely.

Now, for the Italian Government, one of the principal difficulties at the present moment was the financial question, and that was one of the reasons for the journey of the Minister of the Treasury. The question of exchange was becoming almost acute, since, less rich than France and England, Italy was experiencing great difficulties in meeting its payments to foreign countries. Of course, the Italian Government was ready to make every possible effort, but it was necessary for its Allies to come to its aid as well with the help it might require from the financial aspect.

So far as concerned the operations at Salonika, the Senator of the Kingdom of Italy could only express his personal opinion, this question being chiefly within the competence of the military authorities; but he was convinced that the Italian Government would be ready to make the effort asked of it, if it had the assurance that the Russo-Roumanian pressure would be so powerful and continuous that it would be impossible for the Austro-Germans to withdraw troops from the Balkans in order to send them to one of the other fronts. If this condition was not fulfilled, the Allies would be running a great risk in weakening the French, English and Italian Fronts, to any extent, however slight. *An intensification of the effort at Salonika would seem useless, if it were not the consequence and the complement of a great Russo-Roumanian effort.*

It should not be lost sight of that to realise this effort many difficulties would have to be surmounted, not only difficulties of a military order, but economic and financial difficulties as well. It would not be sufficient to send troops; we must also be able to ensure their transport; their artillery supplies, and the provisioning under all heads. The question of the reinforcement of the Eastern Army thus presented very great difficulties.

M. Briand remarked that when the Allies envisaged a plan of campaign, it was, of course, understood to be subject to the reserve that what proves impossible should be abandoned, and that it was precisely the object of the conferences then being held, and of that which would take place in Russia to discover the steps to be taken to secure unity of action on all fronts, regard being had to the resources and the means of each of the Allies.

It would, for instance, be impossible to ask France—which had ten departments invaded, which had mobilised more than 6,000,000 men, which had taken part in the operations in the Dardanelles and at Salonika, and had gone at the outset to the aid of Serbia—it would be impossible to ask her for a greater effort in men. *But if France were asked for artillery, machine-guns, munitions, and if it were in her power to furnish them, she would give them at once.* France had already given a good deal of war material to her Allies, but she was ready to intensify still further her production if this was possible.

The Allies ought to try and fill up the gaps wherever they appeared. If one country was embarrassed in regard to effectives, the others ought to come to her help; if there was another in a difficult financial situation, it was their duty to try to give her the resources which she needed. *In the grave circumstances through which we were passing, all our resources must be pooled without making it a question of* amour propre. That was how the French Government, and assuredly also all the Allied Governments, understood the conduct of the War."

The remainder of the session was devoted to a consideration of the position in Greece. With regard to this country the discussions were confined mainly to the question of the recognition of M. Venizelos's Government. A new factor, which was brought out by M. Briand, was that the King, in his conversations with M. Benazet, had made some remarkable promises. He had said that he was ready to withdraw his troops from Thessaly on condition that the territory evacuated was not occupied by Venizelist troops. He had also offered to give us the whole of the Greek material of war, and even to put his fleet at our disposal. M. Briand said that, if this offer were accepted, the Allies would obtain the use of 200 mountain guns, with 1,000 rounds a gun, as well as a vast amount of other war material.

Mr. Asquith pointed out that if one of the conditions of the King's offer to M. Benazet was the abandonment of M. Venizelos his proposals would have to be rejected. He explained at considerable length the sympathy and respect felt in England for M. Venizelos, and urged that the ideal solution was the reconciliation of the King with M. Venizelos, and that our policy should be directed towards that. He also urged the desirability of the official recognition of the Venizelist Government, particularly owing to the anomalous position of the Venizelist troops, and the danger they ran of not being accorded belligerent rights.

M. Briand did not dispute the desirability of reconciliation between King Constantine and M. Venizelos, and said that in France public opinion was as favourable to M. Venizelos as it is in England. Public opinion, however, he added, was not aware of the difficulties.

The general opinion of the conference was not in favour of the recognition of M. Venizelos at present. It was pointed out that, in order to obtain belligerent rights, it was necessary that the enemy, no less than the Allied Governments, should recognise M. Venizelos.

It was generally agreed, however, that the Allies should not let any opportunity pass to support M. Venizelos and his friends, and to protect them wherever necessary. The friends of the Entente, as

M. Briand said, must not be the victims of their favourable sentiments towards the Allies.

The question was left much where it stood, and no resolution was passed. M. Briand finally summed up the discussion as follows:—

" So the Allies may expect a development which does not seem as though it could be delayed much longer, and which should be of a nature to give them satisfaction; but it still goes without saying that if the King or his Government were to adopt measures against M. Venizelos and his friends, the Allies would intervene immediately with all necessary vigour to defend the great Greek patriot, who has always shown himself favourable to their cause."

Thus ended the first day's conference. Before our meeting on the afternoon of the next day, the military chiefs at Chantilly had completed their deliberations, and had agreed upon a programme which bears evident marks of having been settled for them in advance by the French Headquarters Staff, and which ran as follows:—

" General Headquarters of the
French Armies,
Staff Office, 16th November, 1916.

The members of the Conference give their approval to a plan of action by the Coalition, as it has been defined in the memorandum which has been submitted to them, a plan having for its object to give a decisive character to the campaigns of 1917. They adopt, in consequence, the following resolutions:—

1.

(*a*) During the winter of 1916-17, the offensive operations now being engaged in shall be pursued to the full extent compatible with the climatic conditions on each front.

(*b*) In order to be as much as possible in readiness to face every new situation, and especially in order to prevent the enemy from recapturing in any way the initiative of operations, the armies of the Coalition shall be ready to undertake joint offensives from the first fortnight of February, 1917, with all the means at their disposal.

(*c*) From the time when the armies are ready to attack, the Commanders-in-Chief shall adapt their respective conduct to suit the situation of the moment.

(*d*) If circumstances do not prevent it, the joint offensives carried out with all the means which each army can bring into play, shall be unloosed on all the fronts as soon as they can be synchronised* to dates which shall be fixed by common accord between the Commanders-in-Chief.

---

* It is admitted that synchronisation will be realised if there does not elapse a delay of more than three weeks between the initial dates of the offensives released on the various fronts.

(*e*) With a view to realising all accord necessary between these diverse hypotheses, the Commanders-in-Chief shall not cease to maintain a close contact with each other.

2.   ON THE BALKAN FRONT

(*a*)   The Coalition shall seek to put Bulgaria out of action as soon as possible. The desire of the Russian High Command is to continue and intensify with this object the operations in hand.

(*b*)   Against Bulgaria the Russo-Roumanian forces shall act from the north, and the Allied Army at Salonika from the south, the action of these two groups of forces being closely combined, so as to obtain a decision on one or other front of action, following the development of operations.

(*c*)   The Allied Army of the East shall have its effectives raised as soon as possible to 23 divisions. This figure for effectives corresponds on the one hand to the number of troops which can be manœuvred and supplied with provisions in the theatre of operations in question, and on the other hand to the contingents which can be spared from the Western theatres of operations. With the object of attaining this effective force the British Government will raise without delay its forces to seven divisions, the French Government to six divisions; the Italian Government, having been informed of the intentions definitely affirmed by the Russian High Command, shall be requested to raise to three divisions the Italian forces at Salonika.

(*d*)   The Allied Army of the East shall be carefully maintained at the full complement of its effectives.

3.   SECONDARY THEATRES OF OPERATIONS

On all secondary fronts, actions aiming at the immobilisation of the enemy forces shall be pursued with means as reduced as possible, in order to reserve the maximum forces for the principal theatres.

4.   MUTUAL SUPPORT

(*a*)   The members of the Conference renew the undertaking for mutual assistance adopted by the Conference on 5th December, 1915, and fully observed by all throughout the course of the present year, that is to say : —

If one of the Powers is attacked, the others shall come immediately to its help to the full limit of their resources, whether indirectly by attacks which the armies not assaulted by the enemy will unloose upon prepared zones, or directly by the dispatch of forces between theatres of operations linked by easy communications.

(*b*)   In readiness for this latter eventuality, studies of transport and of the employment of combined forces shall be undertaken between the French, English, and Italian Headquarters Staffs.

5. MAINTAINING THE EFFECTIVES OF THE SERBIAN ARMY

The effectives of the Serbian Army shall be maintained by voluntary enrolments of prisoners of Serbian race, in the hands of Italy and Russia, to the full extent and with all the precautions determined by these two Powers.

Signed by the Representatives of the Commanders-in-Chief of the Allied Armies present at this Conference and designated below: —

For Belgium: —
General Wielemans, Chief of the General Staff of the Belgian Army.

WIELEMANS.

For Great Britain:
General Sir W. Robertson, Chief of the Imperial General Staff of the British Armies.

W. ROBERTSON.

General Sir Douglas Haig, Commander-in-Chief of the British Armies in France.

DOUGLAS HAIG.

For Italy: —
General Porro, Chief of the General Staff of the Italian Army.

PORRO.

For Roumania: —
Colonel Rudeano, Chief of the Roumanian Military Mission at the French G.H.Q.

RUDEANO.

For Russia: —
General Palitzine, representative of His Majesty, the Commander-in-Chief of the Russian Troops, and the Chief of the Russian Military Mission.

PALITZINE.

For Serbia: —
General Rachitch, delegate of the Serbian Army at the French G.H.Q.

RACHITCH.

For France: —
General Joffre, Commander-in-Chief of the French Armies.

JOFFRE."

Accordingly, at our meeting on Thursday, afternoon, 16th November, the representatives of the Allied Governments were joined by the leading generals (Joffre, Robertson, Haig, and Porro), whose report formed the agenda for our discussion, and whose conclusions limited and for practical purposes defined our action. I extract the following passages from the minutes of this session.

After M. Briand, with Mr. Asquith's support, had proposed that for the moment no more could be done than to approve the Chantilly resolutions *ad referendum* to the Petrograd Conference to which the plan of Eastern operations had been referred, I intervened as follows: —

"Mr. Lloyd George wanted to know how the figure of 23 Divisions was arrived at. According to the information supplied, there were only 19—7 English, 6 French, 3 Italian, and 3 Serbian, the effectives in the Serbian Army amounting, according to the information supplied by General Milne, to about 36,000 rifles, which only equalled three divisions on the basis of the standard of the Allied Powers.

General Joffre explained that there was a Russian Division, and that the Serbian Army was counted as six divisions.

Mr. Lloyd George expressed his astonishment at this valuation, and pointed out that the Serb effectives were being reduced all the time. The Serbian soldiers fought with a courage which could not be praised highly enough, but the Serbian Army had no reserves, and its losses were rather high. It was for that reason that he only reckoned there to be three divisions of effectives in that army.

Admiral Lacaze recalled that 140,000 Serbians had been transported from Corfu to Salonika.

General Joffre added that this figure of 23 divisions was the maximum that the Salonika theatre of operations would permit of employment. We could only deal with practical propositions. Besides, to raise the effectives of the Army of the East to this figure would take a good deal more time yet, *for if there were at our disposal a sufficient number of boats, there were still lacking the railways and necessary facilities to enable us to utilise a more numerous army.** This meant that we must immediately intensify the activity at Salonika, and for that it would be preferable to send there one division straight away, rather than to send two or three in January or February.

Mr. Lloyd George asked on what information the opinion was based that this figure of 23 divisions was the maximum that could be used at Salonika, and whether this attitude was shared by the generals commanding the East.

General Joffre replied that this advice was the result of calculations made at General Headquarters.

* The British War Council decided to take steps for this purpose in January, 1915, but the military authorities entirely ignored the decision. See Vol. I, page 235.

General Robertson announced that the British Government had received a *report from General Milne in which he declared that the possibility of utilising thirty divisions at Salonika could only be contemplated if the means of communication, the roads, and railways, could be expanded, and if two new ports could be brought into service.*

General Joffre explained that the military authorities had had to base themselves on the existing state of affairs, *because it would take not less than 12 or 18 months to construct the roads and railways needed to enable thirty divisions to manœuvre.* Replying to Mr. Lloyd George he said that no report had been received from General Sarrail.*

M. Briand pointed out that it was by taking for their basis the position as it stands with its present possibilities that the General Staffs had been led to consider that 23 divisions represented the maximum of what could be absorbed and used this winter on the Salonika Front. That was not to say that they could not, by constructing new roads and new railways, use more important effectives, but that the General Staffs had primarily had in view the realisation as early as possible of the objective set before them —namely the conquest of Monastir, and along all the rest of the front a continuous action designed to retain the enemy forces so as to prevent the Bulgarians from sending troops to the Roumanian Front.

General Joffre added that *the means of communication were not yet sufficient, and before being able to utilise the effectives that had just been spoken of, locomotives and waggons would have to be sent for the Greek railways.*

Mr. Lloyd George paid a tribute to the remarkable skill of the Italian engineers, especially over country of such a character, and wondered whether the Allies could not approach the Cabinet at Rome to ask them for help in this task.

General Porro stated that if necessary the Italian Government would be quite ready to send engineer officers to construct railways in Greece. *He added that the reports from General Pettiti confirmed all that General Joffre had said about the lack of means of communication and about the bad state of the roads, which were almost unusable.*

General Joffre *explained that the roads were so bad that half the fighting troops were being used in maintaining them.*

Mr. Asquith expressed pleasure at the assurance given by General Porro. He considered indeed that Italy could not render a more important service than that of improving the lines of communication in the Balkans.

General Joffre remarked that if the Army of the East had not

* He was Commander-in-Chief of the Salonika Expedition. Decisions had been arrived at without any previous consultation with, or even report from him.

yet reached Monastir, that was largely due to the difficulty of transport of men and materials in those regions, and indeed to the all but impossibility of revictualling them in certain cases. *The first thing to do was to construct roads and railways:* but it must not be lost sight of that, to the extent to which the army advanced, the engineers and workmen would have to make new railways for it. Progress would thus be necessarily very slow, *and that was why the military authorities considered that not more than 23 divisions could be used on the Salonika Front,* and preferred to retain the effectives that were at their disposal for the Western Front.

M. Briand thought the question should be dealt with by stages. For the moment the concern was that the expeditionary corps should be able to realise its objective on the Monastir side, and hold the Bulgarian troops on its front.

If, later on, after the construction of new railways and improvement of the means of communications, it appeared that the expeditionary corps could absorb new troops, the French Government, and no doubt also the other Governments, would be ready to send the necessary troops.

The President of the Council pointed out, in passing, that the conclusions of the military conference were in agreement with the views exchanged on the previous day between the delegates of the Powers. The conclusion of the work of the General Staffs confirmed the importance of intensifying operations in the east, so as to put out of action Bulgaria and Turkey. These conclusions were only adopted, it need hardly be repeated, *ad referendum,* but each group of delegates could forthwith inform its Government, and support at the Petrograd Conference the resolutions which had been proposed.

The President of the Council asked the delegates of the Powers to register the conclusions of the General Staffs while waiting for the possibility of going to meet the Russian Government and get them approved there in definite form."

After this the Italian Representatives gave an interesting account of the economic and financial state of affairs in Italy and its connection with the military situation. They emphasised the vital need of imports and raw materials if the *morale* of the Italian army and people, which remained high, was to be maintained. They described the difficulty of a country whose exports had shrunk to small dimensions, owing to war conditions, in paying for imports unless further financial assistance was forthcoming. Mr. Asquith, while pointing out that our own position was far from easy, promised to examine with the utmost good will any proposals the Italian Government could make for the improvement of the situation, and M. Briand gave a similar undertaking. If the Allies wished to be victorious, he said, it was essential that they should put all their resources into the common stock. Some had reserves of men, others produced a superabundance of war material, others again could dispose of important financial resources. But if the Allies established a balance of their general situation it would be easy for them, or at least possible, to fill up the gaps which might exist by one or the other.

In regard to Poland the Conference discussed the text of a protest to be made by the Allied Governments against the creation by the Central Powers of a Kingdom of Poland.

The text of the draft originally proposed was purely negative in character, merely consisting of a protest, on the grounds of international law, against the German action. Mr. Asquith pressed very strongly that it should not be purely negative in character, but should contain a reference to the promises made by the Grand Duke in regard to Poland in August, 1914.

It will be obvious from the records I have here produced that this conference, on which so much store had been set, turned out from the point of view of securing a genuine examination of the military position and strategy, by a gathering at which both soldiers and statesmen were represented, to be little better than a complete farce. M. Briand's opening speech at the Wednesday afternoon session was characteristic of his strength and weakness—eloquent in phrase, inconclusive in decision—strong in statement, feeble in action. The Allies, he explained, were superior in numbers, equipment and valour to their dispirited foes. We must energise these superior forces of the Allies and promote such a co-ordination of effort as would overwhelm the inferior armies of the enemy. The only danger was that the patience of the Allied nations would be worn out. So we must attack on all sides with all our strength. Our resources were common, so must be the front. The Balkans were the point upon which this united strength should be concentrated in the coming months. He envisaged such energetic action from the Salonika base against Sofia as would free Roumania and put Bulgaria and Turkey out of action before the winter. He pointed the result of this enterprise with a broad brush dipped in radiant colours—public opinion in Germany and Austria would certainly be demoralised, and next spring we should be able to deal our enemies a decisive blow. And he ended up with the proposal of a local operation for the capture of Monastir, a feat achieved later on by the broken army of Serbia alone. He also laid it down in precise terms that the statesmen of the Alliance must make clear to the Chantilly warriors that the strategy and direction came from Governments and not from staffs, and that it was for the latter merely to carry out the instructions framed at the political conference. At that very moment M. Briand had obviously agreed in advance to accept General Joffre's plans which went no further than Monastir! The idea of breaking through the

Bulgarian lines in order to extend effective aid to Roumania was in fact abandoned in the very speech wherein it was advocated with resounding rhetoric.

As for the document submitted to the second session by the generals, setting out their decisions at Chantilly, it was an intimation that the military leaders regarded the determination of the lines of the campaign for 1917 to be a matter for which they had the primary responsibility. To this attitude they adhered in spite of an elaborate appearance of deference to the wishes of the Government. The 1917 campaign was theirs with all its disasters. It repeated all the bloody stupidities of 1915 and 1916 and extinguished finally the *morale* of the Russian Armies, already shaken but not irretrievably shattered. It also temporarily broke the spirit of the French and Italian and British Armies.

The proposal for the conference of responsible political and military leaders to be held immediately on Russian soil to settle the future plans of the Allies was completely ignored by the generals. They had agreed to their plans at Chantilly and they had no intention of allowing General Alexeieff to alter them. Signor Tittoni's objection to agreeing to the meeting, except *ad referendum* to a sick Prime Minister, helped the generals to avoid committing themselves to a conference. As to Salonika they made a concession to civilian obtuseness. An attack was to be staged in that quarter at an early date, but it must be done as cheaply as possible. The stupid politicians must be deluded into the belief that it was a serious operation with a view to crumpling up Bulgaria—a preposterous piece of deception to any one who had made any study of the comparative strength or numbers, equipment and position of the combatants on that front. The generals knew that they had no intention of pressing the attack beyond Monastir. The storming of the Balkans they knew too well was far beyond the power of the badly equipped Salonika Army. But the strength of the Salonika force must be exaggerated for civilian ears. It was, or soon would be, an army of 23 divisions brought up to effective strength. They juggled and shuffled with " divisions " when they knew they were only sham divisions. As a matter of fact it was the equivalent of barely ten divisions, and no effort was contemplated to increase its numbers in offensive efficacy. In the matter of artillery and transport it was hopelessly below the standard of the Western Front. When their attention was called to the inadequacy of the forces, Generals Joffre and Robertson urged that the transport facilities were so defective that you could not feed a larger number of troops, let alone carry the necessary ammunition for more cannon. It would take 12 to 18 months to improve these facilities. The Expeditionary Force had already been at Salonika for that period and these improvements had not been attempted. As I have previously said, a decision had been arrived at by the British War Council as far back as January, 1915, to take immediate steps to increase transport facilities between Salonika and Serbia. Lord Kitchener promised to take the matter in hand at once. Here, at the end of 1916, a campaign which our military advisers considered essential to restore our failures in South-Eastern Europe, could not be attempted because the port, rail and road transport were so inefficient that no effective attack could be staged. It came out in one of the military reports that half the troops were occupied not in fighting but in road repairing. General Milne reported that with 33 divisions the Bulgarian Army could be beaten. Had the necessary 33 divisions been landed, backed by a powerful artillery, what a difference it would have made to the course of events! Bulgaria, now getting tired of the War, would have been eliminated. The Bulgarian peasantry never cared for the side they were forced by their King to take. The road to Roumania would have been reached. The Russian Armies and those of the west would have joined hands. Turkey would have been cut off from the source of her supplies. More heart and spirit would have been given to the depressed and disaffected Russian soldiers. The Revolution would have been further postponed. Austria would have been enveloped on the east, the south and the west and would have fallen to pieces. 1917 might have seen the end of the War. What a difference that would have made to the world!

I left the conference feeling that after all nothing more would be done except to repeat the old fatuous tactics of hammering away with human flesh and sinews at the strongest fortresses of the enemy. If Russia and Roumania fell out, there was nothing more that could be done.

When Mr. Asquith, Sir Maurice Hankey and I returned to the hotel and Mr. Asquith, after a short and perfunctory conversation, retired to his usual rest before dinner, Sir Maurice and I went for a walk together to talk matters over.

We both felt that nothing in the way of a change in the conduct of the War had been accomplished and that in the absence of some dramatic *coup* things would go on as before until we slid into inevitable catastrophe. We felt that if either Russia or Italy collapsed or if the submarine losses could not be checked, the balance of advantage in favour of the Allies would be lost and would pass over to the enemy. I was in favour of an immediate resignation to rouse Allied opinion to the actualities of the position. To this Sir Maurice was opposed until some other means of effecting a change in the War direction had first been attempted. I can recall that as we passed the Vendôme Column, Sir Maurice paused and said " You ought to insist on a small War Committee being set up for the day-to-day conduct of the War, with full powers. It must be independent of the Cabinet. It must keep in close touch with the P.M., but the

Committee ought to be in continuous session, and the P.M., as Head of the Government, could not manage that. He has a very heavy job in looking after the Cabinet and attending to Parliament and home affairs. He is a bit tired, too, after all he has gone through in the last two and a half years. The Chairman must be a man of unimpaired energy and great driving power." We both agreed that it was important that Mr. Asquith should continue to be Prime Minister. His great prestige and his unrivalled authority in the House of Commons would be assets which were regarded as indispensable. It was decided, therefore, that on my return to England I should place the proposition before the Prime Minister; but that before I did so it would be best to sound Bonar Law, whose good will and approval it was essential to secure. I wired from Paris to Lord Beaverbrook, asking him to arrange a meeting between Bonar Law and myself the following evening.

CHAPTER XXXIII

THE FOOD POSITION

By the autumn of 1916 the food position was becoming increasingly alarming and grave, and its handling by the Government was a most conspicuous example of its hesitancies. The increasing shortage of shipping made the food position doubly grave, dependent as we were upon ships for most of our food supplies. As far back as September, 1915, Lord Selborne, in a memorandum which he submitted to the Cabinet, had urged that "we should appoint another committee of the Cabinet to consider the whole question of the food supply of the nation for the next 18 months." In this document he had pleaded the value of an increased wheat production. "It is only about a month," he wrote, "since the Chancellor of the Exchequer [Mr. M'Kenna] showed an invincible repugnance to encourage the growth of wheat in England by offering the farmers a guarantee. It is possible to increase the production of food in the United Kingdom by voluntary effort, but a guarantee of the price of wheat would be by far the most effective measure which the Government would take for that purpose." On 10th March, 1916, I raised this issue anew by urging on the War Committee that the aim we ought to keep in view in the matter of food supplies was that this country should as far as possible be self-contained. To this end the Board of Agriculture ought to be armed with drastic powers to improve the production of food so as to reduce our dependence on imports. Every possible acre ought to be cultivated against the prospective extension of the submarine campaign. I suggested the utilisation of machinery on a large scale. The plan, however, must be a *national* one.

On 23rd March, 1916, I spoke again on the same subject in connection with the problem of the shortage of ships.

In the War Committee of 31st October, 1916, the Prime Minister had read a letter from the Commander-in-Chief of the Grand Fleet who " expressed misgivings regarding the danger to the cause of the Allies from submarine attacks on merchant shipping, *which must be expected to increase in the spring, when the enemy would have more submarines.*" It was known that in this opinion the Admiralty were in complete agreement with the Commander-in-Chief. Lord Crawford was now Minister of Agriculture, and had circulated to the members of the Committee an urgent document showing the seriousness of the situation; and how the outlook grew more difficult as time went on. He pointed out that *our stocks of wheat and flour at that moment (30th October) amounted to four months' consumption, and that there was a world deficit of wheat. The probable wheat requirements of importing countries during the 12 months ending 1st September, 1917, were 72,000,000 quarters, while the total available supplies were estimated at 63,000,000.*

The freight space required to carry the necessary imports of grain and feeding stuffs in the eight months, November-June was 8,981,000 shipping tons. The potato crop, too, had failed in England, as in Germany and France. The forecasts indicated a shortage of some 1,800,000 tons (or 24 per cent.) as compared with 1915. Moreover, the crop was diseased and a shortage of seed potatoes was possible. Fish supplies were some 64 per cent. below normal, and the prices had risen from 100 to 400 per cent. The feeding of live stock was causing anxiety, as foodstuffs were costly and labour scarce.

Lord Crawford stressed the desirability of establishing some central food department to supervise and co-ordinate the varied relations of the State with the import, purchase and distribution of food. The whole field and the general prospects might be suitably submitted to the continuing and comprehensive survey of the central body. (This suggestion had now been before the Committee for at least seven months, but no advance had been made nor decision taken.)

Lord Crawford ended his memorandum by the statement *that not before August, 1917* (i.e., when the harvest of 1917 had been gathered in) *would war policy be free to dissociate itself from the influence of home food supply.*

I supported Lord Crawford whole-heartedly in his efforts to obtain a decision as regard the food supply, and on 10th November I circulated a short memorandum embodying a few concrete suggestions which I thought would materially help in solving the food problem. These were as follows: —

"That someone—who shall not be a member of the Ministry—be immediately appointed to organise the food supplies, including purchase, production, distribution and prices.

That he should be equipped with all the necessary legislative, administrative and financial powers to enable him to utilise to the full the food-producing capacity of the United Kingdom.

That *inter alia* he should direct his attention to:

1. Securing adequate supplies of food, especially from home sources;
2. Keeping prices down.
3. Increasing the acreage of land in this country which produces cereals, potatoes, vegetables, and other food products;

4. The mobilisation and utilisation to the full and in the best way of

(a) All the available mechanical appliances for the cultivation of the soil;

(b) The manufacturing capacity of this country and the United States for the output of machinery for cultivation;

(c) The skilled agricultural labour of the country;

(d) The unskilled male and female labour capacity of the country for agricultural purposes;

5. The utilisation for animal fattening of the enormous waste of food products now consigned to the refuse heaps in the great towns.'

War Office, November 10th, 1916."

The same day (10th November) there was a meeting of the War Committee, at which the question of shipping shortage was discussed. The President of the Board of Trade, in the course of his statement, said that the Wheat Commission were at present unable to find 40 free vessels for the essential service of conveying the Australian wheat supplies. *The conclusion that he drew was that a complete breakdown in shipping would come before June, 1917.*

On 13th November, the War Committee met to discuss the food position again. They had before them Lord Crawford's memorandum. The President of the Board of Agriculture, with the clarity and suavity which he always commands, urged his case. He gave a sketch of the immediate and prospective outlook as regards food. He pointed out that land was going out of cultivation, that labour was scarce. The harvest this year, he said, had been less by half a quarter per acre than had been anticipated, which was equal to a reduction from 12 to 10 weeks' supply. He was apprehensive of next year's harvest unless immediate steps were taken. He again urged the necessity for a Central Food Controlling Authority. I realised that if the submarine menace were not checked (and there seemed at that moment no expectancy that anything could prevent it from increasing in gravity) the War as far as we were concerned might end in starvation for this country. It was now months since the proposition of a central authority had been put before the Government, but we seemed to be no nearer achieving it. I therefore pressed at this meeting for the appointment of a Central Authority (which I had also insisted upon in my memorandum of 10th November). I urged however, *that the President should have real authority with complete control subject only to the War Committee. I considered, moreover, that the person appointed should not be a Minister of the Crown, as his time would largely be taken up with answering questions in Parliament. He need only attend the War Committee whenever he wanted a decision of first-class importance. Above all*

I impressed upon the Committee that the appointment should be made at once. The actual difference between 10 and 12 might seem to be small, but in point of fact it was very serious. I therefore begged the Prime Minister to treat the necessity of obtaining a man to control all food supplies as one of immediate urgency. I said that I attached great importance to machinery and cultivation. I saw no reason why every village in the country should not be self-supporting, just as it was when I was a boy.

The President of the Board of Trade pointed out that nearly all the statutory powers required to carry out my proposals already existed in the Defence of the Realm Act, and that he had recently circulated to the Cabinet new regulations under the Act of a most drastic kind.

In spite of these " full powers " and " drastic regulations," the Government had not sanctioned the measures suggested by the Minister for Agriculture and no progress was being made with the increase of home production.

The War Committee approved of my proposal for a Food Controller, in principle, subject to the right man being found to control the great organisation contemplated.

There were enough provisos in this last paragraph to prevent any action being taken immediately. As a matter fact, no food controller was appointed under Mr. Asquith's Premiership.

On 16th November, the First Sea Lord of the Admiralty and the Chief of the Admiralty War Staff circulated a note to the Cabinet stressing the increasing gravity of the submarine danger. They concluded the note with the following words : —

" The increasing danger to our supplies from the enemy's submarines has recently become so much more evident through their ruthless attacks on neutral shipping as to make this question need more serious reconsideration *before it is too late*."

But no immediate decision was taken. The accumulation of problems requiring urgent attention had indeed become so great that there seemed to be no time for any one of them to be properly thrashed out and a decision to be arrived at. On 22nd November, the matter was still in abeyance. The question of shipping and food supply was reaching a crisis, and the President of the Board of Trade circulated a memorandum complaining that nothing had been decided at the Cabinet meeting on 10th November, and calling attention again to the urgency of the matter from the point of view of tonnage. On the same day the Wheat Commission sent a communication (the memorandum of the President may have been written as a result of this), urging the provision of further tonnage for food supplies. " So far from adding," they said, " to the reserves in the country, the shipments during the last fortnight to arrive this year

have been nearly 200,000 quarters a week less than requirements,
and all the information of the Commission points to the conclusion
that this low rate of shipment will be continued until a further
supply of tramp tonnage has arrived for loading in the Northern
Range."

On the same day (22nd November) the Shipping Control Committee met and discussed the tonnage situation in relation to the
serious position of the wheat supply in this country.

They reported: "The Committee are informed that the stocks
of wheat are running down; that we are living from hand to mouth.
In London there are only two days' supplies, and London has therefore to be fed by rail from other ports. In Bristol there are only
two weeks' supplies. . . .

"The Wheat Commission have purchased 700,000 quarters in
North America, *but there are no steamers to bring the wheat to
England.*

"In normal circumstances there would be ships 'coming free' in
the Mediterranean after discharge of coal." These ships, however,
owing to war conditions, would not become available for four months,
and the wheat position was dangerously acute.

On 23rd November (the next day) three Ministers (the President
of the Board of Trade, Lord Curzon, and the President of the Board
of Agriculture) raised, as a matter of great urgency, our present and
prospective critical situation in regard to grain supplies. They
brought in support the letter from the Wheat Commission and the
report of the Shipping Control Committee; and the President of
the Board of Agriculture pointed out that we were *consuming* 200,000
*quarters a week more than we were receiving; that every week we
were buying sufficient wheat for* 15 *days' consumption, but were
unable to ship it; and that if the wheat we had purchased were not
brought forward it would diminish our power to purchase.*

It was decided that a conference should be held that afternoon
between the Admiralty, Shipping Control Committee, and President
of the Board of Trade, and that they should report next day to the
War Committee.

In spite of these urgent messages showing the critical position of
our food supplies none of the plans suggested either by the Ministry
of Agriculture or myself for dealing with the situation were put into
operation during the lifetime of the First Coalition. A paralysis of
will seemed to have seized the Government. Whatever the subject,
it was impossible to get a move on. I am not sure that this palsy did
not account for the unanimity of the Cabinet on the question of
rejecting overtures for Peace. These would have meant action. The
pacifist element were easily persuaded to do nothing. The Government was getting into that nervous condition where they could
neither wage war nor negotiate peace.

CHAPTER XXXIV

A CABINET OF INDECISION

It is hard for me to convey an adequate picture of the sense of frustration and tangled impotence which oppressed me during those closing months of 1916. There are nightmares in which one welters amid a web of fettering strands and obstacles, and watches, wide-eyed, some doom approaching against which the strangled throat cannot force a sound of protest or appeal. The ineffectiveness and irresolution of our leadership in those dark weeks bred something of this nightmare feeling.

There was at this time a whole series of developments and problems which were being paltered with or shelved. Some of the wider issues of general policy I have already described. Firm handling of them was vital to our prospects of success, and I grew increasingly convinced that it was my duty as a responsible Minister to dispel this miasma of indecision and force these matters to a definite issue, even at the risk of resignation from the Ministry and a subsequent public exposure of the ineptitude of the Allied war direction. I have also told of the way in which two or three important questions were dealt with, and these afford an illustration of the general method of procedure adopted by the Government in an emergency. One of them was the neglect to take competent strong measures to protect our merchant ships against submarine raiders. The alarming rate at which our ships were being sunk was rapidly increasing. The October sinkings had been nearly 70 per cent. above those of September, and the Admiralty wrung their hands in despair when reporting fresh disasters at our meetings, but offered no hope that they could grapple successfully with the rapidly developing catastrophe. Then there was our failure to take steps to co-ordinate our strategy with our Russian Ally —a failure intensified by the refusal of Sir William Robertson, backed and instigated by a member of the War Committee—to represent this country at the proposed Russian Conference. His refusal dealt a death blow to our prospects of saving our Ally from collapse and concerting our military strategy with her. It was prompted by a groundless apprehension that the whole idea was a manœuvre to shift him from his position in the War Office, and that the methods of the intrigue by which he had supplanted Lord Kitchener were to be practised in turn on himself—that Robertson, in fact, was to be "kitchenered" out of his position of high authority. This point of view was pressed upon him by a prominent Cabinet Minister and he was only too ready to listen. It is idle to vow that I had no such purpose in view, and that I had always urged a more authoritative touch between east and west than that which was represented by the appearance at our conference of Russian generals, for whom their own army had no use at home. Those who are capable of such baseness in a great crisis will readily believe that others meditated it. I was pressing on my colleagues what I sincerely believed was the best course in the interest of my country. However, Sir William Robertson would not go and the Prime Minister was not prepared to order him to go. At that time there was no military substitute of sufficient authority. Sir Douglas Haig could not be sent. He was so committed by ideas and loyalty to the front for which he was responsible that he could hardly be expected to review impartially the battlefield as a whole. Sir Henry Wilson was thoroughly disliked and distrusted by the Prime Minister. So that when Sir William Robertson declined to undertake the mission it dealt a sinister blow at the whole project.

The situation in regard to aeroplanes was another of the vital issues which were being muddled and mishandled in a fashion all too symptomatic of the methods of the Government. At that time we had already been discussing for weeks the question of aeroplane production. There was a wasteful rivalry going on between the Army and Navy on the subject. Certain works had been captured by the Navy that ought to be assisting in increasing the much-needed output for the Army. On the Western Front the Germans had regained superiority, especially in attacking and raiding machines, and the military chiefs were clamouring for more aeroplanes of these types.

The Cabinet debates on this issue were so protracted that judgment upon it was never delivered during the lifetime of the Asquith Coalition. The question of responsibility for the manufacture of aeroplanes was raised by Mr. E. S. Montagu on behalf of the Ministry of Munitions in September, 1916. Mr. Montagu was anxious that his Ministry should undertake the manufacture of all the aeroplanes required by both the Army and the Navy. In a memorandum to the Cabinet, he pointed out that: —

"The present organisation, under which the supply of aircraft material is the concern of two bodies—the War Office and the Admiralty—acting under the general supervision of a third—the Air Board—and in constant and inevitable competition with a fourth—the Ministry of Munitions—appears to me to be one for which no arguments can be adduced, and which cannot be expected to obtain satisfactory results. In my opinion it is necessary at once to adopt one of two plans—either to set up a new Supply Department responsible for the entire supply of both Air Services, or to entrust the task of obtaining that supply to the Ministry of Munitions, which was created to meet a situation in regard to munitions similar to that which now appears to exist in regard to aircraft."

The Aviation Board had been set up with a view to co-ordinating the efforts of both Army and Navy. Over this Board Lord Curzon presided. He was strongly opposed to Mr. Montagu's scheme. He admitted that: —

"At this moment a source of urgent anxiety to General Trenchard lies in the appearance on the German Front of two new machines better in certain respects than any which we now possess there. It is not the *number* of these available that concerns him, but the fact of their superiority."

But he claimed that: —

"We are developing fresh engines and fresh aeroplanes which we believe will surpass the recent German production. But the question at issue is, will our machines in fact be superior and will they be developed in time?"

He was clearly of the opinion that a new department should be set up which would have sole and complete control over the production and to a certain extent, the direction of all machinery for aerial warfare.

When Lord Curzon put forward his plan on these lines, he was in turn challenged by Mr. Balfour in a very caustic and amusing memorandum. To this Lord Curzon replied in suitable terms. It was clear that if the controversy did not conduce to the provision of aeroplanes it at least provided excellent entertainment for those who were privileged to read these documents and to hear the discussions. The pleadings took some time. First, the statement of claim by Lord Curzon. Time must be given for the First Lord of the Admiralty to file his defence, then there was a rebutter and surrebutter. An interpleader by the Ministry of Munitions. Then at last the case was set down for trial.

I have a melancholy recollection of Cabinet Committee discussions at this period. The aeroplane case was always first in the list after the usual preliminary reports from the Army and the Navy. Lord Crawford's urgent memorandum on the food position should have come next, and shipping also would have to be discussed, but with such skilled protagonists as Mr. Balfour, Lord Curzon, and Mr. Montagu the time was generally occupied in thrashing out the merits and demerits of the conflicting claims championed by these trained dialecticians. When in despair of conciliating the antagonistic proposals the Prime Minister had a habit of turning round to the mantelpiece to see whether any temporary relief from his perplexities was indicated by the position of the hands on the clock. We all knew what that meant. He was making for a postponement of further discussion to the next meeting. Lord Crawford put in a despairing cry for a few minutes' consideration before lunch of his anxieties about the food of the nation. He pointed out each time that the position was steadily getting worse, that consumption was exceeding supply at a time of the year when the process ought to be reversed. On the other hand, the Prime Minister would point out that it was clear from the hour which had been reached that there was no time left for the discussion of so grave a problem. There was nothing left for Lord Crawford but to plead for a special meeting to consider his difficulties. That meeting never took place in the lifetime of that Administration. At our next meeting came again the aeroplane case (part heard). At the last meeting ever held we all thought that a decision had been arrived at, but as we were dispersing, I saw Lord Curzon standing alongside the Prime Minister and challenging that fact. Mr. Asquith surrendered and said that the case would have to be re-argued at the next meeting. When the next Cabinet meeting took place in Downing Street it was under a different Government.

CHAPTER XXXV

THE CRISIS: DECEMBER 1916

THE upshot of our November peace discussions in the Cabinet had been the decision of the Government not to make peace until the fortunes of the Allies were unchallengeably better than those of the Central Powers. But this decision made it incumbent upon them to take the necessary steps to improve those fortunes before the patience of the Allied nations became exhausted. We had not only to resolve on the prosecution of the War to the utmost limit of our resources, but to take steps to utilise those resources to the best advantage, and especially to see that the great combined strength of all the Allies should not be dissipated and wasted through lack of co-ordinated effort. We had also to make sure that one of the most powerful of the Allies should not retire out of the struggle in a spirit of despair.

At the Paris Conference, M. Briand had pointed to the possibility of exhaustion as one of the perils of the situation. As a matter of fact, we were only a few weeks off the popular uprising in Russia against continuing the sacrifices of the War. Yet in face of this nearing danger there was manifest among our leaders no clearness of vision as to their course, no firmness of leadership and no promptitude or boldness of decision. Their disposition was to leave all vital questions to the Military, Naval or Civilian Organisation in charge of some special war activity, and I felt in my bones that unless some new energy and inspiration were injected into the War direction, we should before long drift into irretrievable disaster. I therefore came to the conclusion that I must act without further delay.

Having regard to the political forces in Parliament, I realised that it was essential that I should carry with me two men—Mr. Bonar Law and Sir Edward Carson. Standing alone I could only bring pressure to bear upon Parliament, and through Parliament upon the Government, by means of a popular agitation conducted with the support of a section of the Press. This would necessarily take time, and might have the effect of discouraging and demoralising public opinion. Russia a few weeks later proved the danger of producing a sense of disillusionment in the public mind, even by justifiable and necessary criticism. It would have reacted on the Army, whose ardour had been temporarily damped by the Somme mud—even more than by the Somme carnage. It was therefore essential that if a change was to be effected in the direction of our war activities it should be achieved with as little disturbance and public agitation as possible.

Of Sir Edward Carson I had seen a good deal through the patriotic good offices of a friend and supporter of his, Sir Arthur Lee—now Lord Lee of Fareham. Sir Edward Carson was convinced that the War was being badly muddled. His few months in the Coalition Cabinet, with its Serbian collapse, its Dardanelles fiasco, and the bloody futilities of our strategy in France and Flanders had the result of deepening his distrust of the Prime Minister's capacity to direct the War. His view was that all the disasters which had befallen the Allies could have been averted but for the Prime Minister's slackness. Mr. Bonar Law on the other hand, having the Scotsman's natural respect for brains, was a great admirer of the Prime Minister, and it took him many months' experience of his obvious tardiness, indecision, and lack of drive in action to come to the conclusion that whatever Mr. Asquith's mental equipment—and of that neither of us had any doubt—he did not possess the qualities that make a great War Minister.

The story of my negotiations with Mr. Bonar Law and Lord Carson has already been told by Lord Beaverbrook in his fascinating book on "Politicians and the War." It is frankly told not from my point of view, but as a vindication of Mr. Bonar Law. Making an allowance for that honourable personal bias, I am prepared on the main facts to accept his narrative. As between Mr. Asquith and myself he is clearly unbiased. He has no personal interest in either of us.

Sir Edward Carson was for pushing Mr. Asquith out of the Premiership. He argued that any shifts like a War Committee, whatever its composition, must necessarily fail so long as the chief responsibility and authority was vested in Mr. Asquith. Certain Ministers whom he named would be constantly at his ear and poisoning him against the new committee, and postponing, modifying, and thwarting its decisions. Mr. Bonar Law was emphatically of the opinion that it was desirable for the sake of preserving the national unity that Mr. Asquith should retain his position of Prime Minister. He dreaded anything like a split in the Cabinet at such a juncture. He was also apprehensive that there might be a division in his own Party if Mr. Asquith were driven out of the Premiership. Most of the Tory Ministers were devoted adherents of Mr. Asquith's leadership in the War. I was also in favour of retaining Mr. Asquith as Prime Minister provided he left the new committee full and unfettered powers to direct the War. It is rather significant that at this stage not one of us (except Sir Edward Carson) contemplated Mr. Asquith's retirement and consequently there was nothing said at any of our interviews as to his possible successor. I wish to confirm Lord Beaverbrook's statement that Lord Northcliffe was never, at any stage, brought into our consultations. He had taken sides with Sir William Robertson against me on my criticism of the military chiefs for the prolongation of the Somme fighting and the failure to avert the Roumanian collapse. He had threatened to attack me in his papers if I continued "to interfere with the soldiers." When he saw that something was going on he made an effort to resume friendly relations. But he was not only left out of the negotiations, but as far as I know he was not informed as to what was actually taking place.

After a good deal of conferring and debating between Mr. Bonar Law, Sir Edward Carson, Lord Beaverbrook and myself, I drew up the following memorandum for submission to the Prime Minister: —

"1st December, 1916.

1.   That the War Committee consist of three members—two of whom must be the First Lord of the Admiralty and the Secretary of State for War, who should have in their offices deputies capable of attending to and deciding all departmental business, and a third Minister without portfolio. One of the three to be Chairman.

2.   That the War Committee shall have full powers, subject to the supreme control of the Prime Minister, to direct all questions connected with the War.

3.   The Prime Minister in his discretion to have the power to refer any question to the Cabinet.

4.   Unless the Cabinet on reference by the Prime Minister reverses decision of the War Committee, that decision to be carried out by the Department concerned.

5.   The War Committee to have the power to invite any Minister, and to summon the expert advisers and officers of any Department to its meetings."

I showed it to Lord Derby who fully approved of its terms.

I then took it to Mr. Asquith, having first of all explained to him fully the reasons that had prompted me to come to the conclusions embodied in my memorandum. He promised to think it over and let me know his views later on in the day. In the evening I received from him the following letter: —

"10 Downing Street.
1st December, 1916.

My dear Lloyd George,
   I have now had time to reflect on our conversation this morning, and to study your memorandum.

Though I do not altogether share your dark estimate, and forecast of the situation, actual and prospective, I am in complete agreement that we have reached a critical situation in the War, and that our own methods of procedure, with the experience which we have gained during the last few months, call for reconsideration and revision.

The two main defects of the War Committee, which has done excellent work, are (1) that its numbers are too large; (2) that there is delay, evasion, and often obstruction, on the part of the Departments in giving effect to its decision. I might with good reason add (3) that it is often kept in ignorance by the Departments of information, essential and even vital, of a technical kind, upon the problems that come before it, and (4) that it is overcharged with duties, many of subordinate bodies.

The result is that I am clearly of opinion that the War Committee should be reconstituted, and its relations to and authority over the Departments be more clearly defined and more effectively asserted.

I come now to your specific proposals. In my opinion, whatever changes are made in the composition or functions of the War Committee, the Prime Minister must be its Chairman. He cannot be relegated to the position of an arbiter in the background or a referee to the Cabinet.

In regard to its composition, I agree that the War Secretary and the First Lord of the Admiralty are necessary members. I am inclined to add to the same category the Minister of Munitions. There should be another member, either without portfolio, or charged only with comparatively light departmental duties. One of the members should be appointed Vice-Chairman.

I purposely do not in this letter discuss the delicate and difficult question of personnel.

The committee should, as far as possible, sit *de die in diem*, and have full power to see that its decisions (subject to appeal to the Cabinet) are carried out promptly and effectively by the Departments.

The reconstitution of the War Committee should be accompanied by the setting up of a Committee of National Organisation to deal with the purely domestic side of war problems. It should have executive powers within its own domain.

The Cabinet would in all cases have ultimate authority.

> Yours always sincerely,
> H. H. ASQUITH."

The reply was entirely unsatisfactory. The Prime Minister's counter proposal would effect no improvement and hardly any change in the position as it stood. The Prime Minister was to preside over the Committee and any Ministers dissatisfied with any of its decisions were entitled to appeal to the Cabinet before any steps were taken to carry them out. Then what about the Committee of National Organisation which was to be set up quite independently of the War Committee to deal with the purely domestic side of War problems?

(1) Would food production and distribution be relegated to it?
(2) What about shipping and ship-building?
(3) Would the question of man-power be left to it?

If these questions were taken out of the cognisance and authority of the War Committee it would have a more limited scope and less power than the existing body of that name.   I felt convinced that Mr. Asquith was resolved not to agree to any change in the War direction. I therefore decided to act without further loss of time and I wrote to Mr. Bonar Law as follows:—

> " War Office,
> Whitehall, S.W.
> 2nd December, 1916.
>
> My dear Bonar,
> I enclose copy of P.M.'s letter.
> The life of the country depends on resolute action by you now.
> Yours ever,
> D. LLOYD GEORGE."

I had seen Mr. Bonar Law late on Friday evening and it was decided that we should go forward with our plan of reorganisation whatever the consequences.   On Saturday and Sunday Mr. Bonar Law was entangled in a series of clumsy manœuvres in which his Conservative colleagues were engaged.   They had lost confidence in Asquith, but they did not want me.   They disliked Carson and had no fanatical belief in Bonar Law.   What were the poor fellows to do?   They had no clear idea themselves.   The story is told in detail by Lord Beaverbrook.   Much of what he relates I learnt for the first time when I read his book.   I could make no further progress until Mr. Bonar Law knew exactly where he stood in reference to the other leaders of his Party.   However, on Sunday afternoon I was asked by the Prime Minister's secretary—Sir Maurice Bonham Carter—to come up from the country to talk things over with his Chief, who was returning from Walmer Castle specially with that object.   At the interview which ensued Mr. Asquith and I discussed the whole situation in the friendliest spirit and ultimately came to a complete understanding. The terms of that arrangement are given by Mr. Asquith in the letter he wrote me the following morning.   As soon as the agreement was reached he sent for Mr. Bonar Law to inform him of the " complete agreement " arrived at.   I met Mr. Bonar Law on my way out.   The Prime Minister and I were to meet on Monday to discuss the personnel of the new committee.   On that question I anticipated no insuperable difficulty.   The Monday meeting never came off and I was never privileged to meet Mr. Asquith as Prime Minister again.

In the Monday morning papers there appeared the following announcement:—

"The Prime Minister, with a view to the most active prosecution of the War, had decided to advise His Majesty the King to consent to a reconstruction of the Government."

Some time in the course of the morning I received the following letter from the Prime Minister:—

> "10, Downing Street, S.W.
> 4th December, 1916.
>
> My dear Lloyd George,
>   Such productions as the first leading article in to-day's *Times*, showing the infinite possibilities for misunderstanding and misrepresentation of such an arrangement as we considered yesterday, made me at least doubtful as to its feasibility. Unless the impression is at once corrected that I am being relegated to the position of an irresponsible spectator of the War, I cannot go on.
>   The suggested arrangement was to the following effect: The Prime Minister to have supreme and effective control of war policy.
>   The agenda of the War Committee will be submitted to him; its Chairman will report to him daily; he can direct it to consider particular topics or proposals; and all its conclusions will be subject to his approval or veto. He can, of course, at his own discretion attend meetings of the Committee.
> > Yours sincerely,
> > H. H. ASQUITH."

When I read that letter I felt the Prime Minister had completely changed his tone. There was none of the cordiality and friendliness which had characterised our Sunday conversation. I had not seen *The Times* article of which he complained, and I certainly had no responsibility for it. I had not communicated any information as to the negotiations which were going on with Mr. Asquith or the agreement arrived at with him, to the proprietor or editor of that paper, either directly or indirectly.* I was frankly too pleased with the idea that a break had been averted on terms which gave some chance of putting new energy into our war activities to do anything that would imperil the completion of the new arrangement. I replied:—

> "War Office,
> Whitehall, S.W.
> December 4, 1916.
>
> My dear Prime Minister,
>   I have not seen *The Times* article. But I hope you will not attach undue importance to these effusions. I have had these misrepresentations to put up with for months. Northcliffe frankly

---

* Lord Beaverbrook makes this quite clear in his narrative of these events. *Vide* "Politicians and the War."

wants a smash. Derby and I do not. Northcliffe would like to make this and any other rearrangement under your Premiership impossible. Derby and I attach great importance to your retaining your present position—effectively. I cannot restrain, or, I fear, influence Northcliffe. I fully accept in letter and in spirit your summary of the suggested arrangement—subject, of course, to personnel.

Ever sincerely,
D. LLOYD GEORGE."

During that Monday I pressed for my promised appointment with the Prime Minister. I was constantly put off by his secretaries. At last I was promised an interview at six o'clock. That interview was never accorded. Here is a facsimile of a note sent in by my private secretary, late in the afternoon to me in my room at the War Office:—

" War Office,
Whitehall, S.W.
Bonham Carter says that the Prime Minister does not think he will trouble you to come over to-night. He is going to write."

Meanwhile the Prime Minister was engaged in a series of interviews with all my colleagues (Liberal and Conservative) who were hostile to the new Committee. He even summoned a formal meeting of all the Liberal Members of the Cabinet to discuss the situation. It was to take place at the hour fixed for my interview. Mr. Arthur Henderson was also invited to attend. I received no invitation to attend that meeting to explain my position, although I was still a member of the Cabinet and had done nothing to forfeit my right to be summoned to a conference of the Liberal Section. My last act had been to agree with the Prime Minister on the very issue which was to be discussed at the meeting.

On Tuesday morning I received the following letter from the Prime Minister:—

" 10, Downing Street, S.W.
December 4, 1916.

My dear Lloyd George,
   Thank you for your letter of this morning.
   The King gave me to-day authority to ask and accept the resignations of all my colleagues, and to form a new Government on such lines as I should submit to him. I start, therefore, with a clean slate.
   The first question which I have to consider is the constitution of the new War Committee.
   After full consideration of the matter in all its aspects, I have come decidedly to the conclusion that it is not possible that such a Committee could be made workable and effective without the Prime Minister as its Chairman. I quite agree that it will be

necessary for him, in view of the other calls upon his time and energy, to delegate from time to time the chairmanship to another Minister as his representative and *locum tenens*; but (if he is to retain the authority, which corresponds to his responsibility, as Prime Minister) he must continue to be, as he always has been, its permanent President. I am satisfied, on reflection, that any other arrangement (such, for instance, as the one which I indicated to you in my letter of to-day) would be found in experience impracticable, and incompatible with the retention of the Prime Minister's final and supreme control.

The other question, which you have raised, relates to the personnel of the Committee. Here again, after deliberate consideration, I find myself unable to agree with some of your suggestions.

I think we both agree that the First Lord of the Admiralty must, of necessity, be a member of the Committee.

I cannot (as I told you yesterday) be a party to any suggestion that Mr. Balfour should be displaced. The technical side of the Board of Admiralty has been reconstituted, with Sir John Jellicoe as First Sea Lord. I believe Mr. Balfour to be, under existing conditions, the necessary head of the Board.

I must add that Sir Edward Carson (for whom, personally, and in every other way, I have the greatest regard) is not, from the only point of view which is significant to me (namely, the most effective prosecution of the War), the man best qualified among my colleagues, present and past, to be a member of the War Committee.

I have only to say, in conclusion, that I am strongly of opinion that the War Committee (without any disparagement of the existing Committee, which, in my judgment, is a most efficient body, and has done, and is doing, invaluable work) ought to be reduced in number; so that it can sit more frequently, and overtake more easily the daily problems with which it has to deal. But in any reconstruction of the Committee, such as I have, and have for some time past had, in view, the governing consideration, to my mind, is the special capacity of the men who are to sit on it for the work which it has to do.

That is a question which I must reserve for myself to decide.

Yours very sincerely,
H. H. Asquith."

The letter was a complete repudiation of the agreement he had entered into with me on Sunday and confirmed in writing on Monday. He had reached his decision to go back on his word without giving me an opportunity of further discussion with him. He saw all the critics. He resolutely refused to see me although he had promised to do so. Had I gone back on my word I know the nature of the comment that would have been passed on me by those who worked with frenzy to persuade Mr. Asquith to break faith. How it would have fitted into that legend of distrust which they so assiduously worked up for years, and which seems to be their sole article of unwavering faith!

I therefore felt bound to send him the following reply:—

> " War Office,
> Whitehall, S.W.
> December 5, 1916.
>
> My dear Prime Minister,
>
> I have received your letter with some surprise. On Friday I made proposals which involved not merely your retention of the Premiership, but the supreme control of the War, whilst the executive functions, subject to that supreme control, were left to others. I thought you then received these suggestions favourably. In fact, you yourself proposed that I should be the chairman of this Executive Committee, although, as you know, I never put forward that demand. On Saturday you wrote me a letter in which you completely went back on that proposition. You sent for me on Sunday and put before me other proposals; these proposals you embodied in a letter to me written on Monday:—
>
>> ' The Prime Minister to have supreme and effective control of war policy;
>>
>> The Agenda of the War Committee will be submitted to him; its chairman will report to him daily; he can direct it to consider particular topics or proposals and all its conclusions will be subject to his approval or veto. He can, of course, at his own discretion attend meetings of the Committee.'
>
> These proposals safeguarded your position and power as Prime Minister in every particular. I immediately wrote you accepting them ' in letter and in spirit.' It is true that on Sunday I expressed views as to the constitution of the Committee, but these were for discussion. To-day you have gone back on your own proposals.
>
> I have striven my utmost to cure the obvious defects of the War Committee without overthrowing the Government. As you are aware, on several occasions during the last two years I have deemed it my duty to express profound dissatisfaction with the Government's method of conducting the War. Many a time, with the road to victory open in front of us, we have delayed and hesitated whilst the enemy were erecting barriers that finally checked the approach. There has been delay, hesitation, lack of forethought and vision. I have endeavoured repeatedly to warn the Government of the dangers, both verbally and in written memoranda and letters, which I crave your leave now to publish if my action is challenged; but I have either failed to secure decisions or I have secured them when

it was too late to avert the evils.   The latest illustration is our lamentable failure to give timely support to Roumania.

I have more than once asked to be released from my responsibility for a policy with which I was in thorough disagreement, but at your urgent personal request I remained in the Government.   I realise that when the country is in peril of a great war, Ministers have not the same freedom to resign on disagreement.   At the same time I have always felt—and felt deeply—that I was in a false position inasmuch as I could never defend in a whole-hearted manner the action of a Government of which I was a member.   We have thrown away opportunity after opportunity, and I am convinced, after deep and anxious reflection, that it is my duty to leave the Government in order to inform the people of the real condition of affairs, and to give them an opportunity, before it is too late, to save their native land from a disaster which is inevitable if the present methods are longer persisted in.   As all delay is fatal in war, I place my office without further parley at your disposal.

It is with great personal regret that I have come to this conclusion. In spite of mean and unworthy insinuations to the contrary—insinuations which I fear are always inevitable in the case of men who hold prominent but not primary positions in any administration—I have felt a strong personal attachment to you as my Chief.   As you yourself said on Sunday, we have acted together for ten years and never had a quarrel, although we have had many a grave difference on questions of policy.   You have treated me with great courtesy and kindness; for all that I thank you.   Nothing would have induced me to part now except an overwhelming sense that the course of action which has been pursued has put the country—and not merely the country, but throughout the world, the principles for which you and I have always stood throughout our political lives—in the greatest peril that has ever overtaken them.

As I am fully conscious of the importance of preserving national unity, I propose to give your Government complete support in the vigorous prosecution of the War; but unity without action is nothing but futile carnage, and I cannot be responsible for that.   Vigour and vision are the supreme need at this hour.

Yours sincerely,
D. Lloyd George."

His reply and the further correspondence that ensued will explain the progress of events that terminated the life of the Asquith Coalition.

" 10 Downing Street, S.W.
December 5, 1916.

My dear Lloyd George,
I need not tell you that I have read your letter of to-day with much regret.

I do not comment upon it for the moment, except to say that I cannot wholly accept your account of what passed between us in regard to my connection with the War Committee. In particular, you have omitted to quote the first and most material part of my letter of yesterday.

Yours very sincerely,

H. H. ASQUITH."

" In the meantime, I feel sure that you will see the obvious necessity in the public interest of not publishing at this moment any part of our correspondence."

" War Office, Whitehall, S.W.

December 5, 1916.

My dear Prime Minister,

I cannot announce my resignation without assigning the reason. Your request that I should not publish the correspondence that led up to and necessitated it places me therefore in an embarrassing and unfair position. I must give reasons for the grave step I have taken. If you forbid publication of the correspondence, do you object to my stating in another form my version of the causes that led to my resigning?

Yours sincerely,

D. LLOYD GEORGE."

" As to the first part of your letter, the publication of the letters would cover the whole ground."

" 10, Downing Street, S.W.

December 5, 1916.

My dear Lloyd George,

It may make a difference to you (in reply to your last letter) if I tell you at once that I have tendered my resignation to the King.

In any case, I should deprecate in the public interest the publication in its present form at this moment of your letters to me of this morning.

Of course, I have neither the power nor the wish to prevent your stating in some other form the causes which have led you to take the step which you have taken.

Yours very sincerely,

H. H. ASQUITH."

On Mr. Asquith's resignation, Mr. Bonar Law was summoned by the King and entrusted with the task of forming an Administration. His first suggestion to the Sovereign was that he should summon some of the leading figures in the recent discussions with Mr. Balfour and Mr. Henderson to Buckingham Palace to see whether it was not possible to avoid any break in the unity of the nation by constituting a National Government under the leadership of Mr. Balfour. It is now a matter of history how we expressed our readiness to serve under Mr. Balfour—all of us except Mr. Asquith, who asked indignantly " What is the proposal? That I who have held first place for eight years should be asked to take a secondary position." This broke up the conference. Mr. Asquith subsequently refused to serve in a Bonar Law Administration. Mr. Bonar Law then declined to undertake the responsibility of forming a Ministry and recommended the King to send for me. This course he took in spite of the advice given him to the contrary by Mr. Balfour, Sir Edward Carson, and myself. I neither sought nor desired the Premiership. I knew that in the circumstances my elevation to that position would be skilfully misrepresented. I also knew that a War Committee in a Bonar Law Administration from which the obstructive elements had been kept out, had an excellent chance of working smoothly and effectively, and I felt confident that Mr. Bonar Law would give me a free hand and extend to me the support of a loyal chief, which was all I desired. However, Mr. Bonar Law refused to listen to our combined entreaties, and I had to undertake the terrible responsibility of Premiership in a muddled war, with at least half my own party and more than half the Labour Party bitterly hostile, and a considerable section of the Tory Party—including most of their leaders—suspicious and distrustful.

I surveyed the possibilities. I was assured of the support of something under one half the Liberal Members in the House. Every Conservative Minister in the Government, except Mr. Bonar Law, and as I subsequently discovered, Mr. Balfour, was hostile to my Premiership. The attitude of Labour was doubtful, but not altogether antagonistic. I was satisfied that I would receive the active co-operation of Mr. Bonar Law and Sir Edward Carson (much the most influential leaders in the Conservative Party as far as its rank and file was concerned) and Lord Milner—who carried great weight with the Tory intelligentsia and Die-Hards (not by any means identical groups). If I secured the adhesion of Mr. Balfour I felt that I could risk the opposition of the other Conservative mandarins. I felt he had neither the energy, initiative, nor the administrative gifts requisite for the position of First Lord of the Admiralty at such a critical moment. His elimination from the Admiralty was an unwritten demand I had submitted to Mr. Asquith. Mr. Balfour had been told by Mr. Asquith of the adverse view I had formed of his administration of the Navy, and of my request for his removal. Nevertheless, I have since discovered that he supported my demand for a change in the War direction and refused to join in a reconstruction of the Ministry under Mr. Asquith.

As he said in letters written at the time to the Prime Minister, after he had been informed of my objection to his retaining Office at the Admiralty: " We cannot, I think, go on in the old way. I still think (a) that the break-up of the Government by the retirement of Lloyd

George would be a misfortune; (*b*) that the experiment of giving him a free hand with the day-to-day work of the War Committee is worth trying; and (*c*) that there is no use trying it except on terms which would enable him to work under conditions which in his own opinion promise the best results." He ended by insisting that his resignation should be accepted and " that a fair trial should be given to the new War Council à la George."

I knew nothing of these letters at the time. I only knew that I tried to get Mr. Balfour out of the Admiralty and that as this disagreeable fact would in all probability be communicated to him, an approach to him under these conditions was not very hopeful. I confess that I underrated the passionate attachment to his country which burnt under that calm, indifferent, and apparently frigid exterior.

Mr. Balfour was then ill in bed. Mr. Bonar Law undertook to sound him. He went to offer him the post of Foreign Secretary. He accepted it without any of the hesitations and portentous declarations of his patriotic duty which smaller and less sincere men might have indulged in—and later on did. But as Mr. Bonar Law was leaving, Mr. Balfour suddenly turned to him and said: " Would you mind telling me why Lloyd George was so anxious to get me out of the Admiralty?" Mr. Bonar Law answered with his usual bluntness:, " You had better ask him yourself."

Quite recently I discovered that my objections to his retaining office at the Admiralty were a source of hurtful perplexity to him up to his last days. He thought I resented the report he issued to the Press of the much debated battle of Jutland. That report undoubtedly conveyed the impression even to friendly minds that the victory was debatable. My reasons for thinking he was not the best selection for the Admiralty had no reference to this episode. The First Lord during a Great War ought to be a man of exhaustless industry and therefore of great physical energy and reserve. It was an office that called for unceasing attention to detail. It meant long hours, early and late. Mr. Balfour was obviously unsuitable for such a post.

As I have mentioned previously, the story of the first five days of December, 1916, and of the efforts I made to bring about a new system in the direction of war—efforts which, quite contrary to my intention, culminated in a change of Government and the retirement of Mr. Asquith—has already been told very graphically and in considerable detail by Lord Beaverbrook in the second volume of his " Politicians and the War." His account presents the story from the point of view of himself and of Mr. Bonar Law. Naturally, the events were seen by me at the time from a somewhat different angle, but there is no difference of substance between us as to the main features and stages of that crisis.

There was a tragic bitterness about the situation which developed through those days, and which forced a cleavage between me and colleagues with most of whom I had for long years been working in the happiest and most fruitful collaboration—a cleavage later on aggravated and perpetuated by the malice of petty-minded men with baneful effects on the future political development of our country. But even at the worst it had its brighter aspects. One was that it brought Mr. Bonar Law and myself into a close partnership, and laid the foundations of a mutual understanding and real friendship which is one of the happiest of my political memories.

From the moment I was invited by the King to form a Government I was so overwhelmed with urgent affairs, which brooked no delay, that I found no opportunity for presenting to the public my reasons for the course of action which ended in the downfall of the Asquith Administration. It was not merely the time occupied in the actual formation of the Government. That took a few days of interviewing, negotiating and adjusting. And here I would like to pay a tribute to the tact, the wisdom and loyalty with which both Mr. Bonar Law and I were assisted in this difficult and even dangerous task by Sir Edmund Talbot (now Lord FitzAlan). He smoothed many difficulties and probably averted many indiscretions.

The moment the Government was formed there were many pressing matters to attend to which ought to have been settled many months ago. The campaign for 1917 had already been settled before I became Prime Minister. But there were many urgent questions which demanded immediate decision and prompt action. The production of aeroplanes—the food supplies of the country—the protection of our ships and the development of ship-building—the better mobilisation of the man-power of this country—the mission to Russia, too long delayed—the German peace move—and afterwards President Wilson's peace notes; these constituted but a part of the calls upon the attention of the War Cabinet. In these circumstances Mr. Bonar Law and I could not enter into a controversy upon the causes that led to the recent crisis. Apart from that consideration, we came to the conclusion that it was not desirable to have discussions upon personal matters which might endanger the national unity and imperil national co-operation. Neither of us therefore issued any statement on the subject. Had we done so we knew we could not have left it there, as we should have been bound to reply to inevitable criticisms and comments from those who were now freed from the cares and burden of office and who had more time, and, as it turned out, more inclination to dwell upon these things.

As far as Mr. Bonar Law was concerned the decision was probably the right one. But there is no doubt that my influence in the Liberal Party suffered severely from my neglect to put my case before opinions had hardened and prejudices had been created. Misrepresentations were soon broadcast throughout the land, and time was given for them to strike root in the soil, and when I regained leisure it was too late to eradicate them. Most of this work was done privately at confidential gatherings of Liberal associations throughout the country. Missionaries were dispatched from Headquarters at Abingdon Street to every district to spread tendentious reports of the origin, motives and methods of the crisis. At secret conclaves much could be said which the presence of a newspaper reporter would have checked. Some salient facts were suppressed; others were distorted, and when I resumed my political activities after the War was over, I was amazed at the beliefs that were current as to what had really happened. When I asked Mr. Asquith for permission to publish the correspondence, he had, as is shown in the above correspondence, refused to accede to my request on public grounds. I was rather surprised to find, when he came to address Liberal Members a few days after his resignation and to explain to them why he resigned, that he summarised some of the passages from his own letters and actually quoted some in full, whilst he omitted altogether to communicate to his hearers the statements I made in reply. His reason for doing so was:—

" I will not read his letter because it is private; it was written very confidentially."

He did not think it necessary in the interest of fair play to explain that I had asked him for permission to publish my letter, and that he had refused. He conveyed the impression to them that the Sunday agreement was not an agreement at all, but merely a proposal for further discussion. He never informed them that he told Mr. Bonar Law after our Sunday interview that he and I had agreed on terms, and that the only question left for further debate was that of personnel; that he had made the same statement that very evening to Mr. Montagu and to Lord Reading. He never informed the meeting that on Monday I had repeatedly asked to see him and that he had declined to give me an interview, nor did he inform them of the important fact that a meeting of all the Liberal Members of the Cabinet had been summoned on Monday night to consider the position and that I had not been invited to attend the meeting. He withheld from them the fact that at a conference at Buckingham Palace presided over by the King he had refused to serve in a National Ministry under the Premiership of Mr. Balfour, although Mr. Bonar Law, Mr. Henderson, and myself were quite prepared to do so. Nor did he tell them that when Mr. Bonar Law was entrusted with the task of forming a National Government he had refused, after consultation with his Liberal colleagues, to join it. It was obvious that, if these vital facts had been communicated to those Members who had assembled at the Reform Club, they would have taken a different view of the transaction. Unfortunately, we allowed a very one-sided statement to go by default, and the truncated statement, because it was unchallenged,

U*

was accepted by the majority of Liberals in the country as a fair account of what had happened.

I will only give one example of the kind of thing which influenced Liberals against me at that time. Here is a speech delivered by Mr. Runciman to his constituents immediately after he left office:—

> "In re-forming the Government the present Prime Minister invited his Unionist colleagues to rejoin him. He invited the Labour Party to join him, and he gave an invitation to one Liberal Minister. I was not that one. I have been asked by my constituents already why I did not join the new Government. I can only make the simple reply that it was impossible to accept an invitation which I had not received."[*]

Surely there never has been a better example of *suppressio veri*. Had Mr. Runciman told his constituents that he was one of those who had agreed at the meeting of Liberal Ministers on Monday night not to take office under anyone except Mr. Asquith, and that at the meeting when that decision was reached the question of my Premiership was discussed as the alternative; had he informed them that he was one of those who advised Mr. Asquith not to serve under any other Premier, quite a different impression would have been conveyed to the minds of his electors. He clearly wished them to believe that whereas I was inviting Conservative and Labour men to join my Government, I wantonly and deliberately ruled out all my former colleagues except one.

[*] How busy I was may be inferred from the fact that I read the speeches of Mr. Asquith and Mr. Runciman for the first time when I came to write this story.

CHAPTER XXXVI

SOME PERSONAL SKETCHES

1. MR. ASQUITH

I RECOLLECT Lord Morley once saying to me: "Asquith ought to have been a judge. He would have made a great one. I remember," he said, " a conversation I had recently with Arthur Acland about early days when Acland, Asquith and I used to meet together often to discuss politics, and I said what a pleasant fellow he was. Acland replied, ' Yes, but did you ever hear him make any suggestion of his own?' I had to confess that although he discussed every proposition advanced by others with great intelligence and force, he never submitted any ideas of his own for our consideration." Asquith undoubtedly had not only the mind, but the temperament of a judge. I hardly ever met him before we entered the same Cabinet together. But during the 11 years we were members of the same Governments —Campbell-Bannerman's and his own Administration—I had ample opportunities of seeing him. I always had an unqualified admiration for his unrivalled gifts of lucid and logical statement—his command of choice words and his sledge-hammer rhetoric. When I came to know him as a colleague, and especially when I served under him as my Chief, my admiration widened and deepened. His massive and well-ordered intellect worked with the precision and directness of a perfect and powerful machine. But he waited until propositions were submitted to him. He never drove or initiated; he decided on schemes when they were placed before him. He never surveyed the needs of the country and devised means for supplying them, in peace or war. He dealt with questions not as they arose but as they were presented to him. But there his judgment was beyond that of any political leader I ever met. He started no new plans, but he was not afraid of examining any projects if they were placed before him clearly, and left on his logical mind an impression of having been well considered beforehand. He was always essentially the judge. When he accepted a plan he used his great authority to obtain for it Cabinet sanction. And when it came to commending the scheme to the acceptance of the House of Commons, there was such inevitability in the presentation that it left critics wondering why they ever doubted. Such a mind was invaluable in the conduct of affairs when peace reigned and there were no emergencies demanding originality, resource and initiative. It was specially useful for a Cabinet where there were several able men full of ideas to which they were anxious to give administrative or legislative effect. But for the deluge, Noah was better adapted than Gamaliel would have been. Had there been no war, the Asquith Administration would to the end have stood as high in the annals of wise, fruitful and beneficent rule as any Government that ever existed in this country, and its capable chief would have been a worthy figure on the pedestal of distinguished achievements, which, by his special gifts, he had made possible. Such a pedestal he will always occupy. The 1906-14 Cabinet was one of the ablest councils that ever directed the affairs of any great country in times of peace.

But war demands other attributes. The part which political chiefs ought to take in the conduct of a war is a very debatable question. The line of demarcation has never been drawn, probably because there ought not to be any rigid line. So much depends on conditions which are never alike in any two wars and vary and fluctuate from time to time in the course of the same war. So much also depends on the personalities engaged, whether civilian or military. Lincoln interfered a good deal with McLellan, but he gave Grant a free hand. There never has been a war where civilian action and impulse was so essential to success as the Great War of 1914-18.

In these volumes I have indicated directions in which civilian aid in the organisation of our military strength was found to be indispensable, and some where civilian advice taken in time might have averted disaster. There are certain indispensable qualities essential to the Chief Minister of the Crown in a great war. I do not propose to give an exhaustive schedule of these essential qualities, but such a Minister must have courage, composure, and judgment. All this Mr. Asquith possessed in a superlative degree. He gave dignified but not rousing and vigorous leadership to the nation. But a War Minister must also have vision, imagination and initiative—he must show untiring assiduity, must exercise constant oversight and supervision of every sphere of war activity, must possess driving force to energise this activity, must be in continuous consultation with experts, official and unofficial, as to the best means of utilising the resources of the country in conjunction with Allies for the achievement of victory. If to this can be added a flair for conducting a great fight, then you have an ideal War Minister. Mr. Asquith at his best did not answer sufficiently to this description to make him a successful Chief Minister in a war which demanded all these qualities strained to the utmost. But apart from these shortcomings the nerve of the Prime Minister at this time was clearly giving out, and he gave the impression of a man who was overwhelmed, distracted and enfeebled not merely by the weight, but by the variety and complexity of his burdens. Whether he was ever fitted for the position of a War Minister in the greatest struggle in the history of the world may be open to doubt, but that he was quite unfitted at this juncture to undertake so supreme a task was not open to any question or challenge on the part of anyone who came constantly in contact with him at the time.

Asquith's will became visibly flabbier, tardier and more flaccid under the strain of the War. Then came the personal tragedy which shattered his nerve. The death of his brilliant son, Raymond, came upon him with stunning effect, and he visibly reeled under the blow. It came at a time when he needed all the calm poise and firmness of mind which man can command. For a crisis had arisen where statesmanship had to intervene, decide and direct. It was a misfortune for Britain that the great statesman who had the supreme responsibility was less equal to his task than he had ever been in the whole course of his distinguished career. Mr. Bonar Law, who was well disposed to him, was of that opinion and expressed it repeatedly in the course of the conversations I held with him.

2. LORD HALDANE

Haldane was a baffling personality. In private he talked incessantly—in public he talked volubly and at interminable length on any subject. His speaking was a rapid, thin stream of involved wordiness tinkling along monotonously. Nevertheless, with all his loquaciousness he was a doer of things. He was essentially a man of ideas which he carried out, but could not explain succinctly. That accounted for his wordiness. In spite of that defect, this garrulous lawyer was a man of action. There was one gathering at which he hardly ever spoke, and that was the Cabinet. He was almost its most silent member. He was by common agreement the best War Minister since Cardwell. He organised the Expeditionary Force which helped to save Paris; he founded the Territorial Army which helped the remnants of our regular army to hold the sodden trenches of Flanders until the new recruits arrived; he was responsible for the Officers' Cadet Corps which gave the Kitchener Army its intelligent young lieutenants; it was he who had the idea that the War Office would be all the better if it had a thinking machine, and so he worked out a General Staff. It was no fault of his that Lord Kitchener decided to dispense with it. On Education he was full of practical suggestions, some of which fructified. He had boundless energy. He always wanted to be doing something. A combination of ideas and energy is tiresome to the complacent. He was, therefore, viewed with distrust by that class of politician. Once Haldane had an idea he worked without cease and resorted to every device and expedient to put it through. The sterile and the indolent cannot distinguish between intrigue and action—so Haldane passed for an intriguer.

Of all the great political personalities he was the kindliest I met. Although I liked him well, I was never one of his special friends. We belonged to different, and at one time, very antagonistic sections of the Party. He was a " Liberal Imp " and I was a " pro-Boer." But his abandonment by men who were his devoted friends—at least by men to whom he was devoted—at the instigation of the fussy and noisy patriots that always dance around the flag as if they owned it, was one of the meanest betrayals in British history.

The British people are fundamentally just. Had his powerful friends stood up for him, pointed out his record of service to his country in this war, shown how flimsy were the imputations of un-patriotic leanings against him, there would have been a reaction in his favour, and the Tory leaders could not have dared to refuse co-operation because the man who organised the Expeditionary Force and the Territorials remained in the Government. Haldane was a brave and unselfish man. He never whined or complained about his treatment. All the same, it shook him. I rarely saw him after he left office. But I have the memory of seeing a man bent and bowed, walking slowly from his house in Queen Anne's Gate towards the Privy Council, where he sat as a Judge.

3. LORD BALFOUR

When I first saw Mr. Balfour he was at the height of his popularity and unpopularity. It was when I entered the House of Commons in 1890. He was then easily the most acclaimed statesman on the Unionist side of the House, and it follows that he was the most detested figure amongst the Home Rulers. To the former he was the embodiment of strength and to the latter the incarnation of brutality. The ruthlessness with which he ruled Ireland would not have given him his Parliamentary pre-eminence had it not been accompanied by consummate dexterity in defending his actions on the floor of the House. He was confronted by a phalanx of brilliant Irish speakers who commanded every weapon of effective Parliamen-tary criticism—eloquence, humour and invective—not forgetting imagination. With these weapons they had pierced and slashed all his predecessors and left them bleeding, exhausted and disfigured. Mr. Balfour proved to be more than a match for the best and for all of them. He beat them at the game at which they were such masters. I am told that on the platform he was always a halting and ineffective speaker, but from 1887 up to the end of his Premiership in 1905 he was the most skilful of all the House of Commons speakers of his day, with the exception of the greatest of all Parliamentary gladiators, Mr. Gladstone. My first encounter with him was in the Session of 1902. He piloted through the House of Commons a measure which provoked the most protracted resistance ever offered up to that time to any Bill, the Education Act of 1902. Day after day for the better part of six months Mr. Balfour piloted this Bill through the House against a pertinacious opposition in which I constituted one of the most tireless and tiresome elements. At the end of the struggle we were friends. That friendship I retained and valued to the end of his days.

His weakness as a democratic leader came out in the Free Trade controversy of 1903-06. His mentality was too detached for the zeal that is born of unquestioning faith without facts. He did not believe that Tariffs would ruin our commerce. Neither had he any fervid conviction that they would enhance our prosperity. In his heart he thought the protagonists on both sides were exaggerating their case. As fully 90 per cent. of his party were enthusiastic supporters of Mr. Chamberlain's protectionist proposals, a statesman who took Mr. Balfour's point of view could offer but indifferent leadership in the raging and tearing propaganda which alone could bring victory to the lot of his party in such a cause. The defeat of 1906 was virtually the end of his leadership. He lingered on as a nominal but distrusted leader until the two disastrous elections of 1910 drove him out, with a savage howl from the die-hard jungle ringing at his heels. He then retired gracefully and finally to the honoured seclusion of Elder Statesmanship. In his capacity he rendered more enduring service to his country than in the more dazzling positions he had hitherto held. His achievements in this rôle culminated with the Washington Conference of 1922, when he represented Britain at the first (and so far the only) Disarmament Conference that ever succeeded in disarming. On many an occasion his vast and varied experience coupled with a discerning and mature intellect illumined counsel in dark days. During the War his unfailing courage steadied faltering spirits in hours of doubt and dread. There were times of weariness, many of depression, a few of genuine dismay during that terrible world conflict. When these occurred I have seen men who were reckoned by their public to be inflexible show signs of bending —but never Mr. Balfour. He was not daunted at the worst moments. It was in council that he revealed his strength and his weakness. He listened intently to all that was said, but since his hearing had been dulled by advancing age he failed sometimes to catch the words of speakers around the table who either pitched their voices too low or articulated indistinctly—a very elementary and painful fault with most English speakers. Mr. Balfour himself was always clear and resonant. Mr. Bonar Law was an egregious example of the first defect. You could barely hear him at the Cabinet a yard off. Mr. Balfour would rise from his place and stand by the speaker, and when the latter finished his observations he returned to his seat. When his turn came to express an opinion he carefully and lucidly marshalled the arguments for taking a given course, and anyone not accustomed to his methods would have thought he was weighing in heavily on that side. Then came the inevitable "but on the other hand" and the Cabinet listened to an equally logical and well-informed presentation of the case against. He then paused, threw up his head, looked vaguely at the window and in hesitant tones would say, "But if you ask me what course I think we ought to take then I must say I feel perplexed." Often have I heard him discuss matters on these lines. He saw both sides too clearly to be able to come readily to a conclusion. He gave the impression of a man who thought it really did not matter so much which of the two courses you took so long as you stuck to it afterwards. So therefore it was for us to choose and he would abide by the decision. This kind of mentality baffled and occasionally fretted Clemenceau, the man who never had doubts, not even about religion. I recollect at the Versailles War Council in 1918 an important question being relegated to the Foreign Secretary for decision. They met and placed Mr. Balfour in the Chair. When the time came for them to report to the Council M. Clemenceau called upon Mr. Balfour. The latter, as was his wont, gave a string of reasons on both sides and then stopped. M. Clemenceau threw up his heavy eyebrows in astonishment, opened his eyes wide, and said, "C'est fini?" Mr. Balfour replied, "Oui, monsieur." Then Clemenceau retorted snappishly in English: "But are you for or against?" Mr. Balfour had evidently not decided and seemed unprepared for an answer. Ultimately he reported against.

I know nothing of his habit of mind in the days of his prime. At the time of his famous Irish Secretaryship he must have been capable of prompt and relentless decision. He then displayed all the highest qualities of a man of action, not only in his repressive but in his constructive measures. On Land Settlement, Cottage Holdings, Harbours and Rural Development he was a man who did bold things in Ireland, and some of the poorest areas bear witness to this day of his beneficent thought and action. I was an opponent of certain parts of his great Education Act of 1902. There can be no doubt as to the determination with which he drove through a measure which revolutionised popular education in England and Wales. Even in the later days, when he had not supreme responsibility for the direction of affairs, and when he therefore took things easily, he could now and again rise to the heights of great decisions. His conduct of the Washington Naval Conference in 1921-22 affords indubitable proof of his capacity to decide when he was confronted with a dilemma which he also had the authority to solve. But at committees and Cabinets, where he was not called upon to act, the picture I have given of him fairly represents his methods of contributing to discussion. It would be a mistake to infer from this that he was worthless in council. You might as well say that the summing-up of an able judge has no value because it is impartial and gives no direction to the jury as to the verdict they should bring in. He often placed before us considerations on both sides which all the rest of us might have overlooked. His summing-up was looked forward to by all his colleagues as a means of understanding the real points at issue and the strength of the arguments for and against any given decision. His was a trained mind of the finest quality, of the ripest experience, of the greatest penetration, piercing and dissecting problems and laying them bare before his colleagues for their examination and judgment.

I can quite understand why the attribute which made him helpful in council completely disqualified him for Party leadership. Yet for all these doubts and hesitancies he was a brave man—and a fearless one. In comparatively small things he shrank from conclusions and thus gave a false impression of irresolution, but on fundamental issues he never flinched or meandered. He was through and through a patriot and never lost confidence in the invincibility of his country. He lacked the physical energy, the fertility of resource and untiring industry for the administration of the Admiralty during the Great War, but even the woeful tale of increasing sinkings of our ships by German submarines and the apparent impotence of the admirals to stop the disastrous process did not daunt him. His one comment after hearing the admirals read out the list of sinkings for the previous day was: " It is very tiresome. These Germans are intolerable." He had no notion how the German attack on our shipping could be circumvented. He only assumed that sooner or later it would be done. Meanwhile, the losses were " tiresome." Clearly he was not the man to stimulate and organise the activity of the Navy in a crisis. But he was an ideal man for the Foreign Office and to assist the Cabinet on big issues. His contributions in the War and afterwards in the making of Peace were of the highest order. In personal charm he was easily first among all the statesmen with whom I came in contact. As to his intellectual gifts I doubt whether I ever met so illuminating an intelligence inside the Council Chamber.

4. LORD CARSON

Driving with Lord Robert Cecil from Paris to Sir Douglas Haig's headquarters, amongst an infinite variety of topics out of which we made conversation, we came to the great advocates of the day. Lord Robert had no hesitation in expressing the opinion that Sir Edward Carson was in his judgment the greatest. I asked him if he had heard Sir Charles Russell. He replied that he had but did not think him equal to Carson. I never heard Sir Edward Carson in the courts, but for nigh unto a generation I saw and witnessed his methods, and felt his personality in the House of Commons. I could well understand his power over a jury. He had the supreme gift of getting

to the point that mattered in the formation of opinion and of presenting and pressing it with the words, voice and emphasis that moved
those who heard him in the direction he wished their sentiments to
travel. I could also appreciate the terrible force of his cross-examination—the penetration which enabled him to see the real weakness of
his opponent's case, the weakness of the story told by the witness and
the weakness of the witness himself, the grim and relentless skill to
pursue until the prey is at his mercy, and the dramatic force which
prostrates or destroys.

I saw something of these gifts in his war contribution. As soon
as he joined the Asquith Coalition in 1915 he penetrated all the
greatest weaknesses of the War administration and was aware of the
fatal defects of the two personalities upon whom the potency of
direction must depend—the Prime Minister and Lord Kitchener.
There was the Prime Minister's lack of initiative and drive, his
inability to apprehend the importance of time in a crisis, Lord
Kitchener's absorption in comparatively unimportant details, his
failure to grasp such of the problems of the War as were not visible
to his eye, the waning of the physical and nervous powers that once
gave him energy, and his concealment of his limitations under a cloak
of professional secrecy. Cabinets, like Boards of Directors, are mostly
composed of those who wish to believe that all is going well with a
concern as long as they are responsible for the direction of its affairs.
Carson's questions cut through complacency and irritated his
colleagues of both parties. He exasperated the Prime Minister,
whose almost morbid shrinking from unpleasantness was placed in
constant jeopardy by the flourish of his deadly scalpel at every meeting
of the Cabinet. Having got rid of the fearfulness of close association
with Sir Edward Carson, Mr. Asquith was reluctant to renew the
torment of his presence at the same Council. This had something
to do with his opposition to the proposals for an independent War
Committee put forward by Mr. Bonar Law and myself in December,
1916. The name of Sir Edward Carson had been mentioned. From
that moment the idea was doomed to immovable dislike.

Carson was very strongly opposed to the Dardanelles expedition
before he entered the Cabinet, and he never changed his opinion
as to the unwisdom of having entered upon that disastrous expedition.
But once he was inside the Government and found how deeply we
were committed to the undertaking, he saw the importance of carrying it right through with all the forces at the disposal of the Allies.
He saw clearly that failure would have a very calamitous effect upon
our prestige in the East; that it would encourage the Turks to
renewed activity against our forces on the Egyptian Fronts and in
Mesopotamia; that it strengthened the hold of the pro-German forces
in Bulgaria and discouraged Roumania. He also realised that now
we had lost Serbia and the Bulgarians had occupied the Balkans,

our only chance of cutting off the communications between Turkey and the Central Powers was to open up the Dardanelles and give our fleet access through the Marmora up to the Bosphorus. He therefore felt that the best thing to be done was to proceed with the campaign with the forces adequate to the accomplishment of our task. Herein he also displayed that instinct for realities which was his conspicuous mental quality.

As an exposer of shams, humbug and pretension Sir Edward Carson had no rival. But he had neither the natural gift nor the experience to make a good administrator. Even as a member of the Cabinet he had the fatal defect ingrained by centuries of habit in all men of his race—he was naturally opposed to every Government. Whether in or out of office he was always " agin the Government " for the time being. Sir Henry Wilson suffered from the same unmanageable contrariness.

The Irish have become through centuries of misrule a race of " Aginners." It will take a long experience of successful self-government to eradicate this germ from their nature. Sir Edward was in this, as in other respects, a typical " Aginner." He resigned from two successive Governments during the War, both of them Governments which at the date of his resignation were receiving the full support of his party. He could not help it. The call of the blood was irresistible.

Still, no one outside the Government could have given criticism such effective voice as he did. Men of less authority, courage and oratorical power would have been brushed aside by Ministers. A whisper as to the obligations of patriotism would have silenced them or deprived them of a hearing. Not so with Sir Edward Carson. I doubt whether Mr. Bonar Law would have taken the final step of threatened disruption had it not been for his fear of the lash of Carson's terrible tongue. Lord Beaverbrook knew this well, and made full use of it to persuade his friend to rise to the greatest opportunity of his career.

5. MR. BONAR LAW

Mr. Baldwin in a recent speech on Bonar Law said that his co-operation with me during the War was the most perfect partnership in political history. This statement must have seemed extravagant to those not intimately acquainted with the facts. I recollect that when I was on the threshold of my official career I was warned by a very shrewd observer, who had been privileged through a long political life to be on intimate terms with some of the greatest figures in the political world, to bear in mind that " there is no friendship at the top." At the time this observation struck me as being the cynicism of a disillusioned man. I wish that after long years of experience I could write with conviction to-day that his comment was unjustifiable. There is rivalry and jealousy in every profession and business. In politics these are stimulated and accentuated by a constant public discussion of the respective and contrasted merits and defects of the prominent figures on the political stage. These discussions are promoted sometimes by genuine interest in a theme which attracts the public—that of the qualities, good and bad, of its well-known personalities—sometimes by sincere admiration for one above all others of the conspicuous political leaders of the day. The virtues and faculties of political leaders constitute an essential item in the assets of the party to which they belong. It is therefore inevitable that exaggeration of the qualities with which their own chieftains are endowed and depreciation of those which characterise the chiefs of rival classes constitute a method of political warfare.

Too often criticisms and panegyrics alike are instigated by sheer mischief and malice—one of the great ones has had the misfortune to attract the dislike of a critic, and an effective method of retaliation by malignity is not only to detract from the abilities and achievements of the object of its hatred, but to laud the personage who is marked for his rival in public favour. All these causes tend to breed intrigues for exalting one or other of the public men at the expense of the others. Friendship cannot thrive in such at atmosphere. For nearly five years Mr. Bonar Law's friendship for me and mine for him not only survived but grew from year to year. When ill-health drove him from collaboration and companionship, I felt the separation more deeply than any I have endured during my political life. At that time the task of Government was so absorbing that those who were not working together soon lost sight of each other and thus drifted apart. Immediately on his retirement he left England for a fairly prolonged stay in the South of France. Neither he nor I ever revelled in the delights of correspondence. When he returned from his health sojourn on the Continent he had fallen back on other associations which were distinctly hostile to our friendship. Had I enjoyed more leisure and he less, this remarkable political partnership would only have ended with his tragic death, and many a chapter in the history of Britain, maybe of the world, would have been different from those which have now been written in indelible ink by the pen of Destiny.

There never were two men who constituted such a complete contrast in temperamental and mental equipment. We had nothing in common, except a lowly origin—his father was a Presbyterian Minister in a humble manse, mine was a school teacher in times when the pay of that profession was equal to half the wages of a town scavenger to-day. We had the same stern puritan upbringing. These early influences differentiated us completely from the other leading figures with whom he and I had to work—Mr. Balfour, Lord Curzon, Lord Lansdowne, Lord Derby, Lord Milner, Mr. Churchill, and Sir

Edward Grey. They had been reared in another planet, and he and I consciously, or rather unconsciously, must have been brought nearer together by that permeating and permanent influence. Although Mr. Asquith had come from similar stock and the like environment, he strove consistently to quit his early past and to surround himself with the appearance of being a native of another world, to which he really never belonged by origin, disposition or pursuits, and to conform as best he could to these new surroundings. Bonar Law would have disdained such contortions to adjust himself to social conditions he detested and despised.

I recollect Lord Morley telling me that a prominent Jew once said to him that he had striven all his life "to get out of the Ghetto, but had utterly failed to do so!" Mr. Asquith strained painfully and patently to get out of "Bethel"; but although he managed to leave it far behind, he was a stranger and a sojourner in any other home. He was ill at ease with either of Disraeli's Two Nations. He shunned direct contact with the people, neither had he the traditions nor the lure of aristocracy. He never appreciated Bonar Law's mental quality, nor the fine but strong fibre of his character. During a gloomy period of the War, I suggested to Mr. Asquith that the leading members of the Cabinet should meet informally one evening to review the situation and consider what could be done to effect an improvement in the Allied position. He acceded to my suggestion. We discussed names. Every peer and aristocrat in the Cabinet was included by him in the list. I suggested the name of Bonar Law, as he was leader of the Tory Party. He snappily answered, " No, he has the intellect of a Glasgow bailie!" So Bonar Law, the trusted leader of the largest party in the British Parliament, was ruled out of an inter-party consultation on events which might decide the fate of the British Empire and the future course of mankind. He was neither a patrician nor an academician. Neither was he troublesome as some of us threatened to be. So why bring in this common person to such a select gathering?

This represented Mr. Asquith's general attitude of mind towards Mr. Bonar Law. He did not under-value his abilities; he placed no value at all upon them. His origin, his training, his equipment, his prejudices, his very appearance and outfit excited every antipathy in Mr. Asquith's mind. When Bonar Law joined the Asquith Coalition Cabinet he did little to dispel impressions of his intellectual inferiority. The problems with which he was confronted were new to him, and at first his comments expressed crudely the opinions of a sensible and able business man on propositions with which he was imperfectly acquainted. It took his virile and logical mind some time to acquire an adequate grip of the terrible complexities of the World War. He did not possess a ready command of the conventional and shallow pomposities with which much less able men cloaked the nakedness of their knowledge and the poverty of their faculties. Mr. Asquith, although himself possessing a powerful and illuminating intelligence and a ready command of adequate phraseology, was always too apt to be impressed by traditional ideas garbed in an appropriate jargon. Bonar Law spoke simply and naturally in the language of a Scottish business man. Thus Mr. Asquith and Mr. Bonar Law never came anywhere near friendly understanding.

There was another reason why Mr. Asquith had a fundamental dislike for Mr. Bonar Law. The latter was by temperament a pessimist. He generally took a gloomy view of the world and its ways. Asquith was a temperamental optimist. " Wait and see! " was the natural expression of a mood confident in the immediate future of all the things in which he was concerned. Things might be obscure and unpleasant for the time being, but wait a little longer and you will see for yourself that all is well even now. He could not bear prophets of gloom anywhere around him.

Bonar rather liked to dwell on the difficulties of a project or a prospect. Pessimist as he was by nature he never despaired of our ultimate success in the War, provided the Allies made effective use of their resources. When, during the Asquith Coalition, a scare was being attempted by the puckish Keynes as to the approximate collapse of our financial credit, Bonar Law's practical sagacity came to the rescue of the timorous, and steadied counsel.

Bonar's first impulse, when a project or a prospect was placed before him, was to dwell on its difficulties and dangers. I found that idiosyncrasy useful and even exhilarating. When I had any plans I took them around to him to test them on his doubting and unenthusiastic nature. I started work very early, and immediately after breakfast I habitually walked along the corridor from No. 10 to No. 11 Downing Street for a smoke and a talk with Bonar. We surveyed the morning news and the business of the day. If I had been thinking out any schemes I invariably unfolded them to him before placing them before the War Cabinet. His reaction was always to array all the difficulties and obstacles (generally political) in the way of operating these ideas successfully. He had an incomparable gift of practical criticism. When he had finished marshalling his objections I knew there was nothing more to be said against my plans. Sometimes I felt the force of his adverse criticisms was so great as to be insuperable, and I abandoned the project altogether; at other times I found it necessary to alter or modify the idea in order to meet some obstacle which I had not foreseen but which he had pointed out. But if I came to the conclusion that his objections were not sufficient to deter the Government from initiating and carrying out the particular scheme, I went away strengthened in my resolve as the result of our conversation. On those occasions I said to him, " Well, Bonar, if there is nothing more to be said against this scheme, then I mean to put it before the War

Cabinet to-day." He usually acquiesced, as he knew that I never failed to listen to his views and to give full weight to them.

Once I had secured his consent I had no more loyal supporter for my plans.

He possessed real courage. It was not the blind dash of the reckless or the buoyant courage of the sanguine. He anticipated trouble everywhere and every time, and mostly exaggerated it. Nevertheless, he faced it without faltering if it came. He was both fearless and apprehensive. His great phrase in beginning and often in ending an interview was " There is lots of trouble ahead!" Any manœuvring in the House of Commons, especially amongst the supporters of the Government, worried him. On these occasions, when he was more miserable than usual, I used to say to him, " Let us swop jobs. You can take mine and I will run yours." That generally put an end to the discussion. He shrank from accepting the supreme responsibility for decisions which might be right but which would, if they turned out to be wrong entail irreparable injury to the interests of the country. During those years, almost every day decisions of that fatefulness had to be taken. A reluctance to decide when there was a serious difference of opinion was a curious defect in so resolute and truly brave a man. But there it undoubtedly was. It was probably due to an inherent diffidence which caused him to distrust his own judgment, coupled with a strong blend of conscientiousness and caution which made him fearful of doing the wrong thing.

His attachment to Lord Beaverbrook was largely although by no means entirely attributable to this natural defect. He found a support and a strength in this resolute friend, whose practical shrewdness gave him confidence and whose personal devotion he knew to be beyond challenge and question. He thus came to rely upon him in every emergency of his public and private life. His remarkable success in so short a time, and in a party so constituted as the Tory Party, was undoubtedly due to Beaverbrook's prompting and management. Mr. Bonar Law was not without ambition, but this motive was not strong enough to overcome the hesitancies of so anxious a temperament. Mr. Asquith once said of him that he was " meekly ambitious." Lord Beaverbrook's forceful insistence and unfailing backing cured all that. He shoved him almost brutally to the front. He firmly believed him to be the best man to succeed Mr. Balfour when the latter was driven out of the leadership of the Conservative Party. I was certainly of the same opinion at the time and I had no reason to change my view afterwards.

Tragedy deepened the pessimism of Bonar Law's later years. Once it took root it certainly spread rapidly over his spirit, like a parasite, until it hid the strength of the granite underneath. It must have come from the shocks of a succession of great sorrows which shattered the joy of life and even the desire for life. He lost a wife to whom he was devoted, and the War bereft him of two fine boys whom he adored. A placid life of unchecked success is the best climate in which to grow the plant of a hopeful disposition. Such had been Mr. Bonar Law's life until fate intervened to shrivel it all up. The brightness of his outlook had seemed unclouded by doubts. I remember meeting him in the corridor of the House of Commons soon after I had introduced my Budget of 1909. He said to me, " Well, you are too late to save your Party. If you had a General Election now not more than 50 Liberal Members would be returned for England, and once a Government begins to go down it never recovers." He was then almost childishly optimistic as to the chances of any ventures in which he was engaged, so different from the stricken Bonar of 1916, with the nerve of hope paralysed by the lightnings from a dark cloud. Then he said to me as soon as we were installed in joint authority, " In six months Asquith will be the most popular man in England." His face was set towards the sunset, and he never swung round to the end.

He never seemed to me to have any appreciation of the brighter side of life. When he and I paid a visit to Paris to confer with the French Government, I took him in the evening to see that joyous comic opera " La Fille de Madame Angot." I have never seen a man so painfully bored at a performance. He continually left the play for the foyer, where I found him smoking his pipe. When I asked him whether he did not enjoy the performance he said : " It would be quite tolerable if it were not for the singing."

I remember before the War, while we were both staying at Cannes, driving with him on a sunny day along the road to the golf course at Cagnes. The sky was cloudless and the sea was blue as only the Mediterranean can be, while on our left was the white-topped amphitheatre of the Maritime Alps. I turned to Bonar and asked him if he did not think it beautiful. " I don't care much for scenery," he replied in his rather toneless voice. The night before I had been to a performance of one of Mozart's operas—I think it was " Il Seraglio." It was the first time I had heard it and I was struck with its exquisite beauty. I mentioned the fact to Bonar Law, but his reaction to my enthusiasm was only to say " I don't care much for music." As we approached the golf course we saw some extremely pretty women also on the way to play golf. I called Bonar Law's attention to them. " Women don't attract me," was his laconic answer. " Will you tell me," I said, exasperated at all this disdain for the attractions of life, " what it is that you do care for? Scenery—music—women—none of them has any meaning for you. What is it that you do like?" " I like bridge," was the reply.

Was he industrious? He was a steady and quiet worker. He took pains to master his case before he expressed an opinion either in council or in public. He read the official papers sent to him carefully, but I never found him searching out extraneous sources of information in order to obtain wider and less official conclusions on the subject under investigation.   He was hard-working when the occasion demanded application, but he was not energetic.   He loved his armchair and he was a slave to his pipe.   He hated a long lunch or dinner, not only because he was an unappreciative eater, but because it delayed the moment when he could pull out his beloved pipe.   I believe it helped to undermine his health.

His method of preparing his speeches was to sit in his armchair with his head well back in the chair and his long legs well up on the mantel-piece.   He loved quiet and ease.   His slogan as Prime Minister was characteristic—" Tranquillity."   He hated not only quarrels and tumults but all that demanded a strenuous life or called for a display of energy and vigour.   He was not exactly lethargic, and certainly not torpid, but he had no constant urge towards action of any kind.   He was in private kindly, good tempered, genial—nay, essentially gentle. His bluntness of speech was all manner and was not attributable in the least to the temper or cold cruelty of disposition that takes pleasure in inflicting hurt.   This impression may serve to explain what follows when I come later on to tell the story of how our partnership began and how it continued unbroken under an unparalleled strain.   It is not too much to claim that the effect it had on the events of that critical period is part of the story of the Empire and of the contribution the Empire made to a struggle which must for generations affect the course of civilisation.

CHAPTER XXXVII

1914-1916: A RETROSPECT

AFTER accepting the Premiership from the King's hands, I proceeded immediately to form my administration. How this Government was formed, the conditions under which it was called upon to undertake its task, the problems which confronted it, and the way in which it proceeded to deal with them, must be the subject of later chapters.

In the foregoing pages I have brought my recollections of the Great War down to the end of 1916. In succeeding chapters I have taken up the tale, and describe the outstanding events with which I was personally connected during the two concluding years of the world conflict. But the month of December, 1916, forms a fitting point at which to pause in my narrative, for it marked, for reasons which I shall proceed to summarise, the end of an epoch in the progress of the War. So far as my own affairs were concerned, it was the point at which, after serving the State in a variety of secondary offices, I was called upon to shoulder the supreme responsibility for administration. I carried that burden throughout the remaining years of the War, and beyond.

In the story of the War, the end of 1916 found the fortunes of the Allies at their lowest ebb, the outlook dark from the open bankruptcy of both their strategy and their diplomacy. Three of the Allied Powers—Belgium, Roumania, Serbia—had been completely knocked out; the fourth—and one of the greatest—had also been practically put out of action. On the other hand the Central Power Federation was intact. The prospect facing us at the moment when I became Prime Minister was enough to daunt any man or group of men. By a succession of incredible blunders we had frittered away one advantage after another possessed by the Allies—in material resources and potential man-power and strategic opportunity—until on balance we were on the wrong side in our comparative strength and strategic position as compared with those enjoyed by the enemy. Even our command of the sea was in jeopardy—and daily increasing jeopardy.

The Allies had originally possessed an immense superiority in man-power, and in all the available and accessible means of equipment. We squandered the former and neglected the latter. At the outbreak of the War the men of military age in Russia, France, the British Empire, Serbia, Roumania, Italy and Belgium outnumbered by many millions those which the Central Powers could call upon. How had we used them? Owing to bad strategy and failure to utilise our vast resources for equipment we threw away our overwhelming surplus of fighting men. For this reason we had left Serbia to be overrun and wiped out. Two-thirds of her resources in fighting men had been one way or another put of action, and the remainder, cut off from their own territory, were unable to draw on their potential reserves and rein-forcements. Roumania had, owing to the same cause, just shared the same fate, and her army of 900,000 (with reserves) had been written off the account. Russia had entered the War with almost illimitable man-power. It was estimated by General Gourko that up to the end of 1916 she had called 14,000,000 men to the colours. In October, 1916, Sir William Robertson estimated that she still had nearly 5,000,000 under arms, and could draw on reserves of a further 6,500,000. The remainder of her troops had disappeared in the shambles of war or were interned in German and Austrian camps supplying the enemy deficiency in labour. But by the end of 1916, Russia through lack of the equipment which France and Britain could easily have furnished, had almost ceased to be an asset on the balance sheet. Her revolution was only a few weeks ahead, and with it her military value to the Allied cause would disappear altogether. Already her troops, dispirited and disaffected, had ceased to be capable of any serious offensive. On the other hand Austria, which could have been disintegrated and destroyed in 1916, was so protected and strengthened that she sur-vived as a formidable opponent in resistance and attack for two more years, while Turkey, which could have been finished off in 1915, had beaten us off in Mesopotamia and Palestine and, her armies re-equipped by Germany, was more redoubtable as a military power than she was in 1914.

Two failures on key questions had completely transformed the military position to our disadvantage. The first was the failure to realise that this was a war of machinery, and the consequent neglect immediately to mobilise our national resources to improve the Allied equipment. The second was our failure until too late to appreciate the fact that the weakest point of the Central Powers was in the Eastern and South-Eastern Fronts. Thus a war of attrition was sub-stituted for a war of intelligence.

Both Lord Kitchener and Sir William Robertson reposed their trust in attrition as a means to victory. How had it worked? I have shown how already we had dissipated our huge surplus of fighting men in the east. What about the west?

The armies of France and Britain were still powerful, but the course of the War up to this date had witnessed a profligate wasting of some of our finest young manhood. In the offensives of the Western Front we had lost three men for every two of the Germans we put out of action. Over 300,000 British troops were being immobilised for lack

of enterprise or equipment or both by the Turks in Egypt and Mesopotamia, and for the same reason, nearly 400,000 Allied soldiers were
for all practical purposes interned by the Bulgarians in the malarial
plains around Salonika.   Altogether the Allied forces which could
still be counted as reliable for energetic campaigning in the future
were facing a foe that was now, for effective purposes, just as powerful
numerically, and was operating on interior lines with all the best
strategic positions in her hands—the Balkans, the Dardanelles, and
the high ground in France and Belgium.   The silly and bloody game
of attrition had already been won by Germany.

    With a criminal prodigality we had squandered the superior man-
power that had been at our disposal.   We had also weakened our
resources and strengthened those of the enemy by our failure to gain
alliances that would have been ours for the asking, and by manœuvring
at least one potential ally to the other side.   Our diplomacy was a
timid and nervous thing, frightened of America, too shy to tackle
Greece, and leaving the Turks and Bulgarians entirely to the allure-
ments of the Germans.   Sir William Robertson complained of the
undoubted fact that the soldiers had received no help from diplomacy.
Bold diplomacy, backed by proper strategy and effective military
action, would have enabled us in the early months of the War to call
into being a great Balkan Confederation on the side of the Allies,
which would have added 1,500,000 to our fighting forces.   With
Bulgaria, Greece and Roumania, in addition to Serbia, on our side,
Turkey would have been cut off and forced to make peace in 1915, or
at latest early in 1916.   And with these forces pressing up on Austria
from the south-east, and with Italy operating from the south, we should
have crushed Austria-Hungary, and compelled Germany to make
peace, particularly if by energetic and early mobilisation of our manufacturing resources we had supplied Russia with the munitions to
make her immense armies effective.

    Peace with victory might have been ours in 1916 if we had pursued
such a course. It would have meant contenting ourselves with holding
the Germans on the Western Front, rather than trying to smash
through there; it would have meant sending the men, who later on
were slain in vain attacks in France and Flanders, to strengthen the
forces of a Balkan Confederation for an assault upon the weakest part
of the Central Powers' defence; it would have meant sending part of
the munitions blazed away in France to assist Russia and the Balkan
States.   Recently I was told in conversation by a distinguished
German who held an exalted position in the government of his
country during the War: " That is what we were always afraid you
would do! "   Nothing pleased them better than to see us mass our
forces for attack in the impregnable west while we allowed ourselves
to be out-manœuvred at every turn in the vulnerable east.   We hammered at the breastplate of Achilles and neglected his heel.   And we

called it sometimes "striking at the vital parts" and sometimes "attrition."

Such was the net result of the diplomacy and the war direction and strategy pursued by the Allies during nearly two and a half years of a war in which they had started with overwhelming advantages, and through which they had been supported by unexampled efforts and sacrifices on the part of their peoples.

Such was the situation I was called upon to face when I took up office as Prime Minister. A few days after I became Prime Minister I invited Sir William Robertson to give me a note on any points connected with the War which particularly required my attention, and I also invited his candid opinion as to our prospects of winning it. The document with which he furnished me was not an encouraging one. There were such phrases as: "The attitude of the British Empire up to the present time has been lamentable." "We are contributing far more to the War than any Power, and we exercise less general control than any."

Later on he says: "At the present time we are practically committing suicide." Then he goes on: "We must considerably enlarge our ideas as to the magnitude of the War. We do not yet nearly realise the stupendous task confronting us."

He prophesied "an increasing strain in every direction. The strain will become greater and greater as time goes on, and we are undoubtedly in for a bad time for the next few months. . . ." Further on he says, "*We can only expect* just *to win through and no more*, and yet things in England are going on much the same to-day as two years ago. It is upon us more than any other Power that the final result depends, and *I cannot hold out any hope of winning until we have been strained to the utmost.* If the nation will not stand that, then the chances are we shall not win. . . ."

Later on he says, ". . . some Members of the late Government had no proper perspective of the War. They lived from telegram to telegram. . . ."

He ends, after saying that Germany is also feeling the strain of the War, "We must learn to set our teeth and refuse to be discouraged; *and, generally, put into our task more spirit, soul, courage and determination to win no matter at what cost, and in any event to go down, if we must, with our colours flying. But there will be no question of going down if we are brave and resolute, and stick to a definite plan once it is made.*"

CHAPTER XXXVIII

FIRST TASKS AS PRIME MINISTER

1. FORMATION OF A NATIONAL THREE-PARTY GOVERNMENT

As soon as the King entrusted me with the task of forming an Administration in succession to the Ministry that had disappeared, I had to survey the tasks awaiting me, political as well as economic, financial, military and naval, and then pass in review the personnel available for such a Government, in order to select men who were suitable for the emergency with which we were confronted. Had my hands been free, the men I thought best fitted to assist me in counsel and in the effective organisation of the Nation for war would have been chosen without reference to Party politics. I should have drawn my Ministers partly from the ranks of the back-benchers, some of whom had made a mark in Parliament, some of whom had no conspicuous Parliamentary gifts, but who possessed, I felt confident, the experience and qualities which would make them good administrators. I should also have looked outside Parliament for men who in their own pursuits had shown faculties of energy, foresight, imagination, judgment and courage, and I should have put them in charge of various branches of Government activity.

But I had to take into account the fundamental fact that I was working under a Parliamentary system, and that it was essential for the Government to secure the support of Parliament during the first testing months, when its schemes were developing but could not hope to fructify in any decisive achievement. Had there been a united party behind me which, with dependable allies, would have commanded in the House of Commons a majority solid and large enough to carry me through the inevitable vicissitudes of evil as well as good tidings for a period of two years and more, I should have had a freer, a wider and a more promising choice. I could then have secured a more homogeneous form of Government and a Government more sympathetic to the War policy in which I believed. I was anxious to change the men and methods which were too much associated with the old war direction.

But the party to which I belonged was divided into two parts. On a canvass undertaken by Dr. Addison with the help of the late Mr. Kellaway, it was ascertained that there were 136 Liberals out of a total 260 who were prepared to support an Administration of which I was the head. That meant that about half of the Party still followed the lead of Mr. Asquith. The Irish Party were on the whole Asquithian, and the Labour Party were divided between supporters of the War and the out-and-out pacifists.

The majority of the Tory Ministers in the Asquith coalition were definitely opposed to my Premiership. When they first realised that it was impending they made hysterical efforts to fend it off. When it became a fact, they accepted the prospect of serving under my leadership with bitter reluctance. As to some of them, there was no time up to the end when they would not have welcomed my resignation. That added to my difficulties in moments calling for critical decision, and their attitude impeded and once or twice thwarted my efforts. To understand their attitude it was necessary to bear in mind that there had never before been a " ranker " raised to the Premiership— certainly not one except Disraeli who had not passed through the Staff College of the old Universities.

As to the attitude of the Labour Party, I had as yet no information, inasmuch as I had not come into contact with them either directly or indirectly during the negotiations. All I knew was that in Asquithian circles there was the most complete confidence that no Tory leader except Bonar Law and Carson would serve under me, and that the Labour Party would have nothing to do with a Lloyd George administration.

The prospect of success in the formation of a Ministry assured of reliable Parliamentary support was therefore at that period not encouraging. The prospect of life for the Government was placed in influential circles at six weeks. However, I decided to undertake the duty entrusted to me by the Sovereign and to do my best to form a Government that would organise the strength of the Nation for victory and thus gradually command its confidence. I felt strongly that failure would mean that the kind of flabby direction which had jeopardised the chance of a favourable issue out of the War would be restored to power with added authority, but with diminished vigour and initiative.

I started by trying to find out what Conservative support was available, and herein I had to depend upon the superior knowledge and experience of Mr. Bonar Law and Lord Edmund Talbot. I have already told the story of how we secured the powerful adhesion of Mr. Balfour, who undertook to fill the position of Foreign Secretary. There were two other able men of great influence in the Party who were also ready to assist the new Administration—Sir Edward Carson and Lord Milner. As soon as I was assured of this support I felt confident that my task would be accomplished. In most Governments there are four or five outstanding figures who by exceptional talent, experience, and personality constitute the inner council which gives direction to the policy of a Ministry. An administration that is not fortunate enough to possess such a group may pull through without mishap in tranquil seasons, but in an emergency it is hopelessly lost. The rest do not count in a crisis. The hummocks that look like eminences in fine weather are quickly submerged in a great flood, when the highest peaks alone are visible above the surface of the waters.

In the Liberal Party there were three or four Ministers, and no more, whose names meant anything to the general public—Mr. Asquith, Lord Grey, and Mr. Winston Churchill. Without any undue presumption I may also add my own name at that date, largely owing to the part I had taken in establishing Old Age Pensions and a national system of Insurance, and to the fact that I had during recent years been in the forefront of all the political controversies of the day. The residue were known to Parliamentarians and to keen politicians outside; but I doubt whether one in ten of the men in the trenches could tell you what office they held or even to what Party they belonged.

The men known to the general public amongst Conservatives were also few. Foremost amongst them were Mr. Bonar Law, Mr. Balfour, and Sir Edward Carson. These were prominent figures as far as the nation at large was concerned. Several others were more or less known to those who were interested in politics; Lord Curzon, Mr. Walter Long, Mr. Austen Chamberlain, and Lord Robert Cecil stood high in the councils of the Party, while Lord Milner made a special appeal to the young intelligentsia. The Diehard element also trusted him in the essentials of the faith. That is more than could be said of Lord Curzon, who inspired a distrust which in some not uninfluential Tory quarters amounted to detestation. Incidentally it was this bloc which ultimately barred his way to Premiership in 1923.

Lord Lansdowne was one of the elder statesmen of the Party who was more respected than followed. His sword was never very formidable in action; it was now only useful to return the salute. The direction in which it was waveringly pointed was no longer heeded by the exclusive regiment he once led. Bonar Law, Carson and Balfour between them commanded the trust and obedience of every section of the Party, and where they went on any patriotic enterprise which did not cross a fundamental Tory principle, the whole Party would follow. The fact that the other leaders, whose names I have given, were not associated with the venture, would not have seriously disturbed Tory sentiment or weakened its adhesion to the new Government. From the point of view of the rigorous and effective prosecution of the War, there was much to be said for leaving them out. Men who come into a joint enterprise reluctantly and resentfully will, if they are honest workers—and these were—fulfil their tasks to the best of their ability, but their doubts usually revive when there are difficulties, and when decision depends on faith in leadership they are a source of irresolution. Many a time during the coming years did I find that this condition of mind in some of my leading lieutenants weakened and postponed and now and again frustrated essential action. This was notably the case in dealing with the vital questions of wasteful offensives and of Unity of Command. I found that the men in question always leant towards support of the military hierarchy in opposition to the view I took. Had they remained outside, their positions could have been filled by men of the type of Maclay, Inverforth, Beaverbrook, Geddes, Lee, Weir, Rhondda, Cowdray, Albert Stanley—men who possessed organising brains of the first order, and whose services to the nation during the War have never been fully appreciated. However, events circumscribed my choice of colleagues.

Mr. Bonar Law, in addition to being a strong Party man, felt that he had a special trust to discharge as the leader of his Party, and that he had not the same freedom to dispense with Party considerations in the choice of Ministers as had been vouchsafed to me by the circumstances of my Party. He therefore felt that in order to avoid splitting his Party he was under an obligation to do all in his power to bring his colleagues, the Conservative ex-Ministers, inside the new Coalition. Of the steps he took to induce them to remain at the posts they held, or their equivalent, I shall give an account later on.

In this connection I quote the following characteristic letter which I received from the late Mr. Leo Maxse. I think there is a good deal in what he said:—

> "*National Review*,
> 43, Duke Street,
> St. James's, London, S.W.
> 8th December, 1916.

Dear Mr. Lloyd George,

I have little hopes of this reaching you or being read by you, but I must write one line because I am appalled by what I hear as to the manner in which you are being blackmailed by Unionist Front Bench politicians, into making numerous undesirable appointments, which when announced cannot fail to cause a great shock to the public by making them feel that the new Government is very little improvement on the old. . . .

Anxious as we are to be quit of the debris which encumbered the late Prime Minister we are hardly less anxious to be rid of the equally useless rubbish by which Bonar Law is surrounded, and there is really no earthly reason from any point of view why politicians whose ' numbers ' have long been ' up ' should be allowed to inflict themselves on the community. All you have to do, if I may say so, is to tell Bonar Law and Co. to go to the devil and they will come to heel. I know these men well—they have not an ounce

x

of pluck and they are only brave when they are successfully applying the squeeze. The public is expecting something much better
than a Cabinet of political hacks who have long been blown upon.

Yours sincerely,

L. J. MAXSE."

This was a shrapnel shot intended to hit Balfour, Curzon, Walter
Long and Robert Cecil.

As the change could not have been effected without the intervention
of Mr. Bonar Law, I felt that I must abide by his decision in the
selection of Conservative Members. Subsequently, I had much reason
to deplore his loyalty to colleagues who were not conspicuously faithful
to him and who, even in these negotiations, had tried to snatch leadership out of his hands.

I felt it was a matter of the first national importance to bring the
Labour Party into active co-operation with the new Government. This
was the first Great War since the American War of the Union in which
whole democracies were engaged in a deadly struggle. As far as the
Western Allies were concerned, this was truly a democratic war. It
was entered into with the full assent of practically the whole of the
people. Their sons without distinction of rank, grade or vocation
fought and suffered. It was necessary in order to win that workers at
home should put forth the whole of their strength. To do so it was
essential that their co-operation should be enlisted and retained right
to the end. I could see no prospect of bringing the War to a satisfactory end for some time to come. War weariness was bound to grow.
The national will was unbroken, but the national ardour did not flame
out as it did during the first months of the War. In these circumstances
it is not surprising that labour troubles were on the increase.

Britain was in this respect no exception to the other belligerent
countries. Allied and enemy countries alike were beginning to
experience the irritation arising from war weariness amongst the
workers. The factories and workshops of Russia were seething with
discontent. The German worker was showing symptoms of the
querulousness of overstrain. In neither of these two countries did the
rulers bring the spokesmen of Labour frankly into active partnership,
and the failure to do so ended in disaster for both, soon in Russia, later
in Germany. I deemed it essential to forestall trouble by bringing
the Labour leaders into more active and effective co-operation with the
Government of the day in the prosecution of the War. In the late
Coalition there was only one Labour Minister—Mr. Arthur Henderson—and he was not a member of the War Committee. I came to the
conclusion that Labour must have a more substantial and effective
representation in the new Government and that one of its most
prominent and respected leaders should be a member of the small
body which had the supreme direction of the War. But first of all it

was necessary that the Labour Party should express its willingness to co-operate.

On the morrow of my visit to the Palace, Mr. Arthur Henderson called on me at the War Office and asked me whether I was prepared to meet a deputation from the Parliamentary Labour Party and the National Labour Executive to discuss the conditions of possible participation in my Government. He had been invited by Mr. Asquith to attend the conclave of Liberal Ministers which decided not to serve in any Government of which the late Prime Minister was not the Chief. Mr. Henderson was the sole dissentient when that resolution was passed. He immediately consulted his Labour colleagues as to the course to be adopted. He informed me that the Labour Executive had discussed the question of whether they should support or oppose the Government, that they were divided on the subject, but that before coming to any final decision on the matter, they were anxious to have my views on two or three issues which particularly concerned them. I readily agreed to meet the representatives of Labour, and later on they came to me at the War Office. All the best known Socialist and Labour leaders were present, including Mr. Ramsay MacDonald, Mr. Snowden, Mr. Henderson, Mr. Sidney Webb, Mr. J. H. Thomas and Mr. Bevin.

I was subjected to a good deal of examination and cross-examination. The Labour Party were by no means completely united in their general attitude towards the War. Broadly speaking, I found at this interview that the Trade Union representatives were in favour of an effective prosecution of the War up to the attainment of victory. On the other hand, there was a strong pacifist element amongst the Socialist section. The spokesmen of the latter—especially Mr. Ramsay MacDonald and Mr. Sidney Webb—took an active part in the process of putting questions which they thought might be embarrassing to the new administration, and the answers to which might ensure a refusal to support the Government. It was apparent to me that their hostility evoked no sympathy amongst their Trade Union colleagues.

I opened the proceedings by addressing them on the position of the War, and upon the general outline of my own policy as Prime Minister.

As there has been a good deal of discussion of a recriminatory character about the conditions under which organised Labour entered the Cabinet, it is only fair to the majority who gave their adhesion to the new Government that I should quote textually from the official record of the proceedings at that fateful interview. The following passage from my speech to the delegation will illustrate the position which I then took, and to which I faithfully adhered.

". . . The War for the moment is going badly; the country and all the nations which hang upon the triumph of Great Britain are in great peril. The fall of Bucharest is not merely a question of one city passing into the hands of the enemy; it means a good deal more than that; it means that for the moment, the blockade is broken, the work of the Fleet to that extent neutralised, and that we are face to face with the grimmest and most perilous struggle in which this country has ever been engaged. I felt that we were not waging this war in the way wars alone can be waged. I hate war; I abominate it. I sometimes think 'Am I dreaming? Is it a nightmare? It cannot be fact.' But these are questions to ask and answer before you go into a war; once you are in it you have to go grimly through it, otherwise the causes which hang upon a successful issue will all perish. Delay in war is as fatal as in an illness. An operation which may succeed to-day is no good six weeks later or, may be, even three days later. So in war. Action which to-day may save the life of a country taken a week late is too late. I thought, rightly or wrongly, that there was delay, hesitation and vacillation, and that we were not waging this war with the determination, promptitude and relentlessness—let us make no mistake about it—with which it must be waged. We cannot send men to carnage without seeing that at any rate everything is being done to give them a fair chance to win through to victory. They are prepared to make the sacrifice, and we, on the other hand, must support them with all the strength and all the will with which we are endowed. So it was I made certain proposals. I do not believe any Prime Minister, whoever he is, if he has the strength of a giant mentally and physically and morally, can possibly undertake the task of running Parliament and running the War. That is the conviction that I have received. I am still of the same opinion, and I shall certainly act upon it if I form an Adminis- tration. Whoever undertakes to run the War must put his whole strength into it and he must make other arrangements with regard to Parliament. The King having failed to secure the adhesion of all parties—I wish myself there were no parties during the War—to the plan of forming a comprehensive national Government, invited me to form an Administration. Mr. Asquith and his colleagues decided that they would not serve under Mr. Bonar Law or under anyone else. I regret that, but I do not wish to criticise it at the present moment. The King's Government must be carried on. You must have an Administration to prosecute the War, and let me say this—it is what I have said to my colleagues and comrades in this office a few minutes ago—politicians make one fundamental mistake when they have been in office. They think that the people who are in office, or who have been in office, are absolutely essential to the Government of the country and that no one else is in the least able to carry on affairs. Well, we are a people of 45,000,000 and really, if we cannot produce at least two or three alternative Cabinets, we must be what Carlyle once called us—' a nation of fools.' I don't believe it and I don't think that is the opinion of the country. We are all very interested in ourselves and each other, but with all respect to ourselves I think the country is looking out for something else; it is looking out for a Government that will prosecute the War efficiently; that is what it is looking for and therefore I am hoping to get the adhesion of men of that character and calibre to form an Administration.

It is obvious that no Government can be carried on in this country, whether during war or peace, without, I won't say the support of Labour, but the co-operation of Labour. Upon its determination to help in winning this War, everything depends, and therefore I invited you here, through Mr. Henderson, who has been my colleague for eighteen months or two years, and let me say at once that I never want a more loyal colleague. He has faced tasks which I thought were difficult, but which were twice as difficult for him because of his association with Labour. He has faced them with courage and very true comradeship and I shall always be grateful to him. I invited him to communicate with the leaders of Labour in this country with a view to inviting their co-operation in the Government of the country—not a subordinate position, but a real share in the War Committee, to direct the War; a real share in the Administration by those who are not members of the War Committee, because those members of the War Committee ought on the whole to be free from the burdens of departmental work. It is absolutely impossible otherwise to give the whole of their mind to the prosecution of the War, and I propose that Labour—as I did propose before I left the late Cabinet—should be represented on that Council, and that it should have its representatives there permanently, taking an equal share of the burdens and contributing to the counsels upon which the success, the life of this country may depend. I propose that Labour should be represented in other Departments. Up to the present we have only one Labour head of a Department. . . . I suggest an absolutely new Department—a Ministry of Labour—that the Labour Department of the Board of Trade and the Labour Department of the Ministry of Munitions should be consolidated under one head. . . . I think it is essential that you should have a Labour Ministry which could incorporate the Labour section of the Board of Trade and Ministry of Munitions under one head. That Department would certainly be one of the most important Departments in the Government because, however important a Labour Ministry would be in time of peace—and it would essentially be a Department whose decisions would very materially affect the lives of millions of people in this country—in times of war it is almost doubly important. It is a War Ministry to that extent as well as a Labour Ministry. I propose that that

Department should have at its head a Labour representative.

Then there is another Ministry which I propose to form, to deal with a subject which, at the present moment, affects hundreds of thousands of households and which, it is sad to reflect, will affect the lives of many hundreds of thousands more. I refer to the Pensions Department. I care not to think how important the Department is and is going to continue to be. It is also a Department which I should suggest should be under the control of a Labour representative.

Then I propose that there should be two Under-Secretaries and a representative of Labour in the Whips' Office as well. That is the suggestion which I put before Mr. Henderson.

With regard to the Cabinet—there is a suggestion which is before us, but I am not in a position to say whether it will be decided upon or not—it is one of the things I shall have to discuss with my colleagues before I give an opinion. I do not think there should be a Cabinet in the ordinary sense of the term. The War Committee should, during the continuation of the War, act as the Cabinet. When a question arises, affecting a particular Department the representatives of that Department would be called in to discuss the matter with the War Cabinet. . .

As regards the question of policy, there are three questions to be dealt with, namely Mines, Food and Shipping.

As regards Mines, there is only one solution and that is that the State should have control over the mines. On this question, however, I shall have to discuss details further with my colleagues. The control of the mines should be nationalised as far as possible. There would be no question of profiting at the expense of the general public; the profits would be reckoned on a pre-War basis.

Personally I am strongly in favour of the same line being taken with Shipping. I have heard of scandalous cases in regard to Shipping—cases of men who at the beginning of the War had practically nothing and who now find themselves not merely with thousands, but very nearly hundreds of thousands, made by the most extravagant freights, which have had the effect of putting up the cost of living throughout the country. I think that is a scandal, and I cannot conceive the Government proceeding without dealing with that matter. There I can only speak for myself and Mr. Bonar Law. The suggestion which I put forward in the late Cabinet was that there should be a Minister to control Shipping and Shipbuilding. As regards Shipping profits, Mr. Bonar Law and three or four of my colleagues are strongly in favour of Railway and Mine terms being applied to Shipping."

On the question of Food Supplies I promised to appoint a Controller to supervise production and distribution.

I then continued : —

" I do not believe there is a country in the world with so much good land which is not producing. I remember talking with a very distinguished German in Strassburg (before the War) and he told me that in going through England, *nothing impressed him so much as the tremendous beauty of the country—except the waste of it.* He said that in England he saw everywhere good land which was producing nothing but neglected grass, and trees which were useless for timber. In Germany every yard of such land was producing food. And during this War at any rate—and we will see afterwards what we shall do—the food capacity of this country ought to be utilised to the very last inch without any regard at all to the uses, ornamental or otherwise, to which it has been hitherto put. At the present moment, I do not believe anyone would object to it.

The second thing is that you cannot do that without a great deal of mechanical appliances for cultivation. You must first of all find out how many steam ploughs there are in this country, and having done this you must see that they are utilised to the best advantage. I mean that a man who has got a plough must use that plough whenever it is needed for the parish. The plough must be used to the fullest possible extent. We must manufacture ploughs, and arrangements will be made with the Ministry of Munitions (this was agreed to in substance by the War Committee) to manufacture ploughs for the purpose of tearing up the soil and making it ready for food production. Agricultural labour has also to be mobilised. I believe there are plenty of skilled men on the soil if you make the best use of them. It is just what you are doing with the Army— making the skilled soldier your non-commissioned officer. Doing that you will be able to increase enormously the produce of the soil.

There is another suggestion I was discussing with Lord Derby the other day. I am told there are 100,000 gardeners in this country. Those are all skilled cultivators of the soil and, I think, in a case of necessity, when the food supply may become absolutely short, if the submarine losses continue, you ought not to allow one of these men to cultivate anything which is ornamental, until they have utilised to the fullest their powers for the production of food. I do not believe any man who is now employed on Agriculture, will object to the mobilisation of those highly skilled men for the purpose, not of tidying up the lawn or even producing flowers, but for the purpose of increasing the food supply of the people. It is better that you should produce it at home. Any man who has lived in the country, knows that the food which is grown at his own door is a luxury compared with what you buy. I do not believe there is a village in this country that ought not to be self-supporting. Go back to the days of your boyhood. Every farmer gave potato ground and vegetable ground to anybody whose wife came and helped on the farm during the harvest. It was a good bargain—there was no need for buying any foodstuffs then, except groceries such as tea and sugar, which came from abroad. Each village was almost entirely self-supporting. I am perfectly certain that if there were a great organisation for the utilisation of the labour of this country in that way, you would be able to make Britain not quite self-supporting, but very near it, with one additional proviso. You must ration. If you don't ration, what happens? The price of food begins to do it for you. What does that mean? The rich man can always buy anything he likes, but the more he buys, the less there will be for the others, and those who are lower down on the scale of comforts will get less than their fair share, whilst the others will get far more. It would be a very good thing to have a National Lent. The Catholic Religion is, I think, the most complete study of human nature that has ever been presented to the world, and when it declares its Lent, there is a good deal of practical common sense in it. It is not merely good morally, but it is good physically, and I am perfectly certain that a rationing system of Lent, which would be appropriate during the horrors of war, would make us feel that at any rate we were making some contribution in suffering discomfort at home. War must be brought home to nations. Everybody must put up with some deprivation, either in the way of discomfort or very often of loss. I would certainly urge that there should be a very complete system of rationing which gives plenty but forbids waste, and everybody must be put on the same footing. I ventured to say in February, 1915, that we were laughing too much at Germany's potato rations. I said then, and I repeat it to-day, that the potato spirit in Germany was more formidable than von Hindenburg's leadership. It was the determination to see their country through, whatever it would cost in discomfort to themselves, in privation, and the same thing must apply to us.

I want to make it quite clear to you what the basis of this new Administration will be. I am prepared to answer any question that it may be in my power to answer, but as you will understand, there are many questions I am not in a position to answer until I have consulted my colleagues. I have given you very fairly and very frankly my own views of the only way in which this War has got to be won. If it is a national war, everyone must contribute, and it is on that basis alone we shall be able to achieve a great triumph."

Then came the process of cross-examination to which I have alluded.

In reply to a question as to the position Labour would take in Peace Negotiations, when the time for such negotiations arrived, I said it seemed inconceivable that any Minister should make terms of Peace without consulting the representatives of Labour.

In reply to a question as to whether the policy of prosecuting small papers for expressing their opinions was to be continued, while the larger papers were allowed to say what they liked, I said that I stated in the House about a week ago that personally I would treat Lord Northcliffe in exactly the same way as I would treat a labourer, and that if Northcliffe were guilty of a breach of the Defence of the Realm Act, I would certainly take exactly the same action as I would in the case of a labourer. I thought that there ought not to be any distinction, and that, if a Government were not administered with complete impartiality, it could not expect to be treated with respect in this country.

As regards German militarism and whether we should substitute English militarism for it, I said that if that were going to be the end of the struggle it would be a tragedy. If militarism were not crushed throughout the whole of Europe, the whole of the British blood spilt in the War would have been shed in vain. It must be put an end to, and I certainly would be no party to anything which would end in having a military system here.

On being asked if I very strongly opposed the continuation of conscription after the War, I said: Certainly, if we win the War. If we did not, we should have to get conscription in order to defend our homes.

On the question of black labour, I said that black labour in this country was never proposed. We were getting black labour in battalions for France, because we could not get enough men behind the line in order to save men in this country. We could not take men from essential labour in this country, so, with the consent of the French Government, we had got battalions from South Africa and the East in order to help in unloading in France and also in road making.

Mr. Sidney Webb asked whether compulsory service applied to labour.

I said there would be no change from the old Administration as regards labour. But it was necessary to have a complete mobilisation of labour in order to utilise to the fullest extent the country's resources.

On being asked whether it was the intention to continue this war until we had obtained a decisive victory which would enable us to dictate our own terms of peace, or whether we would at any time give favourable consideration to reasonable proposals which might be put forward either by neutrals or by the enemy, I said that if the proposals made were reasonable, we would listen to them at this moment, and that surely no one imagined that we wanted to go on with the War and have our own sons killed. Before we entered into negotiations with Germany, we must have a clear idea of what she meant, and I thought every sensible man who wanted a good peace would be of the same opinion.

x*

On being asked if the proposed new Cabinet of four members would mean that we should have four dictators, I said: What is a Government for except to dictate? If it does not dictate, it is not a Government, and whether it is four or twenty-three, the only difference is that four would take less time than twenty-three.

I went on to say that each man in his own Department would be dictator, and the only reason for cutting the Cabinet down to four was because with a larger number of people it meant so many men, so many minds; so many minds, so many tongues; so many tongues, so much confusion; so much confusion, so much delay.

I was asked whether it was understood that in the new Cabinet to be formed, the Labour Party in the House would be represented and whether, when peace negotiations were discussed, it would take part in them.

I said that Mr. Henderson had already answered that question that morning. I thought that peace was a long way off yet, but I sincerely hoped that when the time came there would be a Labour representative at the conference.

Referring to the four members of the Cabinet and the Labour Representative—I said that I had come to the conclusion that there must be a Labour Member of the Cabinet without portfolio in order to give his whole time to the War Council.

The deputation then retired. I understood that subsequently there was a very heated discussion as to whether the Party should accept the invitation which I extended to it, to co-operate actively in the War direction by permitting some of its leading members to join the Government. By a majority of one the Labour Executive decided to join the Administration during the period of the War. I ascertained that Mr. J. H. Thomas, who had voted against Labour joining the Asquith Coalition, on this occasion voted for participation. What made the change in his attitude more significant and honourable was the fact that he refused to accept office himself.

The Labour decision assured the success of my task in the formation of a truly National Ministry. When it became known that the most powerful Conservative leaders had already accepted posts in the Government; that I had assurance of support from one-half of the Liberal Party; and that the Labour Party had decided to come in, Mr. Bonar Law experienced no difficulty in persuading the recalcitrant Conservative Ministers to overcome their reluctance to take office under my Premiership.

Soon after the Labour decision became known, on the evening of the 7th December I received Lord Curzon, Lord Robert Cecil, Mr. Austen Chamberlain, and Mr. Walter Long, at an interview at the War Office—as they put it " to discuss certain matters in connection with the proposed arrangements."

Here is the Minute they subsequently published of what took place at the interview.

"The Unionist ex-Ministers stressed the supreme necessity of setting up a stable Administration, and enquired what support the Prime Minister would count on from Liberal and Labour Parties. The P.M. told them that while the Liberal ex-Cabinet Ministers were understood to have promised Mr. Asquith not to join him, 136 Liberal M.P.'s had promised him their support, and that at least as large a section of the Labour Party had agreed to support the P.M. as had previously backed Mr. Asquith's Coalition. The P.M. gave particulars of his meeting with the Labour Party, and of the agreement he had reached with them, alike as to their representation in the new Government and as to its policy on matters which specially affected their interests. The new Government was assured of a favourable reception from the House of Commons, and if difficulties arose later, he would not shrink from the issue of a General Election.

We discussed in some detail the proposed constitution of the new Government, and reached full agreement as to the principle of making the Cabinet a small War Committee of Ministers without portfolio, sitting daily to deal with the War. The personnel of the proposed Cabinet was also agreed, as were the other Ministerial appointments which the P.M. had in view.

Among other matters discussed were the control of the Press, and our policy regarding Ireland; the extension of the Franchise; and the Army command. He discouraged any hasty measures of Press restriction. He announced that he was free from commitments to the Irish Members, and that the hands of the Government would in no way be tied on this issue, nor on other controversial issues such as the Franchise. *He proposed to make no change in the Army Command for the present.*

At the end of our conversation, the Unionist ex-Ministers stated their willingness to accept office under him, and he told them he could now inform the King forthwith of his readiness to accept the duty of forming an Administration."

Their anxiety that there should be no change in the Army Command was a clear indication of the difficulty I was to experience in controlling the Army Chiefs.

As I pointed out to the Labour deputation, I had decided to make one fundamental change in the constitution of the Cabinet. I had long come to the conclusion that a body of 20 Members was a futile instrument for the conduct of any business which required immediate action. I ultimately resolved to set up a Cabinet of five to whom the whole control of the War should be entrusted. I felt that they must remain in almost constant session to review events from day to day.

Ministers who were in charge of Departments could rarely be available for purposes of consultation, and their minds would naturally be taken up with the innumerable details of their respective Offices. The War Cabinet must therefore consist of men who were free from all departmental cares, and who could devote the whole of their time and thought to the momentous questions which were involved in the successful direction of a world war. When matters arose which affected any particular Department, the Head of that Department could be summoned to attend the Cabinet, bringing with him appropriate experts. It was made quite clear that the Cabinet would have the same direct access to these experts as their Departmental Chiefs; that questions could be addressed to them directly; and that they were to speak their minds freely without awaiting the permission or opinion of their political Chiefs.

I had a painful recollection of the Dardanelles muddle, where distinguished experts sat silent and sullen at the War Committee whilst their Chief was advancing propositions with which they profoundly disagreed. They might as well never have attended our sittings. I felt that it was essential that the Cabinet should know quite as much as the Ministers concerned about the personal opinions of the men who were advising them, and who had a first-hand knowledge of the problems and difficulties.

The first War Cabinet consisted of myself, Lord Curzon, Mr. Henderson, Lord Milner, and Mr. Bonar Law. It was also understood that Mr. Balfour should be called into council not only whenever any question arose which affected the Foreign Office, but regularly when he could spare time from his departmental duties. I felt that his unique experience and penetrating intellect would be invaluable in council and that as far as the details of his office were concerned, they could be effectively discharged by his assistant, Lord Robert Cecil.

I realised that I should have to devote the whole of my time to war problems, and that it would be impossible for me, except on certain occasions, to attend the House of Commons. It was therefore agreed that the leadership of the House should be entrusted to Mr. Bonar Law. As I said in the House of Commons, " there would be a Cabinet of five with one of its Members doing sentry duty outside, manning the walls and defending the Council Chamber against attack while we were trying to do our work inside." That did not mean that I did not put in an appearance in the House of Commons. I attended almost daily to answer important questions, and there was hardly a debate of any consequence at which I was not present and did not take part. But leadership of the House of Commons means a good deal more than that. It calls for constant attendance and attention inside the walls of the Palace of Westminster. This I could not give.

FIRST TASKS AS PRIME MINISTER

2. PERSONNEL

WHEN I came to consider what the Liberal quota of the Ministry was to be, I was confronted with the resolution carried by all the Liberal Ministers at a meeting to which I was not summoned, binding each and all not to serve under me. This decision was responsible for the disastrous split in the Liberal Party which diminished its influence, paralysed its energies, and distracted its purpose for all the years that have ensued since 1916. Even to this day it poisons relations between men whose cordial co-operation is essential to the well-being of Liberalism. It deflects judgment upon every issue. Yet however disastrous it was to the future strength of the Party, from the point of view of the efficiency of the Government as a war instrument, the decision arrived at by the official leaders of the Party to decline association with the new Government was an undoubted advantage. There were only three Liberal ex-Ministers whose assistance would have been of undoubted value. One was the Liberal leader, Mr. Asquith. He lacked the force and initiative essential to leadership of the nation in a great war, but as a member of a War Cabinet his counsel and experience would have been of great value. But as I have already related, at the Buckingham Palace Conference after his resignation, he had refused to serve in any Government in which he was not Premier. He declined to serve under Mr. Balfour (himself an ex-Premier). Subsequently he refused to join a Bonar Law Administration. I could not therefore hope to secure his co-operation.

Another Liberal Minister whose gifts of resource and imagination would have been of service in the prosecution of the War was Mr. Edwin Montagu. Having regard to the close friendship which existed between him and Mr. Asquith, he hesitated to join my Government just then. Later on he came in.

The third ex-Minister who would have been helpful in Council was Mr. Winston Churchill—one of the most remarkable and puzzling enigmas of his time. When I took office he had ceased to be a Minister for some months, but he was still a prominent member of the Liberal Party. His fertile mind, his undoubted courage, his untiring industry, and his thorough study of the art of war, would have made him a useful member of a War Cabinet. Here his more erratic impulses could have been kept under control and his judgment supervised and checked, before plunging into action. Men of his ardent temperament and powerful mentality need exceptionally strong brakes. Unfortunately, the Tory Ministers, with the exception of Mr. Balfour and Sir Edward Carson, were unanimous in their resolve that he should not be a member of the Ministry, and most of them made it a condition precedent to their entry into the Government that he should be excluded.

Mr. Bonar Law had a profound distrust of him. I did my best to persuade him to withdraw his objection and I urged the argument which is usually advanced on these occasions, that Mr. Churchill would be more dangerous as a critic than as a Member of the Government. I remember saying to him that when I was practising as a solicitor one of my most responsible duties was the choice of Counsel in an important case. There was the type of man whom you could always depend upon to do his best for the client—and his best was of the very best at the Bar. On the other hand, there was the man of brilliant parts who on his day was even more formidable. His judgment, however, could never be quite depended upon. He was apt either in cross-examination or in speech to be guilty of an indiscretion which would ruin his client's chances. The difficulty in regard to him always was that if you left him out of your team, the other side might brief him and get the benefit of one of his reliable exhibitions of talent, and then I said the question one always had to put to oneself was this: " Is he more dangerous when he is FOR you than when he is AGAINST you?" When I put it in this way to Mr. Bonar Law, his reply was: " I would rather have him against us every time."

I deeply regretted this attitude, but I could not risk a break up of the political combination which was an essential foundation of the Government, for the sake of an immediate inclusion of Mr. Churchill in the Ministry. A few months later I was able to appoint him to the headship of the Ministry of Munitions. Even then the Tory antipathy to him was so great that for a short while the very existence of the Government was in jeopardy.

Here are some samples of the objections advanced at that later time by my colleagues. One of them wrote: —

" May I again and for the last time urge you to think well before you make the appointment (W. Ch.) which we have more than once discussed? It will be an appointment intensely unpopular with many of your chief colleagues—in the opinion of some of whom it will lead to the disruption of the Government at an early date, even if it does not lead, as it may well do, to resignations now. X— who opened the subject to me of his own accord this evening and who has spoken to you, tells me that it will be intensely unpopular in the Army.

I have every reason to believe the same of the Navy. . . .

He is a potential danger in opposition. In the opinion of all of us he will as a member of the Government be an active danger in our midst."

Another Minister wrote at the same time: " Apart from every other consideration, is it wise for you to have as one of your Ministers, a dangerously ambitious man? . . ." And another important Conservative Minister wrote me in a similar strain: —" As regards W. Churchill and the Government, I have made enquiries and from what Z— tells me I am satisfied it would bring about a very grave situation in our Party. . . ."

Why were they so bitter and implacable? His political record naturally exasperated his old Party. He does nothing by halves, and when he left it he attacked his old associates and condemned his old principles with a vigour and a witty scorn which rankled. When War was declared the national peril constrained all parties into a temporary truce, in which party ranks and party rancours were for the time being overlooked or ignored. But Conservatives could not forgive nor forget Churchill's desertion to their enemies, and his brisk and deadly firing into their ranks at a moment when their rout had begun. Had he remained a faithful son of the political household in which he was born and brought up, his share in the Dardanelles fiasco would have been passed over and another sacrifice would have been offered up to appease the popular anger. There was an abundant choice from which the altar could have been supplied. His mistakes gave resentful Tories an irresistible opportunity for punishing rank treason to their party, and the lash which drove Churchill out of office, although knotted with the insults he had hurled at them, was wielded with an appearance of being applied not by vindictive partisans but by dutiful patriots.

For days I discussed with one or other of my colleagues Churchill, his gifts, his shortcomings, his mistakes, especially the latter. Some of them were more excited about his appointment than about the War. It was a serious crisis. It was interesting to observe in a concentrated form every phase of the distrust and trepidation with which mediocrity views genius at close quarters. Unfortunately, genius always provides its critics with material for censure—it always has and always will. Churchill is certainly no exception to this rule.

They admitted he was a man of dazzling talents, that he possessed a forceful and a fascinating personality. They recognised his courage and that he was an indefatigable worker. But they asked why, in spite of that, although he had more admirers, he had fewer followers than any prominent public man in Britain? They pointed to the fact that at the lowest ebb of their fortunes, Joseph Chamberlain in Birmingham and Campbell-Bannerman in Scotland could count on a territorial loyalty which was unshakable in its devotion. On the other hand, Churchill had never attracted, he had certainly never retained, the affection of any section, province or town. His changes of Party were not entirely responsible for this. Some of the greatest figures in British political life had ended in a different Party from that in which they commenced their political career. That was therefore not an adequate explanation of his position in public confidence. They asked: What then was the reason?

Here was their explanation. His mind was a powerful machine, but there lay hidden in its material or its make-up some obscure defect which prevented it from always running true. They could not tell what it was. When the mechanism went wrong, its very power made the action disastrous, not only to himself but to the causes in which he was engaged and the men with whom he was co-operating. That was why the latter were nervous in his partnership. He had in their opinion revealed some tragic flaw in the metal. This was urged by Churchill's critics as a reason for not utilising his great abilities at this juncture. They thought of him not as a contribution to the common stock of activities and ideas in the hour of danger, but as a further danger to be guarded against.

I took a different view of his possibilities. I felt that his resourceful mind and his tireless energy would be invaluable under supervision. That he had vision and imagination, no one could doubt. The Dardanelles idea (apart from its execution), and his early discernment of the value of tanks clearly demonstrated his possession of these faculties. Men with such gifts are rare—very rare. In an emergency they ought to be utilised to the full, and if you keep a vigilant eye on their activities, they are a greater asset than a legion of the conventional sort.

That is why I thought he ought to be employed. I knew something of the feeling against him amongst his old Conservative friends, and that I would run great risks in promoting Churchill to any position in the Ministry; but the insensate fury they displayed when later on the rumour of my intention reached their ears surpassed all my apprehensions, and for some days it swelled to the dimensions of a grave ministerial crisis which threatened the life of the Government. I took the risk, and although I had occasionally some reason to regret my trust, I am convinced I was right to overrule the misgivings of my colleagues, for Churchill rendered conspicuous service in further increasing the output of munitions when an overwhelming supply was essential to victory. As to Churchill's future, it will depend on whether he can establish a reputation for prudence without losing audacity.

As to the rest of the Liberal Ministers, I felt that none of them could have contributed anything in ideas or energy comparable with the men whom I had in my mind selected to fill the vacancies created by the retirement of these Liberals from office. Mr. M'Kenna would have been plainly impossible, for he was the prime mover in the intrigues that precipitated the break-up of the Asquith Coalition. Apart from that, he had defeatist propensities which would have weakened a Government called into being for the more vigorous prosecution of the War.

This latter observation would have been equally applicable to Mr. Runciman. Moreover, in a Government where prompt and effective action was the dominant aim, he would not have found a suitable niche. Although he is a man of high intelligence, there is a lack of continuity and persistent application which has always accounted for his failure to achieve any distinguished success in any of the various offices which he has held. He never follows through. The energy and mastery which he succeeds in conveying in his speeches evaporate before they are translated into masterful action. His most conspicuous attribute is a glib inefficacy, which can explain and expound with forcible and relevant fluency what he is after and why he has never got it. He has a perfect command of the whole jargon of business, and he flips it about in his speeches with a dexterity which awes the ignorant and impresses even the proficient. There he excels and there he also ends.

After the last Cabinet he ever attended Lord Kitchener walked across with me to the Ministry of Munitions. It was his first and last visit to that Department. Mr. Runciman had taken a conspicuous part in a discussion at the Cabinet meeting. On my referring to the clarity with which he had put his case, Lord Kitchener observed: " No man in the Cabinet has disappointed me as much as Runciman. When I first joined the Cabinet he came to me and said that he would very much like to offer his services to me in any direction where his acquaintance with the commercial community would be helpful. I was very grateful and thought it was exceedingly kind of him to tender his assistance. I had spent most of my life in the East, and therefore I had no opportunity of coming into contact with the industrial activities of this country. I asked him to help me in several matters where I lacked experience and knowledge. He readily agreed to do so. More particularly I remember how I asked him to aid me in organising the engineering capacity of this country for the production of war material. Runciman said: ' You need not bother about that— leave it entirely to me.' So I did. But I always found that in all these cases nothing was really done. No man has disappointed me so completely as Runciman." Lord Kitchener spoke with an unaccustomed note of sadness. I never saw him after that conversation.

As to Lord Grey, he was quite futile in any enterprise that demanded decision and energy, and the tremendous responsibility of action in war had a paralytic effect on his powers. I cannot think of any suggestion of his that contributed in the least to the effective prosecution of the War.

Charles Masterman, whose work on Propaganda had been highly successful, had failed in his efforts to secure a seat in Parliament after his defeat at Bethnal Green, and he had therefore left the Asquith Government. In any case, he unfortunately adopted a very hostile attitude towards my Administration and therefore I could not have availed myself of his services.

In order to test the attitude of my old colleagues towards the Government, I determined to make an offer of office to one of them, who had not displayed any active antagonism to me personally. I therefore invited Sir Herbert Samuel to join the Government. He had taken no part in any of the intrigues that went on. He has always done his own snaring. He was a competent and industrious administrator, and I was persuaded that he could preside with neat efficiency over one of the Offices which owing to the War did not demand exceptional gifts of an original kind. Before the War he had won the reputation of being capable and useful in every official sphere he had occupied. During the War he had done nothing in particular, but he had done it very well. When the crash came in 1914 he was quite anxious to do his bit in the Great War and hit on the idea of organising an immediate provision for the unemployed which his discernment of events foresaw as the urgent home problem we had to think of for the duration of the War. When it was discovered that there were no workless labourers to profit by his benevolent forethought, but that on the contrary there was a labour shortage, his contribution to victory came to an end. He gradually sank out of sight altogether as a man who attended to odd jobs of a minor but serviceable character. I have no recollection of his ever having been called in by Mr. Asquith to any of our consultations on major problems arising out of the War.

I asked Samuel to come and see me at the War Office, and as far as I recollect, offered him the post he had occupied in the preceding Administration. He replied that he did not see any elements of endurance in my Government and therefore must decline. I told him that I thought he was mistaken in his estimate of the vitality of the Government, and that he must not be surprised if that Government were in existence five years from that day. His only reply was an incredulous chuckle. Thus our interview ended. My next meeting with him was at San Remo, four years later, when he came to be offered the Governorship of Jerusalem on my recommendation.

Twelve Liberals who held Office, all minor posts, in the first Coalition, accepted Office in the second. Dr. Addison, who had been very helpful as Parliamentary Secretary of the Ministry of Munitions, was made a Minister. He was a man for whose mental equipment I had a great regard. He possessed both breadth and originality of mind.

As to Labour, positions were offered to and accepted by eight members of that Party, as against three in the late Government.

All the Conservative Ministers in the late Administration occupied positions in the new Government, with the exception of Lord Lansdowne. He had for some time been more in sympathy with a peace than with a war offensive, and when the late Government decided that the time had not arrived for negotiation, he felt that his presence inside a Government constituted to prosecute the War with greater vigour was out of place. Moreover, his health was failing and he decided not to come in. On the other hand there were at least four notable Conservatives who were not in the last Administration, but who accepted the invitation to join my Government. One was Lord Milner. I had been one of his most vigorous critics during the Boer War, but that did not prevent his placing his services at the disposal of the State in a national emergency, although his old assailant was at the head of the Government. Sir Edward Carson also decided to come into the Government once more. It was my original intention to make him a Member of the War Cabinet. He had no administrative experience and I thought that his great talents could be better utilised in a consultative than in an executive position. Conservative Ministers, however, resented his promotion to the Cabinet that directed the War, and I had reluctantly to give way. It was a mistake. He had no aptitude for administrative office, but his keen mind would have been helpful in Council.

The refusal of Liberal Ministers to join the Government enabled me to make an experiment which turned out to be a conspicuous success. I invited from outside a number of men of exceptional capacity who had never held any office in any Government and most of whom were not even in Parliament, to occupy positions of great responsibility. I also decided to place men of this type in charge of some of the new Departments. Shipping was such a vital service for the conduct and continuance of the War that I felt there ought to be a separate Department dealing with it, and that some person experienced in ship management should be put in charge. The very life of the nation depended upon making the best use of our ships—in the transport of food and material from overseas and in the carriage of munitions and men for the various war areas. Had there been a serious breakdown in British shipping the Allies would have been beaten. Our shipping resources were developing a grave deficiency. I therefore decided that a new Ministry should be created whose exclusive function should be their complete reorganisation. I invited a great Glasgow shipowner—Sir Joseph Maclay (afterwards Lord Maclay)—to take the post of Shipping Director. How he discharged the important functions of his office it will be a part of my story to tell and I shall tell it with pride in his great achievement.

A new Department was also created for the purpose of controlling the food supplies of the country. I placed Lord Devonport in charge of it. I had some previous experience of him when I was President of the Board of Trade, and he was Parliamentary Secretary to the Board. I knew all about his clear-headedness and his businesslike and masterful handling of every problem I left to his charge. As far as food distribution was concerned, there was no man in the country who had a wider experience.

Mr. Prothero (afterwards Lord Ernle) was brought in as Minister of Agriculture. Not only was he a man of great ability and culture, but he had acquired a thorough acquaintance with agricultural problems as agent of one of the largest and best managed estates in the country. It is also interesting to recall the fact that this was the first experience in office of a man destined at no remote future to play a notable part in the political life of the country—Mr. Stanley Baldwin. He became one of the Junior Lords of the Treasury, with Mr. James Parker and Mr. Towyn Jones. Up to that time he had been Mr. Bonar Law's Parliamentary Private Secretary.

A new Department was created for the purpose of organising the whole of the man-power of the nation on more systematic and efficacious lines. Up to that time, mobilisation had been rather haphazard and there was a shocking waste of effort and energy in this direction. The result was that there was a shortage in the forces in the field, whilst essential industries suffered from a faulty distribution of the available labour reserves at home. It was decided to form a new Ministry and Mr. Neville Chamberlain was invited to become Director of National Service. He accepted the post. At the time of the appointment I had never seen him and knew very little of him. It was not one of my successful selections.

I resolved to create two other new Ministries. One was for the administration of Pensions. For that I designated Mr. George Barnes, one of the most level-headed and highly respected of the Trade Union Leaders. Another was the Ministry of Labour. I invited Mr. John Hodge to become the first Minister. He had been a conspicuously successful Trade Union leader, one who had succeeded in achieving the maximum of benefit for his men with the minimum of strife in the industry. Lord Cowdray, the famous contractor, accepted the chairmanship of the Air Board. Lord Rhondda took office for the first time as President of the Local Government Board in succession to Mr. Walter Long, who became Colonial Secretary.

I was fortunate enough to persuade Mr. H. A. L. Fisher, the Vice-Chancellor of Sheffield University, to undertake the Board of Education. His tenure of that important Office will ever constitute one of the most outstanding chapters in the annals of our educational history. No Minister since W. E. Forster has left such a mark on our system of education. Sir Albert Stanley (afterwards Lord Ashfield), one of the greatest transport organisers of his time, was appointed to the Board of Trade. How he straightened out the tangle which congested the traffic on our railways will be told in due course.

Another departure from Cabinet traditions which I had decided to initiate was the setting up of a Cabinet Secretariat. Hitherto no written record was ever made of even the most important decisions of the Cabinet, let alone the discussions which preceded them. I have no recollection of Sir Henry Campbell Bannerman or Mr. Asquith ever making a note of the conclusions arrived at, except in very exceptional cases where the decision taken was embodied in the form of an answer to be given to a question about to be put in the House of Commons. The result was that now and again there was a good deal of doubt as to what the Cabinet had actually determined on some particular issue. I came to the conclusion that it was desirable to have a secretary present who would make a short précis of the discussions on all important issues and take a full record of all decisions. Where these decisions affected one of the Departments, a copy of the Minute was immediately sent to the Minister concerned. I thought it was of primary importance that a written intimation of the character and terms of the decision of the Cabinet should be sent formally to the Department, not merely as a reminder to the Minister, but in order that the officials who advised him and carried out his orders should be fully informed. I also thought it not only desirable but imperative, having regard to the number of decisions taken in the past which had not been carried out, to charge the Secretary with the duty of keeping in touch with further developments and of reporting to me from time to time what action had been taken in the various Departments concerned on these Cabinet orders. I subsequently found that these enquiries addressed from the Cabinet Office, and the reports which had to be made in response, were very helpful in keeping the Departments alert and well up to the mark. Where the Secretary reported failure or delay in carrying out decisions, I sent for the Minister, and where unexpected difficulties had arisen, steps were taken to remove them.

The first Secretary appointed to this responsible and confidential position was Sir Maurice Hankey. He discharged his very delicate and difficult function with such care, tact, and fairness that I cannot recall any dispute ever arising as to the accuracy of his Minutes or his reports on the action taken.

I strengthened my own secretariat by adding to my personal staff, Mr. Philip Kerr (now Lord Lothian) and Professor Adams. They were both men of exceptional capacity. Mr. Kerr gave me the assistance of a fine mind in all the work arising out of Imperial and Inter-Allied Conferences. Professor Adams helped over domestic issues like Food Production and Ireland. I found his knowledge and sagacity of great service.

I lost no time in forming the Ministry. We were at war and every hour counted. There were many vital questions overdue for decision. I remembered the leisurely and even dawdling way in which the first

Coalition had been pieced together and the precious days wasted in discussion over appointments to Ministerial posts, whilst important decisions, more particularly over the Dardanelles attacks, had to await the weighing and balancing of personal "claims" rather than merits. This method of doing business during a war was responsible for one of the many delays which proved to be fatal to that particular enterprise.

I was called to the Premiership on the 7th December, and on the 9th the War Cabinet had been constituted and actually met to transact business.

FIRST TASKS AS PRIME MINISTER

3. SURVEY OF THE POSITION

In order to understand the nature and gravity of the undertaking with which the new Government was confronted, it is necessary to make a rapid survey of the position at the end of 1916.

We were on the eve of the fourth campaign of the War. The conditions under which it was to be fought had already been settled by military and naval strategy and by events and circumstances, some of the most fateful of which, as I have already related, I had vainly endeavoured to modify or change. It was my misfortune to be called upon to grapple with the consequences of policies which I had resisted step by step.

Three of the Allied Powers, Belgium, Serbia and Roumania, had been almost completely destroyed as military entities that counted in the struggle. Russia, still huge, was sprawling on the ground, with formidable possibilities if she rose with the remnant of her great strength to face the foe. But no one knew whether she could or would rise. She excited more conjecture than confidence. The overwhelming preponderance in man-power which had given the Allies such a false sense of security and lured them in 1915 and 1916 into enterprises where human life was thrown lavishly and recklessly into the conflagration to feed the flames as if there were an endless store of available men in reserve, had now practically disappeared. From the purely military aspect the Central Powers seemed stronger and more unbreakable than they had ever been.

Most, if not all, opportunities for manœuvring the Central Powers out of their vast stronghold had been closed down one by one. Its weak points had been sought out in order to avoid them as if they were traps for the faint-hearted. The High Commands and the Chiefs of Staffs of the Western Powers had concluded that this was to be a war of attrition, and they had so contrived matters that their strategical notion should be the only one left on the board. It was a pre-planned " I told you so." With these themes I deal later on in my chapter on the military situation. Here I call attention to the fact that the struggle had already become essentially a trial of endurance between nations more than between armies. There were still openings for military skill. Genius can always find or force an opening. The Allies had almost given up looking out for such an instrument of deliverance. The issue of the War now depended on exhaustion. Whose strength would give out first? Morale, food, man-power, war material and transport—the belligerent group that failed first in one of these essential elements would lose the War.

In this devastating struggle the resources of all the warring nations had been wellnigh strained to the utmost limit. The nation that made the most economical and efficient use of its remaining strength, having regard to the strategic and economic position as defined at the end of the third campaign, stood the best chance of winning in the end. The Central Powers were in the best strategical positions on land, on every flank. As they were both in the East and West entrenched on Allied soil, they could not be dislodged without a decisive preponderance in men and machinery on the side of their assailants. The overthrow of Roumania had shortened their line, whilst it had lengthened the Russian line by 500 kilometres. If Russia went out of action, the resources of the combatant groups in men would be equal.

As far as the mechanism of war was concerned, the Allies were making strides towards equality. With a sustained effort, 1917 would see the advantage in this respect inuring to their side. On the French Front the Allies were better off than the Germans in ammunition, but not in guns. The French had neglected the advice given by their ablest artillery officers to them as well as to us to concentrate on heavy artillery, especially howitzers of the latest patterns. We accepted this excellent counsel and acted upon it. The French gunner staffs disliked it, and accordingly delayed action. They regarded this advice as a reflection upon their idol, the *soixante-quinze*—an unpatriotic aspersion on this product of French genius. Later on in the year they realised what Verdun ought to have taught them earlier that in the matter of heavy guns they were inferior to the Germans, and that this inferiority crippled their offensive power.

The Turkish equipment was not comparable to ours. But so far we had made a wretched use of our superiority in men and material in that area. The Staff seemed to discourage victories in the East, regarding them as an exaltation of strategical heresy, and therefore an abomination. On all other fronts the Central Powers were better equipped, having regard to the task in front of them, than the Allied forces. The last remnant of the Roumanian Army was being battered into impotence by a more powerful artillery than their own. The Russians were inferior in every mechanical arm and their transport was deplorable. The army of entrenched Germans, Austrians, Bulgarians, and Turks, looking down from the Balkan heights on their foes in the Macedonian plain, were infinitely better equipped for their purely defensive rôle than were the Allied Expeditionary Army for the offensive they must sooner or later undertake, if victory were ever to be achieved in that battle area. On the Italian Front, Cadorna's artillery was inadequate to the part entrusted to it of shattering defences blasted out of Alpine rocks. The Allies had therefore still a good deal to do before they attained the necessary mechanical advantage over the Central Powers.

The imminent collapse of both Roumania and Russia would give definite advantage to the Central Powers in man-power. To attain an appreciable superiority in equipment, and thus to fill up the deficiency in man-power which would be created by the gaps already yawning in the East, would demand intensified activity on the part of the Allies. The brunt of this burden must fall on the two greatest engineering countries in the Alliance—Britain and France, with such help as we could afford to purchase in America.

An additional reason for increasing the Allied output of munitions in their own factories and workshops, was the growing difficulty experienced in financing Allied orders abroad. The supply of this increasing demand meant a further drain on a diminishing reserve of man-power, at a time when the armies were short of men to fill up their depleted battalions. A survey of our available resources for all these purposes, at and behind the front, left no doubt that the best use was not being made of our manhood, and that a thorough national reorganisation was required if we ever hoped to pull through the years ahead of us with success.

But beyond everything it was becoming a contest of national morale. All the nations involved in this colossal struggle were supremely courageous races with a long military tradition behind them. All their tribes were fighting tribes. Not one of them would give in readily; certainly not as long as their armies presented an unbroken front to the foe. Even a series of shattering military defeats had failed so far to induce Russia, Belgium, Roumania or Serbia to capitulate. A breakdown on one side or the other of the rival nations would come from some cause which would wear out the spirit of their people. Hunger alone could effect such a collapse. Much would depend on the quality and efficacy of the appeals, written and spoken, that would be made in order to stimulate and sustain the courage and constancy of the armies and the people behind them. But the history of sieges demonstrates that it is only a small number of indomitable men and women who can long endure the daily spectacle of privation amongst those whose natural protectors they are. In considering our problems, the question of food supplies therefore took a foremost place in the rank.

The first half of the War demonstrated clearly how vital transport on sea and land and the supply of munitions to a successful prosecution of the War. The second half of the War brought home to all the belligerents the fact which ought to have been obvious before, that an adequate supply of food, not only for the troops, but for the civilian population, was an essential condition of their continuance in the War. The final event depended more on food than on fighting. The drain on man-power, and the concentration of transport on the provision of war material and the carrying of it to the various fronts, were already having a serious effect on food supplies. When I took over the supreme war direction in December, 1916, I found Russia on the point of falling to pieces owing to food shortage. The munition problem there had by no means been solved, but it had considerably improved, and in spite of huge losses there was no lack of fit men to fill up the gaps. But the supply of food for the cities and for certain sectors of the front had broken down completely, and in the grimmest of Russian winters millions of householders from lack of sustenance and fuel, were shivering many degrees below the freezing line. To these hungry and chilled multitudes and their soldier sons, brothers and husbands, revolution was not only acceptable, but inevitable. It was the only alternative to famine. A sufficiency of food and fuel might have kept Russia in the War right to the end, no longer perhaps a steamroller, but at least a stone wall.

Austria was also suffering more and more severely from the lack of food. The Hungarian harvest of 1916 had been a calamitous failure; 1917 did not make up the deficiency. Not only wheat but milk and meat were also becoming scarcer. The shortage contributed to the readiness of Austria to make peace. It was one of the decisive factors in her final surrender. In the field her armies were still unbeaten on foreign soil when the collapse occurred. The turn of Germany was obviously coming. She was passing through the terrible "turnip winter." Her potato crop had failed and the population had to fall back on turnips. The food distributed per head in Germany during this winter had a calorific value of only half the minimum necessary to keep the population in health. We are told that by 1917 the output in the German mines and munition factories was suffering considerably as a result of the decline in the physical fitness of the workers.

It was becoming a war of starvation. In the end meagre and mean feeding at last subdued the spirit that had for four years of sanguinary battles proved indomitable on every battle front. Food in all the belligerent countries was therefore at the end of 1916 becoming a growing, and as it turned out, a paramount element in the chances of victory. They were all beleaguered nations.

So far in Britain, France and Italy, there was no actual privation suffered by any section of the people owing to food shortage. The command of the sea was still in Allied hands and the corn lands of the earth were still open and available to Allied cupboards, not in sufficient quantities to fill them, but just enough to prevent the boards from becoming bare. But the submarine had introduced an element of increasing precariousness to this food supply. Once sea transport failed—and it was failing rapidly—the resistance of the Allied armies would collapse. All nations were becoming rattled and disillusioned by the prolongation of sacrifice and horror with indecisive result. A touch of hunger might convert disillusionment into disaffection. Food was at the very root of national morale, and in a protracted struggle between equally brave nations morale is the decisive factor. That is why, when it became my duty to survey the whole area of the War and the conditions which would determine its final result, I realised that the " feeding of the multitude " was a matter of supreme moment. I had, as a matter of fact, come to that conclusion over a year ago, and quotations I have already given from my interventions and proposals on this question at War Councils in 1915 and 1916, are a proof of my concern that we should take timely steps for the provisionment of the nation.

In a war of this order, sea power was the key to ultimate victory so long as either party could manage just to hold their own on land. If we maintained control of the seas without actually breaking on shore, the Central Powers could in the end be starved into surrender. Before reaching the point of actual starvation, such privations could be inflicted on their population as would destroy their morale. Had our armies been on their soil, the spirit that bids men die rather than give in to the invader of their native land would have sustained them. But no people will die of hunger rather than relinquish conquests of foreign territory. Potential famine was therefore the most powerful weapon in the army of the belligerents. As long as Britain kept her rule over the waves, neither she nor her Allies could be beaten by any shortage of food or essential material for waging war. On the other hand, the Central Powers could not win if they were cut off from the resources of the great world outside. It was a ruthless calculation, but war is organised cruelty. Those who think they can restrict its barbarities will find in the end that savagery is of its essence and that civilised warfare only means that men have changed the instruments and methods of torture. The sum total of the agony inflicted on mankind by war was never as great as it proved to be in the World War of 1914-18. Men, women and children all suffered the horrors of war. The deaths behind the fighting lines owing to the effects of underfeeding and bad feeding were more numerous than those of the slain in the stricken field.

When Verdun and the Somme had both failed to achieve a military decision, the belligerents were confronted with a war of starvation.

For us the most serious and urgent element in this situation was that of our dwindling shipping resources. The sea was the jugular vein of Allied vitality. Once that were cut the Allied strength would soon be drained of its life blood. To quote a contemporary report submitted to the War Cabinet in the first days of its deliberations: " The whole cause of the Allies depends upon the maintenance of sea power. The communications of the Armies in the East and West can only be carried out by sea, and nearly every one of the Allies at the present moment depends upon sea-borne supplies not only for the Armies themselves, but for raw material for munitions, and for the essentials of life of the civil population as well."

There was a serious shortage of shipping for the pressing needs of the Allies. Essential drafts for Allied Armies in Salonika, Egypt and Mesopotamia were held up because there was no transport available. Railway material which was urgently required behind the line in France could not be taken across for lack of ships. Ammunition for some of our armies had to be cut down (although ships had to be found to transport forage for the Cavalry Divisions that were always fit and ready to complete the great rout that was for ever impending on the Western Front). Our food supplies could not be replenished for the same reason. The position in all these respects was precarious. Italy was in dire need of coal for her munition works, but the deliveries were 800,000 tons short of her requirements because we had no available ships to carry the fuel. Italy's already inadequate supply of ammunition was thus still further diminished for lack of British shipping. The submarine attack on our shipping had inflicted serious losses during the last few months. The new submarine monster was gliding everywhere through the deep in search of prey—defenceless prey. Allied ships were being stricken down in increasing numbers. We seemed impotent to protect our ships and their devoted mariners. Since the beginning of August, some 675,000 tons of British shipping had been sent to the bottom of the sea. On the other hand, we were making no real effort to build new vessels and the output of our yards had decreased by 66 per cent. The shortage was not altogether due to the lack of tonnage, but was largely attributable to the fact that the use we made of our available shipping resources was unbusinesslike and consequently very wasteful. The control and distribution of our shipping was exceedingly profitable to certain shipowners, but ruinous to the Allied cause. Whilst we were short of transport for essential war purposes and even for the food of the people, millions of tons were thrown away on superfluous luxuries, carried at ruinous freights. They ought to have been cut out of the national life during a great war. Only half our shipping was under Government control. The rest was left free for the haggling of the market, and in a war-restricted market the haggle became an exaction. One consequence of this was that a very considerable number of our ships were still trading between South American ports, where the freights were extravagantly high because of the scarcity of ships. The ports were also congested and the defective arrangements for loading and discharging cargoes caused considerable delays, thus diminishing still further our transport capacity. The 50 per cent. of our shipping which was under Government control was by no means used to the best advantage, the Admiralty more particularly having far too large a reserve of ships for emergencies which never arose, thus immobilising ships which would have been invaluable if they had been used for urgent war services. The railway system was clogged with non-essential traffic. This got in the way of vital needs, adding to deficiencies and delays. Unless action were immediately taken to improve the transport situation on sea and land, there was a real danger that the maximum effort which was essential to the attainment of victory would never be achieved.

The most serious result of the shipping position was the fact that our food supplies were also in jeopardy. As I have already pointed out, our margin was a very narrow one. Harvests had failed, not merely in this country and on the Continent, but in the Argentine, and the nearest abundant supply was to be found in Australia. That meant long voyages for our dwindling Mercantile Marine. At home, in spite of the appeals made by both Lord Selborne and his successor, Lord Crawford, no steps had been taken by the late Government to increase production. The yield of our soil was steadily diminishing. During the last twelve months the wheat production of this country had fallen off by about one-sixth. Unless some steps were adopted without delay to bring more land into cultivation, and to increase the fertility of that which was capable of cultivation, then there would be a further grave diminution in the quantity of food raised in these islands. That meant either privation or a further inroad on our already overburdened shipping.

As soon as the War Cabinet entered upon its functions, it caused a careful and searching survey to be made of the national position in respect of all these urgent problems. As to many of them, the report presented to us showed that the late Government had decided in principle that some measures should be taken immediately to cope with the difficulty, but in each case the report ended with the words " No Action Taken."

A Government that had surrendered to the Allied military strategy which had decreed a war of attrition had neglected to take the necessary steps to prevent the wearing down process going against us. If it was too late to alter the military strategy, there was yet time to see that we did not fall in the fight through sheer exhaustion, whilst the foe had still enough strength to stand and wield his sword. Our gravest problem was one of reconstruction and concentration so as to make our resources last out longer than those of our adversaries.

CHAPTER XXXIX

THE GERMAN AND WILSON PEACE NOTES
OF DECEMBER, 1916

IN the account I gave in Chapter XXXI of the episode of the Lansdowne Memorandum, I recorded the fact that the Asquith Government had come to the unanimous conclusion that it would be a disastrous mistake to enter into peace negotiations with Germany before inflicting a complete defeat upon her armies.

Although Lord Curzon, in a speech delivered in the House of Lords, referred to " the glorious and noble victory of the Somme," the phrase was recognised at the time, especially by those—soldiers and civilians —who knew the facts, as a merely characteristic piece of fustian. The Allies had completely failed in the main purpose of their attack, and the Germans had actually withdrawn troops from the battlefield at the crisis and climax of the offensive against them, in order to stage a more triumphant offensive of their own in a region which was removed hundreds of miles from the Somme terrain. At best the battle ended in a stalemate, which meant a check for the Allies as far as their main objective was concerned.

Nothing had therefore happened to alter the situation since the Asquith Cabinet decided in November not to encourage or countenance peace negotiations.

An opportunity soon arose for giving a practical application to that decision. Early in December, 1916—a few days after I became Prime Minister—the German Government issued its famous Peace Note.

Although summaries had appeared in the Foreign Press for days, the full text of the Note was not communicated to the Allied Governments until the 18th December, when the American Ambassador delivered it, at the request of the German Government, at the Foreign Office. Lord Robert Cecil, who was acting Foreign Secretary in the absence through illness of Mr. Balfour, reported to the War Council that the American Ambassador, in transmitting the Note on behalf of the German Government, had indicated that the United States Government would deeply appreciate a confidential intimation in advance of the proposed reply by the British Government to the Note, and that his Government itself intended to make representations on the subject at the appropriate moment, and had for some time had such intention independently of the German Note.

As there has been some hostile comment in censorious circles upon the Allied replies to this German Peace approach, it would be well here to reproduce it in full. These replies have been represented as the spurning by the Allies of a favourable opportunity for making a satisfactory peace. Unless the tone and the terms of the document are read carefully, it is not possible for anyone to come to any just conclusion as to the attitude adopted towards it by the Allied Powers.

" Berlin,
12th December, 1916.

Mr. Chargé d'Affaires,

The most formidable war known to history has been ravaging for two and a half years a great part of the world. The catastrophe that the bonds of a common civilisation more than a thousand years old could not stop, strikes mankind in its most precious patrimony; it threatens to bury under its ruin the moral and physical progress on which Europe prided itself at the dawn of the twentieth century. *In that strife Germany and her Allies, Austria-Hungary and Turkey, have given proof of their indestructible strength in winning considerable successes at war. Their unshakable lines resist ceaseless attacks of their enemies' arms. The recent diversion in the Balkans was speedily and victoriously thwarted. The latest events have demonstrated that a continuation of the War cannot break their resisting power. The general situation much rather justified* (sic) *their hope of fresh successes.** It was for the defence of their existence and freedom of their national development that the four Allied Powers were constrained to take up arms. The exploits of their armies have brought no change therein. Not for an instant have they swerved from the conviction that the respect of the rights of other nations is not in any degree incompatible with their own rights and legitimate interests. *They do not seek to crush or annihilate their adversaries.** Conscious of their military and economic strength and ready to carry on to the end if they must the struggle that is forced upon them, but animated at the same time by the desire to stem the flood of blood and to bring the horrors of war to an end, the four Allied Powers propose to enter even now into peace negotiations. They feel sure that the propositions which they would bring forward and which would aim to assure the existence, honour, and free development of their peoples would be such as to serve as a basis for the restoration of a lasting peace.

If, notwithstanding this offer of peace and conciliation the struggle should continue, the four Allied Powers are resolved to carry it on to an end, while solemnly disclaiming any responsibility before mankind and history.

The Imperial Government has the honour to ask through your

* My italics.

obliging medium, the Government of the United States to be pleased to transmit the present communication to the Government of the French Republic, to the Royal Government of Great Britain, to the Imperial Government of Japan, to the Royal Government of Roumania, to the Imperial Government of Russia, and to the Royal Government of Serbia.

I take this opportunity to renew to you, Mr. Chargé d'Affaires, the assurance of my high consideration.

VON BETHMANN HOLLWEG.

To Mr. Joseph Clark Grew,
    Chargé d'Affaires of the United
      States of America.''

This was not the language of an enemy suing for peace after a crushing defeat in the field, or of a foe conscious that on the whole the tide was beginning to turn against him, or even of an adversary who realised that although he had no fear of being beaten, nevertheless, if the War continued both parties in the end would be ruined. It was rather in the nature of an overture from a Power conscious of the unbreakable strength of its armies, boasting of a succession of resounding triumphs against its enemies and of its ability to hold its own in future against every effort to dislodge its grip on the vast territories it had conquered, but anxious to cast upon its enemies the responsibility for prolonging the War. German statesmanship, which was entirely under military control and direction, had three objects in view when it launched this peace offensive. The first was to reconcile that part of the German population who were beginning to feel that brilliant victories without number brought nothing but heavier burdens, more and more privations, and mounting casualties to the triumphant Fatherland. It was necessary to convince these that ultimate victory was the only alternative to an unsatisfying peace. The second was to persuade neutral countries which were becoming increasingly hostile to Germany and also the people behind the Governments of belligerent countries, that the prolongation of the War was due entirely to the bloodthirsty stubbornness and insatiable ambition of Allied Governments. The third was to enter into peace negotiations whilst military conditions were more favourable to Germany than to the Allies, the German Armies being quartered in Allied territory and on the whole having beaten off the assaults made on their positions there on every front.

With a view to enabling the Cabinet to inform itself fully of the position before discussing the character of the reply, the Secretary of the War Cabinet was instructed to circulate to its Members the papers prepared during the discussions of the late Government in connection with possible terms of Peace, conditions of an Armistice, and negotiations at the end of the War. Steps were also taken to ascertain the views of both Allies and Neutrals on the subject of the Note itself. It is interesting now to peruse the reports which came in. They indicate the reaction in each country, and the views and opinions formed at the time by belligerents and neutrals, as to the purport and bona fides of the German communication.

The French attitude was definitely suspicious of the Note. It was expressed by M. Briand in a speech in the Chamber on 13th December, 1916. He declared that it was his bounden duty to put France on her guard against a peace which was really an attempt to split up the Allies. Surveying the situation he showed that, despite German successes in the past year, France, which had supported almost alone the terrible weight of the attack in 1914, had more reasons than ever for confidence in her conviction of the certitude of victory. Germany, in throwing out peace proposals, proclaimed at the same time her victory; and in truth Serbia, Belgium and Roumania were at present invaded and the crime not yet expiated. Germany might declare that she did not want war. But she was the aggressor, and France, victorious at Verdun, would not walk into the trap of these peace proposals.

M. Jules Cambon thought the Allies should traverse the German assertions, and say that a peace offer without terms was not genuine. In his opinion it would be better for France to take the lead in answering, and a conference to settle the reply would be unnecessary and inadvisable.

In view of what happened later, the attitude of Russia towards the German peace overtures has an interest of its own. The Russian answer was inspired by the Duma and not by the Czar alone. The Russian Duma decided in favour of making peace "only after victory." M. Pokrovsky, the Foreign Minister, pointed out that there was nothing in the German Note to suggest that the peace the Central Powers were prepared to make would be satisfactory. "What are the circumstances in which the German proposal was made? The enemy armies have devastated and occupied Belgium, Serbia, and Montenegro, and a part of France, Russia and Roumania. The Austro-Germans have just proclaimed the illusory independence of a part of Poland, and are by this means trying to lay hands on the entire Polish nation. Who then, with the exception of Germany, could derive any advantage under such conditions by the opening of peace negotiations? . . . To attempt at the last moment to profit by their fleeting territorial conquests before their domestic weakness was revealed—that was the real meaning of the German proposal. In the event of failure they will exploit at home the refusal of the Allies to accept peace in order to rehabilitate the tottering morale of their populations."

v

Published on December 20th, 1916.   *Reproduced by courtesy of " Punch."*

" THE NEW CONDUCTOR "
Opening of the 1917 Overture

"Another motive," M. Pokrovsky continued, "might be a hope of exploiting elements of cowardice amongst the Allies. *But Russia would fight on for a peace of victory.* All her sacrifices would be in vain if a premature peace were concluded with an undefeated Germany."

Communications from the Russian Foreign Office to us confirmed this attitude, while suggesting that we should not flatly refuse to make peace, but insist that peace must be made on our terms. Discussion as to the form of the reply could take place in London or Paris.

Baron Sonnino, the Italian Foreign Minister, was of opinion that the Germans hoped for a direct refusal, and suggested that the German claims and assertions should be refuted, and that they should be challenged to declare their terms. The Allies could consent to no annexations by the Central Powers, and Italy would not agree even to the *status quo*.

Belgium favoured a conference to draw up an identical reply. This should not be a flat refusal to make peace, but a refusal to negotiate without knowing the German proposals.

Japan stated that she could not accept the *status quo ante*.

The Neutral countries were all of opinion that it would be a mistake for the Allies to reject outright the German peace offer.

From the United States our Ambassador, Sir C. Spring-Rice, telegraphed, reporting: —

"It is generally felt that Allies should not decline to receive definite terms of peace from the Germans. The German position in the U.S.A. would be much strengthened by such a refusal." He advised "giving expression to strong pacific sentiment but declaring that His Majesty's Government must be guided in their action by the character of the Peace terms proposed and must act in consultation with our Allies." He would further add that pending decision we would continue the War with all our resources until an assured peace was established. If President Wilson should himself put forward any suggestions the British Government should show appreciation non-committally of his friendly gesture. The German party in the United States were clearly hoping for a direct refusal on our part.

Sir C. Spring-Rice suggested "that a statement in the U.S.A. might well be made broadly on the lines of Grey's speech of 22nd March, 1915, stressing the importance of reparation for Belgium. The Government of the United States very much wants to end the War as it fears intensification of the submarine campaign and spread of the War to America."

In Switzerland the Foreign Minister thought that complete rejection might exasperate the German population and intensify the ruthlessness of the War.

Opinion in Holland was to a similar effect.

The Swedish Foreign Minister viewed the German Note as a manœuvre, which should be met by a demand to table proposals, rather than by flat refusal.

At the Vatican, Cardinal Gasparri was of the opinion that the Germans should be asked to state their terms, and if they should prove impossible, the moral advantage would rest with the Allies in continuing the struggle. He said that he had reason to believe that the German terms would be moderate.

The general tenor of opinion among the Allied and Neutral countries was opposed to any reply which would imply a point-blank refusal to negotiate. But opinion was practically unanimous that Germany should be asked to state her terms. It is significant that the Vatican also took this view, and expressed the belief that the terms would be moderate. The Vatican was suspected of being pro-German. It would probably be nearer the truth to say that the majority of the Cardinals had Austrian sympathies. The Vatican reply would therefore be influenced by representations received from Vienna. But Vienna was not Berlin and their interests and ambitions were not identical.

At its meeting on 18th December, 1916, the British War Cabinet had before it all the foregoing information. It was agreed that it would be best for the Allies to concert an identical Note in reply to the German Note, and that this should be signed by them all in Paris, and handed by the representative of France to the American Ambassador. The Note should refute the statements made in the preamble of the German Note, and state that a general offer of peace, without defining terms, was useless. Decision as to its other contents was left over, pending the consideration of a draft reply which M. Briand was reported to be preparing.

As an indication of the attitude of the British Government at that period, I quote two passages bearing on the German Note from the first speech which I delivered in the House of Commons on 19th December, 1916, after a Cabinet discussion of its tenor: —

" Any man or set of men who wantonly, or without sufficient cause, prolonged a terrible conflict like this would have on their soul a crime that oceans could not cleanse. On the other hand, it is equally true that any man or set of men who out of a sense of weariness or despair abandoned the struggle without achieving the high purpose for which we had entered into it being nearly fulfilled would have been guilty of the costliest act of poltroonery ever perpetrated by any statesman. I should like to quote the very well-known words of Abraham Lincoln under similar conditions: —

'We accepted this war for an object, and a worthy object, and the war will end when that object is attained. Under God I hope it will never end until that time.'

Are we likely to achieve that object by accepting the invitation of the German Chancellor? That is the only question we have to put to ourselves. There has been some talk about proposals of peace. What are the proposals? There are none. To enter at the invitation of Germany, proclaiming herself victorious, without any knowledge of the proposals she proposes to make, into a conference, is to put our heads into a noose with the rope end in the hands of Germany.

. . . The mere word that led Belgium to her destruction will not satisfy Europe any more. We all believed it. We all trusted it. It gave way at the first pressure of temptation, and Europe has been plunged into this vortex of blood. We will, therefore, wait until we hear what terms and guarantees the German Government offer other than those, better than those, surer than those, which she so lightly broke, and meanwhile we shall put our trust in an unbroken Army rather than a broken faith. . . ."

The following quotation from Mr. Asquith's reply will demonstrate the unity of the nation on this German move: —

" Peace we all desire. Peace can only come—peace, I mean, that is worth the name and that satisfies the definition of the word— peace will only come on terms that atonement is made for past wrongs, that the weak and downtrodden are restored, that the faith of treaties is observed, and that the sovereignty of public law is securely enthroned over the nations of the world."

No protest was entered from any quarter of the House against the character of our reply. The Pacifist group, led by Mr. Ramsay MacDonald and Mr. Snowden, uttered no word of criticism.

On the following day, the 20th December, the United States Ambassador communicated to the Allied Governments President Wilson's own Peace Note.

This document began, after protestation of its friendly spirit and purpose, with a disclaimer of any association with the peace overtures of the Central Powers. The President then went on to suggest that each of the belligerents should table their views as to the terms on which the War could be concluded, and its recurrence prevented. He said that according to their published declarations, all the belligerent powers had the same object. "Each side desires to make the rights and privileges of weak peoples and small States as secure against aggression or denial in the future as the rights and privileges of the great and powerful States now at war. Each wishes itself to be made secure in the future, along with all other nations and peoples, against

the recurrence of wars like this, and against aggression or selfish interference of any kind. . . ." To attain these and similar ends, a
satisfactory peace must first of all be concluded. The United States
was also vitally interested in an early peace settlement, and the
President therefore urged an exchange of views on peace terms, *which
had not as yet been publicly stated.*

In conclusion, President Wilson stated that he was not himself proposing peace terms, or offering to mediate, but merely proposing the
taking of soundings, to find out how near we might be to attaining
peace.

This document was considered by the War Cabinet on the 21st
December. It was published in the Press on the following day. On
23rd December it was again considered and arrangements made for
drafts of suggested replies to be prepared by Lord Robert Cecil and
Mr. Balfour. There was also before the Cabinet a draft reply prepared by M. Briand to the American Note. But this was set aside as
too vague and too evasive. We were of opinion that the Allied reply
should be explicit and candid. There must be no doubt left in the
minds of belligerents or neutrals as to the objectives for the attainment
of which the Allied countries were prepared to make further sacrifices
if necessary.

It so happened that an Anglo-French Conference was due to be held
three days later in London, to discuss a number of matters connected
with the War, including the situation in Greece and Salonika, and
the problem of unity of command in the West. Advantage was taken
of this occasion to discuss with the representatives of France the replies
to the German and American Peace Notes.

The conference took place on 26th, 27th and 28th December, 1916.
MM. Ribot, Thomas, and Berthelot had come over from France to
confer with us. M. Briand was unable, through indisposition, to be
present. M. Berthelot stated the personal view of the French Premier.

In the discussion on the reply to Germany, doubts were expressed
by us as to certain passages in M. Briand's draft. A fresh text was
submitted by M. Cambon, the French Ambassador, and approved
after revision. This ultimately became the note agreed to by all the
Allies, with the addition of a further passage specially relating to
Belgium.

In its ultimate form, the reply of the Allied Powers to Germany was
handed by the French Government to the United States Ambassador
in Paris on 30th December, 1916. It was signed on behalf of Russia,
France, Great Britain, Japan, Italy, Serbia, Belgium, Montenegro,
Portugal and Roumania.

It began by rebutting the assertions in the German Note that the
Allies were responsible for the War, and that the Central Powers were
now victorious, and it went on to declare the devotion of the Allies
to peace. But, it added : —

"A mere suggestion, without statement of terms, that negotiations should be opened, is not an offer of peace. The putting forward by the Imperial Government of a sham proposal, lacking all substance and precision, would appear to be less an offer of peace than a war manœuvre."

After recapitulating the steps by which the Central Powers had forced on the War, and pointing out that the War map of Europe alone gave no true picture of the strong military position of the Allies, the Note pointed out that penalties, reparations, and guarantees were required from Germany. The German Note was declared to be only a device to stiffen public opinion among the Central Powers, mislead the Neutral Countries and justify in advance fresh crimes of submarine warfare, deportations and forced enlistment of alien peoples. The Note proceeded: —

"Fully conscious of the gravity of this moment, but equally conscious of its requirements, the Allied Governments, closely united to one another and in perfect sympathy with their peoples, refuse to consider a proposal which is empty and insincere."

No peace was possible until reparation could be secured for the violation of national rights, and a settlement achieved which would prevent a repetition of such outrages.

In conclusion, the Note dealt with the case of Belgium, and Germany's violation of its neutrality and cruel treatment of its people. Peace terms must assure that country legitimate reparation, guarantees, and safeguards for the future.

This was the reply to the German Note. The Anglo-French Conference then proceeded to discuss the nature of the reply to be made to the United States President.

The opinion was against separate notes. On this, the French were emphatic. As to the contents of a joint Note, Lord Robert Cecil reported that Mr. Page, the American Ambassador, had told him that morning that the majority of people in America were in reality friendly to the Allies, but that we had not been able to get the spirit in which we were fighting across the Atlantic. Mr. Page urged us to treat the United States Government in the most open way possible.

Mr. Balfour thought we ought to say that if the War were to end without the restoration of Alsace-Lorraine to France, without the union of unredeemed Italy with the Italian Kingdom, without the inclusion of the Serbian people within Serbian boundaries and of the Roumanian population within Roumanian boundaries, without something being done to satisfy Polish aspirations and to free Christian populations from Turkish tyranny, the New Year would begin under unfavourable auspices. He would like to add, as coming especially from Great Britain, that in these results the Government and people of the British Empire had no more direct and immediate interest than had the United States. They would obtain from them neither territory nor revenue; neither military strength nor commercial opportunity. But failure in these matters would imperil the prospects of those great ideas of international relationship to which the President had given so noble an expression.

The joint reply, communicated to the American Government on 10th January, 1917, declared, after expressing respect for the lofty sentiments inspiring the American Note, that the War could be ended satisfactorily only on terms promising a just and durable peace. The suggestion in the American Note that the aims of belligerents on both sides were the same was refuted by the undeniable history of the struggle, and the violation of the rights of small nations in its course by the Central Powers. Reference was made to Belgium and Luxemburg, Serbia, Armenia, Syria, Zeppelin raids, submarine atrocities, Miss Cavell and Captain Fryatt, and other items in the catalogue of German crimes.

In reply to President Wilson's request that the Governments should formulate their peace terms, the Note enumerated the following items as matters which must be dealt with in any settlement: —

The restoration of Belgium, of Serbia, and of Montenegro, with the compensation due to them;

The evacuation of the invaded territories of France, Russia, and Roumania, with fitting reparation;

The reorganisation of Europe, guaranteed by a stable settlement, based alike upon the principle of nationalities, on the right which all people, whether small or great, have to the enjoyment of full security and free economic development, and also upon territorial and international agreements so framed as to guarantee land and sea frontiers against unjust attacks;

The restitution of provinces or territories formerly torn from the Allies by force or contrary to the wishes of their inhabitants;

The liberation of Italians, Slavs, Roumanians, Czechs, and Slovaks from foreign domination;

The liberation of the peoples who now lie beneath the murderous tyranny of the Turks, and the expulsion from Europe of the Ottoman Empire, which has proved itself so radically alien to Western civilisation;

The implementing of the Czar's recent proclamation as to the restoration of Poland;

The rescue of Europe from the brutal encroachments of Prussian militarism.

Belgium, in addition to signing this Note, sent a further reply of her own, drawing attention to the treatment she had received from the Germans, and protesting that she could accept no peace which did not repair these damages and give security for the future.

In conjunction with the dispatch of the Allies' reply, a Note was sent by Mr. Balfour, the Foreign Secretary, to be communicated by the British Ambassador at Washington to the United States Government. This dispatch consisted of an explanation and commentary upon the Allies' Note.

Mr. Balfour emphasised the point that any peace settlement must be of a nature to cure the evil conditions which had precipitated the War. That involved a revision of the map of Europe, the expulsion of the barbaric Turkish Government, and the abolition of the German military machine. If a peace were signed which left German military power unimpaired in the midst of a weakened and exhausted Europe, it would be even less secure than the peace existing before the War.

International treaties were in themselves no remedy, as the fate of Belgium had shown. A powerful nation could stand aloof from or tear up such treaties. If action of that kind were crowned with success in this War, it would be hopeless to try and banish it afterwards by new international treaties.

"Though, therefore, the people of this country share to the full the desire of the President for peace, they do not believe that peace can be durable if it be not based on the success of the Allied cause. For a durable peace can hardly be expected unless three conditions are fulfilled.

The first is that the existing causes of international unrest should be, as far as possible, removed or weakened.

The second is that the aggressive aims and the unscrupulous methods of the Central Powers should fall into disrepute among their own peoples.

The third is that behind international law and behind all the treaty arrangements for preventing or limiting hostilities some form of international sanction should be devised which would give pause to the hardiest aggressor."

Mr. Balfour suggested that this policy was in harmony with the President's declared ideas, and said that we were prepared to go on making unparalleled sacrifices of blood and treasure, not to score a barren triumph over another nation, but to make possible the achievement of such a settlement.

Our replies to America and Germany constituted the first occasion on which the Allies had given to the world a complete outline of the terms of settlement they meant to enforce. The whole of the Versailles conditions were sketched out with unmistakable implication: the restoration by the enemy countries of all provinces conquered by force of arms and annexed against the wishes of the inhabitants; self-determination to be applied to subject races on the basis of nationality;

y*

reparations and indemnities to be claimed from Germany; steps to be taken which should prevent a repetition of the outrage of 1914 upon international right and peace. Mr. Balfour in a pregnant sentence forecast a League of Nations backed by the irresistible might of international sanction.

All the replies made clear to the world the united resolve of the Allied countries not to make peace until the power of Prussian militarism had been broken.

These documents had an undoubted influence on the course which America took during the next few weeks. They brought her intervention on the side of the Allies appreciably nearer. There is no doubt that the Allied answers to the German and Wilson Note favourably impressed American public opinion, and there was a perceptible change in the atmosphere across the Atlantic from that date.

Apart altogether from the intrinsic merits of the Allied demands, there was a personal element which cannot altogether be excluded. President Wilson was a sincere idealist and he was a man of exalted purpose and convictions, but he was also a man of deep and fierce resentments where his pride was offended or his purpose was crossed. There were indications that he was not too well pleased with the way the Germans had anticipated his peace offensive, and cut in front of him with their Note, after he had given them privately an intimation that he meant to approach Europe on the subject of peace negotiations. He was still more ruffled at their scornful neglect to give a considered answer to his Note. On the other hand, there is no doubt that he was propitiated by the trouble the Allies took to send without delay a careful, deliberate and detailed answer to his appeal, first of all by a detached and separate examination and then by summoning into conference the leaders of the Allied nations, to give to his questions the most specific answer that was possible at this stage of the War. One cannot rule out the effect of this personal deference on a man of his temperament and susceptibilities, when we come to examine the motives which prompted him so soon to abandon the attitude of " too-proud " pacifism upon which he had fought and won his way for a second term to the presidential chair.

The German reply to President Wilson's Note was only given on 31st January, 1917, in a confidential Note written by Ambassador von Bernstorff to Colonel House, a month after the publication of the Allied reply. It was as follows: —

> "Washington,
> 31st January, 1917.

My dear Colonel House,

I have received a telegram from Berlin according to which I am to express to the President the thanks of the Imperial Government for his communication made through you. The Imperial

Government has complete confidence in the President and hopes that he will reciprocate such confidence. As proof I am to inform you in confidence that the Imperial Government will be very glad to accept the services kindly offered by the President for the purpose of bringing about a peace conference between the belligerents. My Government, however, is not prepared to publish any peace terms at present, because our enemies have published such terms which aim at the dishonour and destruction of Germany and her Allies. My Government considers that as long as our enemies openly proclaim such terms, it would show weakness which does not exist, on our part, if we publish our terms and we would in so doing only prolong the War. However, to show President Wilson our confidence, my Government through me desires to inform him *personally* of the terms under which we would have been prepared to enter into negotiations, if our enemies had accepted our offer of 12th December.

'Restitution of the part of Upper Alsace occupied by the French.

Gaining of a frontier which would protect Germany and Poland economically and strategically against Russia.

Restitution of Colonies in form of an agreement which would give Germany Colonies adequate to her population and economic interest.

Restitution of those parts of France occupied by Germany under reservation of strategical and economic changes of the frontier and financial compensations.

Restoration of Belgium under special guaranty for the safety of Germany which would have to be decided on by negotiations with Belgium.

Economic and financial mutual compensation on the basis of the exchange of territories conquered and to be restituted at the conclusion of peace.

Compensation for the German business concerns and private persons who suffered by the War. Abandonment of all economic agreements and measures which would form an obstacle to normal commerce and intercourse after the conclusion of peace, and instead of such agreements reasonable treaties of commerce.

The freedom of the seas.'

The peace terms of our Allies run on the same lines.

My Government further agrees, after the War has been terminated, to enter into the proposed second international conference on the basis of the President's message to the Senate.

My Government would have been glad to postpone the submarine blockade, if they had been able to do so. This, however, was quite impossible on account of the preparations, which could not be cancelled. My Government believes that the submarine blockade will terminate the War very quickly. In the meantime my Government will do everything possible to safeguard American interests and begs the President to continue his efforts to bring about peace, and my Government will terminate the submarine blockade as soon as it is evident that the efforts of the President will lead to a peace acceptable to Germany. . . .

Yours sincerely,
J. BERNSTORFF.

P.S.—I could not get the translation of the official answer to the President's message ready in time to send it to you. I was in such a hurry to give you the above most important news, namely that the blockade will be terminated if a conference can be brought about on reasonable terms."

This letter, with its intimation that Germany would demand annexations and indemnities from France and Russia, suzerainty over Belgium, and the cession of part of the French and British colonial Empire, accompanied by an announcement of unrestricted submarine warfare, was no peace overture. Italy was ignored except in so far as it was included in the phrase about Austria demanding similar terms to those upon which Germany insisted. It was a challenge to a fight to a finish, and as such the United States had reluctantly to construe it.

CHAPTER XL

THE PERIL OF THE SUBMARINES

WHAT must be the sensation of a man who took a leading part in the direction of this tremendous War and undertakes to recall these events with their horrors, their perils and their amazing escapes? It is like that of a traveller who revisits dangerous rapids through which once upon a time he helped to pilot a boat without map, without knowledge, and without experience to guide him or any of the crew as to the course of the river, its depth and its shallows, its sharp and unexpected bends, the strength and whirl of its current, or the location of the hidden rocks in its channel.

The stream that had then to be navigated was necessarily one that had been imperfectly explored. In writing these Memoirs I have been walking steadily along the banks from the first speeding of the waters down past the delirious fury of their torrent.

I am now approaching the narrowest and the most threatening gorge in the mad voyage, with one particularly jagged rock right in the middle of the stream and to all appearances barring the way. In the end it was the German boat that crashed against it and was broken to pieces, but I shudder to think that this experience was almost ours. The submarine campaign proved the ruin of Germany. It is a horrifying thought that it very nearly achieved the destruction of Britain's sea power, with all that such a disaster would have meant to the fortunes of the Alliance and of humanity.

We are all too apt, on looking back upon Germany's submarine campaign, to regard it as one of her most fatuous blunders. It is true that it turned out to be the fatal error which precipitated her ultimate defeat. But it was a miscalculation only by a margin which might have been on the other side. There were weeks when the German leaders had truthful reports which gave them confident assurance of success, while giving Britain and her Allies cause for an anxiety which at one stage reached the depths of alarm. There were times when some of our most cautious leaders thought we might be beaten and that we would do well to make peace whilst our ships were afloat.

Soon after the Marne it became evident to the more discerning minds in Germany that complete victory was unattainable as long as the command of the sea was vested in Britain, and that it was not impossible that the Central Powers might be blockaded into premature surrender unless the trident could be wrested out of Britain's hands. Rome understood that supreme factor in a war with a maritime power. Napoleon never quite apprehended it. But in Napoleon's days, Continental populations were smaller and all European countries were more self-sustaining, and the standard of necessaries was much lower. War itself was more intermittent, the material it demanded for its activities was infinitely less. Neither did it absorb as many men on the battlefield or behind the fighting lines. France at that time could not therefore be starved into submission. On the other hand, in this War the Germans began to realise they could not go on indefinitely unless the blockade were broken. They were already restricted in some essentials like copper, oil and rubber for the Army, and in some of the necessaries, many of the comforts and most of the luxuries of life for soldiers and civilians.

Now that, owing to the stupidity of their opponents, the weakest flanks in the defence system of the Central Powers in the East and South-East had been so strengthened as to give Germany confidence that their military situation was established beyond immediate anxiety, both the military and naval authorities turned their thoughts more and more towards the question of blockade. It was a double problem—first that of breaking their own blockade and then that of reversing the situation by becoming the blockaders instead of the blockaded. Had an immediate military decision been within their reach, they need not have worried about the stranglehold of the British Navy. But the failure of the Marne, of the first battle of Ypres, and lastly and notably the check they had sustained at Verdun, had almost convinced their Headquarters that they could not break through the Allied Front in the West. The equally disastrous and much more sanguinary repulses sustained by the Allied forces in their various efforts to rupture the German lines—defended as they were by only two men for every three assailants—strengthened that conviction. It was therefore becoming more and more a struggle of endurance. Here the naval clutch of Britain gave the Allies a decided advantage. The High Command and the Admirals of Germany, therefore, considered separately and together the problem of breaking and if possible of reversing the blockade. Army Headquarters naturally thought first of the possibilities on land. The conquest of Roumania was a definite help. But it did not fill the widening gap between need and supply. It brought the Central Powers oil and corn in great but not sufficient quantities. Russia it is true provided them with unlimited opportunities. Here vast supplies of corn, oil and copper awaited conquest and exploitation. This, however, would take time. The Russian Army had first of all to be cleared out of the way and then some sort of order restored in a revolutionary country. Moreover, Russian transport was very deficient and had to be considerably improved. Something had to be done immediately. The population of Germany was already on diminished and inadequate rations. Whilst German resources were being gradually restricted and German reserves exhausted, the riches and resources of the world were open to the Allies. A blow must therefore be struck at their communications by sea. That was the conclusion to which the German leaders came.

It was some time before the Germans discovered what a formidable weapon they possessed in the submarine. At first, they relied on cruisers and mines and other accepted and established methods of attack on our Mercantile Marine.

I am not sure that the submersible ship was to the Admirals who strode on the quarter deck of mammoth battleships anything more than a fanciful experiment. They never took it very seriously as a real contribution to the struggle for the control of the seas. At best it might perhaps help the ships of the line as an invisible scout, and maybe, by lucky accident, cripple or with extreme luck sink one or two stray enemy warships. When the last roving German cruiser had been beached in a mangrove swamp in Africa, in order to escape capture, the German Admiralty put more faith in the little swordfish which had already destroyed more enemy ships in a month than the cruisers had succeeded in sinking during the whole of their glorious but short-lived career. When they realised the power of this invention they set about building submarines on a great scale and constructing much larger types.

The old type of submarine with its limited oil capacity could not venture much beyond the Channel and the German Ocean. Its voyage was restricted in time as well as distance. The new cruiser type could drive out into and right across the Atlantic. The first example of this new menace was launched in June, 1916, and it crossed the ocean up to American territorial waters. In leaving, it committed the folly of sinking five vessels outside the Nantucket lighthouse. It was a characteristic sample of Prussian psychology. It was meant to intimidate America into complacence. It roused the spirit of growing antagonism to, and apprehension of Germany which ended in war. Germany was elated over the success of her adventure. Her leaders reckoned that the depredations of the new type of submarine would be so successful that, even if America came into the War, by the time she had raised, trained and equipped an army, there would be no shipping available to carry her troops to Europe. Were they so far out in their reckoning?

There can be no doubt about our alarm at this new development. When these bigger boats multiplied, they prowled round all the approaches to Britain's shores, from the Bay of Biscay to Iceland, they glided about in every corner of the Mediterranean, and the sinkings, which were practically all by gunfire, increased at a rate which produced consternation. The Admiralty chart of the waters to the north and south of Ireland, as well as in the chops of the Channel, became blacker and blacker with the plague spots of submarine activity. The sinkings on the Mediterranean route were also on the increase. Our anti-submarine plans were completely baffled and stultified, for the new submarines were able to operate hundreds of miles into the Atlantic beyond the limits of the areas patrolled by our vessels, and we were short of torpedo boats, even for the Narrow Seas. Our great battleships had to be protected from attack and this necessarily absorbed our best destroyers. In those days I could not help thinking of the efforts some of us made before the War to induce the Admiralty to spend some of the large sums they proposed to allocate to the building of super-Dreadnoughts on the construction of more destroyers. During the last four months of 1916, the gross tonnage of our sunken ships totalled 632,000 tons. The German Admiralty reckoned that unrestricted warfare would soon enable them to sink up to 600,000 tons a month and that four months of such losses would find the Allies suppliants for any tolerable peace.

On 1st February, 1917, stimulated by the success of the new type of submarine, the German Government with its new submarine fleet launched its deadliest blow against this country and the Allies which depended on our shipping, by adopting the policy of unrestricted submarine warfare. All mercantile shipping proceeding to and from Allied ports was to be sunk on sight without warning. Germany hoped, and not without reason, that four months of such warfare would make inroads upon the vital sea-borne supplies not only of this country, but of the Allies, on a scale which would force us incontinently to sue for peace.

Was it a wild conjecture at the time? As early as the end of 1915, we were short of sufficient shipping tonnage to transport essential supplies for our forces and those of the Allies and for our own and our Allies' population. During 1916 the position became considerably worse.

As soon as Germany intensified her submarine campaign in the early autumn of 1916 and sinkings began to increase, the prospect became so gloomy that Mr. Runciman, as President of the Board of Trade, warned the Cabinet that at the rate the Allied and Neutral shipping was being swept from the seas, we could not carry on much longer.

At a meeting of the War Committee held on 9th November, 1916, Mr. Runciman told us he had come to the conclusion that "*a complete breakdown in shipping would come before June, 1917.*"

No sooner had the Committee adjourned than he wrote a memorandum in which he said that he had revised his estimate as to the probable date of the breakdown, and that in his judgment he thought it must come much sooner.

In a further memorandum which he sent to the War Committee on 22nd November, 1916, Mr. Runciman pointed out that the urgent need of the moment—so urgent that the feeding of Italy, France and the United Kingdom next summer depended upon it—was sufficient tonnage for the carriage of the Indian and Australian crops.

Then he added the very disquieting sentence: "Free tonnage for this purpose is not in sight." They needed 100 vessels per month during November and during each of the succeeding five months. And yet, he informed us, at the end of four weeks' effort, the Transport Department had succeeded in securing less than 30 vessels.

He also added as an explanation for the desperate view he took of things that all his calculations had been drawn "on the assumption that we should not hesitate to kill commerce in order to make ends meet."

He based his estimates on the further assumption that the losses through submarines next year would continue at the rate of the *first eight months* of 1916. If the import of munitions material were increased, and the losses by enemy action depleted our merchant navy in an increasing degree, our plight would become graver.

As a matter of fact our losses for the *last* four months of 1916 were 632,000 tons gross—more by 32,000 tons than the total losses of the first eight months, and the Germans were every week putting more and more of their new cruising submarines into the sea.

As I have already related, in 1916 we were building new ships at the rate of 52,000 tons per month, and losing through submarine action twice and three times as many per month. From the way things were going, the Allied forces could not be equipped with the overwhelming mechanical superiority which was essential to enable them to smash through fortified positions held by a skilful and brave enemy. Equipment in this country could only barely be kept up, let alone increased, at the expense of adequate food supplies for the Allied population. Italy was suffering severely in the matter of munition supply owing to lack of shipping. The deficiency could not be made up without further imperilling our own food position. It was the failure of the German Government to feed its own people that provoked the discontent which reduced and ultimately broke their morale. The Germans calculated that they could inflict these demoralising privations on the Allies before corresponding hardships had time to disaffect their own civilian population. It was not so rash a calculation when the actual figures of sinkings and resources come to be examined.

Was there anything in the success or efficiency of our naval operations against the new submarine menace up to that date which would justify us in assuming that we could cope with it adequately?

Temporary relief could have been achieved by the withdrawal of all our forces from the Mediterranean and Mesopotamia. The General Staff would have hailed such a movement with joy as a triumphant vindication of their own foresight. Every catastrophe has its compensations for somebody. If the world crashed to its doom according to the Almanac its compiler would have one thrill of satisfaction. But a withdrawal from the Mediterranean, including Egypt, would not have brought much comfort in the end even to the Staffs. We should thus have been saved tonnage equal to one month's sinkings in the unlimited submarine campaign, but at what a cost! The pressure on the Austrian and Bulgarian resources in the Balkans, which with the collapse of Turkey was the beginning of the end in 1918, would have been withdrawn. Austria would have been free to organise, anticipate and exploit Caporetto. We should have withdrawn altogether from our struggle with the Turk. That would mean that we should have acknowledged to the world and in the very eyes of the East that the Turkish Empire with German help had finally beaten the British. The Suez Canal and ultimately Egypt would have been undefended and must have fallen into Turkish hands. In fact, we should have sustained a more disastrous defeat at the hands of the German submarine than Bonaparte endured when the British Fleet cut off the communications between France and Egypt at the Battle of Aboukir. And the sacrifice would not have saved us in the West if the submarine menace had not been overcome. Even if we had been able to guard and secure the passages of the Channel, that would not suffice if we were unequal to the demand for the protection of the ships that brought us food and raw material for our munitions from distant shores to the ports of Britain, France and Italy. America would have been cut off with her essential supplies and later on with her armies.

By the end of 1916 the British mercantile shipping destroyed by enemy action—mainly by submarines—amounted to 738 vessels, with a gross tonnage of over 2,300,000 tons; nearly one-fifth of the total British tonnage existing at the outbreak of the War. At the end of 1916 we were short (as our shipping was then handled) of well over 50 per cent. of the tonnage required for imports of which the President of the Board of Trade reckoned to be our irreducible needs. No wonder he thought we could not continue the War much longer. And in spite of these persistent and heavy losses, in spite of their steady and alarming increase, in spite of the fact that the Admiralty knew they might at any time become very much heavier if the Germans resorted to the unlimited warfare which they had threatened as far back as February, 1915, no counter-measures had been prepared which even began to exercise any restraining effect.

Admiral Jellicoe wrote to the Admiralty towards the end of October, 1916—that is, three months before the date of the German warning of unrestricted sinkings, that there appeared to be

" a serious danger that our losses in merchant ships, combined with the losses in neutral merchant ships, may, by the early summer of 1917, have such a serious effect upon the import of food and other necessaries into the Allied countries as to force us into accepting peace terms which the military position on the Continent would not justify, and which would fall short of our desires."

And Admiral Beatty declared that the danger was

"jeopardising the fate of the nation and seriously interfering with the successful prosecution of the War."

The reports from the First Sea Lord and the President of the Board of Trade at each of our Committees were models of un-relieved dejection. They formed a part of the litany of every War Committee.

How did the Lords of the Admiralty propose to cope with a menace which was gradually strangling the power of the Allies? In another chapter I propose to tell the dismal story of the way the President of the Board of Trade confronted his share of the problem. In a memorandum to the Asquith Government in November, 1916, the Admirals reported: —

" Of all the problems which the Admiralty have to consider, no doubt the most formidable and the most embarrassing is that raised by submarine attack upon merchant vessels. *No conclusive answer has as yet been found to this form of warfare; perhaps no conclusive answer ever will be found. We must for the present be content with palliation.*"

That is to say, we do not see how the patient's life can be saved, but we can prolong his agony—perhaps ease it a little!

This paralytic document was written over two years after the submarine had begun its devastating activities. The Germans had not yet put a great number of these large submarines in the water, neither had they started their campaign of indiscriminate destruction. When the report was penned by a trembling hand we were losing ships at the rate of 175,000 tons a month. When the numbers of the large type had doubled, and the unrestricted sinkings began, the destruction of tonnage mounted up until it reached the figure of 526,000 tons in a single month for British shipping, and 867,000 tons for British, Allied and Neutral shipping together.

What constituted the difference between the selective methods of the submarine campaign as it was prosecuted before February, 1917, and the indiscriminate attack which ensued after February, 1917? When the submarine had to ascertain, before it let loose its destructive charge, the flag under which ships sailed, it took time to make sure of the nationality of a vessel, especially in thick or rough weather. It also involved hesitation and doubt on the part of the commander, who might get into trouble if by chance he sank an American ship whilst he thought he was aiming his shattering torpedo at a British or French vessel.   A few minutes of hesitation and delay often enabled a ship to escape from its assailant.   It also added to the risk of a counter-attack from the guns of the menaced vessel. But when the orders were to sink every vessel that rode the waves under whatever flag it sailed, there was no hesitancy and consequently no time lost.   The result was that three ships were sunk for every one that was destroyed before the new decree came into operation.

It is quite clear that unless some means were adopted, either to protect the ships or to destroy their destroyers, or both, there would hardly be enough vessels afloat at the end of the year to provide the Allied populations with sufficient food to keep them alive, let alone providing the Allied Armies with an adequate equipment to smash the entrenchments of the enemy.   How long would they be able to furnish the means for maintaining their own defences   If Allied shipping continued steadily to disappear at this accelerating rate, the end was not distant. As the Admiralty were in a condition of utter despair at the prospect of either effecting destruction of the submarine or affording protection for our ships, there is nothing surprising in the cry that came from the hearts of men whose caution exceeded their courage: "Let us agree with our adversary quickly."

One of the most lamentable effects of the new submarine campaign was the marked increase in the casualty list amongst our sailors. When a ship was sunk by gunfire the sailors had to take to the boats whatever the weather. Even when the disaster occurred within a few miles of the coast the risks were considerable, but when the ship was sunk in the Bay of Biscay or out in the Atlantic, scores of leagues from any shore, the chances of escape were precarious, and in bad weather few lived to tell the tale. It was one of the new cruelties which this conflict added to the practice of war. The old piratical plank was more humane. The agony was not so prolonged. The German plea in defence of their action was to point to their children starved by our blockade. War is a cruel business.

Was there any justification for the pessimism of British Admirals of high degree? The Official Naval History of the War, in referring to the failure of the Admiralty to hunt down the submarine, states that up to the beginning of 1917, "Our effort, whether considered as attack or defence, had been not only inadequate but wholly ineffective."*   In home waters and the Mediterranean about 3,000 destroyers and auxiliary patrol vessels, trawlers and motor boats had been employed in chasing submarines.   From January, 1916, to February, 1917, they had only caught seven.   A few others had been struck by mines, and lost or disabled through weather conditions. But the total loss of German submarines during the past 12 months from all causes was only 25, almost entirely of the smaller type.   It was known that the Germans had been building more and larger submarines, and that since July they had been putting a succession of submersible cruisers into the seas.   It is not too much to say that our Grand Fleet had a lively apprehension of this hidden terror. It would not put out to sea from its boomed and steel-netted shelters without an adequate escort of destroyers, of which, for all purposes, including the time for refitting, it was considered that at least 100 were required: below this number the Commander-in-Chief said he would be incurring an unjustifiable risk in the event of meeting the German High Seas Fleet.   No capital ship could leave its base without out a patrolling and protecting escort of small craft.   If Britannia ruled the waves, she did it with a shaky trident in the days before the submarine was overcome.   After the Battle of Jutland, Admiral Jellicoe came to the conclusion that it was not safe for his imposing Armada of enormous Dreadnoughts "to undertake prolonged operations to the South of the Dogger Bank," as the risk of mines and submarines was too formidable.   They were not to enter the southern end of the North Sea unless they were forced to do so by direct challenge from the German High Seas Fleet.   Meanwhile, the flag-ship must be interned in safe creeks, the flag had to be carried on the small craft, the nimble destroyers and the weather-beaten trawlers.   Here is the "Nelson touch" up-to-date.

That was the atmosphere of crouching nervousness, even before the Germans had launched more than a few of their latest specimens of submarine cruisers.

No attempt was ever made by our powerful Navy to turn its great guns on the submarine nests of Flanders.   When I ventured to suggest such an idea it was turned down peremptorily.

In the absence of an effective plan for grappling with this threat to our existence as a sea power, there was every reason for Admiral Jellicoe's gloom.   And he certainly had no fresh suggestions for coping with the emergency.   Here are official figures supplied to me from the Shipping Department of the Admiralty in July, 1917, showing the prospect in front of us if the convoy system failed and if the destruction of our shipping continued at the same rate as it had proceeded during the first two quarters of the year: —

* "Naval Operations," Vol. IV, page 337.

				Estimated Loss per annum.	
				(1) On basis of losses during first half of 1917. X2.	(2) On basis of losses during second half of 1917. X4.
VESSELS SUNK.				*Gross Tons.*	*Gross Tons.*
British	...	...	...	4,191,000	5,141,000
Foreign	...	...	...	2,857,000	3,078,000
Total	...	...	...	7,048,000	8,219,000
VESSELS DAMAGED BY TORPEDO OR MINE.					
British	...	...	...	915,000	1,055,000
Foreign*	...	...	...	624,000	631,000
Total	...	...	...	1,539,000	1,686,000
GRAND TOTAL		...	...	8,587,000	9,905,000

According to the President of the Board of Trade we had a serious shortage in November, 1916. Where should we be in November, 1917, if this havoc continued? These figures will show that the submarine was the crucial problem upon which the issue of the War would depend. If we failed to counter its ravages the Allies were irretrievably beaten. And the new submarine cruisers were being turned out rapidly from the German shipyards and launched without delay on their destructive errand. The West Atlantic, the Bay of Biscay, and the Mediterranean became charged with hidden destruction for our merchant ships. A ship passing through the waters surrounding Britain was in the predicament of a swimmer in a shark-infested sea.

At the meeting of the War Cabinet on 25th May, 1917, the First Sea Lords gave information which had been obtained in connection with submarines from the Captain of a German submarine, who stated that the whole of the shipbuilding resources of Germany were now concentrated on the building of submarines; that the output would eventually reach 20 a month; that there were approximately 300 German submarines now in commission; that there were no difficulties as regards obtaining crews for these submarines, which were taken from the men of the High Seas Fleet, trained in a special school for two months, and after three weeks' submarine cruise considered competent.

Had we not found some means of dealing with the menace not then visible to the fear-dimmed eyes of our Mall Admirals, who had before the War been thinking of naval warfare in the terms of gigantic Trafalgars between super-Dreadnoughts (with three to two in our favour), and had we not put into operation ideas which never

* Foreign vessels damaged are assumed to bear same ratio to Foreign vessels sunk as in case of British vessels, actual figures not being available.

emanated from their brains and some of which they resisted, others of which they delayed, the German reckoning would have been accurate. Their 600,000 tons per month estimate of losses was exceeded in April, 1917, when 866,610 tons of Allied and Neutral tonnage were sunk.

As soon as the new Administration was formed, the submarine problem was one of the first we took in hand. It was clear to us that the stunned pessimism of the Admiralty would be justified unless some more effective measures could and would be taken to baffle and quell the submarine. If we failed to achieve this aim, we realised that the War would inevitably be lost to the Allies, and that before long.

We considered several suggestions for coping with the situation, some of which I had already submitted to the War Committee, and which now had the powerful support of the new Shipping Controller: —

(a) The institution of a regular system of convoys for all the merchant shipping from the moment it reached the danger zone;

(b) The construction of new tramp ships on the largest scale attainable consistent with the supply of steel and man-power available;

(c) The reorganisation of our shipping and ports with a view to making better use of our tonnage;

(d) The more rapid and effective arming of merchant ships with guns and howitzers;

(e) Improvement in the methods of hunting down the submarine;

(f) A stern cutting down of non-essential imports; and

(g) A considerable increase in home supplies of food, timber and ore—coupled with a reduction in consumption.

The measures taken under (b), (c), (d), (e), (f) and (g) will be related in other chapters. I propose now to deal with the story of the amazing and incomprehensible difficulties encountered in inducing the Admiralty even to try the convoy system. I take this first because it was the expedient which, when it was ultimately adopted, had the most immediate and ultimate effect in reducing the sinkings. It was also the plan which roused the most implacable and prolonged resistance on the part of the Admiralty. It is especially difficult to understand their prejudices in this respect, because after Trafalgar the main function of our ships-of-war was to convoy our merchant vessels through seas infested with French privateers. Convoying was therefore in accordance with the traditions of our Navy in its greater days.

The first effort made to overcome their blind obstinacy had

occurred on 2nd November, 1916, at a War Committee attended by
Admiral Sir Henry Jackson, who was then First Sea Lord, and Vice-
Admiral Sir H. F. Oliver, then Chief of the War Staff at the
Admiralty. Sir John Jellicoe left the Grand Fleet and travelled
specially to London at the Prime Minister's request to attend this
meeting. The question of submarine attacks by gunfire on merchant
ships was considered, and a statement was made as to the increase in
the loss to Allied and Neutral merchant ships due to submarine
activity. It was stated that the most serious feature in the situation
was that we were not building ships nor obtaining the use of interned
or captured enemy ships rapidly enough to make good our losses.

Then a discussion was initiated by Mr. Bonar Law and myself on
the question of the possibility of establishing a convoy system. Sir
John Jellicoe's answer was that he did not approve of convoys " as
they offered too big a target." In the course of further discussions on
the subject, in reply to Mr. Bonar Law, Admiral Sir Henry Oliver
said that they convoyed in the Mediterranean, so did the French and
the Italians; but that they found it did not do to send more than one
ship at a time under escort. The French had tried more, and lost
two or three of their ships.

I then suggested a dozen ships being convoyed by three ships-of-
war. Sir John Jellicoe said in reply that *they would never be able to
keep merchant ships sufficiently together to enable a few destroyers
to screen them. It was different with warships, which they could
keep in a lock-up formation.* Mr. Runciman added that, *looking at
the principle of convoy from the point of view of tonnage, it was most
wasteful.* There was no advantage in speed, as a convoy must move
at a pace regulated by the slowest ship.*

Here is the official minute of the decision come to by that War
Committee in spite of the protests entered by Mr. Bonar Law and
myself: —

" It was pointed out by the naval experts that the measures
which had hitherto proved comparatively successful in the narrow
waters in which the enemy submarines had mainly operated were
not applicable now that they were able to operate in the open sea
at a greater distance from their base.

The system of convoys had only been found successful where it
was possible to allot a separate escort to each vessel to be protected.
The French had attempted to convoy several ships with one
destroyer, with the result that ships had been lost. Men-of-war,
which were accustomed to cruise in close order, could to a certain
extent be protected by destroyer escorts, but merchant vessels
straggled too much, and the system of convoys was not applicable
to them . *The President of the Board of Trade pointed out that*

* Henry Newbolt, "Naval Operations," Vol. V, pp. 3 and 4.

*from an economical point of view the system of convoys was extremely unsatisfactory since it involved the whole convoy proceeding at the speed of the slowest ship and the simultaneous arrival of all the ships at the port of destination, which would then become congested. The system of convoys was not therefore generally accepted by the War Committee."**

Although the President of the Board of Trade said that convoying would be uneconomical owing to loss of time, he did not mention the loss of time occasioned by ships being held up because there was submarine activity off the ports. Nor did he mention the loss of time by the ships having to steam considerable extra distances to keep out of the submarine danger zone. Incidentally, this made it very difficult to bunker them at Port Said. In effect, his last argument meant that it were better for a ship to be at the bottom of the sea than arrive late, besides which, the more ships that failed to arrive, the less would be the congestion at the ports.

I seem to have asked Sir John Jellicoe if he had any plans against the German submarines that were now working in the open seas. Sir John said that he had not. They had only armed merchant ships and these could not act offensively because they did not see the submarines. He suggested having floating intelligence centres to direct the routes of the shipping if found needful.

There was then a long discussion as to the advisability of the defensive arming of merchant ships. Sir John Jellicoe here was of opinion that it provided the most effective means of protecting merchant ships against submarines. The conclusion we arrived at on this point was that it was a question of the first importance to increase the production of these guns. The Minister of Munitions undertook to make further enquiries on the subject, and it was arranged that a conference should take place between the experts of the Ministry of Munitions and the Admiralty at an early date.

This "question of first importance" remained a question for the next few weeks; after which the new Government took it energetically in hand.

The extent to which the submarine was likely to limit the tonnage at the disposal of the Allies was illustrated by a Report which was communicated to this Committee during its proceedings. Lord Grey informed the War Committee that he had seen the French Minister at Christiania, who had stated that, according to his most recent information, Norway was likely to yield to Germany and was already calling in all her ships. We were told that Norway had already lost $13\frac{1}{2}$ per cent. of her total mercantile marine during the present War. The withdrawal of the Norwegian ships from the transport of Allied material would have been a serious blow, but the incident shows

* War Committee, 31st October, 1916.

clearly the extent to which the fear of the submarine was intimidating even the bravest seafaring nations.

But during the first months of 1917, the Admiralty could not bring itself to change its tactics.

In January, 1917, Admiralty opinion was as emphatic as ever against convoys. An official pamphlet issued on behalf of the Admiralty in that month declared that : —

" Whenever possible, vessels should sail singly, escorted as considered necessary. The system of several ships sailing together in a convoy is not recommended in any area where submarine attack is a possibility. It is evident that the larger the number of ships forming the convoy, the greater is the chance of a submarine being enabled to attack successfully, the greater is the difficulty of the escort in preventing such an attack. . . ."

The " Official History " states that this pamphlet accurately recorded the collective opinion of the Board of Admiralty, " for the minutes of those high officials who were more particularly concerned with the defence of trade are all expressive of the same, or nearly the same, view." The Director of the Trade Division, Sir Richard Webb, was against convoys. The Director of the Operations Division, Sir Thomas Jackson, was inconclusive. Admiral Duff, the Director of the Anti-Submarine Division, was definitely opposed. Sir John Jellicoe agreed with the latter and so did the rest of the Board of Admiralty.

I have since discovered that while the pamphlet referred to above may have represented the view taken by the Admiral in charge of the British Submarine Service, it was written and issued without taking into account the views of serving officers. There were in the Admiralty at the time papers from experienced submarine officers explaining why it was difficult for a submarine to attack a convoy.

The Admiralty regarded the escorting of shipping as quite out of the question, and the only strategy it could devise to oppose the submarines was to arrange for four cone-shaped approach routes for shipping to use when coming to this country, the cones pointing respectively to Falmouth, Berehaven, Instrahull (N. Ireland) and Kirkwall, and the stretch of sea inside each cone near this country being patrolled. The method proved a complete fiasco, and indeed a death-trap. The presence of our patrolling craft notified German submarines of the areas where shipping might be expected, and the concentration of vessels in a comparatively small area enabled the U-boats to reap a rich harvest in a short time. In particular, the cone off the south-west coast of Ireland was rapidly becoming the grave of British shipping.

This is the description given to me by the Shipping Controller of the disastrous plan : —

" Ships would be ordered by the Admiralty to certain points which seemed quite known to the Germans, who had submarines lying in wait, sending down ship after ship.

Possibly it may help your memory if I remind you about the sugar ships which were brought to one point in the Atlantic and sunk one after the other, until (I think I am right) we had not more than one week's supply of sugar in the country."

There were occasions when a ship reached this zone at a point where a naval ship was expected to be awaiting them in order to indicate the exact route, but there was no guiding warship to be found. These were the " floating intelligence centres " alluded to by Sir John Jellicoe at the War Committee. The " centres " were often floating elsewhere than at the point where they were needed, so the " intelligence " was not available. Sometimes wireless messages were sent by perplexed ships asking for directions. These messages were picked up and decoded by the Germans, so that when the poor merchantmen arrived at the point indicated in the wired orders, they found not a guide, but a pirate awaiting their arrival.

In fact, by this egregious plan our ships were in effect often shepherded into the abattoir where the slaughterers lay in wait for them.

Looking back, it seems amazing that the system of escorting our ships in convoys was not adopted earlier. Yet in the teeth of the fact that other methods were proving futile and disastrous, and our sinkings were increasing at an alarming rate, the Admiralty stubbornly refused to consider adopting the convoy system and thus extending to the mercantile marine the same guardianship as that upon which they relied for their own safety in the Grand Fleet.

Several considerations influenced their judgment. Some of them I have already stated. But there were others equally fallacious and more fantastic. The expert advisers of the Admiralty at this time were labouring under a set of surprising delusions. The foremost of these was that the steamers of the mercantile marine could not be relied upon to " keep station." In a convoy they would therefore bump into the escort or each other to the common danger of all, or perhaps in order to avoid this mutual ramming they might disperse, lose sight of each other and of their escort, and in wandering about to recover touch, would become easy victims for the prowling swordfish of the Germany Navy. The seamanship of the experienced mariners who steered the tramp through all weathers across the wild and foggy seas that surround and lead to these islands was completely under-estimated. No voyager who has witnessed a heavily-laden tramp successfully battling through the breakers in a Bay of Biscay storm would doubt the capacity of the sailors who manned these buffeted and swamped vessels to handle them with complete efficiency, whatever the demand. It surprised me to find that the Captains of the liners who were first consulted by the Admiralty shared Sir John Jellicoe's doubts as to the capacity of the small tramp to keep station. It is simply the arrogant sense of superiority which induces the uniformed chauffeur of a Rolls Royce to look down on the driver of what is contemptuously stigmatised as a " tin Lizzie."

The Admirals were thus sure, in defiance of all historic evidence, that vessels travelling together in a convoy would be exposed to greater peril than if they travelled singly. They greatly over-estimated the number of men-of-war that would be needed by a convoy. " The opinion which at the time prevailed at the Admiralty," says the Official History, " was that, if merchantmen were placed under convoy, then the escort would have to be twice as numerous as the ships escorted. The Admiralty's advisers did not share the view, which *was not then uncommon*, that a comparatively weak escort would suffice."* What an amazing miscalculation !

But of all their delusions the most astounding was that which concerned the number of British vessels sailing the high seas and needing escort. This was not some obscure and disputable issue that could be determined only by risky experiment. It was merely a matter of available statistics accurately added up. The blunder on which their policy was based was an arithmetical mix-up which would not have been perpetrated by an ordinary clerk in a shipping office. It nevertheless bewildered the Sea Lords and drove them out of their course for months. Common sense or reference to Lloyd's register and a sum in simple addition would have given them the facts. Up to the middle of 1917 there was no one on the Board of Admiralty who possessed this triple qualification. Here is the fateful error in accountantship which nearly lost us the War, and might have done so had no one pointed it out in time to the Sea Lords.

For some time past the Admiralty had by order of the Government been in the habit of publishing week by week the number of vessels lost by submarine attacks. And in order to make this dismal news sound as hopeful as possible, they had issued with it a return supplied by the Customs Authorities of the number of vessels that had entered and left British ports during the week. To swell this number, every entry and exit was counted, including the numerous going and comings of coastwise small craft of the smallest dimensions, passing from harbour to harbour on the coast, so that it reached a figure of about 2,500 weekly entrances and as many clearances. Probably these figures did not deceive the German High Command, though they doubtless served to encourage neutrals and depress the enemy populations. Unhappily, they also deceived our own Admirals ! A moment's reflection would have told them that nothing approaching 2,500 deep-sea vessels could be concluding voyages to this country

* " Naval Operations," Vol. IV, p. 383.

every week. As a matter of fact, the actual arrivals and departures of ocean-going ships were between 120 and 140 a week. The Admiralty never examined their grotesque figures. On these calculations they were right in concluding that it would be quite impossible to furnish escorts for convoying the merchant shipping that entered and left our ports, as its volume, according to their fantastic estimate, far exceeded anything the Navy could deal with.

Thus, on the one hand we had a confident Germany launching its deadly offensive against our shipping, and on the other hand we had a palsied and muddle-headed Admiralty declaring that nothing effective could be done to counter it.

On 1st February came the announcement by Germany of the policy of unrestricted submarine warfare. It was notified to the U.S.A. in a memorandum which stated that: —

" From 1st February, 1917, sea traffic will be stopped with every available weapon and without further notice in the following blockade zones around Great Britain, France, Italy and the Eastern Mediterranean. . . ."

The zones, as defined in the memorandum, covered all the seas and oceans surrounding the British Isles, France, Belgium, Italy, except a small part of the Mediterranean bordering Spain.

With the effect of this announcement upon America I will deal in another chapter.

During its opening weeks, the new submarine campaign seemed as though it would justify all the hopes of those who had gambled upon it. In the first week of February, 1917, 35 vessels, British and foreign, were sunk in the English Channel and its western approaches. In the course of February and March the number of British merchant vessels lost through enemy action (mainly submarine attacks) was 232, with a gross tonnage of 663,000 tons. In April, our shipping losses for that one month alone were more than 526,000 tons. In addition, upwards of 200,000 tons of Allied and Neutral shipping was being sunk every month.

The effect on the Admiralty was to stun and not to stimulate. But even now they would not listen to the idea of convoying ships. They were like doctors who, whilst they are unable to arrest the ravages of a disease which is gradually weakening the resistance of a patient despite all their efforts, are suddenly confronted with a new unexpected and grave complication. They go about with gloomy mien and despondent hearts. Their reports are full of despair. It is clear that they think the case is now hopeless. All the same, their only advice is to persist in the application of the same treatment. Any other suggestion is vetoed. Their professional honour is involved in not accepting remedies which they have already refused to consider.

What makes it difficult to persuade them to try an obvious cure is
that it had been urged upon them by civilians and turned down by
the experts with scorn and derision. Have you ever heard of doctors
who admitted that physic prescribed by unregistered practitioners
was more efficacious than their own; and that they were wrong all the
time and the quacks right? These specialists were at the head of the
profession. How could you expect them to own up to those who had
called them in and trusted them, that their treatment was inferior
to that which herbalists and bonesetters had recommended? Bearing
this professional sensitiveness in mind, we must not criticise too
harshly their reluctance to admit their well-nigh fatal error in refusing to apply the convoy system. Their stubbornness grew with every
aggravation in the case they were mishandling so crassly and so
cruelly.

But what ought the War Cabinet to have done in the face of this
official refractoriness? When it is a matter of life and death it is a
serious thing for amateurs to interfere, and recklessly exercise their
authority by overriding the opinion of the most famous specialists
that are available in the Kingdom. How much greater an act of
temerity would it be were it a question of the life and death of a
whole nation! You could, of course, call in another specialist. But
who was there whose reputation stood as high in naval councils as
Admiral Jellicoe? Admiral Beatty had won some fame as a first-rate
fighting sailor of the dashing species. He was of the " well done,
Condor " type. But not even to-day would the majority of naval
officers rate his judgment as equal to that of Jellicoe, who had only
just been brought in because his predecessor was not successful in his
anti-submarine measures. Jellicoe had to be given a fair trial. I
decided that it was worth spending some time and patience in winning over Jellicoe to the views held by Mr. Bonar Law, the Shipping
Controller, Sir Maurice Hankey, and myself. We could not take too
long over the process, for our ships were being destroyed at an
alarming rate.

I urged the First Lord of the Admiralty, Sir Edward Carson, to
insist on the convoy system being tried. Personally he favoured a
trial being made, but told me he had no official support from any
quarter in his department. The experts were unanimously and
stubbornly opposed to the experiment. It was the same old story.
Official self-esteem and reputation were involved. The experienced
and distinguished sailors had committed themselves to a definite and
unqualified opinion, not only in their own special sphere of influence,
but outside to all sorts of civilians, shippers, statesmen, and others.
They had delivered to each and all their " considered opinion " that
convoying was impracticable and dangerous to convoyers and convoyed alike. Why waste time on ridiculous and risky experiments?

Sir John Jellicoe and Admiral Oliver were both able men with an unparalleled knowledge of the technique of their profession. They were both men whose caution and prudence gave their judgment weight. To quote the Welsh version of a well-known text, their "slowness was known to all men."* With the phlegmatic Briton, slowness of mind is apt to be taken as an indication of soundness of judgment. But when you are confronted with a situation for which there is no precedent and where therefore experience does not count as much as inventiveness, audacity and celerity of decision, such men are a hindrance to effective action. Their experience often tangles them. And on the other hand, their thorough knowledge of the details of the business and their high reputation give them authority which it is difficult for the amateur to set aside or challenge. In an emergency the able but unimaginative expert is a public danger. In dealing with them Sir Edward Carson's forensic gifts could not be brought into full play. He could hardly cross-examine his First Sea Lord and show him up in the presence of his colleagues as if he were a hostile witness. A peremptory order might produce the resignation of the whole Board. A serious crisis might thus be precipitated. Sir John Jellicoe stood high in the Navy. What was to be done? It was arranged that the First Lord of the Admiralty, the First Sea Lord and I should have a confidential talk on the position. I invited both of them and Admiral Duff, the head of the Anti-Submarine Department, to breakfast at Downing Street on the 13th February, 1917. I submitted to them a memorandum as a basis for our discussion. This memorandum, which was prepared by Sir Maurice Hankey after several consultations we had on the subject, carefully examined the arguments for and against the adoption of the convoy system, and strongly urged that it should be put into practice as the most effective means of combating the acute peril of the German submarine attack. The following are extracts from this document : —

"The general scheme submitted below entails ultimately an entire reorganisation of the Admiralty's present scheme of anti-submarine warfare, although it might, in the first instance, be adopted experimentally on a smaller scale. It involves the institution of a system of scientifically organised convoys, and the concentration on this service of the whole of the anti-submarine craft allotted to the protection of our trade routes, excepting only those vessels devoted to the anti-submarine service of our main fleets. It further involves the concentration on to the convoy system of every means of anti-submarine warfare—the gun, the submarine, the net, the depth charge, the mortar, the hydrophone, and wireless telegraphy. It aims at the effective utilisation of the slower as well as of the faster anti-submarine craft for the convoy system, and it contemplates ultimately the provision of special

* Philippians iv, 5.

salvage and life-saving craft and plant to accompany the convoys.
The memorandum also contains suggestions for investigations of
a technical character for combating the submarine which may or
may not be entirely new. . . ."

The memorandum proceeded to examine the objections to the
convoy system, and to set against them the far more serious objections to the system then practised. It continued: —

" How under this system we are ever to avoid losses limited only
by the number of the enemy's sea-going submarines, and his output
of torpedoes, it is difficult to see. The true strategical principle
would, of course, be to intercept the enemy near his exits from his
ports, and from the very first days of the War the writer has been
an ardent and unceasing advocate of the development of an unrestricted policy of mines, which are ' the trench of the sea.' In the
early part of the War, however, the Admiralty was utterly unsympathetic to submarine mining, with the result that, in the
middle of the third year of the War, our provision for minelaying
is utterly inadequate to the needs of the situation."

Out of 20,000 mines in store at that date, on examination it was
found that only 1,500 were of any use. As one of our sailors said,
when his ship accidentally bumped against one of these dud mines
without an explosion: " Good old Vernon. If hit with a hammer he
won't go off."*
Before the War, the Board of Admiralty had concentrated so much
on big and still bigger ships that they neglected essential weapons
like mines, armour-piercing shells and torpedoes—all of which were
inferior to those manufactured by the German. They neglected even
to provide us with sufficient small craft. The cost of one Dreadnought
spent on the provision of additional destroyers would have made an
appreciable difference at this date, when we were short of patrolling
and coasting vessels.
The memorandum resumes: —

" Over the system described above, the convoy system, if
practicable, appears to offer certain very distinct advantages.
The enemy can never know the day nor the hour when the
convoy will come, nor the route which it will take. The most
dangerous and contracted passages can be passed at night. Routes
can be selected as far as possible in water so deep that submarine
mines cannot be laid. The convoy can be preceded by mine-
sweepers or by vessels fitted with paravanes. The most valuable
vessels can be placed in the safest part of the convoy. Neutrals,

* H.M.S. Vernon was and is a Torpedo and Mining School at Portsmouth.

and other unarmed vessels, can be placed under the protection of armed vessels. The enemy submarine, instead of attacking a defenceless prey, will know that a fight is inevitable in which he may be worsted. All hope of successful surface attack would have to be dismissed at once.

The adoption of the convoy system would appear to offer great opportunities for mutual support by the merchant vessels themselves, apart from the defence provided by their escorts. Instead of meeting one small gun on board one ship the enemy might be under fire from, say, ten guns, distributed among twenty ships. Each merchant ship might have depth charges, and explosive charges in addition might be towed between pairs of ships, to be exploded electrically. One or two ships with paravanes might save a line of a dozen ships from the mine danger. Special salvage ships . . . might accompany the convoy to salve those ships which were mined or torpedoed without sinking immediately, and in any event to save the crews.

Perhaps the best commentary on the convoy system is that it is invariably adopted for our main fleet, and for our transports."

The breakfast discussion, which lasted two hours, evoked a restatement of the Jellicoe objections against convoys with which we were already familiar. The First Lord promised, however, to summon a representative delegation of captains in the mercantile marine in order to ascertain their views as to the practicability of the convoy system. He also undertook to abide by the result of two experiments in escorting which had recently been initiated. The first one was between Britain and the Norwegian ports and the other between British and French ports.

But it took time to establish the efficacy of these experiments. Meanwhile, the Admiralty were confirmed in their views from the fact that the Norwegian experiment in its initial form was not a success.

The fact that the experiment was not a systematic convoy, was imperfectly organised and was therefore not given a fair chance, was not taken into account. It was not a success and the Admirals " had told us so."

On the other hand, the French convoy trial was proceeding satisfactorily. The coal shipments from England to France had been very severely attacked during the latter part of 1916, and the French asked us to arrange for their escort. It was a great piece of luck for Britain that the task of organising the control was entrusted to a very intelligent young officer who had not been afflicted with hardening of the professional arteries. The Allied cause owes much to Commander (now Admiral) Henderson. With the aid of a small force of armed trawlers he carried out a scheme of daily convoys along three routes, making for Brest, Cherbourg, and Havre. The first experiments in this method began on 7th February, 1917, and during the three months March, April and May, 4,013 ships were convoyed across those dangerous waters with a total loss of nine vessels—only one in every 446.

This was a very encouraging result. But the indirect effect of the experiment was still more valuable. In order to carry out his work, Commander Henderson found it necessary to make frequent visits to the Ministry of Shipping to consult its officials about sailing arrangements, and they worked harmoniously and well together. Meantime his practical experience in the organisation of convoys led him to the conviction that they were by far the safest way of bringing ships through the danger zone. He found that the larger target offered by a convoy was no more vulnerable than each single ship would have been. A submarine could not count on firing more than a single " browning shot " as it was at once attacked by the escort and, in addition, if surfaced, by the guns of the convoyed vessels; and wireless warning to the escort would enable the whole convoy to be diverted from a point where a submarine was known to be operating. Further, the convoy also served the purpose of bringing the submarine to the destroyer instead of the destroyer having to range the Atlantic looking for a periscope.

Henderson made various enquiries from several different Departments of the Admiralty in an effort to find out the volume of our overseas trade and the point of origin, but could get no satisfactory information from them. So he tackled the Ministry of Shipping, and was referred to Mr. Leslie (now Sir Norman Leslie, K.B.E.), a shipbroker who had offered his services to the new Ministry, and who, with Mr. (now Sir Arthur) Salter, had built up a card-index system to supply the information about shipping and shipping movements which in peace time is obtainable at Lloyd's. It was Commander Henderson who found, without surprise, that the Admiralty's statistics of the number of vessels arriving and leaving our shores were grotesquely misleading. Arrivals of ocean-going steamers in the United Kingdom and Channel ports were only about 20 a day, of which 15 came to the United Kingdom; that is, there were not 2,500 weekly, only 140. The actual number of ocean-going vessels could easily be handled under convoy arrangements.

The Ministry of Shipping took up with enthusiasm the idea of developing a convoy system, and Mr. Leslie co-operated with Commander Henderson in working out the lines upon which such a scheme could be run. The Shipping Controller, Sir Joseph Maclay, repeatedly pressed that convoys should be given a trial, but the Admiralty persisted in opposing the plan in every shape and form. One morning, as the Controller was entering the Cabinet room, he met Jellicoe coming out. The Admiral stopped him and told him

that he had had a consultation with 12 mercantile captains, and that
not one of them favoured convoys. This step had been taken without
any consultation with the Ministry of Shipping, and without affording
Sir Joseph Maclay any opportunity of advising us as to the choice of
captains, or of meeting the mercantile masters who were chosen and
talking the matter over with them. It was highly probable that the
form in which Admiral Jellicoe put the question might make the
seamen fear that they could never carry out properly the station-
keeping and joint manœuvring that membership of a convoy
demanded, for he himself was firmly convinced that none but naval
men could manage it. When this report was triumphantly presented
to me, I was not told that the Shipping Controller had not been
consulted as to either the names or the class of ship that ought to be
represented at the gathering, and that officers of the smaller tramp
were not deemed fit for so exalted a conclave.

In the spring of 1917 the losses amongst vessels sailing to Norway
were again so serious that early in April a conference was summoned
at Longhope to consider how to protect the Scandinavian trade. The
naval officers at that conference were unanimously of opinion that
instead of the loose and defective system of protected sailings hitherto
adopted for these ships, they ought to be placed in regular convoy.
Their report came to the senior officers, who were by no means so
unanimous; but Admiral Beatty strongly supported them, and urged
the extension of the convoy system to other shipping. The report of
the Longhope Conference was considered by the Admiralty on 11th
April, and they agreed as an exceptional measure to allow convoys
to be run experimentally for the time being in the Scandinavian
trade. Between April and December, 1917, some 6,000 vessels were
convoyed between Norway and the Humber, with a total loss of about
70 ships, or just over 1 per cent. In March and April I awaited the
result of the French experiment and of the arming of merchantmen
in increasing numbers. I was hopeful, after the interview I had with
Jellicoe and Duff, that more energetic steps would be taken. In this
matter I was disappointed.

The attitude of the British Admiralty at that time is well illustrated
by the interview which took place in April between the First Sea
Lord and Admiral Sims, of the United States Navy. When it seemed
probable that the United States would enter the war, Admiral Sims
was dispatched to London to get into touch with the British
Admiralty. He reached Liverpool on the 9th April, and proceeded
at once to London, where he met Admiral Jellicoe. Here is Admiral
Sims' account of the amazing interview which took place between
them:—

    " After the usual greetings, Admiral Jellicoe took a paper out of
his drawer and handed it to me. It was a record of tonnage losses

for the last few months. This showed that the total sinkings, British and neutral, had reached 536,000 tons in February and 630,000 tons in March; it further disclosed that sinkings were taking place in April which indicated the destruction of nearly 900,000 tons. These figures indicated that the losses were three and four times as large as those which were then being published in the Press. It is expressing it mildly to say that I was surprised by this disclosure. I was fairly astounded; for I had never imagined anything so terrible. I expressed my consternation to Admiral Jellicoe.

'Yes,' he said, as quietly as though he were discussing the weather and not the future of the British Empire, 'it is impossible for us to go on with the war if losses like this continue.'

'What are you doing about it?' I asked.

'Everything we can. We are increasing our anti-submarine forces in every possible way. We are using every possible craft we can find with which to fight submarines. We are building destroyers, trawlers, and other like craft as fast as we can. But the situation is very serious and we shall need all the assistance we can get.'

'It looks as though the Germans were winning the war,' I remarked.

'They will win unless we can stop these losses—and stop them soon,' the Admiral replied.

'Is there no solution for the problem?' I asked.

'Absolutely none that we can see now,' Jellicoe announced."

On 22nd April, 1917, Jellicoe submitted to the War Cabinet a long memorandum on "The Submarine Menace and Food Supply." It declared that the increasingly heavy losses of our merchant ships by mine and submarine called for immediate action, and the adoption of such measures as were possible; but when he came to make recommendations for this desperately needed action he declared that "The only immediate remedy that was possible was the provision of as many destroyers and other patrol vessels as could be provided by the United States of America." Pending further means of attacking submarines, the only palliative was more small craft to keep them as much as possible submerged. He did not even hint at convoys as a possible remedy. He enumerated the various methods of attacking submarines that were being attempted, and admitted that the mines then used were worthless.

Meantime, sinkings were proceeding at such a pace that out of every 100 long-voyage steamers which left this country, 25 failed to return. At this rate, Germany's expectation of bringing us to our knees by August did not seem so improbable an inference to be drawn from the actual facts.

Admiral Sims definitely favoured convoys. Writing on 19th April to his Government, he reported the British methods in use and their failure, and expressed his dissent from the Admiralty view that convoys were impracticable.

"They are also insistent that it is impracticable for merchant ships to proceed in formation, at least in any considerable numbers, due principally to difficulty in controlling their speed and to the inexperience of their subordinate officers. With this view I do not personally agree but believe that with a little experience merchant vessels could safely and sufficiently well steam in open formations."

The situation was anxiously discussed by the War Cabinet in three sessions of 23rd and 25th April. In alluding to the recent serious shipping losses, I referred to the possibility of adopting the convoy system, which, I said, was favoured by Admiral Beatty and by Admiral Sims.

The First Sea Lord reported that the matter was under consideration, one of the chief obstacles to adopting such a scheme being the shortage of torpedo-boat destroyers. He stated that there was some prospect of American destroyers being sent to assist us, and that six had already been ordered to leave for this country. A much larger number would, however, be necessary, before any scheme of convoy could be introduced. He mentioned that the trial of the convoy system by the Commander-in-Chief of the Grand Fleet had not been altogether successful, two vessels in separate convoys having already been torpedoed and sunk.*

The First Sea Lord undertook to make a further report on the matter to the War Cabinet.

This shows the characteristic attitude of our naval advisers. The matter was still "under consideration." If two vessels out of some scores or hundreds convoyed were sunk in a month, it seemed a more dreadful thing to the Admiralty than the loss of a score of unescorted vessels in a single day, even though they were just as dependent on our Navy for their protection.

It was clear that the Admiralty did not intend to take any effective steps in the direction of convoying. After first discussing the matter with Sir Edward Carson, I informed the Cabinet that I had decided to visit the Admiralty and there take peremptory action on the question of convoys. Arrangements were made accordingly with the Board that I should attend a meeting to investigate with them all the means at present in use in regard to anti-submarine warfare. I stipulated for the right to send for any officers, whatever their rank, from whom I desired information.

Apparently the prospect of being overruled in their own sanctuary galvanised the Admiralty into a fresh inquisition, and by way of

* This refers to the experiment made on the Scandinavian Front.

anticipating the inevitable they further examined the plans and figures which Commander Henderson had prepared in consultation with Mr. Norman Leslie of the Ministry of Shipping. They then for the first time began to realise the fact which had been ignored by them since August, 1914, that the figures upon which they had based their strategy were ludicrous, and that therefore protection for a convoy system was within the compass of their resources.

Accordingly, when I arrived at the Admiralty I found the Board in a chastened mood. We discussed the whole matter in detail. We agreed to conclusions which I thus reported to the Cabinet.

"I was gratified to learn from Admiral Duff that he had completely altered his view in regard to the adoption of a system of convoy, and I gather that the First Sea Lord shares his views, at any rate to the extent of an experiment. Admiral Duff is not enamoured with the system, but a number of circumstances have combined to bring him to the view, which I believe most of my colleagues share, that, at any rate, an experiment in this direction should be made. One of these reasons is that now that the United States of America have entered the War, he thinks it should be possible to find escorts which were formerly inpracticable. Another is that experience has shown that he cannot rely on merchant ships to find salvation from the submarine by zigzagging and dousing their lights, and he therefore estimates these factors as a means of protection to a single ship lower than he formerly did. Moreover, as a result of an investigation in concert with a representative of the Shipping Controller, he finds that the number of ships for which convoy will have to be supplied is more manageable than he had thought. Further, the losses which he last reported to me on the subject were not in his opinion sufficient to justify the adoption of this experiment, which, he warned me, might involve a great disaster. Now, however, he calculates that he could afford to lose three ships out of every convoy without being worse off than at present, and he therefore thinks the experiment justifiable. . . .

I much regret that some time must elapse before convoys can be in full working order, and I consider that the Admiralty ought to press on with the matter as rapidly as possible.

As the views of the Admiralty are now in complete accord with the views of the War Cabinet on this question, and as convoys have just come into operation on some routes and are being organised on others, further comment is unnecessary. . . ."

The "complete accord" turned out in actual working to be a rather optimistic estimate of the situation. As my minute shows, neither Admiral Jellicoe nor Admiral Duff really believed in the principle of convoys, though they were willing to assent to a cautious trial of this expedient. They had been convinced against their will and at heart remained of the same opinion still.

The High Admirals had at last been persuaded by the "Convoyers" not perhaps to take action, but to try action. But there was a reluctance and a tardiness in their movements. They acted as men whose doubts are by no means removed, and who therefore proceed with excessive caution and with an ill-concealed expectation that their forebodings will be justified by the experience. When anything went wrong with convoyed ships, it was reported with an "I told you so" air to the War Cabinet. I can find no minute where the First Sea Lord reported the unquestionable success of the system in cases where it was fairly tried. There was a Cabinet meeting held a week or two after the decision to experiment in convoying. It was attended amongst others by Admiral Jellicoe, Admiral Duff, Sir William Robertson and Commander Henderson. I listened to the Admiralty argument on the lack of escorts in the form of cruisers and destroyers, but I insisted on their giving a trial to the Gibraltar convoy. The First Sea Lord at this meeting held forth as to the necessity of maintaining the Grand Fleet destroyers up to the number of 100 and the Harwich Force as constituted. He maintained that these destroyers were necessary to fulfil the Cabinet's instructions given to the Admiralty and to the Commander-in-Chief in regard to battle with the German High Seas Fleet, and if destroyers were withdrawn then the general instructions to the higher command must be revised.

Commander Henderson said that he considered that if convoys could be put into being forthwith, it would probably take Germany three months to discover the best method of locating and attacking, during which period we should have further time for thought and for construction.

After this discussion it was decided to try the first experimental convoy from Gibraltar to the United Kingdom. Ships from the Mediterranean to the East Coast were held up for four days from the 6th May, till on the 10th, a convoy of 17 steamers started under the escort of two "Q" ships, the *Mavis* and *Rule*, which had been sent out from this country for the purpose.

It was not until the 17th May—over three weeks after the Cabinet decision—that the Admiralty went so far as to appoint a Committee to study the question of regular convoys. This Committee sat for three weeks and went into the whole question of convoying minutely and with great care. They had to settle routes and the number of ships in each convoy—how to group them according to speed—the sailing instructions to be given. They had also to extort protecting craft from the Admiralty. It was a laborious process, for the Board were convinced that their torpedo boats were more usefully employed on other duties. In arriving at their final recommendations the Committee were helped by the success that attended two experiments.

"During the sittings of the Committee, the convoy from Hampton Roads with H.M.S. *Roxburgh* (Captain Whitehead, R.N.) as ocean escort had sailed on 24th May with 12 ships; two of these vessels, the *Ravenshoe*, with a cargo of sugar, and the *Highbury* with nitrate, were detached, because they could not keep up with the convoy, and sent into Halifax to be routed independently. . . . The convoy arrived safely in 15 days.

Captain Whitehead reported to the First Sea Lord *that the station-keeping was excellent, and that he was prepared to take charge of 30 vessels instead of 12.*"*

The Gibraltar convoy was equally successful. But these disappointing successes simply irritated the Admirals into sullen recalcitrance. The Shipping Controller's report states that: —

"Although Board approval had been vouchsafed to the Committee's scheme on the 14th June, it was in the letter rather than in the spirit, as the indispensable forces were not made available."*

The Controller reported this attitude to me, and I had to convey to the Admiralty in peremptory terms my disapproval of their conduct. They at last "consented to give effect to their own approval."†

On 6th June the Committee presented its report setting out a detailed plan. The report was adopted and Paymaster-Commander Manisty made "Organising Manager of Convoys" (not "Director," as is customary for heads of important Departments): but he was given neither room nor a staff, and had to go round and "scrounge" for these as best he could. And although the report was formally adopted on 14th June, it was some time before the Admiralty could bring itself to scrape together the necessary escorting craft. Regular convoys only began to run from America on 2nd July, from Gibraltar on 26th July, and from Dakar on 11th August. Of the 279 destroyers in Home waters, between 20 and 30 were allotted to convoy duties. The 279 included 100 destroyers attached to the Grand Fleet, to watch over its cold storage at Scapa Flow, and Admiral Jellicoe claims some credit for having allowed from 8 to 12 of these to be used during part of 1917 for trade protection on the convoy routes off the Irish coast. It was a grudging and mean allowance, when we were fighting for bare life against the stranglehold of the U-boats, and when an attack by the German High Seas Fleet upon our vastly stronger Grand Fleet was an extremely remote possibility. But there is no wrath like the cold fury of the professional spirit proved wrong by outsiders, and no folly comparable to its reactions under such conditions. In spite of everything the convoy system proved a brilliant success. The

* Extract from Ministry of Shipping Report on Convoys.
† Ministry of Shipping Report on Convoys.

Admirals were in despair over the refusal of events to follow the lead of professional knowledge.

To quote again from the Official Report of the Shipping Department, in reference to the convoys from the U.S.A.: —

> "*The success of these convoys was phenomenal.* Fourteen convoys comprising 242 steamers were brought in without the loss of a vessel, although the convoys were sometimes attacked, and a tanker, the *Wabasha* in the fourth convoy from Hampton Roads, was hit by a ' browning shot.' With the assistance of the escort on the spot she was brought in with only the loss of part of her cargo, and the offensive side of the system was demonstrated by a heavy attack on the submarine with depth charges. Had she been a solitary ship, even if guarded by several destroyers, it is probable she would have been torpedoed several times until she sank. . . ."

But we were not yet at the end of our troubles with the Admiralty. Here is another illustration of their stubborn hostility and of the effort they expended in circumnavigating it.

> " It was not until the 26th July that the Gibraltar convoy began to run regularly. The reluctance of the Board (of Admiralty) to meet this group of ships with a trawler escort, in the absence of sufficient destroyers, was a stumbling block, but this was ultimately overcome, and the success of this convoy, which was practically never out of the danger zone, and which never had anything but a trawler escort, strengthened with one destroyer, and generally only a ' Q ' ship or an American gunboat for ocean escort, has been wonderful."*

The difficulties experienced by the War Cabinet in handling this problem are inherent in all war operations when civilian opinion clashes with that of the experts. Naval science and strategy are matters very remote from the lay comprehension, and the aura of authority glistened round the heads of the Naval High Command. Whenever I urged the adoption of the convoy system, I was met, as I have related, with the blank wall of assertion that the experts of the Admiralty knew on technical grounds that it was impossible. That is a very difficult argument to counter.

A persistence of a few more weeks in their refusal to listen to advice from outside would have meant irretrievable ruin for the Allies. Neptune's trident would have been snatched out of Britannia's hands by the ravening monster of the great deep. It was not the first time in this War that the lesson was driven home—luckily in time—that no great national enterprise can be carried through successfully in

---

* Extract from Ministry of Shipping Report on Convoys.

peace or in war except by a trustful co-operation between expert and layman—tendered freely by both, welcomed cordially by both.

When individual cases of impeding and blocking were brought to my notice I could exert the necessary pressure, but time was being lost and lost time meant lost ships and lost lives. So I made up my mind to effect a change at the top in the Admiralty. Obviously, unless I were present at the Admiralty every day to supervise every detail of administration, it would be impossible for me promptly to remove all hindrances and speed up action. I therefore contemplated a change in the First Lord, Lord Carson, and the First Sea Lord, Admiral Jellicoe. They were both men of great influence and authority, and both possessed a formidable following, one political, the other naval. I discovered there were Parties in the Navy—the Jellicoe Party and the Beatty Party. Like most Parties their differences of principle were too vague for an outsider to grasp. But the more obscure the doctrine the more fierce the personalities.

As to Lord Carson, he was conscious of half-heartedness in his official associates. Their stubbornness wore him down by wearing him out. They were obstinate, slow and self-willed. Carson was not cut out for a mule driver. That was not his function in life. He had plenty of courage and independence of his own, but being new to Administrative office, and especially to Admiralty business, he was very dependent on his official advisers and he shrank from seeking independent advice. Without that he was lost.

He could have obtained it without going outside the Navy for which he was officially responsible. He might have sought the opinion of men in the service. But his whole training was opposed to such a resort. In his profession he could only call into conference those whose names were on the back of his brief—second leaders, juniors and solicitors. To call another counsellor into the room and to take another into his confidence, was to imply distrust of his colleagues and therefore a professional disloyalty. He therefore only availed himself of the advice of the acknowledged Admiralty chiefs. The perplexity he was in and the impotence in which he was enveloped preyed upon his health. I have never taken the view that the head of a Government Department is forbidden by any rule of honour or etiquette from sending for any person either inside or outside his office, whatever his rank, to seek enlightenment on any subject affecting his administration. If a Minister learns that any subordinate in his Department possesses exceptional knowledge or special aptitude on any question, it is essential he should establish direct contact with him. The political head of a Department has not merely the right, but the duty to send for anyone who will help him to discharge his trust to the public. That principle would apply to both the political and permanent heads of a Department. Lord Carson did not see his way to adopt this point of view. The result

was that although his natural shrewdness and penetration enabled
him to perceive that things were not moving in the right direction,
or as rapidly as they ought, he could not find out exactly the point
where they stuck, how to remove the obstruction or how to speed up.

Before I was called to the Premiership I was not in contact with
the Navy and knew little of what was going on in that sphere.   On
the military side the Ministry of Munitions brought me into direct
touch with the problems of land warfare.   Apart from that I constantly met officers and men home on leave who had spent months
at the battle front and had been taking part daily in the incessant
engagements—great and small—of the campaign in Flanders or
France.   It is not merely a boast but a fact that I had more converse
with fighting officers and men, untabbed with scarlet, straight from
the trenches, than had any member of the Staff either at General
Headquarters or at the War Office.

When I meet men possessing special knowledge and experience on
any subject, it has been my habit through life to question them on
the theme they know and like best.   The information I thus acquire
leaves a deeper and more inerasable impression on my mind than
what is communicated to me in any other way.   Much study is a
weariness to the flesh, but conversations with a knowledgeable person
stimulate and refresh and nourish one's mind.   Had I depended
entirely on departmental chiefs, I could never have carried through
my schemes of Old Age Pensions or Insurance.   I know the importance of maintaining discipline in a Department.   Our public services
are manned by some of the best and most competent men in this
or any country, and it is essential to efficiency that their legitimate
power and prestige in their respective spheres should be fully maintained.   But freedom of access to independent information is quite
compatible with order and due respect for the hierarchy, if that
liberty is tactfully and judiciously exercised by the Minister and
wisely acquiesced in by the service.   There must be no appearance of
flouting the men at the top.   On the other hand, they must not make it
impossible to act without forcing an open disregard of their authority.

When as Prime Minister I became responsible for the efficient
administration of every department of the Government, I took every
opportunity afforded me officially or unofficially of acquainting myself
with the major questions which affected the conduct of the War in
every branch of the public service.   The Admiralty and the Shipping
Controller brought to my notice all the problems arising out of the
struggle on the High Seas.   The Shipping Controller soon formed a
poor opinion of the Admiralty Board.   But my most reliable inside
information on the naval aspect of my problem came from another
source.   I was fortunate enough to obtain the same access to men
who had seen active service on the seas as I had already secured in
land warfare.   I owe much to Commander Kenworthy for making

me acquainted at this critical stage with the views of the younger officers in the Navy. I was introduced to Kenworthy through the good offices of the late Sir Herbert Lewis, who was then Parliamentary Secretary to the Board of Education. I met some of these junior officers and I realised that there was a school of highly intelligent naval men who were very critical of the High Admirals and their methods. They condemned severely their anti-submarine plans. They were scornful of their opinions on the subject of convoys. But what provoked their hostility more than anything was the chilly discouragement accorded by those at Headquarters to any proposals or suggestions from men who were actively engaged in the struggle on the High Seas. When it is borne in mind that the Admirals had themselves filed a petition in bankruptcy to the War Cabinet, as far as their own stock of new ideas was concerned, this lofty disdain of any offer to replenish their mental warehouses was unpardonable. I urged Sir Edward Carson to utilise the services of those men in the Anti-Submarine Department of the Admiralty. He was fully in sympathy with the idea, and undertook to see that their services should be utilised.

At a meeting of the Cabinet War Committee on 20th June, 1917, I asked the First Sea Lord whether the Admiralty were making any progress in the organisation of an Offensive Section of the Operations Division. Admiral Jellicoe said that the First Lord had thought it would be a good plan to assemble some junior officers to form a section for investigating offensive operations. *He himself felt it was not much use putting junior officers there. He could not give the time to examine numbers of projects, and he himself had examined all the possibilities of offensive action.* Captain Richmond's name had been proposed for this section but the First Lord told us that after seeing Captain Richmond he had rejected it. Another officer, selected by himself, was coming up to the Admiralty in his place. He felt, however, *that this section would very likely only waste his time,* though he hoped to be able to refer to them the working out in detail of his own projects.

It is also interesting to record Admiral Jellicoe's opinion as to the offensive value of an overwhelming fleet. I was dissatisfied that our Navy, with all its tremendous power, could do so little against the Belgian harbours which were used as bases for the German submarine and torpedo flotillas, and I asked Jellicoe whether, if the German Fleet had the same preponderance over ours as we and the Americans together now enjoyed over theirs, they could not make Dover or Harwich untenable for our fleets. He denied that we had an overwhelming preponderance, except in battleships, and further stated that even if the Germans held an overwhelming preponderance, they could not render either Harwich or Dover untenable. Harwich was defended by navigational conditions, in which respect it resembled

Zeebrugge and Ostend. Dover could be bombarded, but our ships could come back as soon as the bombardment was over. You could not render a harbour so unpleasant that ships could not use it. Our Grand Fleet could not go nearer to Zeebrugge than 18,000 yards range; and if monitors, which were unarmed, closed to that range, they would be sunk.

This was Jellicoe's view, alike of the possibility of offensive action by the Navy, and of the resource and ability of the younger naval officers. Captain—now Admiral Sir Herbert—Richmond, to whom reference was made, was one of the able young men whom I found helpful in this emergency.

I passed on to the first Lord of the Admiralty the information I derived from these young officers. But he found it impossible to overcome the solid and stolid resistance of his Board of Admirals. I decided, therefore, to put someone in charge who was accustomed to force his will on his subordinates.

When my Administration was formed I was convinced that Sir Edward Carson's great gifts would be better employed by giving him a seat on the War Cabinet. I had designated Lord Milner for the Admiralty. In that choice I was overridden by the personal prejudices of the majority of the Conservative leaders against Carson. They all admired but disapproved of him. Curzon neither admired nor liked him. Long, who magnified his own influence and position in the Conservative Party, was jealous of the idea of including Carson in a War Cabinet from which he was excluded. So Carson had been kept out of a place for which he was qualified and given a post for which he was unsuited. Every Ministry suffers from these misfortunes and misfits.

A few months' experience of an appointment forced on me against my own judgment of its aptness drove me to the conclusion that a change must be effected in the interests of Sir Edward Carson himself. His own exasperation at the obstacles thrown in the path of effective action was visibly telling on his strength. Someone was needed at the head of the Admiralty with a greater reserve of vitality, with more resource and greater mastery of detail. A conversation I had with Sir Douglas Haig in the early summer of 1917 finally decided me. The Commander-in-Chief was also alarmed at the dismaying ravages of the submarine. He was apprehensive that the War might be lost at sea before he had an opportunity of winning it on land. He had great admiration for Jellicoe's knowledge as a technical sailor, but he thought him much too rigid, narrow and conservative in his ideas. As to Sir Edward Carson, I am afraid Sir Douglas Haig had no opinion of his qualities as an administrator. He thought he was distinctly out of place at the Admiralty. He strongly urged upon me the appointment of Sir Eric Geddes to that post. The power, and especially the punch, which Sir Eric had displayed in the reorganisation of transport to and in France had made a considerable impression on the Commander-in-Chief's mind. Geddes was then engaged in the vital task of putting fresh life into the construction of ships to fill up the dark gaps made by the enemy in our Mercantile Marine.

Mr. Bonar Law agreed as to the desirability of effecting a change if it could be done without offending Sir Edward Carson. We had both a great personal regard for Carson and we were anxious not to give him any hurt. But as he knew that we had always been of opinion that he would have rendered greater service to his country in the War Cabinet than in any administrative office, we could honestly present to him the case for a transfer from Admiralty House to the Council Chamber on that ground. Nevertheless, although membership of the War Directorate was a more exalted and powerful position, I am afraid he felt wounded by the change. To him it was an unpalatable proposal, however much we might wrap it up. But his intense patriotic sense prevailed over any personal feeling. So Carson joined the War Cabinet and Geddes went to the Admiralty. The conduct of the War benefited by the double change.

What about Admiral Jellicoe? Sir Eric Geddes, in his acceptance of the position of First Lord, stipulated that Jellicoe should not be immediately removed. Geddes knew that Jellicoe had the confidence of the senior officers in the Navy, and that it would therefore be a distinct advantage to secure his co-operation if that were at all possible. He promised to tell me without delay if he found that he could not work with or through him.

It was not long before he discovered that the proper co-ordination and full efficiency of the Admiralty were being seriously handicapped by personal factors, among which was the lack of sympathetic confidence between Admiral Beatty, Commanding the Grand Fleet, and Admiral Jellicoe, the First Sea Lord. This disagreement had existed since differences had arisen between them about the Battle of Jutland. After consultation with me, Geddes decided to bring in a Deputy First Sea Lord, to facilitate co-operation between the Grand Fleet, the Harwich Force, and the Admiralty. To this post he appointed Admiral Sir Rosslyn Wemyss (afterwards Lord Wemyss). Wemyss, although a good sailor, was not a man of outstanding ability. But he had two special qualities which were conspicuously helpful under the conditions prevailing at that time in the Admiralty. He was not a factionist. He was neither a Jellicoeite nor a Beattyite. He was quite friendly with both. The second attribute which commended him to Geddes was that he was willing to listen to young officers with ideas. He never stared them out of his room. His eyeglass greeted them with a friendly gleam.

Geddes also proceeded to develop a Plans Division of the Admiralty, at the head of which he placed Rear-Admiral Keyes (afterwards Sir Roger Keyes), to study plans for offensive enterprises by the Navy in the Narrow Seas. A " Channel Barrage Committee " was set up on 17th November, 1917, with Admiral Keyes as Chairman.

But the inertia and lack of co-ordination in the Admiralty resisted these measures, and on 21st December, 1917, we found Geddes urging at a Cabinet meeting that he should leave the Admiralty to take charge of the co-ordination of land and sea transport for all the Allies. The Allied Governments were in complete agreement that Geddes was the best man for this important task. Transportation was at that time an acute problem, and the War Cabinet fully recognised that Sir Eric Geddes was by far the best if not indeed the only person qualified to deal effectively with it. But we felt that we could not spare him from the Admiralty. An explanation of his readiness to consider the other post was forthcoming when that afternoon he came to see me at Downing Street and told me that he had come to the conclusion that he could not give of his best at the Admiralty if Admiral Jellicoe remained there as First Sea Lord. Bonar Law, Geddes and I then went into the whole matter, and Geddes explained that while he was on the best of terms with Jellicoe, and had the highest regard for him, and had no intention of trying, as a civilian, to override the Admirals in technical matters, he felt that he could make no progress there with Jellicoe. Wemyss, on the other hand, was a man who would give opportunities to the younger men, and was on the best of terms with Beatty. During the time he had been at the Admiralty as Deputy First Sea Lord, Wemyss had encouraged the active brains in the Planning Division and indeed throughout the Admiralty.

Bonar Law agreed with me that in the circumstances a change was now desirable. We had as a matter of fact thought so for a long time, but had undertaken to give Geddes an opportunity to make up his own mind, and after six months' trial he had come to the same conclusion that we had previously reached—a conclusion shared by Sir Douglas Haig, who had intimate knowledge alike of Admiral Jellicoe's qualities and of the situation at the Admiralty. Haig happened to be in London about this time and expressed his mind freely about the desirability of change.

Sir Eric motored to Sandringham on Christmas Day, where he shared Christmas dinner with the King and Royal Family, and brought back His Majesty's consent to the change at the Admiralty. Jellicoe resigned his post as First Sea Lord on the following day, and was succeeded by Sir Rosslyn Wemyss; and Admiral Keyes replaced Admiral Bacon at Dover. Among the fruits of this rearrangement may be reckoned the carrying through of the attack on Zeebrugge and Ostend by the Dover Patrol Force under Keyes—one of the most gallant and spectacular achievements of the War.

As First Lord of the Admiralty, Geddes' overriding vitality was soon felt in every branch of activity. Difficulties and hesitancies disappeared in every direction. There was a quickening in action all round. The convoy system at last had a fair chance. It was extended, strengthened, improved in every direction. The naval officers who were whole-heartedly for it were encouraged. The attack on the submarine was developed. The Nash invention of the " fish " hydrophone was attached without delay to patrolling vessels. Many other new and ingenious expedients were resorted to for breaking down and destroying the submarine. Best of all, there was real drive put into all these operations. In spite of their increase in power and speed, the enemy submarines began to suffer rapidly growing losses from the effect of the vigorous campaign against them which was now being carried on. The fact is shown by the official German figures of their War Losses in submarines, year by year, which are as follows: —

1914	...	5	submarines	lost by enemy action
1915	...	19	,,	,, ,, ,, ,,
1916	...	22	,,	,, ,, ,, ,,
1917	...	63	,,	,, ,, ,, ,,
1918	...	69	,,	,, ,, ,, ,,

From the end of July, 1917, to the end of October, 1918, we were sinking German submarines at an average rate of seven every month.

In August, convoys were also instituted for outward-bound ships, a measure proposed in the original scheme of the committee, but at first postponed on account of the alleged difficulty of providing escorts. From this time until the end of the War, convoyed ships enjoyed a considerable and growing immunity from submarine attack. As the " Official History " states: —

" The experience gained showed that a convoy had intrinsically great powers of evasion, in that it was almost impossible for a submarine commander to place himself right upon its track, at the right time of the day, and in a good position for attacking it, when its course and time of arrival were completely unknown to him. The great successes of the submarine commanders had hitherto been due to the immensity of their target: they had only to post themselves outside the patrolled routes somewhere between the Fastnets and Scillies, and they were practically certain to sight merchantmen if they waited for them. Some areas were better than others, but as the whole zone was traversed by merchant traffic it was in the German sense productive. The passage of these convoys through the danger area showed that, if the system could be developed and extended, it would alter the whole aspect of submarine warfare. The German submarine commanders would no longer be able to go to a fruitful area and there lie in wait: henceforward they would be compelled to seek out and attack groups of ships of whose movements they knew nothing—a very much more difficult task, and one which in many cases would be quite impossible."*

That verdict was fully confirmed by the statistics of convoys. Between the summer of 1917 and the end of hostilities in November, 1918, some 16,657 vessels were convoyed to or from this country. The total losses, including 16 sunk by marine peril and 36 ships sunk when not in contact with the convoy, amounted to 154 vessels, or less than 1 per cent. of the vessels convoyed. Alike in number and in gross tonnage the total number and tonnage of the ships lost in convoy during nearly a year and a half of unrestricted warfare were considerably less than the losses incurred during the single month of April, 1917, before the first convoys were introduced.

Under Rear-Admiral Duff's leadership the convoy system, benefiting by experience, kept improving each month. The difficulties about varying speeds were adjusted satisfactorily. Hence are some extracts from a Report presented to me after the new regime had been in operation for some time:—

". . . The geographical limits for the various Atlantic Coast convoys were relaxed, and ships were apportioned to the convoys in accordance with their speeds, provided there was no deviation involving delay in reaching this side. . . .

(September) By these means all ships, Allied and Neutral, homeward bound to United Kingdom or French Atlantic ports, whatever their speed, were now brought into convoy."

Neutrals were still suffering heavy losses. Their ships, even when engaged in Allied transport, were not convoyed, either by us or by their own warships. A discussion arose as to whether it was not in our interest to offer them the same protection as was afforded to our own ships. The objection to our doing so lay in the danger of their giving codes and courses away to the enemy—either advertently or inadvertently.

Here are summaries of a few of the Reports which came in to encourage those who believed in the convoy system, and to confute those who predicted that it would turn out to be a failure:—

" Of 115 wheat ships which sailed from Newport News between the 2nd July and the 10th of October, four were sunk out of 18 independent sailings, and only one, the *Noya*, was sunk out of 97 ships in convoys. This ship had got separated from her convoy.

* "Naval Operations," Vol. V, p. 51.

Further figures taken later on showed that the risk of a ship in convoy was only a tenth of that run by a steamer proceeding independently.

There seems no doubt that many of the enemy submarines were afraid to attack a convoy. Not only were they liable to instant counter-attack by the destroyers, but the mere appearance of a convoy of merchant vessels was very unnerving when seen through a periscope. To take up from ahead a suitable position for attack, when some 25 steamers each with a different turning circle were performing a zigzag was more than any but the ablest and most daring German Commander cared to tackle; the larger the convoy, the more unpleasant it looked, and it is the case that in the Atlantic most of the successful attacks were made either by ' browning shots,' or by torpedoes fired at a straggler, who for some reason had failed to maintain his proper situation in the convoy."

.   .   .   .   .   .

" By the middle of August it became very noticeable that the enemy, failing to find the homeward-bound traffic as easily as before, was now devoting more attention to the outward-bound vessels. At the end of April the proportion sunk had been 7 per cent. outward bound as compared with 18 per cent. homeward bound. Now while the numbers of inward-bound losses were rapidly decreasing, the sinkings of outward-bound tonnage were becoming more numerous."

Thereupon, as I have already mentioned, we made arrangements for convoying outward-bound vessels. This threw a great additional strain on the escorting destroyers, and the Report notes that: —

" The crews (of the escorting destroyers) were very hard worked, several of the officers broke down under the constant strain, and the vessels themselves suffered severely as the winter came on."

.   .   .   .   .   .

" By the end of October, 1917, 99 homeward convoys had been brought in, comprising 1,502 steamers of an estimated total dead-weight capacity of 10,656,300 tons, with a loss of 0.66 per cent., or 10 vessels, torpedoed while actually in contact with the convoy. The number of ships which had been sunk after being separated from their convoys by bad weather or the disobedience of their masters was 14. So that the gross total, including these vessels, was only 1.57 per cent. With experience and as masters realised more generally that their safety depended on their continuance with their convoy, the difference between the nett and gross percentage became appreciably less, the figures at the signing of the armistice being 0.78 per cent. lost when in convoy formation and 1.13 per cent. including those which had lost touch with the convoy."

". . . This meant in effect that tonnage being sunk was no longer for the most part large steamers homeward bound with cargoes, but smaller vessels in the coasting trade, and steamers bound round the coast in ballast to load at Cardiff or elsewhere, with a certain number of ships on their way to an assembly port for outward convoy."

" Another notable change produced by the convoy system was the practical disappearance of ' sunk by gunfire ' which had accounted for a large percentage of the vessels lost prior to August-September, 1917.
The statistics for British ships only, at the end of December, 1917, showed that whereas during the five months April to August, the losses over 50 miles from the land were 175, an average of 35 per month; during the period from September to December, the ships sunk at this distance from the land for the whole four months only reached a total of six of which four were sunk in September."

The most gratifying feature of this success was the increased security achieved for the brave mariners who were risking their lives for their country.

" The result of this from the point of view of life saving was enormous; it meant that a crew, even when their ship was torpedoed, and they had to take to their boats, were rarely more than 10 or 20 miles from the land, and probably had a coastal patrol boat to their assistance in less than half an hour. This was a very different ordeal from that which had to be faced in the first six months of 1917, when the ships were sunk 200 and 300 miles from the land, and when the majority of those who managed to get into their boats died from exposure before they reached land or were picked up.
Moreover, it practically eliminated the danger of the master or chief engineer being taken prisoner by the submarine. This was a device which the Germans had adopted with a view of impairing morale, and it is a credit to the Mercantile Marine that they stood for so long the risks to which they were opposed with very little chance of retaliation. How long their courage would have stood the test had the convoy system not altered conditions at sea is a debatable question."

" The possibility of salving a torpedoed ship was also vastly increased by this change of tactics which had been forced on the Bosche."

"In the early days of convoys, the thing was to get the ships and cargoes home, and although many more or less accurate calculations (one very elaborate estimate was drawn up by the Germans and published in their Press) were presented to the Convoy Department to show how delay reduced the amount of imports, it was obvious that a ship ' in being,' however slow, was a better asset than a ship at the bottom of the sea, no matter how quickly she got there.

When the system had thoroughly proved its worth, and experience had been gained of where and how the delays arose, steps were taken to remedy the defects as far as possible. The first step was the formation of convoys of faster speeds which has already been dealt with. . . ."*

The convoy system, supplemented by the arming of merchantmen and the application of new expedients and devices for chasing and chivvying and hunting down the submarines, thus furnished the solution for the submarine problem, and saved the country from this deadly menace. But a system is unavailing without men. No praise can adequately recognise the courage and efficiency of the officers and men who manned the vessels which convoyed our ships through all perils, and those also which were engaged in hunting out and hunting down the piratical craft that lurked in the shadows of the deep. But among all the resources on which Britain was able to draw, in her efforts to meet the challenge of the U-boats, none deserves to be placed higher than the courage and devotion of our merchant seamen and fishermen. These proved to be of a quality far beyond the calculations of the German Admiralty.

The enemy unquestionably reckoned on being able by a campaign of frightfulness to intimidate our sailors from putting to sea. No other explanation is possible of the numerous cases of brutality and outrage that were perpetrated—presumably by express order of the High Command—against defenceless men after their vessels had been torpedoed and sunk. The firing on and scuttling of open boats at sea, and triumphant proclamation of ships " *spurlos versenkt* "—sunk without trace, their whole crews being drowned mercilessly—were all intended to shake the morale of British seamen and make them unwilling to sign on for further voyages. But in this object the German Navy was completely unsuccessful.

I remember meeting an old sea-captain on board the boat in which I was returning from France after one of our Inter-Allied Conferences during the War. I asked him what he was doing there, and the grizzled skipper told me he had just been torpedoed for, I think, the sixth time, and was now making his way back to Liverpool to take charge of another ship and face the U-boats once again.

* Extracts from Ministry of Shipping Report on Convoys.

In a letter written to me on 25th October, 1917, the late Havelock Wilson, Secretary of the National Sailors' and Firemen's Union, said : —

"We have a very large number of the members of the Sailors' and Firemen's Union who have been in as many as five or six ships that have been torpedoed, yet every one of these men the moment they have landed on shore have immediately sought employment on other ships to proceed to sea. I have heard of one man who has been in no less than seven vessels that have been torpedoed and is now away on a voyage. I have also known cases where men have returned to port after having been on vessels torpedoed; they were then entitled to draw from the Union sums varying from £4 to £5 for shipwreck claims, which we invariably settle within 48 hours. These men, however, instead of waiting for their money, have immediately obtained other vessels, and proceeded to sea before their claims were settled; they have often had the misfortune to sign on other vessels which were sunk and on their return to port have drawn accumulative claims for two or three shipwreck benefits. . . .

A large number of men during last winter experienced days of agony and suffering in open boats, many of them have had to have their limbs amputated. On our visits to these men in hospital, each and every one of them have expressed their regret that they were not able to render further assistance to their King and Country.

I have myself been in close touch with the members of the Union, and I have not met one man yet who has expressed a fear to face the dangers, as each and every one of them fully realises how important it is to keep the ships running to meet the needs of the people of these islands and also serve the Army and Navy with men and stores. . . ."

How serious those dangers were is clearly shown by the casualty returns. In the Royal Navy, including Marines, Air Service, the R.N.R. and R.N.V.R. and all other auxiliary branches, the total number of officers and men who were killed in action or died of wounds during the War was 22,811. These include a considerable number of sailors from amongst the fishermen and the Mercantile Marine who were doing naval work and were on the pay-roll of the British Navy. If deaths from other causes are included the total becomes 34,654. The number of lives lost in British Merchant and Fishing vessels between 4th August, 1914, and 11th November, 1918, was 15,313. The deaths in the Royal Navy during the War bore to the total number of those who served in it the proportion of 5.41 per cent. In the Mercantile Marine, the proportion of lives lost was about 7½ per cent. of the persons employed in our merchant shipping. It was a far more dangerous service than was our official fighting service on the sea.   But, as Mr. Havelock Wilson's letter testified, the survivors were as ready as ever to brave the perils of the submarine-infested seas in the service of their country.   Without rank or uniform they ventured as gallantly as any of the men in our fighting services, and it was to their valour and tenacity as much as to the skill and bravery displayed by the crews of our patrolling and escorting craft that we owed our triumph over the deadliest craft that ever menaced our pathways across the deep.

It is perhaps hardly realised how important were the services of our fishing craft and fishermen in maintaining the defence and escort of our merchant shipping.   While we were able to make valuable use of all the destroyers which could be spared from service with the Fleet, and of all that the Americans could furnish, in the task of escorting our shipping convoys, a great deal of the work of watching over the safety of our merchantmen was carried out by armed trawlers.   It is repeatedly stated by apologists for the Admiralty that although convoys were successful when they were eventually introduced, this was only because the advent of America had given us a supply of T.B.D.'s for escort work.   But it must be borne in mind that the first successful line of regular convoys—those organised for the French coal trade by Commander Henderson—made no use of T.B.D.'s at all.   Some of the convoys went without added guard, their strength being their mutual support, manœuvring in rough formation along a specially appointed route.   Mostly, however, they were escorted by armed trawlers, of which Commander Henderson had altogether some 26 available for protecting the three main routes followed by his coal vessels.   The " Official History " remarks that : " the exceptional immunity that the French coal trade enjoyed since it had been placed under this modified system of convoy was certainly remarkable.   During the quarter ending April, 1917, rather fewer than 30 armed trawlers had given protection to over 4,000 cross-Channel voyages."

It cannot be doubted in the face of these experiences that an earlier and fuller use of our armed trawlers in escort work for convoyed vessels would have saved us a very considerable volume of the tonnage which went to the bottom of the sea in 1916 and the earlier part of 1917, before systematic convoys were instituted, or the American Navy became a contributor to our protective forces upon the sea.

The rate at which British vessels were sunk by enemy action showed a steady decline in 1918 from the appalling height which it had reached in the spring of 1917.   The figures of our total tonnage losses from this cause during the War years are as follows : —

						Gross Tonnage of British
Year.						*Vessels sunk by enemy action.*
1914	...	...	...	...	...	252,738
1915	...	...	...	...	...	885,471
1916	...	...	...	...	...	1,231,867
1917	...	...	...	...	...	3,660,054
1918	...	...	...	...	...	1,632,228

The way in which the sinkings were reduced is shown more clearly in the month-by-month totals for 1917 and 1918:—

1917	January	...	153,899 gross tons sunk
	February	...	310,868 ,, ,, ,,
	March	...	352,344 ,, ,, ,,
	April	...	526,447 ,, ,, ,,
	May	...	345,293 ,, ,, ,,
	June	...	398,773 ,, ,, ,,
	July	...	359,539 ,, ,, ,,
	August	...	331,370 ,, ,, ,,
	September	...	186,647 ,, ,, ,,
	October	...	261,873 ,, ,, ,,
	November	...	175,194 ,, ,, ,,
	December	...	257,807 ,, ,, ,,
1918	January	...	173,387 ,, ,, ,,
	February	...	213,045 ,, ,, ,,
	March	...	199,426 ,, ,, ,,
	April	...	214,426 ,, ,, ,,
	May	...	179,395 ,, ,, ,,
	June	...	143,639 ,, ,, ,,
	July	...	163,801 ,, ,, ,,
	August	...	143,944 ,, ,, ,,
	September	...	129,483 ,, ,, ,,
	October	...	56,330 ,, ,, ,,
	November	...	15,352 ,, ,, ,,

Against this record of our decreasing losses can be set the swelling figures for our new construction. The gross tonnage of the British Merchant vessels launched during the War period was as follows:—

Vessels Launched of 100 G.T. and upwards.

1914	...	...	...	...	1,706,000 gross tons
1915	...	...	...	...	664,000 ,, ,,
1916	...	...	...	...	630,000 ,, ,,
1917	...	...	...	...	1,229,000 ,, ,,
1918	...	...	...	...	1,579,000 ,, ,,

BRITISH MERCANTILE SHIPPING LOSSES AUG. 1914–OCT. 1918

| 1,000 G.T. | AUG.-DEC.'14 | 1915 | 1916 | 1917 | JAN.-OCT. 1918 | 1,000 G.T. |

.... = Losses by German raiders and cruisers
———— = Losses by mines
—·—·—·— = Losses by submarines
— — — — — = Losses by marine risk

CHART SHOWING BRITISH SHIPPING LOSSES

Up to the date of the initiation of the convoy the sinkings mounted upwards month by month. As the Germans were increasing the numbers of their more powerful submarines week by week and the long hours of daylight were approaching, there was every reason to apprehend an alarming increase in the rate of destruction of our merchant ships. Instead of that, there was a welcome drop in the casualties at sea; at last the losses were confined to a figure which was about equal to the new tonnage launched from our yards.

British shipbuilding by the end of the War had almost levelled up to the rate at which the submarines were sinking our vessels; the world shipbuilding, including the big output of the United States, had in fact greatly surpassed that rate. Further, the new arrangements made for securing better use of our shipping were beginning to tell, and this reorganisation of our transport caused our shipping to be more effective than the figures for our net balance of available tonnage might imply. Our monthly average of imports during the last half-year of 1917 was 2,968,000 tons a month. During the period July-October, 1918, with a considerably smaller volume of shipping, the average was 3,002,000 tons a month. The story of how this effective use of our tonnage was organised is told in my chapter on the Ministry of Shipping.

It was Britain's grandest struggle on the seas—in its magnitude—in its intensity—in the issues that depended upon it. There were thousands of ships engaged in it, from the great battleships down to the smallest patrol boats—from the stately liners to the dogged tramps and the plucky little trawlers. Even the pleasure boats joined in. The battle was fought in every ocean, and on every trade route. Never were the skill, the daring and the endurance of British sailors put to so stern a test; never was the superiority of their seamanship so triumphantly established. The deadly net that sought to envelop the Allied arms and leave them at the mercy of the Prussian sword was torn to shreds by the mariners of Britain.

The great Allied triumph of 1917 was the gradual beating off of the submarine attack. This was the real decision of the War, for the sea front turned out to be the decisive flank in the gigantic battle-field. Here victory rested with the Allies, or rather with Britain. The moment the War became a struggle, not to beat the foe in a fight, but first to exhaust his strength and then to beat his defences down, the sea became inevitably the determining factor. If Germany was to be weakened it must be in one of two ways: (1) the growing weakness of her Allies; (2) the effect of the blockade on the morale of her people. As far as the first method was concerned, she was using it effectively against us. It was our Allies who were being broken up one by one. But as for the second, whilst she was delivering savage body blows to our Allies which successively knocked four of them out, the grim fingers of the British Navy were tightening around her throat. What mattered most for us on land was that our Army should not let go when it was being battered, until the time came for it to deliver the final punch at its enfeebled opponent.

The repulse of the Allied attacks on the Somme, the Chemin des Dames and the Flanders coast did not bring ultimate victory to Germany. Nor did the defeat of Russia and Roumania. But the frustration of the German effort to destroy the Allied shipping led straight to her ultimate collapse in 1918. Germany's supreme effort to blockade Britain had practically failed by the end of 1917 owing to the growing success of our efforts to protect our shipping, to the increase in our output of new ships, to the better use we were making of our shipping, and to the plans we had put through for adding to the yield of our own soil. The Allied losses were still heavy, but by the end of 1917 we knew that the German effort to blockade us would not succeed. On the other hand, our blockade was gradually breaking down the morale of the German nation. They were not starving, but they were already short of some of the essentials of nutriment. Many comforts and most luxuries had become scarce. Even the soldiers in the field were beginning to feel the effect of our blockade. Their ration was already inferior to that of the men they fought. On land, the Central Powers had the advantage in the campaign of 1917. But they achieved nothing which would bring them final victory. They were beaten at sea and that was decisive. The only chance the Allies ever had of bringing the War to a successful conclusion on land was by breaking up Austria and thus isolating Germany. Failing that, all the Allies had to do was just to hold on until the blockade had completed its terrible work and until the Americans rushed up to help in the final overthrowing of a debilitated enemy. General Pétain was the first General to understand the Allied problem. Whilst the naval blockade was gradually effecting its deadly purpose, the Allies on land had two supreme tasks. One was to hold the Germans on the Western Front, the other to organise on the Eastern Front resistance which would prevent the Central Powers from breaking through to the granaries and oil stores of Russia. The Central Powers were beleaguered. We had to beat off their sorties until the exhaustion of their supplies forced them to surrender. That was the true significance of the virtual failure of the German submarine campaign.

CHAPTER XLI

THE ARMING OF MERCHANT VESSELS

THE carrying of guns during wartime by merchantmen engaged in commerce is a very old practice. Indeed, formerly it was usual for large ships to carry guns in times of peace, as a protection against pirates. In the Napoleonic wars, most British ships carried guns to defend themselves against French privateers, which took the seas as commerce raiders in considerable numbers after the defeat of Trafalgar had finally crushed the naval power of France.

During the Great War, the practice of putting guns on merchant ships was only gradually developed. We were short of guns for our fighting forces. The Admiralty began with the arming of some of the vessels engaged on more important work such as bringing of supplies from America, and in the course of 1915, the provision of guns for merchantmen was steadily developed, so far as guns were available. But the heavy demands of the Army for guns left the supply for shipping very scanty, and as German air-raids developed, the provision of anti-aircraft guns was given priority over other claims for the smaller types of gun. The guns supplied to the merchant ships were mostly of a type which the Army in the field could best spare.

By the autumn of 1916 a considerable number of vessels on the more dangerous routes had been supplied with guns.

On 1st January, 1917, only 1,337 of our merchantmen carried guns.

The Official History records that "During the campaign of 1915, no merchant ships with a defensive armament had been sunk by German submarines; and, up to August, 1916, the number destroyed, though steady, was quite small. In the summer of 1916 the Germans began launching their big submarines. In the autumn of the year, figures showed that the U-boat commanders were beginning to overcome the difficulties they experienced in attacking armed merchant vessels: "Twelve defensively armed merchantmen were sunk in December, 1916 and in January, 1917, the number had risen to twenty. It was true that of the merchantmen which escaped, nine out of ten did so by virtue of their gunfire. . . ."

In the autumn of 1916 the position was that defensive arming of merchantmen had proved itself very useful against gunfire attacks by the older U-boats. The big submarines, however, which the Germans were now beginning to use could outrange the little guns hitherto supplied to merchant ships. And far too few of our ships were carrying any armament at all.

In the spring of 1916 there had been some slight risk of trouble with America over the arming of merchantmen. On January 18th, President Wilson, with the best of intentions for mitigating the horrors of submarine warfare, had issued one of his Notes, proposing to bring this form of war " within the rules of International Law and the principles of humanity." Submarines were not to sink ships without ensuring that all on board were removed to a place of safety, nor to attack them unless they tried to escape or resist. Ships, on the other hand, were to stop and yield if challenged by a submarine, and for this purpose must cease to be armed. He even hinted that America might decide to treat all merchantmen with guns on board as auxiliary cruisers, liable to internment. But this Note was not acceptable in Britain, and had a very mixed reception in the States, where Senators Lodge and Sterling warmly maintained the right of merchantmen to arm for defence, as an established usage of the sea. So the threat of American objection to the arming of merchant ships was dropped, and any fear of its revival disappeared when in March, 1916, the U-boat 29 torpedoed without warning the passenger vessel *Sussex* with 380 passengers aboard, including several American citizens.

The rapid rise in the sinking of merchantmen by U-boats in the late autumn of 1916 roused the War Committee to give its attention to the question of hurrying on the defensive arming of our ships. An alarmist letter from Sir John Jellicoe to the Premier played an important part in bringing up the issue. At their meeting of 31st October, 1916, the War Committee decided to review the whole question two days later with Jellicoe in person, and meantime asked the Admiralty to furnish them " with statistical information regarding the rate of loss from attacks by submarines, and the rate at which measures of defence against submarine attack, particularly guns for use in merchant ships, are being provided."

At the meeting of the War Committee on 2nd November, 1916, at which Admiral Jellicoe was present, it was reported that: —

" The War Committee are of opinion that the protection of shipping and the maintenance of our tonnage is one of the gravest questions at present confronting the Allies. . . .

Admiral Sir John Jellicoe was in complete agreement with the Board of Admiralty that, whatever might be done in the future in the direction of fresh inventions, the defensive arming of merchant ships provides, at present, the most effective means of protecting merchant ships against submarines, as is clear from the statistics supplied to the War Committee.

The War Committee were informed by the representatives of the Admiralty that 3,000 guns, 12-pounder size and upwards, preferably four-inch are required. This estimate is made after allowing for ships engaged on distant voyages to call at some convenient port to land or embark their armament, according as they are leaving or entering the danger zone. 500 guns are on order in America, and some 240 are being obtained from Japan, but at present delivery is only taking place at the rate of eighty guns a month."

At that rate half our mercantile marine might be sunk before the other half was armed.

It was decided that a conference should be held at an early date between experts from the Munitions Ministry and the Admiralty on the subject, as the War Committee considered that the increased production of these guns was a question of the first importance.

As a result of this Inter-Departmental Conference it was recommended that the arming of merchant ships should be entrusted to the Admiralty, the War Office and Ministry of Munitions, the responsibility for initiating action to rest with the Admiralty.

On November 13th another meeting of the War Committee decided: —

" Having regard, first, to the fact that the power of the Allies to continue the War would be materially diminished by continued losses of merchant ships, and second, to the accumulating evidence of the value of guns as a defence for merchant ships against submarine attack, the War Committee decided that, AS A QUESTION OF PRINCIPLE, the arming of merchant ships up to a number considered by the Admiralty as indispensable should be a first charge on our artillery resources."

No immediate action seems to have been taken to carry this decision beyond the establishment of the principle.

Less than four weeks after this Committee, the Second Coalition Government was formed. A fresh energy was infused into the work of arming merchantmen. Lord Jellicoe says in his book, " The Crisis of the Naval War ": —

" The *defensive arming* of merchant ships was a matter which was pressed forward with great energy and rapidity during the year 1917. The matter was taken up with the Cabinet immediately on the formation of the Board of Admiralty presided over by Sir Edward Carson, and arrangements made for obtaining a considerable number of guns from the War Office, from Japan, and from France, besides surrendering some guns from the secondary and anti-torpedo boat armament of our own men-of-war, principally those of the older type, pending the manufacture of large numbers of guns for the purpose. . . ."

Soon after the formation of my Ministry it was decided that the Army should be called upon to give up some of its manufacturing capacity in order to enable the Admiralty to provide some hundreds of four-inch guns and howitzers for the Navy, and as even this provision did not meet the requirements it would be advisable that the Minister of Munitions should be authorised to provide further manufacturing facilities. As the manufacture of these new guns would take time, and the need was urgent, the Army agreed to hand over at once to the Admiralty a considerable number of 15 pounders and 4.7 guns.

Arrangements were approved for suspending the manufacture of 724 guns and howitzers for the Army in order to produce a larger number of four-inch guns for arming merchantmen, and the War Office, Admiralty and Ministry of Munitions were ordered to prepare without delay a scheme for meeting the requirements of the Admiralty for guns for merchantmen by April, 1917. This decision is very significant of the fact that the War Cabinet at that date placed the maritime position first in the order of urgency.

These three Departments met on the same day, and on 29th December, they laid before the War Cabinet a series of proposals for providing the guns wanted, and arrangements were agreed for carrying out most of these plans.

We also took in hand immediately the question of not merely arming our merchant ships but of providing those already armed with guns of a longer range. As I have already stated, this question was raised by Admiral Jellicoe at the War Committee held in November, 1916, and it was then reported by the representatives of the Admiralty that 3,000 guns, 12-pounder size and upwards, preferably four-inch were required. But the guns that had been ordered for the purpose were only being delivered at the rate of 80 a month. This was obviously inadequate and much greater drive had to be put into the supply of the heavier and the longer range type of gun for our merchant ships.

The progress achieved by these measures in the arming of merchantmen can be briefly indicated by the following figures: —

From the outbreak of the Great War until the 9th December, 1916, the date on which the first meeting of my new War Cabinet was held the total number of merchant vessels that had been armed was 1,195. By 1st January, 1917, this number had been increased to 1,420 (of which 83 had been lost). The quarterly increases during 1917 were as follows: —

Number of British Merchant Ships armed with guns [excluding howitzers].

January, 1, 1917 ...	... 1,420
April 1, 1917 ...	... 2,181*
July 1, 1917 ...	... 3,001
October 1, 1917	... 3,763
January 1, 1918	... 4,407

Quite a considerable number of howitzers were also made available for the equipment of the larger steamers. Thus within a year the number of vessels armed was more than trebled and the power of the armament provided was considerably increased. This process gave the convoys greater security by increasing the risks the submarine had to take in its attacks on our shipping.

*From this date many of the guns were of a heavier type in order to cope with the more powerful ones with which the great cruiser submarines were equipped. Several vessels already armed had to be re-armed for this reason.

CHAPTER XLII

ESTABLISHMENT OF THE MINISTRY OF SHIPPING

WHEN the War broke out, Britain occupied a position of overwhelming superiority in the sphere of mercantile shipping. At the beginning of 1914, nearly 40,000 vessels of all kinds flew the British flag. That figure of course included a very large number of small craft—fishing boats, trawlers, drifters, tugs, lighters—which proved to be not without their crucial value in the War. But of steam vessels of over 100 tons there were 10,123 on the registers of Britain and her Dominions, with a total gross tonnage of 20½ million tons. Not far short of one-half of the shipping tonnage in the world was British.

Step by step, as the War developed, as the commitments of the British Government for equipping and reinforcing our armies overseas grew heavier, as the imports of stores to this country for Government purposes increased in volume, as the demands of our Allies for shipping tonnage became heavier, as the inroads of the German U-boat campaign diminished the available tonnage, and as the output of mercantile vessels from our shipbuilding yards dropped, the control by the Government over British shipping was extended, and the need for co-ordinating the various controls and forming a Department for administrative purposes became imperative.

In the early days, most of the work carried out by the Government in respect of British shipping, fell to the Admiralty. The Transport Department of the Admiralty was responsible for chartering the vessels necessary to carry our forces to France, Egypt and subsequently the Dardanelles and other theatres of war in Asia and East Africa, and to maintain them with food, munitions, and reinforcements. The developments of naval warfare also involved a very extensive requisitioning of small craft to act as auxiliaries to the Fleet—for patrol work, minesweeping and message-carrying. Some 1,720 yachts, trawlers, drifters, and motor-boats were secured as auxiliaries for use in home waters within the first ten months of the War. In addition, a number of merchant vessels were converted into armed merchant cruisers.

It must also be pointed out that although Britain owned so large a share of the world's shipping, this country did so much sea carriage for other countries that when the War broke out her shipping was not sufficient to meet our own home needs. A third of the merchant trade done with this country was in goods carried in foreign vessels. Of the imports which reached us in 1913, only 65 per cent. were brought in British bottoms. The shipping problem was thus accentuated on two sides.

Let us examine first of all the vastly increased demands on shipping, owing to the War. There was the immense and continually growing task of transporting men, animals, stores of all kinds from this country to the various fields of war. Like most other services, those of the Army Sea Transport grew beyond all calculation. By the end of the year 1914, 946,000 men had been transported to and fro between the United Kingdom and overseas destinations. By the end of 1915, this figure had grown to over 4,000,000; by the end of 1916, to 9,000,000; by the end of 1917, to 16,000,000, and by the date of the Armistice to about 24,000,000. During the actual period of the War and till November, 1920, the troops and personnel transported to and from all the fighting fronts, including France, Gallipoli, Egypt, Mesopotamia, etc., from and to Great Britain, India and the Dominions and Colonies, amounted to 28,719,315. The total numbers in fact were as follows:—

Troops and personnel	...	...	...	28,719,315
Sick and wounded ...	...	...	...	3,221,992
Nursing sisters and civilians		...	...	929,521
Refugees ...	...	...	...	133,510
Prisoners ...	...	...	...	336,398
TOTAL NUMBERS MOVED				33,340,736
Horses, mules, etc.	...	...	...	2,400,654
Vehicles ...	...	...	...	553,829

To this enormous total must be added the stores and equipment moved for the troops. Up to the Armistice, some 49,000,000 tons by weight, equal to about 122,000,000 shipping tons, were carried. During the later stages of the War, the army stores sent daily to France alone amounted to 90,000 tons.

It is interesting to note how various were the shipments for army account. Camels, for example, were shipped in large numbers. One rather curious shipment was carried out for political purposes arising from our military operations. This was the provision of a vessel to convey the " Holy Carpet " and Moslem pilgrims to Jeddah for their annual pilgrimage to Mecca. The only ship which was at the moment readily available was an ex-German steamer. It was thought inadvisable to use a ship with a German name; so the vessel's name was solemnly changed for the occasion. Nothing untoward happened as a result of the change of name. Thus a superstition of the seas was confuted.

A further task for our shipping imposed by the War was that o
bringing from abroad the raw materials for the manufacture o
munitions and equipment. We also had the task of supplying ou
Allies by means of sea transport, both with munitions and raw
materials for their manufacture, and with many articles of civil use
which they had formerly been able to obtain overland from countrie
now at war with them, or in the case of France, from their own pro
vinces now held by the enemy. Most of the coal and iron mines o
France were in the hands of the enemy, and most of her coal and ore
had therefore to be carried across the seas. France had the equivalen
of over one million tons gross of British shipping set aside exclusivel
for her services, and 43 per cent. of her total imports were carried in
British ships. Of her coal imports, 50 per cent. or 1,600,000 tons a
month, was carried by British ships, and the bulk of her cereals. In
addition, by our practice of refusing bunker coal to vessels not serving
the Allied cause, we forced over 400,000 tons gross of neutral tonnage
into her service.

Italy was during the War period deprived of supplies of coal and
other commodities which she formerly derived from German and
Austrian sources. The deficiency had to be made up by sea-carried
supplies from Britain. Italy had during the War over half a million
tons gross of British shipping set aside for supplying her needs. About
45 per cent. of her total imports, and 75 per cent. of her coal supplie
were carried to her in British ships. And 300,000 tons gross of neutral
tonnage was reserved for her service by us through the exercise of ou
control over bunker supplies.

While our shipping was thus called on to bear a wide range o
additional burdens, the War led to a considerable restriction of th
available tonnage. The German Mercantile Marine, the second
largest in the world, was bottled up in Germany, or, where it had no
been captured by us, interned in neutral harbours. Enemy action
by submarines, mines and surface raiders, was steadily cutting down
the total of available shipping, both Allied and neutral. Ship
building, owing to the need for turning the energies of our yards to
naval demands, fell heavily, and the Board of Trade did not take step
in time to safeguard the interests of mercantile shipbuilding by check
ing the recruitment of skilled workers and by reserving a fair shar
of the berths in the yards for merchant ships. Moreover, whilst th
demand for shipping increased and the number of available ship
diminished without prospect of replenishment, the ships that wer
left could not make as many voyages as usual owing to War condition
The necessity of precautionary measures to avoid danger zones, whic
led to devious routing and to the continual holding-up of vessels whe
a raider or submarine was believed to be operating in the neighbour
hood, had the result of making voyages take much longer, so that th
services which a given volume of shipping could render in a give

time were heavily reduced. There was also a great deal of congestion on the railways and ports which delayed the loading and unloading of ships. Much of that congestion was inevitable, but much of it could have been avoided by businesslike supervision and control.

With the problems which resulted from this growing strain upon our shipping resources I was not myself departmentally concerned during the early part of the War. The one important measure for which I had some responsibility was the scheme of War Risks Insurance which was brought into force at the beginning of August, 1914.

This was one of those financial arrangements with which, as Chancellor of the Exchequer, I was closely occupied during the days immediately preceding and following the outbreak of the War, and of which I have given some account in earlier chapters of these Memoirs. The history of the War Risks Insurance Scheme can be briefly outlined in a few words. For some time past the Huth Jackson Sub-Committee of the Committee of Imperial Defence had been at work upon a scheme for maintaining the shipping services of this country in the event of war by providing State assistance for the underwriting of the special war risks which would arise. Their important task had been completed shortly before the crisis arose. When the Great War threatened, there were immediate signs of panic among shipowners and underwriters. On 30th July, 1914, chartering ceased at North American ports, vessels already loaded with grain being held up owing to the impossibility of insuring except at prohibitive rates, and there appeared a danger that the whole of our import and export trade, vital to maintain our supplies of food and raw materials, might be paralysed.

Urgent representations were made to me as Chancellor of the Exchequer, since the matter was one which could only be remedied by the Government carrying the risk for War losses. As with the cognate questions of credit and finance, which were then deeply preoccupying me, it was a matter of taking State action to restore confidence. So I took steps to have the issue promptly investigated, and a meeting took place around my breakfast table at 11, Downing Street, on Saturday, 1st August, 1914, at which the Ministers and officials most closely concerned were present. Our discussions proving inconclusive, I proceeded to secure the summoning of a special Committee of the Cabinet, to which were invited the late Mr. Huth Jackson and Sir Raymond Beck—two of the leading experts who had been engaged on the question—to expound their views on the situation and on the measures necessary to deal with it. This Committee was held the same day, and debated till nearly midnight without coming to any agreement. It was obviously impossible to leave our shipping hanging on a dead centre whilst politicians wrangled about the ideal nature and extent of State action to set it moving again. I therefore decided that the only possible course was to recommend to the Government the adoption as it stood of the detailed scheme already prepared by the Huth Jackson Sub-Committee. For an imperative need, better an imperfect plan than none at all.

The whole of Sunday was occupied in working out the administrative and other measures for applying the scheme. On Sunday night the War Risks Association of Shipowners were informed of the decision of the Government and invited to submit the proposals to their members. On Monday the Board of Trade took provisional action to furnish cover for the hulls of the vessels held up by war peril. On Tuesday, 4th August, I explained to the House of Commons what had been done and the reasons for our actions, and the scheme was adopted by Parliament and by the shipowners' associations. On the 5th, the first day we were at war, the State Cargo Insurance Office was opened in the public halls of the Cannon Street Hotel by officials of the Board of Trade with the co-operation of the underwriters. Our shipping began to move everywhere and my own immediate concern with this problem was for the time ended.

During the following months, the Departments directly in touch with the shipping situation were those of the Admiralty, War Office, and Board of Trade. The biggest single factor in our problem was the great and growing number of vessels that were being requisitioned by the Transport Department for special war services, and thus withdrawn from general shipping services. By January, 1915, between 1,100 and 1,200 steamships had thus been diverted from their normal employment. Later on, when the Ministry of Munitions had been set up and begun to function actively, its extensive requirements in the shape of imports of raw materials for National Controlled Factories, and of munitions ordered in America, distracted further vessels from general trade.

By degrees the responsibility of the Government for the control of shipping was perforce extended.

Early in 1916 the Departments concerned with sea transport found themselves in a difficulty owing to the growing shortage of tonnage available to meet growing demands.

On 27th January, 1916, the Cabinet set up the Shipping Control Committee, under the Chairmanship of Lord Curzon. This was the first body entrusted with the task of surveying the tonnage situation as a whole. Its main activities were directed to: —

Securing economy in the use of tonnage on naval and military service;

Setting a limit to the amount of tonnage supplied to the Allies whose demands had hitherto been granted as a matter of course

Import restrictions;

Port congestion;

Shipbuilding.

No effective—certainly no adequate—action was taken for over ten months after the appointment of the Committee to achieve any of these aims.

On 10th February, 1916, this Committee presented to Mr. Runciman, the President of the Board of Trade, a Report which showed that whereas the total demands on shipping not as yet requisitioned for war service would require 10,328,000 gross tons of shipping to carry out, the actual tonnage of shipping available for the purpose was only 7,068,803 tons—a deficit of over $3\frac{1}{4}$ million tons. This was after making allowance for the possible services of foreign shipping which we might be able to obtain. The Committee accordingly stated that " the situation is exceedingly grave and calls for immediate and drastic action." They recommended that non-essential imports should be prohibited. " Expressed in terms of tons weight of imports, a deficiency of $3\frac{1}{4}$ million gross tons of shipping means a deficiency of 13 million tons weight of imports, so that . . . the weight of imports . . . must be reduced by more than 25 per cent." The shortage thus envisaged constituted a problem of urgent gravity. We shall however see in the chapter on Imports how utterly we failed to comply with the proposals sketched out by this Committee for dealing with this acute and intensifying crisis by effecting a drastic reduction in our imports.

In the ten months January-October, 1916, the total merchant shipping lost through enemy action (mainly sunk by submarines) was 1,638,460 tons, including Allied and Neutral shipping. Of British shipping alone it was 877,413 tons. And the rate of sinking had begun to mount swiftly with the irruption of the cruiser submarine. It was clear that unless something could be done, and done quickly, to effect a fundamental change in the position, we could not make such a contribution to the War as would enable the Alliance to continue with any hope of success.

Throughout 1916 Mr. Runciman talked in terms of unmitigated pessimism and placed a near limit on the possibility of our continuing the struggle—owing to lack of ships. The Board of Trade declared that : " We have exhausted every civil economy suggested to us or thought of by our experts or by members of the Government and the Departments." Unless, therefore, measures were taken to improve the position by grappling effectively with the submarine menace, by building more ships, and by making the best use of the ships that were left, then the sooner we make tracks for peace the better. That accounted in great measure for the Lansdowne move for immediate peace negotiations. Lord Lansdowne quoted Mr. Runciman's gloomy forecasts in the prelude to his memorandum of November, 1916 (which has been referred to in a previous chapter). Mr. Runciman's prognostications were based on figures which he might have amended by strong and timely action.

In the first week of November, 1916, Mr. Runciman gave to the War Committee a particularly depressing account of the shipping outlook. He subsequently discovered, however, that there were depths of dejection several stages beneath those into which he had plunged us at this meeting. So a few days later he still further darkened the colouring of his picture by warning us that the record of the previous meeting had not been as explicit as he would wish on the gravity of the merchant shipping situation. *His experts had told him that he had been too sanguine in saying that there would be a breakdown of shipping by June, 1917. They considered that the breakdown would come before that time.* He called attention in particular to the demand for additional raw material to the extent of 2,500,000 tons by the Ministry of Munitions. This demand, he said, had been reduced by half. He also drew attention to the difficulties of the Wheat Commission, who were at present unable to find the 40 vessels they required to bring wheat from Australia. They had gone into the neutral market, but had only been able to obtain two ships at reasonable prices. Another neutral ship had been offered at the huge price of 380s. a ton, and this sum would have to be paid. Thus they were nearly 40 ships short on their first allotment.

Further on in the course of our discussions he also pointed out that the balance received from premiums both on ships and cargoes under the Government War Risks Insurance scheme had now for the first time entirely disappeared.

When he came to shipbuilding, he said the situation here was a good deal worse than he had thought. There was no steel available for shipbuilding even on the existing reduced basis.

It is recorded that after the Committee had been drenched with these cumulative jeremiads, I said that "the situation was very serious, and required to be dealt with on broader lines" than those which had been indicated by the President of the Board of Trade. I put forward proposals as to the development of steel production in U.S.A. and Canada, and as to stopping the export of engines.

But the most important proposal I made was: "To appoint a Director of Merchant Shipping under the President of the Board of Trade, with full powers to organise—

(*a*) The merchant shipping available to the best advantage of this country.

(*b*) The building of additional ships in this country and America.

I ended by saying that "in my opinion some such drastic measures as these were absolutely necessary, and any minor suggestions were mere tinkering."

Now that the War had been manœuvred by the Military Command

into a pure war of exhaustion, I felt that our shipping had become the most vital and vulnerable point in the issue of victory or defeat. I was convinced that much more was needed than could be done by the Admiralty and the Board of Trade, separately and in combination, to save us from the desperate position into which we were rapidly drifting through lack of initiative, grasp, and vigour. I thought the handling of our shipping tonnage was so important a matter, involving such unremitting attention to detail in the way of organising voyages, controlling the ports, building new ships, that it was a one-man job, and a task which would absorb the concentrated mind of a whole department, directed and manned by those who had practical experience in the management of our mercantile marine.

With regard to my first two proposals, the President of the Board of Trade said in substance that what I suggested either had been done or could not be done. On the proposition that I put forward about a Shipping Controller, " he had already decided to ask two of the greatest shipping experts of the day *to assist him and take off his shoulders some of the very heavy work connected with shipping. And* AS TIME WENT ON *he hoped to be able to delegate more and more responsibility to them.*" It was all very leisurely. If shipping resources were already inadequate for essential war services and now likely to break down entirely before June—and the Admiralty vowed they could not see how to stop our enormous losses—every hour was precious as blood to a man whose wounds cannot be staunched.

It was also pointed out, in opposition to my proposal, that there was Lord Curzon's Committee on Shipping Control. But it was admitted " that there was no special body outside the Board of Trade for dealing with the building of additional ships in this country and in America."

I explained in reply that I was aware of the splendid work of the Shipping Control Committee, and that it would be necessary for this Committee to continue its work under my scheme in order to assist the Director of Shipping, but the latter would have complete executive authority to an extent not vested in any one person at present. *I urged that no Committee could satisfactorily discharge executive functions,* and that although I had every confidence in the capacity and energy of the chairman, he could not possibly find time for superintending both ships and our air service, each of these demanding the full energies of one man. I pointed out that the present system had not prevented the probability, according to the President of the Board of Trade, of a threatened breakdown next summer.

As success or failure in the War depended upon the maintenance of a sea transport equal to the essential needs of the Allies, I repeatedly urged the Prime Minister and the War Committee to set up a Ministry of Shipping with a Shipping Controller at its head, to deal with this vital problem. The Board of Trade resisted this diminution of its authority, and the Prime Minister's well-known dislike for kicking along laggard colleagues with academic qualifications was growing on him. He always postponed the operation if it was suggested to him that a less drastic remedy would cure the evil. So the time went by, carrying with it every week a mournful diminution in our resources of sea transport.

Nothing was done during the lifetime of the First Coalition Government to establish a thorough and efficient reorganisation and control of our shipping. This problem was therefore left, amongst other embarrassing inheritances, for the new Government to grapple with. I knew it was a whole-time job for a man of practical experience and tried capacity. So pressing did I consider the shipping situation that, as soon as I was invited by the King to form a Government, without even waiting until the principal offices were filled, I invited Sir Joseph Maclay, a well-known Glasgow shipowner of high repute, to take the office of Shipping Controller—a selection which was strongly supported by Mr. Bonar Law. I had never met him, but as Mr. Bonar Law knew him well and had the highest opinion of his capacity and character, I rang Maclay up at his Glasgow office on my first day as Prime Minister. The line was so bad that I could not hear a word he said, so I invited him to come up and see me in London. He travelled up that night and met me the following morning at the War Office—(I had not yet left this office for Downing Street)—and I asked him if he would accept the post of Shipping Controller.

With characteristic modesty Sir Joseph Maclay declined, telling me that in his opinion a man of wider experience and influence should be secured for the position. It required the joint persuasion of Mr. Bonar Law and myself to wring from him a reluctant consent. We had every reason to be proud of the pressure we exerted on the occasion, for no minister ever served his country more effectively in an emergency. The following morning, 9th December, 1916, I informed the War Cabinet at its first meeting that Sir Joseph Maclay was to be appointed Shipping Controller. Until the Shipping Ministry received legislative sanction, he was to take the Presidency of the Shipping Control Committee, but he was to have extended powers, as to which he would himself report after examination.

The War Cabinet directed their Secretary to invite the Admiralty and the Board of Trade to give Sir Joseph Maclay every possible facility and assistance.

The new Ministry was in due course legally authorised by the new Ministries and Secretaries Act, 1916, which received the Royal Assent on 22nd December. But the new Minister of Shipping did not wait for that event. Although on leaving me after accepting the appointment, as he has since confessed to me, " one of the most miserable men in London," he called two leading shipbuilders into conference that same afternoon at his hotel, and arranged with them for an immediate meeting of the Shipbuilders' Association, so that the building of more ships might be pressed on with at once, as the most outstanding need of the country. He also got promptly into touch with the Shipping Control Committee, which was being superseded by the new Ministry. Lord Curzon, its former Chairman, was in any case resigning to join my new War Cabinet, and another member, Lord Farringdon, also withdrew. But the other three members, Sir Thomas Royden, Sir Kenneth Anderson and Mr. Frederick Lewis, three of the ablest ship-owners in the world, agreed to co-operate with Maclay in forming a new Shipping Committee, and thereafter, worked with him closely and with conspicuous loyalty, giving their whole time to the task.

As it was necessary that the Shipping Controller and his staff should be in close and constant touch with the Naval Departments, the Ministry of Shipping was eventually housed in new buildings which were rapidly run up on the only available site near the Admiralty—the lake in St. James's Park, which was drained for the purpose, and transformed into a row of grey, two-storied concrete buildings. Pending the construction of his new quarters, Sir Joseph Maclay was given a room in the Admiralty buildings. Hitherto the Admiralty had exercised a considerable measure of control over sea transport, and the new Ministry was thus relieving them of a very heavy and increasingly difficult task which lay strictly outside their ordinary routine, and for the handling of which they did not possess the appropriate commercial and industrial experience.

Yet here again, as with the War Office when the Ministry of Munitions had been formed, there was little gratitude at the lightening of burdens they were unable to carry. Sir Joseph Maclay got no friendly reception from the Admiralty. He reported that his appointment was resented by them, and as a body they were not out to help.

He is not the kind of man to be deterred by a frosty reception from getting ahead promptly with a duty he has undertaken. Climate and experience had inured him to all weathers. In a few days he had planned a large increase in our shipbuilding output, and in less than a week after his appointment he had secured the agreement of the Admiralty to a programme for constructing a number of tramp steamers of about 8,000 tons each, and came to the War Cabinet with a request for their authority to embark upon the scheme. This permission was immediately given, and at the same meeting (15th December, 1916) he was authorised to go ahead with a scheme he had prepared for purchasing some 77,500 tons of shipping from Japan. A week later, on 22nd December, 1916, the First Sea Lord reported that, according to information received that morning, the rate of output of merchant shipping for next year did not exceed 400,000 tons during the first six months, as compared with submarine losses amounting to about 300,000 tons a month.

The Shipping Controller, however, reported that he had information to the effect that, provided the necessary labour and material

2A*

were available, an output of 1,000,000 tons deadweight capacity might be expected *during the first six months of next year (1917).*

This included a large order given to the U.S.A. When the Americans came into the War all ships in course of construction in their yards were seized for their own use. The ships ordered by the Controller in American yards therefore were not added to our dwindling mercantile fleet. Nevertheless they diminished the sum total of Allied deficiency.

The new Ministry of Shipping took over from the Board of Trade the task of keeping watch on the construction of merchant shipbuilding, embarking in addition upon a programme of direct Government shipbuilding for the standard pattern of ships projected by the new Controller.

Shipbuilding remained in the hands of the Ministry of Shipping until May, 1917. During these five months, Sir Joseph Maclay greatly speeded up the completion of vessels already under construction, and devised a programme that would eventually yield upwards of 3,000,000 tons of merchant shipping a year. There was serious need for some such stimulus, for despite the inroads made by the submarines, our construction of merchant shipping had been falling off heavily since the outbreak of the War. In 1913 there had been completed 1,919,578 tons gross of merchant shipping. In 1915 the total was 688,629 tons, and in 1916 it fell still lower to 538,797 tons. Part of this decline had been due to the much greater output of war vessels and auxiliary craft for the Admiralty, but even after making allowance for this, the total gross tonnage of all kinds completed during these years had shown, too, a heavy falling off from the 1913 figure. During the first five months of 1917, from January to May, the merchant tonnage completed was 376,588 tons. The programme put in hand resulted in the completed tonnage for the whole of 1917 reaching the figure of 1,163,474 gross tons. This result was achieved in spite of the largely increased demands on our iron and steel supplies, as well as on our engineering resources, by the swelling needs of the Army and Navy.

Arrangements were also set on foot for extensive purchases of foreign shipping.

In addition to his efforts to increase our tonnage, the Shipping Controller set to work to organise the more effectual and economic use of the shipping we had. In January, 1917, out of a total of 3,731 passenger and cargo vessels of 1,600 gross tonnage and upwards, flying the British flag, with a gross tonnage totalling 16,591,032 tons, there were 1,500 with a total gross tonnage of 7,082,099 tons not requisitioned by the Admiralty for war services, nor allocated for special purposes, such as supplying the Allies or bringing wheat to this country. The system was wasteful as far as the needs of the nation were concerned. It was grossly unfair as between the owners of requisitioned and unrequisitioned tonnage. The Ministry of Shipping had to see that not only were the requisitioned vessels being worked as efficiently as possible, but that all tonnage not as yet requisitioned was controlled and directed to the most serviceable purposes. To this end the Shipping Controller was given general powers of control over all British shipping. He proceeded to press for the release by the Admiralty of a proportion of the tonnage held by them, which on a careful inquiry he was convinced was being wastefully used. He insisted that $17\frac{1}{2}$ per cent. of the tonnage so requisitioned should be released for carriage of goods, in particular of coal for the Allies. In this demand he received the support of the Cabinet. How promptly the new Controller acted will be seen from the fact that on 22nd December, 1916, it was reported to the War Cabinet that all but 20,000 tons of this percentage had then been released.

The next important step in this connection was taken on 9th February, 1917, when the War Cabinet considered a memorandum prepared by the Shipping Controller making a series of recommendations as to the powers he considered he should possess for the carrying out of his task. Perhaps the most important item in this memorandum was the proposal that the Transport Department of the Admiralty, which was now charged with a multitude of duties in connection with the control and use of shipping, should be transferred to the Ministry of Shipping. This part of the memorandum ran as follows:—

"Attention is called to the present anomalous position of the Transport Department. The Director of Transports is an Admiralty Officer responsible solely to the Board of Admiralty. His Department, however, in practice regulates the distribution of merchant shipping, not merely for Admiralty service, but also under requisition for War Office, Wheat Commission, and other Government services. So long as all Government demands could be met in full, or subject only to minor adjustment, this arrangement might work smoothly; but, as soon as cutting down of requirements in one direction or another becomes necessary, difficulties are bound to arise, and the Director of Transports may find himself involved in a conflict of authority. It is believed that this point has now been reached. The pressure upon available tonnage is now such that it is necessary to weigh against each other the needs of the various Departments, including the Admiralty, and to determine in which direction priority should be given."

This memorandum was originally drawn up by the Shipping Controller after consultation with me and submitted by him to the Admiralty on 12th January, 1917. The reasonableness of the

proposal for the transfer to the Ministry of Shipping of the Department
holding control of merchant shipping was too obvious for dispute.
But on the other hand the Lords of the Admiralty disliked the idea
that a portion of their power should be alienated to another control,
and they were horrified at the notion that brass buttons should be
ordered about by bone. Sir Joseph Maclay appealed to the War
Cabinet.

The fight was thus transferred to the chamber of the War Cabinet.
The Lords of the Admiralty turned up in force to denounce the
impiety of Sir Joseph Maclay's suggestion.

One of the Sea Lords wanted to know how it was possible for senior
officers of the Admiralty engaged on transport to receive orders from
a shipowner. But the War Cabinet decided, in spite of their objections, to approve the proposal of the Shipping Controller, adding
thereto as a rider that if they so desired, the Admiralty could adopt
a suggestion of the Director of Transports about keeping on their
books the part of the staff dealing with Naval and Military shipping.
So ended this naval engagement. The pirates won and the ships of
the line withdrew from these particular waters. The control of our
mercantile marine passed entirely from the Admiralty to the new
Shipping Ministry. The Department of the Director of Transports
and Shipping duly took up its quarters in the desiccated duck-pond
of St. James's Park, under the humble roof of the new Ministry; and
despite the misgivings of the Admiralty chiefs, this arrangement
turned out to be a complete success.

Another matter which engaged the early attention of the Shipping
Controller was one as to which I had given an undertaking as soon as
I took office, namely, a more complete national control of the whole
of our shipping. This, incidentally, involved the question of the
profits earned by British shipowners. Against these profits there had
been a good deal of public outcry. As the demands on shipping grew,
and the progress of requisitioning for Government work diminished
the amount of tonnage available for general commerce, the competition of shippers all over the world had forced up freights to
surprising heights. Thus at the end of 1913 the freight rate for
grain from the Plate to the United Kingdom had been 12s. 6d. At
the end of 1915 it was 115s. and by the end of 1916 it had risen to
145s. Similarly, the rate for coal from Cardiff to Port Said, which
at the end of 1913 had averaged 7s. 9d., rose to 62s. 6d. by the end of
1915 and to 80s. in 1916. The rates for carrying in requisitioned
ships was fixed by the Government and restricted to a scale. As I
have already pointed out, there was thus a grossly unfair discrimination in favour of those ships and shipowners who had successfully
eluded requisition.

These high freights of course tended to force up prices—already
only too much inclined to rise through other causes. And the public

who were called upon to make sacrifices for the sake of their native land were angry when they became painfully aware that their necessities were getting dearer, largely owing to the rapacity of certain shipowners. There was no justification in war risks for these inflated rates. The Government insurance covered losses at sea, and wages had not increased to anything like that extent. The added risk to life did not extend to the owners. It was a scandalous example of war profiteering. Such was the state of things which drove me to the announcement I made to the Labour Deputation that the new Government proposed to bring our shipping under Government control.

There was keen debate about the question whether or not the step should be taken of nationalising all shipping in the sense of transferring it from private ownership altogether. To this course the Shipping Controller was opposed, deeming that the experienced shipowner, subject to an appropriate degree of control, and to excess profits duties or similar methods of diverting the major part of the proceeds of wartime freights into the Exchequer, would be the best person to manage the business side of the shipping. He set out his views in a letter which is not without its bearings on some of the controversies of to-day:—

" 2nd February, 1917.

Dear Prime Minister,

Since the discussion at the War Cabinet last week I have given earnest consideration to the question of the nationalisation of shipping, keeping in view your promises relative thereto.

I think you may justly consider shipping to be nationalised on the lines you aim at when you secure the absolute control of every ship of the British Mercantile Marine and deal with the profits exactly as you elect. Such is the case to-day.

Under the system of requisition and ship licensing, no British vessel can go on any voyage without direct authority from the Government, and the control is thus absolute.

Then with regard to profits, you can deal with these in various ways:—

1. You can give the average of two years before the War plus a percentage on all extra profit earned.

2. You can do as my memorandum suggested, and simply apply the existing machinery of the Excess Profits Tax, making the Exchequer proportion as high as you like.

3. You can give the average of two years before the War and anything more, or nothing.

4. You can deal with shipping on the exact lines of Controlled Establishments, which get the average of two years before the War plus 20 per cent.

My own mind is clear. I believe it is a mistake not to leave an incentive to men to exert themselves to the utmost, however trifling that incentive may be. In my opinion, the definitely fixed figure in Controlled Establishments is a blunder. There is absolutely no incentive to economy, and the results are just as might be expected. In many shops you get neither care of time nor of money, and the same applies very much to railway companies. I therefore specially recommend for your consideration either No. 1 or No. 2 of the above suggestions. Under either you take the two years' pre-War average as your basis, and by granting a percentage, however small, on all extra profit earned, you will secure the whole-hearted effort on the part of shipowners and their staffs, through whom we must continue to work.

I think no greater mistake could be made than by attempting to take over in any other way British shipping. You retain all the advantages of the experience of practical men who know their business, and also, as far as possible all the elaborate system built up by private enterprise and pay nothing for it, and there is the further certainty that, after the War, owners will be able without loss of time, to resume their regular services.

Yours very truly,

J. P. MACLAY."

This letter was laid by me before the War Cabinet on 12th February, 1917, when we gave careful consideration to the question of shipowners' profits and the nationalising of shipping. I was committed to the extent of the pledge I had given to the House of Commons in my speech on 19th December, 1916, which was in the following terms: —

". . . *the Government felt the time had come for taking over more complete control of all the ships of this country and placing them in practically the same position as are the railways of the country at this present moment;* so that during the War shipping will be nationalised in the real sense of the term. The prodigious profits which were made out of freights were contributing in no small measure to the high cost of commodities; and I always found not only that, but that they were making it difficult for us in our task with labour. Whenever I met organised labour under any conditions where I would persuade them to give up privileges, I always had hurled at me phrases about the undue and extravagant profits of shipping. This is intolerable in wartime, when so many are making so great sacrifices for the State."

After some discussion, the War Cabinet decided upon the following course of action: —

(*a*)   The Shipping Controller should extend the requisitioning of tonnage at Blue Book rates so as to make it general and as nearly as possible universal, and that the cases to which requisitioning did not apply were to be justified only by exceptional circumstances.

(*b*)   The Shipping Controller should report to the War Cabinet weekly, or at regular intervals, the progress made in this matter.

(*c*)   The profits should be dealt with in a manner corresponding, *mutatis mutandis*, to that adopted in the case of the railways, i.e., by assessing the profits by the average over a period of time preceding the War, and that the Shipping Controller should be asked to report to the War Cabinet as to the effect of taking for that purpose the average profits made during the two, three, four and five years, respectively, preceding the War.

These decisions brought practically the whole of our shipping under national control for the period of the War.

The Controller's report on the way these decisions had been carried out was considered by the Cabinet on 10th and 17th April. The Controller was able to report that practically all the mercantile fleet of the country was now under requisition at Blue Book rates, and after examining the figures for rates of shipping before the War, the Cabinet decided that: —

" The question of limiting profits should be settled by the Chancellor of the Exchequer and Mr. Henderson, in consultation with the Shipping Controller, the decision to be reported to the War Cabinet at an early date."

An important development took place at the Admiralty in May, 1917, which had a direct influence upon the work of the Ministry of Shipping.

When I paid my visit to the Admiralty at the end of April to confer with the heads there as to measures to be taken to combat the submarine menace, I was told that the Navy could not work a convoy system properly because with all its immense fleet it had not sufficient craft to provide escorts. The excuse was neither adequate nor sincere, for armed trawlers served the purpose. But if it were true, then the task of increasing its resources for this purpose was one which clearly called for immediate supervision and direction by someone of energy and ability. I accordingly recommended to the War Cabinet that there should be appointed, as a member of the Board of Admiralty, a business man to superintend the whole of the ship-building and supply of material for naval purposes. This proposal was not acceptable to the Board. The Cabinet discussed it on 2nd May, 1917. The First Lord pointed out that such functions were already provided for in the duties assigned by Mr. Churchill to the

Additional Civil Lord, although in fact those duties appear to have remained dormant. He stated that the First Sea Lord and himself were in complete agreement with regard to this recommendation, and were prepared to amplify, if necessary, the scope of the duties assigned by Mr. Churchill to such an appointment. They laid stress, however, on the importance of the appointment of someone who had the complete confidence of the War Cabinet.

The War Cabinet considered that the best available man would have to be appointed to this post, and that, in view of the paramount importance of the shipping situation, nothing should stand in the way of this appointment. There was a general agreement that, having regard to his record in this War, Major-General Sir Eric Geddes would be the most suitable person if he were willing to undertake the duties. The War Cabinet saw Major-General Geddes and invited him to accept the appointment. He promised to consider the matter and to reply as soon as possible.

The War Cabinet also felt that, having regard to the intimate connection between shipbuilding for the purposes of the Royal Navy, the Mercantile Marine and the War Office Inland Waterways, there should be a very close association between the holder of the new Office and the shipbuilding side of the Shipping Controller's Committee, and a proposal was made that the new Admiralty Civil Lord should exercise a measure of control over all three departments, after the general policy had been laid down by the War Cabinet.

Sir Eric Geddes consented to undertake this work. Accordingly, on 11th May, 1917, I was able to report his acquiescence, and he was duly appointed.

The War Cabinet decided that on account of his proposed other duties at the Admiralty in connection with supplies of armament, etc., and on account of the complexity of naval design, it was necessary that his touch with the Admiralty should be very close, and it was therefore decided that he should be appointed one of the Lords of the Admiralty.

Sir Eric entered on the office of Controller of the Navy, and was given the rank of Vice-Admiral. He had discovered by bitter experience in France what it meant for an un-uniformed functionary to order about men in uniform. That is why he had been given the rank of a General, for obedience to his orders then became automatic. One rather interesting departure from precedent was occasioned by this further appointment, for by arrangement with Sir Douglas Haig, Sir Eric continued for a couple of months longer in his connection with the transportation branch of the Army, and thus enjoyed the amphibious distinction of being at once both a General and an Admiral—an unprecedented attainment for a civilian. In accordance with the War Cabinet's decision, the control of mercantile shipbuilding was also entrusted to him. It thus passed out of the care of the

Ministry of Shipping. This was not due to any failure of the Ministry to deal energetically and successfully with that part of its task, but to the desirability of placing the whole of ship construction—naval and civil alike—under a single authority specially charged with this vitally important work.

Mention should be made of one important piece of work planned and carried out by the Ministry of Shipping to economise our tonnage in 1917, when losses from submarines were at their worst, when the convoy system had not yet got into working order and the big programmes of new shipping construction had not had time to bear fruit. This was a measure for a large concentration of our shipping in the Atlantic.

The scheme was worked out by Sir Leo Chiozza Money, with the aid of Sir Arthur Salter and Sir Norman Leslie. Briefly, they set themselves to consider how far we could supply our vital needs from countries near at hand, instead of from those which involved a sea voyage lasting twice and thrice as long. Obviously, the same volume of shipping could bring two or three times as much to us from a near as from a distant country in the same space of time. They came to the conclusion that nearly all our essential imports could be secured from the North American Continent, and could easily be carried by the tonnage still available, if it were concentrated on that route instead of being dispersed all over the sea-ways of the world. This concentration would also reduce the amount of miscellaneous patrol work needed for commerce protection, and thus lighten the Navy's task and enable it to carry on a more vigorous campaign against the submarines.

The proposal came at a fortunate moment, when the Admiralty had just consented to approve the introduction of the convoy system. Had it not done so, the concentration of all or a very heavy share of shipping in one ocean and on the constricted routes leading from it to Great Britain, might well have increased our disasters by giving the U-boats a more abundant supply of targets. But the setting-up of the Atlantic convoys enabled a high degree of protection to be assured to shipping using that ocean.

Purchasing Departments were urged in future to order their supplies as far as possible from the United States and Canada, and to limit their commitments in other markets to the lowest possible level. The co-operation of America was essential, and Mr. Balfour could take the matter up with the Government there. A special Committee might be set up to consider the effects of the plan on our export trade, and propose ways and means of keeping the harm done to it as low as possible. A certain amount of import and export trade with India and the Dominions would have to continue.

The War Cabinet considered the idea on 30th May, 1917, and approved it. Our shipping arrangements were thereupon adapted as far as possible to the plan so approved, and during the extremely difficult and anxious time through which we were passing in the summer and autumn of 1917, these arrangements greatly increased the carrying capacity of our shipping, and helped very considerably to bring us through.

Practical measures of this sort, based upon enlightened common sense and carried out by competent business men, were among the measures adopted to increase the effective capacity of our tonnage and thus neutralise the ravages of the submarines. But they by no measure cover the whole of the plans adopted by the Ministry to make a more businesslike use of our tonnage. In the next chapter I propose to describe other steps they took to economise our sea transport.

CHAPTER XLIII

SHIPPING PROBLEMS

I. RELIEVING CONGESTION AT THE PORTS

THE unprecedented activities of the War led to a complete overthrow of the normal organisation and functioning of British ports. This is not surprising in view of the fact that the whole of Britain's war effort had to go through her ports and harbours. Our Navy was using many of our harbours as bases for some of its activities. Southampton was closed to merchant shipping. Prize cargoes of war contraband were being constantly brought into the ports and dumped in the warehouses along the wharves, to wait the adjudication of the Prize Court. Government purchases of supplies arrived in big consignments, and had to wait distribution. This exceptional activity on unusual lines would in any event have created a great deal of confusion and congestion. The problem was intensified by the fact that so many of the regular dock workers had joined up and, as a result, there was a shortage of labour to handle goods.

The steps taken to deal with this problem during the first part of the War can be briefly summarised.

As early as 22nd January, 1915, a deputation of shipowners waited on the President of the Board of Trade to call his attention to the congestion of the ports, and to make a series of recommendations, including the pooling of privately-owned railway trucks; the co-ordination of military and commercial demands; penal rents on goods not promptly removed from quays; and an enquiry into the question of labour at the ports. Strong but unavailing resolutions were also passed by the Diversion of Shipping Committee in the course of 1915 as to the need for dealing with port congestion. Their representations, says Mr. C. E. Fayle* were either ignored or went astray in the mazes of departmental routine. It was nearly ten months after the January deputation before the Port and Transit Executive Committee was set up to deal with the matter. It at once began what developed into a persistent struggle with the recruiting authorities to prevent men being called up for the Army from the ranks of dockworkers.

Among the reasons urged for the restriction of imports by the Shipping Control Committee in their memorandum of 10th February, 1916, on this subject occurs the following statement: —

* "The War and the Shipping Industry," p. 152.

" The reduction in imports would give an opportunity to the ports to clear their congestion and in the meantime the Port and Transit Executive Committee would, it is hoped, be able to reorganise the work of the ports. A number of warehouses and stores in the country would be cleared, and be enabled to take quicker deliveries when the full flow of ordinary traffic is afterwards resumed."

Other suggestions were put forward by the Shipping Committee in their memorandum of 10th February, and discussed from time to time. Some of them reached the formal stage of approval by the Board of Trade and sanction by the War Committee. Only a few travelled any distance beyond that stage.

Mr. Runciman, in his memorandum of 24th October, 1916—that is, nearly two years after the shipowners had called his attention to the congestion at the ports and its causes—said: —

" It is significant that returns obtained by the Port and Transit Executive Committee show that no port claims to be able to give more than a normal rate of discharge to the ships, and many of them report a rate considerably below normal. . . . In view of the fact that the available labour at the ports has with difficulty handled the work in an unusually slack period, it is clear that urgent action is necessary if our ports are not to be blocked during the busier season now commencing."

Mr. Runciman followed this up by a further memorandum on 9th November, in the course of which he said: —

" The effectiveness of our tonnage is diminishing by reason of the slowness of loading and discharging which is intensified as more men are taken away from the docks, harbours, railways, warehouses, carting and wagon industries. We are getting less transport out of each 100 vessels than we got a year ago."

Meantime, a memorandum on 1st November, 1916, submitted by the Shipping Control Committee directed attention to the congestion of our transport in French ports: —

" It is not only at British, but even more at French ports, that the flow of traffic is being impeded. Ships are being delayed in French ports to an extent that is causing serious waste of tonnage. The two following among many similar instances, have recently occurred: —

Thistleard, 7,600 tons d.w.: —
    Arrived in roads, Bordeaux, about 9th October. Docked Bordeaux 27th October. Expected to be discharged 17th November. Say total five weeks, as compared with ten days in normal circumstances.

Algeriana, 7,370 tons d.w. : —
    Arrived in roads, Bordeaux, 13th October. Still waiting berth 30th October.

With a view to preventing these delays, the Committee feel that His Majesty's Government would be well advised to press the French Government to do everything in their power to improve the condition at the ports, in order that vessels may receive prompter dispatch.

Acting upon instruction from the War Committee and with the sanction of the Admiralty and War Office, one of our members, Mr. Royden, made a special visit to certain of the ports in Northern France in June last, and presented a report containing a number of valuable suggestions. Our information is that few of these have been carried into effect, and we again call attention to the matter.

Similar, if not worse conditions prevail in the Bay Ports of France, which, so far as we know, no sustained effort has been made to alleviate."

With regard to the question of importing foreign labour for work at the docks, the Committee's report stated : —

" It is understood that it would not be possible to introduce foreign labour into this country on account of the Trade Unions. No similar difficulty, however, appears to present itself in France. The Committee therefore suggests that foreign labour (e.g., Portuguese) should be imported into France for dock work in order that the British labour battalions now working at the French ports may be released and returned to this country.

The Committee are also disposed to urge that the question of employment of enemy prisoners of war in British docks under conditions analogous to those which have been successfully adopted in French ports should be reconsidered."

These matters were brought forward at the War Committee on 3rd November, 1916, when it was decided to see what could be done in the way of using foreign labour in French ports. But, taking it all in all, no really effective steps were taken in 1915 and 1916 to organise the traffic at the ports, with a view to saving time and tonnage. There was some fumbling about the mobilisation of a Transport Labour Battalion at the ports, but it came to nothing.

When the increase of shipping facilities was becoming more and more a matter of life and death to the nation and its Allies, these removable delays were intolerable. Up to the present, they had been met by facile and fatalistic predictions that we could carry on for a few more months and no longer. The new Government felt it must

cleave a way through all these difficulties and that it could be done.
There were serious obstacles but they must be overcome. The congestion problem is an illustration of the nature of the difficulties and
of the way they were gradually removed.

On 31st January, 1917, the Shipping Controller submitted to the
War Cabinet a memorandum respecting delays at certain ports in
unloading cargoes.

It was suggested that if the railways could handle the cargoes more
expeditiously, the ships would be "turned round" more speedily,
and the result would be an estimated saving in tonnage of 4,000,000
to 5,000,000 tons per annum. At the instance of Sir Albert Stanley
an Inter-Departmental Committee composed of representatives of the
Shipping Controller, Ministry of Munitions and Board of Trade, was
set up to investigate and report what steps, if any, could be taken
which would secure the quicker unloading of the ships.

This Committee produced a first Summary Report on 16th
February, 1917, suggesting a series of drastic measures.

The Report of the Committee was considered by the War Cabinet
on 19th February, and the following conclusions were reached in
respect of the Committee's ten points: —

It was decided that the sale of British railway waggons for export
should be prohibited, except under licence issued by the Board
of Trade.

It was noted that, as stated by the President of the Board of
Trade, machinery was being set up by the Board of Trade for the
pooling of private railway waggons; and it was agreed that the
Board of Trade should seek powers to enable the railway companies
to load empty privately-owned vehicles on the return journey.

It was decided that the Secretary of State for War should be
requested to submit a note explaining why the 10,000 men
promised by the War Office at the meeting of the War Cabinet
held on 21st December, 1916, . . . had not been released for the
Transport Workers' Battalion as arranged, and it should be
pointed out to him that serious difficulties had arisen from the
failure in the supply of these men, of whom the Shipping
Controller stated he had only 6,000 at his disposal.

It was decided that as labour on canals, locomotive repair,
cartage, and loading and unloading of waggons at ports and
destinations, were all questions of shortage of labour, the Secretary
of Mr. Illingworth's Inter-Departmental Committee should confer
or communicate with the Director of National Service and the
War Office on the subject.

It was noted that the President of the Board of Trade stated that
he was preparing machinery to enable the railway companies to
take drastic measures to enforce the prompt unloading of waggons

at destination in order to put a stop to the present practice of utilising waggons at depots.

It was noted that the Shipping Controller stated that he would take up, through the Port and Transit Executive Committee, the question of the possibility of dumping raw and semi-raw materials in the open, where necessary, to relieve congestion, particularly as regards materials belonging to the Ministry of Munitions.

It was decided that the Secretary of Mr. Illingworth's Committee should consult with the Secretary of State for War in regard to the release by the War Office of any transit sheds or dock sites in use by the Government for any other than the purposes for which they had been designed.

All these recommendations were promptly put into operation with almost startling results in the way of releasing tonnage for the High Seas. The submarine was fought on land as well as on sea, and it was the combination that beat off the attack and thus saved the Allies from overwhelming disaster.

Not all the delays suffered by shipping were due to slowness in handling their loading, unloading and bunkering in ports. Frequently they would be held up in port for some days on account of reports of a submarine in the vicinity. It was calculated that during the end of 1916 and the early months of 1917, the Germans had established an efficient outward blockade by this means equivalent to 40 per cent. of the days in a year.

A further complication was added by the fact that with the extension of Government requisitioning the owners ceased to have the same interest in their business. They did not appear to realise that now, if ever, was the time when their utmost efforts should be put forth to get their ships round quickly. They were still working as in peace time, each company with its private berths, and no one working for the common good, to help his neighbours, either by offering the use of an empty berth or by turning over a supply of bunkers which were not immediately required.

The result was that a great deal more time was being spent in Liverpool than was necessary, nor was the situation in America much better. Some of the large, fast ships such as the *Adriatic* were taking 50 to 55 days for the round trip, as against 25 days in 1916. This difficulty had to be dealt with by bringing Government pressure to bear on shipowners who were disposed to take too narrow and selfish a view of their responsibilities in a national emergency.

The difficulties arising out of the grouping of ships under the convoy system were also dealt with.

In January, 1918, a Convoy Committee was formed by the Liverpool shipowners, with the sanction of the Ministry of Shipping, and the Ministry also invited the New York owners to form a similar

committee.   Port convoy officers, similar to those who had been
appointed here, were sent to the United States in the spring of 1918,
and the Ministry of Shipping's Report on Convoys states that: —

" The average total stay of tramps in United States ports fell
from $27\frac{1}{2}$ days in January to $16\frac{3}{4}$ days in September, while that of
liners was reduced from $22\frac{1}{2}$ days to 14 days.   The delay waiting
for convoys which had been $3\frac{1}{2}$ days for tramps, was brought down
to an average of 2 days, and the same cause of detention in the case
of liners, which had averaged as much as 5 days, was in September
only $1\frac{1}{2}$ days.   The time spent in loading was, in the case of tramps,
lessened by nearly 50 per cent., and 20 per cent. was taken off the
loading days of the liners. . . .

In Liverpool the Convoy Committee soon got to work, especially
with the large Atlantic liners, and after the H.X. Convoy for this
type of vessel had been based on New York, they succeeded so well
in their dispatch that aided by the efforts of their counterpart in
New York the goal of a 40 day turn round was attained in 77 per
cent. of the voyages, and a few ships with a cargo of about 3,000
tons, such as the *Melita* did the round trip in 32 days.   The average turn round, taking the bad with the good, for the whole of the
H.X. Convoys was 42.68 days. . . .

All these endeavours undoubtedly effected great improvements
in the dispatch of tonnage, and there is little doubt that the attention devoted to the subject by those interested in the convoys
stimulated those concerned in the loading and discharging to
achieve better results than were the rule in the era when ships ran
independently."

Up to the end of the War it was of course inevitable that the
exceptional difficulties under which all shipping had to operate
should involve a certain measure of delay as compared with peace-
time conditions.   But under the Ministry of Shipping these delays
were thus gradually reduced and avoided in a very high degree.

By these measures the shipping capacity of the country was very
considerably increased at a time when our actual tonnage was being
appreciably reduced by the action of submarines.

2.   CONTROL AND RESTRICTION OF IMPORTS

Now we come to the further measures taken by the Government to
secure the most economical use of our dwindling shipping resources,
and to cut down as fully as possible all non-essential imports, in order
to concentrate upon the supply of the nation's rigidly essential needs.

These measures ought to have been taken systematically as soon
as it became clear—as it certainly did in 1915—that the War might
last for years, and would strain the resources of the belligerent nations

to the utmost, and especially when it became evident that our tonnage was becoming more and more inadequate to the demands made upon it. Whilst our vital war demands were increasing and would continue to increase, our available shipping was diminishing through submarine action and ordinary sea losses and being insufficiently replaced. The measures enforced prior to 1917 for the limitation of imports were of a timid and half-hearted character, and had only a very limited effect in determining which of our imports should be sacrificed to the shipping shortage.

There were two lines of action by which the Government and the nation could adapt themselves to the reduction in their imports forced upon them by shortage of shipping. One was to cut down consumption to the lowest practicable limits, in fact confining it to the barest essentials. The other was to increase to the utmost the home production of commodities formerly imported. Both methods were applied by the Government as fully as possible during the last two years of the War. In this section I deal only with the first.

Economising is always a painful process. Few and exceptionally fortunate are the households that have never come face to face with the necessity for cutting down superfluities and even some comforts, owing to a temporary financial stress. It is always a struggle to begin the process. Afterwards it becomes easier. In practice it is almost invariably put off to the last moment. Experience tends to show that it is often postponed until it is too late to save the family from irretrievable bankruptcy. In this case starvation threatened the whole nation. When at last we grappled with our problem we recognised that stern economy is much easier to achieve if it is universally enforced, for selfishness is not the greatest obstacle to reducing expenditure, but habit and, more particularly, pride. The intervention of a superior authority breaks the force of habit, and pride is mollified by the fact that all one's neighbours are in the same plight. When it is a national necessity, patriotism enlists pride on the side of sacrifice. No one then can point the finger of hurtful pity at the reduced household, for under these conditions it is the extravagant who become objects of public scorn. The gap between the habitual standard of life and the irreducible minimum varies according to countries, and in every country it varies according to classes. But all countries and most classes can sacrifice something without being reduced to a weakening penury. It is only when ingredients essential to sustain vitality are dispensed with that the health of the people begins to suffer. In foodstuffs, drink, clothes, amenities, amusements, there was a good deal that Britain could give up without damage to its health. There were some demands essential to the upkeep and development of a civilised community, e.g., the building of new houses or the repair and decoration of the old, which could be put off for two or three years without inflicting intolerable hardship on the community. The postponement of building operations led to a great deal of overcrowding in munition areas, but at its worst it was not comparable to the insanitary congestion of the slums. It is when deprivation becomes privation—when the cutting down cuts to the quick—that the national strength and morale become impaired. That is what happened in Russia, Germany and Austria. Could we avert a like catastrophe here? This was our problem.

We were faced with an inevitable reduction of our total imports. We had to ask three questions. First: what can the nation do without—that is, without impairing its efficiency? Secondly: how much deprivation will it stand without perilous disgruntlement? Thirdly: to what extent can we produce at home essential commodities hitherto brought across the seas? This last question is dealt with in other chapters. Here we are concerned with the two former questions and with the policy of import restriction framed in relation to them.

A certain restriction of imports was imposed on the country by the reduction in the tonnage available to bring them to our shores. I have spoken elsewhere of the immense demands on our shipping made by our expeditionary forces and by our Allies. Added to this was the reduction in available tonnage caused by war and marine losses, and by the falling-off in the rate of shipbuilding during the first two years of war. When the vessels withdrawn for war services, and those sunk and lost, were subtracted from our original total, there was nothing like enough tonnage left to maintain our imports at the pre-War level. The question was not: shall we have fewer imports? That was inevitable. It was: shall we deliberately cut away the imports we can do without, and concentrate on those that are essential; or shall we leave it to chance, in the hope that without choice or direction the most important commodities will find their way to us?

Nothing could be more significant of the change which the Second Coalition introduced into the handling of our shipping resources than the way in which successive Ministers dealt with this question of imports. Sir Joseph Maclay and Mr. Runciman were both ship-owners; the former by practice, the latter by parentage. While Sir Joseph Maclay grappled with the problem on the principle that complete control was vital, Mr. Runciman's treatment of it suffered from that spirit of procrastination and timidity, from that readiness to assume that something resolved at a Committee was thereby an accomplished fact, which in this and other Departments of State brought us by the end of 1916 perilously near the precipice.

In 1913, the imports into this country totalled nearly 53 million tons in weight. In the first year of the War, despite the enormously increased pressure of demand for goods, they fell to 50 million tons. The main discriminating factor which determined what goods should be left out was the rise in freight rates resulting from that pressure of demand, operating on a reduced supply of tonnage. The goods which could best afford to pay the bigger rates were imported. The others were cut out. This was not a planned process; and there was no guarantee that it would give us the goods we most needed. It was, fortunately, supplemented by other measures. Steps were taken very early to ensure our supplies of meat and wheat by requisitioning refrigerator ships and wheat vessels, and later on the M'Kenna Duties were imposed to restrict luxury imports. In November, 1915, the Ship Licensing Committee began to help the situation by refusing licences where the charters were for the carriage of wasteful and unnecessary imports. But the system of licence could not be pressed far in this service without a plan behind it for the imports which were and those which were not to be permitted.

Speaking of the position at that stage in the War, Fayle says : —

" It was not merely a question of the luxury trades, the volume of which was small, but of a choice between commodities commonly regarded as necessaries; and only the Government were in a position to say, in the light of war requirements, what imports were and what were not essential. The task lay well within their scope; it was capable of administrative solution. . . .

The Government, however, shrank from the responsibility involved. . . ."*

On 10th February, 1916, the Shipping Control Committee presented a report to the President of the Board of Trade, outlining the position with regard to British tonnage available for supplying the needs of this country, and urging the restriction of imports which could best be dispensed with as the only way in which our shipping would be enabled to cope with its task.

The report showed that out of 3,468 steamers of 1,600 tons gross and upwards, with a total tonnage of 15,441,000 tons, the number already requisitioned for war purposes, or trading in other parts of the world (not to and from the United Kingdom), was 1,894, with a tonnage of 8,373,000 tons. Thus, for carrying essential imports for the ordinary needs of the population there were only 1,574 vessels available, with a gross tonnage of 7,068,000 tons—less than half the British mercantile fleet. In this total of 1,574 were included those vessels that had been requisitioned by the Admiralty to bring wheat and sugar to Great Britain.

Figures were submitted to show that 10,328,000 tons gross of British shipping would be needed, after making allowance for the maximum amount of goods that might be carried in foreign vessels, to meet the import trade of the United Kingdom on the level of the first year of the War, and to furnish certain extra tonnage for which

* " The War and the Shipping Industry," p. 156.

our allies France and Italy were making urgent demands. Our available shipping fell short of this by 3¼ million tons gross, representing the carrying capacity for 13 million tons' weight of imports in a year.

The maximum we could hope to obtain by the aid of British and foreign shipping in 1915 would be 37 million tons, and the Committee proceeded to face the question of how we could best arrange to meet the hardship involved in foregoing about 25 per cent. of the imports we had obtained—nearly 50 million tons—in the previous year

The Shipping Control Committee did not put forward a list of the items which should be totally or partially prohibited to achieve this result. They made, instead, a list of the items of food and raw materials and other essential commodities which they considered we should have to import. These, they proposed, should be imported on the 1915 scale, except in the case of timber and paper and paper-making materials, where they suggested definite cuts—of 1,000,000 tons of timber and 800,000 tons of paper and paper-making materials. Subject to these cuts, their list of essential imports totalled 35,375,000 tons. A margin was thus left of 1,635,000 tons to complete the possible 37 million tons of imports, and they proposed that everything outside their list should be prohibited, beyond a few miscellaneous necessary articles which might be covered by the million odd tons of the margin.

The plan was a somewhat blunt and crude one. Sir Arthur Salter says of it:—

" A reduction of this kind and on this scale, effected by direct and absolute prohibition, would have had incalculable results upon the still unexamined and unorganised economic system of the country, and the information and preparatory work behind the recommendation were clearly not sufficient to warrant such drastic action. In particular, later experience showed that while a certain limited number of articles could be excluded altogether as unnecessary, the economy that could be effected in this way was relatively small. The great bulk of any reduction must be made not by the total exclusion of certain articles but by the exclusion of all beyond certain points. . . ."*

As events subsequently proved, the Shipping Control Committee took too pessimistic a view of the importing capacity of our shipping resources. Instead of only 37 million tons, we succeeded in 1916 in importing 42.3 million tons, so that the restriction of our total imports imposed on us by the *force majeure* of shipping shortage was not 13 million but less than 8 million tons.

Unfortunately, however, only a small part of this enforced

* " Allied Shipping Control," p. 65.

reduction was planned for by the Board of Trade. After they had examined the situation in the light of the Committee's report, Mr. Runciman reported to the War Committee, on 8th March, 1916, that the utmost deliberate reduction in non-essential imports which at that moment he could definitely hope to achieve by methods of restriction did not exceed 4,000,000 tons. The War Committee recommended that the President of the Board of Trade should have a free hand to use his discretion in cutting down imports, subject to reference, in particular cases, to the Departments concerned.

How did the 4,000,000 undertaking work out? On 24th October, 1916 (seven months after the undertaking to plan a reduction of 4,000,000 tons), Mr. Runciman presented a memorandum on the subject of Merchant Shipping, in which, speaking of the restriction of imports, he said that the full effect of the restrictions he had devised had not yet been experienced, but it was estimated that the total annual saving would amount to something between 1,500,000 and 1,800,000 tons' weight of imports. He added that after careful inquiry, the Board of Trade were of the opinion that it was not practicable to bring about further material reduction of unessential imports by the instrument of direct prohibition. A further reduction would be secured indirectly by high prices, by the gradual cessation of unessential industries in this country owing to withdrawal of labour, etc., and by the very fact of the shortage of ships.

A very lengthy list had by this time been compiled of provisionally prohibited goods, which could only be imported by permission and licence of the Board of Trade. But such licence was forthcoming freely enough to cut down the possible effect of the prohibition to the slender limits indicated by Mr. Runciman, whose main hope continued to be, not in a fully planned control of imports, but in the undirected and uncontrolled operation of high freights. In the absence both of a considered restriction of imports and of national requisition of all our shipping, tonnage strayed into voyages where the freights were fat. So that while shipping shortage cut down our 1916 imports by between 7 and 8 million tons, not more than 1½ million tons were excluded through deliberate restrictions.

On 15th December, 1916, after the change of Government, the Shipping Control Committee sent a long communication to me in reply to my request for information on merchant shipping, ship-owners' profits, and cutting down of imports. In this letter they said : —

"From the very beginning of their work in January last this Committee have urged the necessity of restricting imports in order to make the supply of tonnage meet the demands made upon it. The Committee's recommendations were set out in a Memorandum to the Board of Trade, dated 10th February. . . . At that time it had been proposed that the importation of particular articles which are not essential should be prohibited or restricted. The Committee suggested that in lieu of a list of articles that may *not* be imported there should be prepared a list of necessary articles that *may* be imported, and that it should be decided for a period to be fixed that nothing but those articles should be allowed to be imported. *This recommendation* was carried out, but in so small a degree that the effect on tonnage was negligible. What seemed to the Committee urgent then applies to-day in a still greater degree."

Ten months' discussion, examination and recommendation by an able and influential Committee had produced " negligible " results, when we were face to face with defeat through lack of sea transport for essentials. Committees are helpful to guide men of action on the right course. But for weak or remiss administrators they only afford an excuse for postponing movement on embarrassing questions.

Following upon this communication, I had an interview with the Shipping Controller and brought the matter to the notice of the War Cabinet on 21st December, 1916. We decided that an Inter-Departmental Committee should be at once assembled to consider and report on the question of the restriction of imports.

An exhaustive examination of all our imports was made, in order to determine where the necessary reductions could best be made. A programme was prepared, based on the assumption of imports being 500,000 tons a month (i.e., six million tons a year) less in 1917 than in 1916. A detailed programme of restrictions was submitted to meet the expected six-million-ton fall in our imports. The cuts proposed affected a large range of commodities. With one of the largest items, timber, and with the way in which we were able to adopt it, I deal in another section. In paper and paper-making materials a cut of 50 per cent. of the 1916 imports was proposed. To ease the strain upon our grain imports, a further drastic reduction of brewing was proposed, of which I gave an account in the chapter on Food. Feeding-stuffs for farm stocks were cut down; and this step, by tending to bring about an earlier and more extensive killing of stock, made possible a reduction in meat imports. Altogether the proposals of the Committee were of a very drastic character, and they were approved with slight modification by the Government.

But meantime the intensive submarine campaign against our shipping had got under way. In the first two months of 1917, 900,000 tons of Allied and Neutral shipping were sent to the bottom, and with them we lost the valuable cargoes of grain and other essential imports they were carrying. It became clear that we should have to reckon on a reduction, not of six million but of eight, ten or more millions of tons of imports. The committee promptly met this challenge by further proposals, which they submitted on 21st February, 1917, for still more drastic cuts in timber, paper, fruit, and vegetables, glass bottles, feeding-stuffs, iron-ore, sugar and other commodities. They suggested that sugar rationing might enable sugar imports to be reduced without serious hardship. The more important of these reductions were approved by the Cabinet.

No time was lost in putting into force these various measures. A report of the Board of Trade, dated 10th May, 1917, on " Imports in Relation to Shipping," showed that by the month of April—the second month after these restrictions were planned—the decrease in the imports of restricted goods, as compared with the volume of imports of these goods in April, 1916, was 499,000 tons for the month. Thus the initial aim of a planned reduction of 500,000 tons a month had in fact been achieved already.

The report said that, " *To meet the necessity of curtailment a policy was adopted which was originally intended to save about 4,500,000 tons in 1917, and there are prospects of its saving more than 6,000,000.*"

Our actual imports in 1917 were 7.9 million tons less than in 1916. In the course of the year, 6,000,000 tons of Allied and Neutral shipping were sunk by the enemy, most of it with cargoes. It is clear that only the careful organisation of our imports, which secured that upwards of 6,000,000 tons of the reductions imposed on us by our shipping losses should fall on classes of goods we could arrange to dispense with, made it possible for the country to carry on its activities effectively in the face of such an attack.

But it is fair to say that the achievement was the result of a co-ordinated effort which made us less dependent on overseas supplies even for essentials. Food production at home was increased by efforts which I describe elsewhere in this volume. Timber felling was organised thoroughly so that we could dispense with the bulky cargoes which took up so much of our tonnage. We opened up disused iron, copper, and manganese mines. We drew more of the necessaries of individual and national existence from our own internal resources than we had done for at least half a century.

The task was immense. Control was extended over practically all commodities. All ships, tramps and liners alike, were brought under requisition. Restriction and economy were enforced in every direction. Sir Arthur Salter gives a description of the process: —

" The ultimate needs of the scores of millions of individuals who required commodities needing transport were sifted many times through a series of sieves of smaller and smaller mesh, but never small enough, before they reached the executive point of requisition and allocation. . . . The total needs for tonnage were received by the Shipping Department, handled and translated

into terms of so many ships at given places and dates by the three
executive branches (Naval, Military and Commercial), and as
such presented as indents on the Requisitioning Branch. . . .
And this indent always exceeded the total in the pool. So each
week the heads of these four branches met in an unofficial committee for a final pruning of the total demand. . . . Even while
the plan was being framed the submarine would be busy, or a
military emergency, or later statistics of food prospects and food
requirements, or . . . [etc., etc.] would require a change in
allocation."

The difficulties of control and restriction are evident in this
picture; but so also is the fact that a system was evolved which during
the last two years of the War exercised a real guiding control over
the whole field of imports, and carried out a flexible, day-to-day
adaptation of its restrictive powers, so as to secure at all times the
exclusion of the less vital in favour of the more vital imports.
Thereby we won through the acute perils of 1917. Had we
continued the haphazard methods of 1916, which offered systematic
planning to cover only 1,500,000 to 1,800,000 tons of the reduction
of imports which we had to face, it needs little foresight to perceive
what disaster would have overtaken us before 1917 was half spent.

3. THE SUPPLY OF HOME-GROWN TIMBER

As the shipping shortage developed and measures had to be
devised to economise our available tonnage, the imports of timber
were regarded as a commodity specially suitable for restriction,
both because timber is very bulky in relation to its value, and
because it was possible to replace for a time a great deal of our
imports by supplies produced at home, from the woods and forests
of Britain and France.

Hitherto the timber of Great Britain had been a very badly
neglected asset. At the outbreak of the War, Britain had a smaller
proportion of wood and forest land than any country in Europe
except Portugal; and the output of our three million acres of wood-
land was about one-third of what it should have been under efficient
management. A beginning had been made with the scientific
development of afforestation by the Development Commissioners
under the Development and Road Improvement Funds Act, which
I carried in 1909, but there had been little time before the War for
the Commissioners to achieve anything definite in a matter such as
afforestation, where time is counted not in years but in decades. Just
before the War the annual felling of British timber was estimated to
amount to about 45,000,000 cubic feet—nearly one million loads—
while our imports in 1913 were 10.4 million loads.

The timber was required for a variety of indispensable uses.

Nearly three million loads consisted of pit-props and pit-wood for use in the coal-mines. A very large quantity was needed for building. Furniture took its share. And a great deal of the imported soft wood was used for making boxes, packing-cases and crates for the dispatch and distribution of manufactured goods.

With the advent of war, the demand for timber grew considerably. Manufacture of armaments and munitions made an increased demand for coal, and so for pit-props. The swelling torrent of supplies which poured overseas to our expeditionary forces called for an immense number of boxes, including ammunition boxes. If private building largely stopped, building of factories, of army hut-ments, both here and in France, went on very rapidly, and for this work wood was in chief demand. Trench warfare again involved wood, as did railway construction behind the lines, with its call for innumerable sleepers, and there were the miles of duckboards needed to cross the sodden and shell-pocked areas.

Wood, in short, was more than ever indispensable. But we could not spare the tonnage space to carry this bulky commodity here from distant countries. As early as 1915, the Government set up the Home-grown Timber Committee to promote the development of timber supplies from our own native resources, and early in 1916, when the first steps were taken to effect a reduction in our imports, it was decided to cut down the imports of pit-props and seek to obtain them more largely from sources in this country.

Timber imports showed an inevitable drop during the first two years of the War, but not so great a drop as might have been expected, in view of the possibility of substituting the home-grown article. The final Report of the Forestry Sub-Committee of the Reconstruction Committee, issued in May, 1917, estimated that the 1915 timber imports represented 75 per cent. and those for 1916, 62 per cent. of the average imports in the five years before the War. But as all our imports were lower in these two years, the proportional reduction was much slighter. In 1909-1913, timber averaged 11.6 per cent. of our total imports; in 1915 it was 11.4 per cent. and in 1916, 10.5 per cent.

The serious shipping situation with which the new War Cabinet was confronted at the beginning of 1917 called, as is told in another section, for further drastic reductions of imports. Lord Curzon's Committee, set up by the Cabinet on 21st December, 1916, to examine this question, recommended that out of a total restriction of 400,000 tons a month, 200,000 tons should be at the expense of timber imports. The War Cabinet examined the Committee's report on 16th February, 1917, and in order to ensure that such a reduction should be carried out without leading to such a timber shortage as would hamper our military efforts, we decided to appoint a Director of Timber Supplies at the War Office, with an Inter-departmental Committee to assist him. The first holder of this post was Sir J. Bampfylde Fuller. On 19th February, we decided at a War Cabinet meeting that timber imports must be cut down by a further 100,000 tons a month—making a total reduction of 300,000 ton a month. The question was further considered by us on 21 February. A memorandum submitted by the Committee o Restriction of Imports pointed out that the reduction of timbe imports by the amount of 200,000 tons a month originally propose would leave the timber imports in 1917 at a rate of 364,000 tons month; a further reduction of 100,000 tons would thus mean cuttin off well over half our 1916 timber imports. There was timber enoug in France and the United Kingdom to replace this amount, bu possibilities of greater home production were limited by labou shortage, scarcity of sawing plant, and difficulties of transport. I this country we could produce a further 1,000,000 tons of pit-prop in addition to the 300,000 tons already allowed for, if labour an transport could be forthcoming. And if large additional supplies labour were made available in France the import of sawn timber f the use of the Expeditionary Force could be considerably reduced.

We asked the War Office to enlist the aid of a timber expert see how far the total requirements of our Army in France could b met from supplies of timber in the vicinity of our front; what labou could be provided by the Army, and what transport was neede there. I may here say that a great deal of timber cutting wa organised in France by the late Lord Lovat, largely with labou furnished by Canadian lumbermen drawn from the Canadia Expeditionary Force in France.

With regard to the problem of increasing our home output timber, we decided to make enquiries of our Dominions to see ho far they could help with skilled men, and also to enquire about th possibility of obtaining Finnish and other foreign labour for the wor

The War Office had already asked the Canadian Government f 5,000 Canadian lumbermen. On 2nd March, 1917, the War Cabin was informed by the Canadian representatives that they would their best to increase this number; it would be easier if the men we not required to wear khaki. Those already being supplied were uniform, and were drawn from the Canadian forces. We also receiv an offer of 1,500 lumbermen from Newfoundland.

One of the difficulties of timber-cutting in this country was th the available woodlands were often individually small, and wid scattered, so that apart from the Royal Forests there were few ac where large scale sawing machinery was either available or capabl of being economically used. But at our meeting of 2nd March I w able to report to the War Cabinet a generous offer by Mr. Alfred Rothschild of his two valuable forests in the Chilterns as a free g to the country. This offer had been communicated to me by him the following letter: —

" 1, Seamore Place,
Mayfair.
28th February, 1917.

My dear Mr. Prime Minister,

I feel that I am hardly justified in troubling you with these lines when you are so overwhelmed with work, but I feel also that you will forgive me when you have read the same.

I am, namely, most anxious to place at your entire disposal the woods which I possess on my Halton Estate, where, as you no doubt know, a very large camp has been in existence since the commencement of the War—the average about 15,000 soldiers and sometimes as many as 20,000.

I am, I must confess, not an expert as regards what sort of timber would be suitable for ' pit-props,' but I cannot help thinking that, as there are so many fine trees in my woods at Halton, some of them at least would be suitable for that purpose. Might I ask you very kindly to send down your own expert who would very easily be able to report fully on the subject, and I should indeed be proud if my offer to you should lead to any practical result.

I hope I have made it perfectly clear, dear Sir, that the offer to you is for your *kind acceptance*, and that it is not at all a question of *selling* a *branch* or a *leaf*.

May I take this opportunity of congratulating you on being Prime Minister. The country congratulates itself.

I remain,
My dear Mr. Prime Minister,
Yours most sincerely,
ALFRED M. S. ROTHSCHILD."

I promptly replied, expressing my appreciation of the generous spirit which prompted him to make this gift, by which the country would greatly benefit; and the War Cabinet also sent him its thanks when I communicated to them the terms of the offer. It was very happily timed to help us in our immediate difficulties, and before long the splendid slopes of beech forest on the Chilterns were laid low by Canadian lumber-jacks.

Scotland was at this time our bright spot for home-produced timber. The trade there was well-organised, and Scotland was not only self-supporting in regard to its chief timber requirements, particularly in pit-props, but was able to send supplies to some of the northern counties of England. It had a highly skilled labour force of 4,500 men, for which its timber merchants put up a most dogged fight when in May, 1917, the War Office proposed to call up a number of them for the Army.

In England and Wales we had at this time no such well-organised body of native foresters, and we had to make use of men rejected for

the Army, of soldiers temporarily released, of Canadian and New
foundland lumbermen, Portuguese, Finnish seamen from torpedoec
ships, prisoners of war and women workers. A contingent of Unitec
States lumbermen came over in 1917, but was presently transferrec
to the American Forestry Corps in France.

This miscellaneous array of labour had a task of vital impòrtanc
to fulfil. For our timber imports in 1917 were perforce cut dow1
very drastically. Whereas in 1913 they had amounted altogethe:
to over 11½ million tons, in 1917 they were reduced to 2,875,00
tons. Part of this reduction was provided for by very carefu
economies. A great deal of our requirements for our Expeditionar
Force was met by forestry work in France. At home we raised th
output of timber of all kinds in the United Kingdom from the pre
War level of about 900,000 tons to 3,000,000 tons in 1917. In 191
this was increased still further to over 4½ million tons, of whic
2,000,000 tons represented mining timber. The imports in 191
were reduced by 1,200,000 tons from the 1917 level.

The nature of the labour used for this work is shown by th
following extract from a Report of the Timber Supply Departmen
at the end of 1918: —

" At 1st October, 1918, the Department employed 8,728 Britis
workmen; 1,740 Portuguese; 1,124 surplus seamen, mostly Finn
from torpedoed ships; 84 Danes; 3,035 prisoners of war; and 2,32
Women Fellers and Measurers. In addition, the Canadian Forestr
Corps in Great Britain at that date comprised 7,518 men and th
Newfoundland Forestry Corps 427 men. . . .

The figures above given for labour have since been increasec
The Department however endeavours as far as possible to us
prisoners of war and other miscellaneous labour of which there i
so pronounced a scarcity that the timber trade is far from bein
able to obtain the number of suitable men needed to yield th
maximum production."

This Report, which was furnished to me by the Department o
28th October, 1918, concluded with the statement that: " The stej
taken are such that there is every hope of tiding over the period o
the War." This hope was splendidly fulfilled.

There was no more useful contribution to our mortal struggle wit
the submarine than this organisation of our home supplies of timbe
It stripped this island of some of its best forest. Alas, the effor
made to replenish the loss have been perfunctory. Not only most
our hill sides, but large areas once clad in fine timber are now ba
and broken. The lesson of the War has not yet been learnt in th
and many other respects. Punishment is apt to teach the wror
lessons to its victims.

CHAPTER XLIV

CONTROLLING THE FOOD SUPPLIES

1. FOOD PRODUCTION

THE established order reacts slowly and reluctantly to the appearance of an unexpected factor. No better illustration of this can be found than the manner in which the war direction of all belligerent countries overlooked the importance of organising during the War food supplies for their citizens. The feeding of armies was of course an important consideration in all wars. But food for non-combatants was their own concern. An army marched on its stomach, but there was no need to trouble about the marching equipment of those who stayed at home.

The food question ultimately decided the issue of this war. It was directly responsible for the downfall of Russia, finally it was the element that led to the collapse of Austria and Germany. Indirectly it was responsible for bringing America into the War, since Germany's indiscriminate submarine warfare was her answer to our blockade. Yet at first, and for some time, Germany was so indifferent to the jeopardy of famine lying in wait for her just below the horizon, that in 1915 she was selling grain to Holland. France had a real excuse in her occupied provinces for the serious deficiency in her wheat supplies. The Russian Government was thinking only of how it could supply forage for its immense cavalry establishment, which rendered no decisive service in the War, and the transport which should have been used to feed the cities was diverted to the feeding of idle horses and useless horsemen. Here in Britain, whilst we were short of shipping for imperative war demands and our food supplies from overseas were becoming more and more precarious, we were allowing our own fertile soil to go out of cultivation without making any effort to keep up its yield of essential food. What is the explanation of so obtuse and general a neglect of this vital war front?

The War, in the view of the experts chiefly concerned with its direction, was an affair of the manœuvring and clashing of armies and navies. The food problem ended with the field kitchen. This was due to the general assumption that war on so colossal a scale could not last long. On that point both pacifist and militarist could agree to sit on the same parapet in complete accord. The pacifist predicted that the financial bankruptcy of nations would quickly supervene, and that the fires of war would soon die down for lack of fuel. He held, too, that the deadliness of modern weapons would effect losses so ghastly that after a short experience men would refuse to face them. The militarist was convinced that the onslaught of his huge armies with their shattering equipment would prove irresistible, and that complete victory could only be a matter of a few months. It is a proof of the tenacity with which a rooted conviction clings that neither the men of peace nor the men of war were able to change their outlook, even after the battles of the Marne and of Ypres had revealed the inconclusive character of the fighting. In 1915 they still believed that a rapid decision was likely—the Germans on the Eastern Front, the French and British on the Western. Why therefore waste energy and man-power on the harvests of 1916, 1917 and 1918? It was a great piece of luck for us that we were not alone in cherishing this dangerous obsession. Neither intelligence nor stupidity are the monopoly of any single nation. Victory is a question of the balance at the critical moment. This fortuitous circumstance constituted an important element in saving us and ruining Germany. Had she devoted a reasonable share of forethought to her precarious food position, and started in 1915 to concentrate her scientific resources and great organising gifts on food production, she might have averted the disasters of 1918 and achieved a less humiliating peace.

The conflict of foresight and obtuseness is clearly shown in the record of our own dealings with this issue. As early as the summer of 1915 a Committee was set up under the presidency of Lord Milner to consider measures for increasing the output of food. It reported that the country must go back to the agricultural system of the 'seventies; it must recover the old arable area by ploughing up the land which in the intervening decades had been laid down to permanent grass. A million more acres should be put under wheat. Guaranteed prices should be accorded for a four-year period to give farmers an inducement to break up their pasture, and better wages should be secured to agricultural workers.

This intelligent and constructive proposal had to wait nearly two years before it was carried into effect. The Government of the day rejected it. Lord Selborne, the Minister of Agriculture, told a meeting of agriculturists on 26th August, 1915, that in view of the favourable reports of the harvests in Canada and Australia, and of the unusually good harvest secured that year in Britain, and

" in view of the fact that it was borne in upon us as the struggle in the East of Europe developed that the call on agricultural labourer for the colours would be very heavy in the coming year; in view of the difficulties with which the farmer would thereby be confronted in view of the superabundant harvest in Canada and Australia, and in view of the great financial stringency which will certainly prevail after the War, the Government decided that they would not incur the additional responsibility involved in the guarantee."

At that period the submarine menace had begun temporarily to slacken down, as the Germans were frightened at the storms of protest raised among neutral nations by their campaign. For the next few months it continued to be at a low ebb, and the alarming heights to which it would rise in the autumn of 1916 were not foreseen. But everywhere in 1916 the seasons were bad. The total cereal crops of Canada, the United States and the Argentine were lower than those for 1915 by nearly 40,000,000 tons. The wheat yield in the United Kingdom fell off by over 400,000 tons. Add to this the sudden and ominous rise in the rate of submarine sinkings, and it will be seen that there was no ground left for complacent optimism.

I had always been concerned about our food supplies. In an earlier chapter of these Memoirs I have described how the steadily growing shortage of food became in the course of 1916 a serious menace, and how Lord Crawford and I urged repeatedly on the Cabinet a programme of food production and the appointment of a Food Controller to supervise distribution. For long I had been of opinion—and still am—that with improved scientific knowledge of soil fertilization and productivity and with mechanical devices we could at least double the yield of our land. I had been in touch for years with the more enlightened agriculturists of the kingdom, and my conviction was based on their experience.

How the situation was viewed by a well-informed observer is shown by the following letter, written to me by one of the foremost of them, Sir Christopher Turnor, in November, 1916, a fortnight before I became Prime Minister:—

> " Stoke Rochford,
> Grantham,
> 23rd November, 1916.
>
> . . . The question of the home production of food is becoming so serious that I beg leave to put before you a few considerations, knowing your deep interest in English agriculture.
>
> Our land is producing less than it did before the War, and in 1917 it will produce still less than in 1916.
>
> Large areas are going out of cultivation. Before we know where we are we shall see a drop of between £300 and £400 millions in the capital value of the land. This will be a great handicap in reconstruction and recuperation after the War.
>
> The fundamental mistake has been that food has not been considered as a munition of war, and that the farm has not been treated as a munition factory. . . .

Had we at the outset come to terms with the farmers and told them definitely what to do, our situation to-day would have been very different.

Yours sincerely,
CHRISTOPHER TURNOR."

Yet our efforts to get this matter dealt with by the First Coalition were disregarded. It was not the fault of the Ministers of Agriculture, who did their best to draw attention to the danger and to urge strong action. Looking back on that period, one could almost imagine that a powerful junta within the Government had made up their minds that we could not win, and that the War must therefore be brought to an end as early as possible, and that for this reason they opposed any plans which might encourage its prolongation—failing to comprehend that an inevitable peace meant a bad peace. Maybe, however, it was just stupidity and inertia on their part. Let us give them the benefit of the doubt whichever plea is put in on their behalf.

When I formed my Administration in December, 1916, I was convinced that if this country should endure to victory, it was essential that both branches of the food problem—production and distribution—should be tackled vigorously and without delay. I therefore regarded the food problem as one of our most important concerns. Food production was entrusted to Mr. Prothero, the Minister of Agriculture, and Sir Richard Winfrey, his Parliamentary Secretary. They were both men who had a thorough practical knowledge of agriculture in all its aspects. As to the distribution and rationing of supplies, I invited Lord Devonport to become the first Food Controller. It was a post for which his long and successful business training as a great food distributor, coupled with his experience in public administration, eminently fitted him. He was the architect of great commercial undertakings dealing with the supply of provisions. He had also been Chairman of the Port of London Authority from 1909. Before that he had been Parliamentary Secretary to the Board of Trade since the end of 1905.

The office of Food Controller was one calling for definite executive ability of a high order. Here was no Department which would run smoothly under a mediocre head on the ball-bearings of an expert permanent staff of civil servants. Someone was needed who would on the one hand take firm and vigorous measures to ensure a sufficient food supply for the needs of the civil population, the armed forces of the Crown, and our Allies on the Continent; and on the other hand, would devise suitable measures of restriction and distribution to make a limited and seemingly inadequate supply stretch out over these demands. It was a double problem, each aspect involving stern interference with some of the most individualistic and conservative industries in the country. The first task involved close co-operation with the Board of Agriculture, Ministry of Shipping, Ministry of National Service and the War Office; the second required a firm and tactful handling of the distributive trades and the general public. As far as distribution was concerned Lord Devonport was well qualified to cope with the complex issues involved.

I felt that as a pre-condition for success it was essential that we should take the public into our confidence by a frank revelation of the facts. It might give temporary encouragement to the enemy. This consideration always arose whenever it was a question of taking the public into your confidence. Sometimes in war there are weaknesses and defects which it is important a nation should keep from the enemy's knowledge, in so far as that is possible. That involves not revealing them to your own nationals. What is known to 46,000,000 people cannot be long preserved as a secret from the knowledge of the world. But if it is withheld from your own nation, then you cannot rouse national apprehension, zeal and energy in the task of remedying the deficiencies. To judge where the balance of advantage lies is one of the most perplexing and responsible tasks of statesmanship. In the matter of munitions I concluded that the advantage to be reaped from willing co-operation at home more than balanced the important drawback of cheering the foe by an exposure of facts of which they were already cognisant. I came to the same conclusion about our food supplies. I therefore gave a clear indication of the nature of these problems and of the methods by which we proposed to deal with them, in my first speech to the House as Prime Minister, on 19th December, 1916. In the course of that speech I said: —

" Now I feel I must say something about the food problem. It is undoubtedly serious, and will be grave unless not merely the Government but the nation is prepared to grapple with it courageously without loss of time. The main facts are fairly well known. The available harvests of the world have failed. Take Canada and the United States of America. As compared with last year the harvests were hundreds of millions of bushels down, and that means that the surplus available for sale abroad is diminished to an extent which is disastrous. In times of peace we can always make up the deficiency in any particular country by resorting to another. If America failed there was Russia or the Argentine. But the Argentine promises badly. Russia is not available. Australia means almost prohibitive transport. When we come to our own harvest, which is not a mean ingredient in the whole, not merely was the harvest a poor one, but, what is still more serious, during the time when the winter wheat ought to have been sown the weather was almost, if not altogether, impossible, and I do not believe that more than three-eighths of the usual sowing has taken place. Let us clearly understand what that means. Let us get to

B*

the bottom of it. Unless the nation knows what it means you cannot ask them to do their duty. It is true that to a certain extent you can make up by the spring sowing, but as any agriculturist knows, that never produces anything comparable to the winter sowing.

Those are the main features so far as the harvest is concerned. But we have also got the submarine menace to think of. Under these conditions, it was decided by the late Government to appoint a Food Controller. We have actually appointed him—an able, experienced administrator, especially in these matters, and a man of great determination and force of character. He is assisted by the ablest experts in this House.. . . The problem is a double one: it is one of distribution and of production. In respect of both, we must call upon the people of this country to make real sacrifices, but it is essential, when we do so, that the sacrifices should be equal. The over-consumption by the affluent must not be allowed to create a shortage for the less well-to-do. I am sure we can depend upon men and women of all conditions . . . to play the game. Any sort of concealment hurts the nation. It hurts it when it is fighting for its life. Therefore we must appeal to the nation as a whole—without the help of the whole nation we can accomplish nothing—to assist us to distribute our resources in such a way that there shall be no man, woman or child who will be suffering from hunger because someone else has been getting too much.

When you come to production, every available square yard must be made to produce food. The labour available for tillage should not be turned to mere ornamental purposes until the food necessities of the country have been adequately safeguarded. The best use must be made of land and of labour to increase the food supplies of this country—corn, potatoes, and all kinds of food products. All those who have the opportunity must feel it is their duty to the State to assist in producing and in contributing to the common stock, upon which everybody can draw. . . . There are hundreds of thousands who have given their lives, there are millions who have given up comfortable homes and exchanged them for a daily communion with death; multitudes have given up those whom they love best. Let the nation as a whole place its comforts, its luxuries, its indulgences, its elegances on a national altar consecrated by such sacrifices as these men have made. Let us proclaim during the War a national Lent. . . ."

This account of the food position did not in any way exaggerate the serious nature of the food problem with which we were now confronted. Government neglect and bad weather had combined to menace our resources. The acreage sown with winter wheat was less than ever. Such as there was had been damaged by weather. It was over-late to prepare additional ground on any considerable scale for spring sowing. The prospects for the 1917 harvest were dark. Our expectation of being able to maintain our food supplies until that harvest was reaped were darkening with every week's returns of ships sunk by the submarines. But if my speech fairly reflected the blackness of the outlook, it reflected no less the practical and energetic policy which the Government had resolved to adopt.

On 13th December, 1916, six days before my speech, and only four since the Government had been formed, the new War Cabinet held a special session to consider the Food question and the organisation of home production. Lord Devonport, the new Food Controller, and Captain Bathurst (now Lord Bledisloe) as centre back of the new Food Department, were present, along with Mr. R. E. Prothero (afterwards Lord Ernle), the President of the Board of Agriculture. The Cabinet reached the following conclusions. They have a bearing on the problems of to-day, for they represent an arrangement between producer and consumer where the interests of both are directly concerned.

(a) The first step to be taken is to define the respective spheres of responsibility of the Food Controller and the President of the Board of Agriculture and Fisheries. Mr. Prothero and Lord Devonport undertook to confer with a view to framing an agreement on this subject, and to report the results of their conference to the War Cabinet.

(b) The principle of fixed prices for the 1917 harvest was approved. The details were left for agreement between the Food Controller and the President of the Board of Agriculture and Fisheries, who were invited, in the case of any difference of opinion, to lay the matter before the War Cabinet.

(c) If, after consultation, the Food Controller and the President of the Board of Agriculture and Fisheries considered it desirable to extend the fixed price beyond the year 1917, the matter should again be brought before the War Cabinet.

(d) In order to maintain the production of milk at a fixed price, it was decided to include in the powers of the Food Controller authority over the prices of feeding-stuffs.

(e) The Food Controller and the President of the Board of Agriculture and Fisheries must be empowered to incur the expenditure necessary for stimulating agricultural production in this country.

Put briefly, these resolutions meant that neither precedent nor price was to be allowed to hinder the production of food for the people. There was no time to lose, for the increase in our home food supplies was not something which could be easily or rapidly achieved. The harvest of 1916 had been poor; cereal crops small, potatoes few and diseased. If food was scarce, labour, owing to injudicious recruiting, was scarcer. There was a shortage of fertilisers, feeding-stuffs and tractors. The land had been badly let down in labour and manure at a time when its help was needed more than ever. The prospect for 1917 was therefore worse than for 1916. Only exceptional measures could hold out a prospect of an increased food production, particularly as the shipping shortage and restriction of imports handicapped the supply of feeding-stuffs for animals and fertilisers for the soil.

An essential preliminary was to create an instrument suitable for carrying out our policy, and on 1st January, 1917, the Board of Agriculture established a Food Production Department, under the direction of Sir T. H. Middleton, to organise the expansion of tillage. The next step was to acquire appropriate powers, and on 10th January, 1917, a Regulation was issued by Order in Council, which gave the Board of Agriculture and Fisheries (and, in Scotland, the Board of Agriculture, Scotland) power to make Orders bearing on the better cultivation of agricultural land. The Regulation empowered the Board to take over any land which they considered was being inadequately cultivated, to commandeer any implements or farm stock required for food production, regulate the use of land and order the ploughing-up of grass-land, dispossess farmers that were not producing enough food from their land, and put someone else in charge. Food was a munition of war and in its production the national interest was asserted as paramount, and no vested interests or class privileges were to be allowed to stand in the way of the safety of the nation, or hamper its successful accomplishment of the terrible enterprise to which it had been committed by events. This Regulation was only the first of a series which we issued from time to time, authorising drastic measures to ensure land cultivation and food production.

These compulsory powers were essential as a weapon to be held in reserve for dealing with individual recalcitrants. But to secure a big food production drive for the 1917 harvest we had to enlist the goodwill and voluntary co-operation of the farmers in general. Early in February, Mr. Prothero and I decided to call into our council to aid our food production the services of Sir Arthur Lee (now Lord Lee of Fareham), who had rendered us such notable assistance in the organisation of munitions. The Food Production Department set up at the beginning of January had already been considerably enlarged and developed. We now made it an independent Department, under a Director-General, responsible to the Minister, but otherwise unrelated to the Board of Agriculture. This post was offered by us to Sir Arthur Lee and in due course accepted by him. Prothero and Lee were an ideal combination for this undertaking. The former with his great agricultural experience, his tact, suavity and persuasive manner and speech; the latter bringing to his task the same persistence, energy and resource that he had already displayed in his work for the Ministry of Munitions, to which I have already referred elsewhere. The new Directorate became responsible for supplying agriculturists with labour, machinery and fertilisers, and for exercising the powers of control conferred by regulations under the Defence of the Realm Act to ensure the maximum production of food.

When his appointment was under consideration, it seemed to me that a lunch at Downing Street would be a suitable occasion to discuss the food problem with him and Prothero. As a result of our talk, Lee worked out his ideas in the form of a memorandum which was carefully considered by the Board of Agriculture, and in substance adopted by them. The resulting document was presented to me by Prothero on 14th February, and considered by the War Cabinet on the same afternoon. Its recommendations formed the basis of our food production policy for the remainder of the War.

After considerable discussion the War Cabinet decided to ensure the co-operation of the farming community by adopting a bold policy of guaranteeing minimum prices for wheat, oats and potatoes. The scales adopted were: —

For Wheat:		
per quarter of 504 lb.	...	60s. in 1917
	...	55s. in 1918 and 1919
	...	45s. in 1920-21-22
For Oats:		
per quarter of 336 lb.	...	38s. 6d. in 1917
	...	32s. 0d. in 1918 and 1919
	...	24s. 0d. in 1920-21-22
For Potatoes:		£6 0s. 0d. in 1917
per ton		£4 10s. 0d. in 1918 and 1919

If the Government should commandeer produce during the first three years, it would give an undertaking to pay not less than 70s. for wheat, and 45s. for oats; while for potatoes it would pay not less than £8 per ton in 1917 and £7 per ton in 1918 and 1919.

We further decided that " as a part of a policy of guaranteed prices, the Government should secure a wage of 25s. a week* to agricultural labourers during the period of the guarantee, and should make provision for the establishment of Wage Boards; for compelling owners and tenants to make the best use of the land under their control; and for preventing rents being raised during the period of the State guarantee, except in special cases, e.g., where the landowner himself pays tithe, such special cases to receive the sanction of the Board of Agriculture." The powers were unprecedented and drastic. But so were the circumstances.

The policy outlined in these decisions: guaranteed prices; guaranteed wages; fixed rents; and compulsory powers to secure good cultivation, was the policy pursued thereafter by the Government in

---

* The average wages of an agricultural labourer in England before the War ranged from 12s. 9d. to 18s. a week. The general average can be put at about 14s. a week.

its treatment of the farming community. Fixed rents, guaranteed wages and compulsory efficient cultivation were always regarded as essential concomitants of guaranteed prices.

A very important further discussion took place three days later, on 17th February. It was reported that the farmers who had been consulted were willing to pay a minimum wage of 25s. a week, if they were guaranteed a minimum price for their produce. Lord Chaplin had called on me and expressed his support for the policy of the minimum price. He was pessimistic as to the prospect of increasing production in 1917, as the land required cleaning, and the farmer would not break up his grass-land until he got his guarantee. The interesting comment on the scheme made by Captain Bathurst, who stated that he represented in the House of Commons a constituency containing some of the worst-paid agricultural labourers in the country, was that among farmers there was an increasing appreciation of the probability that if the labourer were better paid he would give better work. The more enlightened were in favour of a Wage Board, because it would place all the farmers on an equal footing.

At this meeting we also discussed pheasants, and decided that the Board of Agriculture should take any measures necessary to prevent them from making inroads on our grain crops. The destruction of the crops by game in the vicinity of preserves has been treated as a joke by men who can afford to indulge in such humour. During the War, when food was scarce, it was a bad practical joke. The War had almost stopped the usual autumnal massacres of the pheasantry, and the result was that the ravages of the surplus birds were devastating. The Board was authorised to issue an Order empowering tenants to kill pheasants where the landowners had failed to keep them down. The War, which upset so many ancient landmarks, was here making inroads upon those sacred feudal relics, the English Game Laws. It is significant of the temper of the times that this rough interference with privileges which had been guarded for centuries with jealous suspicion should have been passed and practised without audible murmur.

We reviewed and confirmed the decisions made three days earlier, but modified the proposals in regard to prices for commandeered produce in the direction of greater elasticity. Altogether it was a startling series of decisions to be taken by a Government in which there were several great landowners: restriction of rent by law—doubling the wages of the agricultural labourer—compulsory cultivation of land (even of parks!)—power for tenants to kill pheasants which ravaged their crops. While the discussion was going on and the decisions were being taken, Lord Balfour sat in quizzical silence. At last he looked at the clock and said: " As nearly as I can reckon, we have had one revolution every half-hour! "

It remained to secure parliamentary sanction for our policy. I gave

a preliminary description of it in the course of an extensive statement
to the House of Commons on 23rd February, 1917, about the position
of food and shipping. Urging the importance of home food production, I said: —

"Twenty years after the Corn Laws were abolished in this
country we produced twice as much wheat as we imported. . . .
Since then four or five million acres of arable land have been converted into pasture, and about half the agricultural population—
the agricultural labouring population—has emigrated abroad or
into the towns. No doubt the State showed a lamentable indifference to the importance of the agricultural industry and to the very
life of the nation, and that is a mistake which must never be
repeated. No civilised country in the world spent less, or even so
little on agriculture, either directly or indirectly, as we did. I
ventured to call attention to this in 1909, but inasmuch as my statement was mixed up with a good deal of controversial matter, it was
not in the least acceptable to the very people for whom it was
designed. Between 70 and 80 per cent. of our staple cereal for
consumption has been imported yearly, and at the present moment
*I want the country to know our food stocks are low, alarmingly low
—lower than they have been within recollection. . . . It is
essential, therefore, for the safety of the nation . . . that we should
put forth immediately every effort to increase production for this
year's harvest and the next, and that we should do it
immediately. . . ."*

I appealed for support for the hard work being done by the Minister
of Agriculture, and indicated some of the features of the problem
with which he was faced. The difficulties in the way of increasing
cultivation, I pointed out, were not solely those caused by labour
shortage, serious though this was. The greatest obstacle was the
timidity of the farmer when it came to cutting up his pasture.

"He has been caught twice with too much arable land, and
caught very badly—once in 1880 and the other time in 1890—and
then he had years of anxiety, depression, and insolvency, his savings
completely absorbed, and very often he himself for years waterlogged by debt. There is no memory as tenacious as that of the
tiller of the soil, and the furrows are still in the agricultural mind.
Those years have given the British farmer a fright of the plough,
and it is no use arguing with him. You must give him confidence,
otherwise he will refuse to go between the shafts. . . ."

I recounted our reasons for believing that during the War and
for two or three years afterwards agricultural prices were likely to

remain high, and announced our intention of basing on that expectation a Government guarantee of minimum prices to the farmer. There were corollaries to this guarantee. Labour must also have a guaranteed minimum wage. Rents must not be raised. "There must not be any return to what happened during the Napoleonic wars. Then there was an enormous increase in prices; and rents were practically doubled by the end of the war." The landlords must not take advantage of a Government guarantee under which the State might lose money, to raise rents.

I then came to what was the most startling, and may yet turn out to be the most fruitful of these proposals, when its value to the community is appreciated.

"Powers are to be given to the Board of Agriculture to enforce cultivation. It is obvious that it is an injustice to the community that a man should sit on land capable of producing food when he is either too selfish or too indolent to make the best use of it. So the Government must have the right, through the proper Department, to enforce cultivation in these cases."

I reviewed the price question, and announced the prices which had already been agreed to by the Cabinet for wheat, oats and potatoes. And I appealed to the farming community, on the strength of this guarantee, to do their best to increase the 1917 harvest, and to make the best use of the time still available. Somewhat optimistically, as events in the last few years have shown, I declared that "the country is alive now as it has never been before to the essential value of agriculture to the community, and whatever befalls it will never again be neglected by a Government." It is still difficult to wean the urban population from a rooted habit of regarding the countryside as a picnicking ground, whose accessible amenities are restricted by fences and often destroyed by cultivation. They have not yet acquired a real comprehension of the essential importance of the land of the country to its security, its permanent prosperity and contentment.

The legislation foreshadowed in my speech was in due course brought forward in the form of the Corn Production Bill, which was given its first reading on 5th April. The second reading of this measure, on 24th and 25th April, was carried by a majority of more than ten to one, but only after weathering fierce attacks by opponents as diverse as Sir Frederick Banbury, Mr. Runciman, Mr. R. D. Holt, and Mr. Ramsay MacDonald. The measure was in four parts. Part I contained the guarantee of minimum prices for corn, Part II minimum wages for land workers, Part III prohibited rent increases as a result of the guarantees, and Part IV made provision for control and enforcement of cultivation. All these four parts hung together, and as I have shown, they formed a necessary system for ensuring the production of more home-grown food. But each part, taken separately, was of a nature to cause violent offence to the susceptibilities of one class or another of political thought. Mr. Runciman and those of his way of thinking intensely disliked the guaranteed price, which savoured of Protection or Bounties, or at least of a departure from the pure theory of Free Trade, of which he had and has been an intermittent champion and a recurrent adversary. The economic colours he wears depend on his political environment for the time being. He had then thrown off his Parisian blazer and was once more wearing his old Free Trade mantle. Wages boards were denounced by Mr. Holt, who declared in favour of *laissez faire* and perfect freedom of contract between employer and employed. He has always been in favour of leaving the hindmost to the devil in order to speed up the rest. Restrictions on the increase of rents roused the ire of Sir Frederick Banbury (now Lord Banbury), the only perfect specimen of the prehistoric man left in the economic world. He was naturally outraged by nearly everything in the Bill. The insistence on cultivation as a legal obligation stirred a wide range of prejudices, ornamental, artistic, sporting, traditional—every form and species of the human egotism which rebels against doing or submitting to things that inconvenience or interfere with its rights, privileges and amenities.

Criticism was not confined to independent and opposition members. One of the members of the Government, Mr. Walter Long, viewed the measure with most profound distaste, and tried hard to get it dropped or postponed, so strongly did he disapprove of any control over the owners and occupiers of land. I give a letter which I received from him in which he very forcibly states the case against the measure:—

"... There is a very strong feeling among agriculturists of all classes that this Bill is being rushed, and there seems to me to be considerable justification for this view. . . .

The Board of Agriculture have taken powers under the Defence of the Realm Act for which, so far as I know, there is no precedent, and their application may easily lead to disastrous consequences. They have taken power to take the control of a man's land away from him; to turn out the tenant and to compel men to cultivate their land in a manner entirely contrary to what they believe to be in the best interests of food production. They propose, as we understand it, to exercise these powers through certain Local Committees. So far as I know, there is no precedent for giving tremendous powers of this kind to any Local Authority, and I fully share the view that a wholly unfair advantage has been taken of the military situation to pass land legislation which would in quieter time be absolutely impossible.

If the policy is pursued, and sanctioned by Parliament, of entrusting Local Committees, not even composed necessarily of men elected in the locality, with compulsory powers to be exercised against their neighbours, the door is being opened wide to tyrannical action of the most serious character. To my own knowledge, steps of a very questionable character are already being taken in this direction, and I am very strongly of the opinion that the amendments which have been inserted by Lord Lansdowne giving appeal in respect of policy ought to be accepted, and before the Cabinet refuse to do so I ask to be heard.

Representations have already been made to me in several quarters that this Bill is not the result of full consideration by a Cabinet composed of men representing the interests concerned. Whether this is so or not, of course I cannot say, as I have had nothing to do with the Bill from the beginning. I was present at the Cabinet when the present policy was decided, and I concurred, though with some reluctance, as regards parts of it.*

I also unreservedly accepted the policy laid down in the two speeches made by you in the House of Commons and at the Guildhall, but this Bill is a wide departure from anything indicated by you on those occasions, and involves interference with the rights of property of the most grievous kind. I have no hesitation in expressing my disapproval, and must, of course, do so whatever the decision of the Government may be; the fact that land legislation of the future is to be of this very drastic kind is causing a profound amount of irritation among men who have been among the most loyal and devoted supporters of the War from its very commencement."

I passed this letter over to a Conservative Minister for his views. He wrote me as follows in reply: —

"My dear Prime Minister,
It is really very hard to treat this tirade of Long's seriously. He is an awfully good fellow and a friend of mine. But he seems to me to lose his head rather easily, and he has certainly lost his head over this Bill.

This is the landlord's string of objections, to which I have been listening with patience for three days, in their most extreme form.

It is simply out of the question that the Government should, as he suggests, hang up the whole Bill, which is the central pillar of our whole Food Production Policy, now that we have by a considerable effort got it through both Houses, till October!

---

* There were at least three large landowners present at the Cabinet meeting that considered the Bill and assented to its provisos.

The only effect of such a piece of folly would be to give time for all their unreasonable opposition to gather head. Nobody would know where he stood, and the business, difficult enough in any case, of getting a larger quantity of land ploughed up *during the two or three months which are of crucial importance* would be fatally delayed.

I am sure you won't look at it for a moment. . . ."

When the Act was put into operation Mr. Long gave trouble. Although he was a member of the Government, he aspired to play the part of a passive resister.

As this correspondence shows, the opponents of the Bill were supported by a small group of men who could not appreciate the truth that when a nation resorts to war, the traditional privileges of its citizens must give way to the public safety, and that the ordinary laws which guarantee the ordinary attributes of possessive right and amenity must remain silent. At the time this matter of increased food production was absolutely vital. Victory hung on it. Our people were bearing wonderfully well the strain of the prolonged War, and the cheerless military position. But if something near to starvation had assailed them and their children, the firmness of the home front might have crumbled. There were no very rosy prospects abroad to help the nation to endure acute privation at home cheerfully. Our failure to apply a more intelligent strategy had left us in a position where it became a case of holding on until one side or the other should crack. The realisation that our casualties were appalling and that results were not commensurate with sacrifices, together with the fact of the Russian Revolution, combined to create a feeling of uneasiness, especially in the industrial areas. The stories told by the crippled soldiers who had returned home from abroad constituted formidable anti-war propaganda. If hunger had visited every home the consequences might have been as serious here as they now were in Russia and afterwards became in Germany.

The powers we secured under the Corn Production Act and under the various Regulations issued under the Defence of the Realm Acts now gave us authority to insist on a big increase in cultivation of the soil; and this on terms which secured the willing co-operation of the bulk of the agricultural community, landowners, farmers and labourers. The Food Production Department and the organisation, central and local, which it built up in concert with the Ministries of Food and of Agriculture, furnished us with an instrument for carrying through our programme. But there were other serious fences to be cleared in our course. Chief among these were the shortage of labour and of fertilisers.

The problem of agricultural labour might well have been expected to defy solution. For years before the War the countryside had steadily been depopulated, and its landworkers reduced to a minimum. When the War broke out, there was a rush of village lads to the colours. The Army exercised a twofold suction upon farm workers. In the first place, these country-bred men included a much higher average of A category recruits than did the urban workers reared in the slummy and unhealthy back streets of our smoke-poisoned cities. So the military representatives cast covetous eyes on these sturdy sons of the soil, and took every opportunity to slip them into khaki. And in the second place, the wages earned by land-workers were so meagre that army pay, plus family allowance, had an attraction for them which it did not hold out to the well-paid munition worker or city employee. Moreover, the industry was not organised to counteract this allurement. Its workers were not com-bined in strong trade unions that would defend their members, and the farmers had no federation comparable in its strength to those of the great manufacturing industries. Whatever influence the Agricul-tural Labourers' Union or the National Farmers' Union may exercise over Governments to-day, in those days it was negligible.

Thus by 1917 there was far less than the normal pre-War labour force available on the land. And with this decimated army we were proposing to carry out arable cultivation on a scale which had not been attempted for decades.

The thing seemed impossible. Nevertheless, it was achieved. The romance of that triumphant struggle against war and weather, and, not least, against the stubborn prejudices of the countryside, cannot be fully told here. I can only pause to summarise a few of its leading features.

There was first the problem of manual labour. The Army had already absorbed a high proportion of our agricultural workers, and still thirsted impatiently for more. At the beginning of 1917, the War Office notified Mr. Neville Chamberlain, the new Director of National Service, that during the first three months of the year they would require a further 350,000 recruits of category A, as well as 100,000 men of categories B and C. On such terms we had to make up the price for our " victories " on the Somme, and prepare to pay for fresh victories of the same kind, decreed by the military conclave at Chantilly. All industries, however vitally important, had to pay their tribute, agriculture among them. The agricultural quota was fixed at 30,000 men.

The War Cabinet considered this problem, but could find no way of evading the sacrifice. So we decided that an effort should be made to find substitutes for these from among home defence units and surplus recruits, and reinforce them by withdrawing men from gardening and similar occupations, by securing women for land work, and increasing the mobility of labour. We also turned our thoughts to an increase of mechanical appliances for cultivation.

One interesting matter was raised at this discussion. Lord French had pointed out that he could only supply men for agricultural work from his Home Defence forces at the cost of impairing his capacity to resist an enemy raid on our coasts, and the War Cabinet formally decided to relieve him of responsibility by itself taking the decision to authorise the action. The " risk of a raid " was the scare raised at that time by the Admiralty as to the danger of a German landing on our shores. This, the oldest and most profitable bogey in the armoury of our fighting services, is always brought out, dusted, and repainted in flaming red whenever the Generals and Admirals want to retain or increase their estimates of men, money or machinery. For a century the old bogey was dressed in French uniform. For a generation it has been German. The Army now wanted more men, so the Admirals co-operated by saying that they could give no guarantee of being able to prevent the enemy from throwing a force of 160,000 men into England at any time, nor could the Grand Fleet begin to interrupt such an operation until 24 hours or more after the German flotillas appeared off our coasts. It was a sorry exhibition of nervous impotence on the part of the Lord High Admirals of the biggest Navy in the world, by Admirals who were not ashamed to own that they could not get near enough to the coast of Flanders to bombard its submarine refuges without imperilling their warships and who avowed their helplessness to check these submarines. It was obvious that if Germany, without securing the command of the sea, sent such an expeditionary force and if it actually succeeded in getting ashore with its equipment, it would forthwith be cut off by land and sea, compelled to capitulate, and the troopships that conveyed the troops with the flotillas that protected them would be sunk or captured. So the War Cabinet declined to take this attack of nerves too seriously, and Lord French accepted our view that the likelihood of such a raid was extremely remote. The Government held that our need for increased food production was much more real and urgent than the need to hold large forces in readiness to deal with a threadbare fantasy. The provision of farm labour from army sources was therefore duly authorised.

Another source of labour was available in the prisoners of war. This was beset with the twofold difficulty that on the one hand the military authorities insisted on very stringent regulations in regard to their use, to avoid the risk of their escaping, and that on the other hand British farmers were at first very reluctant to avail themselves of this unfamiliar form of assistance. Only by slow degrees was war-prisoner labour introduced; but it proved so satisfactory that the countryside prejudice against it disappeared, and the War Office presently realised that the danger of prisoners escaping was small. As a matter of fact, they showed no eagerness to escape. By the end of 1917, only one officer and two men had actually made good their escape from the country, and accordingly the Cabinet then decided to relax the conditions under which German prisoners were employed by farmers, and leave their surveillance to the local police. By the autumn of 1918, no fewer than 30,000 German prisoners of war were employed on the British countryside, helping us to gather in our harvest.

But the recruit to our agricultural labour force who attracted the liveliest interest was undoubtedly the land girl. Her aid, too, was at first pressed on the farmers in the teeth of a good deal of sluggish and bantering prejudice and opposition. When in 1915 the Board of Agriculture tried to induce the farming community to employ female labour—the " lilac sunbonnet brigade," as they were jocularly hailed in some quarters—it met at first with very little success. There was of course work that had long been done by women on family farms— milking, butter making, poultry keeping, haymaking and the like. But the idea that women could do the ordinary work of a farm called forth bucolic guffaws. This crude merriment roused the ire of the sex, and when a member of the Launceston Board of Guardians publicly declared that women could not do certain forms of farm work, they challenged his statement in the Press, and eight competitors turned up for a public demonstration at which they efficiently carried out all the major operations of a farm. This was in March, 1916, and it aroused such interest that a month later a county demonstration was held in Truro, where 43 female competitors appeared and performed seven types of farm work, including harnessing and driving horses in waggons, ploughing, manure spreading and potato planting. The work chosen as a test was all of a kind only to be performed by skilled and sturdy labourers. One of the judges wrote afterwards:—

" Some of the work was very well done indeed. The dung-spreading and planting were excellent; and the way in which several of the competitors handled the horses on the harrowing and in the waggons was a surprise to many of the spectators. . . . I should like to see some of the men who have been cheaply sneering at the ploughing have a try themselves."*

Still, it took another year to reconcile farmers to this innovation. But at last the really efficient performance of women on the land, of which the Launceston demonstration gave a sample, slowly won them acceptance and recognition by the farmers.

With a view to our big food production drive, we determined to make a more considerable use of this source of land labour, and in January, 1917, the Board of Agriculture set up a Women's Branch, which in March was transferred to the Food Production Department.

* Middleton, " Food Production in War," p. 143.

It set to work to organise women's labour for the farms. This was divided into two classes—casual or part-time work by women in the villages, who could not leave their homes but could help with farm work; and the recruitment of a Land Army of girls and women who would give full-time service and go wherever they were sent.

Of the first type of labour there had always been a fair volume employed. The 1911 Census showed 70,000 women engaged in agriculture. But by means of women's County Committees a greatly increased number were drawn into service, and in 1918 the returns indicated that some 230,000 village women and girls were working on the land in England and Wales.

The recruiting of the Land Army was begun early in 1917 by the National Service Ministry, and then worked jointly by the Ministry of Labour and the Food Production Department. The terms offered at the outset by the Government to recruits included a month's free training at one of the 600 training centres which we arranged on farms where accommodation could be provided; an outfit; a minimum wage of 18s. a week (as compared with the pre-War average wage in England of 14s. a week to men workers); and maintenance at the depots while unemployed. It was of course very important that the new Land Army should create a good impression in the early days, to counteract the general hostility and distrust of the farming community; and the first recruits were most carefully selected. Out of 47,000 applicants who turned up in the first rush, only 7,000 were accepted.

Of the various labour resources applied to agriculture during the War—soldier ploughmen and labour battalions drawn from the home defence forces, prisoners of war, unskilled urban substitutes for farm workers called to the colours—the land girl was certainly the most picturesque figure, and perhaps in some ways the most valuable. Breeched, booted and cropped, she broke with startling effect upon the sleepy traditionalism of the English countryside. She was drawn from a wide range of classes of society, and while as in every large collection of human beings there were included good, bad and indifferent specimens, her general average was high. She brought with her an eager enthusiasm and energy, an alert and unprejudiced mind, that stimulated by example the activity of the men workers.

But when all such sources had been tapped, we could not command anything like enough manual labour to carry through a big increase in cultivation by traditional farming methods, or even maintain cultivation at its previous level. If we were to achieve our big drive, the Government saw clearly that we should have to resort to labour-saving machinery on a large scale, supplementing our limited man-power with the power of petrol and steam.

Here we were up against a twofold difficulty. On the one hand, we had not got the tractors. On the other, the farmers were not at all eager to have them. At that time the agricultural tractor was hardly known in the English countryside, and was regarded with grave suspicion by the farming community as a new-fangled contraption with no manurial utility. Steam ploughing tackle they were in some districts more familiar with; but of the 500 sets which existed in the country, nearly half were idle, as their engine drivers had left for the Army or for munition factories, and many of the sets were out of repair.

Great numbers of farm tractors were needed for ploughing and other tillage operations. These we had either to make in this country or import from America. Lack of shipping made it appear desirable to manufacture them here; but as the firms capable of the work were already fully occupied on munitions and motor transport for the Army, the prospect of getting them to manufacture tractors was gloomy.

At this stage Mr. Henry Ford came to our aid. He was anxious to establish a motor factory in Ireland, and offered, if granted permission and facilities for this, to use the factory during the War for the purpose of making agricultural tractors. The project was sanctioned by the War Cabinet, but was held up through difficulty in securing the necessary structural materials for building the factory. Mr. Ford then came to our help in another way. In April, 1917, he offered to present his "Fordson" tractor to the British Government as a model, together with all drawings, patterns, jigs, etc., needed for its production, free of cost, on condition that the tractors manufactured therefrom should be purchased by the Government, not by private individuals. Arrangements were put in hand to take advantage of this offer, and for 6,000 of the tractors to be manufactured here for us by British firms; but early in June, 1917, we found it necessary to concentrate our motor manufacturing resources on the output of aeroplanes, and all these arrangements went by the board. Ultimately half of the 6,000 Ford tractors were assembled here at a new factory run up at Trafford Park for the purpose, the parts being supplied by Mr. Ford from his American factory. The remainder were imported complete across the Atlantic.

In addition to these 6,000 Ford tractors, the Food Production Department were responsible for securing some 3,262 tractors of other makes. They also hunted out all the sets of steam ploughing tackle in the country, traced their missing engine drivers, and secured the return of some 300 of these from the Army. Further sets to the number of 65 were procured from a British firm.

As an illustration of the achievements of the mechanical power thus made available for our food production campaign, I may say that in the preparations for the 1918 harvest, motor tractors carried out tillage operations equivalent to the ploughing of about 600,000 acres, and the steam tackle ploughed and cultivated about 1,200,000 acres.

Motor and steam power represented only one aspect of the very great resort which we made to mechanical aids in our campaign. The Ministry of Munitions was called on to furnish every kind of improved agricultural implement which would save labour and assist mass production from the soil. Among these may be mentioned such items as 1,000 potato diggers, 5,000 self-binders, more than 3,000 cultivators, and many thousands of harrows, disc harrows, rollers, seed drills, two-furrow ploughs and similar implements. The effect of that wartime campaign was to raise permanently the standard of British farming in respect of mechanical equipment—and seeing the extreme difficulties with which farming has been faced since the War, it was fortunate for it that it was launched on these lean years with at least a more efficient and up-to-date equipment; for despite this advantage agriculture has since then been hard put to it to avoid utter insolvency.

The fertiliser shortage was yet another obstacle to be overcome. This was a difficulty which had confronted us since the outbreak of the War, but it was of course made much more serious when we proposed to effect a vast increase in the cropping area.

The principal artificial manures purchased by farmers here in pre-War days were potash, nitrates and phosphates, the latter two being far the more important. Nine-tenths of the total expenditure before the War on artificials went on nitrates and phosphates. Potash was, however, considered essential for certain crops, notably potatoes. Unfortunately we depended entirely on Germany for our supplies. Despite various experiments, we failed to obtain any considerable output during the War from home sources, and were latterly somewhat handicapped by the lack of this chemical.

As for nitrates, their most popular source before the War was imported nitrate of soda. But munition manufacture combined with the growing shortage of shipping to cut down supplies. Such nitrate as could be imported was wanted for explosives. Accordingly the Acland Committee on Fertilisers, set up by the Ministry of Agriculture in October, 1915, under the chairmanship of Mr. (now Sir Francis) Acland, had to face the difficult task of persuading farmers to use the unfamiliar sulphate of ammonia, which had for years been produced in large quantities at our gas works as a by-product, and exported abroad to appreciative foreigners, who knew its great value as a fertiliser. The Acland Committee carried out useful though tedious spadework in this educational field, and by the time their functions were transferred to the Ministry of Food at the end of 1916, farmers were slowly beginning to use sulphate of ammonia. The Ministry stimulated a larger use of this ingredient.

The growth of the habit is shown by the figures for consumption of this fertiliser in the last three years of the War : —

1916	...	...	...	...	75,000 tons
1917	...	...	...	...	150,000 tons
1918	...	...	...	...	230,000 tons

The provision of phosphatic manures was handicapped by the fact that there was not a convenient home supply of soluble phosphates. Our superphosphate of lime was made by treating imported phosphatic rock with acid, and imports meant shipping, of which we had all too little available. We prohibited the export of basic slag, and the Fertilisers Branch set up at the Ministry of Munitions worked with the Food Production Department to secure the maximum amount possible of superphosphate. These efforts were highly successful, for by the 1918 tillage about 770,000 tons of this manure were provided—a larger quantity than had been used annually before the War. In face of the difficulties to be surmounted this was a remarkable achievement.

It is clear evidence of the restless zeal and energy with which the Food Production Department and the bodies associated with its efforts in the Ministry of Munitions and among some agricultural organisations pursued their task of getting supplies of fertilisers for farmers, that while in 1918 far more land was put under the plough than had been the case in pre-War years, the yield per acre of this increased area was considerably higher than the pre-War average.

In this manner we obtained the powers, set up the administrative machinery, collected the labour, and produced the equipment, the tools and the fertilisers for our great food-growing effort. It remains to summarise the progress of the campaign and its results.

The spring of 1917 remained exceptionally cold and wet till after mid-April, but then a spell of very favourable weather set in, and with the aid of soldiers and with our organisation of machinery the land was ploughed and sown. The severe frosts had given a good tilth for agricultural operations which aided the work. When the preliminary crop returns came in, we were gratified to learn that our hard push was proving successful in getting more land into arable cultivation. Some 975,000 more acres were put under the plough in 1917 than in 1916. Seeing that at the beginning of 1917 it was estimated that the sowing as yet carried out for the 1917 harvest was at least 15 per cent. below that carried out by the corresponding date for the 1916 harvest, the increase eventually compassed was a notable achievement.

The corn crop was of rather poor yield in England and Wales, but fair in Scotland and Ireland. Potatoes cropped better in all countries than they had done the previous year. As compared with 1916, the quantities of produce in 1917 were greater by:—

4,928,000 bushels of wheat;
5,120,000 bushels of barley;
36,700,000 bushels of oats;
41,813,000 sacks of potatoes.

These figures show that despite inevitable war deficiencies in labour, machinery and fertilisers, a truly remarkable beginning had been made with the task of increasing our home-grown food supplies. In addition, the growing army of allotment holders had also been highly successful with their potato and vegetable plantings.

The achievement was a very substantial relief to our overstrained shipping resources. I can hardly describe the relief the figures brought to anxious minds who knew that the battle had resolved itself into a struggle of endurance, and that at the end of 1916 and in the early spring of 1917 it had looked like turning against this country. When I received the statistics of increased production of food, and of shipbuilding, and the returns of diminishing sinkings of our ships which showed that we had checked the submarine depredations, I had a sense that the Allied cause was at last definitely on top, and could not be displaced from that position except by some prodigious act of folly perpetrated by our military leaders. I knew, too, that the food production achieved in so short a time gave promise of infinitely greater results next year.

In this I was not disappointed. The full effect of the work done by the Food Production Department could not be realised until the 1918 harvest. Long preliminary planning was clearly necessary to ensure any extensive inroad upon the permanent pasture of this country, and to secure good cultivation of land that was being neglected.

That programme was set out as early as 7th May, 1917, in a memorandum giving the findings of a Conference of the Agricultural Departments of England and Wales, Scotland and Ireland. Sir Arthur Lee started forthwith to organise the measures for carrying it out. He sent a circular letter to the Agricultural Committee in every county, showing the total area of corn crops suggested for 1918; the additional acreage this represented compared with 1916; the estimated acreage of permanent grass to be broken up; and the percentage of the total arable area of 1918 that would be devoted to corn crops if the programme were carried out in its entirety. These figures were given for each county separately, as well as for the country as a whole. The letter pointed out that it was important for the County Executive Committees to secure as much as possible of their county quotas by agreement, and only to resort to compulsion if all other means failed.

On the whole, these allocations of quota were well received, and the Department then proceeded to recommend the County Executives to set up at least three sub-committees to deal with Labour, Machinery, and Supplies, with the necessary officers and clerks. In most cases these appointments were made before the beginning of the 1917 harvest. A further step in the organisation of the campaign was the division of each county into districts, with district sub-committees in each, forming the final link between the Food Department and the individual farmer.

These sub-committees had the task of investigating and reporting to the County Executives on such matters as: —

Land in the district that was not being put to its best use for the national food supply.

Grass-land that should be ploughed up.

Labour shortage, and the kinds of labour needed.

Difficulties in obtaining supplies of seeds, manures, and other requisites.

They were also charged with the supervision of the work of tractors, steam tackle, horse teams, and gangs of prisoners. They had to keep the farmers informed of the credit facilities we had arranged for them. They were responsible for organising measures against rabbits, rats, rooks, wood-pigeons and other dangers to the crops; for reporting bad drainage; and for assisting allotment holders and seeing that they cultivated their plots well. They rendered very valuable service in carrying out a survey of the land throughout the Kingdom, to ascertain its state of cultivation and what room there was for improvement. This survey was carefully planned in advance by a member of the Land Valuation Staff created under the 1909-10 Budget. Maps were prepared on which every field was shown, and particulars about it could be entered up by the district sub-committees. This kind of work, extended over the country, gave a most valuable picture of our potential resources, and enabled the preparations for the 1918 harvest to be planned on a sound basis.

By this means we learned in October, 1917, through a special return from the County Executive Committees, that the programme for breaking-up of grass-land was making very uneven progress in different parts. It was hampered by the shortage of skilled plough-men. Of 21,500 ploughmen whom the Army had undertaken to supply, only 13,000 had been forthcoming, and most of these turned out to be not really skilled. Only 2,500 knew how to plough! The fact was that Passchendaele was playing havoc with our side of the war of attrition. With its effect on our available man-power in France I deal elsewhere. Here at home it was crippling our food programme. The military chiefs scoffed at the idea that the final issue was being fought in Britain's ploughed fields and on the high seas that surround our islands. Every young ploughman snatched was to them a recruit. In reality he was a casualty before he fell on the battlefield, for he was missing from the front where his services were most needed in the struggle.

It was now too late to proceed with the breaking-up of the heavier clay lands where this had been left undone. So we had to modify our programme. That meant that if we were to get as much land under the plough as we proposed, we should have to encroach on other grass which we had formerly intended to leave alone.

We therefore appealed to all farmers who had any available labour to break up their good grass-land for the national service. The spirit in which this appeal was made is well illustrated by a speech delivered at Darlington on 5th October, 1917, by Mr. Prothero to a meeting of agriculturists. It is an admirable specimen in its clarity and persuasive point of the appeal directed to cultivators, owners and public. Basing his remarks upon the supreme purpose of winning the War, he pointed out the ways in which our agriculture could assist in the task.

". . . First as to bread. The more corn that we can grow in this country, the better able we shall be to feed our people, and the less we shall be forced to buy abroad, the more money we shall keep in these islands, the more ships we shall set free to bring over those raw materials of manufacture on which millions of townsmen depend for their livelihood. . . . It is not a question of policy: it is a matter of necessity—the necessity for essential food in the midst of war and its consequences.

. . . We took the acreage under the plough in 1872. . . . In effect we say to the farmers in each county, ' This is what you were doing 45 years ago when we were less dependent on the foreigner. Take the figures as your goal; get as close to it as you can; make a real, strenuous effort, for the times are critical and the need great.' . . . To attempt ' equality of sacrifice ' is only to make worse inequalities. The ' same for all ' sounds well in theory; in practice it works unfairly. Whether a man should be asked to plough at all, and, if so, how much, is a question which can only be settled on the spot, in view of the nature of the soil, the quality and condition of the grass, the balance of the farm, the necessity of fencing, the farmer's equipment in buildings and implements, or his experience of tillage, and variety of other considerations. . . . The corn is badly wanted; and few farmers, I am confident, will refuse an extra effort and even some sacrifice for the nation's good, provided that they are not asked to do something which they regard as foolish. . . ."

Mr. Prothero went on to speak of the help the Government was seeking to provide for farmers; of guaranteed prices; of seeds, fertilisers, implements, horses, and labour. " From the London Metropolitan Police Force alone we have got 120 skilled ploughmen." He mentioned the training establishments set up to train soldiers and women workers; the arrangements to secure fertilisers; the powers taken to deal with drainage, whereby many thousands of acres were being brought into profitable cultivation. Some 4,500 German prisoners were being employed in drainage works.

In regard to the milk problem, he urged milk farmers to maintain their maximum production. " I know well enough that the labour difficulties of this branch of the industry are greater than in any other branch of it, but none the less stick to it in the dogged spirit of the men who are fighting for us by sea and land." He dealt with the question of the fixed price of milk, and pointed out that if those farmers who found these unprofitable would copy some of the economies in feeding, and in the selection of good cows, adopted by those who were making milk production pay well, they would overcome their difficulties.

" Some dairy farmers must go out of business, or live on their capital, or alter their methods. The only changes of method which will do any good are either to economise in food without reducing the yield of milk or to increase the yield of milk per cow. To do either in ordinary times is the farmers' own affair. But in war time to do one or the other is a duty."

Passing to the question of meat, Mr. Prothero urged the importance of pressing on with winter feeding to maintain the supply of fat stock, and said that as the supply of cake was limited, the farmers should use what could be provided for them chiefly in feeding up the cattle of two years and upwards and reduce consumption when these beasts were exhausted, if meat imports could not supply the deficiency. He also discussed the question of manures, and the position in regard to sheep and pigs.

There was a fine response to these appeals on the part of the farmers. We for our part used all our efforts and persistence to get them the labour they needed. We even managed at the end of 1917, when Passchendaele was over, to get the Army in France to send back 1,500 ploughmen from the ranks for a three months' furlough. With these and German prisoners of war and more land girls and hands from the towns, and an increasing output of tractors we did what we could to eke out the scanty supply of agricultural labour. The spring weather of 1918 was very fine and favourable, and farmers, eager to break up grass-land and plant crops, were clamouring for workers. Then came the German break-through in March, and as a consequence of it, we had to decide in April to claim 30,000 more men from agriculture for the Army!

Happily, by this time the work of preparation for the 1918 harvest was well ahead. The achievements of the autumn campaign and appeal had been remarkable, as is shown by an extract from a letter written to me by Sir Arthur Lee, the Director-General of the Food Production Department, on 15th March, 1918: —

". . . It relates to *Winter Wheat* only, and shows by far the greatest increase ever recorded. The actual percentage of increase over last year's (1917) *Winter* wheat is 45 per cent., and 31 per cent. over *both* winter and spring wheat combined.

The figures are not conjectural estimates, but are based upon actual and compulsory individual returns from every farmer in the country. . . ."

The work thus well begun in the autumn was carried on in the spring with the utmost energy, despite all difficulties. Every fit man, and nearly every unfit man in the countryside was out and at work whenever the weather made farming operations possible. On 21st May, 1918, Sir Arthur Lee wrote me a letter accompanying his Interim Report on the results of the Food Production Campaign, 1917-18, in which he remarked: " I hope you will find them satisfactory. At any rate, they wipe out the losses of 40 years in 15 months."

The Interim Report gave results of a Census of 27th April, 1918, covering England and Wales, which showed the total acreage under corn and potatoes to be larger by 2,142,000 acres than the 1916 level. There was an increase in the acreage under each cereal crop, and in that under potatoes. The wheat area was the highest recorded since 1882; that for oats the highest on record by 20 per cent.; that for potatoes, also the highest on record, by 27 per cent.

The increase in the tillage area was, of course, still greater, because crop rotation compelled a good deal of arable land to be under other crops. The report stated that: —

". . . It is estimated that a total addition of not less than 2,500,000 acres to the tillage area of England and Wales (as compared with 1916) has now been made.

The foregoing figures indicate that the total acreage in the United Kingdom under wheat, barley and oats, in 1918, will be the highest ever recorded in the history of British agriculture. The acreage under potatoes will be the greatest since 1872. Particulars of other crops are not yet available. . . .

Reckoned in tonnage, the *net* saving in shipping resulting from the increased production of corn and potatoes, in England and Wales alone, should amount in the coming year to 1,500,000 tons."

The report added that these figures took no account of the increased production from allotment gardens, of which there were upwards of 800,000 more now than before the War. These might be reckoned to be producing food-stuffs to a total of 800,000 tons above the normal.

This agricultural achievement, it was pointed out, was accomplished in spite of the fact that after reckoning all the military and prisoner labour furnished by the Government, there had been 200,000 fewer male labourers on the land than in the year before the War.

The Agricultural Returns for the year 1918 ultimately showed that the total area in the United Kingdom diverted from grass to arable cultivation was 3,381,000 acres. And the actual realised yields of cereals and potatoes showed a most remarkable and gratifying advance upon those secured in the 1917 harvest. The crop yields in the two successive seasons were as follows:—

Figures in Tons.

CROP.		1917.	1918.	Increase.
Wheat	...	1,757,000	2,579,000	822,000
Barley	...	1,359,000	1,540,000	181,000
Oats	...	3,632,000	4,461,000	829,000
Potatoes	...	8,604,000	9,223,000	619,000

The increase achieved was very striking and immensely valuable. The wheat crop in England and Wales exceeded the average of the last ten years before the War by 59.3 per cent., and the oat crop was similarly greater by 38.5 per cent., and potatoes by 59.2 per cent. For the United Kingdom as a whole, the wheat crop of 1918 was 64.9 per cent. greater than the pre-War average. The 1918 harvest was in fact by far the greatest that has been secured in this country for over the past sixty years.

It would have been far greater still if the weather in the latter part of 1918 had lived up to its early promise. But the early summer was cold and dry. July was very wet, with some damage to crops through the heavy storms. August brought favourable weather in the South of England, where the bulk of the harvest was secured in good season and condition, but September was again very wet, and in the Midlands and North, in Scotland and Ireland, the harvest season turned out to be one of the very worst on record. The corn could not be carried, and a great deal of it sprouted in the fields. Heroic efforts were made to save it. In the crisis, the Home Defence Force was called on for every available man, and the landworkers, reinforced by the help of some 70,000 soldiers and 30,000 prisoners of war, were out whenever weather permitted, aided by all the mechanical resources—tractors, reapers and binders, and so on— that the efforts of the Food Production Department could provide. More than four-fifths of the largest harvest of modern times was thus rescued in the teeth of one of the worst seasons imaginable. If the achievements of the winter and spring sowing and planting had been magnificent, still more magnificent was the triumph of harvesting.

Had Germany carried out our programme of cultivation and rationing, the acute food shortage which provoked revolution and disintegrated the army would not have occurred.

It was the climax of our efforts for home food production. When in the spring of 1918 the programme for the 1919 harvest came to be planned, it was clear that much of the arable which had been so strenuously worked in the last years must now be given a rest unless it was heartened with fertilisers. Of these there was no adequate supply available. Production could therefore only be maintained at the 1918 level if half a million fresh acres could be brought under the plough, to replace land which would have to be let down to rotation grasses or bare fallow. The Food Production Department put forward a programme for ploughing up a further 550,000 acres of " relief land " in order to maintain the corn acreage. But the most convenient grass-land for such a purpose had already been taken, and the carrying out of this further programme would have made inroads upon the remaining pastures, which the farmers would have strongly resented. Any hope of securing their willing concurrence was destroyed by the fact that the German attack in March, 1918, compelled us to call on agriculture to provide a further 30,000 of its fit young men for the Army. The demand was unavoidable. The age limit had been raised, and the age at which recruits were sent to the fighting line had to be lowered. In spite of the urgent demands for coal and munitions, miners and munition workers were being similarly combed. But the withdrawal of more men from the land broke the farmers' spirit. They were already finding it intolerably difficult to keep their cultivation going, and it proved impossible to take away their best men and at the same time call on them to plough up their best pastures.

So when the Corn Production (Amendment) Bill, 1918, was introduced, to give the Food Production Department further powers of compulsion to secure the breaking-up of grass-land, Parliament met it with lively opposition.

Taken as a whole, the agricultural experiment had produced results which definitely helped the nation through a crisis. This fact, however, did not mollify critics who were suffering from a sense of personal grievance or affront to their personal dignity.

The orders issued for breaking up the land were not always acceptable. Although in the main the selection was fair and prudent, there must have been occasions when the choice was doubtful and some perhaps where it was definitely unwise. The instruments used for carrying out this improved programme were by no means the best, but they were the best available under war

2C

conditions. That was inevitable in an organisation which had to be set up in a hurry to meet a pressing emergency. Experts had to be picked from such material as was left after a good deal of the best had either gone to the front or been commandeered for other war work. Mistakes were therefore inevitable and the disgruntled gave them the widest publicity.

Many members of Parliament had experienced in their private capacity as landowners the weight of the Department's hand, and in the House of Lords the majority of members were so hostile that the Bill had to be amended to permit a right of appeal against the Department in cases where it ordered further grass-land to be broken up, or sought to take over land which it held to be mismanaged or under-cultivated. This clipped the wings of the Food Production Department, and made it impossible to hope for the carrying out in full of its proposals for the 1919 harvest.

The strike of the " Junkers " was a serious embarrassment to a Coalition Government, a large and influential section of whose political supporters were drawn from that class. But it was not unexpected. The orders issued for the ploughing of land hitherto kept green and uncultivated for ornamental purposes were received with increasing resentment by some men all-powerful in their domains, who were not accustomed to be ordered about by County Committees as to the use they should make of their park lands and preserves. The grumbling became a growl and at last a snarl with bared teeth. One great landowner who possessed considerable political influence came to me, angrily flourishing a notice which had been served upon him threatening proceedings against him if he did not comply with an order to break up some of his decorative land. He had ignored the order as an impertinence. Hence the threat. When I saw him he was scarlet with fury. He was a man whose patriotism was beyond question. But this proceeding wounded his pride. He had always been one of the most excitable champions of law and order. Nevertheless he told me that he meant to defy this particular order. I reminded him that it was the law of the land he was setting at defiance. That did not appease him. He thought it an unjust law which interfered with the amenities of a man's home. I pointed out to him that he belonged to an order of Society from which magistrates were drawn who administered laws which were rightly or wrongly often regarded by their humbler neighbours as oppressive, but that such a plea was never accepted from offenders summoned before land-owning justices for a breach of those laws. There could not be one interpretation of obedience to law for the rich and another for the poor. He went away more in anger than in sorrow, for he had a great estate, a long pedigree, a vast sense of personal importance, and the doctrine I had expounded was neither palatable nor intelligible to such a man.

It is difficult to understand the limitations put upon patriotic surrender by men several of whom had endured in that war sacrifices much more irreparable and poignant than those they were called upon to make in respect of their lands. But such is human nature. The noble and the petty dwell in the same habitation. They never meet—are not on speaking terms. But they take their turn in running the same soul. When in charge, each of them dominates it to the complete exclusion of the other. The conduct of a man depends on which motive is on the bridge at a given time.

Sir Arthur Lee (who had now become Lord Lee of Fareham) felt so keenly the blow given to his plans by the rebellious Peers that he resigned his post of Director-General of the Department, rather than share responsibility for abandoning the new programme he had drawn up for 1919. I accepted this resignation with sincere regret, not only because I entirely approved of the Lee programme, but because I appreciated the rare ability and the drive with which Sir Arthur Lee had served his country over both Munitions and Food production. The success he had already achieved was the best answer to the apprehensions he now felt. He had helped to carry us through the danger zone.

A small amount of grass-land was broken up for the harvest of 1919, despite the absence of compulsory powers; but the corn area fell by 488,000 acres, thus verifying the forecast of the Food Production Department, that half a million acres would fall out of corn production unless an equivalent area of new ground were brought under the plough. But the Department had done its work with surprising efficiency, and had enabled us to carry on through the most critical moments of the War until we reached victory. Without the extra millions of tons of home-grown food which it secured, the nation would have gone hungry in 1918. It would certainly have been compelled to tighten its belt several holes. The only alternative would have been a peace of failure, preceded or followed by revolution.

Before concluding this account of our Food Production Campaign, I must make special reference to one very important branch of it— important not merely for its material, but perhaps even more for its moral achievements. This was the allotment campaign.

If labour in the countryside was scarce, there was great potential capacity in the spare time of the town workers—those in black coats and those in corduroy trousers alike. They could not get out to help on the farms, but round every town there spreads a devastated area of vacant building plots and other waste land which these men and their families could reach in their leisure hours and during their weekly half-days. Quite early we recognised the possibilities of war time allotments, and even in the first year of the War there was a rapid growth of the movement.

So promising was this development, that towards the end of 1916 Lord Crawford decided to press forward a further extension by the use of his powers under the Defence of the Realm Acts. On 5th December, 1916, a Regulation was issued empowering the Board of Agriculture to requisition any land for cultivation, and to delegate its powers in this respect to local authorities. On 8th December, the day after I took office as Prime Minister, I authorised the Board to issue the Cultivation of Lands Order, 1916, which empowered urban local authorities to take possession of unoccupied land for the purpose of forming allotments, without previously getting the consent of the owner; to set up allotments on common land with the consent of the Board; and to set them up on any occupied land subject to the consent of owner and occupier.

This Order opened the way for a further great allotment advance. Under it, commons, heaths and vacant building plots were commandeered. Hampstead Heath was ploughed up and planted with potatoes. Unsightly wastes were transfigured by fertility, and city dwellers by hundreds of thousands re-discovered the thrill and wonder of making things grow. A new fraternity made itself felt among these amateur cultivators from classes once widely sundered, who found themselves neighbours in the allotment field. There was a kind of brotherhood of the big potato. On his suburban railway platform the bank manager would produce with pride a monstrous tuber, " grown on my allotment!" and challenge his fellow-passengers to show its rival.

No rent was payable by the authorities to owners of unoccupied or common land, and allotment holders were only required to pay such rent as would recoup the cost of providing and preparing the plots. The authorities were empowered to carry out such preparation, and also to supply seeds, manures and implements at cost price, thus simplifying for would-be pilgrims the unfamiliar road back to the land.

Returns collected from 1,161 towns showed that during 1917 there were provided by urban authorities some 19,812 acres of ground, let in 273,822 plots, for which there were 301,359 applicants. The movement was still further extended in 1918, and it was estimated by the Horticultural Division that in that year there existed in the whole country about 1,400,000 allotments, of which 830,000 had come into existence since the outbreak of the War. Some 400,00 of these had been provided since 1916 by local authorities, equipped with the powers given them by the Lands Cultivation Order. The overwhelming majority of these allotments were being worked by urban dwellers; so that this movement, while it contributed perhaps little to the marketed stocks of food-stuffs, had at least the result of bringing scores of thousands of acres of waste land into production, of harnessing the latent horticultural abilities of townsmen to the task of food-growing, and of ensuring a supply of potatoes and fresh vegetables for nearly one and a half million households.

2. RATIONING

The problem of maintaining a sufficient food supply was by no means confined to the task of increasing the home output. At its best —and this best was only reached in the last year of the War—our home production covered only a part of our consumption, and the remainder had to be provided by foreign purchase and importation. Our shipping was shrinking, and the demands of our Allies were increasing, and it became essential for us to exercise a strict supervision over our stocks, and take drastic steps to ration their distribution, so as to ensure that if few enjoyed abundance, none should go hungry.

The policy of food control and rationing was highly uncongenial to our national temper, and had to be developed carefully and cautiously. Probably Mr. Runciman voiced the natural instinctive attitude of most people to the idea when, speaking in a debate on food prices in the House of Commons on 17th October, 1916, he declared : —

". . . The one thing that we ought to avoid in this country is, from any cause whatever, to put ourselves into the position of a blockaded people. Bread tickets, meat coupons, all these artificial arrangements are harmful, and they are harmful to those who have the least with which to buy. . . . We want to avoid any rationing of our people in food."

This was all very well, but if there was only a limited supply, something had to be done to make it go round. Mr. Runciman himself was soon forced by the intensified submarine attacks to take a different view. On 15th and 16th November, 1916, there was another debate in the House on Food Prices and Supplies. Two days previously the War Committee had agreed in principle with the proposal which I had repeatedly urged on them, that a Food Controller should be appointed with drastic powers to deal with the production, supply and price of food-stuffs.* Mr. Runciman accordingly outlined in the course of the Debate the intention of the Government to appoint a Food Controller, and the additional powers it proposed to acquire to enforce economies, and to control manufacture, distribution and sale of food. " If it becomes necessary for us to embark on food tickets," he said, " obviously we must have the power given to us to do it without long and protracted discussion. Directly the need becomes apparent, power ought to be given to us to act." He instanced the working of the Ministry of Munitions as an example of

* See Chapter XXXIII, pp. 577-78.

what could be done in the way of efficient Government control of industry by means of securing the co-operation of able business men, and as some reassurance to those who might share his fear and dislike of systems of control.

On 17th November, 1916, a series of Regulations for the control of food supplies was published. The Board of Trade was authorised to make orders for imposing the most drastic restrictions in respect of food consumption.

Penalties were laid down for resistance to orders of the Board of Trade made under these regulations.

Next day the Board of Trade made two orders, fixing maximum prices for milk and laying down the percentages of flour that must be milled from different qualities of wheat. The Board also made an order prohibiting the use of wheat for brewing, since on account of a shortage of barley, brewers were buying wheat in its place. But any systematic exercise of the further powers acquired by the Government through these regulations was possible only when the Food Controller had been appointed. As I have already shown, that appointment was made when the new Government was formed in December, 1916.

As soon as Lord Devonport, the new Food Controller, took office, he appointed a Committee to study the question of rationing, under the chairmanship of Mr. (now Sir Alfred) Butt, to whose intelligent handling of this troublesome duty we owe a good deal. In three weeks' time this Committee prepared a detailed plan for rationing the food of the nation. It was practically the scheme that was put into operation later on by Lord Rhondda. It was drawn up on the assumption that sooner or later rationing might have to be made compulsory.

For the time being, the Cabinet considered it necessary to hold the scheme in reserve. We recognised the strength of the popular prejudice against compulsory rationing, and decided to approach it —as had previously been done with compulsory service—along the line of first exhausting the possibilities of voluntary control. As a matter of fact, the representatives of Labour in the Government warned us emphatically that the workers would not at that time submit to a compulsory rationing system, and we properly gave due weight to this expert advice.

But detailed rationing of the ultimate consumer was by no means the only way in which control could be exercised. On 14th December, 1916, Lord Devonport stated in the House of Lords that he would take steps, not only to maintain our food supplies, but to ensure that they should be fairly distributed, and with this end in view, would begin by finding out from statistical returns what stocks there were available, with a view to their fair distribution. This he proceeded to do without delay. Meantime, in mid-December, an order was issued through the Board of Trade, which limited meals in clubs, hotels, and other public eating places, to three courses between 6 p.m. and 9.30 p.m. and to two courses at other times, and fixed maximum prices for meals served to soldiers in all licensed premises in London.

On 11th January, 1917, the Food Controller issued six Orders—the first batch of a long series of such Orders issued from time to time in the course of the next two years. To illustrate the nature of the restrictions that were imposed, the purport of some of these Orders may be summarised as follows: —

> *Wheat:* Its use for any other purpose than for seed or flour-milling was prohibited. Millers were required to add to the percentage of flour milled from wheat a further five to ten per cent. obtained either from the offals or from the addition of barley, maize, rice or oat flour. The feeding of game with any grain or grain products required for food or feeding-stuffs was prohibited.
>
> *Sweets, Chocolate and Pastry:* Expensive sweets were forbidden. No manufacturer was to make more than 50 per cent. of the sweet-meats he had made in 1915. Sugar and chocolate coverings of pastries and cakes were forbidden. The use of winter milk in the manufacture of chocolate was prohibited.

At the beginning of February, Lord Devonport issued an appeal for the adoption of voluntary rationing. He stated that compulsory rationing would be avoided as far and for as long as possible, and for the time being he urged the public to limit their purchases of staple foods as follows: Bread, 4 lb. (or, for bread making, its equivalent of 3 lb. of flour) per head per week; meat, 2½ lb.; sugar, ¾ lb. He pointed out that only by such frugality could sufficient be available for all, and ample supplies for our soldiers and sailors.

The Germans unwittingly came to our aid in this appeal by publishing in America a statement that Great Britain had only 30 days' supply of food-stuffs. We promptly sent a contradiction to our Ambassador in the States, but decided not to publish denials at home, since it was important that our people should economise, and the Germans were helping on the good work.

On 3rd February, 1917, I addressed a public meeting at Carnarvon upon the nation's task in the War. In the course of my speech I took advantage of the occasion to add my appeal to that of Lord Devonport for economy in food. I said: —

> " What is the next appeal? It is to the housewife. I want her to read what the Food Controller has got in the papers to-day as to what each of us is to have next week to eat—(laughter)—the national menu. It does not matter how insistent either the husband or the children may be; show them this regulation and say,

No more.   You have had 2½ lb. and not another ounce more! (laughter).   He has made a voluntary appeal, and for a very good reason.   New organisation means energy and labour, and we need them all.   If you had a compulsory system you would need a new organisation, but we want the nation itself to do things.   It would be better for the nation.   The Government has so much to do that really we want the nation to join the Government.   Every house-keeper we want to become a member of the Government, to administer that part of the King's Dominions which is in her immediate sphere.   Let them govern it for the King, and carry out the King's regulations.   There are eight millions of householders. Let them have, if you will, eight million governments, so that each helps to win the War.   That is the appeal I make for the Food Controller.   It all bears on the submarine menace.   Saving of food means the saving of tonnage, and saving tonnage is the very life of the nation at the present moment."

The country took up with a good deal of fine enthusiasm the appeal to them for a voluntary restriction of their use of food. Within a few days Lord Devonport had the gratification of receiving a call from Sir Derek Keppel, who came to tell him on the King's behalf that it was being strictly observed by every member of the Royal Household.

But the growing submarine menace made inroads upon our importing capacity which rapidly threatened to outrun the limit of the economies which could be achieved on a voluntary basis, and in March and April, 1917, a number of compulsory restrictions were imposed on the distribution and sale of foodstuffs.   Bread could not be sold till it was 12 hours old.   Compulsory potato rations were fixed for hotels, clubs and restaurants, and a meatless day was compulsory for them.   Manufacture for sale of light pastries, muffins, crumpets and tea-cakes was prohibited.   The principal flour mills were taken over by the Food Controller, and measures of control imposed in respect of rice, peas, beans and pulse.   An Order was issued prohibiting food hoarding, and drastic action threatened against any individuals who continued to consume more than their proper ration.

Germany was at this time furnishing an illustration of the immense importance of the Cabinet's policy of firmly controlling the supply of food.   In the autumn of 1916 the German Government had over-estimated the yield of its harvest, and did not find out its mistake till February, 1917, when it also discovered that the civilian population had, in fact, been consuming more food than was allotted to them. In a panic the Government drastically cut down the supplies for the towns, with the result that in a few weeks the morale of their urban populations was badly shaken, and their war fervour was being replaced by cries for peace at any price.   Only by drawing on the reserves that had been set aside for feeding the Army did the German Government avert a collapse in the early summer of 1917. How great were the risks they took in cutting down the Army supplies they realised in 1918. For our part, while we maintained our civilian food supply at a sufficient if frugal limit, we resolved even at the worst moment of our food crisis not to reduce the ration of our fighting men. It was never cut down by a single ounce, nor was its quality allowed to deteriorate, to the end of the War, by a single protein, calory or vitamin. But that was a policy we could never have carried through had it not been for our campaign of increased production and stern rationing at home.

By May, 1917, a far-reaching system of control over supplies had been instituted. The rates of distribution and consumption of food had been fixed, though in the main the observance of the limits was left on a voluntary basis. At the end of the month, Lord Devonport found himelf unable to continue his work as Food Controller, owing to a serious breakdown in health. Under imperative orders from his doctor he tendered his resignation. I very regretfully accepted it. He was replaced at the Food Ministry by Lord Rhondda.

Among the wartime measures with which Lord Devonport was associated during his term as Food Controller was the further restriction of liquor. The matter was raised by him in a memorandum to the War Cabinet on 12th January, 1917, in which he urged that a 50 per cent. cut in brewing would preserve home-grown barley for food purposes and set free tonnage used for imported brewing materials. With his memorandum was considered one from the Central Control (Liquor Traffic) Board, which reported the remarkable success which had attended the measures so far taken to restrict and control the sale of alcohol, and urged still further measures, including State Purchase.

The War Cabinet considered these suggestions, but decided that the question of State Purchase should be deferred until other more urgent measures had been settled. The Cabinet on 23rd January, decided that for the time being brewing should be restricted to 60 per cent. of the 1915 output, and that the release of wines and spirits from bond should be cut down proportionately. After enough grain had been malted to supply the brewers for their restricted output, the Food Controller was empowered to stop further malting. A public announcement of this decision was made on 24th January by the Food Controller.

As regards the further developments of this question of liquor restriction, it may be added that on 16th February we decided to make a further reduction of 30 per cent. in the figure of beer permitted under the Output of Beer Restriction Act. The result of this would be that whereas before the War there were about 35,000,000 standard barrels brewed annually, now there would be about

2c*

10,000,000 barrels. On 21st February the Home Secretary was asked to set up a Committee on which the brewers should be represented, to enquire into the position created by these restrictions, and report to the Cabinet.

The Committee's report, which came before the Cabinet on 22nd March, was in favour of State Purchase, although there were difficulties about estimating the price, owing to the complication introduced by the restrictions; and licensed victuallers were not in favour of purchase, except in Ireland. After extended private discussions with leaders of the Trade, we decided on 31st May in favour of assuming Government control over the liquor trade, with a view to probable State Purchase after the War. Committees were set up to examine the situation in England and Wales, Scotland, and Ireland, and report on the terms on which control should be acquired.

But alcohol is a refractory citizen, and as he has a multitude of friends everywhere he soon made trouble. With the arrival of summer weather, widespread discontent began to show itself in munition centres and among landworkers at the scarcity of beer and its high price. It was decided to meet this by brewing light beer, and in place of imposing immediate Government control we arranged on 21st June, 1917, to permit the brewing of $33\frac{1}{3}$ per cent. more beer for the next three months, on condition that its alcoholic strength was reduced, and its price correspondingly modified.

This increase in the amount to be brewed was later made permanent, but subject to restrictions on its specific gravity, and to conditions as to a proportion being placed at the Food Controller's disposal for distribution to munition areas, and to agricultural districts in harvest time. Ultimately, in March, 1918, it was decided that all the beer brewed in Great Britain should be of a specific gravity not exceeding 1030°.

The effect of our successive modifications of the brewing programme can be summarised as follows. The output of beer, calculated in terms of standard barrels, was: —

> In 1913-14, 36,000,000 standard barrels;
> in 1915-16, 30,000,000   „   „   ;
> in 1916-17, 26,000,000   „   „   ;
> in 1917 to the end of the War 12,500,000
>   standard barrels per annum.

Although the innocuous but insipid character of this light beer was the source of a good deal of grumbling at the time, it unquestionably helped to wean millions of the workers of Britain from their pre-War proclivity to unduly heavy drinks. The old habit of stupefaction by strong ales, which led to many being not perhaps drunk, but fuddled, was permanently broken. So was the habit of men getting drunk on Saturday nights which was so prevalent amongst a section of the wage earners before the War. This is one legacy of good from the wartime work of Food Control.

The system of food control which had been inaugurated by Lord Devonport was continued and extended by Lord Rhondda. One of the first decisions of the new Controller was to set up a Costing Department to examine the question of food costs with a view to fixing maximum prices, and on 29th June, 1917, an Order in Council was published under D.O.R.A., giving the Food Controller full powers of requisitioning food and fixing prices. It was necessary to take some strong action of this kind, because by June, 1917, the Board of Trade figures showed that the retail food prices had now risen 102 per cent. above their level in July, 1914, whereas the general cost of living index, including food, had risen only 70 to 75 per cent.

The War Cabinet considered this matter further on 19th July, 1917. The steadily mounting prices for food were producing a good deal of industrial unrest which was interfering with the output of war material. Workers were striking to obtain higher wages with which to meet the higher costs of living. We felt that for the vigorous prosecution of the War a contented working class was indispensable, and we took note of the fact that in France bread was being supplied to the people at rates corresponding to an eightpenny quartern loaf. As wheat and flour were now under full control, we decided to fix the price of bread at ninepence per quartern loaf. This would involve the Treasury in a loss of £33 million. The French were spending £37 million in subsidising their loaf. We also authorised the Food Controller to fix prices for meat, varying with the customs of the different localities.

The decisions reached were announced by Lord Rhondda in the House of Lords on 26th July. He explained that his purpose was to fix the prices of these articles of prime necessity over the supply of which he could obtain effective control at every stage from the producer down to the retailer. He would use every effort to check speculation and eliminate needless middle-men. The work of the Food Ministry would be as far as possible decentralised, and important functions committed to the Local Authorities. Each would be asked to appoint a Food Control Committee, the duties of which would be to enforce the Food Controller's orders; to register the retailers of the various food-stuffs; to recommend variations in the scale of retail food prices; to maintain and extend the economy campaign; and to administer the new scheme of sugar distribution, which would be made by means of sugar cards. He also described the arrangements whereby bread would be subsidised and its price fixed.

In the first week in August, Lord Rhondda circularised the Local

Authorities, laying before them his scheme of food control. The principles of the policy were threefold: to conserve supplies; to ensure that rich and poor shared alike; and to keep down prices. He recommended central kitchens as a means of economising food and fuel. He set out the system of sugar cards that was to be inaugurated, and he notified the authorities of his intention to fix a general scale of prices for all important food-stuffs. Towards the end of August the wholesale and retail prices of meat were fixed by order. On 10th August, the appointment of six Food Commissioners was announced; four for England and Wales; two for Scotland. The Order setting up the Food Control Committees came out in the course of the month.

Thus was set up the machinery which functioned during the remainder of the War to secure the fair distribution and economical use of our limited supplies of food. Bearing in mind that it was a new and inexperienced *ad hoc* machinery, set up to carry through an unprecedented task; that those who had to work it in every town and country district were men already overburdened with duties, and short-handed—the pick of our manhood having already withdrawn to serve their country overseas, and the best brains at home being already requisitioned for munitions or other forms of Government service; and remembering, too, that they were called on to restrict supplies of food, the most vitally indispensable of all commodities, which people will often sacrifice every scruple to obtain for themselves or those who are dependent on their care; considering these facts, it would be hard to praise too highly the fine spirit with which their task was faced, and the good average of efficiency with which it was carried out. We had set up the sternest but the fairest and most effective system of food production and control in any of the belligerent countries. The fact that it was administered with relentless impartiality made it austerely acceptable to all grades of society.

It is hardly necessary to linger long over the further progress of food restriction. In September, orders came into force, fixing the maximum wholesale and retail prices for meat, butter, flour and potatoes, and also for milk; and also wholesale prices for cheese. In November, a new scale of voluntary rations was announced, applying to meat, bread and all other cereals, butter, margarine, lard, fats and oils. Lord Rhondda was able to report that the steep upward motion of food prices had been checked, and that in some cases they had even been reduced. Meat prices had fallen 15 to 20 per cent. in the last few months.

In December, 1917, the growth of food queues outside the shops in London and some provincial centres led to a further Order by the Food Controller to ensure fair distribution and thus to prevent queues. Under the Order, local Food Committees could prohibit the sale of any specified food article except by a licensed or registered retailer; require him only to sell it to customers registered with him for the purpose, and only in quantities within limits laid down by the Committees. And they further had power to prevent any one retailer from taking more registered customers than he could conveniently serve without driving them into queues; to transfer supplies from one retailer to another; and to prescribe manner and time of sale.

With 1st January, 1918, a compulsory meatless day was enforced, and on one day a week no meat, cooked or uncooked, might be sold. Organised Labour, which had hitherto been opposed to compulsory rationing, declared itself at the end of December, 1917, in favour of it as an alternative to food queues, and in January, Mr. Clynes, the Parliamentary Secretary to the Food Ministry, announced that extensive rationing would before long be put into force. A scheme for this had been fully worked out months before by Sir Alfred Butt and a special Rationing Committee under Lord Devonport, before the latter resigned from the Food Ministry. On 25th February, 1918, a system of rationing meat, butter and margarine was put into force in London and the Home Counties, and early in April the rationing of meat was extended to the whole country. In July a new system of ration books was introduced. By this time the foods subject to compulsory rationing were sugar, butter, margarine, meat of all kinds, and lard. Tea was also subject to a system of restriction, and before long, jam and marmalade were added to the list of rationed articles.

So far as the vast bulk of the population was concerned, this rationing system, troublesome though in some respects it was to them, ensured a regular and sufficient food supply; and it made it possible for those in charge to calculate with some precision how best they could make the stocks of available food-stuffs go round equitably. When meat was slightly more plentiful, the ration could be raised. When it grew scarcer, the amount purchasable with each meat coupon was cut down. The steady improvement in our national health figures during and after the War, as compared with pre-War returns, shows that compulsory temperance in eating was in general more beneficial than harmful in its effects. Although there was a degree of scarcity, we were never faced with famine or actual privation. Credit is due to our people for the loyal manner in which they submitted themselves to these strange and unwelcome restrictions. Without general goodwill it would have been impossible to make the regulations effective. That goodwill did not fail. It was not impeded but helped by a few prosecutions for breach of the regulations, for the cases selected demonstrated that the Food Controller was no respecter of persons and that the law was enforced impartially for rich and poor alike.

3. FEEDING OUR ALLIES

The task of Food Control was complicated by the fact that, as the principal shipping Power on the Allied side, we had to take thought not only for ourselves, but also for our Allies. Food cargoes which we urgently needed for our own population we had from time to time to divert to meet the needs of France and Italy, and to save their Governments from having to face dangerous discontent. While this food-importing island not only maintained but increased its home-grown food supplies during the War, France, a food-producing country, much more thinly populated, had to call more and more insistently for outside help. Some of its most fertile provinces were in enemy hands, and as the range and intensity of bombardment lengthened the area of cultivation diminished. Moreover, as nearly half the French Army was drawn from the rural areas, the drain on the man-power of France was telling seriously on the productiveness of the soil.

Soon after America entered the War, Mr. Hoover, who had been in charge of the work of Belgian Relief and had been appointed Food Controller in the U.S.A., had an interview with Lord Robert Cecil and handed him a memorandum, proposing that since all the Allies were seeking to buy food in the States, it would be desirable for them to set up an International Board to co-ordinate their demands, ascertain the available supplies, and allocate them among the Allied countries. He pointed out that " the general outlook from now on is that the available supplies and shipping will be a diminishing, rather than an increasing, quantity; that, in conse-quence, control will need to be exercised in the allocation of these supplies among the Allies." He further pointed out that " the important producing centres having surpluses for export are, with the exception of the Argentine, now under Allied control, and are, therefore, now possible of exclusive distribution and use by the Allies." Coming to the position in America he says: " From a strictly American point of view, the centralisation of buying of any particular staple in one set of hands will promote the regulation of prices, and a knowledge of the amount of food-stuffs required by the Allies will promote any action which may be taken by the American Govern-ment with a view to control of prices, stimulation of production, reduction of consumption of special staples, or the substitution of other American products for them so as to set free such staples for export. It is my impression that the large rise in prices during the last few months has been due in considerable measure to the rivalry of different Allied organisations in the American markets."

The matter was considered at a meeting of the War Cabinet on 18th April, 1917, which Mr. Hoover was invited to attend. He is the only President of the U.S.A. who has taken part in the proceedings of a British Cabinet. We decided: —

(a) To approve the principle of an International Food Board, and we asked Lord Milner first to confer with the Secretary of

State for the Colonies on the subject of the representation of the Dominions.

(b) That Lord Robert Cecil should interview the American Ambassador with the object of securing the adhesion of the United States to the project, and, through the United States, that of France and Italy.

Agreement of the other Allies to this proposal was not speedily obtained, but eventually, on 27th August, 1917, an Inter-Allied Meat and Fats Executive was set up in London to deal with bacon and hams, lard, butter, cheese and meat—including preserved meat. The commission carried on its work in close co-operation with Mr. Hoover, and evolved a scheme by which the requirements of the Allies were purchased on the same basis as those of the United States Army and Navy.

This Commission did not touch the purchase of wheat, which was handled in the United States by the Wheat Export Co., Inc., as agents for the Royal Commission on Wheat Supplies. This Commission worked in with the Wheat Executive, an International body that we had arranged to set up in London to serve the interests of Britain, France and Italy. All wheat supplies for the Allies were procured, so far as American purchases were concerned, through this channel.

On 25th October, 1917, the matter of our Allies' demands for more wheat imports came up before the War Cabinet. Lord Milner reported that M. Clémentel, the French Minister of Commerce, who was in London, was demanding bigger imports of corn into France, and pressing for the adoption of an arrangement which would lay down agreed minimum requirements for the United Kingdom, France and Italy respectively. I had similarly to report that the Italian Ambassador had called on me that morning and handed me an urgent request from Italy in respect of food. He had given me a very bad account, from his personal experience during a recent visit to Italy, of the food situation there.

Members of the War Council pointed out that even if the French harvest was below the normal, there must still be plenty of food in that country. There was no system of distribution in France comparable in its security or imperturbability to that which had been set up and was being applied in this country. The French demands amounted to a request that we should supply their deficiencies because the French Government was too weak to compel its peasantry to stop hoarding. Before long there would no doubt be real need in France, which we should have to help, because the French Government had not established any satisfactory system of control or limitation of consumption which would result in effective economies, even to the same extent as the economies which we were effecting voluntarily in this country. We decided that a careful examination of the facts must be first made before the terms of any pooling of food resources could be determined.

Five days later, on 30th October, 1917, Mr. Balfour reported to the War Cabinet that preliminary investigation showed the food situation in Italy to be really serious. The collapse of Caporetto had taken place while our previous discussion had been in progress, and though we were now arranging for strong military aid to Italy, it would be of little use if through a food shortage her population refused to go on with the War. As to France, M. Clémentel had announced his intention of going back to France to hand in his resignation if nothing satisfactory were settled by the end of the week.

The difficulty was of course primarily one of tonnage. There were so many urgent demands upon our shipping, including demands by our Allies for munitions and coal, that it was a question of how we could maintain our other vitally important commitments in the teeth of the growing shipping shortage, and at the same time increase food imports for the benefit of our Allies. The whole matter hinged on the general military policy, and we considered that we could come to no decision till this, and the general shipping situation in the light of it, had been reviewed.

Eventually we decided that: —

(a) For the next two months certain wheat ships should be diverted from the United Kingdom to France and Italy, these Governments being informed by the Secretary of State for Foreign Affairs of our action in the matter.

(b) The President of the Board of Trade and the Shipping Controller should prepare a statement as to the shipping situation generally and its adequacy to meet the demands of the Allies.

In order to reassure M. Clémentel, an agreement was entered into whereby we expressed our readiness to view the responsibility for the food supplies of France and Italy as being a common charge on all the Allies, including the United States. At the War Cabinet meeting of 6th November, Lord Robert Cecil stressed the importance of this step, saying that Italian fear of food and coal shortage had been used by German propaganda as one means of helping to create the recent debacle of Caporetto. It was pointed out that under this agreement we had decided that the carriage of the food for the Allies, as well as the purchase, should be for joint account. Sir Joseph Maclay said that if we must provide a further 2,000,000 tons of shipping space in 1918 to carry cereals to France and Italy, we must cut our own requirements down by this additional amount. Already he was estimating a cut of 6,000,000 tons in our 1918 imports, and this fresh demand would involve a total cut of over 8,000,000 tons of imports.

We appointed a Committee to go into the question of the imports to be sacrificed in this connection. The task was not made any more welcome by the information laid before the War Cabinet on 14th November, that the French Government had refrained from requisitioning all their available tonnage, and were allowing part of it to be used still for private profit. It also came to our knowledge on the same day that the French had raised an additional 800,000 tons of coal from their collieries in the course of the year, but had omitted to inform us of the fact.

Meantime we were being urged to divert to Italy as many as possible of the cargoes of oats now on their way to us from America, to save the Italian cavalry from being immobilised. The cavalry obsession had crossed the Alps. No General could contemplate the possibility of a war which did not furnish at least one picture of a cavalry charge. The stocks of oats for our own army transports in France were at the time very low, but I recognised that every effort must be made at this critical moment to keep Italy contented, and we accordingly arranged to send to Italy the oats we had purchased from the United States for our own army, and replenish our own supplies in France from such stocks as were available in Great Britain and in Ireland.

There can be little question that our Continental Allies failed to carry out anything in the way of food control at all comparable with the firmly organised measures we adopted in this country. At the War Cabinet for 14th February, 1918, the Secretary of State for Foreign Affairs stated that the French Ambassador had expressed serious misgivings in regard to the British food supply, and doubted whether the British people would be content with the proposed scale of rations. The French had tried the plan of limiting prices, and it had failed completely, with the result that another system had had to be adopted.

On 24th April, 1918, we had to consider an urgent appeal from Italy for more wheat. The situation was that the arrivals of wheat in each of the Allied countries were short of the programme in approximately the same proportion, but that the difference between the French and ourselves on the one hand, and Italy on the other, was that we had begun the year with several weeks' supply in reserve, and that the French had now been obliged to admit that they also had had several, though not quite as many, weeks' stock in reserve. The Italians, on the other hand, had no reserve and had actually impinged on the new harvest before the new cereal year had commenced. They had just enough, if no exceptional losses of wheat in transit, such as had sometimes taken place, occurred.

We decided to send them a special allotment of an extra 25,000 tons of wheat.

In the case of France there is, of course, no doubt that the deadly drain of the War upon its man-power left it very short-handed for the tilling of its fields. In August, 1918, the French went to the length of sending over to Ireland to recruit Irish labourers for work on the land. Yet bearing in mind that nearly half the population of France, and two-thirds that of Italy, obtained their livelihood on the land, as compared with less than a tenth of the population in this country, and that their populations were very much smaller in relation to their agricultural acreage, it is remarkable that we had for the last year of the War to undertake the responsibility of feeding them both. The French and the Italians had not taken the measures adopted here to increase their mechanical powers and their stocks of fertilisers.

Beyond any question, our food organisation both for increasing the yield of our own soil, and for limiting and economically distributing to our own people the available food-stuffs, was superior to that set up by any of the combatant countries.

By the combined measures we took to increase the home production of food whilst restricting consumption beyond the limit of strict necessity, we reached the end of the War without enduring the privations that broke the spirit of other equally brave nations engaged in the struggle. We were able not only to feed ourselves but to help in conveying food for our Allies. The last and most trying year of the War we raised from our own soil more cereals than in the years before the War. If the failure to organise and administer to the best advantage the food resources of Russia and the Central Empires led to their defeat, it will be conceded that the handling of the food problem in this country contributed in no small measure to the attainment of ultimate victory by the Allies. It would be hard to overstate the service rendered by our wartime Ministry of Food, and those who gave—many of them without pay—their services to it, in organising from this side the victory of the Allies.

CHAPTER XLV

A SYSTEM OF NATIONAL SERVICE

In war the ultimate problem is man-power. It was in the last resort the number, calibre, equipment and training of the men that made or worked the machinery of war or sustained the life of the nation during the War, that would decide whether we could endure to the end where victory awaits. It is not necessarily the strongest nation that wins, but the one that has made the best use of its strength.

By the end of the third campaign, man-power in all the countries engaged in the struggle was reaching the point of exhaustion. Germany had made a better use of machinery, engineering skill and intelligent training to save her men than any other nation in the fight. In spite, therefore, of the enormous front on which her armies fought, and the hundreds of battles in which they had been engaged, West, East and South-East, her casualties were lower in proportion to the numbers of her fighting men than those of any other army on either side. The sanguinary attack on Verdun was planned on the principle that the machine was to take the leading part in crushing the defence. The result was that although it was a German offensive against Frenchmen protected by tremendous forts, the defenders lost more men than the assailants. Nevertheless, the German losses were already heavy, and Germany was experiencing a difficulty in filling up gaps in her armies, whilst at the same time meeting the demands for increased equipment on land and sea and for making up the diminishing supplies of food at home. Austria had suffered heavily, not merely from casualties necessarily incurred in fighting so many great battles against Russians, Italians, Serbians, and Roumanians, but even more from the readiness with which her Slavonic troops surrendered on the Russian Front, sometimes by thousands, often by tens of thousands, and in at least one battle by hundreds of thousands. In France and Britain the profligate expenditure of young life in ill-conceived offensives—and, in Russia, in muddle and corruption—had left the belligerents short of the necessary reserves to keep up the prodigious wastage. At this date the warring nations had lost by death or crippling wounds 10,000,000 men in the flower of their strength. The number of prisoners of war ran into millions. Our great volunteer army was not ready for the fighting before 1916.   Our casualties were not therefore comparable to those suffered by France or Germany; but by the end of that year our losses were already over 1,000,000.   The spring offensive had added 200,000 to the melancholy pyre.   As French man-power was on the wane, the burden of the struggle was falling more and more upon us.   At sea the fight was almost entirely ours, and its strain was increasing.   On land the struggle in the West was left gradually to our Army.   In the Far East it was entirely ours.   This meant more and more men for the fighting lines.   But it also meant that the demands behind the lines for supplies to the Army and Navy were rapidly increasing everywhere.   The fulfilment of these requirements involved the employment of more men. The Army and Navy wanted more men—but so did the munition works, to turn out guns, tanks, ammunition, and anti-submarine appliances.   The shipyards had to treble their output in merchant ships and in naval craft and in repair of both, otherwise our sea transport would break down under the exceptional strain of incessant active service, we should lose the command of the sea and the Allies might be starved into surrender.   The Allies were clamouring for more coal: the coal mines demanded more men to increase output. The fields needed more men to increase essential food commodities, so as to satisfy the requirements which hitherto had been supplied from across the seas.   All this complication of urgent demands resolved itself into a problem of making the best use of a reserve of man-power which was not equal to the full need, even with the most efficient and scientific distribution.   And there were limits to the power of any Government to place the manhood of the nation to the best advantage.

The deep-rooted tradition of personal liberty which has long held sway in Britain made it a matter of the greatest difficulty for the Government to secure general consent for the exercise of its common-law right to call on all its citizens to carry out such tasks as it might lay on them for the national security.   You cannot move human beings about with the ease and passive acquiescence of pawns on a chess board.   There is a limit where the most complex and implacable human emotions offer resistance to the demands made on the human will for departure from wont and habit.   Patriotism has eccentric and incalculable limitations in different countries.   It is often the result of some ancient conflict which has left traditional resistance in the very fibre of a nation's mind, just as in deep ploughing you come against boulders deposited in the soil during the glacial period.   In France, where for generations they have been accustomed to being conscripted for military service, no difficulties were encountered in calling up every able-bodied man for the Army.   On the other hand, Governments there shrank from raising money for war purposes by new imposts with which the French citizen was not familiar, and although the young men of France and Germany entered readily at the call into the stern bondage of army discipline in war, and were prepared to face death at an order given to them, no Government would dare enforce the same discipline at the works where war material was produced. The traditions of the workshop were not those of the army.

I have previously described how slowly and unwillingly a system of compulsion for military service was adopted in this country. But military service, while the most spectacular and heroic method of serving the country, was by no means the exclusively important one. Indeed, throughout the War there were at all times more of the male population of Great Britain (as of all other belligerents) employed at home on Government work than there were overseas in the expeditionary forces. Apart from munitions of war on land and sea, which included a large building programme and large repairing establishments for the Navy, there were the ordinary demands of a population of 46,000,000. These had to be supplied by what was left of our workers after 8,000,000 had been taken away either for the Army and Navy or for their munitionment and supply. The task of supreme difficulty for the Government was to secure that every man should be used where he would be of greatest value. It was a task never fully carried out; though in the last two years of the War considerable progress was made towards its achievement. As the War developed, as the military and naval demands became greater and man-power decreased through casualties, the problem in all belligerent countries became more and more urgent.

The ideal would have been for the whole population to be conscripted at the very outbreak of the War, and every man posted forthwith in accordance with a wisely thought-out plan to the job where he would be of most service to our war effort. But such a war as that of 1914-18 had never been experienced or foreseen, much less planned for even by the militarist nations of the Continent. As for us, we had relied on our Navy to keep off the invader. Our Army was just a police force for the Empire. Protected by the moat, our whole national temper had been tuned to the organisation and tasks of peace. So our early war efforts were spasmodic and largely incoherent. Men were allowed to go abroad in our fighting forces who were vitally wanted at home, while others who could far better have been spared for the Army, proceeded to regard themselves as indispensable at home. Indispensability was largely a question of individual choice and disposition and not of national interest. The peace-time organisations of industry, both capital and labour, were maintained for lack of any well-planned system to replace them. As the War went on, Government control and direction were slowly extended. Capital suffered a certain measure of conscription through the Excess Profits Duties and the control of profits in establishments making munitions. Industry experienced a direct overruling, through the conversion of many workshops into controlled establishments and the setting up of National Factories. Railways and shipping, the restriction and licensing of imports, and transport gradually passed more and more under Government control. Labour was in some measure placed under compulsion by the setting up of "reserved occupations," the badging of men engaged on necessary Government work, restrictions on transfer from one establishment to another, and the powers held by the Government under the Military Service Acts of taking men for the Army if they were not doing work of sufficient national importance at home. But some of the most important steps were taken only with great difficulty against the tenacious opposition or the immutable habitude of the vested interests of capital and labour. There was no lack of patriotism. But there were endless prejudices, traditions, jealousies and susceptibilities that impeded its quick and full action.

As regards the control of our man-power, our difficulty throughout the War with the representatives of labour centred round the suspicion of profiteering by the proprietors of works engaged on Government contracts, so that the workers in them had not the same feeling of direct and whole-hearted national service that they developed in the Army or Navy. To conscript men for industry seemed to the workers equivalent to forcing them by law to work for the benefit of private capitalists—a proceeding which they would quite rightly have resisted to the uttermost. Yet much of this work was at least as vital to our national safety as was the maintenance at full strength of our fighting forces. For them we could take men almost at will, fixing our own standards of age and physical fitness. For the home front we had to rely still on the voluntary system, reinforced in some measure by the provisions to which I have already alluded.

It was to deal with this very difficult but essential problem that on setting up my Ministry at the end of 1916 I decided to form a new Department of National Service. The War Committee under the previous Government had already, as one of its last acts, approved in principle on 30th November, 1916, the introduction of a system of National Service, leaving the details to be worked out by a Committee, presided over by Mr. Montagu, then Minister of Munitions. The suggestion was that it should apply to all men up to 60 years of age, and possibly also to women. A first draft for a Bill to enact this system was prepared by the Committee, and came before the new War Cabinet on 14th December, 1916. I was away at the time suffering from an attack of influenza. In my absence the War Cabinet shrank from reaching any final decision on this complex and far-reaching subject, but gave a preliminary survey to the question and provisionally decided that: —

(*a*) A Director of National Service should be appointed who should be in charge both of the Military and Civil side of Compulsory National Service.

(*b*) The Civil and the Military sides of the Directorate of National Service should be entirely separate—that is to say, the Director of National Service would have under him a Military Director and a Civil Director, with a clear line of demarcation between them. The object of this proviso is to allay any suspicion that the adoption of Compulsory National Service for Civil purposes would bring the persons affected under military control.

(*c*) The functions of the Ministry of Labour and the Director of National Service will have to be clearly defined at an early date. Mr. Henderson undertook to discuss this question with the new Labour Minister and his colleagues.

(*d*) No announcement should be made in regard to the Director of National Service until the holder of the post has been nominated and the scope of his duties and responsibilities have been defined.

The War Cabinet were of opinion that Mr. E. S. Montagu would be the best man to undertake the duties of Director. We duly offered him this post, but he did not at the time feel prepared to undertake it, and we eventually fell back upon Mr. Neville Chamberlain. He was appointed in a hurry, as I had to announce the appointment in the House of Commons in my speech on the policy of the new Government. I had never seen him, and I accepted his qualifications for the post on the recommendation of those who had heard of his business and municipal experience.

What ensued from the decision of the Cabinet to extend the principle of compulsion to industries during the War illustrates the insuperable difficulties encountered not only here, but in every belligerent country, in applying conscription to workers in factories and workshops.

The discussions of Mr. Henderson with his colleagues in the Labour Party had important consequences, for when we resumed discussion of the matter on 19th December, he reported to us that the antagonism of organised labour to the proposal of industrial conscription was so strong that it would be very difficult to introduce, and might lead to widespread disturbance and disaffection. We had only with the utmost difficulty succeeded in coaxing the skilled workers of the country to accept measures of dilution of labour and relaxation of their Trade Union restrictions. These concessions had been enshrined in bargains ratified by such measures as the Munitions of War Acts, and the late Government had given pledges against industrial conscription as the price. If the organised skilled workers united to oppose compulsion in industry, it would be a mistaken policy to attempt to carry it out, even had it been feasible to do so. National unity alone could pull us through.   By this step we should encounter the hostility of organised masses.   Accordingly the Cabinet agreed that having regard to the feeling of organised labour on the subject of industrial compulsion, and the pledges given by the late Government, and to the volume of preliminary work necessary for the creation of an adequate and efficient machinery, local and central, it would be necessary to proceed, in the first instance, on the lines of voluntary enrolment and transference of labour without a Bill.

We further agreed that, in the statement to be made to the Houses, an assurance should be given that Labour would be associated with any organisation which it was decided to establish under the Director of National Service, and that no time limit should be fixed for the introduction of compulsion, but that the Prime Minister (in the Commons) and Lord Curzon (in the Lords) should make it clear that, if the voluntary effort failed, the Government would ask Parliament to release them from any pledges heretofore given on the subject of industrial compulsion, and to furnish them with adequate powers for rendering their proposals effective.   In the meantime, it would be the duty of the Director to set up for voluntary enrolment and transference, machinery which might hereafter serve the purpose of compulsion, if compulsion became necessary.

The Secretary of State for War wished to have it put on record that, in order to maintain the drafts, not less than 100,000 men fit for general service must be obtained during January, and that in his opinion it would soon become necessary for the Government to introduce an amending Military Service Bill.

At the disposal of the new Ministry was the experience already accumulated by the recruiting machinery, and by the Man-Power Distribution Board, which had for some time been functioning as an agency for keeping track of the available labour in the country, and furnishing workers to the establishments and departments engaged on Government business.   The business of the new Director was to organise as swiftly and as completely as possible a voluntary enrolment of all the available labour in the country, and at the same time to compile a census of the labour requirements of the nation's industries and activities, tabulating these in order of their importance for our war effort; so that on the one hand we might be able to know exactly where to lay our hands on the men needed for the Army, and on the other hand, might be able promptly to replace any taken from urgently important work by other men or women who were surplus or potentially surplus in less important occupations.

Mr. Neville Chamberlain was in short charged with the task of creating machinery capable of controlling and distributing in the most economical and effective manner the whole man-power of the country.   To begin with, the man-power he would actually have at his disposal would, for civil purposes, be only so much of the whole as could be induced to volunteer, though for military purposes his field covered every fit man of military age. But both the previous Cabinet and my own had approved in principle the introduction of compulsory universal national service, and if voluntary enrolment failed, we were prepared to accord Mr. Chamberlain further powers; so that he was required to construct his machinery in such a way that it could function efficiently as an instrument in charge of all the nation's man-power.

The right to conscript for the Army involved an indirect measure of universal compulsion for all fit men of military age for all national purposes. Unless a man were both needed and actually employed on some essential service at home, he was liable to be drafted into the Army or Navy. Everyone, whatever his avocation or station, knew that, and this knowledge was not without its influence on national discipline and efficiency. It was at the back of men's minds ever since the obligation of military service became compulsory, that if they were not fulfilling their duties as citizens in the spheres where they would be of the greatest use to their country, they would be needed in France or elsewhere in the fighting lines, and would have to go if called up.

The decision having been taken to work the National Service scheme, in the first instance, on a voluntary basis, I did what I could to help Mr. Chamberlain to make a good start. On 10th January, 1917, the War Cabinet decided to dissolve the Man-Power Distribution Board, and transfer all its functions and archives to the new Ministry. At the same time we asked the new Director to prepare for our consideration a statement of the operations he contemplated, the measures he believed necessary for securing co-ordination with the various Departments concerned with labour, and the powers he would require for the purpose. Two days later I called a conference at which Lord Milner, Mr. Henderson and myself with the Director of National Service, met the President of the Local Government Board, the President of the Board of Agriculture and the Minister of Labour, to enable Mr. Chamberlain to review with these Ministers the implications of his task, and the manner in which his organisation could best function. As a result of our discussion, he was asked to prepare a memorandum, setting out: —

(a) His proposals with regard to the organisation, central and local, required for obtaining and enrolling National Service Volunteers;

(b) The method contemplated for allocating volunteers to different branches of National Service, including relations with employers and scales of payment, with special regard to the possibility of the same organisation being hereafter required for compulsory purposes;

(c) The measures to be taken for meeting the requirements of the Army in recruits.

Mr. Neville Chamberlain's Memorandum was forthcoming on 19th January, 1917, on which date it was carefully examined by the War Cabinet. It was in two parts, the first dealing with the supply of men to the Army, and the second with the proposed organisation of the Ministry for enrolling the civil population and allocating labour where it was most wanted. To meet the demands of the Army for recruits, his chief proposal was to withdraw exemptions from all fit men up to the age of 22 by a General Order, to which the fewest possible exceptions should be allowed. There would also have to be a further combing-out of those employed in the less essential industries. For the organisation of National Service he set out a scheme of headquarters staff and District Commissioners, and proposed to take over the Labour Exchanges as his instrument for effecting the actual transfer of volunteers to the industries where they were chiefly needed. As regards further powers, he asked for authority to settle all questions relating to the use and transfer of male and female civilian labour, and for the right to issue Orders and Regulations and create the requisite machinery for the work.

The War Cabinet made several modifications in this scheme. We authorised the calling-up of 30,000 men from Agriculture, 20,000 from Mining and 50,000 semi-skilled and un-skilled workers from Munitions, and outside these groups, the calling-up of all young men from 18 to 22 years of age. But the Employment Exchanges should remain under the Minister of Labour, who would place them at the disposal of the Minister of National Service for organising his scheme. We asked Mr. Chamberlain to revise his scheme along the lines we indicated.

On 6th February, 1917, the national appeal for voluntary enrolment of the population under the National Service scheme was launched at a meeting at the Central Hall, Westminster, where Mr. Neville Chamberlain outlined his proposals, and I delivered a speech warmly endorsing them.

Mr. Chamberlain appealed to the whole civilian population between the ages of 18 and 61 to enrol for National Service (with the exception of doctors and ministers of religion, for whose services special arrangements were being made). A separate department for Women's National Service was being set up under the Ministry, with Mrs. H. J. Tennant at its head. War munition volunteers were included in the appeal, though they would not be transferred as a result of their registration to other work. Volunteers would be allocated to the work for which their training best fitted them—as far as possible in their home district. Rates of pay would be those prevailing in the job they undertook, with a minimum of 25s. a week, and a subsistence grant if they had to live away from home.

Mr. Chamberlain pointed out there were practically no men unemployed, so there would have to be a restriction of non-essential trades to provide workers to take the place of men called to the Army from essential trades. He suggested that without absolutely closing down any trades, such economy might be secured by pooling their resources of machinery, labour and materials as would free men from the less essential trades and yet leave them stronger after the War than before.

On 22nd February the Ministry of National Service Bill was introduced into the House of Commons to define the status and duties of the Director, and give him powers of making orders and regulations. It received the Royal Assent on 28th March. The debates on it showed that there was a great deal of anxiety in some quarters lest any system of industrial compulsion should be imposed, and specific pledges were given and incorporated in the Act that compulsion would not be introduced without further Parliamentary sanction.

A considerable publicity scheme was carried out by Mr. Chamberlain to press home his appeal for volunteers. The fullest Governmental support was accorded to him in the hope that his efforts would succeed in placing our man-power problem upon a satisfactory basis, and constructing an efficient and smooth-running organisation to deal with it.

Our hopes were not realised. The Ministry of National Service was, it must be frankly confessed, a great disappointment, especially during the early months of its existence. Labouring under the handicap of the voluntary system by which it was being operated, it failed to achieve the ends for which it was set up; but more serious was the fact that it showed little sign that it would have worked efficiently if it had been granted compulsory powers.

The difficulties with which it was faced were admittedly immense. The fit men of military age still engaged in civilian occupations had either been exempted because they were engaged in work of vital national importance, or on some special exceptional ground. The employers from whom it was proposed to withdraw them fought to the last ditch for their continued exemption, and were most unwilling to consider taking on other less experienced labour in their stead. The Unions to which they belonged similarly opposed their withdrawal, and the further dilution which substitute labour would involve. To provide such substitute labour meant robbing those industries and employments which were deemed to be less vital to our national effort, and if it was a ticklish matter to make such a black list, it was no less difficult to induce the businesses concerned to accept their own repression. And although Mr. Chamberlain had been accorded the co-operation of the employment exchanges, he was not successful in making smooth-working arrangements by which these should carry out the very important task of placing transferred labour in its new employment.

The result was a great deal of muddle and confusion. Stories got about of men who had volunteered for National Service; had been thereupon instructed to throw up their present jobs, and hold themselves at the disposal of the Director; and having done so, found themselves waiting about for weeks, without work or wages. The effect was, of course, to check voluntary enrolment. Meantime the War Office was complaining that it was not getting the men which it had been promised under the scheme. Nothing like the full number of recruits that had been promised from Agriculture, Railways, Mines and Munitions in January were actually forthcoming by the end of May. Nor, on the other hand, was the substitute labour and the assistance from the forces of the Home Defence Army which had been promised to agriculture actually furnished on the agreed scale.

Voluntary enrolment was definitely disappointing. Of those who put down their names, three-fifths were already engaged in work of vital importance, and less than half of the remainder were suitable for employment in the trades for which workers were most needed by the country. Mr. Chamberlain had appealed in the first instance for the enrolment of at least half a million men. After two months, less than a third of this number had been obtained. On 17th April, 1917, Mr. Bridgeman stated in Parliament in reply to a question: —

"Out of 163,161 Volunteers dealt with by the Employment Exchanges up to 6th April (the latest date for which complete figures are available), 93,622 were definitely known to be in trades of primary importance or otherwise not available for various reasons; 26,873 out of the balance of 69,539 were, from experience or physique, *prima facie* suitable for work in trades of primary importance in which there is a considerable demand for male labour; it cannot at present be stated how many of this total of 26,873 are engaged on work of national importance and are free for transfer. Over 16,000 Volunteers have been offered to employers, of whom 2,804 have started work and 11,826 were awaiting replies from employers. In addition, 5,765 were awaiting decision by National Service Sub-Commissioners of protest against transfer."

There is no disguising the unsatisfactory implication of these figures. The net result to date of the setting-up of a big Department at St. Ermin's, and of the appointment of officials all over the country, and of £60,000 spent on publicity, was the placing in employment of less than 3,000 men. There had been, of course, a good deal of useful work inaugurated by this Department, which was later to bear fruit—

in particular, the organisation of women's service by the Women's Branch under Mrs. Tennant, which gave us the W.A.A.C.'s and the Land Girls. But as an instrument for dealing with our man-power problem, for furnishing the needed recruits for the Army and filling their places at home with substitute labour, the new Ministry of National Service was not a success.

The Cabinet was fully alive to this unsatisfactory state of affairs, and several efforts were made to help the new Department to tackle its job, but they were all futile. A vein of self-sufficient obstinacy in the new Minister contributed to the difficulties that baffled all our endeavours.

There was a general feeling amongst all who were set to investigate the cause of the failure of the new Department that it was being run in a narrow spirit of unimaginative officialism and that its limbs were bound in a tangle of red tape which kept it from getting ahead with its job. Constant attempts were made by me and by others to infuse a new spirit into the Department by the introduction of men of a more suitable type into the work, especially on the publicity side. Mr. Chamberlain regarded these suggestions as involving an aspersion on the men he had chosen for the purpose—all able men for other tasks. He stubbornly resisted every proposal made to him for improving and strengthening the Department in certain directions where it was patently deficient.

The machinery which Mr. Chamberlain created showed itself incompetent to deal even with volunteer recruits, and certainly too unreliable to be entrusted with the administration of dictatorial powers. Possibly the task would have been beyond any man's ability. It called for a great breadth and boldness of conception, a remorseless energy and thoroughness of execution, and for the exercise of supreme tact in dealing with other Departments, notably the recruiting machinery and the Ministries of Labour, Munitions, Agriculture and Trade, in order to avert friction, jealousies and the stranglehold of red tape. We needed, in short, a man of exceptional gifts. A man may possess very considerable ability without qualifying for that definition. Mr. Neville Chamberlain is a man of rigid competency. Such men have their uses in conventional times or in conventional positions, and are indispensable for filling subordinate posts at all times. But they are lost in an emergency or in creative tasks at any time.

On 13th July, 1917, the War Cabinet had under consideration a Report by Mr. Neville Chamberlain, urging the cancellation of Government exemptions to every man in the younger classes; and in support of this proposal he declared that there were at present so few vacancies to fill that if his proposal were not adopted, " he did not see that there was much object in the continued existence of his Department."

On the 13th August, 1917, Mr. C. Beck, the Parliamentary Secretary to the Ministry, stated in reply to a question: —

"The expenditure of the National Service Department from the commencement of the Department to 1st August was £192,709 6s. 1d. Of this, approximately £87,000 was spent on the publicity campaign under the original scheme of National Service. The number of volunteers placed in employment since the commencement of the Department is 19,951. In addition, the services of 9,817 part-time workers have been utilised, and the Department has carried out the distribution of 68,595 soldiers and civilians whose services have been lent for agricultural work. The number of women who have been placed in various forms of employment is 14,256, making a total of 112,609 men and women whose services have been utilised by the Department."

Critically examined, it was not perhaps a very heroic record for the Department, but it had rendered some help in an important need. Parliament did not however deem the help adequate to the need or the cost. A Select Committee appointed by the House of Commons on 25th July, 1917, to consider possible Government economies reported with regard to the Ministry of National Service that its system of filing and correspondence could with advantage be simplified; that its staff could be housed in a smaller area and that some of the salaries were needlessly high; and in general that: —

"The Committee are of opinion that the results obtained were not commensurate with the preparations made and the heavy preliminary outlay of money."

Early in August, Mr. Neville Chamberlain resigned his position at the head of the Ministry of National Service, which was thereupon reconstructed. The organisation of recruiting was transferred to it, and Sir Auckland Geddes was made Director-General in place of Mr. Chamberlain. He brought with him from the War Office General Hutchison (now Lord Hutchison), who afforded him helpful and tactful assistance. Shortly afterwards a clear and definite agreement was reached between the Ministry of National Service and the Ministry of Labour as to the precise division and inter-connection of their functions, and this was set out in a memorandum that was duly examined and approved by Lord Milner's Committee on Man-Power and Recruiting, and was further confirmed by the War Cabinet on 12th September, 1917. The memorandum covered questions such as those of general labour supply, priority, schemes of enrolment, allocation, transfer and substitution of labour, Trade Committees, out-of-work benefit, imported labour, and so on. Lord

Milner's Committee appended a Note on the functions of the Ministry of National Service which may be regarded as describing its operations from this time forward. These functions were:—

(1) To review the whole field of British man-power and to be in a position at all times to lay before the War Cabinet information as to the meaning, in terms of man-power and consequential results, of all Departmental proposals put forward to the War Cabinet and referred to the Ministry for its consideration and for an expression of its opinion.

(2) To make arrangements for the transfer from civil work not declared by the War Cabinet to be of primary importance, or, if ordered by the War Cabinet, from the Navy, Army, or Air Service to urgent national work, of such numbers of men as may be declared by the War Cabinet to be necessary to reinforce the labour already engaged on that work.

(3) Subject to the approval of the War Cabinet, to determine, in consultation with the Departments concerned, the relative importance of the various forms of civil work, and to prepare from time to time lists of reserved occupations with such age and other limitations as may be necessary to secure the preservation of a nucleus of civil occupations and industries.

(4) Within numerical limits imposed by the War Cabinet to obtain for the Army, Navy and Air Service, such men as can be withdrawn from civil life without detriment to the due performance of the civil work necessary to maintain the forces at sea, in the field, and in the air, and any nucleus of civil occupations and industries declared by the War Cabinet to be necessary.

(5) In connection with Function 4, to determine the physical fitness of men available, or possibly becoming available, for withdrawal from civil life.

(NOTE.—Functions 4 and 5 are limited by the action of the Tribunals acting in conformity with regulations and instructions issued to them under authority derived from the War Cabinet, in England and Wales by the Local Government Board, in Scotland by the Scottish Office.)

(6) To make arrangements for the provision, where necessary, of labour (male and female) in substitution for that withdrawn from civil life in accordance with Function 4.

(7) Any other duty which may from time to time be allocated to the Ministry by the War Cabinet.

(8) The above statement of functions is not intended to override in any way any agreement that has been or may be made between the Ministry of National Service and any other Government Department.

Thenceforward the Ministry worked smoothly and efficiently along these lines. Its tasks were of increasing difficulty, as the problems alike of securing fresh recruits for the Army and of maintaining the labour supply of the country grew more acute, and were accentuated by labour unrest. Here is an illustration of some of the difficulties experienced owing to the germs that swept across from Russia and produced feverish symptoms everywhere. In mid-October, 1917, the Cabinet learned that the situation in the South Wales coal-field was serious. Anti-war elements among the miners were organising resistance to the combing-out of recruits for the Army. Sir Auckland Geddes appealed for our help, as the mines represented the last great pool for men both for the Army and for transferable labour. We decided to support his action to the full; and as we learned that the more patriotic leaders of the miners in South Wales had suggested a visit from General Smuts, we asked the General if he would address a meeting at Mountain Ash at an early date. He consented to do so.

General Smuts tells the story of his adventure in the South Wales volcanic area. Before he went, he asked me if I could give him any advice as to the line to take. I seem to have said to him " Remember that my fellow countrymen are great singers!" The hint stuck. It was the only advice I gave him. What followed can perhaps be best told in his own words: —

" I arrived at Cardiff the next morning, where they gave me a great reception. I became a Doctor of the University. That afternoon I went on to the coal-fields where I was due to arrive that night. I found that practically the whole way from Cardiff to the coal-fields was lined by mobs on strike. But they were interested to see this man from South Africa. I really think they expected me to be a black man, and they seemed very much astonished that I was not. I got out everywhere and made little speeches. Finally I arrived at Tonypandy, which was the centre of this great strike. There I had my first meeting of the series which had been arranged for me to address. In front of me there was a vast crowd numbering thousands and thousands of angry miners, and when I got up I could feel the electricity in the air.

I started by saying: 'Gentlemen, I come from far away as you know. I do not belong to this country. I have come a long way to do my bit in this war, and I am going to talk to you to-night about this trouble. But I have heard in my country that the Welsh are among the greatest singers in the world, and before I start, I want you first of all to sing to me some of the songs of your people.'

Like a flash, somebody in that huge mass struck up ' Land of My Fathers.' Every soul present sang in Welsh and with the deepest fervour. When they had finished, they just stood, and I could see that the thing was over. I could judge the effect on myself. I said:

' Well, Gentlemen! It is not necessary for me to say much here
to-night. You know what has happened on the Western Front.
You know your comrades in their tens of thousands are risking
their lives. You know that the Front is not only in France, but that
the Front is just as much here as anywhere else. The trenches are
in Tonypandy, and I am sure you are actuated by the same spirit
as your comrades over in France. It is not necessary for me to add
anything. You know it as well as I do, and I am sure that you are
going to defend the Land of your Fathers of which you have sung
here to-night, and that you will defend it to the uttermost—and
that no trouble you may have with the Government about pay or
anything else will ever stand in the way of your defence of the
Land of your Fathers.'

That was all I said. I do not think I spoke for more than a few
minutes. I went on to the next meeting and repeated the same
thing there, and so right on through the coal-fields. That night I
took the train back to London in time to attend the Cabinet the
next afternoon. They said to me: ' What has happened? All
the men are at work. How did you settle it?' I said, ' Well, it is
news to me that the men are at work.' That great song helped us
to win through at the very moment when a paralysing blow was
being struck at us—when we were being told by our Navy that
they only had reserves of coal for a week, and if this strike went on
for another week, we should be paralysed and finished. It was
then that ' Land of My Fathers ' saved us."

Anxious moments such as this strike outbreak were all too frequent
in our experience during the War, and the Ministry of National
Service had to mingle the utmost tact with its firmness in order to
carry through its essential task.

Strikes and the Labour unrest which characterised 1917 aggravated
our difficulties with man-power. But had there been no labour
troubles, the number of fit men available for indispensable duties
was not equal to every need. It was certainly not commensurate with
the growing demand. The slaughter of Passchendaele added to these
difficulties. As I shall point out when I come to relate the story of
that bloody battle, or series of battles, the French had deliberately
chosen a fighting policy which would save their men for the final
struggle of 1918 when America would be ready to join in. Our
generals had deliberately chosen the opposite policy of flinging
masses of our troops against concrete machine-gun emplacements,
with the result that hundreds of thousands were put out of action.
Then they demanded the replacement of the lost units which ought
not to have been wasted in such a fight. As far back as May, 1917,
we had repeatedly warned our military leaders that we should have
no men available in 1917 for any great enterprises involving heavy

casualties. They disregarded this intimation, and thereby added considerably to the trouble we were experiencing in finding sufficient men for the urgent needs of the nation on land and sea, at home and abroad. How we were hampered by the shortage in our life and death struggle against starvation is told in the chapters on Food and Shipbuilding. Without the Department of National Service we could not have solved the problems of making the best use of our man-power. It made a clumsy start, but when it was reorganised it handled its delicate and troublesome duties efficiently and well.

CHAPTER XLVI

MILITARY OUTLOOK FOR 1917

1. EXISTING STRATEGICAL PLANS

AMONGST the first duties that fell to the Cabinet was a survey of the military position, with a view to deciding whether any reconsideration of the plans agreed to by the late Government for the campaign of 1917 was desirable or possible.

As I have been subjected to much adverse criticism for not insisting upon a complete reversal of the strategical policy hitherto pursued, it is necessary that I should at this stage review the military situation as I found it when I took office.

When I took over the civilian direction of the War as Prime Minister, the conditions under which the struggle was to continue had been already irrevocably fixed by decisions or failures to decide, against which I had made unceasing but unavailing protests at every step.

Our great commanders, having refused or neglected to organise a break-through where and when it was feasible, and having made ineffective attempts on fronts where such rupture was impossible, thereby throwing away myriads of valuable lives and losing inestimable time and opportunity, being unable to think out anything more original, had fallen back on attrition—always the game of the poor player. This is how the proposition presented itself to them: —

" The Allies have five men for every three the enemy can put in the field; therefore, even if we spend four lives in extinguishing three, the foe must be beaten in the end."

The possibility never entered into the computation of these master minds that the survivors might sooner or later object to this method of " forming fours " by taking their turn in the slaughter house from which such multitudes of their comrades never emerged. These arid strategists only saw that the units they commanded had for three consecutive campaigns marched into the death zone without flinching, and that to the very end of the terrible battles of 1916 they never faltered or hesitated, in spite of the fact that already 12 millions of them were dead or mutilated. Why, therefore, should the survivors now shrink from the fate which their fellows had confronted with such fortitude and resignation?

With each campaign, the opportunities for trying the policy of attacking the enemy where he was most vulnerable became bricked up by the enemy, and had now narrowed down to the extreme east and to the Italian Front. Up till the autumn of 1915 the Balkan door was kept wide open by the Serbian Army, one of the best fighting units in the field. The failure of the Dardanelles attack, the refusal to exploit the Salonika base, and the abandonment of Serbia bolted and barred that door: the defeat of Roumania and the impending collapse of Russia would soon eliminate the last possibilities of the Near East. The opportunities—nay, rather the openings— of the Danube Front had been fooled away. The chances of utilising the gigantic man-power of Russia had almost vanished—had in effect gone, although at that date no one grasped the ominous fact. Was there any other chance left except once more to sprinkle the western portal of the temple of Moloch with blood from what remained of the most valiant hearts amongst the youth of France and Britain? I decided to explore every possibility before surrendering to a renewal of the horrors of the West.

At the Chantilly Military Conference in November, 1916, the Generals had gone through the form of pretending that a break through the Balkan barrier was still attainable, and that they contemplated an operation to that end for the early spring. They led the politicians to believe that there was a fair chance even then of breaking through on the South-Eastern Front, and effectively attacking the armies of the Central Powers on their flank, thus driving them out of Roumania, and establishing a clear line of communication with both Roumania and Russia in that quarter. I felt certain that they did not mean it, for they never took any measures to prepare for so formidable a military enterprise. It was all a piece of humbug, written with a chuckle at the thought of the ease with which the politicians assembled at that time in Paris could be taken in. They made no arrangements to send the reinforcements, guns, or munitions essential to a vigorous offensive. They did not even make any effort to fill up the gaps in the units already there.   It was at least nominally part of the Chantilly strategy to undertake an offensive in the Balkans with the Danube as its objective. But although the Paris Conference in November had endorsed the plan proposed by the Allied Military Staffs, no action of any sort or kind had been taken to implement it. In men, guns, ammunition and transport the situation of the Salonika force was if anything worse than it had been before the Chantilly decision. An effort of that kind, had it been made immediately with all the available strength of the Western Powers, might have succeeded. General Milne (now Field-Marshal Lord Milne), who was then in command of the British forces at

Salonika, in a recent speech confirms this appreciation of the military position. He says that "the reason why he had kept them for so long doing nothing on the Salonika Front was because he was not given the means that he considered necessary, and which he had asked for, to enable them to enter into battle with any hope of success. Soldiers could not go into war and expect to win without most fearful sacrifices if the authorities at home did not properly back them up with every means at their disposal."

It was probably too late then to achieve the rescue of Roumania from the wolves that were tearing at her entrails. The Western Allies had almost forced her into the War without taking the trouble of ascertaining whether she was equipped for such an enterprise, and without making any preparations for coming to her aid if she were hard pressed. General Alexeieff was opposed to the Roumanian intervention. He knew how ill-prepared was the Roumanian Army to resist the forces that would be brought to bear upon it by the Central Powers. He also realised that upon his own exhausted armies would fall the work of rescue when Roumania was being crushed by her powerful foes. But although he was more concerned with the decision than any other Allied General, he was not consulted. So much for the common front about which we heard so much at the Paris Conference in the booming rhetoric of M. Briand and Mr. Asquith.

All the same, if timely action had been taken immediately after Chantilly, it might have completely transformed the situation to the advantage of the Allies. Austria, menaced on three flanks, would undoubtedly have collapsed. The Russian Army could have been regenerated and re-inspired. The Germans would have been forced to withdraw masses of their best troops from the Western Front to support a crumbling Austria. As usual, no effort was made to carry out this bold plan. It was nothing more than a show to delude the Ministers into an acceptance of the same old strategy. The only front that was attacked was the political. The moment that was captured, the Staffs reported to each other, to use a military phrase, " Our objectives have been attained." They might have added " The casualties were slight," but that phrase was not to be found in their pigeon-holes. Casualties there were, however; Joffre, who designed this manœuvre, fell as a result of it and the Asquith Government, which acquiesced in it, also went.

By January, 1917, the Roumanian overthrow had entirely altered the Balkan position. The complete defeat of the Roumanian Army and the occupation of the more important Roumanian towns, and especially of the corn fields, demolished the Allied military plans and strengthened the position of the Central Powers, whilst it undoubtedly worsened and weakened the strategical position of the Allies—notably Russia. Her isolation was almost complete at a time when she needed help and comradeship more than ever. Roumania was no longer a menace to an Austrian flank needing cover and protection. Her overthrow was the final and fatal blow to Russia. The prodigious effort put forth by the exhausted Muscovite Army to support its unfortunate ally left Russia prostrate and panting. Her already insufficient transport facilities were still further strained. Her long line of front which she had not enough trained and equipped men to defend, was stretched by hundreds of kilometres. One fourth of Russia's fighting men had to be sent to the Roumanian Front. The last ounce of her fighting strength was spent in the effort, and her strained heart never recovered sufficient vigour to enable her to stand up to her victorious foes. All hope of a Russian revival was buried on the banks of the Pruth, and the Moldavian Delta became the cemetery of the Empire of the Romanoffs. The Roumanian collapse moreover had placed the Central Powers economically in a much better position. It eased the pressure of the blockade and gave them further time and encouragement to push their submarine campaign. Ludendorff points out that the occupation of the Roumanian corn-lands and oil-fields placed the Central Powers " in occupation of an area rich in just those warlike resources which they lacked " and referring to the Roumanian stores they captured he says: " As I saw now quite clearly, we should not have been able to exist, much less carry on the War, without Roumania's corn and oil, even though we had saved the Galician oil-fields of Drohobycz from the Russians." He boasts with justifiable pride of how " a serious crisis in Constantinople was fortunately averted by the timely delivery of Roumanian wheat."

Instead of a road being blasted through by the Allies from Salonika to Galatz and thence to Moscow, a new road had been opened up by the Central Powers through Rustchuck and Adrianople right up to the Ægean. The momentous change which had taken place since Chantilly in the strategic situation in the Balkans was brought home to the Allies by the introduction of a new element and a fresh menace in that quarter. We soon discovered that instead of planning an offensive expedition of a considerable magnitude, we were confronted with a danger to the very existence of our Expeditionary Force at Salonika. Tension with the Greek Government had recently become acute. In Greece, Constantine, the Kaiser's brother-in-law, was once more on top. He had been playing fast and loose with the Allies, and there was good reason to believe that his real sympathies were with Germany, and that he would seize any opportunity that offered to further her interests and incidentally his own. He had a sentimental interest in Monastir, the scene of his easy triumphs in the Balkan War. Venizelos, the loyal friend of the Allies, because of that friendship was a refugee from his country and a rebel against his King. His followers had formed a provisional Government that held sway

in Crete and a number of the Greek islands, and in the Salonika
district; but they were being barbarously treated whenever they
fell into the power of the Royalist Government.   Information reached
the French Staff that the Germans were meditating a coup against
the Salonika Expeditionary Force.   According to the intelligence
reaching their Headquarters, the enemy were organising a combined
attack by Turks, Bulgarians, Germans and Austrians—and most
sinister of all, by Greeks—upon our scattered, depleted, ill-placed
and badly-equipped army. Whilst the victorious forces of the Central
Powers were to dash down from the hills to the north and to the
east, a Greek army was to attack the Allied flank from the south.
There was evidence that could not be disregarded of the substantial
character of this rumour.   Constantine was massing troops in
Northern Thessaly.   For what purpose, unless they meant to attack?
They were not assembled to help the threatened armies of the Allies.
There was a good deal of military activity throughout the Greek
Peninsula. Constantine detested the Allies. His contest with Venizelos
deepened that hatred by making Allied or German sympathies
a party question.   The vulnerability of Greece from the sea kept
him, at an earlier stage, from joining Ferdinand, whose dominions
were immune from naval attack.   A certain clash of ulterior
ambitions about Thrace and Constantinople might also have had a
deterrent effect.   These considerations restrained any impulse he
might feel to allow animosity to ferment into risky action.   But if
the risk were reduced to a minimum by a smashing attack from the
north and the infliction on the Allies at Salonika of another Dardanelles disaster, then Constantine would welcome his friends and in all
probability join their victorious forces.   In Athens and the
Peloponnesus he had a powerful following, and there hostility soon
reached the point of explosion.   It spread up to Athens.   On 11th
December, 1916, there was an attack on British sailors in the Piræus
which resulted in several of our marines being killed.   The French
clamoured, and as General Joffre put it in a message to our War
Office, "emphatically insisted" that we should send a couple of
divisions immediately to Salonika.   Prompt action was essential to
dispel this new threat.   We obviously could take no risk, for the
situation, unless effectively handled, might land the Allies in one of
the worse disasters of the whole War.

    The War Cabinet felt that the Greek menace must be dealt with
firmly and promptly before the Central Powers could disentangle
their troops from the struggle with the remnants of the Roumanian
Army which were, with the help of a few Russian divisions, still
putting up a tenacious resistance in Moldavia, and before the Greek
King could mass a sufficient force in the neighbourhood of Larissa to
enable him to deliver an effective blow on the Allied left.   The
French Government and their military advisers were in a state of

panic about the Salonika force. They were convinced that the
enemy attack was imminent. General Sarrail was all for military
action to clear the Greeks out of Thessaly. The French Staff con
tinued to press us for a reinforcement of two divisions without delay
We pointed out that the force already there was many thousands
below its strength, because the necessary sea transport was not forth
coming, either here or in France. If ships could be found anywhere
and anyhow, let them be used to carry drafts and ammunition to fil
up the divisions and equip the batteries. Meanwhile we advised that
it would be better to anticipate the Constantine manœuvre by forcing
the issue with that potential antagonist before his potential allie
were ready. It was therefore decided by the War Cabinet to deliver
an ultimatum to him demanding the immediate withdrawal of the
whole of the Greek Army in Thessaly to the Peloponnesus. He was
given 24 hours in which to make up his mind. Had he refused he
would have been immediately attacked by land and sea. The threat
answered the purpose. Constantine promised compliance. At first
there was a suspicious tardiness in his redemption of the promise
But a blockade by the British Fleet convinced him that his only
security lay in speeding up the retirement of his Thessaly force. A
portion of our anxiety about the situation at Salonika was thus
relieved. It was, however, still felt that the strength of our force
there was insufficient and the positions they held were too weak
to enable them to resist a serious attack from the victorious forces
of the Central Powers in the Balkan Peninsula.

Consequently we proposed that the Italians, who had a shorter sea
route, should send a couple of divisions across the Adriatic to Sant
Quaranta, and that they should immediately take in hand the
improvement of the communications between that port and Monastir
I record our negotiations on this issue in my account of the Rome
Conference in the next chapter. If the Italians could not see their
way to spare troops for the purpose, we suggested that arrangements
should be made, in the event of a formidable attack by the enemy
for a retirement of the Allied Armies to prepare entrenchments in
front of Salonika. Meanwhile we took steps to send drafts to restore
to full strength units which had been thinned by sporadic fighting
and by disease. The French contingent was short of establishmen
and we pressed General Joffre to fill up the depleted ranks of hi
army. For the time being the idea of an offensive from Salonika
had to be abandoned. When the Roumanian Army of hundreds of
thousands was in being and engaging corresponding enemy forces
a move from Salonika might have been feasible with moderate forces
especially if an earnest endeavour had been made to improve road
rail and dock facilities. But even if steps were taken now to assemble
a much more formidable striking force at Salonika, it was too late
to begin with any hope of accomplishing great results. During the

weeks that had elapsed since Chantilly, the Roumanian Army had become negligible as an offensive force and had been reduced to a condition where a few enemy divisions could have held it in check. The British and French Staffs had not yet given a thought to the essential reconstruction of transport at Salonika except on a strictly limited scale. No survey had been made of what was required in rails and locomotives to improve communications to and behind the lines, consequently no orders had been received for supplying any of these necessaries. Even then success would depend upon the pressure Russia could bring to bear from the north. Until the projected conference at Petrograd took place we knew little of her offensive capacity.

The condition of the Salonika Expeditionary Force several weeks after the great Chantilly project of a Balkan offensive is another indication of the complete lack of unity and energy in the military direction. Joint action on the part of all the Allies was necessary, but was not palatable to the General Staff. A resolution carried at the Allied Conference at Paris approving such a plan was treated as if it were the actual carrying out of the scheme. To that end an old legal maxim was incorporated as a principle of strategy. "Things that ought to be done or are agreed to be done must be taken as done." That probably accounts for the complete neglect by the military Staffs of some of the essential requirements of the Salonika Army. It drove poor Sarrail to his famous *mot*, " Napoleon was not a great general. He only fought a Coalition."

Whilst Joffre was engaged in fighting a rearguard action in Paris against the politicians who sought his life, and whilst Robertson was chuckling at the skilful way in which the British politicians had once more been jockeyed over the Balkans, the Germans, Austrians, Bulgarians and Turks were tearing up the Roumanian Army and pillaging and distributing Roumanian corn. Briand was too busy trying to save the last miserable rags of Joffre's authority to think of the War. The Asquith Government was no more, and the new Government had not had long to study the gigantic problems on sea and land which had been bequeathed to them. What about the military position on other fronts? We were committed by the Chantilly Conference to offensive operations in 1917 on a great scale on the French, Italian and Salonika Fronts. Russia had promised to co-operate by an attack on the Eastern Front. The cutting off of Roumania put the Salonika offensive out of the question. It was now assumed that we were doomed in that quarter to a precarious defensive—certainly until Russia succeeded in restoring the military position in Roumania. That was far beyond her strength to achieve.

But how about the campaign projected for the French and Italian war areas? Were the Chantilly plans still in force there? By these

2D*

schemes another Somme offensive on a wider front was contemplated in France; in Italy there was to be the same old attack on Istria or the Trentino—on both fronts we were doomed to a repetition of the identical denting and chipping tactics to which we were accustomed, with each Ally acting independently on its own front. The only pretence at co-operation was to be found in an effort to time a simultaneous start of the useless slaughter of brave men on each front, each Allied country making its contribution to the holocaust. The campaigns of 1917 were to be another exhibition of platitudes in action, planned by minds too unimaginative or too tired to think of any variation.

It was late in the day to effect a complete change in the plan of campaign for 1917. That ought to have been done at the Paris Conference in November. If a charge of breach of faith was to be avoided (and such a charge, if believed, is fatal to an alliance), nothing could be done without obtaining the assent of the leaders of the four great Allied Armies. This was a hopeless prospect, for the Chantilly plans were their own and they naturally thought them the best. No change could be made without further consultation. How was effective consultation possible at this late hour? Any fundamental alteration of plans involved an admission of error on the part of these great warriors. Pressure from statesmen might force a thorough reconsideration. But was that pressure likely? Not from what I knew of the leading Ministers of France, Italy and Russia. The French Premier was easy-going and indolent—devoid of initiative. If his genius discerned the right road, his temperament led him to acquiesce in the smoothest. The Italian Premier was an honest man of mediocre gifts. His most powerful colleague—Sonnino—was a strong man, but his strength lay entirely in the region of diplomacy. He had no aptitude for conducting a war. He had no special interest in the fighting branch of the business. As to Russia, it was presided over by a weak autocrat, who was ruled by a temperamental and superstitious wife, and internal troubles were surging round both.

In spite of unpropitious conditions I decided to make a much belated effort to save the Alliance from a repetition of the barren and bloody tragedies of 1915 and 1916. As I am bound, in an honest account of the events in which I took part, to tell the story faithfully, whether it ended in success or in failure, I propose now to relate the fruitless efforts I made to avert the horrors of the Chemin des Dames, Passchendaele, and Caporetto—also my last despairing attempt to postpone, if not save, the collapse of Russia.

2. CONDITIONS OF A SUCCESSFUL OFFENSIVE

The only conditions under which a great offensive operation could hope to succeed had been written in scarlet letters by the events of the

War. It needed no special training or intelligence to read the warnings of past disaster.

The first condition was that the morale of the defending troops should have deteriorated, either because it had been undermined by constant defeat or because for one reason or another its ardour was no longer equal to the continued strain upon its courage. This point is put with great force by Falkenhayn in discussing this very problem in reference to the German attacks on the Russian Front: —

" The attack in Galicia was not undertaken until the Germans felt certain that they were opposed by troops whose morale was absolutely rotted by a merciless campaign. In truth, this is the chief factor in the solution of the problem so often discussed during the War, whether attempts to break through with the object of forcing a decision constituted a wise policy or not. Against an enemy in good military and moral condition they were certainly not to be recommended. Accordingly, in the whole course of the War, breaks-through only succeeded where this condition was not present."

Generals on both sides accepted this axiom, but they hardly ever gave it an honest application. When they were anxious to launch an offensive in a particular sector, they always attached undue importance to reports of deterioration in the morale of the enemy on that front. A mass of conflicting gossip and rumours came to the Intelligence Branch from every quarter, often from prisoners trying to deceive or anxious to please. When it was sifted and weighed, human nature being what it is, a bias developed in the direction of the reports that supported the thesis known to have been already formed by the High Command. The subordinate who declines to sacrifice judgment to a mistaken conception of loyalty is rarely acceptable except to the really great. Haig, Robertson and Nivelle all alike professed a conviction that the morale of the German Army had been shaken to such a degree by the raging fires of the Somme that its troops would no longer have the nerve to sustain a similar experience. There was a flood of secret information to that effect, coming mostly from terrified prisoners whose own nerves were temporarily shaken by experiences from which they had only just been rescued by captivity. The effect upon the spirit of the French troops of the repeated failures with numerous losses during 1915 and 1916 was never discussed as an element in the computation of chances. It was assumed that the Allied soldiers were infrangible steel, and enemy soldiers ordinary flesh. And yet in the event, French morale broke first. The two great offensives of 1917 were decided upon what turned out to be an entirely false estimate of the fighting quality of our greatest foe and of the limits of endurance of the Allied troops.

On other fronts, however, there was a distinct falling off in the spirit of the forces that opposed the Allied Armies in the case of two of the belligerents. Speaking of the Turkish Army at the end of 1916, Ludendorff says:—

> "The Turkish Army was exhausted. To begin with, it had not recovered from the Balkan War before it was involved in another. Its wastage from disease and in action was continuously high. The trustworthy, brave Anatolian had vanished from its ranks. The unreliable Arab auxiliaries were playing an increasingly important part everywhere, but especially in Mesopotamia and Palestine. The forces were now below their paper strength and the men were badly fed and still worse equipped. The lack of efficient officers was particularly felt."

It is one of the most serious condemnations of our war direction that we allowed such an army not merely to hold up superior numbers of our troops, but to inflict two serious defeats on them. There can be no doubt that a resolute and well-managed attack on the Turk in 1915 and certainly in 1916 would have crumpled him up and released the considerable forces locked in Egypt and Mesopotamia for a resolute attack on the Balkan Front. The saving in shipping alone would have made a substantial contribution to our resources. A Turkish overthrow in 1916 might have produced decisive results. In 1917 the consequence of such a victory, standing alone, would not have been as far reaching, unless followed by a defeat of the Bulgarian Army.

But if a concentrated attack on Austria-Hungary were considered as a possible objective of the 1917 campaign, the prospect of a triumph which would have a determining effect on the fate of the struggle seemed more promising. The German High Command at this date divided the Austrian troops into "reliable" and "unreliable," the latter being by far the more numerous. In the Brussiloff offensive of 1916, the Austrian Army put up no serious fight. Whole divisions surrendered without striking a blow. The "prisoners" alone numbered over 300,000, Hindenburg said it was not a surrender, but a betrayal. The heart of the Slavs and Roumans who constituted the majority of the Austrian conscripts was not in the struggle. Nor were the Magyars as keen as the Austro-Germans. It is true that the Slavonic regiments preferred fighting Italians to Russians, but they were not specially concerned in the quarrel with either. The Magyar had some reason to dislike the Russian—none to excite his antagonism towards the Italians. There were no memories to inspire their hostility comparable to the secular hatred of Gaul and Teuton that came to a climax in the implacable ferocity of the Verdun battlefield.

The food situation in Austria was also bad. The Hungarian

harvest had failed and there was real starvation in considerable areas of the Austrian Empire. One of our secret agents from Spain, a country which was in close touch throughout the War with Vienna, and especially with the clerical interests in that country, reported that "the Austrians themselves are full of astonishment at the Allies not undertaking a proper offensive against them, as Austria's collapse would then be inevitable." From the same sources our Intelligence Bureau learnt that there was in Austria "great depression and eagerness for peace, even in the highest military circles."

Austria made war to punish Serbia for a crime in which every Austrian and Magyar believed Serbian statesmen to be implicated. Serbia had now been trampled down and every square yard of Serbian territory was in Austrian or Bulgarian occupation. There was thus nothing left for which an Austrian peasant or workman would count it worth the risk of being shot to pieces on the battle-field, or of leaving his wife and children to die of starvation at home. The war objective had been achieved as far as Austria was concerned, and with it went the war spirit. That is why a determined attack on an imperfectly trained army raised from such unpromising material and crowded with "unreliables," had a better chance of success than an offensive against perfectly organised defensive positions, held by the most efficient army in the field—in training, equipment and leadership—and with a morale which, if not unabated, was equal to the best in any other army on any battlefield.

It is said that up to that date the Italian Army had made no extensive progress in its repeated assaults on the Austrian Army. The Italians had in fact advanced much further than we had at Loos or on the Somme, or the French at Artois, Champagne, and the Somme on much more favourable ground. They had lost fewer men, they had made greater progress, they had spent far less ammunition than either the French or British Armies, nevertheless the result was no more decisive than in the French and British offensives. But there was this vital difference, which was an element in any wise consideration of the possibilities of the terrain of the next offensive— the Italian artillery was inferior in every particular to that of their Austrian opponents, especially in heavy guns; and the supply of ammunition was insufficient, even for such guns as they had, to keep up the offensive to the point of decision. Not only was the artillery too light to level trenches hewn into the rocky plateau of the Carso, but it was often not equal to the task of destroying barbed wire defences. There were many critical occasions where "garden pincers" had to be used to make up for deficiencies in artillery preparation. Not even the most reckless and bigoted Western-offensive general would launch an attack on trenches dug in the friable soil of Champagne after a bombardment from artillery so light and so limited in shell supply as that with which the Italian Army had to force its way through defences blasted in the granite of the Julian Alps and the hard porphyry of the Dolomites. Far too little credit is given to the soldiers of the Italian Peninsula for what they achieved with such inadequate mechanical assistance. That they should have accomplished what they did is a proof not only of their own bravery and skill, but of the inferiority in military ardour and discipline of the half-hearted Austrian infantry to the dour and highly trained legionaries of the North German. The Gorizia offensive had to be broken off at the height of its success because the Italian ammunition was exhausted. Many a dominating position stormed by the Alpine troops of Italy had to be abandoned because the supporting artillery could not silence the long range guns of Austria by counter battery work. The Austrian victory of May, 1916, was won because the Austrians concentrated on the Italian line an overpowering fire from a mass of heavy guns which the Italian artillery could not match. It was said at the time that the Italian troops were " unaccustomed " to such fire, and therefore broke. It would be equally correct to say that the Austrians on the whole maintained their defence of the frontier, with forces conspicuously inferior in numbers, because they were not submitted to the shattering bombardments which effaced the German defences on the Somme, and the French forts and trenches at Verdun, and left the respective garrisons without cover on those scarified plateaux.

The Italian Army in 1916 strengthened its heavy artillery considerably by the withdrawal of siege guns from their coast and inland fortifications. But many of the patterns were obsolete. The range and mechanism were not equal to the perfect weapons turned out by Skoda, and such as they were, there was not enough ammunition to keep up a prolonged bombardment of successive positions. The Austrians therefore always experienced a sense of mechanical superiority which sustained their morale. But supposing the position were reversed, and the advantage in artillery were transferred to the Italians, would the unwilling soldiers of the " ramshackle empire " follow the example of the Germans, French and British on the Western Front and lie for hours and days in muddy shell holes to defend their battered defences? I felt confident they would not. Their devotion to the Austrian Empire was not equal to that display of sustained heroism. The pluck of the Croatian and the Czech had been proved in the wars of many centuries, but their hearts were not in this conflict, and it is the heart that gives constancy as well as ardour to courage.

Had the Austrians been beaten on the Italian Front it would have been imperative for them to withdraw several divisions and batteries from their Eastern Front. The Germans would therefore have to extend and thus weaken their lines on the same front. That would have eased the position for the hard-pressed Russians and Roumanians and would have given them time to reform and recover their fighting strength. In the alternative the Germans would have withdrawn divisions from France and made a break-through on that front a more feasible operation.

It is true that the disastrous offensives of the Chemin des Dames and Passchendaele could not have been undertaken, had we moved guns and troops to Italy. The Generals would have been compelled to make that sacrifice to common sense. In what respect would we have been worse off if those sanguinary repulses had been avoided? They cost the Allies well over three-quarters of a million men, an over-strained mettle, shaken nerves and a shattered morale for the survivors. Had the Germans, instead of helping Austria, elected to take advantage of our depleted strength in the West to attack our entrenchments there, they would have been resisted by forces which would still have been superior to their own. All they would have gained by their attack would have been a repetition of Verdun whilst Austria was being abandoned to utter defeat. When the Germans in the summer of 1917, as soon as they heard of the mutinies in the French Army, attacked lines held by troops weakened, depressed and disaffected by their terrible losses, they were beaten off. If the French Army had been depleted by 150,000 efficients sent to Italy, why should it be assumed that the German assault would then have succeeded when it failed after the French numbers had been reduced by 200,000 casualties and the morale of the French Army had been shaken to its foundations? The Allied Staffs always seemed to me to argue with the incoherence and inconsequence with which children reason. What matters with them is the thing they want. Facts, figures, impossibilities are irrelevant things to be used either way and every way according to their desires.

If the Austrians were to be attacked by the Allied forces, the Germans would rush to their aid from the West with men and guns, and they could always send more help than we could. That was one argument. The other was that if the Austrians were subjected to a combined attack, the Germans would take advantage of the temporary improvement in relative strength to break through our reduced garrison in France. Both could not be true. But to the military mind these arguments were not an alternative—they were cumulative. To quote a very pertinent comment from the British Official History of the Macedonian Campaign:—

" There is a great difference in the attitude of a General Staff to arguments according as they fit in or conflict with its own desires."

3. SURPRISE

There was another consideration which in my opinion had not been sufficiently taken into account hitherto—a factor which even in the war of earthworks played a great part several times; this was the element of surprise. It is safe to say that no striking success had hitherto been won except where the victor had managed to surprise the opposite army by an unexpected stroke or a stroke of unexpected strength. It was true up to the very end of the War.

None of the battles of the Great War was decisive in the sense of ending the struggle immediately one way or the other. But many of them were climacteric in their influence on the progress of the campaign, and could be reckoned as turning points, temporary or permanent, in the course of the War. They effected a domination by one contestant over the other in some particular theatre or part of the line; a definite gain of territory, considerable in proportion to the effort put forward and losses incurred; often a break-through and temporary disintegration of hostile defences and forces. While the battles on the Western Front—after the first few weeks of open warfare—had the character of a grim wrestle between forces that moved slowly back or forward and remained substantially intact and invincible, the great battles fought in the Eastern and South-Eastern areas of the struggle ended in one side or the other being thrown into confusion and driven back for leagues in headlong rout.

It is interesting to note the extent to which the element of surprise played a determining part in these critical engagements.

After the Marne, and when the badger tactics on both sides had been inaugurated and established, it was assumed that there would be no room for surprises on a great scale. The forces and resources of the respective combatants at any and every given point and time were known to their adversaries. Modern methods of observation and elucidation, aerial reconnaissance, trench raids, cross-examination of prisoners, highly developed systems of espionage, supplemented the other means of acquiring information as to the movements of each army. There seemed therefore to be no opportunity left for either side to carry out any strategical designs of which the other would be unaware, and against which it would not have timely notice to prepare itself up to the limit of its military resources.

But although the unsuspected blow was difficult to achieve in the Great War, it was attainable. Both sides were able to spring surprises on each other, in regard to the time and place of their attacks, the disposition of their forces, and the weapons they employed. And it is noteworthy that the crucially successful operations of the War were mainly those where one side was not expecting an attack, or at least was unprepared for the enemy's offensive in the matter of its time, its place, or the weapons or weight of troops used. Where each side was fully alive to what the other might be expected to do, and had made such preparation as it could to meet attack, the general result was an indecisive and sanguinary struggle, with no appreciable gain or loss of territory, and no dramatic collapse of the defending troops.

There were many such bloody battles, yielding indeterminate gains. On the other hand, the most striking movements and notable victories were secured with the aid of at least some determining element of surprise.

It is quite impossible to conceal from the enemy every movement on a great scale, but a resourceful General can at any rate organise his activities behind the lines in such a way as to confuse even an intelligent enemy. If he has any knowledge of the mentality of the opposing General—and no man ought to be allowed to lead who does not possess supreme psychological gifts—his task is an easy one. When Joffre, Nivelle and Haig commanded on the Western Front, it needed no special genius to discern the trend of their one-way minds. They were each persuaded at all times that the enemy could not spare a battalion out of the army that was defending its lines against their well-directed and sustained attacks. Thus Serbia, Roumania and Caporetto came to them as a surprise. The Germans were able to withdraw several divisions from France for those attacks, when Joffre and Haig were convinced that the offensive they were then prosecuting had reduced the German Army to a gasping exhaustion. You could have safely depended upon their paying no heed to rumours that would, if true, oblige them to weaken their own forces and thus imperil the chance of winning the dazzling triumph that they felt convinced would soon crown their strategy in the West.

A surprise may therefore be due to the refusal to accept unpalatable warnings—that is, warnings which do not fit into the plans of Headquarters. The classic examples of that are Joffre's conduct at the beginning of the War and subsequently at Verdun; Kitchener's, Robertson's, and Joffre's indifference to the reports of Austro-German and Bulgarian attacks in Serbia in 1915; the assumption by Haig that the Germans were so shattered by Passchendaele that they could not spare a division for the Italian Front; and the refusal of Pétain and Haig in 1918 to pay any attention to the many indications of an attack in front of Amiens. On none of these occasions did it suit these great Commanders to believe in warnings which were subsequently authenticated.

Let us examine two or three of these illustrations of my thesis.

(a) *The German Advance through Belgium in August, 1914.*

Perhaps the most surprising feature of this was the fact that it took the French by surprise at all. But Joffre was taken unawares by the wide northern sweep of encirclement through Belgium which the Germans carried out, and by the number of troops which they concentrated upon the Western Front for the opening move of the War. The result was that they were able to make their advance almost unchallenged, save by the archaic fortifications of Liége and Namur, which their heavy field artillery—another unexpected blow for the Allies—soon reduced. The army under Von Kluck swept through Belgium along a line further north than Joffre had anticipated, and was scarcely checked at all, overwhelming the resistance of the small British force. It swung down to Paris, and very nearly brought to success the German purpose of capturing Paris, sedanising the French Army, and knocking France out of the War.

Thus to the striking advance of the Germans several factors of surprise contributed:—

(1) The German forces mobilised and brought to the Western Front in the first few days of the War were far stronger than Joffre had calculated.

(2) The advance of Von Kluck's Army through Central Belgium to the north of Lanrezac was unexpected.

(3) The Germans used for field warfare guns of a far larger calibre than either the French or the British anticipated or possessed themselves. And yet French Headquarters had been for years in possession of the German plan and had every indication that it was to be carried out. They knew all about the German heavy artillery. The surprise was its mobility.

(b) The Battle of the Marne.

The First Battle of the Marne—second to none in the War for its decisive importance in the course of the world conflict—was in the main a battle of manœuvre and strategy of mobile armies, depending for its issue on the element of surprise. Who was responsible for the Battle of the Marne? When the victor of the Marne is called up for judgment and recompense, there will be the same multitudinous response as Byron predicted when it is the turn of Junius to be summoned to the Bar:—

"The moment that you had pronounced him one,
Presto! his face changed and he was another;
And when that change was hardly well put on,
It varied, till I don't think his own mother
(If that he had a mother) would her son
Have known, he shifted so from one to t'other."

But whoever he was or they were, commentators seem agreed on the factors which determined the issue at the Marne:—

(1) The swing-in of the 6th French Army under Manoury and of Gallieni's Paris Defence Force, against Von Kluck's right flank. Von Kluck was not expecting this attack and was not prepared for it until it was too late.

(2) The weakening of the German forces by the dispatch of two army corps to East Prussia, to counter the unexpected attack by

Samsonoff's army—another surprise—and the leaving of two more army corps in Belgium to mask Antwerp and guard against an alleged Russian Army that was said to be coming to the West through England.

(3) The reappearance of the British Army in full force and vigour. This army was supposed to have been finally dispersed and disposed of.

(c) *The Dardanelles.*

This might have been an unexpected coup. Had we landed troops simultaneously with the naval bombardment, we know now that the Turks would have been taken completely by surprise, and that we could have occupied the Gallipoli Peninsula with hardly any loss. But we made a pyrotechnic and tympanic effort to warn and wake up the enemy and gave him plenty of time to make ready. The result was that we failed to gain Gallipoli.

(d) *Brussiloff's Offensive.*

The offensive carried out by Brussiloff against the Austrians at the beginning of June, 1916, was the most successful battle fought by the Russians throughout the War. It came a month before it was expected. Brussiloff began preparations at over twenty places at once, so that even deserters should not give away the real front of attack. And instead of concentrating his reserves obviously, he distributed them widely. The absence of any obvious concentration was the real secret of his astonishing success. The Austrians were unprepared at that time to meet the impact. Between June and August, the Russians captured more than 350,000 prisoners, nearly 400 guns, 1,300 machine-guns and a tract of ground 200 miles long and in parts nearly 60 miles deep. Had the Russians had the mechanical means to exploit their victory this unforeseen move might have decided the War.

(e) *The Mackensen attack at Gorlice,* which rolled up the Russian Armies in 1915, and *the overthrow of Serbia* in the same year, provide illustrations of the surprises which were due to the refusal of Generals to take heed of intelligence inconsistent with their cherished plans. The Russians had information which ought to have warned them that there was a formidable offensive contemplated by the Germans in the direction of Gorlice. But the Russian High Command had other ideas and other plans, and the information which came to them as to the probable Mackensen offensive was therefore disregarded. Hence although forewarned, the attack had the effect of surprise. The same observation applies to the attack on Serbia.

(f) *The combined Austro-German-Bulgarian invasion of Serbia* in October, 1915, was a strategical surprise in the sense at least that the Allies allowed themselves to be taken unawares and unprepared. It ought to have been foreseen. Ample warning had been given of the

Austro-German plans and of the fact that Bulgaria meant to throw in her lot with them. But the attention of the Western Generals was so focussed on their own great blow in France that they turned their faces away from that impending danger in the East. When it came it had therefore to them all the effect of a surprise.

(g) To a certain extent the *Battle of Verdun* presents another example of this type of surprise. The initial stage of the attack on the Verdun forts was not expected by the French Headquarters, not because they had not been forewarned by German preparations but because it did not suit their plans to believe them. The attack was therefore a great success. When it was pressed on from week to week it ceased to be a surprise and achieved nothing for the assailants.

(h) *The Battle of the Somme.*

The main Battle of the Somme was a perfect illustration of a prolonged effort to inform the enemy beforehand and in time of our intentions—the roads crowded for weeks with columns of marching troops and with heavy guns drawn by caterpillars and huge lorries; the sky throbbing with observing aeroplanes; large numbers of captive balloons floating in the air along the exact line of attack. It was all like an old Chancery suit, where the most detailed pleadings informed the defendant to the minutest particular of every point that would have to be met and fought out. It conduced to protracted and costly litigation which deferred the final decision until both sides were utterly ruined. Our great Generals would have made excellent special pleaders in the days of Jarndyce *v.* Jarndyce. This kind of procedure suited the man in possession. In this case the man in possession of the disputed ground was the German. These elaborate preliminary warnings therefore suited him.

The British attack was supported with colossal artillery preparation—the heaviest that had ever been launched—and it was carried out by the finest flower of our volunteer army. But it was in no way a surprise attack. The enemy were well posted as to how, when, and where the attack was coming. Forewarned, they were forearmed. The result was that such gains as we achieved at the price of ghastly casualty lists during the opening days of the conflict were quite insignificant.

But there was one surprise feature about the opening round of the Somme battle. The French attacked to the south of the British Front with five divisions. The Germans were expecting the British, but not the French attack, and in consequence the French advanced with lightning speed, pushed the line forward five miles on the first day, and within five days could report 9,000 prisoners and 60 guns captured for less than 8,000 total French casualties.

(i) *The defeat of Roumania.*

The swift destruction of Roumania in September-October, 1916, must count as one of the most successful campaigns of the War.

Among the chief determining factors in the German victory were these : —

(1) It was believed that the Carpathian passes at that date were inaccessible to artillery and transport. They were not.

(2) The prompt declaration of war on Roumania by Bulgaria, followed by Mackensen's brilliant advance through the Dobrudja, these were unexpected developments. It had been thought that Bulgaria would delay or avoid open hostilities with Roumania, and that the Bulgaro-German forces would be too much occupied by the Salonika force to intervene.

(3) The Allies were assured that the Germans were so shattered and strained by the tremendous assaults on the Somme that they could not spare a battalion for Roumania. It was indeed a surprise to find that several German divisions were withdrawn from the Western Front at the height of the Battle of the Somme to furnish Falkenhayn with an army to invade Roumania across the Carpathians.

These events prove that trench warfare and aerial observation do not preclude the element of surprise. The question that ought to have been considered by the Allied Military Staffs was whether there existed anywhere at any point of the compass the possibility of bringing off such crashing surprises as those engineered by the Germans. Clearly the enemy was expecting a resumption of the offensive on the Western Front in 1917, for they were making the most elaborate preparations to meet and defeat it. That accounted for the abandonment of the Somme Plateau in March and the retirement to a new and shorter line of defence, which had been carefully prepared. The withdrawal of the line was as a matter of fact a most effective surprise to the Allies. It threw our plans out of gear, and the Germans were enabled to save whole divisions from the trenches and thus accumulate masses of men behind the lines to fill up gaps and build up a reserve for counter-attack. It is inconceivable that these enormous operations should have been made without the knowledge of the French and British Intelligence Departments. Aeroplanes crossed and recrossed over and far beyond the German lines, and if they did observe and report the arrangements, which were in process for weeks running into months, to construct a new and massive line of entrenchments, the Staff do not seem to have attached any importance to the information. There does not seem to have been any aerial observation of the withdrawal of men, guns, munitions and stores that went on for days. The Intelligence Staffs who worked out plans for set offensives in the Allied Headquarters had been taught to believe that no surprises on a great scale were possible on either side in the stabilised West. They had never been able to stage one that misled the Germans. Why then should the Germans be able to deceive them? This was one of the axioms of Allied strategy fermenting under a brass hat. To doubt it, if you were a civilian, was to be an amateur; if a soldier, then a crank only safe to fight in trenches, where to think was a breach of discipline. Surprise was therefore ruled out on the Western Front.

Why not attempt a surprise on the Italian Front? We were assured that nothing of that nature was possible there. The Austrians knew an offensive was coming. They probably did, but they were expecting the same old kind of offensive: a preliminary bombardment in a difficult country of granite trenches by an utterly inadequate artillery, insufficiently supplied with ammunition. Our Staffs knew that nothing could come of such an attack, except the loss by the enemy of a few kilometres which could be easily recovered by a well-timed and well-gunned counter-attack. Such a conventional offensive had its uses in the general scheme of things as ordered at Chantilly: it kept a number of Austrian guns in the Trentino or on the Isonzo so that they should not wander to the Carpathians, or so that the Austrians should not be able to lend their giant guns to the Germans in France. It never occurred to the rigid minds of the two G.H.Q.'s that a kind of attack was possible on the Italian Front which would have taken the Austrians completely unawares and achieved a real break-through and not impossibly a break-up, before the Germans could come in sufficient numbers to the succour of their routed allies. It is fair to point out here that Pétain, Franchet d'Esperey and Micheler suggested a combined offensive in Italy on these lines in March, as an alternative to the attack on the Chemin des Dames. Had this advice been pressed to the point of acceptance and action, Caporetto might have been anticipated and reversed. The Italians had a definite numerical superiority over the Austrians. Had they been equipped with a corresponding superiority in heavy guns and ammunition, the Austrians might have been overwhelmed. They certainly would have been taken completely by surprise. Their soldiers had no experience on any front of that kind of bombardment and it would have completely unnerved them for some time. It would have taken weeks to steady and rally them. If the Italian advance, measured by kilometres, had been comparable to that of the Austrians in the unexpected attack in May, 1916, or to the German break-through at Amiens in March, 1918, or in June, 1918, at Château Thierry, the Istrian Peninsula would have been captured and Pola with its troublesome submarine base would have been cut off. Had it been as great a success as Caporetto was for the Central Powers, the Italians would have reached Laibach and penetrated beyond to the coal basin of Carniola. Why could it not have been done? The Austrians were not better men than the British who fought in front of Amiens, or the French who were driven back to the Marne in 1918.

These were the considerations that led me, on becoming Prime Minister, to make a fresh effort to dissuade the French Government from the contemplated offensive in France and to induce them to join the Italians in launching a great combined attack on the Austrians. If the proposal met with approval at the Rome Conference, then a simultaneous attack on the eastern frontier of Austria could be arranged at the Petrograd Conference. I felt assured that the French and British Military Staffs would be obdurate. Better death (for other soldiers) on the Western Front than victory (for other Generals) on any other flank. The only hope was in the conversion of the French and Italian Governments to the scheme and in an insistence by the three Governments on its adoption by the High Commands. I knew that the Generals would regard the notion as another piece of amateur impertinence. Nevertheless, as I have already indicated, three great French Generals were converted in March to this strategic idea emanating from amateur brains.

CHAPTER XLVII

THE ROME CONFERENCE

WHEN the Anglo-French Conference met in London on 26th December, 1916, to discuss the terms of the Allied reply to the German and Wilson Peace Notes, I proposed to it that representatives of the Governments and of the High Military Commands of Britain, France and Italy should meet together in conference at an early date, in order to have a frank discussion on the whole military and political situation.

There were immediate decisions of great urgency to be taken as to the Balkans, and to suit the convenience of General Sarrail, the Commander-in-Chief of the Allied Forces at Salonika, General Milne, the British Commander, and also the Generals in command of the Serbian and Venizelist forces, whose presence at the discussion of the Greek position was desired, it was ultimately arranged that the conference should be held in Rome.

The Rome Conference met on 5th, 6th and 7th January, 1917. I took with me Lord Milner, Sir William Robertson and Sir Maurice Hankey. The French Premier, M. Briand, was accompanied by MM. Albert Thomas and Berthelot, and General Lyautey, the new French War Minister. The principal Italian Ministers were present in full force with the Commander-in-Chief, General Cadorna, General Sarrail and General Milne, who commanded our Army in the Balkans, crossed over from Salonika. Sir Francis Elliott and Colonel Fairholme, the Military Attaché, came from Athens.

In order to define the aims, and, in so far as I could, direct the discussions of the Conference, I had prepared the following memorandum which I circulated to the delegates. It was designed definitely to raise the important issues as to Allied strategy which I have set forth in the preceding chapter, and if possible to obtain decisions which would release us from the fatal net in which we were enmeshed by the Chantilly plans.

" 1. The Conference was summoned at the desire of the British Government, as we felt that, in the present situation, a very frank discussion was necessary, not only with reference to recent events in the Balkans and in Greece, but also in regard to the whole campaign of 1917.

2. We wish first to ask the permission of the Conference to speak with great frankness, and we invite the representatives of France and Italy to adopt the same course. In the last two and a half years the British and French representatives, owing to the comparative nearness of London and Paris, have been able to meet on very frequent occasions. The result is that we have all got to know one another personally; by degrees formality has been overcome; and at our most recent Conferences we have been able to speak our full minds to one another without reserve, and without causing any friction or misunderstanding. Considerations of distance have unfortunately prevented us from having such frequent meetings with the Italian representatives, but, in view of the traditional friendship between the British and Italian nations, and the racial affinity between the French and the Italians, we feel that we three nations, sitting together in council at this time of tremendous crisis, should speak to one another with the utmost freedom, and endeavour to secure the closest possible understanding. By such an understanding alone can we hope to secure that cordial co-operation which we believe to be essential to the winning of the War.

3. There is, indeed, nothing which the British Government have closer at heart than the concerting of such arrangements for co-operation between the Allies as will enable them to counteract the tremendous advantages which the enemy has obtained from a centralised control.

4. The material and moral resources of the Allies are greatly in excess of those of the enemy. The Entente Powers have more men, more guns, greater resources, and the whole world to draw upon; and yet they have not, up to the present, been able to overcome their common enemy. What is the reason for this? It is that the German Emperor has secured complete control over the resources of all the Central Powers, and is able to use them wherever they can be most effectively employed, having regard to all the circumstances.

5. During the year 1916, each of the Armies of the Entente Powers has conducted a campaign with the utmost skill and courage. We have nothing but admiration for the manner in which each of the Armies has fought. We believe, though, that each nation has concentrated its efforts too much upon its own front, with the result that the advantages which the Allies possess in personnel and resources have not been utilised to their maximum efficiency. The efforts of the British and French Armies on the Western Front; of the Italian Army on the Southern Front; and of the Russians in the East, though latterly co-ordinated in point of time, have not been sufficient to prevent an inferior enemy from overrunning first Serbia and latterly Roumania. This is a

serious reflection on our common efforts, and it behoves each Government to do its utmost to rectify the fundamental error.

6. *This, then, is the primary reason for which we have asked this Conference to assemble, namely, to examine whether some method can be found for focussing the efforts of the Allies in such a manner that, during the year 1917, the enemy can be crushed, and finally defeated.* In fact, we ask that the Conference shall now give expression and find some practical solution to the principle* which was discussed at the Conference held in Paris on the 15th and 16th November last.

7. Assuming, then, that the principle of complete and united co-operation is accepted—and we feel sure that the Governments represented here to-day are bound to accept it—let us examine the present military situation and seek how this principle can best be applied.

8. Unquestionably, the gravest problems confronting the Allies arise from the collapse of Roumania. The Russians have had to extend their front in order that the Roumanian Armies may reform in rear before again coming into the line in full force. This, we fear, may exercise a far-reaching effect on the power of Russia for the offensive during the year 1917. The lack of heavy guns and ammunition which, in 1916, prevented Russia from developing her full strength, and which we had hoped to over-come by the additions to be made to the Russian armament during the next few months may, we fear, again hamper the offensive of our great Eastern Ally, since the additional heavy guns will, for defensive purposes, have to be spread over the greatly increased length of front.

9. The Central Powers, we apprehend, may seek, if they think fit, to pursue their offensive far into the heart of Russia, either in the direction of Odessa or in the direction of Petrograd.

10. Or, alternatively, the Central Powers may prefer, when they have established themselves on the shortest possible defensive line in the East, to transfer a portion of their forces to attack the Allies at Salonika, and to overwhelm us in that theatre. . . . According to our military advisers, the Allies, at their present strength, should be able to maintain themselves against any attack which the enemy can bring against them in the Balkan theatre, but only by the evacuation of Monastir; the consequences of abandoning Monastir, however, are not agreeable to contemplate. It will open the way for direct communication between the Central Powers and Greece, and may lead to the intervention, on the side of the enemy, of yet another Balkan State, a weak one, it is true, but not altogether negligible. Moreover, the evacuation of Monastir

* The principle of the common front and the pooling of Allied resources.

will have a most depressing effect on the morale of the Serbian Army, and it is to be feared that the troops composing this already dwindling force may become so discouraged as to desert the colours and scatter to their homes. In any case, the Serbian Army has always shown itself superior in offence to defence. Thus, by withdrawing to a shorter line, the Allies run the risk not only of a further serious weakening, but possibly of an actual diminution of their forces in the Balkan theatre. Withdrawal from Monastir, and the entry of the enemy into Greece, will inflict a moral blow on the cause of the Allies, which cannot fail to exercise a most unfortunate influence both on our own peoples and on neutral nations.

11. *There is yet another course which the Central Powers may adopt. They may turn the mass of their manœuvre army upon the Italian Front, either before or after they have dealt with the Russians,* or alternatively, with the Army of the East. Are we to look on as anxious but impotent spectators whilst Germany destroys our friends one after another?* This is our present position in reference to Roumania.

12. Now what, I ask, are the plans of the Allies for meeting any of these contingencies? No doubt General Gourko, General Sarrail and General Cadorna has each an admirable plan of his own for meeting the contingency. *But what is the plan of the Allies as a whole? The combined offensive against Bulgaria, planned at Chantilly, is no longer practicable and so far as we know the Allies have absolutely no plan, except for each General to continue ' punching' on his own front.* We do not say that this course is negligible. Unquestionably, operations such as those undertaken on the Somme, or on the Carso, have some considerable effect in drawing in a part of the enemy's manœuvre forces and in exhausting in rotation the troops that are put in to resist, but neither of these operations availed to save Roumania. *In modern war, it seems that the power of the defence, by first-rate and fully-equipped troops, is so considerable that great attacks can be held up by armies inferior numerically.* Unquestionably, also, the enemy has shown very great powers of resistance on the defensive, and extraordinary skill in making the utmost out of, and improving, artificially, such natural defences as are offered by the terrain.

13. We suggest that the Allied Generals should be asked by this Political Conference, to consider some more thorough measures of co-operation and that the Governments should be prepared to give them their support.

14. To give any direct assistance to Russia, except by means of such material equipment as can be passed in through Archangel

---

* This is exactly what happened later on at Caporetto.

and Vladivostock, is, we fear, impossible.* The extent to which material assistance can, and ought to be given to Russia, having regard to the interests of the Allies as a whole, is the primary consideration to be examined at the forthcoming Conference in Russia. If the Russian Conference reports that, by increasing such equipment it is really possible in the year 1917 to put Russia in a position to exert an influence on the War commensurate with her numerical strength, then we think that the Western Allies should themselves be prepared to make sacrifices to render this possible. We are, however, not yet certain that this is the case; we have an open mind on the subject. We think it possible that technical difficulties of communications by sea and rail, lack of communications on the Russian Front, the character of bridges, inadequate facilities for training personnel, and the strategic disadvantages of a greatly extended front already alluded to, may possibly be so serious in their cumulative effect as to prevent a full use being put to the guns given to Russia. These, however, are matters primarily for the Russian Conference, and I will not detain the present Conference with them further.

15. With regard to the Balkans, the British and French Governments are in agreement, in principle, that: —

'The Allies should continue to hold Monastir and the line at present occupied, as long as this can be done without exposing the forces to defeat.

Meanwhile a shorter line should be prepared for occupation, in case of need, which will enable the force to hold its own against any attack which may be made.'

To meet the danger to the Salonika force, the French Government have decided to send two divisions, and have invited the British Government to examine the possibility of sending two divisions.

16. Practical considerations render it extremely difficult for us to comply with this request. The transport of troops from Great Britain to Salonika involves a long sea journey, and locks up shipping for considerable periods. Moreover, every increase of the Army means an increase in the amount of shipping committed, for maintenance purposes, to this long and dangerous line of communications. The increased intensity of the enemy's submarine campaign makes this line of communication dangerous throughout its length. For these reasons we are most unwilling to send any further force to Salonika, at a time when our Allies are making ever-increasing demands on our shipping resources for their essential needs in raw materials, coal, food supplies, and munitions.

* Every other gate had been closed by the enemy.

So serious is the shipping position, so vital a factor it is upon the staying power of the Entente, that we will return to this question later as a separate subject. In the meanwhile, we must ask the Conference to accept our view that after exhaustive examination we have come to the conclusion that the grave shipping situation provides an overwhelming argument against the dispatch of further British divisions to Salonika."

[The chapter on shipping reveals the precarious position we were in at that time. Our measures to deal with the situation had been barely launched. But it is necessary to point out that these difficulties with regard to the supply of shipping had not arisen in an acute form in 1915. Therefore we could then have dispatched to Salonika, and maintained there a sufficient force to prevent the Serbian defeat and the overrunning of the Balkan Peninsula by the Central Powers.]

The next six paragraphs of my memorandum, numbered 17 to 22, urged that Italy should send additional reinforcements to Salonika, and in this connection advocated the development of a route from Santi Quaranta on the Adriatic, straight through to Monastir, and the improvement of railway communications down through Italy, so that supplies and reinforcements could be sent to Salonika overland, save for the short crossing of the Adriatic. Shipping would thus be economised, and the submarine menace to the Salonika communications immensely reduced.

"23. Leaving the Balkans, let us look at the Italian Front. Here there are two possible contingencies: one defensive, the other offensive. If the enemy should, as suggested above, concentrate his manœuvre armies against the Italian Front, it would afford a great opportunity for the Allies. Should the enemy adopt this course, the presumption is that he will gamble upon the stupidity and lack of mobility of the Allies. Unquestionably, he regards us as stupid and lacking in initiative. Let us take advantage of this amiable belief. The enemy will base the plan of attack on the assumption that he has to meet a force of so many Italian heavy guns, some of which he knows to be of old type, and lacking in mobility. If he elects to attack on this front, we propose that the Allies should concert their own plans, so that instead of meeting the artillery armament that he calculates for, he shall find himself confronted with a vastly superior armament of Italian guns reinforced by British, and we should hope, French artillery, with their own personnel. We can put the Germans out of action just as well on the Italian as on the Western Front. By adopting this plan we might well convert a repulse into a rout, just as the Germans, by massing artillery on the Roumanian Front, converted the Roumanian invasion of Transylvania into an utter defeat.

We ask our Allies to examine this proposal in a sympathetic spirit, and, subject to the approval of the Conference, *we propose that orders should be given to our respective General Staffs to work it out in all its technical details, including the elaboration of railway time-tables, and the arrangements for the necessary gun emplacements and communications.*

24. *The second possible contingency is that the Allies themselves should take the offensive in this region.* We consider that the instructions to the Allied Staffs should not be limited to the provision of a purely defensive scheme for the Italian Front, as outlined above. We consider that they should be directed to examine also the possibilities of exploiting the offensive possibilities of this front. *We should like to ask the Generals to report to us whether they cannot devise plans for a surprise artillery concentration for offensive purposes on the Isonzo Front.* If our information is correct, the Italian Army has the strength to conduct offensive operations on a great scale on that relatively narrow front, which is suited to a great offensive, and they have also the *infantry* strength to hold a longer line than the present one. We understand that the reason why they have not yet achieved complete success in their splendid offensive is the lack of sufficient artillery, and more especially heavy artillery and heavy artillery ammunition, to bring about a decisive conclusion. Would it not be possible to make a great and sudden stroke against the enemy by a concentration of British and French artillery on the Isonzo Front, so as not only to ensure the safety of Italy against any enemy concentration, but, what is more important, to shatter the enemy's forces, to inflict a decisive defeat on him, and to press forward to Trieste and to get astride the Istrian Peninsula?

25. The strategical advantages to be gained by such action appear to be very great. It would probably be a great surprise to the enemy. The action would be fought on enemy territory. It would enable the Italians to deploy their full strength. It would compel the enemy to defend a longer line. It should, therefore, have an immediate effect in relieving the Russian, Roumanian, and Balkan Fronts. It might enable the Allies to attack Pola, and probably either to destroy the Austrian Fleet, or to force it to action, or drive it out to become a prey to our submarines. This in turn should hamper the enemy's submarine campaign in the Mediterranean. Moreover, it could be accomplished without any additional strain whatever upon our shipping. It would have a moral and political effect of the greatest consequence, and would be a good counter to the enemy's successes in Roumania. It would enable the Allies to take advantage of a period when the weather

---

* This preparation for a German-Austrian attack on Italy saved the situation after Caporetto.

on the Western Front is unfavourable for the development of a great offensive. It would, however, be absolutely necessary to have a clear understanding that, within a certain period of time, the heavy guns should be withdrawn to enable the British and French Armies to pursue their offensive on the Western Front.*

26.   Such, then, are the problems which we think the Governments and the General Staffs should consider, namely: —

(1)   The desirability of sending guns to Russia, even at a sacrifice, by the Western Powers. This however is a matter on which we must await the report of the Conference in Russia.

(2)   The desirability of the dispatch of two Italian divisions to the Balkan theatre—either through Santi Quaranta or Salonika; in this connection also the development of railway communications through Italy and Greece should be examined.

(3)   The development of defensive and offensive schemes of co-operation on the Italian Front."

Copies of this document were distributed amongst the civilian, military and naval members of the various delegations before the Conference met. It will be noted that this paper forecast accurately the action subsequently taken by the Central Powers, the launching by them of a joint offensive against Italy as soon as they had disposed of Russia. My memorandum urged the Allies to take timely measures to counter the blow when it fell.

After a preliminary meeting, the Conference split up into two sections, Political and Military. The first pre-occupation of both sections was with the situation at Salonika. The military conference on this subject ended in a complete deadlock, for the French military delegates, supported by representatives of Russia, insisted that Britain and Italy should furnish three more divisions for the Salonika Army, without any clear idea in their minds as to the purpose they were intended to serve. For defence they were superfluous; for attack they would be insufficient. The British and Italians were emphatic that they could not do this, and that the few ships available should be utilised to fill up the undoubted weakness of the units already on the spot. If an overwhelming attack came from the North, of which they were doubtful, the forces there should be prepared to withdraw to a shorter line.

General Sarrail's acutest anxiety was about the safety of his left flank in the event of enemy attacks on his front. On 1st December, 1916, parties of Allied troops had been landed in Athens to enforce the fulfilment by the Greek King of Allied demands, and had been attacked by his troops. There was a real danger that any frontal attack by the enemy on the Salonika forces would be the signal for

* When General Cadorna pointed out that this condition vitiated our offer of guns, it was unconditionally withdrawn by me at the Conference.

an outbreak of hostilities by the Greek Royalist troops in their rear, which would make their position one of acute jeopardy.

In view of this situation, General Sarrail came to me on the third morning of the conference for a personal interview.

He was one of those rare personalities of whom no one can form a moderate opinion. To his partisans he was a brilliant general, to his critics he was a bounding charlatan. Joffre said there was nothing he had done in the fight in France that would justify the view that he was an able general. Another distinguished Frenchman that I met said that Sarrail's fight against the Germans in the Nancy area was one of the finest feats of the War. Of one thing I felt certain—the official military clique here and in France " had a down " on him. He was to them a political general, which simply meant that leading politicians believed in him. Better be " a friend of publicans and sinners " than of politicians. To French Headquarters he was therefore a more dangerous foe than Von Kluck. A general who is not in favour with Headquarters has a poorer chance than a politician who is not acceptable to the Party Whips. The obnoxious politician can appeal to the public and thus make himself such a menace that it is safer to conciliate than to crush him; but for a soldier to appeal to any lay tribunal against either the strategy or the competency of his superiors is in itself an offence against professional canons which stamps him as an outsider.

Before I met Sarrail in Rome I had taken my opinions concerning him from official sources, qualified by the eulogies passed upon him by M. Albert Thomas and M. Painlevé. I knew Thomas to be a shrewd judge of men as well as of affairs, and I was therefore quite prepared to find that Sarrail was not the flashy adventurer who subordinated tactics to politics. But I was not quite prepared for the attractive and magnetic personality to whom I was introduced at the Rome Conference.

He was an exceptionally handsome man, with a high forehead, a glittering blue eye, a genial accost and a direct, intelligent and quiet manner of answering all the questions put to him about Salonika.

He demanded a free hand to anticipate the Greek move by an invasion of Greece and an attack on the Royal Army. To this I refused British assent. I was not prepared to allow action which might result in an outbreak of hostilities with the Greek population, which was, on the whole, friendly to the Allies. The affair would, to the outside world, have an unpleasant resemblance to the conduct of the Germans in Belgium. But we were justified in adopting every measure necessary to protect our troops against the danger of sudden attack on their most vulnerable flanks. After the events of 1st December, therefore, we had imposed a severe blockade on Greece, which we were maintaining until we should be satisfied that the King had taken the necessary steps to clear up the position.

I did my best to reassure General Sarrail, and obtained his promise that he would take no action without first communicating with me. It seemed fairly certain that the pressure of our blockade would compel the Greek Government to carry out our terms, even if rather slowly and unwillingly.

I saw a good deal of Sarrail at this Conference. He made no complaint about his superiors, although he might have done so, for no General in the War was accorded meaner treatment. He was landed in an enterprise which could barely have succeeded when he took over the command if there had been abundant resources at his disposal. He was left without a competent Staff, and with a wretched equipment whether for fighting or for transport. His troops were far from being a good specimen of an average French Army. Even thus they were far below strength. He was expected to attack almost inaccessible defiles well entrenched, with a wretched quota of heavy guns and little ammunition. His British Allies were kept in the same condition of inadequacy and unpreparedness for any effective contribution. I was surprised under these conditions that he seemed to preserve his geniality and good temper. But he certainly did. He was completely devoid of any bitterness and he never made a single complaint to me of the shabby treatment accorded to him and to his Army. It is on record that the favourable impression he made upon me was shared by all those who took part in the Rome Conference.

If he did not accomplish anything for two years, it was because it was not intended that he should, and the military junta who managed these things both in France and in England saw to it that every temptation to accomplishment should be withheld from this dashing but obnoxious general. The French General Staff, whilst pursuing a deliberate policy of starving the Salonika force, gave the impression to the Government that Sarrail had been provided with the means which would enable him to carry through a decisive attack on the enemy positions in the Balkans. To do Robertson justice, he never sought to mislead his Government on that point.

But upon the question of further reinforcements for Salonika, no agreement was reached. At the conclusion of the second day's discussion, M. Briand made an impassioned plea for us to send two divisions thither. As a piece of oratory it was the finest exhibition I have ever heard at any Conference. It was delivered in a comparatively small room, at a table around which barely a dozen sat. M. Briand spoke sitting. Voice, gesture, inflection displayed his oratorical powers at their best, as if he were addressing a crowded Chamber of Deputies. He spoke with dramatic force, and yet we never felt anything incongruous in the method of such a deliverance to so small and intimate a gathering. Rhetorically it was a triumph. As soon as he finished, Baron Sonnino turned round to me and said: " That is the finest speech I ever heard." But whilst it was a brilliant

2E

display of M. Briand's powers, it was also a revelation of his defects. There was no attempt to deal with the practical difficulties or to indicate how they were to be overcome. There were two other characteristic touches to follow. We were to dine at the French Embassy that evening. The speech delayed us, and M. Barrère had to postpone the hour of our repast. When M. Briand finished, the tenseness of the face relaxed, the glow in the eye disappeared, and he turned round to us with a smile, and said: "And now for the Embassy!" The following morning Albert Thomas sought to renew the discussion and bring it to some practical point, but his eloquent chief cut him short. He wanted no further debate on the topic. He had come there to deliver a speech and not to obtain a decision. His speech had been delivered; it was a triumph: there was nothing more to be done.

However, I thought it necessary to give practical reasons why we could not comply with the French demand, and I said that "if eloquence would carry two divisions to Salonika, M. Briand's speech at the conclusion of the previous evening's Conference would have accomplished the task. Unfortunately, however, ships were needed and these we had not got." I read a telegram received that morning from the Quartermaster-General of the War Office to the effect that since the previous Thursday the traffic through the Mediterranean had been absolutely closed to our ships, owing to submarines, though it was hoped to resume traffic in a day or two. I had the warmest sympathy with M. Briand's desire to reinforce our Army in the Balkans, particularly if any prospect should be opened of our using it for an effective thrust against the enemy in that region. But our shipping had now been very seriously reduced by submarine attacks, and was in greater demand than ever for carrying supplies, not only for ourselves but for our Allies. We had at the time no less than 1,200,000 tons of shipping occupied with carrying for the French, and several hundred thousand tons carrying for the Italians. Unless they were prepared to forgo the supplies of coal, steel and other commodities which we were shipping for them, we simply could not add to our commitments the task of transporting further forces to Salonika and maintaining them there—certainly not until the submarine crisis had been overcome. We already had more men on that front than either the French or the Italians, and to keep them reinforced with fresh drafts and provisioned with food, equipment and munitions at the other end of the submarine-infested Mediterranean, was a task of no little difficulty.

Besides, the Salonika Front was still unadapted for large-scale offensive operations. Little had been done to improve the transport facilities up country from the ports. The roads were deplorably bad. I urged the Italians, therefore, at the Conference, to supply companies of engineers and workmen for making an additional road from

Santi Quaranta to Monastir and improving the railway lines, so that there might be a line of communication with the Balkans which would run mainly overland, with only a short and easily protected sea trip from Brindisi to Santi Quaranta. But General Cadorna flatly refused to supply engineers, and would give no pledge even to find labourers for the work.

And now we come to the discussions and conclusions on the subject which was to me the main purpose of the Conference—the effort to secure a fundamental reconstruction of Allied strategy on all fronts. I had summarised my views in the memorandum distributed before the meeting and I invited a discussion on my proposals. In opening this discussion I drew particular attention to two questions raised in that memorandum. The first of these was the re-equipment of the Russian Armies, and the second, the question of a combined attack on the Italian Front. Referring to the second of these subjects, I said that the Italian Front appeared to offer an admirable opportunity for breaking fresh ground. The Italian Army, though its equipment had proceeded at a wonderful rate, had not yet reached the stage, particularly in the matter of heavy guns, when it could bring an overwhelming artillery fire to bear on the enemy. But on the Italian Front the Allies had to deal with an enemy who was weaker than elsewhere on the Western Front, where the Allies were opposed by Germans. The Austrians had not the same cohesion as the Germans, and were less redoubtable as a fighting unit. I suggested also that on this front the Central Powers were more vulnerable than on other fronts. If you were to drive the Germans back 20 or 30 miles on our front, you would find them still pivoting on French villages, which would have to be destroyed one by one to ensure a continuance of the advance. On the Italian Front, however, you could reach the enemy's vitals. Here the advance would be in enemy territory, and it would be the enemy's villages that would be destroyed. I laid great stress on the fact that the Austrians were the weakest enemy, and I suggested we ought to strike at the weakest and not at the strongest point in the enemy front. Germany, I pointed out, was formidable so long as she could command an unbroken Austria, but if Austria were beaten Germany would be beaten too. For these reasons I strongly advocated that the question of crushing Austria should be examined. I further pointed out that an incidental advantage would be that an attack on the Italian Front would undoubtedly divert the enemy's attention from the Balkans. If attacked on the Italian Front the Austrians could not carry out an invasion of the Balkans. Possibly, also, action here might have the effect of stopping the Moldavian attack.

I pointed out that the operations on the Somme did not have the effect of withdrawing troops from the East to the West. On the West the enemy sold dearly the land they held. They said that if you wanted to take, for example, Courcelettes, you must pay 10,000 lives for it; Pozières was more important, and for that the enemy demanded 40,000 lives; Combles was more important still, and for this the price paid was perhaps 60,000 lives. Though they ceded these points at a price, the enemy never gave up anything vital on the Western Front.

Shipping was one of our difficulties, but this question did not arise in the matter of assistance to be rendered by the Allies for an Italian offensive. We could supply a certain number of trucks for the transport of guns to the Italian Front, and the operation which I proposed on that front was one which could be carried out without any demand upon shipping.

I therefore strongly urged that my proposal should be examined by the General Staffs. *I pointed out however, that this was not enough, and that it would never be carried out unless Ministers themselves took the matter in hand, and insisted on its being considered favourably.* It was contrary to human nature for General Sir Douglas Haig to say that General Cadorna's front was more important than his own; and conversely, you could not expect General Cadorna to say that the British Front was more important than the Italian.

I then read the following resolution: —

" The Conference are impressed with the advantages afforded by the Italian Front for a combined offensive by the three Western Allies, which are as follows: —

1. It would relieve the pressure on Russia, Roumania and the Balkans.
2. It would attack the enemy on a front where his forces are weaker in numbers, quality, and equipment, than at any other point accessible to the Allied Armies of the West.
3. It might enable the Allies to capture Trieste, which would bring important political advantages.
4. It might enable the Allies to capture Pola, the principal Austrian naval base, thereby reducing the submarine menace in the Mediterranean.
5. No additional demand on shipping transport is involved.
6. The Allies would be fighting on enemy territory.

The Conference refer this question for immediate examination by the Ministers, in conjunction with the military representatives, more particularly from the point of view of the form which the French and British co-operation should take."

I explained that the last sentence referred to the question whether General Cadorna would require guns only or infantry divisions as well.

According to a note taken at the time, M. Briand pointed out

" how great was the organisation needed, under modern conditions, for an offensive. It was, he said, nothing less than a great industrial organisation. *He further pointed out that the Staffs of the Allies had recently worked out their plans at Chantilly; and that the preparations for carrying them out were now far advanced. In view of this he questioned whether it would be wise to change the plan now. M. Briand said that General Nivelle reported that the German forces had, to a considerable extent, been used up, and that they were not nearly so thick on the ground as they used to be. Having regard to the ascendancy recently shown by French troops General Nivelle considered it possible to break through. M. Briand therefore urged that in the examination of this question its repercussion on the offensive, which had been so long prepared, should be carefully considered.* He therefore expressed sympathy with the proposal, but reserved it for technical examination, and at present he would not attempt to anticipate the opinion of the military experts. He urged, however, the importance of the spring offensive being decisive."

Continuing, M. Briand said that,

" if we could really break through to Trieste, he would be quite in accord, and thought that we ought to undertake the operation. *In view, however, of the importance of not unsettling the military plans which were now far advanced, he felt bound to make a reserve in welcoming the proposal.*"

I replied that

" I did not propose for one moment that my plan should be decided on without the fullest examination. I urged, however, that the Government should not take as final a declaration by General Nivelle, or General Douglas Haig, that they could not spare the guns. Of course, the Generals would not allow the guns to go. *I did not deny that the Generals were just as confident now as they had ever been, but I pointed out that they had always been just as confident before previous offensives.* The Central Powers, however, did not confine their efforts to one front as each of the Allied Generals did. They attacked in Roumania, or the Balkans, or wherever they could hit hardest at the moment. *They might very likely strike before long at the Italian Front if they thought they could do any good there.*"

Baron Sonnino said that

" the Italian Government felt it was quite possible that the enemy might come to that front in a month or two."

M. Briand again reverted to the very heavy preparations involve in an attack, under modern conditions.

" There were so many miles of front, so many troops, and s many guns required; all had to be calculated to a nicety, and a kinds of preparations made. He said that, when General Nivell had commanded the armies in the region of Verdun, he had com to M. Briand and proposed an attack. M. Briand had felt som doubt about the question, owing to the *usure*. General Nivell however, had described exactly how he could conduct the opera tion, and had stated that he would send telegrams to him at suc and such an hour from such and such points, which he had cap tured. Eventually, M. Briand sanctioned the attack, and Genera Nivelle carried it out absolutely as he had forecast. This naturall had created a most favourable impression in regard to Genera Nivelle on M. Briand's mind, and made him feel some confidenc in his plans for the future. At Verdun, M. Briand pointed out, th French actually did break right through the German lines, but th country was a *cul de sac* and unfavourable to an advance. Never theless, they gained invaluable experience. *They were inclined t think that an attack, prepared in a certain way, had now a ver good chance of succeeding."*

M. Thomas, while not rejecting my proposal, urged

" that it must be examined to the bottom (*au fond*) particularl in regard to the question of dates and the equilibrium of force o the different fronts."

M. Briand again pressed the contention as to the deterioration i the quality of the German Army. He said

" *there was considerable difference between the character of th enemy's troops now and in the early part of the War. Formerl all the enemy troops consisted of* troupes de choc *but now only portion of the enemy's forces could be regarded as* troupes de cho *Hence, in most parts of the line we should find rather mediocr troops opposed to us. That is how he envisaged the strategic situation of the enemy. He did not dismiss my proposal but onl urged that it required careful examination."*

The Russian Ambassador pointed out that it was very importar to secure concerted plans. He considered my proposal a very sedu tive one.

Baron Sonnino said that there were two ways of presenting th problem for examination : —

1. On the basis that the Italian forces required materi support only; and
2. On the basis that they required troops in addition.

M. Briand said he would be very surprised if General Cadorna had not already had some proposition in view.

I asked that General Cadorna should consider the proposition that evening, and give his views to-morrow.

Baron Sonnino suggested, however, that it would be better for General Cadorna to hear my views at once, and urged that he should be summoned to join the Conference.

At this point General Cadorna entered the Conference and Baron Sonnino explained my proposal to him. General Cadorna said that he had had an opportunity of glancing at my memorandum. As a point of detail he said he did not like the idea of advancing on Pola. To do so would take him away from his main objective, which was Laibach, on the road to Vienna.

I interpolated at this point that I would be quite satisfied if General Cadorna could advance towards Vienna with the reinforcements proposed.

General Cadorna went on to ask

" how long the material would be at his disposal? This was really an essential point. *He gathered from conversations with Generals Lyautey and Robertson that the material would have to be returned by May.* He reminded the Conference that to be useful for offensive operations the material must be back some eight or ten days before the offensive began. Then an allowance had to be made for the time necessary for the transport to and from France. Time also had to be allowed for loading and unloading off the railways. Then there were the different methods of the various nations to be considered in regard to technical matters, such as fire control, the use of metres instead of yards, fire observations, etc.; some time would be required to accustom the British and French artillery to the Italian methods. After you had made allowance for all these things, he asked how much time remained? If he could have the artillery for long enough he would, of course, be delighted."

General Cadorna then alluded to the danger of an offensive from the Trentino, which, he pointed out,

" was very great. So long as the snow was on the mountains the Italians were safe from this menace, but after May he was liable to be attacked from two points."

I said that

" *the conditions as to the return of the guns by May might apply to the French guns, but I myself had not, up to the present, excluded the possibility of allowing British guns to remain for a longer time on the Italian Front.*"

M. Thomas expressed

" considerable surprise at this last remark. He said that I talked as though my resources were unlimited. At one and the same time I talked of sending guns both to Russia and to Italy. *How could this be done without altering the whole equilibrium of the position on the Western Front?*"

I retorted that,

" at the present moment, there were on the British Front twice as many heavy guns as there were at the commencement of the Battle of the Somme. We had given no undertaking that we could allot any specified number of guns to the French Front. At this moment we had three times as much ammunition as we had at the beginning of the Somme offensive. Moreover, if we lent 250 to 300 heavy guns to Italy to-day, by the end of February we should, at our present rate of output, have replaced the whole amount. M. Thomas, no doubt, could speak for the French position, but I knew as much as anyone about the British position in regard to heavy guns."

General Cadorna said that

" he would be only too delighted to have a larger force at his disposal. He would gladly accept heavy guns, but if they were only to be available for some three months from the present time, it was not worth while for him to accept them."

I was disgusted with the lack of enthusiasm displayed by Cadorna over the proposal made by one of the most powerful of the Allies to equip him for a sustained attack on the Austrians by supplying him with his deficiencies in heavy guns, and I turned to Sir Maurice Hankey and said: " The old fellow does not want guns." This provoked a protest from Sonnino, who was utterly bewildered by Cadorna's reluctance to close with our offer.

I replied that,

" of course, General Cadorna would like to have the guns. Every General would like to have more heavy guns. This, however, had not been the motive of my proposal. The question for General Cadorna to consider, and on which the Conference desired his opinion, was, if he were lent the guns, could he carry out a really great, or even decisive, operation on behalf of the Allies?"

General Cadorna replied that

" he could undoubtedly carry out a very great operation with further assistance in heavy guns, but the operation would neces- sarily be a very long one. Referring to my memorandum, *he pointed out that a tactical surprise, under modern conditions, was not practicable.* The enemy would unquestionably discover that the guns were being brought to that front."

I said that,

" nevertheless, it would be a certain surprise to the enemy to see the Allies co-operating closely in this way. I did not intend that the attack would be a surprise in the tactical sense, but that our initiative would necessarily dislocate the enemy's plans. I asked what precisely General Cadorna thought that he could accomplish with the guns. I did not ask for an immediate answer, but I wanted to know what he considered he could do."

General Cadorna stated that undoubtedly he could do a good deal more on a wider front, and he undertook to consider the question. He then withdrew from the Conference.

Lord Milner pointed out,

" *on the question of surprise, that we were always told that we could not surprise the enemy, yet the enemy always surprised us. In support of this he instanced Verdun and the attack on Roumania, both of which were surprises. The fact was that the initiative always rested with the enemy.* General Cadorna had intimated that he could do something if given these guns, but the question we wanted to know was—could he undertake a really great and successful operation? It would not be worth while displacing the guns merely to gain five miles of territory instead of three. But it would be worth while to break right through. In any case, our strategic initiative on this front would be bound to disturb the enemy's plans, even if a tactical surprise were not possible."

The conclusions finally reached by the Rome Conference were set out in the following eight propositions: —

1. The Conference agrees in principle that in future there should be closer co-operation between the Allies than in the past. They further agree that in future more frequent conferences are necessary.

2. The Conference regard as essential to the success of the Allied cause that the Western Powers should take immediate steps to provide the Russian Armies with the necessary guns and ammunition to enable them to make full use of their great resources in men, and to break through the German lines on the Eastern Front.

In order to give practical effect to the above resolution, the Governments represented at the Conference further agree that their representatives at the forthcoming Conference in Russia should be granted full authority to take the necessary decisions, after telegraphic communication with their respective Governments in case of necessity.

3. The Conference approve in principle the development of a new line of communications with Macedonia with the object of diminishing the length of the communications by sea, which are at present seriously threatened by submarine attack, and reducing the dependence on sea transport. With this object in view the Italian Minister of Transport undertook to discuss, with British and French experts to be sent to Rome, the question of the development of transit of Allied troops and material over the Italian railways to the ports of Southern Italy. He indicated that the question depended mainly upon the amount of rolling-stock that could be placed at the disposal of the Italian Government. He suggested that this could best be achieved by diverting to the Italian railways French rolling-stock, which can be attached to the Italian engines more easily than British; British rolling-stock will be sent to France to replace what is taken away, as far as possible. With the object of developing a new line of communications with Monastir from Santi Quaranta, the French Government undertook to supply two companies of field engineers, and the Italian Government undertook to do their best to supply civil engineers and about 2,000 labourers.

4. The Conference approved the immediate presentation to the Greek Government, by the four Governments concerned, of the Declaration in the Appendix.

5. The Conference agreed to the following principles to guide the action of General Sarrail with regard to Greece:—

(*a*) He should take no military action against Greece during the 48 hours covered by the Declaration;

(*b*) If the Declaration should be refused, he should be at liberty to take such military action as he considered necessary for the security of the Allied Army of the East;

(*c*) If the conditions laid down in the Allied Declaration are accepted and carried out by the Greek Government, he should take no military action against Greece without the consent of the Allied Governments;

(*d*) If the Greek Government accept the conditions laid down in the Declaration, but do not carry them out within the fortnight laid down in the Declaration, he should obtain the approval of the British, French, Italian and Russian Governments before taking the initiative in any military action.

6. The Governments represented at the Conference agreed that in future the relations between the Commander-in-Chief of the Allied Army of the East and the Generals commanding the Forces of the different nationalities should be based on the principles

which governed the relations between the British Commander-in-Chief and the Commander of the French Forces in the Gallipoli Expedition, that is to say, the Commander of each of the Allied Forces shall comply with the orders of the Commander-in-Chief as regards military operations, subject to the right of direct communication with, and reference to, his own Government.

7. The Conference are impressed with the opportunities afforded by the Italian Front for a combined offensive by the three Western Allies. They agree that the question of assistance being given by the Western Allies to the Italian Army on the Carso should be referred to the Military Advisers of the various Governments, with a view to a decision by the three Governments concerned.

8. The Conference decided that a technical Naval and Shipping Conference should be held in London at the earliest possible date.

The Appendix, mentioned in the fourth resolution above, contained the French text of the ultimatum to Greece. This document stated that the Allies were determined to protect their armies against the menace created by the presence of the Greek forces in their rear. This could only be done if these forces were, as contemplated in our Note to Greece of 14th December (and in a second Note of 31st December) transported to the Peloponnesus as soon as possible. It was also necessary that the Allies should have full liberty to control the movement. If within 48 hours of the receipt of this declaration it was not agreed to by the Greek Government, the Allies would assume full liberty to safeguard their Armies by other means. For their part, the Allies were prepared to respect the wish of the Greek Government to keep out of the War, and would not allow the Venizelist faction to invade or extend control over any of the territory still under the rule of the Royalist Government. We would also raise the blockade as soon as our demands had been satisfactorily carried out.

This ultimatum proved to be efficacious for its purpose.

I may anticipate the sequel to the Rome Conference as far as Salonika was concerned, to say that although the Greek Government showed an obvious desire to evade fulfilment of the terms of the Allied ultimatum, it found itself compelled to proceed with their observance. By the end of January, Brigadier-General Philipps was able to report to us that while the Greek troops would not all be south of the Isthmus by the appointed day, enough would have gone to render the remnant harmless against us; and the position was by then so satisfactory that we were able to sanction a partial relaxation of the blockade.

The Rome Conference came to subsidiary decisions which had in the sequel important results. It temporarily cleared up the Greek situation. Both at Athens and Salonika it saved us from precipitate action which would have damaged the Allied cause. It initiated transport arrangements for the use of Italian railways to carry troops and material from France to Brindisi. These arrangements relieved the pressure on our shipping, and what is more important, they ultimately enabled French and British troops to rush to the aid of the broken army of Italy after Caporetto without loss of valuable time.

Perhaps one of the most far-reaching decisions of all was that which resolved to summon an Inter-Allied Naval and Shipping Conference to consider the best methods of co-ordinating Allied resources at sea. It is incredible that no such conference had ever been held before. In fact, the Allied War Directors never seemed to have realised that the transport question was at the root of most of their difficulties.

The Central Powers had an undoubted advantage over the Allies in the fact that they were operating on internal lines. We had the paramount advantage of the command of the sea. We ought to have realised both these facts with all their implications, and taken immediate steps to neutralise the enemy superiority due to their central position while profiting more by our own superiority on the sea.

But we were now entering on the fourth campaign of the War, and the Allies had decided for the first time to sit down to a thorough examination of one of the most vital problems with which they were confronted. In that respect the Rome discussions were of great practical value.

I was unable, however, to persuade the French to accept even in principle the idea of a combined spring offensive on the Italian Front, and Cadorna's lukewarmness was fatal to my insistence. In view of the attempt to fasten the whole responsibility for the Nivelle offensive on to me, because of my strenuous effort to make it a success once it was determined upon, I have felt it necessary to quote in full the passages in which early in January I urged the concentration of our offensive gun power on the Italian Front as a substitute for the project of a great spring offensive in France. It will be observed that I failed to persuade our Allies to take that course. The Chantilly plans had been agreed to by all the Allies at the Paris Conference in November. They were in the nature of a military Pact accepted by all the Governments concerned. The consent of all the signatories to the Paris Convention was necessary to secure any important change in its terms. France was implacable, Italy was indifferent. No strategical alteration was therefore possible without a serious conflict between the Allies. Ultimately the Conference agreed to the proposition which I have already quoted as No. 7 of its conclusions. This referred the whole question of a combined offensive on the Italian Front to those military experts who were already committed to the Nivelle plan.

This result was disappointing. When we came to the main purpose

for which the Conference had been summoned—a real and not a
sham co-ordination of strategy—the Conference reached no final
decision and the military staffs were left in possession of the field.
There were many reasons for that. The most important I shall
examine in a separate chapter. I shall here only allude to one of the
chief obstructive elements—the bondage of professional etiquette.
The professional deems it a point of honour to stand by his brethren
against all outsiders, including the facts. I have very little doubt that
this is true of all the Military High Commands. I could see it operate
in Rome. Cadorna, I know, favoured a combined offensive on the
Italian Front, but he put up no fight for his idea, even when a British
Prime Minister offered him an opening and an opportunity. Had
he conducted all his military operations in the same perfunctory spirit,
he would never have captured a single mound on the Austrian frontier.
The reason for his feebleness was that he had been persuaded at
Chantilly to accept a different strategy. His better judgment had
been overridden by men whose prestige was greater, but he had
entered into a definite arrangement with them at the Military Conference, and he was very reluctant to do something which looked like
breaking faith with his brother Commanders. He had been seen by
Robertson and the French Generals before he entered the Conference,
and they had insisted upon his adhering to the letter of his bond, even
though it involved the throwing away of the most promising chance
afforded to him to win a great triumph for his country. Professional
susceptibilities blocked his way. That accounted for his hesitancy,
his raising of objections and obstacles. To justify him in refusing the
powerful aid offered by me to his army, Robertson and Lyautey had
told him that the guns were a temporary loan and would have to be
returned to the French Government in May. After my statement at
the Conference withdrawing this condition, this could no longer be
pleaded as an excuse for declining the offer. When I told Cadorna
that the British guns at least would not be withdrawn, he ignored my
statement. If Cadorna had started a successful offensive in March
or April, no French or British General could or would have insisted
on the withdrawal of a single gun.

What contributed much more to the failure of my effort to induce
a reconsideration of Allied strategy was the fact that the French
Ministers—M. Briand and M. Albert Thomas—gave resolute support
to their military staffs. Their action was incomprehensible to those
who knew their previous attitude. They both were and always had
been zealous advocates of the " way round." They never believed in
the policy of attrition. From January, 1915, onwards they had both
advocated consistently an attack on the weaker enemy front. Why
did they swing round so completely at the Rome Conference? I will
endeavour to give some explanation of this *volte-face* in the ensuing
chapter.

CHAPTER XLVIII

PSYCHOLOGY AND STRATEGY

REFLECTING on the proceedings of the Rome Conference I had an uneasy feeling that the strategy of the Allies was not dictated solely by considerations of military advantage to their cause as a whole. The arguments advanced appeared to me to have very little to do with the various proposals which came before us. The motives that prompted either support or opposition to any particular scheme, arose from incentives that were not revealed in the course of conversation between the Allied representatives. My experience of life has taught me that men and women are not moved so much by argument as by hidden motives which are never exposed in the interchange of words. Once the undisclosed impulses or prejudices are overcome the task of the persuader becomes simpler. The road has then been cleared for reason. The reluctance to help Cadorna with the guns necessary to enable him to stage a powerful offensive, was defended in the Conference room by considerations much too trivial to be genuine. What, then, was the real objection which stood in the way?

Luigi Villari in his fascinating book " The War on the Italian Front," referring to my Rome plan for a combined offensive on the Italian Front, says: —

" The hostility of the British and French military representatives resulted in the abandonment of Lloyd George's scheme. It was not a question of personal or national jealousy on either side, but simply a divergence between two schools of military thought, Cadorna believing in the principle of concentration on the weakest enemy, his British and French colleagues on the strongest."*

This sentiment displays an ingenuousness creditable to the writer's generosity but not to his knowledge of human nature.

It is a commonplace to call attention to the strange mixture of human motive which impels conduct in all manner of men. It is confused and contradictory, selfish and unselfish, generous and mean, noble and petty—sometimes it resolves itself into a struggle between equally exalted passions—all these elements in the same breast and

* " The War on the Italian Front," p. 104.

fermenting in the same heart at the same time. The blend of all with one of the hues predominating is what determines character. In some natures the ingredients constitute a mere blotch or blur of character. It is a mistake to assume that the best are devoid of the worst and that the worst possess no trace of the best. Sometimes a motive which is out of keeping with the general character of a man or a woman gains the ascendancy over reason, baffling and disappointing his or her intimates.

In the Rome discussions, more particularly as to the project of an Italian offensive, were there no personal or national jealousies to deflect judgment? Are men in exalted positions—won by intellectual gifts, high character, and real achievements—quite free from these disturbing elements? I will give an illustration drawn from enemy sources. The great Austrian Commander, Conrad von Hoetzendorff, was a strategist of considerable genius. I have heard and read competent military critics who rank him as the greatest strategist of the War. For the 1916 campaign he conceived a plan to eliminate Italy from the War by an attack from the Trentino. Italian resistance was to be crushed by an overwhelming gun power backed by an adequate force of infantry. It was a feasible operation. Italy was notoriously weak in artillery of the heavier callibres and her supply of ammunition was deficient. Her officers also at that date lacked the necessary training and experience in manœuvring large masses of troops. As long as the Italian Army held strong and fortified positions in the hills, light, and medium artillery might enable them to hold their own in the absence of a surprise attack. Once they were driven into the plains with no time to entrench, their inferiority in guns and manœuvring skill would tell against them.

In the spring of 1916 France and Britain were still inferior to the Central Powers in heavy artillery, and therefore could not, whilst they were undertaking great offensives on their own front, supply the Italians with an equipment which would have enabled them to resist effectively a strong attack by a German-Austrian combination. Had the Germans assisted the project with a few divisions and a complement of heavy guns, the Austrians, in order to create a force of sufficient strength to carry out the operation, need not have weakened their defences in the Carpathians. Von Hoetzendorff placed the scheme before Falkenhayn, who turned it down emphatically. Why? He also had his plan. He proposed to eliminate France by pounding the morale of her fine army into pulp in the mortar of Verdun. Once the fighting quality of the French Army was destroyed there would be nothing left to take its place. Britain was not ready. Her volunteer army was not yet trained. Her equipment of guns and ammunition was not complete. We all know now how disastrously Falkenhayn miscalculated the resisting power of the French soldier. We also know that had the Austrians started their Trentino offensive in March or April instead of at the end of May, which they could have done had the Germans played up, the Russians could not have delivered the famous Brussiloff stroke. Thus the additional weight which the Germans could have brought in guns, troops and quality would have converted the serious Italian defeat of 1916 into a calamitous rout. It would have been a more disastrous Caporetto. It was a more deadly stroke, for its direction was across the rear of the Italian Armies on the Isonzo. Its success must therefore have ended in a complete collapse of the whole Italian system of defence. In 1916 the Allies had made no arrangements such as those they perfected in 1917, as the result of the Rome Conference, to hurry troops to the aid of Italy in the event of a German-Austrian attack. That oversight would have made a difference of weeks—fateful weeks—in the arrival of needful help for the hard-pressed Italians. Even when British and French troops arrived on the scene, they would not then have had such a margin of heavy guns to spare as would have enabled them to rally a broken and demoralised army on the open plains of Lombardy, against the terrible guns that pulverised the forts of Verdun. Italy would not have sued for peace, but her losses in men and material would have been tremendous. Her means of replenishing material losses, which were mainly situated in North Italy, would have largely fallen into the hands of the enemy, and Italian demoralisation would have been general and deep. Recovery would have taken at least a year. As an effective attacking force Italy would have been out of action for the rest of the War. It was a brilliant strategic conception. Why did Falkenhayn refuse to give it a trial?

An examination of the probable effect of success on national and personal values will assist us in finding the true answer to that question.

The complete failure of the plan was out of the question. Partial success was the least that could have happened. Had it realised moderate expectations, the greatest victory of the War would have been Conrad's and not Falkenhayn's. If the destruction of the Italian Army in 1916 had brought the final triumph of the armies of the Central Powers nearer and made it surer, Conrad would have been the Teutonic hero, and not Falkenhayn. On the other hand, had Falkenhayn's Verdun scheme destroyed the French Army, no name in German military history would have stood higher than his. Let us carry our examination of probabilities a step further. Had the Italian Army been smashed, that would have been the achievement of the Austrian Army. The German contingent would have been barely a fourth of the total force of the victors. The prestige of Austrian arms would have out-dazzled that of the invincible legions of Prussia. The struggle between Austria and Prussia for the hegemony of the German Empire had only been provisionally settled in a single battle as late as 1886. It was obviously undesirable that

Austrian military prowess should be elevated above that of the North German. No true Prussian could contemplate such a prospect with equanimity, or help its attainment with any enthusiasm. Falkenhayn was a Prussian from heel to helmet. From the national as well as the personal point of view, a German victory at Verdun was more expedient for his country than an Austrian victory in the Trentino.

Falkenhayn himself came pretty near an admission of this motive in stating his reason for rejecting Conrad's scheme.

" When we come to the question how we are to proceed against England's tools on the Continent, Austria-Hungary is pressing for an immediate settlement of accounts with Italy. We cannot agree with that proposal. If we adopted it, it would advantage Austria-Hungary and her future prospects only, and not directly the prospects of the War as a whole."*

Did Falkenhayn put these considerations frankly before his Staff? I should be surprised if he did. I feel confident that he never put pen to paper to express or marshal those incentives to judgment. Did he ever even avow those motives to himself? Probably not. Their influence was entirely subconscious if not unconscious. Nevertheless they were at the root of decision, a root which had penetrated too deeply into the soil in which it was planted to be visible even to his own eyes. The arguments used by him were purely strategical. The reasons he gives for preferring an offensive at Verdun rather than the Trentino are published in his book. They are obviously inadequate to sway the opinions of so clever a man and so capable a soldier. That does not mean that he had not honestly convinced himself that the Verdun offensive would achieve the aim for which it was designed—the destruction in detail of the most powerful of all the Allied Armies. He was sincerely persuaded that his plan was the best. Had it succeeded it would certainly have been the best. But the chances were against it. These he did not weigh impartially. Where a man is hesitating between two courses, for each of which there is much to be said, his predilections and prejudices weigh in heavily, and

"Where self the wavering balance shakes
'Tis rarely right adjusted."

Where the wider self known as patriotism also comes in, rare indeed (and unpopular) are the men who can preserve an unbiassed judgment.

Falkenhayn was as honourable a man as the War threw up in any camp. His patriotism was just as intense as that of Joffre, Nivelle, Foch, Cadorna, Haig and Robertson, but it was no narrower. Why,

---

* General von Falkenhayn "General Headquarters, 1914-16, and its critical Decisions," pp. 215-216.

therefore, should it be assumed that their decisions on questions of military policy were more free from exotic elements than were Falkenhayn's?

For Falkenhayn substitute Nivelle—for Conrad take Cadorna. For Prussia put France and for Austria write Italy. The analogy will then be complete and the inference irresistible. If Nivelle was persuaded that he would break through the German lines and march in the rear of his victorious armies to the re-conquest of Alsace, why should he forgo that triumph in order to enable Cadorna to redeem Trieste? If the French Army were assured by his scheme of the credit of smashing up at its strongest point the greatest military fortress the world had ever seen, why should that glittering prize be surrendered in order to give the soldiers of Italy the prestige ensuing from making a still wider and wiser gap in the walls of the same fortress elsewhere?

The French jealousy of Italy had in it an element which was lacking in the Prussian envy of Austria. The French regarded the very existence of united Italy as a recent creation, brought into being by the valour of the French Army. For them Italy was still something to be patronised. By implication the French attitude to Italy was " Had we not fought and bled to make you a free country you would still have been an Austrian province." There was always an element of derision in every private reference made by Frenchmen to Italian soldiers and sailors. The French attitude towards Italy was expressed in the cynical comment of a French statesman, when Italy was hesitating as to whether she would throw in her lot with the Allies, or allow Austria to purchase her neutrality by territorial concessions. When asked what Italy was likely to do, he answered: " *Voler au secours du vainqueur.*" The brilliant feats of her soldiers in storming almost inaccessible mountain peaks, their capture of entrenched defiles defended by a superior artillery, the heavy losses they sustained, largely because of their imperfect equipment, the marvellous achievements of her engineers—all these were completely ignored, and every Frenchman greeted any allusion to them with a gibe and a snort.

The following extract from a confidential report which I received from a well-informed official in Italy a few weeks after the Rome Conference has a bearing upon this aspect of Franco-Italian relations: —

". . . Looking ahead, the thing that alarms me most in regard to this country is her relations with France. In spite of all the outward glamour and talk of sister-relationships and the unity of the Latin races, there is little doubt in my mind that the Italians distrust the French profoundly and are thoroughly despised by the sister race. As the Ally of both, our true rôle would seem to be to endeavour to smooth over these exacerbated feelings, and to keep the balance even between the two: but our very evident following of the French lead, whether it be as regards Asia Minor negotiations, Venizelism and Greek politics, blockade matters or what not, tends, I am afraid, to fill the Italian mind with a distrust, not so much of our friendship or loyalty, as of our judgment and sense of proportion. I cannot resist a feeling that they look upon us as the dupes of the French, and to some extent I cannot help wondering whether they are not right. Italians are so level-headed where their interests are concerned that they must necessarily judge us rather by their own standard and criticise our more generous sentimentalism in matters where policy and principle conflict. . . ."

Briand and Thomas, the champions of an attack on Germany through Austria, became rank and almost rancorous Westerners when it was proposed to place Italy in the van of the Allied attack for 1917. Thomas and I were great friends. But he lost his temper with me at the Rome Conference when it was suggested that Italy should occupy the front seat in the 1917 campaign.

It was not altogether attributable to the desire of French statesmen that the weight of the Nivelle offensive should not be diminished by the withdrawal of forces to other fronts. Both Briand and Thomas were eloquently insistent on the need for strengthening our forces at Salonika in men and guns, but when the same process was suggested for the Italian Front then nothing could be spared from the Nivelle offensive. It was my first experience of this envious and supercilious attitude of mind on the part of French generals, statesmen and diplomats towards Italy. It was by no means my last. It is largely the explanation and justification of Mussolini's defiant mien and aggressiveness of tone during the first years of his rule. It is fair to say that the French were ready even to alacrity to rush to the aid of Italy when she was beaten by Austria at Caporetto. That was quite in accord with the historical rôle of France towards Italy. When, however, it was a question of helping Italy to enter first through the portals of the temple of victory and have the laurel wreath placed first on her brow, that prospect could not be endured by any patriotic Frenchman—and all Frenchmen are patriotic. Better a doubtful battle in France with a possible victory, than an assured success in Italy with a probable triumph.

Robertson was not quite in the same position as Nivelle. As between Nivelle and Cadorna he had no prejudices in favour of either. They were both foreigners and consequently needed careful watching. His chronic xenophobia functioned impartially in that respect. Nivelle he actually disliked, Cadorna at that time he viewed with a certain measure of superior contempt. But the main British Army was in France and Flanders and therefore a territorial advance of a few kilometres there (preferably on Flemish soil) was more desirable than a decision elsewhere.

Later on he rested his opposition to a combined offensive on the Italian Front on the plea that if Austria were broken up by such an attack, Italy would make a separate peace with her beaten enemy and leave us in the lurch, with both Austria and Germany on our hands. It was an unworthy and unwarrantable insinuation against the honour of a great people. But the fact that it was in his mind proved that he did not rule out the probability of a complete success for an attack in that quarter.

The French and British Staffs based their objection to concentrating their heaviest blows on the weakest point on the ground that the highest strategical principles demanded an attack on the strongest enemy at his most formidable front. A remarkable doctrine. Had France and Flanders been the weakest front and Italy or the Balkans the strongest, Joffre, Nivelle, Haig and Robertson would have had no difficulty in adapting their principles of strategy to the exigencies of that fact. Then I have no doubt they would have scoffed at the notion that you must seek the foe at his strongest. Robertson would have become a dogmatic and surly Cadornist, and probably Cadorna would have developed into a diffident and courtly Robertsonian.

It is interesting to note that six months after the Rome Conference, General Sir Ian Hamilton, writing on 11th July, 1917, to Mr. Winston Churchill, advanced quite independently the same view which I had urged upon my colleagues in Rome. In the course of his letter he said : —

" Is there no other alternative now that it seems too late to hope to do anything in the East? I have racked my brains over the map and I believe that there is one good chance left (apart from the Russians). Were the Italian Army to be suddenly reinforced so that it could press forward northwards in the direction of Vienna, I believe they might break through and give a final shake to the Austrians. The German preparations, entrenchments and railway communications are not sufficiently good to enable them properly to forestall a thrust in that direction. The stupid idea of Trieste should be used as a pretence until the last moment and then entirely given up—it is a purely political idea and no good as a means of ending the War.

My view throughout has been that no General should attack his enemy where he is strongest. He holds him where he is strongest and attacks him where he is weakest. At the present moment the north of Italy offers the best chance of anything in the nature of a really big gain of ground."

Sir Ian Hamilton was not a civilian politician, but a soldier with a distinguished record. He was perhaps better fitted for a Staff post than for a Commander in the field. He had acted as Chief of Staff to Lord Kitchener in South Africa, had been a member of the Army Council, and for five years, 1910-15, was Inspector-General of our Overseas Forces, in addition to having commanded British forces in many campaigns. He was the only leading soldier who had actually seen and made a careful study of modern warfare. He saw the great battles of the Russo-Japanese War. He was certainly not the sort of person whose considered judgment on questions of military strategy could lightly be brushed aside; and this makes his support for my proposal of an Italian campaign the more impressive.

Pétain and two other French Generals recommended the same plan in March as an alternative to the Nivelle offensive. The Rome proposal is taken out of the category of amateur strategy by the approval of these distinguished military leaders.

CHAPTER XLIX

JOFFRE

A CHANGE in the military leadership of France caused a change not in the strategy, but in the particular French villages where the same old strategy was to be practised. When I came into power Joffre was visibly tottering to his fall. For two and a half years he had been the virtual dictator of France. Governments carried out, or rather provided him with the means of carrying out the decrees he issued from Headquarters. He tolerated no civilian interference or suggestion as to his methods of conducting the War. A threat to resign on his part quelled doubting politicians or journalists and silenced all grumblers. His attitude towards changing Governments was that their sole business in war was to furnish men, munitions, and supplies to enable him to carry through such military dispositions as he, the Commander-in-Chief, ordered. Their functions ended at that point. As the whole strength of France was concentrated on the struggle with the invader, Joffre practically ruled the country. His insolent treatment of the men who warned him in time of the coming attack at Verdun shook his power, and his throne became more and more rickety. The disappointment caused by the sanguinary failure of the Somme to achieve its avowed purpose further weakened his authority. His neglect to make any preparation to support Roumania in her challenge of the Central Powers destroyed what was left of his prestige. As Ludendorff points out, although the Allies had urged the Roumanians to throw in their lot with them, " no common scheme of co-operation had been settled." Although British Generals were just as much to blame as General Joffre, he alone was responsible to French opinion. In Britain the Government fell, in France the military Chief was blamed. The result was that in spite of M. Briand's efforts to protect him, he was gradually stripped of all power and on 12th December, 1916, he resigned the command.

As he was mainly responsible for the military policy of the Allies during the first three campaigns of the War—his ideas dictated even the strategy of the British campaign—I should like to give my estimate of his qualities and defects. No one who ever came in contact with him can doubt that he was a very remarkable man

But his strength lay in character, rather than in capacity. He had the build and the qualities of the peasant breed: powerfully built, he possessed courage, even to recklessness; composure, even to stolidity; craft, even to cunning. Had his mental been equal to his moral equipment, he would have been easily the greatest figure in the War. His patriotism, his uprightness, his courage, his firmness of purpose, and his devotion to duty were all above reproach and without blemish. He was a man of indomitable will and of commonplace mind. He had unbounded confidence but a limited intelligence. The former gave him calm and composure in danger, the latter deprived him of the vision, breadth, and imagination essential to his colossal responsibility. He was faced with a more tremendous military problem than ever confronted Napoleon, and he had to discharge it with the brain of an inferior Wellington or Grant. Like them he was a highly trained professional soldier with excellent abilities. He was like them a pertinacious fighter and an efficient tactician, and given inexhaustible resources he could like them have worn out genius in the end. His mind, as well as that of his British partner Haig, only worked well, like a primitive tank, when the objective was limited, and where the terrain was within the vision of their own eyes. When that objective was reached, they had to re-charge and re-consider for the next move. When either of them had to aim at something wider and more distant and out of sight, they always came to grief. They were not intellectually geared, powered or petrolled for such a purpose.

Where reserves, either of men, material or mind are by no means overwhelming, stubborn perseverance in wasteful tactics may lead to disaster. This is what broke the ardent spirit of French patriotism temporarily in 1917. It broke finally the devoted spirit of Russia. It almost wore down the stubborn spirit of the British troops in 1917. Joffre's generalship, which dominated the Allied strategy for four campaigns (for he shared the responsibility for the campaign of 1917), had an ingenious and superstitious belief in the magic power of a "plan" without reference or adaptation to changing circumstances. A carefully thought out plan of campaign was of course essential. But for the Joffre mind a plan was something to be adhered to whatever new facts were revealed, whatever new conditions arose. A stubborn will, if controlled by a supple and fertile brain, is invaluable in any great enterprise. But if it is wedded to a rigid and narrow mentality, blunders are inevitable. It is always tripping over a new fact, and tumbling into an ignored pitfall. The plan is infallible only if the enemy adapts himself to it. But he sometimes fails to do so. With a perfidy which General Joffre ought to have anticipated in so treacherous a foe, the German refused every time to play the part assigned to him in the plan. Allied Generals were guilty of a very common mistake—they credited their antagonists with possessing merely as good an intelligence as their own, whereas, in fact, they had sometimes a better.

Joffre's plan to counter a German invasion in 1914 was based on the assumption that even if the Germans passed through Belgium, they would march through the Ardennes and not further West. The mistake would not have been disastrous had he adapted his dispositions immediately to meet a move he had not expected. But what would then become of the great " plan "? The whole predestined scheme of salvation could not be thrown over owing to adverse and adventitious circumstances. When it was clear that the German armies meant to outflank French and British by pouring their troops through Maubeuge, the " plan " must by no means be abandoned. Hence the headlong rout and the occupation for over four years of the North-Western provinces of France. Joffre throughout his three campaigns persevered in all his offensives long after it had become clear to every intelligent soldier that he was gaining nothing but casualty lists that deprived his army of some of its best officers and men. He sacrificed the Balkans to one of his conventional offensives and to his obstinate refusal to break off the attack even after it had completely failed. He was the paragon type of those military idols whom the Allied nations worshipped so devotedly, although they suffered so much from their incompetence—the great Generals who never learnt anything from failure except how to stage an even bloodier fiasco.

Joffre, Haig and Robertson had much in common. Joffre was the most forceful personality of the three, and of course had a much wider training and experience in the handling of masses of men. But they had all largely the same qualities and the same limitations. They were genuine patriots. That did not differentiate them from millions of their fellow-countrymen during the War where, in Britain alone, over 4,000,000 young men volunteered to face mutilation and death for their country, without prospect of braid or brass to decorate or distinguish them. The three were industrious workers, who did their duty honestly according to their understanding of it. This also, fortunately for mankind, is a commonplace quality, possessed by the majority of toilers in every sphere to which it has pleased God to call them. They were also men with a knowledge of their craft, acquired by much study and some little experience. In that respect they were inferior to craftsmen in any other trade or art, for their experience before the War had, happily for mankind, been very limited. None of them had taken part in a war under modern conditions, or ever seen one. Their experience, such as it was, was very stale, and quite inapplicable to the job they had in hand. Patriotism, integrity, industry, study, and some grain of experience were essentials of their high responsibility, but by no means the only attributes that leadership in such an immense undertaking demanded. There ought to have been initiative, resource, pliability, vision, imagination, aptitude to learn from experience, courage and skill to profit by, and not to persist in mistakes. In all these respects these honourable men had grave deficiencies, and the world is suffering to-day from the results of their shortcomings.

French statesmen had been quite conscious of Joffre's inadequacy for some time. They had historical precedents which ought to have stimulated them to a quicker decision in disposing of him. The French Revolution was saved by the promptitude with which Generals who failed were removed. The Allies in this war had been beaten in nine out of every ten of the battles that they fought, owing to the reluctance which they displayed to substitute the efficient for the inefficient and the adequate for the misfits. Joffre himself had set an excellent example of the way with Generals who were unequal to their responsibilities, when he dismissed platoons of them after the great retreat. But he got rid of them before they had acquired any public reputation.

Just like the British public with Kitchener, the French public— and that included soldiers—retained their belief in Joffre long after those who transacted business with him had ceased to have any faith in his competence. His resolute countenance inspired a sense of strength. That is what a harried people instinctively seek in trouble. They make the mistake of thinking that the seat of intelligence is in the chin. Great generals, dictators, and bruisers always have that grim feature. It gives confidence to their backers. Joffre was therefore a popular figure.

Why did they not remove him? The victory of the Marne saved him from the consequences of his gravest blunder. That triumph lifted him from penalty to pedestal. Then followed a gruesome series of repulses which by every criterion set up by military history would have been ranked as sanguinary defeats. Why was he not deprived of his command then? Was there anyone who had displayed any greater capacity for command available to replace him? Foch was implicated in most of Joffre's failures from Artois to the Somme. He was therefore ruled out as an eligible successor. Besides, both he and Castelnau were devout and pronounced Catholics, and susceptibilities born of bitter reminiscence had converted that faith into a disqualification for superior command. In France, Pétain, Mangin, and Franchet d'Esperey were successes—but had so far given no indication of the brilliant gifts that make for great military leadership in a World War. Nivelle was Joffre's own choice when he realised that the command of the French Army in the field was to pass from his hands. Statesmen are reluctant to remove officials who are honestly doing their duty to the best of their ability merely because they fail in difficult undertakings, unless they are sure of finding an abler substitute. There was nothing better than Joffre visible to the naked eye of the French politician. So Joffre clung to his exalted office with tarnished glory and waning influence at home and abroad.

And now he had gone entirely. He was given the baton of a Marshal of France to hang in the salon of a Parisian villa, and Nivelle took his place.

CHAPTER L

THE NIVELLE OFFENSIVE

WITH or without Russia the Western Allies were committed to fight out the issue until an honourable peace was attainable. The internecine troubles of the great Eastern Power did not therefore derange or delay the preparations made for a renewal of the struggle on the Western Front. The Chantilly scheme was pressed on according to plan, as if nothing had happened to disturb the calculations upon which it was based. It was assumed by all the commanders in the field, as well as by the Staff advisers of the Governments, that the Russian Army would play the part allotted to it in the campaign, perhaps with renewed energy. Castelnau alone expressed any doubts on the point, and he did not embody his misgivings in his official report.

With the departure of Joffre, many expected a reversal of the profligate strategy of throwing masses of men against an impenetrable labyrinth of trenches, bristling with machine-guns and defended by the most powerful artillery and best trained infantry, on the offchance that some of the assailants might find a way through and out.

Joffre's successor, General Nivelle, was known to be a good soldier with a record of prudent, skilful and successful generalship in the grim struggle around Verdun. Of his endowments as a strategist on a vaster field of operations nothing was proved. But his brilliant record at Verdun and our knowledge of his intellectual quality led us to look forward to a fresh survey, by a fresh mind unhampered by commitments or traditions, of the possibilities of the vast battlefield of the War. Thus might be discovered some wall in the rampart that compassed the Central Powers more vulnerable than the bastion which had so far defied every effort made to reduce it or break through, by the strongest armies and the most formidable machines of the Allies. Our expectations were doomed to disappointment. There is no evidence that General Nivelle gave a thought to any front except the one where he was to command. Unfortunately the French Government, instead of putting him in charge of the whole War—as for all practical purposes was Joffre—limited his sphere to the command of the French Army operating in France. The other fronts were for him " out of bounds " for study and action. When invited to consider other possibilities, he dismissed every suggestion with a curt and peremptory refusal even to enter into a discussion on the subject. It was not his affair, except to the extent that operations on any other battlefield involved a depletion of the resources at his disposal for his own sector of the vast circumvallation. Any project or strategy that took guns and men away from the Armies under his direction must be discouraged. Epauletted egoism is impenetrable to the assault of ideas. The battle front where the *Generalissimo* commanded—there was the War. Every other front or flank was a "side-show." How in 1917 that infatuation led the French Army to the brink of irreparable catastrophe, and the pick of the British Army to a muddy graveyard, is a story which must be told in detail later on. But when it was a question of reconsidering Chantilly tactics, Nivelle was only too ready. He had to justify the change in command. How was that to be done?

To be fair to him, he had some new ideas which were successfully exploited by his successors and opponents at a later stage in the War. But he himself failed to put them into execution through causes for which he was not exclusively responsible. The result was that the slaughter was continued by the same butting and bumping methods as those adopted by his predecessor. The site of Aceldama alone was changed. The field of blood was removed from the Somme Plateau to that of the Chemin des Dames. That was in effect the only gain achieved by the substitution of Nivelle for Joffre.

How came the Allies to slither back into the old sanguinary military ruts? I propose to tell the story without reference to its effect on the reputation of any soldier or statesman who played a part in its construction—whether it be my own or others. It is time the whole of the facts about both the Nivelle and the Passchendaele offensives should be stated without variation or varnish to suit anybody.

The "way round" was for the moment effectively barred. I have already explained why a Balkan operation was, for this year, out of the question. The way through Italy was not available. The timidity of Cadorna and the flabbiness of the Italian Ministry had enabled the French to slam that gate with the greatest ease. There was another circumstance which led to recrudescence of the Western offensive fever. Up to December the French Army and the French people—and they were identical for almost every French home was represented in the Army—were completely disillusioned about the prospect of a break-through on their front. Every French soldier who defended the shell-holes of Verdun or the ruins of one of its shattered forts, and every soldier who had attacked the defended puddles of the Somme, knew that unparalleled gallantry in attack was countered by equal valour in defence, and that neither German nor Frenchman could penetrate even shattered entrenchments defended by the other in time to prevent another line, equally difficult to capture, being thrown up behind. If Joffre had remained at the head of the Army, I doubt whether a French Government or the French people would have agreed to a second Somme campaign. Joffre, who was not without understanding of the temper of his countrymen, realised this to the full, and he imparted the information to Sir Douglas Haig, with a view to inducing him to undertake the heavier and bloodier burden of the 1917 offensive. Haig, who had become a Somme bigot, readily assented. He had a magnificent army of trained volunteers, the flower of Britain's youth. They were backed up by a fine assortment of new guns of the latest pattern. Hence the Chantilly agreement.

Then came one of those sudden changes to which the French are more amenable than their phlegmatic neighbours across the Channel. Joffre went, and Nivelle came. Nivelle had been for five months a successful defender of the Verdun heights. That in itself gave him an assured position in the heart of every Frenchman and Frenchwoman. It is difficult for Britons to realise what Verdun means to France. The world can show no battlefield to correspond to it. On those heights Gaul and Teuton had, from the blizzards of February to the snows of the following December, been fighting out a racial feud which had existed for thousands of years. The concentrated fury of ages raged and tore, shattered and killed for ten months in one intensive struggle which has no parallel in the history of human savagery. The very road that carried the reinforcements, the guns and the shells that redeemed Verdun, is to this hour for Frenchmen the Via Sacra of their country.

The General who had taken a leading and successful part in organising and directing its defence had a place of his own in the affection and admiration of his countrymen. What magnetised his name with a new thrill of hope was a recent episode in the defence of Verdun which established his reputation, not merely as a tenacious defensive, but as a skilful offensive General. To him was attributed the skilful plan which by a dramatic stroke recaptured the fort of Douaumont. The fall of Douaumont to the Germans in February had rankled in the French mind. The Germans had driven the French out of a fortress which was in itself an engineering feat of which they were proud, and in whose strength they reposed the most implicit trust. The man who recaptured Douaumont was therefore a hero. It was a *coup-de-main*, but it was also the result of plans minutely worked out and precisely executed. He had hardly been three days in the saddle as Commander-in-Chief when there was launched another equally well-planned attack on the Verdun Front, securing an element of surprise by the shortness but concentrated power of the artillery bombardment, and the rush of troops advancing behind an effective artillery barrage. In 48 hours he had recovered a further extensive strip of ground and captured 11,000 prisoners. The number of his prisoners alone exceeded that of his total losses in the victorious engagement. Here, indeed, had arisen the long expected military leader for bleeding France—a Captain who could win battles without sacrificing his brave legionaries.

It is interesting, in view of Sir William Robertson's subsequent general attitude towards General Nivelle, to give here his report to the War Cabinet on General Nivelle's successful operation of 16th December, 1916, together with his comments on the strategy of that operation:—

" 21st December, 1916.

The French attack at Verdun appears to have been a complete surprise to the enemy. A heavy bombardment had been maintained for about a week previously on both banks of the Meuse and this probably misled him as to the point of attack. The early capture of the Côte de Poivre seems to have led to considerable numbers of the enemy having their retreat cut off. . . . The enemy's losses, in addition to prisoners, were probably extremely heavy. The actual numbers engaged on each side were approximately equal. . . . Both on 24th October and on 15th December, at Verdun, the enemy were surprised and their resistance was easily overcome by equal or even inferior numbers, and unusually large captures of prisoners and guns were made. In the attack on 15th December, the French took in prisoners about one-third of the total fighting strength of the enemy, a proportion which is greatly in excess of the number of prisoners secured by either side in any previous engagement on the Western Front. . . .

The French success shows once more what can be accomplished at little cost, even by comparatively small numbers, if the attack is thoroughly prepared and organised, *and especially if measures are taken to ensure surprise*. In this case the Germans must have known by the preliminary bombardment that an attack would be made, but the surprise was effected by varying the method of attack, by distributing the bombardment over a much wider front than that selected for the attack, by commencing the intense bombardment on the actual front of attack, before dawn, and by launching the infantry assault before it was expected by the enemy. . . .

A great deal has been written in the press about the 'Nivelle method,' which is sometimes compared favourably with the British tactics on the Somme. The so-called 'Nivelle method' depends mainly upon a meticulously careful artillery preparation, combined with a system of artillery barrage, one line of which moves forward directly in front of the attacking infantry. If this method is to be successful, it is essential that the infantry have complete confidence in the accuracy and timing of the artillery fire. . . ."

These two brilliant victories sent a quiver of joy and expectancy through the whole of France, but the factor that impressed the French mind most of all was that by the suddenness and unexpectedness of his attacks Nivelle had won these triumphs at a low price in casualties. A country desolated and darkened by the sacrifice of Verdun and by the mournful butcheries of Artois, Champagne and the Somme, hailed the appearance of this new leader as they would a deliverer. Public opinion in France was worked up to a pitch of exultation, and was prepared to welcome any plan that emanated from the brain of such a General. When, therefore, there were carefully disseminated rumours that he had a fresh plan and a fresh method for breaking through the German ramparts and driving the hated invader in headlong rout from the soil of France, the demand that this new plan should be at once tried became irresistible. I had noted the change when I met the cautious Ribot at the London Conference, near the end of December. When a few days later I travelled with the French Delegation to Rome, I found the fermentation had touched M. Briand and M. Albert Thomas, who had always hitherto been confirmed believers in the " way round." They had both been accustomed to talk with derision of the expectations of the two G.H.Q.'s that " this time a break-through was inevitable." I was therefore astonished to witness the change that had taken place in their attitude, for now they were ardent advocates of another great offensive on the Western Front, with a view to a rupture of the German line. I have already quoted a passage from M. Briand's speech at the Rome Conference, in which he showed clearly that his change of mind was attributable to the confidence which had been engendered by the Verdun success in the superior military genius of the new Commander-in-Chief. He laid stress on the essential difference between this kind of offensive and all the others with which they had been afflicted, and between the caution of this newly-revealed strategist and the buoyant unreliability of his predecessor. Albert Thomas, who at conferences and private conversations had been an unrelenting critic of the Western offensives, I found now to be an equally implacable advocate of the Nivelle attack. He objected to a single gun being taken away from so promising an operation. It was clear that these two eminent statesmen had been swept off their feet by the torrent of enthusiasm for the new method and the new man.

I realised after the Rome Conference that a rigid opposition to this experiment might have disastrous consequences for the Allies. Had Cadorna and his Ministers shown more enterprise, there was a possibility even then of stemming a current of the result of which I expressed myself at the Rome Conference to be apprehensive. But the moment the combined Italian campaign was ruled out by French resistance and Italian indifference, the only alternative to trying the Nivelle scheme was to do nothing but squat each of us in his own trenches waiting for something to turn up. America had not yet declared war and there was no fresh hope in any quarter of the skies. The Eastern horizon looked dark and stormy. The Western was still

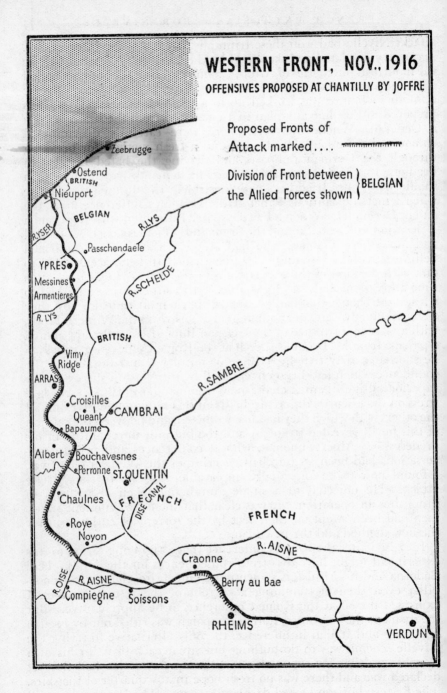

WESTERN FRONT, NOV., 1916
OFFENSIVES PROPOSED AT CHANTILLY BY JOFFRE

Proposed Fronts of
Attack marked....

Division of Front between } BELGIAN
the Allied Forces shown }

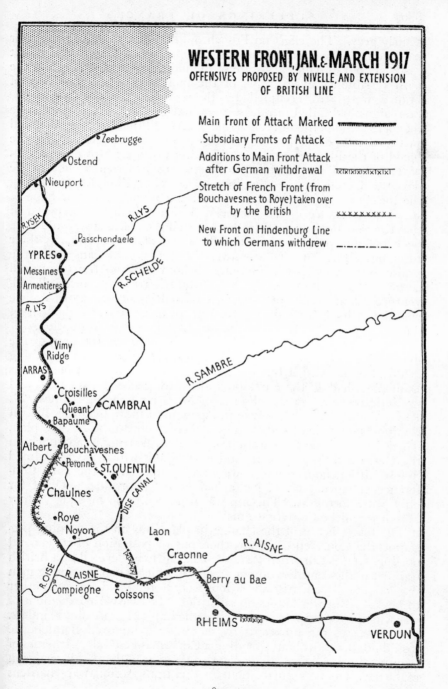

WESTERN FRONT, JAN.& MARCH 1917
OFFENSIVES PROPOSED BY NIVELLE, AND EXTENSION
OF BRITISH LINE

Main Front of Attack Marked

Subsidiary Fronts of Attack

Additions to Main Front Attack
after German withdrawal

Stretch of French Front (from
Bouchavesnes to Roye) taken over
by the British

New Front on Hindenburg Line
to which Germans withdrew

2F

a surly grey. The effect on French opinion of a refusal to play our part would have been calamitous. France was unhappy and might easily get out of hand. In spite of the most enormous efforts and the most terrible sacrifices, some of the most prosperous provinces of France were still occupied by the invader. Three sanguinary campaigns had failed to release the cruel grip of the foe upon more than a few kilometres of French soil. Every millimetre of the liberated earth was rent deeply by the cruel claws of war and reddened by the blood of the liberating troops. Hundreds of the towns and villages of France and thousands of kilometres of her richest fields were devastated. She was bleeding from every vein, still on her feet facing the foe, but staggering. Now there burst upon her a new hope of speedy deliverance. Had she been thwarted in her expectation at that time she might have sulked. As usual the politicians would have been blamed in both countries. To stand blame is primarily their function. The bureaucrats govern and the politicians share the praise, but monopolise the blame. Briand and his Ministers would certainly have disappeared. Who would have come next? Peradventure Clemenceau, but perhaps Caillaux! Peace at this stage would not have been distinguishable from an acknowledgment of defeat, and could only have been concluded on that assumption.

The new hope had gathered such an impetus by the date of the first Allied Conference held in London at Christmas, that nothing could have arrested it but the flaming ramparts of the Chemin des Dames. It had all the unreason and extravagance of a religious and patriotic revival. In the absence of M. Briand through illness, M. Ribot demanded with unwonted peremptoriness that the British Cabinet should there and then give their assent to the Nivelle plan, which involved the co-operation of the British Army in an attack on the German lines at a point and by methods which it was claimed differed from those to which we were committed by the Paris Conference of November. Nivelle had been Commander-in-Chief for only just a fortnight. The ink was scarcely dry on his new Victory March when the Conference met.

The first I heard of the change in plans was on the evening preceding the Conference. I was then put in possession of its general outline. It was Christmas Day. What a day to be devoted by a British Cabinet to the consideration of a plan by which 2,000,000 young men drawn from three Christian nations were to rend and tear each other to pieces! But war knows no sanctities. The barbaric expedient of war which did not spare the stately cathedrals of France and Flanders, and massacres the innocents by bombs in a hundred Bethlehems, would not hesitate about spending a Christmas Festival on schemes of triumphant slaughter. No one gave a thought to the pacific tradition of the day. To quote Burns about another transgression, war " hardens all within and petrifies the feelings."

It appeared that the new plan had been communicated to Sir Douglas Haig on 21st December, 1916, in the following letter, where its leading features are explained with truly French lucidity: —

"My dear General,
     Following on our conversation of 20th December, I have the honour to set out for you as follows my views on the subject of our offensive in 1917, and on the modifications which I think it indispensable to introduce into the original plan of these operations.

Objective.—In the 1917 offensive, the Franco-British Armies must aim at the destruction of the principal mass of the enemy armies in the Western theatre. This result can only be obtained by means of a decisive battle, engaged in with a considerable numerical superiority against all the forces at the disposal of the enemy.

Our concern is then: —

     To retain as important a part as possible of the adverse forces;
     To break the enemy's front under such conditions that the rupture can be immediately exploited;
     To beat down all the available forces which the enemy can bring against us;
     To exploit with all our means the results of this decisive battle.

Necessary means.—To realise this programme, it is indispensable to have at our disposal, apart from the forces destined at the outset to hold the enemy and break his front, a mass of manœuvre powerful enough to be certain of beating down all available hostile forces.

I consider that this mass can only be constituted of homogeneous forces possessing full cohesion and trained for their task by commanders who will have to employ them. It follows that these forces could not be made up by drawing on armies charged with the execution of an offensive of attrition or the rupture of the enemy front.

I estimate that a group of three armies, each consisting of three corps of three divisions apiece is the force necessary for this mass of manœuvre.

General Shape of the Operations.—Starting from these assumptions, I conceive as follows the development of the operations of our armies.

The enemy forces will be *held in the sector Arras-Bapaume* and in that between the Oise and the Somme by means of attacks carried out respectively by the Armies under your orders and by the French forces.

During this time, a sudden attack carried out upon another part of the French Front will lead to a break-through. This will be immediately followed by a broadening out into the decisive battle

This battle, the effects of which will not fail to make themselves felt along the whole extent of our front, will bring about an exploitation over a wide area in which the French Armies and the British Armies will take part with all the means they can bring to bear.

Constitution of the Mass of Manœuvre.—The success of our operations will thus depend essentially upon the mass of manœuvre

For the reasons which I have given you above (homogeneity, cohesion, instruction, command) I consider that this force must be distinct from the large units charged with carrying out the attack to the north of the Oise and with making the break-through.

Now it is impossible for me in the present state of the division of the front between our Allied Armies to form this reserve of 27 divisions.

To allow me to make it, it is indispensable that the British Armies shall relieve an important part of the French troops which hold the front between the Somme and the Oise, and that in this connection they shall put at my disposal the French divisions in position between *Bouchavesnes and the Amiens-Roye road.* I reckon that this front can be held easily by *seven or eight divisions,* which would correspond to the density of the German forces that are facing it

This relief would have to be carried out without any delay unless it is to cause a serious postponement of the preparation for our coming offensive; so I ask you to have it carried out at the latest by 15th January.

Rôle of the British Armies.—Summarily stated, the rôle of the British Armies in our joint offensive should be:—

1. To allow me to constitute without delay the mass of manœuvre indispensable for the decisive battle.

2. To undertake upon the front where you have determined to attack, an offensive large enough and powerful enough to absorb an important part of the German reserves. I consider that your front of attack ought to have an extent of *30 to 40 kilometres,* according to whether you do or do not reckon to leave passive intervals in it.

3. To participate in the general exploitation which will follow the decisive battle delivered in another sector, by achieving the disorganisation of the forces established before your front of attack, and by carrying on the pursuit of the enemy in a zone which we will later on fix by common agreement.

In so defining the task of the British Armies, I wish to make it clear to you that I also envisage the possible employment of my mass of manœuvre on the right wing of our front.

If the enemy attempted an offensive across Switzerland, I should thus not find it necessary to ask you to put a part of your forces at my disposition in order to oppose it.

On the other hand, it is evident that this reserved group of armies will work in the general battle as much for the profit of your armies as for mine.

Further, the extension of front which I am asking from you will in a certain measure dispense your armies from pursuing the execution of the offensive operations which they were due to undertake in the course of the winter, in accordance with the decisions taken at the Conference of Chantilly of 15th November last.

Finally, the plan of operations which I have set before you does not exclude the possibility of carrying out, if the necessity arises, the operation aiming at the conquest of Ostend and Zeebrugge, since this cannot take place before the summer.

This operation can be studied in all its details on the basis of the decision already adopted, and I even consider that our Belgian Allies ought to prepare themselves from now on for the rôle they will have to play in it.

If our big offensive succeeds, it is certain that the Belgian coast will fall into our hands as a result of the retreat of the German Armies, and without a direct attack.

If on the contrary our attacks fail, it will always be possible to carry out in due course the operations projected in Flanders.

In concluding this explanation, I ask you to be so good as to give me, as early as possible, your reply on the subject of the taking over of the front between Bouchavesnes and the Roye road. The constitution of my available troops in view of the various eventualities that may present themselves is really a vital question which I desire to solve without any delay.

Cordially yours,

NIVELLE."

Both the French and the British Armies were to conduct an offensive more or less on the old lines, each on its own front. But a formidable ' mass of manœuvre " was to be constituted behind the French Front, and after the two armies had started their attacks, this mass was without warning to be flung suddenly on the enemy on another part of the French Front.

It will be observed that in its general character it differed fundamentally from the Chantilly scheme. Its success depended on the suddenness of the attack and on misleading the enemy as to the sector where the main effort was to be expected. In no respect was the change more apparent than in the rôle which it assigned to the British Army. To this change more than to any other is attributable the hostility of Sir Douglas Haig. In the Chantilly scheme the main burden of the attack fell upon the British, and Sir Douglas Haig would have played the leading part in the projected offensive. By the Nivelle scheme the French were to bear practically the main burden of the attack, and the part assigned to the British Army was first of all to take over a part of the French line so as to release troops for the attacking force; and to hold the Germans down on their own front by a subordinate offensive, so as to make it impossible for the enemy to spare troops from that sector to rescue their comrades from the plight into which the French surprise assault would plunge them further south. The secondary part allocated to the British Army in this plan was bitterly resented by Sir Douglas Haig. This resentment is apparent in the reply sent by Sir Douglas Haig to General Nivelle's communication:—

> "Montreuil,
> 23rd December, 1916.

In reply to your letter from General Nivelle, General Haig made this morning the following declaration:—

1. The request of the French Command involves the use of ten British divisions; there would only remain eight divisions available, of which the worth of six is very mediocre.*
2. General Haig cannot under present conditions accept a situation which would remove all offensive capacity from his armies.
3. He has accordingly referred the question to the British War Committee, asking it to send to France the necessary divisions to satisfy the request of the French Command.
4. He insistently demands the return of the divisions at Salonika.
5. The relief could be begun 15 days from now, and continued as fast and as far as new divisions arrived, if sent.
6. It is to be anticipated that the British General Staff will raise difficulties about extending relief to the South of the Amiens-Peronne road, desiring to retain the troops at their disposal for offensive action."

Sir Douglas Haig's proposal that the taking over of part of the French line, which was an essential element in the scheme for creating a mass of manœuvre for the attack, should be conditional on British divisions being withdrawn from Salonika to make up the defici created in Sir Douglas Haig's offensive power, was impracticable. I

---

* This is a characteristic objection. When the Commander-in-Chief later on wa persuading the Cabinet to assent to the Passchendaele attack he had 42 divisions avail able for the operations—all of the best. Now he cannot spare 10 divisions for a plan he dislikes.

was a ludicrous proposition, having regard to circumstances which must have been well known to the British Commander-in-Chief. At that moment the French, British and Italian General Staffs were anticipating an overwhelming attack upon the Salonika position from the victorious forces of the Central Powers in the North. There was some ground for apprehending that the Greek Army was very much tempted to join in the enemy attack. General Joffre had urged us to send two more divisions to reinforce our contingent in that sphere. We were pressing the Italians to do the same thing. Sir William Robertson was actually making arrangements for sending a reinforcement of 15,000 men to Salonika. Sir Douglas Haig must have known all that and his proposal must have been made with a view to upsetting the new plan. He must have known that even if ten divisions could have been drawn from Salonika they would not reach France before the middle or the end of February. He also knew that the reason assigned by us for refusing to agree to Joffre's proposal that we should send two divisions to Salonika was that the necessary shipping was not available to transport so many divisions.

How then were we to find ships for ten divisions? As soon as General Nivelle received the communication, he wired to the French Minister of War: —

"24th December, 1916.

Personal.

I have the honour to send you copies of the following: —

1. The letter which I sent to General Haig, Commander-in-Chief of the British Forces in France, to arrange with him the plan of operations to be carried out in 1917.
2. The telegram which General des Vallières, Head of the French Military Mission with the British Army, sent me as an indication of the views of General Haig on this matter.

It appears from the above-mentioned telegram that General Haig has referred the question to the English War Committee, and made it conditional on a reinforcement of the British forces in France.

On the other hand, I saw to-day at my General Headquarters General Davidson, Head of the Operations Branch of the British Army, who repeated to me on behalf of General Haig that *the latter was in full agreement with me about the general plan of the projected operations,* and in consequence upon the necessity of releasing, by taking over their part of the front, the French forces indispensable for this operation, and that he would do all he could to give me entire satisfaction.

This he can do by a combination of three methods: —

(*a*) Extension of the front of the divisions in the line. (The British Army seems to take this course only with a certain timidity, seeing that it counts on holding a front which does not amount to a quarter of the total front, with a number of divisions superior to that which we use ourselves for holding the remainder of the front, although our divisions are much inferior in effectives to the English divisions.)

(*b*) Provisional reduction in their reserves, without there resulting any difficulty for them in taking part in the spring offensives, under the conditions agreed on.

(*c*) Reinforcement by fresh divisions coming from England.

It is undeniable that the co-operation which we are asking from the British Army is relatively much less than that which we are undertaking on our part; it is perfectly reconcilable with the special ulterior projects of the English Command which cannot in any case be put in hand before the summer.

The finding of a solution of these questions becomes a matter of special urgency, since according to the decisions taken at the last meeting of the Inter-Allied General Staffs held at Chantilly, we ought to be ready for any eventuality by the end of the first fortnight of February. The fears which have been manifested with regard to the Swiss Frontier make it necessary for us on the other hand to form as speedily as possible the necessary mass of manœuvre.

So it seemed to me that you might consider it useful as a preliminary measure to entrust to one of the members of the Government who have continually to be going to London, the mission of supporting with his high authority, when meeting the English Prime Minister and General Robertson, the point of view which I have adopted; of insisting on the necessity of giving General Haig the necessary instructions; and of speeding up the dispatch of English Territorial divisions destined for the French Front, so that the relief of our divisions can take place as near as possible to the time I have indicated.

I venture to insist upon the decisive importance of the plan of operations for 1917, and upon the serious inconvenience which would result from undertaking them with insufficient means.

R. NIVELLE."

The purport of these interchanges was communicated to the War Cabinet the evening before the Anglo-French Conference of 26th December. We had no opportunity of conferring upon the subject with either the Chief of Staff or the Commander-in-Chief. This will explain the discussions at this Conference.

Mr. Buchan, in his " History of the War," lapsing into his fictional mood, gives a fanciful picture of my meeting General Nivelle at the Gare du Nord on my way back from the Rome Conference in January, of his seizing the opportunity afforded by the *dix minutes d'arrêt* at the station to unfold to me his great strategical plan, and he proceeds to tell how, having heard it for the first time, I instantly caught fire. When a brilliant novelist assumes the unaccustomed rôle of a historian it is inevitable that he should now and again forget that he is no longer writing fiction, but that he is engaged on a literary enterprise where narration is limited in its scope by the rigid bounds of fact. Had he taken the trouble to read the documents which were in the possession of the War Office and therefore available to him, he would have known, first, that the Nivelle plan had been revealed to me by 25th December, and actually discussed at a War Cabinet on the 26th December, a week before I started for Rome. In the second place he would have known that at the Rome Conference I expressed my doubt about the success of an offensive in France, and suggested an alternative field for operations, and that this alternative had been opposed, as both the British and French military staffs, who were intent on an offensive operation on the French Front, had accepted the general outline of the Nivelle scheme. The précis of the debate on that subject which I have already quoted, amply bears out this statement. And thirdly, he would have known that at the Paris Station I declined to discuss the plan with General Nivelle in the absence of Sir Douglas Haig. That also is officially recorded. Three fundamental inaccuracies in a single sentence are not a bad achievement even for a writer who has won fame by inventing his facts. The real explanation is that Mr. Buchan found it so much less trouble to repeat War Office gossip than to read War Office documents.

And now to revert to the Conference of the 26th to 28th December, at which we had our first discussions on the Nivelle plan.

With the intolerance of a devotee urging the glad tidings of a new evangel, M. Ribot, on behalf of the French Government, urged that we should there and then, without consulting flesh and blood in the shape of military advisers, decide the issues which had been raised in the correspondence between the two Commanders-in-Chief. We, however, insisted upon an opportunity being afforded us for consultation with Sir Douglas Haig. At one of the sittings of the Conference I said that I agreed that the question was very urgent. But General Nivelle had only been in command of the French Armies for a fortnight. The first that His Majesty's Government had heard of this new scheme was on the previous day. It meant a tremendous change in the plan of operations, and His Majesty's Government must really consult not only General Robertson, but also their General in the Field, Sir Douglas Haig. The Cabinet considered that the question must be left for a short time to see whether Sir Douglas Haig and General Nivelle could not arrive at a decision. It looked as if they could, but if that failed, the French Government should then approach His Majesty's Government, who quite agreed as to the necessity of very early decision and action.

2F*

After a good deal of further unreasonable insistence on the part of the French delegates, I replied that I did not think that M. Ribot would ask His Majesty's Government to overrule their General Commanding-in-Chief without at least hearing what he had to say. The Cabinet were sympathetic, but they must first hear Sir Douglas Haig. *" There was no opposition from the Chief of the Imperial General Staff, who was sure that the question could be satisfactorily arranged."*

From this last sentence it is clear that at this meeting Sir William Robertson did not personally object to the Nivelle scheme. He certainly offered no criticism and expressed no doubt. He was only anxious to carry Sir Douglas Haig's assent. According to Nivelle's letter of the 21st December, Sir Douglas Haig had at first notified his approval of the new plan. But Sir William Robertson knew that by this time the Commander-in-Chief was rattled and disappointed by the transference to the French Army of the leading part for which he had been designated by Chantilly. So long, however, as the fight was to be on the Western Front, the C.I.G.S. was satisfied and he thought the Commander-in-Chief could also be reconciled.

This is a minute of the conclusion arrived at : —

" The proposal of the French representatives for an immediate extension of the line held by the British Army on the Western Front was received with complete sympathy by the British War Cabinet, but before a final decision was reached as to exactly how far the British line could be extended, the British War Cabinet felt that the Commander-in-Chief of the British Expeditionary Force must be consulted. The War Cabinet instructed the Chief of the Imperial General Staff to inform General Sir Douglas Haig that they desired him to conform to the wishes of the French Government in this matter to the utmost possible extent.

It was agreed that if an arrangement satisfactory to the French Government could not be reached in the immediate future between General Sir Douglas Haig and General Nivelle, the question should be raised again by the French Government."

I do not propose to give a detailed account of the difficult negotiations that led up to the final arrangements for the Nivelle offensive. That would occupy too much space. I have perused with arduous care the mass of correspondence, memoranda, and minutes which constitute the full record of what took place before the operations of April, 1917, commenced, and I propose to summarise them so as to give a fair and impartial impression of what happened. What in effect was the Nivelle plan and in what respect did it differ from all other " break-through " offensives which had hitherto made such a revolting panorama of gruesome failure? The essential change of policy was in the element of surprise.

Nivelle emphasised this factor as the main idea in his strategical conception of a successful offensive. The enemy must be attacked on an unexpected front at a time when he was not anticipating any operation in that quarter. He would therefore not have any reserves assembled and ready to beat off the attack. A break-through at that point would thus be less difficult, less costly and more easily exploited. The preliminary bombardment at the critical point would be heavy but short and sharp. The offensive as a whole would be on a much wider front than any attack yet staged. But its principal feature was that it would mystify the enemy as to the place of the main attack, and thus take the Germans completely by surprise. It was a brilliant strategical conception. Why did it fail so disastrously? In the main, if not entirely, because in the working out of the plan, surprise, which was the essential condition of its success, totally disappeared. Whose fault was that? It is invidious to distribute blame, and it would be difficult in this case to distribute it fairly. But of this I have no doubt: the fault lies with both parties— French as well as British, British as well as French, but for reasons which will appear in the narrative the failure to conceal the plan from the enemy was attributable to French carelessness. There were two elements in the surprise: one was a change in the terrain of the general attack. The Germans were expecting a renewal of the attack of the Somme plateau mainly from the British Army. That was the Chantilly scheme and the Germans saw the usual preparations made in that area for a great offensive. Nivelle's mass of manœuvre was intended for an attack in a totally different area, where the Germans did not anticipate any assault on their line. The part to be played by the British was that of a " holding " attack. Thus the enemy would be taken unawares, and would have their reserves distributed on a wide front, whilst the point at which the real onslaught was to be made would be without any reserves.

The new sector chosen by Nivelle for his main assault was peculiarly adapted to preparation without being observed. This is admitted by Ludendorff : —

" Thanks to their ample labour supply, the Entente had been in a position to furnish, not only the Verdun sector, but also a large portion of their front with all the means of communication and munitions necessary for an attack. It was, therefore, possible for them in the shortest space of time, and at various parts of the front, to develop an offensive without betraying their plans by their preparations. The photographs of the enemy's field defences and works, and the continual checking and verification by new photographs secured by our aviators, could therefore only give general indications of his intended movements.

The French Front between Vailly on the Aisne and the Argonne was particularly well constructed, so that special preparations for attack were not necessary.   We saw the works that were actually built south of the Chemin des Dames when we advanced in 1918. Their construction seems to have dated from 1915-16. It is possible that the French had intended to make an offensive here in 1916, but were prevented by the German onslaught at Verdun."*

It is acknowledged that the ground thus added to the front which was to be attacked presented exceptional difficulties. It was a plateau which had natural advantages for the construction of a system of defences and the Germans had made the most of their opportunities and converted this high ground into a system of entrenchments which constituted the most formidable fortress on the whole front. But General Nivelle reckoned that even that fact in itself was an element in his favour when a surprise attack was contemplated. The German would not expect that an offensive would be launched on the strongest point in the whole line when there were so many more accessible points on either side. They would therefore take no special precautions either in the way of strengthening the line at that point or of massing guns and reserves behind. The heights and the more formidable defence works could therefore be carried before the Germans could have time to construct a new defence system, or rally sufficient reserves for a counter-attack. That was Nivelle's expectation. But its realisation depended entirely on surprise.

The other element was time. The Germans were accustomed to the heavy-footed and clattering movements of Joffre and Haig—the long laborious and noisy preparations, whose rumble you could hear for leagues with a favourable wind. They knew that not a shot would be fired until the last shell had been pinnacled in the last dump, and the last duckboard had been nailed in the last line of approach. That always meant that the date of attacks was generally postponed and never anticipated, and that the Germans had ample warning and time to make their counter preparations. That is why the " set piece " always failed. The defence gained fourfold as much from time as did the attack. Nivelle was conscious of this. His last success was due to surprise. His next would be planned on the same idea. Had the Nivelle plan been carried out in its integrity, I still believe it would have been an immense success. At the projected date of his offensive there were only eight German divisions—including reserves—in and behind the lines he proposed to attack. At the actual date of advance—about two months later—there were forty. Warning having been given, the Germans massed their reserves behind the point of anticipated attack. Having by that date completed their retirement to the Hindenburg line, they had by that means saved several divisions, which they added to their reserves.

* " My War Memories," General Ludendorff, Vol. II, p. 410.

They threw up fresh entrenchments behind their first system of defence at the point of expected attack. They also accumulated masses of guns and ammunition behind the threatened section. The delay transformed the whole character of the operation. The distinctive features of the Nivelle strategy gradually vanished, and the lumber of the Joffre-Haig military ideas was restored—only with a more difficult terrain substituted. The only point of removing the sphere of attack was not because the ground was more propitious, but because the onslaught if made at this point would not be expected by the enemy. Once that advantage was thrown away there were only two alternatives. One was to seek another terrain of attack on the Western Front. The other was to abandon altogether the idea of a great offensive this year in the France and Flanders areas and concentrate on another theatre or theatres of the War. The final and fatal error committed by France and Britain was not to decide upon one of these alternatives. The second course—a combined Allied offensive against Austria on the Italian Front—was suggested by three eminent French Generals, including General Pétain, but only after the British troops had already started their bombardment. That was one but not the only reason why the idea was not communicated to the British Government.

Who and what was responsible for the delay that wrecked the chances of success? It was largely due to the workings of a divided command. This was my first effort to establish Unity of Command. It was resisted so viciously by Haig and Robertson that the delays caused by the time spent in allaying suspicions and adjusting differences destroyed the effectiveness of the plan. After careful reconsideration of facts and documents it is not too much to say that had the two Allied Armies been as completely under the control of one *Generalissimo* as they became after the Beauvais decision in April, 1918, the Nivelle strategy, while it might not and probably would not have achieved a decision, would have secured a notable success. As it was, the Armies were never given a decent chance. The stubborn mind of Haig was transfixed on the Somme. When a change of terrain was suggested it took him a long time to extricate his mental top boots from the Somme mud. He always moved slowly and heavily when rapid and agile movement was essential. Weeks were wasted in unpleasant and nagging discussions as to the extension of the line to be held by British troops which was essential to the constitution of that mass of manœuvre which was the main feature of the new plan. Then came long delays over questions of transport and co-ordination. A conference of Ministers and Generals had to be summoned to adjust the differences which had arisen on these points. It was held at Calais on the 26th February. *Twelve days before that date, according to the original plan, the attack was due to commence.* The German attack on Verdun had started a week earlier than it was due. That is why it was such a success in its initial stage. Joffre could not believe that their armies were capable of moving at so early a date.

At the Calais Conference M. Briand and General Lyautey represented the French Government, and I myself attended on behalf of the British War Cabinet. General Nivelle was there to put his point of view, and Sir Douglas Haig came to present his case. Sir William Robertson was also there as Chief of the Imperial General Staff. Transport occupied much of our time. The discussion reveals the kind of problem that was responsible for delay. The difficulty ought never to have been allowed to delay matters when time was so vital to success. The British Army demanded 250 trains—an addition of 120 trains over what had been already allocated to them. The French Railways could not spare more than 200 in all, and these with difficulty and only for a short period—for 15 days from 1st April, by the process of stopping supplies for the civilian population during that fortnight. As French Ministers pointed out, the British Army insisted upon twice as many locomotives and waggons as the French Army, and that for half the numbers of troops put into action. General Ragenau stated at Calais that he felt considerable surprise at the size and number of the trains required when compared with the demand of the French Armies, which were being prepared for similar operations. The French, whose striking force consisted of 70 divisions, only required 2,800 waggons a day for two groups of armies. But the requirements of the British striking force of little more than half the size was 8,000 waggons a day. He could not understand how it was that the British Army required so many more waggons, when the French effectives were so much greater.

General Nivelle agreed with General Ragenau. If all the operations were calculated on the same principles as those adopted by the British, no operation, he said, would be possible at all. He could not understand why so many trucks were required during the operation. If we did not succeed within fifteen days we should not continue our offensive. If we failed we should stop. On the other hand, if we did succeed we should get into manœuvre warfare, and the mass of material required for trench warfare would be reduced. As General Officer responsible for the plan he engaged himself that fifteen days should suffice.

Neither Nivelle nor British Ministers were told that, as it turned out, these additional waggons and locomotives were not needed for the Nivelle plan, but were required to carry out the elaborate preparations already being made to stage the tragedy of Passchendaele.

The difficulties created by Haig about taking up more of the line meant delay: discussions about locomotives and waggons were responsible for further delay. There were fresh difficulties in adjusting questions as to the supreme responsibility and direction for the plan of action, and for carrying it out during the course of the battle. Sir Douglas Haig was given the supreme command of the combined British and French troops in the arduous offensive at Passchendaele. But he and Robertson demurred at the idea of a United Command in the spring offensive. In all, three Conferences had to be held, two in London and one in Calais, before an agreement was reached on these questions.

At the Calais Conference on 26th and 27th February, held in consequence of these disputes days after the time originally fixed for the attack, a compromise was reached which was accepted and signed by both Commanders and also by Generals Lyautey and Robertson on behalf of their respective War Offices.

Agreement Signed at Anglo-French Conference held at Calais
26th and 27th February, 1917.

1. The French War Committee and the British War Cabinet approve of the plan of operations on the Western Front as explained to them by General Nivelle and Field-Marshal Sir Douglas Haig on the 26th February, 1917.

2. With the object of ensuring complete unity of command, during the forthcoming military operations referred to above, the French War Committee and the British War Cabinet have agreed to the following arrangements:—

(1) Whereas the primary object of the forthcoming military operations referred to in paragraph 1 is to drive the enemy from French soil, and whereas the French Army disposes of larger effectives than the British, the British War Cabinet recognises that the general direction of the campaign should be in the hands of the French Commander-in-Chief.

(2) With this object in view, the British War Cabinet engages itself to direct the Field-Marshal Commanding the British Expeditionary Force to conform his plans of operation to the General strategical plans of the Commander-in-Chief of the French Army.

(3) The British War Cabinet further engages itself to direct that during the period intervening between the date of the signature of this agreement and the date of the commencement of the operations referred to in paragraph 1, the Field-Marshal Commanding the British Expeditionary Force shall conform his preparations to the views of the Commander-in-Chief of the French Army, except in so far as he considers that this would endanger the safety of his Army, or prejudice its success, and, in any case where Field-Marshal Sir Douglas Haig may feel bound on these grounds to

depart from General Nivelle's instructions, he shall report the action taken together with the reasons for such action, to the Chief of the Imperial General Staff, for the information of the British War Cabinet.

(4)   The British War Cabinet further engages itself to instruct the Field-Marshal Commanding the British Expeditionary Force that, after the date of the commencement of the forthcoming operations referred to in paragraph 1, and up to the termination of these operations, he shall conform to the orders of the Commander-in-Chief of the French Army in all matters relating to the conduct of the operations, it being understood that the British Commander will be left free to choose the means he will employ, and the methods of utilising his troops in that sector of operations allotted to him by the French Commander-in-Chief in the original plan.

(5)   The British War Cabinet and Government and the French Government each so far as concerns its own Army, will be the judge of the date at which the operations referred to in paragraph 1 are to be considered as at an end.   When so ended, the arrangement in force before the commencement of the operations will be established.

M. BRIAND   D. LLOYD GEORGE
LYAUTEY   W. R. ROBERTSON, C.I.G.S.
R. NIVELLE   D. HAIG, F.-M.

When this arrangement was concluded and signed, I thought all disagreement had now been removed and that after this Conference the two armies would move together as a united force.   But you should never put too much trust in the agreements of stubborn men, especially if they think they have been done out of their rights. I ought not, therefore, to have been surprised when three days after the Calais agreement had been reached I received memoranda from both Sir William Robertson and Sir Douglas Haig protesting against the arrangement to which they had attached their signatures. Another Conference had to be summoned, this time in London, to re-bury the resurrected grievances which I thought had been honourably interred.   By this time Haig and Robertson had worked themselves and each other into a condition of personal dislike of Nivelle, and I am afraid that dislike was reciprocated.   It is easier to bury hatchets than hatreds, and old hatreds can always find new hatchets.

Sir William Robertson objected mainly on the ground that if unity of command were established for this battle it might serve as a precedent for future engagements in which both armies were involved.   He was an obdurate opponent of the idea of a United Command, even for a single action in which both armies were involved, if the Supreme Command were vested in the French.   As I have pointed out, the precedent was followed at Passchendaele. I naturally received no protest from Sir William Robertson then.

Sir Douglas Haig's was an elaborate document, suggesting all manner of difficulties as to the practical working of the arrangement, and proposing all kinds of reservations and limitations upon General Nivelle's authority. All these questions ought to have been raised weeks ago and settled. It is right to say that some of the suspicions and apprehensions arrayed in these protests were provoked by a brusque and rather impertinent message sent to the British General from a member of the French Staff, couched in the tones of a peremptory order from a chief to a subordinate. This roused in Sir Douglas Haig's already suspicious breast all manner of forebodings as to the ulterior motives of the French Government and its Generals. He said amongst other things that he " had heard rumours before the Calais Conference of a desire in some quarters in France to gain practically complete control over the British Army and even to break up its unity and sandwich British units and formations between French troops under French control." As a matter of fact this was done in 1918 without presenting any practical difficulties or raising any questions of dignity and personal authority. French divisions were sandwiched in the north between English divisions, all being under the command of Sir Douglas Haig, and British divisions were sandwiched in the Soissons area between French divisions, under the command of General Pétain.

However, I did not apprehend any difficulty in overcoming the objections raised by Sir Douglas Haig. But Sir William Robertson went very much further and objected to the whole agreement on the ground of principle and precedent. Before the Calais Conference he made it clear that he deprecated the plan. At the Calais Conference which he attended he never uttered one word of protest. He confined his dissent to unutterable grunts and groans whenever Nivelle spoke. These inarticulate ejaculations provoked irrepressible merriment in Briand, who was in his most puckish mood. He was in one of those phases of gay detachment which were an infallible sign that he was tired of the whole business and meant soon to resign. This he did shortly afterwards.

Robertson said nothing to me either at the Conference or immediately after it was over. Some days afterwards came his written protest. It is worth quoting because it explains the attitude which he subsequently adopted in 1918 on this question and which led to his resignation: —

". . . It seemed to me that the principle adopted was a dangerous one, because it might prove to be the thin end of the wedge which the French have for long desired to obtain for bringing the British Armies in France under definite French control, and

I suggested to the Prime Minister *that it would be difficult to justify departing from the principle once it is established, because if the arrangement made is the best for one battle, it can be argued that it will be best for all.* I also stated that our officers and men could not be expected to fight nearly as well under a foreign commander; that the Dominion Governments might object; and that entirely to entrust the fortunes of this great battle to a foreign commander, who as yet has had no opportunity of proving his fitness for the position, was a serious step, viewed from the standpoint of the Empire. I also mentioned the legal aspect of the case, which is that no British officer can be placed under the orders of any officer not holding His Majesty's Commission. This, however, may be met by the phrase ' conform to the orders.' I do not know whether this is so or not. . . .''

He excused his assent to the Calais arrangement at the time on the plea that as far as he personally was concerned he had received no previous notification of what was contemplated. He, however, admitted that Sir Douglas Haig had informed him at Calais that he clearly understood the instructions of the War Cabinet regarding the forthcoming operations *as previously communicated to him* and that he would do his best to meet those instructions.

This unfortunate dispute necessitated another Conference, which was held on 12th and 13th March in London, three or four weeks after the date originally fixed for the attack. I made it clear in the course of the discussions that took place that the British War Cabinet resented the tone adopted in the documents sent from the French Headquarters to Sir Douglas Haig. Here is the Minute of my statement; I quote it as one illustration out of many of the support I invariably accorded to the Commander-in-Chief on all questions where his personal authority and prestige were concerned.

" Mr. Lloyd George said that this was another point which had arisen in his discussions with the two Commanders-in-Chief. He had urged that, unless there was goodwill, any agreement would be a failure. He had pointed out that the two first documents sent by General Nivelle to Sir Douglas Haig, after the signature of the Calais Agreement, were couched in rather peremptory tones. As he had expected, however, it had transpired that these letters were not written by General Nivelle himself, but by some subordinate. He had reminded General Nivelle that Field-Marshal Sir Douglas Haig's command extended over more than 1,500,000 men, and was the largest British Army by far that had ever existed. He had further pointed out that Field-Marshal Sir Douglas Haig possessed the full confidence of the War Cabinet, and was regarded with admiration in England, and, he believed, in France also. He had, therefore, told General Nivelle that, in his opinion, these two documents were somewhat brusque. General Nivelle, in reply, had stated that nothing was further from his mind than to show the smallest discourtesy to Field-Marshal Sir Douglas Haig. Mr. Lloyd George himself recognised that General Nivelle was the very last man to do anything discourteous, and everyone in England who had met him had been struck with his great courtesy. The point, therefore, which he wished to impress on the French Government was the danger that subordinate officials are sometimes indiscreet. He further wished to emphasise that it was not only the letter of the Agreement which was of importance, but equally the spirit in which it was carried out."

In the discussion which followed, General Lyautey said that before I wrote, he himself had observed that General Nivelle's communications had a somewhat brusque tone.

M. Thomas said that the whole of the French War Committee were agreed on this point.

General Lyautey said that he had suggested to General Nivelle that he should not send any document to the British General Headquarters without making sure that it was drafted by an officer who was not only a good and competent officer, but one who was careful in the choice of his words in addressing the British Headquarters.

Admiral Lacaze said that what I had said corresponded entirely with the feeling of the French Ministers. For himself, he would like to add that either Commander-in-Chief, in the event of his receiving any document that was perhaps hastily drafted, and was couched in terms calculated to give offence, instead of remaining sullenly dissatisfied, should seek an early interview with the other Commander-in-Chief, in order to clear the matter up.

The Conference was attended by four French Ministers. After a good deal of palavering the trouble was once more arranged. Clumsy dispatches had been reproved and sore heads had been poulticed. As far as I know, there were no further personal embarrassments or misunderstandings in the way of effective co-operation between the two generals. But all this friction made for delay. It was common to both the Chantilly and the Nivelle plans that the Allies should be ready during the first fortnight in February. It was already the first fortnight in March and the Allied Commanders were still wrangling about preliminaries. During this period French Ministers and the French Military Chiefs were quite convinced that the British High Command and the British War Office were deliberately working against the successful achievement of the Nivelle plan. The latter made no concealment of their dislike for the whole scheme. They preferred the old style offensive and they were still fretting about the brunt of the fighting and therefore the sacrifice being shifted from the British to the French Army. So thoroughly convinced was General Nivelle of this antagonism and of its being responsible for British tardiness, that he went to the extent of saying openly that the situation could not improve as long as Sir Douglas Haig remained in command of the British Army. This was conveyed to me indirectly. I promptly discouraged any such notion. But it shows something of the lack of sympathy between men on whose cordial and loyal co-operation so much depended.

We were not yet at the end of delays. This time the enemy was responsible. The enemy had decided to shorten their line in the Somme area. By doing so they gained three advantages. Their new position was considerably stronger than the old. They were also able to defend the new line with fewer troops and thus add several divisions to the reserve army they were building up behind the line in preparation for the offensive which they knew the Allies were contemplating. And thirdly, they dislocated the whole of the elaborate plans made by the Allied Generals just as they were being brought up to starting point.

It is a reflexion on the French and British Staffs that the Germans were able to complete the tremendous arrangements necessary for such a withdrawal without any apprehension of the move on the part of their opponents.

The constant postponements had given the Germans ample opportunity to construct the Hindenburg line and to carry out their scheme of retirement to it at their leisure. The operation was completed to the last detail without a hitch. Whether it ought not to have caused the abandonment of the Nivelle plan is an arguable question. It affected this new scheme in a much lesser degree than it would have affected the old plan for resumption of the Somme offensive. The German retreat involved the whole of that old battlefield. The ground given up by the enemy over which our troops would have to march with all their elaborate equipment was so completely cut up and devastated, in roads, bridges and rails, that it took weeks to re-establish effective contact. An attack on the Somme Front could not have materialised until the end of April.

About the middle of February an incident had occurred which gave the Germans a broad hint not only that an attack was contemplated, but as to the area and time where the blow was to come. Here is Ludendorff's account of the strange accident—if accident it was:—

"In the middle of February, 1917, in order to improve its position, the Third Army had undertaken a local operation on the Champagne battlefields of September, 1915. This operation was successful. Amongst the captured material there was found an order of the 2nd French Infantry Division, dated 29th January, clearly pointing to a great French offensive on the Aisne for April. This gave us an extremely important clue. Little attention was now paid to rumours of attack in Lorraine and the Sundgau."*

That a document of so confidential and momentous a character should have been found lying about in a front trench within reach of the enemy, betrays such inconceivable carelessness that it is difficult to eliminate the idea of treachery. The point has never been cleared up, perhaps it never will be. Although the surprise attack on the right flank was not revealed, the incident apprising the Germans of the sector where the main attack was to be expected, turned out to be very detrimental to the chances of success.

The second incident came later, and was even more serious in its effects. It is established beyond doubt and is recorded by the French Commission of Inquiry appointed by the French War Cabinet after the battle to inquire into its advisability and the tactics adopted during the fight. The Report states:—

" The secrecy of the operations was compromised by regrettable confidences and by the capture on a non-commissioned officer of an order fixing the operations of the third group of armies."

This N.C.O. was taken prisoner by the Germans on the night of 4th April, and the document which he carried gave the order of battle of the troops north of the Aisne and the various corps objectives. Here the whole scheme was given away. It is significant that this kind of thing had never happened on either side before this offensive, and it is difficult to believe that it was altogether fortuitous. For some time French Generals and their Staffs had been conducting a bitter controversy amongst themselves as to the merits and demerits of the new plan. Before the French Army attacked, there had been inside that army what one could call the Great River War, fought between the champions of the Somme offensive and the offensive of the Aisne. There was also much ill-feeling engendered by the promotion of General Nivelle to the High Command over the heads of distinguished and competent seniors. In the course of the internecine conflict between partisans of rival personalities and places, documents seem to have been freely and widely distributed by the excited combatants. The facility with which the most revealing of these secret papers found their way across the line gives rise to a feeling of suspicion which it is difficult altogether to suppress.

The Germans took the warning thus given and prepared to meet it. Had the attack taken place at the date originally fixed, either the German raid would have been anticipated or the French attack, the preparation for which by then would have matured, could have

* " My War Memories," General Ludendorff, Vol. II, p. 410.

been precipitated, so as to afford the enemy no time to adjust and speed up their defensive plans. They would have been still occupying their old positions on the Somme, and the divisions which they reckoned to save by the Hindenburg straightening out would have been still occupied in defending that useless line. There would have been no time to bring up divisions from Russia and Roumania. The tired-out divisions would not have been rested. The Russian Revolution would not yet have occurred, and picked divisions from the East could not therefore have been exchanged for tired divisions from the West.

Before the attack was launched, delays and warnings had already doomed it to failure—so much so that an effort was made by some of Nivelle's leading subordinates, including Pétain, Franchet d'Esperey and Micheler to induce the Commander-in-Chief to abandon it altogether, and think out an effective alternative. It is interesting, and not without consolation to those who have been persistently accused of the crime of amateur strategy, that the first and only alternative that occurred to these eminent Generals was an offensive on the Italian Front. M. Painlevé, who was then War Minister, has put it on record that Pétain, Franchet d'Esperey and Micheler were " unanimous in saying that if we did not attack, we must without delay send an army into the Trentino." The reason why they did not press this idea on the Government was that they had already committed the British Army to the Arras attack (in fact the British bombardment had already commenced). They could not then go back on their agreement with the British. It was too late now to reopen the question. Moreover they felt that French public opinion had for three months been led to expect great things from this offensive, and that the disappointment would be overwhelming if it were suddenly abandoned and the French attacking forces were whisked off to Italy.

It is a sad reflection that had the attack not been put off by difficulties, largely artificial, which genuine good-will would have dissolved, the Allied Armies would have caught the Germans in the act of " moving house " with all the traditional confusion attending that domestic migration. Long before the attack came the Germans had settled comfortably in their new quarters. Before the French attacked the enemy were fully apprised of the locality, direction and weight of the Allied blow. As the preparations for the attack had ceased to have the character attached to surprise, they were given plenty of time to perfect theirs for defence. The " 250 trains " spirit had supervened—slow, methodical and obvious. Time had been given to elaborate guarantees to allay Haig's suspicions as to the effect of Unity of Command on his authority—but time also had been vouchsafed the Germans to perfect their defence. By this time friend and foe alike knew all about the plan; the former gossiping about it, the latter preparing against it. The surprise had developed into the most elaborate and best advertised attack in the War.

The French themselves do not appear to have known at the time about the German capture of their plans in February. The second incident, on 4th April, of the betrayal of their complete plans was fully known to the French General Staff, but not a whisper reached the Cabinet, or for all I know, the British Staff, of the fact that the Germans were already in possession of the French plans. M. Painlevé stated that these momentous incidents, which ought to have constituted overruling considerations, were never revealed to the French Government until after the battle was fought. They changed the whole character of the operation, the success of which depended entirely on surprise. Nivelle was attacking the most formidable bastion on the German Front after the enemy had received ample and accurate knowledge of his intentions, and made the most effective arrangements to baffle them.

Joffre's plan avoided a direct attack on this fortress and proposed to pinch it out without direct assault by attacks on both flanks. Nivelle's idea was that the Germans would never expect a frontal advance on so formidable a position, and would therefore place their reserves opposite more vulnerable sectors of their line. The progress made, even in an attack which had been anticipated and provided against for two months, proved that Nivelle's calculation was not altogether ill-founded. Had this stronghold been captured, Laon was within Nivelle's grasp and the German line would have at last been turned. But what possessed him to persist after the secret had been given away, and the element of surprise upon which he relied had completely disappeared? There is but one answer. These great offensives, once they fired the imagination of a Commander, ceased to be plans for the winning of victory. They became a passion which could not be resisted. Like all passions which possess men, this one banished caution, prudence and fear. The more Joffre, Nivelle and Haig were criticised and opposed, the more fierce became their appetite for their cherished plans. They ignored difficulties, they concealed and suppressed disagreeable facts, even from themselves. We shall see this dementation once more at work when Passchendaele is reached in the course of my narrative. The plan becomes an intoxication and the intoxication a delirium. When the craving is on him the planomaniac is blind. General Nivelle in December was a cool and competent planner. By April he had become a crazy plunger. We have witnessed this process many a time among erring business men who, in a successful, honourable career, have won repute for circumspection and prudence. If they are confronted with an unexpected check in a well-thought-out scheme from which they have a right to anticipate much gain, they suddenly lose control, throw accumulated wisdom to the winds, and decide to smash through

without weighing the hazards.   Many an established fortune has been
squandered and many a respected character has been ruined in that
way.

There was the knowledge that the Germans knew his plans—that
they were proposing to thwart them—that the Russian Revolution
had released many of their best reserves in the East, and that they
had been added to the reserves which were to counter the French
" surprise."   These facts, known to him and urged upon him by the
ablest of his lieutenants, do not seem to have weighed in the estimation of a hair with this General, stimulated to a pitch of infatuation
by constant dram drinking from the inexhaustible puncheons of
anticipated victory.   He was in a state of inebriated exaltation which
destroyed his wonted poise.   The quiet, modest man became
garrulous, boastful and truculent.   This state of mind accounts for
most of the silly offensives of the War, and especially for the way in
which Generals persisted in them after their failure had become
evident to every uncommitted, sane onlooker.

As arranged, the British attack came first.   It was preceded by a
prolonged bombardment which lasted five days.   The infantry
attacked on the 9th April.   In its initial stages the onslaught was a
brilliant success.   The Vimy Ridge was captured, the German
defences were broken through on a front of 18 kilometres to a depth
of six kilometres, 12,000 prisoners and 150 guns were captured, and
we have no less authority than that of General Ludendorff, who was
in command of the German Army, for saying that the situation at the
end of the first day was extremely critical " and might have had
serious consequences if the enemy had pushed further forward."
His further comments on the victory won by the British forces on 9th
April are worth quoting by way of showing how near we were to
achieving a result which, if not decisive, would at least have involved
a rolling up of the German Army to a line far behind that which
they held on the morning of the battle.

" The Battle of Arras on 9th April was a bad beginning for the
decisive struggle of this year.

10th April and the following days were critical.   The consequences of a break-through of 12 to 15 kilometres wide and 6
or more kilometres deep are not easy to meet.   In view of the
heavy losses in men, guns and ammunition resulting from such a
break-through, colossal efforts are needed to make good the damage.   It was the business of G.H.Q. to provide reserves on a large
scale.   But it was absolutely impossible with the troops at our
disposal and in view of the military situation, to have a second
division immediately behind every division that might possibly
fall out.   A day like 9th April threw all calculations to the winds.
Many days had to pass before a new line could really be formed

and consolidated. The end of the crisis, even if the troops were available, depended very largely, as it generally does in such cases, on whether the enemy, after his first victory would attack again, and by further success aggravate the difficulty of forming a new line. Our position having been weakened, such victories were to be won only too easily. The British attacked again at the same spot from the 10th onwards in great strength, but not really on a grand scale."*

The capture of the French document disclosing the Nivelle objective on the Aisne had helped the British Army, for it induced the Germans to concentrate their reserves behind the Chemin des Dames. We were therefore able not only to break the German line but at one point to advance six miles. One officer told me that he marched with his company a quarter of a mile beyond the point at which his battalion was ordered to stop, but found no Germans except a few stragglers who surrendered without a struggle. The following day that evacuated ground was reoccupied by the enemy. The failure to press the attack home with the whole strength of the British forces was probably due to the cavalry obsession which pervaded the hearts as well as the minds of the horse soldiers who commanded the British Army in campaigns where engineering, artillery and infantry tactics meant everything and cavalry charges worse than nothing. Thousands upon thousands of horsemen were assembled at a convenient point behind the line ready to dash through the rent in the German Front. Nothing came of it except the death gallop of Monchy, where horses and horsemen were mown down by a few machine-gunners as soon as they came within range. Infantry had to be called in to capture the village. Cavalry were only an impediment in the advance. They postponed appropriate measures until it was too late to use them. With cavalry the policy of "infiltration" which the Germans used so effectively in March, 1918, was impossible. By that policy, if at one point the opposing line held out, at another it might give way. The Germans with their machine-guns pressed onward where there was an opening. They surrounded the men who held out and forced them either to retreat or to surrender. But cavalry must have a gap wide enough to charge through in masses that will bear down all resistance. The Australian History gives an account of how the Australians, eager to attack the surprised German Army on the right, were kept back for days because no gap had yet been made for the cavalry to get through. When they were allowed to advance the

* " My War Memories," General Ludendorff, Vol. II, pp. 421-422.
    This expression of the German view of the first day's fighting at Arras is confirmed by General von Hindenburg:—" The English attack at Arras on 9th April, 1917, swept over our first three lines. The evening report revealed a dark picture. A ray appeared. The English did not know how to exploit the success to the full. A piece of luck, as so often before. I pressed the hand of my Quartermaster-General with the words, ' We have lived through more critical times.' "

German reserves had arrived, the German resistance had stiffened, and the German line of defence was restored. Hence the bloody and futile attacks on Bullecourt. They ultimately, with infinite courage and tenacity, captured a miserable ruin and created one more salient, but gained no tactical advantage of any sort or kind. A great opportunity was thrown away of winning a reeling and resounding victory which might easily have produced considerable results by compelling the Germans to weaken still further their reserves on the Aisne. As a result of this failure to take full advantage of an opportunity which had been created by the dash and valour of our troops and the negligence of our foes, the Germans found it unnecessary to carry out the operation which at one moment on the 9th they had contemplated—withdrawal to the Wotan position several miles behind their original lines. That was a position which at that date was still under construction and incomplete, and might therefore have been captured in the rout, as our defences in front of Amiens were overrun in the debacle of March, 1918. As it was, the Germans were given plenty of time to rally and to throw in their reserves. By means of counter-offensives they were able to consolidate their defence without very much more loss of ground.

The battle then resolved itself into a series of attacks and counter-attacks on isolated villages and posts—futile and bloody.

On 16th April the French launched their great attack on the plateau above the Aisne. Was it a victory or a defeat? The Germans have no doubt that it was for them a victory. There were many Generals and politicians amongst the Allies who took their view. On the other hand there were distinguished Generals not in the least implicated in the strategy or tactics of the battle, who regarded it as a qualified success for the French. The result is thus summarised by Foch, Gouraud, and Bruyère, who had been appointed by the French Chamber to enquire into the circumstances of the fight and its conduct:—

" It was a success but not a breaking through. . . ."

" To sum up: from 17th to 23rd April, the date at which the investigations of the Commission have to stop, General Nivelle abandoned all idea of breaking through rapidly and violently towards Laon and confined his objective in that direction to the capture of the ridge of the Dames.

All the steps he took were directed to clearing Reims from the enemy, a result which he tried to obtain by joint attacks of the IVth and the Vth Armies. The former was to endeavour by a series of successive efforts to push forward towards the North across the massif of Moronvillers. The latter was to try to advance towards the N.E. after first seizing all the heights of Brimont Spin and Sapegneuil. The battle, of which the object was to break through the enemy's lines, gradually assumed the character of a battle of long duration with the object of using up the enemy's troops. This process developed rapidly in the enemy's ranks. On the 1st April the enemy had on the Western Front 50 fresh divisions in reserve, i.e. a third of his total forces on that front. By the end of April all these reserves had been absorbed. He was compelled to draw upon quiet sectors of the front to maintain the fight. At first the divisions withdrawn from the front lines could have some days' rest before returning to their sectors. Soon this was no longer possible. The process of exhaustion quickened at a rate impossible to believe. The remnants of the troops brought back from the front line were thrown directly into quiet sectors such as the Argonne or the heights of the Marne. It is thus that the second division of the Guards, which had been cut up at Harazoe from the 5th to the 16th May, as well as the 28th Division, are identified on the 25th at the hill of the Talon.

The only rest these divisions enjoyed was the time occupied in moving from one place to another.

On the English Front the same results were observed."

It all sounds very much like the official explanation for the failure of Passchendaele. There was no break through, but part of a desirable ridge was captured and for the rest the enemy divisions had been used up.

The conditions under which the final arrangements for the attack were completed, and the atmosphere in which it was launched, were not conducive to that composure and concentration which are essential in the execution of a critical enterprise.

The view taken by the French Government of the progress and results of the Nivelle offensive was not formally communicated to the British Government. But information percolated through as to the atmosphere of dubiety that was thickening around the offensive.

During the progress of the fight the British War Cabinet took note of the situation. On 16th April I informed the War Cabinet that I had heard from M. Thomas some further details of the attitude recently assumed by the French Government towards General Nivelle. This was supplemented by information furnished by the Chief of the Imperial General Staff. It appeared that General Nivelle had summoned a meeting of his Army commanders, at which his plan of operations for the future had been criticised by General Pétain, who, though his senior in service, was now subordinate to him. As a result of what occurred, General Pétain communicated direct with the French War Cabinet, and General Nivelle was summoned to a Conference, at which he refused to explain or justify his plan before one of his own subordinates. After this certain French

Ministers had proceeded to the French Front to discuss the situation.

The Chief of the Imperial General Staff pointed out to the Cabinet that, after having approved the plan adopted by the French Commander-in-Chief in its initial stage, the French Government had proceeded to throw doubt on its soundness, though nothing had occurred in between to justify this change of attitude, and that such conduct was hardly fair to the man who had to execute the operations.

I said that I was of opinion that it must have been difficult for the French Government to ignore any arguments put before them by an officer of such high position as General Pétain.

It was no doubt very disconcerting for a General on the eve of a great attack to have conclaves of politicians and of subordinate generals challenging, questioning and doubting his dispositions. Sometimes the debates were held at General Nivelle's Headquarters, sometimes he was hiked off to Paris, to explain and defend his dispositions. Not only must it have rattled the Commander-in-Chief, but it must also have had the effect of unnerving all the Generals who were to take part in the attack, and the atmosphere of distraction and divided counsel must have spread far and wide amongst those who had the responsibility for leading the attack on strongly entrenched positions.

The battle was viewed by a delegation of Members from the French Parliament, and there is no doubt that the break-off, which was the consequence of the failure to break through, was attributable to their intervention. Some of the horrors inseparable from a great battle were witnessed by them and excited them to a wail of exaggeration as to the numbers of the fallen.

The Generals appointed by the French Government to enquire into the battle summarised their view of what had been achieved by the combined attack which constituted the Nivelle scheme in the following words:—

" However this may be, if the offensive was far from obtaining the results hoped for, it is none the less true that it constituted a real success for our armies. Under the menace of its preparation the enemy refused to fight on a portion of his front and had evacuated 2,000 square kilometres of ground, thus setting free one-eighth part of the invaded territory. As for the attack itself, it had procured 55,000 prisoners, 800 guns, and 1,000 mitrailleuses.

Apart from this result as regards material, thanks to the rapid using up of the enemy's reserves, it cleared the Italian Front in the Trentino, got rid of all danger from the Russian Front and gave the initiative in the operations into our hands."

The French members had exaggerated very considerably the

casualties sustained by the French Army. These extravagant estimates were commented upon very adversely by the French Committee of Enquiry, and in dealing with the question of casualties they say : —

> " as for the losses themselves which public opinion spoke of as particularly heavy, they did not exceed those which had occurred in previous great battles. The battle of April, 1917, may be compared to the battle in Champagne in September, 1915. The object of both was to pierce the enemy's front. Now the losses in Champagne in September, 1915, on a front of 40 kilometres were 125,000. Those on the Aisne during a similar period on a front of 80 kilometres did not exceed 117,000 men."*

> " To understand the bearing of the advantages that it produced, it is enough to recall the impressions which would have been produced in France if the same result had been gained by our adversary. It is easy to imagine the tone of triumph which would have been adopted in their *communiqués,* all Germany would have been beflagged."

This report came too late to dissipate rumours which had been partly due to the Lobby gossip set going and stimulated by the excitable Deputies who had viewed the battle. Rumour doubled and even trebled the actual casualty figures, and the popular imagination was staggered by the reports that were circulated. The revulsion of feeling was all the greater because of the altitude of hope from which France had been flung into despond by this shock.

When Nivelle succeeded Joffre, as I have already pointed out, every Frenchman, soldier and civilian, said, " Here is something different at last." When they discovered that they had only substituted King Cormorant for King Stork, despair kindled into anger and anger into mutiny in trench and Parliament.

Rumours that had been disseminated amongst the civilian population behind the lines soon spread into the camps where soldiers were awaiting their time to be flung into the shambles. The result was widespread disaffection, and here and there mutiny amongst the troops which at one time was so serious as to threaten revolution. The French Chamber was in revolt against the High Command. The French Government demanded the resignation of General Nivelle. General Pétain was appointed in his place. He was specially qualified to deal with the situation. He was a man of great calm and common sense, and it was probably known by this time throughout

---

* A similar contrast might have been drawn between the losses and gains of this battle and that of the Somme, much to the advantage of the Nivelle offensive.

The Committee proceed to cast discredit upon the efforts made by General Nivelle's enemies to treat the Battle of the Chemin des Dames as if it were a great defeat.

the Army that he was opposed to the attack which had miscarried with such heavy losses. The French soldiers knew, therefore, that General Pétain's appointment was a guarantee that there would be no more of these sanguinary offensives which for three years had so recklessly squandered the youth of France in experiments or schemes prepared by Staffs, most of whom had never seen any actual fighting in or over the trenches.

Pétain's tact, judgment, and firmness re-established confidence in the armies of France. But it meant that for attack on any considerable scale these armies had ceased at any rate for a whole year to be an effective fighting machine.

CHAPTER LI

SEQUEL TO NIVELLE OFFENSIVE

To clear up the doubt that existed in the minds of our Commander-in-Chief and C.I.G.S. as to French intentions, it was finally decided at the end of April that a Conference should be held in Paris at which the political and military Chiefs should be present. It was fixed for 4th May. On the 1st May the Imperial War Cabinet considered very carefully the line which the British representatives should take at the Conference. Some days before the meeting General Smuts paid a special visit to Headquarters in France in order to ascertain the exact position. Sir Douglas Haig seems to have taken advantage of the visit to impress upon General Smuts the importance of an offensive to clear the Flanders coast. He came back full of the idea. At my request, he put the whole of his views upon the military situation into writing. As the document is an interesting survey of the position as it appeared at that time to a competent and independent observer, it is worth quoting literally the views he expressed.

" THE GENERAL AND MILITARY SITUATION
AND
PARTICULARLY THAT ON THE WESTERN FRONT

1. *General.*

The present strategic and military situation is determined not only by the previous course of the War but to a large extent also by our conception of general policy, by the political aims we are fighting for, and the possibility of vigorously defining and limiting those aims.

A military situation which is hopeless in view of a large and ambitious political programme may yet be quite hopeful and reassuring if that programme is severely cut down to the essential minimum of our war aims and of the victory we consider necessary to realise them. Such a definition and limitation of our war aims has now become quite necessary at this very late stage of this long and exhausting struggle and has been carried out by two committees of the War Cabinet. Apart from the subsidiary recommendations of those committees our war aims are now limited to the following four : —

(*a*) Destruction of the German colonial system with a view to the future security of all communications vital to the British Empire. This has already been done—an achievement of enormous value which ought not to be endangered at the peace negotiations.

(*b*) Tearing off from the Turkish Empire all parts that may afford Germany opportunity of expansion to the Far East and of endangering our position as an Asiatic Power. This has essentially been achieved, although the additional conquest of Palestine may be necessary to complete this task.

(*c*) Evacuation by the enemy of Belgium, Northern France, Serbia, Montenegro, and Roumania, and compensation to Belgium and perhaps France and Serbia.

(*d*) A settlement of Europe which will limit or destroy the military predominance of the Germanic powers, though the actual details of such a settlement may be left open for the peace conference.

The last two aims have still to be achieved. The net result of the War so far may be stated as follows: while all other parties have been heavy losers in territory both the German and the British Empires have been winners, the one in Central Europe, the other over the rest of the globe. While our gains have immensely strengthened our position the risk remains that the German Empire may have gained even more relatively and, unless defeated now, will become again at some future date an even more serious menace to us than it has been in the past. How has this defeat to be brought about?

I have already told the War Cabinet and I repeat here my frank opinion that that will not be merely or even entirely a military defeat. A certain substantial measure of military success will be necessary and must be achieved not only because it is necessary for our ends but also as a lasting lesson to Prussian militarism.

But greater forces are fighting for us than our armies. This War will be settled largely by the imponderables—by the forces of public opinion all over the world which have been mobilised by German outrages, by fear on the part of the governing classes of Central Europe of the dark forces of revolution already gathering in the background, by the gaunt spectre of want or even starvation already stalking through the land: and by all those consequential factors of morals to which even Napoleon attached more military importance than to the prowess of his armies. Thus the present impotence of the Russian Army is almost balanced and in the end may be more than balanced by the dread which this example of successful revolution is inspiring in the rulers of Central Europe. And the coming in of even pacific America shows the growing force of the imponderables set free by this War in the minds of the nation.

In this connection two considerations cannot be too clearly realised by us. First, that in our diplomacy and our conduct of the War we should ever strive to keep this world opinion on our side and not be deflected by German methods of barbarism or in any other way from our true course. This affects such questions as the severer forms of reprisals, our coercion of small neutral nations, and even an added emphasis to our traditional generous policy in purely domestic affairs, and similar questions. Second, that the imponderables will continue to act beyond the duration of this War and produce greater changes than any which we will be able to achieve or even contemplate in the peace treaty. It appears now fairly probable that the democratisation of Central Europe, which will be an inevitable consequence of this War, will go further to achieve our war aim (d) than any measures we could devise. But, even so, a substantial measure of military success will be necessary for the attainment of our ends (c) and (d). How is this to be achieved? And this brings me to the consideration of the present strategic and military situation.

2. *Salonika.*

In this connection the dominant fact that emerges is that our scope for military operations has become considerably narrowed down as the War has progressed. Possibilities of offensive action which at earlier stages of the War were open to us are no longer possible and several brilliant ideas will not now be put to the test of trial. On the contrary even our present fields of operation may have to be revised and contracted. The warnings of the First Sea Lord as to the naval and shipping position have become so grave and insistent that it would be dangerous in the extreme to continue to ignore them indefinitely. The question therefore arises, which of our overseas campaigns is the least promising to the attainment of our ends and makes the heaviest demands on our shipping. This undoubtedly is the Salonika campaign, which has failed in its original intention, and will more and more become not only a military and naval but possibly also a political embarrassment. Apart from a victorious offensive which may seriously threaten Sofia I can only see two advantages arising from this campaign: (a) it may support our diplomacy in endeavouring to detach Bulgaria from the Central Powers, (b) it may serve as a cover to Greece and prevent the Germans from reaching it and gathering fresh resources in men and submarine bases and lairs on the Greek coast and islands.

With our present forces on that front I consider a real threat to Bulgaria out of the question. The strategic geographical position in Central Europe is such that the Balkan Front should either be one of our most formidable in men and guns or should be left alone altogether. Any middle course such as we have adopted is either futile or dangerous. . . .

The question for immediate consideration of the Foreign Office is whether the detachment of Bulgaria is possible: if it can be and is brought about the Salonika campaign would not remain as a further addition to our list of failures. And a Bulgaria which is not only powerful and nationally satisfied but which has played Germany false at the most critical stage of the War will be a great factor in the future settlement of the Balkans, quite apart from the immediate military advantages. If possible the effort should be made. If not, then I can only advise a change of our plans, and our retirement from this front in such stages as will not endanger the position of our Allies who will remain on the contracted front. The Balkan situation has now become primarily a diplomatic one, and our military policy should be revised accordingly.

Next in importance to the detachment of Bulgaria from Central Europe would be the detachment of Turkey which might become feasible if the Russian Government would definitely waive their rights under the Bosphorus agreement. The danger, however, of Russia going out of the War on some pretext or other is so serious and would have such far-reaching consequences that I do not think we should moot the question with her at present, but leave the situation to clear up of itself in the course of events. Nagging is the worst form of dealing with a patient. I therefore proceed on the assumption that our campaign against the Turkish Empire will continue in full vigour.

3. *Mesopotamia.*

As regards Mesopotamia, we have achieved all that we were aiming at and can now consolidate our position and make it impregnable to any future counter-attacks. General Maude should at the most convenient point on this front select and prepare a strong defensive position for any future emergency, while continuing the pressure against the enemy further afield. . . .

4. *Palestine.*

This Palestine campaign presents very interesting military and even political possibilities. As it progresses to Jerusalem and Damascus, it will threaten the Turkish Empire far more gravely than anything we have so far undertaken except the Dardanelles and Gallipoli campaign. We should therefore be prepared for the most obstinate resistance, and it is essential for us to contemplate the gradual but complete withdrawal of our forces from Salonika to this front. This transfer will also have the effect of our making less use of the dangerous Mediterranean for our overseas operations, as the Palestine Army could be largely supplied from the East, Australia, and South Africa, and the ships now used in East Africa will also soon be set free for this purpose. The contraction of the Salonika Front and the increasing pressure in Palestine must obviously have the effect of bringing the whole of the Turkish forces to the Asiatic fronts of the Turkish Empire. It must be clearly realised that unless the Russians are made to pull their full weight in Armenia and General Maude continues to threaten the enemy on his front the Palestine force is certain to meet with the most formidable opposition even before it reaches Jerusalem. In any case, if we adopt a vigorous offensive we must be prepared to face the fact that this front will in all probability assume an importance eventually second only to that of the Western Front. The coming campaign must be judged and appreciated from that point of view to prevent future surprises or disappointments.

5. *Western Front.*

THERE REMAINS FOR CONSIDERATION THE FAR MORE IMPORTANT AND COMPLICATED QUESTION OF THE WESTERN FRONT. I HAVE ALWAYS LOOKED UPON IT AS A MISFORTUNE, NO DOUBT INEVITABLE UNDER THE CIRCUMSTANCES, THAT THE BRITISH FORCES HAVE BECOME SO ENTIRELY ABSORBED BY THIS FRONT. THE RESULT NOW IS THAT IN A THEATRE MAINLY OF THE ENEMY'S CHOOSING, THE TWO MOST IMPORTANT ARMIES OF THE ENTENTE ARE LOCKED UP IN FRONT OF ALMOST IMPREGNABLE POSITIONS. It is essential to our ends that we should keep the initiative and offensive, but both are enormously difficult in the situation in which we are placed on this front. I have no confidence that we can break through the enemy line on any large scale. No doubt with our predominance of heavy artillery we can batter in any selected portion of the enemy line, but in every case so far we have been unable to advance for more than a comparatively short distance, and there is no reason to think that this state of affairs will materially alter in the near future unless some unforeseen calamity overtakes the enemy. I found the spirit of both our officers and men on this front magnificent in its confidence and determination. But my visit has only strengthened my impression that a decision on this front can only be reached by a process of remorselessly wearing down the enemy. And that is a very slow, costly and even dangerous process for us no less than for the enemy and threatening both with exhaustion of man-power as the process of attrition goes on. Victory in this kind of warfare is the costliest possible to the victor.

My visit to this front has also impressed me with the undesirability of the present position both as regards the supreme military direction and the state of our strategic reserves. On both these points I wrote my views immediately after my return to the Chief of the Imperial General Staff and they have been largely incorporated into his important memorandum of the 17th April to the War Cabinet (O.I.-95/274) which has no doubt received the most careful consideration. These views I shall briefly repeat here: —

We entered the War in a very small way with a small military force and not as a principal combatant but rather as an auxiliary to France. This fact was reflected in our general military policy which was of necessity one of great modesty and almost complete subordination to that of France. Our Army took its position side by side with the French Army in defence of French soil, and as our forces continued to grow, we proceeded to take over more and more of the French line. The modesty of our policy and the subordination of our rôle to that of France have continued notwithstanding the fact that during the last two years the whole situation has been transformed and we are now the principal opponent of the Central Empires and the financial, naval and, to a large extent, the military mainstay of the Entente. This anomalous situation is now reflected in three curious respects. . . .

.   .   .   .   .

The most serious result of all is that our whole Army (with the exception of the Forces conducting campaigns elsewhere) has been locked up on the Western Front and we have no great strategic reserve left for any unforeseen contingencies. For no doubt good and sufficient reasons we have gradually shouldered more and more of the burden of defending France and so both the French and English Armies have become pinned down along the present Western Front. The Germans probably have great reserve forces which they could fling either against one of the existing fronts or into some new diversion into which they may be driven in order to achieve success. . . .

I consider the time has come for us to aim resolutely at the removal of these three anomalies. We should endeavour to recover the diplomatic lead, especially in the Balkans; we should, after the present offensive, resume the independence of our military direction; and, above all, we should aim at the liberation from the Western Front at an early date of at least one of our armies, which should remain in the north of France or the neighbourhood of the Belgian border as a strategic reserve to be used only when necessary in the case of grave contingencies. A great force such as ours, which has no strategic reserve, is running grave risks. The German strategic reserve last December could deal with Roumania as soon as the danger of her invading Transylvania arose, and we should be in a similar position of security against unforeseen developments.

These impressions which I brought from the Front have since been reinforced by the rumour that several important members of the French Government do not approve of General Nivelle's present offensive and consider a defensive policy the wisest one for the French Army to pursue. If this policy is carried out and is applied also to the British Army, it means that, towards the end of the third year of the War, the enemy has still succeeded in reducing us to the defensive. This, coupled with the fact that the enemy forces are now more numerous than ever before, that they have conquered large parts of Entente territory, which they are still holding, and that the submarine campaign, already so grave, is growing in violence, would look very much like our defeat, would dishearten all the Entente nations whose discouragement might precipitate serious peace movements among one or more of them. And once the rot sets in it might be difficult to stop it. No doubt the weight of America would be felt in 1918, but the danger is that we may not get there, unless active operations are presented and a continuance of military success buoys up the spirit of the nations to fight on till America can come in as a decisive factor. I feel the danger of a purely defensive policy so gravely that I would make the following suggestions in case the French carry out such a policy. In that case we should make them take back a substantial part of their line now occupied by us. As they would require no great reserve for offensive purposes, they would be in a position to do so. Our forces should then be concentrated towards the north, and part should go to the rear as a strategic reserve, while the rest should endeavour to recover the northern coast of Belgium and drive the enemy from Zeebrugge and Ostend. This task will be most formidable, especially if both the Russian and French lines remain passive, and every pressure should be exerted to induce them to be as aggressive as possible, even if they cannot actually assume the offensive. But, however difficult the task, something will have to be done to continue our offensive, and I see more advantages in an offensive intended to recover the Belgian coast and deprive the enemy of two advanced submarine bases, than in the present offensive, which in proportion as it succeeds in driving the enemy out of France will make the French less eager to continue the struggle beyond the goal. If the French are determined to go on the defensive, our (British) task on the Western Front may become so difficult that the Cabinet may decide to abandon the further prosecution of the Palestine campaign and to bring our Salonika troops as reinforcements to our Western Front.

I mention this here because I consider the time is now rapidly

approaching when the military situation as a whole will have to be
most carefully reviewed by the War Cabinet and circumstances
may force them to contract their military fronts even more than
was above suggested. We are approaching the final stage of this
long-drawn-out struggle, when we cannot afford to make any more
mistakes, and when any false move made by either side may well
prove decisive and fatal to it.

6. *Contingencies.*

All this is the reason why I am anxious to see a proper strategic
reserve established. The chapter of accidents in war is a long and
curious one, and many a struggle has been settled by something
unforeseen happening near the end. We want a reserve force to
provide against surprises and accidents and also to be in a position
to make use of any good opportunity which may present itself for
offensive action on our part. . . .

7. *Review of policy necessary.*

The point I would emphasise finally for the attention of the War
Cabinet is that the time has come, or is coming soon, when the
strategic situation, both military and naval, in relation to our
resources and diplomacy, should be reviewed as a whole, and, so
far as is possible, a definite policy should be laid down on the
points raised in this memorandum as well as on others which I
have refrained from referring to. Unless the First Sea Lord and
the Chief of the Imperial General Staff have the clear guidance of
the War Cabinet on general questions of policy, it is impossible for
them to obtain the highest and most efficient power out of the war
machine they are directing.

29th April, 1917.   J. C. S."

Sir William Robertson sent in to the War Cabinet his comment
upon the Smuts document:

"Operations on West Front

1. The French Government is apparently unwilling to continue
serious offensive operations. This, if true, means a drastic change
in the military situation. Local offensive operations, which the
French are said to be contemplating will have no real effect. In
war there is no half-way house between fighting a battle through
with the determination to beat the enemy, and acting defensively.
Such phrases as ' active defensive ' and ' offensive defensive ' are
mere words without any meaning in practice.

2. If the French stop now and once get away from the idea of
heavy fighting and heavy losses, it will be difficult, if not impossible,
to persuade them to undertake a big offensive again. At the best

the stop may mean that they will not begin again till the spring of 1918, as, until the arrival of an American Army in France, there is no reason to suppose that the Allies will be in a better position to fight on the Western Front than they are now.

3. The advantages which the French may claim for inaction are: Germany may be starved out (which we certainly cannot rely upon, especially as she already has Roumania to draw upon and may later have Russia); loss of life will be less and therefore the policy of less fighting will be popular in France (this being the most futile of all arguments); America may help with troops. But is it certain that shipping can be found in nine to twelve months' time for the transport of, say, 500,000 Americans to France and maintain them there?* Is it certain that our own shipping will hold out for another year, and that the French and British peoples will stand the strain of a year of inactivity while they have to endure continually increasing privations?

4. Can we be sure of keeping Russia and Italy in the War if Germany is free to strike hard at them? At the present time Russia is an easy prey, and cannot stand up to a formidable attack. What will be the attitude of the new Russian Government to us if we allow their country to be overrun once more? The Italian danger is notorious and nothing more need be said about it.

5. The above are briefly the dangers of inaction. What are the advantages of continuing the battle?

In every great battle a time of extreme stress arrives and the side which sets its teeth the hardest usually wins.

Again, before any considerable success can be gained in battle the enemy's reserves have to be exhausted. This used to be a matter of hours, now is a matter of weeks and months. The Commander with the last reserves usually wins.

When General Nivelle's plan was presented to the War Cabinet I said I did not believe in an early break-through such as he anticipated. I never have believed in a break-through of that kind, nor is an absolute break-through necessarily a preliminary to satisfactory terms of peace. If we sufficiently exhaust the enemy's reserves we may hope to attain such a measure of success as will persuade him that worse things are in store for him and that it is useless to continue the struggle.

6. *In the present battle we have done more than we expected (e.g. captured about 250 guns) and if the French have not done what they expected it is chiefly because their hopes were foolishly extravagant. They have not gained much ground, but between us we have made a much bigger hole in the German reserves than we thought was possible in the time. Out of 49 divisions originally*

* Britain alone found shipping to convey a million American troops to France in 1918. American ships carried another million.

available, 20 have been drawn into the fight on the French Front and 16 on ours. The fighting, though undoubtedly very heavy, is going slowly and steadily in our favour, and if the enemy were pushing us back every day and had already taken over 40,000 prisoners and 400 guns, I think we should not be without anxiety. Nor is he, as is shown by information received from Germany and the tone of recent German communiqués. For the first time in the War Germany is faced with really serious labour troubles at home. General Groener's proclamation (Sir W. Townley's telegram of 27th April) is clear evidence of this. Germany's plan is quite obviously to act defensively in the West and hold us up until her submarine campaign has had time to take effect. She is hopeful that this will happen before next harvest, for in the interval between this and then the privations of her people will be severe. If we can add anxiety regarding the military situation to anxiety as to food, we may bring her to terms. We are making her fight against her wishes, and that of itself justifies continued prosecution of the offensive.

On the other hand, if we, by our inaction, leave her free to win easy successes on fronts other than the Western, and allow her to proclaim to the world that we have failed, she will certainly keep both her people and her Allies together, and with these advantages and a harvest, the yield of which will be increased by the Roumanian crops, she will, in 1918, be in a military position which will allow her to regard calmly the arrival of a dozen or so American Divisions on the Western Front, even if shipping is available to send and maintain them.

7. My opinion is that the risks of waiting are too great, and that we must bring every possible pressure to bear on the French to make them fight. General Smuts in a paper just circulated to the War Cabinet supports this view. He says, speaking of the Western Front, ' It is essential to our ends that we should keep the initiative and offensive, but both are enormously difficult in the situation in which we are placed on this front. . . . These impressions which I brought from the Front have since been reinforced by the rumour that several important members of the French Government do not approve of General Nivelle's present offensive, and consider a defensive policy the wisest one for the French Army to pursue. If this policy is carried out and is applied also to the British Army it means that towards the end of the third year of war the enemy has still succeeded in reducing us to the defensive. This, coupled with the fact that the enemy forces are now more numerous than ever before, that they have conquered large parts of Entente territory, which they are still holding, and that the submarine campaign, already so grave, is growing in violence, would look very much like our defeat, would dishearten all the Entente

nations, whose discouragement might precipitate serious peace movements among one or more of them. And once the rot sets in, it might be difficult to stop it. No doubt the weight of America would be felt in 1918, but the danger is that we may not get there unless active operations are prosecuted, and a continuance of military success buoys up the spirit of the nations to fight on till America can come in as a decisive factor.'

8. If it should prove that we cannot persuade the French to fight, or if they agree to fight but we are not adequately satisfied that they really mean to do so and to the full extent of their power, we should as a *pis-aller* insist on their taking over a large part of our front and should continue our preparations for attacking in Belgium. I am by no means prepared to recommend now that that operation should be carried out if the French do nothing and if as many German troops are on the Western Front as are there now, as I doubt if it would be feasible in these circumstances.* But it is very important that it should be undertaken if reasonably practicable, and as the enemy may give us a chance we should be ready to take advantage of it. When all is said and done, there is really no satisfactory alternative to continuing the battle we and the French have started.

9. I have for a long time past urged on the War Cabinet the necessity of our taking much greater control over the War, for I have always felt that a time would come when the French Government would break down. They have broken down and the only remedy is for us to take charge and at once. I attach a note by Lieut.-General Wilson which supports this view."

In view of the scornful references to " the failure of the Nivelle offensive," which afterwards became one of the clichés of the Staff, it is interesting to record Sir William Robertson's deliberate summary of the result obtained, which he put on record a fortnight after the battle had been fought. In his opinion we have achieved " more than he had expected." Between the French and ourselves we had " made a much bigger hole in the German reserves than we had thought was possible in the time." So pleased was he with the progress made in this particular offensive that he was anxious to continue it. As to our general policy, he was back at the strategy of attrition. He had no other idea in his head except exhausting the enemy's reserves. He does not seem to have contemplated the possibility that we might at the same time be wasting our own men and that the success of attrition is a question of the balance of wastage. He was very pessimistic, even contemptuous, about American help. He also took a gloomy view of the prospects and

* The opinions expressed by the C.I.G.S. in this paragraph are quite inconsistent with the attitude he adopted in June when the question of a tremendous offensive to clear the Belgian coast was discerned and determined.

effect of the submarine attack. He thought that by 1918 the Allies could not spare the necessary shipping to bring over more than half a million Americans " and maintain them here." He contemplated that by that time we might have been starved into a bad peace. Robertson was a close friend of Jellicoe, and they worked in the most intimate co-operation. Both Jellicoe and Robertson took the German estimate of the probable outcome of the German submarine attack. That is the real significance of Robertson's references to shipping. It may account for his adhesion to the project of a Flanders campaign. In this memorandum he is not sanguine about its possibilities, but he regards it almost as a last desperate throw. He can think of no other. Meanwhile let the Nivelle offensive proceed.

I must add a word as to my own attitude at the time towards this offensive.

At the Rome Conference I tried in vain to dissuade my French colleagues from attempting another great offensive in France this year and I indicated clearly what the result would be. I urged an attack in another quarter, on the Italian Front. When they insisted on the redemption of our Chantilly bond, I could not withdraw the British signature and risk what might have been a rupture in the Alliance, especially as all our own military advisers took the French view. When Robertson supported the French thesis at Rome, he was in full possession of the detailed Nivelle modifications of the Chantilly scheme. At that Conference he was one of its most strenuous and stubborn advocates. When the Nivelle operation was the only one left on the board I did my utmost to make it a success in transport, material and men—to the limit of our resources. I urged Unity of Command as an essential condition of success. That the first experiment was not a success was unfortunate. The facts I have related will enable those who have perused the miserable tale of folly, bickering, jealousy, tactlessness and sullenness to distribute the blame for failure to achieve a better result. Unity of Direction had to be postponed until events compelled Generals to subordinate personal pride and national susceptibilities to the exigencies of a common cause in straits. It needed a greater disaster than the Nivelle disappointment to achieve this end. In spite of all that happened this offensive was for the British Army a distinct success—a much greater success than the Somme. It might have ended in a triumph had it been skilfully and resolutely exploited. But once more the " angels on horseback " had spoilt the feast.

Whether there was anything more to be gained by pressing on the attack which had commenced so auspiciously in our sector, was a question upon which I was not competent to express an opinion. I was strongly inclined to take the Pétain view that nothing considerable could be achieved by continuing the offensive on any considerable scale. But I knew that other Members of the

Cabinet were of a different opinion, notably General Smuts, who had been sent over to the front by the Cabinet to report on the situation and who came back from his visit to Headquarters persuaded the Western offensive was the only military operation which was now open to us. I subsequently found that the majority of the Members of the War Cabinet were impressed by his ardent support of the Staff's estimate and advice.

At this time no rumours had reached us of serious trouble in the French Army. Its worst developments came later. Had he known what the exact condition of the French Army was at this date, I am convinced that General Smuts would have hesitated to throw over Pétain's sagacious counsel.

Both the Smuts and Robertson documents were circulated to the Cabinet and were considered at the meeting of 1st May. In the course of the discussion, the Chief of the Imperial General Staff read a letter from Sir Douglas Haig, in which he pointed out that at the moment some doubt existed as to who was the *de facto* Commander-in-Chief of the French Army, since General Nivelle was still the titular Commander-in-Chief, while General Pétain had been appointed as Chief of the Staff at the French Ministry of War. However this might be, the Field-Marshal had little doubt that the French Government was in control, and that their policy was defensive in character. He considered it would be useless for him to continue to press his present offensive vigorously if the French did not co-operate actively, and he proposed a modification in his plans to meet this situation.

The questions raised for decision at the War Cabinet were as follows: —

1. Should the British representatives at the forthcoming Anglo-French Conference press the French Government to pursue the policy of an active offensive?
2. What attitude should the British representatives adopt if the French should decline to take the offensive, or alternatively, if they should accept the obligation to undertake it, but show by their attitude that they did not intend to give full effect to their undertaking?

I summed up the arguments against further offensives on the Western Front this year, which weighed with Pétain and the French Government. The French, I pointed out, could claim that two very great Generals were opposed to the policy of a great offensive, namely, Generals Alexeieff and Pétain. The former had given his opinion that Russia could not undertake any large offensive this year, and consequently the Allies in the West would find themselves opposed to the great bulk of the German reserves, and by attacking would exhaust their man-power in an operation offering no prospect of success, thereby weakening their offensive capacity for 1918. General Pétain, the French could say, had accurately forecast the failure of General Nivelle's offensive, and believed in repeated surprise attacks designed on a less ambitious scale. The French would ask what prospect there was of a successful offensive on the Western Front this year. They would produce figures to show that the Germans had a superiority in heavy artillery, and that in numbers the Allies had no considerable superiority; in short, that the superiority of men and material necessary for a successful offensive was lacking. They would further urge that the blockade was telling on the enemy; that by 1918 the Russian situation would have cleared up definitely one way or the other, and that the United States of America would be able to put half a million men in the field. Even if the shipping conditions did not enable the American Army to be transported to the Western Front, it could be sent to Russia, where American organisation would by that time have effected improvements in Russian transport conditions. They would advocate that for the present our policy on the Western Front should be defensive, and that in the meantime we should use our surplus strength to clear up the situation elsewhere—in Syria, for example—and to eliminate first Turkey, then Bulgaria, and finally, perhaps even Austria, from the War. They would urge that, if the British Generals were confident now both they and the French Generals had time after time expressed confidence before previous offensives in the West, which had never yet succeeded. These, I pointed out, were considerations which could not lightly be dismissed, and I felt bound to admit that they made some appeal to me. Moreover, we could not disregard the possibility that in a few months' time we might be confronted with an insistent demand for peace. If Russia collapsed it would be urged that it might be beyond our power to beat Germany, as the blockade would become to a great extent ineffective, and the whole of the enemy's forces would soon become available to oppose the Western Allies. We could not contemplate with equanimity the prospect of entering a Peace Conference with the enemy in possession of a large slice of Allied territory, and before we had completed the conquest of Mesopotamia and Syria. General Pétain was said to be a very resolute and determined man, and he would be strongly supported by M. Painlevé. If they declined to co-operate they would practically take it out of our power to continue the offensive, and we could not succeed unless a substantial part of the German reserves were drawn off. Finally, I reminded the War Cabinet that we had no reserve of man-power sufficient to sustain a combat with the bulk of the German reserves, until the United States of America could bring their strength to bear. I also reminded the War Cabinet that, to maintain our shipping at the barest minimum required to sustain the War, we required to realise a building programme of 3,000,000 gross tons, and we could not afford that men should be recruited from this or from the connected trades.   Shipping was at present our weakest flank, and we could not afford to take men from shipbuilding.   On the contrary, I had almost come to the conclusion, as the result of my enquiries during the past week, that we should be obliged to withdraw men from the Army for this purpose.

In stating the case as above, against the continuation of our offensive in the West, I made it clear that I was not myself committed to the arguments that I had expressed, but I considered that they required earnest consideration.   This statement represented the view I then took of the military position and possibilities for 1917.   I had, however, no support for this attitude and policy amongst my colleagues. In the course of the discussion that followed it was evident that the Cabinet as a whole took a different view from the one I stated.

It was pointed out that, if the Allies contented themselves with a defensive policy in the West, or with the policy of small offensives generally attributed to General Pétain, which the Chief of the General Staff and General Smuts characterised as equivalent to a defensive policy, the Germans would be able to release reserves for operations against Russia or Italy.   Russia, it was generally agreed, was the weak point of the Alliance, but some difference of opinion was expressed as to whether the effect of a German offensive against Russia would be advantageous or the reverse.   One view was that an attack might stiffen the Russian resistance and pull the whole nation together.   Even admitting that the Allies had not much chance of breaking the German line this year, it was urged, nevertheless, that by continuing to hammer the enemy, we might bring them to a frame of mind in which they would agree to a peace on terms acceptable to the Allies.   In this connection it was pointed out that Germany would probably reach almost the lowest point of depression and misery between now and the next harvest.   The Allies, on the other hand, were still capable of making a great military effort.   Later on, after a long continuance of submarine losses, though we probably should not be starved, we should be compelled, in order to supply the essential needs of the nation, to withdraw shipping from military purposes and consequently to reduce our military effort.   To desist now would be to lose the moment when our own force was at a maximum and when the enemy's anxieties were most acute.   It was further suggested that to relinquish our efforts at this period of the War would be to deal a fatal blow at the morale of the Allies.   In this connection it was pointed out that the French Socialists had by only two votes rejected the invitation to an International Socialist Conference at Stockholm, to be attended by German Socialists, and summoned in the interests of peace.   It is interesting to note that all the arguments for a strong offensive were based on the implicit assumption that America would not be in a position next year to render the Allies such military assistance as to influence a decision.

General Smuts was very insistent on the moral aspect of the question. He considered that to relinquish the offensive in the third year of the War would be fatal, and would be the beginning of the end. It would be impossible to keep up the spirits of the people, and pessimism and despair would be rife among the Allies, while the Germans would be correspondingly cheered, and would have time to recover their spirits. He did not foresee any likelihood of our breaking the German line, but by remorselessly hammering away we might expect ultimately to bring the enemy to terms. If we could not break the enemy's front we might break his heart. It was hard on us and would involve heavy casualties, but, though it was a great misfortune, the Western Front was our problem and it could only be solved by this policy. For replacing losses we must rely ultimately on the United States of America, but to delay action until the United States could bring their strength to bear, that is to say, until the year 1918, might be a disastrous policy. Even if the French refused to take the offensive, we ought to be prepared to continue, and should insist on the French taking over the section of the line recently occupied by us to enable General Nivelle to take the offensive. Moreover, General Smuts assumed that the French would not remain entirely passive in any case. He considered that from a purely British point of view it would be better to attack in Flanders, where very important objects of British policy were to be achieved, in order to leave to the French the incentive to clear the enemy from France, an incentive which would be lacking if the recent operations had resulted in driving the enemy across the Meuse.

The First Sea Lord pointed out that shipping might prove the decisive factor and undertook to investigate the transport facilities likely to be available to the United States in 1918.

On a review of the foregoing considerations the War Cabinet decided: —

    1. That the British representatives at the Conference should press the French to continue the offensive.

    2. If, after hearing General Pétain's views or after a conference between the Chief of the Imperial General Staff and General Pétain, they were not satisfied that the French offensive would prove effective, they should insist on our entire freedom of action and on the French Army reoccupying the trenches recently taken over by the British forces.

The Imperial War Cabinet was influenced by these considerations to support the advice given by the British military leaders that the best course to pursue in the immediate future was to continue the pressure on the Germans in France, in order to prevent them from releasing their troops for an offensive which would finally put a distracted Russia out of action, and also to make it impossible for Germany to send any divisions to the aid of the Austrians in the impending attack upon them by the Italians. In the sequel we found that the policy of an active offensive in the West achieved neither of these results, whilst it ended in colossal losses for our Army.

At the request of Sir Douglas Haig and Sir William Robertson I accompanied them to Paris for the Conference held on 4th May, to discuss the whole situation with the French Government and the new Commander-in-Chief. Before the ministers and generals met, there was a military Conference held at the Ministry of War. At that Conference an agreement was reached, and a statement of the results was read at the mixed Conference of Ministers and Generals in the afternoon.

Here follows the copy of the statement by Sir William Robertson:

" 4th May, 1917.

I conferred this morning with Generals Pétain and Nivelle and Field-Marshal Sir Douglas Haig. We reviewed the whole situation including the situation in Russia and Italy, and the entry of America into the War, and we arrived at the unanimous opinion that it is essential to continue offensive operations on the Western Front. A large portion of the enemy's reserves have already been exhausted by the French and British attacks. If the enemy is given time to recover, the fruits of this success will be lost. He will be free to attack either Russia or Italy, neither of whom are at present in a condition to resist an attack in great force. His present object is certainly to encourage his people to hold out until the submarine warfare has taken effect, and if he is left free to gain easy successes where he can, and allowed to proclaim to the world that he has defeated his two principal enemies, he will obtain this object. This might be fatal to our chance of winning the War. We are, however, unanimously of opinion that the situation has changed since the plan for the offensive begun in April was agreed upon by the two Governments, and that this plan is no longer operative. It is no longer a question of aiming at breaking through the enemy's front and aiming at distant objectives. It is now a question of wearing down and exhausting the enemy's resistance, and if and when this is achieved, to exploit it to the fullest extent possible. In order to wear him down we are agreed that it is absolutely necessary to fight with all our available forces with the object of destroying the enemy's divisions. We are unanimously of opinion that there is no half-way between this course and fighting defensively, which, at this stage of the War, would be tantamount to acknowledging defeat. We are all of opinion that our object can be obtained by relentlessly attacking with limited objectives, while making the fullest use of our artillery. By this means we hope to gain our ends with the minimum loss possible.

Having unanimously agreed to the above principles, we consider that the methods to be adopted to put them into practice, and the time and place of the various attacks, are matters which must be left to the responsible Generals, and that they should at once be examined and settled by them."

Then followed a discussion which in effect emphasised the agreement which had been reached.

General Pétain expressed entire concurrence, and said that the Generals were in agreement in detail as well as on general principle. Very shortly, the position was to maintain an offensive by limited action with definite objectives, and the British Generals made it clear that the full forces of the French and British Armies were to be employed for this end. This point was very emphatically elaborated by me. I pointed out that both France and Great Britain were apt to underestimate the measure of success already achieved, because their standard of comparison was the high and possibly exaggerated hopes with which their offensive began.

I asked what would our feelings be if we had lost 45,000 prisoners, that is to say, practically five divisions of fighting men, 450 guns, including some of the heaviest calibre, about 800 machine-guns, had had 36 reserve divisions put out of action, and had lost 70 square miles of territory. Such a feeling of pessimism would have gone through both countries that it might have been difficult to keep the fighting spirit up. Captured documents showed that the Germans were short of material, and we knew that the food problem was much more serious for them than for us. We must go on hitting and hitting with all our strength until the German ended, as he always did, by cracking.

M. Ribot accepted my points. He said that to shut ourselves up on the defensive after three years of war would be a reckless and imprudent policy. We must press on with all our forces. But the question of effectives was really serious, especially for France, who had stood the brunt of the War practically alone until the British Army was ready. Therefore France must, although putting forth her full strength, guard against excessive losses.

I repeated that we were ready to put the full strength of the British Army into the attack, *but it was no good doing so unless the French did the same. Otherwise, the German would bring his best men and guns and all his ammunition against the British Army and then later against the French.* Tentative and feeble attacks were really more costly in the end.

M. Painlevé said that the French Government were in complete agreement with my opinions, but thought the idea, which had grown since the last offensive, that France now contemplated a passive offensive in order to save lives, should be put right. What the French Government really intended was to adopt the best method for using the full effect of the French resources and sacrifices with the minimum of loss, and he thought that the opinion of the Conference was unanimous to continue to do the enemy the greatest possible amount of damage. The discussion ended by a mutual assurance of complete confidence in the British and French intentions to use their full strength.

General Pétain adhered firmly to his policy of " limited " offensives. The strategy of the rupture which was the idea of the Champagne, Somme, Chemin des Dames and afterwards of the Flanders offensive, was thus definitely thrown over in favour of the policy of limited offensives with a definite objective, which was subsequently practised with such success by General Pétain at Moronvilliers and Verdun.

It will be noted that Sir William Robertson, at the Conference and after, accepted unreservedly the Pétain policy of " making the fullest use of our artillery "—that meant the Pétain scheme of saving your own men and wasting the enemy by heavy bombardment. The C.I.G.S. stated categorically that " it is no longer a question of aiming at breaking through the enemy front and aiming at distant objectives." He thus by clear implication ruled out the project of an offensive on a large scale to rupture the German lines in Flanders and clear the Belgian coast. That certainly could not be described as a limited offensive, with no distant objectives.

This is how matters were left as the result of the Paris Conference.

CHAPTER LII

THE PETROGRAD CONFERENCE

As indicated previously, I had made repeated efforts to induce the British Government to establish more direct and authoritative contact with Russia in order to ascertain the real position in that country, and to discover what was wrong in its equipment and organisation. I had also urged the holding of Allied Conferences at which Russia should be represented by her most responsible statesmen and soldiers. That was only possible by holding these gatherings occasionally in the East. With a retreating Army important Generals could not have spared the time to visit Paris. And the Czar, with whom rested the final decision, could not have left Russia. At last, at the Paris Conference held on the 15th and 16th November, 1916, it had been decided that, subject to the Czar's approval, such a Conference should be held at Petrograd in time to discuss and make the final arrangements for the 1917 campaign. The Government instructions to the Allied Delegations were to be " the united front," which included community of resources.

At the second meeting of the War Cabinet on 11th December, 1916, the question was discussed of making quite definite arrangements for a Conference of the Allied Governments and Military Staffs to be held in Russia, as agreed at the Paris Conference in November. Our Foreign Office was instructed to inform our Allies that the British representatives would be ready to start immediately after Christmas.

Delays occurred however in settling the personnel of the delegations from the different countries. I attached great importance to securing an authoritative and impressive British delegation, whose representation would command respectful attention in Russia. On the civilian side I nominated Lord Milner. The only other alternative would have been Mr. Balfour, but he had not recovered from a severe attack of influenza. On the military side Sir Douglas Haig could not leave his command in France, and Sir William Robertson, who was the alternative to Haig, would have gone sullenly and reluctantly, if at all. There was no other General available who had the necessary qualifications except Sir Henry Wilson, so he was chosen. He was a man of brilliant gifts but he had obvious defects which gave the impression of unreliability. Had his force of character been equal to the subtlety of his brain, he would have deserved and probably attained the highest position in the British Army. His complete knowledge of both the British and French Armies on the Western Front specially qualified him for this Mission.

I urged the French Government to select a General whose status would be recognised by the Russians. Here is an extract from the Minutes of a discussion on the subject which took place at the London Inter-Allied Conference on December 28th: —

" THE PRIME MINISTER referred to the Petrograd Conference. It was proposed to leave this country on the 9th January. His Majesty's Government hoped to be represented by a member of the War Cabinet and by one of their ablest Generals. They desired that the whole deputation should be as strong as possible, so as to bring Russia into line and secure *real* co-operation between the East and the West. He therefore hoped that the French Government would send a strong deputation.

M. RIBOT said that they would send a Cabinet Minister and a General of the first rank. General Castelnau had exhibited so marked a desire to be in active touch with the Army that there was no question of his going, and the French Government had thought that General Roques, the late Minister of War, might go.

THE PRIME MINISTER said that he was going to speak quite frankly and openly; it was the only way to ensure complete confidence between the Allies. He felt that a merely complimentary deputation was useless. There had been many of them sent to Russia already. The representatives who were going on this occasion must not only have full powers, subject, of course, to the final decision of their Government, but be capable of exercising their full powers. Was General Roques being sent because he was the best man to discuss the 1917 campaign, or because the best men were busy elsewhere? In the latter case the deputation would be a pretence and useless. It must have authority and capacity.

LORD CURZON said that, while appreciating the attitude of General Roques at previous Conferences, he was bound to say that the General had taken no very active part. What was wanted now was the military mind of France, and he endorsed the wish of the Prime Minister to see a fighting General appointed to the deputation.

THE PRIME MINISTER said that it must be someone whom the Emperor of Russia and his advisers would listen to. There were unpleasant things that would have to be said and they must be said by someone who would be taken seriously. He begged the French Government to treat the deputation as a really serious matter.

The General should be somebody of the status and prestige of General Castelnau. We were sending a Cabinet Minister and one of our most brilliant Generals. Unless the French deputation was of equal strength the onus of the discussions would fall on us, and the Conference might fail in its purpose. If the French Government did not assist to the utmost of their power, our difficulties would be greatly added to.

M. RIBOT was not afraid that the Russian Government would not listen. He feared that they would not execute their promises once the deputation had left Russia.

THE PRIME MINISTER said that they would not even listen unless those who spoke to them were people who could speak with authority. The only chance of a really great success in 1917 was completely effective co-operation with Russia, and the whole campaign might depend on the authority of the deputation now sent.

M. RIBOT said that he would inform his colleagues and he thanked the Prime Minister for the complete frankness that had been shown."

As a result of this short discussion, the French Government dropped the idea of sending General Roques and chose General Castelnau as the head of the military section of their mission.

Then came a series of postponements—all of them ominous of trouble. The subterranean fires in Russia had already begun to break through the crust. News came of the assassination of Rasputin —the Czar's protégé and the Czarina's friend—by a cabal of young aristocrats. The anger of the Court found vent in a shifting of Ministers who had failed to protect the favourite. The rumbling underneath became louder, and the seething and spluttering of steam and boiling mud became everywhere more apparent and disquieting.

At the request of the Russian Government, the start of the Allied Mission was put off to the middle of January in the vain hope that the volcanic fires might subside. The next postponement was significant of further trouble. The Russians expressed the desire that the visit should be further postponed, on the ground that the Duma was due to meet on 25th January, and as its first sessions were expected to be stormy the Russian Government therefore preferred that the Allied Conference should not begin its deliberations till at least three or four sessions of the Duma had taken place. In fact, the air of the Russian capital became so charged with sulphurous exhalations that the opening of the Duma was postponed for a month, to keep out the lava from surging in hot fury around the Conference doors. Its first meeting was actually held on 27th February, a week after the Allied Conference had concluded. In another fortnight the revolutionary crater had opened, and the fires are still reddening the Eastern sky.

The representatives of Britain, France and Italy foregathered in England on 19th January, 1917, and sailed from Oban for Russia two days later. At this first Conference on the Eastern side of the battlefield, the Western Powers were represented by able men on the civilian side and by at least two men of distinction on the military side. The principal British representatives were Lord Milner, a member of the War Cabinet; General Sir Henry Wilson for the Army; Lord Revelstoke, as an authority on Finance, and Sir Walter Layton on Munitions. Sir George Buchanan, the British Ambassador in Russia, attended the Conference as a diplomatic representative. In addition there were a number of special delegates to discuss different problems. The French delegation was led by M. Doumergue, an ex-Premier and a future President of the Republic, and again a Premier, and General Castelnau, one of France's greatest soldiers. The Italian delegation had Signor Scialoja at its head. It was the first time during the War that the Allies had conferred together on the Eastern Front. It was the first time after these years of war that East, as well as West, had been authoritatively represented at a Conference on any front. And now, alas, it was too late as far as Russia was concerned, to repair the blunders due to lack of co-ordination.

The party reached Petrograd on 29th January, and the Commission on Supplies started work the following afternoon. The first plenary session of the Conference was held on 1st February. Altogether the various meetings of the full conference and of the separate Commissions were spread out over three weeks, the concluding session being held on the afternoon of 20th February, 1917. In the intervals between their meetings the members of the Allied Mission travelled about in Russia and tried to get a first-hand impression of its conditions, discussing matters with leading Russians and with their own agents and representatives in the country.

The Mission re-embarked at Romanoff on the Murmansk coast on 25th February, reaching Scapa Flow on 2nd March. Ten days later the Russian Revolution began, and on 15th March, Czar Nicholas II abdicated.

The evidence collected by our representatives and the points which emerged in the course of the Conference show forcibly how great was the need for a closer co-operation between Russia and her Western Allies, and how deplorable were the consequences of Russian ineptitude and Western selfishness. The casual and inefficient methods of the Russian autocracy were well known to the West; but the Mission now realised fully for the first time how the selfish and stupid concentration of the military authorities of France and Britain on their own fronts, and their consequent neglect to give studied and timely thought to the difficulties and deficiencies of their Eastern Ally, had contributed to the confusion and ruin which was so soon to end in the utter collapse of Russia.

They found Russia in a deplorable state of disorganisation, muddle and disorder, rent with faction, permeated with German propaganda and espionage, eaten up with corruption. As to the Conference itself, Lord Milner reported in a confidential note to the War Cabinet that: —

"The proceedings of the plenary meetings of the Conference were of the most jejune and superficial character. . . . The whole thing was exceedingly ill-arranged."

A large and miscellaneous crowd of people was allowed to be present, and perhaps the most ominous note in Milner's report is the reason he assigns for their inability to discuss things seriously at the Conference—the lack of secrecy and the prevalence of espionage.

"It was obviously impossible to discuss anything of a confidential nature before more than forty persons, many of whom we did not know at all, and one or two of whom we had a certain amount of reason to suspect. . . ."

A report made by another member of the Delegation noted that there were three groups of opinion in the country, of which the first was the pro-Germans,

"whose sympathies and interests are entirely German. These people are recruited from the Court, the Civil Service, and the business community. If they could they would end the War to-morrow. They belong to the reactionaries, and profess to believe that Russian and German interests are identical, and must always remain so."

This observer also noted that: —

"While goods are still being imported into Russia from enemy countries, it is just as certain that sums of money are being paid by German agents to Government officials. Probably this was done in the case of the Murman Railway, where the conflicting interests of the Archangel railway and port, assisted by German money, contrived to prevent the construction of an efficient railway to Kola."

In explanation of this point it may be said that our representatives found the port of Kola or Romanoff had an unloading capacity of 1,500 tons a day, but the railway could not move 600 tons a day from it, and in mid-May it would have to be closed for the summer for repairs.

This evidence shows the comparative freedom with which German agents and propaganda were able to operate in the country.

During the discussions it became clear from the outset that the Russians had decided to place in the forefront of their demands at the Conference the implementing of M. Briand's phrase about " the common front " and " the pooling of resources." They crystallised their plea into a request for the fixation, for each of the Allies, of " a minimum equipment " on the condition of carrying out their part of the general offensive. A reasonable and practical proposition, but coming—oh, so late. Why was it not made at the very beginning of the War? But one of the unsolved mysteries of this War will always be—why those who were responsible for directing it never met to confer as to their strategy until February, 1917, when it was too late to amend the most calamitous strategical errors. M. Pokrovski, the Russian Foreign Minister, opened the proceedings with a formulation of the new Russian claim upon the Allies:—

" Our [the Allied] joint resources in men, in material, in products of every kind," he said, " exceed too obviously those of our enemy for victory to be uncertain. All the same, our military situation is as yet far from being all that it ought to be. . . . It is essential that the initiative in operations shall be captured from the enemy and maintained by the Allies. We shall only keep it by an activity that is continuous and incessant on all fronts. For that we have got to distribute as usefully and intelligently as possible all our resources—men and materials—and thus assure from them the biggest return. *That, gentlemen, is one of the objects, in fact the principal object, of our meetings.*"

General Alexeieff, the ablest strategist of all the Russian Generals, was unable to be present, partly through ill-health. His place was taken by General Gourko, the Russian Chief of Staff. He also was reputed to be a good soldier. He spoke next after M. Pokrovski, and stressed the same point:—

" The Russian High Command regards the co-ordination of the Allied efforts as the essential and necessary condition of success. . . . To enable the Allies to carry to success the operations which will be decided on, they will have to investigate and discover how to distribute as usefully as possible the resources at their disposal. In this connection it is impossible to emphasise enough the importance of the principle of pooling our resources."

The importance of this principle was clearly recognised by Lord Milner, and he underlined it in a Confidential Note which he prepared while in Russia and passed over to Pokrovski and to the Czar, for the purpose of intimating to them his view on matters which it had been difficult to thrash out in the crowded open session. In this Note he said:—

> " The way I look at it is this: we are face to face with a supreme emergency; we are all absolutely in one boat, and have got to sink or swim together. There can be no thought of the individual interests of the Allied nations—they have all one supreme interest: Victory. . . .
>
> The only point from which we ought to look at the matter is that of the total strength of the Allies. Subject to the inexorable physical necessities governing the transfer of men and things, all the men, all the material, all the money at the disposal of any of the Allies ought to be employed at that point where they can be employed with the most effect. . . . *It might be good policy to sacrifice some addition of strength on the Western Front for the purpose of supplying Russia's urgent needs. For it is at least possible that an amount of material which would not make any vital difference to the result of the clash of enormous armaments on the Western Front might make the whole difference between success and failure on the Eastern Front.** This is a consideration of great weight, and one which would naturally incline us to give priority of consideration to Russia's needs at the present time. . . ."

These quotations show how firmly Lord Milner had come to support the view which, as documents I have quoted previously in these Memoirs show, had long been urged by me, that if a share of the ammunition blazed away in France on senseless and sanguinary attacks, and of the transport material rendered necessary by these tremendous offensives, had been given to the Russians, Serbians and Roumanians, it would have enabled them to roll back the foe and produce decisions.

The neglect to give to Russia some part of the supplies wasted by the Allies on their own Front seems to have sunk deep into the Russian mind and produced a sense of general irritation with the West.

In his report to the War Cabinet, Milner said:—

> " I feel it to be necessary that my colleagues should realise—as I certainly did not myself realise till I went to Petrograd—the Russian attitude of mind with regard to the failures and losses of the War. There can be no doubt that there is just now a feeling of considerable discouragement. Reckless as the Russians are of human life, their enormous losses—at least 6,000,000 men, up to date, killed, captured, or permanently disabled—are beginning

* My italics.

to prey upon their minds. More than this, they feel bitterly that these exceptional losses were not inevitable, but that the Russian soldiers, whose gallantry is undoubted, never have had in this war, and still have not, anything like a fair chance, owing to their lamentable deficiency in equipment. . . . They certainly do feel intensely that the Allies, in view of their much more fortunate position in regard to material of war, are bound to do everything that is humanly possible, and even at some sacrifice to themselves, to redress this great inequality."

When I come to the chapter on the Revolution I shall deal more fully with the effect on the Russian mind of our imprudent stinginess in the matter of sharing supplies.

In pressing for the consideration of some real measure of resource-pooling, the Russians urged again and again their interesting practical suggestion, that account should be taken of the *minimum requirements* necessary to enable an army to carry out the operations expected from it. General Gourko said in his address: —

"The Russian Army cannot carry out successfully an offensive action on a wide front until it possesses an agreed minimum of technical equipment. . . . It hopes that the Allied Governments will, on behalf of our common aim of victory, find means to furnish the Russian Army with what it lacks. Only on this condition can it bring to bear its whole weight against the adversary. It goes without saying that if the minimum in question can be exceeded, the hour of final success would be brought much nearer."

The proposition he lays down is unchallengeable; and had it been discussed in a friendly manner between the Allies in 1914 or even in 1915, and accepted and acted upon as a cardinal principle of their strategical combination, it would have enabled them to achieve victory before the end of 1916, if not sooner. It is incredible that this Conference was the first occasion on which so obvious a principle had ever been seriously advanced and considered fully. It had not even been urged at any Conference before November, 1916.

When at the conclusion of the first plenary session, M. Pokrovski submitted a series of questions which the Conference was to discuss at its subsequent meetings and commissions, he specifically included this issue, setting it out in the following terms: —

"On what principle will be settled the quantity of material that will be furnished to Russia? Will it be judged possible—in order to obtain the best results—to distribute the available munitions in such a way as to assure to each of the Allied Armies a certain minimum? In this event, ought not this minimum of material to be proportioned to the number of active units and to the importance of each front, alike in respect of its length and in respect of the problem which confronts it?"

The carrying into effect of this proposition was, as it turned out in the subsequent discussions, handicapped by the difficulty of getting goods into Russia, and, once they were in Russia, of transporting them promptly to the requisite destination.   There was first the shortage of shipping tonnage, resulting from the activity of German submarines; then the congestion and bad management of the few Russian ports; the shortage of railway lines and rolling stock, and inefficient management of existing facilities for getting the goods from the ports to the interior and the front.   Added to this was the consideration that the Russians sometimes failed to assemble correctly the articles sent them, or to use them properly when they had them.

Thus our representatives reported that there was at Vladivostock an accumulation of essential war stores, estimated at 400,000 to 500,000 tons, much of it lying about in the open, through failure of the Trans-Siberian Railway to clear it.   At Kola the congestion was such that tonnage was being held up in the port for weeks, and sometimes for months, waiting to be unloaded.   As there were no exports to place on returning vessels, and no ballasts available for them,

"coal was put on board to serve this purpose which had only just been shipped out from England."

Although there was a shortage of rolling stock to move these goods we learnt that in addition to the rolling stock used for carrying supplies and munitions for the Army,

" a large amount of rolling stock is improperly used for other subsidiary purposes, such as the housing of soldiers and the storing of supplies.   It is also asserted that the strategic reserve of rolling stock is far in excess of military requirements, and that some of the railways are so congested with waggons that at times they cannot be used at all."

Similarly as regards the railway rolling stock used to carry supplies for the civilian population,

" The methods of allocation adopted by these bodies [local distribution Commissions] are slow and cumbersome, with the result that thousands of waggons are often held up at various points waiting to be distributed.   Sometimes they are delayed in this way for weeks and months."

Private traders would circumvent this by bribing railway officials to let them have waggons. But as no one was bribing in the interests of the Government, Government stores remained stationary for long periods. Bribery is always an anti-social weapon.

These circumstances ought not to have been a surprise to anyone who knew Czarist Russia. In fact it was always a subject of gossip and jest whenever and wherever Russian needs were discussed. But the Allies ought to have made a common effort to grapple with these conditions years ago. The organisation of Russia for waging effective war ought to have been one of the first concerns of the Western Allies.

At this Conference arrangements were made to reorganise transport and distribution. In determining what supplies to send to Russia, discussion proceeded partly upon the principle of the maximum amount which it was thought could be brought to the country and distributed there in the course of 1917. In this connection, Lord Milner reported to the War Cabinet: —

> " I think we have done two things: —
> 1. We have worked out a practical scheme for the supply of war material, based on the principle of using the available tonnage to give the Russian the largest possible quantities of the types of which they stand most in need.
> 2. We have done what lay in our power to ensure this material being turned to the best account."

It cannot be denied that there was real force behind the contention of the Allies that transport difficulties would handicap the allotment of large supplies to Russia. But that ought to have been ascertained and set right years ago: the defect in Russian efficiency was well known before the war. Had there been such an authoritative Conference in Russia in 1915 as the one the proceedings of which I am now summarising, deficiencies could have been made up, shortcomings could have been rectified—and all in time, before Russian nerve, patience and endurance had been exhausted and before despair and hunger had bred disaffection. The Russians were so frightened by their defeats in 1915 that they would have agreed to any system of supervision and control in return for assured supplies. They were quite accustomed to the spectacle of foreigners organising industries and enterprises for them in their own country. Before the War there were German engineers in every branch of the metal industries and there were Welsh settlements in the iron and steel districts and in the coal areas. Sir John Hanbury-Williams reported in 1916 that the Czar had looked forward to the visit of Lord Kitchener as an opportunity for overhauling and reorganising the transport system in Russia.

General Hanbury-Williams was a soldier perfectly adapted to represent the country at a Headquarters where the Commander-in-Chief was a Grand Duke, followed by an Emperor. He had enough intelligence to perceive that things were going wrong—he was enough of a soldier to feel that he must call attention to muddles and break-downs—he was enough of a courtier to be able to do so without offence or effect. His deferential criticisms gave the Czar the requisite impression of the blunt and straightforward Englishman doing his duty to his own Army Chiefs, whilst the way it was said caused no irritation, left no uneasiness and produced no results. That is why I was anxious that Sir William Robertson and Lord Reading should be sent on a special mission to Russia in September, 1916. Even at that late hour something might have been achieved in the way of reorganisation which would have sufficiently improved transport to carry hundreds of thousands more tons of food and fuel to towns and trenches in the hardest days of a cruel winter and thus have averted revolution.

The plan adopted at the Conference for re-equipping the Russian Army and replenishing the meagre provisionment of the towns promised immediate improvement. Whether it was or was not adequate and whether it would have been honestly operated, are questions no one can now answer.

If the Duma leaders had been brought into active co-operation, I believe the plan would have worked reasonably well. But it was too late to put it into operation. The Revolution was crouching just round the corner, and, as soon as the delegates left, it leapt up with a furious spring.

What was the state of the Russian Army? At the beginning of 1917, despite the terrible experiences it had suffered, it was still a force of great numerical strength and of fine material. Its weakness was mainly behind the front. At the front its chief deficiency was munitions, but the requisite supplies of food and clothing were also lacking. Sir Henry Wilson noted in his diary that: —

" The Russian original positions were very strong, and in several lines with a good deal of wire. Miles and miles of corduroy roads, several light railways, and a fine bridge, 2,000 yards long, over a river. Altogether I was much more pleased with the front system and organisation than I had thought to be. The men were well fed and clothed*—the little horses in perfect condition. . . .

An army which completely recovered from the disasters of 18 months ago may, and will, do good things. Neither the French nor our Army could have made such a recovery. Then, the Boches are very thin opposite to the Russians, and I can quite imagine a crack in the Boche lines and then masses of Cossacks. The

* In this respect he was misled.

Russians have 52 Cavalry Divisions. My own opinion is that, with luck, the Russians may do great things. . . ."

In his report to the War Cabinet, Wilson said: —

"The men are wonderful. For the most part big, powerful, cheery children and wonderfully brave and patient. On the other hand, they are illiterate and stupid, and quite devoid of enterprise and initiative. They are well clothed (except on the Roumanian Front), well booted,* well fed, and well cared for—the standard being Russian, not English. The Russian private is more punctilious in saluting than the private of any army I have seen in this War. . . .

So far as I could see and hear, I should think the morale of the Russian Army is good, and the officers and men are less depressed by their lack of guns, of ammunition, and of aeroplanes, than any other Army of the Alliance in a similar situation."

But where did Sir Henry Wilson ever see any other army of the Alliance "in a similar situation"? An incident which was not recorded in his report, but which so impressed him that he frequently spoke of it afterwards, occurred at one point of his visit to the front. Through an interpreter he was chatting with some soldiers in a trench, and was surprised to find that the question they chiefly wanted to ask him, with a quite particular insistence, was "whether the British soldiers fighting on the Western Front were called upon to tear down barbed-wire entanglements with their hands!"

Lord Milner could not shut his eyes to the scantiness of the help we were arranging to offer to Russia. He stated in his report: —

"Of course, when all is said and done, the amount of assistance which we are offering to give to Russia, even if it all materialises, falls very far short of her undoubted requirements."

But if the soldiers were short of arms and ammunition, our Mission found that the civil population was becoming no less short of enthusiasm for a prolonged conflict. Lord Milner reported: —

"The Russians are in an unhappy frame of mind just now——thoroughly disgruntled, from domestic causes quite as much as from war-weariness. So far from being the stolid, unmovable, irresistible 'steam-roller' of popular imagination, they are a very sensitive, impressionable, and almost mercurial people. . . . What I do feel is that the general discontent and vague unhappiness might

---

* He was not well informed as to boots and food. On some fronts there was a lamentable deficiency in both these respects.

easily turn into disgust with the War. In short, I think the Russians just now need to be very carefully handled, especially by the English. . . . Such an attitude is all the more called for in view of Russia's internal troubles. These are indeed intimately connected with her ill-success in the War, but I am not sure that Russians themselves are always quite conscious of this. . . . When one comes to analyse these matters, it is soon apparent that the root cause, even of the domestic discontent, is dissatisfaction with the course of the War, and bitter resentment of the mismanagement—for which the Government is held responsible—that has been the cause of so many failures."

The incompetence of the Government was, it is true, a byword.

The depression which Lord Milner felt on coming into contact with the deplorable conditions in Russia attacked his Allied colleagues in similar fashion. General Wilson records in his diary that when he met General Castelnau, the French military delegate, after returning on 14th February from a trip to the front, he found the General,

"very down on his luck. He saw no way by which these Russians could take the offensive this year, and he did not believe that they could do anything before May at the earliest, and not very seriously even then. He was not impressed by their men, nor officers, nor Staff, nor by such of their lines as he had seen; but he said that he had not been up in the front line. He thought the railways were in a hopeless mess, and, in short, he did not think they were in a position to hold the Boche divisions in front of them; so he doubted the success of our offensive."

Two days later Wilson met Milner, and recorded:

"I find Milner in depression, tired and worried and listless. . . . Castelnau had depressed him beyond words."

General Wilson tried to cheer him up, but evidently was not successful, for he notes after a discussion with Milner, Castelnau and others of the Mission who had been comparing notes and reflections during the return journey after the Conference that:—

"Milner considers the defeat of the Boches in the field as impossible, and therefore he is prepared to consider terms of peace."

Lord Milner's dejection over the state of things he found in Russia must have been deep indeed for him to voice so gloomy a sentiment. The outbreak of the Russian Revolution, which followed so swiftly on the heels of the Allied Conference, destroyed the value of all the work it had accomplished. The shadow of this rapidly approaching political collapse overhung all the deliberations of the Conference. The minutes of the proceedings, and still more the memoranda and confidential reports prepared by the British delegates, convey to their reader the impression of a general state of chaos and disorganisation, of open corruption and incompetent leadership, which made most of the work which the Conference attempted to carry out as futile as cultivating a quicksand.

The murder of Rasputin had taken place on 31st December, 1916, a month before the Mission reached Petrograd, and instead of closing accounts between Court and people, it had only stirred up the latent discontents to franker and freer expression. Throughout their stay in Russia, our delegates heard quite open discussion, even in the highest circles of Petrograd society, as to the probability of the Czar and Czarina being assassinated. Indeed, it transpired that in some quarters the highest hope entertained in regard to the Allied Conference was that it might produce some arrangement which would on one pretext or other remove Nicholas and his wife out of Russia, and leave affairs there to a Regent who might be able to pull things together.

Curiously enough, the British delegates could not bring themselves to take this talk quite seriously. Apart from these reports, the British Delegation had been informed by Sir George Buchanan that the Czar was hesitating between the grant of a Liberal Constitution and the dissolution of the Duma, with definite leanings towards the latter course. Rodzianko, the President of the Duma, had also told Lord Milner that the majority of the members of the Duma had definitely decided to defy the Czar's decree to dissolve. That meant the beginning of a conflict between the Emperor and the popular leaders.

They had received a still more significant piece of information from Colonel Knox—the plain-spoken officer who not only saw things as they were, but reported and recorded them without gloss to his superiors. According to Knox, the Czar, anticipating trouble when the Duma was dispersed, ordered two crack regiments (including the Guards) to leave the front and proceed at once to Petrograd to preserve order and overawe treason. All the officers of these regiments signed a round robin begging to be allowed to remain at the front. And yet our Delegation, knowing this, did not anticipate any immediate convulsion.

They were given another warning. The Duma was to meet in a week after the close of the Conference. The Delegation asked permission to remain in Russia to witness the meeting. A Court official intimated to them that if they stayed, the assembling of the Duma would be put off for another fortnight. That portended mischief. The delegates ought to have known that it indicated the Czar's resolve to suppress all efforts at co-operation with the Liberal leaders (the

Socialists had not yet appeared on the scene) and that such a course would end in anarchy. All the same they came away fully convinced there would be no revolution till after the War. Sir Walter Layton was perhaps an exception. When asked on his return, " Are they keen on the War?" he replied, " No, they are much too busy thinking of the coming revolution." His official report, however, dealt only with Munitions—and properly so—and the War Cabinet were therefore not informed of the conclusion to which he personally had come.

The Head of the British Delegation, Lord Milner, was by training and temperament a bureaucrat. He knew nothing of the populace that trod the streets outside the bureau. He did not despise them. He just left them out of his calculations. A study of the ways and thoughts of the crowd constituted no part of the preparation for entry into the civil service or for success afterwards. The more you meddled with that side of Government, the less chance there was for promotion. It was for the politicians to deal with these things, and he was not and never became a politician. Henry Wilson was every inch of him—and he had many more inches than the average—a professional soldier. The soldiers were not supposed to take cognisance of the people, except the specimens who joined the Army. He judged these entirely by the canons of discipline. The supreme test of discipline was saluting the officers. He saw with his own eyes that the Russian soldiers passed that test superbly. Mutiny in the Army was therefore remote, and if the Army could be depended upon, " the frocks " (as he always nicknamed politicians) who babbled in the Duma did not matter. He had strong political prejudices, but they were sectarian in their origin and all irrelevant to the Russian situation. He hated Papists and Irish Patriots and he encountered neither amongst the Russian soldiers or civilians. So he quite independently and from another angle supported Milner in the conclusion that there was no danger of any upheaval in the immediate future. The chief missioners therefore were unanimously of opinion that although revolution was inevitable, it would be postponed till after the War. After comparing notes on their way home, Lord Milner on his own and their behalf reported to the Cabinet: —

" As far as the purely political aspect of the matter is concerned, I have formed the opinion that there is a great deal of exaggeration in the talk about revolution, and especially about the alleged disloyalty of the army. That the army should be very dissatisfied with the way in which the War has been conducted is only natural. But there is a long distance separating dissatisfaction in the army and the nation, and even the loud public expression of it (for astonishing freedom of speech is allowed in Russia), from a genuine revolutionary movement. And, assuming for a moment that a revolution were successful, I should regard with great apprehension its effect on the conduct of the War. For though autocracy is a bad form of government, it will take something like a generation to organise anything in its place."

Having regard to the warnings which were blaring at them in every direction, it is incomprehensible that they should have been so deaf and blind. It is one more proof of the way in which the most intelligent human judgment has always been misled by the tapestries of an established order without paying sufficient regard to the condition of the walls they hide and on which they hang. Everything they saw, most of what they heard, pointed to revolution, and immediate revolution. Even Sir Henry Wilson wrote in his private diary:—

"It seems as certain as anything can be that the Emperor and Empress are riding for a fall. Everyone—officers, merchants, ladies —talk openly of the absolute necessity of doing away with them. . . . They have lost their people, their nobles, and now their army, and I see no hope for them; there will be terrible trouble one day here."

Mr. G. R. Clerk (now Sir George Clerk) the British Ambassador in Paris, then an experienced Foreign Office official who accompanied the Mission to Russia, presented to Lord Milner a report of his impressions from which I give the following extract:—

"When the Mission left England on 21st January, the position in Russia appeared to be dominated by the possible effects of the assassination of Rasputin. When we arrived in Petrograd, we found that, beyond a general feeling of relief that there was one obnoxious and noisome personality the less in the world, nothing had really been changed by the murder, and the only definite result appeared to be an inclination to doubt the value of assassination as tempering autocracy. This situation is typical of the whole position in Russia to-day. Every member of the Mission heard from all sides, Russian and foreign, of the inevitability of something serious happening; the only question was whether the Emperor, the Empress, or M. Protopopoff would be removed, or perhaps all three. Meanwhile, it was generally agreed that there must be no revolution during the War, and short of revolution, or more murders, no one could say how the power for evil of the Empress was to be broken. The open way in which people of all classes, including those nearest the throne and officers holding high military commands, spoke against the Empress and her two blind tools—the Emperor and M. Protopopoff —was, to one who knew anything at all of Russia, extraordinary. *But what to me was almost more remarkable was the manner in which the Mission was kept in a sort of ring fence and prevented* *from hearing any defence or serious explanation of the Emperor's policy.** To some extent this was no doubt due to the reluctance of the reactionaries to give the Mission any excuse for discussing the internal affairs of Russia, but that in turn was, to my mind, largely due to the way in which the liberal and anti-governmental faction endeavoured, and I think with some success, to use the Mission as a demonstration in favour of the principles for which they are fighting. Meanwhile the fact remains, that until the present Minister of the Interior loses the Emperor's favour, he is the most powerful man in Russia, and it is with him, or a successor of like tendencies, that we shall have to reckon until the War ends.

I do not believe that there will be a revolution before the War is over, unless maladministration and happy-go-luckiness succeed in producing a jacquerie, which is most unlikely. I must, however, admit that I am probably in a minority in this opinion, certainly in Russia. (See the annexed record of your Lordship's conversations with M. Chelnokoff and Prince Lvoff at Moscow.) . . ."

The interview to which he alludes ought to have convinced Lord Milner of the danger of an imminent upheaval. Those who still cherish the belief—of these Mr. Churchill is the most eloquent—that the Czarist regime had at this time by heroic efforts overcome most of the difficulties under which Russia laboured and was stricken down in the hour of impending achievement, ought to read this confidential report of a conversation between Lord Milner and two of the most moderate leaders on the Russian Duma. It took place immediately after the arrival of Lord Milner on 11th February : —

" M. Chelnokoff, owing to his position as Mayor of Moscow, and the active and able manner in which he has fulfilled the duties of the post during the War, is one of the best-known figures in Russia to-day; and the work which Prince Lvoff has done, as President of the All Russia Zemstvos Union, has made him universally recognised as, perhaps, the ablest organiser whom Russia possesses.

The conversation was entirely confidential on both sides, and was marked by great openness of speech. The essence of it lay in an effort on the part of the two distinguished Russians to impress upon Lord Milner that the present state of things could not possibly continue. They said that maladministration had reached such a pitch that, although in the country itself there was no real dearth of provisions, and abundance of fuel, yet parts of the country were within measurable distance of starvation. Hitherto the Government had at least provided, though after perpetual delay, the funds which enabled the Zemstvos and Cities Unions to carry on the work which had proved of such inestimable value to the Russian Army

* My italics.

during the War. There were, however, signs that the Minister of the Interior, in his blind anxiety to destroy any and every organisation that could be held to contain the germs of a possible liberal political tendency, would try to withhold the necessary funds. To do so would literally be fatal to the Russian Army, and possibly that fact might yet save the work of the Unions, but they were already meeting with every sort of difficulty and obstruction short of actual refusal to pay the money.

Another instance of the complete absence of efficiency lay in the indiscriminate way in which hundreds of thousands of men had been called up from all sorts of useful work for the Army, and were now quartered for instance, in thousands in Moscow without arms, useless, militarily speaking, for the War; while, at the same time, the shortage of labour in Moscow itself was, coupled with the lack of fuel, etc., leading to a closing of factories, and, even where factories were working, there was no labour to transport the material from and to the railways. *Seventeen million men had been called to the colours, without any sort of discrimination, more than half of them were without arms, and were left hanging about doing nothing.*

A few months ago, one word from the Emperor to his people to show that he appreciated the situation and meant to meet it would have changed all this, and would have united Russia in an enthusiastic effort to carry through the War with every ounce of energy that her people possessed, but to-day the Emperor's position as Father of his people was shaken to an extent that no Russian would have thought possible. It was not so much that he was disliked or unpopular, as that the people of Russia had grown completely indifferent to the person of their Emperor. It was typical of this feeling that now it was quite a common thing for the peasants to leave the churches when the prayers for the Emperor were being uttered.

Unless something was done to remedy the present state of things, Prince Lvoff feared that nothing could avert the revolution that was threatening. Every day the position grew more difficult, and every day the disorganisation that wanted putting in order became more pronounced, and the remedy, therefore, required to be more drastically applied. Prince Lvoff himself most earnestly hoped that it might be possible to effect some change for the better, anyhow sufficient to ensure a relatively decent administration during the War, without a revolution; but with every day his hopes grew less, and though he did not say so, he gave the impression of feeling that the presence of the Allied Mission offered perhaps the last chance of opening the Emperor's eyes before it was too late. The only definite suggestion that Prince Lvoff made as to the action that might be taken to this end by the Mission was that the Allies should only grant their further supplies on condition that they were used, or some of them, by organisations in which the Allies had confidence, such as the Unions presided over by himself and M. Chelnokoff respectively. . . .

Lord Milner said that . . . the Allied Mission was not here to discuss the internal affairs of Russia, but the conduct of the War, and it was only in so far as the conduct of the War was adversely affected by the internal conditions that the Allied representatives could even indirectly approach a political problem. But Lord Milner made it quite clear that his sympathies were entirely with Prince Lvoff and M. Chelnokoff, that he would take the opportunity of letting the Emperor know of the favourable impression of their work which he had derived from his visit to Moscow, and he added he would like to say, though he should not do so, that His Majesty had better make Prince Lvoff Minister of the Interior. Prince Lvoff at once said that he would not be able to take such a post, but he quite understood Lord Milner's point of view, and said that all that he and M. Chelnokoff either expected or desired was that Lord Milner should have a clear understanding of the actual position in Russia, and they were now quite satisfied that this was the case."

The appeal which two of the most influential Duma leaders thus made to Lord Milner was that the Allied Mission should exercise the whole of their influence with the Czar to inaugurate the necessary reforms and to work in completer harmony with the chosen representatives of his people; a similar appeal was made to the French Delegation. There is something poignant in their entreaty to M. Doumergue and his colleagues to do something at once to save their country from imminent disruption. Miliukoff, the eminent Russian jurist, and Maklakoff, the great Duma orator, made a passionate protest against the counsel of patience given them on this occasion: —

"At the very mention of the word 'patience,' Maklakoff burst out: —

'We've had quite enough patience! . . . Our patience is utterly exhausted! Besides, if we don't act soon, the masses won't listen to us any longer.'

Maklakoff went on to remind us of Mirabeau's remark: 'Beware of asking for time! Disaster never gives it!'"*

The delegates, however, seemed to have felt some delicacy as to bringing pressure to bear upon the Czar in reference to the internal administration of the country of which he was the autocratic ruler. Sir George Buchanan had talked to him with great candour. His

* "An Ambassador's Memoirs," M. Paléologue, p. 188.

straightforwardness was rewarded with a reply the arrogance of which will always be quoted as one of the best examples of that haughtiness of spirit which prefaces a bad fall.* But there is nothing in the reports which indicate that any of the Allied delegates challenged a similar snub. The French civilian delegates appeared to be more preoccupied with the extension of the French frontiers after victory than with securing conditions which alone made victory possible.

Paléologue gives in his entrancing Diary an astonishing account of his first interview with Doumergue. The latter first enquired about the internal condition of Russia and on being assured that " Russia was walking straight into the abyss and that we must make haste," he promptly took the Ambassador's advice by asking him to take steps without delay to obtain from the Emperor a written record of his promise to help France to secure in the Peace Treaty the left bank of the Rhine. The French Premier had given definite instructions to his Delegation on this subject, but apparently on no other. The Czar was giving an official reception to all the Inter-Allied delegates. An interview was arranged to take place at that reception between him and the heads of the French Delegation. When the opportunity came in the course of the evening, M. Doumergue seized it with true French élan. A jejune sentence from him about the desirability of simultaneous offensives began the conversation. This was assented to by the Czar. Then the French delegate plunged into real business by " broaching the topic of the left bank of the Rhine." Alsace-Lorraine was to be restored to France and it must be the ancient Lorraine of the ninth century. The rest of the German territories on the left bank of the Rhine were to be severed from Germany and suitable arrangements made for their administration. M. Doumergue examined each of these questions " in the greatest detail " and obtained the Emperor's unqualified assent. There was obviously no time to discuss Russia's internal difficulties, the lack of food and fuel that was starving the crowded and crowding populations of the great towns into a state of universal sedition, nor the absence of effective equipment at the front to enable the Army to take its part in the all-round offensive. The Czar feared, so the French Ambassador tells us, " that the delegates would give him unwanted advice on internal politics." He was now reassured on the point. You must not presume too much on an Emperor's courtesy in granting at a ceremonial reception such a prolonged interview; and to requite such a civility by introducing unpleasant topics, and especially after he had conceded the main purpose and petition of the delegates, would have been untactful and discourteous in the extreme.

* Sir G. Buchanan: " Your Majesty, if I may be permitted to say so, has but one safe course open to you, namely to break down the barrier that separates you from your people and to regain their confidence." The Emperor: " Do you mean that I am to regain the confidence of my people or that they are to regain *my* confidence?" " My Mission to Russia," Sir G. Buchanan, Vol. II, p. 46.)

It is recorded that the Emperor showed his relief at French forbear-
ance by lighting a cigarette and passing on to other groups. He was
not sure that conversation with the British and Italian delegates
would turn out to be quite as agreeable. He therefore decided to
take no risks. The report states that " all had a kind word from him,
but nothing more; he did not linger to talk to anyone."

And at this time " Russia was walking straight into the abyss " and
a few weeks later fell into it, dragging with her the amiable and
assenting Czar and his pledge to France.

At that time it was taken for granted that a revolution would be
confined to the deposition of Czar Nicholas and the substitution of
his son. Pledges given by the former would bind his successor. Hence
the anxiety of the French Ministry to extract this understanding
before the present Czar disappeared through the oubliette. The
Regent and his advisers might not be so obliging.

So as to leave no doubt on the supreme question of France's dominance over the left bank of the Rhine, M. Briand issued definite
instructions to the Ambassador to reduce the French demands to
writing. And here is his record of the action Paléologue took : —

> " Wednesday,
> 14th February, 1917.

Acting on instructions received from Briand, I have just sent the
following letter to Pokrovski : —

> I have the honour to inform the Imperial Government that
> the Government of the Republic is proposing to incorporate the
> following territorial claims and guarantees in the terms of peace
> to be imposed on Germany.
>
> (1) Alsace-Lorraine shall be returned to France; (2) its
> frontiers shall extend at the least to the limits of the former Duchy
> of Lorraine; they will be drawn in such a way as to provide for
> strategic necessities and include the whole of the coal basin in
> the valley of the Sarre in French territory; (3) the other territories
> on the left bank of the Rhine, which are now incorporated in the
> German Empire, shall be completely severed from Germany and
> liberated from any political and economic dependence upon her;
> (4) the territories on the left bank of the Rhine which are not
> incorporated in French territory shall form an autonomous and
> neutralised State; they will be occupied by French troops until
> the enemy States shall have completely carried out all the terms
> and guarantees stipulated for in the peace treaty.
>
> The Government of the Republic will, therefore, be glad to
> be able to count on the support of the Imperial Government in
> realising its projects. . . ."*

* " An Ambassador's Memoirs," M. Paléologue, p. 192.

As a comment on the fraternity and good faith that characterised relations between the Allies, it is worth while mentioning the fact that the Government of "perfidious Albion" was kept completely in the dark about these secret discussions and pledges concerning the terms of the Peace Treaty. The promise was extracted from the Czar in the presence, but not in the hearing, of the British and Italian representatives at Petrograd, and not a hint was given them of the clandestine and underhanded transaction. When the Revolutionaries later on revealed the existence of this secret Treaty between two Allies, the French Government explained privately to our Ambassador that Doumergue had exceeded his instructions on this occasion.

The preoccupation of the French Delegation with a topic not relevant to the effective prosecution of the War diverted them from the essential common effort to persuade the Emperor and his Government to take the necessary steps to set their chaotic house in order. Even the bold Buchanan had to be careful not to press his diplomatic candour too far. After the famous interview in which he had spoken plainly to the Emperor as to the danger that he might lose the confidence of his people, there came a dinner to the Inter-Allied Delegates, at which Sir George, as the *doyen*, sat next to the Emperor. His account of it, in a letter I have seen, is instructive. He was apprehensive as to the treatment which the Czar would accord him after the last audience, but he " was glad to find no trace of resentment at what he had said." He then proceeds " As I was anxious to regain my old footing with His Majesty, I was careful to keep off dangerous topics." Such is the paralysing fear created by awe of kingship in the boldest and most accustomed minds. If the Ambassador of another and a vaster Empire could not speak freely, how could one expect the poor Ministers of his will " who to-day are and to-morrow are cast into the oven " to face his wrath? The clouds and darkness that surround a throne may inspire awe, but they also obscure perils.

The efforts made by the Mission to bring pressure to bear on the Czar to set things right at the top and to co-operate with patriotic and loyal but independent Russians in doing so, were sporadic, timid and consequently unimpressive. That is why they failed. Had Milner, Doumergue and Scialoja made united and insistent representations, and declared that help would be withheld unless the Czar and his Ministers were prepared to work loyally with the Duma, the situation might have been saved.

A week after they returned to London, serious trouble broke out in Russia. There were riots in the streets and mutinies in the ships. Although Sir George Buchanan, with his clear and discerning eyes, had foreseen trouble, when it actually arrived he did not recognise it for the events he had so steadily foretold. From day to day disturbances, strikes and bread riots were reported. From day to day they appeared to get worse. The streets were thronged with workmen who struck work because they were starving. Trains were wrecked, there were conflicts with the police, and the Cossacks were called out to preserve order. Then came shots and casualties, and still there came the reassuring sentence: "If order is more or less kept to-night and to-morrow without serious loss of life, the Counsellor of the Embassy is inclined to think trouble will blow over, as it has done before." There is certainly a proviso about "the food problem being solved" and the political problem—less important—not to be lost sight of.

On the very day of the revolution, when the Military Attaché wired that all the Guards at Petrograd had mutinied, killed their officers, broken into the artillery departments and appropriated the guns: when mutineers were in complete control of the situation, and the soldiers without leaders or officers, we had a sentence from the Ambassador: "Excitement will probably quieten down for the present if there is no active provocation to-day." Why not? It had all happened before—perhaps not in a form quite as aggravated, but still bad enough—and relapsed into sullen acquiescence.

But there was a point when it became quite clear that this outbreak was of a different character and had attained graver dimensions than anything that had occurred in the past. The Petrograd garrison deserted the Czar. All now depended upon the Army at the Front. Were they loyal to Nicholas II? If they were, the situation could be re-established. For days we were in a state of doubt. As I shall point out later on, the attachment of even the superior officers to the present occupants of the Throne had been completely alienated. No one at Petrograd knew what had happened to the Czar. Two days after the Revolution had broken out, the Minister for Foreign Affairs "did not believe it would be difficult to put down the rising, as the insurgents would before long get tired out and run short of provisions." And even M. Gutchkoff, of the Executive Committee, told Sir George Buchanan that "he did not regard the situation as desperate, if only the Emperor would follow the advice tendered to him and reconstruct the Government."

But on 15th March, Sir George Buchanan, wiring to Mr. Balfour, says that "nothing is known as to where the Emperor actually is at present or as to when he is likely to arrive at Tsarskoe Selo." He points out that "the delay may have most serious consequences, as the extreme Socialist Party is gaining ground everywhere." They were agitating for a Republic and there was a strong Peace Party in their ranks. A Provisional Government was then set up with only one Social-Democrat, Kerensky, in it, and they decided to demand the abdication of the Emperor.

The most serious factor of all was the conflict between the Duma and the Throne. Almost from the outset the soldiers and sailors took the side of the popular Assembly. In a few days the Czar had abdicated. There was some idea of appointing the Czarevitch as his successor, with the Grand Duke Michael as Regent, but the fond and anxious parents declined to put their son in that jeopardy. The Czar nominated his brother the Grand Duke Michael, but the nation declined to ratify that appointment. When the Duma set up a Provisional Government, the reign of the Romanoffs was at an end.

And then came the deluge. A deluge with an unseaworthy Ark. The timbers were rotten and most of the crew not much better. The Captain was suited for a pleasure yacht in still waters, and his sailing master had been chosen by his wife, reclining in the cabin below. The rudder was seized by a disorderly rabble of counsellors, drawn at random from Duma, soldiers, sailors and workers' Committees, political organisations of every colour and creed, who spent most of their time and energies in quarrelling as to the direction in which the ship ought to be sailed, until at last it was captured and sunk by a piratical crew who knew their destination.

2H*

CHAPTER LIII

THE RUSSIAN REVOLUTION

I FEEL it would be impossible to explain to those who have forgotten the pre-revolutionary conditions, the attitude adopted by the British and French governments towards the revolutionary governments that were set up immediately after the fall of the Czar, unless I state here some of the causes which led to the crash. Moreover, the Russian Revolution is in itself such a tremendous fact in world history that a fuller knowledge of its origin must always be of interest to every student of great human movements. As it fell to my lot to deal with it from this end, some account of its origin is not out of place in these Memoirs.

I had striven in 1915 and 1916 to induce the Allies to take steps to remove defects and deficiencies which ultimately precipitated the Revolution. The Petrograd Conference was the last—it would be more accurate to say the first—genuine organised effort made by the Allies to avert or postpone this cataclysm by removing the evils that caused its precipitation during and into the War.

The effort came much too late to save the Czar. It came too late to save Russia as an effective Ally. A similar conference after the 1915 disaster might have produced decisive results. A conference of the same character in 1916 would have effected certain imperative changes in organisation which would have enabled Russia to lumber through 1917 and, if necessary, 1918 as a still serious menace to the armies of the Central Powers, sufficiently serious to make it imprudent on their part to withdraw their good troops from the Eastern Front to France. But the recommendations of the conference were not given enough time to bring an additional waggon load of bread to the hungry queues of Petrograd.

Mr. Churchill says: " It is the shallow fashion of these times to dismiss the Czarist regime as a purblind, corrupt, incompetent tyranny." Talking of Czarist Russia, he said: " With victory in her grasp, she fell upon the earth, devoured alive, like Herod of old, by worms." The worms that ate into the vitals of the old regime and devoured its strength, were bred out of its own corruption. It fell because every fibre of its power, influence and authority had rotted through and through. It therefore tumbled to pieces at the first shock of insurrection. There was not enough strength left in its arm even to lift the sceptre when its decrees were challenged by a hungry Petrograd mob.

Mr. Churchill in describing the catastrophe says: "The ship sank in sight of port." A ludicrous picture this, made attractive only because of the glittering rhetoric in which it is framed by a great colour artist.

He continues: "She had weathered the storm." Yes, a battered hulk, with her engines neglected and out of repair, tossed about helplessly in the breakers with a feeble and foolish captain, a scratch lot of officers, and a crew some on the brink of mutiny and the rest steeped in the spirit of discontent, rapidly fermenting into mutiny. General Castelnau thought them incapable of another offensive in the state he found them at the time of the Petrograd Conference and he ruled out their active help during the 1917 campaign.

Mr. Churchill's morbid detestation of the Revolution that in 1919 baffled his most ingenious military dispositions in Russia has rendered him incapable of weighing fairly the causes that led to the downfall of autocracy. The Revolution was the inevitable consequence of the failure of Czardom and not its cause. Bolshevism had practically nothing to do with the events of March, which ended in the abdication of the Czar. When the Revolution started, Lenin was a refugee in Switzerland, Trotsky was earning a precarious living as a writer on the staff of an unprofitable Communist journal in New York. The conspirators who overthrew Czardom were the Czarina and Rasputin, with the help of inept Ministers they promoted and favoured.

The unconscious head of that conspiracy was the Czar himself. For all this gigantic Continent, inhabited by scores of millions of emotional but rather primitive humanity, confronted with the greatest crisis in the history of their country, there was no leader. There was only a crown without a head—a ruler who, according to Mr. Churchill, was "only a true simple man of average ability and of merciful disposition," but who, he admits, had not the qualities fitting him for his job. He would never have been chosen by any responsible board of directors to manage any business of any magnitude, and certainly not a business confronted with a serious emergency. It was hard on him that he should have been called upon to be the supreme ruler of a gigantic country in the most terrible days that ever befell it. Moreover, Mr. Churchill's phrase is not an exhaustive, and, in one respect, not an accurate, description of the Czar's qualities in action. "Merciful disposition" is not strictly applicable at all times to the character of his dealings with some of the worthiest of his subjects. There are incidents in his reign for which he was directly and personally responsible, which will always cast a doubt upon his possession of the quality of mercy. The blood-stained squares of Petrograd, the howling wastes of Siberia, bore witness to other and more merciless attributes. The horror of his end tempers criticism. But if it is to remain silent it must not be provoked by truculent challenge.*

Had there been no Revolution or had it been postponed, Russia could only have just pulled through by the active intervention of her Allies in formulating and carrying through a complete programme of reconstruction. Nothing else could have saved the Empire from the chaos and muddle in which it had been landed by its ruler and his minions. The Allies could not have accomplished this object had the most powerful Ministers chosen by the Czar been retained in their positions. The only hope of success was in the unequivocal surrender of his autocratic authority to the Duma, and the appointment of Ministers who had the confidence of that body and were in essence its nominees. Czarism had completely broken down in peace and war as an instrument of government for so great a country. The manhood of the nation was uneducated, illiterate and untrained for anything except the most primitive tasks by the most primitive methods. Their great natural gifts had not been developed. Every effort in that direction was regarded as a menace to autocracy. The rich natural resources of this immense country in water power, in timber and in cultivable land had only received elementary development. Its mineral wealth and its manufactures depended for their exploitation mainly on the skill of foreigners. The means of communication and transport were utterly inadequate for the needs of so vast a land, so numerous a population and so opulent a soil. How utterly the Czarist autocracy had failed in peace to make the best use of the splendid men and material at its disposal was quickly revealed by the ruthless hand of war.

What was the result? The facts are well known; they have been told by reputable men of every shade of opinion, who had a horror of Bolshevism, its principles and its methods. A virtuous and well-meaning Sovereign became directly responsible for a regime drenched in corruption, indolence, debauchery, favouritism, jealousy, sycophancy, idolatry, incompetence and treachery—an accumulation of all those vices that make for utter misgovernment and inevitably

---

* Princess Radziwill in her book, " Nicholas II, last of the Czars," says (p. 197):—
    " I will here say something that may surprise my readers. I feel convinced the hatred for Rasputin which was openly expressed in the best society of Petersburg and Moscow, was but a blind to hide a campaign for the overthrow of the Emperor himself! A plausible pretext was essential, but the more serious aim was cherished by a considerable number of those sick of the graft, corruption and complete disorder of the administration, and disgusted with the shallow, false and unreliable character of Nicholas II, and the cold-blooded cruelty with which he was trying to suppress every aspiration and movement towards reform. The torrents of blood shed since he ascended the Throne had alienated all respect and affection, and his subjects had come to look upon him as an impediment to the development and the prosperity of Russia."

end in anarchy. Too narrow a definition of virtue has many a time been responsible for a multitude of errors and mischiefs. The tragedies of Charles I of England and Louis XVI of France, now reinforced by the downfall of Nicholas II of Russia, afford terrible illustrations of that truth.

The men who gave the Russian Revolution its first impulse were not the Bolsheviks, but disgusted aristocrats and bourgeois—princes, merchants and lawyers. Then followed the riots of the half-starved workers and the mutiny of the soldiers and the sailors. But they had endured their miseries for year without a murmur. Rodzianko, the President of the Duma and the head and front of the constitutional movement, was the Emperor's Chamberlain. He was an aristocrat, a considerable landowner, and an officer of the Household Cavalry. Prince Lvoff belonged to the same class. Miliukoff was a Conservative lawyer and Gutchkoff was a manufacturer. They all belonged to the propertied classes. They were devoutly attached to the Monarchy, but they belonged to that Russian intelligentsia which, ever since the days of Alexander I. had believed in a constitutional rather than an autocratic sovereignty. They were more conservative in their fundamental attitude towards social and economic questions than the leaders of Disraelian Toryism who were my colleagues in the War Cabinet. Had the Czar been endowed with the wisdom to make the moderate concession they asked for, he might still have been the proud sovereign of a victorious, powerful and prosperous empire. It was his stubborn clutching at an unchecked authority that he was less qualified to wield than almost any of his predecessors, which antagonised solid and reliable elements in his Empire and drove them to the despair of Revolution.

Kerensky, the Socialist who followed, represented a new and more advanced phase of opinion than the Duma had done. He was a lawyer of bureaucratic lineage, who held moderate Socialist opinions. It was the Bolsheviks who later on converted an accomplished revolution into a subversive reality. Whether it will develop into a constructive triumph, history, which is in the making, alone will tell. But the first impetus which started the wild whirl of Russian autocracy down the slopes of revolution came from misgovernment so intolerable that loyal Imperialists (outside the governing clique) could no longer endure its continuance. It is a fatal hour for monarchy when men and women who are both patriotic and loyal are compelled to choose between Throne and Country. It is that choice which destroyed Czardom. Rasputin and Protopopoff were the most effective propagandists for revolution, and not Lenin. Lenin was the exploiter: Rasputin was the originator. He was a man of the people, and even his lurid obscenities served them well, for they rotted the last strand of the bonds that held down the Russian toilers from whom he had sprung. They rose from bondage to power, and as is the wont of reactionaries, transferred their concentrated miseries to their oppressors.

I asked a distinguished Russian refugee whom I recently met what or who in his opinion was most responsible for the fall of Czarism. His reply was: Rasputin. Why was that so? He led no armies, he intervened in no military movements. He did not meddle with transport or the manufacture of munitions, nor did he directly interfere with those who directed these operations of war. How came he, then, to be the malignant influence that was the chief agent in precipitating chaos? It is a unique story in the annals of squalid tragedy. Probably the whole truth has not yet been revealed.

Rasputin was a religious satyr of hypnotic powers. He established indirect dominion over a highly domesticated autocrat through the control he acquired over a perfectly virtuous consort by means which are entirely creditable to her as an affectionate mother. Rasputin repeatedly saved her son, the heir to the throne, from death by his remarkable mesmeric gifts. Thenceforward his sway over the Court was unchallengeable. His orgies of unbridled lust were disbelieved or ignored by his Imperial patrons. This evil monster could do no evil in their sight. The relations which won the sinister libertine power over this simple and pure-minded couple he preserved to the end of the great tragedy. A whisper from his libidinous lips into the ear of the infatuated Czarina, passed on to her fond but feeble husband, was enough to undermine confidence in the most loyal and serviceable officials, civil or military. Anyone who protested against the regime of ineptitude and turpitude that was driving Russia into the abyss was liable to be suspected and ultimately removed on a word from Rasputin. His selections for removal or promotion were impelled not by questions of disservice or usefulness to the Empire, but of hostility or servility displayed towards himself. " Whom he would, he set up, and whom he would, he put down." Honest and capable but intractable Ministers he put down, and worthless Ministers were substituted. He must have been a man of exceptional qualities, for in spite of his loathsome debauchery he held converse on equal terms with statesmen of unchallengeable capacity and character. He was on friendly terms even with a man of the high repute of Count Witte. And he exerted undoubted influence over many virtuous priests, some of high, some of lowly rank, who believed in the saintliness of his life and leadership. He was possessed of an uncanny discernment of men, women and events. When war was declared, he had retired to his village in a remote Siberian province. As soon as he heard that hostilities were imminent, he sent a message to the Czar, warning him not to permit Sazonov and the Grand Duke Nicholas to persuade him to embark on a conflict with Germany, as it would inevitably end in the downfall of the Empire. He imbued the Czarina with the idea that the safety of her children lay not in a doubtful and precarious victory at the end of a prolonged war; but in peace at the earliest opportunity. Her apprehension bred hesitancies which must have been communicated to her all-powerful husband. She therefore viewed with distrust all those who were intent on prosecuting the War to the unknown end. This mental or rather nervous attitude originated and gave colour to the rumour universally believed in Russia, that she was at heart a pro-German. There was no foundation for that suspicion. Some time after her deposition she was reported to have said to one of the friendliest of her guards: " They said I was pro-German; I hate the Germans. I am English. I speak English and I love England."

But the pacifism of Rasputin was not what constituted the principal factor in the downfall of the Empire. There was another and a still more potent reason. Rasputin destroyed that idolatrous reverence which surrounded the person as well as the throne of the Czar, and which was essential to sustain the spirit of endurance and sacrifice which alone could carry the nation through a succession of calamitous defeats accompanied by unparalleled loss of young lives. As the War went wrong, the Czar's power came to depend more upon fear than upon worship. As long as that fear remained, his authority was paramount. Then came the death of Rasputin to shatter the delusion of his irresistible power. The assassination of his intimate friend by men who boasted openly of their crime without anyone daring to punish them extinguished the lightnings of authority. Dread of the thunders of Imperial Jove quickly disappeared once their futility was exposed. In his lifetime Rasputin undermined all respect for the Czar. In death he swept away the last remnant of fear of that potentate. The bullet that killed him penetrated the heart of Czarism. He predicted not only his own violent death, but also that his murder would bring down the Empire in less than six months. And so it did.

The Czar was insane with anger at the murder, and stimulated by his wife he sank into a mood of infatuated hostility against all those who did not attempt to conceal their delight at the event. It widened the already yawning crevasse between him and the intelligentsia which was represented by the Duma. The Duma had at its first meetings exhibited a flaming enmity towards Rasputin. Through Rodzianko it had made representations to the Czar about the danger of harbouring him any longer at the Palace. The Duma leaders rejoiced ostentatiously in his violent removal. The Czar's fury was therefore concentrated on them, and he turned a sullen face and a deaf ear to all their wise counsel. On the other hand, the crazy Protopopoff, who affected to be in occult converse with the spirit of the departed prophet, was listened to with a new respect and an increased deference. The influence of Rasputin was more potent and pernicious than ever after his death. In life he was a shrewd villain, but when his ideas had to pass through an imbecile they partook of the addled quality of the medium's brain.

What about the Army?

The night that the news of the murder of the Court favourite reached the Army, every officer toasted the assassins amidst scenes of savage joy. The Czar of all the Russias was flouted by the leaders of his people and by the officers of his Army. With the fall of Rasputin fell the autocracy of the Romanoffs, and it fell without a friend to regret the dismissal of its last representative.

The old Russia was Czarism. In no land was the mystic power and authority of kingship so potent and so pervasive. Nowhere has kingly power much reference to the particular occupant of the throne for the time being. A great monarch at distant intervals preserves and infuses new vitality into, and strengthens and prolongs the life of this indefinable influence, but on his death it passes on to and through worthless successors. How few really great Sovereigns has Europe seen during the last two centuries, and how many commonplace and inept specimens has it endured during the same period! In this country Queen Victoria was a remarkable personality, but she was no more firmly established on the throne than was her dissolute and worthless uncle, George the Fourth. In a Constitutional Monarchy the weaknesses of the Sovereign can be checked or controlled by Parliament. That takes away from his personal power but adds to his personal security. With an autocracy, however, deposition, which in Russian meant assassination, was the only corrective. As long as Nicholas II remained Czar of all the Russias, then all the Russians obeyed his decrees, whether they approved of them or not. Approval was immaterial to the validity of the *ukase*. In the Czar was vested all the powers of King, Cabinet and Legislature. That is why the only effective opposition in Russia took the form of a conspiracy against the occupant of the Throne. Hence the military plot to remove Czar Nicholas and substitute another Emperor. The conspirators meant to follow precedent by changing Czars; they blundered into a change of systems.

The facts which have been revealed since the Revolution clear up a situation which at that time was obscure. The rumours which filled the air, and which were heard by the well-chaperoned members of the Inter-Allied Delegation, were rooted in a subsoil of undoubted conspiracy. The Army Chiefs had already practically decided to depose the Czar. All the generals are supposed to have been in it. The Chief of the Staff, General Alexeieff, was certainly in the plot; Russky, Ivanoff and Brussiloff were also sympathetic. When the question of getting rid of the Czar was put to the latter, he is reported to have said: " If I have to choose between the Czar and my country, I shall decide for the latter." The temper of the officers of the Army was made clear in those exuberant demonstrations when

the news came of the murder of Rasputin. As a further proof of the
complicity of the Army Chiefs, there is the fact that the regiments
left at Petrograd were composed of young recruits only just called up
from works, seething with discontent, led by officers inadequate in
numbers, broken down through wounds and ill-health, many of them
only just discharged from hospitals. One of the most level-headed of
the Russian refugees whom I met was convinced that this was
deliberately arranged by highly placed Generals who were preparing
the *coup d'état*, in order to ensure that it should not be suppressed
before it became effective. They had resolved to get rid of
Nicholas II. It is significant that when the news of the outbreak at
Petrograd reached General Headquarters, and the Czar immediately
returned to his capital to take command, he was detained at Pskow
by General Russky. The crisis exploded prematurely, owing to an
unexpected outbreak amongst the miserable standing army of the
bread queues who could bear their wretchedness no longer, and it
detonated before the military fuse was quite ready to be fired. The
explosion blew up Czardom, but it also incidentally shattered the
well-organised plot of the Generals. The fire which broke out too
soon got beyond the control of those who had laid the train. Instead
of a well-ordered *coup d'état* of Generals, directed from Headquarters
and following well-established tradition, there was substituted an
insurrection of the proletariat with no precedent to guide its course
except the French Revolution.

The evidence on which I base the foregoing conclusions as to the
causes of the revolution, is drawn almost exclusively from official
reports which I have in my possession.

It was not a sudden and unexpected eruption of a mountain that
had given no warning or shown no symptoms of disturbance. Every
visitor to Russia from 1915 onwards heard the rumbling and felt the
ground trembling under his feet. Here are extracts from a letter
which I received in November, 1915, from Sir Ian Malcolm, who was
then Conservative M.P. for Croydon. He was touring Russia from
North to South in connection with the Red Cross: —

"... I don't think the seriousness of the social situation here
can be exaggerated: it is perfectly frightful. Where shall I begin?
Food and fuel are already becoming extinct commodities: of the
latter, which consists entirely of wood, our Embassy (among others)
and many manufacturing houses have not nearly enough to last
them through the winter and don't know where to turn for more.
Food is exorbitantly high and the richest are beginning to feel
it. . . .

Besides the existing corruption in high places and apparent
indifference among the middle classes, there lies the further complicating problem: about 400,000 refugees from Poland and the

Baltic provinces, and an immense aggregation of soldiers, centred in the capital—over a million new inhabitants in the last 12 months, less food than in normal times and not one single new house built since the War began! The condition of the refugees is quite indescribably bad. I have been to see them in their misery: there they lie, serried ranks of emaciated huddled humanity, brutalised by their abject surroundings, corroded by disease, men, women and children of different races and languages crowded and congested like litters of pigs in an asphyxiating sty; no order is kept by the police or anybody else, daughters outraged under their mothers' eyes night after night, children naked and hungry: and there are as many sleeping in the streets as there are in these barracks. . . .

The Opera and the Ballet go on every night: yesterday there was an order that all restaurants, etc., were to be closed at 11—and the cries of the well-to-do were heart-rending! It was high time. Everything and everybody presages a terrible future for the now governing classes when the War is over, *but not before*—on that they are equally unanimous. *The Emperor and family and Court have not a single friend. It is said they have made every possible mistake.* . . . And, when the Revolution—that is what it is openly called—comes, I am told that at least half the Army is so enraged at the massacre of their fellows, consequent on the lack of munitions, that they will side with the rebellion. Imagine one whole Division, one of whose chief officers I saw, going into action with three rifles for every ten men and the remaining seven instructed to clap their hands to *sound* as though they were shooting from the trenches! ! ! Of course this is much better now and there are plenty of munitions at last. . . . They simply don't know, and, not knowing, are inclined to think we are doing nothing and leaving it all to them. You may say that is childish, but you will remember that the Russians are essentially children. . . ."

A careful and considered report on the situation came from the pen of Professor Bernard Pares, a distinguished scholar who knew Russia and Russian thoroughly. He visited Petrograd in 1915 as official Correspondent with the Russian Army, and on his return presented to the Government a very remarkable account of the state of things in Russia. It has not yet been published and is an impartial and at the same time a vivid and accurate picture, and so prophetic a forecast of the wrath to come that it is worth quoting at some length as an explanation of the causes which generated the trouble.

". . . I have to submit my strong opinion that the unfortunate failure of Messrs. Vickers, Maxim and Co. to supply Russia with munitions, which were to have reached that country five months ago, is gravely jeopardising the relations of the two countries and in particular their co-operation in the work of the present War.

The Russians have so far put in line 7,000,000 men. Their losses when I left Petrograd (11th July) had reached the enormous figure of 3,800,000. . . . The Russian authorities and the public opinion of the country has always looked to the Western Allies, and particularly to England for the supply to the common cause of munitions in general, and more particularly of those which Russia is not itself able to manufacture.

I am definitely told that so far no supplies of munitions whatever have reached Russia from England. . . . We (Colonel Knox and myself) represented that the arrangement made by the Russian Government with Messrs. Vickers, Maxim & Co. was not made through the British Government. But we could in no way remove the grave impression caused by the failure of the British firm to supply the munitions which it had promised under different dates from December last, a failure which all Russians who are aware of it associate intimately with the crushing losses in recent fighting and the obvious necessity of almost indefinite retreat until this crying deficiency has been made good. . . .

The present military crisis in Russia has led, among other things, to the sending under fire even of large units entirely unequipped with rifles and to restrictions in certain cases of the amount of ammunition discharged to two shells per day, or in the case of infantry ten rounds per man. *This has inevitably raised the widest feeling of vexation among the troops and—through the return of vast numbers of wounded—all over the country.* This strong and general feeling (especially in view of the defaults of Messrs. Vickers, Maxim & Co.) cannot fail to be gravely prejudicial to the confidence so far placed by Russia in her Western Allies. *It has also led to threatening signs of resentment against the Russian authorities, which in my judgment must lead if continued to grave internal complications. Momentous developments in the internal affairs of Russia seem in any case inevitable."*

After conference with leading members of a Committee selected by the Sovereign from members of the two Legislative Houses and of the Moscow Munitions Committee, Professor Pares was requested to submit for the consideration of the authorities in Great Britain certain suggestions. Here is one of them. It has a special significance because it reappeared in the demand made upon the Allied Delegation in February, 1917, by both the Army and the Duma leaders. It was in essence a demand that the vaunted "common front" should be made a reality:—

"It was considered highly desirable that if possible some assurance should be given that this country is making and will continue to make similar efforts for the supply of the Russian Army with munitions as it is making for the supply of its own."

Here is Professor Pares' note on the request: —

"In view of information given me at the British War Office, such a statement is no more than an assertion of existing fact; but it would carry to Russians great comfort in the difficult months which we have to expect."

Existing fact? At that date, the summer of the great retreat (1915), we had supplied the Russians with hardly any munitions. The report continues: —

". . . It is the Russian opinion that the most valuable of contributions is men and that their enormous sacrifices were substantially instrumental in saving Paris, and in giving the British Army time to organise and to provide itself with the necessary equipment. In continuing these sacrifices they will expect such assistance from their Allies as will make the Russian numbers effective and reduce their losses. Under the existing conditions each engagement allows the enemy an opportunity of destroying our superiority in numbers without the corresponding loss to himself. . . ."

Here is an extract from a letter written about this date to Professor Pares by Mr. Nicholas Homyakov, formerly President of the Russian Duma.

"In Russia, I think that we have now set to work in the right way, but I doubt whether Russia alone could satisfy the deficiencies of the Army in guns, shells, and in the equipment of new workshops with machinery and implements. In this matter we feel we have a right to count on the help of our Allies. They must regard the equipment of the Russian Army as an affair of their own, as a task on the successful accomplishment of which will depend the issue of this great War—which we must in the interests of the whole world bring to the wished for end as soon and as completely as possible.

Exactly what it is necessary to make, I will not take it on myself to enumerate. This is better known to those who are responsible for the equipment of our Army. *But for me one thing is quite clear. The Armies of the Allies must be one; their needs must be the common care of all the Allies; and only with this unity will victory be on our side. You are going to England; try to enable your Government and your public to realise the necessity of full*

*unity of action in all Departments of the present work of war. Let
everyone remember that in this War there are no reverses of the
Russians, of the English, or of the French alone, and that success or
failure is one and the same thing for all of us. . . ."*

I have no recollection that Sir Edward Grey, to whom these
communications were addressed, took any steps to bring this important message to the notice of the British Cabinet. He took refuge
in that aloofness that detached him from all concern for the efficient
conduct of a war he had advised the Government to declare.

Professor Pares writes later on, in September, 1916, to give
amongst other things an account of the suspicions attaching to the
Jews in Russia. He then proceeds: —

"The best elements of the Russian public are either in
the Army, or at present, in the country. These have a
strong antipathy to the political atmosphere of Petrograd, which
is at present a nest of bureaucratic intrigues and financial
corruption. . . .

The reactionary Ministry is universally condemned. This is not
on the ground of political programmes. It is on the contrary the
Court and Ministry that are themselves regarded as having forced
internal politics into the midst of the national war task. This feeling has culminated with the dismissal of M. Sazonov. Till then it
was thought that at least foreign affairs, of which the substance is
the close co-operation of the Allies in the War, would have been
reserved from the influence of what is regarded as simply internal
political intrigue. . . .

The reconstruction of the Ministry is not merely a refusal to the
national request of last winter for a Ministry possessing the public
confidence. The public would for the present at least be content
with able Ministers who knew their work. The choices made have
been ruled by two principles: the dismissal of all Ministers who
signed last October a request for a Ministry of public confidence;
selection only from the very limited number of extreme Russian
Conservatives. These last formerly worked with the German elements in the Court for reaction against the Duma. The Emperor
wishes to fight the Germans but to retain the unnational system of
representation, and the two objects cannot possibly be harmonised;
hence the dangerous significance of an attempt to bring foreign
policy into line with home policy. Able men cannot be found in
this small group and men of principle are rare. . . ."

Apologists for the ancient regime urge that the efforts that were
put forth by the Russian Government to remedy the defects which
led to the calamities of 1915 had completely changed the situation, so

that the real justification for the Revolution had long ago disappeared. The answer to these contentions is to be found in some of the reports I have already quoted as to the appalling conditions both at the front and in the Russian towns during the winter of 1916-17. The Czar in the autumn of 1915, with his confidence unnerved by calamity, was in a mood to make terms with the popular leaders in Petrograd, Moscow and the provinces. The Duma was called into consultation and as an essential condition of their co-operation, reactionary Ministers like Sukhomlinoff, the Secretary for War, were reluctantly, and after considerable pressure from their Liberal colleagues, dismissed and men of more liberal views were substituted. The Zemstvos, representing all classes of the community, including workmen, were also mobilised for assistance, and voluntary committees were set up in all parts of the Empire to raise and provide essentials for the Army. A great deal of useful work was done in the way of organising an increased supply of munitions, and it looked as if the Czar and his people would henceforth work together to a victorious end. Then reactionary influences once more asserted themselves. The men who had failed so conspicuously to provide equipment for the Army regarded the effort made by unofficial bodies to supply deficiencies for which they were responsible as a censure upon their own maladministration. The spectacle of an energy which they never displayed, and of efforts which they never put forth, being made by others, in a sphere which they regarded as peculiarly their own, became unendurable. That was an experience which was by no means confined to Russia. We passed through it in Britain, but there the authority of Parliament was paramount, and in the last resort any Minister who was prepared to stand up on behalf of the nation against professional incompetence was bound to secure constitutional support, which was omnipotent in a country where constitutional Government was established. That was not the case in Russia, where, as the Czar assured General Hanbury-Williams, his word was final. That the reactionaries knew only too well, so they used all the means and agencies with which they were only too familiar, to capture that Imperial word. Gradually they succeeded. They ultimately paid the penalty of their success, but unfortunately they entangled multitudes of better men and women in the ruin which they had wrought. They resolved to use the first opportunity that presented itself to thwart the demonstrations of irregular and unprofessional activity which were producing supplies which they had failed to provide, and which were a constant rebuke to their incapacity and corruption. They found that opportunity when the Czar removed from the capital to command the Army in the field. It was a task for which he was utterly unfitted by capacity and experience. All the Czar's Ministers unanimously entreated him not to undertake this position. The Prime Minister on their behalf represented to him that it might well be fatal to the Empire, having regard to the inferiority of equipment in his Army. Every defeat would henceforth be inflicted not on the Russian Army, but on the Russian throne, and would inevitably diminish its prestige amongst his people. The Czar rudely brushed this protest aside by informing Goremykin, the Prime Minister, that it was none of the business of Ministers to consider or decide that question. It was entirely a matter for himself. Goremykin informed him that all the Ministers had decided to resign if he took command of the Army in the field. He replied that they had no right to give up their posts in the middle of a great war, and that he insisted upon their remaining.

Nevertheless the reactionaries urged his acceptance of this responsibility, which they knew only too well would not be additional but alternative to his other functions. As soon as he left Petrograd he was no longer in contact with events or with those who controlled them behind the lines. Once he was removed from Petrograd and from daily contact with the more liberal-minded amongst his Ministers, mischief and intrigue had full play. At Headquarters he was so overwhelmed with the details of his gigantic task—a task which would have been a whole time job for a bigger mind than his —that he was unable to inform himself as to what was happening in the vast country behind the front. That was the opportunity of the intriguers of the Court, including the Empress and her spiritual confessor. The Czar's mind was filled with suspicions about the Duma, the municipalities, and the Munition Committees upon which workmen were represented. Rasputin, through the Empress, worked upon these suspicions. The Duma was adjourned. Independent Ministers were gradually eliminated. Inefficient Ministers like Sturmer, with pro-German sympathies, and weak-headed Ministers under the influence of Rasputin like Protopopoff were left in control of affairs. As soon as the panic of 1915 had subsided, reaction once more resumed its sway. The recommendations made by the Duma and the Municipal Committees for Reforms and Improvements in organisation and control, were ignored one after another, until by the end of 1916 matters were in a worse state than ever before. In the winter of 1916-17, when conditions were becoming alarming and all intelligent Russians who were not dazzled by the splendour of autocracy foresaw impending disaster, the Duma appointed a Committee to investigate causes and to suggest remedies for the trouble of the nation. I quote a few passages from the evidence that was given before this Committee by men of moderate views whose loyalty to the Czar was beyond doubt or dispute.

" Sitting, 1st February, 1917.

M. V. Rodzianko, President of the Imperial Duma, pointed out that the question of the possibility of the crisis that had now arisen was raised by the Special Conference on Defence already in 1915, when a special commission was dispatched for the inspection of the Donetz region. This commission formulated a whole series of measures of a preventative character, which apparently remained unrealisable. Similarly, the Conference pointed out the necessity for a rational use of the available transport capacity of the railway network and for the requisite increase of rolling stock. Lastly, the Conference gave directions for the timely regularisation of the victualling question. The wishes expressed by the Conference, however, remained unfulfilled. As a result, a situation has been created which had been characterised by the President of the Conference as evoking the most serious apprehensions. *To these apprehensions there is further added the alarm for the fate of our army which is beginning to experience a considerable shortage of articles of material supplies and particularly of food-stuffs, owing to the disorganisation of railway transport. According to information in the possession of M. V. Rodzianko the Armies on the South-Western and Southern Fronts are only fed on lentils.* If these difficulties are not removed then we cannot reckon upon a successful issue for us of the campaign. Such a threatening state of affairs impels the members of the Conference called together at the will of the Emperor, for participation in the matter of supplies for the Army, to request the President of the Conference to report to His Imperial Majesty the most devoted application of the members of the Conference for the appointment of a joint Meeting of the Special Conferences under the personal Presidency of His Imperial Majesty. In supporting this proposal, submitted by P. N. Krupenski, at the preceding sittings, the members of the Conference are actuated by the desire to report to the Emperor all that is troubling them at the present time. . . ."

" Sitting, 4th February, 1917.

The meeting opened with a resumption of an exchange of views in regard to the proposal submitted by the member of the Imperial Duma, P. N. Krupenski, as to the most devoted application to the Emperor for the appointment of a Joint Meeting of the Special Conferences under the personal Presidency of His Imperial Majesty.

In supporting this proposal, the member of the Imperial Duma, A. I. Shingareff, stated that at the present time the situation appeared to be more serious than in the summer of 1915. Then during our retreat from Galicia and Poland the healthy and unbroken rear had sufficient strength for affording moral and material existence to the Army and the enemy was held up. Now, however, we are in a period of serious disorganisation of the rear; food-stuffs, transport and the supply of fuel to the works—in all these most important spheres for defence exceptional difficulties, involving serious consequences, are experienced. Meanwhile, the decisive moment of the whole campaign is drawing near. In order to find an outlet from the crisis that has arisen and to produce a revival of spirits among the population, in whose midst alarm is beginning to penetrate, immediate and extraordinary measures are necessary. A conscientious duty impels the members of the Conference to express this personally to the Emperor. . . .

N. E. Markoff, Member of the Imperial Duma, pointed out that he adheres to a political tendency, the motto of which is: power— to the Czar, opinion—to the people. From the point of view of the convictions shared by N. E. Markoff, loyal subjects should go to the Czar and tell him the whole truth, but at the same time they should know what to say. . . .

M. V. Chelnokoff, Member of the Imperial Duma, reported to the Conference the serious position of Moscow as regards the delivery of food-stuffs and fuel. According to information in the possession of M. V. Chelnokoff, up to 50 large towns in the Empire are in the same difficult position. . . .

S. F. Oldenberg, Member of the State Council, in the capacity of a delegate of the Petrograd Municipal Duma, thought it necessary to place on record that even in November, 1916, the Petrograd Municipal Self-Administration considered the position of Petrograd threatening as regards its security for food-stuffs, and formulated regulations for the distribution of food products. Those regulations, however, were not realised and the responsibility for this must be imposed on the organs of the Government authorities.

A. I. Guchkoff, Member of the State Council, expressed the opinion that since the commencement of the War there had not been such a critical moment for Russia as that which it is experiencing at present. The crisis that for a long time had been coming on in this sphere, of the satisfaction of our requirements in food-stuffs, fuel and raw materials, had set in. The consequences thereof would be very serious: the stoppage of many factories, among them also those working on defence, serious victualling difficulties, a depressed state of spirits in wide spheres of the population—all this would not only cause material damage to this matter of supplies for the Army, but besides that would also be a heavy moral blow for the Army.

A. I. Guchkoff arrived at the conclusion that the monarch was not acquainted with the true state of affairs. At present, in face of the arrival of a terrible danger, A. I. Guchkoff experiences the greatest alarm at the thought as to whether the Emperor is aware of the full seriousness of the situation, as to whether he has been informed of the extent and significance of the crisis that the country is experiencing. This alarm impels A. I. Guchkoff to support wholly the wish expressed by P. N. Krupenski as to the appointment of a joint meeting of the Special Conferences under the personal presidency of the Emperor."

To this reasonable proposal the Czar refused acceptance.

" Sitting, 8th February, 1917.

. . . According to information in A. I. Shingareff's possession, the reserves of the Department *cannot be regarded as adequate even for the satisfaction of the needs of the Army.* At the present time the Western Front is already experiencing an acute shortage of food-stuffs, as is clear from the telegram of the Chief Field Commissary, Lieutenant-General Egorieff. The position appears to be threatening as so far as A. I. Shingareff is aware, *an adequate quantity of bread for the Army has not yet been prepared;* the distribution undertaken by the Ministry of Agriculture has so far given unsatisfactory results—meanwhile in a few weeks the transmission of grain will become impossible in many places. . . .

In A. I. Guchkoff's opinion the Government should take upon itself to supply food-stuffs, not only for the Army but also for the large urban centres and the factories working on defence. . . ."

" Sitting, 15th February, 1917.

. . . The stocks of grain in the country and the Army were being gradually exhausted. Upon the Steward of the Household, A. A. Rittich, taking up the administration of Agriculture, i.e. by the middle of November of the past year, an extremely serious situation had arisen. The stocks of bread on all the fronts were alarmingly small: there was bread for a few days. To avoid a catastrophe such a situation demanded the adoption of immediate and decisive measures. . . ."

This testimony does not bear out the theory that Czardom had overcome Russia's worst difficulties, and that the country had emerged into a period of growing efficiency just at the moment when the Czar was stricken down by a felon blow. Things were going from bad to worse as far as the internal conditions of every belligerent country were concerned. But in Russia there was no one in authority who had the capacity to handle the aggravating crisis. Those who were competent were ruled out of authority by the Head of the State, who was the fountain head of all official power in Russia. In these circumstances Revolution was not only inevitable—it was imperative. This will explain the attitude adopted towards the news of the Revolution by the leaders of all parties in the House of Commons.

On Sir George Buchanan's advice the Cabinet decided to recognise the new Government. On the 16th it was known in Petrograd that the Emperor had abdicated, and soldiers marched through the town " tearing down the Imperial Eagles."

When the Revolution was an accomplished fact, the British Cabinet considered its attitude towards the Russian Provisional Government, and decided to invite the House of Commons to send a resolution of fraternal greeting to the Duma. There is no more painful and difficult problem for a man than to know what to do with a good friend who has made a thorough mess of a concern in which they are jointly concerned. If you do not stand by him you feel you are abandoning a loyal comrade in his trouble. If you do, then what is left is inevitably lost. Luckily this question did not arise. The Czar had already abdicated. There was therefore no question of personal disloyalty to one who had stood faithfully by the Allies through good and evil report. Mr. Bonar Law, as leader of the House of Commons, on 22nd March, moved the following Resolution in the House of Commons : —

" That this House send to the Duma its fraternal greetings and tenders to the Russian people its heartiest congratulations upon the establishment among them of free institutions in full confidence that they will lead not only to the happy and rapid progress of the Russian nation, but to the prosecution with renewed steadfastness and vigour of the War against the stronghold of an autocratic militarism which threatens the liberty of Europe."

In supporting that resolution he made use of words which faithfully represented the feeling of every party in the House of Commons and in the country towards the changes which had taken place in the Government of a great Allied people : —

" It is not, I think, for us to judge, much less to condemn, those who have taken part in the Government in an Allied country, but I hope I may be permitted to express a feeling which I believe will be shared by the vast majority of the members of this House, and which I, at least, hold strongly, a feeling of compassion for the late Czar, who was for three years, or nearly three years, as I believe, our loyal Ally, and who had laid upon him by his birth a burden which has proved too heavy for him. But we cannot forget that one of the issues, and the greatest of all the issues of this War, is whether or not free institutions can survive against the onslaught of military despotism, and we cannot but rejoice in the hope that in the final stages of this world conflict all the Allied Powers will be under the direction of Governments which represent their peoples. The Government, in putting down this Motion for the consideration of the House of Commons, were well aware that it might be considered premature, but we have submitted it to the House in the hope and in the belief that if sent now, it may strengthen the hands of the Russian Government in their difficult task."

As Mr. Asquith, who seconded, well said: —

" The Resolution which my right honourable friend has proposed expresses, in my belief, the opinion not only of the House of Commons, but of all the peoples of the constituent parts of the United Kingdom and of the whole British Empire. . . . An autocracy which notwithstanding the strange mutations in its history, in the personal fortunes of the occupants of the Throne, seemed to have become an integral part of Russian life, and beyond the reach of possible attack, has, in the course of a few days, without effective resistance, or even defence, been blotted out of existence. The form of Russia's future Government is to be submitted, as we are glad to know, to the free judgment of an enfranchised people. Whatever their ultimate decision may be, at this moment, by that very fact, Russia takes her place by the side of the great Democracies of the world. We, here, as my right honourable friend has reminded us, the first home, the original home, of Parliamentary institutions and of popular election, feel that it is not only our privilege, but that we have a special claim of our own to be the first to rejoice in her emancipation, and to welcome her into the fellowship of free peoples."

On 24th March I wired the following message to Prince Lvoff, the new Russian Premier: —

" It is with sentiments of the most profound satisfaction that the people of Great Britain and of the British Dominions across the seas, have learned that their great Ally Russia now stands with the nations which base their institutions upon responsible Government. Much as we appreciate the loyalty and steadfast co-operation which we have received from the late Emperor and the Armies of Russia during the last two and a half years, yet we believe that the Revolution whereby the Russian people have placed their destinies on the sure foundation of freedom, is the greatest service which they have yet made to the cause for which the Allied peoples have been fighting since August, 1914. It reveals the fundamental truth that this War is at bottom a struggle for popular Government as well as for liberty. It shows that through the War the principle of liberty, which is the only sure safeguard of Peace in the world, has already won one resounding victory. It is the sure promise that the Prussian military autocracy which began the War and which is still the only barrier to Peace will itself before long be overthrown. Freedom is the only warranty of Peace, and I do not doubt that as a result of the establishment of a stable Constitutional Government within their borders the Russian people will be strengthened in their resolve to prosecute this War until the last stronghold of tyranny on the Continent of Europe is destroyed and the free peoples of all lands can unite to secure for themselves and their children the blessings of fraternity and of Peace."

I stand by every word of that declaration to-day.

A few days later, Sir George Buchanan wired to Mr. Balfour: —

" Message from the Premier cabled by you to Russian Prime Minister created extremely good impression and its reference to the Czar caused no difficulty. But I am sorry to say that the sympathy expressed by Mr. Bonar Law in his speech has given rise to unfriendly criticism in various journals, particularly in the Labour Party's official organ. . . ."

We all felt, nevertheless, that Mr. Bonar Law was bound to utter the sentiments he expressed about the Czar and that his words had been well and wisely chosen.

There was no doubt that the Russian Revolution was an accomplished fact, but it was by no means completed. It was quite clear in the first few days that this Revolution was to follow the usual course of all revolutions. The Government might decree, but it was the Jacobins that determined the course of events; deep was calling unto deep, and already the answer was beginning to resound on the surface.

Before concluding this chapter on the tragic end of the Czarist regime in Russia, I must refer to the causes which prevented the Imperial family from gaining an asylum in this country, and escaping the final horror of the Ekaterinberg cellar. Several writers have alleged that the determining factor was a refusal on the part of the British Government to permit the Czar to take refuge here. That is untrue. The fact is that at no time between his abdication and his murder was he free to leave Russia. An invitation to take refuge here was extended by the British Crown and Government. The Czar was unable in the event to avail himself of it, even had he been anxious to do so—and of that we had no evidence.

That statement is amply corroborated by the official records. Not all of them, even at this interval of time, am I free to publish. But I propose to quote such extracts from them as will give the reader an accurate picture of the march of events in relation to this painful episode.

On 19th March, 1917, a telegram arrived from our Ambassador in Russia, Sir George Buchanan, saying that M. Miliukoff had asked him whether he knew of any arrangements being made for the Czar to go to England. To this he had replied in the negative. Two days later he wired us again as follows:—

" Petrograd,
21st March, 1917.

Most Urgent
(Paraphrased)

This morning I asked the Foreign Minister about the announcement in the papers that the Czar had been placed under arrest. I was informed by His Excellency that this was not strictly accurate. The position was that the Emperor was no longer allowed his liberty, and that a delegation of the Duma and an escort provided by General Alexeieff would accompany him to Tsarskoe Selo.

Pointing out to the Minister that the Czar was closely related to our own King and on intimate terms of friendship with him, I urged that I wished to be in a position to reassure His Majesty that the Emperor's safety would be fully safeguarded. I enquired if the Russian Government would agree to the Czar being accompanied by our Military Representative as a further precaution. I was answered that there was not the slightest need for this and that the Government would much rather it was not done. His Excellency proceeded to enquire whether we were making any plans for the Czar to stay in England, and when I said not, he declared himself most anxious for His Majesty to leave Russia, and said he would be most glad if our King and Government would invite the Czar to take refuge with them. Should such invitation be made, it should include condition that the Emperor would be kept in England for the remainder of the War. He wishes for an answer to this without avoidable delay."

On the following day, 22nd March, the question of allowing the Russian Imperial Family to come to this country was discussed at the Imperial War Cabinet, and it was decided that in the interests of his personal safety, it was of the first importance that the Czar should leave Russia at the earliest possible date. On a review of the political considerations involved, and more particularly of the desirability of avoiding the risk of his being exposed to hostile intrigue in the event of residence in neutral countries, we reached the conclusion that the best plan would be to invite the Czar, together with the Empress and their family, to take up residence in this country, on the distinct understanding that they should not leave this country during the War except with the consent of the British Government.

Accordingly the Imperial War Cabinet " authorised the Secretary of State for Foreign Affairs to send a telegram in this sense to the British Ambassador at Petrograd."

Mr. Balfour, therefore, wired to Sir George Buchanan:—

(Paraphrased)

" Foreign Office,
22nd March, 1917.

Responding to the suggestion put forward by the Russian Government, His Majesty and the British Government are glad to invite the Czar and Czarina to take sanctuary in this country and to stay here for the duration of the War. In conveying this message to the Russian Government you are to make it clear that they must be responsible for providing for the maintenance of their Majesties here in a suitable manner."

To which Sir George Buchanan replied:—

(Paraphrased)   " 24th March.

Yesterday I told the Foreign Minister the purport of your message, and to-day I communicated to him the contents of your telegram of the 22nd about this matter and stressed the point that our invitation was made solely in response to the suggestion of his Government.

He was very anxious that this fact should not be made public because the extreme Left Wing were stirring up opinion against letting the Czar leave Russia. While he was hopeful that this opposition could be surmounted by the Government, they had not yet made a final decision. In any case, the Czar could not set out until his children had got over the measles. When I hinted at the question of the Czar's means I was informed that according to the Foreign Minister's information he had ample private resources. The financial issue would in any case be handled generously. . . .

He was emphatic that in regard to His Majesty's safety there was no ground at all for anxiety."

Already there appears in the foregoing telegram a warning about the opposition to the Czar's leaving the country being so strong inside Russia as to delay decision on this point. On the following day a further telegram from Buchanan again insisted upon this.

On 26th March, the Ambassador made a further reference in a cable to the Czar's departure for England and added that he and General Hanbury-Williams concurred in the opinion that if it were settled for the Emperor to make the journey, General Headlam might go with him. He adds:—

" According to what I learned this morning from the Foreign Minister, His Majesty has not yet been approached about it by the

Government, as they want first of all to get rid of left-wing opposition to the proposal."

On 2nd April, Sir George Buchanan wrote to the Foreign Secretary in the following strain:—

" *Nothing has yet been decided about the Emperor's journey to England.* He is living with the Empress and his children at Tsarskoe under a strong guard, and is allowed to walk in the park but is always kept under observation. From a private and confidential source I hear he is perfectly happy and takes exercise by clearing the paths in the park of snow. He does not yet realise that he will not be allowed to go as he had hoped to Livadia, but the loss of his throne does not seem to have depressed him. The Empress, on the other hand, is said to feel the humiliation of her present position deeply. *She is, I hear, averse to the idea of going to England.* Some telegrams have just been published in the Press, which were sent by her to the Emperor before and after Rasputin's murder, which show clearly that he did everything she told him to. There was also published a hysterical letter from the Empress to Rasputin, in which she wrote as if she were addressing a saint, saying that she only found comfort when leaning on his shoulder, and praying him to bless ' thy child.' She has been the Emperor's evil genius even since they married, and nobody pities her. . . ."

Owing to the illness of the Grand Duchesses (they had measles, and two of them were very ill for some time) nothing could at that moment be done in the matter of the removal of the Imperial Family. Before this delay had ceased to operate, a fresh hindrance arose. On 9th April, Sir George Buchanan wired us reporting a conversation he had held with M. Kerensky, in the course of which he had asked if anything was yet settled about the Emperor. M. Kerensky had replied:—

" that on the following day he would be going himself to Tsarskoe Selo, but that *he was of opinion that the Czar would be unable to set out for England within the next month. Until they had finished their examination of the documents they had seized, they could hardly permit him to leave, and M. Kerensky urged me not to use any pressure to try to induce the Government to let him go earlier.* I assured him that I had no such intention, although of course we were anxious that everything should be done to ensure the Emperor's safety. . . ."

The Ambassador further told us in this wire that he had pleaded for permission to hand the Empress Marie some letters for her from her sister, Queen Alexandra, but had been begged by Kerensky not to do so, as if the Government allowed it they would be charged by the extremists with encouraging intrigues.

It was clear from this cable that the net around the Imperial family was being drawn tighter, and that feeling was already hardening in Russia against the policy of allowing the Czar to leave Russia. M. Kerensky was obviously not prepared to accept the responsibility of permitting the Czar to leave Russia at that date.

On receipt of Sir George Buchanan's telegram the War Cabinet conferred about the matter. The difficulty of keeping our invitation open was growing. Opinion in France was opposed to the Czar taking up his residence in any Allied country. It was felt there that it might tend to create a feeling of suspicion amongst the revolutionary elements in Russia, whose support was essential for the effective co-operation of the Russian Army in the War. To illustrate and confirm this statement as to the French attitude I may quote a letter written on 22nd April by Lord Bertie, our Ambassador in Paris, to the Foreign Secretary, in which he expressed satisfaction that the proposal to welcome the ex-Emperor and his family in England had not materialised, and said that:—

" the Germans would have given out and the Russian extreme Socialists might have believed that the British Government were keeping the ex-Emperor in reserve to be used for a restoration if it would suit the selfish policy of England to promote discord in Russia in the future.

I do not think that the ex-Emperor and his family would be welcome in France. The Empress is not only a Boche by birth but in sentiment. She did all she could to bring about an understanding with Germany. She is regarded as a criminal or a criminal lunatic and the ex-Emperor as a criminal from his weakness and submission to her promptings.

Yours ever,
BERTIE."

An agitation had also started in this country, which indicated that there was a strong feeling in extensive working-class circles, hostile to the Czar coming to Great Britain. However, the invitation was not withdrawn. The ultimate issue in the matter was decided by the action of the Russian Government, which continued to place obstacles in the way of the Czar's departure.

On 15th April, 1917, Sir George Buchanan wired us at some length about the situation. He expressed grave doubts about the wisdom of bringing the Czar to England, and said he had asked the Russian Premier on the previous day why they would not let the Emperor go to Livadia, his palace in the Crimea, where it would surely be easy both to isolate and to protect him. The Premier

" answered that the journey would involve far too serious risks. He wished that he could get the Emperor out of Russia soon, because all the time he was there a possibility existed of a restoration movement, and if any sign of counter-revolution appeared there would be deadly danger for the Czar. The Premier still understands that we should allow the Czar to come to England. . . ."

But on this prospect, the Ambassador noted that

" the parties of the Extreme Left, who are far from friendly to us, and the agents of Germany, would certainly use his presence in England as an excuse for rousing public opinion against us. . . ."

and he suggested that it would be better if the Emperor went to France. On the following day he sent us a letter in which he said he had suggested to Prince Lvoff that the Czar should be allowed to go to Livadia; but the Prince had expressed the fear that the train would be held up by workmen and the Czar's life endangered.

It was in fact clear that the Russian Government was held irresolute by divided counsels—anxious on the one hand to be quit of responsibility for the Czar, and on the other, dreading the anger of the extreme left wing if an attempt were made to remove him to safety. They dared not attempt to transfer him even to the comfortable Crimea. Much less were they prepared to take the risk of trying to send him out of the country. Nothing could be done about it unless the Russian Government changed their attitude.

Sir George Buchanan, in his book " My Mission to Russia," sums up the matter when he says that : —

" We had offered the Emperor an asylum, in compliance with the request of the Provisional Government; but as the opposition of the Soviet, which they were vainly hoping to overcome, grew stronger, they did not venture to assume responsibility for the Emperor's departure, and receded from their original position. . . .

It was they who took the initiative in the matter by asking us to offer the Emperor and his family an asylum in England. We on our part at once complied with their request, and at the same time pressed them to make the necessary arrangements for the journey to Port Romanoff. More than this we could not do. *Our offer remained open and was never withdrawn.** If advantage was not taken of it, it was because the Provisional Government failed to overcome the opposition of the Soviet."

That statement, as the extracts I have quoted show, sums up the real history of the issue. The end was tragedy, the details of which will horrify endless generations of mankind. But for that tragedy this country cannot be in any way held responsible.

* My italics.

CHAPTER LIV

AMERICA ENTERS THE WAR

AT the beginning of 1917, the entry of the United States into the War seemed more remote and improbable than at any time since the first outbreak of world hostilities. Although the bulk of public opinion in the States was all along pro-Ally, its attitude was one of detached and bored sympathy rather than of any strong desire to join in the conflict on our side. As the months of the War lengthened into years, and the struggle developed into a confusing scrimmage out of which nothing emerged but a growing mass of crushed, bruised and blood-stained humanity, pro-Ally sentiment tended to settle down resignedly into a rut of benevolent but horrified neutrality. America was prospering more and more by the conflict, but getting less and less reconciled to battening on the ghastly heap of bleeding horror. The best wanted peace as soon as a reasonably satisfactory one could be patched up.

The Presidential election at the beginning of November, 1916, emphasised this attitude. Woodrow Wilson secured his re-election on the slogan that he was the man who kept America out of the European slaughter house. Theodore Roosevelt, the one leading figure in the States who was openly and emphatically in favour of intervention on the Allied side, felt himself to be in so small a minority that he did not attempt to secure nomination. Hughes, who stood against Wilson as the Republican nominee, was anxious to secure the German-American vote, and that of such stray Irishmen as might wander from the Democratic fold. He therefore took care to dissociate himself from the fiery expressions of his more famous, but less timorous, co-Republican. The possibility of entry into the War was not an issue in the Presidential election. Both candidates ostentatiously dissociated themselves from the idea. Here is a letter from a prominent and well-informed American sent to me by the late Sir Gilbert Parker, the well-known Canadian novelist who organised Intelligence from America for the British Government, which gives a fair summary of the Allied view of the election.

"... From the point of view of international politics, I am inclined to think that things are much safer in the hands of Mr. Wilson than they would have been in the hands of Mr. Hughes. ...

We know how Mr. Wilson stands and we may feel very sure that he will do nothing of a serious nature to interfere with the blockade or the export of munitions which are the two vital points. . . . The most satisfactory feature of the election has been the fact that the German-American vote did not materialise. The German-American Alliance and all the German papers with hardly an exception were rampant for Hughes and yet Mr. Wilson carried Milwaukee and St. Louis, two German strongholds. It seems pretty certain that the Germans voted according to their Party affiliations or at all events according to their inclinations, and not according to the way the German-American Alliance or the Kaiser wanted them to vote. I regard this as a very important and significant feature of the campaign because it proves that the great effort which has been made by the Pan-German leaders for the last six or seven years in this country to create a solid German-American vote which might in time of need obey the Kaiser, has completely failed. . . .

Incidentally, I hear on very good authority that Bernstorff was strongly inclined to Wilson. I think this is because Bernstorff is a good deal cleverer than some of his colleagues in the Wilhelmstrasse, and he also feels that he is safer with Wilson because he knows what to expect. There is pending a critical issue between this country and Germany on account of the sinking of the *Marina*, and I suppose that Bernstorff feels that as usual Wilson will do no more than make a protest in words. But his greatest reason for being inclined to Wilson, I imagine, is that he will find in Wilson the best chance of some effort at mediation. Wilson owes his victory in the election very largely to the fact that he has kept the country out of the War, and I have not a doubt that his greatest ambition during the next four years will be to act as mediator. Therefore we have constantly to be on the look-out for some steps in this direction at Washington. I imagine that the next big effort to be made by the Germans in their propaganda will be to influence this country towards an early peace . . . now that the election is over and they know that they have to deal with Wilson for the next four years, and they must know that an embargo is practically out of the question and that Wilson will do nothing to interfere with the blockade, their great effort must be directed towards peace propaganda. For they know that it is just here that Mr. Wilson is most likely to help them. . . .

I don't think there is anything more to say about the present situation except to point out that the defeat of Mr. Hughes in no way signifies a cooling-off of the pro-Ally sentiment or a repudiation of Mr. Roosevelt's ideas concerning the German attack on Belgium. The fact of the matter is that there was no real issue in the campaign. Mr. Roosevelt created a clear issue between himself and Mr. Wilson, and on this issue he might have won or he might have been defeated. Personally, I think he would have won, because he would have carried all the States that Mr. Hughes carried and he would undoubtedly have carried California, where his recent running mate, Mr. Johnson, was returned by an enormous majority to the Senate. But in any case, whether he was successful or not, we should have had an expression of opinion from the American people about the great issues of the War. As it is the election returns indicate nothing in this respect. They simply show that the big manufacturing and financial interests were for Hughes and that the progressive element in the country inclined towards Wilson. It is not necessary to tell you that in a national election the democratic candidate starts with 170 electoral votes in his favour whatever he says or does. The solid South was bound to vote for Mr. Wilson whether it liked his foreign policy or not, and when we consider this fact, the small majority which Mr. Wilson maintained in the electoral college cannot possibly be taken as an endorsement, though it cannot be taken as a repudiation either. The whole campaign was a muddle and the returns show that the voter was a good deal confused."

This was an accurate summary of the position as it stood, or at least as it appeared to discerning eyes, at and immediately after the election. But it is almost a classic example of the happening of the unexpected. Here was an election fought when both parties were convinced that the idea of intervention in the War was universally unpopular. The only contention between them in their rival appeals was as to which of them was the less likely to be tempted to join in the fray. Hughes' friends said that he loved the Germans more than Wilson did. Wilson replied by pointing to the fact that he had already successfully kept the country out of war for over two years. Who would have predicted at that date that Germany would have deliberately provoked the pacific and hesitating Wilson to gird on his sword and after an interval to unsheath it? Colonel House records that on 14th November, 1916, President Wilson was planning to use his newly confirmed authority to propose peace negotiations—a course which House opposed, because he felt that Germany would, at this stage, insist on terms which America could not recommend to the Allies, and that any attempt to force peace at this stage would be playing the game of German militarism. The President took a different view. He earnestly wished for peace, and was anxious to precipitate negotiations.

I have already told how the Kaiser irritated the President by forestalling him with a German Peace Note, and how Wilson issued his own Note six days later, fearful lest the Allies should close the door to negotiations before he could get in his appeal to them. In face of the tenor of the German Note, arrogant and confident, which showed clearly that the only terms the Germans would contemplate would be terms based on the assumption of substantial victory already achieved by them, President Wilson's intervention emphasises his painful anxiety for peace at any price.

A further proof of the fact that President Wilson was up to the last determined not to contemplate any departure from neutrality is afforded by the total lack of any sort or kind of military or naval preparation for the possible contingency of war. His view was that a messenger of peace should only be armed with an olive branch, not realising that a whole grove of olives at that stage of the War would make no impression on either side unless the combatants knew that guns were hidden by the foliage. This is the more noteworthy, since as far back as 18th April, 1916, after the sinking of the *Sussex* by a German submarine, the President had found himself compelled to address an ultimatum to Germany, in which he had declared that : —

"Unless the Imperial Government should now immediately declare and effect an abandonment of its present methods of submarine warfare against passenger and freight-carrying vessels, the Government of the United States can have no choice but to sever diplomatic relations with the German Empire altogether."

Germany had on that occasion climbed down to the extent of stating that she was ordering her submarines not to sink merchantmen without warning, and without saving human lives, unless the ship attempted to escape or offer resistance. But her covering Note stated clearly that she made this concession merely as a matter of expediency, reserving in principle her right to resume grimmer methods if she thought it would pay her to do so. If the U.S.A. failed to induce Britain to abandon her blockade of Germany, " the German Government would then be facing a new situation in which it must reserve itself complete liberty of decision."

It is incomprehensible why Wilson took no measures to strengthen the naval and military forces of America when two things must have been made clear to him by the course of the War : —

1. That one or other or both of the belligerent parties were constantly interfering with the rights of American subjects and one of them actually sacrificing American lives.

2. That America was bound sooner or later to intervene and propose peace. There was no other country left with sufficient authority and influence to demand negotiation amongst the belligerents. Her intervention would not be heeded by a winning Power unless there was force behind it. As things stood in the War, both parties thought that victory was in the end assured to their side, and therefore the War might go on for many more years.

The President had already been driven to issue one ultimatum to Germany and he had also sent repeated warnings to the Allies about their interference with his cargoes. Yet through the intervening months he took no steps whatever, despite Colonel House's frequent urgings, to prepare the country so that a threat of intervention by her might not ring hollow. A movement had sprung up in the States for "national preparedness," of which the chief advocate was the National Security League, that carried on a vigorous publicity campaign on behalf of military training. But Wilson withheld his blessing from the movement, and it gradually fizzled out. He honestly thought that he was serving the cause of Peace by an ostentatious display of his impotence for war. Had he issued no threats, there was an exalted precedent for his demeanour. But he did not turn the other cheek to the smiter, he just rushed to his typewriting machine to record his feelings about the blow. Such an attitude was neither divine nor dignified. In effect, his action prolonged the War by its most destructive years. The attitude of the President was such as to breed in Germany the not unnatural conviction that while there might be limits to America's neutrality, there was no fear that even if she declared war, she would or could really fight. Wilson, if annoyed, would simply put a little more sulphur in his ink: that would be all. He had no troops, no guns, no aeroplanes, only a portable typewriting machine which clicked harmlessly and heedlessly. In 1916, a big addition to the Navy was voted by Congress; but the programme was to be spread over several years, and no part of it had materialised when America actually entered the War in 1917. They had not built a single additional torpedo-boat to protect their own shipping. No steps were taken to increase the Army in numbers or effectiveness.

The failure of the German and Wilson Peace Notes brought no change in the President's attitude. Throughout the last weeks of 1916 and the month of January, 1917, omens were increasing that a ruthless intensification of the German submarine warfare was in prospect. Yet on 4th January, 1917, Colonel House records that Wilson declared to him: "There will be no war. This country does not intend to become involved in this War." Refusal to contemplate the growing danger of being driven into war had become with him not an issue of fact but an article of religious faith.

On 22nd January, 1917, President Wilson made his famous "Peace without Victory" speech to Congress. Dealing with his own peace move of December and its outcome, he developed in this speech his ideas as to the kind of peace settlement America would support. From first to last his speech contained no hint that America could possibly be drawn into the struggle. On the contrary, he suggested that while the conclusion of peace was not far away ("We are much nearer a definite discussion of the peace which will end the present War"), it would be one in settling the terms of which the United States, as a non-combatant, would be able to take no part. "We shall have no voice," he declared, "in determining what those terms shall be."

He outlined the main principles of what he would regard as a desirable and lasting peace, on lines which foreshadowed his subsequent "Fourteen Points." He proposed a concert of the nations, general disarmament, the independence of a united Poland, democratic Governments, universal civil and religious liberty, self-determination of the peoples, freedom of the seas. And of these ideas, he asserted that "They imply, first of all, that it must be a peace without victory." He never condescended to explain how he thought Poland could be freed and self-determination won for the subject races of Turkey, Austria and Germany, without victory, and Allied victory. Without an Allied triumph, there was no faintest hope of realising any of the ideals he was advancing so eloquently. Germany was in possession of vast territories, much of which she had no intention of surrendering after the War—some of which she did not intend to restore without imposing conditions of practical vassalage. To talk of self-determination of the peoples, an independent Poland, democratic Governments, universal liberty, with an undefeated Imperial Germany was a mockery. Peace without victory? The President's detachment from realities was more than ever obvious. To the Allies the phrase was an offence—to the Germans a jest.

Nine days later, his balloon was shot down by a German shell. On 31st January, 1917, the German Ambassador, Von Bernstorff, handed to Mr. Lansing, the American Secretary of State, a letter announcing that:—

"The Imperial Government—in order to serve the welfare of mankind in a higher sense and not to wrong its own people—is now compelled to continue the fight for existence, again forced upon it, with the full employment of all the weapons which are at its disposal."

Attached to the letter were two memoranda, one of which stated in the following terms that Germany would no longer be bound by the pledge she had given America after the sinking of the *Sussex,* to practise her submarine warfare subject to humane restrictions:—

"The Government of the United States will further realise that the now openly disclosed intention of the Entente Allies gives back to Germany the freedom of action which she reserved in her note addressed to the Government of the United States on 4th May, 1916. Under these circumstances, Germany will meet the illegal measures of her enemies by forcibly preventing after 1st February, 1917, in a zone around Great Britain, France, Italy, and in the Eastern Mediterranean, all navigation, that of neutrals included, from and to England and from and to France, etc. All ships met within the zone will be sunk."

The second memorandum set out closer details of the areas within which vessels would be sunk without warning, and made the concession that if the United States were prepared to carry out certain elaborate arrangements dictated by Germany, they might send one ship a week as far as Falmouth without having it sunk.

This was a bitter blow to the President. Not only did it smash all his hopes of remaining on good neutral terms with both belligerent sides, but it more than hinted that Germany was contemptuous of America's power. She had made her calculation, and concluded that the United States were so impotent for effective intervention that they would be less dangerous to her as an enemy she could disregard, than as a neutral with authority to hold up her submarine campaign. Germany reckoned that six months of unrestricted submarine warfare would force Britain to her knees, and that America would be unable to intervene actively on the Allied side for a year. Long before then, the War would have been won. If a German peace had not been attained by that time, America would be safely isolated, for there would be no shipping available to transport her armies to the battle area.

In addition, Bernstorff wrote a private letter to Colonel House,* apprising him of the German Government's decision, and confiding to him in general outline the peace terms which Germany would consider—terms which showed what "a Peace without Victory" would have brought to Europe. He explained that these were not being made public, because "our enemies have published such terms which aim at the dishonour and destruction of Germany and her allies. My Government considers that as long as our enemies openly proclaim such terms, it would show weakness, which does not exist, on our part, if we publish our terms, and we would in so doing only prolong the War."

The German Peace terms were such as only a complete German victory could wring out of defeated Allies. Bluntly, they amounted to a demand for German suzerainty over a dismantled and defenceless Belgium; annexation of the iron mines of French Lorraine; parts of Russia and all Poland to be incorporated in the German Empire; and an indemnity from France to cover "financial losses." In addition to that, the Allies were to cover all German commercial losses through the War; there was to be a return of all the captured German colonies, and cession of further colonial territory by ourselves and our Allies; and similar restitutions, concessions and indemnities to Austria, Turkey, and Bulgaria. It was the detailed and explicit interpretation of the arrogant note in the German Peace Despatch.

The President's course now was clear. The Allied terms approximated to his Fourteen Points. The German conditions traversed his principles at every section. And these conditions were accompanied

* The full text of this letter is given on pp. 664-66.

by a threat to sink his ships at sight.   His only choice was between a break with Germany and abject surrender.   In view of the statements he had made to Germany in his ultimatum after the *Sussex* incident, their blunt repudiation of the undertaking then given, and their declaration of ruthless and indiscriminate submarine warfare, there was no option but to sever diplomatic relations.

Accordingly, on 3rd February, 1917, President Wilson appeared before Congress, and after recapitulating the recent course of negotiations, announced: —

" I have therefore directed the Secretary of State to announce to His Excellency the German Ambassador that all diplomatic relations between the United States and the German Empire are severed and that the American Ambassador to Berlin will immediately be withdrawn; and, in accordance with this decision, to hand to His Excellency his passports."

Yet the president's hopes died hard, for he proceeded while deploring the attitude of the German Government, to assert that notwithstanding their action,

" I refuse to believe that it is the intention of the German Authorities to do in fact what they have warned us they will feel at liberty to do.   I cannot bring myself to believe that they will indeed pay no regard to the ancient friendship between their people and our own. . . .   Only actual overt acts on their part can make me believe it even now."

At the same time he felt himself compelled to sound a warning note, in a final forlorn hope of deterring Germany from driving him from his neutral position.   If American ships and lives were in fact sacrificed by German submarines, he said: —

" I shall take the liberty of coming again before Congress to ask that authority be given me to use any means that may be necessary for the protection of our seamen and our people in the prosecution of their peaceful and legitimate errands on the high seas."

President Wilson's announcements were warmly approved by public opinion in the United States.   But they were not followed by any preparation for action.   The President excused his inaction by a statement that he would give Germany no provocation which would deter her from reconsidering her threat.

A graphic description of the state of things in America at this time was given in the following letter from our Ambassador in the States, Sir Cecil Spring-Rice: —

" 23rd February, 1917.

The situation is much that of a soda-water bottle with the wires cut but the cork unexploded. The President appears to be watching. There are two currents of opinion. One is, has the President lost ground by delay? The other is, has he gained it? His policy has always been to wait for an uncontrollable outburst of public opinion. The question naturally is, has public opinion grown stronger or weaker in consequence of the action of Germany and the inaction of the United States? Germany has declared that she will destroy United States ships if found in the War zone. The United States has declared that Germany will do so at her peril. But so far no United States ship has been destroyed. Is this because no United States ship has been sent into the War zone or because no United States ship has been found there? American ships have certainly passed these waters. Others are on their way. But the great majority have remained in port and the German threat appears to have been entirely effective. She has not committed murder, but the threat of murder has kept America off the seas. The result is a stoppage of trade, a congestion in the ports, widespread discomfort and even misery on the coast and inland, even bread riots and a coal famine. These seem to be overt acts. They are at any rate overt facts. But they are not it seems of a sufficiently spectacular character. What is required to arouse the American people is the destruction of an American ship with American passengers. Mr. Franklin, a very energetic man, who is in control of the American line, wanted to send his ships in the danger zone with passengers on board if he was allowed to arm them. The Secretary of the Navy told him that to provide guns to a private ship would be an unneutral act, although if he could get them from private sources he was welcome to use them. Mr. Franklin said that he knew of no store in New York where six-inch guns were on sale. He then went back and ordered his crews to be disbanded and the ships unloaded. It was said in the Press that they were to be used for War purposes but this the Navy Department emphatically denied. The fact is that the United States Government is firmly resolved to give Germany no excuse whatever for saying that America took the first step to bring on war. Bernstorff, when he left, announced his firm conviction that the German Government would take no aggressive action and would leave the initiative to the United States. This may mean that the initiative is sending a ship into the forbidden zone. It may also mean sending an armed ship.

There seems to be little doubt that although the pacifist party in Congress is very strong, Congress will follow the initiative of the President and give him any powers he may desire to have. The country generally is convinced that the President will avoid war if it is possible to avoid it and that any steps which he takes will be purely defensive. The spirit of the country is rising. This does not mean that the desire for peace is less, but that the sense that something must be done to unify the nation and to prepare for war is growing. The celebrations on Washington Day, yesterday, were characterised by a great deal of enthusiasm. In the President's presence in this city a Senator declared most emphatically the necessity for union and for defence and denounced the action taken by Germany. The attitude of Congress is mixed because the members reflect the very mixed sentiment of their constituents. But I hear from the Middle States that there is a growing feeling and that there is a strong desire to follow the President's lead whatever that may be.

Before you get this letter you will know what action has been taken, if any. Unless an incident has occurred in the interval there will certainly not be war. The preparations here are being actively pushed forward mainly in the form of very large money votes and of the constant meeting of committees. I hear that a state of disorganisation has been discovered which might have been expected after a long peace in a Democratic country. Congress however seems ready to go to any length in the way of naval credits. The difficulty is in proceeding with the actual work of construction and with enlistment. With regard to the army, many people like Colonel Roosevelt have offered to raise large volunteer forces. It would be unpopular to send a large force abroad in case of war and I think this would be wholly out of the question. The utmost the United States would do would be to encourage enlistment. With regard to ourselves the courts have refused to give any decision as to the interpretation of the neutrality act and all our operations are hung up in spite of our protests. The general feeling is first of all that the United States should take no action except of a purely defensive character; secondly, that if this action leads to war the war should be an American war in defence of American interests, and thirdly, that no general compact should be made with any European Power. The competent authorities are perfectly aware of the vital necessity of not interfering with our supplies and as a matter of fact should war take place a close understanding will naturally ensue. It will be closer with France than with the other belligerents. Most people would be glad to have paid the debt owed by the United States to France both in money and in men, but an understanding with England or Russia would certainly not be liked. There appears to be an immense amount of indifference in the country at large; and in California, the only country which excites the fear or dislike of the population of Japan. In the West they have no pecuniary or other interests in the War and the West has much influence in Washington. The Middle West seems to be waking up and the East is undoubtedly in a considerable state of excitement. But on the whole the President will do all he can to maintain peace and it will be extremely unwise to count with any certainty on the United States entering into the War."

As this letter shows, the situation in America was rapidly becoming impossible. The President was waiting for Germany to declare herself by some " overt act " which would serve as a pretext for resolving his perplexities. Meantime American shipping congestion grew worse, and important branches of commerce and industry were at a standstill. The President however was reluctant to take any action which would look as if he contemplated war.

Germany quickly showed that she was in no way deterred by Wilson's vague menace of further action from carrying out her policy of unrestricted sinking. Indeed, on the very day when the President was delivering his address to Congress, an American vessel, the *Housatonic,* was sunk by a submarine, and it was followed to the bottom ten days later by the *Lyman M. Law.* But a more serious result, both to American merchants and to British imports, was the extent to which the German submarine threat kept United States vessels in harbour.

On 26th February, 1917, President Wilson appeared before Congress and asked its sanction for the arming of United States merchantmen. Diplomatic means of safeguarding American rights, he said had broken down, and

"there may be no recourse but to an armed neutrality, which we shall know how to maintain, and for which there is abundant American precedent.

It is devoutly to be hoped, that it will not be necessary to put armed forces anywhere into action. . . . I am a friend of peace and mean to preserve it for America as long as I am able. . . .

I am not now proposing or contemplating war or any steps that would lead to it. I merely request that you will accord me by your own vote the definite bestowal of means of authority to safeguard in practice the right of a great people who is at peace. . . .

It is in that belief that I request that you will authorise me to supply our merchant ships with defensive arms, should that become necessary, and with means of using them, and to employ any other instrumentalities or methods that may be necessary and adequate to protect our ships and people in their legitimate peaceful pursuits on the seas. . . ."

The House of Representatives carried the Bill to accord these powers with an overwhelming majority. But in the Senate a group of twelve Senators, led by Senators Stone and La Follette, took advantage of the rules of the House and of the fact that Congress was adjourning on 4th March, to block and hold up the Bill so that the House could not come to a vote on it. The immense majority of the Senators supported it, and 75 of them signed a manifesto desiring it to to be recorded that the Senate favoured the proposed legislation, and would have carried it if a vote could have been secured.

Several events occurred at about this time to stir public opinion in the States, and to stiffen the President's resolve. The first of these was in connection with Mexico. President Wilson had been in trouble throughout a good part of his administrative course with this country, and latterly the Germans had been fomenting trouble there in order to harass and pre-occupy the American Government, and keep its hands too full for it to intervene in Europe. They were suspected of stimulating General Villa to his insurrection in the spring of 1916, which forced the States to intervene with an armed force in Mexico, and to call out the National Guard to line the frontier.

On 19th January, 1917, Zimmermann, the German Foreign Secretary, sent a secret note to Von Eckhardt, the German Minister in Mexico, in the following terms: —

" On the first of February we intend to begin submarine warfare unrestricted. In spite of this it is our intention to endeavour to keep the United States of America neutral.

If this attempt is not successful, we propose an alliance on the following basis with Mexico.

That we shall make war together and together make peace. We shall give general financial support and it is understood that Mexico is to reconquer her lost territory of New Mexico, Texas and Arizona. The details are left to you for settlement.

You are instructed to inform the President of Mexico of the above in the greatest confidence as soon as it is certain that there will be an outbreak of war with the United States, and suggest that the President of Mexico, on his own initiative, should communicate with Japan suggesting adherence at once to this plan; at the same time offer to mediate between Germany and Japan.

Please call to the attention of the President of Mexico that the employment of ruthless submarine warfare now promises to compel England to make peace in a few months.

ZIMMERMANN."

This telegram was intercepted and deciphered by the British Naval Intelligence, the head of which, Admiral Hall, set up a special Department under Mr. W. H. L. Ewart (of the British Diplomatic Service) and a staff of University dons, who organised and conducted this Department with brilliant success during the War, and developed an uncanny efficiency in the unearthing of German secrets. The contents of the telegram were quietly communicated on 26th February to the American Government, and although Wilson was rather doubtful about publishing it, fearing it might over-excite popular feeling, it was given to the Press on 28th February. It roused a great deal of indignation in the States, and strongly reinforced the popular backing for strong measures by the President.

On 27th February, while the Bill to arm merchantmen was before Congress, the Cunarder *Laconia* was sunk without warning, and two American women lost their lives. On 12th March, the American *S.S. Algonquin* was sunk without warning, and on the same day the Secretary of State, Mr. Lansing, issued an announcement that the American Government had decided to place an armed guard upon all American ships passing through the danger zone. Thus the advance to " armed neutrality " proposed by the President on 26th February was definitely made. The further inevitable step to open hostilities was merely a matter of time—dependent upon Wilson's choice of the decisive " overt act " for which he had declared he would wait. The atmosphere during those days is reflected in the despatches which the British Government received from its Washington Embassy. On 21st March, the following cable was received: —

" Naval Attaché sent for last night by Beverley* who told him that while Cabinet is for war and is trying to force the issue, Wilson is rather hesitating about the attitude the new Congress may adopt. Beverley is loth to advise President as if he goes wrong he will lose influence with him. Briefly his whole conversation was to the effect that they are uncertain of Congress, and on the other hand they are anxious about danger of cooling down of public feeling. This would appear another example of the hesitation which throughout has marked the President's actions but every indication shows that war is inevitable."

Two or three days earlier, three American ships had been sunk within 24 hours, and 15 lives lost. House confirms in his Memoirs that at this time the American Cabinet was eager for a declaration of war without further delay, but that the President could not be induced to make up his mind. But on 21st March he determined to summon a special session of Congress for 2nd April in order to agree on future policy. On 23rd March a letter was written by one of our representatives in America who was in close touch with events at Washington: —

" It looks as if W. [Wilson] would in fact help us *pretty* well: almost all he can; but I think he will try not to be *technically* an ally. He's the most agile pussy-footer ever made, and when any

* Colonel House.

serious decision is taken, always tries to unload the responsibility on to someone else, and has been doing so this time again. But it does seem as if the Huns had fairly driven him into a corner out of which he can't possibly wriggle!

Unpreparedness, except as far as money goes, is quite complete. . . ."

This picture, as indeed all the accounts we received at this time from Washington, showed the President as being aware that before long he would be compelled to take sides with the Allies, but holding on until he was finally driven to action. House records that on 24th March, 1917, Mr. Lansing, the Secretary of State, came to see him in desperation, saying that he—

" Has no idea what the President has in mind to say in his address to Congress when it convenes. He saw the President yesterday, and tried in several ways to get some line upon his thoughts, but failed."

And on 27th March, when House went to tackle Wilson at Washington, and make certain that he was going to announce a state of war with Germany—which by now virtually existed—the President cried despairingly, " What else can I do? Is there anything else I can do?"

There was by this time no shortage of " overt acts " to determine the issue. On 21st March, the same day as Wilson issued his summons for a special session of Congress, another American vessel, the *S.S. Healdton,* was torpedoed and sunk with a loss of seven lives. The final problem which the President had to decide was whether to ask Congress to sanction a Declaration of War, or to put it to them that a state of war already existed, and ask them to sanction the necessary measures for carrying it on. House advised the second course, which Wilson in the end adopted.

On 2nd April, 1917, the President addressed the special session of Congress, and declared : —

" With a profound sense of the solemn and tragical character of the step I am taking, and of the grave responsibilities which it involves, but in unhesitating obedience to what I deem my con-stitutional duty, I advise that Congress declare the recent course of the Imperial German Government to be in fact nothing less than war against the Government and people of the United States; that it formally accept the status of belligerent which has thus been thrust upon it; and that it take immediate steps not only to put the country in a more thorough state of defence, but also to exert all its power and employ all its resources to bring the Government of the German Empire to terms and end the War."

Thus at last, more than $2\frac{1}{2}$ years after the World War broke out, Germany succeeded in forcing the United States to take sides against her. It must be conceded that the States had clung to their neutrality with almost incredible patience and persistence. Had it been possible, they would have stood aside from the conflict until the end. The unwavering stupidity of Imperial German statesmanship since the dismissal of Bismarck can have no more illuminating testimonial than this, that it brought a reluctant America into the War against her in the third year of the fight, as it had brought a reluctant Britain into action against her at the very commencement.

From the moment when Germany declared her unrestricted submarine warfare, America's entry was a foregone conclusion. That she waited two months before she would admit this fact must be attributed to the attitude of her President. The delay did not avert the issue. It only made it two months later before she began to prepare herself for the defence of her interests or the support of her associates in the struggle. And this was at a time when days were of vital importance; when it was becoming a matter of touch and go whether the cause which America was driven to espouse might not be finally defeated before she could put into the field an effective contingent for its defence. Had those two months been utilised for preparation, the American Army would have been adequately represented in the trenches in France at the end of March, 1918, and the Ludendorff coup would have failed at the outset.

When at last President Wilson made his declaration to Congress on 2nd April, 1917, he showed no uncertainty as to the issues. In the course of his speech he said : —

" We are accepting this challenge of hostile purpose because we know that in such a government, following such methods, we can never have a friend; and that in the presence of its organised power, always lying in wait to accomplish we know not what purpose, there can be no assured security for the democratic governments of the world. We are now about to accept the gage of battle with this natural foe to liberty and shall, if necessary, spend the whole force of the nation to check and nullify its pretensions and its power. We are glad, now that we see the facts with no veil of false pretence about them, to fight thus for the ultimate peace of the world and for the liberation of its peoples, the German peoples included; for the rights of nations, great and small, and the privilege of men everywhere to choose their way of life and of obedience. The world must be made safe for democracy. Its peace must be planted upon the tested foundations of political liberty."

These principles were excellent, and excellently expressed. The Allied democracies of France and the British Commonwealth had already borne the burden and been scorched by the heat of a thousand days in the "battle with this natural foe to liberty." They rejoiced at the advent of this powerful help from the greatest democracy in the world, at a time when troubles were multiplying. They perhaps might be excused for thinking that issues so clear now to President Wilson ought to have been apparent earlier to his eyes. They felt grateful in their hearts to the great American (Theodore Roosevelt) whose vision was so undimmed and whose sympathies were so sure from the outset of this grim struggle for international right.

During these last two months, while President Wilson was making up his mind, the Allies were naturally very anxious to keep in touch with the American movements of opinion. Among my papers is a letter sent to the British Government by Mr. J. Allen Baker,* the idealist Quaker who had devoted his life to the cause of Peace and who had just returned at the end of March, 1917, from a visit to the States. He gives an account of various interviews he had had during this critical time with leading people in the States, in particular with Colonel House, who expressed warm sympathy with the cause of the Allies, and was reassuring as to the certainty of America joining in with all her strength. "We want to be your reservoir for everything that America can supply—food, munitions, money and men—the latter to volunteer and go over as soon as wanted, or can be carried, and they can be trained on your side, if wanted."

"We are ready also to exchange inventions, naval or otherwise, and to co-operate with our United States Navy to rid the seas of submarines."

At an interview on 10th March, the Colonel gave Mr. Baker the following message for Mr. Balfour and me:—

"Tell your people to take no steps to hasten matters directly or indirectly; it only hinders instead of helping us. Let us alone and we will go all the faster. The only thing I fear is your trying to push us—the strongest pro-allies resent this."

To this he added a further message, reiterating what he had said at previous interviews:—

"Tell them we are with you to the finish of our resources in supplies, money and men. We are prepared to go the whole hog. They have no idea how soon we can raise a big army; many thousands of young men already have the necessary training— cadets in our military schools and State institutions. Texas alone, where I come from, has 200,000 men who can ride and shoot, and other Western States are in proportion. They are men of the calibre of your Canadians and Australians.

* The father of Mr. Noel Baker, M.P.

Give my warmest regards to my friends over there, Lloyd George, Balfour, Asquith and Grey. Tell them all I am thinking of them all every hour."

We had shown the greatest reticence in our references to America. We fully realised that Americans would resent any appearance of our trying to lure them into the War. This was appreciated on the other side.

We made preparations for joint action if and when the moment should have arrived for America to come into the conflict. I invited the War Cabinet to make such arrangements as were possible for securing the most effective co-operation with America if and when she came into the War. We decided that it was desirable that, in the event of intervention in the War by the United States of America, a special Mission should proceed to the United States for the purpose of notifying the relative importance of the various forms in which co-operation could be given. The War Cabinet recognised however, that it was essential for such a Mission to have at its head some individual of the highest consequence and authority, who would carry great weight with the United States Government, and that the dispatch of this Mission was contingent on the selection of such a leader.

When the news came through of President Wilson's decision, I read a summary of his Congress statement to the Imperial War Cabinet of 3rd April, and repeated to this larger meeting, which included the Dominion Premiers, my suggestion of sending a Special Mission to America. The Imperial War Cabinet agreed that the Secretary of State for Foreign Affairs should, in the same afternoon, sound the United States Ambassador in London as to the desirability of sending a special Mission to Washington, and should, in addition, explain to him the views of the War Cabinet as to the most effective form which the co-operation of the United States of America could take, laying special stress on the importance of putting into service the enemy ships in their ports, and of stimulating ship-building to the utmost possible extent.

It is difficult at this date to recall the effect which the accession of the United States to the anti-German forces had upon public opinion in the belligerent countries. The Allied countries were naturally heartened. The Allied cause was not prospering. The streets of Petrograd and Moscow were crowded with revolutionary workmen chanting endlessly a monotonous demand for Peace. The chant was murmured by the Russian soldiers behind and even in the trenches. On sea the submarine peril was at its height and the heart of our Admirals at its lowest. The knowledge that the great Republic had decided to throw her might into the struggle on our side lightened the deepening gloom. German opinion was curiously undismayed.

It was even contemptuous. The submarine attack was fulfilling the most sanguine expectations and they had complete confidence in its ultimate and speedy success. America had no army and before it could raise and train an army there would be no ships to carry it to Europe. What a joke! Germany laughed. War is an intoxication where the judgment of man reels like a drunkard from side to side. One moment it is exhilarated without reason to a pitch of delirious joy—the next it staggers with just as little reason into the ditch of despair on the other side. German public opinion, inebriated by truthful accounts of submarine triumphs, was now enjoying a moment of rapture. In such a mood an American Declaration of War did not count.

Arrangements were carried further at the War Cabinet meeting of 4th April, where Mr. Balfour was able to report that the American Ambassador, Mr. Page, had welcomed the idea of the dispatch of the contemplated mission. It was decided that the Head of the Mission must be someone of high status, well known to the American people, and that he should be accompanied by representatives of the Admiralty, War Office, Ministries of Munitions, Food and Shipping, and by the Governor of the Bank of England. On the following day it was settled that Mr. Balfour, the Foreign Secretary, should be the Head of the Mission. It was also decided to include representatives of British Labour in the Mission.

As to the terms of reference of this Mission, they were widely drawn to cover all negotiations with the Government of the United States about possible forms of assistance. On 10th April, at the request of the Cabinet, Mr. Balfour undertook to ask the President of the United States for assistance in the following ways.

He undertook to call the President's attention to the need of developing to the full the shipbuilding capacity of the United States of America. He would explain to the President the difficulty of inducing neutral vessels, even by insurance, to keep in our trade, and he would therefore ask the President whether the American vessels now engaged in coastal trade could not be diverted to the service of the Allies, and their places taken by neutrals.

In view of the desirability of getting as many troops as possible for the Western Front in a few months' time, and some troops immediately in order to show the United States flag and give the public in the United States of America a definite stake in the War, Mr. Balfour was requested to ask President Wilson:—

1. To send at once a few trained troops from the regular Army, amounting in numbers to a brigade, or, better still, a division, if that be possible.

2. To train as many troops as possible with a view to having an advance force to proceed to France, in say, August or September,

to occupy a quiet part of the line as part of the final stages of its training.

3. To consider the question of training in the later stages, whether in France or elsewhere. It was agreed that the early training should be done in the United States of America, having regard to the difficulties of shipping food on this side, and that the complete units should not come over until they are, at any rate, partly trained.

4. To consider whether it will be possible to send any drafts of recruits at once to join (a) British, (b) Canadian, or (c) French units. The War Cabinet realise that this may be impossible, but they regard it as the most valuable form of assistance that could be given, and one likely to lead to the most rapid conclusion of the War.

In addition Mr. Balfour was authorised to offer every possible assistance in training the new levies in accordance with experience gained in the present War, and he undertook to suggest to the United States Government that advantage might also be taken of French experience.

At the request of the Minister of Munitions, and with the concurrence of the Chief of the Imperial General Staff, Mr. Balfour undertook to impress on the United States Government the adoption of British type of guns, with a view to rapid production, closer co-operation, and facility of supply of ammunition.

Mr. Balfour undertook to impress on the United States Government the importance, with a view to meeting the increased requirements due to the formation of their own Army, of increasing the output and reducing civilian demands for steel.

Mr. Balfour would point out the desirability of not recruiting steel and other skilled workers. Dr. Addison undertook to send Mr. Balfour, before his departure, a list of difficulties encountered and surmounted by the Ministry of Munitions, including labour difficulties.

Mr. Balfour undertook to make special enquiry, and to telegraph to the War Cabinet, as to the importance of the Irish question in connection with our relations with the United States of America.

It will be seen that a good deal of care was devoted, not only to considering what help we could ask for the Allied cause from the United States, but what information from our own experience we could place at their disposal to help them in organising themselves for war.

The French Government also decided to send a Mission to America, with M. Viviani at its head. At the request of the French, we concerted with them arrangements for the visit of the two missions to the States.

Meantime, Admiral Sims had arrived in this country to discuss combined naval policy with the British Admiralty. He came in response to an informal and confidential invitation from us, sent as a result of discussions between the American Government and our Naval Attaché at Washington, and left America on 31st March, 1917, reaching this side on 9th April. When he left the States, they were nominally at peace with Germany. When he arrived here, they were at war. The Resolution of Congress, declaring a state of war, had, in the meantime, been carried by both Houses, and been signed on 6th April, 1917, by President Wilson. Admiral Sims therefore was able to enter forthwith upon serious and official discussions with our naval authorities at the Admiralty about combined naval strategy, in which he showed a clear intelligence and a practical ability and, what was just as important, an eagerness to co-operate, which were of the greatest assistance. He subsequently admitted that before he came over, Admiral Benson, the American Chief of Naval Operations, said to him: " Don't let the British pull the wool over your eyes. It is none of our business pulling their chestnuts out of the fire. We would as soon fight the British as the Germans!" Benson had a double dose of Anglophobia and it afflicted him and embarrassed us right through the War. But Sims himself did not share Benson's disease. Fortunately for both countries, he was not only a warm friend of this country, but he was a man of judgment and tact, and he got on extremely well with our sailors and statesmen. It is not too much to say that he won the confidence and affection of all with whom he came in contact. His advice was always timely and practical and as such highly valued.

On 10th April, the day after Sims arrived at Liverpool, another step towards naval co-operation with the States was taken, when an International Naval Conference took place at Hampton Roads, attended by the British and French Admirals of the Allied Fleets in the Atlantic. It was followed next day by a further conference at the Navy Department at Washington, and was a pronounced success. Every phase of the naval situation was discussed, and decisions were reached by which the United States Navy would take over the patrolling of the American Atlantic coast from Canada to South American waters, and protect the Pacific coast from Canada to Columbia; would hold squadrons in readiness to operate against any surface raiders; would at once send six destroyers to assist the anti-submarine campaign on the European side of the Atlantic; would detail armed naval transports to carry needed railway material to France; and would undertake several other special tasks of patrol and supervision. Admiral Jellicoe reported to the War Cabinet meeting on 16th April, that he had received a communication from the British Naval Attaché at Washington to the effect that the International Conference had been a great success, very largely owing to the efforts of Admiral Browning. He now anticipated that the naval co-operation of the United States of America would be whole-hearted and more effective than had been anticipated.

Mr. Balfour and the British Mission reached America on 21st April, 1917. The principal representatives with him were Lord Cunliffe of the Bank of England; Rear-Admiral Sir Dudley de Chair to represent the Admiralty and Major-General G. T. M. Bridges for the Army; while Sir Walter Layton represented the Ministry of Munitions. In response to a cabled enquiry about their progress, the following telegram dated 26th April, 1917, records their first impressions on the other side: —

" Our problem was that administration here was found to be in a very chaotic state. It has, therefore, not been possible to set on foot any formal discussions, and it was clearly intimated to us that, for the present, we were not desired to put forward any precise demands, but merely announce our readiness to give any information wanted on particular points. The actual arrival of the Mission, we are told, has been of very great service. As a consequence committees have been appointed to handle all the matters which our mission wants to deal with. Discussion is being urged by the State Department, and will, we hope, take place at latest on Monday. A review of the general situation and what progress has been made on various questions is being sent by Secretary of State.

I am confident that the Americans will take every possible step to help, but political considerations greatly hamper them and *they are quite unprepared.*

We continue to receive a welcome which surpasses the expectations of our best friends, and the personality of Balfour is carrying immense weight. It is, of course, a great asset to us.

I am of the opinion that we cannot force the pace any more at present and it might be harmful to try to do so, but we shall insist without hesitation on the urgency and importance, particularly of shipping issues."

This First British Mission to the States was in fact mainly concerned with preparing the ground for full co-operation and stimulating interest and good will. Mr. Balfour visited Chicago, Boston, and other great centres, and was everywhere received with enthusiasm. A letter from one of the members of the Mission to a colleague in this country describing their experiences, was passed on to me, and as it is interesting for its sidelights I take from it the following extract: —

" A list of the dinners and receptions would bore you, but two items on the programme stand out. The Mount Vernon expedition to George Washington's tomb where we went with the French, and Mr. B.'s speech to Congress yesterday. The first was remarkable, apart from the occasion and from one or two amusing little incidents between Viviani and Joffre (who quite eclipsed Viviani, much to the latter's visible annoyance), for the great attention paid in the Press to the significance of a British homage to G. W. I expect Mr. B.'s speech was reported in the *Times*. Viviani is a fine orator and perspired freely, but Mr. B. was splendid too and was a remarkable contrast by his quietness and distinction. People here still feel that England is the England of the War of Independence, and such animosity as there is is based more on old history than on, say, the Irish Question or our supposed airs. We missed the speech to Congress. I hear however, that Mr. B. was at his very best. His delivery and voice enchanted them, and it is the first time in history that the President has come down to the House on such an occasion. As he did not do this for the French it is certainly a hopeful sign of his attitude in the future. . . .

You hear a terrific amount of the Irish Question discussed and we get shoals of letters about it. With perhaps three or four exceptions they are most friendly in tone and take the line that the settlement of the Home Rule question will sweep away the last obstacle to a perfect unity between the U.S. and us. . . . The prosperity and wealth flabbergast you coming straight from England.

The French had a great reception but I think they were regarded more as a travelling circus than anything else. Kissing babies played a large part in their programme. Thank Heaven we held rather aloof from it all, as now people realise we are here on a serious job and appear to be cutting far more ice than the French.

I used to dislike this country, but now I am really converted. With all their defects they are very little different from us—whether they come of Irish or Italian stock. Even the Irish though pronounced Home Rulers, are not as bad as I imagined. Congress was, I hear, rather hesitating about asking Mr. B. down on account of the Irish members, but the latter went *en bloc* to the Speaker and told him they all very much hoped to see Mr. B. address Congress from the floor of the House and gave him an excellent reception. Even the Irish Deputation to whom he said nothing in particular, were enormously pleased at his receiving them, so Quinn told the Ambassador. . . ."

Perhaps the chief interest of this letter is the light it throws, not on the activities of the British Mission, but on the fact—a fact of the deepest historical significance—that this Mission began the process of filling up the chasm of suspicion and resentment rent between

England and the States by the great convulsion of the eighteenth century, and kept wide and deep ever since by political interests. It was the beginning of a real friendship and fellowship between us which had never existed before. But the letter I have just quoted shows that the attitude of semi-hostility in America had some justification and nourishment in British arrogance and affectation of superiority.

British democracy had a genuine admiration for the' great Republic—its struggle for freedom against the statesmen who successfully held the people down in Britain, as they failed to do in America —its heroes, notably Abraham Lincoln, as revered a name here as in America, its amplitude and equality of opportunity for all those who toiled and wrought intelligently. America was regarded by the British people as a whole with a wistfulness rooted in a consciousness of their own more restricted conditions. Dislike of America was confined to the snobocracy of Britain. Unfortunately, it was more vocal and quotable. John Bright alone amongst the statesmen of the past impressed America with the warmth of his appreciation for her qualities and for the importance of the part she must play in the progress of humanity. But Bright in the days of his famous American orations was just as detestable to our governing classes as George Washington or a Western tail twister.

The dawn of mutual appreciation which this letter reflects was one of the most valuable gains resulting from the World War, and may yet prove an asset of vital importance for achieving international order and securing the foundations of world peace.

Both President Wilson and Colonel House spent a good deal of time discussing war aims with Mr. Balfour.

Mention was made of the various secret treaties which had been concluded with Russia and Italy about territorial changes which it would be the Allied purpose to effect if successful, and Mr. Balfour described in detail these agreements and offered repeatedly to supply copies of the treaties to the President. This fact is very fully acknowledged in the contemporary notes of Colonel House, reproduced in his " Intimate Papers," and they placed beyond dispute the fact that Wilson was fully apprised by Balfour of the nature of these arrangements. Wilson was unwilling to discuss them in detail, because on the one hand it was not at that stage possible to modify the terms of the secret treaties, and on the other, he clearly hoped that by the time peace was made, America would have established herself firmly enough inside the counsels of the victorious Powers to be able to secure modifications if she so willed. He was obviously anxious not to be informed in writing of the details as he did not wish to be embarrassed by being " affected with notice." But the statement subsequently made by President Wilson before the Senate Foreign Relations Committee on 19th August, 1919, that " the whole series of understandings were disclosed to me for the first time when I arrived in Paris for the Peace Conference," is a palpable misrepresentation of the true facts. By that time however his health was seriously undermined and he was on the brink of his tragic breakdown. A lapse of memory was therefore pardonable. As it affects the relations between two great countries I feel bound to correct the mistake. Good faith is essential to good understanding between nations as well as individuals.

On 23rd May, 1917, Mr. Balfour and his party left Washington for Canada, where they made a short visit before starting back to England on 31st May. Before leaving the States, Mr. Balfour suggested that it would be desirable to establish a permanent British Mission there, to maintain liaison with the American Government, and co-ordinate the activities of the various British agencies at work in the States. For this post he suggested Viscount Grey. On 11th May the War Cabinet approved of my approaching Grey with this proposal. I did so, but was not able to induce him to accept the position. He urged that his eye trouble disqualified him for the discharge of the duties of so strenuous and responsible a post. The matter was therefore reconsidered on 25th May by the War Cabinet, who felt it was desirable to proceed as early as possible to reach a decision with regard to a business man being appointed as the head of all the Missions representing the different Departments concerned, such as the Admiralty, War Office, the Ministry of Munitions, the Shipping Controller, and the Food Controller.

It was pointed out that these Missions were at present without a responsible Head, with the result that there was some conflict of interests, and that, by co-ordinating their action, thus preventing overlapping and one Department bidding against another, far better results might be expected to ensue. Although the person selected would no doubt have a great deal to do with Americans, his primary duty would be to control our own operations, including recruiting, production, purchase, manufactures, transport, and the priority of the various claims.

Those Heads of Departments concerned who were present were of opinion that Lord Northcliffe might be a very suitable person for this appointment, and the War Cabinet decided that a telegram should be transmitted to the British Ambassador at Washington as well as to Mr. Balfour, asking them for an early expression of their views on the proposed appointment.

A satisfactory response was cabled by Mr. Balfour on 28th May, and Lord Robert Cecil was also able to report to the War Cabinet on 30th May that Mr. Page, the American Ambassador, was enthusiastically in favour of the suggestion that Lord Northcliffe should be appointed. Accordingly it was decided on that day that the Prime Minister should invite Lord Northcliffe to proceed to the

United States of America, not as a diplomatic representative, but as the Head of the Mission representing the different Departments concerned, for the purpose of co-ordinating their action.

Lord Northcliffe accepted the appointment without any fuss, and was anxious to start with the least possible delay. It was decided that before doing so he should have interviews with the Heads of the Departments whose affairs he would be watching over in the States, and that instructions should be drafted for his guidance. These instructions were considered and approved by the War Cabinet on 31st May, 1917. They were as follows: —

TERMS OF REFERENCE FOR LORD NORTHCLIFFE ON HIS APPOINTMENT AS HEAD OF THE BRITISH WAR MISSION IN THE UNITED STATES OF AMERICA

1. Several Government Departments—the Treasury, Admiralty, War Office, Ministry of Munitions, Ministry of Shipping, and Ministry of Food—have Missions representing their interests in the United States of America. These Missions are acting, more or less, independently, with the result that there is conflict of interests, and loss of effort.

2. The War Cabinet have decided that a man of high business qualifications, wide knowledge, experience, and energy, shall be appointed with direct responsibility to them as Head of a British War Mission, comprising the existing Departmental Missions, so that by generally supervising and co-ordinating their action he may prevent overlapping and secure better results. He will have full authority over all the Departmental Missions, and will have the right to dispense with the services of any member whom he may consider unsuitable.

3. His primary duty will be to control our own operations, e.g. the recruiting of British citizens, and the manufacture, purchase, and transport over land and sea of all supplies. He will determine the priority of conflicting claims among different Departments in these and kindred matters.

4. As Great Britain is not the only purchaser of supplies in the United States of America, it will be necessary for the Head of the Mission to establish and maintain the friendliest possible relations, not only with the United States Authorities, but also with the representatives of our Allies in the United States of America, to promote co-operation between them and to use his utmost endeavours to avoid competition between them, and the raising of prices.

5. On questions of importance arising directly out of his Mission, the Head of the Mission will have the right to communicate direct with the Prime Minister; on matters of less importance, or of Departmental detail, he will communicate to the head of the

Department concerned, either direct or through the Department's representative in the United States of America.

6. The Head of the British War Mission will keep the British Ambassador at Washington generally informed of the main lines of his action, and will profit by the Ambassador's advice and assistance, whenever these may be required.

7. The Head of the British War Mission will have full authority to establish Central Offices; to engage such staff as his experience may show to be necessary; and to concentrate or group in one or more buildings such of the Departmental Missions as, after investigation, he considers desirable.

8. The expenses of the Head of the British War Mission will be borne on the Treasury Vote. Arrangements will be made forthwith and communicated to the Head of the Mission by the Treasury for placing the necessary credits at his disposal.

The appointment of Lord Northcliffe was, of course, bound to raise a storm of criticism in certain quarters. There were considerable sections of orthodox and tabulated opinion in this country, not altogether confined to one party, to which he had long been a name of reproach for the dash and novelty of his journalistic methods. His newspaper circulations alone condemned him. There could not be a million genteel readers in the whole Kingdom—certainly not a million over and above the regular readers of the reputable Press. His appeal was to the " ha'penny public," that is, the common people, and must therefore be by methods not sanctioned by convention. The appointment of such a person to a highly honourable and responsible position therefore shocked many worthy people of conventional outlook. I observed the same shiver pass through orthodox circles when Lord Beaverbrook and Lord Rothermere were given important positions in the Government.

Overseas opinion was more friendly. But Northcliffe's scornful criticisms in the papers he controlled had also made him personal enemies, and even in high quarters in America grave doubts were felt as to the wisdom of the Cabinet's choice. One of our representatives in the States wrote to Mr. Balfour on 22nd June, and remarked in the course of his letter : —

" Incidentally, whatever induced the Government to send Lord Northcliffe here? May I explain, hastily, that this is not a question to which I expect an answer. It is merely a horrified note of exclamation. . . . The fact is, if I may say so, that I should think a man less a *persona grata* it would have been difficult to find, nor is it very wise, surely, to have as a governing representative, in any way, a man with a journalistic claque always rubbing the skin off its hands, in its exertions. I am quite sure of this, that there is in certain high quarters here a tendency to make a grimace, and ask what on earth he was selected for. I know I am not making a guess at this."

This last sentence was understood to refer to the President, who had an instinctive and cultivated aversion for men of the Northcliffe type.

Among those who took this view of the appointment was the British Ambassador, Sir Cecil Spring-Rice. He, in fact, nursed a personal grievance against the great newspaper proprietor, who had criticised him with unwelcome and perhaps unjust frankness. On 20th June, 1917, a few days after he arrived in the States, Northcliffe sent a letter for my information giving his first impressions and a note of his initial activities, and in this he recorded the reception he had received from our diplomatic representatives as follows:—

" My reception at Washington from the President downwards could not have been better.

My reception at the hands of the British Ambassador could not have been worse.

I was not received here on my arrival even by the British Consul, who excused himself by telling me that, although he knew I was coming, he had not been formally notified by the Embassy. The Embassy excused themselves by saying that they were told from London to keep the matter entirely secret.

It was not a secret, because I was met by the usual gang of reporters, photographers and cinematographers.

That didn't matter, but it necessitated my reading to the Members of the Commission my agreement with the Government* to prove my authority.

Sir Cecil Spring-Rice is an odd person. He is under the impression that anybody who comes here is a reflection on himself. He was rude to Sir Hardman Lever and ruder to me.

Here is an account of an amazing scene which took place in his room at the Embassy. . . .

In the evening—after introducing me all day to a number of the Ministers—Sir Cecil gave a dinner to me at the Embassy. He asked me in the afternoon to come a little beforehand as he wished to go into a few private matters. I went.

He was sitting at a table before his red boxes, and, suddenly looking up, produced a cutting from the pro-German *Evening Post* which had appeared prior to my arrival and which said, as far as I can remember, that it was odd that a man who had criticised the Ambassador in scare-heads and articles (a concoction) should be coming to this appointment.

* A characteristic interpretation of his instructions which could not have been incompatible with his status as an independent sovereign.

He then suddenly rose, looked at me in a very queer way, and pointing his finger at me, said: ' You are my enemy. Apart from these criticisms, you inserted four years ago an anonymous attack in the *Times* which nearly *killed me; and Lady Spring-Rice declines to receive you on that account.*' (There are, fortunately, other charming ladies in Washington!)

I replied that I had never criticised him. He rejoined that he was criticised in a letter to the *Times* for his prolonged absence from the Embassy and for travelling on German ships; that his absence was due to his health, and to diplomatic circumstances which he could not publicly explain.

I observed that as this was his view of my visit I proposed to leave the house, and I walked towards the door with the intention of so doing, when he rushed after me, put out his hand, and said: ' We have to work together whatever we may feel about each other.'

I accepted his hand and the incident was fortunately closed at that moment by the announcement of the French Ambassador. . . ."

It is fair to the British Ambassador's memory that I should give his own account of this exchange of civilities: —

" When Lord Northcliffe arrived he sent for Gaunt and Wiseman and complained very bitterly that the Embassy had not sent to meet him at the dock. He said it was an intentional insult and that he felt inclined to go home again. They explained to him that strict orders had been given to keep his movements secret. I had written him a letter to be delivered to him on his arrival, care of the Consul-General. As soon as Clive Bayley heard that he had arrived he delivered the letter, but he took care, according to our invariable practice, not to send any official to the dock. . . . I arranged that the President should receive him in audience. I could not accompany him myself as with other Allied representatives I was going to Princeton to receive a degree the day appointed for the audience. . . . On the day of his arrival Tom Spring-Rice and Gaunt met him at the station with a message from me that I was attending an entertainment in honour of the French Scientific Mission but would go at once to his lodging if he wished to see me that night. He preferred, according to his habit, to go early to bed. . . .

I hear he made an extremely favourable impression. He asked me how it was that the opinion seemed to prevail that there was hostility between himself and the Embassy. I told him that as far as I knew no one in the Embassy was responsible for this impression which certainly prevailed in the Press. The cause of it was no doubt the attacks made in his papers on several occasions against the Embassy. Before the War he had made in the *Times* an anonymous and libellous attack on myself which, being an official, I was unable to resent in the manner which my solicitors had informed me was open to me if I desired. During the War his paper in conjunction with the *Tribune,* had attacked the Embassy for not having imitated Count Bernstorff's policy as regards the Press. This also we had not resented and had made no reply, but of course the impression prevailed that his attitude towards the Embassy was as hostile now as it had been before I said that under present circumstances it would be childish and wicked to allow personal antagonisms to prevail over the public advantage. He entirely agreed and our relations have been very pleasant and friendly."

Because of the attack Northcliffe had already made on the Ambassador, the latter expected antagonism from Northcliffe. For the same reason Northcliffe was on the look-out for hostility on the part of Spring-Rice. Anticipated antagonisms do not make for cordiality. That explains the misunderstanding.

I have given these quotations because the incidents they describe are typical of the acute criticism which Lord Northcliffe's appointment called forth, and of the susceptibilities with which he had to contend. The critics did not sufficiently appreciate the fact that the very qualities of aggressive energy and self-assertion, which might have led Lord Northcliffe in his rôle of universal stirrer-up to lay about and prod far and wide, to the general exasperation of all in authority, might prove a useful stimulus to a nation in an emergency calling for a doubling of its energies. It was an occasion that gave scope to his great powers of organisation and drive. It is the wisdom of successful Government that it should harness powerful but unruly natural elements to some beneficent task.

In the event, Lord Northcliffe proved to be a striking success in his new rôle. Colonel House, who at first had his anxieties when he heard of the appointment, established with him from the outset of his visit a personal friendship which lasted till Northcliffe's death. In his " Intimate Papers " House says that : —

" To this task Northcliffe brought interminable energy and complete disregard of the impossible, gilded with never-failing good temper. ' You may rely upon me never to use minatory language,' Northcliffe cabled to Mr. Balfour towards the close of his mission. ' I have been dealing with these people for thirty years. Nothing can be gained here by threats, much by flattery and self-abnegation.' With all his experience in a life well stocked with problems he confessed that he had never confronted a task crammed with so many difficulties. ' The task is immense,' he cabled home, ' and ever growing. I have never worked so hard before.' . . ."

The references to Northcliffe in House's papers in the summer of 1917 all reflect increasing admiration and affection. " Northcliffe is doing good work," he cabled to England on 11th August, " and is getting along well with everyone."

Even Spring-Rice and the Embassy Staff found themselves getting on with Northcliffe far better than they had feared, and learned to modify their resentful prejudices against him. Just at the outset, when he was building up the organisation of the British Mission, and clearing out superfluous members of the staffs of the already established agencies, he perhaps roused more apprehension than confidence. But the keen spirits among our representatives soon learnt to appreciate the increased efficiency and smoother working of the machine under his powerful direction; and if Northcliffe could be ruthless, he could also be big-hearted and magnificently encouraging.

Among his most difficult problems was that of making satisfactory financial arrangements with America. By this time Britain had used up practically all the external credits which could easily be mobilised, and with the restriction alike of shipping and of civilian industry, our exports had fallen off very considerably. But our external purchases of munitions and supplies had vastly increased, and by this time we were also providing very extensive equipment and stores for our Allies on the Continent. American finance was not as yet accustomed to floating huge loans to the credit of foreigners. I have no doubt that as the money was being spent on purchases in the States, the sellers would have found means of raising adequate funds on the credit of such sound concerns as the British Empire and France, but there would have been difficulties and injurious delays. When America came into the War the financial situation was eased and we were enabled to borrow on credit from the States, without hypothecating our securities, but their Government, unused as yet to the immense expenditure of war were slow to realise how vast a financial support would have to be provided.

On 17th July, 1917, Northcliffe wrote to me as follows: —

" My dear Prime Minister,
    As you have landed me in the most difficult job I have ever had in my life, I want you to help me in every way in your power.
    Members of the Cabinet should understand that our attitude towards the United States Government is that of beggars. The majority of people with whom one comes in contact (though not the President or Colonel House) have no notion of the immense sacrifices we have made and are making. I do not know who was

responsible for the suppression of this information in the early days of the War, but whoever he was he has rendered our position here as beggars on behalf of the British nation, most difficult.*

It does not require any imagination to foresee great difficulty in obtaining money from the United States in the future. When we come to the actual point of contact with members of the Government and others from whom we have to ask, all that we have done seems, even if they know it, to be ignored by them. Such a strong partisan of ours as Higginson, the head of Lee, Higginson, the great bankers of Boston had no idea that we had advanced £1,000,000,000 to the Allies and that without prescription that they were to spend the money in England.

Mr. McAdoo and subsequently Colonel House plainly told us that they insist on knowing whether or not the supplies for which we are asking are of strict military necessity. The question has been put to Tardieu, the French Commissioner and myself—' Can you assure us that steel plates for England, wheat for France, coal for Italy, locomotives and railway material for Russia are essential to winning the War? If so what authority have you for saying so? We cannot go to Congress and ask for money unless we are able to assure them that every dollar is being spent for victory.' There is a general suspicion that much of the huge Russian locomotive and general railway order is in the nature of a ' job ' to put the Russian railways in order after the War.

Tardieu and I have had two long conferences on the subject and a further conference with Bakhnetieff, the Russian. Tardieu, as a Frenchman, is in a far better position to obtain money than are the English, but he sees the coming danger.

The Americans are not accustomed to our huge financial operations and it will be a very long time before they are. They regard the appropriation of one hundred and eighty-five million dollars which we have secured each month for four months as a tremendous sum. When I repeat the Chancellor's statement that war is costing us fifty million of dollars a day they are aghast.

Mr. Phillips, who brings this, knows the situation here better than any person I have met, and I part with him with the greatest reluctance. His going considerably weakens our organisation in Washington. I send him for two reasons: Firstly, in order that he may urge upon you the necessity of insisting that the British Government sets up a co-ordinating War Council, which shall state why each article of supply the Allies require is needed. If that Council be not set up, we shall one day be face to face with one of those abrupt actions on the part of the United States with which by this time we are, I presume, becoming accustomed. I

---

* It had been the policy of every belligerent Government including ours from the commencement of the War to withhold the publication of casualties.

refer to the denial of their promise as to the $400,000,000 loan and the seizure of the ships we are building here. . . .

Yours very sincerely,

NORTHCLIFFE."

He was naturally impatient of even inevitable delays. Not accustomed to being thwarted or to have his decision questioned or delayed, in his experience an order rung down the telephone had to be executed forthwith and he expected a report on the same telephone at latest in an hour's time. He had thus acquired a telephone mentality. He was now in a world where the autocrat had to submit to being an all-round subordinate. He was subject to approval of the Home Government—to acceptance or acquiescence by the American Government; to protracted conversations and negotiations —palavering instead of commanding.

In politics and diplomacy long intricate persuasion is an essential prelude to action. Lord Northcliffe had not even the experience of a provincial Mayor to guide him in the activities which depend more on co-operation than on dictation. For a man of his dictatorial temperament and experience he did well. He was not always ready to make allowances for conditions which neither he nor the British Government had power to control. There was a President waging reluctant war. To Wilson war was an abomination from which he had failed to escape. So it was to most of us. But his hatred of war took the form of throwing as little of his spirit, zeal and force into its prosecution as he could consistently with his responsibility as the chief executive officer of the Republic. He recoiled from any display of exceptional energy for accelerating the time when he could fling masses of American young men into deadly contact with the youth of Germany. To do so was to him to show indecent haste for the slaughter he had perforce ordained. Such a man was not easily dealt with by a dynamic and impatient personality like Northcliffe who had gone over to America purposely to help in the speeding up. There was therefore some friction and occasional misunderstanding. Northcliffe fretted and fumed and grizzled. But fortunately he directed his complaints to his own Government and restrained his impatience wonderfully when he came to deal with the proud, susceptible and unwarlike President. It is to the credit of Northcliffe's fundamental commonsense that he succeeded in winning the confidence and goodwill of a man with a temper as autocratic as his own, but with a mind, training, character and outlook essentially different from his own. His work in America exposed some of his pettiness but it also revealed something of his greatness. The fact that he did not permit his weaknesses to impair his work or imperil his mission is a proof of his genuine strength.

President Wilson, when he decided to declare war, had not yet resolved that it would be necessary for him to make war. I cannot help thinking that in his heart he hoped that the mere act of ranging the States with their infinite resources on the side of the Allies would lead to Peace before any American blood was shed. He thought Germany and her Confederates must now realise that he meant to fight if they did not give in and that it was hopeless for them to triumph against such a combination. He wanted that knowledge to sink well into their consciousness. I have no right to say that he deliberately dawdled his preparations in order to give the Central Powers full opportunity for reconsidering their attitude in view of the new fact. But that must have been an element in the otherwise inexplicable delay which occurred in preparing American troops for the battle line and throwing them into the fight when they were ready. The British Empire with a small regular army, when war was declared, contrived in six months to send 500,000 men into the battle-fields of East and West Most of these at the declaration of war had either received no military training at all or only training of the most elementary character. In six months and a bit the first American Division occupied a trench in a quiet sector of the line. Twelve months after the American entry into the War there was only that one divisional unit confronting the enemy. Within a year of Britain's declaration of war she had sent 900,000 men into action and her casualties numbered 170,000. Had it not been for the disaster of March, 1918, there is no one who can tell what President Wilson's notion was as to the time when his huge army should start fighting. He certainly could not have intended it to take any part in the actual struggle of 1918, for he had not provided it with the necessary weapons for that purpose. When his troops were compelled to fight owing to the critical situation created by the defection of Russia and the exhaustion of France, they did so with borrowed guns, for they had few of their own up to the end of the War. Aeroplanes and other essential equipment had also to be lent them. This is all the more inexplicable, having regard to the fact that the Allies had already organised a great deal of the industrial resources of America for the production of war material. Abraham Lincoln was a lover of peace. He was one of the most humane rulers that ever presided over the destiny of any nation. It must have wrung his kindly heart to shoot down honest men, especially amongst his own countrymen, in any quarrel. But having been forced into war, he concentrated all his energy and genius on the measures that could alone ensure victory for the sacred cause he had undertaken to champion. But Wilson was not a Lincoln.

The shipping matter referred to in Lord Northcliffe's letter was the decision of the American Government to commandeer a number of ships then building in the States to the orders of the British Government, and others that had been ordered by the Australian

Government. The incident illustrated the complex issues which arose between our two countries during the War. Our own shipping was being rapidly sunk, and there was no question of increasing our mercantile marine, but merely of replacing a part of our war losses. But there were in the States powerful influences which had long been jealous of our shipping supremacy, and saw in the large shipbuilding orders we had placed there the menace of a still further increase in our mercantile fleet. While America was neutral there was no excuse for refusing our orders for ships. But as soon as she entered the War, they saw a good pretext for retaining these vessels under the American flag, by requisitioning them for the carriage of supplies and troops.

On 21st August, 1917, Lord Northcliffe sent me a long cable about this matter. It was as follows:—

" With reference to the threat of immediate confiscation of the ships building for us here, I should not interfere with a question properly concerning the Ambassador, but Spring-Rice is absent on holiday at Woodshole, Mass.

A crisis has now been reached in the situation. The *War Sword* at the Union Iron Works, San Francisco, is one of our steamers and will be ready for delivery on Saturday. Food-stuffs and fuel oil have been procured as cargo for her and are waiting to be put on board. Her skipper and officers were sent out from England and they are now ready to join the ship.

The Shipping Board were asked by Royden to order the builders to hand the vessel over to us. He is afraid, however, that their answer may be nothing more than a temporising one, as the question is still unsettled whether we shall be allowed to take possession.

There are several other vessels also nearing completion in regard to which this question will very soon arise. . . ."

Northcliffe proceeds to quote a characteristic protest which Hughes, Premier of Australia, had sent to Colonel House. It was as follows:—

" 1. The ships in question are for the Commonwealth Government and not for private firms.

2. For all practical purposes Australia is an independent nation.

3. During the War it has played a distinguished part and has now a large force at the Front.

4. The intention is to use these vessels exclusively for War work and for trade between Australia and America, and for carrying wheat and flour to Britain and the Allies.

5. That it would be an unfriendly act to confiscate these ships which belong to another nation, which for three years has been gallantly fighting, and the act would be so regarded by Australia.

6. That we cannot agree to lease these vessels as this is not an acceptable alternative.

7. That trade developments between the two countries would be impaired if American Government refuses to exempt these vessels from requisition." (ends)

Northcliffe ends his message by saying that: —

" If H.M. Government were to send a strong and earnest protest to the United States I cannot believe that America would perpetrate a deed which would always be regarded as an example of unfriendly commercialism.

A splendid fight at Washington has been put up by Royden who assures me that if the President were emphatically told than confiscating Allies' ships purely to gain commercial advantage is an action not in conformity with the best traditions of civilised States, Wilson might alter his opinion.

The emphasis he lays on moral issues is well known to those about him. The issue is entirely in his hands. Without a doubt he is much under the influence of McAdoo, his son-in-law, who is trying hard to secure political prestige as he may possibly in 1920 stand for the Presidency.

If we act at all we must act quickly. Anti-British prejudice in America has to be met and the Germans are directing powerful propaganda against our ships. There is great ignorance at Washington of the enormous sacrifices which the British mercantile marine has made during the War. If affairs were in my hands I would lodge an urgent protest with the President without delay.

I hope you will pardon me for exceeding my proper functions as this matter is urgent and our Ambassador is, as I said, twelve hours distant from Washington.

Even if our protest is unsuccessful, we shall at least have placed it on record and the next time the United States will not I think attempt to take such action without very careful consideration.

In considering this matter, I think you might have before you a list of the ships which are built and are being built in the U.S.A. similar to the one supplied to Caird by the Ministry of Shipping early in June.

There is the prospect of several other difficulties in the future. For example, our retention of the German African Colonies is an anxious point. It would be well to send Smuts here to state our case as otherwise Americans may fail to understand why the retention of these colonies is essential for us."

This telegram was considered by the War Cabinet on 22nd August, 1917. As regards Lord Northcliffe's suggestion of an earnest and vigorous protest from me to President Wilson, Lord Robert Cecil urged that in his opinion it would be unwise to adopt Lord North-cliffe's suggestion, having regard to the pledges given by Mr. Balfour when in America. Moreover, if the United States had decided to take over the ships, a protest might not prove effective and might only cause irritation and friction. He continued that Mr. Balfour believed that the best chance of persuading the United States Government to allow us to keep the ships was to appeal to their sense of justice and goodwill, as had been done in his letter of the 16th August to the American Ambassador.

The Shipping Controller pointed out the very serious blow to our prospective tonnage programme—amounting to a loss of some 4,000,000 tons carrying capacity a year—if we failed to get delivery of the steamers. Recent public pronouncements as to our prospective gains in tonnage had taken full account of the American ships. The ships were urgently needed during the critical period between now and next year's harvest.

The possibility was suggested of negotiating with the United States Government on the basis of our giving back the vessels after the War.

Mr. Salter, of the Ministry of Shipping, who had just returned from Washington, where he had had an interview with President Wilson on this subject, said that the President was at that time in favour of requisitioning the ships, but had come to that conclusion under pressure from Mr. Denman, the ex-head of the American Shipping Board, and on grounds that were not really relevant, and he had promised to reconsider the question. It must be remembered that there was an element in the United States of America that was very jealous of our Mercantile Marine, and also that the United States Army and Navy were anxious to carry their troops and stores to France in their own ships.

The War Cabinet decided to support the policy expressed in Mr. Balfour's letter of the 16th August to the American Ambassador, of appealing to the American sense of justice and goodwill. They asked the Acting Secretary of State for Foreign Affairs after consultation with the Ministry of Shipping, to telegraph in this sense to His Majesty's Ambassador at Washington, at the same time pointing out the serious blow that would be caused to our tonnage programme in the event of requisition.

At the War Cabinet meeting of 24th August the matter was further discussed, and we decided to put forward in the last resort the suggestion of restoring the ships to America after the War, or of time-chartering them. A communication in this sense was wired to Northcliffe, who replied: —

" I hear from House that he is corresponding with the President about confiscation of the ships.

Your letter and parts of one which I wrote to House have been handed to President. Untiring work being done by Royden. Should the vessels be saved in part or entirely, it will all be due to his tireless efforts and unquenchable good humour. He is a tower of strength to this mission, and I trust I may keep him permanently with us."

Unhappily, despite our appeals and the strenuous efforts of Northcliffe and Royden in America, the influences antagonistic to British shipping interests won the day with the President, and 150 ships which were then building to British orders in the States were confiscated by the American Government and added to its Government Fleet. The authorities there cherished an ambitious project of developing a large, nationally-owned mercantile marine. Before the War, America possessed about one-eighth the sea-going merchant tonnage that Britain had, but during the latter part of the War the Emergency Fleet which she constructed grew until it was far greater, alike in numbers and in tonnage, than the privately-owned American shipping. But the post-War history of this fleet has not been very cheerful. The American Shipping Board retained it for a time after the War, and suffered very serious losses through the slump of ship-values and the cost of operation. Even when full allowance had been made for the strategic or economic value of a national fleet, it was still more of a liability than an asset. After the War the Hudson River became a knackers' yard.

Reverting to Lord Northcliffe's letter of 17th July, 1917, it may be of interest to note the position of the other principal matter he there dealt with, viz., the financial arrangements between Britain and America.

The Allies encountered two obstacles in their financial dealings with the American Government. The first difficulty was to bring the American Government to appreciate the scale upon which war expenditure was being incurred. They had some notion that considerable orders had been and were being placed with factories, workshops, grain merchants, but they had never totalled it up or considered how the money was found to pay the contractors. The Administration deliberately turned a blind eye to these profitable transactions which made America prosper and the revenue swell. When the Allies came to ask the American Treasury for credit to pay the enormous weekly bills run up for war material in the States, that Department was shocked at the amount that was being spent. It suspected not only extravagance but something worse. It was convinced that the Allies under the guise of war expenditure meant to equip themselves for future trade and industry at the expense of the American lender. They were especially jealous of orders for railway material and locomotives or anything to do with ships. It was difficult to persuade them that Russia was on the verge of irreparable catastrophe for lack of the former and that the whole of the Allies might be beaten owing to the shipping shortage, long before America was ready to fight.   Allies have always been mistrustful of each other's ulterior motives.   I was told during the War that one distinguished Frenchman was convinced that the English having once again recovered possession of Calais never intended to surrender it at the end of the War.   An equally distinguished Englishman was just as firmly persuaded that the French meant to annex Greece in order completely to dominate the Mediterranean and place the British communications to the East at the mercy of France.   Jealousy is a foolish monster.   America was altogether doubtful of Europe.   She had a romantic affection for France because of the memories of Lafayette and Rochambeau.   The shades of these champions of American liberty constituted an important part of the theatrical properties of every French Mission to the States and assured to every French envoy a favourable reception.   But historical memories of England were not such as conduced to any sentimental glow.   For Russia, democratic America had a definite repugnance.   The Russian autocracy was a tyranny of the worst kind.   France was a Republic and therefore free, but Russia and Italy and ourselves were classed with Germany and Austria in a favourite demagogic phrase as " the effete Monarchies of Europe."   As we had to take the leading part in the borrowing for our Allies even more than for ourselves, there was a reluctance to be in any hurry to accommodate us.   France might have fared better had she taken the lead.   But although they had never shown any disposition to recoil when there was fighting to be done, they are more inclined to hang back when there are any debts to be incurred or paid.   We were therefore in the forefront of the Treasury queue and American opinion was apprehensive of our designs.

But there was another difficulty of a practical rather than a sentimental kind.   America had never lent money abroad on any considerable scale.   When Lord Reading visited the States in 1915 to raise a loan for the purpose of financing our contracts, these American financiers shuddered at his proposal to fix the amount borrowed at £100,000,000.   They regarded it as an example of megalomania which sprang from War fever.   When he succeeded, with much help as to a substantial portion from the contractors who would ultimately receive all, it was regarded as one of the greatest British triumphs in the War.   Now the foreign borrowings were to reach $4,000,000,000 and the Treasury at Washington shrank from the magnitude of the loan.

On 5th July, 1917, our Ambassador at Washington, Sir Cecil Spring-Rice, wrote a letter which throws a light not only on the financial difficulties, but on others which were impeding action at that date : —

" The situation here is much as it was in London in Canning's time when the Russian Ambassador used to call at the Foreign Office being ignorant of French and slap his pockets and say ' aurum aurum.' As England was the sole financial resource of the Allies in the war against Napoleon so the United States are our sole resource from the financial point of view at the present moment. The Secretary of the Treasury has had several conversations with Crawford, Northcliffe and myself recently. He says that Congress authorised the loan of three billions immediately after the declaration of war. The country did not realise the necessity of this vast expenditure but accepted the President's recommendation. The idea was to help the Allies in buying supplies for the continuation of the War. The country did not realise the situation in which the Allies actually were and that financial help was needed not only for future expenditure but for the obligations incurred in the past. The time was rapidly approaching when the sum authorised would be expended. The Secretary thought that it would be a very difficult matter to get a new appropriation from Congress. It would be absolutely impossible unless he were able to explain exactly how the money already voted had been expended. This he was totally unable to do at the present as full explanations had not been afforded to him. Furthermore, he felt that loans should be utilised like battalions in a battle where they were most needed and where they would have the greatest effect. This was impossible unless he knew accurately what was the actual state of affairs from the military, naval, political and financial points of view. I said that I believed a request had already been made to the United States Government to send someone of high authority to take part in the deliberations of the Allies. He said that besides this it would be desirable for the British Government to send someone of authority over here. I pointed out that Sir Hardman Lever was Financial Secretary of the Treasury, that Lord Northcliffe came here with full powers for general discussions and that Sir Richard Crawford was Financial Adviser to the Embassy with the rank of Minister. It is clearly undesirable that anyone should be sent whose presence is not definitely asked for by the President himself. Lord Northcliffe is making an excellent impression and is seeing a great number of prominent persons here. He must be collecting a great deal of valuable information. There is no objection to him on the part of any official and the President has given him a very favourable reception. . . . The fact remains that the President did not ask for his appointment, and being known here not as a statesman but as a very influential proprietor of newspapers his opinion would not carry very great weight in itself, however much he may be liked and respected. He is on very good terms with M. Tardieu, who is an old friend, and this is a very important matter at the present moment. This is written to show you that the question of the direct representation of the British Government here is not entirely solved by sending Lord Northcliffe. The only way it could be solved is by taking the President's wishes which it will be extremely difficult to do. As I have reported to you by telegraph Crawford and I were received in audience by the President who treated us with great kindness. He impressed on us the importance of making absolutely full and frank explanations to Mr. McAdoo in whose hands lay the administration of finance. He used the same arguments as have been used by Mr. McAdoo to show the necessity of having full knowledge of the situation. I told him how conscious we were of the immense importance of the rôle which would now have to be played by the President of the United States. He admitted the fact, which he regretted. He said he had not wished it. I imagine that what he said represents very much the feeling of thinking men here. The United States entirely against its own will has been driven into the War, partly by the peril in which the cause of democracy was placed and partly by the individual wrongs perpetrated by Germany against the United States. Suddenly after going into war the United States realises the immense importance and the great gravity of the situation. A very strong element in the public is urging the Government that it is hopeless to fight against the predominance of Germany in Europe, that the United States should keep all their resources for their own defence and assume in the new world the same predominance assumed by Germany in the Old. Voices came from some of the Allies claiming that they had borne the burden and heat of the day for the sake of the United States Government and that the United States Government was under the sacred obligation of repaying the debt. To this it is urged in reply that it would have been perfectly easy for the United States to admit the legality of submarine warfare as a new form of warfare for which there was no precedent and to hold aloof from the European contest. It is to be expected that at the first disaster these voices will become louder and more insistent. The extraordinary openness and boldness of the German language Press leaves no room for doubt what will be the attitude of Germans and pro-Germans here. Their power is already shown in the outbreaks in the labour world. A Senator from Arizona told me that the copper workers are receiving more than $5 a day with a rise in pay dependent on the rise in the price of copper. The I.W.W. acting on the instigation of Sinn Feiners, led by Larkin, were organising strikes. Strikes also threatened among the dockers and shipping men. The Mexicans working in Texas are being urged to quit for fear of enlistment, leaving the cotton fields without the necessary labour. The Irish are especially active under the leadership of

priests who for instance are warning the Irish cooks not to economise food because it would help the English.

Congress is very reluctant to pass a Food Control Bill and there
is every prospect of a long delay. *There seems no likelihood that
Congress will adjourn at any near date. There is much uncertainty
still as to the form of organisation which will be adopted in many
Departments most important in the conduct of the War. There
seems to be a general agreement that public opinion is still largely
apathetic as to the War and that it is not yet realised what are the
obligations incurred by the U.S.G.* We cannot explain this matter
which it is for the Americans themselves to explain to each other.
But we should realise the great difficulty in which the Government
is placed and especially with regard to public opinion and Congress.
The President so far has been able to induce Congress to accept
his measures in the main because Public opinion is on his side. But
he cannot go further than public opinion wants him to. The
situation may change when the casualty lists arrive. They may
serve as an incentive or as a deterrent. You will have seen the
situation as it existed when you were here and the Government
seems to have implicit confidence in your thorough sympathy and
understanding."

A letter from Sir William Wiseman to the Foreign Office, dated
7th August, 1917, contained notes of a recent conversation he had
held with President Wilson. Sir William Wiseman was a young
officer who, after being invalided from the Western Front, was
attached to our Embassy in Washington, where he developed remarkable ability as a diplomat. By this time he was beginning to play a
considerable part in smoothing over relations with the American
Government. On the financial issue, these notes ran as follows: —

" With reference to finance, the President expressed his opinion
that *the recent crisis* looks as though it was capable of solution.
He urged strongly that more information, both as to actual
financial needs and general policy of the Allies, must be given to the
U.S.G. He pointed out that there was much confusion and some
competition in the demands of the various Allies. Specifically, as
far as the British are concerned, he pointed out that there was no
one who could speak with sufficient financial authority to discuss
the whole situation, both financial and political, with the Secretary
of the Treasury. All these things should be remedied as soon as
possible."

This question of some distinguished representative proceeding to
America to discuss finance became increasingly important, and after
further consultations with Colonel House, Lord Northcliffe cabled
us as follows on the 15th August: —

" I learned from House that a very warm welcome will be given to Bonar Law if he can pay a long enough visit to discuss financial future of War, and make settlement. His coming would be held a great compliment by U.S.A. Recent British differences are blamed for tardiness in reaching decision on this issue.

If delay continues I think we shall have a sharp conflict with McAdoo. . . .

Bonar Law or else Reading should come as early as possible with full power to act. I can settle the whole matter alone with Crawford, Lever and Blackett, but House demands the presence of a politician.

Enemies of McAdoo complain that, to use an American phrase ' He is spending money like a drunken sailor.' His political future absolutely depends on handling successfully this financial situation, especially loans to Great Britain."

Bonar Law being unable to leave his Parliamentary responsibilities, the Cabinet suggested Reading should be invited to go. Bonar Law cabled Lord Northcliffe as follows: —

" The suggestion that I should go arrived yesterday from Lever but it would be very hard for me to absent myself and in any case I could not stay more than a week or so. I think in view of your message the best plan is to arrange if possible for Reading to go and as soon as I hear that you agree I will see him about it. The Premier went off to-day for a week's rest."

The matter was further discussed at the Cabinet Meeting of 28th August, 1917. A telegram was dispatched to the British Ambassador intimating that the War Cabinet had decided in view of the difficulties which had arisen in connection with the financial situation, to ask Lord Reading to go out on special mission to the United States. He would have their full authority to negotiate with the Administration and to decide on behalf of His Majesty's Government any questions that might be raised. Though primarily concerned with finance, he would be authorised to deal with any subject which he considered desirable for the proper discharge of his mission.

Meanwhile the tension in our financial relations with the States was increasing, and on 7th September, 1917, Lord Northcliffe sent me the following cable: —

" May I suggest that the Press be circularised with a warning of the very delicate condition of Anglo-American finance at present and urged to make any reference to Reading's visit as tactfully as possible.

If you let Press know that funds are dealt to us by U.S.A. in driblets and that our allowance was suddenly cut down this week, they would fully understand the essential importance of Reading's mission. If I myself were in charge I should publish the whole truth. The difficulties of Reading's task are as great as those of Royden whose success is undoubtedly due to the fact that he is liked by Americans and is the sort of Englishman who can talk bluntly to them without offence.

The present agitation in the minds of the public here over the enormous sums which the Allies and particularly England require must have been foreseen by Colonel House, who always sees three months ahead.

The subject of the loans to the Allies and particularly those to England is being given much space by current newspapers.

It was obviously foreseen by House that the only Englishman who could succeed would be someone popular with Americans.

I am sure I shall have Balfour's support for stating that the personal equation is everything in this country. The presence of the Lord Chief Justice will give pleasure in America. I hope very much that his very difficult work will not be hampered by blunders in England."

The financial problem which had arisen in our relations with America can be briefly summarised. During the period between the outbreak of the Great War and America's entry in April, 1917, Britain had carried out very extensive purchases in the States, of food, munitions and other war supplies needed by herself and her Allies. These had been paid for in part by British exports, in part by exports of gold, of which we sent £190,000,000 to America before 1st April, 1917, in part by mobilising American securities held in this country and sending them to the States. Altogether in the course of the War we sent gold and securities to America totalling £600,000,000 in value. When these ran out, we arranged to borrow money in the commercial loan market in the States, the total of which amounted to over £300,000,000. These loans we have since repaid.

By the time America came into the War, our capacity to produce further securities to sell in the States to pay for our purchases there was approaching the end. We had not only been required to buy our own equipment; we had also been the main financial resource of our Allies, and up to the time when America joined in, we had advanced to them sums totalling £827,000,000. Including these advances, our total expenditure during the War, up to April, 1917, amounted to £4,300,000,000. By this time the War was costing us at the rate of seven million pounds a day.

The United States, on entering the War, were quite unprepared to take any large share in military operations, but they declared themselves ready and eager to place their immense financial resources at the service of the common cause. We were given to understand that until their men were ready they would fight with their money, and we naturally welcomed the prospect of their taking over from us the task of financing the external purchases of our Allies and ourselves. Our own capacity for mobilising credit for them and for ourselves had been strained almost to breaking point. We had hitherto been finding both men and money to the limit of our available resources.

President Wilson asked Congress to sanction liberal loans to the Allies, and Congress promptly passed the first Liberty Loan Act, for raising a loan of £1,000,000,000, of which £600,000,000 were to be used to lend to the Allies. But America declined our suggestion that she should take over from us the whole responsibility for financing the foreign purchases of our Continental Allies. She would only lend money to finance their expenditure in the States, and we had to continue to find credits for their other external purchases, including those from Britain. Much of what we ourselves supplied them we had to replace by fresh purchases in the States, so that the strain on us continued to be very severe, and consequently the credits we were forced to ask for from America were on a large scale.

Prior to America's entry, we had arranged our financial matters in the States, including the raising of loans on the American market through the firm of J. P. Morgan & Co. When the American Government became the new source of credits, the problem arose of arranging our transactions through this new agency, which was inexperienced in its task. After much discussion, the Government of the States decided to set up a special Commission at Washington, through which all purchases made in the States by ourselves and by the other Allies should proceed. An agreement to this effect was signed by the Secretary of the Treasury, and the representatives of Great Britain, France and Russia, on 24th August, 1917. The arrangement greatly eased the situation. Prior to finding this solution the American Treasury had been irritable with anxiety about the complexities of their new, unwonted and unaccustomed responsibilities.

Lord Reading reached America in mid-September, and his arrival made a further marked improvement in the Anglo-American financial relations, Lord Northcliffe cabling home on 21st September, 1917, the results of an interview with Colonel House about the situation, said:—

" House told me in the course of an interview of one and a half hours that the financial situation would eventually be eased by the coming of Reading and his experts.

There is gratification also in Government circles here at the quality of the experts sent by us to aid their Air Department, which is the object of great interest to both Government and people.   . .

House was most emphatic that we should arrange British representation here so as to avoid all risk of friction by strengthening either the Embassy or Mission.

I recommended him to talk the matter over with Reading, which he will probably do. He will be in New York all the winter and I expect to see him constantly.

Tireless work being done by Reading under heavy handicaps. I had to see McAdoo and Crosby in Washington about the trouble which has cropped up between newspapers of America and Canada about their raw material supplies. U.S.A. journals declare that they are being overcharged by Canada in contradiction of the spirit of U.S.A. which is making one price for materials, whether for America or the Allies.

Reading's advice and assistance cordially acknowledged by both men but Crosby complains that by obtaining $50,000,000 for purchase of Canadian wheat Reading has made a breach of their fundamental principle that all the money advanced to the Allies should be expended in the States.

In my opinion anyone not possessed of Reading's charm, ability and tact in dealing with these difficult people could not have brought off this achievement. By his frankness and lack of concealment, his sympathy and understanding for their worry over the daily Allied demands for money, and trouble with politicians and Press, Reading will, I am convinced, do all that any man can for us. The official visit to Canada which I spoke of in previous messages will take place on Tuesday."

In November, 1917, Lord Northcliffe returned to this country in order to attend the Conference of the Allies which opened in Paris on 29th November, and Lord Reading also came back for this Conference. By this time the multitudinous arrangements between the Allies and America had got into fairly smooth working order. The first detachments of United States troops were now in France.

The actual military effort of America took place mainly in the following year; but a beginning was made in 1917 which furnished to the Allies, and particularly to the French, a visible proof that their expectation of American help was not groundless. The first United States division reached France on 25th June, 1917. By 30th September, the strength of the American Expeditionary Force in France had reached 61, 531 (i.e. 4,406 officers and 57,125 men). Their training for the warfare of the Western Front went on behind the lines, and in October the 1st Division was advanced enough to be placed, on 21st October, 1917, in the line on a quiet sector of the French Front, between Nancy and Luneville. It suffered its first casualties on 3rd November, 1917, when the Germans raided one of its posts, and three Americans were killed, five wounded and twelve captured. By 31st December, 1917, the total strength of the American Expeditionary Force that had reached Europe was 9,804 officers and 165,080 men. These included four divisions in various stages of organisation and training. For their heavier equipment they had for some time to rely mainly on the French and British. On 28th February, 1918, General Pershing pointed out in a telegram to his Government that " as a matter of fact there is not to-day a single American-made plane in Europe." And until a much later date, practically all their artillery was supplied by the French and ourselves. Partly this was due to their complete lack of equipment for war on a European scale, and partly to the acute shortage of shipping, which hampered the bringing of supplies across the Atlantic. How the situation was transformed by the time that hostilities ceased belongs to a later stage of my narrative.

CHAPTER LV

THE IMPERIAL WAR CABINET AND CONFERENCE

BEFORE the end of October, 1916, the Dominions had raised 673,808 men for the service of the Empire in the War. India brought this figure to well over a million. Had it not been for the readiness with which Dominion and Dependency sprang to our aid in the lean years of 1914-15, the Allies would have been hard put to it to pull through before Italy came in, and at a time when the forces at the disposal of the Central Powers were at their best. Apart from the contingents sent from the Indian Regular Army, this impressive Imperial contribution was voluntary. Not a squad would have appeared in response to any order issued from Downing Street. It was a spontaneous rally to the flag which was marching to battle in a war when the whole Empire felt our cause was just. The Dominions even anticipated every appeal for help. So did some of the Princes of India. These great countries had no responsibility for the policy or diplomatic methods that preceded the War. They were, therefore, free to judge for themselves whether they were under any moral obligation to risk the lives of their citizens in an active participation in the conflict.

The Canadian Government, watching events from thousands of miles away, foresaw that war was inevitable, and on the 31st July, the day before Germany declared war on Russia, began to lay its plans for the mobilisation of its forces. On 3rd August, the enrolment of volunteers began. As soon as our ultimatum expired, a message was sent on behalf of the Canadian Ministry: " Canada stands united from the Pacific to the Atlantic in her determination to uphold the honour and traditions of the Empire." Party conflicts immediately ceased. Sir Robert Borden, the Premier, of British stock, and Sir Wilfrid Laurier, the veteran leader of the Opposition, of French lineage, joined hands. The official call for troops was promulgated throughout the Dominion on 5th August, and in one week recruiting had to be stopped because more than 100,000 men had already offered themselves. The alacrity and enthusiasm shown by the premier Dominion were repeated in Australia and New Zealand.

South Africa had difficulties of her own. It was only 12 years since the Boer War—a fierce struggle between two white races, which devastated South Africa—had been brought to an end. The defeated race were in power and their gallant Commander in the field was Premier of the new South African Commonwealth. Germany had sympathised openly with the Boers in their desperate fight against the British Empire. When war was declared by the Empire against Germany, General Botha had to cope with formidable dissensions amongst his own people. A rebellion led by some of the most cherished and trusted leaders of the Dutch population broke out against his decision to take sides with the Empire. I recollect a meeting I had with General Botha during the Imperial Conference of 1911 in London. He represented the South African Union as Prime Minister. One morning he breakfasted with me, and after some interchange of reminiscence about the old pro-Boer controversies, he expressed deep gratitude and admiration for the fullness with which the British Government had granted self-government and freedom to a people so recently in arms against them. He then expressed a very definite opinion that sooner or later there would be war with Germany. He thought everything pointed in that direction. I then said to him, " If there is trouble, what will you do?" He said, " I will keep my word and stand by the Empire. As soon as war is declared I will lead 40,000 horsemen into German South-West Africa and clear out the Germans." I knew Botha meant it, and if the occasion arose, would do it. The occasion arrived sooner than most observers anticipated. When it came, Botha stood by his word in the letter and in the spirit. He did more than he had promised. He not only cleared the Germans out of South-West Africa, but helped us in the campaign in German East Africa and sent a contingent to the battlefields of Europe.

As for India, as soon as war was declared, the 27 larger native States, which maintained Imperial Service troops, tendered the help of their armies, and several Indian rulers offered to lead their troops in person.

During the four years of war they all had their full share of the hard fighting and privations. The Indians helped us to defend the waterlogged trenches of Flanders through the miserable winter of 1914-15, and contributed to our victories in Mesopotamia; Canadians, Australians and New Zealanders took a valiant part in some of the bloodiest encounters of the War, and they all suffered heavily. South Africans took an effective lead in the attack on the German Colonial Empire. They had all won their right, long before 1917, to an honoured seat at the War Council of Empire. Some of the most notable victories of the War were won largely owing to the dash and courage of the fine troops from the Dominions who had come voluntarily to our aid. They won a fame of their own, gratefully and proudly conceded by their British comrades, chivalrously acknowledged by their German foes. Had they stayed at home, the issue of the War would have been different and the history of the world would have taken a different course. It was a near thing, with all the help we got. If a million men—and such men—had been detached from our armies in the first three critical years of the War, Britain would not have been beaten, but she would not have won. On the continent of Europe, Prussian military autocracy would not have been overthrown finally without them. On the contrary, it would have ended the War with the stride of a Colossus—a bleeding Colossus—with one foot firmly planted on a devastated France and the other on a prostrate Russia.

But the accession of these leaders to our Council in 1917 was not a recognition, least of all a reward: it was a distinct and special contribution to our usefulness as a War Directory. In the great experiment there were difficulties to be surmounted and dangers to be avoided. The Imperial Cabinet must be allowed to discuss every circumstance connected with the conduct of the War. On the other hand, we would have to steer clear of any decisions which would impinge upon the complete independence of any of the contributory States. For instance, no direction could come from this body to the United Kingdom or to any Dominion as to the contribution in men and money each had to make, and certainly not as to the best means of raising soldiers or funds. Then there was also the colour difficulty, which affected all the Dominions in a greater or less degree, with the possible exception of New Zealand.

But we had no desire to confine discussions to the War. Any question affecting Imperial relations should be examined if anyone raised it. The future constitution of the Empire and trade relations were subjects bristling with controversial possibilities. But obviously they ought not to be ruled out. We decided that rigid rules should not be laid down, but that the best thing to do was to meet on terms of perfect freedom and equality, and trust to the common sense and Imperial patriotism of the delegates, whether they came from Britain or elsewhere.

The first public mention of the decision to hold an Imperial Conference—in connection with which the Imperial War Cabinet ultimately took shape—was in my speech to the House of Commons of 19th December, 1916.

" We feel that the time has come when the Dominions ought to be more formally consulted as to the progress and course of the War, as to the steps that ought to be taken to secure victory, and as to the best methods of garnering in the fruits of their efforts as well as of our own. We propose, therefore, at an early date to summon an Imperial Conference, to place the whole position before the Dominions, and to take counsel with them as to what further action they and we can take together in order to achieve an early and complete triumph for the ideals they and we have so superbly fought for."

Previous to this there had been an exchange of correspondence between Mr. Walter Long, the Colonial Secretary, and myself, on 12th December, 1916.

Mr. Walter Long was rather piqued at his exclusion from the War Cabinet. He was always conscious of the fact that he was regarded by a large section of the Conservative Party as the most eligible successor to the leadership vacated by Balfour. There is no greater calamity that can befall a public man than that he should be constantly aware of some personal achievement or position in the past which others have completely forgotten. Long was convinced that his resentment at being left out of the War Cabinet would be shared by the Dominions. Lest, therefore, irreparable harm be done, he felt I should send to every Dominion a telegram (of which he enclosed draft) assuring them that the establishment of a small Cabinet of five that did not include the Colonial Secretary would in no way prejudice the interests of the Dominions, and promising them a weekly letter that would give them confidential news of all important matters.

I thought a weekly report was by no means an adequate recognition of the magnitude of the contribution made by them to the effort put forth by the Empire in the War. I had already decided to propose to the War Cabinet that we should set up an Imperial War Cabinet in which the Dominions and India should be represented. I therefore sent the following answer to his suggestion : —

"12th December, 1916.

My dear Colonial Secretary,

I propose to say something about the Empire in my speech on Thursday The more I think about it, the more I am convinced that we should take the Dominions into our counsel in a much larger measure than we have hitherto done in our prosecution of the War. They have made enormous sacrifices, but we have held no conference with them as to either the objects of the War or the methods of carrying it out. They hardly feel that they have been consulted. As we must receive even more substantial support from them before we can hope to pull through, it is important that they should feel that they have a share in our councils as well as in our burdens. We want more men from them. We can hardly ask them to make another great recruiting effort unless it is accompanied by an invitation to come over to discuss the situation with us.

Please let me know what you think about it.

Thanks for inquiries. I hope to be all right by Thursday.

Ever sincerely,

D. LLOYD GEORGE.

The Rt. Hon. Walter Long, M.P."

The first reference to the Imperial Conference in the discussions of the War Cabinet was on 20th December, 1916, when I informed the Cabinet with reference to the statement I had made to the House on the previous day that I proposed to ask the Dominions to send representatives as soon as possible.

On 22nd December the matter was further discussed, and it was agreed to send telegrams to the Dominion Premiers inviting them to a gathering which should not be an ordinary Imperial Conference, but a series of Cabinet meetings of which they would form members with the British War Cabinet, to discuss urgent matters arising out of the War.   On 23rd December the discussion was pushed further, and it was suggested that the Dominion Premiers might wish when they were together here to deal with other matters than those that would be laid before them in the War Cabinet.   It was accordingly decided that if the Dominion Premiers wanted to raise other points they could have a separate Conference to deal with these issues, but that the prime object of inviting them should be the constitution of an Imperial War Cabinet.

Accordingly, a telegram was sent to the Dominion Premiers in the following terms: —

" I wish to explain that what His Majesty's Government contemplate is not a session of the Ordinary Imperial Conference, but a special War Conference of the Empire.   They therefore invite your Prime Minister to attend a series of special and continuous meetings of the War Cabinet in order to consider urgent questions affecting the prosecution of the War, the possible conditions on which, in agreement with our Allies, we could assent to its termination, and the problems which will then immediately arise.   For the purpose of these meetings, your Prime Minister would be a member of the War Cabinet.

In view of the extreme urgency of the subjects of discussion, as well as of their supreme importance, it is hoped that your Prime Minister may find it possible, in spite of the serious inconvenience involved, to attend at an early date, not later than the end of February.   While His Majesty's Government earnestly desire the presence of your Prime Minister himself, they hope that if he sees insuperable difficulty he will carefully consider the question of nominating a substitute, as they would regard it as a serious misfortune if any Dominion were left unrepresented."

The Colonial Secretary had promptly sent a preliminary notification to the Dominion Premiers after the War Cabinet meeting of 20th December, but the above telegram gave authoritative definition of the nature of the consultation to which they were being summoned. It was important not to announce it as a regular Imperial Conference, since the constitution of such a conference was already firmly defined by precedent, and what was desired on this occasion was something definitely simpler and more direct in character.

On 1st January, 1917, the matter again came before the War Cabinet, when it was agreed that Dominion Premiers should be invited to bring with them any of their Ministers whose presence might be necessary in connection with discussion of special issues; such Ministers not to become actual Members of the War Cabinet, but to be available for consultation as wanted. It was reported at this meeting that the Australian Premier had sent word that he would not be able to come over, as the lack of a settlement in Ireland was causing trouble in Australia.

A further telegram was sent to the Dominions in the following terms: —

" I wish to make it clear that if your Prime Minister desires the presence at the War Cabinet of colleagues, of whose special knowledge he wishes to avail himself, the latter will be welcome, though of course the Prime Minister alone will be a member of the War Cabinet. Further, if your Ministers should desire to discuss other questions of common interest not directly affecting the conduct of the War, or less appropriate for discussion at the War Cabinet, His Majesty's Government are prepared to arrange facilities for conferring on any other questions awaiting decision between the Imperial Government and the Dominions, although it may not be possible for the Prime Minister to preside."

The cautious wording of this telegram was dictated by the wish to give full opportunities for conference, while avoiding any appearance of summoning a normal Imperial Conference, and becoming subject to the technical limitations which the official constitution of an Imperial Conference would impose.

On 10th January, 1917, it was decided that the Maharajah of Bikanir should be invited to attend the Imperial War Cabinet gathering as a third Assessor to the Secretary of State for India, representing the Indian Native Princes.

This question was further discussed on 19th January, and the Indian Secretary was authorised to publish a statement about the Indian representation at the Imperial Cabinet in the following terms: —

" As already announced, the Secretary of State for India, when representing India at the special sittings of the War Cabinet, will have the assistance of two gentlemen specially selected for the purpose. In pursuance of this decision, the Secretary of State has, with the advice of the Governor-General in Council, selected Sir

James Meston, K.C.S.I., Lieutenant-Governor of the United Provinces of Agra and Oudh, and Sir Satyendra Prasanna Sinha. In accordance with a further decision of His Majesty's Government, the Secretary of State for India will also have the assistance of one of the Ruling Chiefs of India. With the advice of the Governor-General in Council, he has invited His Highness the Maharajah of Bikanir, G.C.S.I., G.C.I.E., A.D.C., to accompany him, and His Highness has accepted the offer."

In noting the amount of care and caution bestowed on the question of Indian representation at this gathering, it must be borne in mind that hitherto India had not participated in the Imperial Conferences. The constitution of the Imperial Conference had been settled in 1907, when the first was held. Prior to 1907, there had been a couple of "Colonial Conferences" the last of them taking place in 1902, when the Colonial Prime Ministers had been invited to London to consult with the Imperial Government on colonial matters. In 1907, Sir Henry Campbell-Bannerman, when summoning a Colonial Conference, decided to take the step in advance of establishing this as a definitely constituted Imperial Conference, to be held every four years, and attended by the Premiers of the Self-Governing Dominions, under the presidency of the British Premier. A permanent Imperial Conference Secretariat was set up, as a department of the Colonial Office, to keep the records of the Conferences and make the arrangements for them. But India, not being a self-governing Dominion, was at that time outside the purview of the Conference constitution. She was not represented at the Imperial Conference of 1911, the first to be summoned under the new constitution.

There was, therefore, no authority by which India could be invited to an Imperial Conference, and no understanding with the Dominion Premiers to permit of such a new development. But India had made a large contribution of men and money to the carrying on of the War, and her troops were fighting alongside white soldiers and against white enemies. This fact had created a new self-consciousness among the Indians that showed itself in a demand for greater recognition, and it also made consultation with them about the further conduct of the War, just and desirable. Hence the Imperial Conference of 1917 was summoned on a special basis, outside the official constitution. The representation of India in the Imperial War Cabinet was the beginning of the open recognition of India's new status. The precedent was followed in the conferences and discussion of 1919 regarding the peace settlement, and since then India has had her place in every Imperial Conference. The two Imperial Conferences of 1923 —the regular quadrennial Conference and the special Imperial Economic Conference—found India's representatives at the table alongside the Dominion Premiers.

Two letters I received during the War from the recent Viceroy, Lord Willingdon (he was then Governor of Bombay), give a new idea of the changes effected in enlightened British opinion by India's loyalty during the War.

The first I received in January, 1916.

"22/1/16.

My dear Lloyd George,

Can you, amid all your preoccupation, give a minute to this letter coming from one who is trying to do his bit out here and has after three years got a profound and certain belief in the necessity for a big and generous move in the way of legislation both in economic and administrative matters by the Home Government?

I won't go into any details, but I wish to preface my remarks by saying that I have written to various of our leaders on this and either got no answer or no encouragement. What the position here wants is courage and the readiness to take chances. If this is done by some leader after this war is over, it is my conviction that India will prove to be in every way one of the most loyal and productive parts of the Empire.

The Indian's point of view is 'You English have educated us: You have brought us to an intense desire to look after ourselves: when you want us you call us fellow citizens of a Great Empire, but when it comes to business you give us nothing but "concessions." We love our country, we want you to give us a real chance of doing something for it.'

The Englishman replies: 'You are not ready for any more: We must have efficiency in our administration, and you can't come in and really help us administer until you can show more character and honesty.'

But the Englishman will not realise that the Indian can't learn unless he is given a chance to do so. Of course, it is true that the advance of the Indian means the gradual disappearance of this great Civil Service out here, but *that*, if the Indians are given a real chance to progress, is inevitable. I only write this outline of view to ask you to keep in mind this great country after the War is over. India has done her part nobly during the War, and while she asks for nothing *because of that*, I think she deserves to be generously treated. It is such an opportunity for a statesman to bind, I believe for long years, this great people in the bonds of amity and Imperial Unity, that I hope you may remember this outburst, for the question is one of real Imperial concern.

I am afraid we are in for a bad time up the Gulf; why is it that somebody blunders so often? We want a victory badly out here— Gallipoli and this last business in the Gulf have unsettled people a bit, but I think that bar Bengal, India will be staunch.

All good wishes to you, and all congratulations on your munition efforts. I only hope the result may be the pulverisation of our foe before long.

Yours sincerely,

WILLINGDON."

The next came to me immediately after my appointment as Premier.

"Bombay,

10/12/16.

My dear Lloyd George,

I must write you a line to congratulate you warmly on being Prime Minister and on taking over the greatest responsibility for the Empire that has ever been borne by a British Statesman. Here we have wondered for some time why our proceedings have been characterised by so much leisurely statesmanship. While the Germans push on and seem to achieve their purposes because they show force and determination, we want to get a move on, a move that will show the Germans we mean business, a move that will hearten us all out here, and make us all feel that we are not allowing the enemy to run rings round us in the way of making up our minds and on our decisions.

I think you may be quite happy about the position in India on the whole, though until we have settled Turkey, the Mohammedan uneasiness is sure to continue. Personally, I have never liked the Government's action with regard to the Sherif of Mecca which has been resented out here and is, I think, not going to be of much value to us.

It is, I know, impossible for you to have much time to consider the future policy of this country, but I do trust that you will call to mind a letter I wrote to you many months ago suggesting that our policy should be conceived in a really generous spirit, for India has done, is doing, and will continue to do her part. It is, I am certain, a magnificent opportunity for securing the faithful loyalty of India for all time, to give her substantial advance and to give it generously. We must run a certain amount of risk in so doing, but I believe the risk should be run and I am confident the result will be satisfactory. Forgive my bothering you, but I wanted to write you these few lines to wish you Godspeed in your great task and to express a hope that politicians will put aside party and support you in your endeavour through thick and thin until you have achieved the great result.

With all good wishes,

Yours sincerely,

WILLINGDON."

These were the first communications I received from any authoritative source in India which definitely indicated that the time had arrived when Great Britain should contemplate an advance on the lines of self-government for the Indian people.

I had several discussions more especially with Lord Milner, Mr. Philip Kerr (now Lord Lothian) and Sir Maurice Hankey as to the Agenda for the coming Conference. As a result of these talks the Secretary prepared a Memorandum which appears in Appendix B. It gives a good idea of the wide scope which we had arranged for the proceedings and the importance we attached to this unique gathering.

Sir Maurice Hankey's Note was considered at a meeting of the War Cabinet on 15th February, and the proposals as to information to be prepared in the various Departments were generally approved. With regard to the procedure at the meetings, the War Cabinet inclined to the view that the proceedings should open by a general synopsis by the Prime Minister of the military effort made by the United Kingdom, which should include a general review of the naval and military situation, and that the First Sea Lord and the Chief of the Imperial General Staff should be prepared either to answer questions at the meeting or to give the representatives of the Dominions and India any special information that they might require. The War Cabinet further considered that the Secretary of State for Foreign Affairs should be prepared to give a general review of foreign policy.

The Imperial War Cabinet in its personal composition was the most remarkable Council of War in the whole vast battlefield.

Canada was represented by Sir Robert Borden, who was the very quintessence of common sense. Always calm, well-balanced, a man of co-operating temper, invariably subordinating self to the common cause, he was a sagacious and helpful counsellor, never forgetting that his first duty was to the people of the great Dominion he represented, but also realising that they were engaged in an Imperial enterprise and that an insistent and obstructive particularism would destroy any hope of achieving success in the common task.

South Africa was represented by General Smuts, the gifted and versatile Dutchman. He had made a study of war and had no mean experience of it. He had just conducted a successful campaign in the vast jungles of tropical Africa, where he fought the most resourceful of all the German Generals—von Lettow-Vorbeck.

Smuts is one of the most remarkable personalities of his time. He is that fine blend of intellect and human sympathy which constitutes the understanding man. Although he had proved his courage in many enterprises which demanded personal valour, and although he had shown his powers in many a fight which had called for combative qualities, his sympathies were too broad to make of him a mere fighting man. His rare gifts of mind and heart strengthened those finer elements which are apt to be overwhelmed in an hour of savage temper

ASQUITH: " David, talk to him in Welsh and pacify him."

Mr. Hughes at a Cabinet Conference, 1916.

and pitiless carnage. Of his practical contribution to our counsels during these trying years, it is difficult to speak too highly.

The Dutch statesman was a complete contrast to the pugnacious little Welshman—W. M. Hughes—who directed so effectively the contribution of Australia to the War, but who, having only just returned to Australia, was unable to attend the Imperial Conference. He concentrated the whole of his acute mind and of his phenomenal energy on beating down the foe. Smuts and Hughes had nothing in common except an indomitable courage. They were both essential to the tasks of Empire at this grave juncture in its history. Hughes had been to England in 1916 and then did his fiery best to stir things up. He and Asquith did not get on too well. They would not. They were antipathetic types. As Hughes was never over-anxious to conceal his feelings or restrain his expression of them, and was moreover equipped with a biting tongue, the consultations between these two were not agreeable to either.

Massey, the burly son of an Ulster stock, led the New Zealand delegation. Shrewd, sensible, direct and single-minded, his very appearance inspired a feeling of strength in the fight. He was a complete answer to the foolish notion inculcated by Carlyle, that strong men are always silent. Once he started, his speech was a rapid torrent, but the waters were clear and they always dashed along in the right direction. His partner, Sir Joseph Ward, was a more finished, if equally galloping speaker. But although neither of them had an oratorical speed limit, their contributions were lucid, invariably directed to the point at issue and had a note of practical good sense which was always helpful.

"Bikanir" as he was familiarly and affectionately called—the Indian Prince—was a magnificent specimen of the manhood of his great country. We soon found that he was one of "the wise men that came from the East." More and more did we come to rely on his advice, especially on all questions that affected India.

Apart from the aggregate numbers that these men represented, their very presence gave confidence in the most depressing and dreary moments. The Imperial Contingent came into our counsels with minds not staled and stunted by years of thinking and toiling in departmental dug-outs and deep trenches where progress was barred by entanglements of all kinds. It was a distinct advantage to have these fresh and untrammelled brains and these virile personalities with whom to interchange ideas. They had an invigorating and emancipating effect on our worn nerves and shackled minds.

On 2nd March, the date for opening the Imperial War Cabinet Meetings and the sessions of the Imperial War Conference was discussed. By mid-March the representatives of India and of all the Dominions except Australia would be present. Mr. Hughes, of Australia, could not be expected before 9th April at the earliest. It was agreed that the meetings could not wait till that date, but that matters specially affecting Australia could be held up till Mr. Hughes' arrival. The ultimate decision of the Cabinet was that the Special Imperial Sittings of the War Cabinet should begin about the 20th March, but the discussion of peace terms, and similar urgent matters of common interest, should be postponed until Mr. Hughes' arrival. Meanwhile a number of questions, such as, for instance, man-power, timber supply, mineral production, etc., could be discussed before the 20th March between His Majesty's Government and the Dominion Representatives, either outside or at the meetings of the War Cabinet, on the distinct understanding, however, that no decision affecting the Commonwealth of Australia should be taken.

On 17th March, the War Cabinet discussed the failure of Australia to send a representative to the Imperial War Cabinet. General Smuts had urged telegraphing Hughes that an Imperial consultation would be unreal without Australia's participation. But in view of the extremely difficult political situation in Australia, it was felt that such a message could do no good and might only embarrass Hughes; and it was decided that the best thing would be to pass a resolution at the first meeting of the Imperial War Cabinet regretting Australia's absence. I dwell on this incident as it affords an illustration of one of the practical difficulties experienced by so far-flung an Empire in securing authoritative consultation leading to action.

The Imperial discussions began on 20th March. As has been indicated in some of the foregoing extracts, it had been arranged for them to take two concurrent forms. On the one hand, there were the meetings of the Imperial War Cabinet, at which the representatives of the Dominions and of India joined with the British Cabinet to handle the daily administrative Cabinet problems, and also to decide on executive measures for the Imperial conduct of the War; and on the other hand, there were the meetings of an Imperial War Conference at the Colonial Office, presided over by the Secretary of State for the Colonies, to discuss a number of problems which either arose out of the War or had been accentuated by it. The two series of meetings, in both of which the same representatives of the Empire overseas were taking part, were mainly held on alternate days.

I opened the Conference with a general exposition as to the progress of the War and the aims for which it was undertaken—aims which would have to be realised before a stable peace could be secured. I reproduce that statement in an Appendix* as it indicates the view taken by the War Cabinet at that time of the military position and of the allied objectives. It was delivered in secret session and therefore the situation and prospect could be reviewed without the reticence necessarily imposed on public utterances in a state of war.

Altogether there were fourteen sessions of the Imperial War

* See Appendix A.

Cabinet, the first being on 20th March, 1917, and the last on 2nd May. There were fifteen sessions of the Imperial War Conference, the first on 21st March, and the last on 27th April.

At the meetings of the Imperial War Cabinet, those present in full session were:—

THE PRIME MINISTER OF THE UNITED KINGDOM (*in the Chair*);

The Rt. Hon. A. BONAR LAW, M.P., Chancellor of the Exchequer;

The Rt. Hon. the EARL CURZON OF KEDLESTON, K.G., G.C.S.I., G.C.I.E., Lord President of the Council;

The Rt. Hon. VISCOUNT MILNER, G.C.B., G.C.M.G.;

The Rt. Hon. A. HENDERSON, M.P.;

The Rt. Hon. A. J. BALFOUR, O.M., M.P., Secretary of State for Foreign Affairs;

The Rt. Hon. W. H. LONG, M.P., Secretary of State for the Colonies;

The Rt. Hon. A. CHAMBERLAIN, M.P., Secretary of State for India;

The Rt. Hon. SIR ROBERT L. BORDEN, G.C.M.G., K.C., Prime Minister of Canada;

The Hon. SIR GEORGE H. PERLEY, K.C.M.G., Minister of the Overseas Military Forces of Canada;

The Rt. Hon. W. F. MASSEY, Prime Minister of New Zealand;

The Rt. Hon. SIR J. G. WARD, Bt., K.C.M.G., Minister of Finance and Posts, New Zealand;

Lt.-Gen. the Rt. Hon. J. C. SMUTS, K.C., Minister for Defence, Union of South Africa;

The Rt. Hon. SIR E. P. MORRIS, K.C.M.G., Prime Minister of Newfoundland.

When the subjects under discussion made it desirable, the C.I.G.S. and Sir John Jellicoe attended the Imperial Conference. Occasionally the War Secretary, the Food Controller, Shipping Controller, the President of the Board of Agriculture and other Ministers were summoned.

At the subsequent meetings of the Imperial War Cabinet, in addition to dealing with immediate war issues which arose from day to day, the Cabinet discussed the broader aspects of the War and the problems arising out of it. At the second Session on 22nd March, statements on Foreign Affairs were made by the Secretary of State for Foreign Affairs and the Secretary of State for India. Shipping and food problems, finance, the war effort of the Dominions and India and their capacity for further effort, were dealt with on different days, as also the relations with Russia and Greece.

As regards peace terms, two Sub-Committees were set up under the chairmanship respectively of Lord Curzon and Lord Milner, to discuss territorial and non-territorial desiderata of a peace settlement. On each of these Committees the Dominions were represented. They held prolonged sittings. Ultimately they came to conclusions as to the Peace aims of the British Empire. (The non-territorial peace terms are embodied in Appendix D.)

Lord Curzon's Committee dealing with territorial questions recommended that so far as the British Empire was concerned, territorial settlement after the War should leave in British hands the German colonies and Turkish territory that we had captured or occupied. This was the first occasion on which any indication was given that Britain meant as a condition of peace to retain its conquests in the German Colonial Empire. So far the British Government had formulated no such demand. It was mainly due to the insistence of the Dominion representatives. They made it quite clear that they had no intention of restoring to Germany after the War the territories they had conquered. The British members of the Sub-Committees took the same view concerning German East Africa and Mesopotamia. It was agreed that British delegates to a Peace Conference should take these proposals as a guide, but it was pointed out that if peace were negotiated while Allied territory was still held by the Central Powers, it might prove necessary to hand back some of our gains to secure satisfactory terms for our Allies.

In its final decision the Imperial War Cabinet, whilst accepting the Report of the Committee as an indication of the objects to be sought by the British Representatives at the Peace Conference and of their relative importance, rather than as definite instructions from which they are not intended in any circumstances to depart, noted that the demands of the British Empire would require to be correlated at the Conference with those of our Allies.

Mr. Henderson dissented from this resolution, as he said that the Labour Party could not agree to any annexations after the War.

The report of Lord Milner's Committee on non-territorial peace issues raised much more far-reaching questions, such as Disarmament, the League of Nations, Indemnity, Trade arrangements after the War. These provoked a remarkable discussion at two successive meetings of the Imperial War Cabinet and the summary of these discussions as recorded in the Minutes of the Cabinet is perhaps worth transcription. These deliberations have their special value at the present time as they indicate how the statesmen of the British Empire in their first collective examination of proposals for Disarmament and the establishment of the League of Nations foresaw all the practical difficulties that have since arisen to thwart the exalted purpose of peace lovers throughout the world.

With reference to Conclusion 6 of Lord Milner's Committee (*vide* Appendix D), I expressed the view that the Committee had rather thrown cold water on the idea of a League of Nations, and had not dealt at all with the question of disarmament or limitation of armaments, or of the sanctions by which the conclusions of a League of

Nations, or the provisions of any agreement for the limitation of armaments, should be enforced. I thought that there would be great disappointment if it were thought that at the end of the War nothing could be done in these directions.

With regard to the limitation of armaments, Lord Robert Cecil pointed out that he had submitted a memorandum in which this was advocated, but confessed that he had been driven out of his position by the criticisms contained in an examination of that memorandum by Sir Eyre Crowe. Crowe's powerfully written document took a pessimistic view of the prospects of post-War disarmament. It is summarised in Appendix C, and is worth reading as an accurate account of difficulties actually experienced.

In the discussion which ensued it was pointed out that one of the first difficulties in the way was that of the standard of armaments to be allowed for each nation. The existence of our own dominating sea-power, coupled with the sea-power of America, was undoubtedly the best guarantee for peace; but it was probably one of the very first things which the members of an international body would agree should be cut down.

Then, again, there was the difficulty of the manner in which any limitation could be prescribed. Napoleon's attempt to limit the Prussian Army to a definite numerical strength had been directly responsible for the creation of the Prussian military system.

Further, it was impossible to draw the line as to what constituted armaments. In the present war, Germany had been able for two years and more to hold her own against the rest of the world in armaments, owing to her effective industrial organisation. That organisation had not been purely planned for war; its adaptation to military purposes had been a matter of improvisation in Germany as well as in Allied countries. But the fact remained that it was an essential part of Germany's military strength.

Lastly, there was the difficulty that the Powers who were most likely to use their armaments in order to forward their ambitions were the ones who would be least willing to fall in whole-heartedly and honestly with any scheme of limitation of armaments that might be agreed upon.

With regard to the question of a League of Nations, Lord Robert Cecil pointed out that there were really two main alternatives, namely, an International Court of Arbitration or a system of International Conference and Consultation. He did not believe that matters affecting the vital interests of the British Empire could possibly be submitted to the decisions of an International Tribunal. On the other hand, he did believe that a great deal could be effected if the habit of conference and consultation could once be firmly established. He thought one of the chief causes of international conflict lay in the fact that treaty terms attempted to settle for all time matters that were inherently subject to variation and development. Under a system of International Conferences the situation could be periodically reviewed. To begin with, at any rate, the most hopeful plan probably was to say that no one should declare war till a conference of all the Powers had been summoned, the summoning and decision of such a conference taking place within a reasonable time.

In the discussion which ensued it was pointed out that a periodical conference to readjust the map of Europe might possibly create causes of friction as well as allay them.

There was the further difficulty that, under any procedure which could be suggested for a League of Nations, or for a Conference of Nations, called together to deal with such problems as those of nationality, a United Italy could never have come into being, or the subject races of the Ottoman Empire have been delivered from Turkish oppression.

Lord Milner said that he did not believe that any attempt to establish an International Court would be successful or be a good thing in itself; but he did believe that a great advance could be made if the nations who entered into the next Treaty of Peace bound themselves not to go to war without submitting their cause to a conference. Failure to do so should be a case of war for all the Powers who were party to the Treaty. The conference, however, could not be a Court binding nations who took part in it to enforce its decisions. Such a conference, in his opinion, would, in all probability, have prevented the outbreak of the present war.

Sir Robert Borden expressed the view that the real basis of future peace must be the public opinion of the world. The present war had demonstrated the futility of treaties and conventions when nations were determined to violate them. He laid particular stress on the last sentence in Conclusion 6 of Lord Milner's Committee—that which referred to discussion with our Allies and with the United States. He considered that the United States and the British Empire in agreement could do more than anything else to maintain the peace of the world.

Such was, in sum, the nature of the discussion on 26th April, 1917. At the next meeting of the Imperial War Cabinet on 1st May, a further discussion took place with reference to a League of Peace and the problem of disarmament. With regard to the possibility of a League of Peace, Lord Milner again expressed the view that the most that could be done would be for the Powers concerned in the Treaty of Peace to bind themselves not to go to war without previous conference, and all to go to war against any Power that violated this agreement.

Lord Robert Cecil read to the Imperial War Cabinet a suggested clause in the terms of peace by which it was agreed that, in case

2L

of any difference or controversy, a conference should be forthwith summoned, and no action taken until that conference had considered the matter, or for three months after the meeting of the conference. Each of the high contracting Powers should bind itself to enforce this agreement by cutting off all financial and commercial intercourse from an offending Power.

General Smuts suggested that the precise nature of the sanction to be imposed would have to be worked out later. It would be sufficient if the Imperial War Cabinet expressed itself in general terms in favour of the principle of a sanction.

The Imperial War Cabinet concurred in this view.

This discussion has considerable interest as evidence of the way in which the scheme for a League of Nations was at this time beginning to take definite form. It has all the more importance because it was found at the date of the Peace Conference that the British Government alone had taken measures to work out a practical scheme for the constitution of a League of Peace. President Wilson had not gone beyond the vague idea and the striking phrase. He had not attempted to develop his thoughts into any concrete plan.

On the subject of disarmament this meeting of the Imperial War Cabinet continued its discussion and Lord Robert Cecil briefly explained to the Imperial War Cabinet the difficulties in the way of any agreement, either between the Powers collectively or between individual Powers, with regard to disarmament. These difficulties, as set forth in Sir Eyre Crowe's Memorandum had convinced him that disarmament was not a hopeful line of progress. It is fair to point out that Sir Eyre Crowe's arguments made only a temporary impression on Cecil's opinions, and that he soon reverted to the conclusion he had formed that without disarmament there would be no secure peace.

In continuing the debate, I stated that I was not quite convinced that Sir Eyre Crowe's arguments had quite exhausted the subject. In my opinion, the War had been largely due to the existence of a great, highly-trained and professionalised army exciting public opinion, and eager to test its strength. I thought it might be possible to have an agreement in favour of setting up, in place of this provocative system based on the spirit of offensive, a militia system essentially non-provocative, and based on the idea of defence.

Against this it was argued that it was extremely difficult to get rid of the professional element altogether, and that the conditions of different countries differed so widely that it would in practice be impossible to find a system on which everybody could be agreed. Moreover, the greatest existing guarantee of peace—the British Navy—was undoubtedly a highly professionalised institution, and it would be impossible to ask for a general reduction of military efficiency on land without raising the question of naval disarmament. It was, indeed, suggested by General Smuts that if the European Powers by agreement debarred themselves from spending money on their land defence they would have much more to spend on big navies.

Mr. Henderson considered that Lord Milner's Committee, in framing paragraph 6 of their report, while they had excluded complete disarmament as a counsel of perfection, were quite prepared to consider any reasonable means for reducing armaments and preventing the recurrence of war. Personally, he held very strong views on the subject of disarmament, but was convinced that it was necessary first of all to see what result could be achieved in the direction of a League of Nations. The policy with regard to disarmament would have to depend on the nature of the international relations set up after the conclusion of peace.

Mr. Chamberlain confessed to feeling that any attempt to lay down restrictions on armaments was bound to give rise to opportunities for fraud. Public opinion in this country would insist that any British Government should be bound, both in the letter and in the spirit, by the restrictions. In a country such as Germany, public opinion would be entirely in favour of the restrictions being tacitly broken or evaded. He considered, however, that the suggestion contained in Lord Milner's report, of communications with America, might be followed up, and that we might endeavour to see whether Americans, who had given a great deal of time to discussing these subjects, could formulate any workable scheme.

Sir Robert Borden said he was certainly quite willing that the question of limitation of armaments should be included in the details for discussion with the United States, which had been suggested in the last sentence of paragraph 6 of the Committee's Report. He adhered to his opinion that really the public opinion of the world was the only sure guarantee of peace.

The Imperial War Cabinet were of the opinion that the question of the limitation of armaments should also be discussed with the United States in connection with any discussion of this question of a League of Peace.

In connection with Imperial development after the War, the Imperial War Cabinet discussed ways and means of linking the Dominions and Motherland more closely. Mr. Massey put forward a resolution in the following terms: —

" That the time has arrived when all possible encouragement should be given to the development of Imperial resources, and (consistent with the resolution of the Paris Conference) especially to making the Empire independent of other countries for the food supplies of its population and raw materials for its manufactures.

With these objects in view this Conference expresses itself in favour of : —

1.   A system by which each country of the Empire will give preference through its Customs to the goods produced or manufactured in any other British country; and

2.   An arrangement by which, in the case of intending emigrants from the United Kingdom, inducements may be offered to such emigrants to settle in countries under the British Flag."

In the discussion on this resolution, Sir Robert Borden urged that Customs Preference was not only an Imperial, but also a domestic matter for Britain, and " no one in Canada would desire a Preference that was felt to be oppressive or unjust by the population of these islands.   Any such feeling would injure the Imperial aspect of ' Preference.' "   But the Empire could produce all its own food, if the cost of transport were reduced, and he suggested that " it might be possible for the United Kingdom and the Dominions to get together in some great enterprise which would restrict the cost of transportation within the Empire.   Transportation was quite as important to all the Dominions as Customs Preference."

My contribution to the discussion was on the following lines: I began by saying that I was speaking not in my official capacity but as one who had taken a leading part in discussions on this question. My general attitude had been altered by things which had happened since the War.   The War had undoubtedly revealed certain fundamental facts which it was necessary to take cognisance of in our Imperial and domestic arrangements.   There were industries essential to defence which we had been compelled to build up at great cost in the middle of the War, and which might not be able to hold their own unassisted at the end of the War.   It would be great folly, in view of the expenditure we should still have to incur upon the Army and Navy, if we neglected to maintain industries essential to the efficiency of those Forces.

Again, there was the Imperial point of view.   The value of cohesion and co-operation between the nations of the British Commonwealth had been revealed in an extraordinary way; it had been the great surprise of the War to our enemies and largely to ourselves, and had made us the most important factor in the War.   Consequently, from the selfish point of view of the United Kingdom alone, the development of the Empire would be an essential motive in British policy.   The figures Mr. Massey had quoted (about the direction of pre-War British emigration) showed that if more trouble had been taken over the development of the Empire in the past, the Dominions might possibly have had double their present population and proportionately increased the strength of the British contribution to the present war. These were fundamental facts which were bound to produce an essential change in the policy of the United Kingdom with regard to the Dominions, and vice versa.

With regard to the methods to be adopted, I wished to point out that the War had revealed, more particularly in the case of Russia, the peril which might arise from dear food. That issue was one which had somehow or other obsessed the minds of the working classes in the United Kingdom ever since the Corn Laws, and the memories of the present war would revive that dread. I concurred in Sir Robert Borden's statesmanlike view, that it would not do for the prosperity of Canada to be based on the want of the workmen in England. I wished the working-classes to regard the Empire as something that meant not only glory, but also material advantage.

I was all for Preference, and would personally assent to any resolution laying down the principle, but I asked Mr. Massey to leave out the three words: " through its Customs," which specified a particular method. I was inclined to consider that Sir Robert Borden's method of subsidised transit through the Empire would give a more substantial Preference. I was all for the old Roman method of binding an Empire together by its roads—in our case by shipping. Another argument in favour of this particular method was that the principal meat and wheat producing countries besides the Empire were not our present enemies, but our Allies, Russia and the United States, and a Declaration in favour of a Customs Preference might look as if we were attempting to do them an injury. It was quite true that improved shipping would also take trade away from them, but that was a matter which could be justified on grounds of Imperial defence, and was a recognised method of development employed by the United States, Russia and France.

I did not rule out the remission of dues on the Suez Canal, or the possibility of subsidy on the actual goods sent over, but trusted that for the moment the precise method should be left open for future discussion. The United Kingdom had got to consider the question of its own industries after the War. This was not a matter of Free Trade or Protection, but of stern Imperial necessity for defence. Subject to this, I would personally agree with the resolution.

After general discussion the Cabinet agreed in principle with the resolution, subject to elimination of the words about Customs. As finally approved after a further discussion on 26th April, the resolution ran: —

" The time has arrived when all possible encouragement should be given to the development of Imperial resources, and especially to making the Empire independent of other countries in respect of food supplies, raw materials and essential industries. With these objects in view this Conference expresses itself in favour of: —

1. The principle that each part of the Empire, having due regard to the interests of our Allies, shall give specially favourable treatment and facilities to the produce and manufactures of other parts of the Empire.

2. Arrangements by which intending emigrants from the United Kingdom may be induced to settle in countries under the British Flag."

At the concluding session of the Imperial War Cabinet I expressed the satisfaction of the British Cabinet with the experiment, and proposed that it should be repeated and incorporated in the machinery of the British Empire. To this effect they considered that Sessions of the Imperial Cabinet, as distinct from the British Cabinet, should be convened annually, and that as an institution the Imperial Cabinet should have an Annual Session, though that did not preclude the summoning of a Special Session if questions of urgency arose in the interval. While the War was in progress the main business of such a Session would be to review the position of the War; apart from that it would naturally review questions of foreign policy, Imperial defence, and other matters of common concern. It was to me inconceivable that in the future the Dominions should be neither fully informed nor consulted on questions which might lead to war.

This proposal was heartily endorsed by the Dominion representatives.

Concurrently with this Imperial War Cabinet, there took place at the Colonial Office a series of meetings of an Imperial War Conference. It was presided over by Mr. Walter Long, the Secretary of State for the Colonies, and attended by all the representatives of India and the Dominions that were in London for the Imperial War Cabinet. Leading Civil Servants were present for consultation, and when the subjects under discussion made it desirable, the Ministers of Departments concerned attended the sessions.

Discussion ranged at the Conference over a large number of topics connected with the War—equipment and training of men, care of soldiers' graves, demobilisation arrangements, naval defence, control of natural resources, munitions, post-War trade. Two of the resolutions adopted deserve mention as having a wider and more permanent bearing upon Imperial affairs. These were the resolutions upon Indian representation, and upon the future Constitution of the Empire.

The resolution with regard to the Representation of India at a future Imperial Conference ran as follows:—

" That the Imperial War Conference desires to place on record its view that the Resolution of the Imperial Conference of 20th April, 1907, should be modified to permit of India being fully represented at all future Imperial Conferences, and that the necessary steps should be taken to secure the assent of the various Governments in order that the next Imperial Conference may be summoned and constituted accordingly."

This resolution was important, not merely because it opened the door for the future appearance of India alongside the Dominions at Imperial Conferences, but because it marked the first Imperial recognition of the altered status of India. It was one of the preliminary stages of the reforms on Indian administration, which started that great country on the pathway towards full self-government within the British Commonwealth. And in view of the controversies that have arisen over the development of that idea, it is worth noting that its inception was not the whim of any individual, but was attributable largely to the cordial welcome accorded by the Heads of the Dominions to the representatives of India as equals in the Council Chamber of the Empire in its greatest emergency.

The Imperial War Conference also gave careful thought to the question of the Constitution of the Empire. The very grave issues which the War had brought to the fore, and the critical effects of partnership within the British Empire which it had demonstrated, made this a major problem. At the same time, it was not one to be dealt with hastily, and the resolution of the Imperial War Conference on this matter was as follows: —

"The Imperial War Conference are of opinion that the readjustment of the constitutional relations of the component parts of the Empire is too important and intricate a subject to be dealt with during the War, and that it should form the subject of a special Imperial Conference to be summoned as soon as possible after the cessation of hostilities.

They deem it their duty, however, to place on record their view that any such readjustment, while thoroughly preserving all existing powers of self-government and complete control of domestic affairs, should be based upon a full recognition of the Dominions as autonomous nations of an Imperial Commonwealth, and of India as an important portion of the same, and should recognise the right of the Dominions and India to an adequate voice in foreign policy and in foreign relations, and should provide effective arrangements for continuous consultation in all important matters of common Imperial concern, and for such necessary concerted action, founded on consultation, as the several Governments may determine."

This resolution was a formal interpretation of the meaning which underlay the convention and consultations of the Imperial War Cabinet.

Considerations of space have prevented me from doing more than summarise in the foregoing pages a few of the outstanding matters of permanent interest which were dealt with in the course of this momentous and historic Conference. Every aspect of our far-ranging war interests came up for review before this, the first Empire Cabinet which ever assembled.

But the value of the Cabinet and Conference were vastly greater than their immediate utility as an instrument for discussing our common war problems, and with the extent and method of the help which the Dominions could supply. The meetings had an immense importance for the consolidation of the British Empire. The Imperial Cabinet did not end with a discussion of common problems; it directed common action in events of solemn magnitude which were shaking the earth and shaping the destinies of the people in every clime and continent. The fact bred alike a new individual dignity, and a more conscious solidarity. In our discussions there was less concentration, in the minds of the Dominion Premiers, on the sectional interests of the part of the Empire which each represented, and more eagerness to pull together to secure the maximum achievement in our joint effort. We were partners, not only in a Commonwealth, but in a Crusade. And the fine spirit thus engendered proved to be of critical value when, after the War, we came to complete that review of the Empire's constitution which had received its preliminary survey while we were in such temper.

Nor was the work confined to our discussions round the conference table. The visiting Dominion Premiers took advantage of their presence here to travel round the country, to meet with the people of the Homeland, and deepen by speech and interview our sense of common purpose and Imperial Unity. Mr. Hughes, of Australia, had done some invaluable work of this order when he was here in 1916. Meantime, his work was continued by Sir Robert Borden, of Canada, and Mr. Massey, of New Zealand.

So deep was the impression that General Smuts made at this time upon his colleagues, nay, upon the nation, that we would not let him leave us when the Conference was ended. We insisted on keeping him here to help us at the centre with our war efforts. In every aspect of our multifarious tasks he was a valuable helper. He took his full share of the numerous committees set up to investigate, to advise, and subject to Cabinet assent, to direct action on vital issues of policy and strategy. He became and remained until the end of the War, an active member of the British Cabinet for all the purposes of war direction.

APPENDIX A

You will permit me, on behalf of the British Government, to give the representatives of the great Dominions and of the Indian Empire welcome to the first Imperial Cabinet ever held in the British Empire. I need not dwell upon the essential distinction between this gathering and any other Imperial gathering we have ever held of representatives of the Empire. Previous gatherings were very properly characterised as Conferences, but this is a Cabinet in the real sense of the term, with power to take decisions and to give effect to them. And it is held to take counsel about the utilisation of the resources of the British Empire to the best advantage in the fulfilment of the most terrible duty ever imposed upon any Empire—a duty upon the proper and effective discharge of which not merely the destiny of the Empire depends, but, I think, the destiny of civilisation for many ages to come.

I do not know that it is necessary for me to say—because the fact is thoroughly well known to us all—that we were precipitated into this war before any opportunity could have been afforded us to consult first the Dominions or the Empire as a whole. A few days before war became inevitable, there were many well-informed statesmen in this country—I am not sure that it is not true of the majority —who thought it could be avoided; and even when a European war seemed to be inevitable, there were still very many statesmen peculiarly qualified by their knowledge to judge of events, who even then thought that we need not necessarily be involved in it. And it only became clear a very short time before the declaration of war that Germany meant deliberately to provoke it for sinister ends which have since become even more clear—to impose, first upon Europe, and, through Europe, upon the world, a military despotism; and I am sure that the representatives of the Empire will recognise that if they were not consulted before we had engaged ourselves in this war, it was due entirely to circumstances, not merely over which we had no control, but which many statesmen with an intimate knowledge of the facts did not at the time even foresee. However, we entered into it, as we conceived, for the defence of liberty, for the protection of weak nationalities who were threatened by a powerful autocracy, and we took for granted that the Dominions and the rest of the Empire would take exactly the same view as we did, that the very highest traditions of the British Empire made it imperative upon us to accept the challenge the moment it was thrown down. And the sequel proves that we were right in that assumption; for all parts of the Empire have nobly come to our aid—spontaneously and with a good heart, recognising that our quarrel in this is the quarrel of the whole Empire, and, through the Empire, the quarrel of humanity.

The Imperial Staff and the advisers of the great Navy of Britain will present their views as to the military and naval situation, and therefore it will not be for me even to attempt to give any sketch of the position from a military or naval point of view. The Foreign Secretary will, if not this morning, at any rate I hope to-morrow morning, give to the Cabinet a review of our foreign relations in respect both of our Allies and of neutrals, and also of the obligations into which we have entered. We shall have from the Chancellor of the Exchequer a review of the financial position in this country. The Minister of Blockade will give a summary of the actual position with regard to the blockading operations of Germany. The Secretary of State for India is here also, and will submit to the War Cabinet a document in which he will review the financial position, and the position in regard to military assistance and assistance in supplies—a most important matter for the consideration of this Cabinet. The Shipping Controller will also furnish us with a paper on the shipping position—a most vital element when we come to weigh and estimate the prospects of this country in the War.

I can only give a bare sketch of the task which I conceive is in front of us, and for the efforts which it will be essential for us to make in order to accomplish our purpose. We ought, in my judgment, to have, in the first place, a very frank discussion as to peace terms—such a discussion as would be impossible in public, and such a discussion as would not at present be possible in the first instance even with our Allies—a free, sincere, candid discussion amongst ourselves of what we conceive the peace terms ought to be. That is essential, not merely in order to equip those who will enter the Peace Conference, which will come sooner or later, with a knowledge of what the Empire as a whole desires to be achieved at that Conference. It is more than that. We cannot really measure the effort which we have still got to put forth until we have a clear comprehension of what we are aiming at, and what we conceive to be the essentials of any satisfactory peace. I think it is too early to lay down in rigid detail even our minimum demands. The War is not over, and although things for the moment may be going our way, the enemy is by no means exhausted. His army is greater than ever; he is in possession of hundreds of thousands of square miles of Allied territory; his power is still unbroken; he is still a very formidable, dangerous, and incalculable foe. And, therefore, whatever consideration, whatever attention we may give to the subject, however long we may deliberate, for us now to lay down, even in our own mind, in any rigid way, even the outlines of the terms without which we could not assent to signing a treaty of peace, is something, I think, which is beyond the determination of any human council at this stage. But we ought to have a very clear idea what it is we are aiming at, what we should like to achieve, what we hope to achieve. We ought to go beyond that: we should also dwell upon what we think we must achieve unless the blood which has been spilt is to be spilt in vain, and unless the world is to be plunged once more at no distant date into the same welter of destruction.

Let us then consider the things which surely must be essential to any rational, acceptable peace. In the first place the Germans must be driven out of the territories which they have invaded. They must abandon the lands which they have overrun—in France, Belgium, Russia, Serbia, Roumania, Montenegro. The freedom and independence of those countries must be restored, and Poland must not be merely restored, but restored under conditions which will give freedom to its oppressed population, and the events of the last few days in Russia have brought that possibility nearer to realisation than it ever was before. Compensation must be demanded for the damage done to these ravaged countries. It is undoubtedly desirable that there should also be such a geographical adjustment of the map of Europe, on the basis of recognising national rights, as will prevent trouble in future, secure a more permanent peace, and also make firmer and more solid the foundations of democratic freedom in Europe.

That surely is the very least which we ought to achieve in a peace. But if we only accomplished so much, we should have failed in some of the main purposes to which we have set ourselves in this terrible struggle. There are at least four or five other essential aims to be striven for, and the first is this: the conviction must be planted in the minds of the civilised world—a conviction that will ripen into an instinct—that all wars of aggression are impossible enterprises; that they accomplish nothing but the destruction of the aggressor. Men must in future be taught to shun war as every civilised being shuns a murder; not merely because it is wrong in itself, but because it leads to inevitable punishment. That is the only sure foundation for any league of peace. There has been a good deal of discussion lately about leagues of peace, and there is no doubt at all that we should endeavour to establish a league of that kind. But unless you drive that conviction into the human mind in every land, the league of peace will be built on a foundation of sand; and therefore the first thing to accomplish in this War is to make every country feel that in future, if it attempts to repeat the outrage perpetrated by Germany upon civilisation, it will inevitably encounter dire and destructive punishment. That, I think, is essential to the peace of the world. I will come later on to consider how far we have accomplished that.

The second aim which I hope will be achieved by this war is the democratisation of Europe. It is the only sure guarantee of peaceful progress. The menace to Europe did not come from its democratic countries; it came from a military autocracy. France, before the War, had just elected a peace Parliament. The majority had been elected on a peace ticket. It was the most peaceable and peace-loving Parliament that had ever been chosen in France. The election was fought on a military issue where the peace party won, because the French electors regarded the proposals that were set before them by the militarist party as provocative. It was essentially a peace Parliament. Rightly or wrongly, it was an extreme peace Parliament. In spite of dubious leadership, the French democracy were so bent on peace that they preferred choosing bad leaders who were for peace to choosing men of much greater power and genius who they thought were associated with militarist proposals. That was the case with France. Italy—well, Italy was so reluctant to wage war that she was months late in coming in, and it was with great difficulty that the most powerful statesman in that country was able to persuade the Italian Parliament, even in the end, to declare war. The Italian democracy was very loath to embark on war, and if it had not been for the appeal of their unredeemed territory in Austria, and the opportunity which presented itself of recovering it, they would never have come in. Then, as for ourselves, we have been reproached, and probably rightly reproached for our unreadiness. That is a very different reproach from that of provoking war. The only rebuke which can be justly levelled against the British Government was that they were not ready for war. That, in effect, was the spirit that animated the democracies of Europe, and if Germany had had a democracy like France, like ourselves, or like Italy, we should not have had this trouble. Liberty is the only sure guarantee of peace and goodwill amongst the peoples of the world. Free nations are not eager to make war. The democratisation of Europe has come nearer within the last few days. In fact, if there is wisdom amongst the democratic rulers of Russia, not merely will Russia become a great democratic State, but Germany must follow her example inevitably; and the speech of the German Chancellor within the last few days indicates that clearly.

What is the third aim? The disruption of the Turkish Empire as an Empire. The Turks have been ruling, or rather misruling, the most fertile and the most favoured lands in the world. They have not ruled successfully any of the lands they have conquered, and I am not sure that they are not the only race in the world of whom that can be said. They are ruling lands which were the cradle of civilisation, the seminary of civilisation, the temple of civilisation, and, from the material point of view, lands which at one time were the granary of civilisation; and now those fair lands are a blighted desert, although once upon a time they were the richest in the world. The Mesopotamia expedition and its history is in itself the greatest reflection upon Turkish misgovernment. It proceeded through lands which were at one time about the richest under the sun, and yet we found them so swept of all fertility by hundreds of years of Turkish misrule that India had to supply practically everything for our military expedition. We could only proceed slowly, after making railways and getting transport facilities for carrying there every provision for feeding an army. And yet this was a country that at one time maintained countless millions of people, and even countless armies. The history of the Mesopotamia expedition is the condemnation of Turkish misrule in that quarter of the world. The same applies to Syria, the same applies to Palestine, the same applies to Armenia—it applies to all those famed lands. The Turk must never be allowed to misgovern these great lands in future. We owe it to these countries, for the gifts with which they have enriched mankind, that we should do something to restore their glory. There have been many expeditions from Christendom into that part of the world to wrest them from the grip of the destroyer. I believe this will be the last, because it is the one which is going to be successful, and completely successful. It is impossible that we should permit these lands longer to remain under Turkish government. Under Turkish rule they have been a constant source of irritation, and friction, and war. There has been no one cause which has been more fruitful of bloodshed in Europe than the misgovernment of the Turkish Empire and its results. I am not sure that even this war had not something to do with German ambition in the East; in fact, as the Secretary for India was pointing out to us yesterday, there is a good deal to be said for the point of view that this was one of the main motives which inspired Germany in plunging the world into this chaos of blood. She had made up her mind to open up the road to the East, and probably to establish her dominion in the East. We are blocking that road, and the abolition of the Turkish Empire as an Empire, will to a very large extent settle the European mind, and it will give the energies of these great nations something to operate on which will be beneficent to mankind as a whole. It will be a great achievement to restore these famous territories to the splendour they enjoyed in the past, and to enable them once more to make their contribution to the happiness and prosperity of the world. You will hear from the Staff, I hope, how far we have proceeded with this task. I believe we have advanced already about forty or fifty miles beyond Baghdad.

As to another war-aim which concerns ourselves alone, I shall be very disappointed if this war does not lead to a reconstruction of our own country in many respects, economic and industrial—local government, the relation of capital and labour, the condition of life amongst the people, and generally in an improvement, in a raising of the standard of life of the vast multitudes of this kingdom; and finally, to a greater solidarity of aim and action as far as the British Empire is concerned. This war is already making of it a great and effective democratic commonwealth of nations which will exercise a real, a beneficent, and I think a permanent influence upon the course of human affairs. It is becoming more and more consolidated without in the least impinging on the freedom of the constituent parts.

I do not know that I should at this stage say anything about the German colonies which have been conquered so very largely, and in some cases entirely, through the efforts of our self-governing Dominions. All I would like to say at this stage would be this—that I hope we will treat this question as part of the whole problem of the settlement of the War, and not consider it merely from the point of view of any particular part of the Empire. We shall consider it, I trust, not merely as members of the same Empire, but also in reference to the great Alliance into which the Dominions as well as ourselves entered when they embarked with us upon this War. The extent to which we can establish permanently our dominion in those colonies must depend very largely upon the measure of success we achieve in the War, because if the success were partial we could not expect our Allies to bear their share of the sacrifice whilst we were enjoying practically the whole of the advantage. That is all I would like to say at the present stage on that question.

I have only given a rough sketch of what I consider to be the main aims of this country and of the British Empire in the prosecution of this war. Are we anywhere near attaining these objects? We are getting nearer. No doubt the War has been a great disappointment to Germany—a very, very great disappointment to Germany. She reckoned upon the knowledge that she had the most perfect military machine in the world. So she had. And she reckoned upon France being far inferior, not merely in numbers, but in equipment, in discipline, and in leadership. She regarded the Russian Army as an ill-equipped mob, very badly provided with transport, and therefore unable to bring up her millions to the point of conflict with Germany. As for us, they thought that, from a military point of view, we were contemptible, and they said so. And they calculated—and with some show of reason—upon being able to bring this war to a triumphant conclusion, in a very few months. There is no doubt about it—that was their reckoning, and there was a good deal to be said for their point of view. There were many soldiers to whom I had the privilege of talking before the War—not German soldiers, but soldiers in this country—who, looking at the condition of the French Army and contrasting it with that of the German, thought that Germany would just walk through it without the slightest difficulty, and for the first few weeks, it looked as if that calculation was justified. Now all that has gone, and the result of the War has undoubtedly been a great surprise and a great disappointment to Germany. We know now that her casualties exceed the number of her army on a war footing before the War,* and I think if she could have foreseen what was going to happen she would have hesitated a good deal; and I think she would have hesitated long enough not to have taken the step which, in a fatal moment, she took when she declared war, first against Russia, and then against Belgium, thus bringing the British Empire into action against her. Still, her punishment is not sufficiently severe, even now, to create that essential conviction in the mind of all military autocracies without which peace is impossible.

I dwell on this because I want later on to come to the question of what is still left to be done, and that is the question to which I hope this Cabinet will address itself. Germany has failed, but we have not yet succeeded. She is retreating in the West, but she is retreating with a purpose.† All you can say is, she would not have retreated if she had been strong enough to hold her own, and she would certainly not have retreated if she had been strong enough to advance.

But let us look quite frankly at the position. She has more men in the field now than ever she had. Her equipment is more powerful. She is in possession of scores of thousands of square miles of Allied territory. She is in a very powerful military position, acting as she is on interior lines; and the enormous casualties which we have had to sustain before we could force Germany to take this last step show that Germany still possesses enormous resources. I would not like to embark upon a prediction, but looking at all those objects which, I have ventured to submit, constitute the main purpose of our engaging in this war, although I am very hopeful, I should still say it would be a fatal error to reckon upon our being able to so destroy the *military power of Germany as to be able to achieve those aims in 1917.* They are purposes which Germany cannot possibly assent to unless she feels thoroughly beaten. *It would be a mistake for us to assume that we can beat her in 1917.* If we can, all the better; *but for us to base the whole of our action, the whole of our arrangements upon the anticipation that in 1917 we are going to inflict such a military defeat upon a Power which in 1917 is at its strongest, might be a miscalculation which would be fatal to the whole of our purpose.*

* This estimate, based on figures supplied by the General Staff, was considerably exaggerated.
† I referred to the retirement to the Hindenburg line.

To attempt less than those aims which I have indicated would mean the renewal of the conflict at no distant date, the throwing away of the great sacrifices which have been made, and the postponing of the great struggle for the elimination of war and of the military autocracy which means war, until another generation arrives, perhaps sterner, more purposeful, more tenacious in the prosecution of its ideals than the one to which Providence has first entrusted the accomplishment of this great task.

The Allies are depending more and more upon the British Empire. Ministers who have visited other countries will bear me out in saying that each time they go to those countries they feel that there is on their part a greater and a greater dependence upon the strength of the British Empire. We started with 100,000 men, we have now 3,000,000 in the field; but that is not all, as I shall point out. Lord Milner has just returned from Russia, and that is the tale he tells of it; they are all looking to Great Britain, and that is the case now more than ever after this revolution. The autocracy there was probably looking to us less than the people; but now that the people are on top their whole hope is centred in Great Britain. Lord Milner and I went to Rome, as you know, and we found exactly the same attitude of mind there. Many a time the Foreign Secretary and I have had to visit France, but invariably we have found, each succeeding time, a growing reliance on the strength of Great Britain. And that is inevitable, because it is not merely that we have increased thirtyfold, with the magnificent help which has been given us by the Dominions and by India, the numbers of our armies—they are depending upon us for other things which are just as essential to the waging of a successful war. Our finance is their very life-blood. They could not have tottered along and staggered so far on the way had it not been for the financial support which Great Britain had given them. Then there is our shipping—they would starve without it. It is not merely that they would not have their cannon and their shell, because we are bringing them steel and ore and material for both, but their people and their armies would actually starve. France, a great wheat-producing country, has to depend upon the fleets of Great Britain for her daily bread. The same thing applies to Italy; the millions of Italy would have died of starvation had it not been for the British Empire. Then there is coal—they have got to get their coal from here. The mines of France are in the hands of the enemy, and we have to supply French workshops and hearths with fuel. In men, in materials, in food, and I think I should add in morale, more and more they are depending upon the physical, the material, the moral support which the British Empire is giving to the whole of its Allies in this gigantic world struggle. The sense that we are getting more and more behind them is sustaining their courage, and that sense is increasing.

I say at once we could not have done it without the help the Empire has given us. It is impossible in words to describe our sense of gratitude and the thrill of pride with which we always think about the way in which the Empire came to our assistance when we risked the life of these islands upon the struggle for liberty in Europe. We could only spare 100,000 men to send to France at the beginning. The Dominions and India have practically given us a million already. It is very difficult to dwell upon what we feel about that; and the achievements of their valour—well, they are just a household tale on every hearthstone in these little islands. We know what we owe to the Dominions—how, in the first Battle of Ypres, when our little army had all been practically thrown in, and there was nothing left between the powerful military machine of Germany and our shores (and if they could have conquered the Channel, Heaven knows what would have happened then), the gallant soldiers who had come from India were thrown in, and helped to turn the scale. And in the second struggle, when for a second time, by a diabolical device— we knew about poisoned gases too, but we disdained to even discuss them at this table, and when the matter was mentioned we said " No, we won't look at that " and we absolutely refused to debate it even in this room—when I say, by a diabolical device the French lines were broken, and the Germans for a second time nearly succeeded in their attempt upon the Channel upon which we depend so much, we shall never forget how the valiant sons of Canada helped us. Australia last but not least—the glorious fights of the Australian troops in the Dardanelles and Pozières, and many another field where they sustained heavy casualties and achieved ringing triumphs by their valour.

And so I might go through the whole list; it is no use beginning to select instances; New Zealand, South Africa, Newfoundland, India, all have played their part, and here, last of all, we see how the brave sons of India are sweeping the Turks before them in the land of Mesopotamia. We all know these things, and it is the fact that the Dominions and India have come in, and come in not merely to show that they are contributing, but come in with the whole of their might and strength—it is that fact which has turned the scale in this great struggle. We wish to acknowledge that. It depends upon what we all continue to do together how this struggle is going to turn out; whether it is going to be a sort of half success which will mean a repetition of the struggle, or whether it is going to end in a victory which will create a new world such as has been the vision of many of us for years. Our army—a great citizen army—has become a veteran army. Its amateur officers are becoming skilful, trained leaders of men. But if this struggle goes on, we shall have to depend more and more upon the British Empire.

Now, what is it necessary for us to do? That is what I want to put before this gathering. What is it necessary for us to do in order to achieve the very sublime purpose which we have set before us? The first thing is this: we must get more men. Germany this year has put every available man into her army, relying undoubtedly upon our not being able to carry the conflict beyond 1917. She has therefore made the most amazing effort. She has called up men from unessential trades, she has organised the whole of her civilian population, and practically all her able-bodied men have been flung into the conflict in 1917. If the War goes beyond 1917, France has nothing to spare. France has already put one out of six of the whole of her population into this terrible conflict. It is a most wonderful effort, and she cannot do more. Next year she has got 200,000 or 300,000 coming on—boys of 17; she can do that next year, and that is about all she can do. Then Russia. Well, Russia is Russia. You never can tell what she can do; and the trouble of Russia is that if she could put men in, she has not got the lines of communication, the transport, which would enable her to make use of those men. And, therefore, the winning of this war in the real sense of the term, depends upon the efforts which the British Empire is able to put forward.

You will have figures circulated which will show exactly what we have all done—Great Britain, Ireland, and the rest of the Empire. We are relying upon getting a good deal more assistance from India, especially in the breaking up of Turkish power. I am sure that the resources of India, which have been willingly and enthusiastically placed at the disposal of the Empire in this struggle, will be available for any further efforts that it may be called upon to make; but undoubtedly it would enable us to concentrate far more upon the struggle in the West if India were to be able to undertake the larger share of the effort which is to be made in the fights in Mesopotamia and Egypt more especially. Efforts have been made to secure more labour from India—because in that respect we have a great scarcity. There is a great shortage of labour behind the lines in France, and this struggle is becoming very largely a matter of making roads, constructing railways, and generally making and improving the access to the front, so as to enable us to bring up our ammunition and men. There, undoubtedly, India could render us enormous assistance in the way, not merely of helping us with labour for that purpose, but, subject to what the War Office say, I personally think there are many men now engaged upon work behind the lines, and altogether right up to the lines, who I think might be replaced by men from India. I think we might incorporate into our armies men from the great Empire of the East who would release other men for other purposes—men not merely from the Army Service Corps, but I have also asked the War Office to consider whether even in the artillery it is not possible to utilise very large bodies of men from

India for the purpose of bringing ammunition up and for other purposes. There are scores of thousands of men absorbed in these tasks in our artillery; they are not all gunners.

I have to apologise for taking up a very much longer time than I had anticipated in placing these considerations before the Cabinet. To be ready for 1918 means victory, and it is a victory in which the British Empire will lead. It will easily then be the first Power in the world. And I rejoice in that not merely for selfish reasons, but because with all its faults, the British Empire is the truest representative of freedom—in the spirit even more than in the letter, of its institutions. We are here representing a great many races. Even in the United Kingdom there are three or four different races, and the Dominions and more especially India, represent a very considerable number of races. Of their free will they have come together to tender spontaneously their assistance to the Empire in this great struggle. That I regard as the triumph of the spirit and tradition of British institutions; and therefore, when I foresee that in 1918, with a special effort on the part of all of us, we shall be able to win not merely a great triumph, but to win it through the agency of the British Empire, I feel that it is worth our while to take steps to organise the Empire now, and to enable it to attain the heights of noble achievement and influence in the glorious task which is set before it.

APPENDIX B

Note by the Secretary.

THE Colonial Office telegrams indicate that the Special War Cabinet Meetings with representatives of the Dominions and India may commence about the second week in March. I venture to submit some preliminary observations for the consideration of the War Cabinet with a view, more particularly, to the preparation of materials required for the Conference.

The telegram sent by the Colonial Office and India Office on the subject of the Agenda is reproduced in the Appendix.

2. From this it will be seen that the Deliberations of the War Cabinet will fall broadly under three heads: —

(1) Increased effort during the War.
(2) The Terms of Peace.
(3) *Post Bellum* Conditions.

3. As regards the first, it is presumed that the War Cabinet will, in the first instance, wish to place the representatives of the Dominions and India in full possession of all the facts regarding the Naval, Military, Political and Economic situation, both of the enemy and of the Allies. It is submitted, however, that a great deal of this information would better be communicated verbally rather than in the form of memoranda, partly owing to its secrecy and partly owing to the desirability of not flooding the Overseas representatives with a mass of literature which they will find it difficult to read and digest.

4. As a basis for this part of the discussion, it is suggested that the memoranda should be confined in the main to questions of fact, which can be used, as it were, as works of reference during the Cabinet meetings. The information might be set forth under the following heads: —

(1) The facts regarding naval co-operation rendered by the Dominions and India, with indications of further directions in which co-operation might be given. This would be prepared by the Admiralty.

(2) The facts regarding the military co-operation of the Dominions and India, with indications of any directions in which further co-operation might be given. This would be prepared by the General Staff.

(3) The facts regarding co-operation in shipbuilding, with indications as to further possible developments. This would be provided by the Shipping Controller.

(4) The facts regarding co-operation in the production of food, with suggestions by the Food Controller and the President of the Board of Agriculture and Fisheries.

(5) The facts regarding financial assistance given by the Dominions and India, with suggestions by the Treasury.

(6) The facts regarding co-operation by the Dominions and India in the provision of munitions, with suggestions by the Minister of Munitions.

(7) The facts regarding any other form of co-operation by the Dominions and India outside the above headings might be given by the Colonial Office and India Office respectively.

(8) The facts regarding the co-operation of the Crown Colonies, Dependencies, etc. This would be prepared by the Colonial Office.

It is for consideration also whether, conversely, the facts under each heading regarding Imperial assistance to the Dominions and India should not be given.

5. It is suggested that, following the highly successful precedent of the meetings at the Committee of Imperial Defence in 1911, the first meeting should open with a series of general statements regarding the strategical, political, and economic situation, which might be made by the Prime Minister (whose statement might usefully include a recapitulation of the far-reaching economic and other measures taken in this country), the First Sea Lord, the Chief of the Imperial General Staff, the Secretary of State for Foreign Affairs, and the Minister of Blockade, respectively. Perhaps also Lord Curzon would make a statement on such matters as mercantile shipping, restriction of imports, and aerial warfare, and Lord Milner might say something about Russia. These statements might be followed up by a summing-up by the Prime Minister of the particular questions which on our part we wish the Dominions to consider; and an invitation for them to offer suggestions to us, after which, no doubt, a general discussion would ensue.

6. Probably a large number of the suggestions would have to be remitted, either to Special Sub-Committees or Conferences, or to the Parallel Conferences proceeding at the Colonial Office and the India Office.

7. With regard to the second group of questions relating to Peace,

it is suggested that the only memoranda to be furnished should be the following: —

A translation of the reply by the Allies to President Wilson.
Sir Louis Mallet's Interim Report and Final Report on Territorial Changes outside Europe.
The Board of Trade Memorandum on Economic Desiderata in the Terms of Peace, and Professor Ashley's Memoranda on Indemnities.
The Report of Lord Balfour of Burleigh's Economic Sub-Committee of the Reconstruction Committee.
The Reconstruction Committee's Report on Germany's after-war policy.

8. It is suggested, however, that early in these discussions the Prime Minister or the Secretary of State for Foreign Affairs should make a full verbal statement covering the following subjects: —

The Agreements made in regard to Constantinople and Turkey.
The Agreement with Italy.
The Agreement with Roumania.
The desiderata of the Allies, so far as they are known, and of ourselves in regard to territorial and economic changes, more particularly those affecting Belgium, Alsace-Lorraine, Poland, and the Balkans.

9. There are several matters which the Government itself has not yet considered in relation to the terms of peace. For example, there is the big question of policy as to whether we are to aim at some sort of international organisation, such as a league to enforce peace, or a league of the character of the Concert of Europe formed after 1815; or alternatively, something in the nature of a balance of power; the financial arrangements between the Allies and ourselves, and the question whether we should use these as a lever to bargain for territorial or other advantages; the question of ton for ton, and any naval desiderata. It would seem very probable that some of these questions will be raised at the Conference. I should like the instructions of the War Cabinet as to whether any material should be prepared in connection with any of them.

10. As regards the third group of *post bellum* problems, it is understood that they will probably, to a large extent, be discussed outside the Imperial War Cabinet, and that the Colonial Office have already been in communication with other Departments on the various subjects. Perhaps the most immediate of these is Demobilisation. The Demobilisation Sub-Committee of the Reconstruction Committee is, I understand, at present in abeyance, pending a decision

on the future work of the Reconstruction Committee, but both the Ministry of Labour and the War Office are actively at work. One question which may have to be discussed in the War Cabinet is that of the constitution of the British Empire, if it is raised by any of the Dominions and it is included in the general programme sent to the Dominions and India; but I would submit that, in the first instance, it would be more usefully raised at the Special War Conference at the Colonial Office, which is fully conversant with the past history of this question and its difficulties.

11. Other questions which would, in the first instance at any rate, fall rather within the scope of the special War Conference at the Colonial Office would include: Commercial, industrial and shipping policy after the War, emigration (including coloured emigration), Imperial communications, All-Red Route, cables, etc., naturalisation, organisation of Consular and Intelligence Services, and any other subjects which the Colonial Office and the Dominion Governments may consider it desirable to raise, and finally the constitutional problem itself.

I have already written informally to the Chancellor of the Exchequer, Secretary of State for Foreign Affairs, Secretary of State for the Colonies, Secretary of State for India, Minister of Blockade, First Sea Lord, Chief of the Imperial General Staff, Minister of Munitions, Shipping Controller, Food Controller, and President of the Board of Agriculture and Fisheries, suggesting, for their consideration, the desirability of getting together the material for the various documents suggested in this note, and I should be glad to have the approval of the War Cabinet, in order to place the matter on a more formal footing, and also to receive any further instructions.

M.P.A.H.

2 Whitehall Gardens, S.W.
10th February, 1917.

APPENDIX C

In a memorandum dated 12th October, 1916, Sir Eyre Crowe made a critical examination of the scheme which had been put forward by Lord Robert Cecil for a League to enforce peace.

Analysing this scheme, he noted that it proposed a joint association of all the Powers signing the Peace Treaty:—

(1) To guarantee the territorial settlement it imposed;

(2) To settle in conference any question of modifying that settlement;

(3) To enforce their decisions by united action against a recalcitrant State;

(4) To carry out general disarmament under cover of the foregoing guarantees.

As regards the nature and constitution of the Conference of Nations which should be set up to deal with these issues, he observed:—

(a) That it must include not only the Powers signing the Peace Treaty, but also the Neutral Powers; in fact, every Sovereign State would have to be included.

(b) That it would have to possess a permanent headquarters and organisation, so as to deal at once with every concrete issue arising.

(c) That it would work as a formidable means of obstruction and delay, but would be feeble in promoting definite progress.

(d) That the readiness of all countries to join in and pledge themselves to united action could not be taken as certain.

Assuming that all nations united in such a solemn league and covenant, would they keep it? Taking first the case of a violation or attempted violation of the territorial settlement, they would only be willing to enforce it as long as they felt it to be a just one. No territorial settlement could be permanently just, even if it was so at the outset. By degrees some Powers would feel it to be unjust, and there would be a division of Powers into two groups. If the revisionist group grew strong enough, it would force an alteration, whether the Conference approved as a whole or not. "When a combination of Powers commands a preponderance of force—using the word 'force'

...d the necessary means of aggression, there can ...ᴛ that an effort on its part to alter the territorial settlement for its own benefit will be actively resisted by the rest of the world."

Failing active resistance, would the rest of the world impose a blockade and economic boycott? Probably not, if they were in any danger of being overrun in consequence by powerful neighbours. The economic as much as the military weapon would be powerless against a strong combination of Powers. At most, the proposed conference would be a mitigating influence against hasty aggression. It could not abolish it.

Further, wars do not always arise out of territorial disputes, even though they frequently end in territorial changes. Even the Great War did not so arise, for Austria explicitly disavowed any territorial ambition when she invaded Serbia. Even if the Conference could ensure counter-action against a war of territorial aggression, it could not compel nations to compromise on issues they felt vital to their national existence or interests. The only way in which agreement could be reached in a general conference would be by an evasion of the issue, or by accepting a majority vote. A majority vote on the vital issues would not be acceptable to a Great Power. "Great Britain in particular would be exposed to special and grave dangers; for a substantial majority among the Powers could at almost any time be found for measures ostensibly designed to favour the general cause of peace, but in effect calculated to curtail British supremacy at sea."

A settlement of a dispute means that either one party gives way to the other, or that a compromise is agreed. A satisfactory settlement means that both sides are satisfied as to the general justice of the solution agreed. Failing this, the issue is not settled; it is only postponed. Such postponement means that the unsatisfied side reckons it would lose more by going to war than the achievement of its aim is worth. This again means that it does not consider itself strong enough to win, or to win cheaply, in relation to the importance of the issue involved.

So to attain ends which a nation regards as vital, it will continue to seek alliances and to develop understandings with useful neighbours, as in the past. And when once it has secured sufficient backing for its side, a Conference cannot hold it back; a Conference would only reveal its strength and the measure of support it possessed. All that can be said in favour of the Conference is that it introduces a pause, and makes the issue clear, thus enabling outside nations to decide their verdict as to its justice.

But in the last resort, everything depends upon the "sanction" that can be applied; and this means military force. The forces of the League Powers must be such that in any dispute they can bring overwhelming pressure promptly to bear on any possible recusants before the smallest of their members can be overrun. If not, little Powers will not dare to act with the League in taking economic measures against a Great Power.

"The balance of power reappears as the fundamental problem. To prevent the possibility of any one State or group of States pursuing, through war and bloodshed a policy of aggression and domination, nothing will serve but adequate force." The effectiveness of a League of Nations is ultimately a military problem.

This leads Sir Eyre Crowe to discuss the possibility of limitation of armaments as a means of reducing the horrors of war and increasing the power of a League of Nations as against any individual nation. Such limitation must be in terms of quantity of arms; kinds of arms; or expenditure of arms; or all three.

None of these methods is effective by itself. The possible size of armies is limited only by national man-power. Lack of it can be met by using more potent weapons, and the prohibition of certain categories would only stimulate invention of new types; and even financial limitation may be defeated by discovery of cheaper and more deadly weapons.

Suppose all three were used together; even then certain further conditions are essential if genuine disarmament is to be carried out.

The first condition is confidence in the good faith of all parties. This does not exist and is not likely to. Any nation could evade disarmament agreements, and none will trust its neighbour not to attempt evasion.

The second and fundamental condition is for each State to accept for itself a standard of force which it will not exceed. Since nations differ widely in size, defensibility of frontiers, and responsibilities, the standard must be different for each. What shall the comparative standard be? Not that existing before the War, which has proved itself a danger to world peace. Not that which we can impose on the Central Powers after the War if we defeat them, for they will not submit permanently to helpless inferiority. We cannot stereotype the relative armament strength of nations because they grow and decline and change, as do their relations with each other. "Who will undertake to fix the standard of armed strength for China, for Holland, for Mexico, for the United States? Can it be seriously believed that standards so fixed now could survive a general revolution in China, a quarrel over the Dutch Indies between Holland and Japan, or an American invasion of Mexico? Such events—none of them improbable—would scatter to the winds the papers on which the agreements for fixing the proportionate amounts of armaments had been written."

Finally, Sir Eyre Crowe examined the prospects of an agreement about arms limitations between a few countries only. This, while apparently the simplest, he held to be really the most dangerous, because any alteration in the armament of other powers standing

...nt would upset its basis and stimulate a new ...race between its signatories.

. . . . .

In a footnote to Sir Eyre Crowe's Memorandum, Lord Robert Cecil said: —

"The objections to any attempt to limit armaments are powerfully put. On the whole I agree that nothing can be done at present. But it is possible that in future ages a public opinion will develop so strong against the settlement of disputes by war that armament will be reduced by common consent. The history of feudalism in England illustrates my meaning. The catastrophe of the Wars of the Roses led to the supremacy of the law.

R. C."

APPENDIX D

THE findings of the Committee were set out under the following seven heads:—

1. Paris Resolutions.
2. Control of Imperial Resources.
3. Renewal of Treaties.
4. Indemnities.
5. Settlement of private claims arising out of the War.
6. The League of Nations.
7. The Freedom of the Seas.

The Committee held that the Paris Resolutions were no longer applicable to the situation, but they commended that feature in them which supported a refusal to grant the enemy countries a renewal of most-favoured-nation treatment when making peace. The peace terms should impose no limits on the freedom of the governments within the Empire to develop its natural resources for national purposes. No general renewal of pre-War treaties and conventions with the enemy Powers should be made.

On indemnities the Committee felt unable to prophesy just how much we could hope to get. Indemnities in kind would probably be more practical than money, though this also should be exacted as far as feasible. Shipping, railway material and natural products like potash, the last over a period of years, might be claimed; and money payments should also be spread over some years.

"The greatest difficulty connected with an indemnity is to determine which are the parties possessing the strongest claim to the benefit of it, having regard to the fact that even all justified claims cannot possibly be satisfied." Belgium should be given priority, and after her, France in respect of her north-eastern provinces, and Serbia. Britain had an equal claim with these in respect of her shipping. If France secured the rich iron fields of Lorraine, it would go some way to compensate her for the destruction wrought in her territory. The Committee doubted whether the transfer of the German Navy would have much practical value.

For the settlement of private debts the Committee suggested that each Government should pay to its creditor citizens the sums due to them from enemy nationals, and collect from them debts they owed. Any balance could be settled between the Governments. The validity of action taken under Emergency Acts and regulations with respect to enemy property should be insisted on by us in the peace settlement. The conclusion on the League of Nations ran as follows: —

" The Committee were deeply impressed with the danger of the complete destruction of civilised society which threatens the world if the recurrence of a war like the present cannot be prevented, and with the necessity of devising means which would tend, at any rate, to diminish the risk of such a calamity. They felt, however, that any too comprehensive or ambitious project to ensure world peace might prove not only impracticable, but harmful. The proposal which seems to promise the best results proceeds along the path of consultation and conference for composing differences which cannot otherwise be adjusted. The Treaty of Peace should provide that none of the parties who are signatories to that Treaty should resort to arms against one another without previous submission of their dispute to a Conference of the Powers. The Committee think that the details of such a scheme should be discussed with our Allies and especially with the United States of America, before the conclusion of the War."

No fundamental change was thought to be necessary in the British policy regarding the Freedom of the Seas.

END OF VOLUME ONE